PEARSON

Foundations and Pre-calculus Mathematics 10

Garry Davis
David Ellis
Jack Hope
Delcy Rolheiser
David Sufrin
Chris Van Bergeyk
David Van Bergeyk
David Zimmer

PEARSON

Publisher
Mike Czukar

Research and Communications Manager
Barbara Vogt

Design and Art Direction
Zena Denchik

Composition
Lapiz Digital Services, India

Photo Research
Carrie Gleason

Cover Image
Chad Baker/The Image Bank/GettyImages

ISBN-13 978-0-321-62684-4
ISBN-10 0-321-62684-2

Printed and bound in the United States

4 5 —CC— 14 13 12 11

Publishing Team
Enid Haley
Lesley Haynes
Claire Burnett
Stephanie Boragina
Ioana Gagea
Alison Rieger
Lynne Gulliver
Ellen Davidson
David Liu
May Look
Alison Dale
Cheri Westra
Carolyn Sebestyen
Jane Schell
Karen Alley
Judy Wilson

PEARSON

Advisors and Reviewers

Pearson Canada thanks its advisors and reviewers who helped shape the vision for *Foundations and Pre-calculus Mathematics 10* through discussions and reviews of prototype materials and manuscript.

Advisors

Bob Berglind
Calgary Board of Education
Calgary, AB

Marc Garneau
Surrey School District No. 36
Surrey, BC

Susan Ludwig
Edmonton Catholic Separate School District No. 7
Edmonton, AB

Christine Ottawa
Mathematics Consultant
Winnipeg, MB

Robert Sidley
Burnaby School District No. 41
Burnaby, BC

Francophone Advisors

Nathalie Houle
Winnipeg School Division
Winnipeg, MB

Danielle Lamoureux
Conseil scolaire centre-nord no. 2
Edmonton, AB

Northern Advisor

Peter Maguire
Yellowknife Education District No. 1
Yellowknife, NT

FNMI Advisors

Edward Doolittle
First Nations University of Canada
Regina, SK

Shirley A. Mykituk
Edmonton Catholic Separate School District No. 7
Edmonton, AB

Reviewers

Joe Beaudin
Calgary Board of Education
Calgary, AB

Rhonda German Hawthorne
St. James-Assiniboia School Division
Winnipeg, MB

Andrew Hirst
River East Transcona School Division
Winnipeg, MB

Terry Kaminski
Northern Lights School Division No. 69
Bonnyville, AB

Ryan Mann
Parkland School Division
Stony Plain, AB

Chad Raible
Maple Ridge-Pitt Meadows School District No. 42
Maple Ridge, BC

Ralph R. Schmidt
Elk Island Public Schools
Sherwood Park, AB

Contents

5 Relations and Functions

6 Linear Functions

7 Systems of Linear Equations

Your Book at a Glance

This book organizes your grade 10 course into three major topics. By focusing on one topic at a time, you can:

- spend more time on new concepts
- develop deeper understanding
- improve your recall of math concepts and strategies
- make connections across topics

MEASUREMENT

1. Measurement

2. Trigonometry
Project: Ramp It Up!
Cumulative Review: Chapters 1 and 2

Apply and extend what you know from previous grades as you investigate and solve real-world problems involving measurement.

ALGEBRA AND NUMBERS

3. Factors and Products

4. Roots and Powers
Project: Human Calculators
Cumulative Review: Chapters 1 – 4

Extend your work with patterning, algebra, and number concepts as you develop tools for solving new types of problems.

RELATIONS AND FUNCTIONS

5. Relations and Functions

6. Linear Functions

7. Systems of Linear Equations
Project: Exercise Mind and Body
Cumulative Review: Chapters 1 – 7

Build on what you have learned about algebra to study graphs and explore patterns.

Projects after Chapters 2, 4, and 7 have you solve applied problems while you reinforce your learning.

Cumulative Reviews cover all the content up to that point in the book.

Chapter Opener

Each chapter is organized around a few key **Big Ideas** of mathematics. Learning through the **Big Ideas**:

- lets you make sense of math topics
- helps you understand how the topics are related
- lets you learn more efficiently

Look for an illustration where the math of the chapter is applied. The caption describes the application.

3 Factors and Products

AERIAL PHOTO OF MANITOBA
The Dominion Land Survey divides much of western Canada into 1-mile square sections. This photo shows canola fields around Shoal Lake, located in western Manitoba.

BUILDING ON

- determining factors and multiples of whole numbers to 100
- identifying prime and composite numbers
- determining square roots of rational numbers
- adding and subtracting polynomials
- multiplying and dividing polynomials by monomials

BIG IDEAS

- Arithmetic operations on polynomials are based on the arithmetic operations on integers, and have similar properties.
- Multiplying and factoring are inverse processes, and a rectangle diagram can be used to represent them.

NEW VOCABULARY

prime factorization
greatest common factor
least common multiple
perfect cube, cube root
factoring by decomposition
perfect square trinomial
difference of squares
radicand, radical, index

Building on...
tells you what you need to know before learning new concepts.

Big Ideas...
tell you the learning goals for the chapter.

New Vocabulary...
identifies the new terms you will use as you work through the chapter.

Numbered Lessons

Each lesson links to the **Big Ideas** stated at the start of the chapter.

Lesson Focus...
states the learning goal for the lesson.

Make Connections...
presents previous content, or an application, so you can make connections between what you already know, and what you are about to learn.

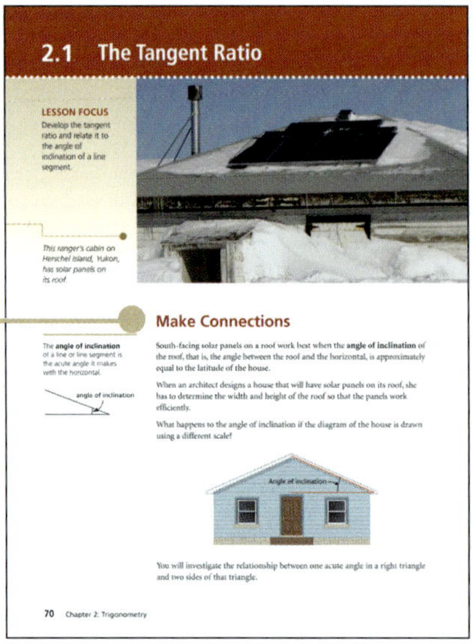

In each lesson you **Construct Understanding**, then apply what you have learned.

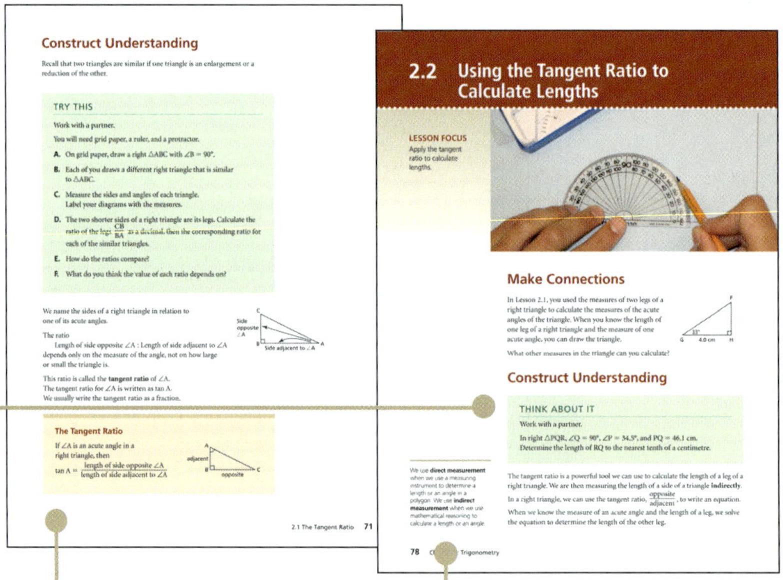

Try This or **Think About It...**
presents an activity or a problem that uses ideas from **Make Connections**.

The activity or problem leads you to new concepts.

Colour boxes highlight important rules, formulas, or definitions.

Look for margin notes that define or explain a key term.

Examples...
model strategies for solving problems.

Check Your Understanding
gives you an opportunity for immediate reinforcement after each **Example**.

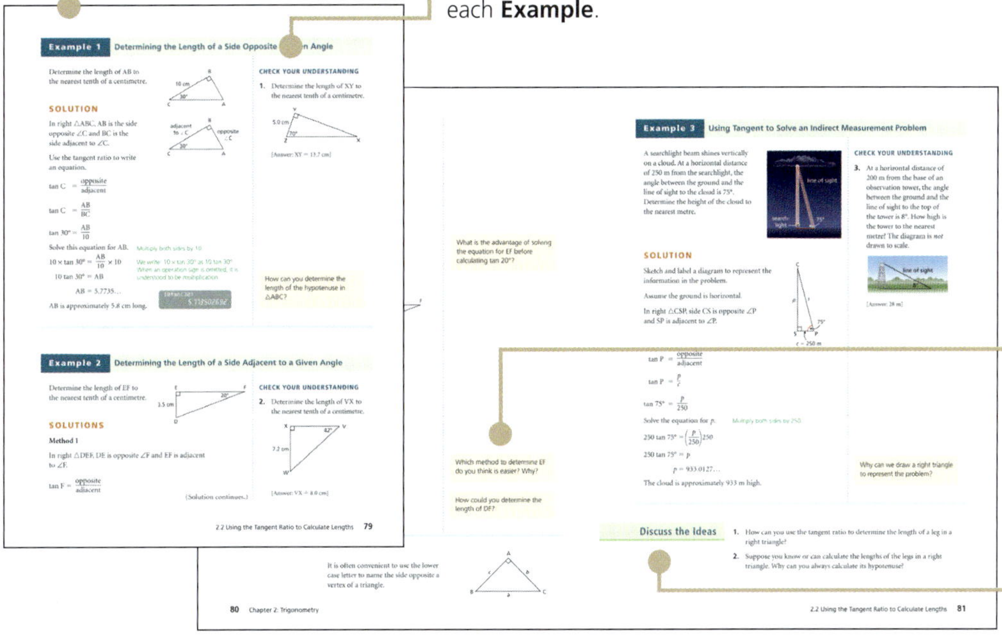

Margin questions extend your thinking, or ask you to think about key points.

Discuss the Ideas...
after working through the Examples, and before starting the Exercises.

Each lesson provides practice for the concepts you've been working with.

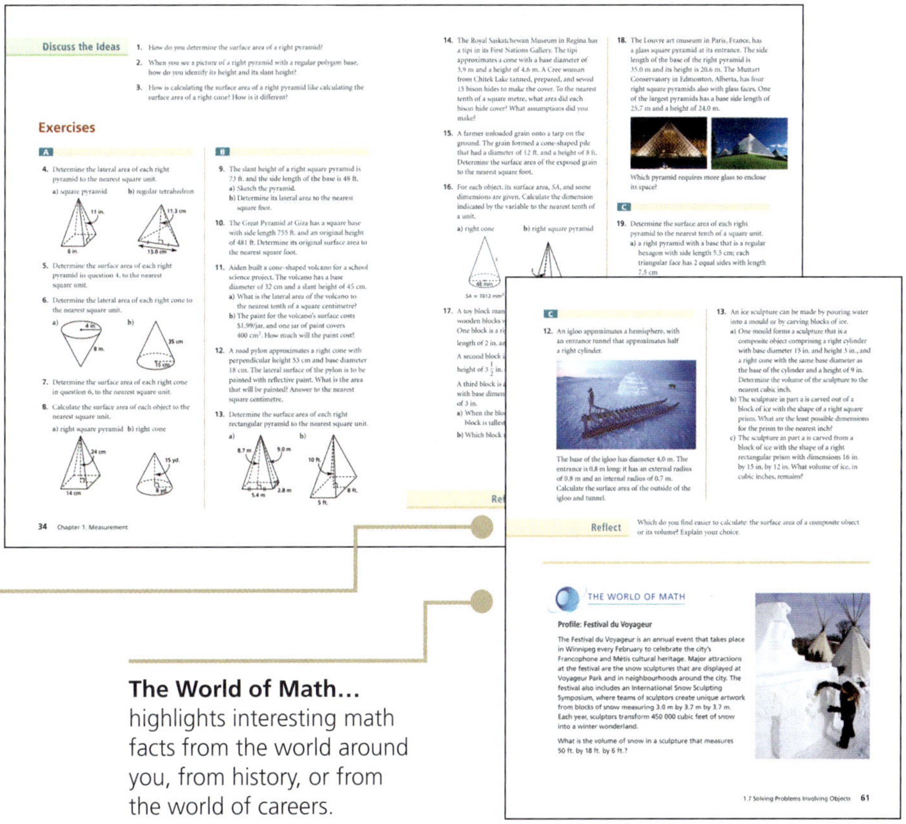

Exercises...
are organized by A/B/C levels of difficulty and allow you to check your skills and understanding.

Reflect...
prompts you to think about, and record, what you learned.

The World of Math...
highlights interesting math facts from the world around you, from history, or from the world of careers.

Math Lab Lessons

Math Lab lessons provide more time to explore the math using materials or technology.

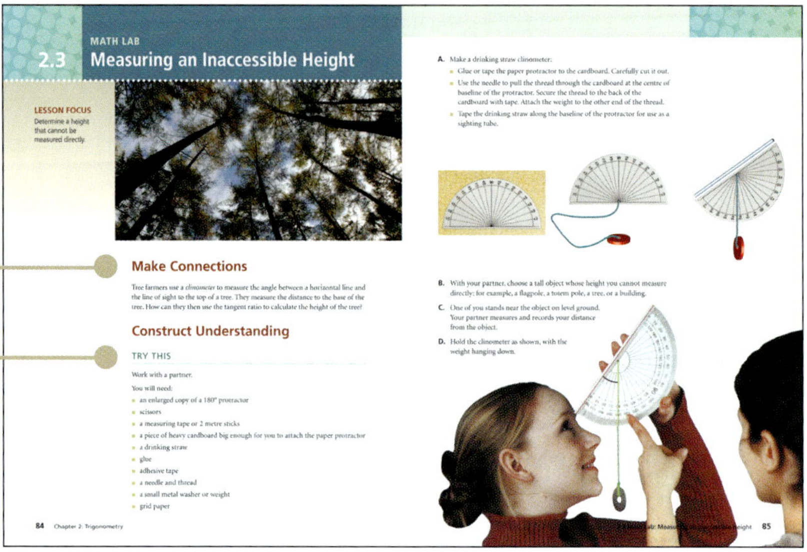
MATH LAB

2.3 Measuring an Inaccessible Height

LESSON FOCUS
Determine a height that cannot be measured directly.

Make Connections

Tree farmers use a *clinometer* to measure the angle between a horizontal line and the line of sight to the top of a tree. They measure the distance to the base of the tree. How can they then use the tangent ratio to calculate the height of the tree?

Construct Understanding

TRY THIS

Work with a partner.

You will need:

- an enlarged copy of a 180° protractor
- scissors
- a measuring tape or 2 metre sticks
- a piece of heavy cardboard big enough for you to attach the paper protractor
- a drinking straw
- glue
- adhesive tape
- a needle and thread
- a small metal washer or weight
- grid paper

84 Chapter 2: Trigonometry

A. Make a drinking straw clinometer:
- Glue or tape the paper protractor to the cardboard. Carefully cut it out.
- Use the needle to pull the thread through the cardboard at the centre of baseline of the protractor. Secure the thread to the back of the cardboard with tape. Attach the weight to the other end of the thread.
- Tape the drinking straw along the baseline of the protractor for use as a sighting tube.

B. With your partner, choose a tall object whose height you cannot measure directly: for example, a flagpole, a totem pole, a tree, or a building.

C. One of you stands near the object on level ground. Your partner measures and records your distance from the object.

D. Hold the clinometer as shown, with the weight hanging down.

85

As in other lessons, you'll find the **Lesson Focus** and **Make Connections**.

Try This...
presents an extended activity.

After completing **Try This**, check if you're on the right track.

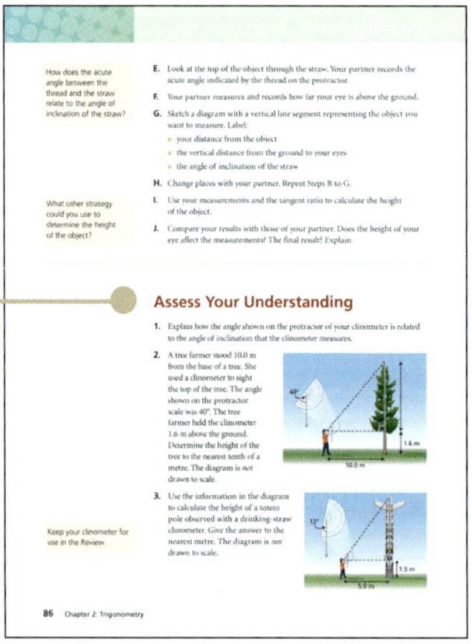
How does the acute angle between the thread and the straw relate to the angle of inclination of the straw?

E. Look at the top of the object through the straw. Your partner records the acute angle indicated by the thread on the protractor.

F. Your partner measures and records how far your eye is above the ground.

G. Sketch a diagram with a vertical line segment representing the object you want to measure. Label:
- your distance from the object
- the vertical distance from the ground to your eyes
- the angle of inclination of the straw

H. Change places with your partner. Repeat Steps B to G.

What other strategy could you use to determine the height of the object?

I. Use your measurements and the tangent ratio to calculate the height of the object.

J. Compare your results with those of your partner. Does the height of your eye affect the measurements? The final result? Explain.

Assess Your Understanding

1. Explain how the angle shown on the protractor of your clinometer is related to the angle of inclination that the clinometer measures.

2. A tree farmer stood 10.0 m from the base of a tree. She used a clinometer to sight the top of the tree. The angle shown on the protractor scale was 40°. The tree farmer held the clinometer 1.6 m above the ground. Determine the height of the tree to the nearest tenth of a metre. The diagram is *not* drawn to scale.

3. Use the information in the diagram to calculate the height of a totem pole observed with a drinking-straw clinometer. Give the answer to the nearest metre. The diagram is *not* drawn to scale.

Keep your clinometer for use in the Review.

86 Chapter 2: Trigonometry

Assess Your Understanding...
provides a few key questions so you can apply what you learned in **Try This**.

Review and Study Features

Checkpoints occur at key intervals in the chapter, so you can reflect on Big Ideas as they've been developed. Checkpoints let you check your understanding so far.

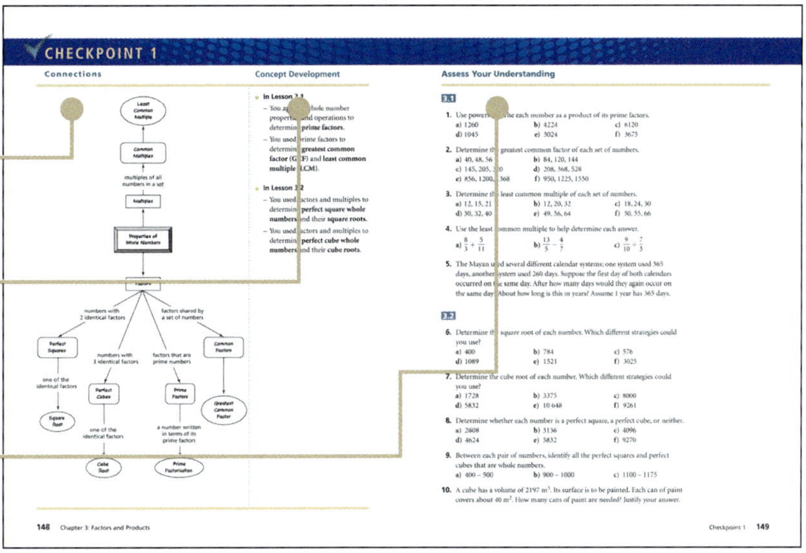

Connections...
gives a picture of what you've been learning.

Concept Development...
summarizes important content.

Assess Your Understanding...
provides questions related to each lesson.

At the end of each chapter:

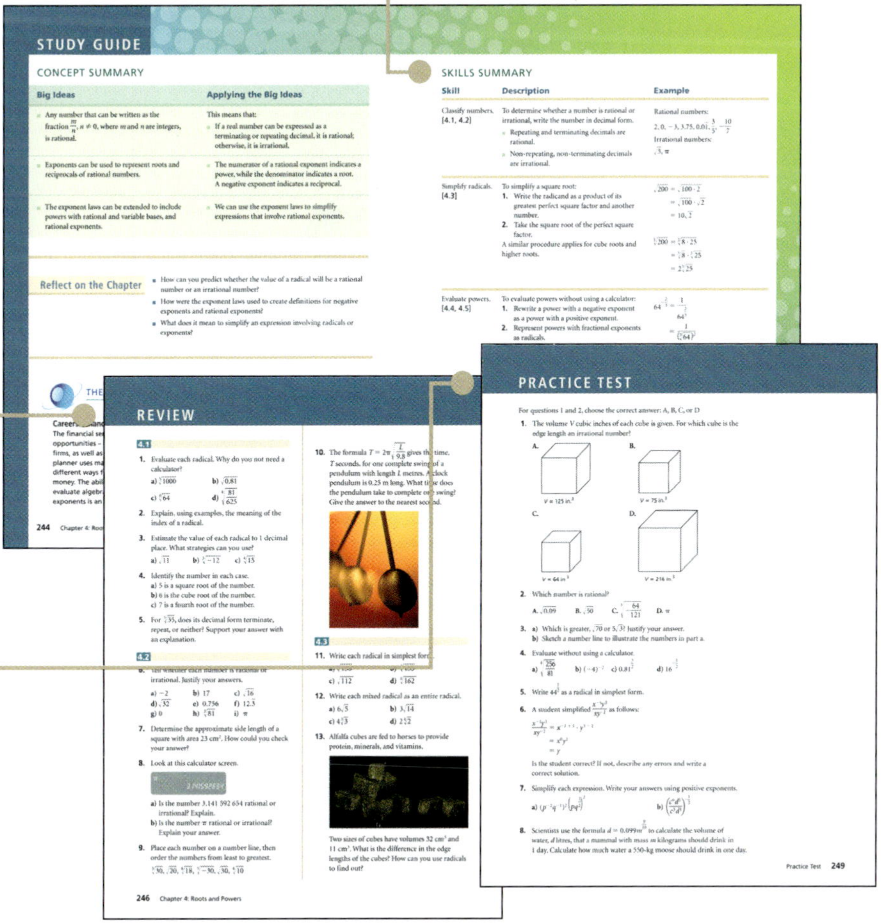

Study Guide...
summarizes the important concepts and skills from the chapter.

Review...
pages provide additional practice.

Practice Test...
lets you try a sample test before you take a class test.

Cumulative Reviews and Projects

After 2 or 3 chapters, these book features support your learning.

Cumulative Reviews…
help you recall content from earlier in the course.

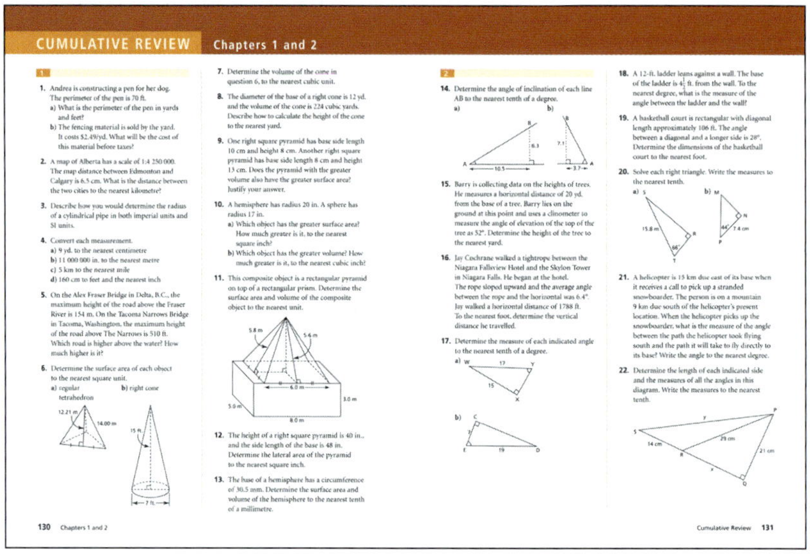

Projects…
present applications where you can use the math you have learned to solve problems.

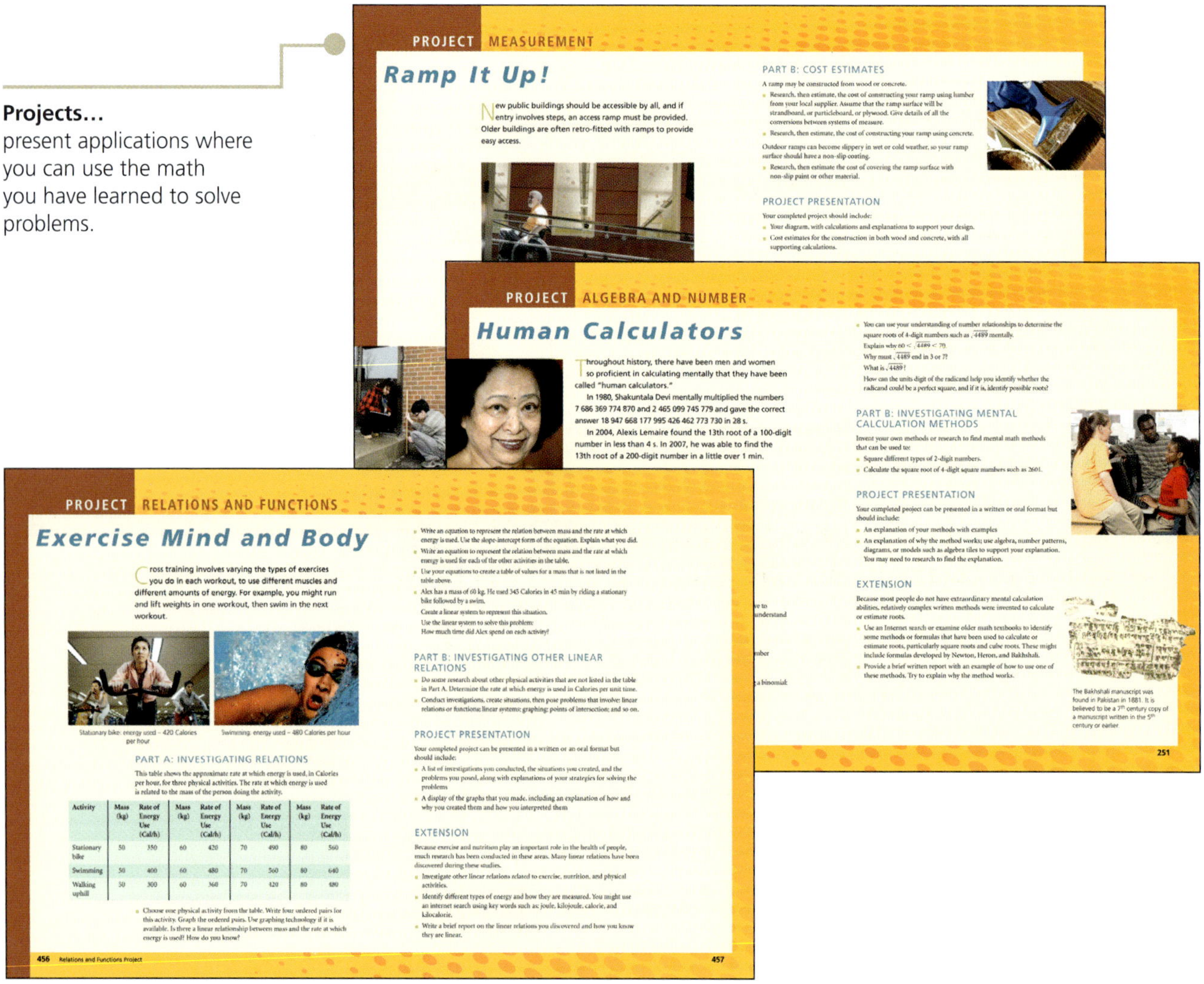

End of Book Features

This book provides supports you can use to learn on your own, or with others. In addition to the Chapters, you'll find these tools for learning:

- A **Glossary** of key math terms, so you can check the meaning of new math vocabulary
- **Answers** to exercise questions so you can check your work
- An **Index** to let you locate where a topic is covered

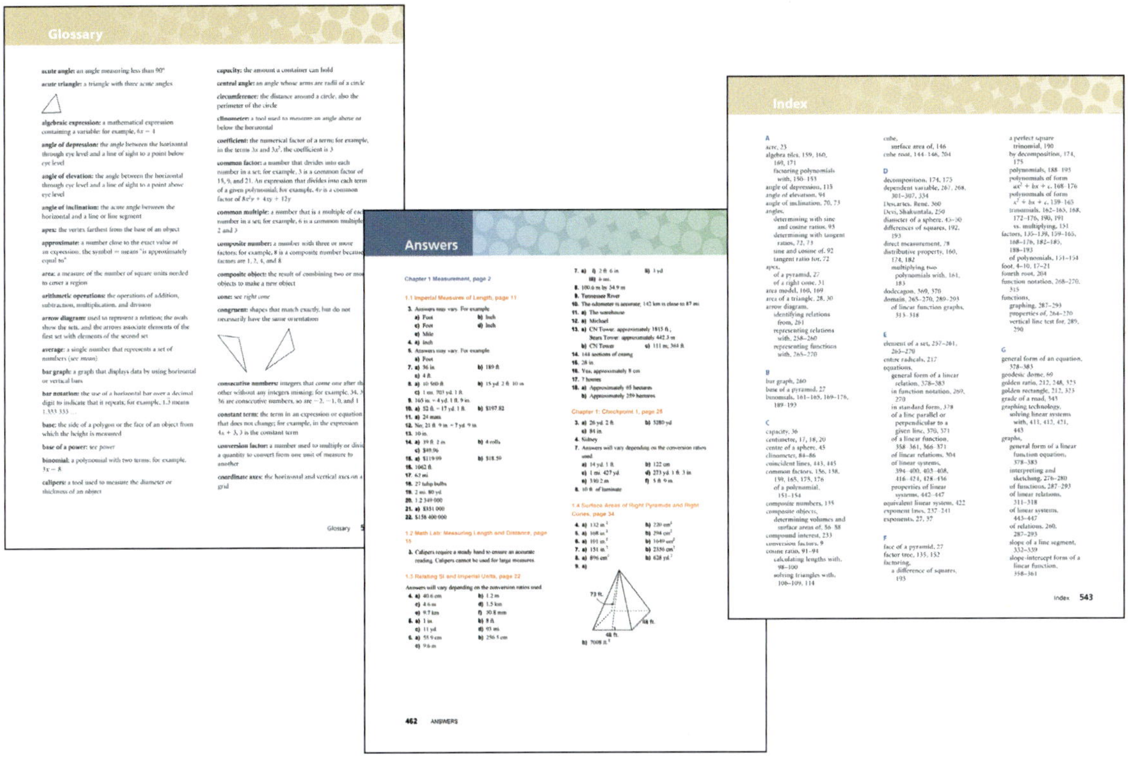

Use these book features throughout the course. They will help you locate material, interpret examples, and check your work as you practise.

1 Measurement

BUILDING ON

- working with metric units of measure
- determining the surface areas and volumes of right prisms and cylinders

BIG IDEAS

- You can use proportional reasoning to convert measurements.
- The volume of a right pyramid or cone is related to the volume of the enclosing right prism or cylinder.
- The surface area of a right pyramid or cone is the sum of the areas of the faces and the curved surfaces.
- The surface area of a sphere is related to the curved surface area of the enclosing cylinder.

NEW VOCABULARY

imperial units
unit analysis
SI system of measures
apex
right pyramid and right cone
slant height
lateral area
sphere

STARSHIP ENTERPRISE

A replica was constructed in Vulcan, Alberta, in June 1995. The base is part of a pyramid and it supports a 31-ft. long spacecraft. Visitors are welcomed in 3 languages: English, Vulcan, and Klingon.

1.1 Imperial Measures of Length

LESSON FOCUS

Develop personal referents to estimate imperial measures of length.

Make Connections

The **SI system of measures** is an abbreviation for *Le Système International d'Unités.* Since 1960, this form of the metric system has been adopted by many countries, including Canada.

Some **imperial units** of measure are the inch, the foot, the yard, and the mile.

In 1976, Canada adopted SI units to measure length. However, construction and manufacturing industries continue to use **imperial units**. Many Canadians use imperial units to measure their height.

What is your height?

Look around the classroom.
Which object has a length of about one foot?
Which object has a length of about one inch?
Which object has a length of about one yard?

Construct Understanding

Many units in the imperial system are based on measurements of the human body.

TRY THIS

Work with a partner.

You will need a ruler and measuring tape with imperial units, string, and scissors.

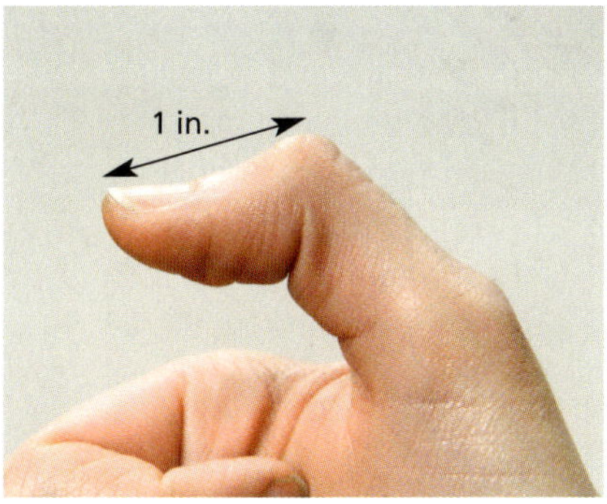

A. Use the length of your thumb from its tip to the first joint as a measuring instrument.
Use your thumb to estimate then record the length of your pencil and the dimensions of your textbook, in thumb units.
Use a ruler or measuring tape to measure each length.
For which imperial unit could you use your thumb length as a referent?

B. Use your foot length to estimate then record the length and width of a bookcase, in foot units.
Use a ruler or measuring tape to measure each length.
For which imperial unit could you use your foot length as a referent?

C. Hold a piece of string from your nose to the longest finger of an outstretched arm. Have your partner cut the string to this length.
Use this string to estimate then record the length and width of the classroom, in arm spans. Use a measuring tape to measure each length.
For which imperial unit could you use your arm span as a referent?

D. Determine approximately:

- how many thumb lengths equal one foot length
- how many foot lengths equal one arm span
- how many thumb lengths equal one arm span

E. Compare the measures in your personal units with those of your partner. Why is it necessary to have standard units of length?

F. What other referents could be used for each length?

- one inch
- one foot
- one yard

People have been measuring for thousands of years. Early trades people created their own measuring devices and units. For example, people measured the distance between two places by the number of days it took to travel from one place to the other. Over time, these units were standardized as imperial units, and relationships between the units were determined.

The imperial unit for measuring long distances is the mile. The length of one mile was first established as the distance a Roman soldier could walk in 1000 paces. One pace is 2 steps.

On maps and scale diagrams, you may see symbols for imperial units instead of abbreviations. One inch is 1″ and one foot is 1′.

Imperial Unit	Abbreviation	Referent	Relationship between Units
Inch	in.	Thumb length	
Foot	ft.	Foot length	1 ft. = 12 in.
Yard	yd.	Arm span	1 yd. = 3 ft. 1 yd. = 36 in.
Mile	mi.	Distance walked in 20 min	1 mi. = 1760 yd. 1 mi. = 5280 ft.

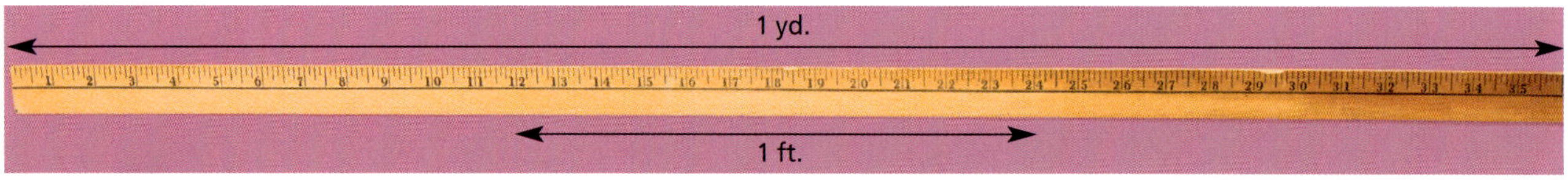

Many rulers marked with imperial units show one inch divided into eighths, tenths, or sixteenths. To measure the length of an object, you must first determine the smallest indicated unit by counting the number of divisions between two adjacent inch marks. The ruler below has 16 divisions between two adjacent inch marks, so the smallest indicated unit is $\frac{1}{16}$ of an inch, which is written as $\frac{1}{16}$ in.

The pencil point is closest to the 7th division mark between 3 in. and 4 in., so its length is $3\frac{7}{16}$ in.

A fraction of an imperial measure of length is usually written in fraction form, not decimal form.

Example 1 Converting between Imperial Units

a) Convert 5 yd. to:

i) feet ii) inches

b) Convert 51 in. to:

i) feet and inches ii) yards, feet, and inches

SOLUTION

a) i) Since 1 yd. = 3 ft., to convert yards to feet multiply by 3.

5 yd. = 5(3 ft.)

5 yd. = 15 ft.

ii) Since 5 yd. = 15 ft. and 1 ft. = 12 in., to convert feet to inches multiply by 12.

5 yd. = 15(12 in.)

5 yd. = 180 in.

b) i) Since 12 in. = 1 ft., to convert inches to feet, divide by 12.

51 in. = $\frac{51}{12}$ ft. Write this improper fraction as a mixed number.

51 in. = $4\frac{3}{12}$ ft.

51 in. = 4 ft. 3 in.

ii) 51 in. = 4 ft. 3 in.

Since 3 ft. = 1 yd.

4 ft. = 1 yd. 1 ft.

and 51 in. = 1 yd. 1 ft. 3 in.

CHECK YOUR UNDERSTANDING

1. a) Convert 7 yd. to:

i) feet ii) inches

b) Convert 62 in. to:

i) feet and inches

ii) yards, feet, and inches

[Answers: a) i) 21 ft. ii) 252 in.
b) i) 5 ft. 2 in. ii) 1 yd. 2 ft. 2 in.]

When you convert a measurement from a larger unit to a smaller unit, do you expect the number of units to increase or decrease? Why?

There are 3 ft. in 1 yd. so, in *Example 1*, we multiply by 3 to convert a measurement in yards to a measurement in feet; this is one type of *proportional reasoning*.

Similarly, we use proportional reasoning when we divide by 12 to convert a measurement in inches to a measurement in feet.

We also use proportional reasoning when we write then solve a proportion, as illustrated on the next page.

Example 2 Solving a Problem Involving Converting between Units

Anne is framing a picture.
The perimeter of the framed picture will be 136 in.

a) What will be the perimeter of the framed picture in feet and inches?

b) The framing material is sold by the foot. It costs $1.89/ft. What will be the cost of material before taxes?

SOLUTIONS

a) Method 1

To convert inches to feet, divide by 12.

$$136 \text{ in.} = \frac{136}{12} \text{ ft.}$$

$$136 \text{ in.} = 11\frac{4}{12} \text{ ft.}$$

So, 136 in. = 11 ft. 4 in.

The perimeter of the framed picture will be 11 ft. 4 in.

Method 2

Use a proportion. Let x represent the length in feet.

The ratio of x feet to 136 in. is equal to the ratio of 1 ft. to 12 in. Write a proportion.

$$\frac{x}{136} = \frac{1}{12}$$ Multiply each side by 136.

$$136\left(\frac{x}{136}\right) = 136\left(\frac{1}{12}\right)$$

$$x = \frac{136}{12}$$

$$x = 11\frac{4}{12}$$

$11\frac{4}{12}$ ft. is 11 ft. 4 in.

The perimeter of the framed picture will be 11 ft. 4 in.

b) The perimeter of the framed picture is greater than 11 ft., so Anne must buy 12 ft. of framing material.

The cost, C, is:
$C = 12(\$1.89)$
$C = \$22.68$

Before taxes, the material will cost $22.68.

CHECK YOUR UNDERSTANDING

2. Ben buys baseboard for a bedroom. The perimeter of the bedroom, excluding closets and doorway, is 37 ft.

a) What length of baseboard is needed, in yards and feet?

b) The baseboard material is sold by the yard. It costs $5.99/yd. What is the cost of material before taxes?

[Answers: a) 12 yd. 1 ft. b) $77.87]

How could you use mental math and estimation to check that your answer is reasonable?

We can use **unit analysis** to verify a conversion between units.

Unit analysis is one method of verifying that the units in a conversion are correct.

For *Example 2*, we can write the relationship between feet and inches as a fraction in two ways: $\frac{1 \text{ ft.}}{12 \text{ in.}}$ and $\frac{12 \text{ in.}}{1 \text{ ft.}}$

These fractions are *conversion factors*. Each fraction is equal to 1, so we can multiply any number by the fraction and not alter its value.

Since we are converting 136 in. to feet, we use the conversion factor with feet in the numerator. We write:

$$136 \text{ in.} \times \frac{1 \text{ ft.}}{12 \text{ in.}} = \frac{136 \text{ in.}}{1} \times \frac{1 \text{ ft.}}{12 \text{ in.}}$$

Eliminate corresponding units.

$$= \frac{136 \cancel{\text{in.}}}{1} \times \frac{1 \text{ ft.}}{12 \cancel{\text{in.}}}$$

$$= \frac{136}{12} \text{ ft.}$$

$$= 11\frac{4}{12} \text{ ft.}$$

Since this measurement is equal to the measurement in *Example 2*, the conversion is verified.

Example 3 Solving a Problem Involving Two Unit Conversions

The school council has 6 yd. of fabric that will be cut into strips 5 in. wide to make decorative banners for the school dance.

a) How many banners can be made?

b) Use unit analysis to verify the conversions.

SOLUTION

a) Since the width of a banner is measured in inches, convert the length of the material to inches.
Convert 6 yd. to inches.

1 yd. = 3 ft.

6 yd. = 6(3 ft.)

6 yd. = 18 ft.

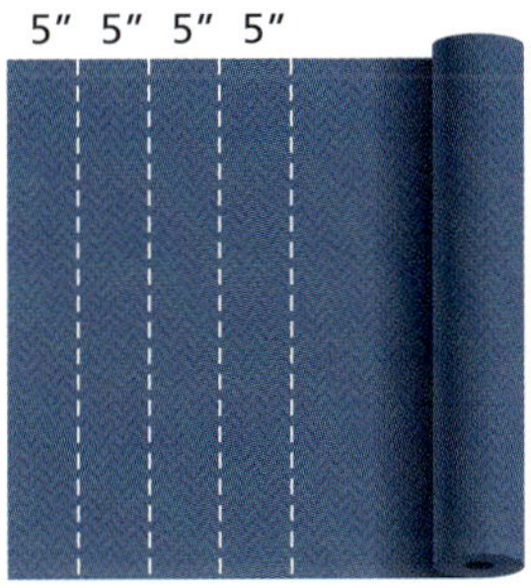

1 ft. = 12 in.

18 ft. = 18(12 in.)

18 ft. = 216 in.

(Solution continues.)

CHECK YOUR UNDERSTANDING

3. Tyrell has 4 yd. of cord to make friendship bracelets. Each bracelet needs 8 in. of cord.

a) How many bracelets can Tyrell make?

b) Use unit analysis to check the conversions.

[Answer: a) 18]

The number of banners is: $\frac{216}{5} = 43.2$

43 banners can be made.

b) To convert yards to inches, first convert yards to feet, then convert feet to inches.

Write a conversion factor for yards and feet, with feet in the numerator: $\frac{3 \text{ ft.}}{1 \text{ yd.}}$

Write a conversion factor for feet and inches, with inches in the numerator: $\frac{12 \text{ in.}}{1 \text{ ft.}}$

$$\text{Then, } 6 \text{ yd.} \times \frac{3 \text{ ft.}}{1 \text{ yd.}} \times \frac{12 \text{ in.}}{1 \text{ ft.}} = \frac{6 \cancel{\text{yd.}}}{1} \times \frac{3 \cancel{\text{ft.}}}{1 \cancel{\text{yd.}}} \times \frac{12 \text{ in.}}{1 \cancel{\text{ft.}}}$$

$$= (6 \times 3 \times 12) \text{ in.}$$

$$= 216 \text{ in.}$$

Since this measurement is equal to the measurement in part a, the conversion is verified.

What conversion factor could you use to convert the units in one step?

Example 4 Solving a Problem Involving Scale Diagrams

A map of Alaska has a scale of 1:4 750 000. The distance on the map between Paxson and the Canadian border is $3\frac{11}{16}$ in. What is this distance to the nearest mile?

SOLUTION

The map scale is 1 in. represents 4 750 000 in.

$3\frac{11}{16}$ in. represents

$3\frac{11}{16}(4\,750\,000 \text{ in.}) = 17\,515\,625 \text{ in.}$

Divide by 12 to convert 17 515 625 in. to feet:

$$\frac{17\,515\,625}{12} = 1\,459\,635.417\ldots$$

Divide by 5280 to convert 1 459 635.417… ft. to miles:

$$\frac{1\,459\,635.417\ldots}{5280} = 276.446\ldots$$

The distance between Paxson and the Canadian border is approximately 276 mi.

CHECK YOUR UNDERSTANDING

4. On the map with a scale of 1:4 750 000, the distance between Seward and Anchorage in Alaska is $1\frac{3}{4}$ in. What is the distance between these two towns to the nearest mile?

[Answer: approximately 131 mi.]

Discuss the Ideas

1. Why is it important to measure with standard units? Give an example.

2. When might you use referents to estimate a measure?

Exercises

A

3. Which imperial unit is the most appropriate unit to measure each item? Justify your choice.
   a) the height of your desk
   b) the thickness of a mattress
   c) the width of a car
   d) the length of a flat panel TV
   e) the distance from the school to your home

4. a) Which imperial unit is most appropriate to measure the length of a piece of notepaper? Why?
   b) Use a referent to estimate the length of a piece of notepaper. Explain the process. Measure to check your estimate.

5. a) Which imperial unit is most appropriate to measure the height of the door in your classroom? Why?
   b) Use a referent to estimate the height of the door. Explain the process. Measure to check your estimate.

6. Estimate each measurement in imperial units.
   a) the length of your arm from wrist to elbow
   b) the height of your classroom
   c) the distance from your classroom to the school office
   d) the perimeter of your school grounds

7. Convert:
   a) 3 ft. to inches
   b) 63 yd. to feet
   c) 48 in. to feet

B

8. Convert:
   a) 2 mi. to feet
   b) 574 in. to yards, feet, and inches
   c) 7390 ft. to miles, yards, and feet

9. Explain how to convert a measurement of 165 in. to a measurement in yards, feet, and inches.

10. Carolyn is building a pen for her dog. The perimeter of the pen is 52 ft.
    a) Explain how you can use a proportion to convert the perimeter to yards and feet.
    b) The fencing material is sold by the yard. It costs \$10.99/yd. What is the cost of material before taxes?

11. David has 10 yd. of material that he will cut into strips 15 in. wide to make mats.
    a) How many mats can David make?
    b) Use unit analysis to verify the conversions.

12. Pierre-Marc converted 21 ft. 9 in. into yards, feet, and inches. His answer was 7 yd. 1 ft. 6 in. Is his answer correct? If your answer is no, show the correct conversion.

13. In 2008, Sandy Allen and Leonid Stadnyk were the world's tallest living woman and man. Their respective heights are 7 ft. 7 in. and 8 ft. 5 in. How many inches shorter is Sandy than Leonid?

14. A wallpaper border is to be pasted halfway up the wall around a child's bedroom.

a) What is the total length of border needed?

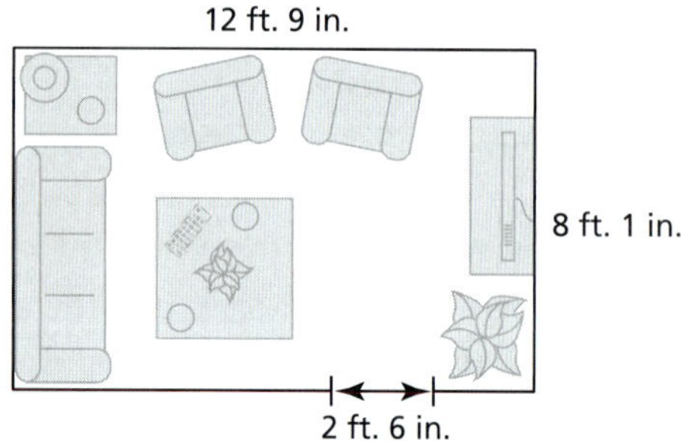

b) The border is purchased in 12-ft. rolls. How many rolls are required?

c) Each roll of border costs $12.49. How much will the border cost, before taxes?

15. a) In a basement renovation, the contractor measured the length of a wall in a square room as 18 ft. 4 in. The width of the doorway is 3 ft. The contractor plans to place wood trim along the bottom of each wall. The trim costs $1.69/ft. What is the cost of the trim for the room, before taxes?

b) The contractor uses the same trim around this window.

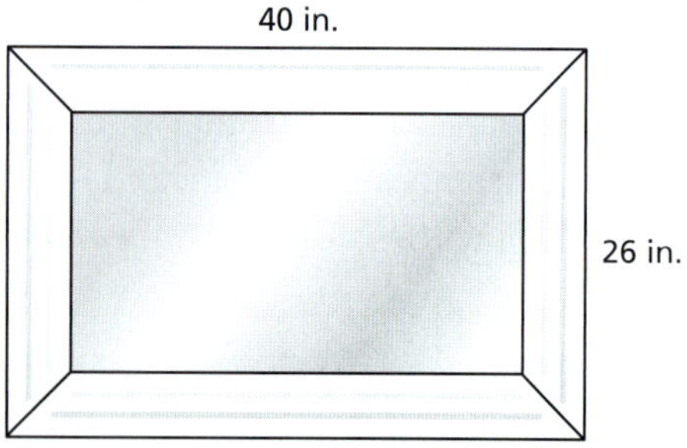

Determine the cost of the trim for the window, before taxes.

16. A 3-D puzzle of the Eiffel Tower has a scale of 1:360. In the puzzle, the tower is $35\frac{2}{5}$ in. tall. What is the height of the Eiffel Tower in feet?

17. A map of Québec has a scale of 1:1 500 000. On the map, the distance between Trois-Rivières and Québec City is $2\frac{5}{8}$ in. What is the distance between these cities to the nearest mile?

18. A gardener recommends planting tulip bulbs 8 in. apart. Erica follows the gardener's advice and plants tulips beside her 18-ft. sidewalk. How many tulip bulbs will Erica need?

C

19. A student can walk 30 ft. in 10 s. How far could she walk in 1 h? Write the answer in miles and yards.

20. On a map of British Columbia and Alaska, the distance between Prince Rupert, B.C., and Ketchikan, AK, is $2\frac{9}{16}$ in. The actual distance between these towns is 95 mi. What is the map scale, to the nearest thousand?

21. Twenty reams of paper form a stack 40 in. high. Each ream costs $3.

a) What is the value of a stack that has the same height as Mount Logan, which is 19 500 ft. high?

b) How can you use mental math and estimation to determine if your answer is reasonable?

22. Five toonies form a stack that is $\frac{2}{5}$ in. high. What is the approximate value of a stack of toonies that spans the 100 mi. between Plamondon and Bonnyville, AB?

Reflect

How would you use a referent to estimate a length? How do you determine the appropriate imperial unit to record the measure of that length?

MATH LAB

1.2 Measuring Length and Distance

LESSON FOCUS

Use measuring instruments and personal strategies to determine linear measures.

Make Connections

How do you think the person who makes these glass vases checks that the dimensions of each vase are correct?

Construct Understanding

TRY THIS

Work with a partner.

You will need:

- rulers and measuring tapes in both SI and imperial measures, metre stick, and yard stick
- string
- calipers
- 3 objects with different sizes and shapes, such as a can, a bottle, an eraser, a paper clip, a sunflower seed, a desk

How can you measure the perimeter of a can without using the formula for the circumference of a circle?

Repeat the following steps for each object:

A. Sketch each object.
Use a referent to estimate all possible linear measures of the object in:

- imperial units
- SI units

Record these estimates on the sketch.
Justify your choice of units.

B. Choose appropriate measuring instruments. Use both imperial units and SI units to measure the object in as many ways as you can. Record the measurements on the sketch.

C. Describe any problems you had making the measurements and the strategies you used to solve the problems.

THE WORLD OF MATH

Historical Moment: The Origin of the Inch

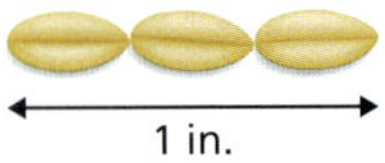

The word *inch* may be derived from the Latin word *uncia* meaning "one-twelfth part," referring to one-twelfth the length of a man's foot. Alternatively, the Anglo-Saxon term *inch* was defined as the length of 3 corns of barley. King David I of Scotland described an *ynche* as the width of a man's thumb at the base of the nail; this is supported by the similarity of the word "inch" to the word "thumb" in several languages. For example, in French, *pouce* means inch and also means thumb. In Swedish, *tum* is inch and *tumme* is thumb.

Assess Your Understanding

1. Describe a referent you could use for each SI measure.
   a) 1 m b) 1 cm c) 1 mm
2. What referent could you use for 1 km?
3. What are the limitations of the use of calipers?
4. Describe a strategy you would use to estimate and then measure each length.
   a) the circumference of a cylindrical garbage can
   b) the thickness of your hand
   c) the distance between your home and the closest store
   d) the distance between two cities on a map
   e) the distance around an oval running track
   f) the length of an eyelash
5. What referents would you use to estimate the length, in both SI units and imperial units, of the Lion's Gate Bridge in Vancouver, B.C.? Explain how you could measure the length in both units.

6. Look around the classroom.
   a) Identify objects that were built using imperial measures. Justify your choice.
   b) Identify objects that were built using SI measures. Justify your choice.

1.3 Relating SI and Imperial Units

LESSON FOCUS

Convert measurements between SI units and imperial units.

The driver of this solar powered car was at a Canada/U.S. border crossing during the North American Solar Challenge in July 2005.

Make Connections

Two cars are driven in opposite directions from a Canada/United States border crossing.

In one hour, Hana drove 62 mi. south while Farrin drove 98 km north.

How could you determine which vehicle travelled farther from the border?

Construct Understanding

TRY THIS

Work on your own.

You will need a ruler, metre stick, or measuring tape that has both SI and imperial units.

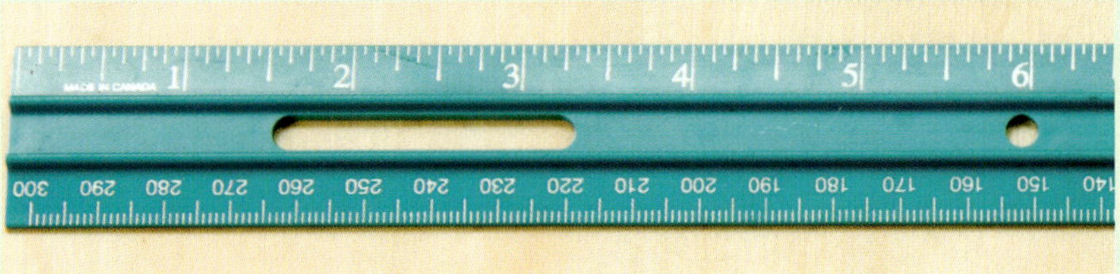

A. Look at the SI and imperial scales on the ruler.
Estimate the length of 1 in. to the nearest tenth of a centimetre.
Estimate the length of 1 cm to the nearest fraction of an inch.

B. Copy this table. Use the results from Step A to complete the table. In the first column, write the numbers as decimals to the nearest tenth. In the second column, write the numbers as fractions or mixed numbers.

Imperial Units to SI Units	SI Units to Imperial Units
1 in. ≐ cm	1 cm ≐ in.
1 ft. ≐ cm	1 m ≐ in. 1 m ≐ ft. in. 1 m ≐ yd. ft. in.
1 yd. ≐ cm 1 yd. ≐ m	1 km ≐ yd.
1 mi. ≐ m	

C. Choose 3 different objects in the classroom. For each object:

- Measure its length in SI units.
- Use the completed table in Step B to write the measurement in imperial units.
- Check your answer by measuring the length in imperial units.

D. Choose 3 more objects in the classroom. For each object:

- Measure its length in imperial units.
- Use the completed table in Step B to write the measurement in SI units.
- Check your answer by measuring the length in SI units.

Each measurement in the imperial system relates to a corresponding measurement in the SI system.

This table shows some approximate relationships between imperial units and SI units.

SI Units to Imperial Units	Imperial Units to SI Units
$1 \text{ mm} \doteq \frac{4}{100}$ in.	1 in. $\doteq 2.5$ cm
$1 \text{ cm} \doteq \frac{4}{10}$ in.	1 ft. $\doteq 30$ cm 1 ft. $\doteq 0.3$ m
$1 \text{ m} \doteq 39$ in. $1 \text{ m} \doteq 3\frac{1}{4}$ ft.	1 yd. $\doteq 90$ cm 1 yd. $\doteq 0.9$ m
$1 \text{ km} \doteq \frac{6}{10}$ mi.	1 mi. $\doteq 1.6$ km

Some conversions are exact; for example,
1 in. = 2.54 cm
1 yd. = 91.44 cm

We can use the data in the table above to convert between SI and imperial units of measure.

Example 1 Converting from Metres to Feet

A bowling lane is approximately 19 m long.

What is this measurement to the nearest foot?

SOLUTION

From the table, $1 \text{ m} \doteq 3\frac{1}{4}$ ft.

$$\text{So, } 19 \text{ m} \doteq 19(3\tfrac{1}{4} \text{ ft.})$$

$$19 \text{ m} \doteq 19\left(\frac{13}{4}\right)\text{ft.}$$

$$19 \text{ m} \doteq \frac{247}{4} \text{ ft.}$$

$$19 \text{ m} \doteq 61\tfrac{3}{4} \text{ ft.}$$

A length of 19 m is approximately 62 ft.

CHECK YOUR UNDERSTANDING

1. A Canadian football field is approximately 59 m wide.

   What is this measurement to the nearest foot?

   [Answer: approximately 192 ft.]

Example 2 Converting between Miles and Kilometres

After meeting in Emerson, Manitoba, Hana drove 62 mi. south and Farrin drove 98 km north. Who drove farther?

SOLUTIONS

To compare the distances, convert one measurement so the units are the same.

Method 1

Convert the distance Hana drove from miles to kilometres.

$1 \text{ mi.} \doteq 1.6 \text{ km}$

So, $62 \text{ mi.} \doteq 62(1.6 \text{ km})$

$62 \text{ mi.} \doteq 99.2 \text{ km}$

Since $99.2 \text{ km} > 98 \text{ km}$, Hana drove farther.

Method 2

Convert the distance Farrin drove from kilometres to miles.

$1 \text{ km} \doteq \frac{6}{10} \text{ mi.}$

So, $98 \text{ km} \doteq 98\left(\frac{6}{10} \text{ mi.}\right)$

$98 \text{ km} \doteq 58\frac{8}{10} \text{ mi., or } 58\frac{4}{5} \text{ mi.}$

Since $58\frac{4}{5} < 62$, Hana drove farther.

CHECK YOUR UNDERSTANDING

2. After meeting in Osoyoos, B. C., Takoda drove 114 km north and Winona drove 68 mi. south. Who drove farther?

[Answer: Takoda]

THE WORLD OF MATH

Historical Moment: The Decimal System of Measurement

Gabriel Mouton, who lived in Lyons, France from 1618 – 1694, was the first person to propose a decimal system of measurement. In 1670, he created a unit equal to the length of 1° of longitude on Earth's surface. Mouton suggested that this unit, the *milliare*, be successively further divided by 10 to produce these units: *centuria*, *decuria*, *virga*, *virgula*, *decima*, *centesima*, and *millesima*.

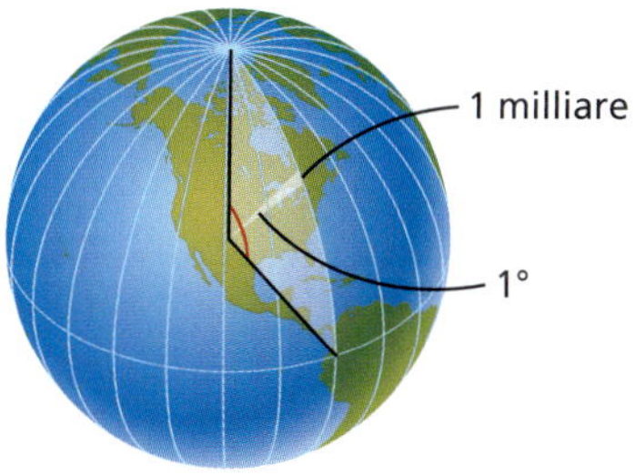

Mouton's ideas were studied at the time but it was more than 100 years later that the French Academy of Sciences adopted a decimal system of measurement. Mouton's milliare corresponds to 1 nautical mile that is used in the shipping and aviation industries today.

Example 3 Solving a Problem that Involves Unit Conversions

Alex is 6 ft. 2 in. tall. To list his height on his driver's license application, Alex needs to convert this measurement to centimetres.

a) What is Alex's height to the nearest centimetre?

b) Use mental math and estimation to justify that the answer is reasonable.

SOLUTION

a) Convert 6 ft. 2 in. to inches.

1 ft. = 12 in.

So, 6 ft. = 6(12 in.)

6 ft. = 72 in.

And, 6 ft. 2 in. = 72 in. + 2 in.

6 ft. 2 in. = 74 in.

Write a proportion to convert 74 in. to centimetres.
Let h represent Alex's height in centimetres.
The ratio of h centimetres to 74 in. is approximately equal to the ratio of 1 cm to $\frac{4}{10}$ in.

Write $\frac{4}{10}$ as 0.4.

$$\frac{h}{74} \doteq \frac{1}{0.4}$$

Multiply each side by 74.

$$74\left(\frac{h}{74}\right) \doteq 74\left(\frac{1}{0.4}\right)$$

$$h \doteq \frac{74}{0.4}$$

$$h \doteq 185$$

Alex is approximately 185 cm tall.

b) To check:

1 ft. $\doteq$ 30 cm

6 ft. $\doteq$ 180 cm

So, 6 ft. 2 in. $\doteq$ 185 cm is reasonable.

CHECK YOUR UNDERSTANDING

3. Nora knows that she is 5 ft. 7 in. tall.

a) What height in centimetres will she list on her driver's license application?

b) Use mental math and estimation to justify that the answer is reasonable.

[Answer: a) 168 cm]

What other strategy could you use to determine Alex's height in centimetres?

Example 4 Estimating and Calculating Using Unit Conversions

A truck driver knows that her semitrailer is 3.5 m high. The support beams of a bridge are 11 ft. 9 in. high. Will the vehicle fit under the bridge? Justify the answer.

SOLUTION

Write a proportion to convert 3.5 m to feet.

Let h represent the height of the vehicle in feet.

The ratio of h feet to 3.5 m is approximately equal to the ratio of 1 ft. to 0.3 m.

$$\frac{h}{3.5} \doteq \frac{1}{0.3}$$

Multiply each side by 3.5.

$$3.5\left(\frac{h}{3.5}\right) \doteq 3.5\left(\frac{1}{0.3}\right)$$

$$h \doteq \frac{3.5}{0.3}$$

$$h \doteq 11.\overline{6}, \text{ or } 11\frac{2}{3}$$

The vehicle is approximately $11\frac{2}{3}$ ft., or 11 ft. 8 in. high; so it should fit under the bridge.

This height is an estimate that is very close to the bridge height. To be sure the vehicle will fit, calculate an exact conversion. Convert the height of the vehicle in centimetres to inches.

Use the conversion: 2.54 cm = 1 in.
So,

$$350 \text{ cm} = \frac{350}{2.54} \text{ in.}$$

Converting 3.5 m to 350 cm

$$350 \text{ cm} = 137.7952\ldots \text{ in.}$$

Convert inches to feet.

$$350 \text{ cm} = \frac{137.7952\ldots}{12} \text{ ft.}$$

$$350 \text{ cm} = 11.4829\ldots \text{ ft.}$$

This measurement is a little less than $11\frac{1}{2}$ ft. or 11 ft. 6 in., so the vehicle will fit under the bridge.

CHECK YOUR UNDERSTANDING

4. A truck driver knows that his load is 15 ft. wide. Regulations along his route state that any load over 4.3 m wide must have wide-load markers and an escort with flashing lights. Does this vehicle need wide-load markers? Justify your answer.

[Answer: Yes, the load is approximately 4.6 m wide.]

Discuss the Ideas

1. When might you want to convert:
   - a measurement in SI units to imperial units?
   - a measurement in imperial units to SI units?
2. What relationships can help you check that an answer is reasonable when you convert between systems of measurement?
3. When you use unit analysis to verify an answer, how do you decide which conversion factor to use?

Exercises

A

4. Convert each measurement. Answer to the nearest tenth.
   a) 16 in. to centimetres
   b) 4 ft. to metres
   c) 5 yd. to metres
   d) 1650 yd. to kilometres
   e) 6 mi. to kilometres
   f) 2 in. to millimetres
5. Convert each measurement.
   a) 25 mm to the nearest inch
   b) 2.5 m to the nearest foot
   c) 10 m to the nearest yard
   d) 150 km to the nearest mile
6. Convert each measurement. Answer to the nearest tenth.
   a) 1 ft. 10 in. to centimetres
   b) 2 yd. 2 ft. 5 in. to centimetres
   c) 10 yd. 1 ft. 7 in. to metres

B

7. a) Convert each measurement.
      i) 75 cm to feet and the nearest inch
      ii) 274 cm to yards, feet, and the nearest inch
      iii) 10 000 m to the nearest mile
   b) Use mental math and estimation to justify that each answer in part a is reasonable.
8. The dimensions of a lacrosse field are 110 yd. by 60 yd. What are these dimensions to the nearest tenth of a metre?
9. The Fraser River is approximately 1375 km long. The Tennessee River is approximately 886 mi. long. Which river is longer? Justify your answer.
10. On a road trip in Montana, USA, Elise sees this road sign:

Elise tests the accuracy of her car's odometer and tracks the distance she drove from that sign to Helena's city limits. Her odometer showed 142 km. Is the odometer accurate? Explain.

11. A retail fabric store advertises a storewide sale. It lists a certain material for \$0.89/yd. A fabric warehouse is selling the same material for \$0.93/m.
    a) Which store has the better price?
    b) Use mental math and estimation to justify that the answer is reasonable.
12. In preparation for les Jeux de la francophonie canadienne, Jean-Luc ran two laps around a 400-yd. track. Michael did seven 110-m hurdle practice races.
    a) Who ran farther?
    b) Use unit analysis to verify the conversion.

13. The tallest structure in Canada is the CN Tower in Toronto. It is 553.3 m tall. The tallest structure in the United States is the Willis Tower, previously known as the Sears Tower, in Chicago. It is 1451 ft. tall.

a) Determine the height of the CN Tower in feet and the height of the Willis Tower in metres.

b) Which structure is taller? Explain how you know.

c) Determine the difference in the heights of the structures, in metres and to the nearest foot.

14. On a lease site, an oil company determined that there was an oil reserve 1400 m beneath the surface. While the crew drilled, it lined the hole with casing. Each 32-ft. piece of casing was welded to the previous piece to prevent the hole from collapsing. How many sections of casing did the crew need to reach the oil reserve?

C

15. The rim of a basketball net is mounted 10 ft. off the ground. A basketball player has a maximum reach of 2.5 m. How high, in inches, does the player need to jump to reach 6 in. above the rim?

16. An electrician was hired to run the wires for a surround-sound stereo speaker system. She purchased 2 rolls of 14-gauge speaker wire. Each roll contains 4 m of wire. For each of 2 speakers, 2 ft. of wire are required. For each of the other 2 speakers, 11 ft. of wire are required. Will the electrician have enough wire? If your answer is no, what length of wire in centimetres will she need? If your answer is yes, what length of wire in centimetres will be left over?

17. A real-estate developer purchased a 30-m by 50-m plot of land to create a mobile home park. The developer sketched this plan:

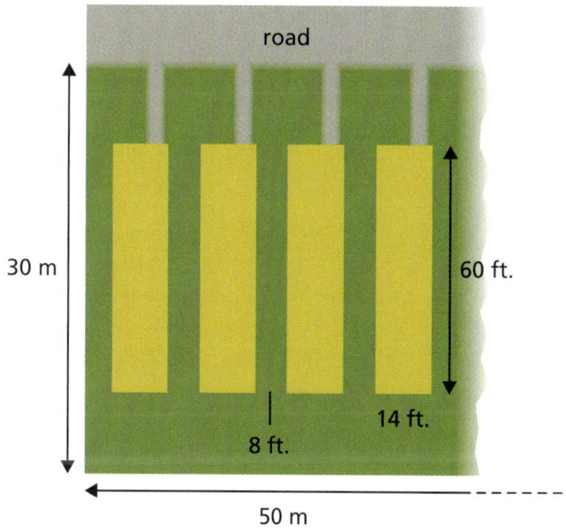

What is the maximum number of homes the developer can fit on this land?

18. The imperial unit to measure an area of land is the *acre*. During the initial agricultural expansion of the western provinces, the Canadian government offered 160 acres of land free to settlers who were willing to immigrate to Canada. Today, Canada uses the *hectare* to measure land area:

1 hectare $\doteq$ 2.471 acres

a) How many hectares did each settler receive?

b) One hundred sixty acres is a square with a side length of one-half a mile. How many hectares are in one square mile?

Reflect What strategies do you know for converting a measure in imperial units to a measure in SI units? Include examples in your explanation.

CHECKPOINT 1

Connections

Imperial Units of Length

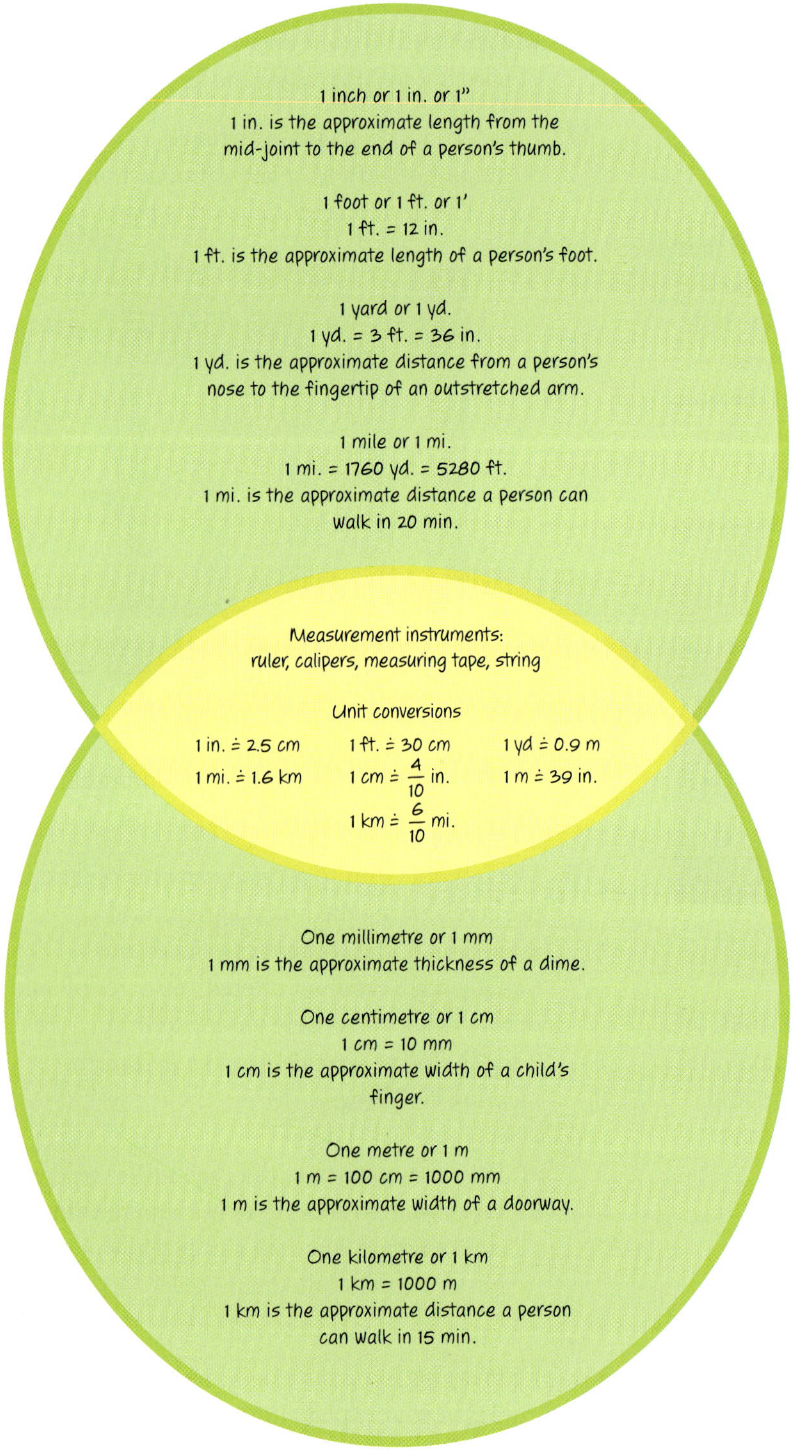

SI Units of Length

Concept Development

- **In Lesson 1.1**
  - You developed **referents** for units of linear measure in the **imperial system**.
  - You **converted between units** within the imperial system.
  - You used conversion factors and **proportional reasoning** to solve problems.
  - You used **unit analysis** to verify conversions.

- **In Lesson 1.2**
  - You **estimated and measured** dimensions of objects using both the **imperial** and **SI systems.**
  - You developed **personal strategies** and used measuring instruments to **determine linear measurements.**

- **In Lesson 1.3**
  - You established approximate **relationships between SI and imperial units** of length.
  - You used conversion factors and **proportional reasoning** to solve problems.
  - You used **unit analysis** to verify conversions.

Assess Your Understanding

1.1

1. Use imperial units to estimate each measure. State the referent you used in each case.
   a) the distance from your elbow to your wrist
   b) the length of a cell phone
   c) the width of a twin bed
   d) the height of the ceiling in the gymnasium

2. Choose the most appropriate imperial unit, then measure the items in question 1 parts a and b.

3. Convert:
   a) 80 ft. to yards and feet
   b) 3 mi. to yards
   c) 2 yd. 1 ft. to inches

4. Lindsay is 51 in. tall. Sidney is 3 ft. 11 in. tall. Who is shorter? How do you know?

1.2

5. Measure each item in both SI and imperial units:
   a) the perimeter of your classroom
   b) the width of a car
   c) the circumference of a dinner plate

6. Describe how you would determine the diameter of a marble. State the measuring instrument and the unit you would use.

1.3

7. Convert each measurement.
   a) 13 m to yards and the nearest foot
   b) 4 ft. to the nearest centimetre
   c) 2 km to miles and the nearest yard
   d) 25 000 cm to yards, feet, and the nearest inch
   e) 13 000 in. to the nearest tenth of a metre
   f) 1750 mm to feet and the nearest inch

8. A thin strip of wood laminate is to be glued to the edges of a table. The length of laminate required is equal to the perimeter of the table, which has dimensions 30 cm by 115 cm. The laminate can only be bought in lengths of whole numbers of feet. What length of laminate is needed?

1.4 Surface Areas of Right Pyramids and Right Cones

LESSON FOCUS

Solve problems involving the surface areas of right pyramids and right cones.

Make Connections

The ancient pyramids at Giza, Egypt, were built about 4500 years ago.

The pyramid above has a square base with a side length of 755 feet. The original height of the pyramid was 481 feet. Archeologists believe that the pyramid was once covered with a white limestone casing. How could you calculate the area that was once covered with limestone?

Construct Understanding

TRY THIS

Work in a group.

You will need a right pyramid and a ruler with SI units and imperial units.
You may need 1-cm grid paper and 1-in. grid paper.
One-half of the group will use imperial units and the other half will use SI units.

A. Estimate the surface area of the pyramid, including its base. Describe your strategy for estimating.

B. Determine the surface area of the pyramid. Describe the measurements you made and the strategies you used.

C. Compare your strategies with those of another group that measured a different type of pyramid. Did the strategy depend on the type of pyramid? Explain.

We use exponents when we write units for area; for example, five square inches is 5 in.^{2} and five square centimetres is 5 cm^2.

A **right pyramid** is a 3-dimensional object that has triangular faces and a base that is a polygon. The shape of the base determines the name of the pyramid. The triangular faces meet at a point called the **apex**. The *height* of the pyramid is the perpendicular distance from the apex to the centre of the base.

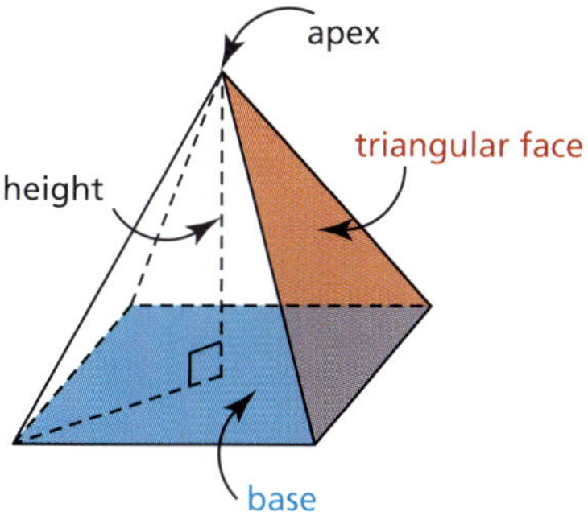

When the base of a right pyramid is a regular polygon, the triangular faces are congruent. Then the **slant height** of the right pyramid is the height of a triangular face.

A *tetrahedron* is a triangular pyramid.

A *regular tetrahedron* has 4 congruent equilateral triangular faces.

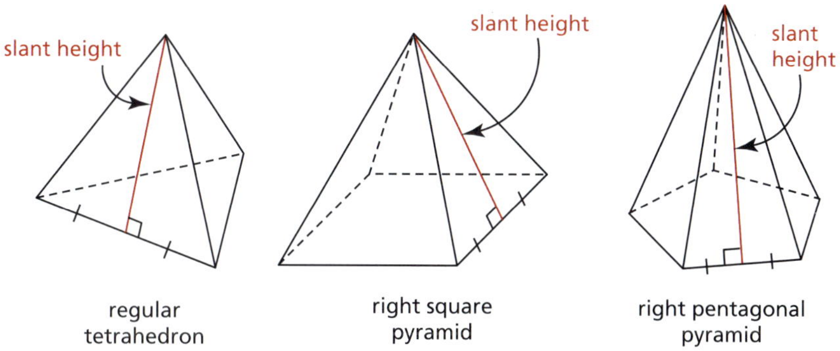

The surface area of a right pyramid is the sum of the areas of the triangular faces and the base.

This right square pyramid has a slant height of 10 cm and a base side length of 8 cm.

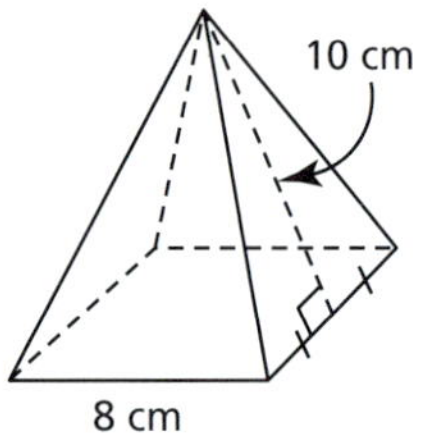

This net shows the faces and base of the pyramid.

The area, A, of a triangle with base, b, and height, h, is:

$A = \frac{1}{2}bh$

The area, A, of each triangular face is:

$A = \frac{1}{2}(8)(10)$

$A = 40$

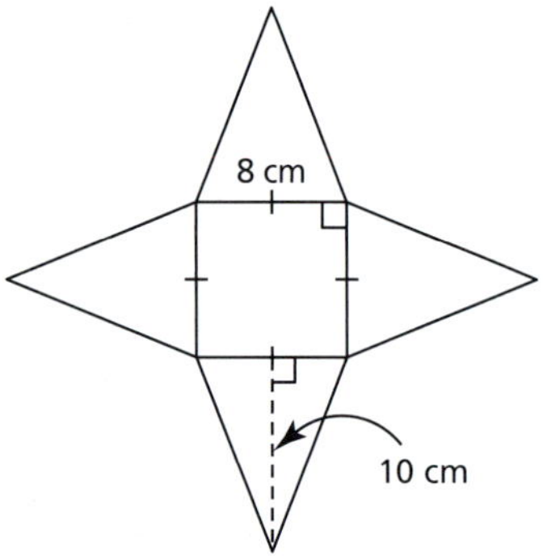

The area, B, of the base is:

$B = (8)(8)$

$B = 64$

So, the surface area, SA, of the pyramid is:

$SA = 4A + B$

$SA = 4(40) + 64$

$SA = 224$

The surface area of the pyramid is 224 cm^2.

Example 1 Determining the Surface Area of a Regular Tetrahedron Given Its Slant Height

Jeanne-Marie measured then recorded the lengths of the edges and slant height of this regular tetrahedron. What is its surface area to the nearest square centimetre?

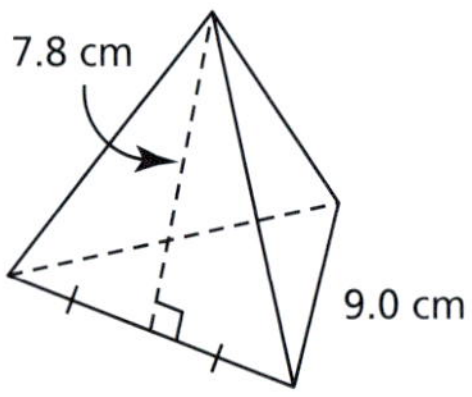

SOLUTION

The regular tetrahedron has 4 congruent faces. Each face is a triangle with base 9.0 cm and height 7.8 cm.

The area, A, of each face is:

$A = \frac{1}{2}(9.0 \text{ cm})(7.8 \text{ cm})$

The surface area, SA, is:

$SA = 4\left(\frac{1}{2}\right)(9.0 \text{ cm})(7.8 \text{ cm})$

$SA = 140.4 \text{ cm}^2$

The surface area of the tetrahedron is approximately 140 cm^2.

CHECK YOUR UNDERSTANDING

1. Calculate the surface area of this regular tetrahedron to the nearest square metre.

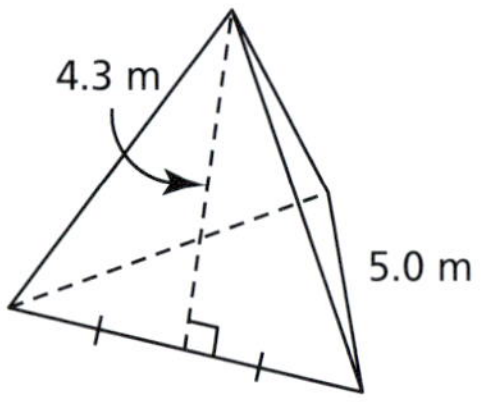

[Answer: 43 m^2]

Example 2 Determining the Surface Area of a Right Rectangular Pyramid

A right rectangular pyramid has base dimensions 8 ft. by 10 ft., and a height of 16 ft. Calculate the surface area of the pyramid to the nearest square foot.

SOLUTION

There are 4 triangular faces and a rectangular base.
Sketch the pyramid and label its vertices. Opposite triangular faces are congruent.
Draw the heights on two adjacent triangles.

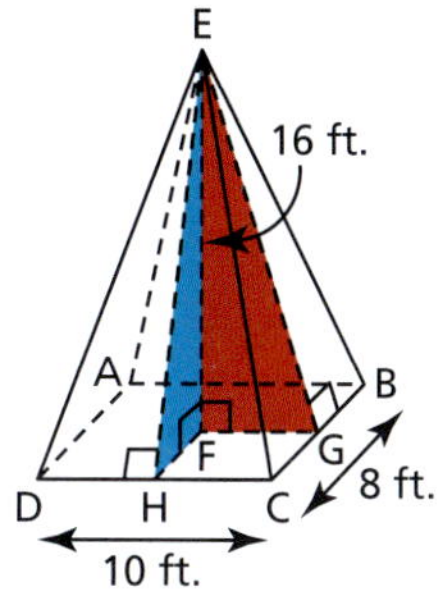

In $\triangle$EFH, FH is $\frac{1}{2}$ the length of BC, so FH is 4 ft.

EF is the height of the pyramid, which is 16 ft.

Use the Pythagorean Theorem in right $\triangle$EFH.

$$\text{EH}^2 = \text{EF}^2 + \text{FH}^2$$

$$\text{EH}^2 = 16^2 + 4^2$$

$$\text{EH}^2 = 272$$

$$\text{EH} = \sqrt{272}$$

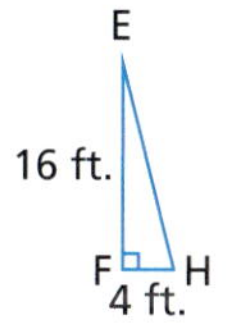

Area, A, of $\triangle$EDC is:

$$A = \frac{1}{2}(10)(\sqrt{272})$$

$$A = 5(\sqrt{272})$$

Since $\triangle$EDC and $\triangle$EAB are congruent, the area of $\triangle$EAB is $5(\sqrt{272})$.

In $\triangle$EFG, FG is $\frac{1}{2}$ the length of DC, so FG is 5 ft.
Use the Pythagorean Theorem in right $\triangle$EFG.

$$\text{GE}^2 = \text{EF}^2 + \text{FG}^2$$

$$\text{GE}^2 = 16^2 + 5^2$$

$$\text{GE}^2 = 281$$

$$\text{GE} = \sqrt{281}$$

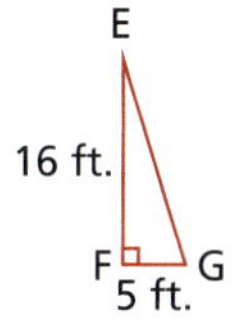

Area, A, of $\triangle$EBC is:

$$A = \frac{1}{2}(8)(\sqrt{281})$$

$$A = 4(\sqrt{281})$$

(Solution continues.)

CHECK YOUR UNDERSTANDING

2. A right rectangular pyramid has base dimensions 4 m by 6 m, and a height of 8 m. Calculate the surface area of the pyramid to the nearest square metre.

[Answer: approximately 108 m^2]

What is an advantage of using EH = $\sqrt{272}$ and GE = $\sqrt{281}$, instead of writing these square roots as decimals?

Since $\triangle$EBC and $\triangle$EAD are congruent, the area of $\triangle$EAD is $4(\sqrt{281})$.

Area, B, of the base of the pyramid is:
$B = (8)(10)$
$B = 80$

Each of two triangles has area $5(\sqrt{272})$, and each of the other two triangles has area $4(\sqrt{281})$.

Surface area, SA, of the pyramid is:
$SA = 2(5)(\sqrt{272}) + 2(4)(\sqrt{281}) + 80$

$SA = 379.0286\ldots$
The surface area of the pyramid is approximately 379 square feet.

We can determine a formula for the surface area of any right pyramid with a regular polygon base. Consider this right square pyramid. Each triangular face has base ℓ and height s.

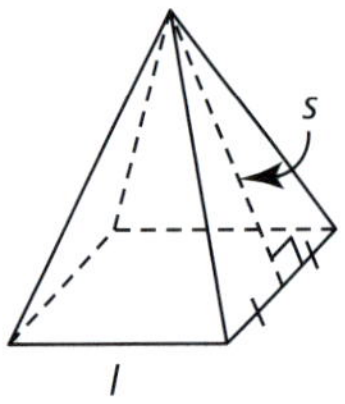

The area, A, of each triangular face is:

$A = \frac{1}{2}(\text{base})(\text{height})$

$A = \frac{1}{2}\ell s$

So, the area of the 4 triangular faces is:

$4\left(\frac{1}{2}\ell s\right) = 4\left(\frac{1}{2}\right)\ell s$ Rearrange the numbers and variables.

$= \left(\frac{1}{2}s\right)(4\ell)$

The area of the triangular faces of a pyramid is called the **lateral area**, denoted A_L.

We use A_L to represent the lateral area so it is not confused with A, which represents the area of a triangular face.

$A_L = \left(\frac{1}{2}s\right)(4\ell)$

The term 4ℓ is the perimeter of the base of the pyramid, so

Surface area of the pyramid $= (\frac{1}{2}$ slant height)(perimeter of base) + base area

Since any right pyramid with a regular polygon base has congruent triangular faces, the same formula is true for any of these pyramids.

Surface Area of a Right Pyramid with a Regular Polygon Base

For a right pyramid with a regular polygon base and slant height s,

Surface area $= \frac{1}{2}s(\text{perimeter of base}) + (\text{base area})$

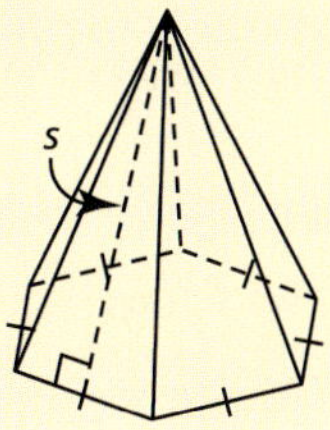

A right circular cone is usually called a **right cone**.

A *right circular cone* is a 3-dimensional object that has a circular base and a curved surface. The *height* of the cone is the perpendicular distance from the apex to the base. The *slant height* of the cone is the shortest distance on the curved surface between the apex and a point on the circumference of the base.

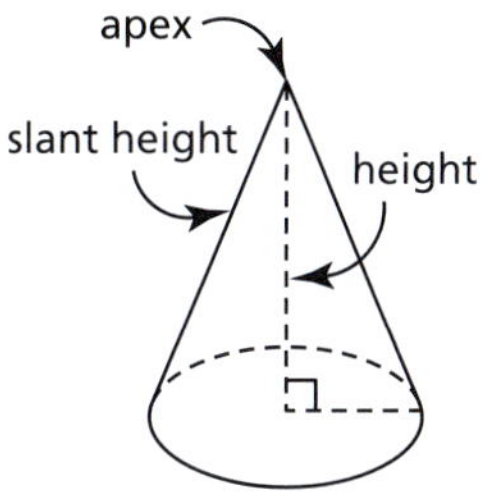

One way to derive a formula for the surface area of a right cone is to consider the surface area of a right pyramid with a regular polygon base. Visualize the pyramid as the number of sides of the base increases.

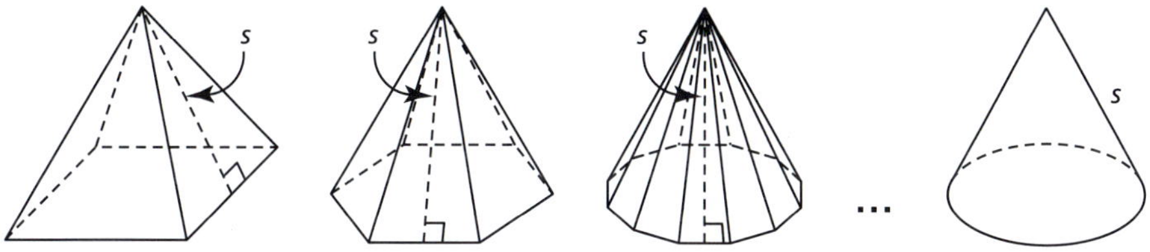

The number of triangular faces increases. The lateral area of the right pyramid approaches the lateral area of a right cone.

Lateral area of a right pyramid $= \frac{1}{2}s(\text{perimeter of base})$

For a right cone, the perimeter of the base is the circumference of the circle.

So, for a right cone with slant height s and base radius r:

Lateral area $= \frac{1}{2}s(\text{perimeter of base})$

Lateral area $= \frac{1}{2}s(\text{circumference of base})$

$A_L = \frac{1}{2}s(2\pi r)$

$A_L = \pi rs$

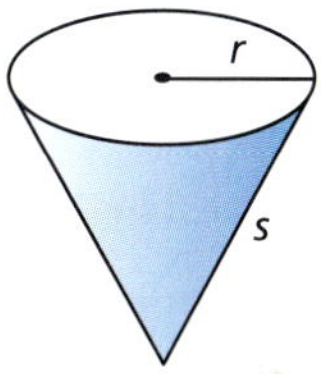

Surface Area of a Right Cone

Surface area = lateral area + base area

For a right cone with slant height s and base radius r:

$SA = \pi rs + \pi r^2$

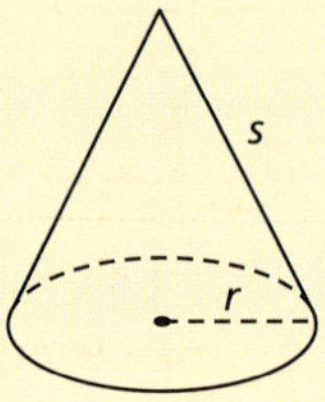

Example 3 Determining the Surface Area of a Right Cone

A right cone has a base radius of 2 ft. and a height of 7 ft. Calculate the surface area of this cone to the nearest square foot.

SOLUTION

Sketch a diagram.

Let s represent the slant height.

Visualize cutting the cone in half through a diameter of its base. This produces an isosceles triangle with a base that is equal to the diameter of the cone and a height that is equal to the height of the cone.

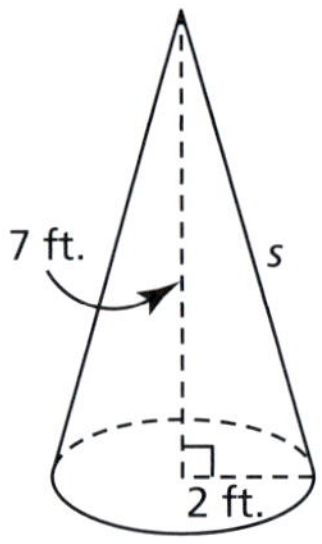

Use the Pythagorean Theorem in right △ACD.

$s^2 = 7^2 + 2^2$

$s^2 = 49 + 4$

$s^2 = 53$

$s = \sqrt{53}$

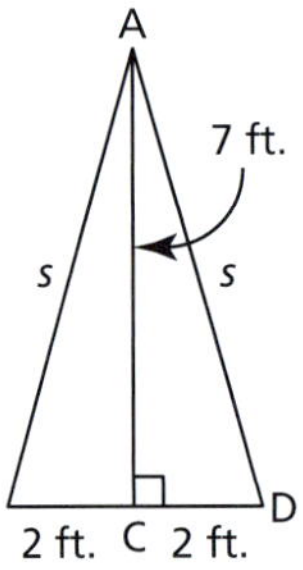

Use the formula for the surface area of a right cone:

$SA = \pi rs + \pi r^2$ Substitute: $r = 2$, $s = \sqrt{53}$

$SA = \pi(2)(\sqrt{53}) + \pi(2)^2$

$SA = 58.3086\ldots$

The surface area of the cone is approximately 58 square feet.

CHECK YOUR UNDERSTANDING

3. A right cone has a base radius of 4 m and a height of 10 m. Calculate the surface area of this cone to the nearest square metre.

[Answer: approximately 186 m^2]

In *Example 3*, which part of the formula represents the lateral area of the cone? How do you know?

We can use the formula for surface area to determine unknown measurements.

Example 4 Determining an Unknown Measurement

The lateral area of a cone is 220 cm^2. The diameter of the cone is 10 cm. Determine the height of the cone to the nearest tenth of a centimetre.

SOLUTION

Sketch a diagram.

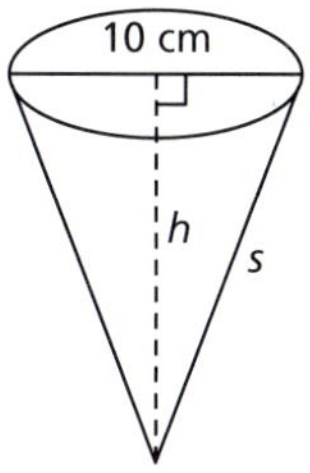

Let h represent the height of the cone and s the slant height.

The radius of the cone is 5 cm.

Use the formula for the lateral area, A_L, of the cone and solve for s.

$A_L = \pi rs$ Substitute: $A_L = 220$ and $r = 5$

$220 = \pi(5)s$ Divide both sides of the equation by 5π.

$\frac{220}{5\pi} = \frac{5\pi s}{5\pi}$

$s = \frac{220}{5\pi}$

$s = 14.0056\ldots$

To determine the height of the cone, use the Pythagorean Theorem in right $\triangle ABC$.

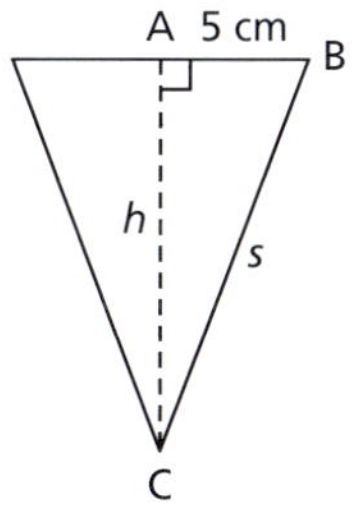

$5^2 + h^2 = s^2$ Substitute for s.

$25 + h^2 = (14.0056\ldots)^2$ Solve for h^2.

$h^2 = 196.1578\ldots - 25$

$h^2 = 171.1578\ldots$ Solve for h.

$h = \sqrt{171.1578\ldots}$

$h = 13.0827\ldots$

The height of the cone is approximately 13.1 cm.

CHECK YOUR UNDERSTANDING

4. A model of the Great Pyramid of Giza is constructed for a museum display. The surface area of the triangular faces is 3000 square inches. The side length of the base is 50 in. Determine the height of the model to a tenth of an inch.

[Answer: approximately $16\frac{3}{5}$ in.]

Discuss the Ideas

1. How do you determine the surface area of a right pyramid?
2. When you see a picture of a right pyramid with a regular polygon base, how do you identify its height and its slant height?
3. How is calculating the surface area of a right pyramid like calculating the surface area of a right cone? How is it different?

Exercises

A

4. Determine the lateral area of each right pyramid to the nearest square unit.

   a) square pyramid

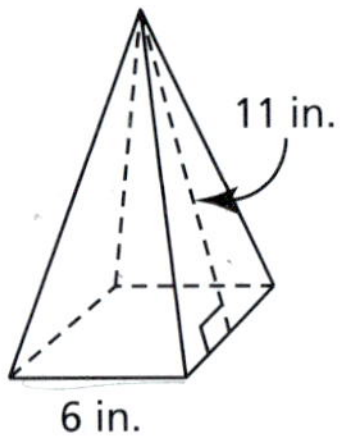

   b) regular tetrahedron

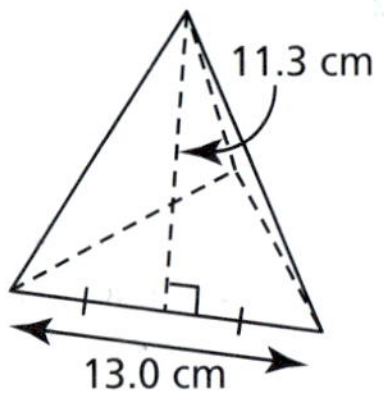

5. Determine the surface area of each right pyramid in question 4, to the nearest square unit.

6. Determine the lateral area of each right cone to the nearest square unit.

   a)

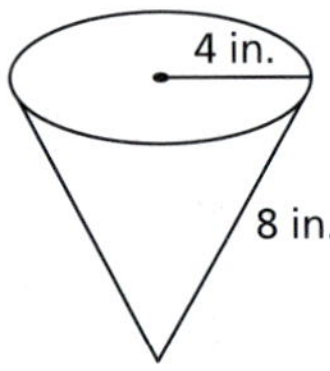

   b)

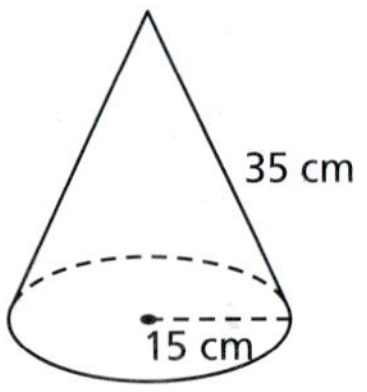

7. Determine the surface area of each right cone in question 6, to the nearest square unit.

8. Calculate the surface area of each object to the nearest square unit.

   a) right square pyramid

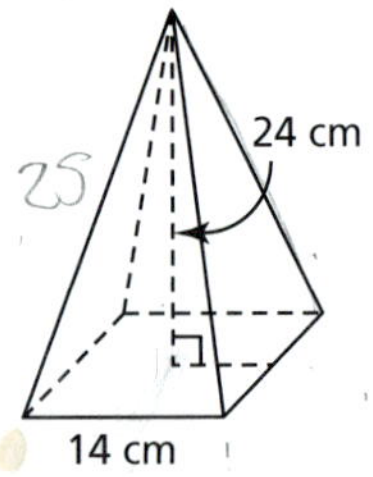

   b) right cone

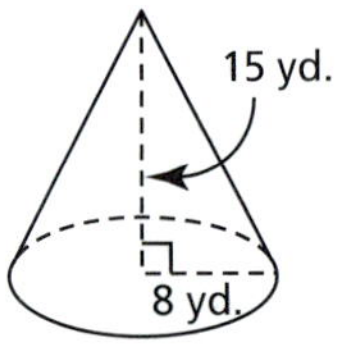

B

9. The slant height of a right square pyramid is 73 ft. and the side length of the base is 48 ft.
   a) Sketch the pyramid.
   b) Determine its lateral area to the nearest square foot.

10. The Great Pyramid at Giza has a square base with side length 755 ft. and an original height of 481 ft. Determine its original surface area to the nearest square foot.

11. Aiden built a cone-shaped volcano for a school science project. The volcano has a base diameter of 32 cm and a slant height of 45 cm.
    a) What is the lateral area of the volcano to the nearest tenth of a square centimetre?
    b) The paint for the volcano's surface costs \$1.99/jar, and one jar of paint covers 400 cm^2. How much will the paint cost?

12. A road pylon approximates a right cone with perpendicular height 53 cm and base diameter 18 cm. The lateral surface of the pylon is to be painted with reflective paint. What is the area that will be painted? Answer to the nearest square centimetre.

13. Determine the surface area of each right rectangular pyramid to the nearest square unit.

    a)

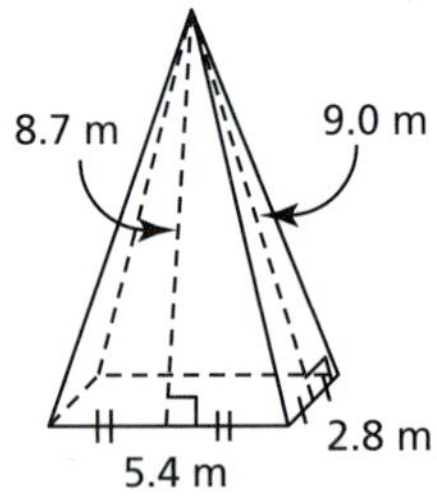

    b)

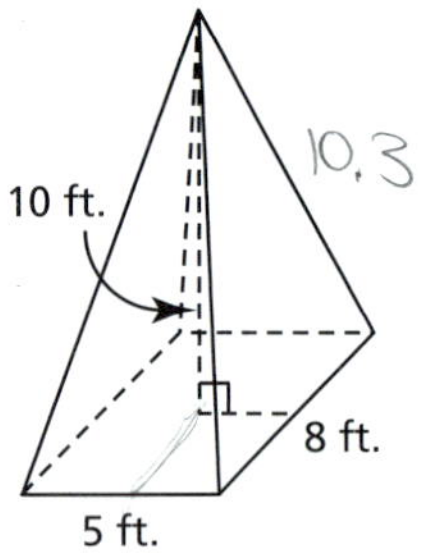

14. The Royal Saskatchewan Museum in Regina has a tipi in its First Nations Gallery. The tipi approximates a cone with a base diameter of 3.9 m and a height of 4.6 m. A Cree woman from Chitek Lake tanned, prepared, and sewed 15 bison hides to make the cover. To the nearest tenth of a square metre, what area did each bison hide cover? What assumptions did you make?

15. A farmer unloaded grain onto a tarp on the ground. The grain formed a cone-shaped pile that had a diameter of 12 ft. and a height of 8 ft. Determine the surface area of the exposed grain to the nearest square foot.

16. For each object, its surface area, *SA*, and some dimensions are given. Calculate the dimension indicated by the variable to the nearest tenth of a unit.

a) right cone

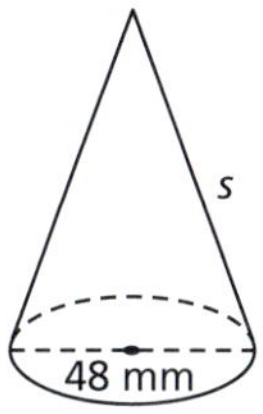

$SA = 7012\ \text{mm}^2$

b) right square pyramid

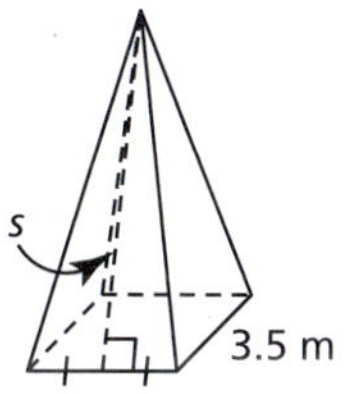

$SA = 65.5\ \text{m}^2$

17. A toy block manufacturer needs to cover its wooden blocks with a non-toxic paint.
One block is a right square pyramid with a base length of 2 in. and a slant height of $3\frac{1}{2}$ in.
A second block is a right cone that has a slant height of $3\frac{1}{2}$ in. and a base radius of 1 in.
A third block is a right rectangular prism with base dimensions 2 in. by 1 in. and a height of 3 in.

a) When the blocks rest on their bases, which block is tallest? How do you know?

b) Which block requires the most paint?

18. The Louvre art museum in Paris, France, has a glass square pyramid at its entrance. The side length of the base of the right pyramid is 35.0 m and its height is 20.6 m. The Muttart Conservatory in Edmonton, Alberta, has four right square pyramids also with glass faces. One of the largest pyramids has a base side length of 25.7 m and a height of 24.0 m.

Which pyramid requires more glass to enclose its space?

C

19. Determine the surface area of each right pyramid to the nearest tenth of a square unit.

a) a right pyramid with a base that is a regular hexagon with side length 5.5 cm; each triangular face has 2 equal sides with length 7.5 cm

b) a right pyramid with a base that is a regular pentagon with side length 2.4 m and the distance of each vertex from the centre of the base is 2.0 m; the height is 3.9 m

20. A right cone has a height of 8 ft. and a base circumference of 12 ft. Determine the surface area of the cone to the nearest square foot.

21. A right pyramid has a surface area of 258 cm^2. A right cone has a base radius of 4 cm. The cone and pyramid have equal surface areas. What is the height of the cone to the nearest tenth of a centimetre?

Reflect

What do you need to know to be able to calculate the surface areas of a right pyramid and a right cone? Include labelled diagrams in your explanation.

1.5 Volumes of Right Pyramids and Right Cones

LESSON FOCUS

Solve problems involving the volumes of right pyramids and right cones.

Volume is the amount of space an object occupies. It is measured in cubic units.

Capacity is the amount of material a container holds. It is measured in cubic units or capacity units.

Make Connections

Right pyramids and right cones are related to right prisms and right cylinders.
Look at the objects above.
How do you determine the volume of a right prism?
How do you determine the volume of a right cylinder?

Construct Understanding

TRY THIS

Work in a group.

You will need:

- a right cone and a right cylinder with equal bases and equal heights
- a right pyramid and a right prism with equal bases and equal heights
- a container of sand
- an empty container

A. Predict the relationship between the volume of the prism and the volume of the pyramid.

B. Fill the pyramid with sand; do not overfill. Pour the sand from the pyramid into the prism. How many full pyramids fill the prism?

C. What conclusion can you make about the relationship between the volumes of a right prism and a right pyramid with equal bases and equal heights?

D. Repeat Steps A to C for the cone and cylinder.

We use exponents when we write units for volume; for example, four cubic yards is 4 $yd.^3$ and four cubic metres is 4 m^3.

The volume of a right prism is 3 times the volume of a right pyramid with the same base and the same height.

Or, the volume of a right pyramid is $\frac{1}{3}$ the volume of the right prism with the same base and the same height.

Volumes of a Right Prism and a Right Pyramid

The volume of a right prism is:
Volume = (base area)(height)

$V = Ah$

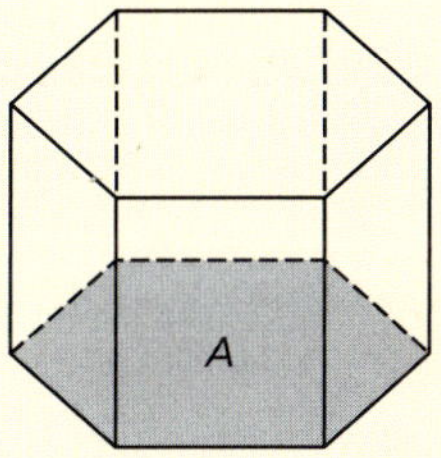

The volume of a right pyramid with the same base and the same height is:

Volume $= \frac{1}{3}$(base area)(height)

$V = \frac{1}{3}Ah$

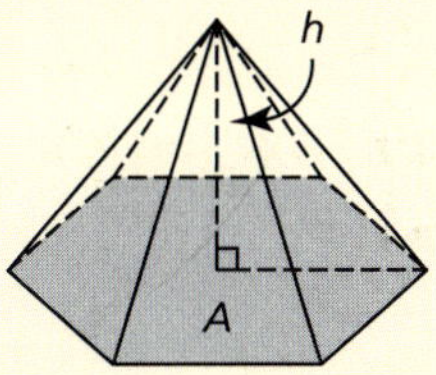

Example 1 Determining the Volume of a Right Square Pyramid Given Its Slant Height

Calculate the volume of this right square pyramid to the nearest cubic inch.

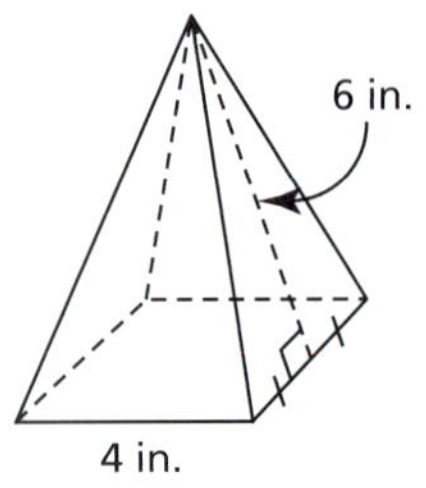

SOLUTION

Calculate the height of the pyramid.
Let h inches represent the height.

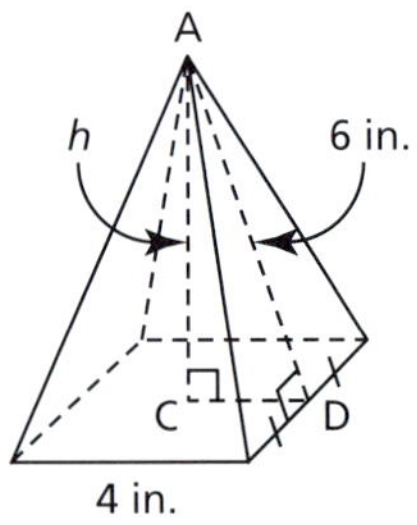

In right $\triangle$ACD, CD is $\frac{1}{2}$ the side length of the base, so CD = 2 in.

Use the Pythagorean Theorem in right $\triangle$ACD to calculate h.

$h^2 + 2^2 = 6^2$ Solve the equation for h^2.

$h^2 + 4 = 36$

$h^2 = 36 - 4$

$h^2 = 32$ Solve the equation for h.

$h = \sqrt{32}$

The height is $\sqrt{32}$ in.

Use the formula for the volume of a right pyramid:

$$\text{Volume} = \frac{1}{3}(\text{base area})(\text{height})$$

$$V = \frac{1}{3}(4)^2(\sqrt{32})$$

$$V = 30.1698\ldots$$

The volume of the pyramid is approximately 30 cubic inches.

CHECK YOUR UNDERSTANDING

1. Calculate the volume of this right square pyramid to the nearest cubic foot.

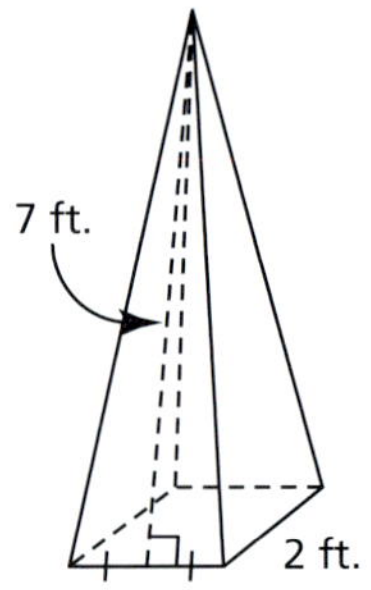

[Answer: approximately 9 ft.^{3}]

We can write algebraic formulas for the volumes of right rectangular prisms and right rectangular pyramids with the same base and the same height.

Volumes of a Right Rectangular Prism and a Right Rectangular Pyramid

A right rectangular prism with length l, width w, and height h, has volume:

$V = lwh$

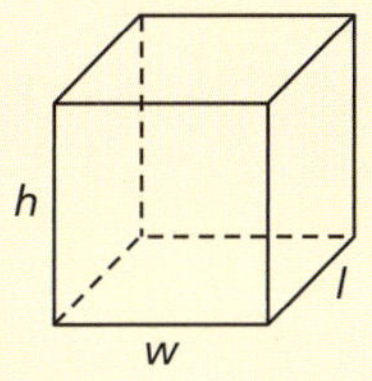

A right rectangular pyramid with base length l, base width w, and height h, has volume:

$V = \frac{1}{3}lwh$

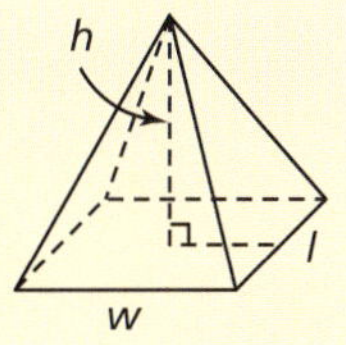

Example 2 Determining the Volume of a Right Rectangular Pyramid

Determine the volume of a right rectangular pyramid with base dimensions 5.4 cm by 3.2 cm and height 8.1 cm.
Answer to the nearest tenth of a cubic centimetre.

SOLUTION

Sketch and label a diagram.

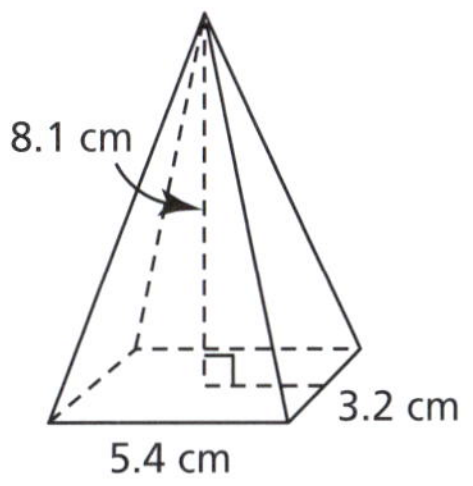

Use the formula for the volume of right rectangular pyramid.

$V = \frac{1}{3}lwh$ Substitute: $l = 5.4$, $w = 3.2$, $h = 8.1$

$V = \frac{1}{3}(5.4)(3.2)(8.1)$

$V = 46.656$

The volume of the pyramid is approximately 46.7 cm^3.

CHECK YOUR UNDERSTANDING

2. Determine the volume of a right rectangular pyramid with base dimensions 3.6 m by 4.7 m and height 6.9 m. Answer to the nearest tenth of a cubic metre.

[Answer: approximately 38.9 m^3]

The volume of a right cylinder is 3 times the volume of a right cone with the same base and the same height.

Or, the volume of a right cone is $\frac{1}{3}$ the volume of a right cylinder with the same base and the same height.

We can write algebraic formulas for the volumes of right cylinders and right cones with the same base and the same height.

Volumes of a Right Cylinder and a Right Cone

A right cylinder with base radius r and height h has volume:

$V = \pi r^2 h$

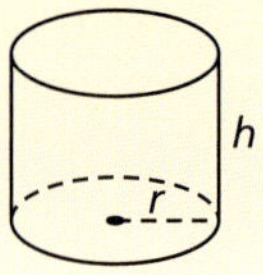

A right cone with base radius r and height h has volume:

$V = \frac{1}{3}\pi r^2 h$

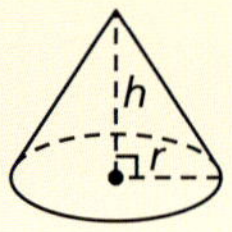

Example 3 Determining the Volume of a Cone

Determine the volume of this cone to the nearest cubic inch.

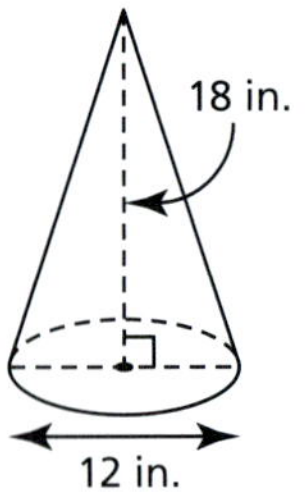

SOLUTION

The radius, r, of the base of the cone is $\frac{1}{2}$ the diameter.

$r = \frac{1}{2}(12 \text{ in.})$

$r = 6$ in.

Use the formula for the volume of a cone.

$V = \frac{1}{3}\pi r^2 h$ Substitute: $r = 6$, $h = 18$

$V = \frac{1}{3}\pi(6)^2(18)$

$V = 678.5840\ldots$

The volume of the cone is approximately 679 cubic inches.

CHECK YOUR UNDERSTANDING

3. Determine the volume of this cone to the nearest cubic millimetre.

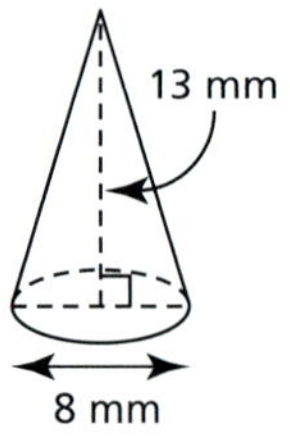

[Answer: approximately 218 mm^3]

How can you determine if your answer is reasonable?

Example 4 Determining an Unknown Measurement

A cone has a height of 4 yd. and a volume of 205 cubic yards. Determine the radius of the base of the cone to the nearest yard.

SOLUTION

Sketch a diagram.

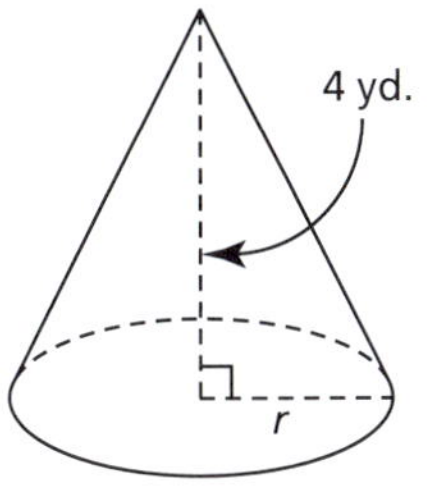

Use the formula for the volume of a cone.

$$V = \frac{1}{3}\pi r^2 h$$ Substitute: $V = 205$, $h = 4$

$$205 = \frac{1}{3}\pi r^2(4)$$ Solve for r^2. Multiply both sides by 3.

$$3(205) = 3\left(\frac{1}{3}\pi r^2(4)\right)$$

$$615 = 4\pi r^2$$ Divide both sides by 4π.

$$\frac{615}{4\pi} = \frac{4\pi r^2}{4\pi}$$

$$\frac{615}{4\pi} = r^2$$ Solve for r.

$$\sqrt{\frac{615}{4\pi}} = r$$

```
√(615/(4π))
        6.995723336
```

$$r = 6.9957\ldots$$

The radius of the base of the cone is approximately 7 yd.

CHECK YOUR UNDERSTANDING

4. A cone has a height of 8 m and a volume of 300 m^3. Determine the radius of the base of the cone to the nearest metre.

[Answer: approximately 6 m]

Discuss the Ideas

1. How are the volumes of a right pyramid and right cone related to the volumes of a right prism and right cylinder, respectively?

2. How are the formulas for the volumes of a right cone and a right pyramid alike? How are the formulas different?

3. Suppose you cannot remember the formula for the volume of a right cone or a right pyramid. What strategy could you use to determine the volume?

Exercises

A

4. Calculate the volume of each right prism.

a) square prism

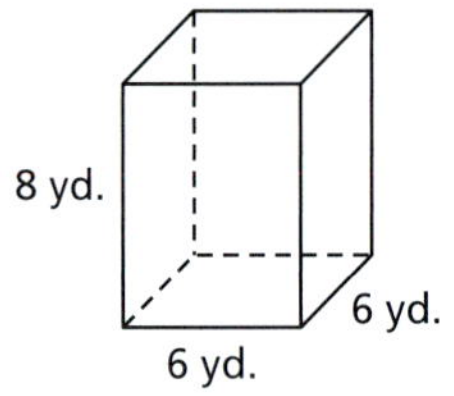

b) rectangular prism

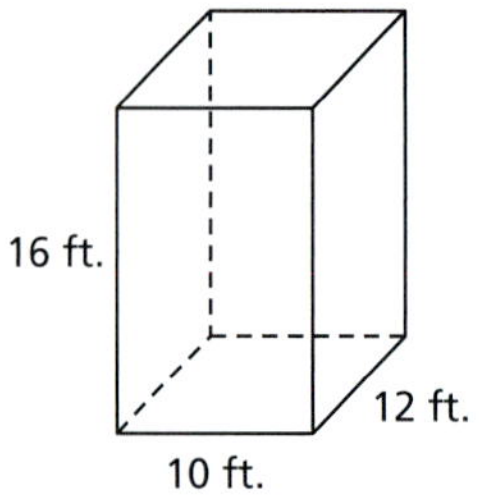

5. For each prism in question 4, sketch a right pyramid with the same base and same height. Calculate the volume of each pyramid.

6. Calculate the volume of each right cylinder to the nearest cubic unit.

a)

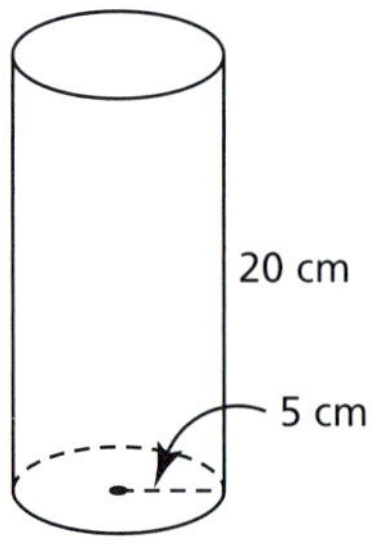

b)

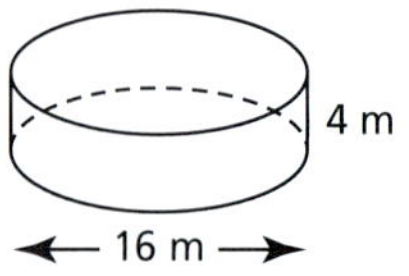

7. For each cylinder in question 6, sketch a right cone with the same base and same height. Calculate the volume of each cone to the nearest cubic unit.

8. Calculate the volume of each right pyramid.

a) square pyramid

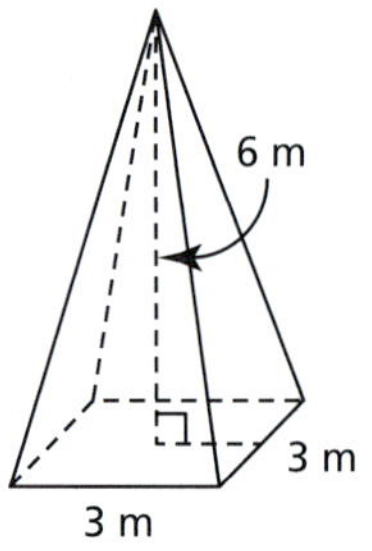

b) rectangular pyramid

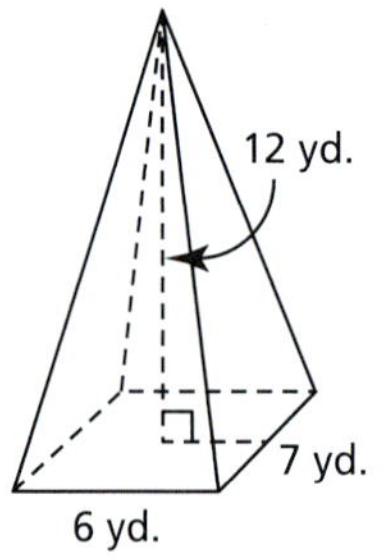

9. Calculate the volume of each right cone. Write the answer to the nearest tenth of a cubic unit.

a)

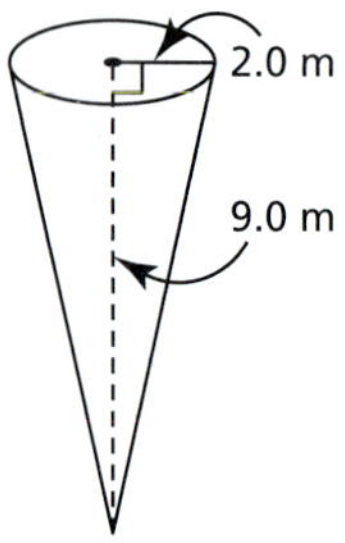

b)

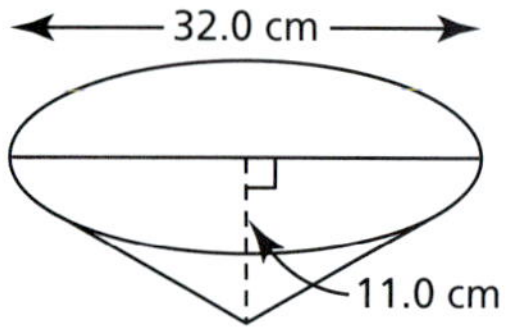

B

10. A regular tetrahedron has base area $68.0\ m^2$ and height 10.2 m.

a) Sketch the tetrahedron.

b) Determine its volume to the nearest tenth of a cubic metre.

11. A right cone has slant height 12 yd. and base diameter 4 yd.

a) Sketch the cone.

b) Determine its volume to the nearest cubic yard.

12. A stone monument has the shape of a square pyramid. Its slant height is 1.6 m and the side length of its base is 0.8 m. Determine the volume of the monument to the nearest tenth of a cubic metre.

13. Annika has a wooden right rectangular pyramid. She measures the dimensions of the base as 10.4 cm by 8.6 cm, and the height as 14.8 cm.

a) Explain how Annika can use these measurements to calculate the volume of the pyramid.

b) What is the volume of the pyramid to the nearest tenth of a cubic centimetre?

14. An ice cream shop in Bellevue, Alberta, created a new dessert. It is a waffle cone with a height of 5 in. and a base diameter of 2 in., filled with ice cream. Then whipped topping and sprinkles are added.

a) The ice cream is level with the top of the cone. How much ice cream can the cone hold? Write the answer to the nearest cubic inch.

b) One cubic inch of soft ice cream costs 55¢, the waffle cone costs 35¢, and the whipped topping and sprinkles cost 10¢ per dessert. How much will this dessert cost to produce?

c) Suppose the cone had the shape of a right square pyramid with base side length 2 in. and height 5 in. How much ice cream would it hold?

15. A right square pyramid has a base side length of 3.5 m. Each triangular face has two equal sides of length 4.5 m.

a) Sketch and label the pyramid.

b) Calculate the height of the pyramid to the nearest tenth of a metre.

c) Calculate the volume of the pyramid to the nearest tenth of a cubic metre.

16. Determine the volume of a right rectangular pyramid with base dimensions 6 ft. by 12 ft. For each triangular face, the equal sides have length 6 yd. Write the answer to the nearest cubic foot.

17. A tea bag has the shape of a regular tetrahedron. Each edge is 5.8 cm long. The height of the tetrahedron is approximately 4.7 cm.

a) Calculate the area of the base of the tetrahedron to the nearest square centimetre.

b) What is the volume of the tea bag to the nearest cubic centimetre?

c) Do you think the volume of tea in the bag is equal to your answer from part b? Explain.

18. For each object, its volume, V, and some dimensions are given. Calculate the dimension indicated by the variable. Write each answer to the nearest tenth of a unit.

a) right rectangular prism

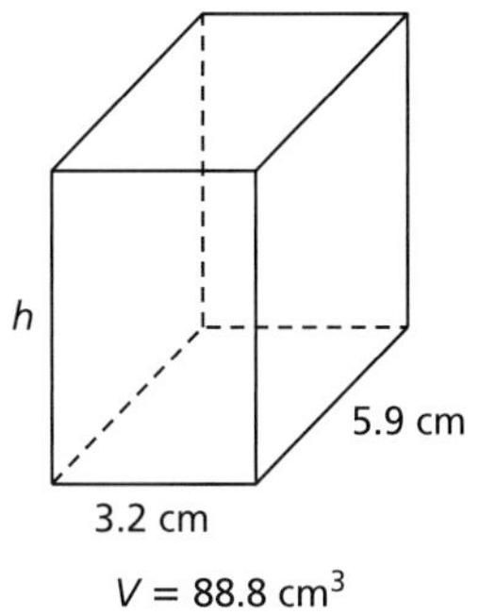

b) right square pyramid

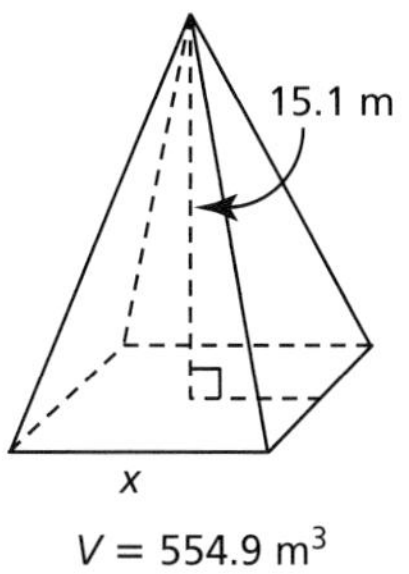

c) right cylinder

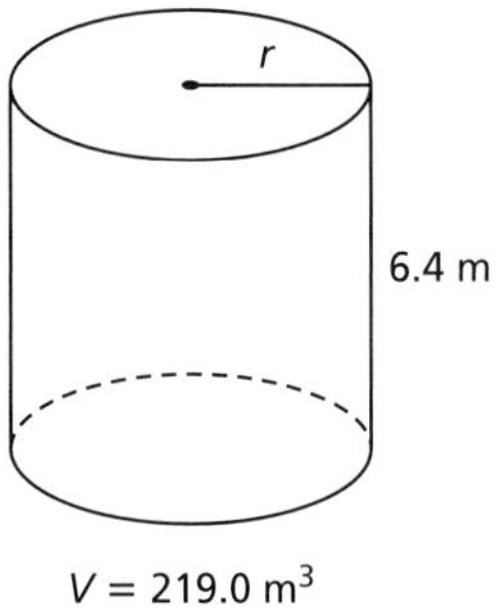

d) right cone

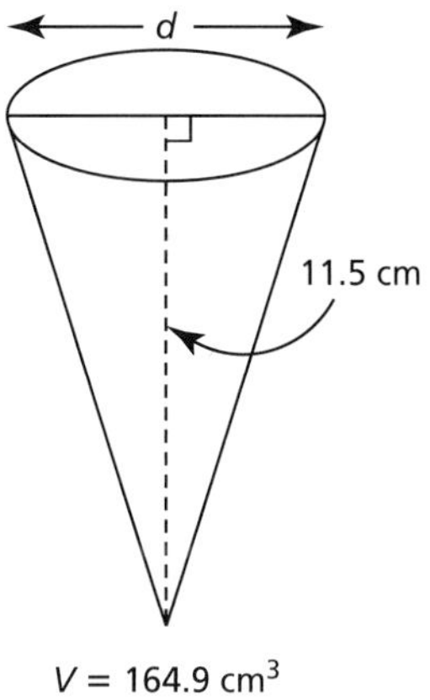

19. Sunil immersed a right plastic cone in a measuring cylinder containing water and determined that the volume of the cone was 33.5 cm^3. He measured the diameter of the base of the cone as 4.0 cm.

a) With these data, how could Sunil calculate the height of the cone?

b) What is the height of the cone to the nearest tenth of a centimetre?

C

20. An underground tank has the shape of a right cone, supported with its apex beneath its base. The tank collects the water run-off for a three-storey parking garage. The cone has a base diameter of 5.0 m and a height of 3.5 m. ($1 \text{ m}^3 = 1 \text{ kL}$)
   a) What is the capacity of this tank to the nearest tenth of a kilolitre?
   b) How much water is in the tank when the water level is 1 m below the top of the tank?

21. A right square pyramid has a volume of 111 cubic yards. The base has a side length of 6 yd. Determine the slant height of the pyramid to the nearest yard.

22. A right rectangular pyramid has base dimensions 5 m by 3 m, and a height of 10 m. A horizontal cut is made through the pyramid 2 m from its apex and this smaller right rectangular pyramid is removed. What is the volume of the remaining piece?

Reflect

How are a cone and a pyramid alike? How are they different? Explain how these similarities and differences account for the formulas for the volume of each object.

THE WORLD OF MATH

Careers: Petroleum Engineer

Petroleum engineers work closely with geologists, geophysicists, and oilfield operating personnel. Their primary job is to analyze drilling data to determine if wells contain significant quantities of oil and gas. The engineers estimate the costs of developing a drilling location and its potential profits. After a site has been selected for drilling, a petroleum engineer designs and implements appropriate drilling, processing, and transportation for the oil or gas. To do this, petroleum engineers must be able to measure lengths and distances accurately, estimate the recoverable volumes of oil and gas based on seismic data, and determine the most efficient methods for storage and transportation to minimize any environmental impact.

1.6 Surface Area and Volume of a Sphere

LESSON FOCUS

Solve problems involving the surface area and volume of a sphere.

Make Connections

The sphere above is in Winnipeg, Manitoba. It contains methane and carbon dioxide that is produced during the treatment of waste water. How could you estimate the volume of gas the sphere could hold?

A **sphere** is the set of points in space that are the same distance from a fixed point, which is the *centre*. A line segment that joins the centre to any point on the sphere is a *radius*. A line segment that joins two points on a sphere and passes through the centre is a *diameter*.

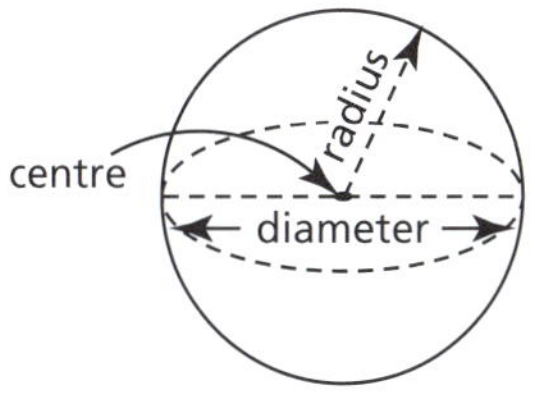

Construct Understanding

TRY THIS

Work with a partner.

You will need:

- an orange
- calipers or a ruler
- a compass

A. An orange approximates a sphere and the area of its peel represents the surface area of the sphere.
Measure and record the diameter of the orange in 3 different places.
Calculate the mean diameter of the orange.

B. Draw 6 circles with diameter equal to the mean diameter of the orange.

C. Peel the orange and arrange the peel within the circles. Completely fill one circle before moving to the next one. (Hint: It is easiest to use small pieces of peel).

D. Continue filling the circles until all the peel has been used. About how many circles did you cover with orange peel?

E. Use the filled circles and the formula for the area of a circle to estimate the surface area of the orange.

F. Compare your answer for part D with those of your classmates. Work together to create a formula for determining the surface area of a sphere.

The surface area of a sphere is related to the curved surface area of a cylinder that encloses it. The cylinder has the same diameter as the sphere, and a height equal to its diameter.

If the curved surface of the cylinder is made from paper, it can be cut and pasted on the surface of the sphere to cover it.

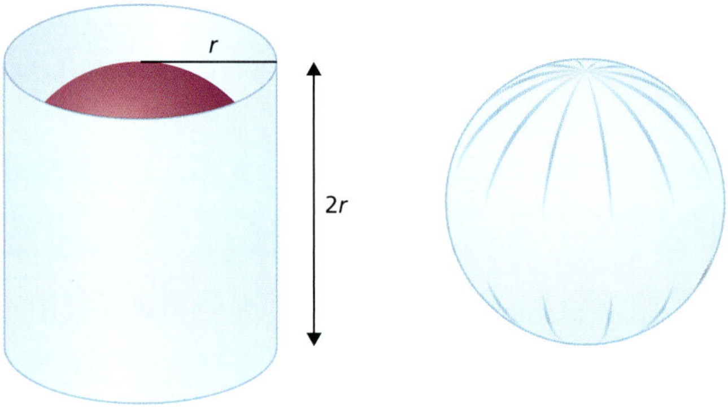

The curved surface area, SA_C, of a cylinder with base radius r and height h is:
$SA_C = 2\pi rh$

When a cylinder has base radius r and height $2r$:

$SA_C = 2\pi r(2r)$

$SA_C = 4\pi r^2$

So, this is also the formula for the surface area of a sphere with radius r.

Surface Area of a Sphere

The surface area, SA, of a sphere with radius r is:
$SA = 4\pi r^2$

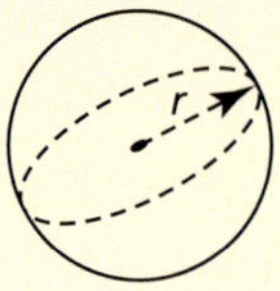

Example 1 Determining the Surface Area of a Sphere

The diameter of a baseball is approximately 3 in. Determine the surface area of a baseball to the nearest square inch.

SOLUTION

Use the formula for the surface area of a sphere.

The radius is:

$\frac{1}{2}(3 \text{ in.}) = 1.5 \text{ in.}$

$SA = 4\pi r^2$ — Substitute $r = 1.5$.

$SA = 4\pi(1.5)^2$

$SA = 28.2743\ldots$

The surface area of a baseball is approximately 28 square inches.

CHECK YOUR UNDERSTANDING

1. The diameter of a softball is approximately 4 in. Determine the surface area of a softball to the nearest square inch.

[Answer: approximately 50 in.^{2}]

What happens to the surface area of a sphere when its radius is doubled?

Example 2 Determining the Diameter of a Sphere

The surface area of a lacrosse ball is approximately 20 square inches. What is the diameter of the lacrosse ball to the nearest tenth of an inch?

SOLUTION

Let r represent the radius of the lacrosse ball.

Use the formula for the surface area of a sphere.

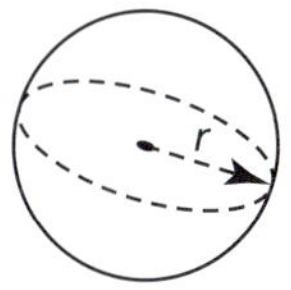

$SA = 4\pi r^2$ — Substitute $SA = 20$.

$20 = 4\pi r^2$ — Divide both sides of the equation by 4π.

$\frac{20}{4\pi} = \frac{4\pi r^2}{4\pi}$

$\frac{20}{4\pi} = r^2$ — Solve for r.

$r = \sqrt{\frac{20}{4\pi}}$

$r = 1.2615\ldots$

(Solution continues.)

CHECK YOUR UNDERSTANDING

2. The surface area of a soccer ball is approximately 250 square inches. What is the diameter of a soccer ball to the nearest tenth of an inch?

[Answer: approximately $8\frac{9}{10}$ in.]

The diameter is:

$2r = 2(1.2615\ldots)$

$2r = 2.5231\ldots$

The diameter of the lacrosse ball is approximately $2\frac{5}{10}$ in., or $2\frac{1}{2}$ in.

We can use the formula for the surface area of a sphere to develop a formula for the volume of a sphere.

Visualize a sphere covered with very small congruent squares, and each square is joined by line segments to the centre of the sphere to form a square pyramid. The volume of the sphere is the sum of the volumes of the square pyramids.

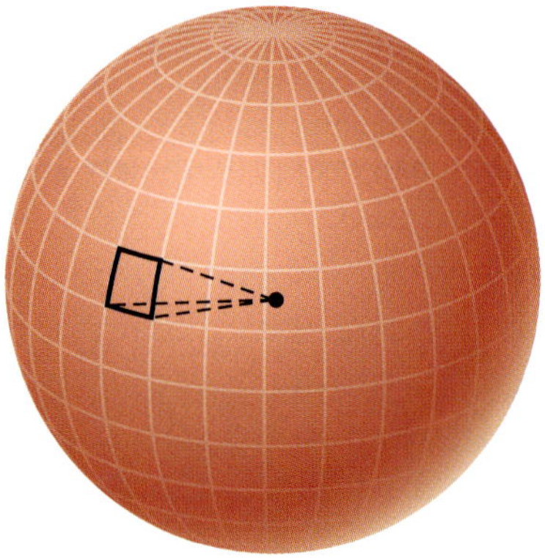

Volume of sphere = sum of volumes of pyramids

Volume of sphere = sum of all the $\left[\frac{1}{3}(\text{base area})(\text{height})\right]$

The height of a pyramid is the radius of the sphere.

Volume of sphere $= \frac{1}{3}$(sum of all the base areas)(r)

The sum of all the base areas is the surface area of the sphere: $4\pi r^2$

$V = \frac{1}{3}(4\pi r^2)(r)$

$V = \frac{4}{3}\pi r^3$

Volume of a Sphere

The volume, V, of a sphere with radius r is:

$V = \frac{4}{3}\pi r^3$

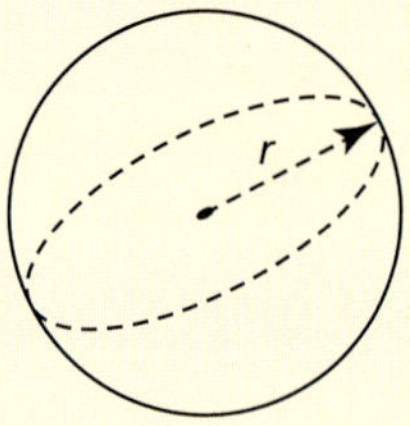

Example 3 Determining the Volume of a Sphere

The sun approximates a sphere with diameter 870 000 mi. What is the approximate volume of the sun?

SOLUTION

Use the formula for the volume of a sphere.

The radius, r, is:

$$r = \frac{1}{2}(870\,000 \text{ mi.})$$

$$r = 435\,000 \text{ mi.}$$

$$V = \frac{4}{3}\pi r^3$$

Substitute $r = 435\,000$.

$$V = \frac{4}{3}\pi(435\,000)^3$$

$$V = 3.4479\ldots \times 10^{17}$$

This number is too large for the calculator display, so it is displayed as the product of a number and a power of 10.

The volume of the sun is approximately 3.4×10^{17} cubic miles.

CHECK YOUR UNDERSTANDING

3. The moon approximates a sphere with diameter 2160 mi. What is the approximate volume of the moon?

[Answer: approximately 5.3×10^9 mi.^{3}]

When a large number is displayed as the product of a power of 10 and a number between 1 and 10, the number is written in *scientific notation*.

When a sphere is cut in half, two *hemispheres* are formed.

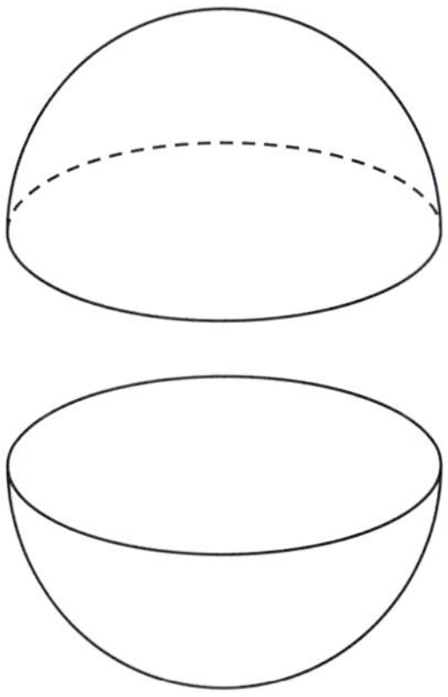

hemispheres

Why is a globe constructed from two hemispheres?

Example 4 Determining the Surface Area and Volume of a Hemisphere

A hemisphere has radius 8.0 cm.

a) What is the surface area of the hemisphere to the nearest tenth of a square centimetre?

b) What is the volume of the hemisphere to the nearest tenth of a cubic centimetre?

SOLUTION

a) SA of a hemisphere = SA of one-half a sphere + area of a circle

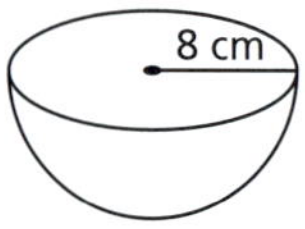

$SA = \frac{1}{2}(4\pi r^2) + \pi r^2$

$SA = 2\pi r^2 + \pi r^2$

$SA = 3\pi r^2$ Substitute: $r = 8.0$

$SA = 3\pi(8.0)^2$

$SA = 603.1857\ldots$

The surface area of the hemisphere is approximately 603.2 cm^2.

b) Volume of a hemisphere = volume of one-half a sphere

$V = \frac{1}{2}\left(\frac{4}{3}\pi r^3\right)$

$V = \frac{2}{3}\pi r^3$ Substitute: $r = 8.0$

$V = \frac{2}{3}\pi(8.0)^3$

$V = 1072.3302\ldots$

The volume of the hemisphere is approximately 1072.3 cm^3.

CHECK YOUR UNDERSTANDING

4. A hemisphere has radius 5.0 cm.

a) What is the surface area of the hemisphere to the nearest tenth of a square centimetre?

b) What is the volume of the hemisphere to the nearest tenth of a cubic centimetre?

[Answers: a) approximately 235.6 cm^2 b) approximately 261.8 cm^3]

In *Example 4a*, why can we write $2\pi r^2 + \pi r^2$ as $3\pi r^2$?

Discuss the Ideas

1. A sphere is cut in half. How is the surface area of the sphere related to the area of the circular face on one hemisphere?

2. Visualize a sphere with radius *r* that fits in a cylinder with base radius *r* and height 2*r*.
How is the volume of the sphere related to the volume of the cylinder?
How could you use this relationship to help you remember the formula for the volume of a sphere?

Exercises

A

3. Determine the surface area of each sphere to the nearest square unit.

a) 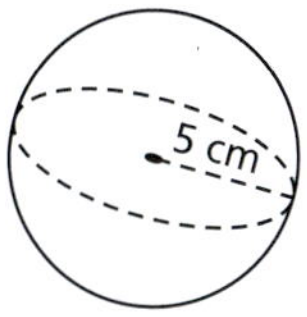

b) 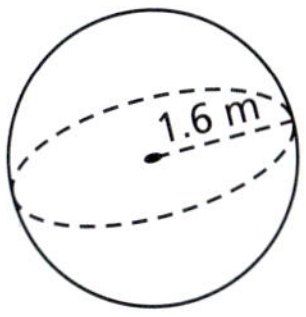

c) 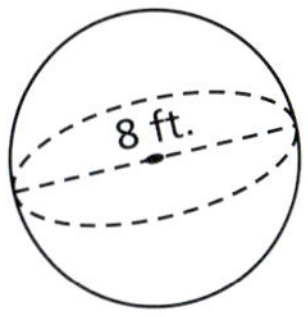

d) 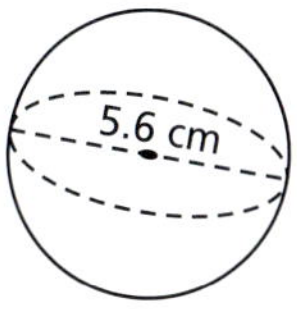

4. Determine the volume of each sphere in question 3 to the nearest cubic unit.

5. Determine the surface area and volume of each hemisphere. Write your answers to the nearest whole unit.

a) 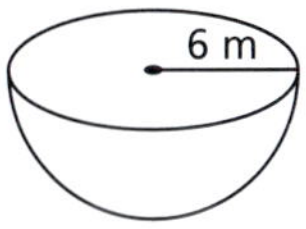

b) 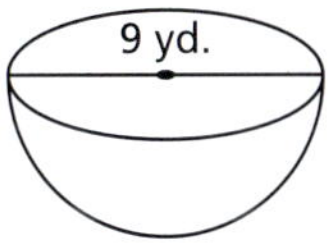

B

6. Use a marble or other sphere. Measure its diameter. Calculate its volume and surface area.

7. A sphere has a radius of 8.4 m. Determine its surface area and volume to the nearest tenth of a unit.

8. The surface area of a tennis ball is approximately 127 cm^2. What is the radius of the tennis ball to the nearest tenth of a centimetre?

9. A sphere has a surface area of 452 square inches. What is the diameter of the sphere to the nearest inch?

10. A glass bowl approximates a hemisphere with diameter 20 cm.
    a) What is the capacity of the bowl to the nearest tenth of a litre? ($1000 \text{ cm}^3 = 1 \text{ L}$)
    b) One cup is 250 mL. How many cups of punch can the bowl hold?

11. A sphere has a diameter of 12 cm. A hemisphere has a radius of 8 cm.
    a) Which object has the greater surface area?
    b) Which object has the greater volume?

12. The gas storage sphere on page 45 has diameter 15.8 m.
    a) What is the surface area of the sphere to the nearest square metre?
    b) What is the capacity of the sphere to the nearest kilolitre? ($1 \text{ kL} = 1 \text{ m}^3$)

13. Earth approximates a sphere but its diameter varies. The mean diameter of Earth is approximately 12 756 km.
    a) Determine the surface area of Earth to the nearest square kilometre.
    b) About 70% of Earth's surface is covered in water. What is this area in square kilometres?
    c) Determine the volume of Earth to the nearest thousand cubic kilometres.
    d) The inner core of Earth has a radius of approximately 1278 km. Determine, to the nearest thousand cubic kilometres, the volume of Earth that is *not* part of the inner core.

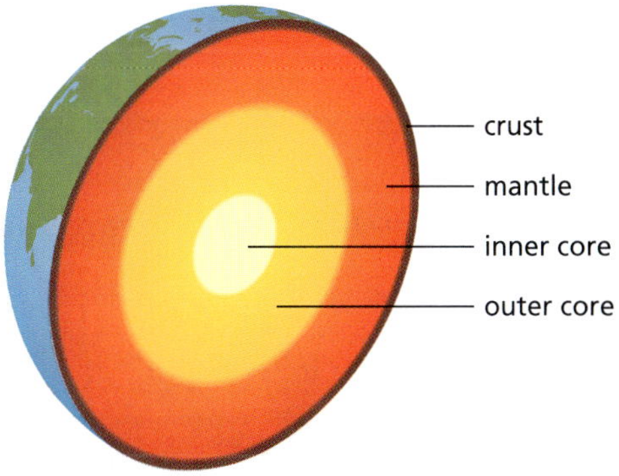

14. The diameter of Earth through the North and South poles is 16 km less than its mean diameter, approximately 12 756 km. The diameter of Earth at the equator is 26 km greater than its mean diameter. Determine the approximate volume of Earth using the polar radius and equatorial radius.

15. The centre of a doughnut is removed and formed to make a sphere of dough with diameter 2.5 cm. A batch of these spheres is to be covered in a sugar glaze. There is enough glaze to cover an area of 4710 cm^2. How many spheres can be glazed?

16. The size of a ball used in sport is often described by the measure of its circumference. The circumference of a ball is the length of the longest circle that can be drawn on the surface of the ball. A volleyball has a circumference of 66 cm and a basketball has a circumference of $29\frac{1}{2}$ in.
   a) Determine the radius of each ball to the nearest unit.
   b) Determine the surface area of each ball to the nearest square unit.
   c) Determine the volume of each ball to the nearest cubic unit.
   d) Which ball is larger? Justify your answer.

17. In the rain forests of Vancouver Island, there are tree houses shaped like spheres. One spherical shell has outside diameter 3.20 m and inside diameter 3.15 m.
   a) Calculate the volume of the inside of the shell to the nearest tenth of a cubic metre.
   b) What is the difference between the outside and inside surface areas, to the tenth of a square metre?

18. A hemisphere has a circumference of 47.1 m. Determine the surface area and volume of the hemisphere to the nearest tenth of a unit.

19. A fitness ball is delivered in a flat package with a hand pump. The pump inflates the ball at a rate of 280 cm^3 per pump, to a diameter of 28 cm. How many pumps are needed to inflate the ball? Justify your answer.

20. A pail of cookie dough is cylindrical, with diameter 17 cm and height 13 cm. A scoop makes a sphere of cookie dough with diameter 5 cm. How many cookies can be made from this pail of dough?

C

21. Giselle has a block of wood that measures 14 cm by 12 cm by 10 cm. She is making a wooden ball in tech class.
   a) What percent of the wood is wasted?
   b) What assumptions are you making?

22. Derive formulas for the surface area and volume of a sphere in terms of its diameter *d*. Check your formulas by using them to calculate the surface area and volume of the sphere in question 3c.

23. A beach ball that was deflated to 70% of its maximum volume now has a volume of 420 cubic inches. What is the radius of the beach ball when it is at its maximum volume?

24. A spherical balloon has a radius of 10 cm. It is blown up until its radius is three times the original radius. For the inflated balloon and the original balloon:
   a) How do the circumferences compare?
   b) How do the surface areas compare?
   c) How do the volumes compare?

Reflect

What strategies do you have for remembering the formulas for the volume and surface area of a sphere?

CHECKPOINT 2

Connections

Volume

Surface Area

Right pyramid with regular polygon base

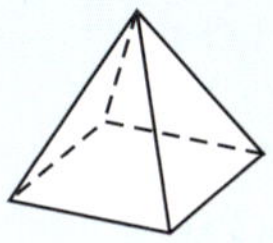

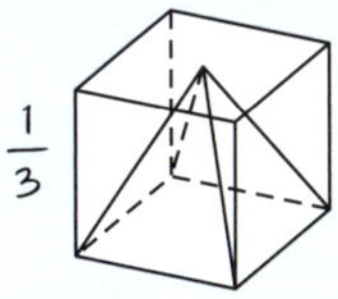

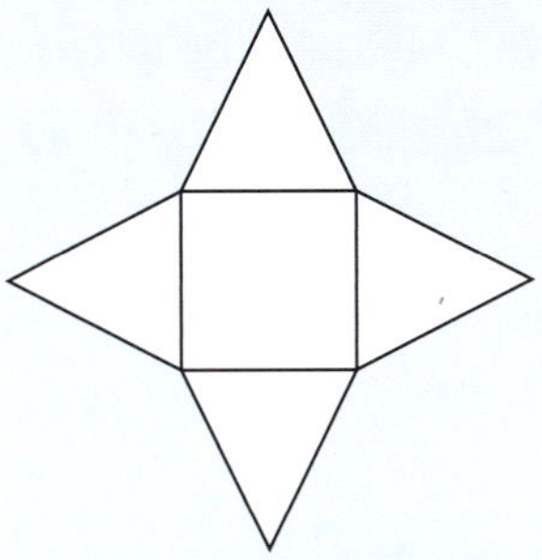

$SA = \frac{1}{2}$(slant height)(perimeter of base) + base area

Right cone

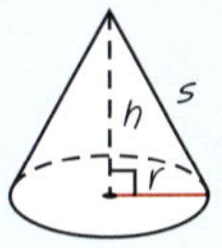

SA = lateral area + base area

$SA = \pi rs + \pi r^2$

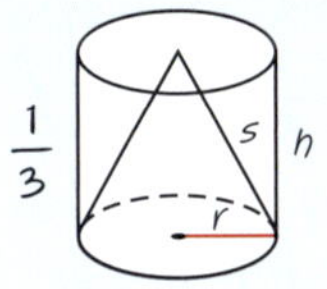

Sphere

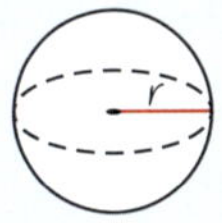

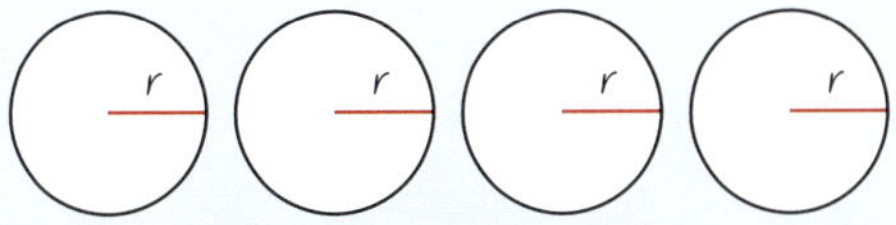

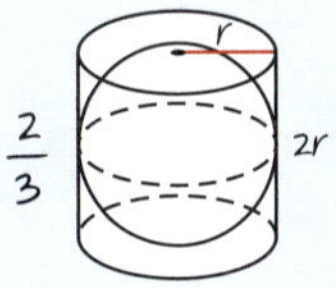

Concept Development

- **In Lesson 1.4**
  - You developed and applied formulas for the **surface areas of a right pyramid and a right cone**.
  - You **determined an unknown dimension** given the surface area of a right cone or a right pyramid, and sufficient other information.
- **In Lesson 1.5**
  - You described the **volume relationships between a right prism and a right pyramid, and between a right cylinder and a right cone.**
  - You developed and applied formulas for the **volumes of a right pyramid and a right cone.**
  - You **determined an unknown dimension** given the volume of an object and sufficient other information.
- **In Lesson 1.6**
  - You developed and applied formulas for the **surface area and volume of a sphere**.
  - You **determined an unknown dimension** given the surface area of a sphere and sufficient other information.

Assess Your Understanding

1.4

1. Determine the surface area of each object to the nearest square unit.

a) right square pyramid

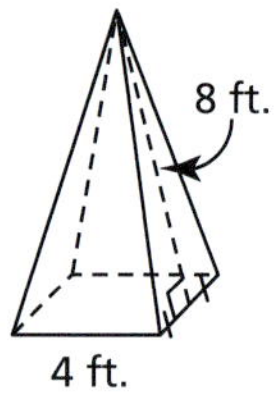

b) right rectangular pyramid

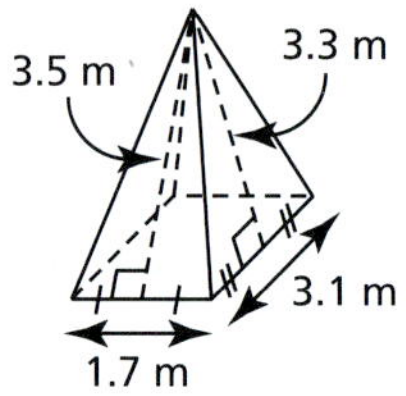

c) right cone

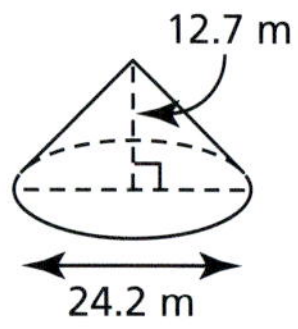

2. The top of a clock tower has the shape of a right square pyramid, with base side length 15 m and height 12 m. The roofing tiles on the tower need to be replaced. Determine the area that needs to be re-covered, to the nearest square metre.

3. A sector of a circle is used to make a hat shaped like a right cone. The cone has a height of 14 in. and a base diameter of 8 in. The outside of the hat is to be covered in red crepe paper. Determine the area that will be covered in crepe paper to the nearest square inch.

1.5

4. Determine the volume of each object in question 1 to the nearest cubic unit.

5. For each object, its volume, V, and some dimensions are given. Calculate the dimension indicated by the variable to the nearest tenth of a unit.

a) right square pyramid

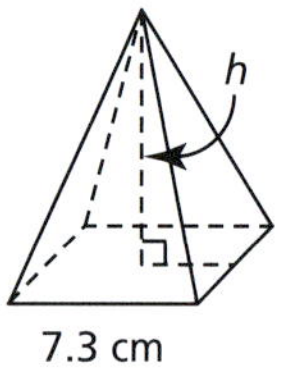

$V = 168.8\text{ cm}^3$

b) right cone

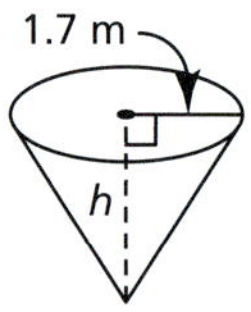

$V = 8.2\text{ m}^3$

c) right square pyramid

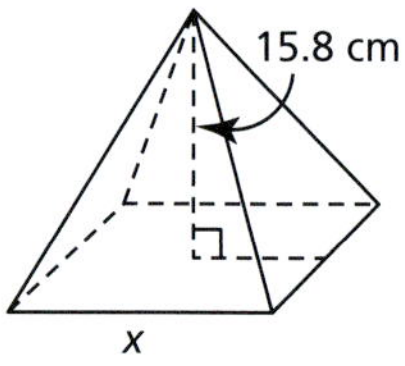

$V = 1594.5\text{ cm}^3$

1.6

6. Determine the surface area and volume of each object with the given dimension. Write the answers to the nearest tenth of a unit.

a) sphere, radius 8.8 km

b) hemisphere, diameter 6.8 cm

7. A spherical globe has circumference 158 cm. The surface of the globe is to be painted with a high-gloss varnish. What is the area to be painted to the nearest square centimetre?

1.7 Solving Problems Involving Objects

LESSON FOCUS

Solve problems involving the surface area and volume of composite objects.

Make Connections

A farmer is constructing a new grain bin. The bin she would like to build has a cylindrical body and a cone-shaped roof. The farmer knows the dimensions of the bin she wants to build.

How can the farmer determine the amount of material she will need to build the bin?

Construct Understanding

THINK ABOUT IT

Here is a sketch of a grain bin. The farmer's grain truck can hold 550 cubic feet of barley. How many truckloads are required to fill the bin?

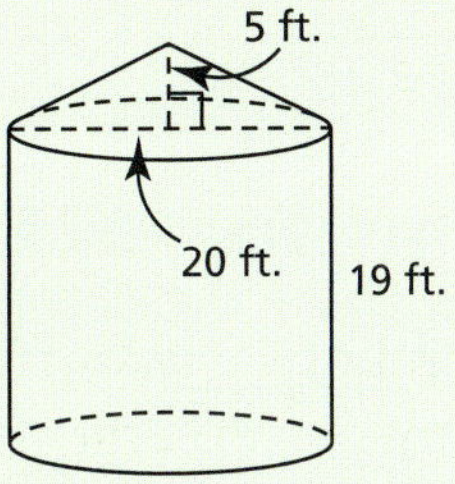

A *composite object* comprises two or more distinct objects.
To determine the volume of a composite object, identify the distinct objects, calculate the volume of each object, then add the volumes.

Example 1 Determining the Volume of a Composite Object

Determine the volume of this composite object to the nearest tenth of a cubic metre.

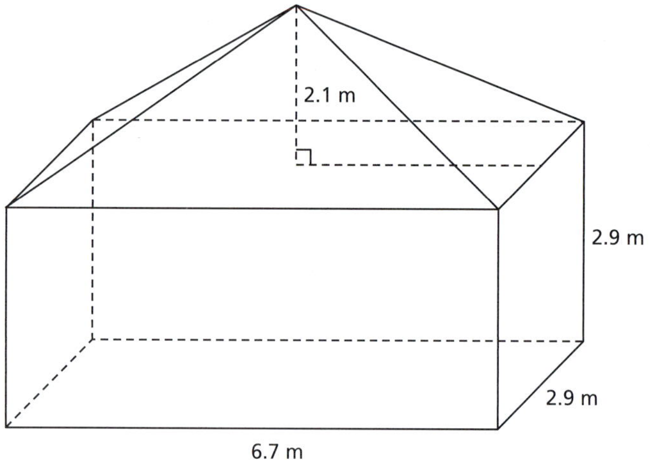

SOLUTION

The object comprises a right rectangular prism and a right rectangular pyramid.

Use the formula for the volume of a right rectangular prism.

$V = lwh$ Substitute: $l = 6.7$, $w = 2.9$, $h = 2.9$

$V = (6.7)(2.9)(2.9)$

$V = 56.347$

Use the formula for the volume of a right rectangular pyramid.

$V = \frac{1}{3}lwh$ Substitute: $l = 6.7$, $w = 2.9$, $h = 2.1$

$V = \frac{1}{3}(6.7)(2.9)(2.1)$

$V = 13.601$

Volume of the composite object is:

$56.347 + 13.601 = 69.948$

The volume of the composite object is approximately 69.9 m^3.

CHECK YOUR UNDERSTANDING

1. Determine the volume of this composite object to the nearest tenth of a cubic centimetre.

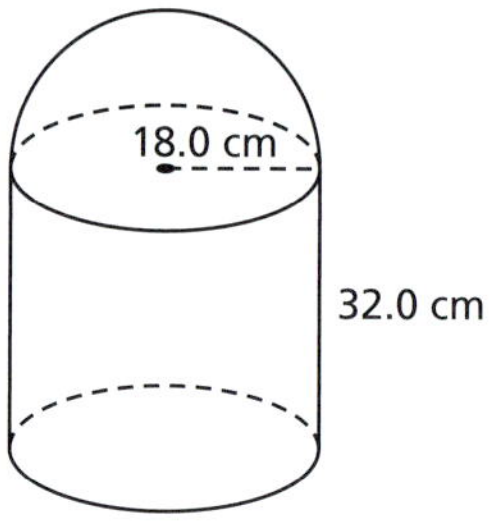

[Answer: approximately 44 786.5 cm^3]

To calculate the surface area of a composite object, the first step is to determine the faces that comprise the surface area. Then calculate the sum of the areas of these faces.

Example 2 Determining the Surface Area of a Composite Object

Determine the surface area of this composite object to the nearest square foot.

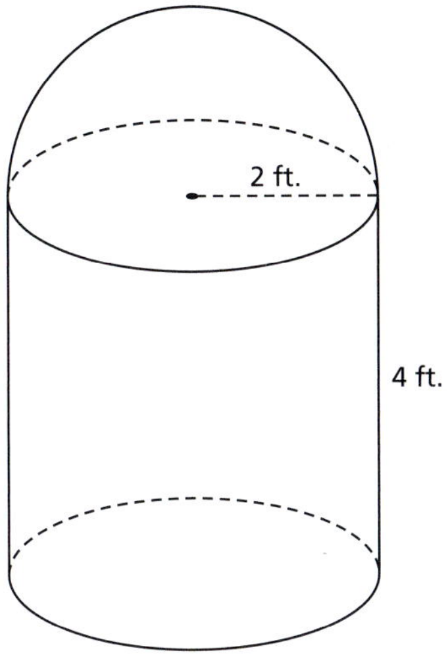

SOLUTION

The curved surface of the hemisphere, one base of the cylinder, and the curved surface of the cylinder comprise the surface area.

The cylinder and hemisphere have equal radii.

Surface area of composite object is:
Area of curved surface of hemisphere + area of base of cylinder + area of curved surface of cylinder

Use the algebraic formulas for surface area.

$SA = 2\pi r^2 + \pi r^2 + 2\pi rh$

$SA = 3\pi r^2 + 2\pi rh$ Substitute: $r = 2$, $h = 4$

$SA = 3\pi(2)^2 + 2\pi(2)(4)$

$SA = 87.9645...$

The surface area of the composite object is approximately 88 square feet.

CHECK YOUR UNDERSTANDING

2. Determine the surface area of this composite object.

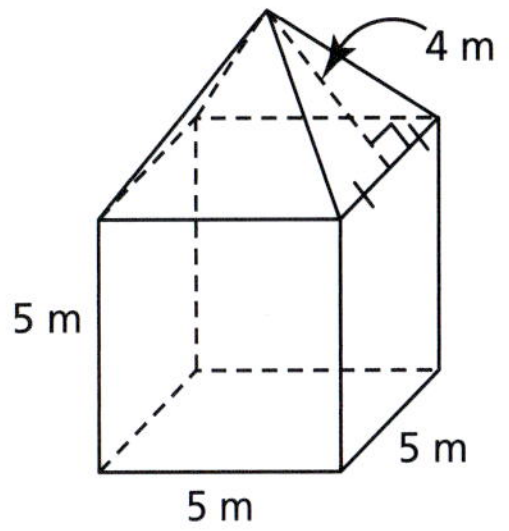

[Answer: 165 m^2]

Example 3 Solving a Problem Related to a Composite Object

A cabane à sucre is a composite object formed by a rectangular prism with a right triangular prism as its roof. Determine the surface area of the cabane à sucre in square yards.

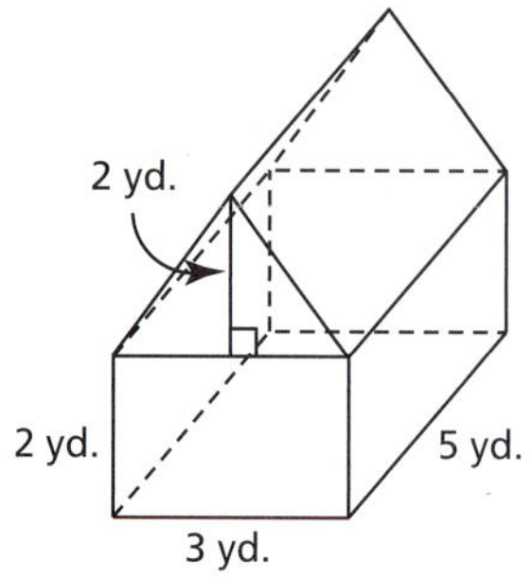

SOLUTION

The surface area of the cabane is the sum of the areas of the 4 walls, plus the areas of the 2 rectangular faces and 2 triangular faces of the roof.

The area of the 4 walls, in square yards, is:
$A = 2(3)(2) + 2(5)(2)$
$A = 32$

To determine the surface area of the roof, calculate the width of a rectangular face.
Sketch a triangle to represent a triangular face of the roof.

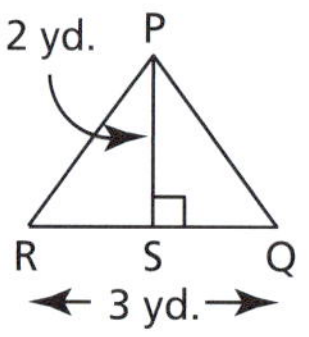

Use the Pythagorean Theorem in right △PSQ.

$PQ^2 = PS^2 + SQ^2$ Substitute the known values.
$PQ^2 = 2^2 + 1.5^2$
$PQ^2 = 6.25$
$PQ = \sqrt{6.25}$
$PQ = 2.5$

Area of the 2 rectangular faces of the roof, in square yards, is:
$A = 2(2.5)(5)$
$A = 25$

Area of the 2 triangular faces of the roof, in square yards, is:
$A = 2\left(\frac{1}{2}\right)(3)(2)$
$A = 6$

Surface area of the cabane à sucre, in square yards, is:
$SA = 32 + 25 + 6 = 63$

The surface area of the cabane à sucre is 63 square yards.

CHECK YOUR UNDERSTANDING

3. A tool shed is formed by a rectangular prism with a triangular prism as its roof. Determine the surface area of the tool shed to the nearest square foot.

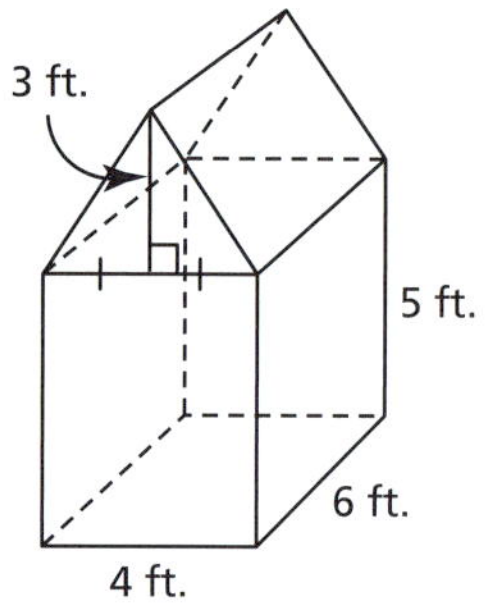

[Answer: approximately 155 ft.^{2}]

Discuss the Ideas

1. When you determine the surface area of a composite object, how do you identify the faces that comprise the surface area?

2. When might you use the Pythagorean Theorem in a calculation of the surface area or volume of a composite object? How do you know your answer is reasonable?

Exercises

A

3. Determine the surface area of each composite object to the nearest square unit.

a) right cylinder and right cone

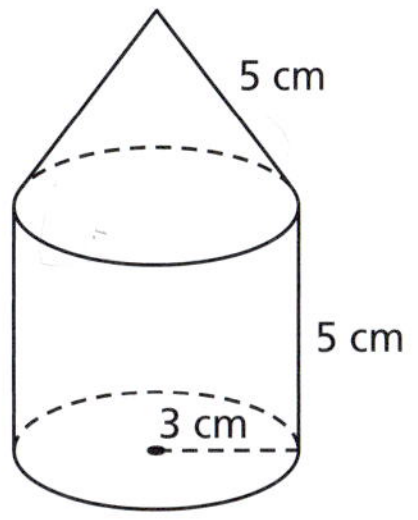

b) right square prism and right square pyramid

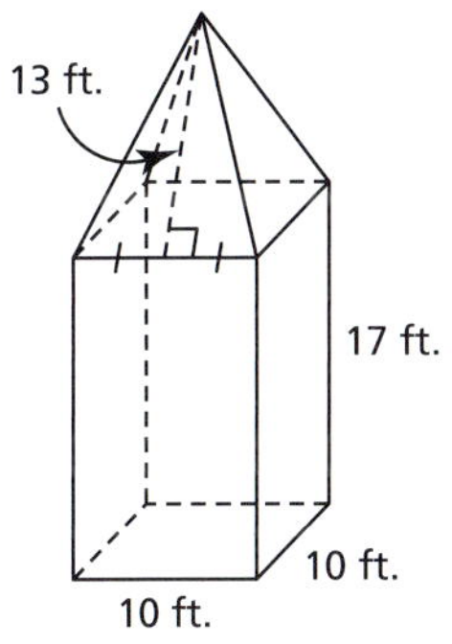

c) right square prism and right cylinder

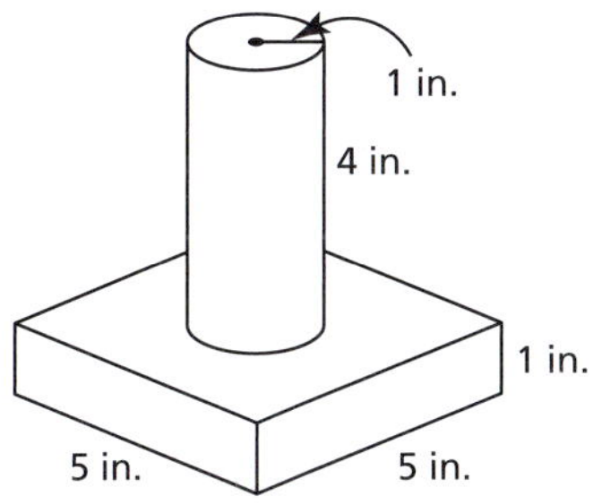

d) right cone and hemisphere

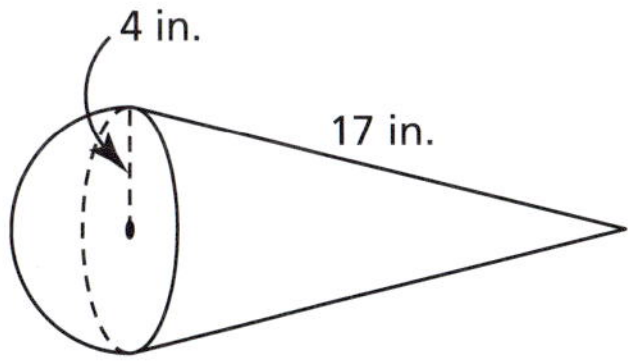

4. a) For which composite objects in question 3 could you calculate the volumes without determining any further dimensions?

b) Determine the volume of each composite object you identified in part a.

B

5. Determine the surface area and volume of each composite object. Write the answers to the nearest tenth of a unit.

a) right cylinder and hemispheres

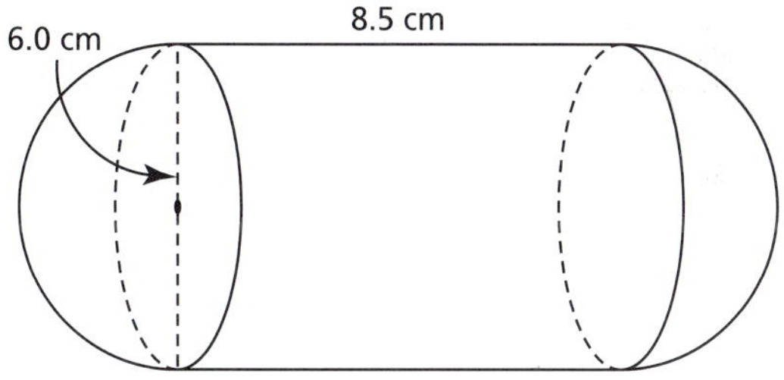

b) right square prism and right square pyramid

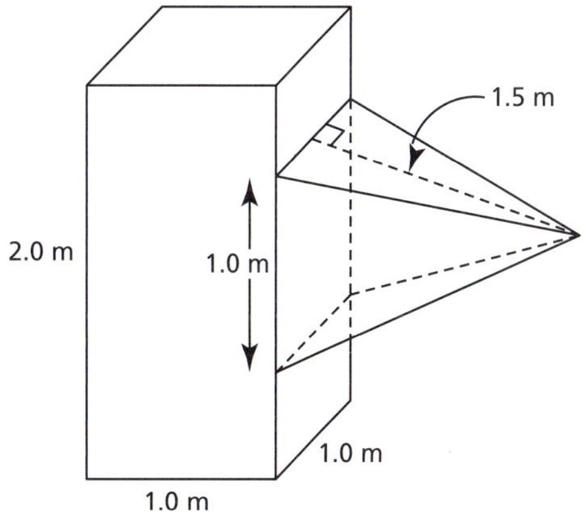

6. For each object, its surface area, SA, and some dimensions are given. Calculate the dimension indicated by the variable. Write each answer to the nearest tenth of a unit.

a) right cylinder

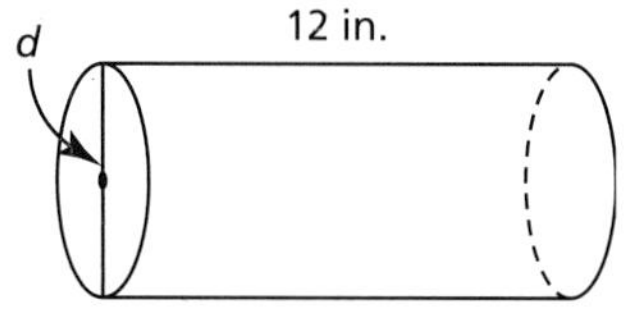

b) right cylinder

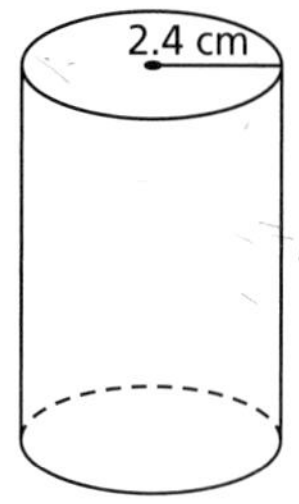

7. A rocket has a cylindrical body and a cone-shaped nose. The cylinder is 55 cm long with a radius of 6 cm. The cone has a slant height of 12 cm and has the same radius as the cylinder.

a) Sketch and label a diagram of the rocket.

b) Determine the surface area of the rocket to the nearest square centimetre.

c) Determine the volume of the rocket to the nearest cubic centimetre.

d) One-third of the interior space of the rocket is used for fuel storage. How much fuel can the rocket hold?

8. A solid sphere just fits inside a cube that has an edge length equal to the diameter of the sphere. The edge length of the cube is 5.8 cm. What is the volume of air in the cube to the nearest cubic centimetre?

9. Here are two different grain storage bins.

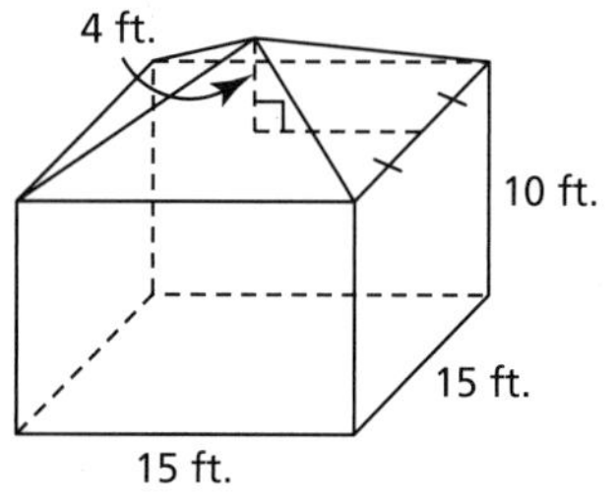

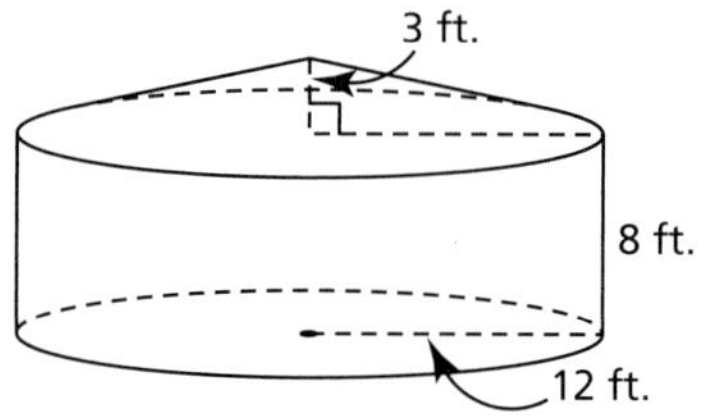

a) Which storage bin holds more grain?

b) Each storage bin has a cement base. The materials for the walls and roof of the square-based bin cost $10.49 per square foot. The materials for the walls and roof of the circular-based bin cost $9.25 per square foot. Which bin is cheaper to build? Justify your answer.

10. Determine the volume of each object to the nearest tenth of a cubic unit.

a) a right square prism with a right square pyramid removed

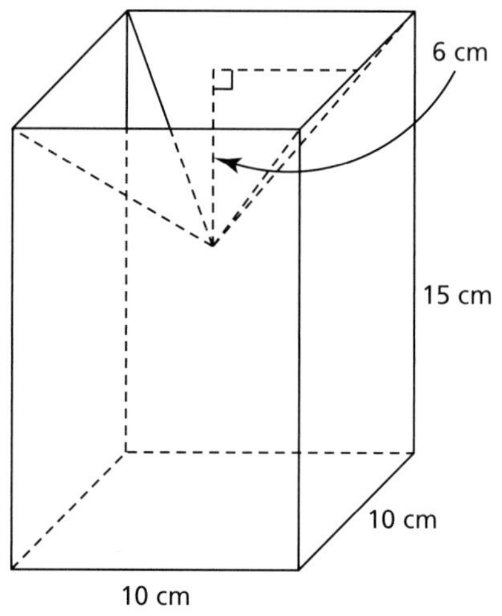

b) a right cylinder with a hemisphere removed

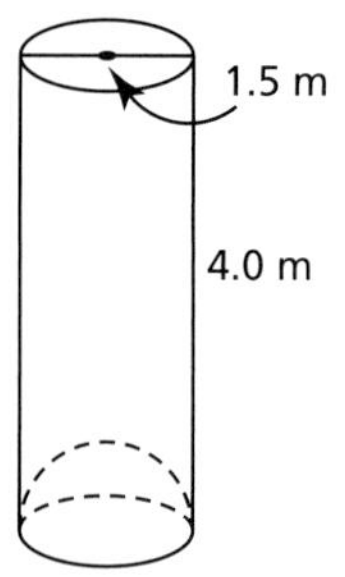

11. Determine the surface area of each object in question 10 to the nearest tenth of a square unit.

C

12. An igloo approximates a hemisphere, with an entrance tunnel that approximates half a right cylinder.

The base of the igloo has diameter 4.0 m. The entrance is 0.8 m long; it has an external radius of 0.8 m and an internal radius of 0.7 m. Calculate the surface area of the outside of the igloo and tunnel.

13. An ice sculpture can be made by pouring water into a mould or by carving blocks of ice.

a) One mould forms a sculpture that is a composite object comprising a right cylinder with base diameter 15 in. and height 3 in., and a right cone with the same base diameter as the base of the cylinder and a height of 9 in. Determine the volume of the sculpture to the nearest cubic inch.

b) The sculpture in part a is carved out of a block of ice with the shape of a right square prism. What are the least possible dimensions for the prism to the nearest inch?

c) The sculpture in part a is carved from a block of ice with the shape of a right rectangular prism with dimensions 16 in. by 15 in. by 12 in. What volume of ice, in cubic inches, remains?

Reflect

Which do you find easier to calculate: the surface area of a composite object or its volume? Explain your choice.

THE WORLD OF MATH

Profile: Festival du Voyageur

The Festival du Voyageur is an annual event that takes place in Winnipeg every February to celebrate the city's Francophone and Métis cultural heritage. Major attractions at the festival are the snow sculptures that are displayed at Voyageur Park and in neighbourhoods around the city. The festival also includes an International Snow Sculpting Symposium, where teams of sculptors create unique artwork from blocks of snow measuring 3.0 m by 3.7 m by 3.7 m. Each year, sculptors transform 450 000 cubic feet of snow into a winter wonderland.

What is the volume of snow in a sculpture that measures 50 ft. by 18 ft. by 6 ft.?

STUDY GUIDE

CONCEPT SUMMARY

Big Ideas	Applying the Big Ideas
■ You can use proportional reasoning to convert measurements.	■ Converting within and between two systems of measurement allows you to measure lengths using the most appropriate unit from either system.
■ The volume of a right pyramid or cone is related to the volume of the enclosing right prism or cylinder.	■ The volume of a right pyramid or a right cone is $\frac{1}{3}$ the volume of its enclosing right prism or right cylinder.
■ The surface area of a right pyramid or cone is the sum of the areas of the faces and the curved surfaces.	■ You can determine the surface area of a right pyramid by sketching a labelled diagram of its net and then calculating the area of each triangle and polygon that forms the net. For a right pyramid with a regular polygon base, the triangular faces are congruent. ■ For a right pyramid with a regular polygon base and for a right cone, the surface area is: $\frac{1}{2}$(slant height)(perimeter of base) + (base area)
■ The surface area of a sphere is related to the curved surface area of the enclosing cylinder.	■ The surface area of a sphere is equal to the curved surface area of the cylinder that encloses it.

Reflect on the Chapter

- Why do we need a standard system of measurement?
- What strategies do you have for using a referent to estimate a length?
- What is surface area? Describe how to determine the surface areas of three different shaped objects.
- What is volume? Choose two objects. Explain how their volumes are related.

SKILLS SUMMARY

Skill	Description	Example
Convert within and between systems of measurement. [1.1, 1.3]	Use proportional reasoning to convert. Use unit analysis to check the conversion.	Convert 2 mi. to feet. Use the table on page 6. There are 5280 ft. in 1 mi. So, 2 mi. = 2(5280 ft.) = 10 560 ft.
Choose an appropriate measuring instrument and unit to measure an object. [1.2]	The measuring device could be a ruler, calipers, or tape measure. The units could be imperial or metric.	Which measuring device is most appropriate for measuring the length of your index finger? Which unit would you use? I would use a ruler and measure in centimetres.
Calculate the surface area of a right prism, right pyramid, right cylinder, right cone, sphere, or a composite object. [1.4, 1.6, 1.7]	To determine surface area: **1.** Identify the faces that comprise the surface area. **2.** Calculate the area of each face. **3.** Add the areas. You may need to use the Pythagorean Theorem to determine any dimension that is not given.	Determine the surface area of this cone. 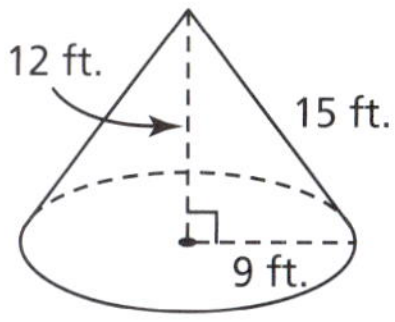 $SA = \pi r^2 + \pi rs$ $SA = \pi(9)^2 + \pi(9)(15)$ $SA = 678.5840\ldots$ Surface area is approximately 679 square feet.
Calculate the volume of a right prism, right pyramid, right cylinder, right cone, sphere, or a composite object. [1.5, 1.6, 1.7]	To determine volume: **1.** Identify the objects. **2.** Use a formula to determine the volume of each object. **3.** Add the volumes, if necessary. You may need to use the Pythagorean Theorem to determine any dimension that is not given.	Determine the volume of the cone above. $V = \frac{1}{3}\pi r^2 h$ $V = \frac{1}{3}\pi(9)^2(12)$ $V = 1017.8760\ldots$ The volume is approximately 1018 cubic feet.

REVIEW

1.1

1. Which imperial unit is the most appropriate unit to measure each item? Justify your choice.

a) the length of your arm
b) the width of the classroom
c) the distance you ran in gym class

2. For each item in question 1a and b:

a) Use a referent to estimate its measure.
b) Use a ruler or tape measure to check your estimate.

3. Convert:

a) 14 yd. to feet
b) 5 mi. to yards
c) 6 ft. 3 in. to inches
d) 123 in. to yards, feet, and inches

4. The scale of a model airplane is 1 in. to 40 in. The model is 8 in. long. How long is the actual plane?

1.2

5. Describe a strategy you would use to estimate then measure each length in imperial units and in metric units.

a) the diameter of a car tire
b) the length of a car
c) the radius of a marble

1.3

6. Convert each measurement:

a) 261 cm to feet and the nearest inch
b) 125 m to yards, feet, and the nearest inch
c) 6 km to miles and the nearest yard
d) 350 mm to feet and the nearest inch

7. Convert each measurement. Answer to the nearest tenth.

a) 13 yd. 2 ft. to metres
b) 4 mi. 350 yd. to kilometres
c) 1 ft. 7 in. to centimetres
d) $8\frac{1}{2}$ in. to millimetres

8. The length of Vancouver Island from the north to the south is approximately 460 km. Sarah has an average stride length of 27 in. How many strides would Sarah take to walk from the northernmost tip to the southernmost tip?

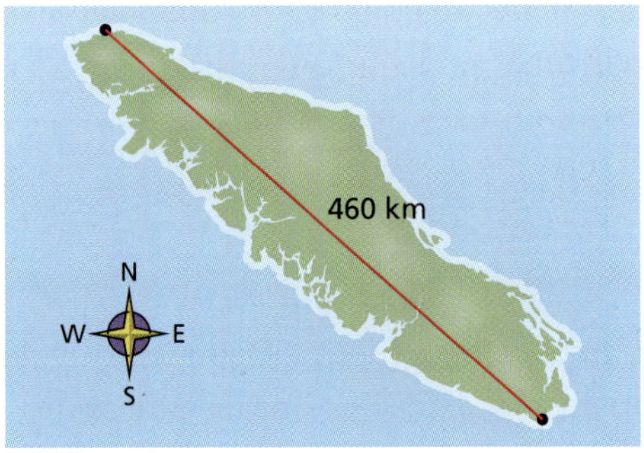

1.4

9. Determine the surface area of each object to the nearest square unit.

a) right cone

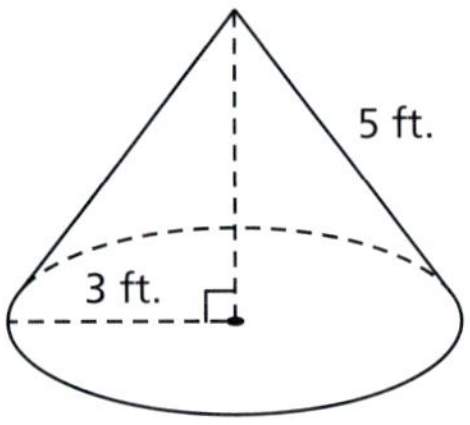

b) regular tetrahedron

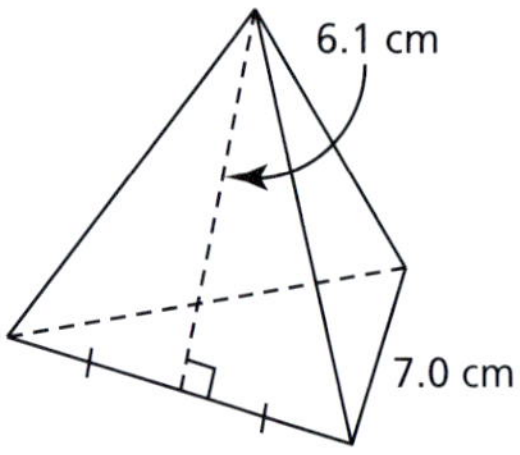

c) right cone

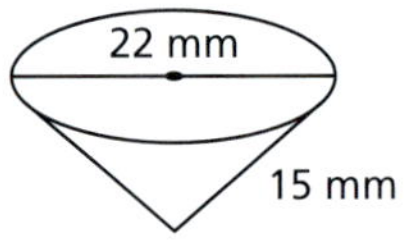

d) right rectangular pyramid

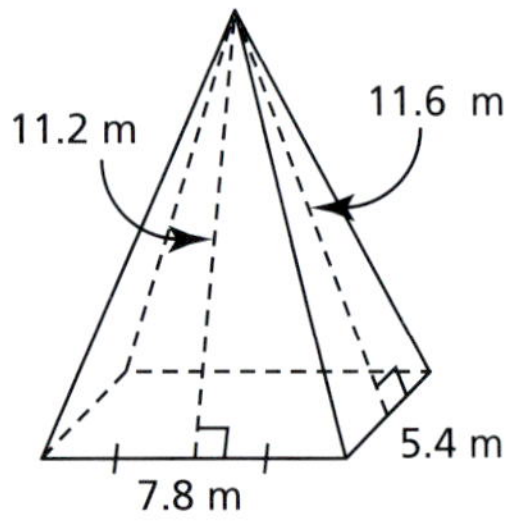

10. A right rectangular pyramid has base dimensions 7 yd. by 5 yd. and a height of 10 yd. Determine the surface area of the pyramid to the nearest square yard.

11. Julie is constructing a tent in the shape of a right square pyramid. She uses 4 poles, each 2.1 m long, for the edges that form the triangular surfaces. The side length of the base of the tent is 1.5 m.
    a) Sketch a diagram of the tent.
    b) What is the slant height of the tent to the nearest tenth of a metre?
    c) What is the lateral surface area of the tent to the nearest square metre?

12. A regular tetrahedron has edge length 10 in.
    a) What is the slant height of the tetrahedron to the nearest tenth of an inch?
    b) What is the surface area of the tetrahedron to the nearest square inch?

13. An ice-cream cone is to be coated with chocolate on the inside. The cone has an interior diameter of 7.5 cm and an interior height of 10.0 cm. What is the area to be coated? Write the answer to the nearest tenth of a square unit.

14. The Summerhill Pyramid Winery in Kelowna, B.C., has a pyramid that is a replica of the Great Pyramid in Egypt. The Summerhill pyramid has base side length 60 ft. and height 38 ft. The pyramid is to be coated with polished white limestone. What area of limestone is needed to the nearest square foot?

1.5

15. Determine the volume of each object to the nearest cubic unit.
    a) right rectangular pyramid

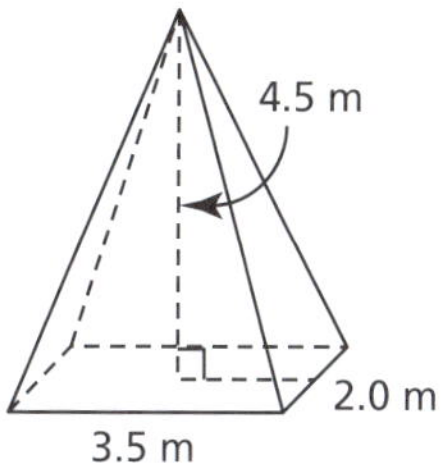

    b) right cone

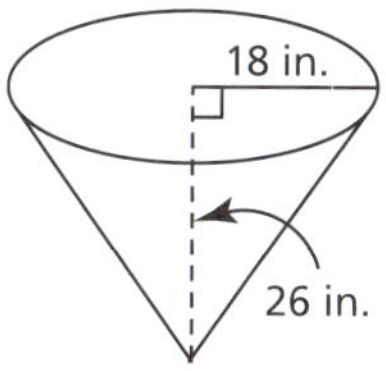

    c) right square pyramid

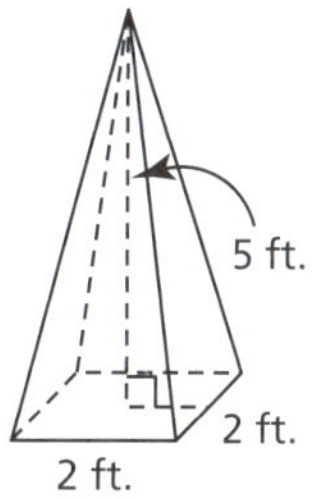

    d) right cone

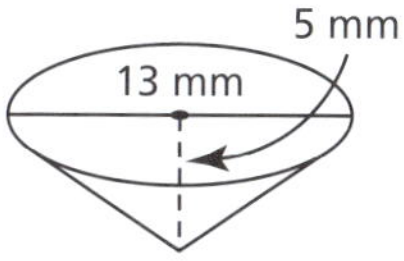

16. To determine the volume of a cone, Owen measured its slant height as 7.3 cm and its base diameter as 9.6 cm. Can Owen determine the volume of the cone with only these measurements? If your answer is yes, show your solution. If your answer is no, explain what Owen needs to do to determine the volume, then calculate the volume.

17. Emma used water displacement in a large measuring cylinder to determine that the volume of a right square pyramid was 400 cm^3. Emma measured the side of the base as 10 cm. What was the height of the pyramid?

18. a) A solid iron garden ornament has the shape of a right square pyramid. The slant height of the pyramid is 8 in. and the side length of the base is 3 in. Determine the volume of the garden ornament to the nearest cubic inch.
    b) Another garden ornament has volume 96 cubic inches. It has the same shape and the same height as the ornament in part a. What is the side length of its base to the nearest inch?

19. For each object, its volume, V, and some dimensions are given. Calculate the dimension indicated by the variable. Write each answer to the nearest tenth of a unit.

a) right cone

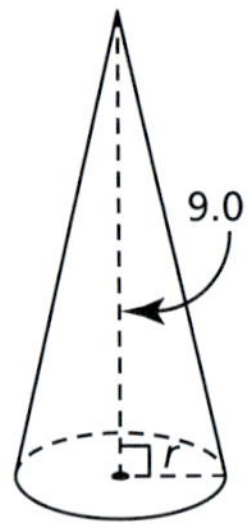

$V = 41.6\ m^3$

b) right rectangular pyramid

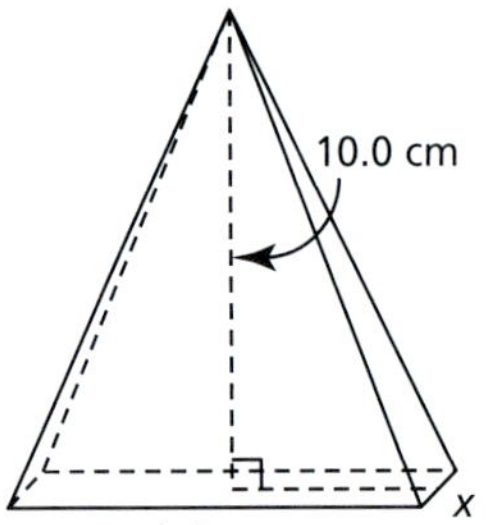

$V = 68.4\ cm^3$

1.6

20. Determine the surface area and volume of each sphere. Write the answers to the nearest whole unit.

a)

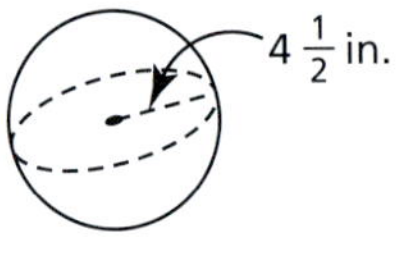

b)

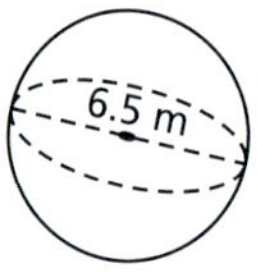

21. Sketch a hemisphere with diameter 18 ft.

a) What is the surface area of the hemisphere to the nearest square foot?

b) What is the volume of the hemisphere to the nearest cubic foot?

22. The surface area of a sphere is approximately 66 square inches. What is the diameter of the sphere to the nearest tenth of an inch?

23. A handful of snow is compressed into a spherical snowball. The snowball has circumference 18 cm. What is its volume?

24. A "gazing ball" is a spherical garden ornament with a mirrored surface that reflects its surroundings. The surface area of the ball is approximately 314 square inches. What is its volume to the nearest cubic inch?

1.7

25. Determine the surface area and volume of each composite object to the nearest whole unit.

a) right square prism and right square pyramid

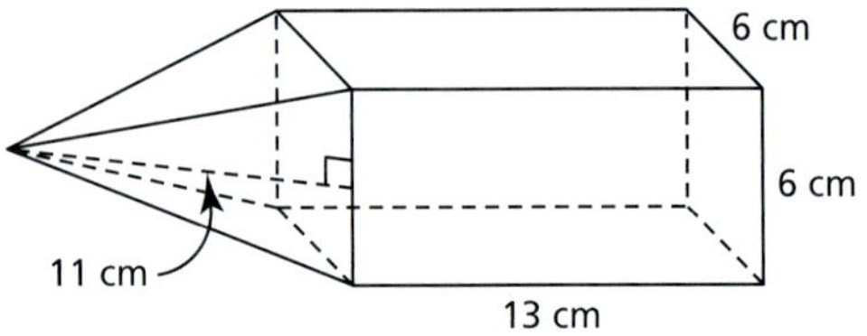

b) right cylinder and right cones

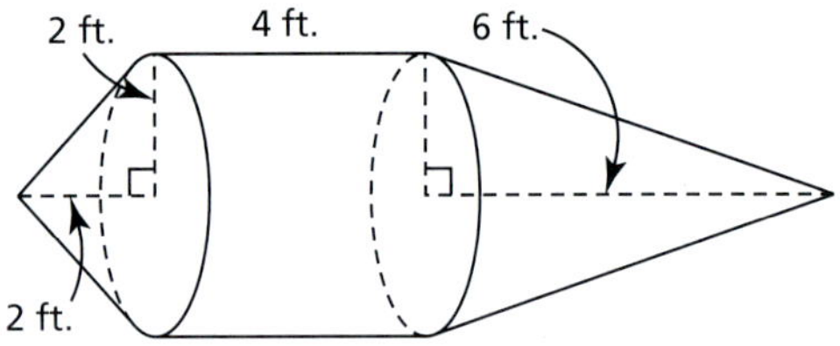

26. A sandcastle comprises a right rectangular prism with base dimensions 75 cm by 50 cm, and height 30 cm. There are 4 congruent cones on the top surface of the prism. Each cone has base diameter 10 cm and slant height 15 cm.

a) Determine the volume of sand required to construct this castle. Write the answer to the nearest cubic centimetre.

b) Determine the surface area of the castle. Write the answer to the nearest square centimetre.

27. For each object, its surface area, SA, and some dimensions are given. Calculate the dimension indicated by the variable. Write each answer to the nearest whole unit.

a) right square pyramid

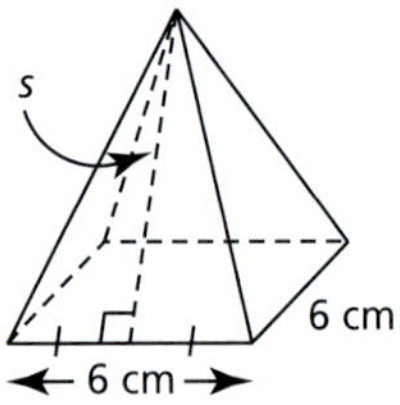

$SA = 132\ cm^2$

b) right cone

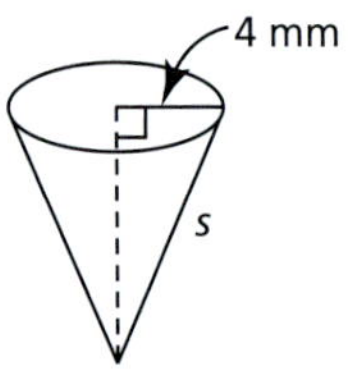

$SA = 176\ mm^2$

PRACTICE TEST

For questions 1 and 2, choose the correct answer: A, B, C, or D

1. Which expression represents an approximate measure of 3 cm in inches?

A. $\frac{3}{0.4}$ **B.** $3(0.4)$

C. $\frac{0.4}{3}$ **D.** $\frac{1}{3(0.4)}$

2. Which expression represents the volume of a sphere with radius r?

A. $\frac{4}{3}\pi^3 r$ **B.** $4\pi r^2$

C. $\frac{4}{3}\pi r^3$ **D.** $\frac{4}{3}\pi r^2$

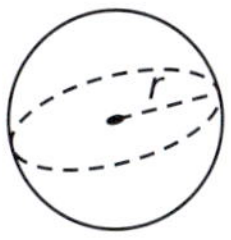

3. A right cylinder and a right cone have the same base radius and the same height. How are their volumes related?

4. Determine the volume and surface area of each composite object. Write your answers to the nearest tenth of a unit.

a)

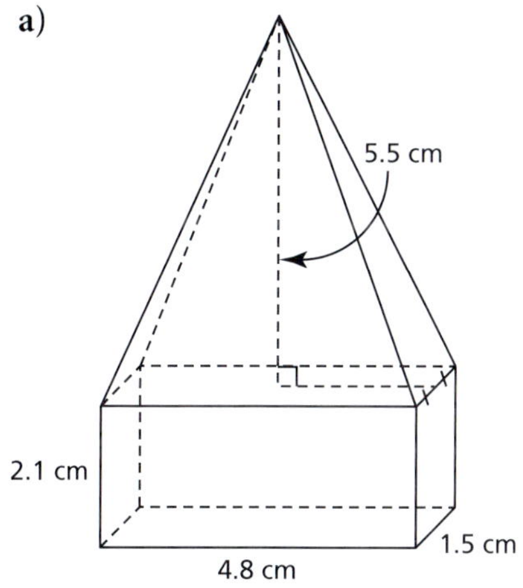

b)

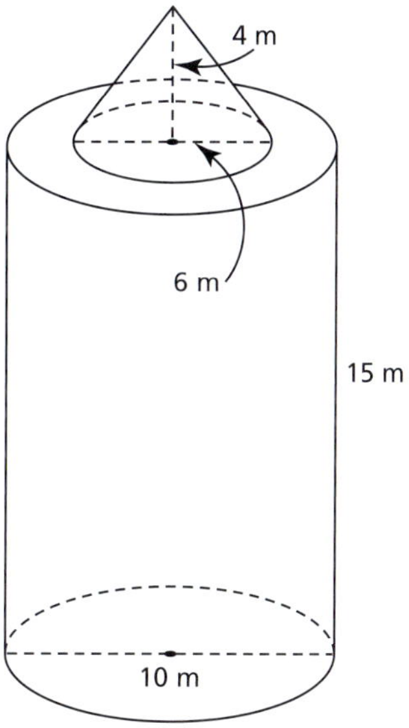

5. A student measured the height of a right square pyramid as 3 in. and the side length of its base as 2 in.

a) Which measuring instrument do you think the student used? Justify your answer.

b) Explain how the student could use these measurements to determine the volume and surface area of the pyramid.

6. A sphere has a radius of 5.0 cm. What is the radius of a hemisphere that has the same surface area as the sphere? Write the answer to the nearest tenth of a centimetre.

2 Trigonometry

BUILDING ON

- applying the Pythagorean Theorem
- solving problems using properties of similar polygons
- solving problems involving ratios

BIG IDEAS

In a right triangle,

- The ratio of any two sides remains constant even if the triangle is enlarged or reduced.
- You can use the ratio of the lengths of two sides to determine the measure of one of the acute angles.
- You can use the length of one side and the measure of an acute angle to determine the length of another side of the triangle.

NEW VOCABULARY

angle of inclination
tangent ratio
indirect measurement
sine ratio
cosine ratio
angle of elevation
angle of depression

SCIENCE WORLD *This building was constructed for the Expo '86 World Fair held in Vancouver, British Columbia. The structure is a geodesic dome containing 766 triangles.*

2.1 The Tangent Ratio

LESSON FOCUS

Develop the tangent ratio and relate it to the angle of inclination of a line segment.

This ranger's cabin on Herschel Island, Yukon, has solar panels on its roof.

Make Connections

The **angle of inclination** of a line or line segment is the acute angle it makes with the horizontal.

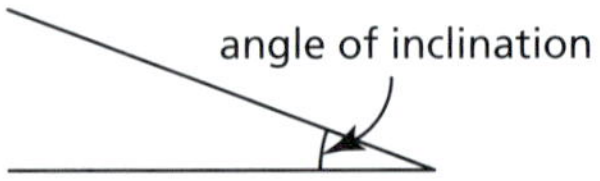

South-facing solar panels on a roof work best when the **angle of inclination** of the roof, that is, the angle between the roof and the horizontal, is approximately equal to the latitude of the house.

When an architect designs a house that will have solar panels on its roof, she has to determine the width and height of the roof so that the panels work efficiently.

What happens to the angle of inclination if the diagram of the house is drawn using a different scale?

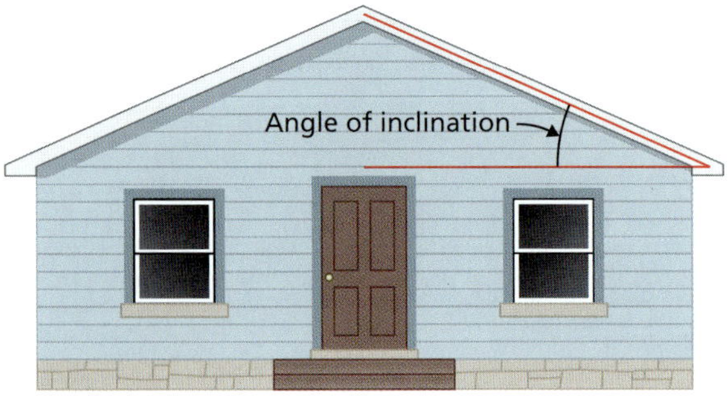

You will investigate the relationship between one acute angle in a right triangle and two sides of that triangle.

Construct Understanding

Recall that two triangles are similar if one triangle is an enlargement or a reduction of the other.

TRY THIS

Work with a partner.

You will need grid paper, a ruler, and a protractor.

A. On grid paper, draw a right $\triangle ABC$ with $\angle B = 90°$.

B. Each of you draws a different right triangle that is similar to $\triangle ABC$.

C. Measure the sides and angles of each triangle. Label your diagrams with the measures.

D. The two shorter sides of a right triangle are its legs. Calculate the ratio of the legs $\frac{CB}{BA}$ as a decimal, then the corresponding ratio for each of the similar triangles.

E. How do the ratios compare?

F. What do you think the value of each ratio depends on?

We name the sides of a right triangle in relation to one of its acute angles.

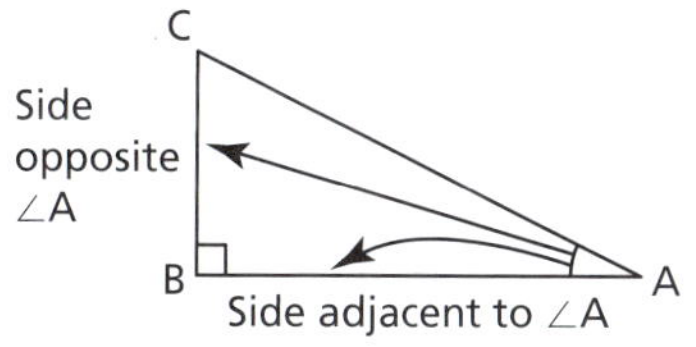

The ratio

Length of side opposite $\angle A$: Length of side adjacent to $\angle A$

depends only on the measure of the angle, not on how large or small the triangle is.

This ratio is called the **tangent ratio** of $\angle A$.
The tangent ratio for $\angle A$ is written as tan A.
We usually write the tangent ratio as a fraction.

The Tangent Ratio

If $\angle A$ is an acute angle in a right triangle, then

$$\tan A = \frac{\text{length of side opposite } \angle A}{\text{length of side adjacent to } \angle A}$$

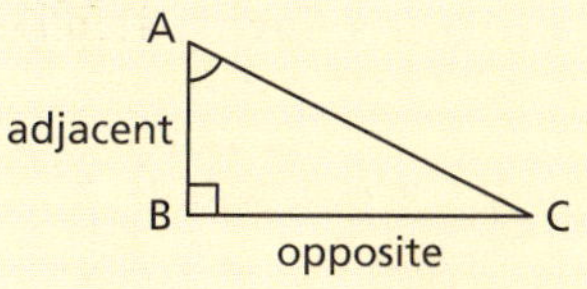

As the size of ∠A increases, what happens to tan A?

The value of the tangent ratio is usually expressed as a decimal that compares the lengths of the sides.

For example, if tan A = 1.5; then, in any similar right triangle with ∠A, the length of the side opposite ∠A is 1.5 times the length of the side adjacent to ∠A.

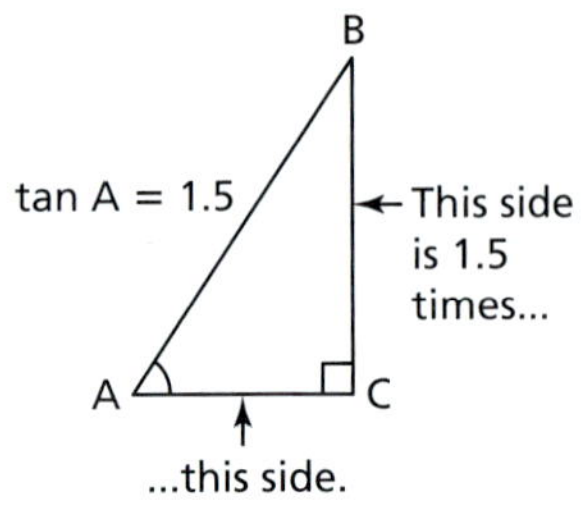

Example 1 Determining the Tangent Ratios for Angles

Determine tan D and tan F.

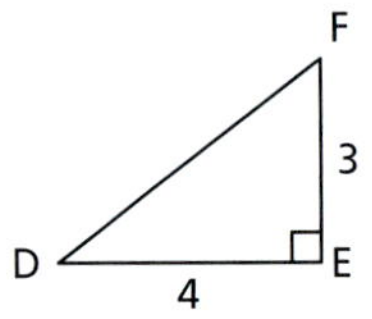

SOLUTION

$$\tan D = \frac{\text{length of side opposite } \angle D}{\text{length of side adjacent to } \angle D}$$

$$\tan D = \frac{EF}{DE}$$

EF is opposite ∠D, DE is adjacent to ∠D.

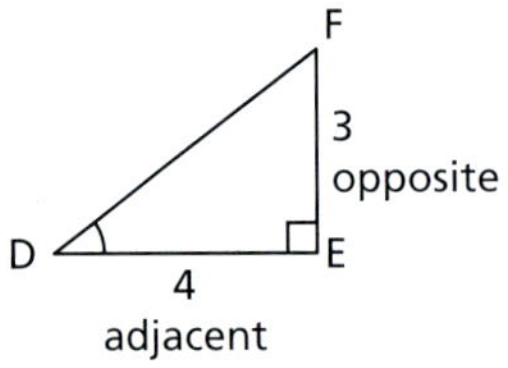

$$\tan D = \frac{3}{4}$$

$$\tan D = 0.75$$

$$\tan F = \frac{\text{length of side opposite } \angle F}{\text{length of side adjacent to } \angle F}$$

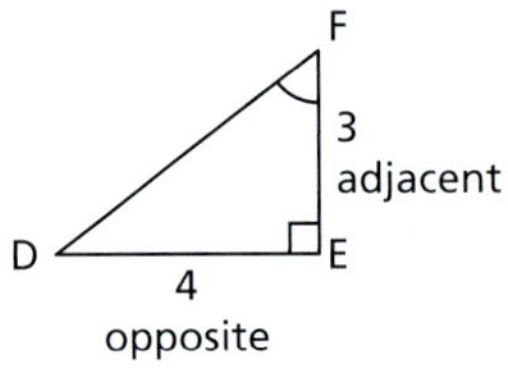

$$\tan F = \frac{DE}{EF}$$

$$\tan F = \frac{4}{3}$$

$$\tan F = 1.\bar{3}$$

CHECK YOUR UNDERSTANDING

1. Determine tan X and tan Z.

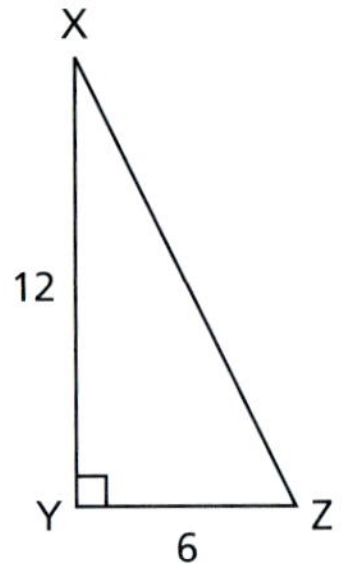

[Answer: tan X = 0.5; tan Z = 2]

How are the values of tan D and tan F related? Explain why this relation will always be true for the acute angles in a right triangle.

You can use a scientific calculator to determine the measure of an acute angle when you know the value of its tangent. The $\tan^{-1}$ or InvTan calculator operation does this.

Example 2 Using the Tangent Ratio to Determine the Measure of an Angle

Determine the measures of ∠G and ∠J to the nearest tenth of a degree.

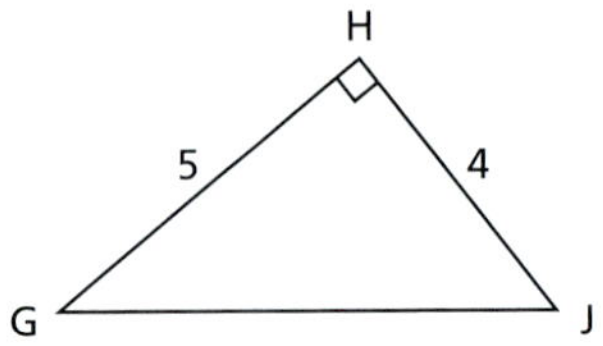

SOLUTION

In right $\triangle GHJ$:

HJ is opposite $\angle G$, HG is adjacent to $\angle G$.

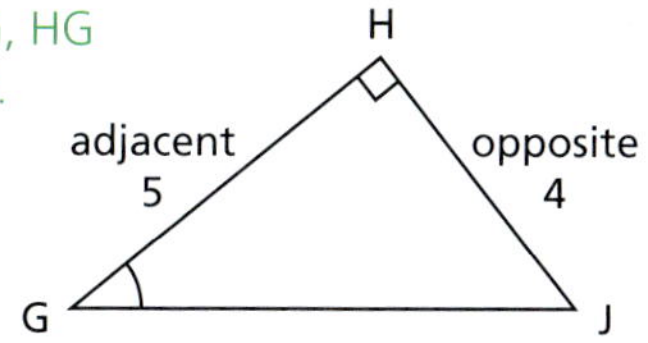

$$\tan G = \frac{\text{opposite}}{\text{adjacent}}$$

$$\tan G = \frac{HJ}{GH}$$

$$\tan G = \frac{4}{5}$$

$$\angle G \doteq 38.7°$$

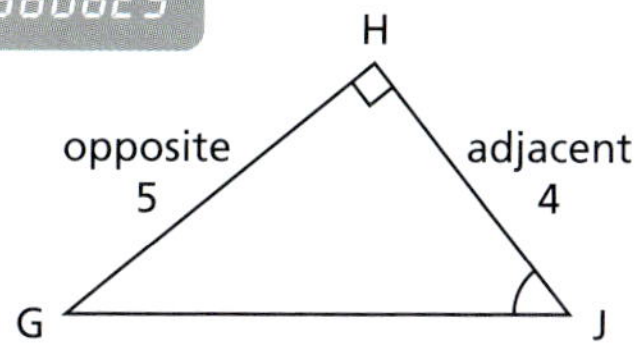

$$\tan J = \frac{\text{opposite}}{\text{adjacent}}$$

$$\tan J = \frac{GH}{HJ}$$

$$\tan J = \frac{5}{4}$$

$$\angle J \doteq 51.3°$$

CHECK YOUR UNDERSTANDING

2. Determine the measures of $\angle K$ and $\angle N$ to the nearest tenth of a degree.

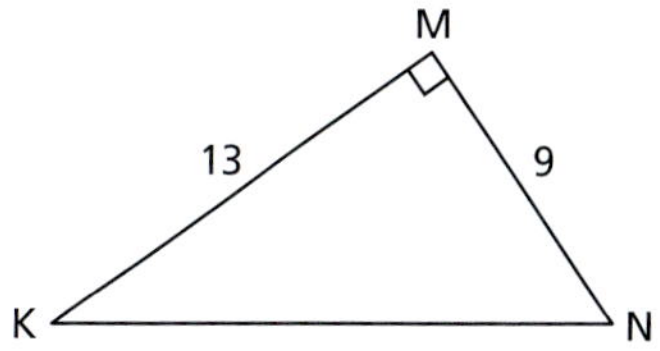

[Answer: $\angle K \doteq 34.7°$; $\angle N \doteq 55.3°$]

What other strategy could you use to determine $\angle J$?

Example 3 Using the Tangent Ratio to Determine an Angle of Inclination

The latitude of Fort Smith, NWT, is approximately 60°. Determine whether this design for a solar panel is the best for Fort Smith. Justify your answer.

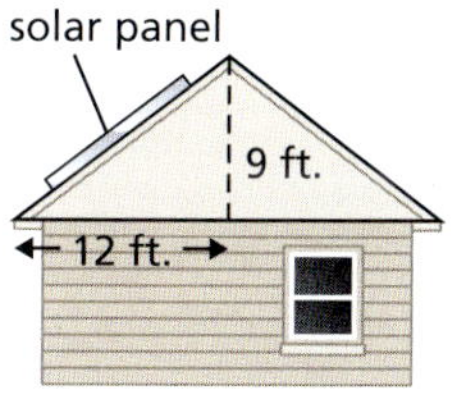

SOLUTION

The best angle of inclination for the solar panel is the same as the latitude, 60°. Draw a right triangle to represent the cross-section of the roof and solar panel. $\angle C$ is the angle of inclination. In $\triangle ABC$:

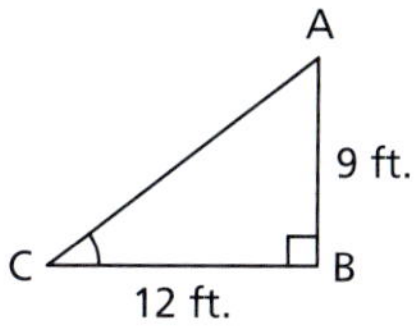

$$\tan C = \frac{\text{opposite}}{\text{adjacent}}$$

$$\tan C = \frac{AB}{BC}$$

AB is opposite $\angle C$, BC is adjacent to $\angle C$.

$$\tan C = \frac{9}{12}$$

$$\angle C \doteq 37°$$

The angle of inclination of the solar panel is about 37°, which is not equal to the latitude of Fort Smith. So, this is not the best design.

CHECK YOUR UNDERSTANDING

3. Clyde River on Baffin Island, Nunavut, has a latitude of approximately 70°. The diagram shows the side view of some solar panels. Determine whether this design for solar panels is the best for Clyde River. Justify your answer.

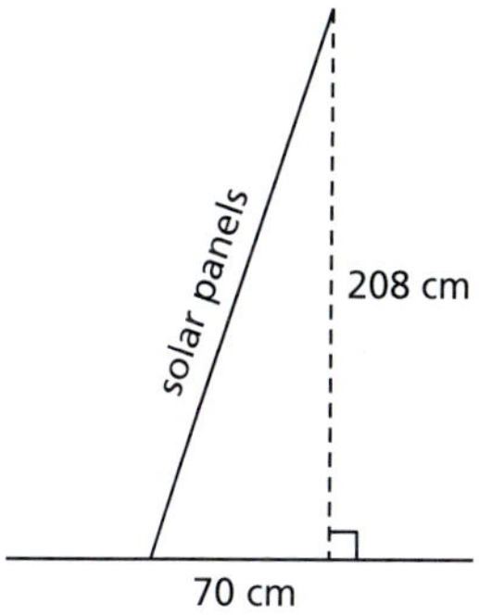

[Answer: The angle of inclination is approximately 71°. So, the design is the best.]

Example 4 Using the Tangent Ratio to Solve a Problem

A 10-ft. ladder leans against the side of a building with its base 4 ft. from the wall.

What angle, to the nearest degree, does the ladder make with the ground?

SOLUTION

Draw a diagram.

Label the vertices of the triangle PQR.

Assume the ground is horizontal and the building vertical.

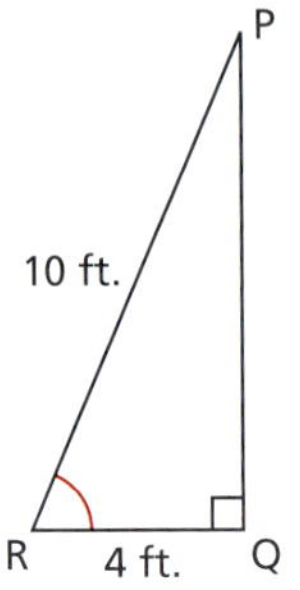

To use the tangent ratio to determine $\angle R$, we first need to know the length of PQ.

Use the Pythagorean Theorem in right $\triangle PQR$.

$PR^2 = PQ^2 + QR^2$ Isolate the unknown.

$PQ^2 = PR^2 - QR^2$

$PQ^2 = 10^2 - 4^2$

$= 84$

$PQ = \sqrt{84}$

Use the tangent ratio in right $\triangle PQR$.

$\tan R = \dfrac{PQ}{QR}$ PQ is opposite $\angle R$, QR is adjacent to $\angle R$.

$\tan R = \dfrac{\sqrt{84}}{4}$

$\tan R = 2.2913\ldots$

$\angle R \doteq 66°$

tan⁻¹(Ans)
66.42182152

The angle between the ladder and the ground is approximately 66°.

Suppose you used $PQ \doteq 9.2$, instead of $PQ = \sqrt{84}$. How could this affect the calculated measure of $\angle R$?

CHECK YOUR UNDERSTANDING

4. A support cable is anchored to the ground 5 m from the base of a telephone pole. The cable is 19 m long. It is attached near the top of the pole. What angle, to the nearest degree, does the cable make with the ground?

[Answer: The angle is approximately 75°.]

Discuss the Ideas

1. Why does the value of the tangent ratio of a given angle not depend on the right triangle you use to calculate it?

2. How can you use the tangent ratio to determine the measures of the acute angles of a right triangle when you know the lengths of its legs?

Exercises

A

3. In each triangle, write the tangent ratio for each acute angle.

a)

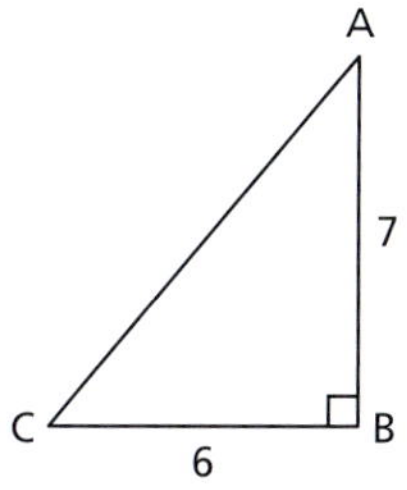

b)

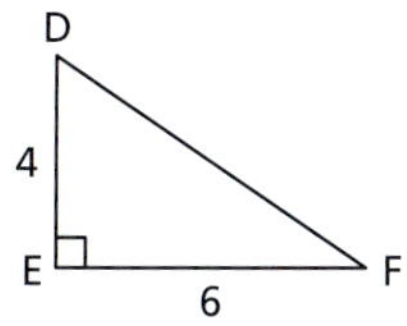

c)

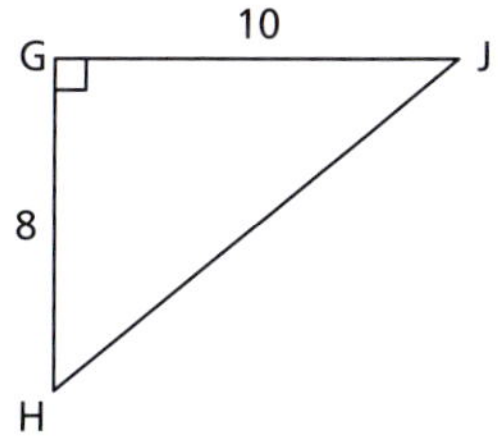

d)

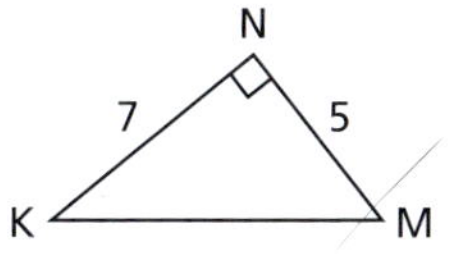

4. To the nearest degree, determine the measure of $\angle X$ for each value of tan X.

a) $\tan X = 0.25$ **b)** $\tan X = 1.25$

c) $\tan X = 2.50$ **d)** $\tan X = 20$

5. Determine the measure of each indicated angle to the nearest degree.

a)

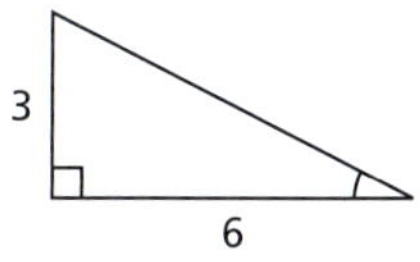

b)

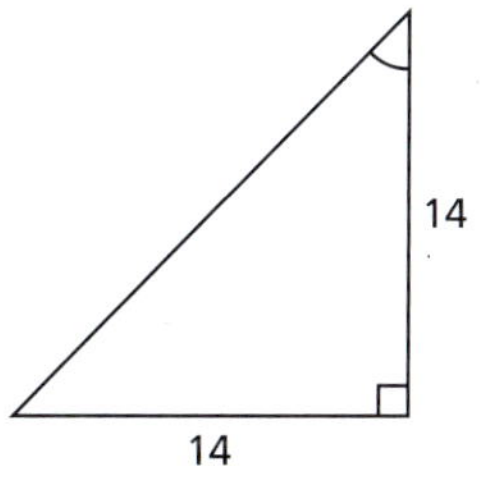

c)

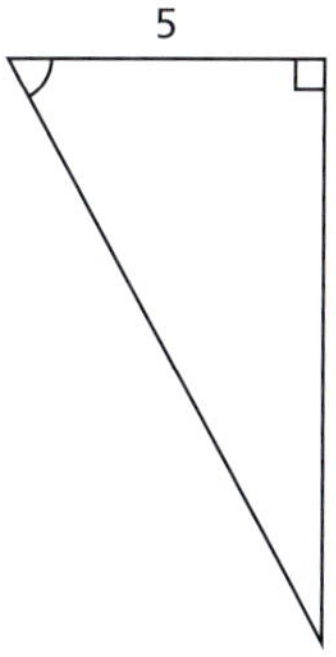

d)

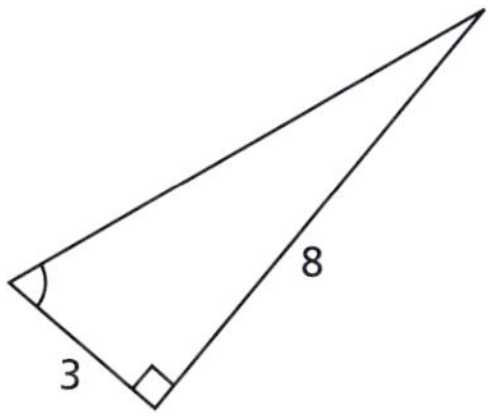

B

6. Use grid paper. Illustrate each tangent ratio by sketching a right triangle, then labelling the measures of its legs.

a) $\tan B = \frac{3}{5}$ **b)** $\tan E = \frac{5}{3}$ **c)** $\tan F = \frac{1}{4}$

d) $\tan G = 4$ **e)** $\tan H = 1$ **f)** $\tan J = 25$

7. a) Is tan 60° greater than or less than 1? How do you know without using a calculator?

b) Is tan 30° greater than or less than 1? How do you know without using a calculator?

8. Determine the measure of each indicated angle to the nearest tenth of a degree. Describe your solution method.

a)

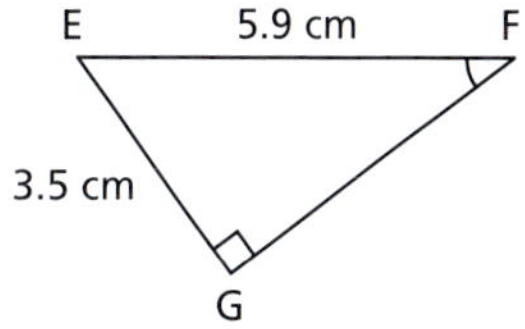

b)

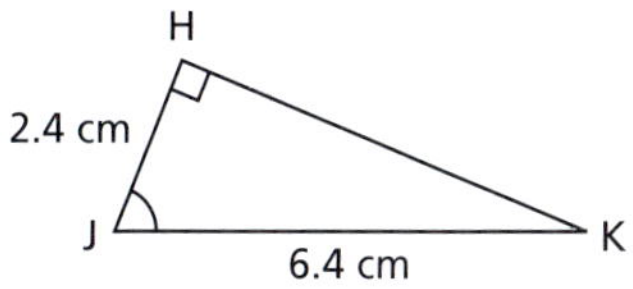

9. a) Why are these triangles similar?

i)

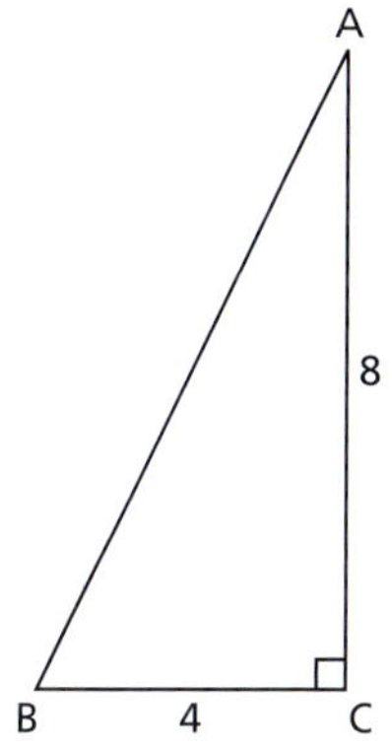

ii)

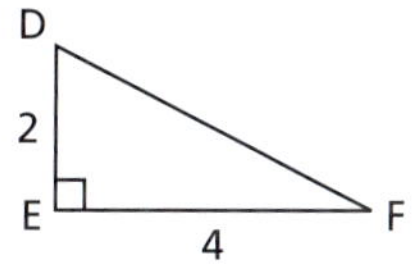

iii)

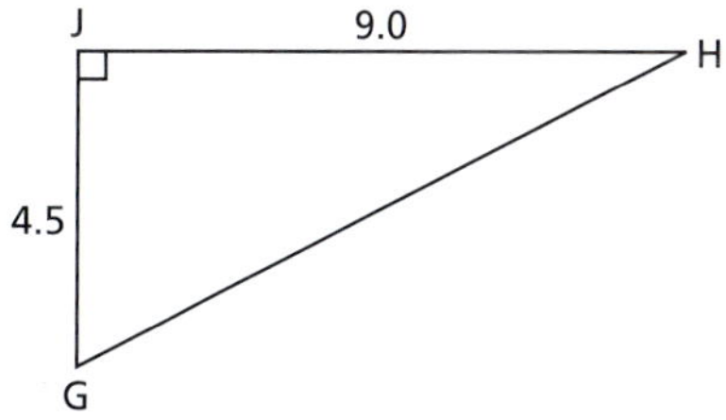

b) For each triangle in part a, determine the measures of the acute angles to the nearest tenth of a degree.

c) To complete part b, did you have to calculate the measures of all 6 acute angles? Explain.

10. Determine the angle of inclination of each line to the nearest tenth of a degree.

a)

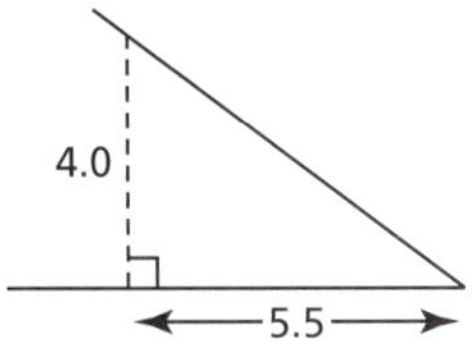

b)

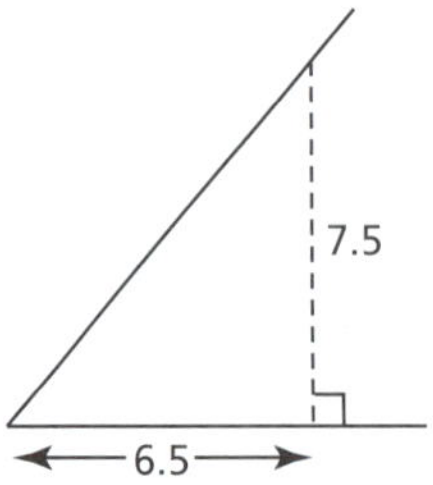

c)

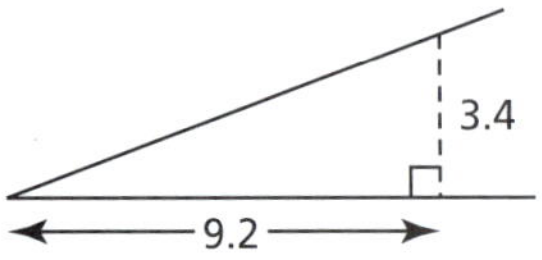

d)

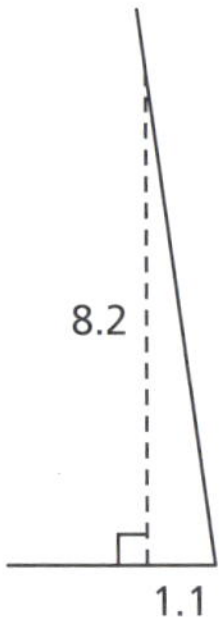

11. The grade or inclination of a road is often expressed as a percent. When a road has a grade of 20%, it increases 20 ft. in altitude for every 100 ft. of horizontal distance.

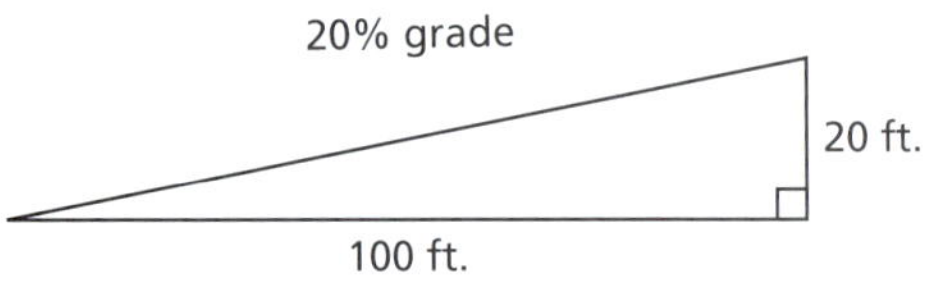

Calculate the angle of inclination, to the nearest degree, of a road with each grade.

a) 20% **b)** 25% **c)** 10% **d)** 15%

12. The approximate latitudes for several cities in western and northern Canada are shown.

Calgary	51.1°	Edmonton	53.5°
Fort McMurray	56.5°	Inuvik	68.4°
Kamloops	51.2°	Saskatoon	52.2°
Victoria	48.4°	Whitehorse	60.7°

For which locations might the following roof design be within 1° of the recommended angle for solar panels? Justify your answer.

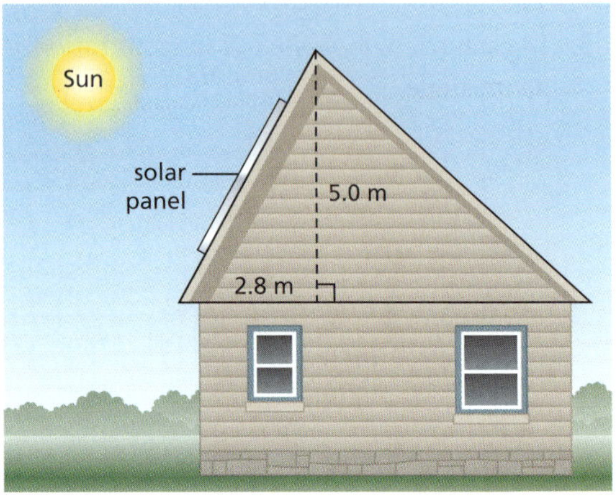

13. Determine the measures of all the acute angles in this diagram, to the nearest tenth of a degree.

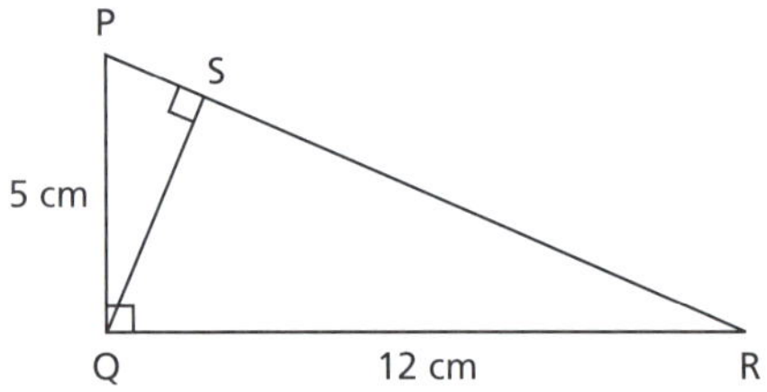

14. A birdwatcher sights an eagle at the top of a 20-m tree. The birdwatcher is lying on the ground 50 m from the tree. At what angle must he incline his camera to take a photograph of the eagle? Give the answer to the nearest degree.

15. A rectangle has dimensions 3 cm by 8 cm. What angles does a diagonal of the rectangle make with the sides of the rectangle? Give the measures to the nearest tenth of a degree.

16. In a right isosceles triangle, why is the tangent of an acute angle equal to 1?

17. A playground slide starts 107 cm above the ground and is 250 cm long. What angle does the slide make with the ground? Give the answer to the nearest degree.

18. The Pioneer ski lift at Golden, B.C., is 1366 m long. It rises 522 m vertically. What is the angle of inclination of the ski lift? Give the answer to the nearest degree.

19. From a rectangular board, a carpenter cuts a stringer to support some stairs. Each stair rises 7.5 in. and has a tread of 11.0 in. To the nearest degree, at what angle should the carpenter cut the board?

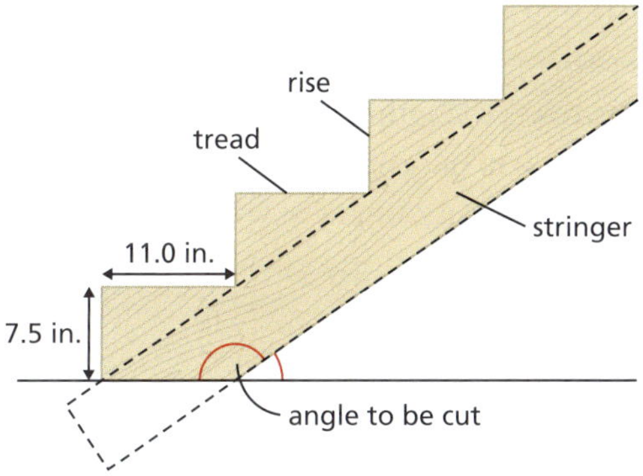

20. For safety reasons, a ladder is positioned so that the distance between its base and the wall is no greater than $\frac{1}{4}$ the length of the ladder. To the nearest degree, what is the least angle of inclination allowed for a ladder?

C

21. In isosceles △XYZ, XY = XZ = 5.9 cm and YZ = 5.0 cm. Determine the measures of the angles of the triangle to the nearest tenth of a degree.

22. For the tangent of an acute angle in a right triangle:

a) What is the least possible value?

b) What is the greatest possible value?

Justify your answers.

23. A Pythagorean spiral is constructed by drawing right triangles on the hypotenuse of other right triangles. Start with a right triangle in which each leg is 1 unit long. Use the hypotenuse of that triangle as one leg of a new triangle and draw the other leg 1 unit long. Continue the process. A spiral is formed.

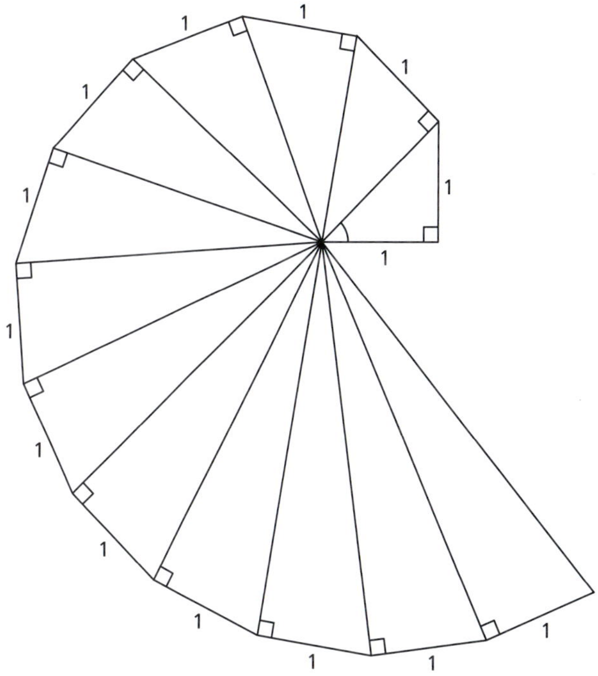

a) Determine the tangent of the angle at the centre of the spiral in each of the first 5 triangles.

b) Use the pattern in part a to predict the tangent of the angle at the centre of the spiral for the 100th triangle. Justify your answer.

Reflect

Summarize what you have learned about the tangent ratio and its relationship to the sides and angles of a right triangle.

2.2 Using the Tangent Ratio to Calculate Lengths

LESSON FOCUS

Apply the tangent ratio to calculate lengths.

Make Connections

In Lesson 2.1, you used the measures of two legs of a right triangle to calculate the measures of the acute angles of the triangle. When you know the length of one leg of a right triangle and the measure of one acute angle, you can draw the triangle.

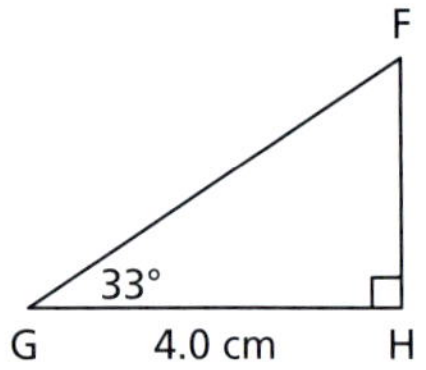

What other measures in the triangle can you calculate?

Construct Understanding

THINK ABOUT IT

Work with a partner.

In right △PQR, ∠Q = 90°, ∠P = 34.5°, and PQ = 46.1 cm.
Determine the length of RQ to the nearest tenth of a centimetre.

We use **direct measurement** when we use a measuring instrument to determine a length or an angle in a polygon. We use **indirect measurement** when we use mathematical reasoning to calculate a length or an angle.

The tangent ratio is a powerful tool we can use to calculate the length of a leg of a right triangle. We are then measuring the length of a side of a triangle **indirectly**.

In a right triangle, we can use the tangent ratio, $\frac{\text{opposite}}{\text{adjacent}}$, to write an equation. When we know the measure of an acute angle and the length of a leg, we solve the equation to determine the length of the other leg.

Example 1 Determining the Length of a Side Opposite a Given Angle

Determine the length of AB to the nearest tenth of a centimetre.

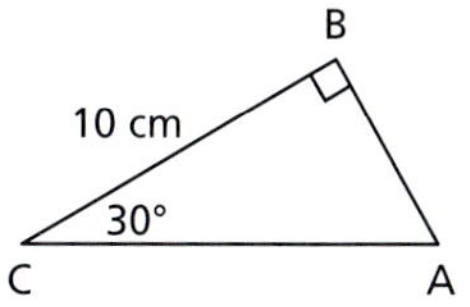

SOLUTION

In right $\triangle ABC$, AB is the side opposite $\angle C$ and BC is the side adjacent to $\angle C$.

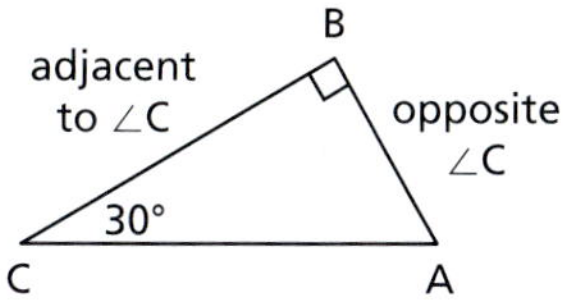

Use the tangent ratio to write an equation.

$$\tan C = \frac{\text{opposite}}{\text{adjacent}}$$

$$\tan C = \frac{AB}{BC}$$

$$\tan 30° = \frac{AB}{10}$$

Solve this equation for AB.

Multiply both sides by 10.

$$10 \times \tan 30° = \frac{AB}{10} \times 10$$

$$10 \tan 30° = AB$$

We write: $10 \times \tan 30°$ as $10 \tan 30°$
When an operation sign is omitted, it is understood to be multiplication.

$$AB = 5.7735\ldots$$

AB is approximately 5.8 cm long.

CHECK YOUR UNDERSTANDING

1. Determine the length of XY to the nearest tenth of a centimetre.

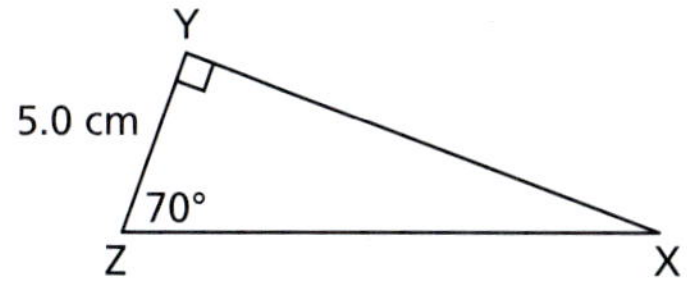

[Answer: XY ≐ 13.7 cm]

How can you determine the length of the hypotenuse in $\triangle ABC$?

Example 2 Determining the Length of a Side Adjacent to a Given Angle

Determine the length of EF to the nearest tenth of a centimetre.

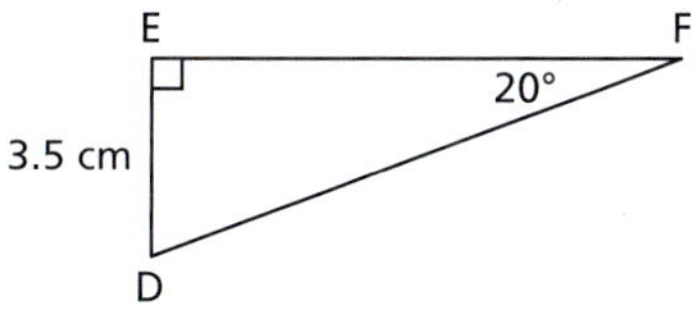

SOLUTIONS

Method 1

In right $\triangle DEF$, DE is opposite $\angle F$ and EF is adjacent to $\angle F$.

$$\tan F = \frac{\text{opposite}}{\text{adjacent}}$$

(Solution continues.)

CHECK YOUR UNDERSTANDING

2. Determine the length of VX to the nearest tenth of a centimetre.

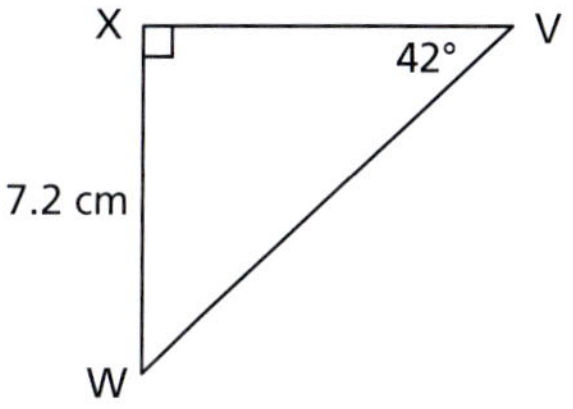

[Answer: VX ≐ 8.0 cm]

$$\tan F = \frac{DE}{EF}$$

$$\tan 20° = \frac{3.5}{EF}$$

Solve the equation for EF. Multiply both sides by EF.

$$EF \tan 20° = EF\left(\frac{3.5}{EF}\right)$$

$$EF \tan 20° = 3.5$$ Divide both sides by tan 20°.

$$\frac{EF \tan 20°}{\tan 20°} = \frac{3.5}{\tan 20°}$$

$$EF = \frac{3.5}{\tan 20°}$$

```
3.5/tan(20)
     9.616170968
```

$$EF = 9.6161\ldots$$

EF is approximately 9.6 cm long.

What is the advantage of solving the equation for EF before calculating tan 20°?

Method 2

In right △DEF:

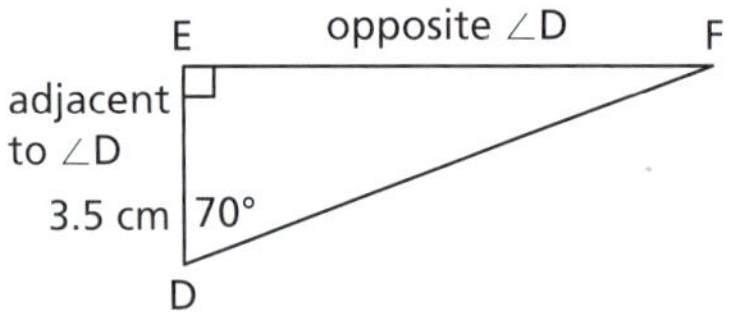

$$\angle D + \angle F = 90°$$

$$\angle D + 20° = 90°$$

$$\angle D = 90° - 20°$$

$$\angle D = 70°$$

EF is opposite ∠D and DE is adjacent to ∠D.

$$\tan D = \frac{\text{opposite}}{\text{adjacent}}$$

$$\tan D = \frac{EF}{DE}$$

$$\tan 70° = \frac{EF}{3.5}$$

Solve the equation for EF. Multiply both sides by 3.5.

$$3.5 \tan 70° = \frac{(EF)(3.5)}{3.5}$$

$$3.5 \tan 70° = EF$$

$$EF = 9.6161\ldots$$

EF is approximately 9.6 cm long.

Which method to determine EF do you think is easier? Why?

How could you determine the length of DF?

It is often convenient to use the lower case letter to name the side opposite a vertex of a triangle.

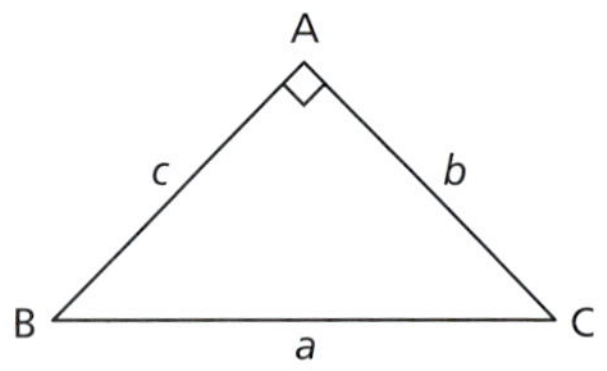

Example 3 Using Tangent to Solve an Indirect Measurement Problem

A searchlight beam shines vertically on a cloud. At a horizontal distance of 250 m from the searchlight, the angle between the ground and the line of sight to the cloud is 75°. Determine the height of the cloud to the nearest metre.

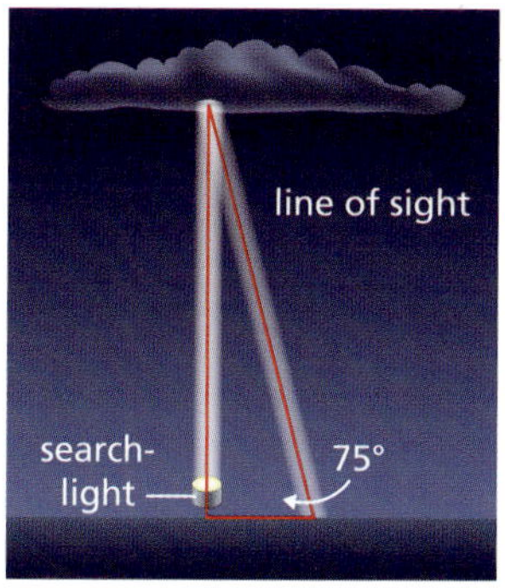

SOLUTION

Sketch and label a diagram to represent the information in the problem.

Assume the ground is horizontal.

In right △CSP, side CS is opposite ∠P and SP is adjacent to ∠P.

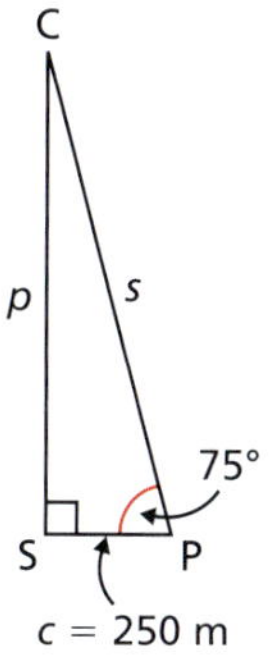

$$\tan P = \frac{\text{opposite}}{\text{adjacent}}$$

$$\tan P = \frac{p}{c}$$

$$\tan 75° = \frac{p}{250}$$

Solve the equation for p. Multiply both sides by 250.

$$250 \tan 75° = \left(\frac{p}{250}\right)250$$

$$250 \tan 75° = p$$

$$p = 933.0127\ldots$$

The cloud is approximately 933 m high.

CHECK YOUR UNDERSTANDING

3. At a horizontal distance of 200 m from the base of an observation tower, the angle between the ground and the line of sight to the top of the tower is 8°. How high is the tower to the nearest metre? The diagram is *not* drawn to scale.

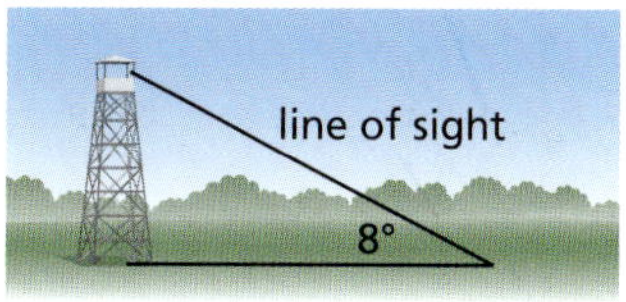

[Answer: 28 m]

Why can we draw a right triangle to represent the problem?

Discuss the Ideas

1. How can you use the tangent ratio to determine the length of a leg in a right triangle?

2. Suppose you know or can calculate the lengths of the legs in a right triangle. Why can you always calculate its hypotenuse?

Exercises

A

3. Determine the length of each indicated side to the nearest tenth of a centimetre.

a) 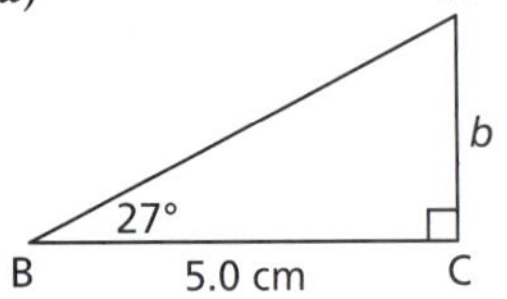

b) 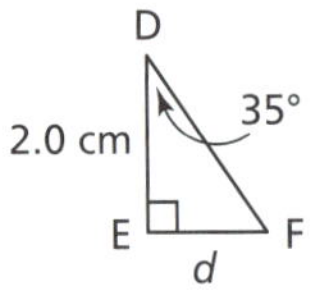

c) 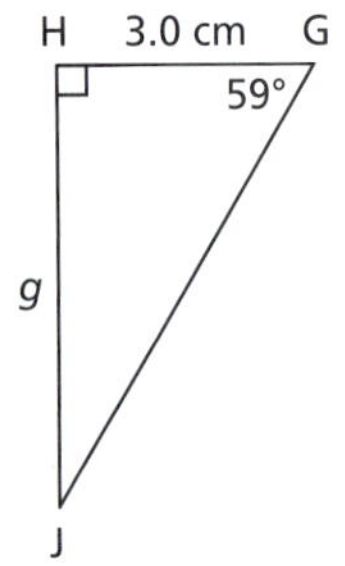

d) 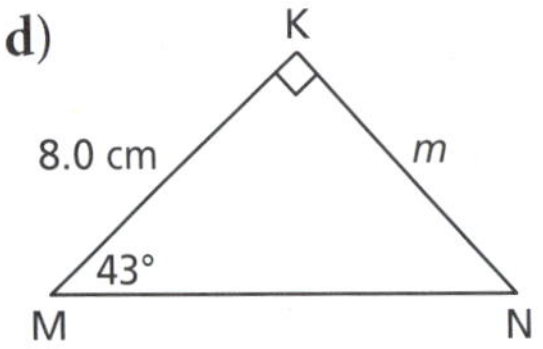

4. Determine the length of each indicated side to the nearest tenth of a centimetre.

a) 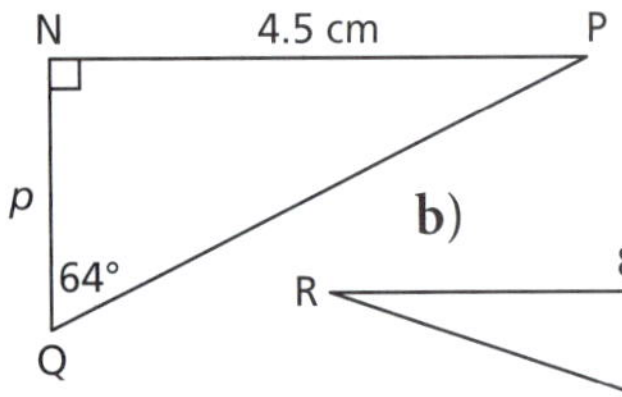

b) 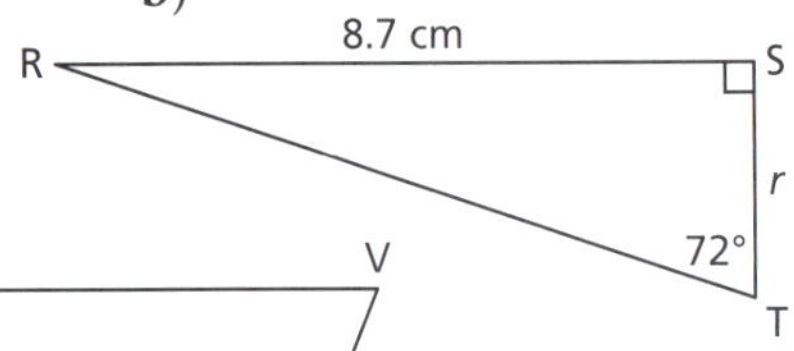

c) 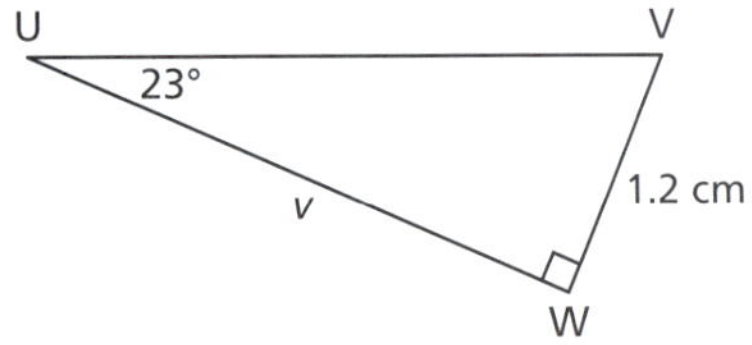

5. Determine the length of each indicated side to the nearest tenth of a centimetre.

a) 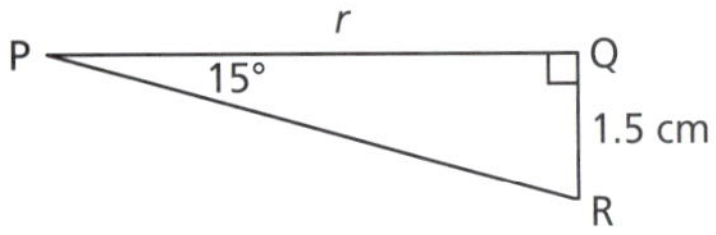

b) 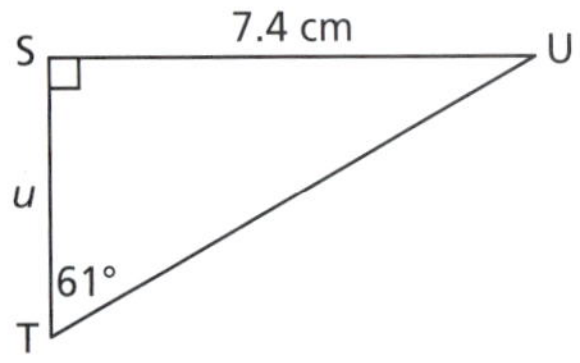

c) 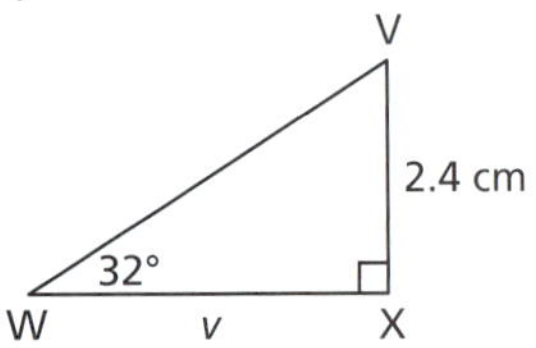

B

6. A guy wire helps to support a tower. The angle between the wire and the level ground is 56°. One end of the wire is 15.4 m from the base of the tower. How high up the tower does the wire reach to the nearest tenth of a metre?

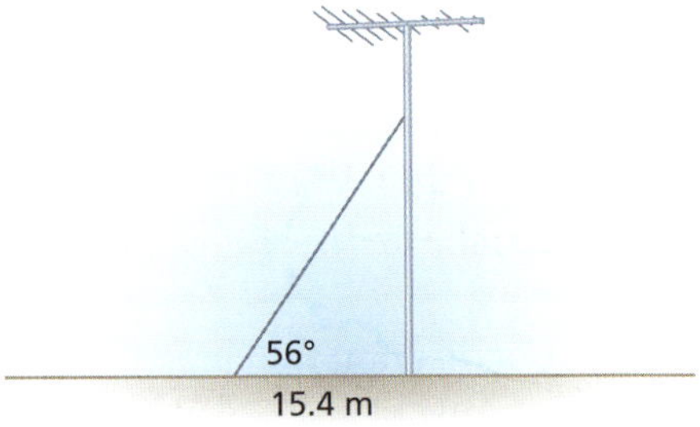

7. The base of a ladder is on level ground 1.3 m from a wall. The ladder leans against the wall. The angle between the ladder and the ground is 71°. How far up the wall does the ladder reach to the nearest tenth of a metre?

8. A helicopter is descending vertically. On the ground, a searchlight is 200 m from the point where the helicopter will land. It shines on the helicopter and the angle the beam makes with the ground is 43°. How high is the helicopter at this point to the nearest metre?

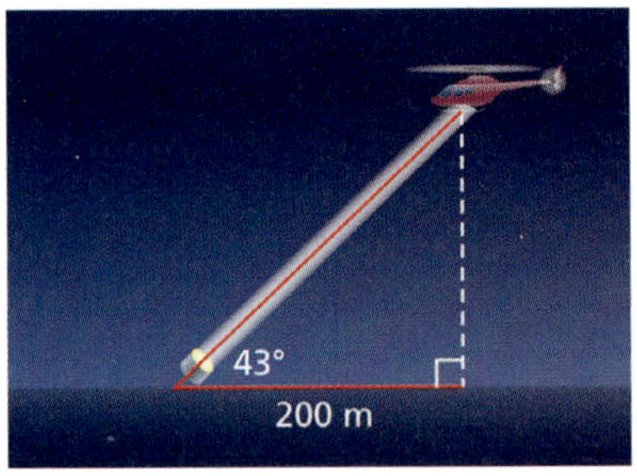

9. Determine the length of the hypotenuse of each right triangle to the nearest tenth of a centimetre. Describe your strategy.

a)

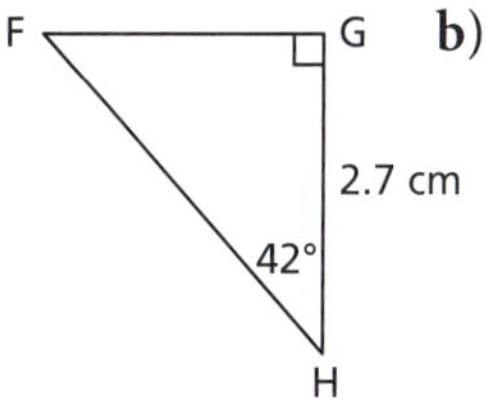

b)

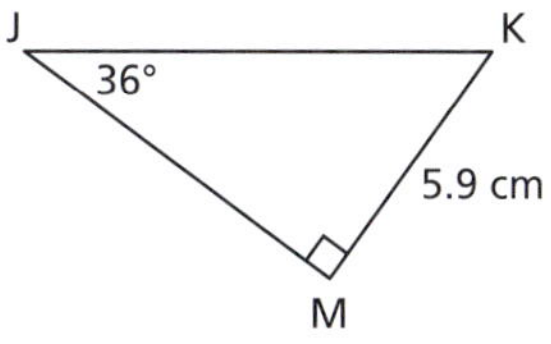

10. Claire knows that the Calgary Tower is 191 m high. At a certain point, the angle between the ground and Claire's line of sight to the top of the tower was 81°. To the nearest metre, about how far was Claire from the tower? Why is this distance approximate?

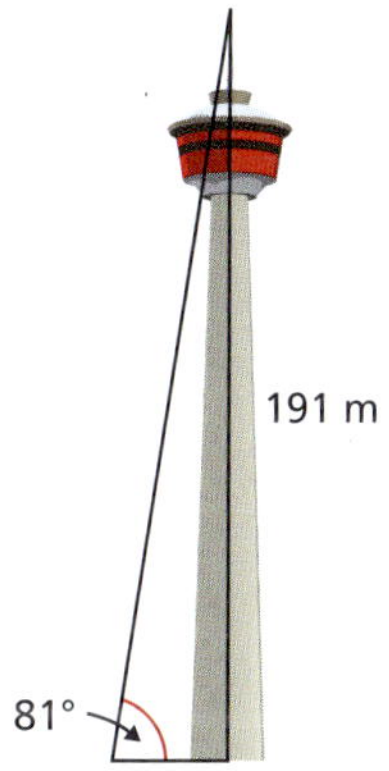

11. The angle between one longer side of a rectangle and a diagonal is 34°. One shorter side of the rectangle is 2.3 cm.

a) Sketch and label the rectangle.

b) What is the length of the rectangle to the nearest tenth of a centimetre?

12. In $\triangle PQR$, $\angle R = 90°$, $\angle P = 58°$, and $PR = 7.1$ cm. Determine the area of $\triangle PQR$ to the nearest tenth of a square centimetre. Describe your strategy.

13. The height of the Manitoba Legislature Building, from the ground to the top of the Golden Boy statue, is about 77 m. Liam is lying on the ground near the building. The angle between the ground and his line of sight to the top of the building is 52°. About how far is Liam from a point on the ground vertically below the statue? How do you know?

14. Janelle sees a large helium-filled balloon anchored to the roof of a store. When she is 100 m from the store, the angle between the ground and her line of sight to the balloon is 30°. About how high is the balloon? What assumptions are you making?

C

15. In kite PQRS, the shorter diagonal, QS, is 6.0 cm long, $\angle QRT$ is 26.5°, and $\angle QPT$ is 56.3°. Determine the measures of all the angles and the lengths of the sides of the kite to the nearest tenth.

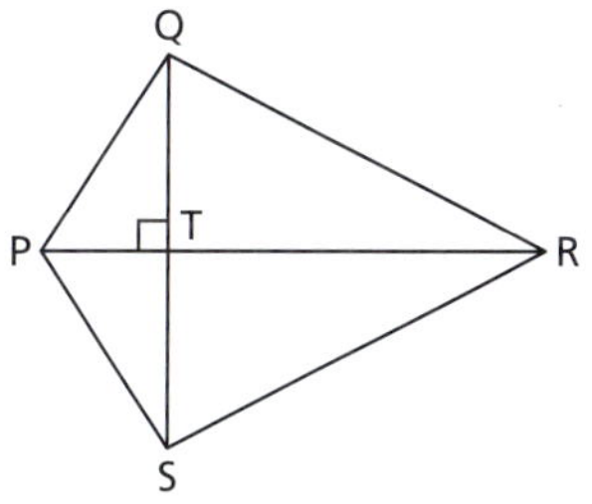

16. On a coordinate grid:

a) Draw a line through the points A(4, 5) and B(−4, −5). Determine the measure of the acute angle between AB and the y-axis.

b) Draw a line through the points C(1, 4) and D(4, −2). Determine the measure of the acute angle between CD and the x-axis.

Reflect Summarize what you have learned about using the tangent ratio to determine the length of a side of a right triangle.

MATH LAB

2.3 Measuring an Inaccessible Height

LESSON FOCUS

Determine a height that cannot be measured directly.

Make Connections

Tree farmers use a *clinometer* to measure the angle between a horizontal line and the line of sight to the top of a tree. They measure the distance to the base of the tree. How can they then use the tangent ratio to calculate the height of the tree?

Construct Understanding

TRY THIS

Work with a partner.

You will need:

- an enlarged copy of a 180° protractor
- scissors
- a measuring tape or 2 metre sticks
- a piece of heavy cardboard big enough for you to attach the paper protractor
- a drinking straw
- glue
- adhesive tape
- a needle and thread
- a small metal washer or weight
- grid paper

A. Make a drinking straw clinometer:

- Glue or tape the paper protractor to the cardboard. Carefully cut it out.
- Use the needle to pull the thread through the cardboard at the centre of baseline of the protractor. Secure the thread to the back of the cardboard with tape. Attach the weight to the other end of the thread.
- Tape the drinking straw along the baseline of the protractor for use as a sighting tube.

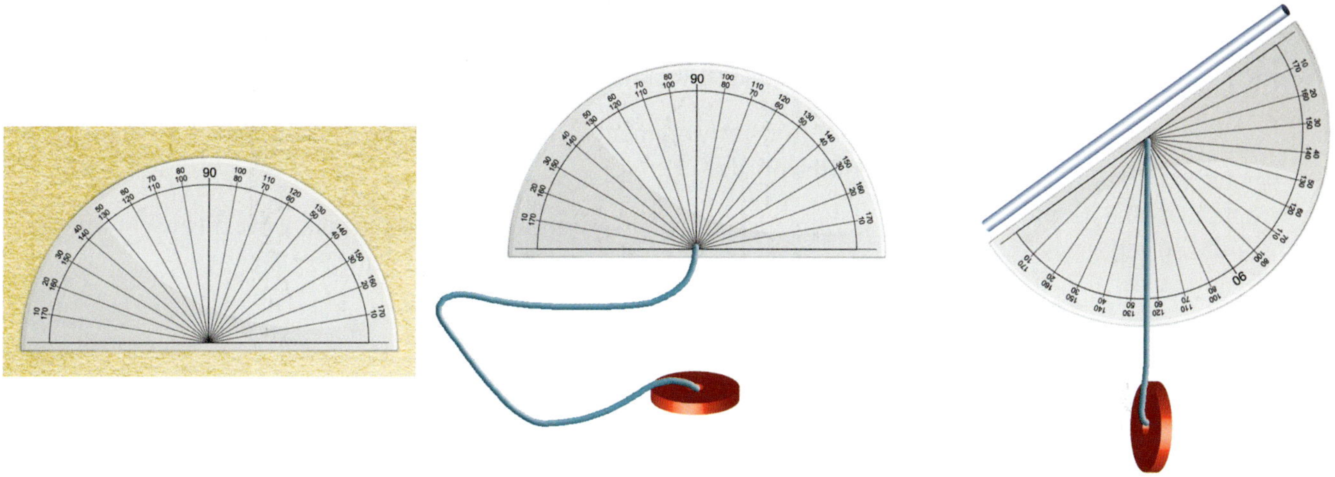

B. With your partner, choose a tall object whose height you cannot measure directly; for example, a flagpole, a totem pole, a tree, or a building.

C. One of you stands near the object on level ground. Your partner measures and records your distance from the object.

D. Hold the clinometer as shown, with the weight hanging down.

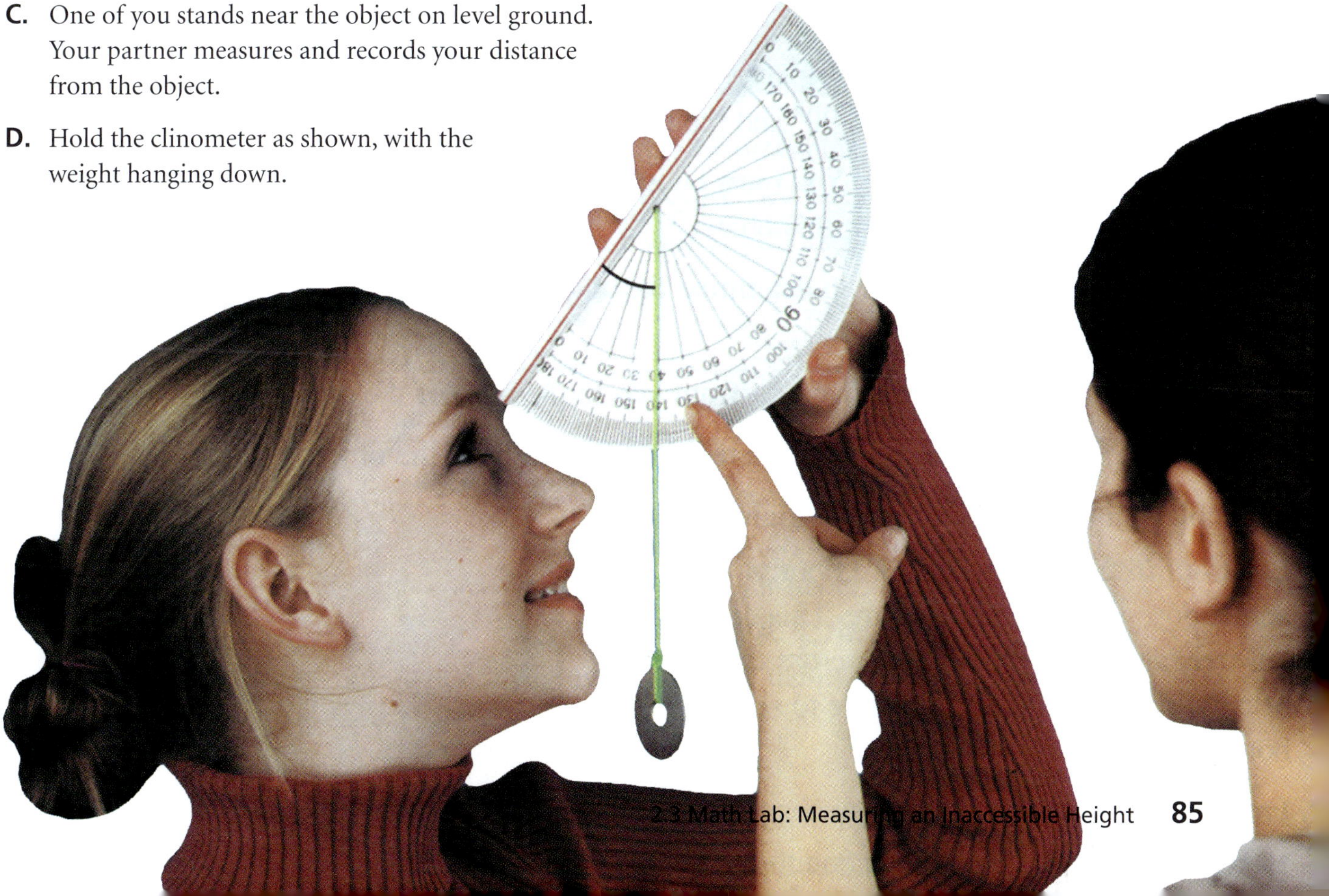

How does the acute angle between the thread and the straw relate to the angle of inclination of the straw?

E. Look at the top of the object through the straw. Your partner records the acute angle indicated by the thread on the protractor.

F. Your partner measures and records how far your eye is above the ground.

G. Sketch a diagram with a vertical line segment representing the object you want to measure. Label:

- your distance from the object
- the vertical distance from the ground to your eyes
- the angle of inclination of the straw

H. Change places with your partner. Repeat Steps B to G.

What other strategy could you use to determine the height of the object?

I. Use your measurements and the tangent ratio to calculate the height of the object.

J. Compare your results with those of your partner. Does the height of your eye affect the measurements? The final result? Explain.

Assess Your Understanding

1. Explain how the angle shown on the protractor of your clinometer is related to the angle of inclination that the clinometer measures.

2. A tree farmer stood 10.0 m from the base of a tree. She used a clinometer to sight the top of the tree. The angle shown on the protractor scale was 40°. The tree farmer held the clinometer 1.6 m above the ground. Determine the height of the tree to the nearest tenth of a metre. The diagram is *not* drawn to scale.

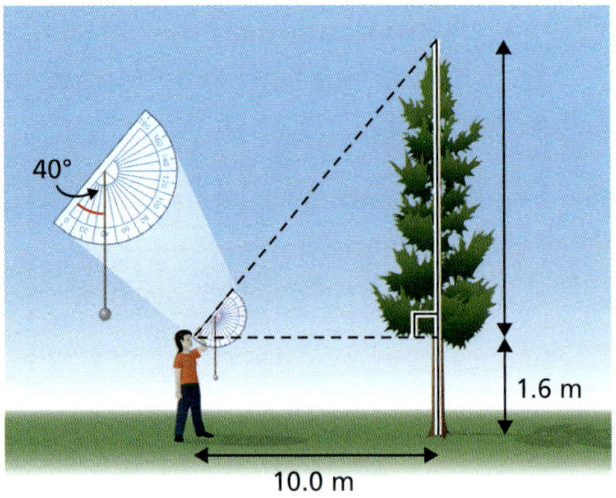

3. Use the information in the diagram to calculate the height of a totem pole observed with a drinking-straw clinometer. Give the answer to the nearest metre. The diagram is *not* drawn to scale.

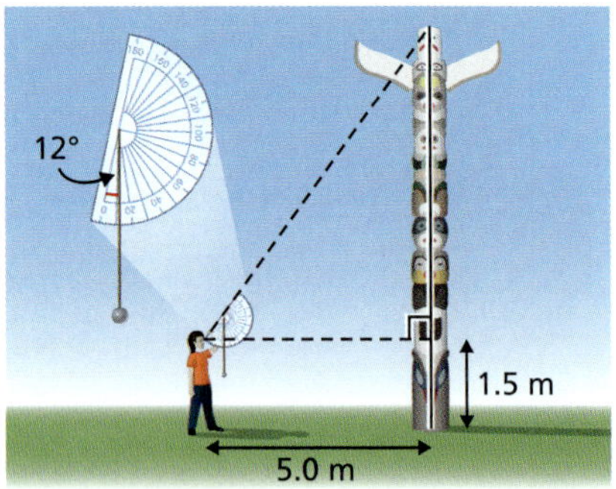

Keep your clinometer for use in the Review.

CHECKPOINT 1

Connections

Similar Right Triangles

$\triangle ABC \sim \triangle XYZ$

Corresponding angles are equal. | Corresponding sides are proportional.

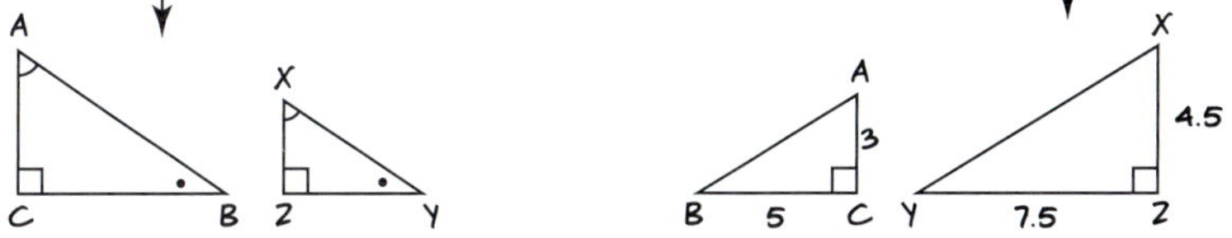

Tangent Ratio

$\tan B = \dfrac{\text{opposite}}{\text{adjacent}}$

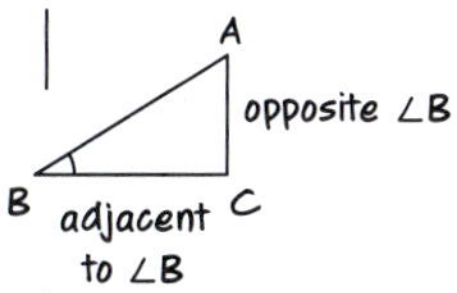

Determine an angle given two legs. | Determine a side given an angle and a leg.

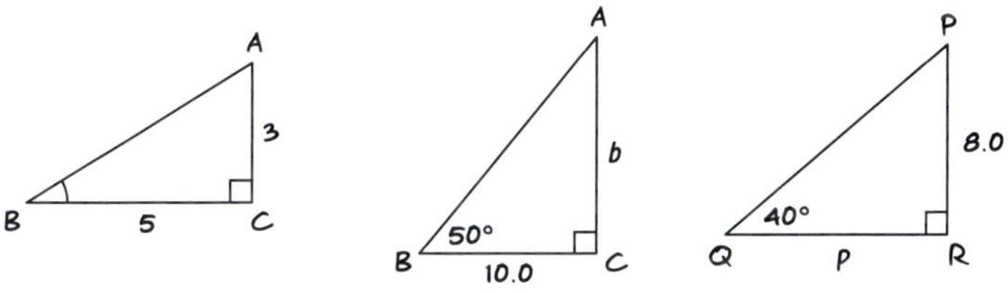

$\tan B = \dfrac{\text{opposite}}{\text{adjacent}}$

$\tan B = \dfrac{3}{5}$

$\tan B = 0.6$

$\angle B \doteq 31°$

$\tan B = \dfrac{\text{opposite}}{\text{adjacent}}$

$\tan 50° = \dfrac{b}{10}$

$b = 10 \tan 50°$

$b \doteq 11.9$

$\tan Q = \dfrac{\text{opposite}}{\text{adjacent}}$

$\tan 40° = \dfrac{8}{p}$

$p = \dfrac{8}{\tan 40°}$

$p \doteq 9.5$

or

$\angle P = 90° - \angle Q$

$\angle P = 50°$

$\tan P = \dfrac{\text{opposite}}{\text{adjacent}}$

$\tan 50° = \dfrac{p}{8}$

$p = 8 \tan 50°$

$p \doteq 9.5$

Concept Development

- **In Lesson 2.1**
  - You applied what you know about similar right triangles to develop the concept of the **tangent ratio**.
  - You used the tangent ratio **to determine an acute angle** in a right triangle when you know the lengths of the legs.
- **In Lesson 2.2**
  - You showed how to determine the **length of a leg** in a right triangle when you know the measures of an acute angle and the other leg.
- **In Lesson 2.3**
  - You applied the tangent ratio to a real-world measurement problem.

Assess Your Understanding

2.1

1. Determine the measure of each indicated angle to the nearest degree.

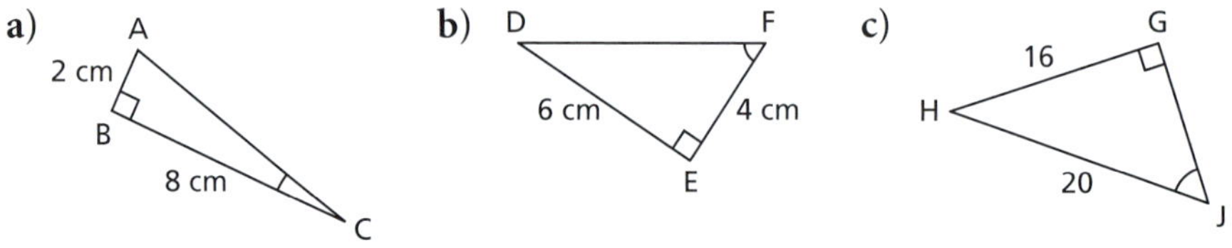

2. Why does the tangent of an angle increase as the angle increases?

3. A small plane is flying at an altitude of 1000 m and is 5000 m from the beginning of the landing strip. What is the angle between the ground and the line of sight from an observer at the beginning of the landing strip? Give the measure to the nearest tenth of a degree.

2.2

4. Determine the length of each indicated side to the nearest tenth of a centimetre.

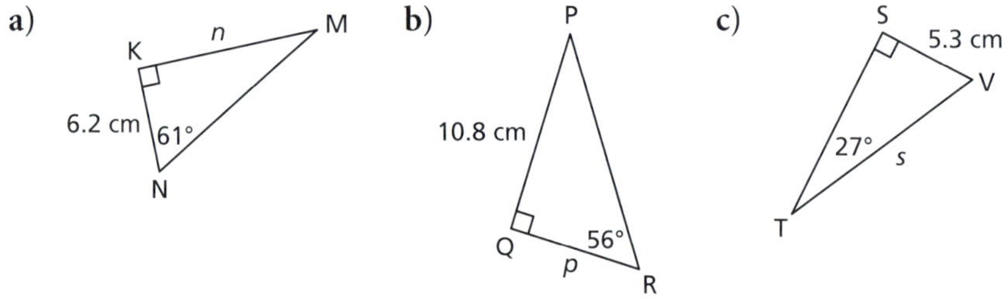

5. A hiker saw a hoodoo on a cliff at Willow Creek in Alberta's badlands. The hiker was 9.1 m from the base of the cliff. From that point, the angle between the level ground and the line of sight to the top of the hoodoo was 69°. About how high was the top of the hoodoo above the level ground?

2.4 The Sine and Cosine Ratios

LESSON FOCUS

Develop and apply the sine and cosine ratios to determine angle measures.

Make Connections

The railroad track through the mountains between Field, B.C., and Hector, B.C., includes spiral tunnels. They were built in the early 1900s to reduce the angle of inclination of the track between the two towns. You can see a long train passing under itself after it comes out of a tunnel before it has finished going in.

Visualize the track straightened out to form the hypotenuse of a right triangle. Here is a diagram of the track before the tunnels were constructed. The diagram is *not* drawn to scale.

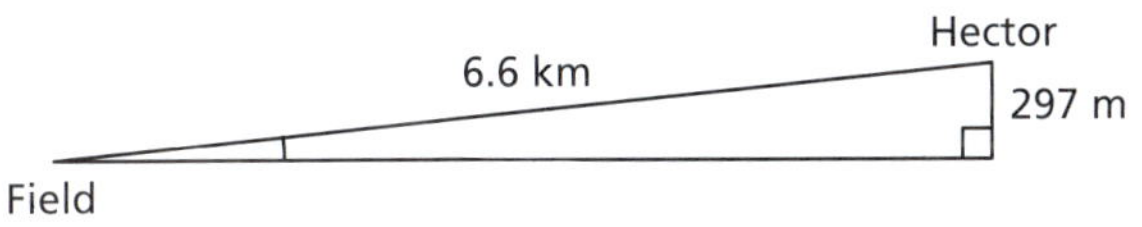

How could you determine the angle of inclination of the track?

Construct Understanding

We defined the tangent ratio for an acute angle in a right triangle. There are two other ratios we can form to compare the sides of the triangle; each ratio involves the hypotenuse.

TRY THIS

Work with a partner.

You will need grid paper, a ruler, and a protractor.

A. Examine the nested right triangles below.

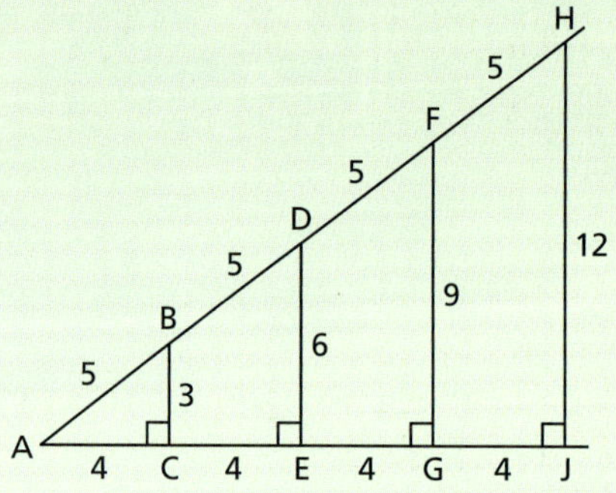

∠A is common to each triangle. How are the other acute angles in each triangle related? How do you know? How are the triangles related?

B. Copy and complete this table.

Triangle	Measures of Sides			Ratios	
	Hypotenuse	Side opposite ∠A	Side adjacent to ∠A	$\frac{\text{Side opposite } \angle A}{\text{Hypotenuse}}$	$\frac{\text{Side adjacent to } \angle A}{\text{Hypotenuse}}$
△ABC					
△ADE					
△AFG					
△AHJ					

C. Draw another set of nested right triangles that are not similar to those in Step A.

D. Measure the sides and angles of each triangle. Label your diagram with the measures, as in the diagram above.

E. Complete a table like the one in Step B for your triangles.

F. For each set of triangles, how do the ratios compare?

G. What do you think the value of each ratio depends on?

In a right triangle, the ratios that relate each leg to the hypotenuse depend only on the measure of the acute angle, and not on the size of the triangle. These ratios are called the **sine ratio** and the **cosine ratio**.

The sine ratio for ∠A is written as sin A and the cosine ratio for ∠A is written as cos A.

The Sine Ratio

If ∠A is an acute angle in a right triangle, then

$$\sin A = \frac{\text{length of side opposite } \angle A}{\text{length of hypotenuse}}$$

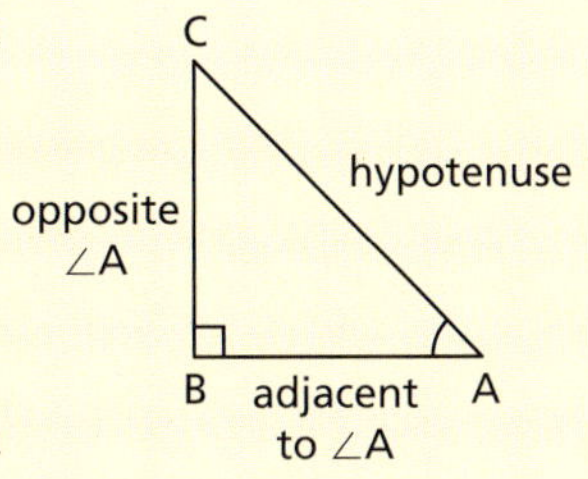

The Cosine Ratio

If ∠A is an acute angle in a right triangle, then

$$\cos A = \frac{\text{length of side adjacent to } \angle A}{\text{length of hypotenuse}}$$

The tangent, sine, and cosine are called the **primary trigonometric ratios.** The word **trigonometry** comes from three Greek words "tri + gonia + metron" that together mean "three angle measure."

The branch of math that deals with the relations between the sides and angles of triangles is called **trigonometry**.

The values of the sine and cosine that compare the lengths of the sides are often expressed as decimals. For example, in right △ABC,

If sin A = 0.5, then in any similar right triangle, the length of the side opposite ∠A is 0.5 times the length of the hypotenuse.

What happens to sin A as ∠A gets closer to 0°?

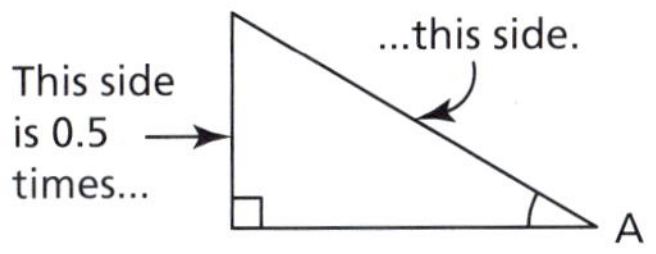

sin A = 0.5

If cos A = 0.7, then in any similar right triangle, the length of the side adjacent to ∠A is 0.7 times the length of the hypotenuse.

What happens to cos A as ∠A gets closer to 0°?

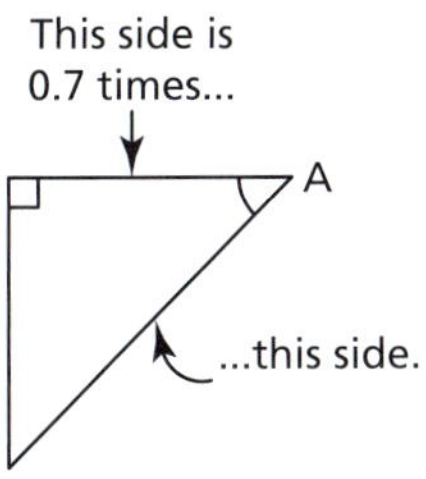

cos A = 0.7

Example 1 Determining the Sine and Cosine of an Angle

a) In $\triangle$DEF, identify the side opposite $\angle$D and the side adjacent to $\angle$D.

b) Determine sin D and cos D to the nearest hundredth.

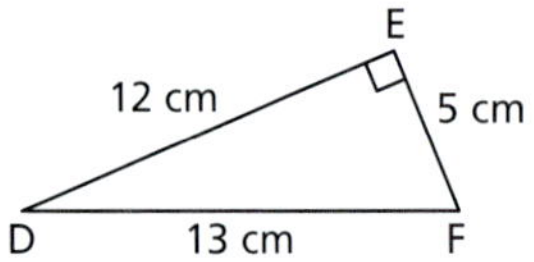

SOLUTION

a) In right $\triangle$DEF,
DF is the hypotenuse.
EF is opposite $\angle$D and
DE is adjacent to $\angle$D.

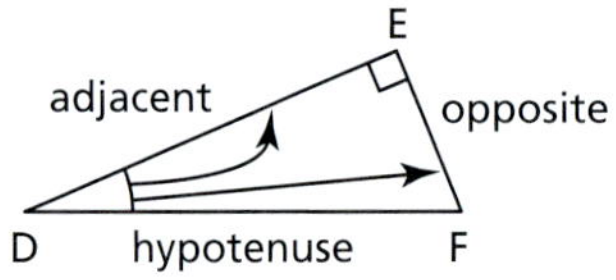

b) $\sin D = \dfrac{\text{opposite}}{\text{hypotenuse}}$

$\sin D = \dfrac{EF}{DF}$ EF is opposite $\angle$D, DF is the hypotenuse.

$\sin D = \dfrac{5}{13}$

$\sin D = 0.3846\ldots$

$\sin D \doteq 0.38$

$\cos D = \dfrac{\text{adjacent}}{\text{hypotenuse}}$

$\cos D = \dfrac{DE}{DF}$ DE is adjacent to $\angle$D, DF is the hypotenuse.

$\cos D = \dfrac{12}{13}$

$\cos D = 0.9230\ldots$

$\cos D \doteq 0.92$

CHECK YOUR UNDERSTANDING

1. a) In $\triangle$GHJ, identify the side opposite $\angle$G and the side adjacent to $\angle$G.

b) Determine sin G and cos G to the nearest hundredth.

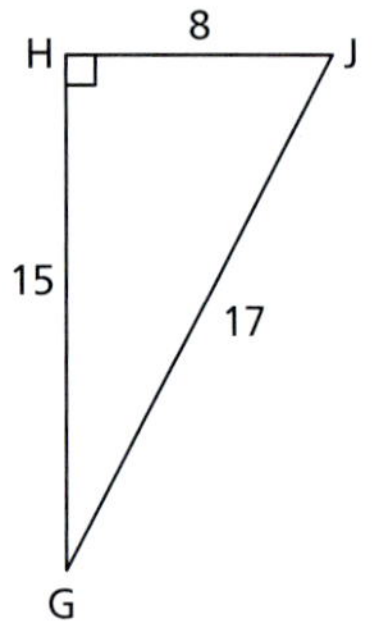

[Answers: a) HJ, HG
b) $\sin G \doteq 0.47$; $\cos G \doteq 0.88$]

Determine sin F and cos F. How are these values related to sin D and cos D?

You can use a scientific calculator to determine the measure of an angle:

- When you know its sine, use $\sin^{-1}$ or InvSin
- When you know its cosine, use $\cos^{-1}$ or InvCos

Example 2 Using Sine or Cosine to Determine the Measure of an Angle

Determine the measures of $\angle G$ and $\angle H$ to the nearest tenth of a degree.

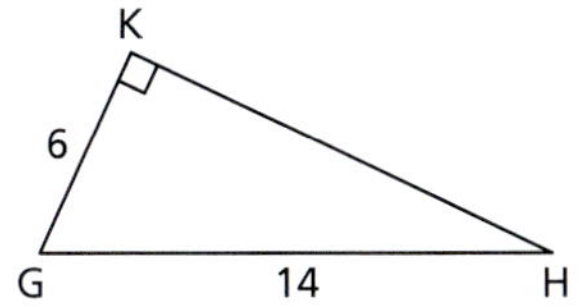

SOLUTIONS

Method 1

Determine the measure of $\angle H$ first.

In right $\triangle GHK$:

$$\sin H = \frac{\text{opposite}}{\text{hypotenuse}}$$

GK is opposite $\angle H$, GH is the hypotenuse.

$$\sin H = \frac{GK}{GH}$$

$$\sin H = \frac{6}{14}$$

$$\angle H = 25.3769\ldots°$$

sin⁻¹(6/14)
25.37693353

$$\angle G + \angle H = 90°$$

$$\angle G = 90° - \angle H$$

The angle sum of any triangle is 180°, so the two acute angles in a right triangle have a sum of 90°.

So, $\angle G = 90° - 25.3769\ldots°$

$$\angle G = 64.6230\ldots°$$

Method 2

Determine the measure of $\angle G$ first.

In right $\triangle GHK$:

$$\cos G = \frac{\text{adjacent}}{\text{hypotenuse}}$$

GK is adjacent to $\angle G$, GH is the hypotenuse.

$$\cos G = \frac{GK}{GH}$$

$$\cos G = \frac{6}{14}$$

$$\angle G = 64.6230\ldots°$$

cos⁻¹(6/14)
64.62306647

$$\angle G + \angle H = 90°$$

The two acute angles have a sum of 90°.

So, $\angle H = 90° - 64.6230\ldots°$

$$\angle H = 25.3769\ldots°$$

$\angle G$ is approximately 64.6° and $\angle H$ is approximately 25.4°.

CHECK YOUR UNDERSTANDING

2. Determine the measures of $\angle K$ and $\angle M$ to the nearest tenth of a degree.

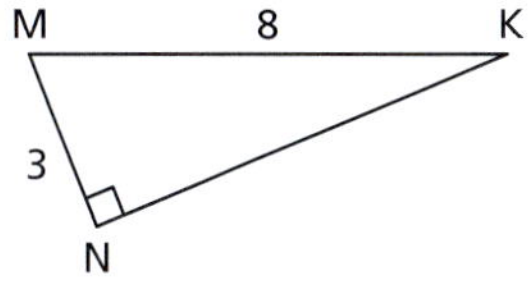

[Answer: $\angle K \doteq 22.0°$, $\angle M \doteq 68.0°$]

How are cos G and sin H related? Explain why this relationship occurs.

We can use the sine or cosine ratio to solve problems that can be modelled by a right triangle when we know the length of the hypotenuse, and the length of a leg or the measure of an acute angle.

Example 3 Using Sine or Cosine to Solve a Problem

A water bomber is flying at an altitude of 5000 ft. The plane's radar shows that it is 8000 ft. from the target site. What is the **angle of elevation** of the plane measured from the target site, to the nearest degree?

SOLUTION

Draw a diagram to represent the situation.
Altitude is measured vertically.
Assume the ground is horizontal.

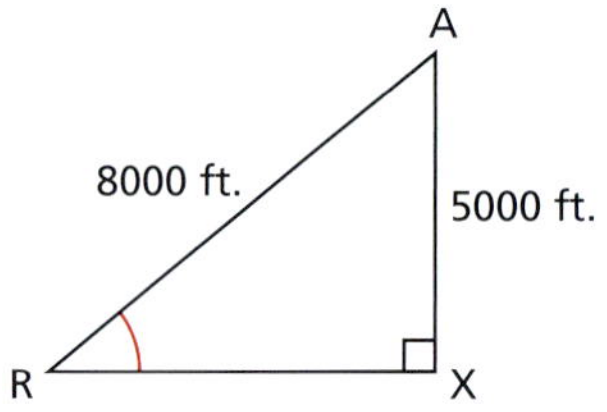

∠R is the angle of elevation of the plane.

AX is the altitude of the plane.

RA is the distance from the target site to the plane.

In right △ARX:

$\sin R = \frac{AX}{RA}$

AX is opposite ∠R, RA is the hypotenuse.

$\sin R = \frac{5000}{8000}$

$\angle R \doteq 39°$

The angle of elevation of the plane is approximately 39°.

CHECK YOUR UNDERSTANDING

3. An observer is sitting on a dock watching a float plane in Vancouver harbour. At a certain time, the plane is 300 m above the water and 430 m from the observer. Determine the angle of elevation of the plane measured from the observer, to the nearest degree.

[Answer: approximately 44°]

The **angle of elevation** of an object above the horizontal is the angle between the horizontal and the line of sight from an observer.

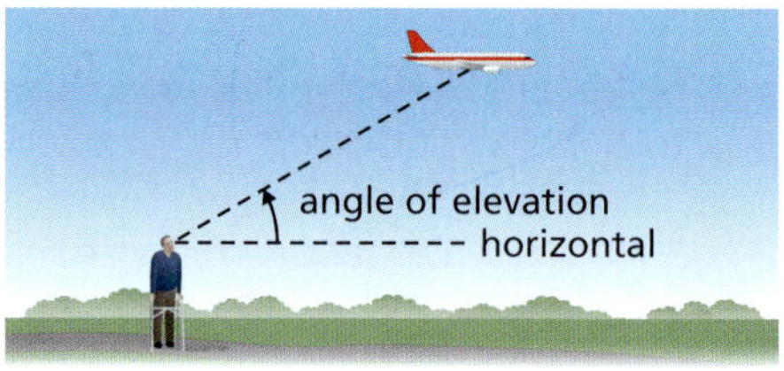

Discuss the Ideas

1. When can you use the sine ratio to determine the measure of an acute angle in a right triangle? When can you use the cosine ratio?
2. Why is it important to draw a sketch before you start to solve a problem?
3. Why are the values of the sine of an acute angle and the cosine of an acute angle less than 1?

Exercises

A

4. **a)** In each triangle below:

- Name the side opposite ∠A.
- Name the side adjacent to ∠A.
- Name the hypotenuse.

i)

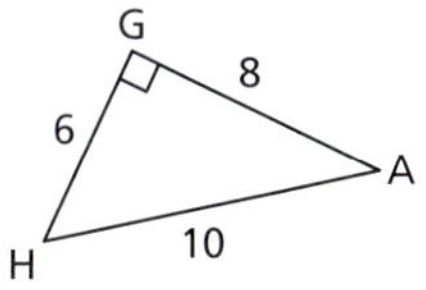

ii)

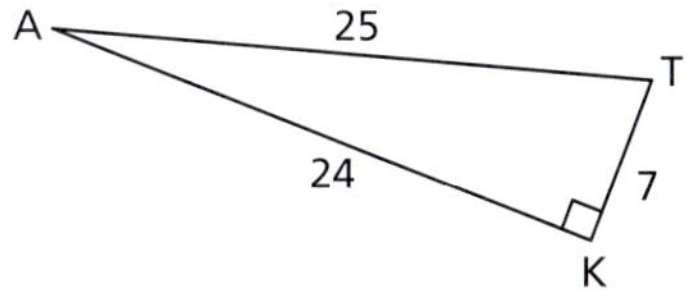

b) For each triangle in part a, determine sin A and cos A to the nearest hundredth.

5. Determine the sine and cosine of each angle to the nearest hundredth.

a) 57° **b)** 5° **c)** 19° **d)** 81°

6. To the nearest degree, determine the measure of each ∠X.

a) sin X = 0.25 **b)** cos X = 0.64

c) $\sin X = \frac{6}{11}$ **d)** $\cos X = \frac{7}{9}$

B

7. Determine the measure of each indicated angle to the nearest degree.

a)

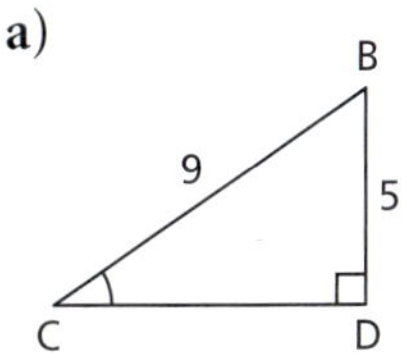

b)

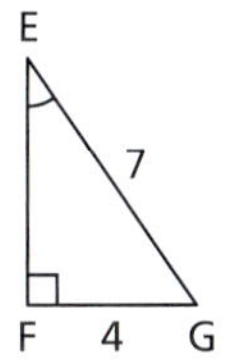

c)

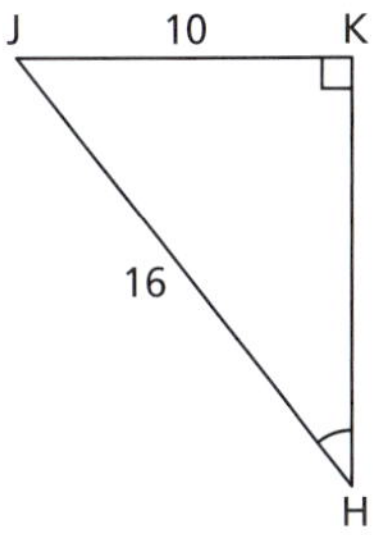

d)

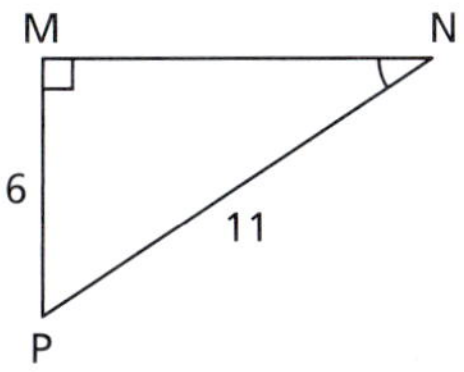

8. Determine the measure of each indicated angle to the nearest degree.

a)

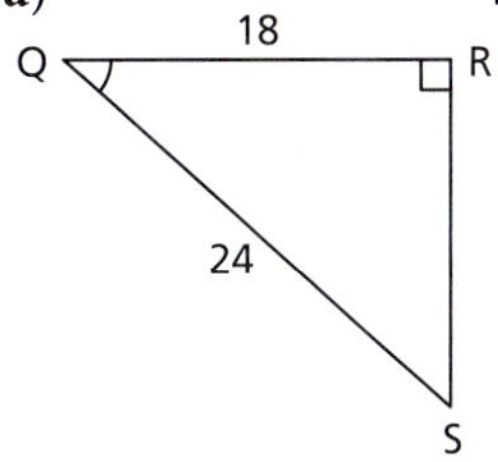

b)

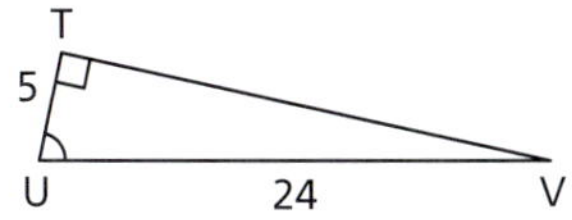

c)

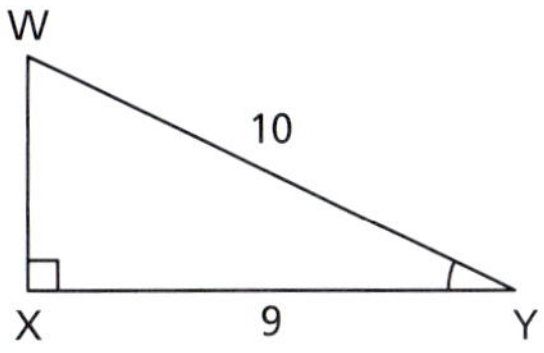

d)

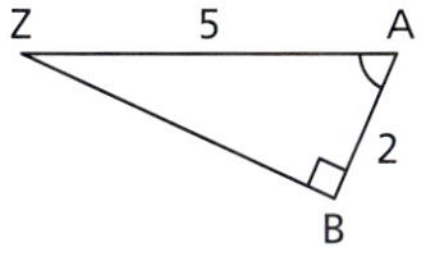

9. For each ratio below, sketch two different right triangles and label their sides.

a) $\sin B = \frac{3}{5}$ **b)** $\cos B = \frac{5}{8}$

c) $\sin B = \frac{1}{4}$ **d)** $\cos B = \frac{4}{9}$

10. Use the sine or cosine ratio to determine the measure of each acute angle to the nearest tenth of a degree. Describe your strategy.

a)

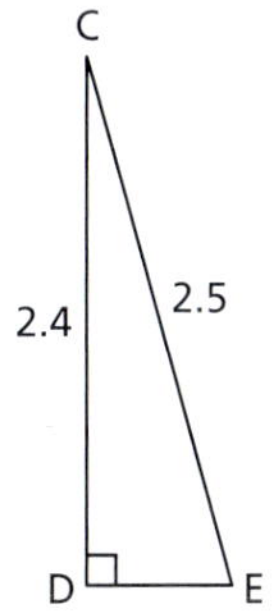

b)

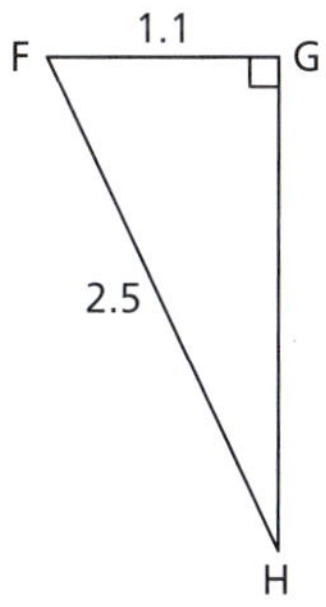

c)

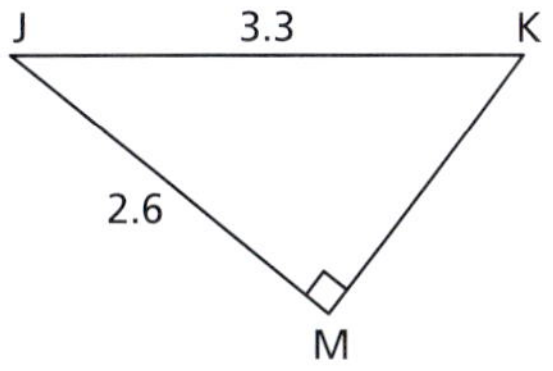

d)

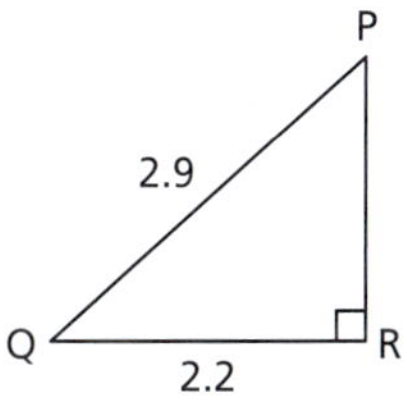

11. Suppose the railroad track through the spiral tunnels from Field to Hector were straightened out. It would look like the diagram below. The diagram is *not* drawn to scale. What is the angle of inclination of the track to the nearest tenth of a degree?

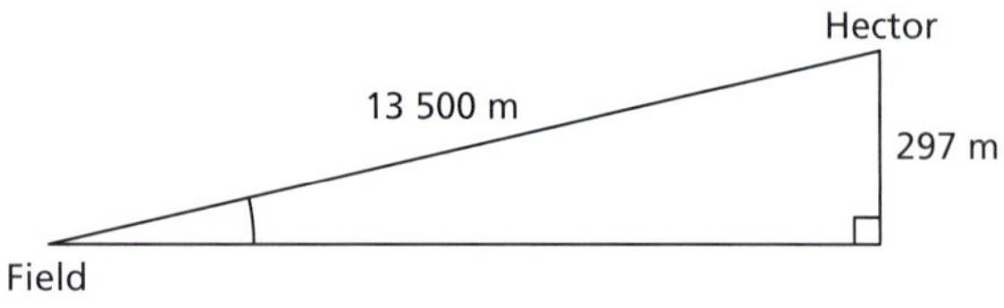

12. A ladder is 6.5 m long. It leans against a wall. The base of the ladder is 1.2 m from the wall. What is the angle of inclination of the ladder to the nearest tenth of a degree?

13. A rope that supports a tent is 2.4 m long. The rope is attached to the tent at a point that is 2.1 m above the ground. What is the angle of inclination of the rope to the nearest degree?

14. A rectangle is 4.8 cm long and each diagonal is 5.6 cm long. What is the measure of the angle between a diagonal and the longest side of the rectangle? Give the answer to the nearest degree.

15. **a)** Calculate:

i) sin 10° **ii)** sin 20° **iii)** sin 40°
iv) sin 50° **v)** sin 60° **vi)** sin 80°

b) Why does the sine of an angle increase as the angle increases?

16. Sketch a right isosceles triangle. Explain why the cosine of each acute angle is equal to the sine of the angle.

C

17. A cylindrical silo is 37 ft. high and has a diameter of 14 ft. The top of the silo can be reached by a spiral staircase that circles the silo once. What is the angle of inclination of the staircase to the nearest degree?

18. **a)** We have defined the sine and cosine ratios for acute angles. Use a calculator to determine:

i) sin 90° **ii)** sin 0° **iii)** cos 90° **iv)** cos 0°

b) Sketch a right triangle. Use the sketch to explain the results in part a.

Reflect

Explain when you might use the sine or cosine ratio instead of the tangent ratio to determine the measure of an acute angle in a right triangle. Include examples in your explanation.

THE WORLD OF MATH

Careers: Tool and Die Maker

A tool and die maker constructs tools and prepares dies for manufacturing common objects, such as bottle caps. A *die* is made up of two plates that stamp together. A tool and die maker uses trigonometry to construct a die. She works from blueprints that show the dimensions of the design. To cut the material for a die, a tool and die maker must set the milling machine at the precise angle.

2.5 Using the Sine and Cosine Ratios to Calculate Lengths

LESSON FOCUS

Use the sine and cosine ratios to determine lengths indirectly.

Make Connections

A surveyor can measure an angle precisely using an instrument called a *transit*. A measuring tape is used to measure distances. How can the surveyor use these measures and her knowledge of trigonometry in a right triangle to calculate the lengths that cannot be measured directly?

Construct Understanding

THINK ABOUT IT

Work with a partner.

The diagram shows measurements taken by surveyors. How could you determine the distance between the transit and the survey pole?

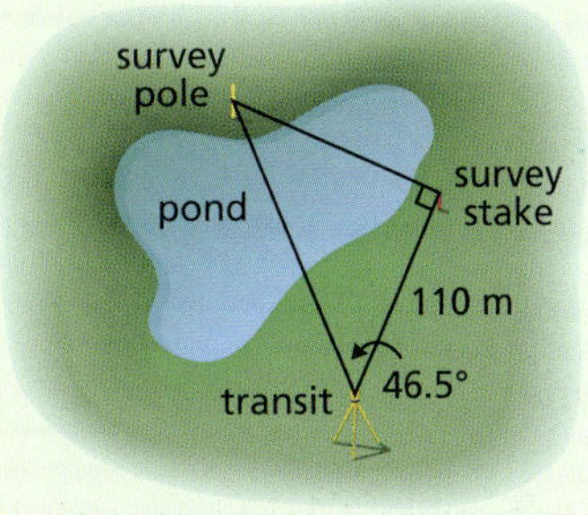

We can use the sine ratio or cosine ratio to write an equation that we can solve to calculate the length of a leg in a right triangle when the measure of one acute angle and the length of the hypotenuse are known.

Example 1 Using the Sine or Cosine Ratio to Determine the Length of a Leg

Determine the length of BC to the nearest tenth of a centimetre.

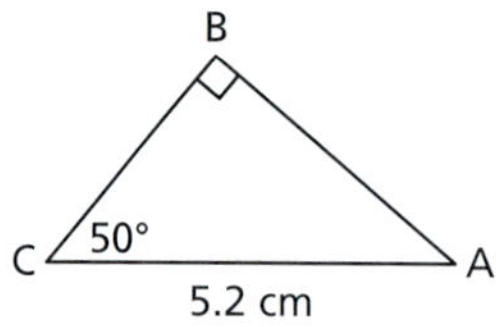

SOLUTION

In right $\triangle$ABC, AC is the hypotenuse and BC is adjacent to the known $\angle$C.

Choose the ratio that compares the adjacent side to the hypotenuse.

Use the cosine ratio to write an equation.

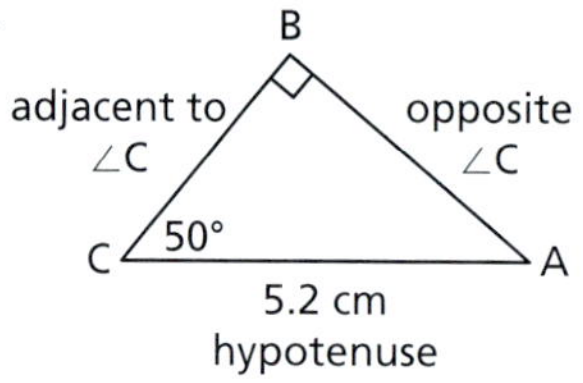

$$\cos C = \frac{\text{adjacent}}{\text{hypotenuse}}$$

$$\cos C = \frac{BC}{AC}$$

$$\cos 50° = \frac{BC}{5.2}$$

Solve this equation for BC. Multiply both sides by 5.2.

$$5.2 \cos 50° = \frac{(5.2)(BC)}{5.2}$$

$$5.2 \cos 50° = BC$$

$$BC = 3.3424\ldots$$

```
5.2cos(50)
                3.34249557
```

BC is approximately 3.3 cm long.

CHECK YOUR UNDERSTANDING

1. Determine the length of PQ to the nearest tenth of a centimetre.

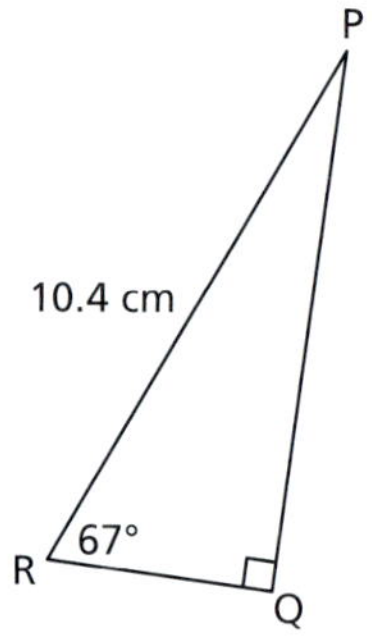

[Answer: PQ $\doteq$ 9.6 cm]

How could you have used the sine ratio to solve this problem?

The sine and cosine ratios can be used to calculate the length of the hypotenuse when the measure of one acute angle and the length of one leg are known.

Example 2 Using Sine or Cosine to Determine the Length of the Hypotenuse

Determine the length of DE to the nearest tenth of a centimetre.

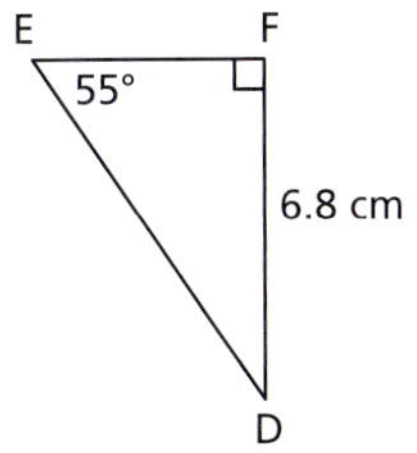

SOLUTION

In right △DEF, DE is the hypotenuse and DF is opposite the known ∠E.

The sine ratio compares the opposite side to the hypotenuse. Use lower case letters to label the lengths of the sides.

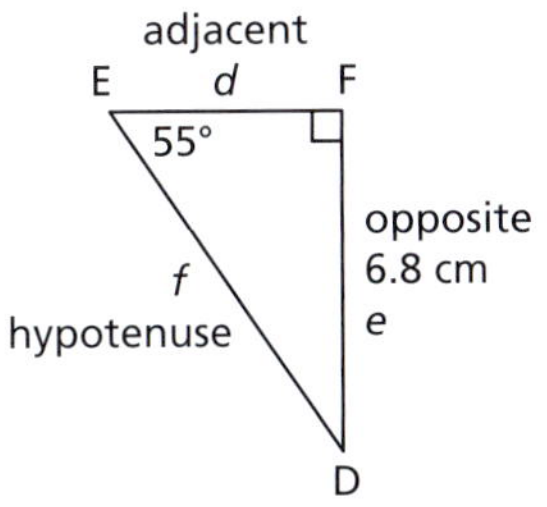

Use the sine ratio to write an equation.

$$\sin E = \frac{\text{opposite}}{\text{hypotenuse}}$$

$$\sin E = \frac{e}{f}$$

$$\sin 55° = \frac{6.8}{f}$$

Solve for f. Multiply both sides by f.

$$f \sin 55° = \frac{6.8f}{f}$$

$$f \sin 55° = 6.8$$

Divide both sides by sin 55°.

$$\frac{f \sin 55°}{\sin 55°} = \frac{6.8}{\sin 55°}$$

$$f = \frac{6.8}{\sin 55°}$$

$$f = 8.3012\ldots$$

DE is approximately 8.3 cm long.

CHECK YOUR UNDERSTANDING

2. Determine the length of JK to the nearest tenth of a centimetre.

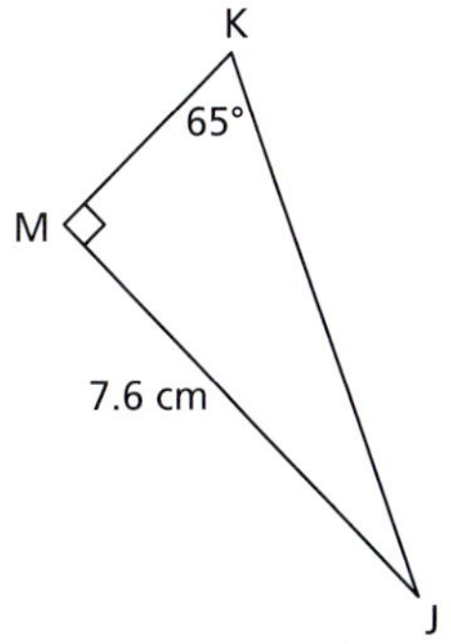

[Answer: JK ≐ 8.4 cm]

Example 3 Solving an Indirect Measurement Problem

A surveyor made the measurements shown in the diagram. How could the surveyor determine the distance from the transit to the survey pole to the nearest hundredth of a metre?

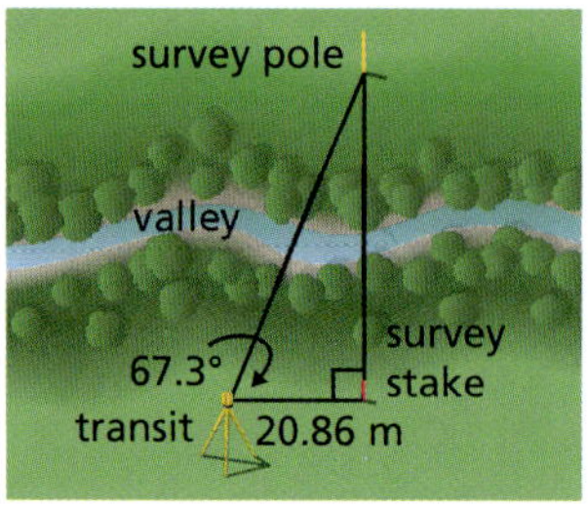

SOLUTION

Label a diagram to represent the problem.

The required distance is the hypotenuse of right △PST.

In right △PST, TP is the hypotenuse and TS is adjacent to ∠T.

Use the cosine ratio to write an equation.

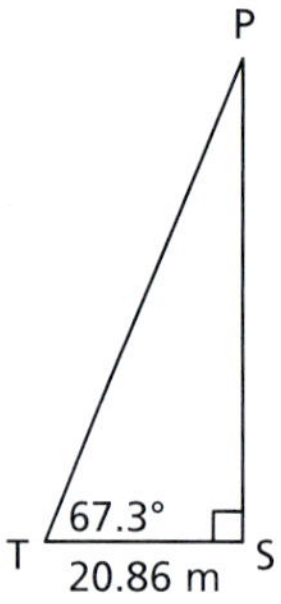

$$\cos T = \frac{\text{adjacent}}{\text{hypotenuse}}$$

$$\cos T = \frac{TS}{TP}$$

$$\cos 67.3° = \frac{20.86}{TP}$$

Solve this equation for TP.

Multiply both sides by TP.

$$TP \cos 67.3° = \frac{(TP)(20.86)}{TP}$$

$$TP \cos 67.3° = 20.86$$

Divide both sides by cos 67.3°.

$$\frac{TP \cos 67.3°}{\cos 67.3°} = \frac{20.86}{\cos 67.3°}$$

$$TP = \frac{20.86}{\cos 67.3°}$$

$$TP = 54.0546\ldots$$

The distance from the transit to the survey pole is approximately 54.05 m.

CHECK YOUR UNDERSTANDING

3. From a radar station, the angle of elevation of an approaching airplane is 32.5°. The horizontal distance between the plane and the radar station is 35.6 km. How far is the plane from the radar station to the nearest tenth of a kilometre?

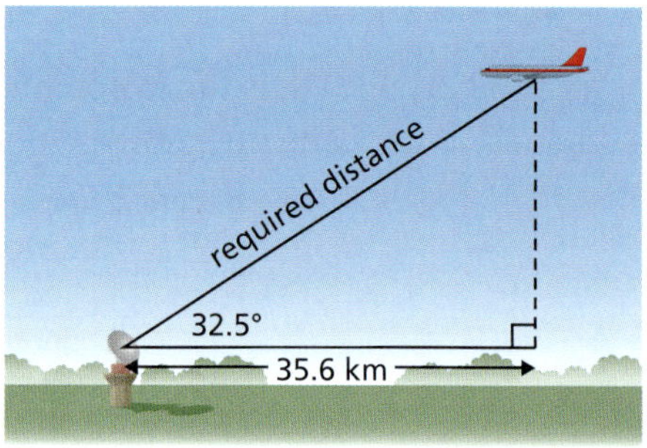

[Answer: 42.2 km]

How could you use the sine ratio instead of the cosine ratio to solve Example 3?
How could you use the tangent ratio?

Discuss the Ideas

1. What are the advantages of using a trigonometric ratio instead of an accurate drawing to solve a measurement problem?

2. When would you use the sine ratio to determine the length of a side of a right triangle? When would you use the cosine ratio?

Exercises

A

3. Determine the length of each indicated side to the nearest tenth of a centimetre.

a) 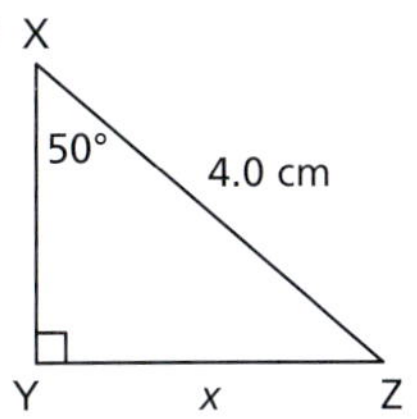

b) 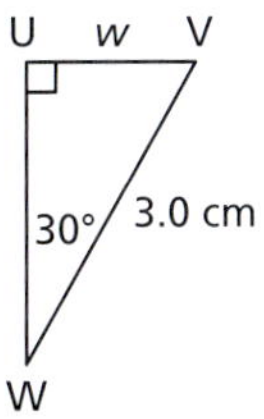

c) 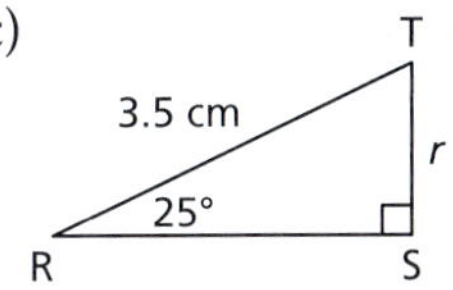

d) 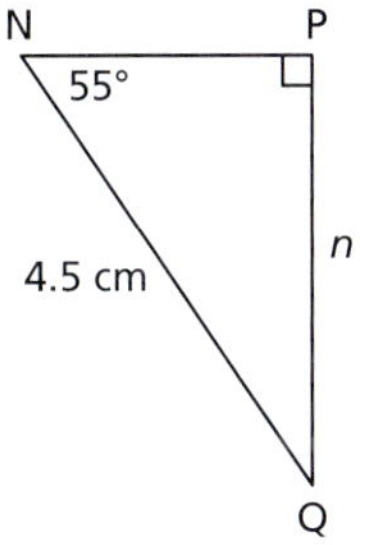

4. Determine the length of each indicated side to the nearest tenth of a centimetre.

a) 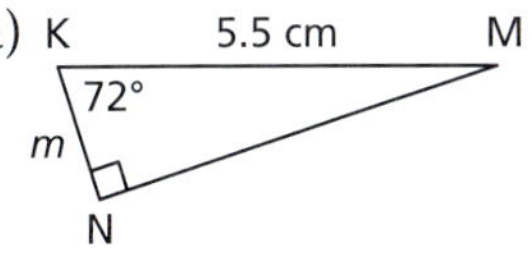

b) 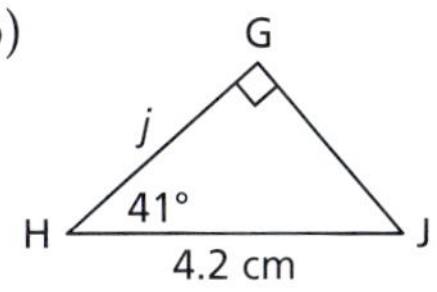

c) 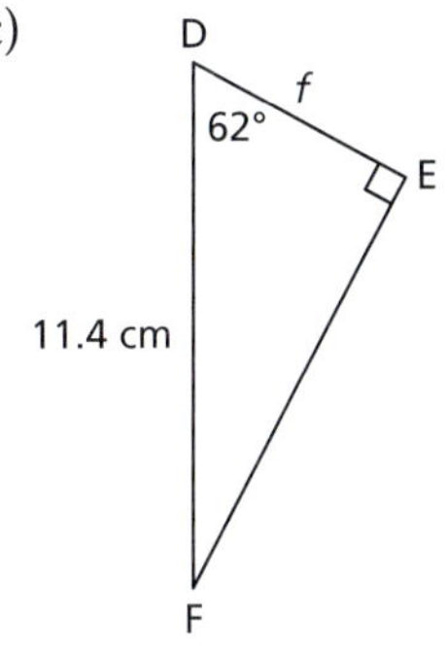

d) 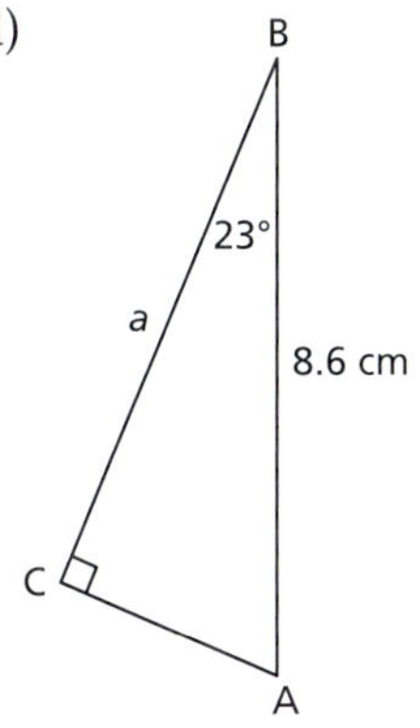

B

5. Determine the length of each indicated side to the nearest tenth of a centimetre.

a) 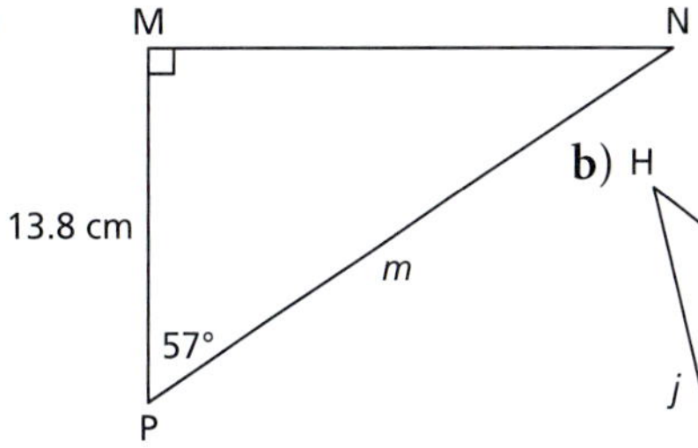

b) 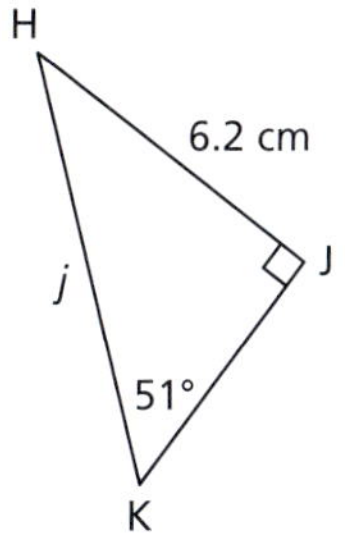

c) 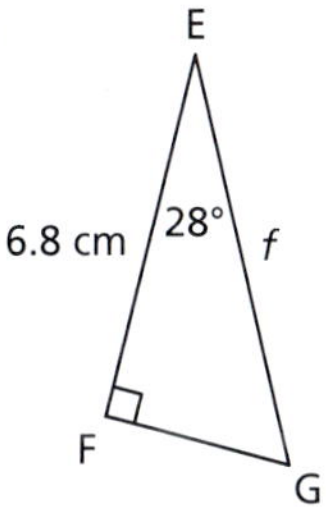

d) 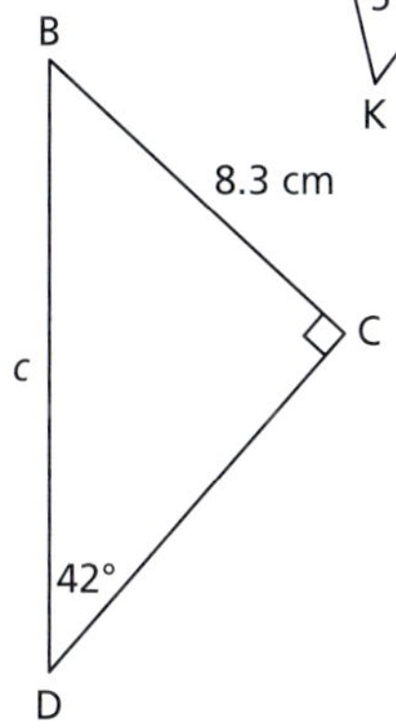

6. A fire truck has an aerial ladder that extends 30.5 m measured from the ground. The angle of inclination of the ladder is 77°. To the nearest tenth of a metre, how far up the wall of an apartment building can the ladder reach?

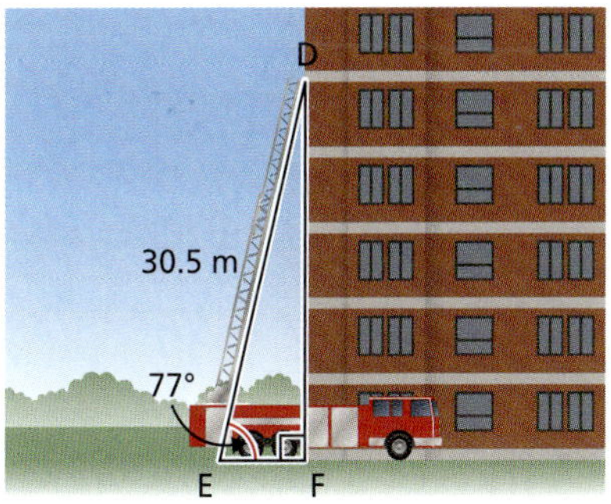

7. A surveyor makes the measurements shown in the diagram to determine the distance from C to E across a gorge.

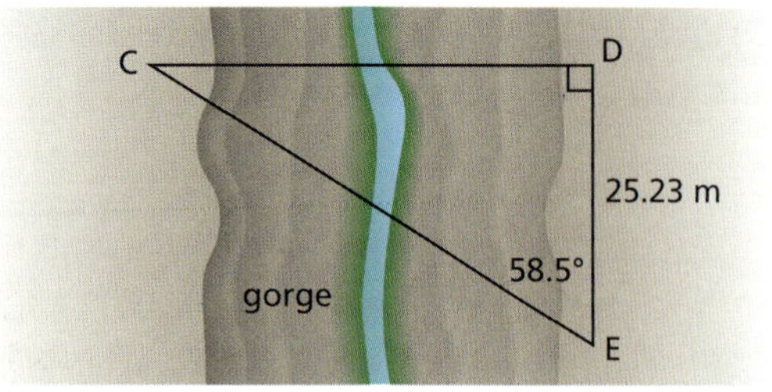

a) To the nearest tenth of a metre, what is the distance from C to E?

b) How could the surveyor calculate the distance from C to D?

8. A ship is sailing off the north coast of the Queen Charlotte Islands. At a certain point, the navigator sees the lighthouse at Langara Point, due south of the ship. The ship then sails 3.5 km due east. The angle between the ship's path and the line of sight to the lighthouse is then 28.5°. To the nearest tenth of a kilometre, how far is the ship from the lighthouse?

9. An airplane approaches an airport. At a certain time, it is 939 m high. Its angle of elevation measured from the airport is 19.5°. To the nearest metre, how far is the plane from the airport?

10. Calculate the dimensions of this rectangle to the nearest tenth of a centimetre.

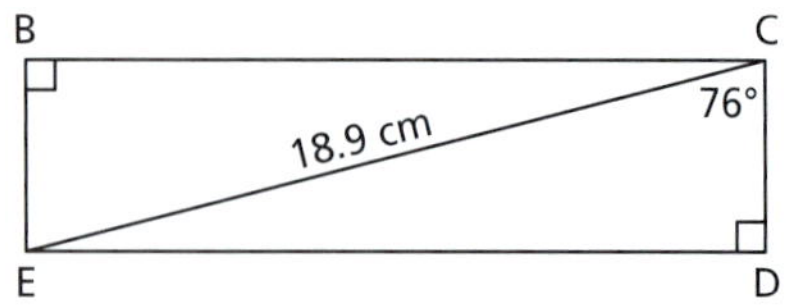

11. A bookcase is built against the sloping ceiling of an attic. The base of the bookcase is 3.24 m long. The angle of inclination of the attic ceiling is 40°.

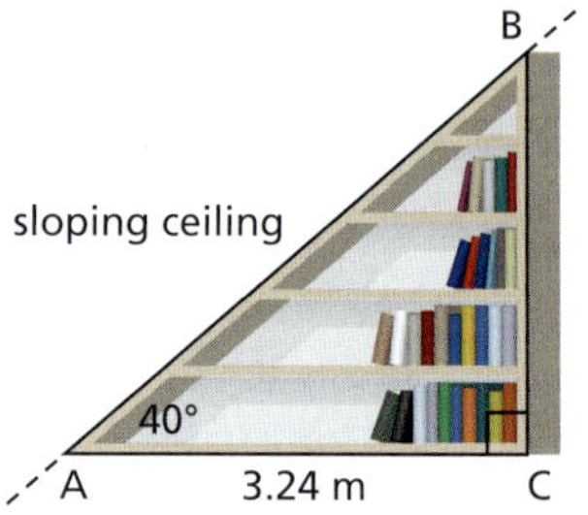

a) What is the length of the top of the bookcase, measured along the attic ceiling?

b) What is the greatest height of the bookcase?

Give the answers to the nearest centimetre.

12. a) Determine the perimeter of each shape to the nearest tenth of a centimetre.

i)

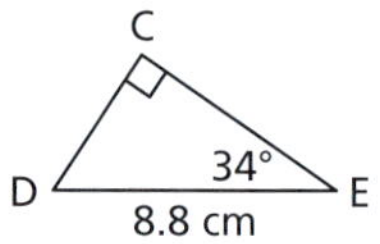

ii)

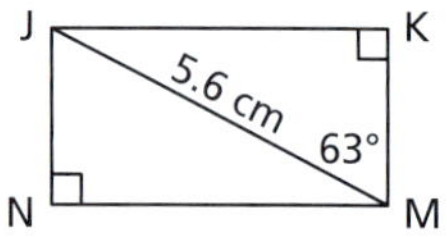

b) What strategies did you use to complete part a? What other strategies could you have used instead?

C

13. In trapezoid CDEF, $\angle D = \angle E = 90°$, $\angle C = 60°$, EF = 4.5 cm, and DE = 3.5 cm. What is the perimeter of the trapezoid to the nearest millimetre? Describe your strategy.

14. A survey of a building lot that has the shape of an acute triangle shows these data:

- Two intersecting sides are 250 ft. and 170 ft. long.
- The angle between these sides is 55°.

a) Use the 250-ft. side as the base of the triangle. What is the height of the triangle?

b) Determine the area of the lot to the nearest square foot.

Reflect

Explain when you might use the sine or cosine ratio instead of the tangent ratio to determine the length of a side in a right triangle. Include examples.

CHECKPOINT 2

Connections

Similar Right Triangles

△ABC ~ △XYZ

Corresponding angles are equal. | Corresponding sides are proportional.

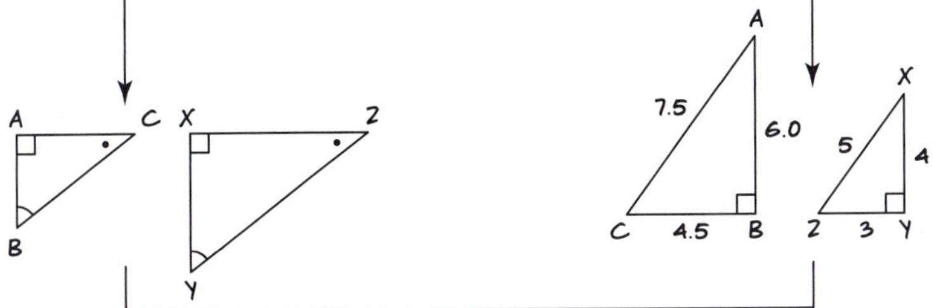

Sine and Cosine Ratios

$\sin C = \frac{\text{opposite}}{\text{hypotenuse}}$

$\cos C = \frac{\text{adjacent}}{\text{hypotenuse}}$

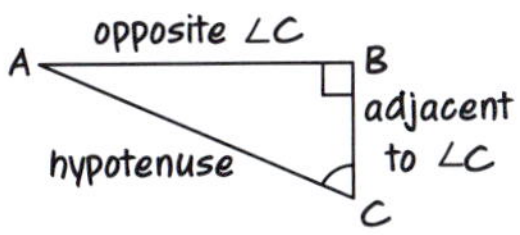

Determine an angle given one leg and the hypotenuse.

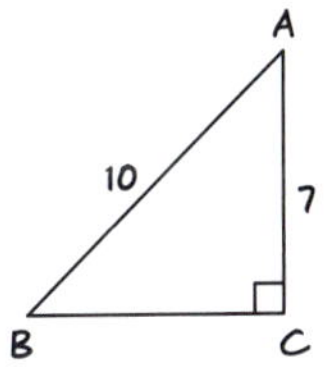

$\sin B = \frac{\text{opposite}}{\text{hypotenuse}}$

$\sin B = \frac{7}{10}$

$\sin B = 0.7$

$\angle B \doteq 44°$

$\cos A = \frac{\text{adjacent}}{\text{hypotenuse}}$

$\cos A = \frac{7}{10}$

$\cos A = 0.7$

$\angle A \doteq 46°$

Determine a side given an angle and a side.

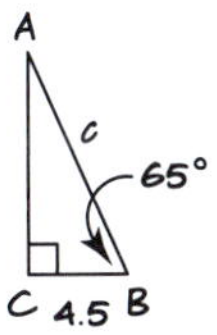

$\cos B = \frac{\text{adjacent}}{\text{hypotenuse}}$

$\cos 65° = \frac{4.5}{c}$

$c \cos 65° = 4.5$

$c = \frac{4.5}{\cos 65°}$

$c \doteq 10.6$

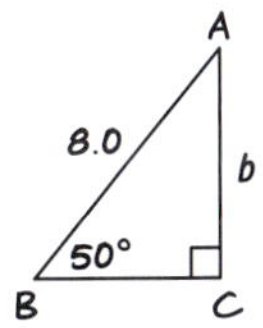

$\sin B = \frac{\text{opposite}}{\text{hypotenuse}}$

$\sin 50° = \frac{b}{8}$

$b = 8 \sin 50°$

$b \doteq 6.1$

Concept Development

- **In Lesson 2.4**
  – You applied what you know about similar right triangles to develop the **sine and cosine ratios.**
  – You used the sine or cosine ratio **to determine an acute angle** in a right triangle when you know the lengths of one leg and the hypotenuse.

- **In Lesson 2.5**
  – You showed how to determine the **length of a leg** in a right triangle when you know the measure of an acute angle and the length of the hypotenuse.
  – You showed how to determine the **length of the hypotenuse** when you know the measure of an acute angle and the length of one leg.

Assess Your Understanding

2.4

1. Determine the measure of each indicated angle to the nearest degree.

a)
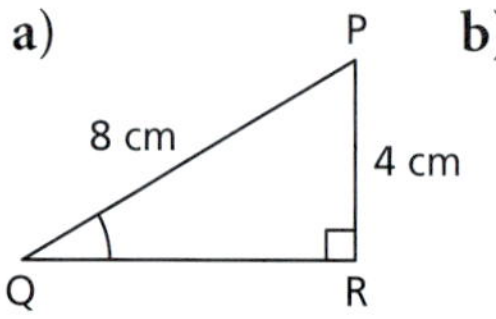

b)
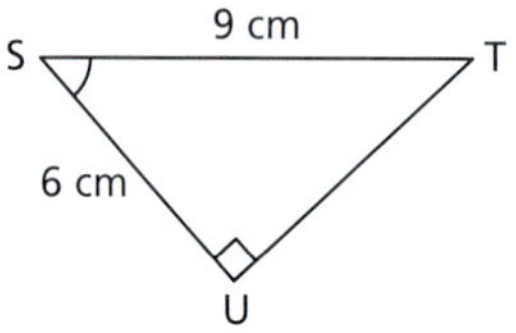

c)
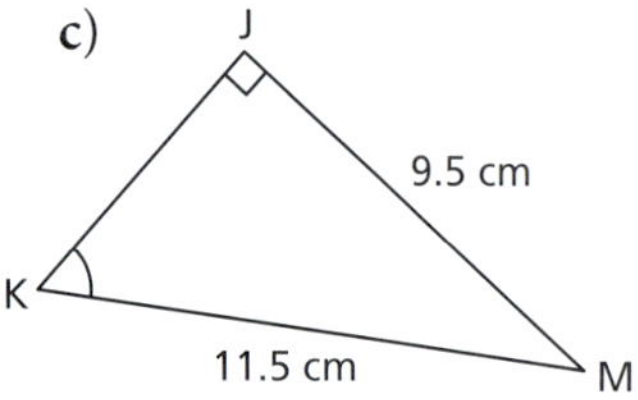

2. A factory manager plans to install a 30-ft. long conveyor that rises 7 ft. from the road to a loading dock. What is the angle of inclination of the conveyor to the nearest degree?

3. **a)** Calculate the cosine of each angle:
   i) 10° **ii)** 20° **iii)** 30° **iv)** 40° **v)** 50° **vi)** 60° **vii)** 70° **viii)** 80°
   b) Explain why the cosine of an angle decreases as the angle increases.

2.5

4. Determine the length of each indicated side to the nearest tenth of a centimetre.

a)
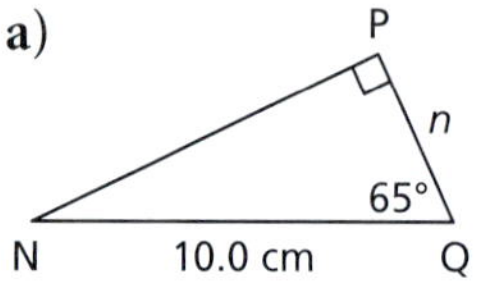

b)
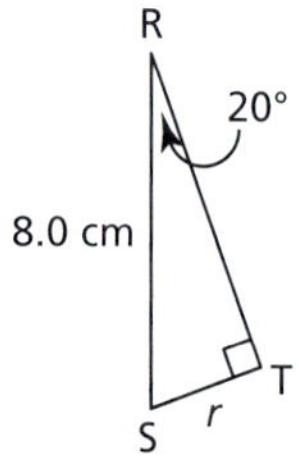

c)
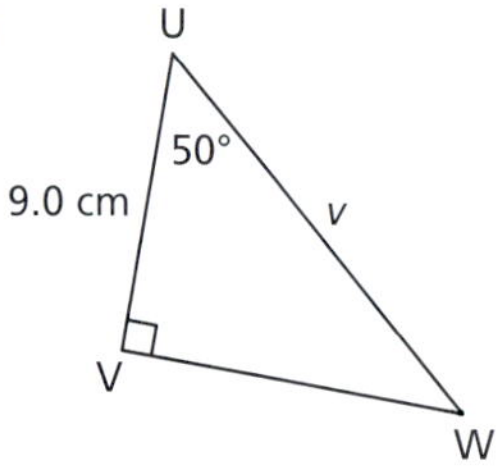

5. A ship is sailing off the south coast of the Queen Charlotte Islands. At a certain point, the navigator sees the beacon at Cape St. James, due north of the ship. The ship then sails 2.4 km due west. The angle between the ship's path and the line of sight to the beacon is 41.5°. How far is the ship from the beacon?

2.6 Applying the Trigonometric Ratios

LESSON FOCUS

Use a primary trigonometric ratio to solve a problem modelled by a right triangle.

Make Connections

Double-decker buses with wheelchair access ramps are used in Victoria, BC. When the bus is lowered, the extended ramp allows entry to the bus at about 4 in. above the sidewalk level. The ramp is about 3 ft. 3 in. long. How could you determine the angle of inclination of the ramp?

Construct Understanding

THINK ABOUT IT

Work with a partner.

Anwar is designing a wheelchair accessibility ramp for his sister. He knows these data:

- The ramp will rise 1 ft. from the level ground to the door of the house.
- The horizontal distance from the start of the ramp at the sidewalk to the door is 20 ft.
- The building code states that the angle of inclination of the ramp must be less than 5°.

Determine whether Anwar's design will comply with the building code.

Solving a triangle means to determine the measures of all the angles and the lengths of all the sides in the triangle.

When we calculate the measures of all the angles and all the lengths in a right triangle, we **solve the triangle**. We can use any of the three primary trigonometric ratios to do this.

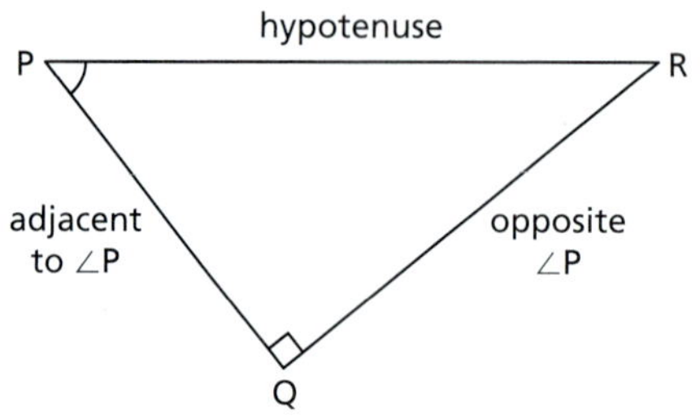

$$\tan P = \frac{\text{opposite}}{\text{adjacent}}$$

$$\sin P = \frac{\text{opposite}}{\text{hypotenuse}}$$

$$\cos P = \frac{\text{adjacent}}{\text{hypotenuse}}$$

Example 1 Solving a Right Triangle Given Two Sides

Solve △XYZ. Give the measures to the nearest tenth.

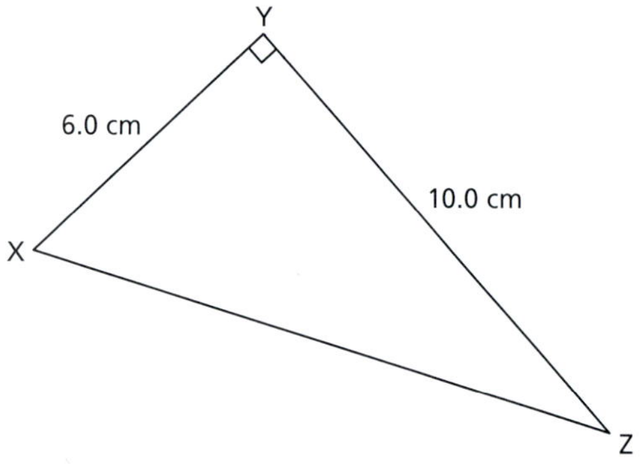

SOLUTIONS

Method 1

Determine the length of XZ first.
Use the Pythagorean Theorem in right △XYZ.

$XZ^2 = 6.0^2 + 10.0^2$

$XZ^2 = 36.00 + 100.00$

$XZ^2 = 136.00$

$XZ = \sqrt{136}$

$XZ = 11.6619\ldots$

XZ is approximately 11.7 cm.

CHECK YOUR UNDERSTANDING

1. Solve this triangle. Give the measures to the nearest tenth.

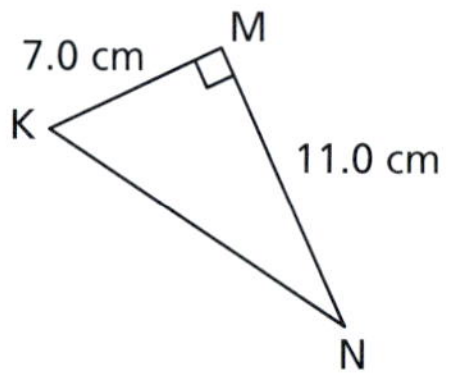

[Answers: KN ≐ 13.0 cm; ∠K ≐ 57.5°; ∠N ≐ 32.5°]

Determine the measure of ∠Z.

Since YZ is adjacent to ∠Z and XZ is the hypotenuse, use the cosine ratio.

$$\cos Z = \frac{\text{adjacent}}{\text{hypotenuse}}$$

$$\cos Z = \frac{YZ}{XZ}$$

$$\cos Z = \frac{10.0}{\sqrt{136}}$$

$$\angle Z = 30.9637\ldots°$$

So, $\angle X = 90° - \angle Z$

The acute angles in a right triangle have a sum of 90°.

$$\angle X = 59.0362\ldots°$$

Which other trigonometric ratio could you have used in Method 1? Why might it be better to use this ratio?

Method 2

Determine the angle measures first. Determine the measure of ∠Z in right △XYZ.

Since YZ is adjacent to ∠Z and XY is opposite ∠Z, use the tangent ratio.

$$\tan Z = \frac{\text{opposite}}{\text{adjacent}}$$

$$\tan Z = \frac{XY}{YZ}$$

$$\tan Z = \frac{6.0}{10.0}$$

$$\tan Z = 0.6$$

$$\angle Z = 30.9637\ldots°$$

```
tan⁻¹(0.6)
        30.9637565
```

So, $\angle X = 90° - \angle Z$

The acute angles in a right triangle have a sum of 90°.

$$\angle X = 59.0362\ldots°$$

Determine the length of XZ.

Since YZ is adjacent to ∠Z and XZ is the hypotenuse, use the cosine ratio.

$$\cos Z = \frac{\text{adjacent}}{\text{hypotenuse}}$$

$$\cos Z = \frac{YZ}{XZ}$$

$$\cos 30.9637\ldots° = \frac{10.0}{XZ}$$

Solve the equation for XZ.
Multiply both sides by XZ.

$$XZ \cos 30.9637\ldots° = 10.0$$

Divide both sides by cos 30.9637…°

$$XZ = \frac{10.0}{\cos 30.9637\ldots°}$$

$$XZ = 11.6614\ldots$$

XZ is approximately 11.7 cm.
∠X is approximately 59.0° and
∠Z is approximately 31.0°.

Example 2 Solving a Right Triangle Given One Side and One Acute Angle

Solve this triangle. Give the measures to the nearest tenth where necessary.

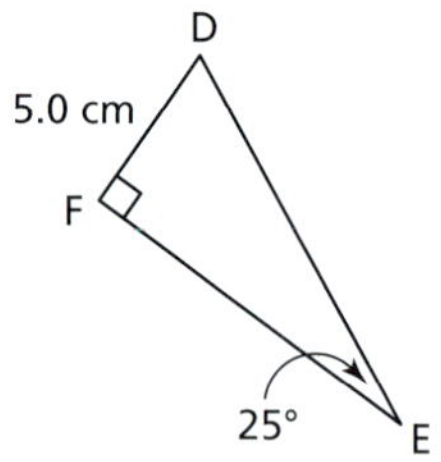

SOLUTION

Label a diagram.
Determine the measure of ∠D first.
In right △DEF:

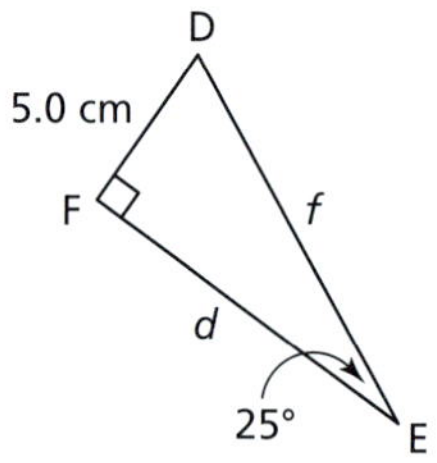

$$\angle D + \angle E = 90°$$

$$\angle D = 90° - 25°$$

$$\angle D = 65°$$

Determine the length of EF.

Since EF is opposite ∠D and DF is adjacent to ∠D, use the tangent ratio.

$$\tan D = \frac{\text{opposite}}{\text{adjacent}}$$

$$\tan D = \frac{d}{e}$$

$$\tan 65° = \frac{d}{5.0}$$

Solve the equation for *d*. Multiply both sides by 5.0.

$$5.0 \tan 65° = d$$

$$d = 10.7225\ldots$$

EF is approximately 10.7 cm.

Use the sine ratio to calculate the length of DE.

$$\sin E = \frac{\text{opposite}}{\text{hypotenuse}}$$

$$\sin E = \frac{e}{f}$$

$$\sin 25° = \frac{5.0}{f}$$

Solve the equation for *f*. Multiply both sides by *f*.

$$f \sin 25° = 5.0$$

Divide both sides by sin 25°.

$$f = \frac{5.0}{\sin 25°}$$

$$f = 11.8310\ldots$$

DE is approximately 11.8 cm.

CHECK YOUR UNDERSTANDING

2. Solve this triangle. Give the measures to the nearest tenth where necessary.

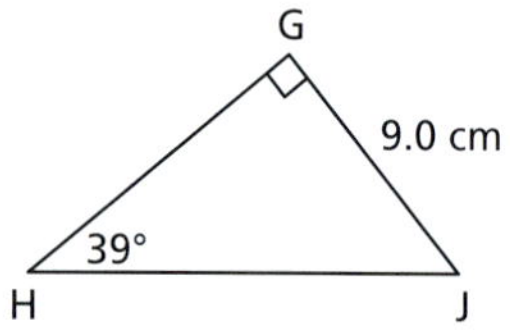

[Answers: ∠J = 51°; GH ≐ 11.1 cm; HJ ≐ 14.3 cm]

What is the advantage of determining the unknown angle before the unknown sides?

Example 3 Solving a Problem Using the Trigonometric Ratios

A small table has the shape of a regular octagon. The distance from one vertex to the opposite vertex, measured through the centre of the table, is approximately 30 cm. There is a strip of wood veneer around the edge of the table. What is the length of this veneer to the nearest centimetre?

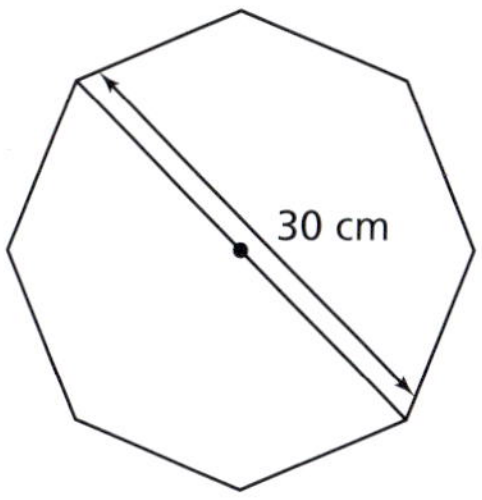

SOLUTION

To determine the length of veneer, calculate the perimeter of the surface of the table.

Since the surface of the table is a regular octagon, congruent isosceles triangles are formed by drawing line segments from the centre of the surface to each vertex.

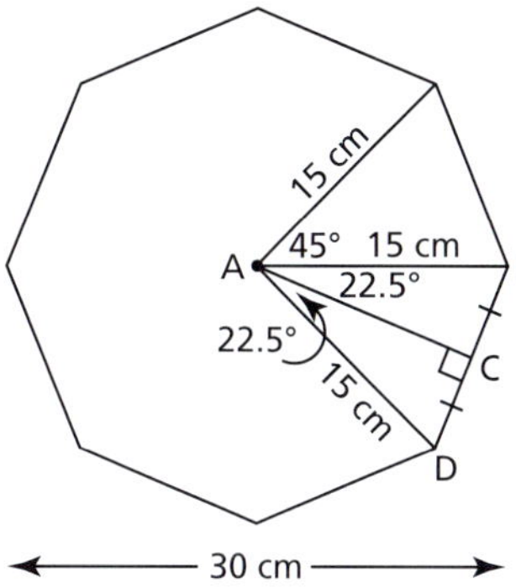

In each triangle, the angle at the centre is:

$360° \div 8 = 45°$

The line segment from the centre of the octagon to the centre of each side of the octagon bisects each central angle and is perpendicular to the side.

So, in right $\triangle ABC$,

$$\angle A = 22.5° \text{ and } AB = 15 \text{ cm}$$

$$\sin A = \frac{BC}{AB}$$

Solve the equation for BC.
Multiply both sides by 15.

$$\sin 22.5° = \frac{BC}{15}$$

$$15 \sin 22.5° = BC$$

Since $BC = 15 \sin 22.5°$, then $BD = 2(15 \sin 22.5°)$, and $BD = 30 \sin 22.5°$

And, the perimeter of the octagon is:
$8(BD) = 8(30 \sin 22.5°)$
$8(BD) = 91.8440\ldots$

The length of veneer required is approximately 92 cm.

CHECK YOUR UNDERSTANDING

3. A window has the shape of a regular decagon. The distance from one vertex to the opposite vertex, measured through the centre of the window, is approximately 4 ft. Determine the length of the wood moulding material that forms the frame of the window, to the nearest foot.

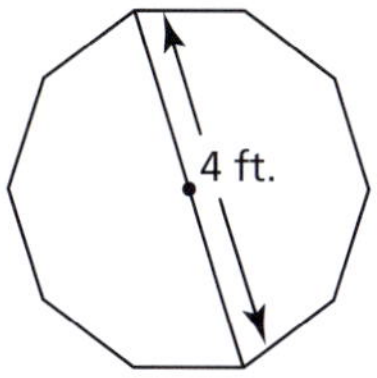

[Answer: approximately 12 ft.]

THE WORLD OF MATH

Profile: Renewable Energy

Aboriginal and northern communities are committed to developing sustainable energy from sources such as wind turbines, solar panels, geothermal, and hydroelectric projects.

Weather Dancer 1 is a 900 KW wind turbine situated on Piikani Nation land in southern Alberta. First commissioned in 2001, it was developed and is run as a joint venture by the Piikani Indian Utility Corporation and EPCOR, a City of Edmonton power company. Weather Dancer 1 generates 9960 MWh of carbon-dioxide free power each year. It was named in honour of Okan (Sun Dance), a traditional ceremony of the Blackfoot that renews their relationship with the life forces of nature.

How could you use trigonometry to determine the length of a blade of a wind turbine?

Discuss the Ideas

1. When we solve a right triangle, sometimes we determine the measure of an unknown angle before we determine the length of an unknown side and sometimes we reverse these calculations. How would you decide which measure to calculate first?

2. Can we solve a right triangle if we are given only the measures of the two acute angles? Explain.

Exercises

A

3. To determine the measure of each indicated angle, which trigonometric ratio would you use? Why?

a) 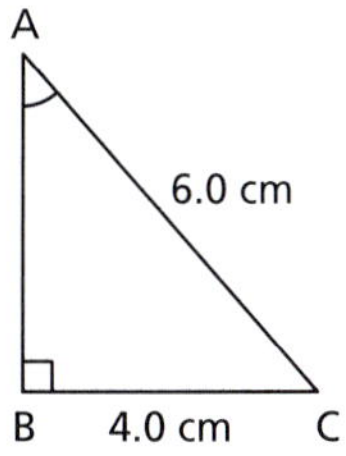

b) 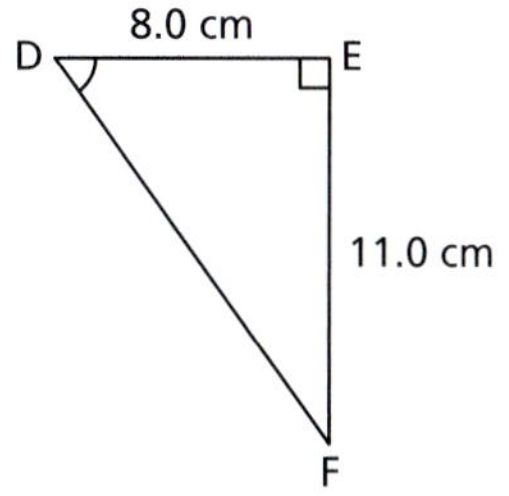

c) 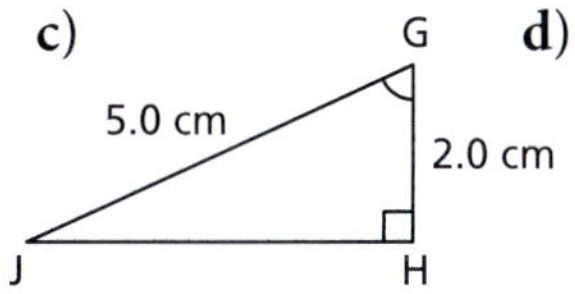

d) 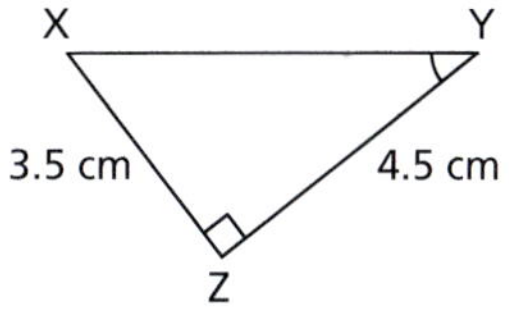

4. Determine the length of each indicated side to the nearest tenth of a centimetre. Which trigonometric ratio did you use? Why?

a) 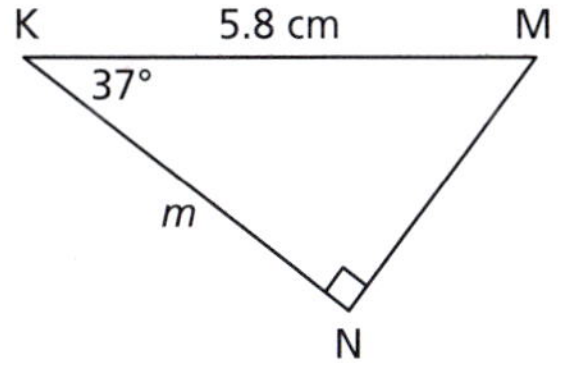

b) 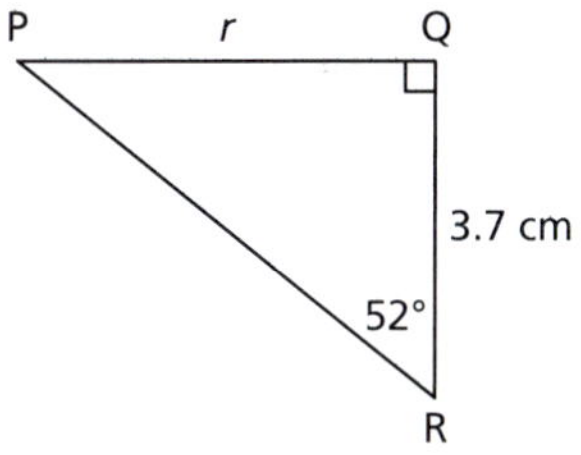

c) 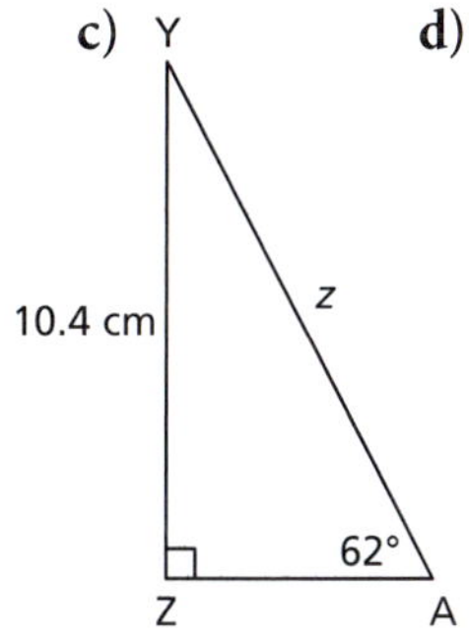

d) 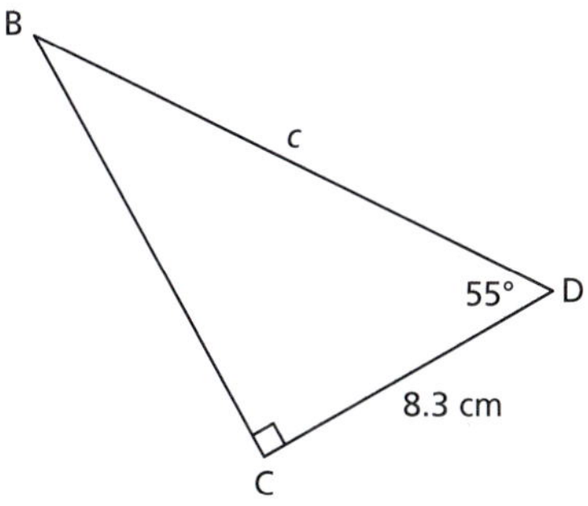

5. To determine the length of each indicated side, which strategy would you use? Why?

a) 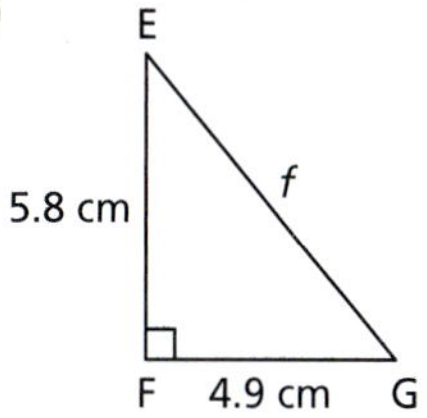

b) 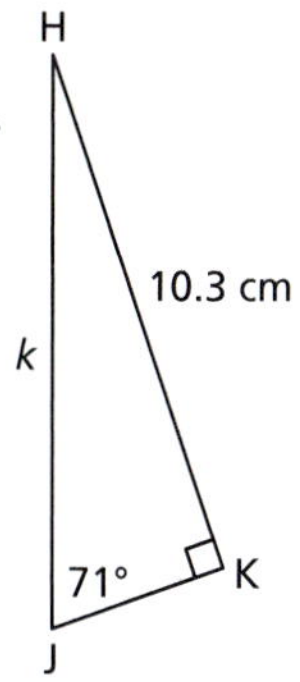

c) 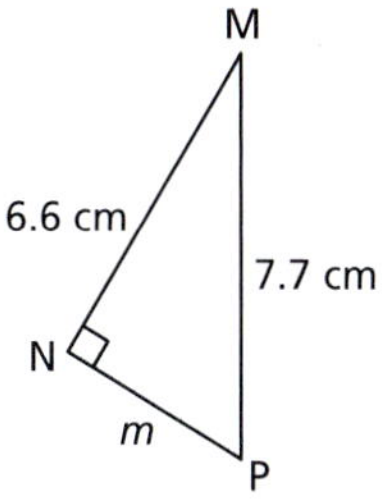

d) 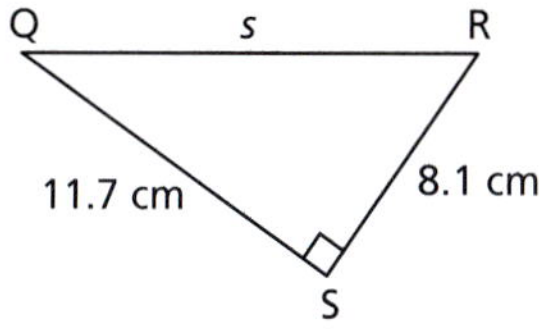

B

6. Solve each right triangle. Give the measures to the nearest tenth.

a) 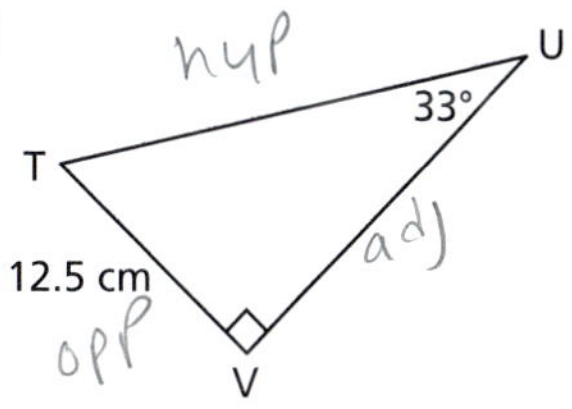

b) 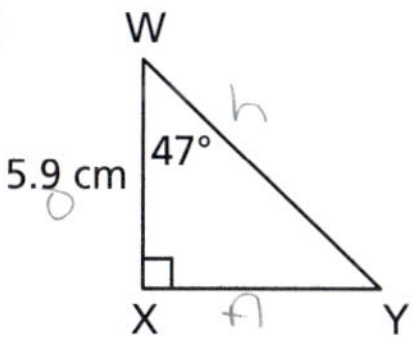

c) 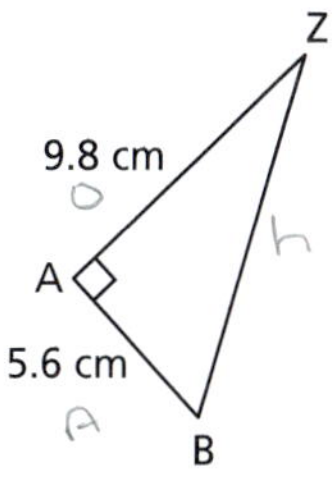

d) 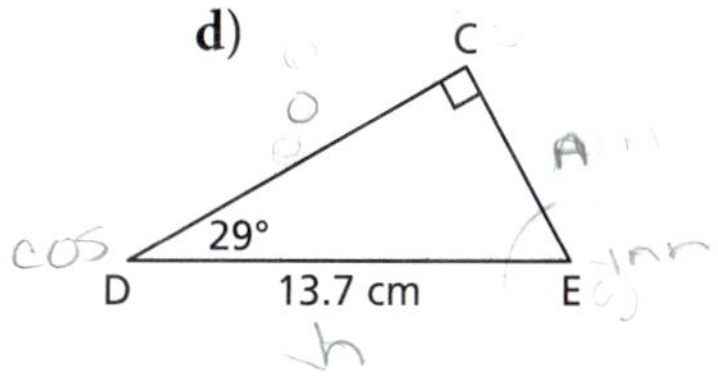

7. An architect draws this diagram of a wheelchair entrance ramp for a building.

a) Determine the length of the ramp.
b) Determine the horizontal distance the ramp will take up.
Give the measures to the nearest centimetre.

8. The world's tallest totem pole is in Alert Bay, B.C., home of the Nimpkish First Nation. Twenty feet from the base of the totem pole, the angle of elevation of the top of the pole is 83.4°. How tall is the totem pole to the nearest foot?

9. A helicopter leaves its base, and flies 35 km due west to pick up a sick person. It then flies 58 km due north to a hospital.
   a) When the helicopter is at the hospital, how far is it from its base to the nearest kilometre?
   b) When the helicopter is at the hospital, what is the measure of the angle between the path it took due north and the path it will take to return directly to its base? Write the angle to the nearest degree.

10. A road rises 1 m for every 15 m measured along the road.
   a) What is the angle of inclination of the road to the nearest degree?
   b) How far does a car travel horizontally when it travels 15 m along the road? Give the answer to the nearest tenth of a metre.

11. A roof has the shape of an isosceles triangle with equal sides 7 m long and base 12 m long.
   a) What is the measure of the angle of inclination of the roof to the nearest degree?
   b) What is the measure of the angle at the peak of the roof to the nearest degree?

12. Determine the perimeter and area of each shape. Give the measures to the nearest tenth.
   a)

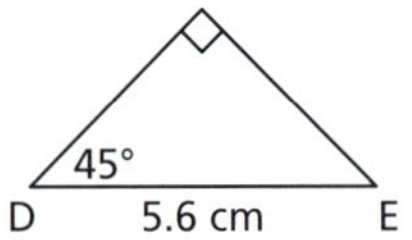

   b)

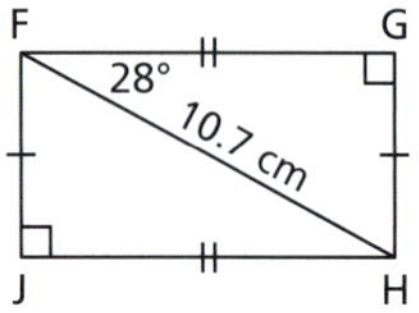

13. Determine the perimeter of this rhombus to the nearest tenth of a centimetre.

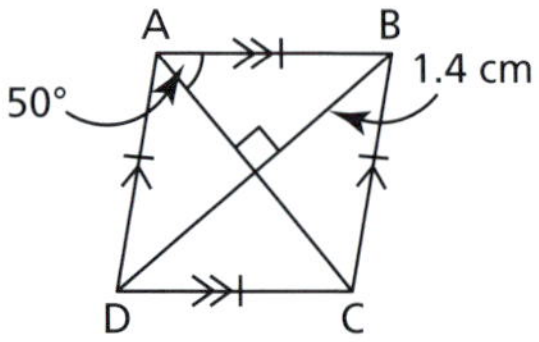

14. A candle has the shape of a right prism whose bases are regular polygons with 12 sides. On each base, the distance from one vertex to the opposite vertex, measured through the centre of the base, is approximately 2 in. The candle is 5 in. high.
   a) What is the area of the base, to the nearest square inch?
   b) What is the volume of wax in the candle, to the nearest cubic inch?

C

15. To irrigate crops, a farmer uses a boom sprayer pulled by a tractor. The nozzles are 50 cm apart and spray at an angle of 70°. To the nearest centimetre, how high should the sprayer be placed above the crops to ensure that all the crops are watered?

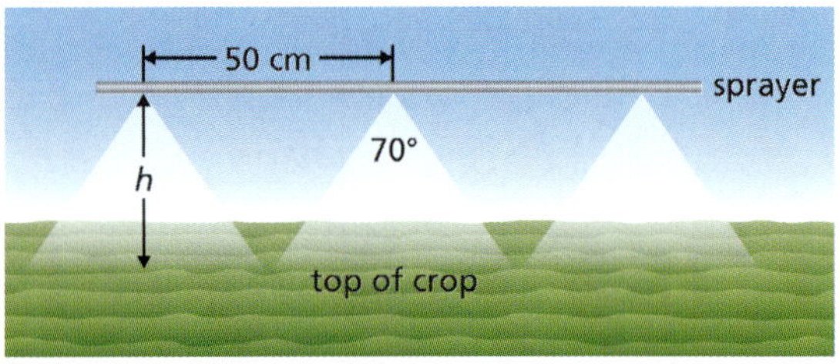

16. Determine the perimeter and area of this isosceles trapezoid. Give the measures to the nearest tenth.

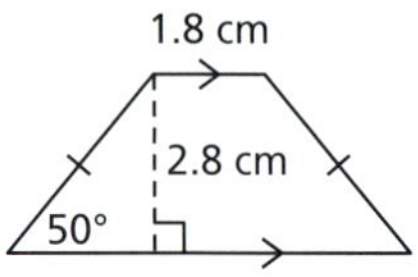

Reflect

How does the information you are given about a right triangle determine the steps you take to solve the triangle? Include examples with your explanation.

2.7 Solving Problems Involving More than One Right Triangle

LESSON FOCUS

Use trigonometry to solve problems modelled by more than one right triangle.

Make Connections

The Muttart Conservatory in Edmonton has four climate-controlled square pyramids, each representing a different climatic zone. Each of the tropical and temperate pyramids is 24 m high and the side length of its base is 26 m. How do you think the architects determined the angles at which to cut the glass pieces for each face at the apex of the pyramid?

Construct Understanding

THINK ABOUT IT

Work with a partner.

Sketch a square pyramid.
Label its height and base with the measurements above.
Draw right triangles on your sketch that would help you determine the angle between the edges of the pyramid at its apex.

How could you use trigonometry to help you determine this angle?

We can use trigonometry to solve problems that can be modelled using right triangles. When more than one right triangle is involved, we have to decide which triangle to start with.

Example 1 Calculating a Side Length Using More than One Triangle

Calculate the length of CD to the nearest tenth of a centimetre.

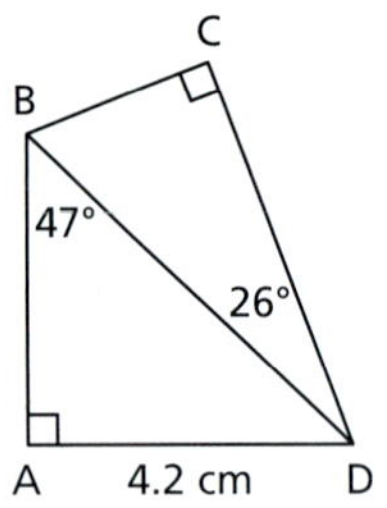

SOLUTION

The length of CD cannot be determined in one step because we know only the measure of one angle in △BCD. So, use △ABD to calculate the length of BD.

In right △ABD, AD is opposite ∠ABD and BD is the hypotenuse.

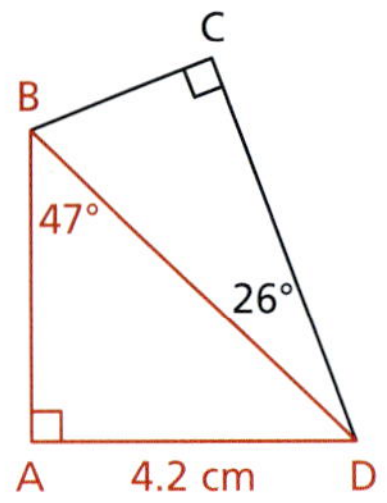

Use the sine ratio in △ABD.

$$\sin B = \frac{\text{opposite}}{\text{hypotenuse}}$$

$$\sin B = \frac{AD}{BD}$$

$$\sin 47° = \frac{4.2}{BD}$$ Solve for BD. Multiply both sides by BD.

$$BD \sin 47° = 4.2$$ Divide both sides by sin 47°.

$$BD = \frac{4.2}{\sin 47°}$$

$$BD = 5.7427\ldots$$

In right △BCD, CD is adjacent to ∠BDC and BD is the hypotenuse. Use the cosine ratio in △BCD.

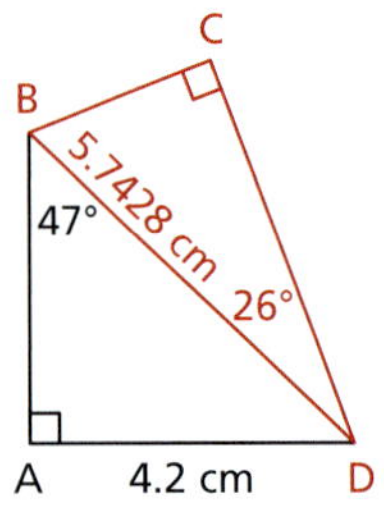

$$\cos D = \frac{\text{adjacent}}{\text{hypotenuse}}$$

$$\cos D = \frac{CD}{BD}$$

$$\cos 26° = \frac{CD}{5.7427\ldots}$$ Solve for CD. Multiply both sides by 5.7427...

$$(5.7427\ldots)\cos 26° = CD$$

$$CD = 5.1615\ldots$$

CD is approximately 5.2 cm.

CHECK YOUR UNDERSTANDING

1. Calculate the length of XY to the nearest tenth of a centimetre.

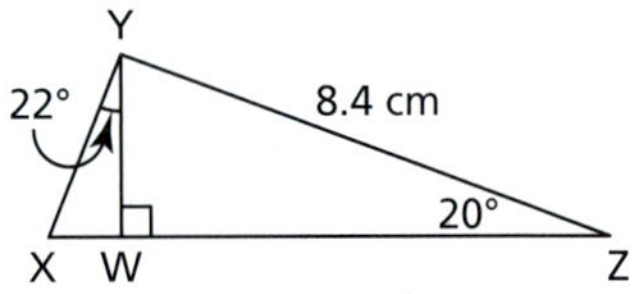

[Answer: XY ≐ 3.1 cm]

Explain how you could calculate all the unknown sides and angles of quadrilateral ABCD.

Example 2 Solving a Problem with Triangles in the Same Plane

From the top of a 20-m high building, a surveyor measured the angle of elevation of the top of another building and the **angle of depression** of the base of that building.

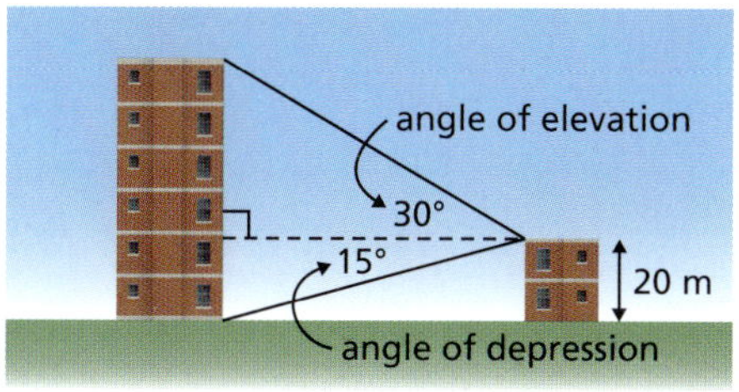

The surveyor sketched this plan of her measurements. Determine the height of the taller building to the nearest tenth of a metre.

SOLUTION

Draw and label a diagram. The height of the building is represented by PR.

We cannot calculate PR in one step because it is not a side of a right triangle.

PR = PS + SR

In △PQS, we know only the measure of ∠PQS. So, use right △QRS to calculate the length of SQ. QSRT is a rectangle, so SR = QT = 20 m.

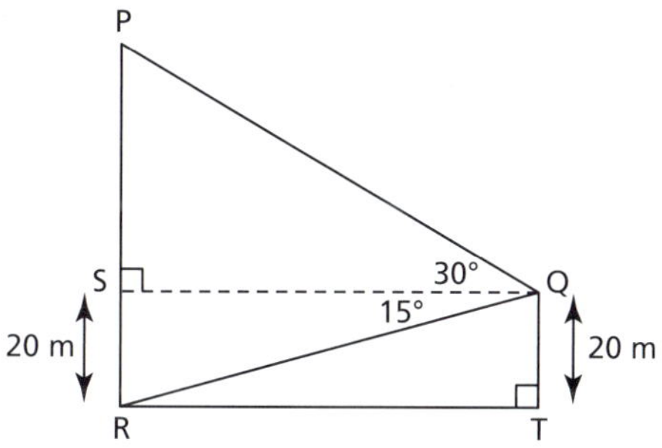

Use the tangent ratio in △QRS.

$$\tan Q = \frac{\text{opposite}}{\text{adjacent}}$$

$$\tan Q = \frac{SR}{QS}$$

$$\tan 15° = \frac{20}{QS}$$

Solve the equation for QS. Multiply both sides by QS.

$$QS \tan 15° = 20$$

Divide both sides by tan 15°.

$$QS = \frac{20}{\tan 15°}$$

$$QS = 74.6410\ldots$$

(Solution continues.)

CHECK YOUR UNDERSTANDING

2. A surveyor stands at a window on the 9th floor of an office tower. He uses a clinometer to measure the angles of elevation and depression of the top and the base of a taller building. The surveyor sketches this plan of his measurements. Determine the height of the taller building to the nearest tenth of a metre.

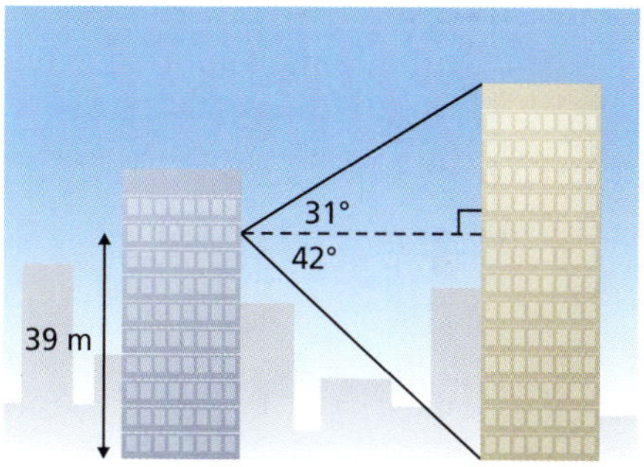

[Answer: Approximately 65.0 m]

The **angle of depression** of an object below the horizontal is the angle between the horizontal and the line of sight from an observer.

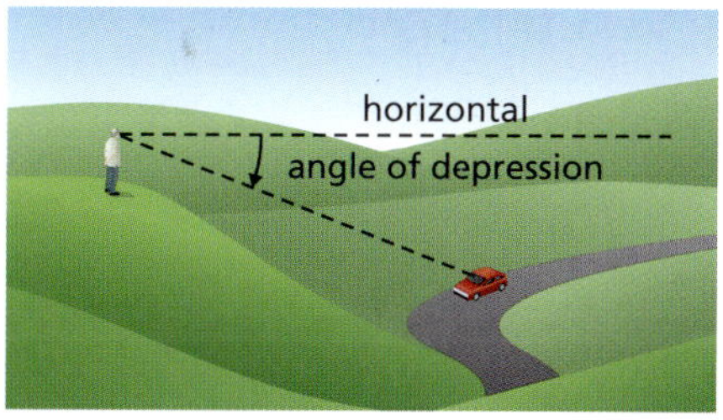

Use the tangent ratio in $\triangle PQS$.

$$\tan Q = \frac{\text{opposite}}{\text{adjacent}}$$

$$\tan Q = \frac{PS}{QS}$$

$$\tan 30° = \frac{PS}{74.6410\ldots}$$

Solve the equation for PS. Multiply both sides by 74.6410…

$$(74.6410\ldots)\tan 30° = PS$$

$$PS = 43.0940\ldots$$

So, $PR = PS + SR$

$$PR = 43.0940\ldots + 20$$

$$= 63.0940\ldots$$

The taller building is approximately 63.1 m high.

Suppose you did not evaluate a decimal equivalent for QS. What expression would you need to use to determine the length of PS?

Sometimes the right triangles we solve are not in the same plane.

Example 3 Solving a Problem with Triangles in Different Planes

From the top of a 90-ft. observation tower, a fire ranger observes one fire due west of the tower at an angle of depression of 5°, and another fire due south of the tower at an angle of depression of 2°. How far apart are the fires to the nearest foot? The diagram is *not* drawn to scale.

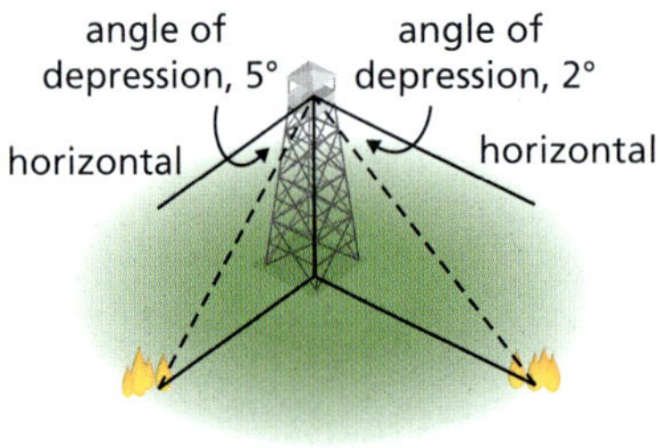

SOLUTION

Label a diagram.

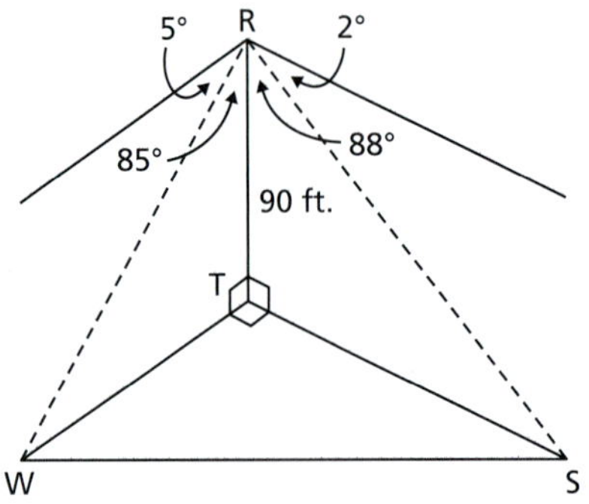

The fires are due south and due west of the tower, so the angle between the lines of sight, TW and TS, to the fires from the base of the tower is 90°.

Since the angles of depression are 5° and 2° respectively, the angles between the tower, RT, and the lines of sight are 85° and 88° respectively.

To calculate the distance WS between the fires, first calculate the distances, TW and TS, of the fires from the base of the tower.

Use the tangent ratio in right △RTW.

$$\tan R = \frac{\text{opposite}}{\text{adjacent}}$$

$$\tan R = \frac{WT}{RT}$$

$$\tan 85° = \frac{WT}{90} \quad \text{Solve for WT. Multiply both sides by 90.}$$

$$90 \tan 85° = WT$$

$$WT = 1028.7047...$$

Use the tangent ratio in right △RTS.

$$\tan R = \frac{\text{opposite}}{\text{adjacent}}$$

$$\tan R = \frac{TS}{RT}$$

$$\tan 88° = \frac{TS}{90} \quad \text{Solve for TS. Multiply both sides by 90.}$$

$$90 \tan 88° = TS$$

$$TS = 2577.2627...$$

In right △STW, use the Pythagorean Theorem.

$$SW^2 = WT^2 + TS^2$$

$$SW^2 = 1028.7047...^2 + 2577.2627...^2$$

$$SW = \sqrt{1028.7047...^2 + 2577.2627...^2}$$

$$= 2774.9805...$$

The distance between the fires is approximately 2775 ft.

CHECK YOUR UNDERSTANDING

3. A communications tower is 35 m tall. From a point due north of the tower, Tannis measures the angle of elevation of the top of the tower as 70°. Her brother Leif, who is due east of the tower, measures the angle of elevation of the top of the tower as 50°. How far apart are the students to the nearest metre? The diagram is *not* drawn to scale.

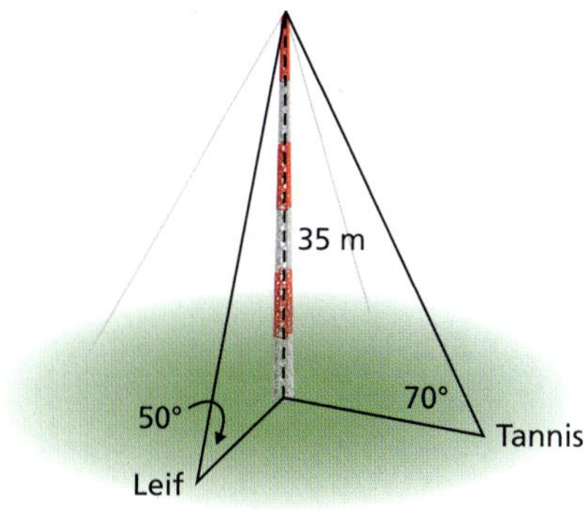

[Answer: About 32 m]

Solve Example 3 using your calculator only once. Explain why this might be more efficient and accurate than calculating intermediate lengths.

Discuss the Ideas

1. What do you have to think about when you draw a diagram with triangles in three dimensions?

2. When you have to solve a problem that involves two right triangles, how do you decide where to begin?

Exercises

A

3. In each triangle, determine the length of JK to the nearest tenth of a centimetre.

a)

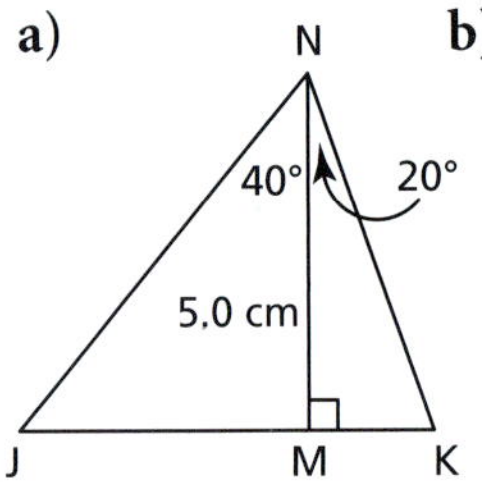

b)

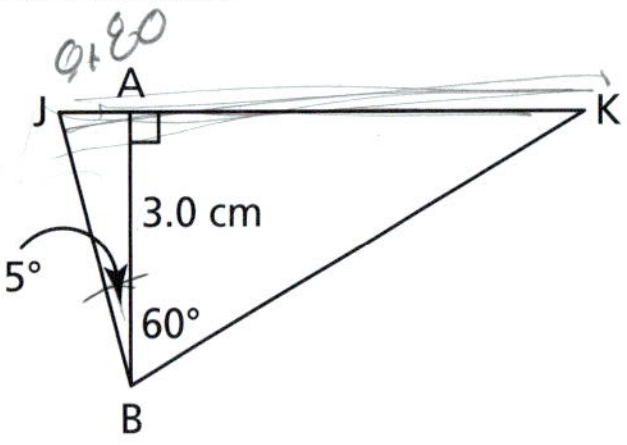

c)

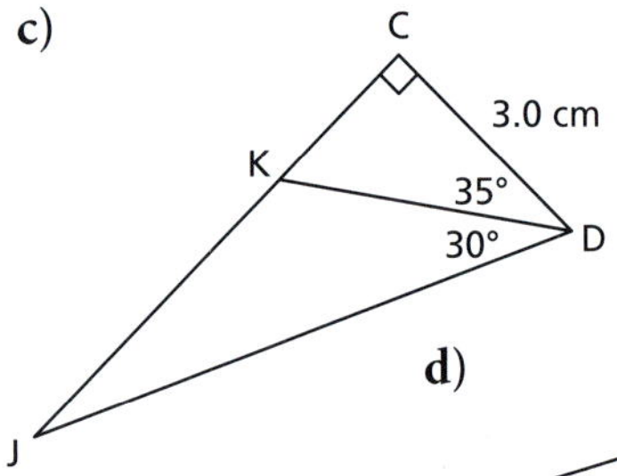

d)

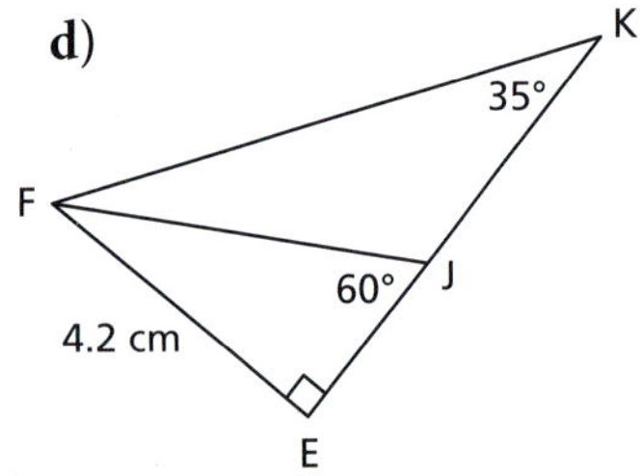

4. In each quadrilateral, calculate the length of GH to the nearest tenth of a centimetre.

a)

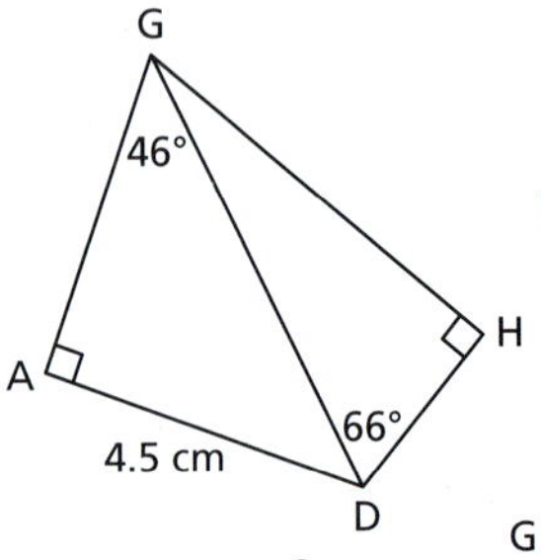

b)

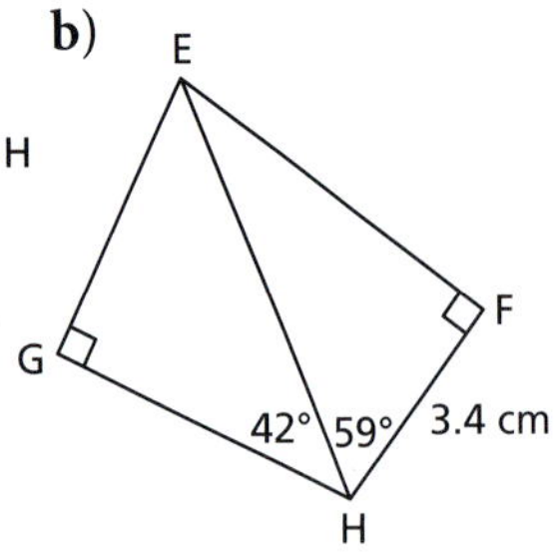

c)

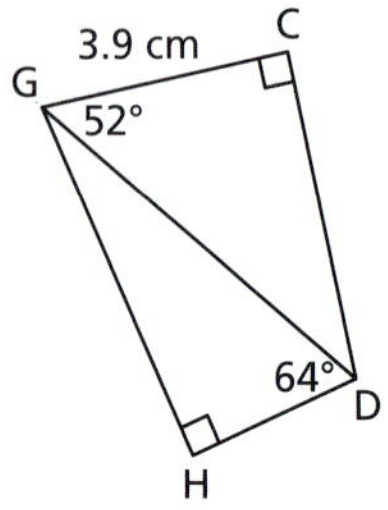

B

5. In each diagram, calculate the measure of each ∠XYZ to the nearest tenth of a degree.

a)

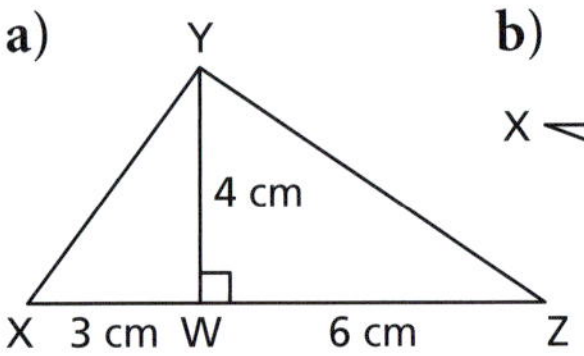

b)

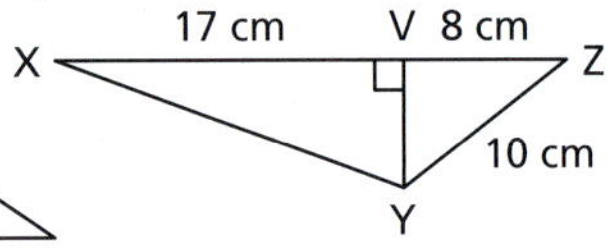

c)

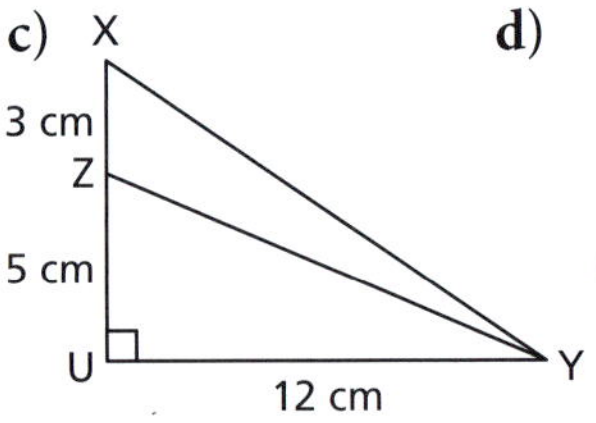

d)

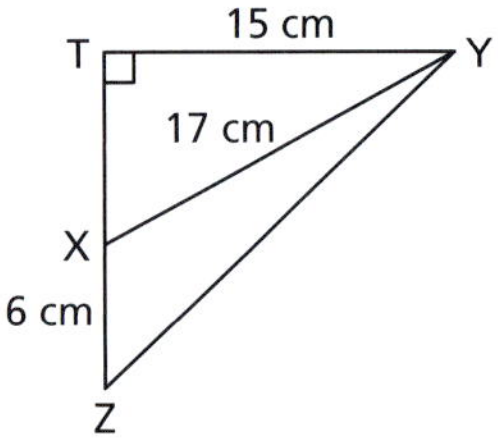

6. Two trees are 80 m apart. From a point halfway between the trees, the angles of elevation of the tops of the trees are measured. What is the height of each tree to the nearest metre?

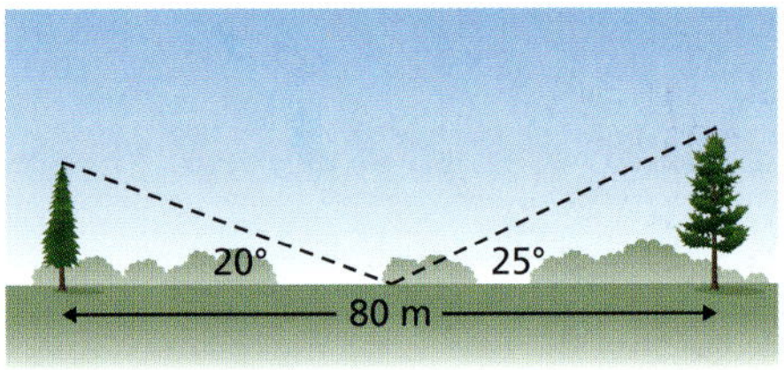

7. At the Muttart Conservatory, the arid pyramid has 4 congruent triangular faces. The base of each face has length 19.5 m and the slant height of the pyramid is 20.5 m. What is the measure of each of the three angles in the face? Give the measures to the nearest degree.

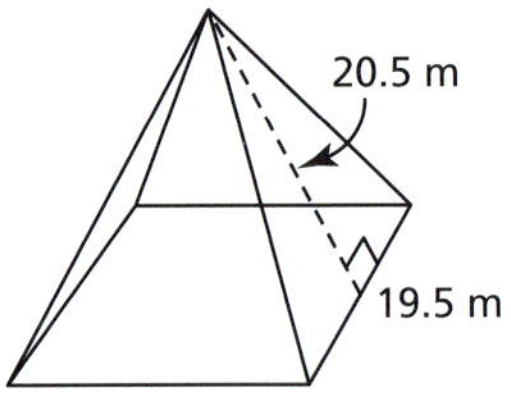

8. From a window on the second floor of her house, a student measured the angles of elevation and depression of the top and base of a nearby tree. The student knows that she made the measurements 16 ft. above the ground.

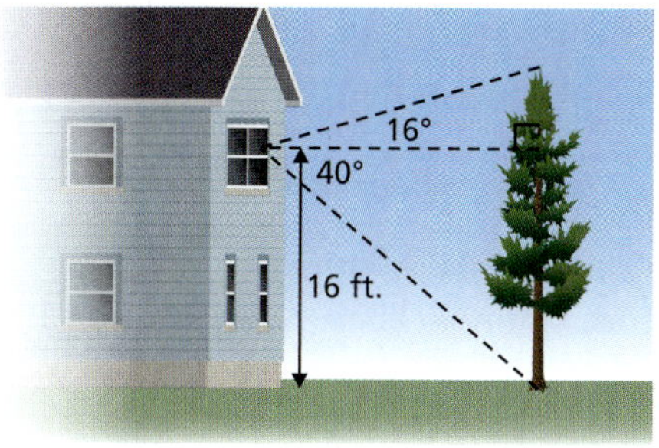

a) What is the horizontal distance between the student and the tree?

b) How tall is the tree?

Give the measures to the nearest foot.

9. Two office towers are 50 m apart. From the top of the shorter tower, the angle of depression of the base of the taller tower is 35°. The angle of elevation of the top of this tower is 25°. Determine the height of each tower to the nearest metre.

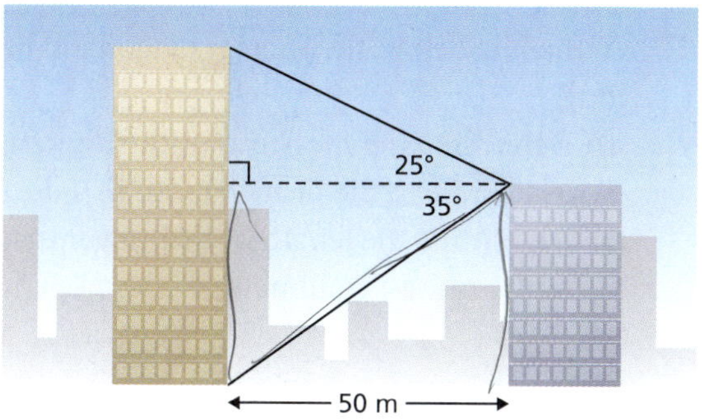

10. A rectangle has dimensions 5.5 cm by 2.8 cm. Determine the measures of the angles at the point where the diagonals intersect. What strategy did you use? Could you have determined the angle measures a different way? Explain.

11. A student wanted to know the distance between two particular carvings on a spirit pole. She measured the angle of elevation of each carving 15.0 m from the base of the pole. The student drew the sketch below. What is the distance between the carvings to the nearest tenth of a metre?

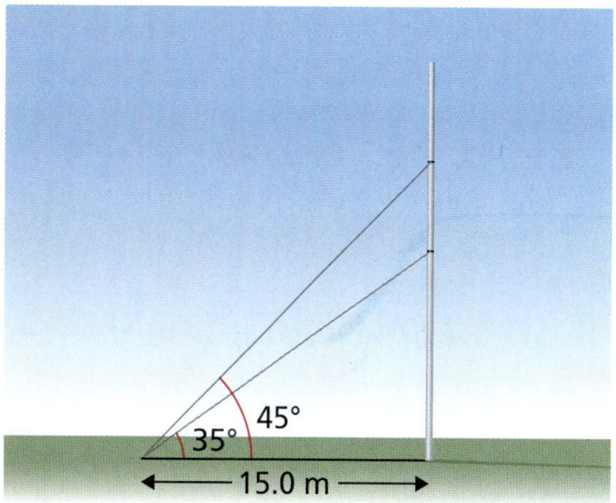

12. The Legislative Building in Wascana Park, Regina, has a domed tower at its centre.

Janelle stood due south of the tower, 40 m from a point directly beneath the dome, and measured the angle of elevation of the top of the dome as 53°. Troy stood due east of the tower and measured the angle of elevation of the top of the dome as 61°.

a) How high is the top of the dome?

b) How far is Troy from a point directly beneath the dome?

c) How far apart are Janelle and Troy?

Give the measures to the nearest metre.

13. A communications tower has many guy wires supporting it. Two of these guy wires are 10.0 m and 8.0 m long. They are attached at the same point on the ground. The longer wire has an angle of inclination of 60°.

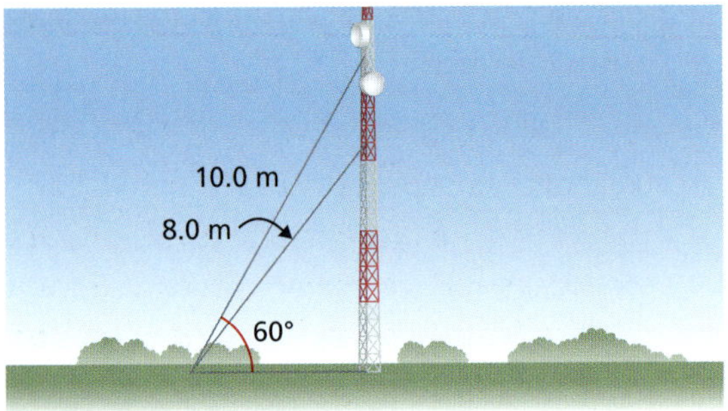

a) How far from the base of the tower are the wires attached on the ground?

b) What is the angle of inclination of the shorter guy wire?

c) How far apart are the points where the guy wires are attached to the tower?

Give the measures to the nearest tenth.

14. A surveyor drew the sketch below to show the measurements he took to determine the width and depth of a gorge.

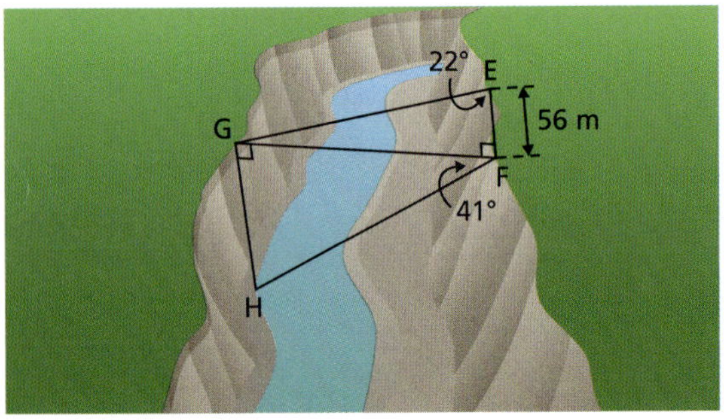

a) Determine the width, GF, of the gorge.

b) Determine the depth, GH, of the gorge.

Give the measures to the nearest metre.

15. A surveyor wants to determine the height of a cliff on the other side of the river from where she is standing. The surveyor cannot cross the river. She has a clinometer and a measuring tape. Describe how she can calculate the height of the cliff.

16. The Gastown Steam clock in Vancouver has been chiming since 1977. From a point on the ground, Connor measured the angle of elevation of the top of the clock tower as 59.5°. Monique was 3.5 m from Connor. The line joining them formed a right angle with the line joining Connor and the base of the tower. The angle between Monique's lines of sight to Connor and to the base of the tower was 40.6°.

a) Sketch a diagram.

b) Determine the height of the tower to the nearest tenth of a metre.

C

17. In the kite below, the shorter diagonal is 6.8 cm long.

a) Determine the measures of the four angles of the kite to the nearest tenth of a degree.

b) Determine the length of the longer diagonal to the nearest millimetre.

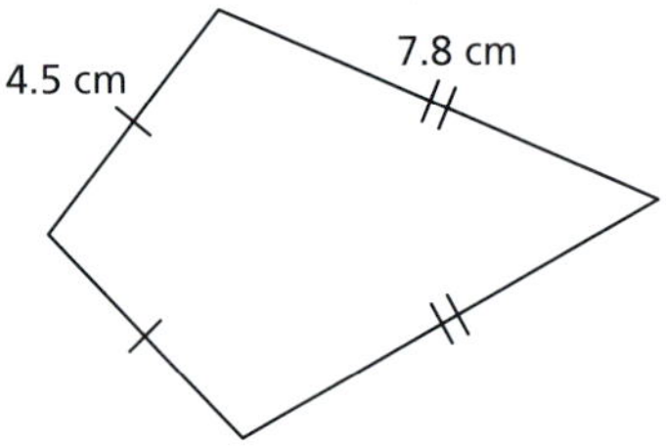

18. At the Muttart Conservatory, the tropical pyramid has 4 congruent triangular faces. The base of each face has length 25.7 m and the slant height of the pyramid is 27.2 m.

a) Sketch and label the pyramid.

b) What is the height of the pyramid to the nearest tenth of a metre?

19. a) What is the length of the body diagonal in this rectangular prism?

b) What is the measure of ∠AFH, the angle between the body diagonal and a diagonal of the base of the prism?

Give the measures to the nearest tenth.

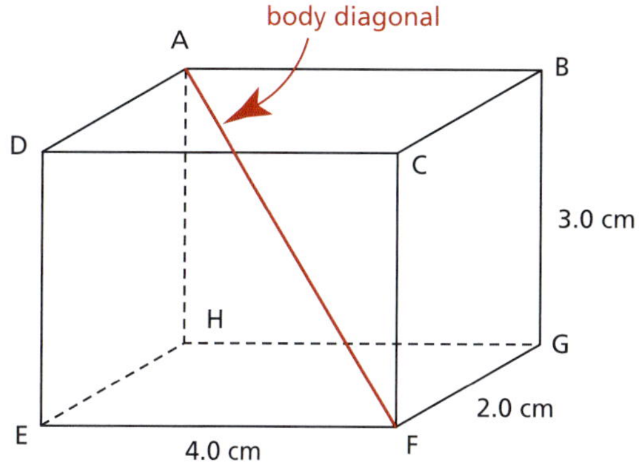

20. A communications tower is supported by guy wires. One guy wire is anchored at a point that is 8.9 m from the base of the tower and has an angle of inclination of 36°. From this point, the angle of elevation of the top of the tower is 59°. How far from the top of the tower is the guy wire attached to the tower?

21. A geodesic dome is constructed by bolting together many pentagonal pyramids. Each triangular face of a pyramid is formed with two struts, each 54 in. long, and one strut that is 60 in. long. Determine the height of one of these pyramids.

Reflect Summarize the different steps used to solve right triangle problems.

THE WORLD OF MATH

Historical Moment: Claudius Ptolemy

Claudius Ptolemy, who died in 161 CE, was a mathematician, an astronomer, and a geographer. He lived in Alexandria in Roman Egypt, and wrote in Greek. As part of his interest in astronomy, he extended the tables of trigonometric ratios started by Hipparchus of Bythnia (190 – 120 BCE) and studied triangles. Ptolemy's first major work, the *Almagest,* is the only ancient comprehensive material on astronomy that survives today. His other major works were *Geographia, Harmonics*, and *Optics*.

STUDY GUIDE

CONCEPT SUMMARY

Big Ideas	Applying the Big Ideas
In a right triangle: ■ The ratio of any two sides remains constant if the triangle is enlarged or reduced.	This means that: ■ The size of the triangle does not affect the value of any trigonometric ratio of an acute angle in the triangle.
■ You can use the ratio of the lengths of two sides to determine the measure of one of the acute angles.	■ If the tangent ratio, sine ratio, or cosine ratio of an angle is known, the related inverse operation — $\tan^{-1}$, $\sin^{-1}$, or $\cos^{-1}$ — on a scientific calculator can be used to determine the measure of the angle.
■ You can use the length of one side and the measure of an acute angle to determine the length of another side of the triangle.	■ You can use the definition of the tangent ratio, sine ratio, or cosine ratio to create an equation. You can then solve this equation to determine the unknown side length.
■ You can use the primary trigonometric ratios to solve problems that can be represented using right triangles.	■ You can solve problems that involve more than one right triangle by applying the trigonometric ratios to one triangle at a time.

Reflect on the Chapter

- How were the properties of similar triangles used to establish the meaning of the sine, cosine, and tangent ratios?
- When you used the trigonometric ratios to solve a problem, why was it important to be able to sketch the situation to show the given information?

SKILLS SUMMARY

Skill | **Description** | **Example**

Calculate a trigonometric ratio. [2.1, 2.4]

Description

$$\tan A = \frac{\text{opposite}}{\text{adjacent}}$$

$$\sin A = \frac{\text{opposite}}{\text{hypotenuse}}$$

$$\cos A = \frac{\text{adjacent}}{\text{hypotenuse}}$$

Example

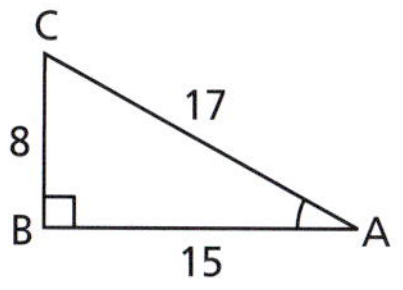

$$\tan A = \frac{\text{opposite}}{\text{adjacent}}$$

$$\tan A = \frac{BC}{BA}$$

$$\tan A = \frac{8}{15}, \text{ or } 0.5\bar{3}$$

Determine the measure of an angle. [2.1, 2.4]

Description

In right $\triangle ABC$, to determine the measure of acute $\angle A$ when you are given:

- the length of the adjacent leg, AB
- the length of the hypotenuse, AC

1. Determine cos A using the given lengths.
2. Use $\cos^{-1}$ on a scientific calculator to determine the measure of $\angle A$.

Example

In $\triangle ABC$ above,

$$\cos A = \frac{\text{adjacent}}{\text{hypotenuse}}$$

$$\cos A = \frac{AB}{AC}$$

$$\cos A = \frac{15}{17}$$

$$\angle A \doteq 28°$$

Determine the length of a side. [2.2, 2.3, 2.5]

Description

In right $\triangle PQR$, to determine the length of the hypotenuse QP when you are given:

- the measure of $\angle P$ and
- the length of the leg QR

1. Identify the trigonometric ratio to use, then write an equation.
2. Substitute the known values.
3. Solve the equation for the unknown length.

Then, if you need to determine the length of the leg PR:

4. Use a trigonometric ratio, or use the Pythagorean Theorem.

Example

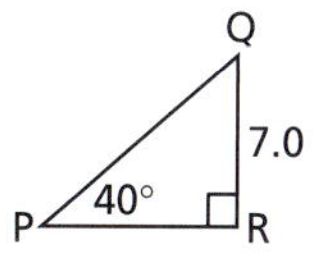

$$\sin P = \frac{\text{opposite}}{\text{hypotenuse}}$$

$$\sin P = \frac{QR}{QP}$$

$$\sin 40° = \frac{7}{QP}$$

$$QP = \frac{7}{\sin 40°}$$

$$QP \doteq 10.9$$

REVIEW

2.1

1. Determine each indicated angle to the nearest degree.

   a) 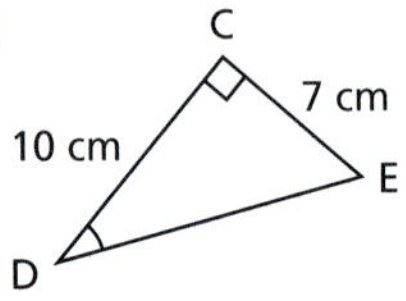

   b) 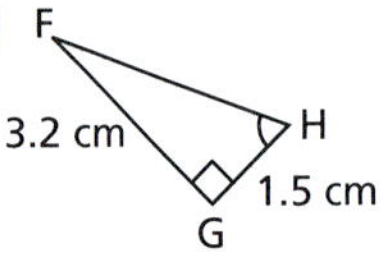

2. a) Is tan 20° greater than or less than 1?
   b) Is tan 70° greater than or less than 1?
   c) How could you answer parts a and b if you did not have a calculator? Sketch a right triangle to illustrate your answer.

3. A road rises 15 m for each 150 m of horizontal distance. What is the angle of inclination of the road to the nearest degree?

4. Sketch a triangle to show that tan 45° = 1. Describe the triangle.

2.2

5. a) Determine the length of each indicated side to the nearest tenth of a centimetre.

   i) 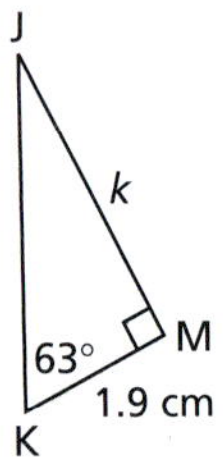

   ii) 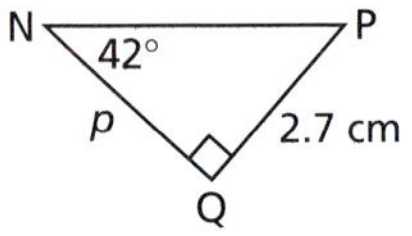

   b) Use the Pythagorean Theorem to determine the length of the hypotenuse of each triangle in part a. What other strategy could you have used to determine each length?

6. At a point 100 m from the base of the Eiffel tower, the angle of elevation of the top of the tower is 73°. How tall is the tower to the nearest metre?

7. The shorter side of a rectangle is 5.7 cm. The angle between this side and a diagonal is 64°.
   a) Determine the length of the rectangle.
   b) Determine the length of a diagonal.
   State the answers to the nearest tenth of a centimetre.

8. A tree casts a shadow that is 31.5 m long when the angle between the sun's rays and the ground is 29°. What is the height of the tree to the nearest tenth of a metre?

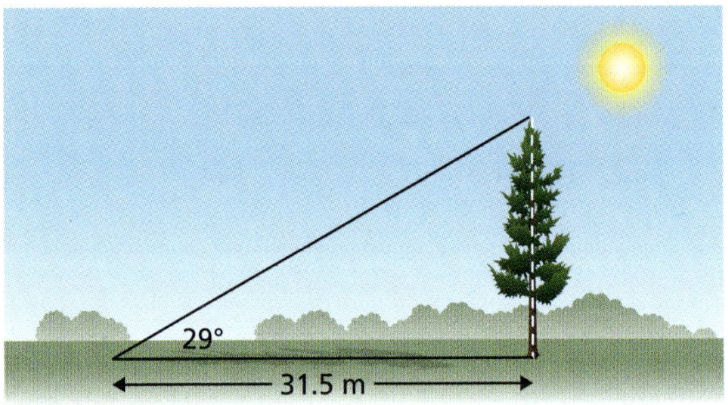

9. Aidan knows that the observation deck on the Vancouver Lookout is 130 m above the ground. He measures the angle between the ground and his line of sight to the observation deck as 77°. How far is Aidan from the base of the Lookout to the nearest metre?

2.3

10. Use your drinking-straw clinometer to measure the height of your gymnasium to the nearest tenth of a metre. Explain your strategy. Include a sketch that shows all the measurements you made or calculated.

2.4

11. Determine the measure of each indicated angle to the nearest degree. Which trigonometric ratio did you use each time? Explain why.

a)
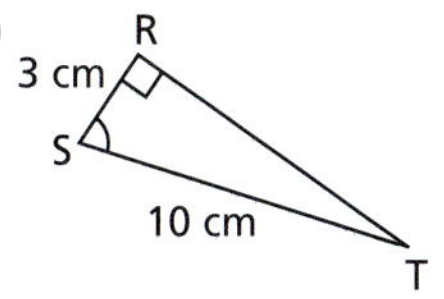

b)
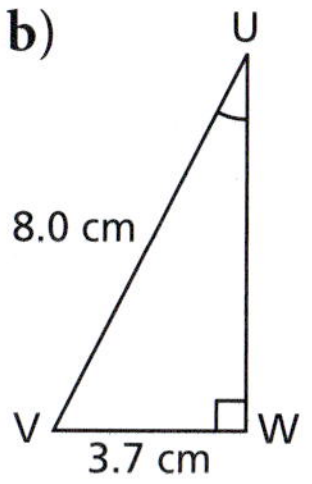

12. Sketch and label right △BCD with BC = 5 cm, CD = 12 cm, and BD = 13 cm.

a) What is the value of each ratio?

i) sin D **ii)** sin B

iii) cos B **iv)** cos D

b) How are the ratios in part a related? Explain why this relationship occurs.

13. During a storm, a 10.0-m telephone pole was blown off its vertical position. The top of the pole was then 9 m above the ground. What was the angle of inclination of the pole to the nearest tenth of a degree?

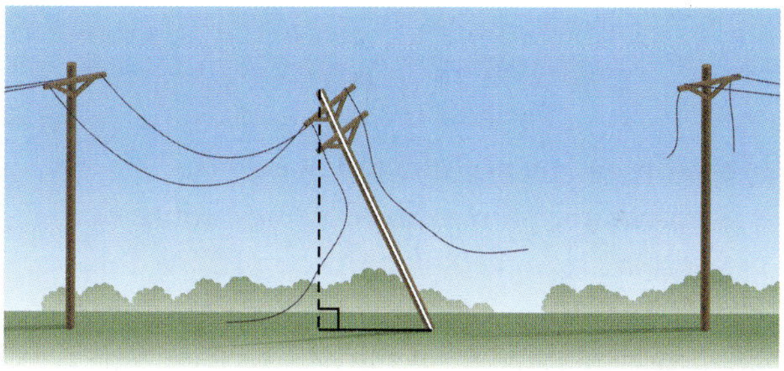

14. Determine the measure of ∠C in this trapezoid. Give your answer to the nearest tenth of a degree. Describe your strategy.

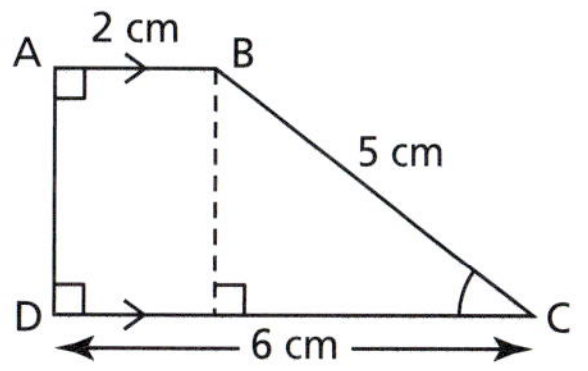

2.5

15. Determine the length of each indicated side to the nearest tenth of a centimetre. Which trigonometric ratio did you use each time? Explain why.

a)
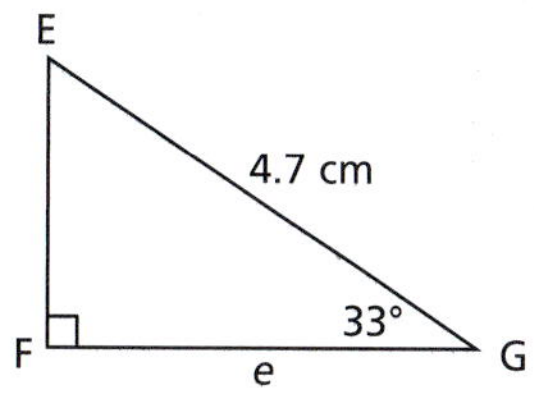

b)
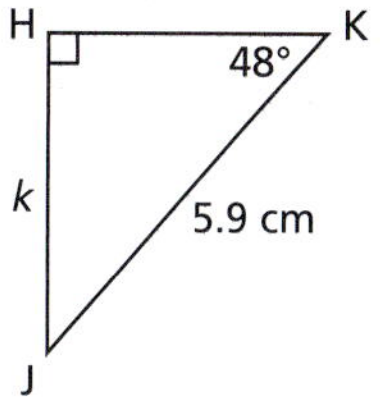

c)
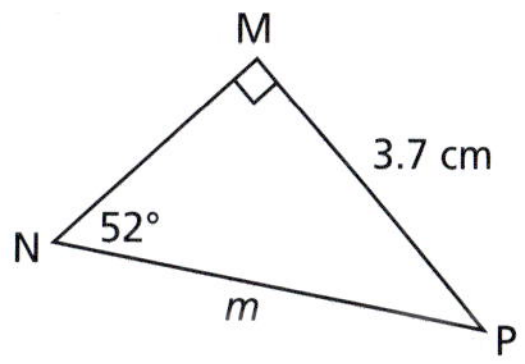

d)
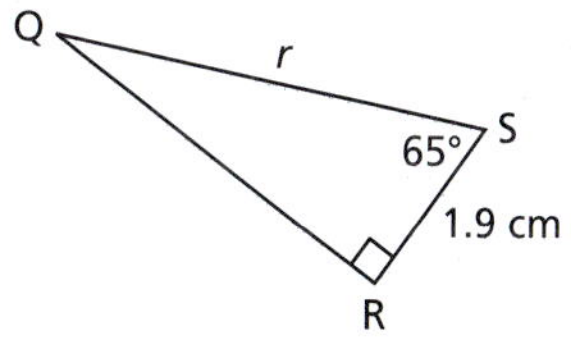

16. A ship is sailing off the west shore of Hudson Bay. At a certain point, the ship is 4.5 km due east of the town of Arviat. The ship then sails due north until the angle between the path of the ship and the line of sight to Arviat is 48.5°. How far is the ship from Arviat? State the answer to the nearest tenth of a kilometre.

17. Determine the dimensions of this rectangle to the nearest tenth of a centimetre.

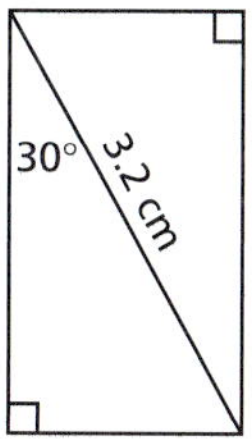

2.6

18. Solve each right triangle. State the measures to the nearest tenth.

a)

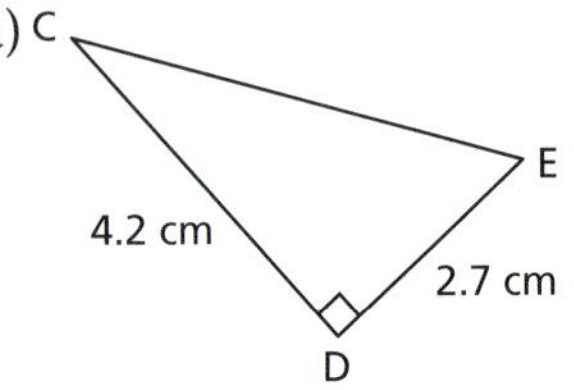

b)

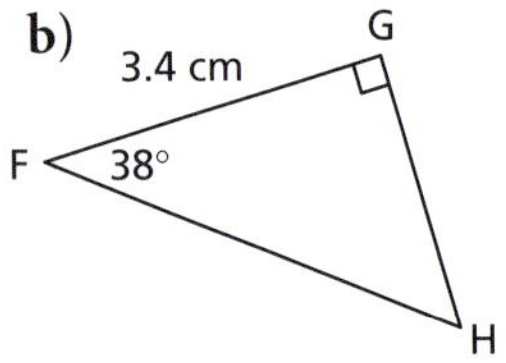

c)

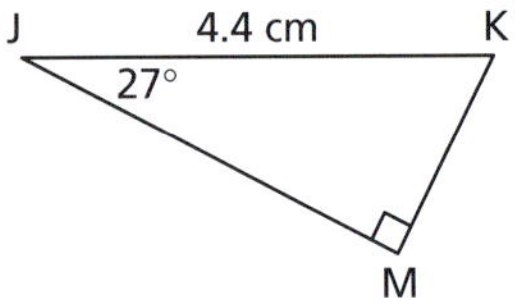

19. In Italy, the Leaning Tower of Pisa currently leans 13 ft. off the vertical. The tower is 183 ft. tall. What is its angle of inclination to the nearest tenth of a degree?

20. Determine the perimeter and area of each shape. Give the measures to the nearest tenth.

a)

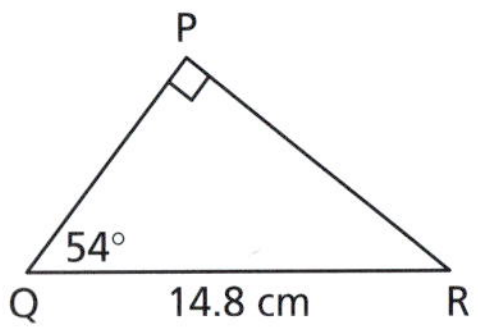

b)

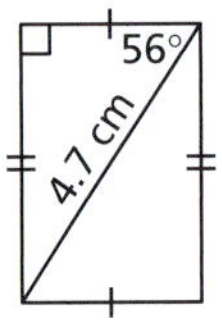

21. Cars are parked at an angle to the street. The diagram shows a parking space.

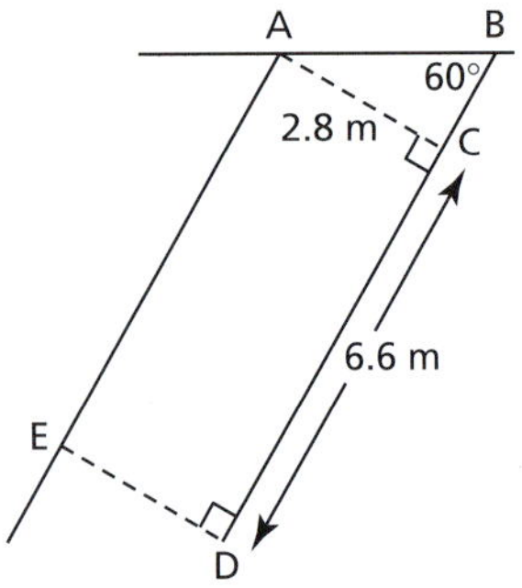

a) What is the length, AB?
b) What is the length, BD?
Give the measures to the nearest tenth of a metre.

2.7

22. In the diagram below, determine each measure.
a) KJ **b)** HK **c)** ∠HKJ
Give the measures to the nearest tenth.

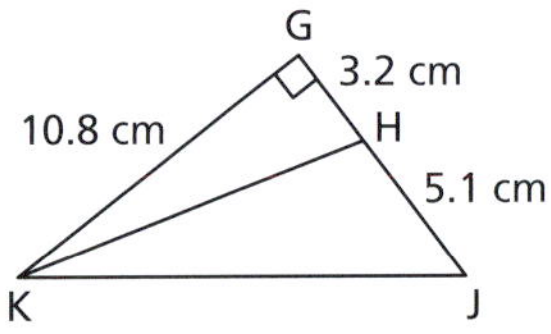

23. A fire ranger is at the top of a 90-ft. observation tower. She observes smoke due east at an angle of depression of 5° and due west at an angle of depression of 4°. How far apart are the fires to the nearest foot? The diagram is *not* drawn to scale.

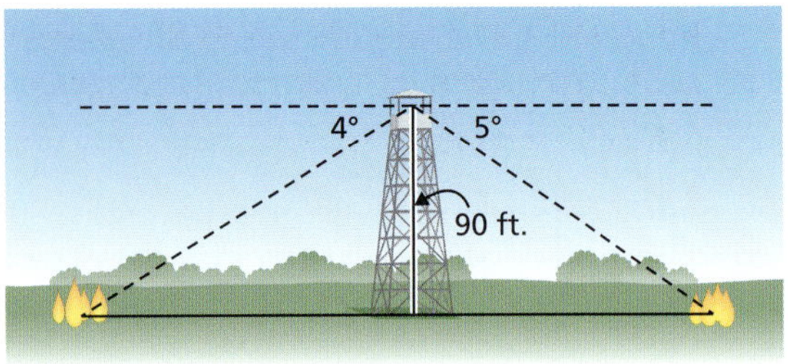

PRACTICE TEST

For questions 1 and 2, choose the correct answer: A, B, C, or D

1. For $\triangle PQR$, how many of these statements are true?

$\tan Q = \frac{3}{4}$ $\qquad \sin P = \frac{3}{5}$

$\sin Q = \frac{3}{5}$ $\qquad \tan P = \frac{4}{3}$

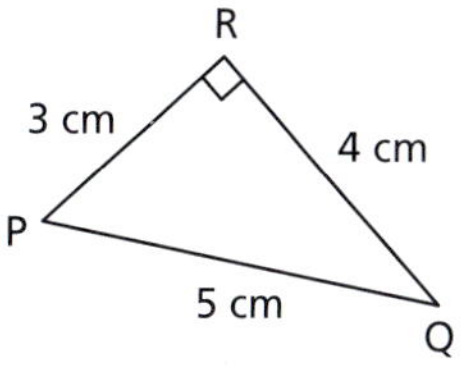

A. All are true. **B.** 3 are true. **C.** 2 are true. **D.** 1 is true.

2. In right $\triangle PQR$, with $\angle Q = 90°$, which statement is true?
As $\angle P$ increases:

A. tan P decreases **B.** sin P decreases

C. cos P decreases **D.** cos P increases

3. Triangle ABC is similar to $\triangle XYZ$ and $\angle A = \angle X = 90°$.
Use a diagram to explain why sin B = sin Y.

4. In right $\triangle DEF$, $\angle E = 90°$, $\angle F = 63°$, and DF = 7.8 cm. Solve this triangle. State the measures to the nearest tenth.

5. A ramp is used to load a snowmobile onto the back of a pickup truck. The truck bed is 1.3 m above the ground. For safety, the angle of inclination of the ramp should be less than 40°. What is the shortest possible length of the ramp to the nearest centimetre? Explain why.

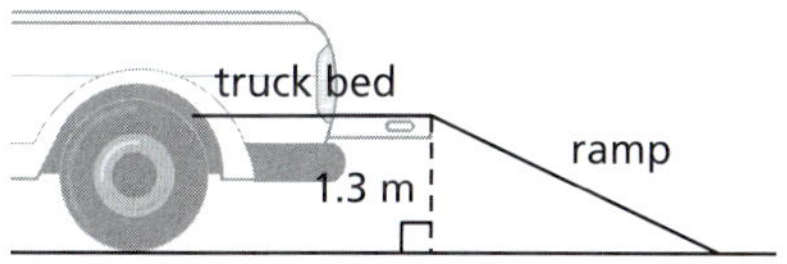

6. A student uses a clinometer to measure the angle of elevation of a sign that marks the point on a tower that is 50 m above the ground. The angle of elevation is 37° and the student holds the clinometer 1.5 m above the ground. She then measures the angle of elevation of the top of the tower as 49°. Determine the height of the tower to the nearest tenth of a metre. The diagram is *not* drawn to scale.

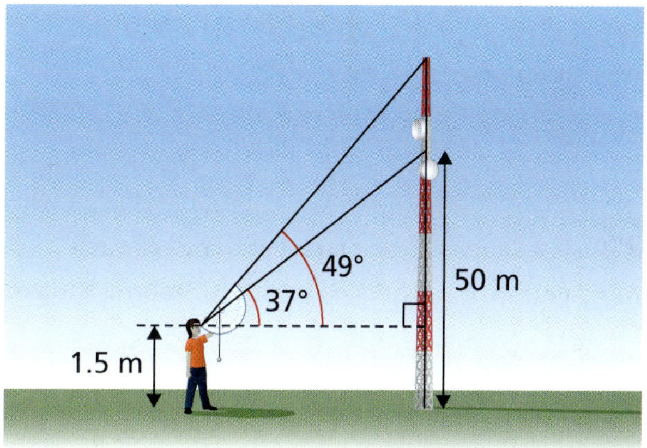

Ramp It Up!

New public buildings should be accessible by all, and if entry involves steps, an access ramp must be provided. Older buildings are often retro-fitted with ramps to provide easy access.

PART A: DESIGN

Choose a doorway to your school or to a building in your neighbourhood for which a wheelchair ramp could be constructed.

- Measure or use trigonometry to determine the height of the doorway above the ground.

Most building codes require the slope of an access ramp to be no greater than 1:12; that is, for a rise of 1 cm, the ramp must be 12 cm long. Slopes of 1:15 or 1:20 are preferable. A ramp should be at least 915 mm wide.

- Determine the minimum length of ramp required.
- Draw a labelled diagram of your ramp that shows all required lengths and angle measures.

PART B: COST ESTIMATES

A ramp may be constructed from wood or concrete.

- Research, then estimate, the cost of constructing your ramp using lumber from your local supplier. Assume that the ramp surface will be strandboard, or particleboard, or plywood. Give details of all the conversions between systems of measure.
- Research, then estimate, the cost of constructing your ramp using concrete.

Outdoor ramps can become slippery in wet or cold weather, so your ramp surface should have a non-slip coating.

- Research, then estimate the cost of covering the ramp surface with non-slip paint or other material.

PROJECT PRESENTATION

Your completed project should include:

- Your diagram, with calculations and explanations to support your design.
- Cost estimates for the construction in both wood and concrete, with all supporting calculations.

EXTENSION

Access ramps may have level landings with an area of at least 1.525 m^2. These landings are often at the top and bottom, but a long ramp may have a landing as a rest spot. Because of space consideration, long ramps may change direction. Ramps that rise more than 15 cm or have a horizontal distance of more than 1.83 m require a handrail.

- Design and cost your ramp to meet the requirements above with a landing at the top and bottom.

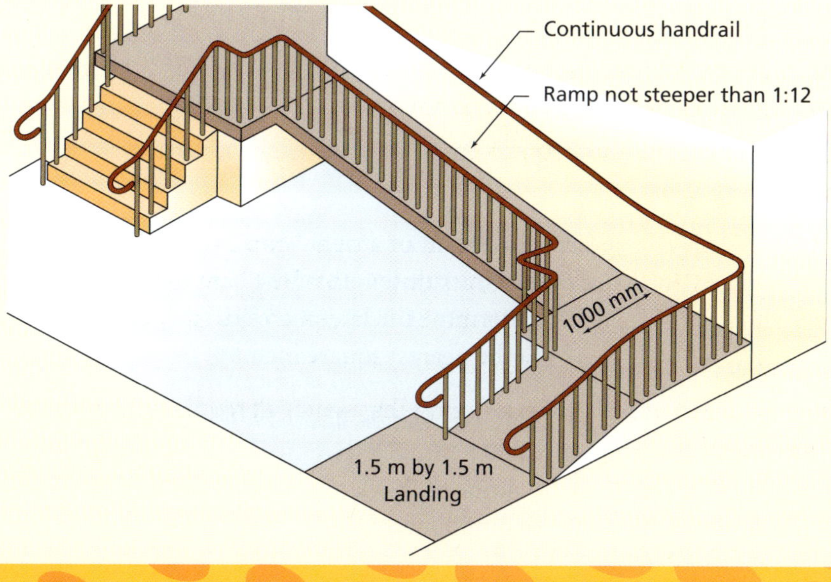

CUMULATIVE REVIEW Chapters 1 and 2

1

1. Andrea is constructing a pen for her dog. The perimeter of the pen is 70 ft.
  a) What is the perimeter of the pen in yards and feet?
  b) The fencing material is sold by the yard. It costs \$2.49/yd. What will be the cost of this material before taxes?

2. A map of Alberta has a scale of 1:4 250 000. The map distance between Edmonton and Calgary is 6.5 cm. What is the distance between the two cities to the nearest kilometre?

3. Describe how you would determine the radius of a cylindrical pipe in both imperial units and SI units.

4. Convert each measurement.
  a) 9 yd. to the nearest centimetre
  b) 11 000 000 in. to the nearest metre
  c) 5 km to the nearest mile
  d) 160 cm to feet and the nearest inch

5. On the Alex Fraser Bridge in Delta, B.C., the maximum height of the road above the Fraser River is 154 m. On the Tacoma Narrows Bridge in Tacoma, Washington, the maximum height of the road above The Narrows is 510 ft. Which road is higher above the water? How much higher is it?

6. Determine the surface area of each object to the nearest square unit.
  a) regular tetrahedron

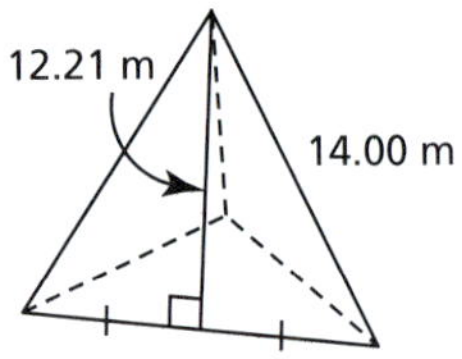

  b) right cone

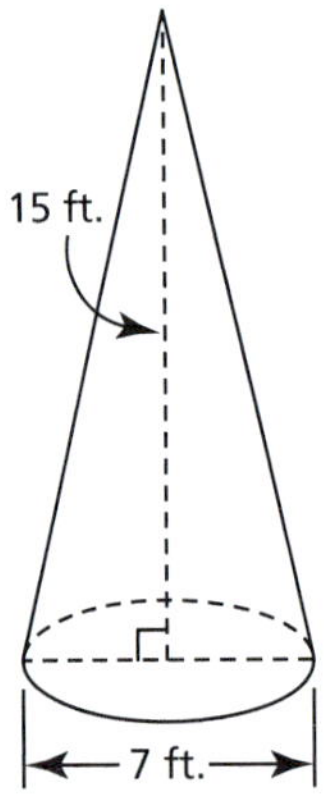

7. Determine the volume of the cone in question 6, to the nearest cubic unit.

8. The diameter of the base of a right cone is 12 yd. and the volume of the cone is 224 cubic yards. Describe how to calculate the height of the cone to the nearest yard.

9. One right square pyramid has base side length 10 cm and height 8 cm. Another right square pyramid has base side length 8 cm and height 13 cm. Does the pyramid with the greater volume also have the greater surface area? Justify your answer.

10. A hemisphere has radius 20 in. A sphere has radius 17 in.
  a) Which object has the greater surface area? How much greater is it, to the nearest square inch?
  b) Which object has the greater volume? How much greater is it, to the nearest cubic inch?

11. This composite object is a rectangular pyramid on top of a rectangular prism. Determine the surface area and volume of the composite object to the nearest unit.

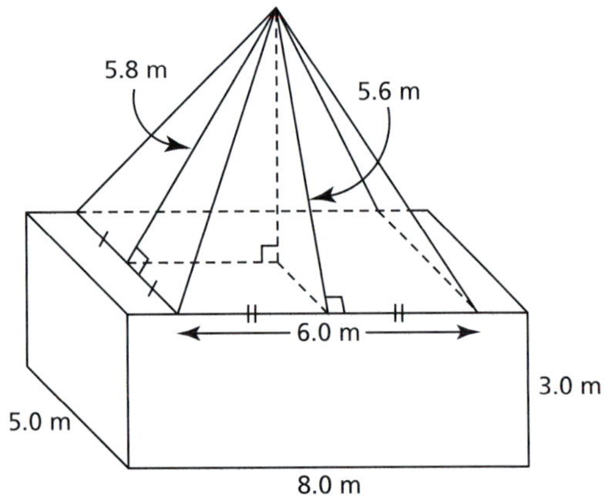

12. The height of a right square pyramid is 40 in., and the side length of the base is 48 in. Determine the lateral area of the pyramid to the nearest square inch.

13. The base of a hemisphere has a circumference of 30.5 mm. Determine the surface area and volume of the hemisphere to the nearest tenth of a millimetre.

2

14. Determine the angle of inclination of each line AB to the nearest tenth of a degree.

a)

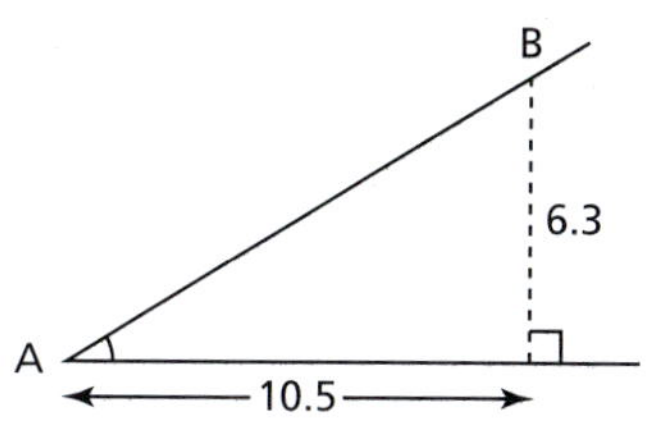

b)

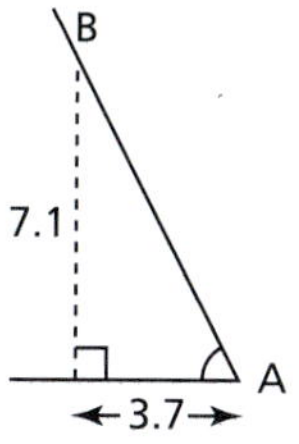

15. Barry is collecting data on the heights of trees. He measures a horizontal distance of 20 yd. from the base of a tree. Barry lies on the ground at this point and uses a clinometer to measure the angle of elevation of the top of the tree as 52°. Determine the height of the tree to the nearest yard.

16. Jay Cochrane walked a tightrope between the Niagara Fallsview Hotel and the Skylon Tower in Niagara Falls. He began at the hotel. The rope sloped upward and the average angle between the rope and the horizontal was 6.4°. Jay walked a horizontal distance of 1788 ft. To the nearest foot, determine the vertical distance he travelled.

17. Determine the measure of each indicated angle to the nearest tenth of a degree.

a)

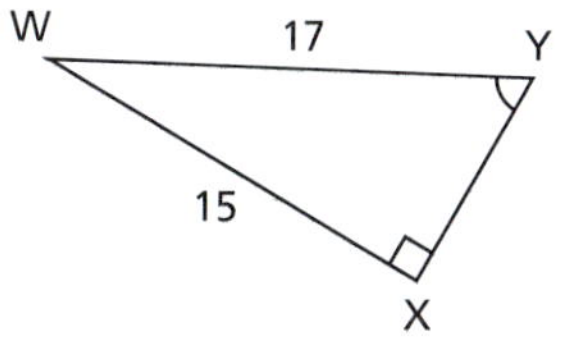

b)

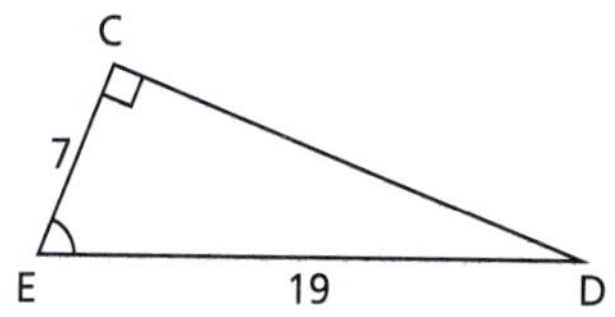

18. A 12-ft. ladder leans against a wall. The base of the ladder is $4\frac{1}{2}$ ft. from the wall. To the nearest degree, what is the measure of the angle between the ladder and the wall?

19. A basketball court is rectangular with diagonal length approximately 106 ft. The angle between a diagonal and a longer side is 28°. Determine the dimensions of the basketball court to the nearest foot.

20. Solve each right triangle. Write the measures to the nearest tenth.

a)

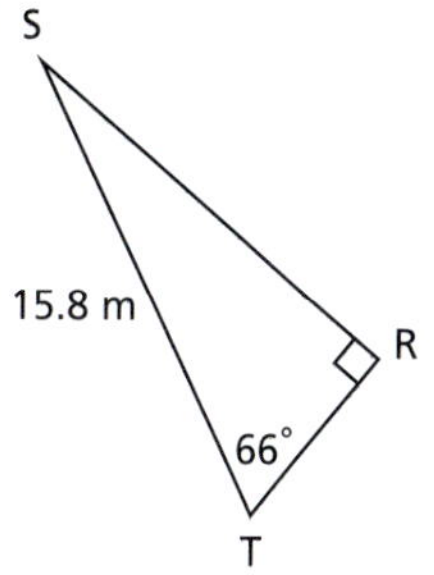

b)

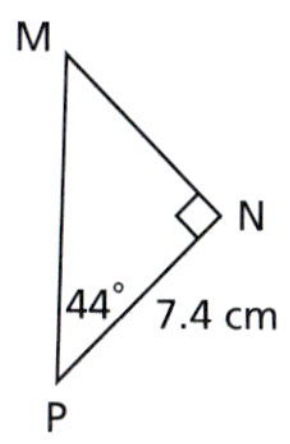

21. A helicopter is 15 km due east of its base when it receives a call to pick up a stranded snowboarder. The person is on a mountain 9 km due south of the helicopter's present location. When the helicopter picks up the snowboarder, what is the measure of the angle between the path the helicopter took flying south and the path it will take to fly directly to its base? Write the angle to the nearest degree.

22. Determine the length of each indicated side and the measures of all the angles in this diagram. Write the measures to the nearest tenth.

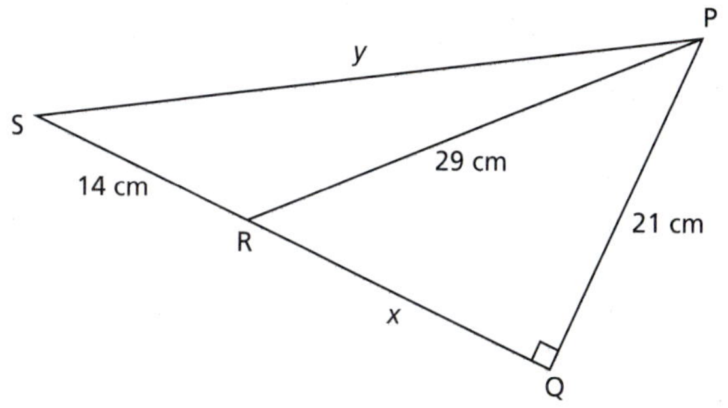

3 Factors and Products

BUILDING ON

- determining factors and multiples of whole numbers to 100
- identifying prime and composite numbers
- determining square roots of rational numbers
- adding and subtracting polynomials
- multiplying and dividing polynomials by monomials

BIG IDEAS

- Arithmetic operations on polynomials are based on the arithmetic operations on integers, and have similar properties.
- Multiplying and factoring are inverse processes, and a rectangle diagram can be used to represent them.

NEW VOCABULARY

prime factorization
greatest common factor
least common multiple
perfect cube, cube root
radicand, radical, index
factoring by decomposition
perfect square trinomial
difference of squares

AERIAL PHOTO OF MANITOBA

The Dominion Land Survey divides much of western Canada into 1-mile square sections. This photo shows canola fields around Shoal Lake, located in western Manitoba.

3.1 Factors and Multiples of Whole Numbers

LESSON FOCUS

Determine prime factors, greatest common factors, and least common multiples of whole numbers.

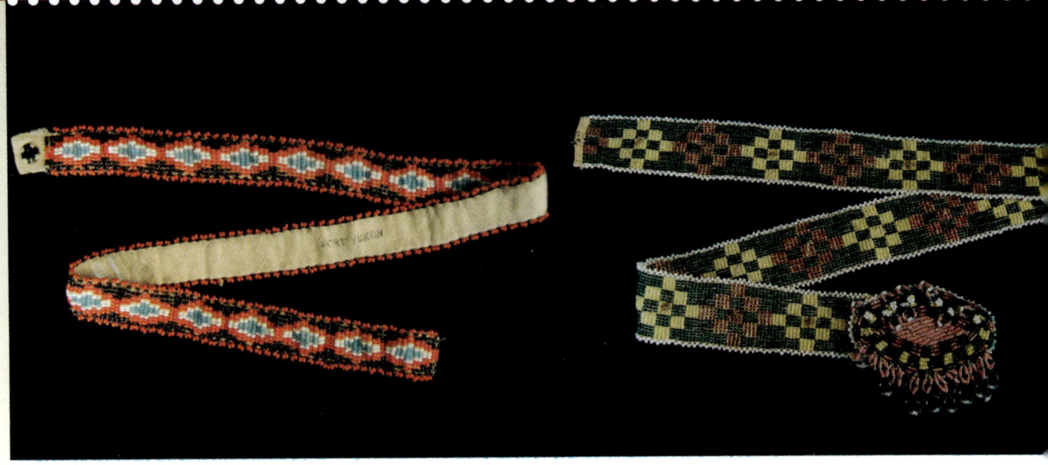

The origins of these belts are unknown. They are on display in the MacBride museum in Whitehorse, Yukon.

Make Connections

In the belts above, the patterns are 12 beads long and 40 beads long. How many beads long must a belt be for it to be created using either pattern?

Construct Understanding

TRY THIS

Work with a partner.

A. List some powers of 2. Make another list of powers of 3. Pick a number from each list and multiply them to create a different number. What are the factors of this number? What are some multiples of this number?

B. Compare your number to your partner's number. Which factors do the two numbers have in common? Which factor is the greatest?

C. What are some multiples the two numbers have in common? Which multiple is the least?

D. How can you use the product of powers from Step A to determine the greatest factor and the least multiple that the numbers have in common?

When a factor of a number has exactly two divisors, 1 and itself, the factor is a *prime factor*. For example, the factors of 12 are 1, 2, 3, 4, 6, and 12. The prime factors of 12 are 2 and 3. To determine the **prime factorization** of 12, write 12 as a product of its prime factors: $2 \times 2 \times 3$, or $2^2 \times 3$

To avoid confusing the multiplication symbol with the variable x, we use a dot to represent the multiplication operation: $12 = 2 \cdot 2 \cdot 3$, or $2^2 \cdot 3$

The first 10 prime numbers are: 2, 3, 5, 7, 11, 13, 17, 19, 23, 29
Natural numbers greater than 1 that are not prime are *composite*.

The **prime factorization** of a natural number is the number written as a product of its prime factors.

Every composite number can be expressed as a product of prime factors.

Example 1 Determining the Prime Factors of a Whole Number

Write the prime factorization of 3300.

SOLUTIONS

Method 1

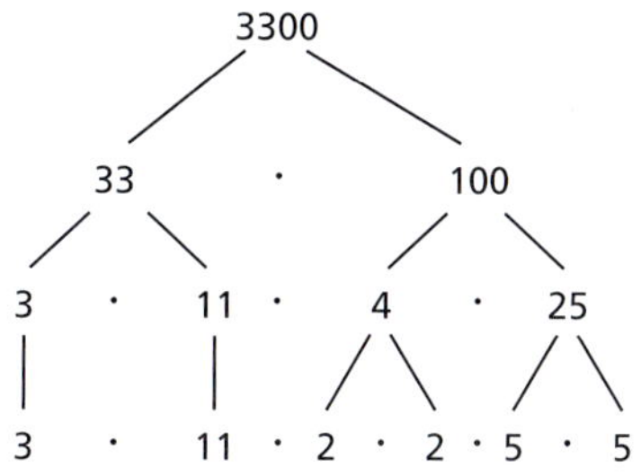

Draw a factor tree.
Write 3300 as a product of 2 factors.
Both 33 and 100 are composite numbers, so we can factor again.
Both 3 and 11 are prime factors, but 4 and 25 can be factored further.
The prime factors of 3300 are 2, 3, 5, and 11.
The prime factorization of 3300 is: $2 \cdot 2 \cdot 3 \cdot 5 \cdot 5 \cdot 11$, or $2^2 \cdot 3 \cdot 5^2 \cdot 11$

Method 2

Use repeated division by prime factors.
Begin by dividing 3300 by the least prime factor, which is 2.
Divide by this prime factor until it is no longer a factor.
Continue to divide each quotient by a prime factor until the quotient is 1.

$3300 \div 2 = 1650$
$1650 \div 2 = 825$
$825 \div 3 = 275$
$275 \div 5 = 55$
$55 \div 5 = 11$
$11 \div 11 = 1$

The prime factors of 3300 are 2, 3, 5, and 11.

The prime factorization of 3300 is: $2 \cdot 2 \cdot 3 \cdot 5 \cdot 5 \cdot 11$, or $2^2 \cdot 3 \cdot 5^2 \cdot 11$

CHECK YOUR UNDERSTANDING

1. Write the prime factorization of 2646.

[Answer: $2 \cdot 3^3 \cdot 7^2$]

What other factor trees could you draw?

Could we have divided by the prime factors in a different order? If so, which order do you think is best? Why?

The **greatest common factor** of two or more numbers is the greatest factor the numbers have in common.

For 2 or more natural numbers, we can determine their **greatest common factor**.

Example 2 Determining the Greatest Common Factor

Determine the greatest common factor of 138 and 198.

SOLUTIONS

Method 1

Use division facts to determine all the factors of each number.
Record the factors as a "rainbow."

$138 \div 1 = 138$
$138 \div 2 = 69$
$138 \div 3 = 46$
$138 \div 6 = 23$

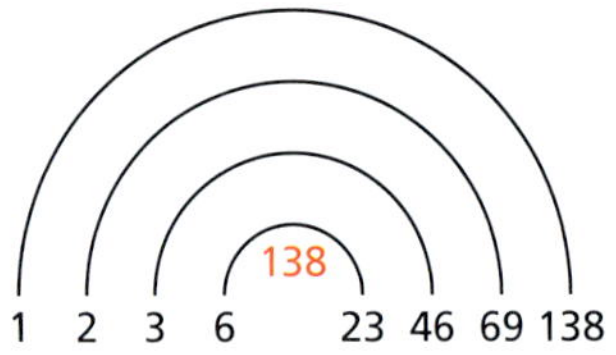

Since 23 is a prime number, there are no more factors of 138.

$198 \div 1 = 198$
$198 \div 2 = 99$
$198 \div 3 = 66$
$198 \div 6 = 33$
$198 \div 9 = 22$
$198 \div 11 = 18$

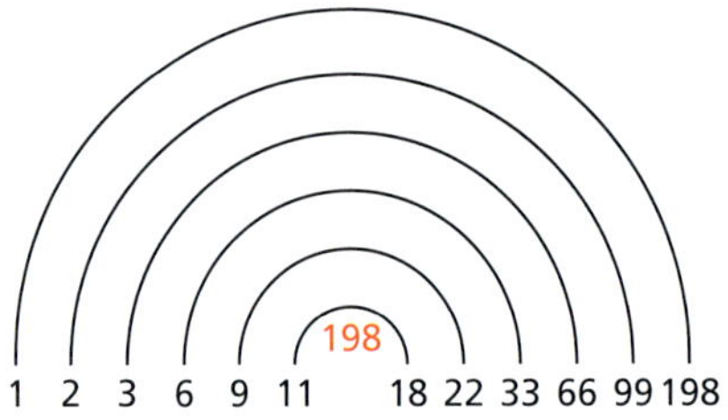

There are no more factors of 198 between 11 and 18.
The common factors of 138 and 198 are: 1, 2, 3, and 6.
So, the greatest common factor is 6.

Method 2

Check to see which factors of 138 are also factors of 198.
Start with the greatest factor.
The factors of 138 are: 1, 2, 3, 6, 23, 46, 69, 138
198 is not divisible by 138, 69, 46, or 23.
198 is divisible by 6: $198 \div 6 = 33$
The greatest common factor is 6.

Method 3

Write the prime factorization of each number.
Highlight the factors that appear in each prime factorization.

$138 = \mathbf{2} \cdot \mathbf{3} \cdot 23$
$198 = \mathbf{2} \cdot \mathbf{3} \cdot 3 \cdot 11$

The greatest common factor is $2 \cdot 3$, which is 6.

CHECK YOUR UNDERSTANDING

2. Determine the greatest common factor of 126 and 144.

[Answer: 18]

How would you determine the greatest common factor of 3 numbers?

To generate multiples of a number, multiply the number by the natural numbers; that is, 1, 2, 3, 4, 5, and so on. For example, some multiples of 26 are:

$26 \cdot 1 = 26$ $26 \cdot 2 = 52$ $26 \cdot 3 = 78$ $26 \cdot 4 = 104$

For 2 or more natural numbers, we can determine their **least common multiple**.

The **least common multiple** of two or more numbers is the least number that is divisible by each number.

We can determine the least common multiple of 4 and 6 by combining identical copies of each smaller chain to create two chains of equal length.

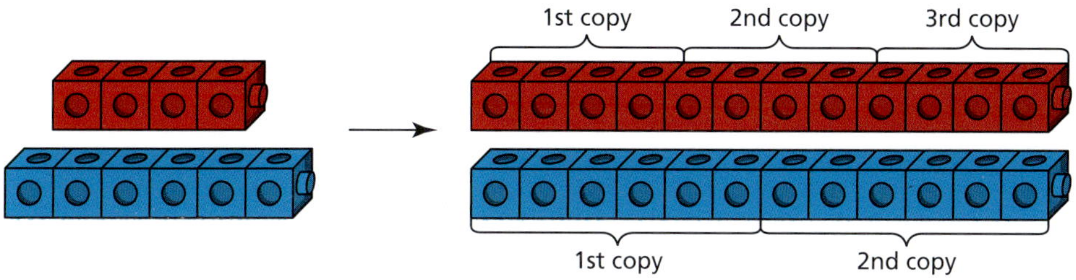

The shortest chain possible is 12 cubes long.
So, the least common multiple of 4 and 6 is 12.

Example 3 Determining the Least Common Multiple

Determine the least common multiple of 18, 20, and 30.

SOLUTIONS

Method 1

List the multiples of each number until the same multiple appears in all 3 lists.

Multiples of 18 are: 18, 36, 54, 72, 90, 108, 126, 144, 162, **180**, …
Multiples of 20 are: 20, 40, 60, 80, 100, 120, 140, 160, **180**, …
Multiples of 30 are: 30, 60, 90, 120, 150, **180**, …

The least common multiple of 18, 20, and 30 is 180.

Method 2

Check to see which multiples of 30 are also multiples of 18 and 20.

The multiples of 30 are: 30, 60, 90, 120, 150, 180, …

18 divides exactly into: 90, **180**, …
20 divides exactly into: 60, 120, **180**, …

The least common multiple of 18, 20, and 30 is 180.

(Solution continues.)

CHECK YOUR UNDERSTANDING

3. Determine the least common multiple of 28, 42, and 63.

[Answer: 252]

Method 3

Write the prime factorization of each number.
Highlight the greatest power of each prime factor in any list.

$18 = 2 \cdot 3 \cdot 3 = 2 \cdot \mathbf{3^2}$ — The greatest power of 3 in any list is 3^2.

$20 = 2 \cdot 2 \cdot 5 = \mathbf{2^2} \cdot 5$ — The greatest power of 2 in any list is 2^2.

$30 = 2 \cdot 3 \cdot \mathbf{5}$ — The greatest power of 5 in any list is 5.

The least common multiple is the product of the greatest power of each prime factor:

$$2^2 \cdot 3^2 \cdot 5 = 4 \cdot 9 \cdot 5$$
$$= 180$$

The least common multiple of 18, 20, and 30 is 180.

Are there any pairs of numbers for which the least common multiple and greatest common factor are the same number? Explain.

Example 4 Solving Problems that Involve Greatest Common Factor and Least Common Multiple

a) What is the side length of the smallest square that could be tiled with rectangles that measure 16 cm by 40 cm? Assume the rectangles cannot be cut. Sketch the square and rectangles.

b) What is the side length of the largest square that could be used to tile a rectangle that measures 16 cm by 40 cm? Assume that the squares cannot be cut. Sketch the rectangle and squares.

SOLUTION

a) In the square, arrange all the rectangles with the same orientation.

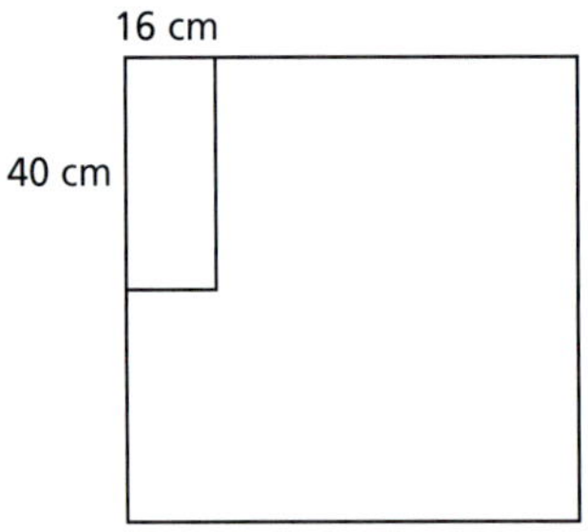

The shorter side of each rectangle measures 16 cm. So, the side length of the square must be a multiple of 16.

The longer side of each rectangle measures 40 cm. So, the side length of the square must be a multiple of 40.

So, the side length of the square must be a common multiple of 16 and 40.

(Solution continues.)

CHECK YOUR UNDERSTANDING

4. a) What is the side length of the smallest square that could be tiled with rectangles that measure 8 in. by 36 in.? Assume the rectangles cannot be cut. Sketch the square and rectangles.

b) What is the side length of the largest square that could be used to tile a rectangle that measures 8 in. by 36 in.? Assume that the squares cannot be cut. Sketch the rectangle and squares.

[Answers: a) 72 in. b) 4 in.]

The side length of the smallest square will be the least common multiple of 16 and 40.

Write the prime factorization of each number. Highlight the greatest power of each prime factor in either list.

$16 = \mathbf{2^4}$
$40 = 2^3 \cdot \mathbf{5}$

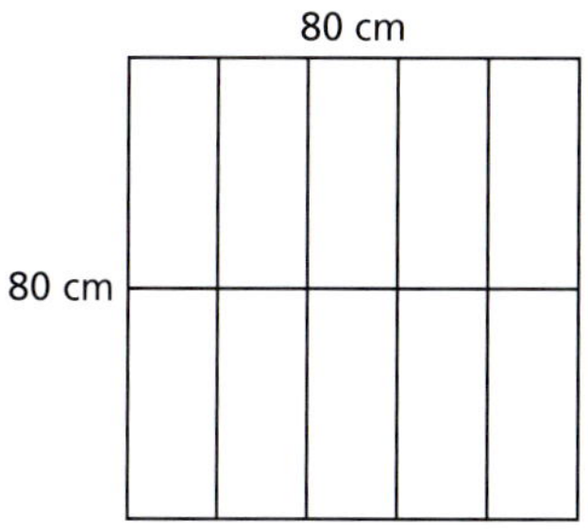

The least common multiple is:
$2^4 \cdot 5 = 80$

The side length of the smallest square is 80 cm.

b) The shorter side of the rectangle measures 16 cm. So, the side length of the square must be a factor of 16.

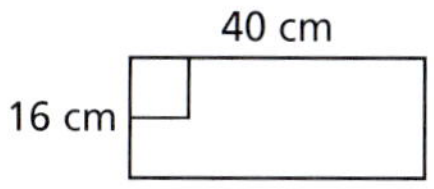

The longer side of the rectangle measures 40 cm. So, the side length of the square must be a factor of 40.

So, the side length of the square must be a common factor of 16 and 40.

The side length of the largest square will be the greatest common factor of 16 and 40.

Write the prime factorization of each number.
Highlight the prime factors that appear in both lists.

$16 = \mathbf{2} \cdot \mathbf{2} \cdot \mathbf{2} \cdot 2$
$40 = \mathbf{2} \cdot \mathbf{2} \cdot \mathbf{2} \cdot 5$

The greatest common factor is:
$2 \cdot 2 \cdot 2 = 8$

The largest square has side length 8 cm.

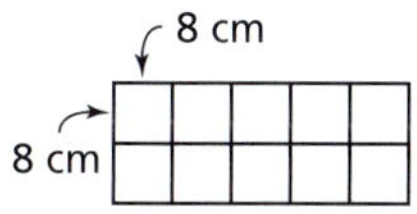

In *Example 4a*, would the answer change if the rectangles could be oriented in any direction? Explain.

Why is it helpful to write the prime factorization of 16 and 40 as a product of powers in part a and as an expanded product in part b?

Discuss the Ideas

1. What strategies can you use to determine the prime factorization of a whole number?

2. How can you use the prime factorization of a number to determine all the factors of that number?

Exercises

A

3. List the first 6 multiples of each number.
a) 6 b) 13 c) 22
d) 31 e) 45 f) 27

4. List the prime factors of each number.
a) 40 b) 75 c) 81
d) 120 e) 140 f) 192

5. Write each number as a product of its prime factors.
a) 45 b) 80 c) 96
d) 122 e) 160 f) 195

B

6. Use powers to write each number as a product of its prime factors.
a) 600 b) 1150
c) 1022 d) 2250
e) 4500 f) 6125

7. Explain why the numbers 0 and 1 have no prime factors.

8. Determine the greatest common factor of each pair of numbers.
a) 46, 84 b) 64, 120
c) 81, 216 d) 180, 224
e) 160, 672 f) 220, 860

9. Determine the greatest common factor of each set of numbers
a) 150, 275, 420 b) 120, 960, 1400
c) 126, 210, 546, 714 d) 220, 308, 484, 988

10. Determine the least common multiple of each pair of numbers.
a) 12, 14 b) 21, 45
c) 45, 60 d) 38, 42
e) 32, 45 f) 28, 52

11. Determine the least common multiple of each set of numbers.
a) 20, 36, 38 b) 15, 32, 44
c) 12, 18, 25, 30 d) 15, 20, 24, 27

12. Explain the difference between determining the greatest common factor and the least common multiple of 12 and 14.

13. Two marching bands are to be arranged in rectangular arrays with the same number of columns. One band has 42 members, the other has 36 members. What is the greatest number of columns in the array?

14. When is the product of two numbers equal to their least common multiple?

15. How could you use the greatest common factor to simplify a fraction? Use this strategy to simplify these fractions.
a) $\frac{185}{325}$ b) $\frac{340}{380}$ c) $\frac{650}{900}$
d) $\frac{840}{1220}$ e) $\frac{1225}{2750}$ f) $\frac{2145}{1105}$

16. How could you use the least common multiple to add, subtract, or divide fractions? Use this strategy to evaluate these fractions.
a) $\frac{9}{14} + \frac{11}{16}$ b) $\frac{8}{15} + \frac{11}{20}$
c) $\frac{5}{24} - \frac{1}{22}$ d) $\frac{9}{10} + \frac{5}{14} + \frac{4}{21}$
e) $\frac{9}{25} + \frac{7}{15} - \frac{5}{8}$ f) $\frac{3}{5} - \frac{5}{18} + \frac{7}{3}$
g) $\frac{3}{5} \div \frac{4}{9}$ h) $\frac{11}{6} \div \frac{2}{7}$

17. A developer wants to subdivide this rectangular plot of land into congruent square pieces. What is the side length of the largest possible square?

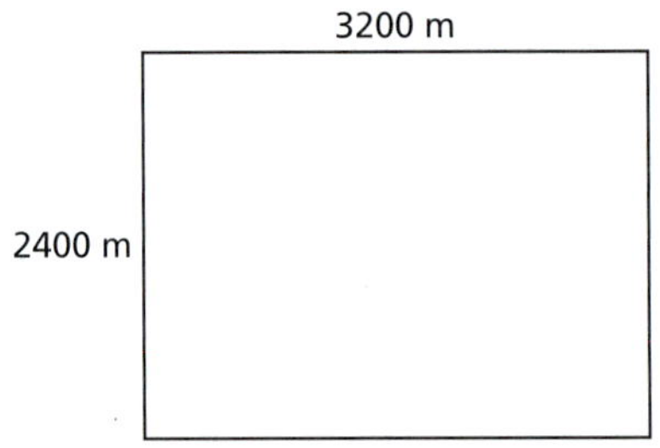

18. Do all whole numbers have at least one prime factor? Explain.

19. a) What are the dimensions of the smallest square that could be tiled using an 18-cm by 24-cm tile? Assume the tiles cannot be cut.
b) Could the tiles in part a be used to cover a floor with dimensions 6.48 m by 15.12 m? Explain.

20. The Dominion Land Survey is used to divide much of western Canada into sections and acres. One acre of land is a rectangle measuring 66 feet by 660 feet.

a) A section is a square with side length 1 mile. Do the rectangles for 1 acre fit exactly into a section? Justify your answer. [1 mile = 5280 feet]

b) A quarter section is a square with side length $\frac{1}{2}$ mile. Do the rectangles for 1 acre fit exactly into a quarter section? Justify your answer.

c) What is the side length of the smallest square into which the rectangles for 1 acre will fit exactly?

C

21. Marcia says that she knows that 61 is a prime number because she tried dividing 61 by all the natural numbers up to and including 7, and none of them was a factor. Do you agree with Marcia? Explain.

22. A bar of soap has the shape of a rectangular prism that measures 10 cm by 6 cm by 3 cm. What is the edge length of the smallest cube that could be filled with these soap bars?

Reflect

Describe strategies you would use to determine the least common multiple and the greatest common factor of a set of numbers.

THE WORLD OF MATH

Math Fact: Cryptography

Cryptography is the art of writing or deciphering messages in code. Cryptographers use a key to encode and decode messages. One way to generate a key is to multiply two large prime numbers. This makes it almost impossible to decipher the code without knowing the original numbers that were multiplied to encipher the message.

In 2006, mathematicians announced they had factored a 274-digit number as the product of a 120-digit prime number and a 155-digit prime number.

3.2 Perfect Squares, Perfect Cubes, and Their Roots

LESSON FOCUS

Identify perfect squares and perfect cubes, then determine square roots and cube roots.

Kubiks were temporary structures built in Barcelona, Berlin, and Lisbon in 2007.

Make Connections

The edge length of the Rubik's cube is 3 units.

What is the area of one face of the cube? Why is this number a *perfect square*?

What is the volume of the cube? This number is called a **perfect cube**. Why do you think it has this name?

Competitors solve a Rubik's cube in the world championships in Budapest, Hungary, in October 2007.

Construct Understanding

TRY THIS

Work in a group.

You will need: 100 congruent square tiles, 100 linking cubes, grid paper, and isometric dot paper.

A. Use the tiles to model all the perfect squares from 1 to 100. Sketch each model on grid paper and record the corresponding perfect square.

B. Use the cubes to model all the perfect cubes from 1 to 100. Sketch each model on isometric dot paper and record the corresponding perfect cube.

C. Which numbers from 1 to 100 are perfect squares and which are perfect cubes?

D. Join with another group of students. Take turns to choose a number between 101 and 200. Determine if it is a perfect square or a perfect cube.

E. Suppose you did not have tiles or cubes available. How could you determine if a given number is a perfect square? How could you determine if a given number is a perfect cube?

Any whole number that can be represented as the area of a square with a whole number side length is a *perfect square.*
The side length of the square is the *square root* of the area of the square.

The *square root* of a number n, denoted $\sqrt{n}$, is a positive number whose square is n.

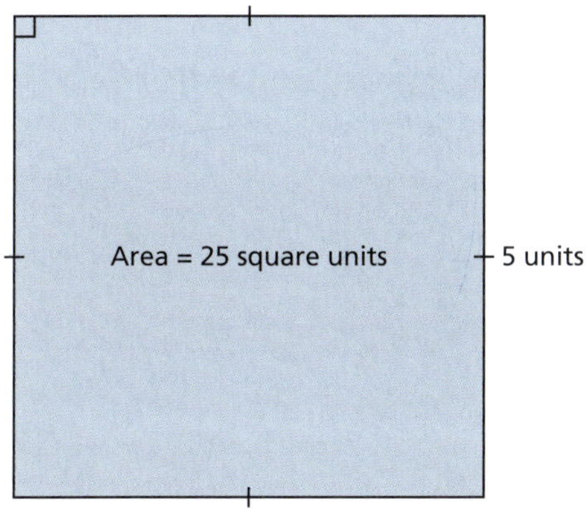

We write: $\sqrt{25} = 5$

25 is a perfect square and 5 is its square root.

The **cube root** of a number n, denoted $\sqrt[3]{n}$, is a number whose cube is n.

Any whole number that can be represented as the volume of a cube with a whole number edge length is a **perfect cube**. The edge length of the cube is the **cube root** of the volume of the cube.

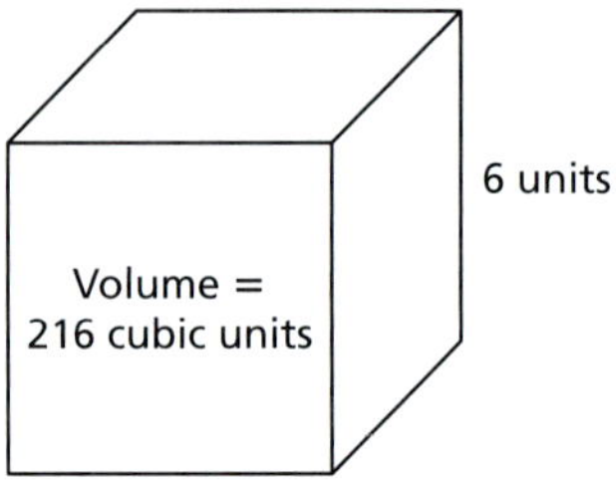

We write: $\sqrt[3]{216} = 6$

216 is a perfect cube and 6 is its cube root.

Example 1 Determining the Square Root of a Whole Number

Determine the square root of 1296.

SOLUTIONS

Method 1

Write 1296 as a product of its prime factors.

$1296 = 2 \cdot 2 \cdot 2 \cdot 2 \cdot 3 \cdot 3 \cdot 3 \cdot 3$

$= (2 \cdot 2)(2 \cdot 2)(3 \cdot 3)(3 \cdot 3)$ — Group the factors in pairs.

$= (2 \cdot 2 \cdot 3 \cdot 3)(2 \cdot 2 \cdot 3 \cdot 3)$ — Rearrange the factors in 2 equal groups.

$= 36 \cdot 36$

Since 1296 is the product of two equal factors, it can be represented as the area of a square.

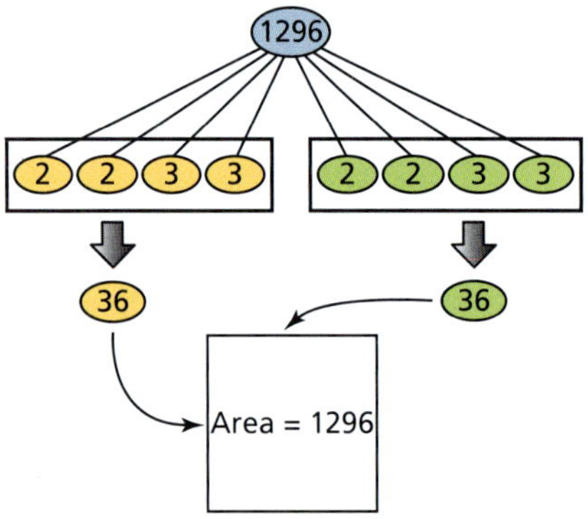

So, the square root of 1296 is 36.

Method 2

Estimate:

$30^2 = 900$ and $40^2 = 1600$

$900 < 1296 < 1600$

So, $30 < \sqrt{1296} < 40$

1296 is about halfway between 900 and 1600.

So, $\sqrt{1296}$ is about halfway between 30 and 40.

Use guess and test to refine the estimate.

Try 35: $35^2 = 1225$ (too small, but close)

Try 36: $36^2 = 1296$

So, the square root of 1296 is 36.

CHECK YOUR UNDERSTANDING

1. Determine the square root of 1764.

[Answer: 42]

What if the prime factors cannot be grouped into pairs? What can you say about the number?

Example 2 Determining the Cube Root of a Whole Number

Determine the cube root of 1728.

SOLUTIONS

Method 1

Write 1728 as a product of its prime factors.

$1728 = 2 \cdot 2 \cdot 2 \cdot 2 \cdot 2 \cdot 2 \cdot 3 \cdot 3 \cdot 3$ Group the factors in sets of 3.

$= (2 \cdot 2 \cdot 2)(2 \cdot 2 \cdot 2)(3 \cdot 3 \cdot 3)$ Rearrange the factors in 3 equal groups.

$= (2 \cdot 2 \cdot 3)(2 \cdot 2 \cdot 3)(2 \cdot 2 \cdot 3)$

$= 12 \cdot 12 \cdot 12$

Since 1728 is the product of three equal factors, it can be represented as the volume of a cube.

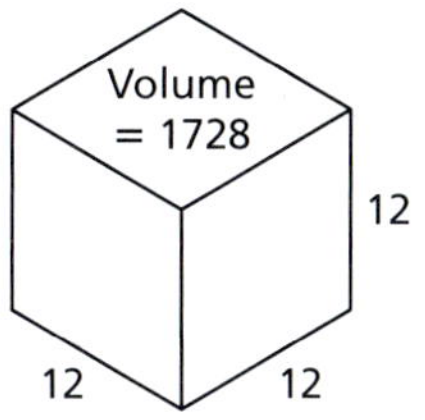

So, the cube root of 1728 is 12.

Method 2

Estimate:
$10^3 = 1000$ and $20^3 = 8000$

$1000 < 1728 < 8000$

So, $10 < \sqrt[3]{1728} < 20$

1728 is closer to 1000 than to 8000.

So, $\sqrt[3]{1728}$ is closer to 10 than to 20.

Use guess and test to refine the estimate.
Try 11: $11^3 = 1331$ (too small, but close)
Try 12: $12^3 = 1728$

So, the cube root of 1728 is 12.

CHECK YOUR UNDERSTANDING

2. Determine the cube root of 2744.

[Answer: 14]

How could you use this strategy to show a number is not a perfect cube?

Can a whole number be both a perfect square and a perfect cube? Explain.

In *Example 1*, $\sqrt{1296}$ is a radical with radicand 1296. The square root can be written as $\sqrt[2]{1296}$, with index 2, but the index on a square root is implied and often not written.

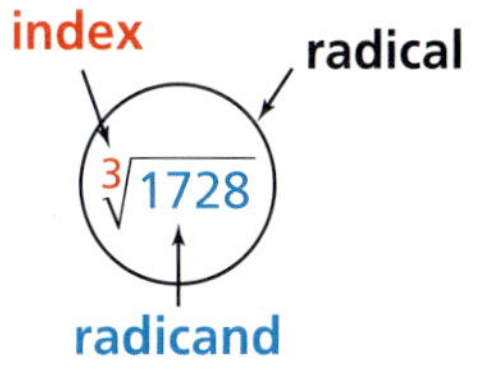

Example 3 Using Roots to Solve a Problem

A cube has volume 4913 cubic inches. What is the surface area of the cube?

SOLUTION

Sketch a diagram.

To calculate the surface area, first determine the edge length of the cube.

The edge length e, of a cube is equal to the cube root of its volume.

$e = \sqrt[3]{4913}$

$e = 17$

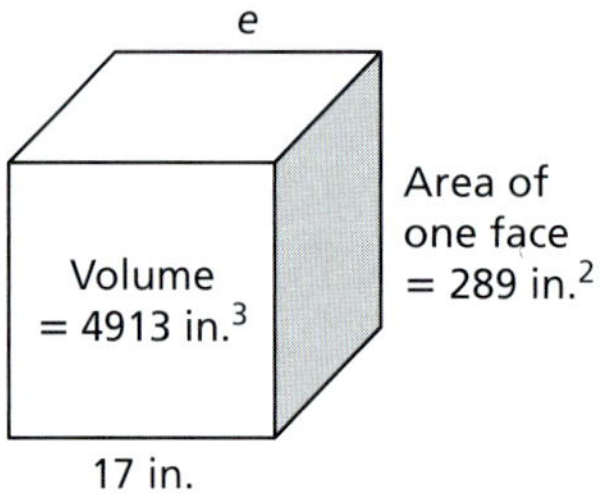

The surface area, SA, of a cube is the sum of the areas of its 6 congruent square faces.

$SA = 6(17 \cdot 17)$

$SA = 6(289)$

$SA = 1734$

The surface area of the cube is 1734 square inches.

CHECK YOUR UNDERSTANDING

3. A cube has volume 12 167 cubic feet. What is the surface area of the cube?

[Answer: 3174 square feet]

Discuss the Ideas

1. What strategies might you use to determine if a number is a perfect square or a perfect cube?

2. What strategy could you use to determine that a number is not a perfect square? Not a perfect cube?

3. What strategies can you use to determine the square root of a perfect square?
What strategies can you use to determine the cube root of a perfect cube?

Exercises

A

4. Determine the square root of each number. Explain the process used.
a) 196 **b)** 256 **c)** 361 **d)** 289 **e)** 441

5. Determine the cube root of each number. Explain the process used.
a) 343 **b)** 512 **c)** 1000 **d)** 1331 **e)** 3375

B

6. Use factoring to determine whether each number is a perfect square, a perfect cube, or neither.
a) 225 **b)** 729 **c)** 1944
d) 1444 **e)** 4096 **f)** 13 824

7. Determine the side length of each square.

a)

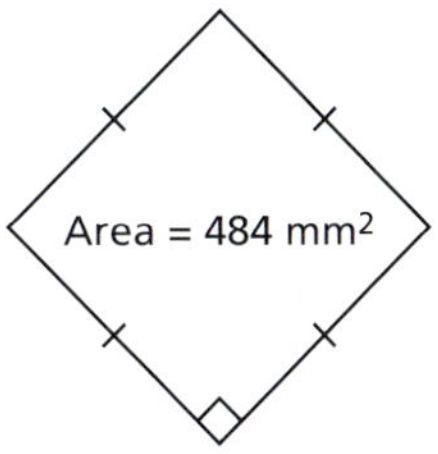

b)

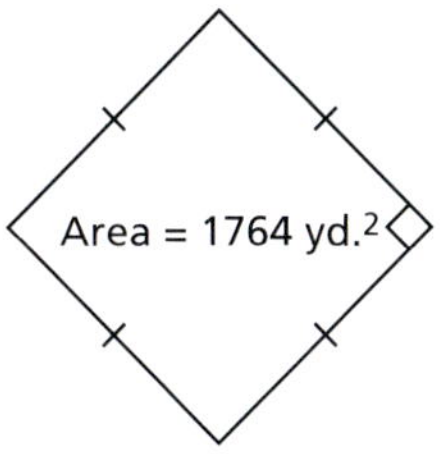

8. Determine the edge length of each cube.

a)

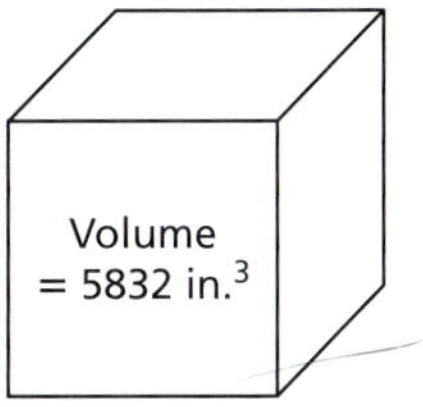

b)

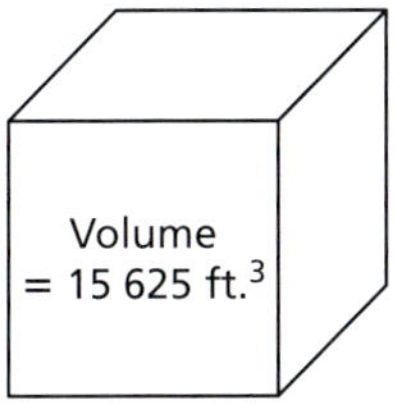

9. In February 2003, the Battlefords Chamber of Commerce in Saskatchewan placed a cage containing a 64-cubic foot ice cube along Yellowhead Highway. Local customers were asked to predict when the ice cube would melt enough for a ball above the ice cube to fall through it. What was the surface area of the cube?

10. A cube has surface area 6534 square feet. What is its volume?

11. Is it possible to construct a cube with 2000 interlocking cubes? Justify your answer.

12. Determine all the perfect square whole numbers and perfect cube whole numbers between each pair of numbers:

a) 315 − 390 b) 650 − 750
c) 800 − 925 d) 1200 − 1350

13. Write 3 numbers that are both perfect squares and perfect cubes.

14. During the Festival du Voyageur in Winnipeg, Manitoba, teams compete in a snow sculpture competition. Each team begins with a 1440-cubic foot rectangular prism of snow. The prism has a square cross-section and height 10 ft. What are its length and width?

C

15. a) Write an expression for the surface area of this tent. Do not include the floor.

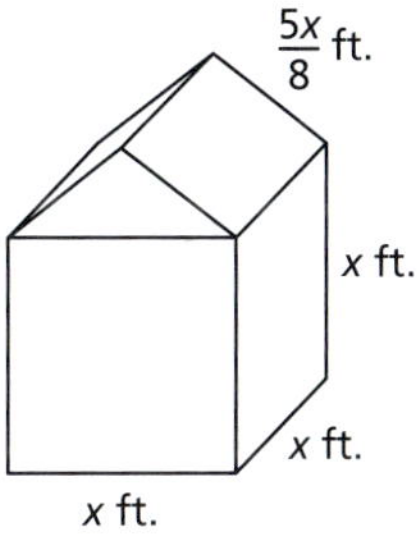

b) Suppose the surface area of the tent is 90 square feet. Calculate the value of x.

16. Determine the dimensions of a cube for which its surface area is numerically the same as its volume.

17. a) Determine the side length of a square with area $121x^4y^2$.

b) Determine the edge length of a cube with volume $64x^6y^3$.

18. Which pairs of perfect cubes have a sum of 1729?

Reflect How is determining the square root of a number similar to determining its cube root? How are the strategies different?

CHECKPOINT 1

Connections

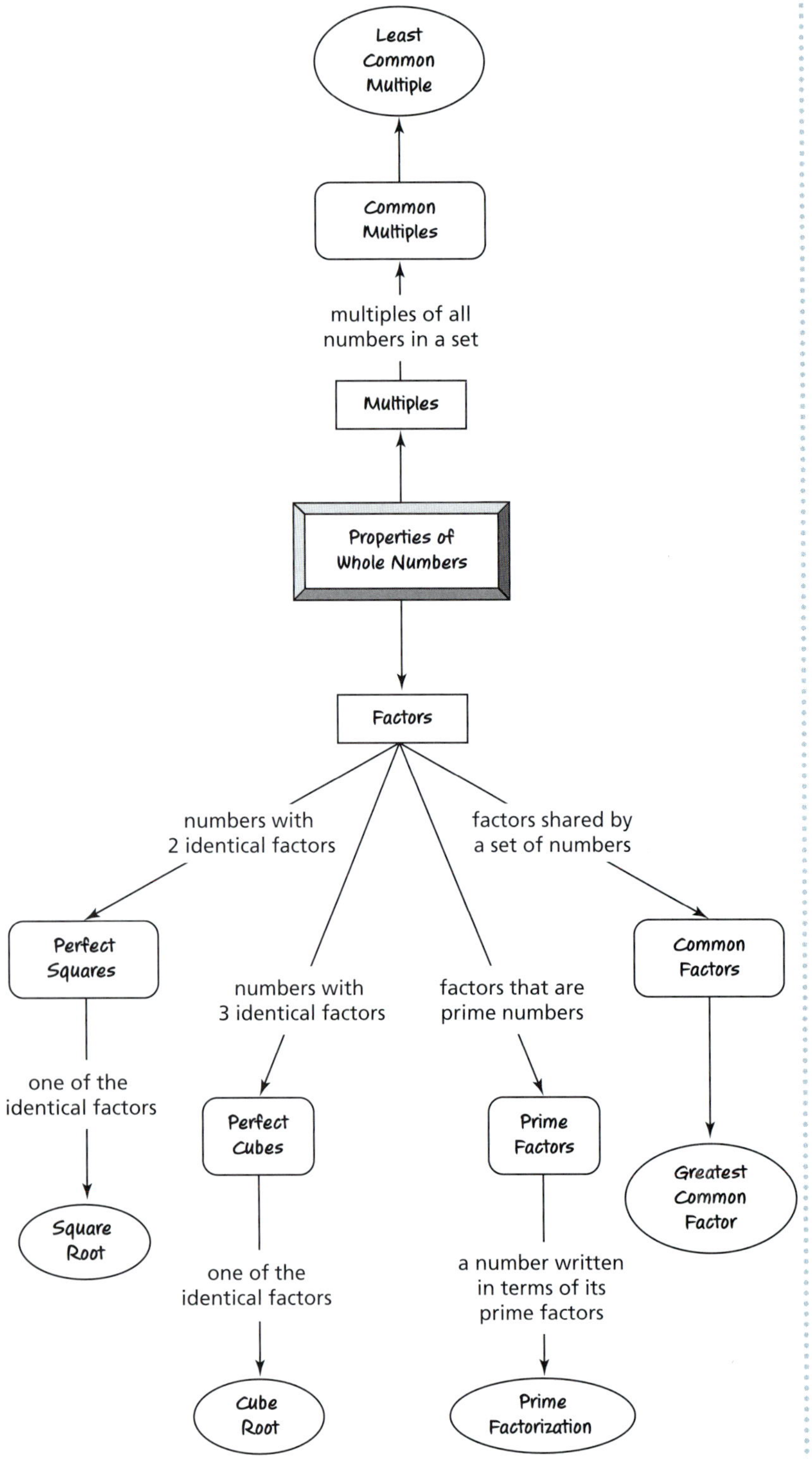

Concept Development

- **In Lesson 3.1**
  - You applied whole number properties and operations to determine **prime factors.**
  - You used prime factors to determine **greatest common factor** (GCF) and **least common multiple** (LCM).
- **In Lesson 3.2**
  - You used factors and multiples to determine **perfect square whole numbers** and their **square roots.**
  - You used factors and multiples to determine **perfect cube whole numbers** and their **cube roots.**

Assess Your Understanding

3.1

1. Use powers to write each number as a product of its prime factors.
   a) 1260 b) 4224 c) 6120
   d) 1045 e) 3024 f) 3675

2. Determine the greatest common factor of each set of numbers.
   a) 40, 48, 56 b) 84, 120, 144
   c) 145, 205, 320 d) 208, 368, 528
   e) 856, 1200, 1368 f) 950, 1225, 1550

3. Determine the least common multiple of each set of numbers.
   a) 12, 15, 21 b) 12, 20, 32 c) 18, 24, 30
   d) 30, 32, 40 e) 49, 56, 64 f) 50, 55, 66

4. Use the least common multiple to help determine each answer.
   a) $\frac{8}{3} + \frac{5}{11}$ b) $\frac{13}{5} - \frac{4}{7}$ c) $\frac{9}{10} \div \frac{7}{3}$

5. The Mayan used several different calendar systems; one system used 365 days, another system used 260 days. Suppose the first day of both calendars occurred on the same day. After how many days would they again occur on the same day? About how long is this in years? Assume 1 year has 365 days.

3.2

6. Determine the square root of each number. Which different strategies could you use?
   a) 400 b) 784 c) 576
   d) 1089 e) 1521 f) 3025

7. Determine the cube root of each number. Which different strategies could you use?
   a) 1728 b) 3375 c) 8000
   d) 5832 e) 10 648 f) 9261

8. Determine whether each number is a perfect square, a perfect cube, or neither.
   a) 2808 b) 3136 c) 4096
   d) 4624 e) 5832 f) 9270

9. Between each pair of numbers, identify all the perfect squares and perfect cubes that are whole numbers.
   a) 400 – 500 b) 900 – 1000 c) 1100 – 1175

10. A cube has a volume of 2197 m^3. Its surface is to be painted. Each can of paint covers about 40 m^2. How many cans of paint are needed? Justify your answer.

3.3 Common Factors of a Polynomial

LESSON FOCUS

Model and record factoring a polynomial.

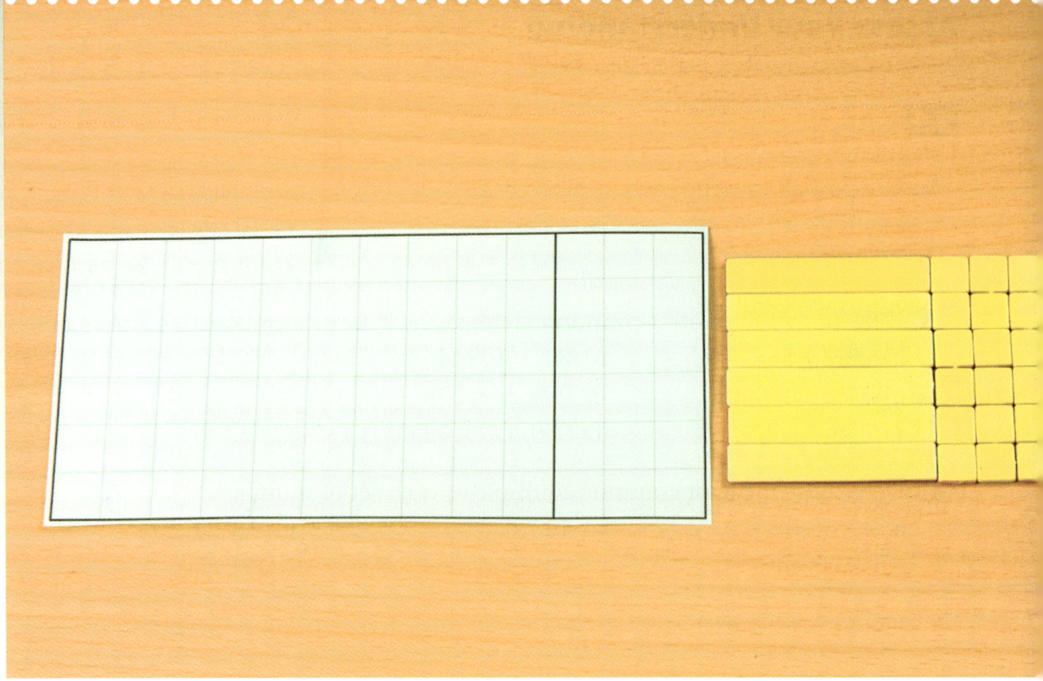

Make Connections

Diagrams and models can be used to represent products.

What multiplication sentences are represented above?

What property do the diagrams illustrate?

Construct Understanding

The variable algebra tile can represent any variable we like. It is usually referred to as the *x*-tile.

THINK ABOUT IT

You may need algebra tiles.

Sketch all the ways you can arrange these tiles to form a rectangle.

Beside each sketch, write the multiplication sentence it represents.

Each set of tiles below represents the polynomial $4m + 12$.

The dimensions of each rectangle represent the *factors* of the polynomial.

- $1(4m + 12) = 4m + 12$

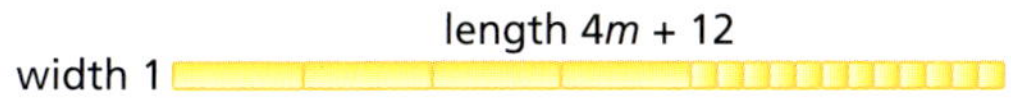

- $2(2m + 6) = 4m + 12$

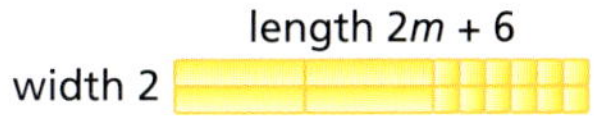

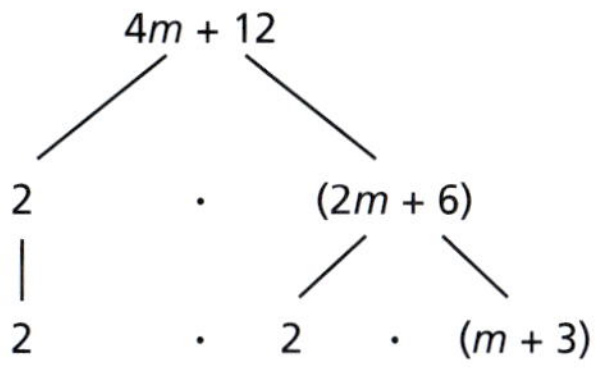

- $4(m + 3) = 4m + 12$

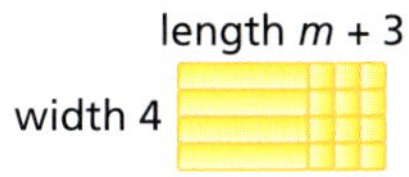

When we write a polynomial as a product of factors, we *factor* the polynomial.

The diagrams above show that there are 3 ways to factor the expression $4m + 12$.

The first two ways: $4m + 12 = 1(4m + 12)$ and $4m + 12 = 2(2m + 6)$ are incomplete because the second factor in each case can be factored further. That is, neither 1 nor 2 is the greatest common factor of $4m$ and 12.

The third way: $4m + 12 = 4(m + 3)$ is complete. The greatest common factor of $4m$ and 12 is 4.

We say that $4m + 12$ is *factored fully* when we write $4m + 12 = 4(m + 3)$; that is, the polynomial cannot be factored further.

Compare multiplying and factoring in arithmetic and algebra.

Factoring and expanding are inverse processes.

In Arithmetic	**In Algebra**
Multiply factors to form a product. $(4)(7) = 28$	*Expand* an expression to form a product. $3(2 - 5a) = 6 - 15a$
Factor a number by writing it as a product of factors. $28 = (4)(7)$	*Factor* a polynomial by writing it as a product of factors. $6 - 15a = 3(2 - 5a)$

Example 1 Using Algebra Tiles to Factor Binomials

Factor each binomial.

a) $6n + 9$ **b)** $6c + 4c^2$

SOLUTIONS

a) $6n + 9$

Method 1

Arrange algebra tiles in a rectangle.

The dimensions of the rectangle are 3 and $2n + 3$.
So, $6n + 9 = 3(2n + 3)$

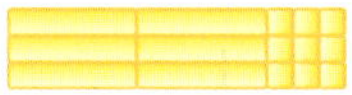

Method 2

Use a factor tree.

$6n + 9 = 3(2n + 3)$

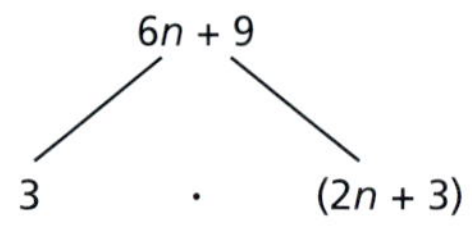

b) $6c + 4c^2$

Method 1

Use algebra tiles.

$6c + 4c^2 = 2c(3 + 2c)$

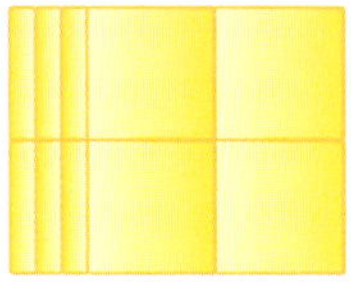

Method 2

Use the greatest common factor.
Factor each term of the binomial.

$6c = 2 \cdot 3 \cdot c$

$4c^2 = 2 \cdot 2 \cdot c \cdot c$

The greatest common factor is $2c$.

Write each term as a product of $2c$ and another monomial.

$6c + 4c^2 = 2c(3) + 2c(2c)$

Use the distributive property to write the sum as a product.

$6c + 4c^2 = 2c(3 + 2c)$

CHECK YOUR UNDERSTANDING

1. Factor each binomial.

a) $3g + 6$ **b)** $8d + 12d^2$

[Answers: a) $3(g + 2)$
b) $4d(2 + 3d)$]

How can you check that your answer is correct?

When a polynomial has negative terms or 3 different terms, we cannot remove a common factor by arranging the tiles as a rectangle. Instead, we can sometimes arrange the tiles into equal groups.

Example 2 Factoring Trinomials

Factor the trinomial $5 - 10z - 5z^2$.

Verify that the factors are correct.

SOLUTIONS

$5 - 10z - 5z^2$

Method 1

Use algebra tiles. Arrange five 1-tiles, 10 negative z-tiles, and 5 negative z^2-tiles into equal groups.

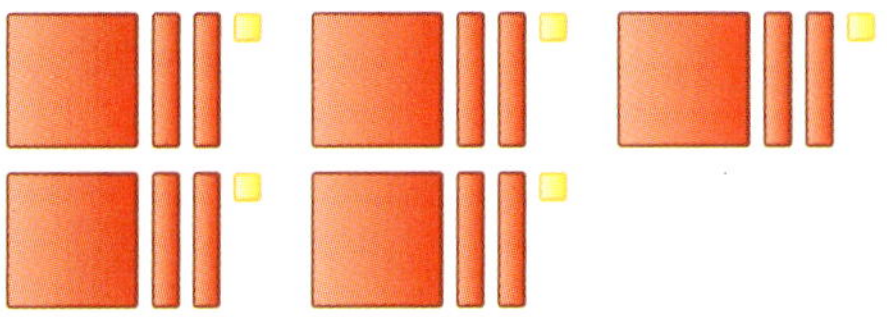

There are 5 equal groups and each group contains the trinomial $1 - 2z - z^2$.
So, the factors are 5 and $1 - 2z - z^2$.

$5 - 10z - 5z^2 = 5(1 - 2z - z^2)$

Method 2

Use the greatest common factor.
Factor each term of the trinomial.

$5 = 5$

$10z = 2 \cdot 5 \cdot z$

$5z^2 = 5 \cdot z \cdot z$

The greatest common factor is 5. Write each term as a product of the greatest common factor and another monomial.

$5 - 10z - 5z^2 = 5(1) - 5(2z) - 5(z^2)$

Use the distributive property to write the expression as a product.

$5 - 10z - 5z^2 = 5(1 - 2z - z^2)$

Check: Expand $5(1 - 2z - z^2) = 5(1) - 5(2z) - 5(z^2)$

$= 5 - 10z - 5z^2$

This trinomial is the same as the original trinomial, so the factors are correct.

CHECK YOUR UNDERSTANDING

2. Factor the trinomial $6 - 12z + 18z^2$
Verify that the factors are correct.

[Answer: $6(1 - 2z + 3z^2)$]

When you have factored an expression, why should you always use the distributive property to expand the product?

Another strategy used in factoring polynomials is to identify and factor out any common factors.

Example 3 Factoring Polynomials in More than One Variable

Factor the trinomial. Verify that the factors are correct.

$-12x^3y - 20xy^2 - 16x^2y^2$

SOLUTION

$-12x^3y - 20xy^2 - 16x^2y^2$

Factor each term of the trinomial.

$12x^3y = \mathbf{2} \cdot \mathbf{2} \cdot 3 \cdot x \cdot x \cdot \boldsymbol{x} \cdot \boldsymbol{y}$

$20xy^2 = \mathbf{2} \cdot \mathbf{2} \cdot 5 \cdot \boldsymbol{x} \cdot \boldsymbol{y} \cdot y$

$16x^2y^2 = \mathbf{2} \cdot \mathbf{2} \cdot 2 \cdot 2 \cdot x \cdot \boldsymbol{x} \cdot \boldsymbol{y} \cdot y$

The greatest common factor is: $2 \cdot 2 \cdot x \cdot y = 4xy$

Write each term as a product of the greatest common factor and another monomial.

$-12x^3y - 20xy^2 - 16x^2y^2$

$= 4xy(-3x^2) - 4xy(5y) - 4xy(4xy)$ Write the expression as a product.

$= 4xy(-3x^2 - 5y - 4xy)$

$= 4xy(-1)(3x^2 + 5y + 4xy)$

$= -4xy(3x^2 + 5y + 4xy)$

Check: Expand $-4xy(3x^2 + 5y + 4xy)$

$= (-4xy)(3x^2) + (-4xy)(5y) + (-4xy)(4xy)$

$= -12x^3y - 20xy^2 - 16x^2y^2$

This trinomial is the same as the original trinomial, so the factors are correct.

CHECK YOUR UNDERSTANDING

3. Factor the trinomial. Verify that the factors are correct.
$-20c^4d - 30c^3d^2 - 25cd$

[Answer: $-5cd(4c^3 + 6c^2d + 5)$]

What other strategies could you use?

In *Example 3*, the common factor -1 was removed because every term was negative. When we factor a polynomial that has negative terms, we usually ensure that the first term inside the brackets is positive.

Discuss the Ideas

1. How is using an algebra tile model to multiply a polynomial by a monomial like using an area model to multiply two whole numbers?

2. How are the strategies used to factor a polynomial like those used to determine the prime factorization of a whole number?

3. Can every binomial be factored? Explain.

Exercises

A

4. For each arrangement of algebra tiles, write the polynomial they represent and identify its factors.

a)

b) 

c) 

5. Factor the terms in each set, then identify the greatest common factor.

a) $6, 15n$ b) $4m, m^2$

6. Use the greatest common factors from question 5 to factor each expression.

a) i) $6 + 15n$ ii) $6 - 15n$
iii) $15n - 6$ iv) $-15n + 6$

b) i) $4m + m^2$ ii) $m^2 + 4m$
iii) $4m - m^2$ iv) $m^2 - 4m$

B

7. Use algebra tiles to factor each binomial. Sketch the tiles you used.

a) $5y + 10$ b) $6 + 12x^2$
c) $9k + 6$ d) $4s^2 + 14s$
e) $y + y^2$ f) $3h + 7h^2$

8. Factor each binomial. Why can you not use algebra tiles? Check by expanding.

a) $9b^2 - 12b^3$ b) $48s^3 - 12$
c) $-a^2 - a^3$ d) $3x^2 + 6x^4$
e) $8y^3 - 12y$ f) $-7d - 14d^4$

9. Use algebra tiles to factor each trinomial. Sketch the tiles you used.

a) $3x^2 + 12x - 6$ b) $4 - 6y - 8y^2$
c) $-7m - 7m^2 - 14$ d) $10n - 6 - 12n^2$
e) $8 + 10x + 6x^2$ f) $-9 + 12b + 6b^2$

10. Factor each trinomial. Why can you not use algebra tiles? Check by expanding.

a) $5 + 15m^2 - 10m^3$ b) $27n + 36 - 18n^3$
c) $6v^4 + 7v - 8v^3$ d) $-3c^2 - 13c^4 - 12c^3$
e) $24x + 30x^2 - 12x^4$ f) $s^4 + s^2 - 4s$

11. a) Write the polynomial these algebra tiles represent.

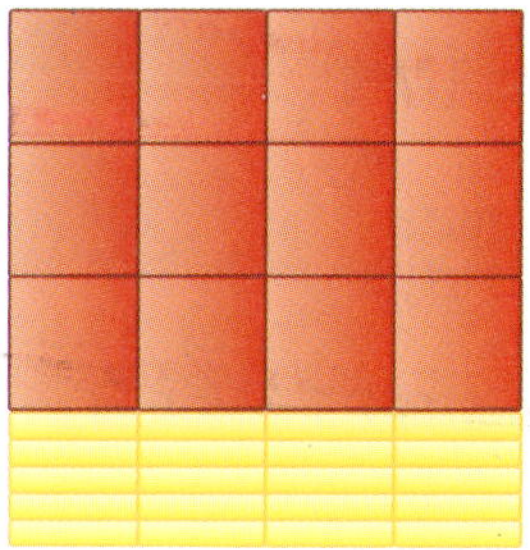

b) Factor the polynomial.

c) Compare the factors with the dimensions of the rectangle. What do you notice?

12. a) Here are a student's solutions for factoring polynomials. Identify the errors in each solution. Write a correct solution.

i) Factor: $3m^2 + 9m^3 - 3m$
Solution: $3m^2 + 9m^3 - 3m = 3m(m + 3m^2)$

ii) Factor: $-16 + 8n - 4n^3$
Solution: $-16 + 8n - 4n^3 = -4(4 + 2n + n^2)$

b) What should the student have done to check his work?

13. Suppose you are writing each term of a polynomial as the product of a common factor and a monomial. When is the monomial 1? When is the monomial -1?

14. Simplify each expression by combining like terms, then factor.

a) $x^2 + 6x - 7 - x^2 - 2x + 3$
b) $12m^2 - 24m - 3 + 4m^2 - 13$
c) $-7n^3 - 5n^2 + 2n - n^2 - n^3 - 12n$

15. a) Factor the terms in each set, then identify the greatest common factor.
   i) $4s^2t^2$, $12s^2t^3$, $36st^2$
   ii) $3a^3b$, $8a^2b$, $9a^4b$
   iii) $12x^3y^2$, $12x^4y^3$, $36x^2y^4$

b) Use the greatest common factors from part a to factor each trinomial.
   i) $4s^2t^2 + 12s^2t^3 + 36st^2$
   ii) $12s^2t^3 - 4s^2t^2 - 36st^2$
   iii) $-3a^3b - 9a^4b + 8a^2b$
   iv) $9a^4b + 3a^3b - 8a^2b$
   v) $36x^2y^4 + 12x^3y^2 + 12x^4y^3$
   vi) $-36x^2y^4 - 12x^4y^3 - 12x^3y^2$

16. Factor each trinomial. Check by expanding.
   a) $25xy + 15x^2 - 30x^2y^2$
   b) $51m^2n + 39mn^2 - 72mn$
   c) $9p^4q^2 - 6p^3q^3 + 12p^2q^4$
   d) $10a^3b^2 + 12a^2b^4 - 5a^2b^2$
   e) $12cd^2 - 8cd - 20c^2d$
   f) $7r^3s^3 + 14r^2s^2 - 21rs^2$

17. A formula for the surface area, *SA*, of a cylinder with base radius *r* and height *h* is:
$SA = 2\pi r^2 + 2\pi rh$
   a) Factor this formula.
   b) Use both forms of the formula to calculate the surface area of a cylinder with base radius 12 cm and height 23 cm. Is one form of the formula more efficient to use than the other? Explain.

18. A formula for the surface area, *SA*, of a cone with slant height *s* and base radius *r* is:
$SA = \pi r^2 + \pi rs$
   a) Factor this formula.
   b) Use both forms of the formula to calculate the surface area of a cone with base radius 9 cm and slant height 15 cm. Is one form of the formula more efficient to use than the other? Explain.

19. A silo has a cylindrical base with height *h* and radius *r*, and a hemispherical top.

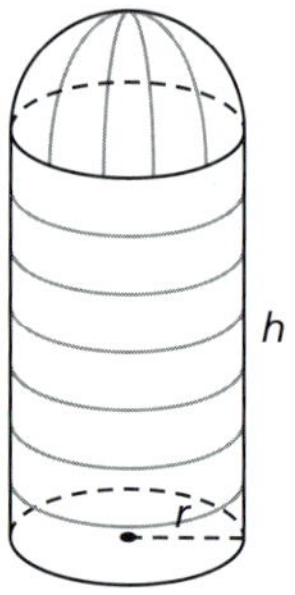

   a) Write an expression for the surface area of the silo. Factor the expression. Determine the surface area of the silo when its base radius is 6 m and the height of the cylinder is 10 m. Which form of the expression will you use? Explain why.
   b) Write an expression for the volume of the silo. Factor the expression. Use the values of the radius and height from part a to calculate the volume of the silo. Which form of the expression will you use? Explain why.

20. Suppose *n* is an integer. Is $n^2 - n$ always an integer? Justify your answer.

C

21. A cylindrical bar has base radius *r* and height *h*. Only the curved surface of the cylindrical bar is to be painted.
   a) Write an expression for the fraction of the total surface area that will be painted.
   b) Simplify the fraction.

22. A diagonal of a polygon is a line segment joining non-adjacent vertices.
   a) How many diagonals can be drawn from one vertex of a pentagon? A hexagon?
   b) Suppose the polygon has *n* sides. How many diagonals can be drawn from one vertex?
   c) The total number of diagonals of a polygon with *n* sides is $\frac{n^2}{2} - \frac{3n}{2}$. Factor this formula. Explain why it is reasonable.

Reflect If a polynomial factors as a product of a monomial and a polynomial, how can you tell when you have factored it fully?

MATH LAB

3.4 Modelling Trinomials as Binomial Products

LESSON FOCUS

Explore factoring polynomials with algebra tiles.

Make Connections

We can use an area model and the distributive property to illustrate the product of two 2-digit numbers.

$$\begin{aligned} 12 \times 13 &= (10 + 2)(10 + 3) \\ &= 10(10 + 3) + 2(10 + 3) \\ &= 10(10) + 10(3) + 2(10) + 2(3) \\ &= 100 + 30 + 20 + 6 \\ &= 156 \end{aligned}$$

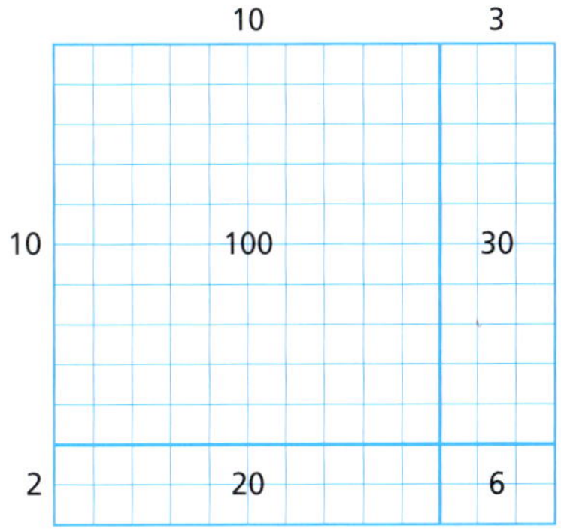

How could you use an area model to identify the binomial factors of a trinomial?

Construct Understanding

TRY THIS

You will need algebra tiles. Use only positive tiles.

A. Use 1 x^2-tile, and a number of x-tiles and 1-tiles.

- Arrange the tiles to form a rectangle. If you cannot make a rectangle, use additional x- and 1-tiles as necessary. For each rectangle, sketch the tiles and write the multiplication sentence it represents.
- Choose a different number of x-tiles and 1-tiles and repeat until you have 4 different multiplication sentences.

B. Use 2 or more x^2-tiles and a number of x-tiles and 1-tiles.

- Arrange the tiles to form a rectangle. Use additional x- and 1-tiles if necessary. For each rectangle, sketch the tiles and write the corresponding multiplication sentence.
- Repeat with different numbers of tiles until you have 4 different multiplication sentences.

C. Share your work with a classmate. What patterns do you see in the products and factors?

Assess Your Understanding

1. Which of the following trinomials can be represented by a rectangle? Use algebra tiles to check. Sketch each rectangle.

a) $y^2 + 4y + 3$ b) $d^2 + 7d + 10$ c) $m^2 + 7m + 7$
d) $r^2 + 14r + 14$ e) $t^2 + 6t + 6$ f) $p^2 + 9p + 2$

2. Which of the following trinomials can be represented by a rectangle? Use algebra tiles to check your answers. Sketch each rectangle.

a) $2s^2 + 7s + 3$ b) $3w^2 + 5w + 2$ c) $2f^2 + 3f + 2$
d) $2h^2 + 10h + 6$ e) $4n^2 + 2n + 1$ f) $6k^2 + 11k + 3$

3. Suppose you must use 1 x^2-tile and twelve 1-tiles. Which numbers of x-tiles could you use to form a rectangle?

4. Suppose you must use 2 x^2-tiles and 9 x-tiles. Which numbers of 1-tiles could you use to form a rectangle?

THE WORLD OF MATH

Math Fact: Taylor Polynomials

A certain type of polynomial is named for the English mathematician Brook Taylor, 1685–1731. Taylor polynomials are used to determine approximate values.

When you use the square root key on a scientific calculator, you are seeing Taylor polynomials in action. The square root of a number between 0 and 2 can be approximated using this polynomial:

$$\sqrt{x} \doteq 1 + \frac{1}{2}(x - 1) - \frac{1}{8}(x - 1)^2 + \frac{1}{16}(x - 1)^3 - \frac{5}{128}(x - 1)^4$$

Use the polynomial to estimate the value of $\sqrt{1.5}$.
Use a calculator to determine how many digits of your answer are correct.

3.5 Polynomials of the Form $x^2 + bx + c$

LESSON FOCUS

Use models and algebraic strategies to multiply binomials and to factor trinomials.

Make Connections

How is each term in the trinomial below represented in the algebra tile model above?

$(c + 3)(c + 7) = c^2 + 10c + 21$

Construct Understanding

TRY THIS

Work with a partner.

- Sketch a rectangle to illustrate each product. Write a multiplication sentence that relates the factors to the final product.

  $(c + 4)(c + 2)$ $(c + 4)(c + 3)$ $(c + 4)(c + 4)$ $(c + 4)(c + 5)$
- Describe a pattern that relates the coefficients of the terms in the factors to the coefficients in the product.
- Use the patterns you identified. Take turns to write two binomials, then sketch a rectangle to determine their product.
- Describe a strategy you could use to multiply two binomials, without sketching a rectangle.

When two binomials contain only positive terms, here are two strategies to determine the product of the binomials.

Use algebra tiles.

To expand: $(c + 5)(c + 3)$
Make a rectangle with dimensions $c + 5$ and $c + 3$.
Place tiles to represent each dimension, then fill in the rectangle with tiles.

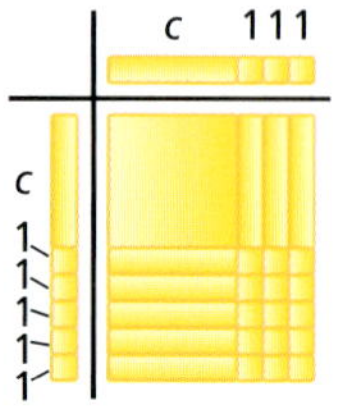

The tiles that form the product are: 1 c^2-tile, 8 c-tiles, and fifteen 1-tiles.
So, $(c + 5)(c + 3) = c^2 + 8c + 15$

Use an area model.
To expand: $(h + 11)(h + 5)$
Sketch a rectangle with dimensions $h + 11$ and $h + 5$.
Divide the rectangle into 4 smaller rectangles and calculate the area of each.

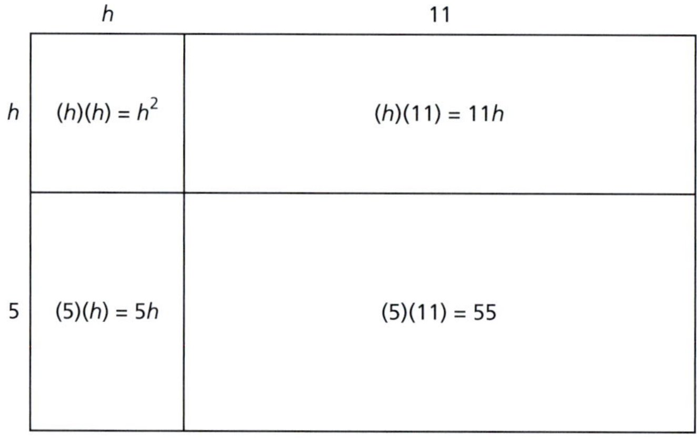

So, $(h + 11)(h + 5) = h^2 + 5h + 11h + 55$ Combine like terms.
$= h^2 + 16h + 55$

Note that $(h + 11)(h + 5) = (h + 5)(h + 11)$ since both products represent the area of the same rectangle.

This strategy shows that there are 4 terms in the product. These terms are formed by applying the distributive property and multiplying each term in the first binomial by each term in the second binomial.

$$(h + 11)(h + 5) = h^2 + 5h + 11h + 55$$

When binomials contain negative terms, it is not easy to determine their product using algebra tiles. We cannot determine the product using an area model because a negative area does not exist, but we can use a rectangle diagram. We can also use the distributive property.

Example 1 Multiplying Two Binomials

Expand and simplify.

a) $(x - 4)(x + 2)$ **b)** $(8 - b)(3 - b)$

SOLUTIONS

a) $(x - 4)(x + 2)$

Method 1

Use a rectangle diagram.

	x	2
x	$(x)(x) = x^2$	$(x)(2) = 2x$
-4	$(-4)(x) = -4x$	$(-4)(2) = -8$

$$\begin{aligned}(x - 4)(x + 2) &= x^2 + (-4x) + 2x + (-8) \quad \text{Combine like terms.}\\ &= x^2 - 2x - 8\end{aligned}$$

Method 2

Use the distributive property.

$$\begin{aligned}(x - 4)(x + 2) &= x(x + 2) + (-4)(x + 2)\\ &= x(x) + x(2) + (-4)(x) + (-4)(2)\\ &= x^2 + 2x - 4x - 8 \quad \text{Combine like terms.}\\ &= x^2 - 2x - 8\end{aligned}$$

b) $(8 - b)(3 - b)$

Use the distributive property.

$$\begin{aligned}(8 - b)(3 - b) &= 8(3 - b) + (-b)(3 - b)\\ &= 8(3) + 8(-b) + (-b)(3) + (-b)(-b)\\ &= 24 - 8b - 3b + b^2\\ &= 24 - 11b + b^2\end{aligned}$$

CHECK YOUR UNDERSTANDING

1. Expand and simplify.

a) $(c + 3)(c - 7)$

b) $(5 - s)(9 - s)$

[Answers: a) $c^2 - 4c - 21$
b) $45 - 14s + s^2$]

How do the constant terms in the binomial factors relate to the middle term and the last term in the trinomial product? How can you use these relationships to determine the product?

Factoring and multiplying are inverse processes. We can use this to factor a trinomial.

When a trinomial contains only positive terms, we may use algebra tiles to factor it.

For example: to factor $v^2 + 12v + 20$, arrange the tiles that represent these terms in a rectangle. Place the v^2-tile in the top left, then arrange the v-tiles to the right and beneath this tile so the 1-tiles fit in the space that is left.

How does the use of algebra tiles for factoring relate to the area model for multiplication?

So, $v^2 + 12v + 20 = (v + 2)(v + 10)$

We say that the factors of $v^2 + 12v + 20$ are $v + 2$ and $v + 10$.

Look at the numbers in the trinomial and the binomial.

$$v^2 + 12v + 20 = (v + 2)(v + 10)$$

12 is the sum of 2 and 10.

20 is the product of 2 and 10.

How could you complete this factorization?

Factoring a Trinomial

To determine the factors of a trinomial of the form $x^2 + bx + c$, first determine two numbers whose sum is b and whose product is c. These numbers are the constant terms in two binomial factors, each of which has x as its first term.

Example 2 Factoring Trinomials

Factor each trinomial.

a) $x^2 - 2x - 8$

b) $z^2 - 12z + 35$

SOLUTION

a) $x^2 - 2x - 8$

Since factoring and expanding are inverse processes, there will be two binomial factors.
They will have the form: $(x + \text{an integer})(x + \text{an integer})$
The two integers in the binomials have a sum of -2 and a product of -8.
To determine the integers, list pairs of factors of -8, then add the factors in each pair.
Since the product is negative, the factors have different signs.

Factors of −8	Sum of Factors
$-1, 8$	$-1 + 8 = 7$
$1, -8$	$1 - 8 = -7$
$-2, 4$	$-2 + 4 = 2$
$2, -4$	$2 - 4 = -2$

The factors that have a sum of -2 are 2 and -4.
Write these integers as the second terms in the binomials.

$x^2 - 2x - 8 = (x + 2)(x - 4)$

b) $z^2 - 12z + 35$

Find two integers whose sum is -12 and whose product is 35.
Since the product is positive, the factors have the same sign.

Factors of 35	Sum of Factors
$1, 35$	$1 + 35 = 36$
$-1, -35$	$-1 - 35 = -36$
$5, 7$	$5 + 7 = 12$
$-5, -7$	$-5 - 7 = -12$

The factors that have a sum of -12 are -5 and -7.

$z^2 - 12z + 35 = (z - 5)(z - 7)$

CHECK YOUR UNDERSTANDING

2. Factor each trinomial.

a) $x^2 - 8x + 7$

b) $a^2 + 7a - 18$

[Answers: a) $(x - 7)(x - 1)$
b) $(a + 9)(a - 2)$]

Does the order in which the binomial factors are written affect the solution? Explain.
Why do we list all the factors for the given product rather than all the numbers that have the given sum?

We should always check that the binomial factors are correct by expanding the product.

For *Example* 2*b*, expand $(z - 5)(z - 7)$.

$$(z - 5)(z - 7) = z(z - 7) - 5(z - 7)$$
$$= z^2 - 7z - 5z + 35$$
$$= z^2 - 12z + 35$$

Since this trinomial is the same as the original trinomial, the factors are correct.

The trinomials in *Example 2* are written in *descending order*; that is, the terms are written in order from the term with the greatest exponent to the term with the least exponent.

When the order of the terms is reversed, the terms are written in *ascending order*.

Example 3 Factoring a Trinomial Written in Ascending Order

Factor: $-24 - 5d + d^2$

SOLUTIONS

Method 1

$-24 - 5d + d^2$

The binomials will have the form:
(an integer + d)(an integer + d)

Find two integers whose product is -24 and whose sum is -5.

The integers are -8 and 3.

So, $-24 - 5d + d^2 = (-8 + d)(3 + d)$

Method 2

Rewrite the polynomial in descending order.

$-24 - 5d + d^2 = d^2 - 5d - 24$

Find two integers whose product is -24 and whose sum is -5.

The integers are -8 and 3.

$d^2 - 5d - 24 = (d - 8)(d + 3)$

CHECK YOUR UNDERSTANDING

3. Factor: $-30 + 7m + m^2$

[Answer: $(-3 + m)(10 + m)$]

Is the answer obtained in Method 1 equivalent to that obtained in Method 2? Does the order we write the terms of the binomial matter? Why or why not?

A trinomial that can be written as the product of two binomial factors may also have a common factor.

Example 4 Factoring a Trinomial with a Common Factor and Binomial Factors

Factor.

$-4t^2 - 16t + 128$

SOLUTION

$-4t^2 - 16t + 128$

The greatest common factor is 4. Since the coefficient of the first term is negative, use –4 as the common factor.

$-4t^2 - 16t + 128 = -4(t^2 + 4t - 32)$

Two numbers with a sum of 4 and a product of -32 are -4 and 8.

So, $t^2 + 4t - 32 = (t - 4)(t + 8)$

And, $-4t^2 - 16t + 128 = -4(t - 4)(t + 8)$

Since factoring and expanding are inverse processes, check that the factors are correct. Multiply the factors.

$$-4(t - 4)(t + 8) = -4(t^2 + 4t - 32)$$
$$= -4t^2 - 16t + 128$$

This trinomial is the same as the original trinomial, so the factors are correct.

CHECK YOUR UNDERSTANDING

4. Factor.

$-5h^2 - 20h + 60$

[Answer: $-5(h - 2)(h + 6)$]

What other ways can you write the trinomial as a product of 3 factors?

When we compare factors of a trinomial, it is important to remember that the order in which we add terms does not matter, so $x + a = a + x$, for any integer a. Similarly, the order in which we multiply terms does not matter, so $(x + a)(x + b) = (x + b)(x + a)$.

Discuss the Ideas

1. How is representing the product of two binomials similar to representing the product of two 2-digit numbers?

2. How does a rectangle diagram relate binomial multiplication and trinomial factoring?

3. For the multiplication sentence $x^2 + ax + b = (x + c)(x + d)$, what relationships exist among a, b, c, and d?

Exercises

A

4. Write the multiplication sentence that each set of algebra tiles represents.

a) 

b) 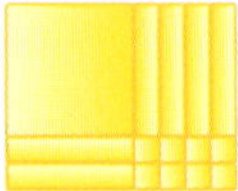

c) 

d) 

5. Use algebra tiles to determine each product. Sketch the tiles you used.

a) $(b + 2)(b + 5)$
b) $(n + 4)(n + 7)$
c) $(h + 8)(h + 3)$
d) $(k + 1)(k + 6)$

6. For each set of algebra tiles below:

i) Write the trinomial that the algebra tiles represent.
ii) Arrange the tiles to form a rectangle. Sketch the rectangle.
iii) Use the rectangle to factor the trinomial.

a)

b) 

c) 

d) 

7. a) Find two integers with the given properties.

	a	b	Product ab	Sum $a + b$
i)			2	3
ii)			6	5
iii)			9	10
iv)			10	7
v)			12	7
vi)			15	8

b) Use the results of part a to factor each trinomial.

i) $v^2 + 3v + 2$ ii) $w^2 + 5w + 6$
iii) $s^2 + 10s + 9$ iv) $t^2 + 7t + 10$
v) $y^2 + 7y + 12$ vi) $h^2 + 8h + 15$

B

8. a) Use algebra tiles to factor each trinomial. Sketch the tiles you used.

i) $v^2 + 2v + 1$ ii) $v^2 + 4v + 4$
iii) $v^2 + 6v + 9$ iv) $v^2 + 8v + 16$

b) What patterns do you see in the algebra tile rectangles? How are these patterns shown in the binomial factors?

c) Write the next 3 trinomials in the pattern and their binomial factors.

9. Multiply each pair of binomials. Sketch and label a rectangle to illustrate each product.

a) $(m + 5)(m + 8)$ b) $(y + 9)(y + 3)$
c) $(w + 2)(w + 16)$ d) $(k + 13)(k + 1)$

10. Copy and complete.

a) $(w + 3)(w + 2) = w^2 + \square w + 6$
b) $(x + 5)(x + \square) = x^2 + \bigcirc x + 10$
c) $(y + \bigcirc)(y + \square) = y^2 + 12y + 20$

11. Factor. Check by expanding.

a) $x^2 + 10x + 24$ b) $m^2 + 10m + 16$
c) $p^2 + 13p + 12$ d) $s^2 + 12s + 20$
e) $n^2 + 12n + 11$ f) $h^2 + 8h + 12$
g) $q^2 + 7q + 6$ h) $b^2 + 11b + 18$

12. Expand and simplify. Sketch a rectangle diagram to illustrate each product.

a) $(g - 3)(g + 7)$ b) $(h + 2)(h - 7)$
c) $(11 - j)(2 - j)$ d) $(k - 3)(k + 11)$
e) $(12 + h)(7 - h)$ f) $(m - 9)(m + 9)$
g) $(n - 14)(n - 4)$ h) $(p + 6)(p - 17)$

13. Find and correct the errors in each expansion.

a) $(r - 13)(r + 4) = r(r + 4) - 13(r + 4)$
$= r^2 + 4r - 13r + 52$
$= r^2 + 9r + 52$

b) $(s - 15)(s - 5) = s(s - 15) + 15(s + 5)$
$= s^2 - 15s + 15s + 75$
$= s^2 + 75$

14. Factor. Check by expanding.

a) $b^2 + 19b - 20$ b) $t^2 + 15t - 54$
c) $x^2 + 12x - 28$ d) $n^2 - 5n - 24$
e) $a^2 - a - 20$ f) $y^2 - 2y - 48$
g) $m^2 - 15m + 50$ h) $a^2 - 12a + 36$

15. Factor. Check by expanding.

a) $12 + 13k + k^2$ b) $-16 - 6g + g^2$
c) $60 + 17y + y^2$ d) $72 - z - z^2$

16. a) Simplify each pair of products.

i) $(x + 1)(x + 2)$ and $11 \cdot 12$
ii) $(x + 1)(x + 3)$ and $11 \cdot 13$

b) What are the similarities between the two answers for each pair of products?

17. Find and correct the errors in each factorization.

a) $m^2 - 7m - 60 = (m - 5)(m - 12)$
b) $w^2 - 14w + 45 = (w + 3)(w - 15)$
c) $b^2 + 9b - 36 = (b + 3)(b - 12)$

18. a) Expand each product, then write it as a trinomial.

i) $(t + 4)(t + 7)$ ii) $(t - 4)(t - 7)$
iii) $(t - 4)(t + 7)$ iv) $(t + 4)(t - 7)$

b) i) Why are the constant terms in the trinomials in parts i and ii above positive?
ii) Why are the constant terms in the trinomials in parts iii and iv above negative?
iii) How could you determine the coefficient of the t-term in the trinomial without expanding?

19. Find an integer to replace □ so that each trinomial can be factored.
How many integers can you find each time?

a) $x^2 + \square x + 10$
b) $a^2 + \square a - 9$
c) $t^2 + \square t + 8$
d) $y^2 + \square y - 12$
e) $h^2 + \square h + 18$
f) $p^2 + \square p - 16$

20. Find an integer to replace □ so that each trinomial can be factored.
How many integers can you find each time?

a) $r^2 + r + \square$ b) $h^2 - h + \square$
c) $b^2 + 2b + \square$ d) $z^2 - 2z + \square$
e) $q^2 + 3q + \square$ f) $g^2 - 3g + \square$

21. Factor.

a) $4y^2 - 20y - 56$ b) $-3m^2 - 18m - 24$
c) $4x^2 + 4x - 48$ d) $10x^2 + 80x + 120$
e) $-5n^2 + 40n - 35$ f) $7c^2 - 35c + 42$

C

22. In this lesson, you used algebra tiles to multiply two binomials and to factor a trinomial when all the terms were positive.

a) How could you use algebra tiles to expand $(r - 4)(r + 1)$?
Sketch the tiles you used. Explain your strategy.

b) How could you use algebra tiles to factor $t^2 + t - 6$?
Sketch the tiles you used. Explain your strategy.

23. a) Factor each trinomial.

i) $h^2 - 10h - 24$
ii) $h^2 + 10h - 24$
iii) $h^2 - 10h + 24$
iv) $h^2 + 10h + 24$

b) In part a, all the trinomials have the same numerical coefficients and constant terms, but different signs. Find other examples like this, in which all 4 trinomials of the form $h^2 \pm bh \pm c$ can be factored.

Reflect Suppose a trinomial of the form $x^2 + ax + b$ is the product of two binomials. How can you determine the binomial factors?

3.6 Polynomials of the Form $ax^2 + bx + c$

LESSON FOCUS

Extend the strategies for multiplying binomials and factoring trinomials.

Make Connections

Which trinomial is represented by the algebra tiles shown above?

How can the tiles be arranged to form a rectangle?

Construct Understanding

THINK ABOUT IT

Work with a partner.

You will need algebra tiles.

For which of these trinomials can the algebra tiles be arranged to form a rectangle? For those that can be represented by a rectangular arrangement, write the multiplication sentence.

$2x^2 + 15x + 7$	$2x^2 + 5x + 2$	$6x^2 + 7x + 2$
$5x^2 + 4x + 4$	$2x^2 + 9x + 10$	$5x^2 + 11x + 2$

To multiply two binomials where the coefficients of the variables are not 1, we use the same strategies as for the binomials in Lesson 3.5.

Example 1 Multiplying Two Binomials with Positive Terms

Expand: $(3d + 4)(4d + 2)$

SOLUTIONS

Method 1

Use algebra tiles.

Make a rectangle with dimensions $3d + 4$ and $4d + 2$.

Place tiles to represent each dimension, then fill the rectangle with tiles.

The tiles that form the product represent $12d^2 + 22d + 8$.

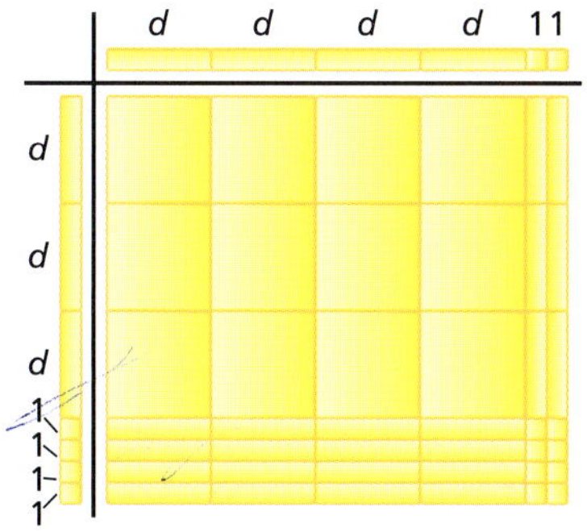

So, $(3d + 4)(4d + 2) = 12d^2 + 22d + 8$

Method 2

Use an area model.

To expand: $(3d + 4)(4d + 2)$, draw a rectangle with dimensions $3d + 4$ and $4d + 2$. Divide the rectangle into 4 smaller rectangles then calculate the area of each.

	$3d$	4
$4d$	$(4d)(3d) = 12d^2$	$(4d)(4) = 16d$
2	$(2)(3d) = 6d$	$(2)(4) = 8$

The area of the larger rectangle is the sum of the areas of the smaller rectangles.

$$\begin{aligned} \text{So, } (3d + 4)(4d + 2) &= 12d^2 + 16d + 6d + 8 \\ &= 12d^2 + 22d + 8 \end{aligned}$$

CHECK YOUR UNDERSTANDING

1. Expand: $(5e + 3)(2e + 4)$

[Answer: $10e^2 + 26e + 12$]

This rectangle diagram shows the relationship between the coefficients in the product and the coefficients in the factors for $(ax + b)(cx + d)$.
$(ax + b)(cx + d) = acx^2 + adx + bcx + bd$

	cx	d
ax	$(ax)(cx) = acx^2$	$(ax)(d) = adx$
b	$(b)(cx) = bcx$	$(b)(d) = bd$

When binomials contain negative terms, it can be difficult to model their product with algebra tiles. We can use the distributive property to determine their product.

Example 2 Multiplying Two Binomials with Negative Coefficients

Expand and simplify: $(-2g + 8)(7 - 3g)$

SOLUTIONS

Method 1

Use a rectangle diagram.

Write $(-2g + 8)(7 - 3g)$ as $[(-2g) + 8][7 + (-3g)]$.

Draw a rectangle with dimensions $(-2g) + 8$ and $7 + (-3g)$.

Divide the rectangle into 4 smaller rectangles and label each one.

	7	$-3g$
$-2g$	$(-2g)(7) = -14g$	$(-2g)(-3g) = 6g^2$
8	$(8)(7) = 56$	$(8)(-3g) = -24g$

$$\begin{aligned}(-2g + 8)(7 - 3g) &= -14g + 6g^2 + 56 - 24g\\ &= 6g^2 - 14g - 24g + 56\\ &= 6g^2 - 38g + 56\end{aligned}$$

Method 2

Use the distributive property.

$$\begin{aligned}(-2g + 8)(7 - 3g) &= (-2g)(7 - 3g) + 8(7 - 3g)\\ &= -14g + 6g^2 + 56 - 24g\\ &= -38g + 6g^2 + 56\\ &= 6g^2 - 38g + 56\end{aligned}$$

CHECK YOUR UNDERSTANDING

2. Expand and simplify: $(6t - 9)(7 - 5t)$

[Answer: $-30t^2 + 87t - 63$]

Which terms of the binomial factors determine the value of each term in the trinomial? How can you use this to simplify the calculation?

We can use algebra tiles to factor a trinomial when its terms are positive.

For example, to factor $2x^2 + 5x + 3$, arrange the tiles that represent these terms in a rectangle.

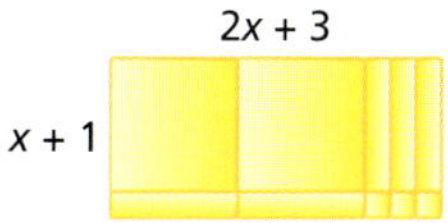

This algebra-tile model illustrates how the terms in the two binomial factors are related to the terms in the trinomial.

$2x^2 + 5x + 3 = (2x + 3)(x + 1)$

$2x^2$ is the product of the 1st terms in the binomials.

$2x^2 + 5x + 3 = (2x + 3)(x + 1)$

$5x$ is the sum of these products: $2x(1) + 3(x)$

$2x^2 + 5x + 3 = (2x + 3)(x + 1)$

3 is the product of the 2nd terms in the binomials.

When we use algebra tiles to factor a trinomial with negative terms, we may have to use the Zero Principle and add pairs of opposite tiles to form a rectangle. For example, to model the factoring of the trinomial $3x^2 + 5x - 2$, first arrange the tiles to attempt to form a rectangle. To complete the rectangle, we need two x-tiles. So, add one positive x-tile and one negative x-tile. Place them so that all the positive x-tiles are together.

What do you know about a polynomial for which you can never form a rectangle?

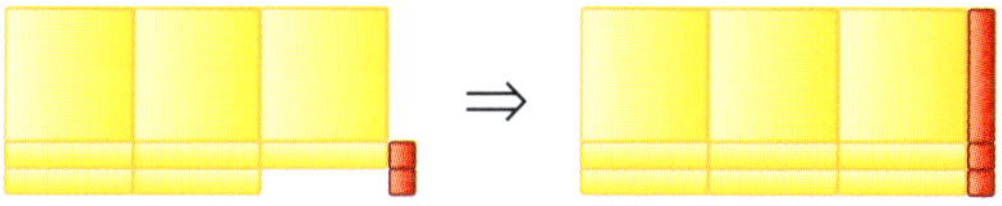

So, $3x^2 + 5x - 2 = (3x - 1)(x + 2)$

Some trinomials, for example $2x^2 + x + 1$, cannot be factored. You cannot add pairs of opposite x-tiles to form a rectangle.

We can use the patterns on page 171 and logical reasoning to factor without algebra tiles. Often, by looking carefully at the relative sizes of the coefficients, we can estimate which factors of the coefficients of the trinomial to try first.

Example 3 Factoring a Trinomial Using Logical Reasoning

Factor.

a) $4h^2 + 20h + 9$ **b)** $6k^2 - 11k - 35$

SOLUTIONS

a) Method 1

$4h^2 + 20h + 9$

To factor this trinomial, find factors of the form $(ah + b)(ch + d)$.

The coefficient of h^2 is 4, so the coefficients of the 1st terms in the binomial are factors of 4, which are 1 and 4, or 2 and 2.

So, the binomials have the form

$(h + b)(4h + d)$ or $(2h + b)(2h + d)$

The constant term in the trinomial is 9, so the 2nd terms in the binomial are factors of 9, which are 1 and 9, or 3 and 3.

So, the binomials could be:

$(h + 1)(4h + 9)$ or $(2h + 1)(2h + 9)$ or

$(h + 9)(4h + 1)$ or $(2h + 9)(2h + 1)$ or

$(h + 3)(4h + 3)$ or $(2h + 3)(2h + 3)$

Check which of the 6 binomial products above has its h-term equal to $20h$.

$(h + 1)(4h + 9) = 4h^2 + 13h + 9$
$(2h + 1)(2h + 9) = 4h^2 + 20h + 9$

This is the correct trinomial so we need not check any further.

$4h^2 + 20h + 9 = (2h + 1)(2h + 9)$

(Solution continues.)

CHECK YOUR UNDERSTANDING

3. Factor.

a) $4g^2 + 11g + 6$

b) $6m^2 - 7m - 10$

[Answers: a) $(4g + 3)(g + 2)$
b) $(6m + 5)(m - 2)$]

In *Example 3a*, why did we not need to list or check the negative factors of 4?

Method 2

$4h^2 + 20h + 9$

Use number sense and reasoning, with mental math.

The factors of $4h^2$ are $4h$ and $1h$, or $2h$ and $2h$.

The factors of 9 are 9 and 1, or 3 and 3.

The coefficient of the middle term of the trinomial, 20, is greater than the coefficients of the other two terms, so try the greater factors. Arrange the factor combinations vertically.

$4h \quad 9$	$2h \quad 9$	Form the products, then add.
$1h \quad 1$	$2h \quad 1$	
$4h + 9h = 13h$	$2h + 18h = 20h$ ←	This is the correct combination of factors.

So, $4h^2 + 20h + 9 = (2h + 9)(2h + 1)$

b) Method 1

$6k^2 - 11k - 35$

Find factors of the form $(ak + b)(ck + d)$.

The coefficient of k^2 is 6, so the coefficients of the 1st terms in the binomial are factors of 6, which are 1 and 6, or 2 and 3.

The constant term in the trinomial is -35, so the 2nd terms in the binomial are factors of -35, which are 1 and -35, or -1 and 35, or -5 and 7, or 5 and -7.

The coefficient of the middle term of the trinomial, -11, is between the coefficients of the other two terms, so try combinations of the lesser factors first; that is, try combinations of 2 and 3 with combinations of ± 5 and ± 7.

So, the binomials could be:

$(2k + 5)(3k - 7)$ or $(2k - 7)(3k + 5)$ or
$(2k - 5)(3k + 7)$ or $(2k + 7)(3k - 5)$

Check if any of the 4 binomial products above has its k-term equal to $-11k$.

$(2k + 5)(3k - 7) = 6k^2 + k - 35$
$(2k - 7)(3k + 5) = 6k^2 - 11k - 35$

This is the correct trinomial so we need not check any further.

$6k^2 - 11k - 35 = (2k - 7)(3k + 5)$

(Solution continues.)

In *Example 3b*, why did we not need to list or check the negative factors of 6?

Method 2

$6k^2 - 11k - 35$

Use number sense and mental math, with guess and test.
The factors of $6k^2$ are $1k$ and $6k$, or $2k$ and $3k$.
The factors of -35 are 1 and -35, or -1 and 35, or -7 and 5, or 7 and -5.
The coefficient of the middle term of the trinomial, -11, is between the coefficients of the other terms, so try factors of these coefficients that would be in the middle if the factors were listed in numerical order. Arrange the factor combinations vertically:

$2k \quad 7$	$2k \quad -7$
$3k \quad -5$	$3k \quad 5$
$-10k + 21k = 11k$	$10k - 21k = -11k$

Form the products, then add.

This is the correct combination of factors. (arrow points to the second combination, $2k$, -7 and $3k$, 5)

$6k^2 - 11k - 35 = (2k - 7)(3k + 5)$

Factoring by decomposition is factoring after writing the middle term of a trinomial as a sum of two terms, then determining a common binomial factor from the two pairs of terms formed.

Another method of factoring is **factoring by decomposition**.

Consider the binomial product: $(3h + 4)(2h + 1)$

We can use the distributive property to expand:

$$\begin{aligned}(3h + 4)(2h + 1) &= 3h(2h + 1) + 4(2h + 1)\\ &= 6h^2 + 3h + 8h + 4\\ &= 6h^2 + 11h + 4\end{aligned}$$

To factor $6h^2 + 11h + 4$ by decomposition, we reverse the steps above.

Notice that the coefficients of the h-terms have the product: $3(8) = 24$

This is equal to the product of the coefficient of the h^2-term and the constant term: $6(4) = 24$

So, to factor $6h^2 + 11h + 4$, we *decompose* the h-term and write it as a sum of two terms whose coefficients have a product of 24.

Why don't we need to list the negative factors of 24?

Factors of 24	Sum of Factors
1, 24	$1 + 24 = 25$
2, 12	$2 + 12 = 14$
3, 8	$3 + 8 = 11$
4, 6	$4 + 6 = 10$

The two coefficients that have a sum of 11 are 3 and 8,
so we write the trinomial $6h^2 + 11h + 4$ as $6h^2 + 3h + 8h + 4$.

We remove a common factor from the 1st pair of terms, and from the 2nd pair of terms: $6h^2 + 3h + 8h + 4 = 3h(2h + 1) + 4(2h + 1)$

Each product has the common binomial factor $2h + 1$.

$6h^2 + 11h + 4 = (2h + 1)(3h + 4)$

Example 4 Factoring a Trinomial by Decomposition

Factor.

a) $3s^2 - 13s - 10$ b) $6x^2 - 21x + 9$

SOLUTION

a) $3s^2 - 13s - 10$

Check for common factors; there are none.

The product of the coefficient of s^2 and the constant term is: $3(-10) = -30$

Write $-13s$ as the sum of two terms whose coefficients have a product of -30.

Factors of −30	Sum of Factors
$1, -30$	$1 - 30 = -29$
$-1, 30$	$-1 + 30 = 29$
$2, -15$	$2 - 15 = -13$
$-2, 15$	$-2 + 15 = 13$
$3, -10$	$3 - 10 = -7$
$-3, 10$	$-3 + 10 = 7$
$5, -6$	$5 - 6 = -1$
$-5, 6$	$-5 + 6 = 1$

The two coefficients are 2 and -15, so write the trinomial $3s^2 - 13s - 10$ as $3s^2 + 2s - 15s - 10$.

Remove a common factor from the 1st pair of terms, and from the 2nd pair of terms:

$3s^2 + 2s - 15s - 10 = s(3s + 2) - 5(3s + 2)$

Each product has a common binomial factor.

$3s^2 + 2s - 15s - 10 = (3s + 2)(s - 5)$

So, $3s^2 - 13s - 10 = (3s + 2)(s - 5)$

b) $6x^2 - 21x + 9$

Check for common factors; 3 is a common factor.

So, $6x^2 - 21x + 9 = 3(2x^2 - 7x + 3)$

Factor $2x^2 - 7x + 3$.

(Solution continues.)

CHECK YOUR UNDERSTANDING

4. Factor.

a) $8p^2 - 18p - 5$

b) $24h^2 - 20h - 24$

[Answers: a) $(2p - 5)(4p + 1)$
b) $4(2h - 3)(3h + 2)$]

When we write the middle term as the sum of two terms, could we write $3s^2 - 15s + 2s - 10$ instead? Justify your answer.

The product of the coefficient of x^2 and the constant term is: $2(3) = 6$

Write $-7x$ as the sum of two terms whose coefficients have a product of 6.

Factors of 6	Sum of Factors
1, 6	$1 + 6 = 7$
−1, −6	$-1 - 6 = -7$
2, 3	$2 + 3 = 5$
−2, −3	$-2 - 3 = -5$

The two coefficients are −1 and −6, so write the trinomial $2x^2 - 7x + 3$ as $2x^2 - 1x - 6x + 3$.

Remove a common factor from the 1st pair of terms, and from the 2nd pair of terms:

$2x^2 - 1x - 6x + 3 = x(2x - 1) - 3(2x - 1)$

Each product has a common binomial factor.

$2x^2 - 1x - 6x + 3 = (2x - 1)(x - 3)$

So, $2x^2 - 7x + 3 = (2x - 1)(x - 3)$

And, $6x^2 - 21x + 9 = 3(2x - 1)(x - 3)$

When would you use decomposition to factor a trinomial?

To check that the factors are correct, multiply them.
In *Example 4b*, multiply:

$$\begin{aligned}3(2x - 1)(x - 3) &= 3(2x^2 - 6x - x + 3)\\ &= 3(2x^2 - 7x + 3)\\ &= 6x^2 - 21x + 9\end{aligned}$$

Since this trinomial is the same as the original trinomial, the factors are correct.

Discuss the Ideas

1. How are the strategies for multiplying binomial factors of the form $(ax + b)(cx + d)$ like the strategies you used in Lesson 3.5 for products of the form $(x + a)(x + b)$? How are they different?

2. How can you use the coefficients of a trinomial to determine the coefficients of its binomial factors?

3. How can you tell when a trinomial cannot be factored?

4. How can you use logical reasoning to reduce the number of possible combinations of coefficients you have to consider in the guess-and-test or the decomposition methods of factoring a trinomial?

Exercises

A

5. Write the multiplication sentence that each set of algebra tiles represents.

a) 

b) 

c) 

d) 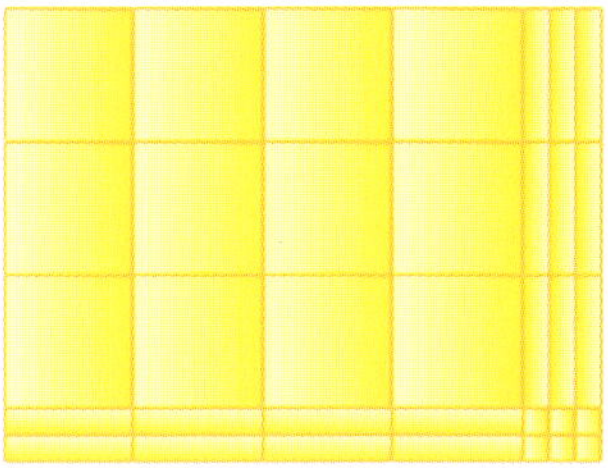

6. Use algebra tiles to determine each product.

a) $(2v + 3)(v + 2)$ b) $(3r + 1)(r + 4)$

c) $(2g + 3)(3g + 2)$ d) $(4z + 3)(2z + 5)$

e) $(3t + 4)(3t + 4)$ f) $(2r + 3)(2r + 3)$

7. For each set of algebra tiles below:

i) Write the trinomial that the algebra tiles represent.

ii) Arrange the tiles to form a rectangle. Sketch the rectangle.

iii) Use the rectangle to factor the trinomial.

a) 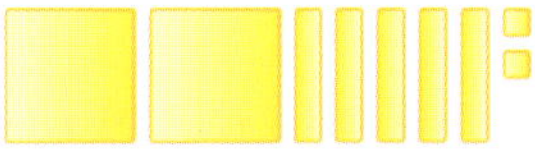

b) 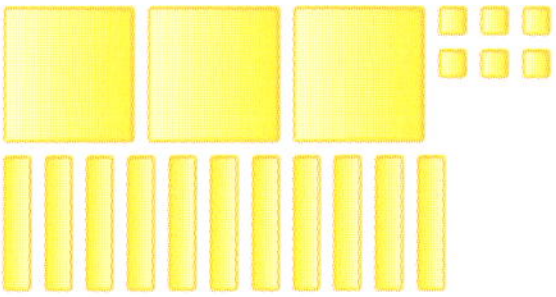

c) 

d) 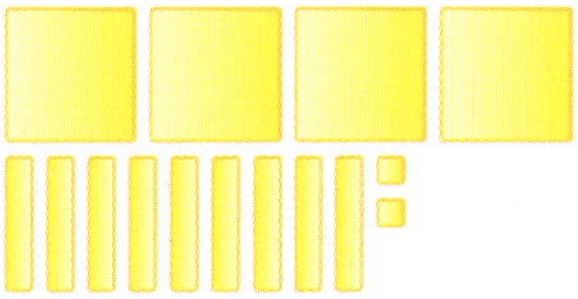

B

8. Copy and complete each statement.

a) $(2w + 1)(w + 6) = 2w^2 + \square w + 6$

b) $(2g - 5)(3g - 3) = 6g^2 + \square + \bigcirc$

c) $(-4v - 3)(-2v - 7) = \square + \bigcirc + 21$

9. Expand and simplify.

a) $(5 + f)(3 + 4f)$

b) $(3 - 4t)(5 - 3t)$

c) $(10 - r)(9 + 2r)$

d) $(-6 + 2m)(-6 + 2m)$

e) $(-8 - 2x)(3 - 7x)$

f) $(6 - 5n)(-6 + 5n)$

10. Expand and simplify.

a) $(3c + 4)(5 + 2c)$

b) $(1 - 7t)(3t + 5)$

c) $(-4r - 7)(2 - 8r)$

d) $(-9 - t)(-5t - 1)$

e) $(7h + 10)(-3 + 5h)$

f) $(7 - 6y)(6y - 7)$

11. a) Use algebra tiles to factor each polynomial. Sketch the tiles you used.

i) $3t^2 + 4t + 1$

ii) $3t^2 + 8t + 4$

iii) $3t^2 + 12t + 9$

iv) $3t^2 + 16t + 16$

b) What patterns do you see in the algebra-tile rectangles? How are these patterns shown in the binomial factors?

c) Write the next 3 trinomials in the pattern and their binomial factors.

12. Factor. What patterns do you see in the trinomials and their factors?

a) i) $2n^2 + 13n + 6$ ii) $2n^2 - 13n + 6$

b) i) $2n^2 + 11n - 6$ ii) $2n^2 - 11n - 6$

c) i) $2n^2 + 7n + 6$ ii) $2n^2 - 7n + 6$

13. Factor. Check by expanding.

a) $2y^2 + 5y + 2$ b) $2a^2 + 11a + 12$

c) $2k^2 + 13k + 15$ d) $2m^2 - 11m + 12$

e) $2k^2 - 11k + 15$ f) $2m^2 + 15m + 7$

g) $2g^2 + 15g + 18$ h) $2n^2 + 9n - 18$

14. a) Find two integers with the given properties.

	Product	Sum
i)	15	16
ii)	24	14
iii)	15	8
iv)	12	7
v)	12	13
vi)	24	11

b) Use the results of part a to use decomposition to factor each trinomial.

i) $3v^2 + 16v + 5$ ii) $3m^2 + 14m + 8$
iii) $3b^2 + 8b + 5$ iv) $4a^2 + 7a + 3$
v) $4d^2 + 13d + 3$ vi) $4v^2 + 11v + 6$

15. Factor. Check by expanding.

a) $5a^2 - 7a - 6$ b) $3y^2 - 13y - 10$
c) $5s^2 + 19s - 4$ d) $14c^2 - 19c - 3$
e) $8a^2 + 18a - 5$ f) $8r^2 - 14r + 3$
g) $6d^2 + d - 5$ h) $15e^2 - 7e - 2$

16. Find and correct the errors in each factorization.

a) $6u^2 + 17u - 14 = (2u - 7)(3u + 2)$
b) $3k^2 - k - 30 = (3k - 3)(k + 10)$
c) $4v^2 - 21v + 20 = (4v - 4)(v + 5)$

17. Find and correct the errors in this solution of factoring by decomposition.

$$15g^2 + 17g - 42 = 15g^2 - 18g + 35g - 42$$
$$= 3g(5g - 6) + 7(5g + 6)$$
$$= (3g + 7)(5g + 6)$$

18. Factor.

a) $20r^2 + 70r + 60$ b) $15a^2 - 65a + 20$
c) $18h^2 + 15h - 18$ d) $24u^2 - 72u + 54$
e) $12m^2 - 52m - 40$ f) $24g^2 - 2g - 70$

19. Factor.

a) $14y^2 - 13y + 3$ b) $10p^2 - 17p - 6$
c) $10r^2 - 33r - 7$ d) $15g^2 - g - 2$
e) $4x^2 + 4x - 15$ f) $9d^2 - 24d + 16$
g) $9t^2 + 12t + 4$ h) $40y^2 + y - 6$
i) $24c^2 + 26c - 15$ j) $8x^2 + 14x - 15$

20. Find an integer to replace □ so that each trinomial can be factored.
How many integers can you find each time?

a) $4s^2 + \square s + 3$ b) $4h^2 + \square h + 25$
c) $6y^2 + \square y - 9$ d) $12t^2 + \square t + 10$
e) $9z^2 + \square z + 1$ f) $\square f^2 + 2f + \square$

C

21. a) Factor, if possible.

i) $4r^2 - r - 5$ ii) $2t^2 + 10t + 3$
iii) $5y^2 + 4y - 2$ iv) $2w^2 - 5w + 2$
v) $3h^2 - 8h - 3$ vi) $2f^2 - f + 1$

b) Choose two trinomials from part a: one that can be factored and one that cannot be factored. Explain why the first trinomial can be factored and the second one cannot be factored.

22. a) Factor each trinomial.

i) $3n^2 + 11n + 10$ ii) $3n^2 - 11n + 10$
iii) $3n^2 + 13n + 10$ iv) $3n^2 - 13n + 10$
v) $3n^2 + 17n + 10$ vi) $3n^2 - 17n + 10$

b) Look at the trinomials and their factors in part a. Are there any other trinomials that begin with $3n^2$, end with +10, and can be factored? Explain.

23. Find all the trinomials that begin with $9m^2$, end with +16, and can be factored.

Reflect Which strategies can you use to factor a trinomial? Give an example of when you might use each strategy to factor a trinomial.

CHECKPOINT 2

Connections

Type of Factor	Patterns Relating Factors and the Product	Example
Monomial x Polynomial	The monomial factor is the greatest common factor of the terms of the product polynomial.	$5x^2 - 10xy + 15x$ $= 5x(x - 2y + 3)$
$(x + a)(x + b)$	$(x + a)(x + b)$ $= x^2 + (a + b)x + ab$	$(x + 2)(x - 8)$ $= x^2 + 2x - 8x - 16$ $= x^2 - 6x - 16$
$(ax + b)(cx + d)$	$(ax + b)(cx + d)$ $= (ac)x^2 + (ad + bc)x + bd$	$(3x - 2)(2x + 5)$ $= 6x^2 - 4x + 15x - 10$ $= 6x^2 + 11x - 10$

Concept Development

- **In Lesson 3.3**
  - You applied an area model for the product of whole numbers to develop models and strategies to determine **common factors** in the terms of a polynomial.
- **In Lesson 3.4**
  - You used algebra tiles to **multiply binomials** and to **factor trinomials.**
- **In Lesson 3.5**
  - You used diagrams and algebraic strategies to **multiply binomials** and to **factor trinomials** of the form $x^2 + bx + c$.
- **In Lesson 3.6**
  - You extended the strategies from Lesson 3.5 to **multiply binomials** and to **factor trinomials** of the form $ax^2 + bx + c$.

THE WORLD OF MATH

Careers: Computer Graphics Artist

If you have played a video game or been to a movie recently, you may have seen special effects created by a computer graphics artist. To create an image in virtual space, the artist may take measurements from a model and make many calculations to ensure the objects look and move realistically on the screen. Computer graphics artists use their knowledge of algebra and geometry to help produce visually attractive and entertaining material.

Assess Your Understanding

3.3

1. For each set of algebra tiles, write the polynomial they represent and identify its factors. Sketch the tile arrangement that illustrates the factors.

a)

b)

2. a) Factor each polynomial. Use algebra tiles when you can. Sketch the tiles you used.

i) $4a + 8$

ii) $3c - 6$

iii) $-2v^2 - 5v$

iv) $2x^2 + 14x + 6$

v) $-3r^2 + 15r - 3$

vi) $15a^3 - 3a^2b - 6ab^2$

vii) $12 - 32x + 8x^2$

viii) $12x^2y - 8xy - 16y$

b) For which polynomials in part a could you not use algebra tiles? Explain why you could not use them.

3.4

3. Use 1 x^2-tile. Choose x-tiles and 1-tiles to make a rectangle. Sketch your arrangement and write the multiplication sentence it represents.

4. Use 2 or more x^2-tiles. Choose x-tiles and 1-tiles to make a rectangle. Sketch your arrangement and write the multiplication sentence it represents.

3.5

5. Expand and simplify. Use an area model or a rectangle diagram to illustrate each product.

a) $(x + 1)(x + 4)$

b) $(d - 2)(d + 3)$

c) $(x - 4)(x - 2)$

d) $(5 - r)(6 + r)$

e) $(g + 5)(g - 1)$

f) $(2 - t)(10 - t)$

6. Factor each trinomial. Check by expanding.

a) $s^2 + 11s + 30$

b) $n^2 - n - 30$

c) $20 - 9b + b^2$

d) $-11 - 10t + t^2$

e) $z^2 + 13z + 30$

f) $-k^2 + 9k - 18$

7. Factor.

a) $3x^2 + 15x - 42$

b) $-2y^2 + 22y - 48$

c) $-24 - 11m - m^2$

d) $50 - 23y - y^2$

3.6

8. Expand and simplify.

a) $(2c + 1)(c + 3)$
b) $(-m + 5)(4m - 1)$
c) $(3f - 4)(3f + 1)$
d) $(6z - 1)(2z - 3)$
e) $(5 - 3r)(6 + 2r)$
f) $(-4 - 2h)(-2 - 4h)$

9. Factor each trinomial. Check by expanding.

a) $2j^2 + 13j + 20$
b) $3v^2 + v - 10$
c) $5k^2 - 23k + 12$
d) $9h^2 + 18h + 8$
e) $8y^2 - 2y - 1$
f) $6 - 23u + 20u^2$

THE WORLD OF MATH

Historical Moment: François Viète

François Viète (1540–1603) was a lawyer who worked at the court of Henri III and Henri IV of France. In addition to offering legal advice, he was a cryptanalyst, deciphering messages intercepted between enemies of the king, but his hobby was mathematics. He was one of the first people to use letters to represent numbers. In his work *Prior Notes on Symbolic Logistic*, written toward the end of the sixteenth century but not published until 1631, he showed how to operate on symbolic quantities and derived many algebraic results. He applied his algebra to many different fields of mathematics, publishing work on trigonometry and what he viewed as his most elegant, the analysis of equations.

3.7 Multiplying Polynomials

LESSON FOCUS

Extend the strategies for multiplying binomials to multiplying polynomials.

Make Connections

The art work above was a design for a stained glass panel. How could you use the length and width of each small rectangle to determine the area of the large rectangle without first finding its overall length and width?

Construct Understanding

THINK ABOUT IT

Work with a partner.

- Draw a rectangle diagram to determine the product $(a + b + 2)(c + d + 3)$.
- Draw a rectangle diagram to determine the product $(a - b + 2)(c + d - 3)$.
- Use a different strategy to check the products.

Would the product have been different if you reversed the order of the factors? Explain.

The distributive property can be used to perform any polynomial multiplication. Each term of one polynomial must be multiplied by each term of the other polynomial.

Example 1 Using the Distributive Property to Multiply Two Polynomials

Expand and simplify.

a) $(2h + 5)(h^2 + 3h - 4)$ **b)** $(-3f^2 + 3f - 2)(4f^2 - f - 6)$

SOLUTION

a) Use the distributive property. Multiply each term in the trinomial by each term in the binomial.
Write the terms in a list.

$$(2h + 5)(h^2 + 3h - 4)$$
$$= (2h)(h^2 + 3h - 4) + 5(h^2 + 3h - 4)$$
$$= (2h)(h^2) + (2h)(3h) + 2h(-4) + 5(h^2) + 5(3h) + 5(-4)$$
$$= 2h^3 + 6h^2 - 8h + 5h^2 + 15h - 20$$
$$= 2h^3 + 6h^2 + 5h^2 - 8h + 15h - 20 \quad \text{Combine like terms.}$$
$$= 2h^3 + 11h^2 + 7h - 20$$

b) Use the distributive property. Multiply each term in the 1st trinomial by each term in the 2nd trinomial.
Align like terms.

$(-3f^2 + 3f - 2)(4f^2 - f - 6)$:

$-3f^2(4f^2 - f - 6)$:	$-12f^4$	$+ 3f^3$	$+ 18f^2$		
$3f(4f^2 - f - 6)$:		$12f^3$	$- 3f^2$	$- 18f$	
$-2(4f^2 - f - 6)$:			$-8f^2$	$+ 2f$	$+ 12$
Add:	$-12f^4$	$+ 15f^3$	$+ 7f^2$	$- 16f$	$+ 12$

CHECK YOUR UNDERSTANDING

1. Expand and simplify.

a) $(3k + 4)(k^2 - 2k - 7)$

b) $(-2t^2 + 4t - 3)(5t^2 - 2t + 1)$

[Answers: a) $3k^3 - 2k^2 - 29k - 28$
b) $-10t^4 + 24t^3 - 25t^2 + 10t - 3$]

Both solutions to parts a and b use the distributive property. Which strategy for recording the products of terms do you prefer, and why?

One way to check that a product is likely correct is to substitute a number for the variable in both the trinomial product and its simplification. If both expressions are equal, the product is likely correct.
In *Example 1a*, substitute $h = 1$.

$(2h + 5)(h^2 + 3h - 4) = 2h^3 + 11h^2 + 7h - 20$

Left side: $(2h + 5)(h^2 + 3h - 4) = [2(1) + 5][(1)^2 + 3(1) - 4]$
$= (7)(0)$
$= 0$

Right side: $2h^3 + 11h^2 + 7h - 20 = 2(1)^3 + 11(1)^2 + 7(1) - 20$
$= 2 + 11 + 7 - 20$
$= 0$

Since the left side equals the right side, the product is likely correct.

In *Example 1b*, substitute $f = 1$.

$(-3f^2 + 3f - 2)(4f^2 - f - 6) = -12f^4 + 15f^3 + 7f^2 - 16f + 12$

Left side: $(-3f^2 + 3f - 2)(4f^2 - f - 6)$

$= [(-3)(1)^2 + 3(1) - 2)\ [(4(1)^2 - (1) - 6]$

$= (-2)(-3)$

$= 6$

Right side: $-12f^4 + 15f^3 + 7f^2 - 16f + 12$

$= -12(1)^4 + 15(1)^3 + 7(1)^2 - 16(1) + 12$

$= -12 + 15 + 7 - 16 + 12$

$= 6$

Since the left side equals the right side, the product is likely correct.

Example 2 Multiplying Polynomials in More than One Variable

Expand and simplify.

a) $(2r + 5t)^2$ **b)** $(3x - 2y)(4x - 3y + 5)$

SOLUTION

a) $(2r + 5t)^2 = (2r + 5t)(2r + 5t)$

$= 2r(2r + 5t) + 5t(2r + 5t)$

$= 2r(2r) + 2r(5t) + 5t(2r) + 5t(5t)$

$= 4r^2 + 10rt + 10rt + 25t^2$ Combine like terms.

$= 4r^2 + 20rt + 25t^2$

b) $(3x - 2y)(4x - 3y + 5)$

$= 3x(4x - 3y + 5) - 2y(4x - 3y + 5)$

$= 3x(4x) + 3x(-3y) + 3x(5) - 2y(4x) - 2y(-3y) - 2y(5)$

$= 12x^2 - 9xy + 15x - 8xy + 6y^2 - 10y$ Collect like terms.

$= 12x^2 - 9xy - 8xy + 15x + 6y^2 - 10y$ Combine like terms.

$= 12x^2 - 17xy + 15x + 6y^2 - 10y$

CHECK YOUR UNDERSTANDING

2. Expand and simplify.

a) $(4k - 3m)^2$

b) $(2v - 5w)(3v + 2w - 7)$

[Answers: a) $16k^2 - 24km + 9m^2$
b) $6v^2 - 11vw - 14v - 10w^2 + 35w$]

Look at the factors and product in part a. How could you write the product without using the distributive property?

Example 3 Simplifying Sums and Differences of Polynomial Products

Expand and simplify.

a) $(2c - 3)(c + 5) + 3(c - 3)(-3c + 1)$

b) $(3x + y - 1)(2x - 4) - (3x + 2y)^2$

SOLUTION

Use the order of operations. Multiply before adding and subtracting. Then combine like terms.

a) $(2c - 3)(c + 5) + 3(c - 3)(-3c + 1)$

$= 2c(c + 5) - 3(c + 5) + 3[c(-3c + 1) - 3(-3c + 1)]$

$= 2c^2 + 10c - 3c - 15 + 3[-3c^2 + c + 9c - 3]$

$= 2c^2 + 7c - 15 + 3[-3c^2 + 10c - 3]$

$= 2c^2 + 7c - 15 - 9c^2 + 30c - 9$

$= -7c^2 + 37c - 24$

b) $(3x + y - 1)(2x - 4) - (3x + 2y)^2$

$= 3x(2x - 4) + y(2x - 4) - 1(2x - 4) - (3x + 2y)(3x + 2y)$

$= 6x^2 - 12x + 2xy - 4y - 2x + 4 -$
$[3x(3x + 2y) + 2y(3x + 2y)]$

$= 6x^2 - 14x + 2xy - 4y + 4 - [9x^2 + 6xy + 6xy + 4y^2]$

$= 6x^2 - 14x + 2xy - 4y + 4 - [9x^2 + 12xy + 4y^2]$

$= 6x^2 - 14x + 2xy - 4y + 4 - 9x^2 - 12xy - 4y^2$

$= -3x^2 - 14x - 10xy - 4y + 4 - 4y^2$

CHECK YOUR UNDERSTANDING

3. Expand and simplify.

a) $(4m + 1)(3m - 2)$
$+ 2(2m - 1)(-3m + 4)$

b) $(6h + k - 2)(2h - 3)$
$- (4h - 3k)^2$

[Answers: a) $17m - 10$
b) $-4h^2 - 22h + 26hk - 3k + 6 - 9k^2$]

Discuss the Ideas

1. How is the process for multiplying polynomials with more than 2 terms like multiplying binomials? How is it different?

2. What strategies can you use to check that you have correctly multiplied two polynomials?

3. When you substitute a number for a variable to check that a polynomial product is correct, would 0 be a suitable number to substitute? Would 9 be a suitable number? Explain.

Exercises

A

4. Expand and simplify.

a) $(g + 1)(g^2 + 2g + 3)$

b) $(2 + t + t^2)(1 + 3t + t^2)$

c) $(2w + 3)(w^2 + 4w + 7)$

d) $(4 + 3n + n^2)(3 + 5n + n^2)$

5. Expand and simplify.

a) $(2z + y)(3z + y)$

b) $(4f - 3g)(3f - 4g + 1)$

c) $(2a + 3b)(4a + 5b)$

d) $(3a - 4b + 1)(4a - 5b)$

e) $(2r + s)^2$

f) $(3t - 2u)^2$

B

6. a) Expand and simplify.

i) $(2x + y)(2x + y)$

ii) $(5r + 2s)(5r + 2s)$

iii) $(6c + 5d)(6c + 5d)$

iv) $(5v + 7w)(5v + 7w)$

v) $(2x - y)(2x - y)$

vi) $(5r - 2s)(5r - 2s)$

vii) $(6c - 5d)(6c - 5d)$

viii) $(5v - 7w)(5v - 7w)$

b) What patterns do you see in the factors and products in part a? Use these patterns to expand and simplify each product without using the distributive property.

i) $(p + 3q)(p + 3q)$

ii) $(2s - 7t)(2s - 7t)$

iii) $(5g + 4h)(5g + 4h)$

iv) $(10h - 7k)(10h - 7k)$

7. a) Expand and simplify.

i) $(x + 2y)(x - 2y)$

ii) $(3r - 4s)(3r + 4s)$

iii) $(5c + 3d)(5c - 3d)$

iv) $(2v - 7w)(2v + 7w)$

b) What patterns do you see in the factors and products in part a? Use these patterns to expand and simplify each product without using the distributive property.

i) $(11g + 5h)(11g - 5h)$

ii) $(25m - 7n)(25m + 7n)$

8. Expand and simplify.

a) $(3y - 2)(y^2 + y - 8)$

b) $(4r + 1)(r^2 - 2r - 3)$

c) $(b^2 + 9b - 2)(2b - 1)$

d) $(x^2 + 6x + 1)(3x - 7)$

9. Expand and simplify.

a) $(x + y)(x + y + 3)$

b) $(x + 2)(x + y + 1)$

c) $(a + b)(a + b + c)$

d) $(3 + t)(2 + t + s)$

10. Expand and simplify.

a) $(x + 2y)(x - 2y - 1)$

b) $(2c - 3d)(c + d + 1)$

c) $(a - 5b)(a + 2b - 4)$

d) $(p - 2q)(p + 4q - r)$

11. Find and correct the errors in this solution.

$$\begin{aligned} & (2r - 3s)(r - 5s + 6) \\ &= 2r(r - 5s + 6) - 3s(r - 5s + 6) \\ &= 2r^2 - 5rs + 12r - 3rs - 15s^2 - 18s \\ &= 2r^2 - 8rs + 12r - 33s^2 \end{aligned}$$

12. The area of the base of a right rectangular prism is $x^2 + 3x + 2$. The height of the prism is $x + 7$. Write, then simplify an expression for the volume of the prism.

13. Expand and simplify. Substitute a number for the variable to check each product.

a) $(r^2 + 3r + 2)(4r^2 + r + 1)$

b) $(2d^2 + 2d + 1)(d^2 + 6d + 3)$

c) $(4c^2 - 2c - 3)(-c^2 + 6c + 2)$

d) $(-4n^2 - n + 3)(-2n^2 + 5n - 1)$

14. Find and correct the errors in this solution.

$$\begin{aligned} & (3g^2 + 4g - 2)(-g^2 - g + 4) \\ &= -3g^4 - 3g^3 + 12g^2 - 4g^3 + 4g^2 + 8g \\ &\quad + 2g^2 + 2g + 8 \\ &= -3g^4 + 5g^3 + 6g^2 + 10g + 8 \end{aligned}$$

15. Expand and simplify.

a) $(3s + 5)(2s + 2) + (3s + 7)(s + 6)$

b) $(2x + 3)(5x + 4) + (x - 4)(3x - 7)$

c) $(3m + 4)(m - 4n) + (5m - 2)(3m - 6n)$

d) $(4y - 5)(3y + 2) - (3y + 2)(4y - 5)$

e) $(3x - 2)^2 - (2x + 6)(3x - 1)$

f) $(2a + 1)(4a - 3) - (a - 2)^2$

16. A box with no top is made from a piece of cardboard 20 cm by 10 cm. Equal squares are cut from each corner and the sides are folded up.

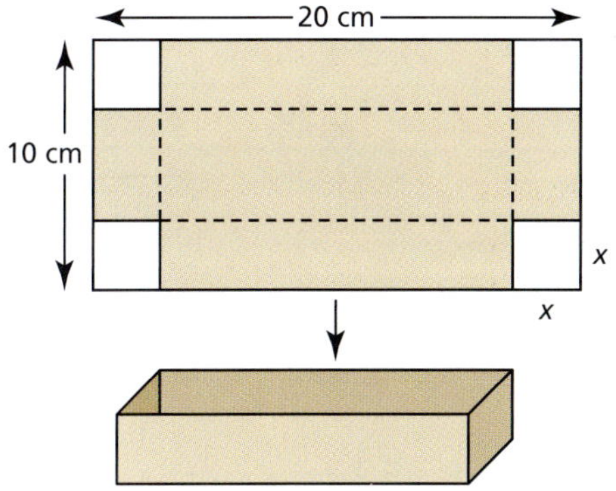

Let x centimetres represent the side length of each square cut out. Write a polynomial to represent each measurement. Simplify each polynomial.

a) the length of the box
b) the width of the box
c) the area of the base of the box
d) the volume of the box

17. Each shape is a rectangle. Write a polynomial to represent the area of each shaded region. Simplify each polynomial.

a)

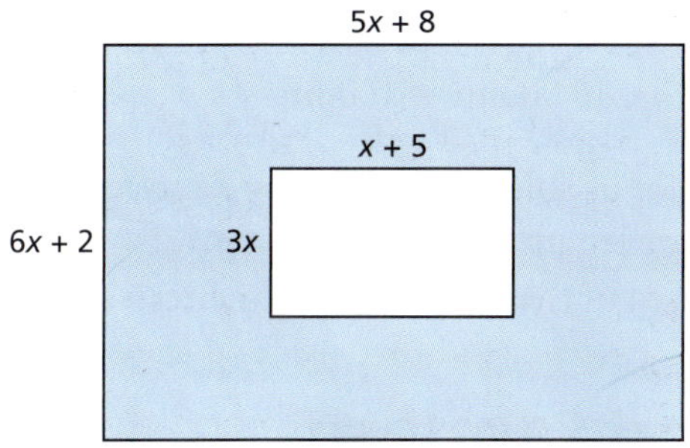

b)

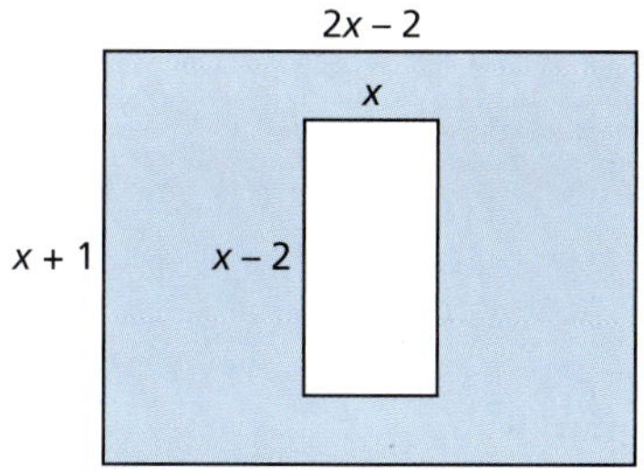

C

18. Expand and simplify.
a) $(x - 2)^3$
b) $(2y + 5)^3$
c) $(4a - 3b)^3$
d) $(c + d)^3$

19. Expand and simplify.
a) $2a(2a - 1)(3a + 2)$
b) $-3r(r - 1)(2r + 1)$
c) $5x^2(2x - 1)(4x - 3)$
d) $-xy(2x + 5)(4x - 5)$
e) $2b(2b - c)(b + c)$
f) $y^2(y^2 + 1)(y^2 - 1)$

20. A cube has edge length $2x + 3$.
a) Write then simplify an expression for the volume of the cube.
b) Write then simplify an expression for the surface area of the cube.

21. Expand and simplify.
a) $(3x + 4)(x - 5)(2x + 8)$
b) $(b - 7)(b + 8)(3b - 4)$
c) $(2x - 5)(3x + 4)^2$
d) $(5a - 3)^2(2a - 7)$
e) $(2k - 3)(2k + 3)^2$

22. Expand and simplify.
a) $(x + y + 1)^3$
b) $(x - y - 1)^3$
c) $(x + y + z)^3$
d) $(x - y - z)^3$

Reflect

What strategies do you know for multiplying two binomials? How can you use or adapt those strategies to multiply two trinomials? Include examples in your explanation.

3.8 Factoring Special Polynomials

LESSON FOCUS

Investigate some special factoring patterns.

Make Connections

The area of a square plot of land is one hectare (1 ha).

1 ha = 10 000 m^2

So, one side of the plot has length $\sqrt{10\,000}$ m = 100 m

Suppose the side length of the plot of land is increased by x metres.
What binomial represents the side length of the plot in metres?
What trinomial represents the area of the plot in square metres?

Construct Understanding

THINK ABOUT IT

Work with a partner.

You may need algebra tiles.

- Determine each product.

$(x + 1)^2$	$(x + 2)^2$	$(x + 3)^2$
$(x - 1)^2$	$(x - 2)^2$	$(x - 3)^2$
$(2x + 1)^2$	$(3x + 1)^2$	$(4x + 1)^2$
$(2x - 1)^2$	$(3x - 1)^2$	$(4x - 1)^2$

- What patterns do you see in the trinomials and their factors above?
  How could you use the patterns to factor these trinomials?
  $4x^2 + 20x + 25$ $\qquad$ $9x^2 - 12x + 4$
- Write two more polynomials that have the same pattern, then factor the polynomials.
  Write a strategy for factoring polynomials of this type.

Here is a square with side length $a + b$:

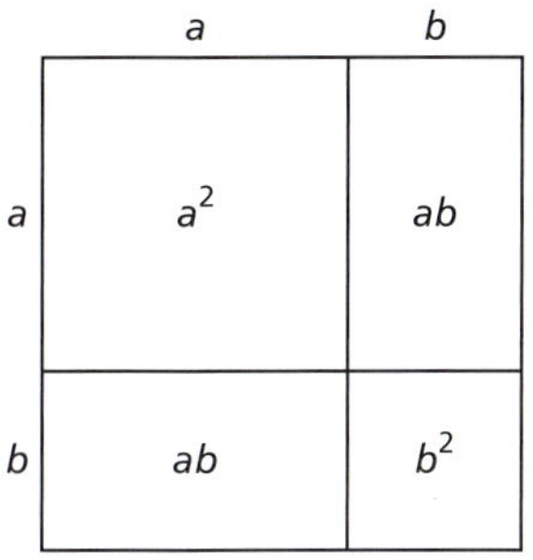

Its area is: $(a + b)^2 = (a + b)(a + b)$

$$= a(a + b) + b(a + b)$$

$$= a^2 + ab + ab + b^2$$

$$= a^2 + 2ab + b^2$$

We say that $a^2 + 2ab + b^2$ is a **perfect square trinomial.**

The square of the 1st term in the binomial

Twice the product of the first and second terms in the binomial

The square of the 2nd term in the binomial

$$(a + b)^2 = a^2 + 2ab + b^2$$

Perfect Square Trinomial

The area model of a perfect square trinomial results in a square.

In factored form, a perfect square trinomial is:
$a^2 + 2ab + b^2 = (a + b)(a + b)$, or $(a + b)^2$

And, $a^2 - 2ab + b^2 = (a - b)(a - b)$, or $(a - b)^2$

We can use these patterns to factor perfect square trinomials.

Example 1 Factoring a Perfect Square Trinomial

Factor each trinomial. Verify by multiplying the factors.

a) $4x^2 + 12x + 9$ **b)** $4 - 20x + 25x^2$

SOLUTION

a) $4x^2 + 12x + 9$

Arrange algebra tiles to form a rectangle.

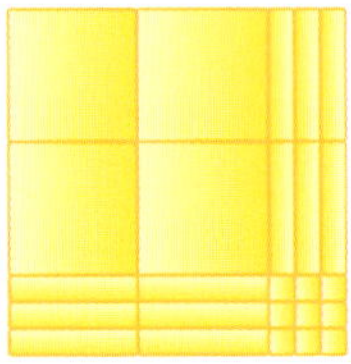

The rectangle is a square with side length $2x + 3$.

$4x^2 + 12x + 9 = (2x + 3)^2$

To verify, multiply:

$$\begin{aligned}(2x + 3)(2x + 3) &= 2x(2x + 3) + 3(2x + 3)\\ &= 4x^2 + 6x + 6x + 9\\ &= 4x^2 + 12x + 9\end{aligned}$$

Since this trinomial is the same as the original trinomial, the factors are correct.

b) $4 - 20x + 25x^2$

The 1st term is a perfect square since $4 = (2)(2)$
The 3rd term is a perfect square since $25x^2 = (5x)(5x)$
The 2nd term is twice the product of $5x$ and 2:
$20x = 2(5x)(2)$

Since the 2nd term is negative, the operations in the binomial factors must be subtraction.

So, the trinomial is a perfect square and its factors are:
$(2 - 5x)(2 - 5x)$, or $(2 - 5x)^2$

To verify, multiply:

$$\begin{aligned}(2 - 5x)(2 - 5x) &= 2(2 - 5x) - 5x(2 - 5x)\\ &= 4 - 10x - 10x + 25x^2\\ &= 4 - 20x + 25x^2\end{aligned}$$

Since this trinomial is the same as the original trinomial, the factors are correct.

CHECK YOUR UNDERSTANDING

1. Factor each trinomial. Verify by multiplying the factors.

a) $36x^2 + 12x + 1$

b) $16 - 56x + 49x^2$

[Answers: a) $(6x + 1)^2$
b) $(4 - 7x)^2$]

When $ax^2 + bx + c$ is a perfect square trinomial, how are a, b, and c related?

In Lesson 3.7, you multiplied two binomials in two variables. We can use the inverse process to factor trinomials of this form. We can use the strategy of logical reasoning or decomposition.

Example 2 Factoring Trinomials in Two Variables

Factor each trinomial. Verify by multiplying the factors.

a) $2a^2 - 7ab + 3b^2$ **b)** $10c^2 - cd - 2d^2$

SOLUTION

a) $2a^2 - 7ab + 3b^2$

Use logical reasoning. Since the 3rd term in the trinomial is positive, the operations in the binomial factors will be the same. Since the 2nd term is negative, these operations will be subtraction.

The two binomials will have the form: $(?a - ?b)(?a - ?b)$

List the possible factors of $2a^2$ and $3b^2$, then use guess and test to determine which combination of products has the sum of $-7ab$.

$1a$ ╳ $-1b$	$1a$ ╳ $-3b$
$2a$ ╳ $-3b$	$2a$ ╳ $-1b$
$-3ab - 2ab = -5ab$	$-1ab - 6ab = -7ab$ ← This is the correct combination of factors.

Form the products, then add.

So, $2a^2 - 7ab + 3b^2 = (2a - b)(a - 3b)$

To verify, multiply:

$$\begin{aligned}(2a - b)(a - 3b) &= 2a(a - 3b) - b(a - 3b)\\ &= 2a^2 - 6ab - ab + 3b^2\\ &= 2a^2 - 7ab + 3b^2\end{aligned}$$

Since this trinomial is the same as the original trinomial, the factors are correct.

b) $10c^2 - cd - 2d^2$

Use decomposition. Since the 3rd term in the trinomial is negative, the operations in the binomial factors will be addition and subtraction.

The two binomials will have the form: $(?c + ?d)(?c - ?d)$

The product of the coefficients of c^2 and d^2 is: $10(-2) = -20$

Write $-1cd$ as a sum of two terms whose coefficients have a product of -20.

(Solution continues.)

CHECK YOUR UNDERSTANDING

2. Factor each trinomial. Verify by multiplying the factors.

a) $5c^2 - 13cd + 6d^2$

b) $3p^2 - 5pq - 2q^2$

[Answers: a) $(5c - 3d)(c - 2d)$ b) $(3p + q)(p - 2q)$]

Factors of −20	Sum of Factors
1, −20	1 − 20 = −19
−1, 20	−1 + 20 = 19
2, −10	2 − 10 = −8
−2, 10	−2 + 10 = 8
4, −5	4 − 5 = −1
−4, 5	−4 + 5 = 1

The two coefficients are 4 and −5, so write the trinomial $10c^2 - cd - 2d^2$ as $10c^2 + 4cd - 5cd - 2d^2$.

Remove a common factor from the 1st pair of terms, and from the 2nd pair of terms:

$10c^2 + 4cd - 5cd - 2d^2 = 2c(5c + 2d) - d(5c + 2d)$

Remove the common binomial factor.

So, $10c^2 - cd - 2d^2 = (5c + 2d)(2c - d)$

To verify, multiply:

$$\begin{aligned}(5c + 2d)(2c - d) &= 5c(2c - d) + 2d(2c - d)\\ &= 10c^2 - 5cd + 4cd - 2d^2\\ &= 10c^2 - cd - 2d^2\end{aligned}$$

Since this trinomial is the same as the original trinomial, the factors are correct.

Another example of a special polynomial is a **difference of squares**.

A difference of squares is a binomial of the form $a^2 - b^2$.

We can think of it as a trinomial with a middle term of 0.

That is, write $a^2 - b^2$ as $a^2 + 0ab - b^2$.

Consider the binomial $x^2 - 25$.

This is a difference of squares because $x^2 = (x)(x)$ and $25 = (5)(5)$.

We write $x^2 - 25$ as $x^2 - 0x - 25$.

To factor this trinomial, look for 2 integers whose product is −25 and whose sum is 0.

The two integers are 5 and −5.

So, $x^2 - 25 = (x + 5)(x - 5)$

This pattern is true for the difference of any two squares.

Difference of Squares

A difference of squares has the form $a^2 - b^2$.

In factored form, $a^2 - b^2 = (a - b)(a + b)$

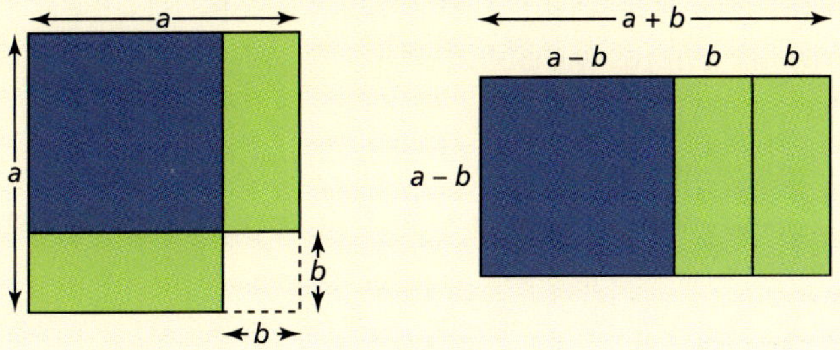

Example 3 Factoring a Difference of Squares

Factor each binomial.

a) $25 - 36x^2$ **b)** $5x^4 - 80y^4$

SOLUTION

a) $25 - 36x^2$

Write each term as a perfect square.

$$25 - 36x^2 = (5)^2 - (6x)^2$$

Write these terms in binomial factors.

$$= (5 + 6x)(5 - 6x)$$

b) $5x^4 - 80y^4$

As written, each term of the binomial is not a perfect square. But the terms have a common factor 5. Remove this common factor.

$$5x^4 - 80y^4$$

Now write each term in the binomial as a perfect square.

$$= 5(x^4 - 16y^4)$$

$$= 5[(x^2)^2 - (4y^2)^2]$$

Write these terms in binomial factors.

$$= 5(x^2 - 4y^2)(x^2 + 4y^2)$$

The 1st binomial is also a difference of squares.

$$= 5(x + 2y)(x - 2y)(x^2 + 4y^2)$$

CHECK YOUR UNDERSTANDING

3. Factor each binomial.

a) $81m^2 - 49$

b) $162v^4 - 2w^4$

[Answers: a) $(9m - 7)(9m + 7)$
b) $2(3v - w)(3v + w)(9v^2 + w^2)$]

Does a sum of squares factor? Explain.

Discuss the Ideas

1. How do the area models and rectangle diagrams support the naming of a perfect square trinomial and a difference of squares binomial?
2. Why is it useful to identify the factoring patterns for perfect square trinomials and difference of squares binomials?
3. Why can you use the factors of a trinomial in one variable to factor a corresponding trinomial in two variables?

Exercises

A

4. Expand and simplify.
   a) $(x + 2)^2$ b) $(3 - y)^2$
   c) $(5 + d)^2$ d) $(7 - f)^2$
   e) $(x + 2)(x - 2)$ f) $(3 - y)(3 + y)$
   g) $(5 + d)(5 - d)$ h) $(7 - f)(7 + f)$

5. Identify each polynomial as a perfect square trinomial, a difference of squares, or neither.
   a) $25 - t^2$
   b) $16m^2 + 49n^2$
   c) $4x^2 - 24xy + 9y^2$
   d) $9m^2 - 24mn + 16n^2$

6. Factor each binomial.
   a) $x^2 - 49$ b) $b^2 - 121$
   c) $1 - q^2$ d) $36 - c^2$

B

7. a) Factor each trinomial.
   i) $a^2 + 10a + 25$ ii) $b^2 - 12b + 36$
   iii) $c^2 + 14c + 49$ iv) $d^2 - 16d + 64$
   v) $e^2 + 18e + 81$ vi) $f^2 - 20f + 100$
   b) What patterns do you see in the trinomials and their factors in part a? Write the next 4 trinomials in the pattern and their factors.

8. Factor each trinomial. Verify by multiplying the factors.
   a) $4x^2 - 12x + 9$ b) $9 + 30n + 25n^2$
   c) $81 - 36v + 4v^2$ d) $25 + 40h + 16h^2$
   e) $9g^2 + 48g + 64$ f) $49r^2 - 28r + 4$

9. a) Cut out a square from a piece of paper. Let x represent the side length of the square. Write an expression for the area of the square.
   Cut a smaller square from one corner. Let y represent the side length of the cut-out square. Write an expression for the area of the cut-out square.
   Write an expression for the area of the piece that remains.

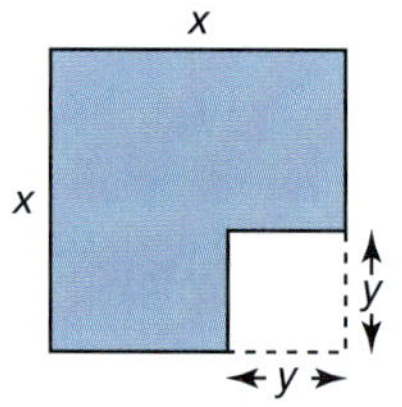

   b) Cut the L-shaped piece into 2 congruent pieces, then arrange as shown below.

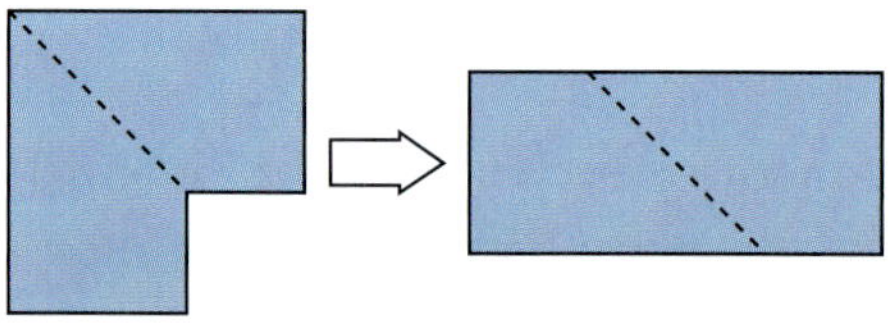

   What are the dimensions of this rectangle, in terms of x and y?
   What is the area of this rectangle?
   c) Explain how the results of parts a and b illustrate the difference of squares.

10. Factor each binomial. Verify by multiplying the factors.

a) $9d^2 - 16f^2$ b) $25s^2 - 64t^2$
c) $144a^2 - 9b^2$ d) $121m^2 - n^2$
e) $81k^2 - 49m^2$ f) $100y^2 - 81z^2$
g) $v^2 - 36t^2$ h) $4j^2 - 225h^2$

11. Factor each trinomial.

a) $y^2 + 7yz + 10z^2$ b) $4w^2 - 8wx - 21x^2$
c) $12s^2 - 7su + u^2$ d) $3t^2 - 7tv + 4v^2$
e) $10r^2 + 9rs - 9s^2$ f) $8p^2 + 18pq - 35q^2$

12. Factor each trinomial. Which trinomials are perfect squares?

a) $4x^2 + 28xy + 49y^2$ b) $15m^2 + 7mn - 4n^2$
c) $16r^2 + 8rt + t^2$ d) $9a^2 - 42ab + 49b^2$
e) $12h^2 + 25hk + 12k^2$ f) $15f^2 - 31fg + 10g^2$

13. Factor.

a) $8m^2 - 72n^2$ b) $8z^2 + 8yz + 2y^2$
c) $12x^2 - 27y^2$ d) $8p^2 + 40pq + 50q^2$
e) $-24u^2 - 6uv + 9v^2$ f) $-18b^2 + 128c^2$

14. A circular fountain has a radius of r centimetres. It is surrounded by a circular flower bed with radius R centimetres.

a) Sketch and label a diagram.
b) How can you use the difference of squares to determine an expression for the area of the flower bed?
c) Use your expression from part b to calculate the area of the flower bed when $r = 150$ cm and $R = 350$ cm.

15. a) Find an integer to replace □ so that each trinomial is a perfect square.

i) $x^2 + \square x + 49$
ii) $4a^2 + 20ab + \square b^2$
iii) $\square c^2 - 24cd + 16d^2$

b) How many integers are possible for each trinomial in part a? Explain why no more integers are possible.

16. Find consecutive integers a, b, and c so that the trinomial $ax^2 + bx + c$ can be factored. How many possibilities can you find?

17. Use mental math to determine (199)(201). Explain your strategy.

18. Determine the area of the shaded region. Simplify your answer.

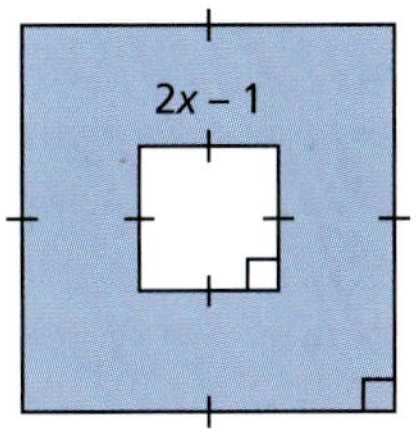

C

19. a) Identify each expression as a perfect square trinomial, a difference of squares, or neither. Justify your answers.

i) $(x^2 + 5)^2$
ii) $-100 + r^2$
iii) $81a^2b^2 - 1$
iv) $16s^4 + 8s^2 + 1$

b) Which expressions in part a can be factored? Factor each expression you identify.

20. Factor fully.

a) $x^4 - 13x^2 + 36$
b) $a^4 - 17a^2 + 16$
c) $y^4 - 5y^2 + 4$

21. Factor, if possible. For each binomial that cannot be factored, explain why.

a) $8d^2 - 32e^2$
b) $25m^2 - \frac{1}{4}n^2$
c) $18x^2y^2 - 50y^4$
d) $25s^2 + 49t^2$
e) $10a^2 - 7b^2$
f) $\frac{x^2}{16} - \frac{y^2}{49}$

Reflect

Explain how a difference of squares binomial is a special case of a trinomial. How is factoring a difference of squares like factoring a trinomial? How is it different? Include examples in your explanation.

STUDY GUIDE

CONCEPT SUMMARY

Big Ideas	Applying the Big Ideas
▪ Arithmetic operations on polynomials are based on the arithmetic operations on whole numbers, and have similar properties.	This means that: ▪ Factors and multiples can be found for both whole numbers and polynomials.
▪ Multiplying and factoring are inverse processes, and a rectangle diagram can be used to represent them.	▪ We multiply factors to determine their product. ▪ For trinomials, the factors can be constant terms, monomials, binomials, or trinomials. When we multiply the factors, we expand. ▪ We factor a polynomial by writing it as a product of its factors. ▪ Algebra tiles or a rectangle diagram can represent a product of polynomials.

Reflect on the Chapter

- Describe how the operations of addition, subtraction, and multiplication on whole numbers are similar to these operations on polynomials. Include examples in your description.
- Explain how a rectangle diagram is used to multiply and factor whole numbers and to multiply and factor polynomials. Why can the rectangle diagram be used for both multiplying and factoring?

SKILLS SUMMARY

Skill	Description	Example
Determine prime factors, greatest common factor (GCF), and least common multiple (LCM). [3.1]	Express a whole number as the product of its prime factors, using powers where possible. Use the prime factors to determine GCF and LCM.	As a product of prime factors: $64 = 2^6$ and $80 = 2^4 \cdot 5$ The GCF of 64 and 80 is: $2^4 = 16$ The LCM of 64 and 60 is: $2^6 \cdot 5 = 320$
Determine whether a number is a perfect square or a perfect cube. [3.2]	Use prime factors to check for perfect squares and perfect cubes.	$4225 = 5^2 \cdot 13^2$ Since the factors occur in pairs, 4225 is a perfect square and $\sqrt{4225}$ is: $5 \cdot 13 = 65$ 4225 is not a perfect cube because the factors do not occur in sets of 3.
Determine common factors for a polynomial. [3.3]	Look at the terms and determine their greatest common factor. Multiply the factors to verify.	$3x^2y - 21xy + 30y^2$ $= 3y(x^2 - 7x + 10y)$
Multiply binomials of the form $(x + a)(x + b)$ and $(ax + b)(cx + d)$. [3.4, 3.5, 3.6]	Use algebra tiles, diagrams, and the distributive property to multiply.	$(3d + 2)(4d - 5)$ $= 12d^2 - 15d + 8d - 10$ $= 12d^2 - 7d - 10$
Factor polynomials of the form $x^2 + bx + c$ and $ax^2 + bx + c$. [3.4, 3.5, 3.6]	Use algebra tiles, diagrams, and symbols to factor. Look for common factors first. Multiply the factors to verify.	$5x^2 - 9x - 2$ $= 5x^2 - 10x + x - 2$ $= 5x(x - 2) + 1(x - 2)$ $= (x - 2)(5x + 1)$
Multiply polynomials. [3.7]	Use the distributive property to multiply each term in the first polynomial by each term in the second polynomial.	$(x - 4)(3x^3 + 5x - 2)$ $= 3x^4 + 5x^2 - 2x - 12x^3 - 20x + 8$ $= 3x^4 - 12x^3 + 5x^2 - 22x + 8$
Factor special polynomials. [3.8]	Factor a perfect square trinomial and a difference of squares binomial. Look for common factors first. Multiply the factors to verify.	$25x^2 - 49y^2$ $= (5x + 7y)(5x - 7y)$ $4x^2 + 16xy + 16y^2$ $= 4(x + 2y)(x + 2y)$

REVIEW

3.1

1. Determine the prime factors of each number, then write the number as a product of its factors.

a) 594 **b)** 2100
c) 4875 **d)** 9009

2. Determine the greatest common factor of each set of numbers.

a) 120, 160, 180 **b)** 245, 280, 385
c) 176, 320, 368 **d)** 484, 496, 884

3. Determine the least common multiple of each set of numbers.

a) 70, 90, 140 **b)** 120, 130, 309
c) 200, 250, 500 **d)** 180, 240, 340

4. A necklace has 3 strands of beads. Each strand begins and ends with a red bead. If a red bead occurs every 6th bead on one strand, every 4th bead on the second strand, and every 10th bead on the third strand, what is the least number of beads each strand can have?

5. Simplify. How did you use the greatest common factor or the least common multiple?

a) $\frac{1015}{1305}$ **b)** $\frac{2475}{3825}$

c) $\frac{6656}{7680}$ **d)** $\frac{7}{36} + \frac{15}{64}$

e) $\frac{5}{9} \div \frac{3}{4}$ **f)** $\frac{28}{128} - \frac{12}{160}$

3.2

6. How do you know that the area of each square is a perfect square? Determine the side length of each square.

a)

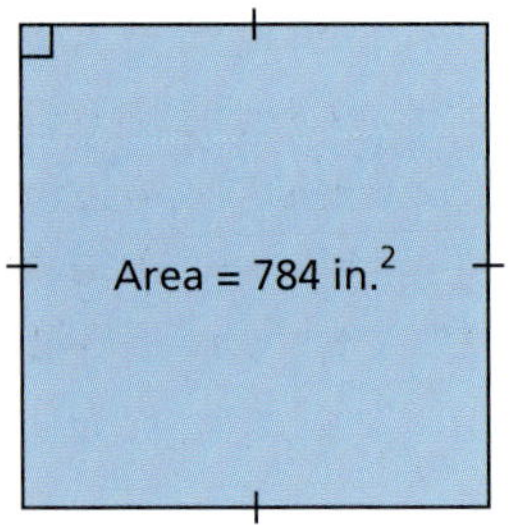

b)

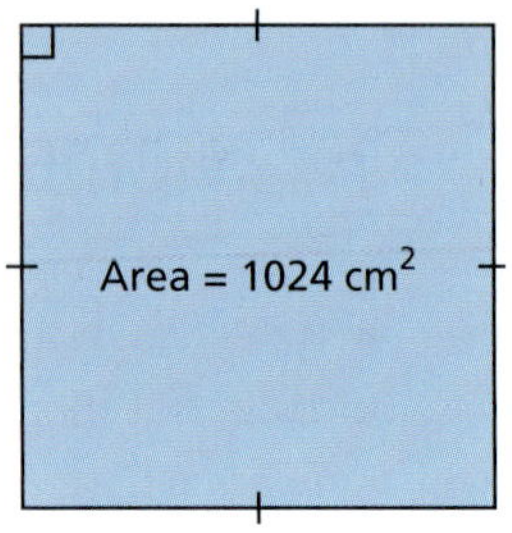

7. How do you know that the volume of each cube is a perfect cube? Determine the edge length of each cube.

a)

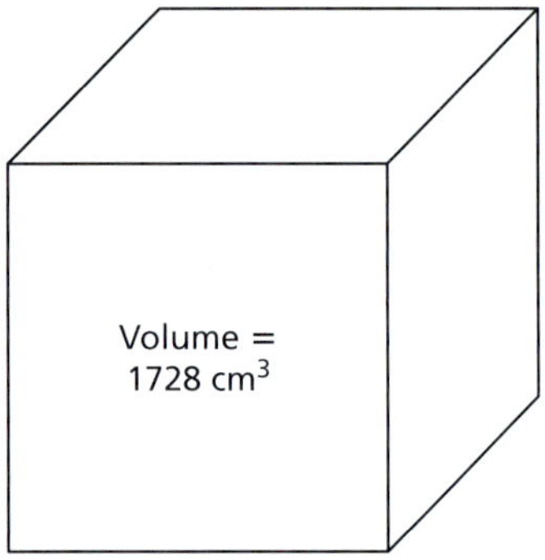

b)

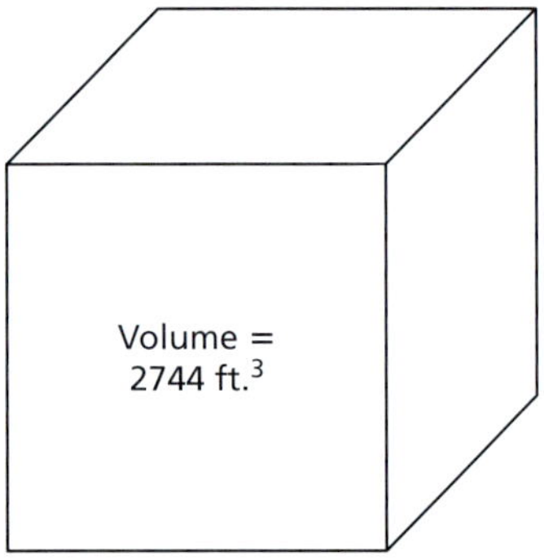

8. Is each number a perfect square, a perfect cube, or neither? Determine the square root of each perfect square and the cube root of each perfect cube.

a) 256 **b)** 324
c) 729 **d)** 1298
e) 1936 **f)** 9261

9. A square has area 18 225 square feet. What is the perimeter of the square?

10. A cube has surface area 11 616 cm^2. What is the edge length of the cube?

3.3

11. Factor each binomial. For which binomials could you use algebra tiles to factor? Explain why you could not use algebra tiles to factor the other binomials.

a) $8m - 4m^2$
b) $-3 + 9g^2$
c) $28a^2 - 7a^3$
d) $6a^2b^3c - 15a^2b^2c^2$
e) $-24m^2n - 6mn^2$
f) $14b^3c^2 - 21a^3b^2$

12. Factor each trinomial. Verify that the factors are correct.

a) $12 + 6g - 3g^2$
b) $3c^2d - 10cd - 2d$
c) $8mn^2 - 12mn - 16m^2n$
d) $y^4 - 12y^2 + 24y$
e) $30x^2y - 20x^2y^2 + 10x^3y^2$
f) $-8b^3 + 20b^2 - 4b$

13. Factor each polynomial. Verify that the factors are correct.

a) $8x^2 - 12x$
b) $3y^3 - 12y^2 + 15y$
c) $4b^3 - 2b - 6b^2$
d) $6m^3 - 12m - 24m^2$

14. Find and correct the errors in each factorization.

a) $15p^2q + 25pq^2 - 35q^3$
$= 5(3p^2q + 5pq^2 - 7q^3)$
b) $-12mn + 15m^2 + 18n^2$
$= -3(-4mn + 15m^2 + 18n^2)$

3.4

15. Use algebra tiles. Sketch the tiles for each trinomial that can be arranged as a rectangle.

a) $x^2 + 8x + 12$
b) $x^2 + 7x + 10$
c) $x^2 + 4x + 1$
d) $x^2 + 8x + 15$

16. Use algebra tiles. Sketch the tiles for each trinomial that can be arranged as a rectangle.

a) $2k^2 + 3k + 2$
b) $3g^2 + 4g + 1$
c) $2t^2 + 7t + 6$
d) $7h^2 + 5h + 1$

17. Suppose you have one x^2-tile and five 1-tiles. What is the fewest number of x-tiles you need to arrange the tiles in a rectangle?

3.5

18. Expand and simplify. Sketch a rectangle diagram to illustrate each product.

a) $(g + 5)(g - 4)$
b) $(h + 7)(h + 7)$
c) $(k - 4)(k + 11)$
d) $(9 + s)(9 - s)$
e) $(12 - t)(12 - t)$
f) $(7 + r)(6 - r)$
g) $(y - 3)(y - 11)$
h) $(x - 5)(x + 5)$

19. Factor. Check by expanding.

a) $q^2 + 6q + 8$
b) $n^2 - 4n - 45$
c) $54 - 15s + s^2$
d) $k^2 - 9k - 90$
e) $x^2 - x - 20$
f) $12 - 7y + y^2$

20. a) Factor each trinomial.

i) $m^2 + 7m + 12$
ii) $m^2 + 8m + 12$
iii) $m^2 + 13m + 12$
iv) $m^2 - 7m + 12$
v) $m^2 - 8m + 12$
vi) $m^2 - 13m + 12$

b) Look at the trinomials and their factors in part a. Are there any other trinomials that begin with m^2, end with $+12$, and can be factored? If your answer is yes, list the trinomials and their factors. If your answer is no, explain why there are no more trinomials.

21. Find and correct the errors in each factorization.

a) $u^2 - 12u + 27 = (u + 3)(u + 9)$
b) $v^2 - v - 20 = (v - 4)(v + 5)$
c) $w^2 + 10w - 24 = (w + 4)(w + 6)$

3.6

22. Use algebra tiles to determine each product. Sketch the tiles to show how you used them.

a) $(h + 4)(2h + 2)$
b) $(j + 5)(3j + 1)$
c) $(3k + 2)(2k + 1)$
d) $(4m + 1)(2m + 3)$

23. For each set of algebra tiles below:

i) Write the trinomial that the algebra tiles represent.

ii) Arrange the tiles to form a rectangle. Sketch the tiles.

iii) Use the rectangle to factor the trinomial.

a) 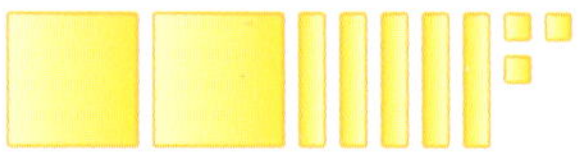

b) 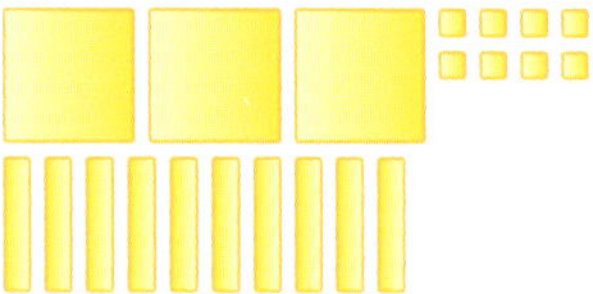

24. Expand and simplify. Sketch a rectangle diagram to illustrate each product.

a) $(2r + 7)(3r + 5)$ b) $(9y + 1)(y - 9)$

c) $(2a - 7)(2a - 6)$ d) $(3w - 2)(3w - 1)$

e) $(4p + 5)(4p + 5)$ f) $(-y + 1)(-3y - 1)$

25. Factor. Check by expanding.

a) $4k^2 - 7k + 3$ b) $6c^2 - 13c - 5$

c) $4b^2 - 5b - 6$ d) $6a^2 - 31a + 5$

e) $28x^2 + 9x - 4$ f) $21x^2 + 8x - 4$

26. Find and correct the errors in each factorization.

a) $6m^2 + 5m - 21 = (6m - 20)(m + 1)$

b) $12n^2 - 17n - 5 = (4n - 1)(3n + 5)$

c) $20p^2 - 9p - 20 = (4p + 4)(5p - 5)$

3.7

27. Expand and simplify. Check the product by substituting a number for the variable.

a) $(c + 1)(c^2 + 3c + 2)$

b) $(5 - 4r)(6 + 3r - 2r^2)$

c) $(-j^2 + 3j + 1)(2j + 11)$

d) $(3x^2 + 7x + 2)(2x - 3)$

28. Expand and simplify.

a) $(4m - p)^2$

b) $(3g - 4h)^2$

c) $(y - 2z)(y + z - 2)$

d) $(3c - 4d)(7 - 6c + 5d)$

29. Expand and simplify. Check the product by substituting a number for the variable.

a) $(m^2 + 3m + 2)(2m^2 + m + 5)$

b) $(1 - 3x + 2x^2)(5 + 4x - x^2)$

c) $(-2k^2 + 7k + 6)(3k^2 - 2k - 3)$

d) $(-3 - 5h + 2h^2)(-1 + h + h^2)$

30. Expand and simplify.

a) $(5a + 1)(4a + 2) + (a - 5)(2a - 1)$

b) $(6c - 2)(4c + 2) - (c + 7)^2$

31. Suppose n represents an even integer.

a) Write an expression for each of the next two consecutive even integers.

b) Write an expression for the product of the 3 integers. Simplify the expression.

3.8

32. Factor.

a) $81 - 4b^2$ b) $16v^2 - 49$

c) $64g^2 - 16h^2$ d) $18m^2 - 2n^2$

33. Factor each trinomial. Check by multiplying the factors.

a) $m^2 - 14m + 49$ b) $n^2 + 10n + 25$

c) $4p^2 + 12p + 9$ d) $16 - 40q + 25q^2$

e) $4r^2 + 28r + 49$ f) $36 - 132s + 121s^2$

34. Factor each trinomial. Which strategy did you use each time?

a) $g^2 + 6gh + 9h^2$

b) $16j^2 - 24jk + 9k^2$

c) $25t^2 + 20tu + 4u^2$

d) $9v^2 - 48vw + 64w^2$

35. Determine the area of the shaded region. Write your answer in simplest form.

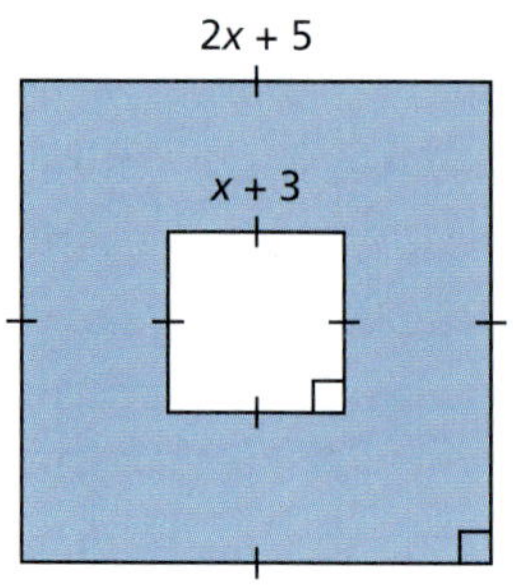

PRACTICE TEST

For questions 1 and 2, choose the correct answer: A, B, C, or D

1. For the number 64, which statement is not true?

A. It has only one factor.

B. It is a perfect square.

C. It is a perfect cube.

D. Its prime factor is 2.

2. The factorization of the trinomial $2x^2 + 7x + 6$ is:

A. $(2x + 1)(x + 6)$ **B.** $(2x + 2)(x + 3)$

C. $(2x + 3)(x + 2)$ **D.** $(2x + 6)(x + 1)$

3. Write each number below as a product of its prime factors, then determine the least common multiple and the greatest common factor of the 3 numbers.

20 45 50

4. Look at the numbers in question 3.

a) What would you have to multiply each number by to produce a number that is:

i) a perfect square? **ii)** a perfect cube?

b) Why is there more than one answer for each of part a?

5. Expand and simplify, using the strategy indicated.
Sketch a diagram to illustrate each strategy.

a) Use algebra tiles: $(2c + 5)(3c + 2)$

b) Use an area model: $(9 + 4r)(8 + 6r)$

c) Use a rectangle diagram: $(4t - 5)(3t + 7)$

6. Expand and simplify.

a) $(2p - 1)(p^2 + 2p - 7)$

b) $(e + 2f)(2f^2 + 5f + 3e^2)$

c) $(3y + 2z)(y + 4z) - (5y - 3z)(2y - 8z)$

7. Factor each polynomial. For which trinomials could you use algebra tiles? Explain.

a) $f^2 + 17f + 16$ **b)** $c^2 - 13c + 22$

c) $4t^2 + 9t - 28$ **d)** $4r^2 + 20rs + 25s^2$

e) $6x^2 - 17xy + 5y^2$ **f)** $h^2 - 25j^2$

8. A cube has edge length $2r + 1$. A right square prism with dimensions r by r by $2r + 1$ is removed from the cube.
Write an expression for the volume that remains. Simplify the expression.

9. Write all the trinomials that begin with $8t^2$, end with $+3$, and can be factored.
How do you know you have found all the trinomials?

4 Roots and Powers

BUILDING ON

- determining the square root of a positive rational number
- applying the exponent laws for powers with integral bases and whole number exponents

BIG IDEAS

- Any number that can be written as the fraction $\frac{m}{n}$, $n \neq 0$, where m and n are integers, is rational.
- Exponents can be used to represent roots and reciprocals of rational numbers.
- The exponent laws can be extended to include powers with rational and variable bases, and rational exponents.

NEW VOCABULARY

irrational number
real number
entire radical
mixed radical

YUKON QUEST *This is a sled dog race from Whitehorse, Yukon, to Fairbanks, Alaska.*

MATH LAB

4.1 Estimating Roots

LESSON FOCUS

Explore decimal representations of different roots of numbers.

Make Connections

Since $3^2 = 9$, 3 is a square root of 9.

We write: $3 = \sqrt{9}$

Since $3^3 = 27$, 3 is the cube root of 27.

We write: $3 = \sqrt[3]{27}$

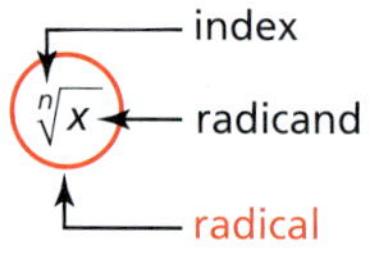

Since $3^4 = 81$, 3 is a fourth root of 81.

We write: $3 = \sqrt[4]{81}$

How would you write 5 as a square root?
A cube root? A fourth root?

Construct Understanding

TRY THIS

Work with a partner.

You will need a calculator to check your estimates.

A. Write the two consecutive perfect squares closest to 20. Estimate the value of $\sqrt{20}$. Square your estimate. Use this value to revise your estimate. Keep revising your estimate until the square of the estimate is within 1 decimal place of 20.

B. Write the two consecutive perfect cubes closest to 20. Estimate the value of $\sqrt[3]{20}$. Cube your estimate. Use this value to revise your estimate. Keep revising your estimate until the cube of the estimate is within 1 decimal place of 20.

C. Write the two consecutive perfect fourth powers closest to 20.
Use a strategy similar to that in Steps A and B to estimate a value for $\sqrt[4]{20}$.

D. Copy and complete this table. Use the strategies from Steps A to C to determine the value of each radical.

Radical	Value	Is the Value Exact or Approximate?
$\sqrt{16}$	4	Exact
$\sqrt{27}$	5.1962	Approximate
$\sqrt{\frac{16}{81}}$	$\frac{4}{9}$ or $0.\overline{4}$	Exact
$\sqrt{0.64}$		
$\sqrt[3]{16}$		
$\sqrt[3]{27}$		
$\sqrt[3]{\frac{16}{81}}$		
$\sqrt[3]{0.64}$		
$\sqrt[3]{-0.64}$		
$\sqrt[4]{16}$		
$\sqrt[4]{27}$		
$\sqrt[4]{\frac{16}{81}}$		
$\sqrt[4]{0.64}$		

Choose 3 different radicals.
Extend then complete the table for these radicals.

E. How can you tell if the value of a radical is a rational number? What strategies can you use to determine the value of the radical?

F. How can you tell if the value of a radical is *not* a rational number? What strategies can you use to estimate the value of the radical?

Assess Your Understanding

1. **a)** Give 4 examples of radicals. Use a different index for each radical.
b) Identify the radicand and index for each radical.
c) Explain the meaning of the index of each radical.

2. Evaluate each radical. Justify your answer.

a) $\sqrt{36}$ **b)** $\sqrt[3]{8}$ **c)** $\sqrt[4]{10\,000}$ **d)** $\sqrt[5]{-32}$

e) $\sqrt[3]{\frac{27}{125}}$ **f)** $\sqrt{2.25}$ **g)** $\sqrt[3]{0.125}$ **h)** $\sqrt[4]{625}$

3. Estimate the value of each radical to 1 decimal place.
What strategy did you use?

a) $\sqrt{8}$ **b)** $\sqrt[3]{9}$ **c)** $\sqrt[4]{10}$ **d)** $\sqrt{13}$

e) $\sqrt[3]{15}$ **f)** $\sqrt[4]{17}$ **g)** $\sqrt{19}$ **h)** $\sqrt[3]{20}$

4. **a)** What happens when you attempt to determine the square root of a number such as –4? Explain the result.
b) For which other radical indices do you get the same result with a negative radicand, as in part a?
c) When a radicand is negative:
i) Which types of radicals can be evaluated or estimated?
ii) Which types of radicals cannot be evaluated or estimated?

5. For each number below, write an equivalent form as:
i) a square root **ii)** a cube root **iii)** a fourth root

a) 2 **b)** 3 **c)** 4 **d)** 10 **e)** 0.9 **f)** 0.2

6. Choose values of n and x so that $\sqrt[n]{x}$ is:
a) a whole number **b)** a negative integer
c) a rational number **d)** an approximate decimal
Verify your answers.

4.2 Irrational Numbers

LESSON FOCUS

Identify and order irrational numbers.

The room below the rotunda in the Manitoba Legislative Building is the Pool of the Black Star. It has a circular floor.

Make Connections

The formulas for the area and circumference of a circle involve π, which is not a rational number because it cannot be written as a quotient of integers.

What other numbers are not rational?

Construct Understanding

TRY THIS

Work with a partner.

These are rational numbers.	These are not rational numbers.
$\sqrt{100}$ $\sqrt{0.25}$ $\sqrt[3]{8}$ 0.5	$\sqrt{0.24}$ $\sqrt[3]{9}$ $\sqrt{2}$
$\frac{5}{6}$ $\sqrt{\frac{9}{64}}$ 0.8^2 $\sqrt[5]{-32}$	$\sqrt{\frac{1}{3}}$ $\sqrt[4]{12}$

A. How are radicals that are rational numbers different from radicals that are not rational numbers?

B. Which of these radicals are rational numbers?
Which are not rational numbers? How do you know?

$\sqrt{1.44}$, $\sqrt{\frac{64}{81}}$, $\sqrt[3]{-27}$, $\sqrt{\frac{4}{5}}$, $\sqrt{5}$

C. Write 3 other radicals that are rational numbers.
Why are they rational?

D. Write 3 other radicals that are not rational numbers.
Why are they not rational?

Radicals that are square roots of perfect squares, cube roots of perfect cubes, and so on are rational numbers. Rational numbers have decimal representations that either terminate or repeat.

Irrational Numbers

An **irrational number** *cannot* be written in the form $\frac{m}{n}$, where m and n are integers, $n \neq 0$. The decimal representation of an irrational number neither terminates nor repeats.

When an irrational number is written as a radical, the radical is the *exact value* of the irrational number; for example, $\sqrt{2}$ and $\sqrt[3]{-50}$. We can use the square root and cube root keys on a calculator to determine *approximate values* of these irrational numbers.

There are other irrational numbers besides radicals; for example, π.

We can approximate the location of an irrational number on a number line. If we do not have a calculator, we use perfect powers to estimate the value. For example, to locate $\sqrt[3]{-50}$ on a number line,
we know that $\sqrt[3]{-27} = -3$ and $\sqrt[3]{-64} = -4$.

Guess: $\sqrt[3]{-50} \doteq -3.6$ Test: $(-3.6)^3 = -46.656$

Guess: $\sqrt[3]{-50} \doteq -3.7$ Test: $(-3.7)^3 = -50.653$

This is close enough to represent on a number line.

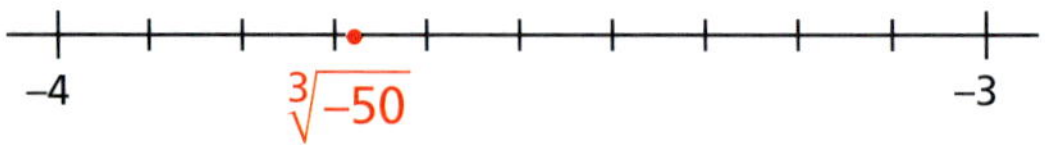

Since $(-3.7)^3 = -50.653$, then $\sqrt[3]{-50}$ is slightly greater than -3.7, so mark a point to the right of -3.7 on the number line.

Example 1 Classifying Numbers

Tell whether each number is rational or irrational. Explain how you know.

a) $-\frac{3}{5}$ b) $\sqrt{14}$ c) $\sqrt[3]{\frac{8}{27}}$

SOLUTION

a) $-\frac{3}{5}$ is rational since it is written as a quotient of integers.

Its decimal form is -0.6, which terminates.

b) $\sqrt{14}$ is irrational since 14 is not a perfect square.

The decimal form of $\sqrt{14}$ neither repeats nor terminates.

c) $\sqrt[3]{\frac{8}{27}}$ is rational since $\frac{8}{27}$ is a perfect cube.

$\sqrt[3]{\frac{8}{27}} = \frac{2}{3}$ or $0.\overline{6}$, which is a repeating decimal

CHECK YOUR UNDERSTANDING

1. Tell whether each number is rational or irrational. Explain how you know.

a) $\sqrt{\frac{49}{16}}$ b) $\sqrt[3]{-30}$

c) 1.21

[Answers: a) rational
b) irrational c) rational]

Together, the rational numbers and irrational numbers form the set of **real numbers**.

This diagram shows how these number systems are related.

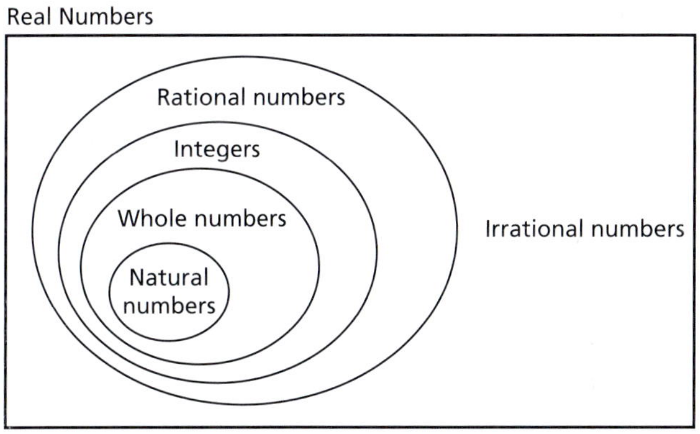

Example 2 Ordering Irrational Numbers on a Number Line

Use a number line to order these numbers from least to greatest.

$\sqrt[3]{13}$, $\sqrt{18}$, $\sqrt{9}$, $\sqrt[4]{27}$, $\sqrt[3]{-5}$

(Solution continues.)

SOLUTION

13 is between the perfect cubes 8 and 27, and is closer to 8.

$\sqrt[3]{8}$	$\sqrt[3]{13}$	$\sqrt[3]{27}$
$\downarrow$	$\downarrow$	$\downarrow$
2	?	3

Use a calculator.

$\sqrt[3]{13} = 2.3513\ldots$

18 is between the perfect squares 16 and 25, and is closer to 16.

$\sqrt{16}$	$\sqrt{18}$	$\sqrt{25}$
$\downarrow$	$\downarrow$	$\downarrow$
4	?	5

Use a calculator.

$\sqrt{18} = 4.2426\ldots$

$\sqrt{9} = 3$

27 is between the perfect fourth powers 16 and 81, and is closer to 16.

$\sqrt[4]{16}$	$\sqrt[4]{27}$	$\sqrt[4]{81}$
$\downarrow$	$\downarrow$	$\downarrow$
2	?	3

Use a calculator.

$\sqrt[4]{27} = 2.2795\ldots$

-5 is between the perfect cubes -1 and -8, and is closer to -8.

$\sqrt[3]{-1}$	$\sqrt[3]{-5}$	$\sqrt[3]{-8}$
$\downarrow$	$\downarrow$	$\downarrow$
-1	?	-2

Use a calculator.

$\sqrt[3]{-5} = -1.7099\ldots$

Mark each number on a number line.

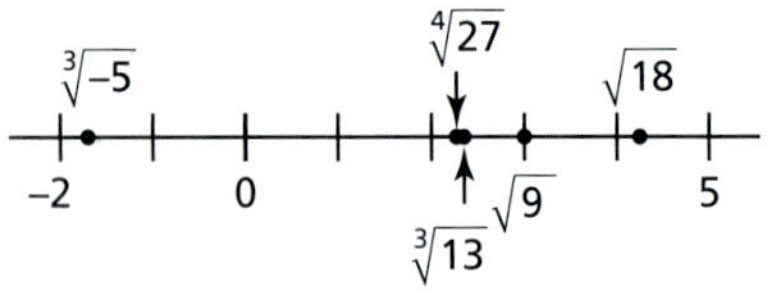

From least to greatest: $\sqrt[3]{-5}, \sqrt[4]{27}, \sqrt[3]{13}, \sqrt{9}, \sqrt{18}$

CHECK YOUR UNDERSTANDING

2. Use a number line to order these numbers from least to greatest.

$\sqrt{2}, \sqrt[3]{-2}, \sqrt[3]{6}, \sqrt{11}, \sqrt[4]{30}$

[Answer: $\sqrt[3]{-2}, \sqrt{2}, \sqrt[3]{6}, \sqrt[4]{30}, \sqrt{11}$]

How can you order a set of irrational numbers if you do not have a calculator?

Discuss the Ideas

1. How do you determine whether a radical represents a rational or an irrational number? Use examples to explain.

2. How can you determine whether the decimal form of a radical represents its exact value?

Exercises

A

3. Tell whether each number is rational or irrational.

   a) $\sqrt{12}$ b) $\sqrt[4]{16}$

   c) $\sqrt[3]{-100}$ d) $\sqrt{\frac{4}{9}}$

   e) $\sqrt{1.25}$ f) 1.25

4. Classify each number below as:

   a) a natural number b) an integer

   c) a rational number d) an irrational number

   $\frac{4}{3}, 0.3\overline{4}, -5, \sqrt[4]{9}, -2.1538, \sqrt[3]{27}, 7$

B

5. a) Why are $\sqrt{49}$ and $\sqrt[4]{16}$ rational numbers?

   b) Why are $\sqrt{21}$ and $\sqrt[3]{36}$ irrational numbers?

6. Look at this calculator screen.

   √(150)
   12.24744871

   a) Is the number 12.247 448 71 rational or irrational? Explain.

   b) Is the number $\sqrt{150}$ rational or irrational? Explain.

7. a) Sketch a diagram to represent the set of rational numbers and the set of irrational numbers.

   b) Write each number that follows in the correct set.

   $\frac{1}{2}, -\sqrt{3}, \sqrt{4}, \sqrt[4]{5}, -\frac{7}{6}, \sqrt[3]{8}, 10.12, -13.\overline{4}, \sqrt{0.15}, \sqrt{0.16}, 17$

8. For which numbers will the cube root be irrational? Use 2 different strategies to justify your answers.

   a) 8 b) 64 c) 30 d) 300

9. Sketch a number line for each irrational number and label its approximate location. Explain your reasoning.

   a) $\sqrt{5}$ b) $\sqrt[3]{12}$ c) $\sqrt[4]{25}$ d) $\sqrt[3]{-12}$

10. Use a number line to order the irrational numbers in each set from greatest to least.

    a) $\sqrt[3]{70}, \sqrt{50}, \sqrt[4]{100}, \sqrt[3]{400}$

    b) $\sqrt{89}, \sqrt[4]{250}, \sqrt[3]{-150}, \sqrt[3]{150}$

11. Use a number line to order these numbers from least to greatest. How can you verify your answer?

    $\sqrt{40}, \sqrt[3]{500}, \sqrt{98}, \sqrt[3]{98}, \sqrt{75}, \sqrt[3]{300}$

12. Use a number line to order these numbers from least to greatest. Identify which numbers are irrational and which are rational.

    $\frac{-14}{5}, \frac{123}{99}, -2, \sqrt[3]{-10}, \sqrt{4}$

13. How do you use irrational numbers when you calculate the length of the hypotenuse of a right triangle with legs 5 cm and 3 cm?

14. a) Which of the following statements are true? Explain your reasoning.

    i) All natural numbers are integers.

    ii) All integers are rational numbers.

    iii) All whole numbers are natural numbers.

    iv) All irrational numbers are roots.

    v) Some rational numbers are natural numbers.

    b) For each statement in part a that is false, provide examples to explain why.

15. Write a number that is:

    a) a rational number but not an integer

    b) a whole number but not a natural number

    c) an irrational number

16. a) Create a diagram to show how these number systems are related: irrational numbers; rational numbers; integers; whole numbers; and natural numbers.
Write each number below in your diagram.
$\frac{3}{5}$, 4.91919, 16, $\sqrt[3]{-64}$, $\sqrt{60}$, $\sqrt{9}$, -7, 0
b) Choose 3 more numbers that would be appropriate for each number system in your diagram. Include these numbers.

17. This diagram shows a cube with volume V cubic units and edge length s units.

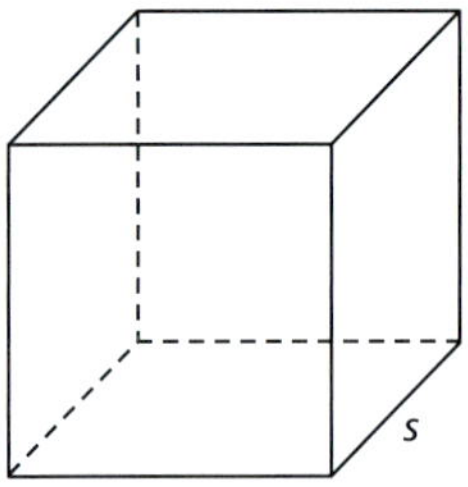

Provide a value of V for which s is:
a) irrational
b) rational

18. The *golden rectangle* appears in art and architecture. It has the property that the ratio of its length to width is $\frac{1+\sqrt{5}}{2}$ to 1. The shape of the front of the Parthenon, in Greece, is a golden rectangle.

a) Use a calculator. Write the value of $\frac{1+\sqrt{5}}{2}$ to the nearest tenth.
b) Use the number from part a as the length in inches of a rectangle. Draw a golden rectangle.
c) Measure other rectangles in your classroom. Do any of these rectangles approximate a golden rectangle? Justify your answer.

19. The ratio $\frac{1+\sqrt{5}}{2}$: 1 is called the *golden ratio.*
Use the dimensions of the Great Pyramid of Giza, from Chapter 1, page 26. Show that the ratio of its base side length to its height approximates the golden ratio.

20. Determine whether the perimeter of each square is a rational number or an irrational number. Justify your answer.
a) a square with area 40 cm^2
b) a square with area 81 m^2

C

21. Suppose you know that $\sqrt[n]{\frac{a}{b}}$ is a rational number and that a and b have no common factors. What can you say about the prime factorizations of a and b?

22. For each description, sketch and label a right triangle or explain why it is not possible to create a triangle.
a) All sides have rational number lengths.
b) Exactly 2 sides have rational number lengths.
c) Exactly 1 side has a rational number length.
d) No sides have rational number lengths.

23. a) Can the square root of a rational number be irrational? Show your reasoning.
b) Can the square root of an irrational number be rational? Show your reasoning.

24. Describe strategies to generate numbers with the property that their square roots, cube roots, and fourth roots are all rational numbers. Support your strategies with examples.

Reflect

Describe strategies you can use to determine if a radical represents a rational number or an irrational number.

4.3 Mixed and Entire Radicals

LESSON FOCUS

Express an entire radical as a mixed radical, and vice versa.

This quilt represents a Pythagorean spiral. The smallest triangle is a right isosceles triangle with legs 1 unit long.

Make Connections

We can name the fraction $\frac{3}{12}$ in many different ways:

$\frac{1}{4}$ $\quad \frac{5}{20}$ $\quad \frac{30}{120}$ $\quad \frac{100}{400}$

How do you show that each fraction is equivalent to $\frac{3}{12}$?
Why is $\frac{1}{4}$ the simplest form of $\frac{3}{12}$?

Construct Understanding

TRY THIS

Work with a partner.

You will need 1-cm grid paper and a calculator.

A. On grid paper, draw an isosceles right triangle with legs 1 cm long.
Write the length of the hypotenuse as a radical.
Label the lengths of the sides on the triangle.

B. Draw an isosceles right triangle with legs 2 cm long.
Write the length of the hypotenuse as a radical.
Label the lengths of the sides on the triangle.

C. Explain why the triangle in Step B is an enlargement of the triangle in Step A.
What is the scale factor of the enlargement?
How is the length of the hypotenuse in the larger triangle related to the corresponding length in the smaller triangle?

D. Draw isosceles right triangles with legs: 3 cm long; 4 cm long; and 5 cm long. For each triangle, write the length of the hypotenuse in 2 different ways.

E. Describe any relationships in the lengths of the sides of the triangles. Which form of the radical makes the relationships easier to see?

Just as with fractions, equivalent expressions for any number have the same value.

- $\sqrt{16 \cdot 9}$ is equivalent to $\sqrt{16} \cdot \sqrt{9}$ because:

$\sqrt{16 \cdot 9} = \sqrt{144}$ and $\sqrt{16} \cdot \sqrt{9} = 4 \cdot 3$

$= 12$ $= 12$

- Similarly, $\sqrt[3]{8 \cdot 27}$ is equivalent to $\sqrt[3]{8} \cdot \sqrt[3]{27}$ because:

$\sqrt[3]{8 \cdot 27} = \sqrt[3]{216}$ and $\sqrt[3]{8} \cdot \sqrt[3]{27} = 2 \cdot 3$

$= 6$ $= 6$

Multiplication Property of Radicals

$\sqrt[n]{ab} = \sqrt[n]{a} \cdot \sqrt[n]{b}$,
where n is a natural number, and a, b, $\sqrt[n]{a}$, and $\sqrt[n]{b}$ are real numbers

We can use this property to simplify square roots and cube roots that are not perfect squares or perfect cubes, but have factors that are perfect squares or perfect cubes.
For example, the factors of 24 are: 1, 2, 3, 4, 6, 8, 12, and 24.

- We can simplify $\sqrt{24}$ because 24 has a perfect square factor of 4.
Rewrite 24 as the product of two factors, one of which is 4.

$$\begin{aligned}\sqrt{24} &= \sqrt{4 \cdot 6}\\ &= \sqrt{4} \cdot \sqrt{6}\\ &= 2 \cdot \sqrt{6}\\ &= 2\sqrt{6}\end{aligned}$$

We read $2\sqrt{6}$ as "2 root 6."

- Similarly, we can simplify $\sqrt[3]{24}$ because 24 has a perfect cube factor of 8. Rewrite 24 as the product of two factors, one of which is 8.

$$\begin{aligned}\sqrt[3]{24} &= \sqrt[3]{8 \cdot 3}\\ &= \sqrt[3]{8} \cdot \sqrt[3]{3}\\ &= 2 \cdot \sqrt[3]{3}\\ &= 2\sqrt[3]{3}\end{aligned}$$

We read $2\sqrt[3]{3}$ as "2 cube root 3."

- However, we cannot simplify $\sqrt[4]{24}$ because 24 has no factors (other than 1) that can be written as a fourth power.

We can also use prime factorization to simplify a radical.

Example 1 Simplifying Radicals Using Prime Factorization

Simplify each radical.

a) $\sqrt{80}$ **b)** $\sqrt[3]{144}$ **c)** $\sqrt[4]{162}$

SOLUTION

Write each radical as a product of prime factors, then simplify.

a)

$$\begin{aligned}\sqrt{80} &= \sqrt{8 \cdot 10}\\ &= \sqrt{2 \cdot 2 \cdot 2 \cdot 5 \cdot 2}\\ &= \sqrt{(2 \cdot 2) \cdot (2 \cdot 2) \cdot 5}\\ &= \sqrt{2 \cdot 2} \cdot \sqrt{2 \cdot 2} \cdot \sqrt{5}\\ &= 2 \cdot 2 \cdot \sqrt{5}\\ &= 4\sqrt{5}\end{aligned}$$

Since $\sqrt{80}$ is a square root, look for factors that appear twice.

b)

$$\begin{aligned}\sqrt[3]{144} &= \sqrt[3]{12 \cdot 12}\\ &= \sqrt[3]{2 \cdot 2 \cdot 3 \cdot 2 \cdot 2 \cdot 3}\\ &= \sqrt[3]{(2 \cdot 2 \cdot 2) \cdot 2 \cdot 3 \cdot 3}\\ &= \sqrt[3]{2 \cdot 2 \cdot 2} \cdot \sqrt[3]{2 \cdot 3 \cdot 3}\\ &= 2 \cdot \sqrt[3]{2 \cdot 3 \cdot 3}\\ &= 2\sqrt[3]{18}\end{aligned}$$

Since $\sqrt[3]{144}$ is a cube root, look for factors that appear 3 times.

c)

$$\begin{aligned}\sqrt[4]{162} &= \sqrt[4]{81 \cdot 2}\\ &= \sqrt[4]{3 \cdot 3 \cdot 3 \cdot 3 \cdot 2}\\ &= \sqrt[4]{(3 \cdot 3 \cdot 3 \cdot 3) \cdot 2}\\ &= \sqrt[4]{3 \cdot 3 \cdot 3 \cdot 3} \cdot \sqrt[4]{2}\\ &= 3\sqrt[4]{2}\end{aligned}$$

Since $\sqrt[4]{162}$ is a fourth root, look for factors that appear 4 times.

CHECK YOUR UNDERSTANDING

1. Simplify each radical.

a) $\sqrt{63}$

b) $\sqrt[3]{108}$

c) $\sqrt[4]{128}$

[Answers: a) $3\sqrt{7}$ b) $3\sqrt[3]{4}$ c) $2\sqrt[4]{8}$]

Some numbers, such as 200, have more than one perfect square factor.
The factors of 200 are: 1, 2, 4, 5, 8, 10, 20, 25, 40, 50, 100, 200
Since 4, 25, and 100 are perfect squares, we can simplify $\sqrt{200}$ in these ways.

$$\sqrt{200} = \sqrt{4 \cdot 50} = \sqrt{4} \cdot \sqrt{50} = 2\sqrt{50}$$

$$\sqrt{200} = \sqrt{25 \cdot 8} = \sqrt{25} \cdot \sqrt{8} = 5\sqrt{8}$$

$$\sqrt{200} = \sqrt{100 \cdot 2} = \sqrt{100} \cdot \sqrt{2} = 10\sqrt{2}$$

$10\sqrt{2}$ is in simplest form because the radical contains no perfect square factors other than 1.

To write a radical of index n in simplest form, we write the radicand as a product of 2 factors, one of which is the greatest perfect nth power.

Example 2 Writing Radicals in Simplest Form

Write each radical in simplest form, if possible.

a) $\sqrt[3]{40}$ b) $\sqrt{26}$ c) $\sqrt[4]{32}$

SOLUTION

Look for perfect nth factors, where n is the index of the radical.

a) The factors of 40 are: 1, 2, 4, 5, 8, 10, 20, 40
The greatest perfect cube is $8 = 2 \cdot 2 \cdot 2$,
so write 40 as $8 \cdot 5$.

$$\sqrt[3]{40} = \sqrt[3]{8 \cdot 5} = \sqrt[3]{8} \cdot \sqrt[3]{5} = 2 \cdot \sqrt[3]{5} = 2\sqrt[3]{5}$$

b) The factors of 26 are: 1, 2, 13, 26
There are no perfect square factors other than 1.
So, $\sqrt{26}$ cannot be simplified.

c) The factors of 32 are: 1, 2, 4, 8, 16, 32
The greatest perfect fourth power is $16 = 2 \cdot 2 \cdot 2 \cdot 2$,
so write 32 as $16 \cdot 2$.

$$\sqrt[4]{32} = \sqrt[4]{16 \cdot 2} = \sqrt[4]{16} \cdot \sqrt[4]{2} = 2 \cdot \sqrt[4]{2} = 2\sqrt[4]{2}$$

CHECK YOUR UNDERSTANDING

2. Write each radical in simplest form, if possible.

a) $\sqrt{30}$

b) $\sqrt[3]{32}$

c) $\sqrt[4]{48}$

[Answers: a) cannot be simplified b) $2\sqrt[3]{4}$ c) $2\sqrt[4]{3}$]

Radicals of the form $\sqrt[n]{x}$ such as $\sqrt{80}$, $\sqrt[3]{144}$, and $\sqrt[4]{162}$ are **entire radicals.**

Radicals of the form $a\sqrt[n]{x}$ such as $4\sqrt{5}$, $2\sqrt[3]{18}$, and $3\sqrt[4]{2}$ are **mixed radicals.** Entire radicals were rewritten as mixed radicals in *Examples 1* and *2*.

Any number can be written as the square root of its square; for example, $2 = \sqrt{2 \cdot 2}$, $3 = \sqrt{3 \cdot 3}$, $4 = \sqrt{4 \cdot 4}$, and so on. Similarly, any number can be written as the cube root of its cube, or the fourth root of its perfect fourth power. We use this strategy to write a mixed radical as an entire radical.

Example 3 Writing Mixed Radicals as Entire Radicals

Write each mixed radical as an entire radical.

a) $4\sqrt{3}$ **b)** $3\sqrt[3]{2}$ **c)** $2\sqrt[5]{2}$

SOLUTION

a) Write 4 as: $\sqrt{4 \cdot 4} = \sqrt{16}$

$$4\sqrt{3} = \sqrt{16} \cdot \sqrt{3}$$

Use the Multiplication Property of Radicals.

$$= \sqrt{16 \cdot 3}$$

$$= \sqrt{48}$$

b) Write 3 as: $\sqrt[3]{3 \cdot 3 \cdot 3} = \sqrt[3]{27}$

$$3\sqrt[3]{2} = \sqrt[3]{27} \cdot \sqrt[3]{2}$$

$$= \sqrt[3]{27 \cdot 2}$$

$$= \sqrt[3]{54}$$

c) Write 2 as: $\sqrt[5]{2 \cdot 2 \cdot 2 \cdot 2 \cdot 2} = \sqrt[5]{32}$

$$2\sqrt[5]{2} = \sqrt[5]{32} \cdot \sqrt[5]{2}$$

$$= \sqrt[5]{32 \cdot 2}$$

$$= \sqrt[5]{64}$$

CHECK YOUR UNDERSTANDING

3. Write each mixed radical as an entire radical.

a) $7\sqrt{3}$

b) $2\sqrt[3]{4}$

c) $2\sqrt[5]{3}$

[Answers: a) $\sqrt{147}$ b) $\sqrt[3]{32}$ c) $\sqrt[5]{96}$]

How would rewriting mixed radicals as entire radicals help you to order a set of mixed radicals with the same index?

Discuss the Ideas

1. How can you determine if an entire radical can be written as a mixed radical?

2. Suppose an entire radical can be simplified. How do you use the Multiplication Property of Radicals to write it in simplest form?

Exercises

A

3. List all the perfect squares up to 400, and their square roots.

4. Write each radical in simplest form.
   a) $\sqrt{8}$ b) $\sqrt{12}$ c) $\sqrt{32}$ d) $\sqrt{50}$
   e) $\sqrt{18}$ f) $\sqrt{27}$ g) $\sqrt{48}$ h) $\sqrt{75}$

5. Write each mixed radical as an entire radical.
   a) $5\sqrt{2}$ b) $6\sqrt{2}$ c) $7\sqrt{2}$ d) $8\sqrt{2}$
   e) $5\sqrt{3}$ f) $6\sqrt{3}$ g) $7\sqrt{3}$ h) $8\sqrt{3}$

6. a) List all the perfect cubes up to 1000, and their cube roots.
   b) List all the perfect fourth powers up to 1000, and their fourth roots.

B

7. a) Use the diagram to explain why $\sqrt{45} = 3\sqrt{5}$.

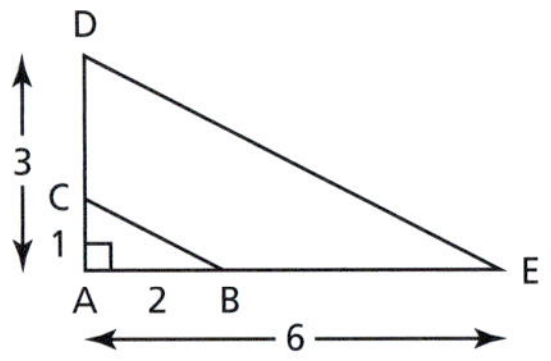

   b) Use algebra to verify that $\sqrt{45} = 3\sqrt{5}$.

8. a) Use the diagram to explain why $\sqrt{40} = 2\sqrt{10}$.

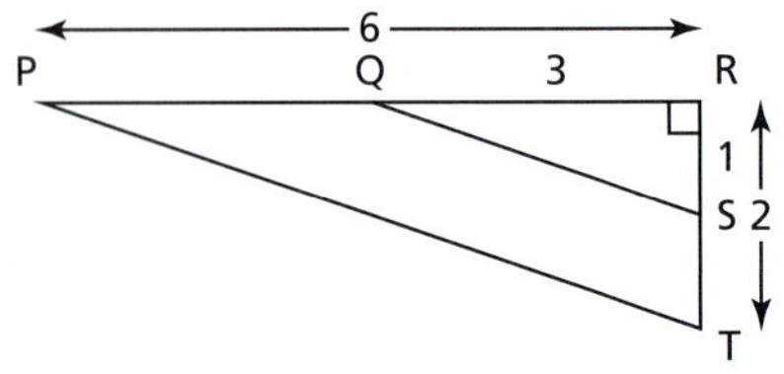

   b) Use algebra to verify that $\sqrt{40} = 2\sqrt{10}$.

9. Explain why rewriting $\sqrt{50}$ as $\sqrt{25} \cdot \sqrt{2}$ helps you simplify $\sqrt{50}$, but rewriting $\sqrt{50}$ as $\sqrt{10} \cdot \sqrt{5}$ does not.

10. Write each radical in simplest form, if possible.
   a) $\sqrt{90}$ b) $\sqrt{73}$ c) $\sqrt{108}$
   d) $\sqrt{600}$ e) $\sqrt{54}$ f) $\sqrt{91}$
   g) $\sqrt{28}$ h) $\sqrt{33}$ i) $\sqrt{112}$

11. Write each radical in simplest form, if possible.
   a) $\sqrt[3]{16}$ b) $\sqrt[3]{81}$
   c) $\sqrt[3]{256}$ d) $\sqrt[3]{128}$
   e) $\sqrt[3]{60}$ f) $\sqrt[3]{192}$
   g) $\sqrt[3]{135}$ h) $\sqrt[3]{100}$
   i) $\sqrt[3]{500}$ j) $\sqrt[3]{375}$

12. Write each mixed radical as an entire radical.
   a) $3\sqrt{2}$ b) $4\sqrt{2}$
   c) $6\sqrt{5}$ d) $5\sqrt{6}$
   e) $7\sqrt{7}$ f) $2\sqrt[3]{2}$
   g) $3\sqrt[3]{3}$ h) $4\sqrt[3]{3}$
   i) $5\sqrt[3]{2}$ j) $2\sqrt[3]{9}$

13. a) Can every mixed radical be expressed as an entire radical?
   b) Can every entire radical be expressed as a mixed radical?
   Give examples to support your answers.

14. Express the side length of this square as a radical in simplest form.

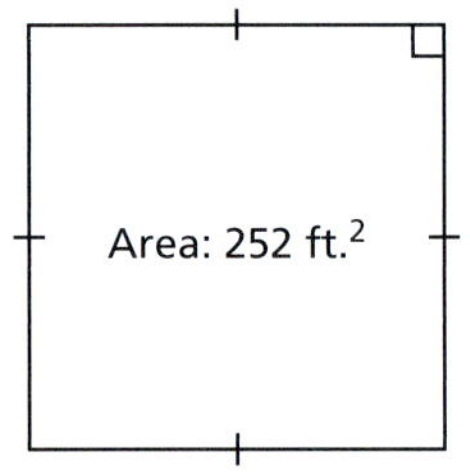

15. A cube has a volume of 200 cm^3. Write the edge length of the cube as a radical in simplest form.

16. A square has an area of 54 square inches. Determine the perimeter of the square. Write the answer as a radical in simplest form.

17. Write each radical in simplest form.
   a) $\sqrt[4]{48}$ b) $\sqrt[4]{405}$
   c) $\sqrt[4]{1250}$ d) $\sqrt[4]{176}$

18. Write each mixed radical as an entire radical.
   a) $6\sqrt[4]{3}$ b) $7\sqrt[4]{2}$
   c) $3\sqrt[5]{4}$ d) $4\sqrt[5]{3}$

19. The quilt on page 213 is made from right triangles. In Chapter 2, page 77, you determined the tangents of the angles at the centre of the spiral. The first triangle is a right isosceles triangle with legs 1 unit long. The hypotenuse of this triangle is one leg of the second triangle, with its other leg 1 unit long. This pattern continues.

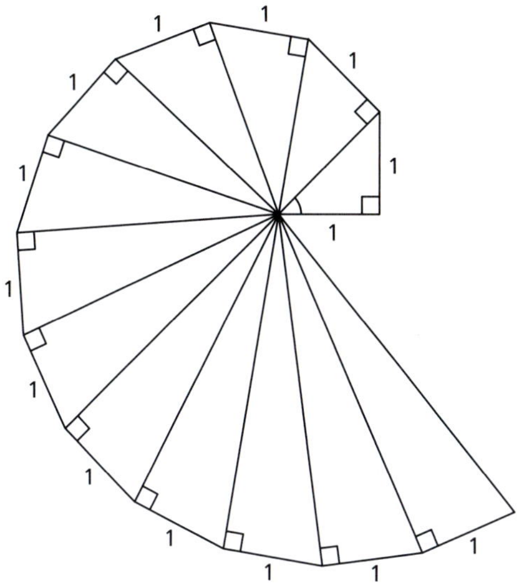

a) Calculate the length of the hypotenuse of each triangle. Write each length as an entire radical.

b) **i)** What pattern do you see in the lengths?
ii) Use this pattern to predict the length of the hypotenuse of the 50th triangle.
iii) How many of the first 100 triangles have hypotenuse lengths that can be written as mixed radicals? Justify your answer.

20. Here is a student's solution for writing $8\sqrt[3]{2}$ as an entire radical.

$$8\sqrt[3]{2} = 8 \cdot \sqrt[3]{2}$$
$$= \sqrt[3]{2} \cdot \sqrt[3]{2}$$
$$= \sqrt[3]{2 \cdot 2}$$
$$= \sqrt[3]{4}$$

Identify an error the student made, then write the correct solution.

21. A student simplified $\sqrt{96}$ as shown:

$$\sqrt{96} = \sqrt{4} \cdot \sqrt{48}$$
$$= 2 \cdot \sqrt{48}$$
$$= 2 \cdot \sqrt{8} \cdot \sqrt{6}$$
$$= 2 \cdot 4 \cdot \sqrt{6}$$
$$= 8\sqrt{6}$$

Identify the errors the student made, then write a correct solution.

22. Arrange in order from greatest to least. What strategy did you use each time?

a) $9\sqrt{2}, 2\sqrt{6}, 8\sqrt{3}, 4\sqrt{5}, 6\sqrt{2}$

b) $4\sqrt{7}, 8\sqrt{3}, 2\sqrt{13}, 6\sqrt{5}$

c) $7\sqrt{3}, 9\sqrt{2}, 5\sqrt{6}, \sqrt{103}, 3\sqrt{17}$

23. Simplify the radicals in each list. What patterns do you see in the results? Write the next 2 radicals in each list.

a) $\sqrt{4}$
$\sqrt{400}$
$\sqrt{40\,000}$

b) $\sqrt[3]{27}$
$\sqrt[3]{27\,000}$
$\sqrt[3]{27\,000\,000}$

c) $\sqrt{8}$
$\sqrt{800}$
$\sqrt{80\,000}$

d) $\sqrt[3]{24}$
$\sqrt[3]{24\,000}$
$\sqrt[3]{24\,000\,000}$

C

24. The largest square in this diagram has side length 8 cm. Calculate the side length and area of each of the two smaller squares. Write the radicals in simplest form.

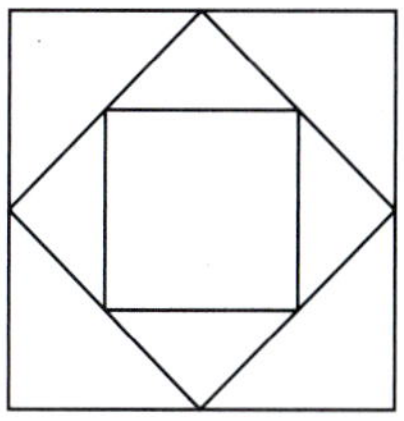

25. Given that $\sqrt{2} \doteq 1.4142$, determine a decimal approximation for each radical, without using a calculator.

a) **i)** $\sqrt{200}$ **ii)** $\sqrt{20\,000}$

b) **i)** $\sqrt{8}$ **ii)** $\sqrt{18}$ **iii)** $\sqrt{32}$ **iv)** $\sqrt{50}$

Reflect

How do you use the index of a radical when you simplify a radical, and when you write a mixed radical as an entire radical? Use examples to support your explanation.

CHECKPOINT 1

Connections

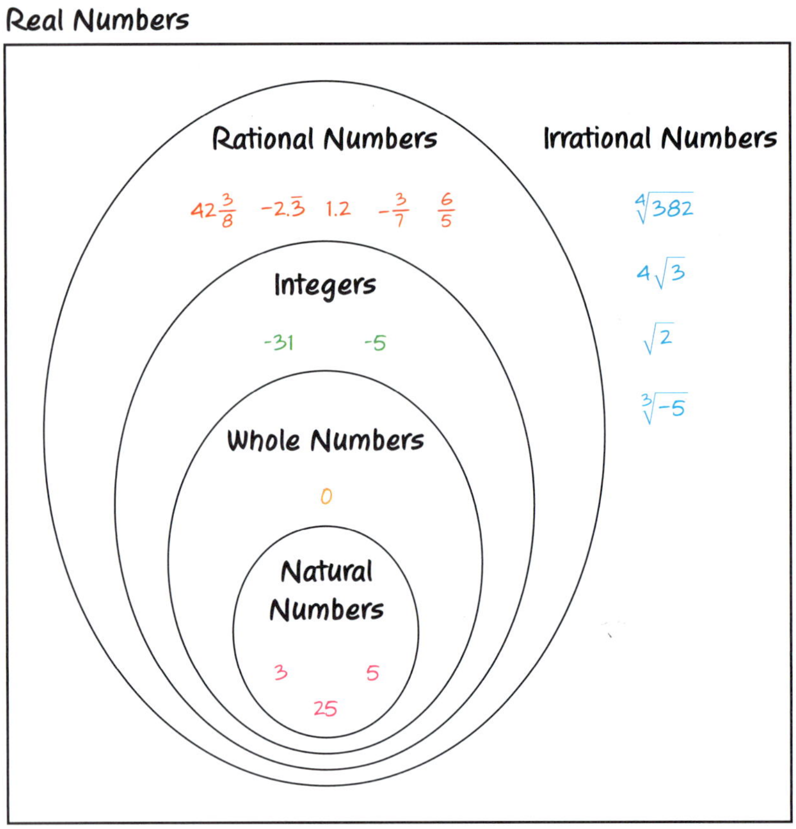

Concept Development

- **In Lesson 4.1**
  – You applied what you know about **square roots** to explore **decimal approximations of cube roots and fourth roots.**
  – You determined that **some radicals** can be represented as **rational numbers** and other radicals cannot.
- **In Lesson 4.2**
  – You defined **irrational numbers**, and represented these numbers and **rational numbers as the set of real numbers.**
  – You **identified** conditions for which a **radical** has a **rational number value**, and **estimated** the values of **radicals that are irrational.**
- **In Lesson 4.3**
  – You defined **mixed radicals** and **entire radicals**, and used factoring to simplify radicals.

Assess Your Understanding

4.1

1. Evaluate each radical. How did you use the index of the radical in your work?

a) $\sqrt{81}$ b) $\sqrt[3]{-125}$ c) $\sqrt[4]{256}$ d) $\sqrt[5]{243}$

2. Estimate the value of each radical to 2 decimal places.
How can you do this without using the root keys on a calculator?

a) $\sqrt{10}$ b) $\sqrt[3]{15}$ c) $\sqrt[4]{9}$ d) $\sqrt[5]{23}$

3. Does the decimal representation of $\sqrt[4]{60}$ repeat, terminate, or neither?
Justify your answer.

4.2

4. Tell whether each number is rational or irrational. Justify your answers.

a) $\sqrt{11}$ b) $\sqrt[3]{16}$ c) $\sqrt[3]{-16}$ d) $\sqrt{121}$ e) $\sqrt{\frac{121}{16}}$ f) $\sqrt{12.1}$

5. For each irrational number, sketch a number line and label its approximate location. Describe your strategies.

a) $\sqrt{19}$ b) $\sqrt[3]{-20}$ c) $\sqrt[4]{30}$ d) $\sqrt[3]{36}$

6. a) Draw a diagram to illustrate the real number system.
Write the numbers below in the appropriate places on your diagram.

i) $3\frac{1}{3}$ ii) -42 iii) 4.5 iv) $-4.\overline{5}$

v) 0 vi) 14 vii) $\sqrt{7}$ viii) π

b) Choose 1 more number for each section of your diagram, where possible. Write each number in the correct place on your diagram.

7. a) Sketch a number line and mark each number on it.

i) $\sqrt{32}$ ii) $\sqrt[3]{72}$ iii) $\sqrt[4]{100}$ iv) $\sqrt[3]{50}$ v) $\sqrt{65}$ vi) $\sqrt[4]{60}$

b) Order the numbers in part a from greatest to least.

8. Sketch a square. Label its area so that:

a) The perimeter of the square is a rational number.

b) The perimeter of the square is an irrational number.

4.3

9. Write each radical in simplest form, if possible.

a) $\sqrt{45}$ b) $\sqrt[3]{96}$ c) $\sqrt{17}$ d) $\sqrt[4]{48}$ e) $\sqrt[3]{80}$ f) $\sqrt[4]{50}$

10. Choose one radical from question 9 that can be simplified.
Write a set of instructions for simplifying the radical.

11. Rewrite each mixed radical as an entire radical.

a) $3\sqrt{7}$ b) $2\sqrt[3]{4}$ c) $7\sqrt{3}$ d) $2\sqrt[4]{12}$ e) $3\sqrt[3]{10}$ f) $6\sqrt{11}$

4.4 Fractional Exponents and Radicals

LESSON FOCUS

Relate rational exponents and radicals.

Make Connections

Coffee, tea, and hot chocolate contain caffeine. The expression $100(0.87)^{\frac{1}{2}}$ represents the percent of caffeine left in your body $\frac{1}{2}$ h after you drink a caffeine beverage.

Given that $0.87^1 = 0.87$ and $0.87^0 = 1$, how can you estimate a value for $0.87^{\frac{1}{2}}$?

Construct Understanding

TRY THIS

Work with a partner.

A. Copy then complete each table. Use a calculator to complete the second column.

x	$x^{\frac{1}{2}}$
1	$1^{\frac{1}{2}} =$
4	$4^{\frac{1}{2}} =$
9	
16	
25	

x	$x^{\frac{1}{3}}$
1	
8	
27	
64	
125	

Continue the pattern. Write the next 3 lines in each table.

B. For each table:

- What do you notice about the numbers in the first column? Compare the numbers in the first and second columns. What conclusions can you make?
- What do you think the exponent $\frac{1}{2}$ means? Confirm your prediction by trying other examples on a calculator.
- What do you think the exponent $\frac{1}{3}$ means? Confirm your prediction by trying other examples on a calculator.

C. What do you think $a^{\frac{1}{4}}$ and $a^{\frac{1}{5}}$ mean?
Use a calculator to test your predictions for different values of a.

D. What does $a^{\frac{1}{n}}$ mean? Explain your reasoning.

In grade 9, you learned that for powers with integral bases and whole number exponents:
$a^m \cdot a^n = a^{m+n}$

To multiply powers with the same base, add the exponents.

We can extend this law to powers with fractional exponents with numerator 1:

$$5^{\frac{1}{2}} \cdot 5^{\frac{1}{2}} = 5^{\frac{1}{2}+\frac{1}{2}} \quad \text{and} \quad \sqrt{5} \cdot \sqrt{5} = \sqrt{25}$$
$$= 5^1 \qquad\qquad = 5$$
$$= 5$$

$5^{\frac{1}{2}}$ and $\sqrt{5}$ are equivalent expressions; that is, $5^{\frac{1}{2}} = \sqrt{5}$.

Similarly, $5^{\frac{1}{3}} \cdot 5^{\frac{1}{3}} \cdot 5^{\frac{1}{3}} = 5^{\frac{1}{3}+\frac{1}{3}+\frac{1}{3}}$ and $\sqrt[3]{5} \cdot \sqrt[3]{5} \cdot \sqrt[3]{5} = \sqrt[3]{125}$

$$= 5^1 \qquad\qquad = 5$$
$$= 5$$

$5^{\frac{1}{3}} = \sqrt[3]{5}$

These examples indicate that:

- Raising a number to the exponent $\frac{1}{2}$ is equivalent to taking the square root of the number.
- Raising a number to the exponent $\frac{1}{3}$ is equivalent to taking the cube root of the number, and so on.

Powers with Rational Exponents with Numerator 1

When n is a natural number and x is a rational number, $x^{\frac{1}{n}} = \sqrt[n]{x}$

Example 1 Evaluating Powers of the Form $a^{\frac{1}{n}}$

Evaluate each power without using a calculator.

a) $27^{\frac{1}{3}}$ b) $0.49^{\frac{1}{2}}$ c) $(-64)^{\frac{1}{3}}$ d) $\left(\frac{4}{9}\right)^{\frac{1}{2}}$

SOLUTION

The denominator of the exponent is the index of the radical.

a) $27^{\frac{1}{3}} = \sqrt[3]{27}$
$= 3$

b) $0.49^{\frac{1}{2}} = \sqrt{0.49}$
$= 0.7$

c) $(-64)^{\frac{1}{3}} = \sqrt[3]{-64}$
$= -4$

d) $\left(\frac{4}{9}\right)^{\frac{1}{2}} = \sqrt{\frac{4}{9}}$
$= \frac{2}{3}$

CHECK YOUR UNDERSTANDING

1. Evaluate each power without using a calculator.

a) $1000^{\frac{1}{3}}$ b) $0.25^{\frac{1}{2}}$

c) $(-8)^{\frac{1}{3}}$ d) $\left(\frac{16}{81}\right)^{\frac{1}{4}}$

[Answers: a) 10 b) 0.5 c) -2 d) $\frac{2}{3}$]

How could you check your answers?

A fraction can be written as a terminating or repeating decimal, so we can interpret powers with decimal exponents; for example, $0.2 = \frac{1}{5}$, so $32^{0.2} = 32^{\frac{1}{5}}$.

We can evaluate $32^{\frac{1}{5}}$ and $32^{0.2}$ on a calculator to show that both expressions have the same value.

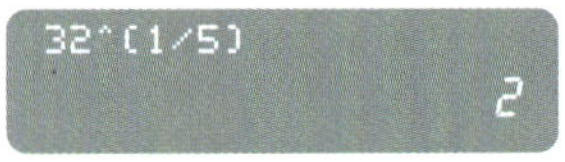

Why do we use brackets to evaluate when the exponent is a fraction, but not when the exponent is a decimal?

To give meaning to a power such as $8^{\frac{2}{3}}$, we extend the exponent law $(a^m)^n = a^{mn}$ so that it applies when m and n are rational numbers.

We write the exponent $\frac{2}{3}$ as $\frac{1}{3} \cdot 2$, or as $2 \cdot \frac{1}{3}$.

So, $8^{\frac{2}{3}} = 8^{\frac{1}{3} \cdot 2}$
$= \left(8^{\frac{1}{3}}\right)^2$
$= \left(\sqrt[3]{8}\right)^2$

Take the cube root of 8, then square the result.

So, $8^{\frac{2}{3}} = 2^2$
$= 4$

or

$8^{\frac{2}{3}} = 8^{2 \cdot \frac{1}{3}}$
$= (8^2)^{\frac{1}{3}}$
$= \sqrt[3]{8^2}$

Square 8, then take the cube root of the result.

$8^{\frac{2}{3}} = \sqrt[3]{64}$
$= 4$

These examples illustrate that the numerator of a fractional exponent represents a power and the denominator represents a root. The root and power can be evaluated in any order.

Powers with Rational Exponents

When m and n are natural numbers, and x is a rational number,

$$x^{\frac{m}{n}} = \left(x^{\frac{1}{n}}\right)^m = \left(\sqrt[n]{x}\right)^m \quad \text{and} \quad x^{\frac{m}{n}} = (x^m)^{\frac{1}{n}} = \sqrt[n]{x^m}$$

Example 2 Rewriting Powers in Radical and Exponent Form

a) Write $40^{\frac{2}{3}}$ in radical form in 2 ways.

b) Write $\sqrt{3^5}$ and $\left(\sqrt[3]{25}\right)^2$ in exponent form.

SOLUTION

a) Use $a^{\frac{m}{n}} = \left(\sqrt[n]{a}\right)^m$ or $\sqrt[n]{a^m}$.

$$40^{\frac{2}{3}} = \left(\sqrt[3]{40}\right)^2 \text{ or } \sqrt[3]{40^2}$$

b) Use $\sqrt[n]{a^m} = a^{\frac{m}{n}}$.

$$\sqrt{3^5} = 3^{\frac{5}{2}}$$

The index of the radical is 2.

Use $\left(\sqrt[n]{a}\right)^m = a^{\frac{m}{n}}$.

$$\left(\sqrt[3]{25}\right)^2 = 25^{\frac{2}{3}}$$

CHECK YOUR UNDERSTANDING

2. a) Write $26^{\frac{2}{5}}$ in radical form in 2 ways.

b) Write $\sqrt{6^5}$ and $\left(\sqrt[4]{19}\right)^3$ in exponent form.

[Answers: a) $\left(\sqrt[5]{26}\right)^2$ or $\sqrt[5]{26^2}$
b) $6^{\frac{5}{2}}$, $19^{\frac{3}{4}}$]

Example 3 Evaluating Powers with Rational Exponents and Rational Bases

Evaluate.

a) $0.04^{\frac{3}{2}}$ b) $27^{\frac{4}{3}}$
c) $(-32)^{0.4}$ d) $1.8^{1.4}$

SOLUTION

a) $0.04^{\frac{3}{2}} = \left(0.04^{\frac{1}{2}}\right)^3$
$= \left(\sqrt{0.04}\right)^3$
$= 0.2^3$
$= 0.008$

b) $27^{\frac{4}{3}} = \left(27^{\frac{1}{3}}\right)^4$
$= \left(\sqrt[3]{27}\right)^4$
$= 3^4$
$= 81$

(Solution continues.)

CHECK YOUR UNDERSTANDING

3. Evaluate.

a) $0.01^{\frac{3}{2}}$ b) $(-27)^{\frac{4}{3}}$

c) $81^{\frac{3}{4}}$ d) $0.75^{1.2}$

[Answers: a) 0.001 b) 81
c) 27 d) 0.7080…]

c) The exponent $0.4 = \frac{4}{10}$ or $\frac{2}{5}$

So, $(-32)^{0.4} = (-32)^{\frac{2}{5}}$

$= \left[(-32)^{\frac{1}{5}}\right]^2$

$= (\sqrt[5]{-32})^2$

$= (-2)^2$

$= 4$

d) $1.8^{1.4}$

Use a calculator.

```
1.8^1.4
        2.277096874
```

$1.8^{1.4} = 2.2770\ldots$

The powers in parts a to c were evaluated by taking the root first. Evaluate each power by raising the base to the exponent first. Which strategy is more efficient? Justify your answer.

Example 4 Applying Rational Exponents

Biologists use the formula $b = 0.01m^{\frac{2}{3}}$ to estimate the brain mass, b kilograms, of a mammal with body mass m kilograms. Estimate the brain mass of each animal.

a) a husky with a body mass of 27 kg

b) a polar bear with a body mass of 200 kg

SOLUTION

Use the formula $b = 0.01m^{\frac{2}{3}}$.

a) Substitute: $m = 27$

$b = 0.01(27)^{\frac{2}{3}}$

$b = 0.01(\sqrt[3]{27})^2$

Use the order of operations. Evaluate the power first.

$b = 0.01(3)^2$

$b = 0.01(9)$

$b = 0.09$

The brain mass of the husky is approximately 0.09 kg.

b) Substitute: $m = 200$

$b = 0.01(200)^{\frac{2}{3}}$

Use a calculator.

```
0.01(200)^(2/3)
        0.341995189
```

The brain mass of the polar bear is approximately 0.34 kg.

CHECK YOUR UNDERSTANDING

4. Use the formula $b = 0.01m^{\frac{2}{3}}$ to estimate the brain mass of each animal.

a) a moose with a body mass of 512 kg

b) a cat with a body mass of 5 kg

[Answers: a) approximately 0.64 kg b) approximately 0.03 kg]

Why did we use mental math to evaluate part a, but a calculator to evaluate part b?

Discuss the Ideas

1. When a is a rational number and n is a natural number, what does $a^{\frac{1}{n}}$ represent?

2. When a is a rational number and m and n are natural numbers, what does $a^{\frac{m}{n}}$ represent?

Exercises

A

3. Evaluate each power without using a calculator.
   a) $16^{\frac{1}{2}}$ b) $36^{\frac{1}{2}}$ c) $64^{\frac{1}{3}}$
   d) $32^{\frac{1}{5}}$ e) $(-27)^{\frac{1}{3}}$ f) $(-1000)^{\frac{1}{3}}$

4. Evaluate each power without using a calculator.
   a) $100^{0.5}$ b) $81^{0.25}$
   c) $1024^{0.2}$ d) $(-32)^{0.2}$

5. Write each power as a radical.
   a) $36^{\frac{1}{3}}$ b) $48^{\frac{1}{2}}$ c) $(-30)^{\frac{1}{5}}$

6. Write each radical as a power.
   a) $\sqrt{39}$ b) $\sqrt[4]{90}$
   c) $\sqrt[3]{29}$ d) $\sqrt[5]{100}$

7. Evaluate each power without using a calculator.
   a) 8^0 b) $8^{\frac{1}{3}}$ c) $8^{\frac{2}{3}}$
   d) $8^{\frac{3}{3}}$ e) $8^{\frac{4}{3}}$ f) $8^{\frac{5}{3}}$

B

8. Write each power as a radical.
   a) $4^{\frac{2}{3}}$ b) $(-10)^{\frac{3}{5}}$ c) $2.3^{\frac{3}{2}}$

9. A cube has a volume of 350 cm^3. Write the edge length of the cube as a radical and as a power.

10. Write each power as a radical.
   a) $48^{\frac{2}{3}}$ b) $(-1.8)^{\frac{5}{3}}$ c) $\left(\frac{3}{8}\right)^{2.5}$
   d) $0.75^{0.75}$ e) $\left(-\frac{5}{9}\right)^{\frac{2}{5}}$ f) $1.25^{1.5}$

11. Write each radical as a power.
   a) $\sqrt{3.8^3}$ b) $\left(\sqrt[3]{-1.5}\right)^2$ c) $\sqrt[4]{\left(\frac{9}{5}\right)^5}$
   d) $\sqrt[3]{\left(\frac{3}{8}\right)^4}$ e) $\left(\sqrt{\frac{5}{4}}\right)^3$ f) $\sqrt[5]{(-2.5)^3}$

12. Evaluate each power without using a calculator.
   a) $9^{\frac{3}{2}}$ b) $\left(\frac{27}{8}\right)^{\frac{2}{3}}$ c) $(-27)^{\frac{2}{3}}$
   d) $0.36^{1.5}$ e) $(-64)^{\frac{2}{3}}$ f) $\left(\frac{4}{25}\right)^{\frac{3}{2}}$

13. Write an equivalent form for each number using a power with exponent $\frac{1}{2}$, then write the answer as a radical.
   a) 2 b) 4 c) 10 d) 3 e) 5

14. Write an equivalent form for each number using a power with exponent $\frac{1}{3}$, then write the answer as a radical.
   a) -1 b) 2 c) 3 d) -4 e) 4

15. Arrange these numbers in order from least to greatest. Describe your strategy.
   $\sqrt[3]{4}, 4^{\frac{3}{2}}, 4^2, \left(\frac{1}{4}\right)^{\frac{3}{2}}$

16. a) Evaluate.
   i) $16^{1.5}$ ii) $81^{0.75}$
   iii) $(-32)^{0.8}$ iv) $35^{0.5}$
   v) $1.21^{1.5}$ vi) $\left(\frac{3}{4}\right)^{0.6}$

   b) Which powers in part a could you have evaluated without a calculator? How can you tell before you evaluate?

17. The height, h metres, of a certain species of fir tree can be estimated from the formula $h = 35d^{\frac{2}{3}}$, where d metres is the diameter at the base. Use the formula to determine the approximate height of a fir tree with base diameter 3.2 m.

18. Here is a student's solution for evaluating a power.

$$1.96^{\frac{3}{2}} = (\sqrt[3]{1.96})^2$$
$$= (1.2514\ldots)^2$$
$$= 1.5661\ldots$$

Identify the errors the student made. Write a correct solution.

19. A formula for the approximate surface area, SA square metres, of a person's body is $SA = 0.096m^{0.7}$, where m is the person's mass in kilograms. Calculate the surface area of a child with mass 40 kg.

20. Here is an expression for the percent of caffeine that remains in your body n hours after you drink a caffeine beverage:

$100(0.5)^{\frac{n}{5}}$

a) Show that this expression and the expression on page 222 give the same result, to the nearest whole number, for the percent of caffeine that remains after $\frac{1}{2}$ h.

b) Use the expression above to determine the percent of caffeine that remains after 1.5 h.

c) After how many hours does 50% of the caffeine remain? Explain how you know.

21. In the late 1500s, Johannes Kepler developed a formula to calculate the time it takes each planet to orbit the sun (called the *period*). The formula is $T \doteq 0.2R^{\frac{3}{2}}$, where T is the period in Earth days and R is the mean distance from the planet to the sun in millions of kilometres.

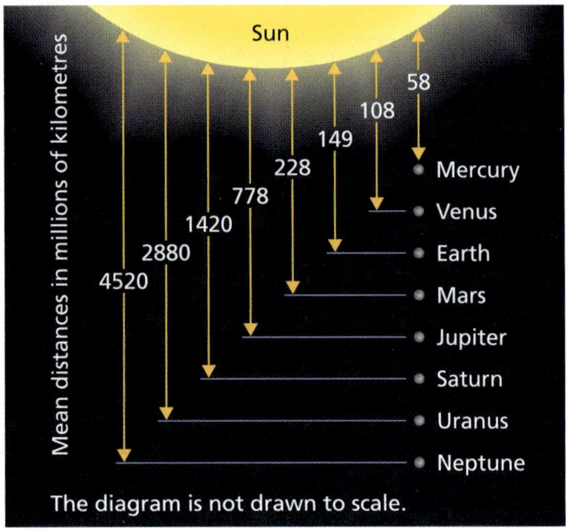

The mean distance of Earth from the sun is about 149 million kilometres. The mean distance of Mars from the sun is about 228 million kilometres. Which planet has the longer period, Earth or Mars? Justify your answer.

C

22. Two students discussed the meaning of the statement $3.2^{4.2} = 132.3213...$

Luc said: It means 3.2 multiplied by itself 4.2 times is about 132.3213.

Karen said: No, you can't multiply a number 4.2 times. $3.2^{4.2}$ can be written as $3.2^{\frac{42}{10}}$. So the statement means that 42 factors, each equal to the tenth root of 3.2, multiplied together will equal about 132.3213.

Which student is correct? Explain.

Reflect

In the power $x^{\frac{m}{n}}$, m and n are natural numbers and x is a rational number. What does the numerator m represent? What does the denominator n represent? Use an example to explain your answer.

What must be true about x for $x^{\frac{m}{n}}$ to be a rational number?

4.5 Negative Exponents and Reciprocals

LESSON FOCUS

Relate negative exponents to reciprocals.

Scientists can calculate the speed of a dinosaur from its tracks. These tracks were found near Grand Cache, Alberta.

Make Connections

A rectangle has area 1 square foot.
List 5 possible pairs of lengths and widths for this rectangle.
What is the relationship between the possible lengths and widths?

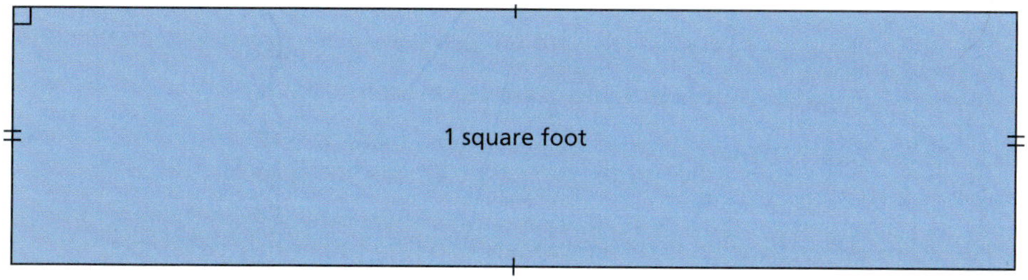

Construct Understanding

TRY THIS

Work with a partner.

You will need grid paper and scissors.

A. Cut out a 16 by 16 grid. Determine the area of the grid in square units and as a power of 2. Record your results in a table like this:

Cut	Area (units^2)	Area as a Power of 2
Start	256	
1		
2		
3		

B. Cut the grid in half and discard one piece.
In the table, record the area of the remaining piece in square units and as a power of 2.

C. Repeat Step B until the paper cannot be cut further.

D. Use patterns to extend the second and third columns of the table to Cut 13.

E. Compare the areas for each pair of powers in the table:
- 2^{-1} and 2^1
- 2^{-2} and 2^2
- 2^{-3} and 2^3

What relationships do you notice?

Two numbers with a product of 1 are reciprocals.
Since $4 \cdot \frac{1}{4} = 1$, the numbers 4 and $\frac{1}{4}$ are reciprocals.

Similarly, $\frac{2}{3} \cdot \frac{3}{2} = 1$, so the numbers $\frac{2}{3}$ and $\frac{3}{2}$ are also reciprocals.

We define powers with negative exponents so that previously developed properties such as $a^m \cdot a^n = a^{m+n}$ and $a^0 = 1$ still apply.

Apply these properties.

$$\begin{aligned} 5^{-2} \cdot 5^2 &= 5^{-2+2} \\ &= 5^0 \\ &= 1 \end{aligned}$$

Since the product of 5^{-2} and 5^2 is 1, 5^{-2} and 5^2 are reciprocals.

So, $5^{-2} = \frac{1}{5^2}$ and $\frac{1}{5^{-2}} = 5^2$

That is, $5^{-2} = \frac{1}{25}$

This suggests the following definition for powers with negative exponents.

Powers with Negative Exponents

When x is any non-zero number and n is a rational number, x^{-n} is the reciprocal of x^n.

That is, $x^{-n} = \frac{1}{x^n}$ and $\frac{1}{x^{-n}} = x^n, x \neq 0$

Why can't x be 0?

Example 1 Evaluating Powers with Negative Integer Exponents

Evaluate each power.

a) 3^{-2} **b)** $\left(-\frac{3}{4}\right)^{-3}$ c) 0.3^{-4}

SOLUTION

a) $3^{-2} = \frac{1}{3^2}$

$= \frac{1}{9}$

b) $\left(-\frac{3}{4}\right)^{-3} = \left(-\frac{4}{3}\right)^3$

$= -\frac{64}{27}$

c) 0.3^{-4}

Use a calculator.

```
0.3^-4
          123.4567901
```

$0.3^{-4} = 123.4567\ldots$

CHECK YOUR UNDERSTANDING

1. Evaluate each power.

a) 7^{-2} **b)** $\left(\frac{10}{3}\right)^{-3}$

c) $(-1.5)^{-3}$

[Answers: a) $\frac{1}{49}$ b) $\frac{27}{1000}$ c) $-0.2962\ldots$]

We can apply the meaning of rational exponents and negative exponents to evaluate powers with negative rational exponents. For example, the rational exponent in the power $8^{-\frac{2}{3}}$ indicates these operations at the right.

reciprocal ↓ $8^{-\frac{2}{3}}$ 2 ←square, 3 ←cube root

Since the exponent $-\frac{2}{3}$ is the product: $(-1)\left(\frac{1}{3}\right)(2)$, and order does not matter when we multiply, we can apply the three operations of reciprocal, cube root, and square in any order.

Example 2 Evaluating Powers with Negative Rational Exponents

Evaluate each power without using a calculator.

a) $8^{-\frac{2}{3}}$ **b)** $\left(\frac{9}{16}\right)^{-\frac{3}{2}}$

(Solution continues.)

SOLUTION

a) $8^{-\frac{2}{3}} = \frac{1}{8^{\frac{2}{3}}}$ — Write with a positive exponent.

$= \frac{1}{(\sqrt[3]{8})^2}$ — Take the cube root.

$= \frac{1}{2^2}$ — Square the result.

$= \frac{1}{4}$

b) $\left(\frac{9}{16}\right)^{-\frac{3}{2}} = \left(\frac{16}{9}\right)^{\frac{3}{2}}$ — Write with a positive exponent.

$= \left(\sqrt{\frac{16}{9}}\right)^3$ — Take the square root.

$= \left(\frac{4}{3}\right)^3$ — Cube the result.

$= \frac{64}{27}$

CHECK YOUR UNDERSTANDING

2. Evaluate each power without using a calculator.

a) $16^{-\frac{5}{4}}$ **b)** $\left(\frac{25}{36}\right)^{-\frac{1}{2}}$

[Answers: a) $\frac{1}{32}$ b) $\frac{6}{5}$]

What other strategies could you use to evaluate the powers?

Example 3 Applying Negative Exponents

Paleontologists use measurements from fossilized dinosaur tracks and the formula $v = 0.155\,s^{\frac{5}{3}}f^{-\frac{7}{6}}$ to estimate the speed at which the dinosaur travelled. In the formula, v is the speed in metres per second, s is the distance between successive footprints of the same foot, and f is the foot length in metres.
Use the measurements in the diagram to estimate the speed of the dinosaur.

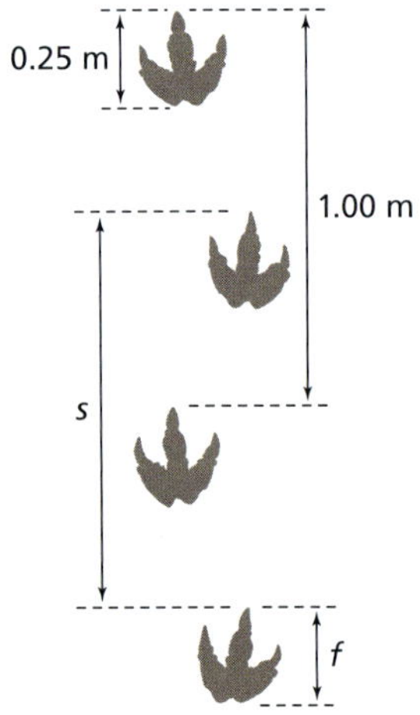

SOLUTION

Use the formula: $v = 0.155\,s^{\frac{5}{3}}f^{-\frac{7}{6}}$

Substitute: $s = 1$ and $f = 0.25$

$v = 0.155\,(1)^{\frac{5}{3}}\,(0.25)^{-\frac{7}{6}}$

$v = 0.155\,(0.25)^{-\frac{7}{6}}$

$v = 0.7811\ldots$

The dinosaur travelled at approximately 0.8 m/s.

CHECK YOUR UNDERSTANDING

3. Use the formula $v = 0.155\,s^{\frac{5}{3}}f^{-\frac{7}{6}}$ to estimate the speed of a dinosaur when $s = 1.5$ and $f = 0.3$.

[Answer: approximately 1.2 m/s]

What is the speed of the dinosaur in kilometres per hour?

Discuss the Ideas

1. When m is an integer, describe the relationship between a^m and a^{-m}.

2. Why is there usually more than one way to determine the value of a power of the form $a^{-\frac{m}{n}}$? Use examples to justify your answer.

Exercises

A

3. Copy then complete each equation.

a) $\frac{1}{5^4} = 5^{\square}$ b) $\left(-\frac{1}{2}\right)^{-3} = (-2)^{\square}$

c) $\frac{1}{3^{\square}} = 3^2$ d) $\frac{1}{4^{-2}} = 4^{\square}$

4. Evaluate the powers in each pair without a calculator.

a) 4^2 and 4^{-2} b) 2^4 and 2^{-4}

c) 6^1 and 6^{-1} d) 4^3 and 4^{-3}

Describe what is similar about the answers, and what is different.

5. Given that $2^{10} = 1024$, what is 2^{-10}?

6. Write each power with a positive exponent.

a) 2^{-3} b) 3^{-5} c) $(-7)^{-2}$

7. Write each power with a positive exponent.

a) $\left(\frac{1}{2}\right)^{-2}$ b) $\left(\frac{2}{3}\right)^{-3}$ c) $\left(-\frac{6}{5}\right)^{-4}$

8. Evaluate each power without using a calculator.

a) 3^{-2} b) 2^{-4} c) $(-2)^{-5}$

d) $\left(\frac{1}{3}\right)^{-3}$ e) $\left(-\frac{2}{3}\right)^{-2}$ f) $\frac{1}{5^{-3}}$

B

9. Evaluate each power without using a calculator.

a) $4^{-\frac{1}{2}}$ b) $0.09^{-\frac{1}{2}}$

c) $27^{-\frac{1}{3}}$ d) $(-64)^{-\frac{1}{3}}$

e) $(-0.027)^{-\frac{2}{3}}$ f) $32^{-\frac{2}{5}}$

g) $9^{-\frac{3}{2}}$ h) $0.04^{-\frac{3}{2}}$

10. Use a power with a negative exponent to write an equivalent form for each number.

a) $\frac{1}{9}$ b) $\frac{1}{5}$ c) 4 d) -3

11. When you save money in a bank, the bank pays you *interest*. This interest is added to your investment and the resulting amount also earns interest. We say the interest *compounds*. Suppose you want an amount of \$3000 in 5 years. The interest rate for the savings account is 2.5% compounded annually. The money, P dollars, you must invest now is given by the formula: $P = 3000(1.025)^{-5}$. How much must you invest now to have \$3000 in 5 years?

12. Here is a student's solution for evaluating a power. Identify any errors in the solution. Write a correct solution.

$$\left(-\frac{64}{125}\right)^{-\frac{5}{3}} = \left(\frac{64}{125}\right)^{\frac{5}{3}}$$
$$= \left(\sqrt[3]{\frac{64}{125}}\right)^5$$
$$= \left(\frac{4}{5}\right)^5$$
$$= \frac{1024}{3125}$$

13. Evaluate each power without using a calculator.

a) $27^{-\frac{4}{3}}$ b) $16^{-1.5}$ c) $32^{-0.4}$

d) $\left(-\frac{8}{27}\right)^{-\frac{2}{3}}$ e) $\left(\frac{81}{16}\right)^{-\frac{3}{4}}$ f) $\left(\frac{9}{4}\right)^{-\frac{5}{2}}$

14. Michelle wants to invest enough money on January 1st to pay her nephew \$150 at the end of each year for the next 10 years. The savings account pays 3.2% compounded annually. The money, P dollars, that Michelle must invest today is given by the formula $P = \frac{150\left[1 - 1.032^{-10}\right]}{0.032}$. How much must Michelle invest on January 1st?

15. The intensity of light at its source is 100%. The intensity, I, at a distance d centimetres from the source is given by the formula $I = 100d^{-2}$. Use the formula to determine the intensity of the light 23 cm from the source.

16. Which is greater, 2^{-5} or 5^{-2}? Verify your answer.

17. a) Identify the patterns in this list.
$16 = 2^4$
$8 = 2^3$
$4 = 2^2$
b) Extend the patterns in part a downward. Write the next 5 rows in the pattern.
c) Explain how this pattern shows that $a^{-n} = \frac{1}{a^n}$.

18. How many times as great as 3^{-5} is 3^3? Express your answer as a power and in standard form.

19. What do you know about the sign of the exponent in each case? Justify your answers.
a) $3^x > 1$ b) $3^x < 1$ c) $3^x = 1$

C

20. A number is raised to a negative exponent. Is it always true that the value of the power will be less than 1? Use an example to explain.

21. There is a gravitational force, F newtons, between Earth and the moon. This force is given by the formula $F = (6.67 \times 10^{-11})Mmr^{-2}$, where M is the mass of Earth in kilograms, m is the mass of the moon in kilograms, and r is the distance between Earth and the moon in metres. The mass of Earth is approximately 5.9736×10^{24} kg. The mass of the moon is approximately 7.349×10^{22} kg. The mean distance between them is approximately 382 260 km.
a) What is the gravitational force between Earth and the moon?
b) The value r is actually the distance between the centres of Earth and the moon. Research to find the diameters of Earth and the moon. Calculate the gravitational force with this new value of r.

Reflect Explain what a negative exponent means. Use examples to demonstrate your thinking.

THE WORLD OF MATH

Math Fact: Computers and π

The most famous irrational number of all, π, was not proved irrational until the 18th century. Throughout history, many mathematicians have spent much time manually calculating the decimal digits of π. This had no practical value, but did provide motivation for some discoveries that have been influential in modern mathematics. In 1949, an early computer calculated π to 2000 digits, which was many more digits than any previous manual calculations. Today, calculating digits of π is a test of the power, speed, and accuracy of supercomputers. Computers have calculated π to more than 6 billion digits, and even a home computer can be programmed to calculate π to millions of digits in a few hours. This T-shirt shows the first 100 digits of π.

CHECKPOINT 2

Connections

$(a^m)^n = a^{mn}$

↓ When $m = \frac{1}{n}$

$(a^{\frac{1}{n}})^n = a^{\frac{1}{n} \cdot n}$
$= a^1$
$= a$

↓ Definition of a radical

$a^{\frac{1}{n}} = \sqrt[n]{a}$

↓ $a^{\frac{m}{n}} = \left(a^{\frac{1}{n}}\right)^m$ and $a^{\frac{m}{n}} = (a^m)^{\frac{1}{n}}$

$a^{\frac{m}{n}} = (\sqrt[n]{a})^m$
$a^{\frac{m}{n}} = \sqrt[n]{a^m}$

$a^n \cdot a^m = a^{n+m}$

↓ When $m = -n$

$a^n \cdot a^{-n} = a^{n+(-n)}$
$= a^0$
$= 1$

↓ Definition of a reciprocal

$a^{-n} = \frac{1}{a^n}$

↓ When n is a rational number

$a^{-\frac{m}{n}} = \frac{1}{a^{\frac{m}{n}}}$

↓ Reciprocal of a fraction

$\left(\frac{a}{b}\right)^{-\frac{m}{n}} = \left(\frac{b}{a}\right)^{\frac{m}{n}}$

Concept Development

- **In Lesson 4.4**
  - You used patterns to explain a meaning for an exponent of the form $\frac{1}{n}$.
  - You applied the exponent law for the power of a power to justify why a **power with exponent $\frac{1}{n}$ is the nth root of the base of the power.**
- **In Lesson 4.5**
  - You used patterns to explain a meaning for a negative exponent.
  - You applied the exponent law for multiplying powers to justify why a **power with a negative rational exponent is written as a reciprocal.**

Assess Your Understanding

4.4

1. Evaluate each power without using a calculator.

   a) $16^{\frac{1}{4}}$ b) $49^{0.5}$ c) $(-64)^{\frac{2}{3}}$ d) $\left(\frac{49}{9}\right)^{1.5}$ e) $(-8)^{\frac{5}{3}}$

2. a) Write each power as a radical.

   i) $35^{\frac{2}{3}}$ ii) $32^{\frac{3}{2}}$ iii) $(-32)^{\frac{2}{5}}$

   iv) $400^{1.5}$ v) $(-125)^{\frac{1}{3}}$ vi) $\left(\frac{8}{125}\right)^{\frac{2}{3}}$

   b) Evaluate each radical in part a without using a calculator, if possible. Explain why you could not evaluate some radicals.

3. Write each radical in exponent form.

   a) $\sqrt[3]{4}$ b) $\sqrt{9}$ c) $\sqrt[4]{18}$ d) $\left(\sqrt{10}\right)^3$ e) $\left(\sqrt[3]{-10}\right)^2$

4. The circulation time is the average time it takes for all the blood in the body to circulate once and return to the heart. The circulation time for a mammal can be estimated from the formula $T \doteq 17.4m^{\frac{1}{4}}$, where T is the circulation time in seconds and m is the body mass in kilograms. Estimate the circulation time for a mammal with mass 85 kg.

5. Arrange these numbers in order from least to greatest.

   $3^{\frac{3}{2}}, \sqrt[3]{3}, \left(\sqrt{3}\right)^5, 3^{\frac{2}{3}}, \left(\sqrt[3]{3}\right)^4$

6. An AudioCube creates sounds and musical patterns. Each cube exchanges musical information wirelessly with nearby cubes. The volume of an AudioCube is 421 875 mm^3. Write the edge length of the cube as a radical and as a power, then calculate the edge length.

4.5

7. Evaluate each power without using a calculator.

   a) $\left(\frac{2}{3}\right)^{-4}$ b) 0.5^{-2} c) $(-1000)^{-\frac{2}{3}}$

   d) $\left(\frac{1}{4}\right)^{-\frac{1}{2}}$ e) $\left(\frac{1}{10}\right)^{-2}$ f) $(-0.008)^{-\frac{4}{3}}$

8. Suppose you want \$5000 in 3 years. The interest rate for a savings account is 2.9% compounded annually. The money, P dollars, you must invest now is given by the formula: $P = 5000(1.029)^{-3}$
   How much must you invest now to have \$5000 in 3 years?

4.6 Applying the Exponent Laws

LESSON FOCUS
Apply the exponent laws to simplify expressions.

We can use a measuring cylinder to determine the volume of a sphere. Then we can use the exponent laws to help calculate the radius.

Make Connections

Recall the exponent laws for integer bases and whole number exponents.

Product of powers: $a^m \cdot a^n = a^{m+n}$

Quotient of powers: $a^m \div a^n = a^{m-n}, a \neq 0$

Power of a power: $(a^m)^n = a^{mn}$

Power of a product: $(ab)^m = a^m b^m$

Power of a quotient: $\left(\frac{a}{b}\right)^m = \frac{a^m}{b^m}, b \neq 0$

What other types of numbers could be a base? An exponent?
How would you use the exponent laws to evaluate an expression with these numbers?

Construct Understanding

THINK ABOUT IT

Work on your own.

What is the value of $\left(\frac{a^6b^9}{a^5b^8}\right)^{-2}$ when $a = -3$ and $b = 2$?

Compare strategies with a classmate.
If you used the same strategy, find a different strategy.
Which strategy is more efficient, and why?

We can use the exponent laws to simplify expressions that contain rational number bases. It is a convention to write a simplified power with a positive exponent.

Example 1 Simplifying Numerical Expressions with Rational Number Bases

Simplify by writing as a single power. Explain the reasoning.

a) $0.3^{-3} \cdot 0.3^5$

b) $\left[\left(-\frac{3}{2}\right)^{-4}\right]^2 \cdot \left[\left(-\frac{3}{2}\right)^2\right]^3$

c) $\frac{(1.4^3)(1.4^4)}{1.4^{-2}}$

d) $\left(\frac{7^{\frac{2}{3}}}{7^{\frac{1}{3}} \cdot 7^{\frac{5}{3}}}\right)^6$

SOLUTION

a) $0.3^{-3} \cdot 0.3^5$

Use the product of powers law:
When the bases are the same, add the exponents.

$0.3^{-3} \cdot 0.3^5 = 0.3^{(-3)+5}$
$= 0.3^2$

b) $\left[\left(-\frac{3}{2}\right)^{-4}\right]^2 \cdot \left[\left(-\frac{3}{2}\right)^2\right]^3$

First use the power of a power law:
For each power, multiply the exponents.

$$\left[\left(-\frac{3}{2}\right)^{-4}\right]^2 \cdot \left[\left(-\frac{3}{2}\right)^2\right]^3 = \left(-\frac{3}{2}\right)^{(-4)(2)} \cdot \left(-\frac{3}{2}\right)^{(2)(3)}$$

Then use the product of powers law.

$$\left[\left(-\frac{3}{2}\right)^{-4}\right]^2 \cdot \left[\left(-\frac{3}{2}\right)^2\right]^3 = \left(-\frac{3}{2}\right)^{-8} \cdot \left(-\frac{3}{2}\right)^{6}$$

$= \left(-\frac{3}{2}\right)^{-2}$ Write with a positive exponent.

$= \left(-\frac{2}{3}\right)^{2}$

c) $\frac{(1.4^3)(1.4^4)}{1.4^{-2}}$ Use the product of powers law.

$= \frac{1.4^{3+4}}{1.4^{-2}}$

$= \frac{1.4^7}{1.4^{-2}}$ Use the quotient of powers law.

$= 1.4^{7-(-2)}$
$= 1.4^9$

(Solution continues.)

CHECK YOUR UNDERSTANDING

1. Simplify by writing as a single power. Explain your reasoning.

a) $0.8^2 \cdot 0.8^{-7}$

b) $\left[\left(-\frac{4}{5}\right)^2\right]^{-3} \div \left[\left(-\frac{4}{5}\right)^4\right]^{-5}$

c) $\frac{(1.5^{-3})^{-5}}{1.5^5}$

d) $\frac{9^{\frac{5}{4}} \cdot 9^{-\frac{1}{4}}}{9^{\frac{3}{4}}}$

[Answers: a) $\frac{1}{0.8^5}$ b) $\left(-\frac{4}{5}\right)^{14}$ c) 1.5^{10} d) $9^{\frac{1}{4}}$]

d) $\left(\dfrac{7^{\frac{2}{3}}}{7^{\frac{1}{3}} \cdot 7^{\frac{5}{3}}}\right)^6$ Use the product of powers law.

$= \left(\dfrac{7^{\frac{2}{3}}}{7^{\frac{1}{3}+\frac{5}{3}}}\right)^6$

$= \left(\dfrac{7^{\frac{2}{3}}}{7^{\frac{6}{3}}}\right)^6$ Use the quotient of powers law.

$= \left(7^{\frac{2}{3}-\frac{6}{3}}\right)^6$

$= \left(7^{-\frac{4}{3}}\right)^6$ Use the power of a power law.

$= 7^{\left(-\frac{4}{3}\right)(6)}$

$= 7^{-\frac{24}{3}}$

$= 7^{-8}$ Write with a positive exponent.

$= \dfrac{1}{7^8}$

In part d, what other strategy could you use? Which strategy is more efficient?

Example 2 Simplifying Algebraic Expressions with Integer Exponents

Simplify. Explain the reasoning.

a) $(x^3y^2)(x^2y^{-4})$

b) $\dfrac{10a^5b^3}{2a^2b^{-2}}$

SOLUTION

a) $(x^3y^2)(x^2y^{-4}) = x^3 \cdot y^2 \cdot x^2 \cdot y^{-4}$ x^3y^2 means $x^3 \cdot y^2$

$= x^3 \cdot x^2 \cdot y^2 \cdot y^{-4}$ Use the product of powers law.

$= x^{3+2} \cdot y^{2+(-4)}$

$= x^5 \cdot y^{-2}$ Write with a positive exponent.

$= x^5 \cdot \dfrac{1}{y^2}$

$= \dfrac{x^5}{y^2}$

b) $\dfrac{10a^5b^3}{2a^2b^{-2}} = \dfrac{10}{2} \cdot \dfrac{a^5}{a^2} \cdot \dfrac{b^3}{b^{-2}}$ Use the quotient of powers law.

$= 5 \cdot a^{5-2} \cdot b^{3-(-2)}$

$= 5 \cdot a^3 \cdot b^5$

$= 5a^3b^5$

CHECK YOUR UNDERSTANDING

2. Simplify. Explain your reasoning.

a) $m^4n^{-2} \cdot m^2n^3$

b) $\dfrac{6x^4y^{-3}}{14xy^2}$

[Answers: a) m^6n b) $\dfrac{3x^3}{7y^5}$]

Example 3 Simplifying Algebraic Expressions with Rational Exponents

Simplify. Explain the reasoning.

a) $(8a^3b^6)^{\frac{1}{3}}$

b) $(x^{\frac{3}{2}}y^2)(x^{\frac{1}{2}}y^{-1})$

c) $\dfrac{4a^{-2}b^{\frac{2}{3}}}{2a^2b^{\frac{1}{3}}}$

d) $\left(\dfrac{100a}{25a^5b^{-\frac{1}{2}}}\right)^{\frac{1}{2}}$

SOLUTION

a) $(8a^3b^6)^{\frac{1}{3}} = 8^{\frac{1}{3}} \cdot a^{3\left(\frac{1}{3}\right)} \cdot b^{6\left(\frac{1}{3}\right)}$ Using the power of a power law.

$= (2^3)^{\frac{1}{3}} \cdot a^1 \cdot b^2$

$= 2ab^2$

b) $(x^{\frac{3}{2}}y^2)(x^{\frac{1}{2}}y^{-1}) = x^{\frac{3}{2}} \cdot x^{\frac{1}{2}} \cdot y^2 \cdot y^{-1}$ Use the product of powers law.

$= x^{\frac{3}{2}+\frac{1}{2}} \cdot y^{2+(-1)}$

$= x^2y$

c) $\dfrac{4a^{-2}b^{\frac{2}{3}}}{2a^2b^{\frac{1}{3}}} = \dfrac{4}{2} \cdot \dfrac{a^{-2}}{a^2} \cdot \dfrac{b^{\frac{2}{3}}}{b^{\frac{1}{3}}}$ Use the quotient of powers law.

$= 2 \cdot a^{(-2)-2} \cdot b^{\frac{2}{3}-\frac{1}{3}}$

$= 2 \cdot a^{-4} \cdot b^{\frac{1}{3}}$ Write with a positive exponent.

$= \dfrac{2b^{\frac{1}{3}}}{a^4}$

d) $\left(\dfrac{100a}{25a^5b^{-\frac{1}{2}}}\right)^{\frac{1}{2}} = \left(\dfrac{100}{25} \cdot \dfrac{a^1}{a^5} \cdot \dfrac{1}{b^{-\frac{1}{2}}}\right)^{\frac{1}{2}}$ Simplify inside the brackets first. Use the quotient of powers law. Write with a positive exponent.

$= \left(4 \cdot a^{1-5} \cdot b^{\frac{1}{2}}\right)^{\frac{1}{2}}$

$= \left(4 \cdot a^{-4} \cdot b^{\frac{1}{2}}\right)^{\frac{1}{2}}$ Use the power of a power law.

$= 4^{\frac{1}{2}} \cdot a^{(-4)\left(\frac{1}{2}\right)} \cdot b^{\left(\frac{1}{2}\right)\left(\frac{1}{2}\right)}$

$= 2 \cdot a^{-2} \cdot b^{\frac{1}{4}}$ Write with a positive exponent.

$= \dfrac{2b^{\frac{1}{4}}}{a^2}$

CHECK YOUR UNDERSTANDING

3. Simplify. Explain your reasoning.

a) $(25a^4b^2)^{\frac{3}{2}}$

b) $(x^3y^{-\frac{3}{2}})(x^{-1}y^{\frac{1}{2}})$

c) $\dfrac{12x^{-5}y^{\frac{5}{2}}}{3x^{\frac{1}{2}}y^{-\frac{1}{2}}}$

d) $\left(\dfrac{50x^2y^4}{2x^4y^7}\right)^{\frac{1}{2}}$

[Answers: a) $125a^6b^3$ b) $\dfrac{x^2}{y}$ c) $\dfrac{4y^3}{x^{\frac{11}{2}}}$ d) $\dfrac{5}{xy^{\frac{3}{2}}}$]

Example 4 Solving Problems Using the Exponent Laws

A sphere has volume 425 m^3.
What is the radius of the sphere to the nearest tenth of a metre?

SOLUTION

The volume V of a sphere with radius r is given by the formula: $V = \frac{4}{3}\pi r^3$. Substitute $V = 425$, then solve for r.

$$425 = \frac{4}{3}\pi r^3$$

Multiply each side by 3.

$$3(425) = 3\left(\frac{4}{3}\pi r^3\right)$$

$$1275 = 4\pi r^3$$

Divide each side by 4π.

$$\frac{1275}{4\pi} = \frac{4\pi r^3}{4\pi}$$

$$\frac{1275}{4\pi} = r^3$$

To solve for r, take the cube root of each side by raising each side to the one-third power.

$$\left(\frac{1275}{4\pi}\right)^{\frac{1}{3}} = (r^3)^{\frac{1}{3}}$$

Use the power of a power law.

$$\left(\frac{1275}{4\pi}\right)^{\frac{1}{3}} = r$$

```
3√(1275/(4π))
     4.664088405
```

$$r = 4.6640\ldots$$

The radius of the sphere is approximately 4.7 m.

CHECK YOUR UNDERSTANDING

4. A cone with height and radius equal has volume 18 cm^3. What are the radius and height of the cone to the nearest tenth of a centimetre?

[Answer: approximately 2.6 cm]

How do you know that the length of the radius is an irrational number?

Discuss the Ideas

1. Suppose you want to evaluate an algebraic expression for particular values of the variables. Why might it be helpful to simplify the expression first?

2. When you simplify an expression, how do you know which exponent law to apply first?

Exercises

A

3. Simplify.

a) $x^3 \cdot x^4$ b) $a^2 \cdot a^{-5}$

c) $b^{-3} \cdot b^5$ d) $m^2 \cdot m^{-3}$

4. Write as a single power.

a) $0.5^2 \cdot 0.5^3$ b) $0.5^2 \cdot 0.5^{-3}$

c) $\frac{0.5^2}{0.5^3}$ d) $\frac{0.5^2}{0.5^{-3}}$

5. Simplify.

a) $\frac{x^4}{x^2}$ b) $\frac{x^2}{x^5}$

c) $n^6 \div n^5$ d) $\frac{a^2}{a^6}$

6. Simplify.

a) $(n^2)^3$ b) $(z^2)^{-3}$

c) $(n^{-4})^{-3}$ d) $(c^{-2})^2$

7. Write as a single power.

a) $\left[\left(\frac{3}{5}\right)^3\right]^4$ b) $\left[\left(\frac{3}{5}\right)^3\right]^{-4}$

c) $\left[\left(\frac{3}{5}\right)^{-3}\right]^{-4}$ d) $\left[\left(-\frac{3}{5}\right)^{-3}\right]^{-4}$

8. Simplify.

a) $\left(\frac{a}{b}\right)^2$ b) $\left(\frac{n^2}{m}\right)^3$

c) $\left(\frac{c^2}{d^2}\right)^{-4}$ d) $\left(\frac{2b}{5c}\right)^2$

e) $(ab)^2$ f) $(n^2m)^3$

g) $(c^3d^2)^{-4}$ h) $(xy^{-1})^3$

B

9. Simplify. State the exponent law you used.

a) $x^{-3} \cdot x^4$ b) $a^{-4} \cdot a^{-1}$

c) $b^4 \cdot b^{-3} \cdot b^2$ d) $m^8 \cdot m^{-2} \cdot m^{-6}$

e) $\frac{x^{-5}}{x^2}$ f) $\frac{s^5}{s^{-5}}$

g) $\frac{b^{-8}}{b^{-3}}$ h) $\frac{t^{-4}}{t^{-4}}$

10. Evaluate.

a) $1.5^{\frac{3}{2}} \cdot 1.5^{\frac{1}{2}}$ b) $\left(\frac{3}{4}\right)^{\frac{3}{4}} \cdot \left(\frac{3}{4}\right)^{\frac{5}{4}}$

c) $(-0.6)^{\frac{1}{3}} \cdot (-0.6)^{\frac{5}{3}}$ d) $\left(\frac{4}{5}\right)^{\frac{4}{3}} \cdot \left(\frac{4}{5}\right)^{-\frac{4}{3}}$

e) $\frac{0.6^{\frac{1}{2}}}{0.6^{\frac{3}{2}}}$ f) $\frac{\left(-\frac{3}{8}\right)^{\frac{2}{3}}}{\left(-\frac{3}{8}\right)^{-\frac{1}{3}}}$

g) $\frac{0.49^{\frac{5}{2}}}{0.49^4}$ h) $\frac{0.027^{\frac{5}{3}}}{0.027^{\frac{4}{3}}}$

11. Simplify. Explain your reasoning.

a) $(x^{-1}y^{-2})^{-3}$ b) $(2a^{-2}b^2)^{-2}$

c) $(4m^2n^3)^{-3}$ d) $\left(\frac{3}{2}m^{-2}n^{-3}\right)^{-4}$

12. A cone with equal height and radius has volume 1234 cm^3. What is the height of the cone to the nearest tenth of a centimetre?

13. A sphere has volume 375 cubic feet. What is the surface area of the sphere to the nearest square foot?

14. Simplify. Which exponent laws did you use?

a) $\frac{(a^2b^{-1})^{-2}}{(a^{-3}b)^3}$ b) $\left(\frac{(c^{-3}d)^{-1}}{c^2d}\right)^{-2}$

15. Evaluate each expression for $a = -2$ and $b = 1$. Explain your strategy.

a) $(a^3b^2)(a^2b^3)$ b) $(a^{-1}b^{-2})(a^{-2}b^{-3})$

c) $\frac{a^{-4}b^5}{ab^3}$ d) $\left(\frac{a^{-7}b^7}{a^{-9}b^{10}}\right)^{-5}$

16. Simplify.

a) $m^{\frac{2}{3}} \cdot m^{\frac{4}{3}}$ b) $x^{-\frac{3}{2}} \div x^{-\frac{1}{4}}$

c) $\frac{-9a^{-4}b^{\frac{3}{4}}}{3a^2b^{\frac{1}{4}}}$ d) $\left(\frac{-64c^6}{a^9b^{-\frac{1}{2}}}\right)^{\frac{1}{3}}$

17. Identify any errors in each solution for simplifying an expression. Write a correct solution.

a) $(x^2y^{-3})(x^{\frac{1}{2}}y^{-1}) = x^2 \cdot x^{\frac{1}{2}} \cdot y^{-3} \cdot y^{-1}$
$= x^1 \cdot y^3$
$= xy^3$

b) $\left(\frac{-5a^2}{b^{\frac{1}{2}}}\right)^{-2} = \frac{10a^{-4}}{b^{-1}}$
$= \frac{10b}{a^4}$

18. Explain how to use a measuring cylinder containing water to calculate the diameter of a marble that fits inside the cylinder.

19. Identify the errors in each simplification. Write the correct solution.

a) $\frac{(m^{-3}.\ n^2)^{-4}}{(m^2.\ n^{-3})^2} = (m^{-5}.\ n^5)^{-6}$
$= m^{30}.\ n^{30}$
$= (mn)^{30}$

b) $\left(r^{\frac{1}{2}}.\ s^{-\frac{3}{2}}\right)^{\frac{1}{2}}.\left(r^{-\frac{1}{4}}.\ s^{\frac{1}{2}}\right)^{-1} = r^1.\ s^{-1}.\ r^{-\frac{5}{4}}.\ s^{-\frac{1}{2}}$
$= r^{1-\frac{5}{4}}.\ s^{-1-\frac{1}{2}}$
$= r^{-\frac{1}{4}}.\ s^{-\frac{3}{2}}$
$= \frac{1}{r^{\frac{1}{4}}.\ s^{\frac{3}{2}}}$

20. ISO paper sizes A0, A1, A2, …, are commonly used outside of North America. For any whole number n, the width, in metres, of a piece of An paper is $2^{-\frac{2n+1}{4}}$ and its length, in metres, is $2^{-\frac{2n-1}{4}}$.

a) Write, then simplify expressions to represent the dimensions of each piece of paper. Evaluate each measure to the nearest millimetre.
  i) A3 ii) A4 iii) A5

b) Suppose each piece of paper from part a is folded in half along a line perpendicular to its length. Write, then simplify expressions to represent the dimensions of each folded piece.

c) Compare your results in parts a and b. What do you notice?

C

21. Simplify. Show your work.

a) $\left(\dfrac{a^{-3}b}{c^2}\right)^{-4} \cdot \left(\dfrac{c^5}{a^4b^{-3}}\right)^{-1}$ b) $\dfrac{(2a^{-1}b^4c^{-3})^{-2}}{(4a^2bc^{-4})^2}$

22. If $x = a^{-2}$ and $y = a^{\frac{2}{3}}$, write each expression in terms of a.

a) $\left(x^{\frac{1}{2}}y^{\frac{2}{3}}\right)^2$ b) $\left(x^{\frac{3}{4}} \div y^{-\frac{1}{2}}\right)^3$

23. Write 3 different expressions for each result.

a) $x^{\frac{3}{2}}$ is the product of two powers with rational exponents.

b) $x^{\frac{3}{2}}$ is the quotient of two powers with rational exponents.

c) $x^{\frac{3}{2}}$ is the result of raising a power with a rational exponent to a rational exponent.

24. A regular tetrahedron has edge length 1 cm. It is placed inside a sphere so that all its vertices touch the surface of the sphere. Point D is the centre of the sphere. The measures, in centimetres, of 3 line segments are:

$$AB = \left(\frac{2}{3}\right)^{\frac{1}{2}};\ AC = \frac{3}{2}\left(\frac{1}{3}\right)^{\frac{1}{2}};\ AE = \left(\frac{1}{3}\right)^{\frac{1}{2}}$$

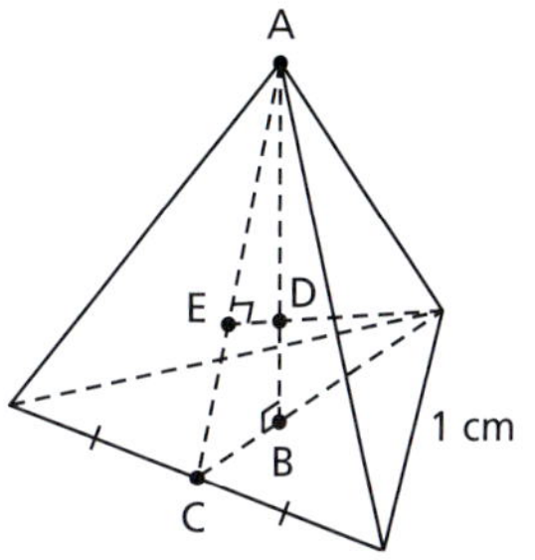

Given that $\triangle$ABC is similar to $\triangle$AED and $\dfrac{AC}{AB} = \dfrac{AD}{AE}$; determine the length of AD.

Reflect

Explain how to apply the exponent laws to simplify algebraic expressions. Use examples to illustrate the types of expressions you can simplify.

THE WORLD OF MATH

Math Fact: Platonic Solids

Platonic solids are the only regular polyhedra that can be placed in a sphere so that each vertex touches the surface of the sphere. In about 300 B.C.E, Euclid used trigonometry, similar triangles, and the Pythagorean Theorem to show the ratio of the edge length of each Platonic solid to the diameter of the sphere:

Tetrahedron Cube Octahedron Dodecahedron Icosahedron

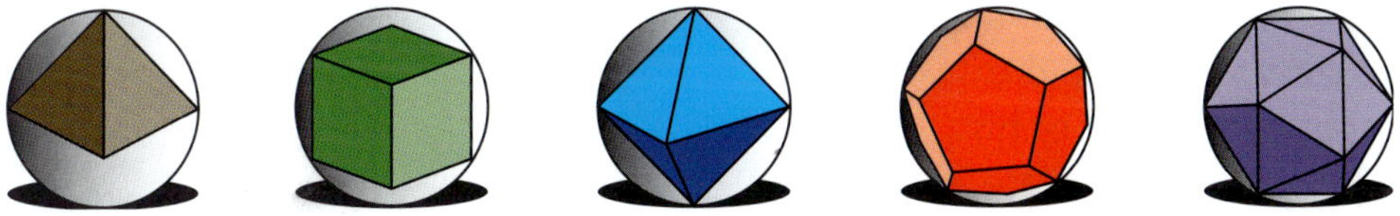

$1 : \left(\frac{3}{2}\right)^{\frac{1}{2}}$ $1 : 3^{\frac{1}{2}}$ $1 : 2^{\frac{1}{2}}$ $1 : \frac{1}{2}\left(3^{\frac{1}{2}} + 15^{\frac{1}{2}}\right)$ $1 : \frac{1}{2}\left(10 + 2(5)^{\frac{1}{2}}\right)^{\frac{1}{2}}$

STUDY GUIDE

CONCEPT SUMMARY

Big Ideas	Applying the Big Ideas
■ Any number that can be written as the fraction $\frac{m}{n}$, $n \neq 0$, where m and n are integers, is rational.	This means that: ■ If a real number can be expressed as a terminating or repeating decimal, it is rational; otherwise, it is irrational.
■ Exponents can be used to represent roots and reciprocals of rational numbers.	■ The numerator of a rational exponent indicates a power, while the denominator indicates a root. A negative exponent indicates a reciprocal.
■ The exponent laws can be extended to include powers with rational and variable bases, and rational exponents.	■ We can use the exponent laws to simplify expressions that involve rational exponents.

Reflect on the Chapter

- How can you predict whether the value of a radical will be a rational number or an irrational number?
- How were the exponent laws used to create definitions for negative exponents and rational exponents?
- What does it mean to simplify an expression involving radicals or exponents?

THE WORLD OF MATH

Careers: Financial Planner

The financial services industry offers many career opportunities – in banking, insurance, investment firms, as well as private practice. A personal financial planner uses math and technology to explore different ways for a person to invest her or his money. The ability to understand, manipulate, and evaluate algebraic formulas that involve rational exponents is an essential skill.

SKILLS SUMMARY

Skill	Description	Example
Classify numbers. [4.1, 4.2]	To determine whether a number is rational or irrational, write the number in decimal form. ■ Repeating and terminating decimals are rational. ■ Non-repeating, non-terminating decimals are irrational.	Rational numbers: $2, 0, -3, 3.75, 0.0\overline{1}, \frac{3}{5}, -\frac{10}{7}$ Irrational numbers: $\sqrt{3}, \pi$
Simplify radicals. [4.3]	To simplify a square root: **1.** Write the radicand as a product of its greatest perfect square factor and another number. **2.** Take the square root of the perfect square factor. A similar procedure applies for cube roots and higher roots.	$\sqrt{200} = \sqrt{100 \cdot 2}$ $= \sqrt{100} \cdot \sqrt{2}$ $= 10\sqrt{2}$ $\sqrt[3]{200} = \sqrt[3]{8 \cdot 25}$ $= \sqrt[3]{8} \cdot \sqrt[3]{25}$ $= 2\sqrt[3]{25}$
Evaluate powers. [4.4, 4.5]	To evaluate powers without using a calculator: **1.** Rewrite a power with a negative exponent as a power with a positive exponent. **2.** Represent powers with fractional exponents as radicals. **3.** Use mental math to evaluate the powers and/or simplify the roots.	$64^{-\frac{2}{3}} = \frac{1}{64^{\frac{2}{3}}}$ $= \frac{1}{(\sqrt[3]{64})^2}$ $= \frac{1}{4^2}$ $= \frac{1}{16}$
Apply the exponent laws to simplify expressions. [4.6]	To simplify expressions involving powers: **1.** Remove brackets by applying the exponent laws for products of powers, quotients of powers, or powers of powers. **2.** Write the simplest expression using positive exponents.	$\left(\frac{(xy^2)^3}{x^5y}\right)^{-4} = \left(\frac{x^3y^6}{x^5y}\right)^{-4}$ $= \left(\frac{x^5y^1}{x^3y^6}\right)^4$ $= (x^{5-3}y^{1-6})^4$ $= (x^2y^{-5})^4$ $= x^8y^{-20}$ $= \frac{x^8}{y^{20}}$

REVIEW

4.1

1. Evaluate each radical. Why do you not need a calculator?

a) $\sqrt[3]{1000}$ b) $\sqrt{0.81}$

c) $\sqrt[6]{64}$ d) $\sqrt[4]{\frac{81}{625}}$

2. Explain, using examples, the meaning of the index of a radical.

3. Estimate the value of each radical to 1 decimal place. What strategies can you use?

a) $\sqrt{11}$ b) $\sqrt[3]{-12}$ c) $\sqrt[4]{15}$

4. Identify the number in each case.

a) 5 is a square root of the number.
b) 6 is the cube root of the number.
c) 7 is a fourth root of the number.

5. For $\sqrt[3]{35}$, does its decimal form terminate, repeat, or neither? Support your answer with an explanation.

4.2

6. Tell whether each number is rational or irrational. Justify your answers.

a) -2 b) 17 c) $\sqrt{16}$
d) $\sqrt{32}$ e) 0.756 f) $12.\overline{3}$
g) 0 h) $\sqrt[3]{81}$ i) π

7. Determine the approximate side length of a square with area 23 cm^2. How could you check your answer?

8. Look at this calculator screen.

π
3.141592654

a) Is the number 3.141 592 654 rational or irrational? Explain.
b) Is the number π rational or irrational? Explain your answer.

9. Place each number on a number line, then order the numbers from least to greatest.

$\sqrt[3]{30}, \sqrt{20}, \sqrt[4]{18}, \sqrt[3]{-30}, \sqrt{30}, \sqrt[4]{10}$

10. The formula $T = 2\pi\sqrt{\frac{L}{9.8}}$ gives the time, T seconds, for one complete swing of a pendulum with length L metres. A clock pendulum is 0.25 m long. What time does the pendulum take to complete one swing? Give the answer to the nearest second.

4.3

11. Write each radical in simplest form.

a) $\sqrt{150}$ b) $\sqrt[3]{135}$

c) $\sqrt{112}$ d) $\sqrt[4]{162}$

12. Write each mixed radical as an entire radical.

a) $6\sqrt{5}$ b) $3\sqrt{14}$

c) $4\sqrt[3]{3}$ d) $2\sqrt[4]{2}$

13. Alfalfa cubes are fed to horses to provide protein, minerals, and vitamins.

Two sizes of cubes have volumes 32 cm^3 and 11 cm^3. What is the difference in the edge lengths of the cubes? How can you use radicals to find out?

14. A student simplified $\sqrt{300}$ as shown:

$$\begin{aligned}\sqrt{300} &= \sqrt{3}\cdot\sqrt{100}\\ &= \sqrt{3}\cdot\sqrt{50}\cdot\sqrt{50}\\ &= \sqrt{3}\cdot\sqrt{2}\cdot\sqrt{25}\cdot\sqrt{2}\cdot\sqrt{25}\\ &= 3\cdot 5\cdot\sqrt{2}\cdot 5\\ &= 75\sqrt{2}\end{aligned}$$

Identify the errors the student made, then write a correct solution.

15. Arrange these numbers in order from greatest to least, without using a calculator. Describe your strategy.

$5\sqrt{2}, 4\sqrt{3}, 3\sqrt{6}, 2\sqrt{7}, 6\sqrt{2}$

4.4

16. Show, with examples, why $a^{\frac{1}{n}} = \sqrt[n]{a}$, when n is a natural number and a is a rational number.

17. Express each power as a radical.

a) $12^{\frac{1}{4}}$ b) $(-50)^{\frac{5}{3}}$

c) $1.2^{0.5}$ d) $\left(\frac{3}{8}\right)^{\frac{1}{3}}$

18. Express each radical as a power.

a) $\sqrt{1.4}$ b) $\sqrt[3]{13^2}$

c) $\left(\sqrt[5]{2.5}\right)^4$ d) $\left(\sqrt[4]{\frac{2}{5}}\right)^3$

19. Evaluate each power without using a calculator.

a) $16^{0.25}$ b) $1.44^{\frac{1}{2}}$

c) $(-8)^{\frac{5}{3}}$ d) $\left(\frac{9}{16}\right)^{\frac{3}{2}}$

20. Radioactive isotopes decay. The half-life of an isotope is the time for its mass to decay by $\frac{1}{2}$. For example, polonium-210 has a half-life of 20 weeks. So, a sample of 100 g would decay to 50 g in 20 weeks. The percent, P, of polonium remaining after time t weeks is given by the formula $P = 100(0.5)^{\frac{t}{20}}$. What percent of polonium remains after 30 weeks?

21. Arrange these numbers in order from greatest to least. Describe the strategy you used.

$\sqrt[4]{5}, 5^{\frac{2}{3}}, \sqrt[3]{5}, 5^{\frac{3}{4}}, \left(\sqrt{5}\right)^3$

22. Kleiber's law relates a mammal's metabolic rate while resting, q Calories per day, to its body mass, M kilograms:

$q = 70M^{\frac{3}{4}}$

What is the approximate metabolic rate of each animal?

a) a cow with mass 475 kg

b) a mouse with mass 25 g

4.5

23. a) Identify the patterns in this list.

$81 = 3^4$

$27 = 3^3$

$9 = 3^2$

b) Extend the patterns in part a downward. Write the next 5 rows in the pattern.

c) Explain how this pattern shows that $a^{-n} = \frac{1}{a^n}$ when a is a non-zero rational number and n is a natural number.

24. Evaluate each power without using a calculator.

a) 2^{-2} b) $\left(\frac{2}{3}\right)^{-3}$ c) $\left(\frac{4}{25}\right)^{-\frac{3}{2}}$

25. Kyle wants to have \$1000 in 3 years. He uses this formula to calculate how much he should invest today in a savings account that pays 3.25% compounded annually: $P = 1000(1.0325)^{-3}$

How much should Kyle invest today?

26. A company designs a container with the shape of a triangular prism to hold 500 mL of juice. The bases of the prism are equilateral triangles with side length s centimetres. The height, h centimetres, of the prism is given by the formula:

$h = 2000(3)^{-\frac{1}{2}}s^{-2}$

What is the height of a container with base side length 8.0 cm? Give your answer to the nearest tenth of a centimetre.

27. When musicians play together, they usually tune their instruments so that the note A above middle C has frequency 440 Hz, called the *concert pitch*. A formula for calculating the frequency, F hertz, of a note n semitones above the concert pitch is:

$F = 440(\sqrt[12]{2})^n$

Middle C is 9 semitones below the concert pitch. What is the frequency of middle C? Give your answer to the nearest hertz.

4.6

28. Simplify. Explain your reasoning.

a) $(3m^4n)^2$ b) $\left(\frac{x^2y}{y^{-2}}\right)^{-2}$

c) $(16a^2b^6)^{-\frac{1}{2}}$ d) $\left(\frac{r^3s^{-1}}{s^{-2}r^{-2}}\right)^{-\frac{2}{3}}$

29. Simplify. Show your work.

a) $(a^3b)(a^{-1}b^4)$ b) $\left(x^{\frac{1}{2}}y\right)\left(x^{\frac{3}{2}}y^{-2}\right)$

c) $\frac{a^3}{a^5}\cdot a^{-3}$ d) $\frac{x^2y}{x^{\frac{1}{2}}y^{-2}}$

30. Evaluate.

a) $\left(\frac{3}{2}\right)^{\frac{3}{2}} \cdot \left(\frac{3}{2}\right)^{\frac{1}{2}}$ b) $\frac{(-5.5)^{\frac{2}{3}}}{(-5.5)^{-\frac{4}{3}}}$

c) $\left[\left(-\frac{12}{5}\right)^{\frac{1}{3}}\right]^6$ d) $\frac{0.16^{\frac{3}{4}}}{0.16^{\frac{1}{4}}}$

31. A sphere has volume 1100 cm^3. Explain how to use exponents or radicals to estimate the radius of the sphere.

32. Identify any errors in each solution, then write a correct solution.

a) $\left(s^{-1}t^{\frac{1}{3}}\right)(s^4t^3) = s^{-1}\cdot s^4 \cdot t^{\frac{1}{3}} \cdot t^3$
$= s^{-4}t$

b) $\left(\frac{4c^{\frac{1}{3}}}{d^3}\right)^{-3} = \frac{-12c^{-1}}{d^0}$
$= -12c^{-1}$
$= \frac{1}{12c}$

THE WORLD OF MATH

Historical Moment: The Golden Ratio

The ratio, $\frac{1+\sqrt{5}}{2}$: 1, is called the *golden ratio*.

Buildings and pictures with dimensions in this ratio are often considered visually pleasing and "natural." The Greek sculptor Phidias used the golden ratio for the dimensions of his sculptures. His 42-ft. high statue of the Greek god Zeus in the temple in Olympia, created in about 435 B.C.E., was one of the Seven Wonders of the Ancient World. The number $\frac{1+\sqrt{5}}{2}$ is often called "phi" after the first Greek letter in "Phidias."

PRACTICE TEST

For questions 1 and 2, choose the correct answer: A, B, C, or D

1. The volume V cubic inches of each cube is given. For which cube is the edge length an irrational number?

A.

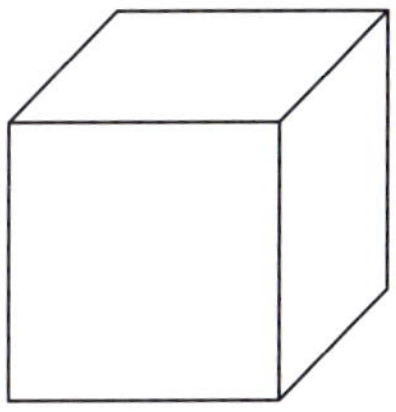

$V = 125$ in.^{3}

B.

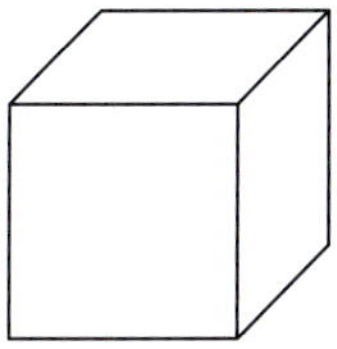

$V = 75$ in.^{3}

C.

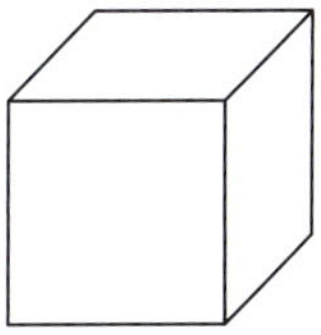

$V = 64$ in.^{3}

D.

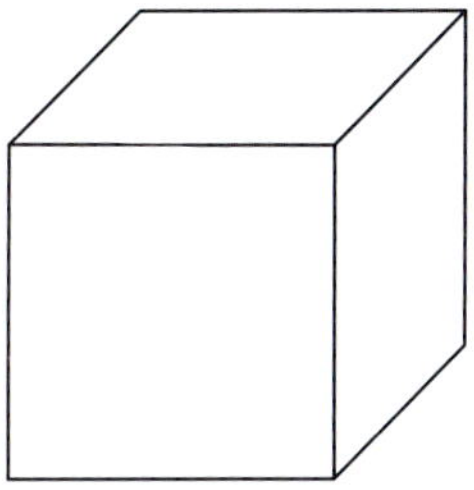

$V = 216$ in.^{3}

2. Which number is rational?

A. $\sqrt{0.09}$ **B.** $\sqrt{50}$ **C.** $\sqrt[3]{-\frac{64}{121}}$ **D.** π

3. **a)** Which is greater, $\sqrt{70}$ or $5\sqrt{3}$? Justify your answer.
b) Sketch a number line to illustrate the numbers in part a.

4. Evaluate without using a calculator.

a) $\sqrt[4]{\frac{256}{81}}$ **b)** $(-4)^{-2}$ **c)** $0.81^{\frac{3}{2}}$ **d)** $16^{-\frac{1}{2}}$

5. Write $44^{\frac{1}{2}}$ as a radical in simplest form.

6. A student simplified $\frac{x^{-1}y^3}{xy^{-2}}$ as follows:

$$\frac{x^{-1}y^3}{xy^{-2}} = x^{-1+1} \cdot y^{3-2}$$
$$= x^0y^1$$
$$= y$$

Is the student correct? If not, describe any errors and write a correct solution.

7. Simplify each expression. Write your answers using positive exponents.

a) $(p^{-2}q^{-1})^2\left(pq^{\frac{1}{2}}\right)^2$ **b)** $\left(\frac{c^6d^5}{c^3d^4}\right)^{-\frac{1}{3}}$

8. Scientists use the formula $d = 0.099m^{\frac{9}{10}}$ to calculate the volume of water, d litres, that a mammal with mass m kilograms should drink in 1 day. Calculate how much water a 550-kg moose should drink in one day.

Human Calculators

Throughout history, there have been men and women so proficient in calculating mentally that they have been called "human calculators."

In 1980, Shakuntala Devi mentally multiplied the numbers 7 686 369 774 870 and 2 465 099 745 779 and gave the correct answer 18 947 668 177 995 426 462 773 730 in 28 s.

In 2004, Alexis Lemaire found the 13th root of a 100-digit number in less than 4 s. In 2007, he was able to find the 13th root of a 200-digit number in a little over 1 min.

PART A: CALCULATING MENTALLY

To calculate squares and square roots using mental math, you have to recognize number patterns, know some elementary algebra, and understand number relationships.

- Use a calculator to evaluate 15^2, 25^2, 35^2, 45^2, and 55^2.
  What patterns do you notice?
  How can you use the patterns to determine the square of a number that ends in 5?
  Use the patterns to evaluate 75^2 and 105^2.
- To square a 2-digit number, you can use the patterns for squaring a binomial:
  $$\begin{aligned}41^2 &= (40 + 1)^2\\ &= 40^2 + 2(40)(1) + 1^2\\ &= 1600 + 80 + 1\\ &= 1681\end{aligned}$$
  Adapt this method to determine 39^2 mentally.

- You can use your understanding of number relationships to determine the square roots of 4-digit numbers such as $\sqrt{4489}$ mentally.

  Explain why $60 < \sqrt{4489} < 70$.

  Why must $\sqrt{4489}$ end in 3 or 7?

  What is $\sqrt{4489}$?

  How can the units digit of the radicand help you identify whether the radicand could be a perfect square, and if it is, identify possible roots?

PART B: INVESTIGATING MENTAL CALCULATION METHODS

Invent your own methods or research to find mental math methods that can be used to:

- Square different types of 2-digit numbers.
- Calculate the square root of 4-digit square numbers such as 2601.

PROJECT PRESENTATION

Your completed project can be presented in a written or oral format but should include:

- An explanation of your methods with examples
- An explanation of why the method works; use algebra, number patterns, diagrams, or models such as algebra tiles to support your explanation. You may need to research to find the explanation.

EXTENSION

Because most people do not have extraordinary mental calculation abilities, relatively complex written methods were invented to calculate or estimate roots.

- Use an Internet search or examine older math textbooks to identify some methods or formulas that have been used to calculate or estimate roots, particularly square roots and cube roots. These might include formulas developed by Newton, Heron, and Bakhshali.
- Provide a brief written report with an example of how to use one of these methods. Try to explain why the method works.

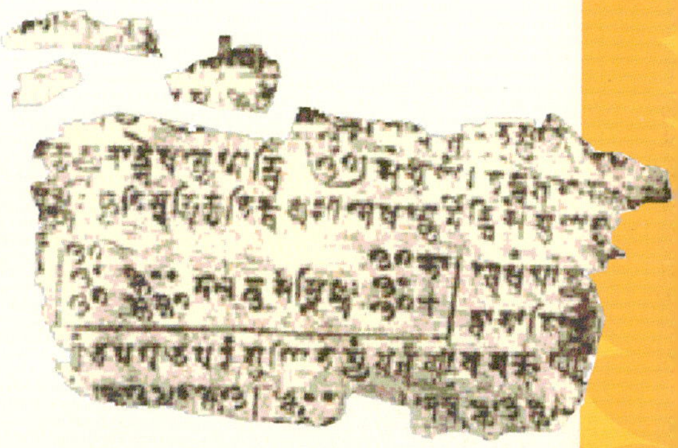

The Bakhshali manuscript was found in Pakistan in 1881. It is believed to be a 7th century copy of a manuscript written in the 5th century or earlier.

CUMULATIVE REVIEW Chapters 1–4

1

1. A right rectangular pyramid has base dimensions of 6 m by 4 m and a height of 9 m. Determine the surface area of the pyramid to the nearest square metre.

2. A right cone has a slant height of 12 in. and a base diameter of 9 in. Determine the volume of the cone to the nearest cubic inch.

3. The surface area of a sphere is 86 cm^2.
a) Calculate the diameter of the sphere to the nearest tenth of a centimetre.
b) What is the radius of the sphere to the nearest inch?

2

4. A tree casts a shadow that is 15 yd. long when the angle between the sun's rays and the ground is 32°. What is the height of the tree to the nearest foot?

5. In this trapezoid, determine the measure of ∠W to the nearest tenth of a degree.

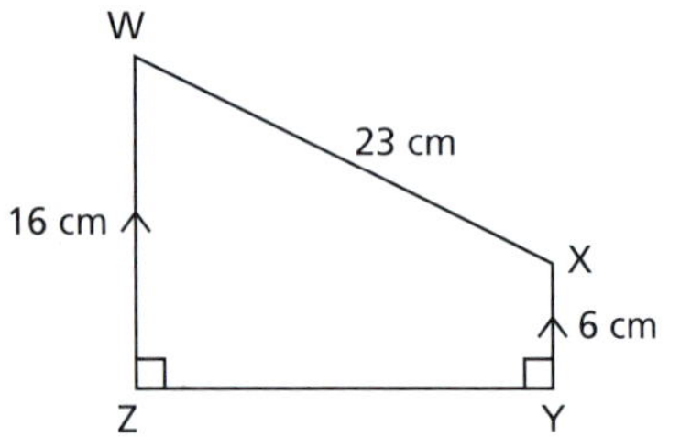

6. a) Determine the perimeter of △ABC to the nearest tenth of an inch.

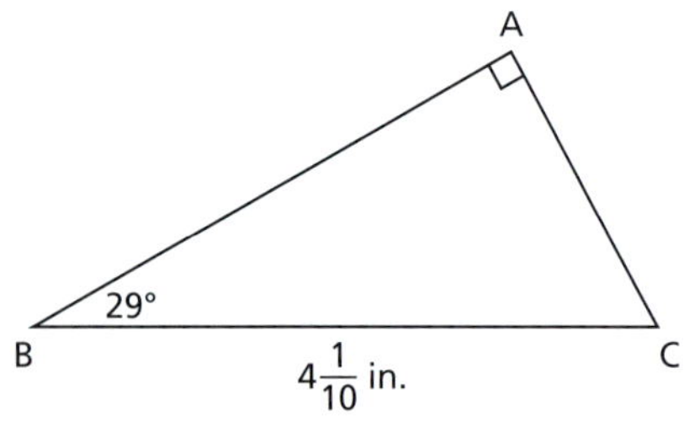

b) Determine the area of △ABC to the nearest square inch.

3

7. Determine the greatest common factor and least common multiple of each set of numbers.
a) 45, 117
b) 84, 154
c) 63, 90, 150
d) 42, 132, 140, 330

8. A cube has volume 50 653 cubic inches. What is its surface area?

9. a) List the first ten perfect squares.
b) List the first ten perfect cubes.
c) Which of the perfect cubes in part b are also perfect squares?

10. Factor each polynomial.
a) $15a^2 - 27a$
b) $4p + 12p^3 - 6p^2$
c) $-8d^4 - 14d$
d) $21w - 28 + 14w^2$
e) $18x^4y^2 - 4x^3y^3 + 10x^2y^4$
f) $33n^4p^3 + 11n^2p^2 - 121np^4$

11. Which trinomials can be represented as a rectangle of algebra tiles? What does that tell you about the trinomials?
a) $t^2 + 8t + 7$
b) $c^2 + 16c + 4$
c) $3s^2 + 4s + 6$
d) $2m^2 + 11m + 15$

12. Expand and simplify. Sketch a rectangle diagram to illustrate each product.
a) $(d + 5)(d - 3)$
b) $(5 - s)(9 - s)$
c) $(-7 + 4g)(7 + 4g)$
d) $(3k - 7)(2k + 9)$

13. Find an integer to replace □ so that each trinomial can be factored.
a) $x^2 + \square x + 14$
b) $b^2 - 5b + \square$
c) $y^2 + \square y - 18$
d) $a^2 + 4a + \square$

14. Factor. Check by expanding.
a) $n^2 + 9n - 22$
b) $60 - 19m + m^2$
c) $6r^2 + 23r + 20$
d) $10n^2 + n - 2$

15. Factor.

a) $3c^2 - 24c - 60$
b) $-5h^2 - 20h + 105$
c) $24c^2 - 87c - 36$
d) $100 - 155a + 60a^2$
e) $4t^2 - 48t + 144$
f) $64 + 8w - 2w^2$
g) $108r^2 - 147s^2$
h) $-70x^2 + 22xy + 12y^2$

16. Expand and simplify.

a) $(2x - 3)(x^2 + 3x - 5)$
b) $(a + 2b)(2a - 5b - 6)$
c) $(4 + t + 3s)(3 - t)$
d) $(n^2 + 2n - 1)(2n^2 - n - 4)$

17. Expand and simplify. Substitute a number for the variable to check each product.

a) $(2c - 5)(c + 6) + (c + 6)(3c - 2)$
b) $(2t - 5)^2 - (2t + 5)(3t - 1)$
c) $(3w + 4)(2w + 7) - (5w + 3)(2w - 6)$
d) $(6d + 3)(2d - 3) - (3d - 4)^2$

18. Factor. Verify by multiplying the factors.

a) $25n^2 + 40n + 16$
b) $24v^2 + 14vw - 3w^2$
c) $81c^2 - 169d^2$
d) $9a^2 - 30ab + 25b^2$

4

19. Use the two consecutive perfect cubes closest to 40 to estimate a value for $\sqrt[3]{40}$. Revise your estimate until its cube is within two decimal places of 40.

20. Locate each number on a number line. Then order the numbers from least to greatest.
$\sqrt[3]{90}, \sqrt{30}, \sqrt[4]{150}, \sqrt[3]{-90}, \sqrt[4]{250}$

21. a) Write each entire radical as a mixed radical.

i) $\sqrt{96}$ ii) $\sqrt[3]{108}$ iii) $\sqrt[4]{144}$
iv) $\sqrt{425}$ v) $\sqrt[3]{648}$ vi) $\sqrt[4]{352}$

b) Write each mixed radical as a entire radical.

i) $5\sqrt{3}$ ii) $2\sqrt[3]{5}$ iii) $11\sqrt[4]{2}$
iv) $3\sqrt{7}$ v) $9\sqrt[3]{4}$ vi) $2\sqrt[5]{3}$

22. a) Write each power as a radical.

i) $50^{\frac{3}{4}}$ ii) $(-2.5)^{\frac{2}{3}}$ iii) $\left(\frac{3}{4}\right)^{1.6}$

b) Write each radical as a power.

i) $\sqrt[3]{8.9^2}$ ii) $\left(\sqrt[4]{\frac{7}{4}}\right)^3$ iii) $\sqrt[5]{(-4.8)^6}$

23. Evaluate each power without using a calculator.

a) $81^{0.75}$ b) $\left(\frac{36}{49}\right)^{\frac{3}{2}}$ c) $(-0.027)^{\frac{5}{3}}$
d) $\left(\frac{4}{9}\right)^{-2}$ e) $16^{-\frac{3}{4}}$ f) $\left(\frac{25}{64}\right)^{-\frac{3}{2}}$
g) $243^{0.6}$ h) $(-0.064)^{-\frac{2}{3}}$ i) $\left(\frac{49}{121}\right)^{-\frac{3}{2}}$

24. Suppose an investor wants to have \$30 000 in 7 years. The interest rate for a savings account is 2.7% compounded annually. The money, *P* dollars, that she should invest today is given by the formula $P = 30\,000(1.027)^{-7}$. How much money should the investor invest today?

25. Evaluate

a) $\left(\frac{2}{5}\right)^{1.5}\left(\frac{2}{5}\right)^{0.5}$ b) $\dfrac{0.25^{-\frac{2}{3}}}{0.25^{-\frac{5}{3}}}$

c) $\dfrac{\left(0.36^{\frac{5}{2}}\right)\left(0.36^{\frac{3}{2}}\right)}{0.36^{\frac{9}{2}}}$ d) $\dfrac{\left(-\frac{1}{8}\right)^{\frac{7}{3}}\left(-\frac{1}{8}\right)^{\frac{2}{3}}}{\left(-\frac{1}{8}\right)^{\frac{5}{3}}\left(-\frac{1}{8}\right)}$

26. Simplify.

a) $\dfrac{(a^{-2}b^{-1})^{-3}}{a^3b}$ b) $\left(\dfrac{2x^{-4}y^{-3}}{4x^2y^{-5}}\right)^{-4}$

c) $\dfrac{-15a^{-\frac{1}{2}}b}{5ab^{-\frac{3}{2}}}$ d) $\left(\dfrac{x^6z^{-\frac{1}{3}}}{-125y^{-9}z^{\frac{8}{3}}}\right)^{-\frac{1}{3}}$

5 Relations and Functions

BUILDING ON

- writing equations to represent patterns in tables
- graphing and analyzing linear relations

BIG IDEAS

- A relation associates the elements of one set with the elements of another set.
- A function is a special type of relation for which each element of the first set is associated with a unique element of the second set.
- A linear function has a constant rate of change and its graph is a non-vertical straight line.

NEW VOCABULARY

relation
arrow diagram
function
domain
range
function notation
rate of change
linear function
vertical intercept
horizontal intercept

PAULATUUQ *(place of coal) is in the Northwest Territories, north of the Arctic Circle. Here, on June 21st, the longest day of the year, the sun never sets.*

5.1 Representing Relations

LESSON FOCUS

Represent relations in different ways.

Make Connections

This family tree shows relations within a family.

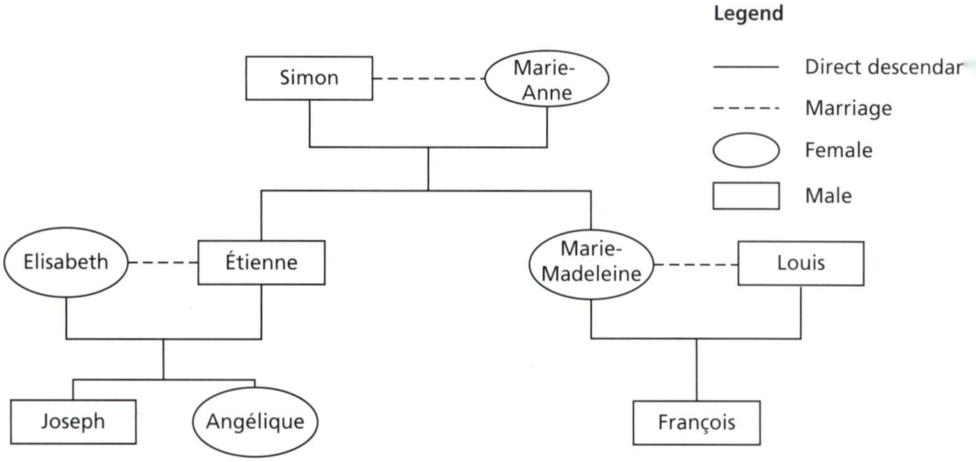

How is Joseph related to Simon?

How are Angélique and François related?

How does the family tree show these relations?

Construct Understanding

TRY THIS

A. Use the letters in the square below to write as many words as you can with 3 or more letters.

- Each word must contain the letter in the centre square.
- A letter can only be used once in each word.
- Plurals cannot be used.

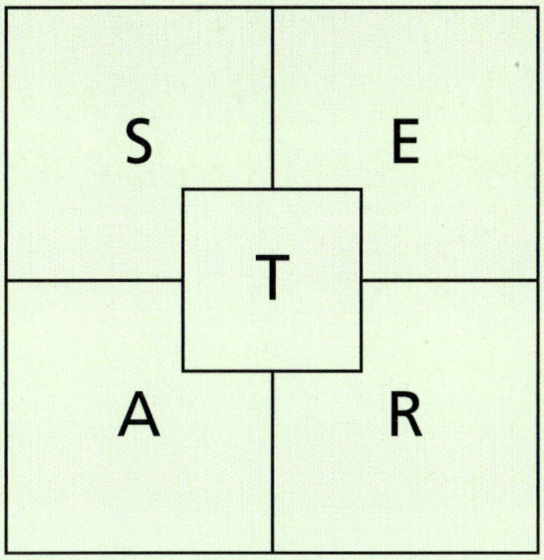

B. Use the letters in the square and the words you wrote. Pair a letter with a word to show the association "is a letter of the word." Write as many pairs as you can.

C. Use the same association. Suppose you reverse the order of the items in the pairs. Does the association make sense? Explain.

A *set* is a collection of distinct objects.
An *element* of a set is one object in the set.
A **relation** associates the elements of one set with the elements of another set.

One way to write a set is to list its elements inside braces.
For example, we can write the set of natural numbers from 1 to 5 as:
$\{1, 2, 3, 4, 5\}$

The order of the elements in the set does not matter.

Consider the set of fruits and the set of colours.
We can associate fruits with their colours.
For example:

An apple	may have the colour	red.
↑	↑	↑
element of first set	association	element of second set

What other relations could you create using the same association between fruits and colours?

So, this set of ordered pairs is a relation:

{(apple, red), (apple, green), (blueberry, blue), (cherry, red), (huckleberry, blue)}

Here are some other ways to represent this relation:

- a table

Fruit	Colour
apple	red
apple	green
blueberry	blue
cherry	red
huckleberry	blue

  The heading of each column describes each set.

- an **arrow diagram**

  The two ovals represent the sets.
  Each arrow associates an element of the first set with an element of the second set.

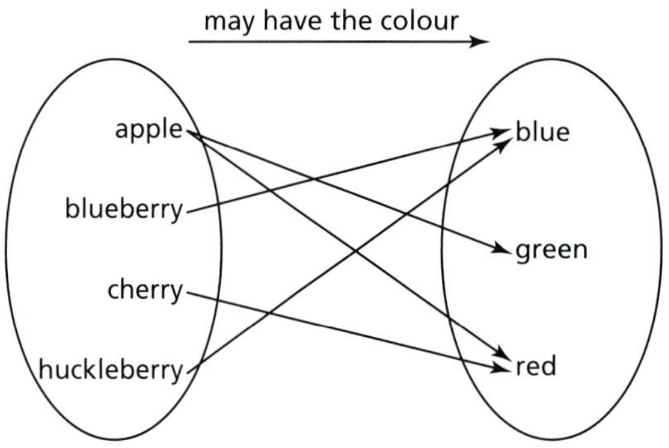

The order of the words in the ordered pairs, the columns in the table, and the ovals in the arrow diagram is important. It makes sense to say, "an apple may have the colour red," but it makes no sense to say, "red may have the colour apple." That is, a relation has direction from one set to the other set.

Example 1 Representing a Relation Given as a Table

Northern communities can be associated with the territories they are in. Consider the relation represented by this table.

Community	Territory
Hay River	NWT
Iqaluit	Nunavut
Nanisivik	Nunavut
Old Crow	Yukon
Whitehorse	Yukon
Yellowknife	NWT

a) Describe this relation in words.

b) Represent this relation:
   i) as a set of ordered pairs
   ii) as an arrow diagram

SOLUTION

a) The relation shows the association "is located in" from a set of northern communities to a set of territories. For example, Hay River is located in the NWT.

b) i) The communities are the first elements in the ordered pairs. The territories are the second elements in the ordered pairs. The ordered pairs are: {(Hay River, NWT), (Iqaluit, Nunavut), (Nanisivik, Nunavut), (Old Crow, Yukon), (Whitehorse, Yukon), (Yellowknife, NWT)}

ii) The communities are written in the first set of the arrow diagram.

The territories are written in the second set; each territory is written only once.

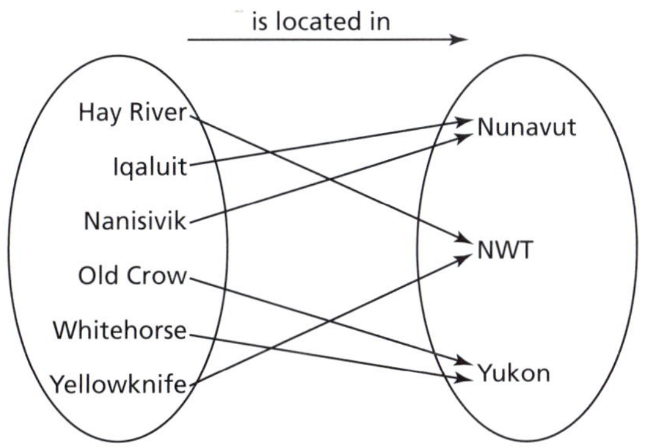

CHECK YOUR UNDERSTANDING

1. Animals can be associated with the classes they are in.

Animal	Class
ant	Insecta
eagle	Aves
snake	Reptilia
turtle	Reptilia
whale	Mammalia

a) Describe this relation in words.

b) Represent this relation:
   i) as a set of ordered pairs
   ii) as an arrow diagram

[Answers: a) The relation shows the association "belongs to the class" between a set of animals and a set of classes. b) i) {(ant, Insecta), (eagle, Aves), (snake, Reptilia), (turtle, Reptilia), (whale, Mammalia)}]

Why is the direction of the arrows in the arrow diagram important?

How are the representations the same?

When the elements of one or both sets in a relation are numbers, the relation can be represented as a bar graph.

Example 2 Representing a Relation Given as a Bar Graph

Different breeds of dogs can be associated with their mean heights. Consider the relation represented by this graph. Represent the relation:

a) as a table

b) as an arrow diagram

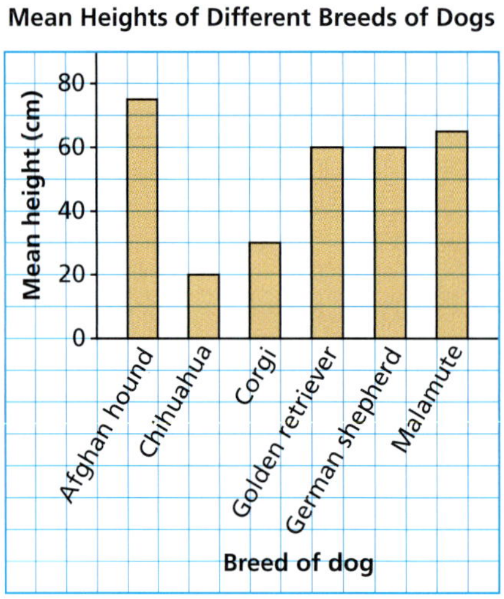

SOLUTION

a) The association is: "has a mean height of"

In the table, write the breeds of dogs in the first column and the mean heights in centimetres in the second column.

Breed of Dog	Mean Height (cm)
Afghan hound	75
Chihuahua	20
Corgi	30
Golden retriever	60
German shepherd	60
Malamute	65

b) In the arrow diagram, write the breeds of dogs in the first set and the mean heights in centimetres in the second set.

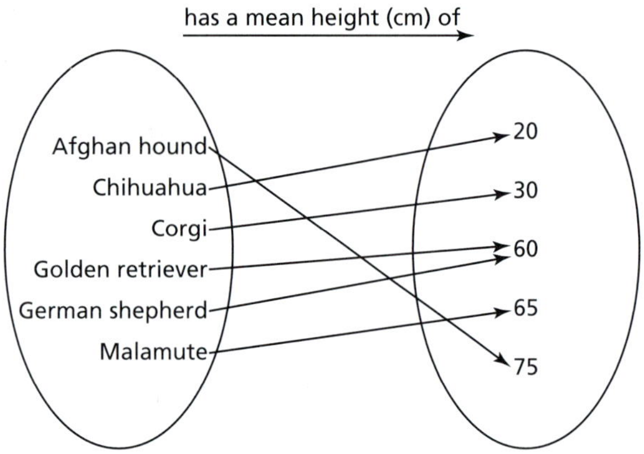

CHECK YOUR UNDERSTANDING

2. Different towns in British Columbia can be associated with the average time, in hours, that it takes to drive to Vancouver. Consider the relation represented by this graph.

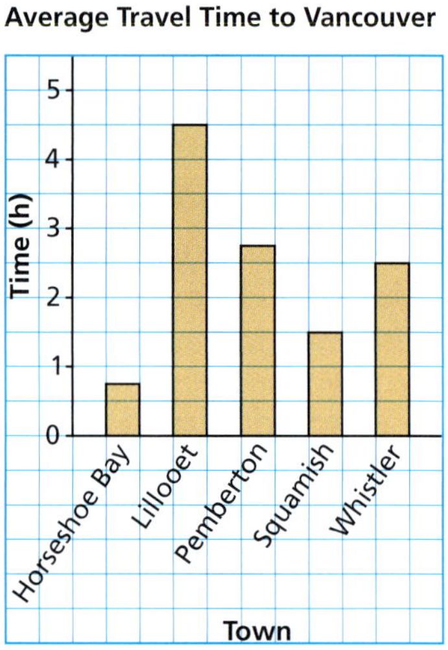

Represent the relation:

a) as a table

b) as an arrow diagram

Answer: a)

Town	Average Time (h)
Horseshoe Bay	0.75
Lillooet	4.5
Pemberton	2.75
Squamish	1.5
Whistler	2.5

Sometimes a relation contains so many ordered pairs that it is impossible to list all of them or to represent them in a table.

Example 3 Identifying a Relation from a Diagram

In this diagram:

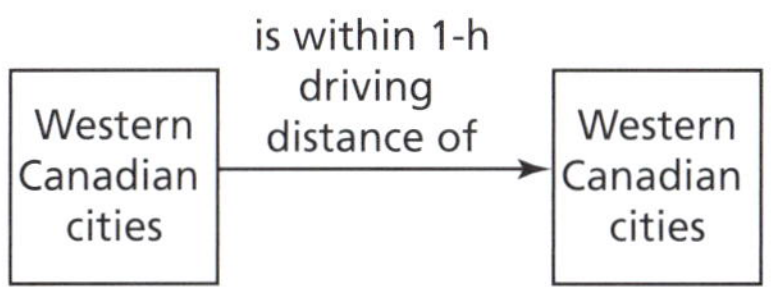

Both sets in a relation can be the same.

a) Describe the relation in words.

b) List 2 ordered pairs that belong to the relation.

SOLUTION

a) The relation shows the association "is within 1-h driving distance" from a set of cities in Western Canada to a set of cities in Western Canada.

b) Two ordered pairs that belong to the relation are:
(Innisfail AB, Olds AB), (Kelowna B.C., Vernon B.C.)

CHECK YOUR UNDERSTANDING

3. In the diagram below:

a) Describe the relation in words.

b) List 2 ordered pairs that belong to the relation.

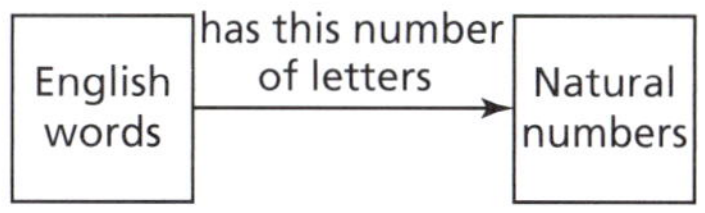

[Sample Answers: a) The relation shows the association "has this number of letters" from a set of English words to a set of natural numbers. b) (mathematics, 11) and (language, 8)]

Discuss the Ideas

1. What are the advantages and disadvantages of the different ways you can represent a relation?

2. Why is the order of the elements in an ordered pair important? Give an example.

Exercises

A

3. For each table below:
   i) Describe the relation in words.
   ii) Represent the relation:
   - as a set of ordered pairs
   - as an arrow diagram

a)

Coin	Value ($)
penny	0.01
nickel	0.05
dime	0.10
quarter	0.25
loonie	1.00
toonie	2.00

b)

Sport	Equipment
badminton	shuttlecock
badminton	racquet
hockey	puck
hockey	stick
tennis	ball
tennis	racquet
soccer	ball

4. Consider the relation represented by this graph.

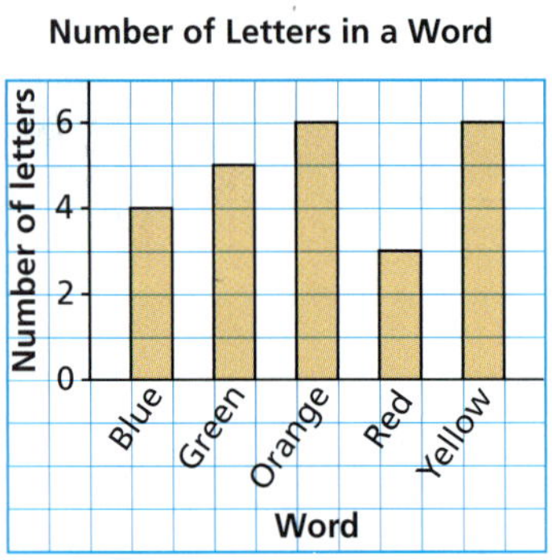

Represent the relation:
a) as a table
b) as an arrow diagram

B

5. This table shows some of Manitoba's francophone artists and the medium they use.

Artist	Medium
Gaëtanne Sylvester	sculpture
Hubert Théroux	painting
Huguette Gauthier	stained glass
James Culleton	painting
Nathalie Dupont	photography
Simone Hébert Allard	photography

a) Describe the relation in words.
b) Represent this relation:
   i) as a set of ordered pairs
   ii) as an arrow diagram

Burning Sunset Detail by James Culleton

6. a) Describe the relation represented by this bar graph.

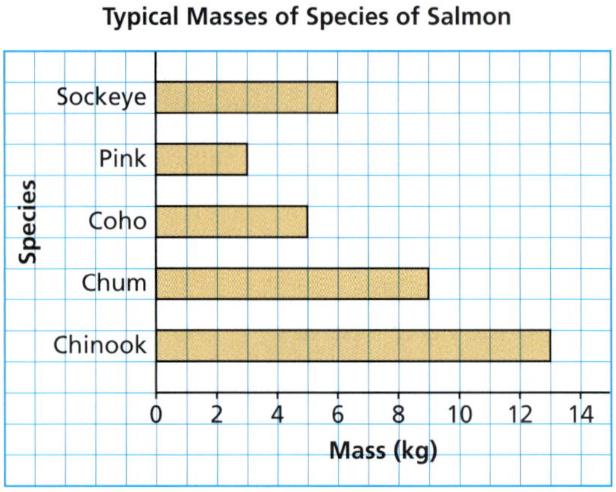

b) Represent the relation as a set of ordered pairs.
c) Represent the relation in a different way.

7. For a word game, words that begin with the letter Z can be difficult to find.

a) What does this arrow diagram represent?

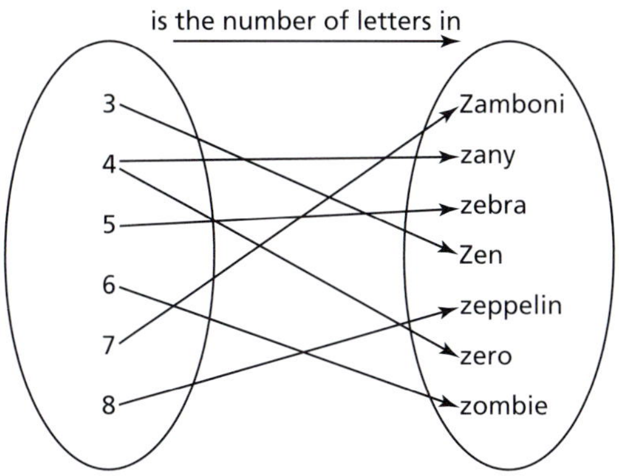

b) Represent this relation in two different ways.

c) Create an arrow diagram for words beginning with the letter X, then represent the relation in two different ways.

8. In the diagram below:

a) Describe the relation in words.

b) List two ordered pairs that belong to the relation.

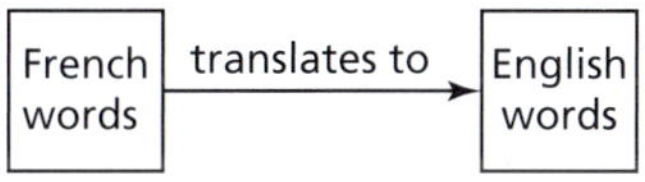

9. A digital clock displays digits from 0 to 9 by lighting up different segments in two squares. For example, the digit 2 needs 5 segments to light up, as shown.

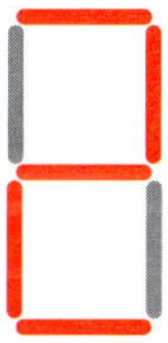

a) List the set of ordered pairs of the form: (digit, number of segments lit up)

b) Represent this relation in two different ways.

10. Here are some Canadian hockey players and the year they were born.
Jennifer Botterill (1979); Jonathan Cheechoo (1980); Roberto Luongo (1979); Jordin Tootoo (1983); Hayley Wickenheiser (1978)
For each association below, use these data to represent a relation in different ways.

a) was born in

b) is the birth year of

11. Choose five people in your class.

a) Use the association "is older than" to write a relation. Represent the relation using a set of ordered pairs.

b) Create your own association for these five people, then describe the relation in words. Represent this relation in different ways.

C

12. Two dice are rolled and the numbers that show are recorded.

a) Use each association below to create a relation as a set of ordered pairs.

i) The sum of the numbers is even.

ii) The difference between the numbers is a prime number.

b) In part a, does the order of the numbers in each ordered pair matter? Explain.

13. The association "is the parent of" is shown in the diagram. Each dot represents a person and each arrow maps a parent to her or his child.

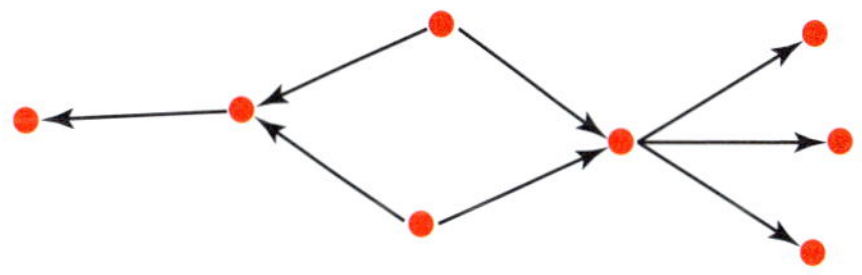

In this relation:

a) How many children are shown?

b) How many parents are shown?

c) How many grandparents are shown?

Justify your answers.

14. The association "is the sister of" is shown in the diagram. Each dot represents a person and each arrow maps a sister to a sibling.

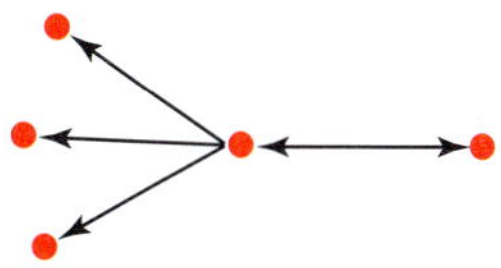

In this relation:

a) How many females are shown?

b) How many males are shown?

Justify your answers.

Reflect Create a relation that you can describe in words. Show two different ways to represent your relation.

5.2 Properties of Functions

LESSON FOCUS

Develop the concept of a function.

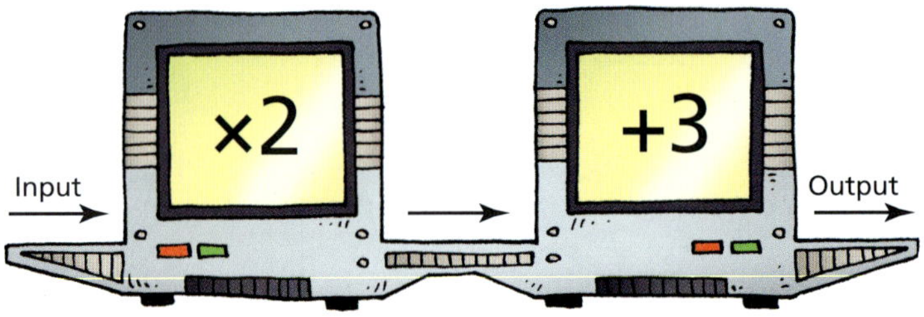

Make Connections

What is the rule for the Input/Output machine above?
Which numbers would complete this table for the machine?

Input	Output
1	5
2	7
	9
4	
	13

Construct Understanding

THINK ABOUT IT

	David	Gina	Sara	Emily	Jack	Helen
Height (m)	1.8	1.6	1.5	1.5	1.7	1.6
Age (years)	40	38	12	10	65	67

Work in a group of 3.
Use the picture above.

Each of you chooses one of the relations below.

- *name* related to *age*
- *name* related to *height*
- *height* related to *name*

Represent the relation you chose. Compare the relations.
How are they alike? How are they different?

The set of first elements of a relation is called the **domain.**
The set of related second elements of a relation is called the **range.**
A **function** is a special type of relation where each element in the domain is associated with exactly one element in the range.

Here are some different ways to relate vehicles and the number of wheels each has.

This relation associates a number with a vehicle with that number of wheels.

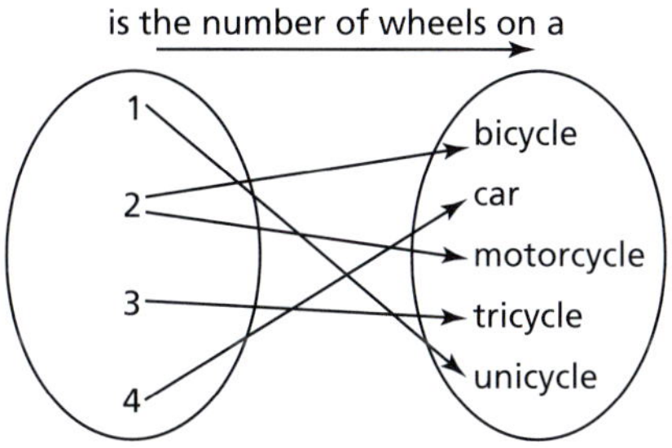

This diagram does not represent a function because there is one element in the first set that associates with two elements in the second set; that is, there are two arrows from 2 in the first set.

{(1, unicycle), (2, bicycle), (2, motorcycle), (3, tricycle), (4, car)}

The set of ordered pairs above does not represent a function because two ordered pairs have the same first element.
The domain is the set of first elements: {1, 2, 3, 4}
The range is the set of associated second elements: {unicycle, bicycle, motorcycle, tricycle, car}

This relation associates a vehicle with the number of wheels it has.

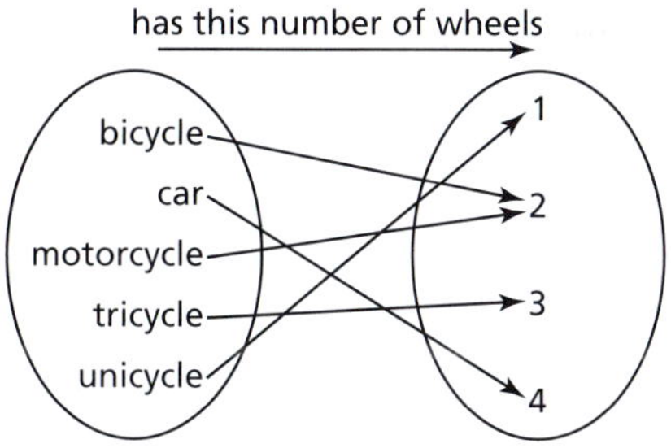

This diagram represents a function because each element in the first set associates with exactly one element in the second set; that is, there is only one arrow from each element in the first set.

{(unicycle, 1), (bicycle, 2), (motorcycle, 2), (tricycle, 3), (car, 4)}

The set of ordered pairs above represents a function because the ordered pairs have different first elements.
The domain is the set of first elements: {unicycle, bicycle, motorcycle, tricycle, car}
The range is the set of associated second elements: {1, 2, 3, 4}

When we list the elements of the range, we do not repeat an element that occurs more than once.

Example 1 Identifying Functions

For each relation below:

- Determine whether the relation is a function. Justify the answer.
- Identify the domain and range of each relation that is a function.

a) A relation that associates given shapes with the number of right angles in the shape: {(right triangle, 1), (acute triangle, 0), (square, 4), (rectangle, 4), (regular hexagon, 0)}

b)

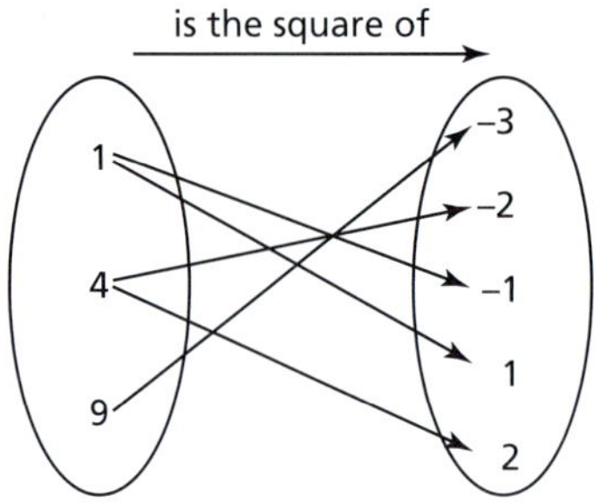

SOLUTION

a) Check to see if any ordered pairs have the same first element: {(right triangle, 1), (acute triangle, 0), (square, 4), (rectangle, 4), (regular hexagon, 0)}
Each ordered pair has a different first element, so for every first element there is exactly one second element. So, the relation is a function.

The domain is the set of the first elements of the ordered pairs: {right triangle, acute triangle, square, rectangle, regular hexagon}
The range is the set of second elements of the ordered pairs: {0, 1, 4}

b) Check to see if any element in the first set associates with more than one element in the second set.

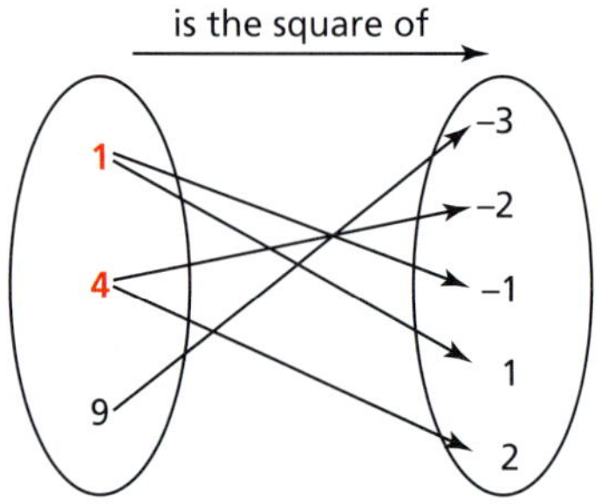

This relation is not a function because each of the numbers 1 and 4 in the first set associates with more than one number in the second set.

CHECK YOUR UNDERSTANDING

1. For each relation below:

- Determine whether the relation is a function. Justify your answer.
- Identify the domain and range of each relation that is a function.

a) A relation that associates a number with a prime factor of the number: {(4, 2), (6, 2), (6, 3), (8, 2), (9, 3)}

b)

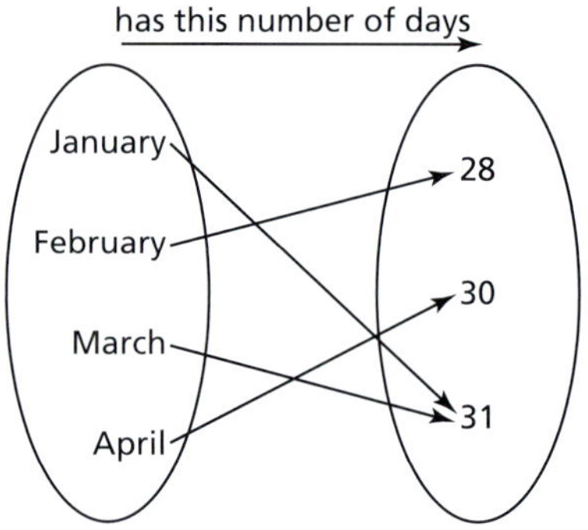

[Answers: a) no b) yes; domain: {January, February, March, April}; range: {28, 30, 31}]

What other strategies could you use to determine whether each relation is a function?

If (a, b) and (a, c) are ordered pairs in a function, what can you say about b and c?

In the workplace, a person's gross pay, P dollars, often depends on the number of hours worked, h.
So, we say P is the *dependent variable*. Since the number of hours worked, h, does not depend on the gross pay, P, we say that h is the *independent variable*.

independent variable ⟶ (Hours Worked, h) — dependent variable ⟵ (Gross Pay, P)

Hours Worked, h	Gross Pay, P ($)
1	12
2	24
3	36
4	48
5	60

domain (first column) — range (second column)

A table of values usually represents a sample of the ordered pairs in a relation.

The values of the independent variable are listed in the first column of a table of values. These elements belong to the domain.

The values of the dependent variable are listed in the second column of a table of values. These elements belong to the range.

Example 2 Describing Functions

The table shows the masses, m grams, of different numbers of identical marbles, n.

Number of Marbles, n	Mass of Marbles, m (g)
1	1.27
2	2.54
3	3.81
4	5.08
5	6.35
6	7.62

a) Why is this relation also a function?

b) Identify the independent variable and the dependent variable. Justify the choices.

c) Write the domain and range.

(Solution continues.)

CHECK YOUR UNDERSTANDING

2. The table shows the costs of student bus tickets, C dollars, for different numbers of tickets, n.

Number of Tickets, n	Cost, C ($)
1	1.75
2	3.50
3	5.25
4	7.00
5	8.75

a) Why is this relation also a function?

b) Identify the independent variable and the dependent variable. Justify your choices.

c) Write the domain and range.

[Answers: b) n; C c) {1, 2, 3, 4, 5,...}; {1.75, 3.50, 5.25, 7.00, 8.75,...}]

SOLUTION

a) For each number in the first column, there is only one number in the second column. So, the relation is a function.

b) From an understanding of the situation, the mass of the marbles, m, depends on the number of marbles, n. So, m is the dependent variable and n is the independent variable.

c) The first column of the table is representative of the domain.
The domain is: {1, 2, 3, 4, 5, 6,...}; that is, all natural numbers

The second column of the table is representative of the range.
The range is: {1.27, 2.54, 3.81, 5.08, 6.35, 7.62,...}; that is, the product of each natural number and 1.27

We can think of a function as an input/output machine. The input can be any number in the domain, and the output depends on the input number. So, the input is the independent variable and the output is the dependent variable.

Consider two machines that both accept quarters. Machine A calculates the value of the quarters. Machine B weighs the quarters. Each machine performs a different operation, so the machines represent two different functions.

- Machine A

Function V

When the input is q quarters, the output or value, V, in dollars is: $0.25q$
The equation $V = 0.25q$ describes this function.

Since V is a function of q, we can write this equation using **function notation**:
$V(q) = 0.25q$
We say: "V of q is equal to $0.25q$."

This notation shows that V is the dependent variable and that V depends on q.

$V(3)$ represents the value of the function when $q = 3$.

$V(3) = 0.25(3)$

$V(3) = 0.75$

So, the value of 3 quarters is \$0.75.

- Machine B

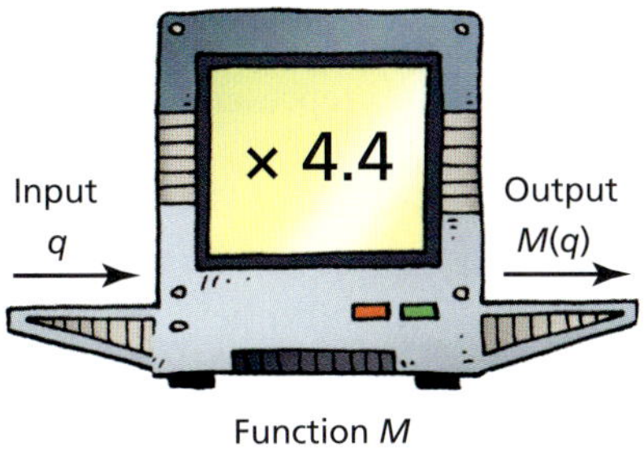

The mass of 1 quarter is 4.4 g.

When the input is q quarters, the output or mass, M, in grams is: $4.4q$
The equation $M = 4.4q$ describes this function.
Since M is a function of q, we can write this equation using function notation:
$M(q) = 4.4q$
This notation shows that M is the dependent variable and that M depends on q.

Any function that can be written as an equation in two variables can be written in function notation. For example, to write the equation $d = 4t + 5$ in function notation, we may write $d(t) = 4t + 5$. t represents an element of the domain and $d(t)$ represents an element of the range.

When we write an equation that is not related to a context, we use x as the independent variable and y as the dependent variable. Then an equation in two variables such as $y = 3x - 2$ may be written as $f(x) = 3x - 2$.

We can use any other letter, such as g or h or k, to name a function.

Conversely, we may write an equation in function notation as an equation in two variables.
For example, for the equation $C(n) = 300 + 25n$, we write $C = 300 + 25n$.
And, for the equation $g(x) = -2x + 5$, we write $y = -2x + 5$.

Example 3 Using Function Notation to Determine Values

The equation $V = -0.08d + 50$ represents the volume, V litres, of gas remaining in a vehicle's tank after travelling d kilometres. The gas tank is not refilled until it is empty.

a) Describe the function.
Write the equation in function notation.

b) Determine the value of $V(600)$.
What does this number represent?

c) Determine the value of d when $V(d) = 26$.
What does this number represent?

(Solution continues.)

CHECK YOUR UNDERSTANDING

3. The equation $C = 25n + 1000$ represents the cost, C dollars, for a feast following an Arctic sports competition, where n is the number of people attending.

a) Describe the function.
Write the equation in function notation.

(Question continues.)

SOLUTION

a) The volume of gas remaining in a vehicle's tank is a function of the distance travelled. In function notation:
$V(d) = -0.08d + 50$

b) To determine $V(600)$, use:

$$
\begin{aligned}
V(d) &= -0.08d + 50 && \text{Substitute: } d = 600\\
V(600) &= -0.08(600) + 50\\
V(600) &= -48 + 50\\
V(600) &= 2
\end{aligned}
$$

$V(600)$ is the value of V when $d = 600$.
This means that when the car has travelled 600 km, the volume of gas remaining in the vehicle's tank is 2 L.

c) To determine the value of d when $V(d) = 26$, use:

$$
\begin{aligned}
V(d) &= -0.08d + 50 && \text{Substitute: } V(d) = 26\\
26 &= -0.08d + 50 && \text{Solve for } d.\\
-24 &= -0.08d && \text{Divide each side by } -0.08.\\
d &= 300
\end{aligned}
$$

$V(300) = 26$ means that when $d = 300$, $V = 26$; that is, after the car has travelled 300 km, 26 L of gas remains in the vehicle's tank.

b) Determine the value of $C(100)$. What does this number represent?

c) Determine the value of n when $C(n) = 5000$. What does this number represent?

[Answers: a) $C(n) = 25n + 1000$ b) $3500 c) 160]

What values of d do not make sense as possible domain values?

Discuss the Ideas

1. How can you tell whether a set of ordered pairs represents a function?

2. When a function is completely represented using a set of ordered pairs or a table of values, how can you determine the domain and range of the function?

3. Why are some relations not functions? Why are all functions also relations?

Exercises

A

4. Which arrow diagrams represent functions?

a)

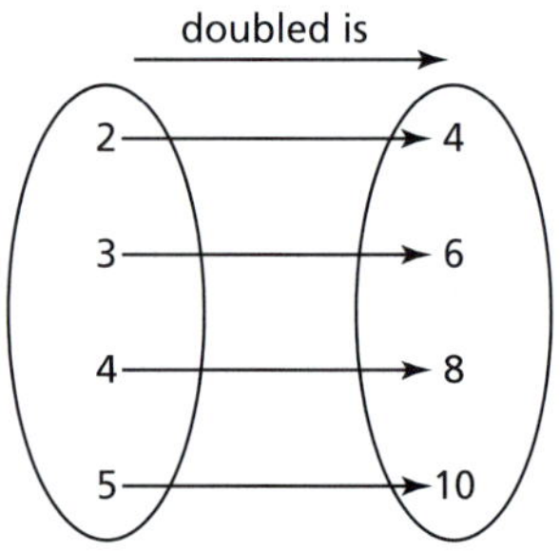

b)

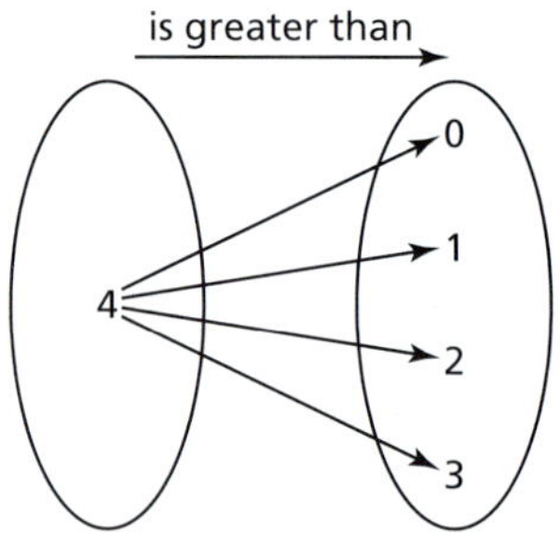

c)

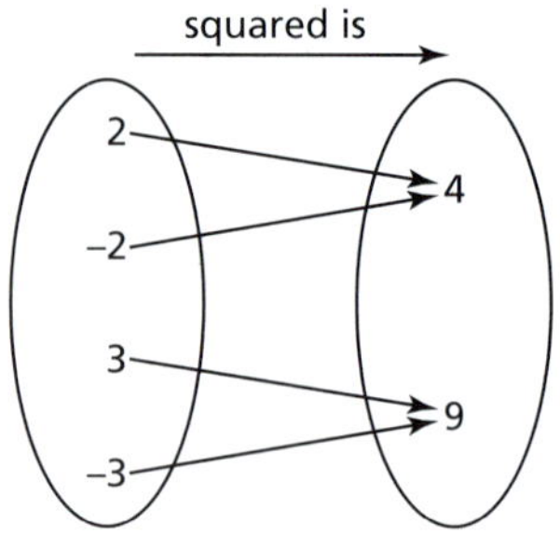

5. Which sets of ordered pairs represent functions? Identify the domain and range of each set of ordered pairs.

a) $\{(1, 3), (2, 6), (3, 9), (4, 12)\}$
b) $\{(1, 0), (0, 1), (-1, 0), (0, -1)\}$
c) $\{(2, 3), (4, 5), (6, 7), (8, 9)\}$
d) $\{(0, 1), (0, 2), (1, 2), (0, 3), (1, 3), (2, 3)\}$

6. Write in function notation.

a) $C = 20n + 8$
b) $P = n - 3$
c) $t = 5d$
d) $y = -x$

7. Write as an equation in two variables.

a) $d(t) = 3t - 5$
b) $f(x) = -6x + 4$
c) $C(n) = 5n$
d) $P(n) = 2n - 7$

B

8. For each relation below:

- Determine whether the relation is a function. Justify your answer.
- Identify the domain and range of each relation.

a) $\{(1, 1), (2, 8), (3, 27), (4, 64)\}$
b) $\{(3, 4), (3, 5), (3, 6), (3, 7)\}$

9. For each table of values below:

i) Explain why the relation is a function.
ii) Identify the independent variable and the dependent variable. Justify your choices.
iii) Write the domain and range.

a)

Number of Cans of Juice Purchased, n	Cost, C ($)
1	2.39
2	4.00
3	6.39
4	8.00
5	10.39
6	12.00

b)

Altitude, A (m)	Temperature, T (°C)
610	15.0
1220	11.1
1830	7.1
2440	3.1
3050	−0.8
3660	−4.8

10. This set of ordered pairs associates a number with a polygon that has that number of sides: {(3, isosceles triangle), (3, equilateral triangle), (3, right triangle), (3, scalene triangle), (4, square), (4, rectangle), (4, rhombus), (4, trapezoid), (4, parallelogram), (5, pentagon), (6, hexagon)}

a) Does the set of ordered pairs represent a function? Explain.
b) Suppose the elements in the ordered pairs were reversed. Use the association "has this number of sides." Would the new relation be a function? Explain.
c) Identify the domain and range of each relation in parts a and b.

11. The Rassemblement jeunesse francophone in Alberta brings together French language high school students from all over the province for a day of activities. Use two columns in this table to represent a relation.

a) Name two relations that are functions.
b) Name two relations that are not functions.

Justify your answers.

Name	From	Age	Gender
Marie	Edmonton	13	F
Gabriel	Falher	16	M
Élise	Bonnyville	14	F
Christophe	Calgary	13	M
Jean	Edmonton	15	M
Mélanie	Edmonton	15	F
Nicole	Red Deer	17	F
Marc	Légal	13	M

12. Which statement is true? Give an example to justify your choice.

a) All functions are relations, but not all relations are functions.

b) All relations are functions, but not all functions are relations.

13. In a crossword game, each letter is worth a certain number of points. Here are some letters and their points.

a) Create two different tables to represent relations that associate these letters and their points.

b) Which table in part a represents a function? Justify your choice.

14. For the function $f(x) = -5x + 11$, determine:

a) $f(1)$ b) $f(-3)$

c) $f(0)$ d) $f(1.2)$

15. a) For the function $f(n) = 2n - 7$, determine n when:

i) $f(n) = 11$ ii) $f(n) = -6$

b) For the function $g(x) = -5x + 1$, determine x when:

i) $g(x) = 41$ ii) $g(x) = -16$

16. The function $C(i) = 2.54i$ converts a measurement of i inches to a measurement of C centimetres.

a) Write the function as an equation in 2 variables.

b) Determine the value of $C(12)$. What does this number represent?

c) Determine the value of i when $C(i) = 100$. What does this number represent?

17. A car is travelling toward Meadow Lake Park, Saskatchewan. The equation $D = -80t + 300$ represents the distance, D kilometres, to Meadow Lake after t hours of driving.

a) Describe the function. Write this equation in function notation.

b) How far away from Meadow Lake Park was the car at the start of its journey? How do you know?

18. Anthropologists who study human remains have developed equations for estimating the height of a person from a measure of her or his bones. The height in centimetres is a function of the length, l centimetres, of the humerus (the upper arm bone).

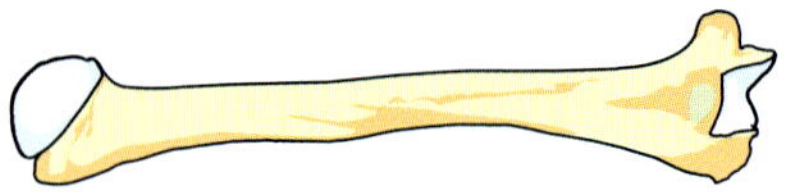

For a female: $f(l) = 2.754l + 71.475$

For a male: $m(l) = 2.894l + 70.641$

a) Determine each value. What does each number represent?

i) $f(15)$ ii) $m(20)$

b) Determine each value of l. What does each number represent?

i) $f(l) = 142$ ii) $m(l) = 194$

c) Measure the length of your humerus. Use an equation to estimate your height. How close was your answer to your actual height?

19. The function $C(f) = \frac{5}{9}(f - 32)$ converts a temperature, f degrees Fahrenheit, to C degrees Celsius.

a) Determine:

i) $C(50)$ ii) $C(-13)$

b) Determine each value of f when:

i) $C(f) = 20$ ii) $C(f) = -35$

c) Write an equation in function notation to relate the temperatures in each fact.

i) Pure water freezes at 0°C or 32°F.

ii) Pure water boils at 100°C or 212°F.

iii) Cookies are baked at 180°C or 356°F.

C

20. To convert a temperature in degrees Celsius to degrees Fahrenheit, multiply the Celsius temperature by $\frac{9}{5}$ then add 32. Use these instructions to write an equation in function notation for this conversion.

21. The area of a rectangle with length l centimetres and width w centimetres is 9 cm^2. Express the perimeter of the rectangle as a function of its length.

22. A rectangle with length l centimetres and width w centimetres has a perimeter of 12 cm. Use function notation to express the length of the rectangle as a function of its width. What are the domain and range of the function?

23. The lengths of the sides of a triangle, in units, are s, $s + 5$, and t. Its perimeter is 16 units. Use function notation to express t as a function of s. What are the domain and range of the function?

Reflect Describe how you can determine if a relation is a function. Use an example to illustrate each strategy you might use.

THE WORLD OF MATH

Careers: Forensic Anthropologist

Forensic anthropologists study human remains to understand more about how people develop, both as individuals and as societies. They collect data on bones and teeth to identify the sex, height, mass, race, and age at death. Forensic anthropologists work in crime labs, law enforcement agencies, museums, or at archaeological sites; and may give expert testimony in court. They may identify bones and bone fragments that have been in storage for many years.

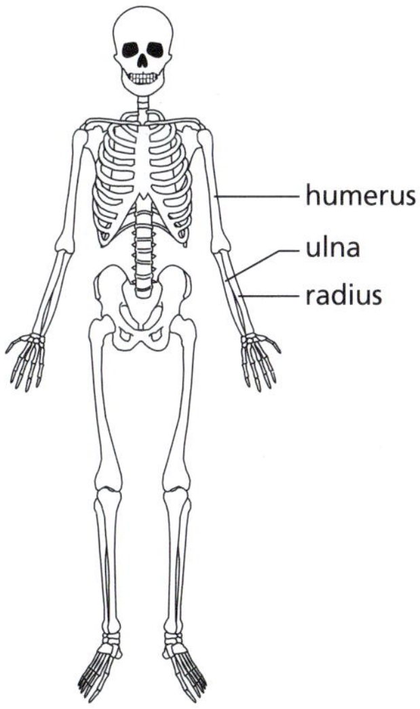

Specimens must be cleaned, accurately measured, and catalogued. Measurements of the skull and teeth can help to estimate the age of a person. When the length of the humerus, radius, or ulna is known, then a person's height can be approximated.

Here are some typical equations used to estimate the height of a person from the length of her or his radius.

For a female: $h = 3.343r + 81.224$
For a male: $h = 3.271r + 89.925$,

where h is the height of the person in centimetres and r is the length of the radius in centimetres.

CHECKPOINT 1

Connections

Here is a Frayer model for a function.

Definition

A function is a relation where each element in the first set is associated with exactly one element in the second set.

Essential Characteristics

The domain is the set of first elements in the ordered pairs. These are the values of the independent variable.
The range is the set of second elements in the ordered pairs. These are the values of the dependent variable.

Function

Example

x	y
0	4
1	5
2	6
3	7

{(0, 4), (1, 5), (2, 6), (3, 7)}

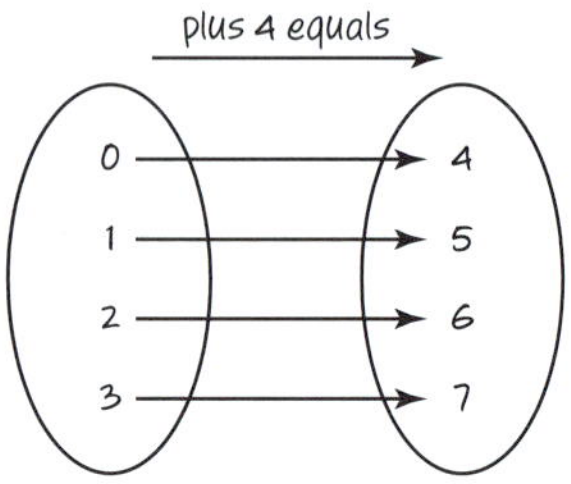

Non-examples

Number of Faces	Object
4	triangular pyramid
5	square pyramid
6	cube
6	rectangular prism

{(4, triangular pyramid),
(5, square pyramid),
(6, cube),
(6, rectangular prism)}

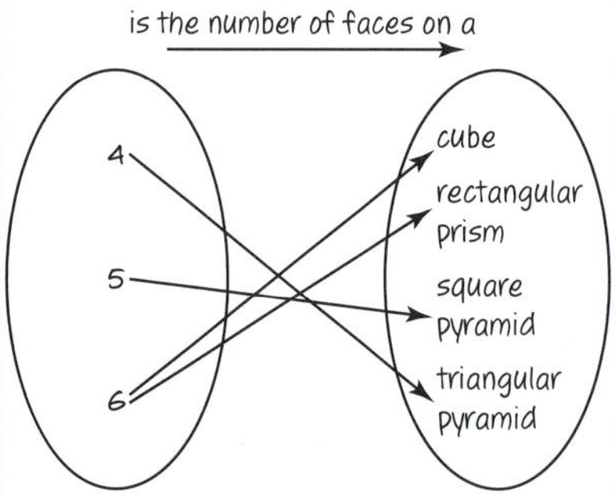

Concept Development

- **In Lesson 5.1**
  - You described a relation in words and represented it using: a set of ordered pairs, an arrow diagram, a table, and a bar graph.
- **In Lesson 5.2**
  - You identified a function by checking to see whether its ordered pairs had different first elements.
  - You listed the elements of the domain and of the range.
  - You related the elements of the domain to the independent variable and the elements of the range to the dependent variable.
  - You described functions in words, and algebraically using function notation.

Assess Your Understanding

5.1

1. Copy and complete this table for different representations of relations.

	Description in Words	Set of Ordered Pairs	Arrow Diagram	Table or Graph
a)		{(skin, drum), (skin, kayak), (bark, basket), (stone, inukshuk), (stone, carving)}		
b)				Number / Number of Factors 1 / 1 2 / 2 3 / 2 4 / 3
c)			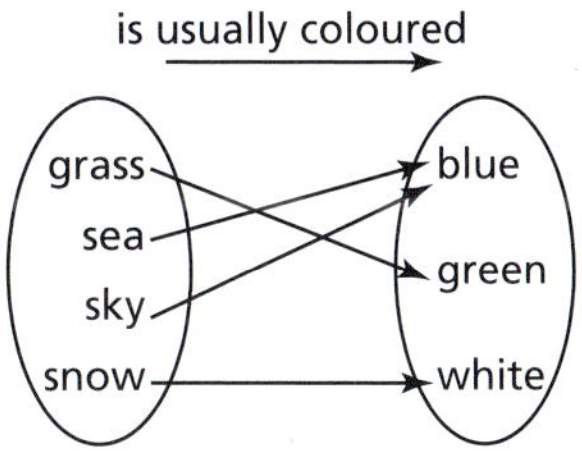	
d)	For the numbers 1 to 4, the first number in an ordered pair is greater than the second number.			

5.2

2. **a)** Which relations in question 1 are functions? Justify your answers.
b) State the domain and range of each function.

3. **a)** Think about two sets of numbers and an association.
i) Create a relation that is not a function.
ii) Create a function.
b) Represent each relation in part a in different ways.

4. The temperature, T degrees Celsius, of Earth's interior is a function of the distance, d kilometres, below the surface: $T(d) = 10d + 20$
a) Identify the dependent and independent variables.
b) Write this function as an equation in two variables.
c) Determine the value of $T(5)$. Describe what this number represents.
d) Determine the value of d when $T(d) = 50$. Describe what this number represents.

5.3 Interpreting and Sketching Graphs

LESSON FOCUS

Describe a possible situation for a given graph and sketch a possible graph for a given situation.

Make Connections

In math, a graph provides much information.
This graph shows the depth of a scuba diver as a function of time.

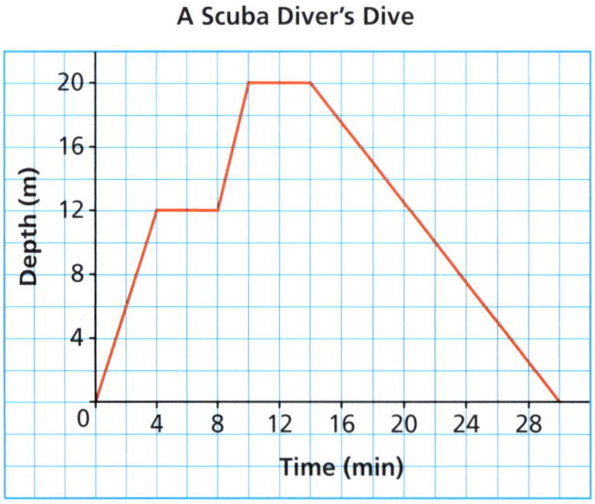

How many minutes did the dive last?

At what times did the diver stop her descent?

What was the greatest depth the diver reached? For how many minutes was the diver at that depth?

Construct Understanding

TRY THIS

Work with a partner.
You will need grid paper.

This graph shows the depth of water in a bathtub as a function of time.

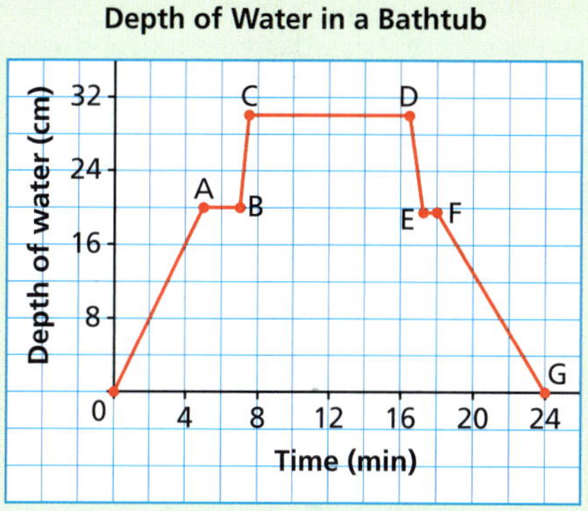

A. What does each segment of the graph represent? Compare your description with that of your partner. Are both your stories the same? Should they be? Explain.

B. Sketch a graph to represent this situation:

You put the plug in the bath and turn on the taps.
You leave the bathroom and return to discover that the bath has overflowed.
You turn off the taps and pull out the plug to let out some water. You put the plug back in.

C. Compare your graph with that of your partner. How are the graphs the same? How are they different?

The properties of a graph can provide information about a given situation.

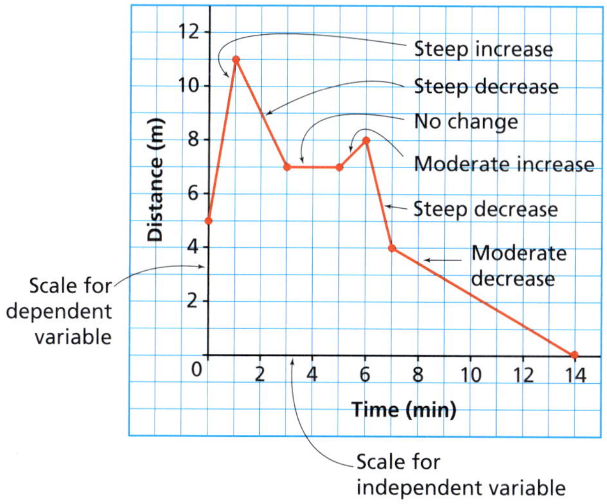

Example 1 Interpreting a Graph

Each point on this graph represents a bag of popping corn. Explain the answer to each question below.

a) Which bag is the most expensive? What does it cost?

b) Which bag has the least mass? What is this mass?

c) Which bags have the same mass? What is this mass?

d) Which bags cost the same? What is this cost?

e) Which of bags C or D has the better value for money?

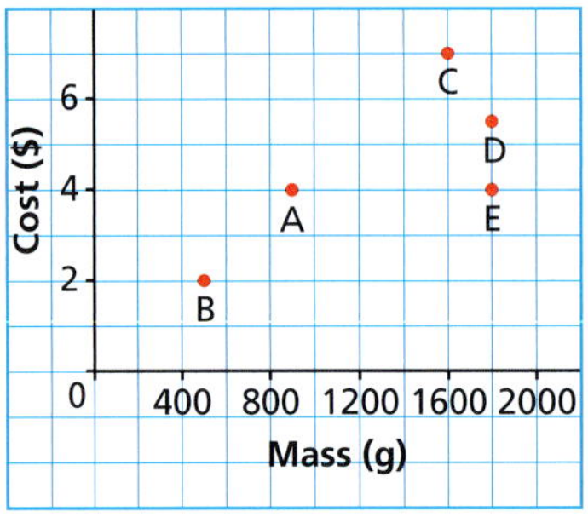

SOLUTION

a) Bag C is most expensive because it is represented by the highest point on the graph and the vertical axis represents cost. It costs $7.00.

b) Bag B has the least mass because it is represented by the point on the graph farthest to the left and the horizontal axis represents mass. The mass appears to be 500 g.

c) Bags D and E have the same mass because the points that represent them lie on the same vertical line and it passes through 1800 on the *Mass* axis. The mass is 1800 g.

d) Bags A and E cost the same because the points that represent them lie on the same horizontal line and it passes through 4 on the *Cost* axis. The cost is $4.00.

e) Bag D has the better value for money because it has a greater mass than bag C and costs less than bag C.

CHECK YOUR UNDERSTANDING

1. Each point on this graph represents a person. Explain your answer to each question below.

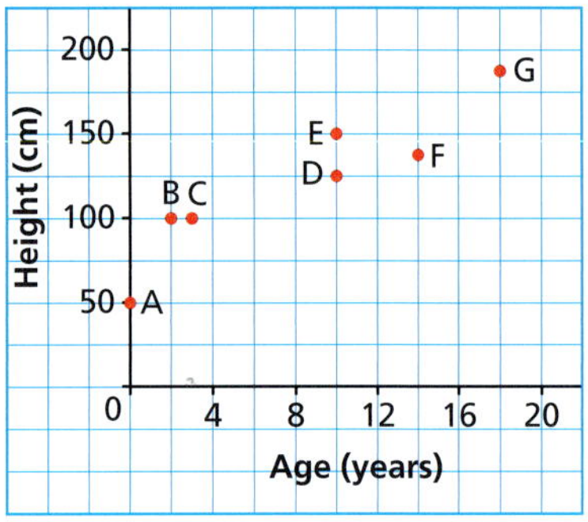

a) Which person is the oldest? What is her or his age?

b) Which person is the youngest? What is her or his age?

c) Which two people have the same height? What is this height?

d) Which two people have the same age? What is this age?

e) Which of person B or C is taller for her or his age?

[Answers: a) G, 18 years
b) A, newborn
c) B and C, 100 cm
d) D and E, 10 years
e) B]

Does this graph represent a function? Explain.

Why do you think bag D is more expensive than bag E?

The graph shows how the volume of water in a watering can changes over time.
The starting volume is 1 L, which is the volume at point A.
Segment AB goes up to the right, so the volume of water is increasing from 0 s to 30 s.
Segment BC is horizontal, so the volume is constant from 30 s to 70 s.
Segment CD goes down to the right, so the volume is decreasing from 70 s to 90 s.
At point D, the volume is 0 L after 90 s.

Volume of Water in a Watering Can

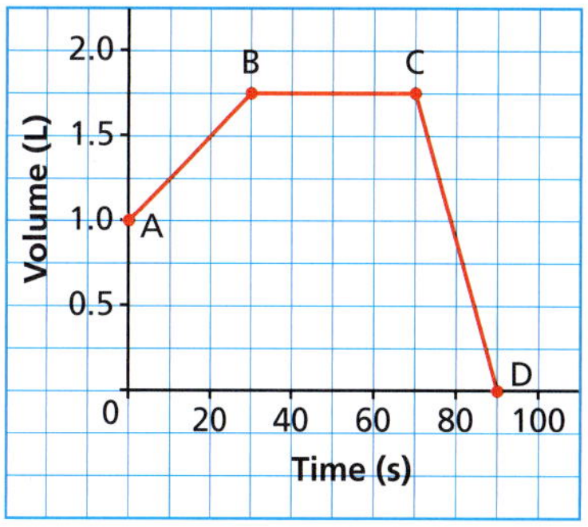

Example 2 Describing a Possible Situation for a Graph

Describe the journey for each segment of the graph.

Day Trip from Winnipeg to Winkler, Manitoba

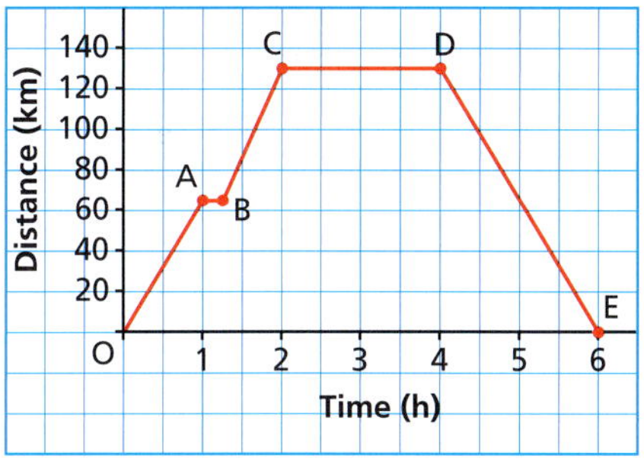

The distance between Winnipeg and Winkler is 130 km.

SOLUTION

Segment	Graph	Journey
OA	The graph goes up to the right, so as time increases, the distance from Winnipeg increases.	In the first hour, the car leaves Winnipeg and travels approximately 65 km toward Winkler.
AB	The graph is horizontal, so as time increases, the distance stays the same.	The car stops for approximately 15 min.
BC	The graph goes up to the right, so as time increases, the distance increases.	The car travels approximately 65 km toward Winkler.
CD	The graph is horizontal, so as time increases, the distance stays the same.	At C, the car has travelled 130 km so it has reached Winkler, where it stops for 2 h.
DE	The graph goes down to the right, so as time increases, the distance decreases.	The car returns to Winnipeg and takes 2 h to travel 130 km.

CHECK YOUR UNDERSTANDING

2. This graph represents a day trip from Athabasca to Kikino in Alberta, a distance of approximately 140 km.

Describe the journey for each segment of the graph.

Day Trip from Athabasca to Kikino

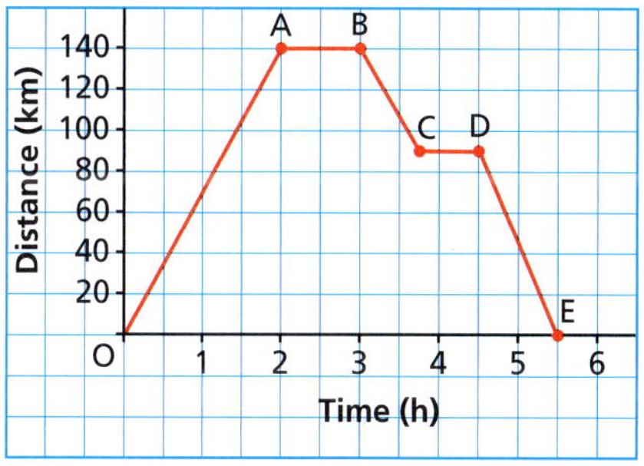

[Answer: The car takes 2 h to travel 140 km to Kikino; the car stops for 1 h: the car takes approximately 45 min to travel 50 km toward Athabasca; the car stops for approximately 45 min; the car takes 1 h to travel approximately 90 km to Athabasca]

What was the total driving time? Explain.

What are the dependent and the independent variables?

Example 3 Sketching a Graph for a Given Situation

Samuel went on a bicycle ride. He accelerated until he reached a speed of 20 km/h, then he cycled for 30 min at approximately 20 km/h. Samuel arrived at the bottom of a hill, and his speed decreased to approximately 5 km/h for 10 min as he cycled up the hill. He stopped at the top of the hill for 10 min.

Sketch a graph of speed as a function of time. Label each section of the graph, and explain what it represents.

SOLUTION

Draw and label axes on a grid. The horizontal axis represents time in minutes. The vertical axis represents speed in kilometres per hour.

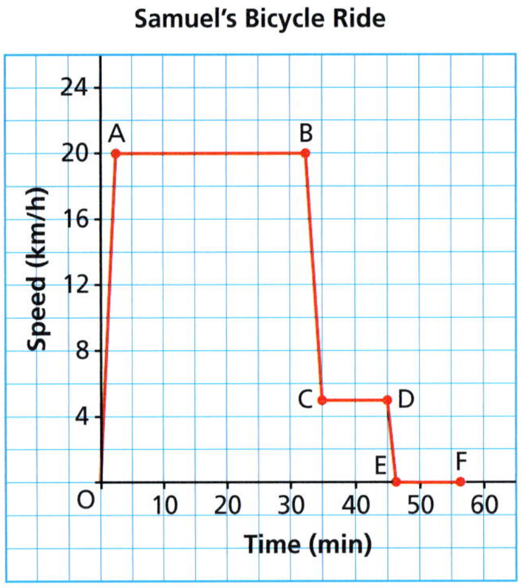

Segment	Journey
OA	Samuel's speed increases from 0 to 20 km/h, so the segment goes up to the right.
AB	Samuel cycles at approximately 20 km/h for 30 min. His speed does not change, so the segment is horizontal.
BC	Samuel's speed decreases to 5 km/h, so the segment goes down to the right.
CD	Samuel cycles uphill at approximately 5 km/h for 10 min. His speed does not change, so the segment is horizontal.
DE	Samuel slows down to 0 km/h, so his speed decreases and the segment goes down to the right.
EF	Samuel remains stopped at 0 km/h for 10 min, so the segment is horizontal.

CHECK YOUR UNDERSTANDING

3. At the beginning of a race, Alicia took 2 s to reach a speed of 8 m/s. She ran at approximately 8 m/s for 12 s, then slowed down to a stop in 2 s. Sketch a graph of speed as a function of time. Label each section of your graph, and explain what it represents.

Answer:

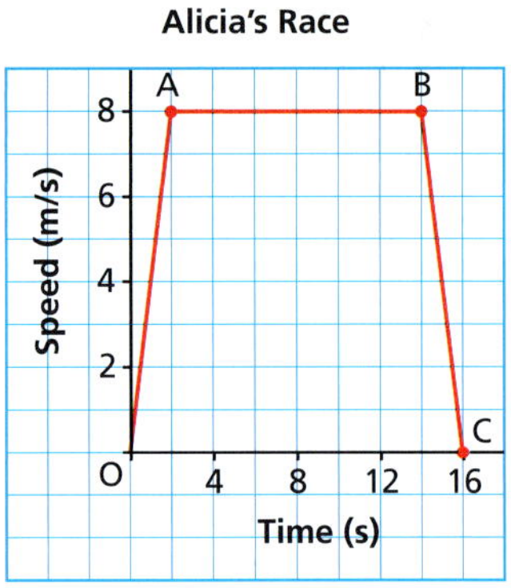

Why does the graph not end at point E?

Discuss the Ideas

1. For a graph of distance as a function of time, what does each segment represent?
   - a horizontal line segment
   - a segment that goes up to the right
   - a segment that goes down to the right
2. For a graph of speed as a function of time, what does each segment represent?
   - a horizontal line segment
   - a segment that goes up to the right
   - a segment that goes down to the right

Exercises

A

3. Each point on the graph represents a polar bear. Explain the answer to each question below.

Heights and Masses of 8 Polar Bears

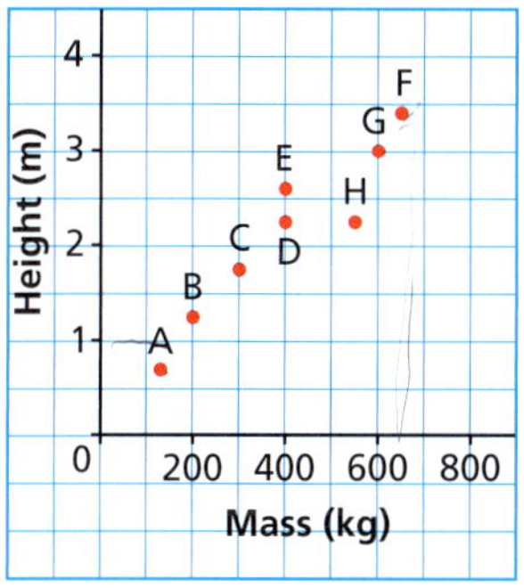

a) Which bear has the greatest mass? What is this mass?
b) Which bear is the shortest? What is its height?
c) Which two bears have the same mass? What is this mass?
d) Which two bears have the same height? What is this height?

B

4. This graph shows the height of the tide in a harbour as a function of time in one day. Explain the answer to each question below.

Height of the Tide in a Harbour

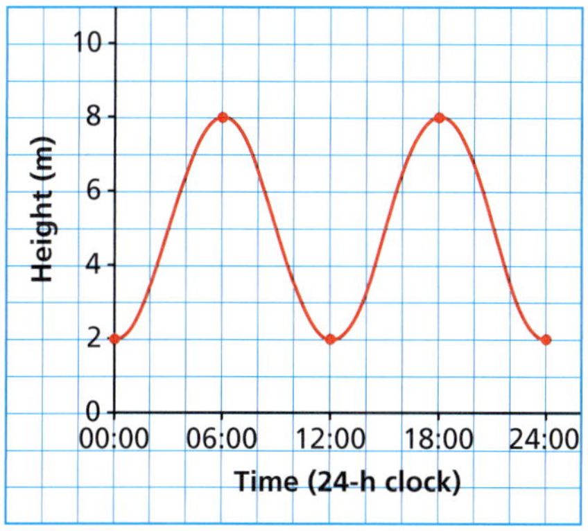

a) What is the greatest height? At what times does it occur?
b) What is the least height? At what times does it occur?
c) How high is the tide at 04:00?
d) When is the tide 4 m high?

5. To raise a flag, Sepideh pulls the rope steadily with both hands for a short time, then moves both hands up the rope and pulls again. She does this until the flag has been raised. Which graph best represents the height of the flag? Give reasons for your choice.

Graph A

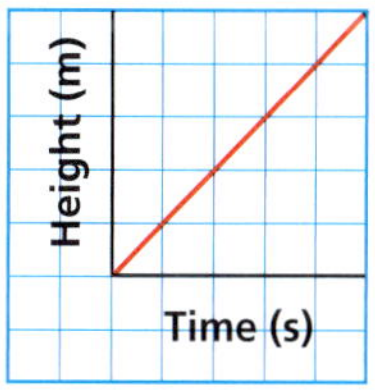

Graph B

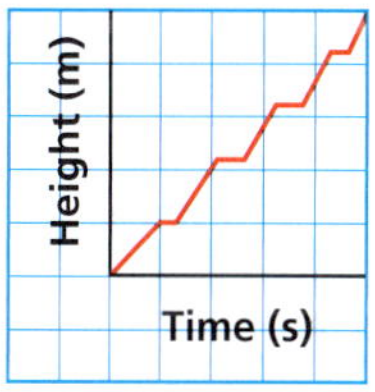

Graph C

Graph D

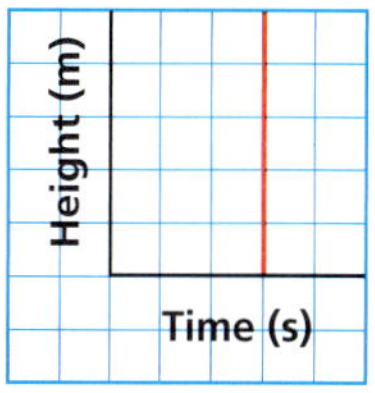

6. Gill runs for exercise. This graph shows her distance from home during one of her runs. Describe Gill's run for each segment of the graph.

Gill's Run

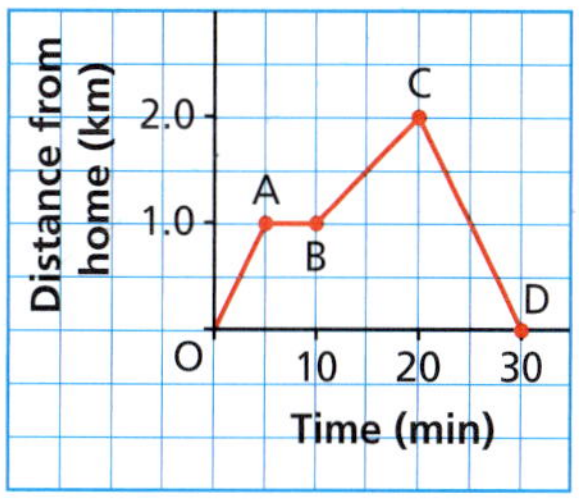

7. Katanya went scuba diving in Egypt. This graph shows her depth below sea level as a function of time on one of her dives.

Depth of Katanya's Scuba Dive

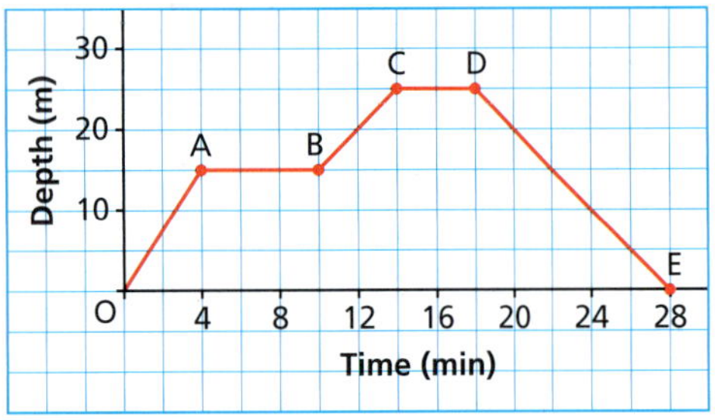

Write all that you know about the dive from the graph.

8. Point A and Point B represent the same helicopters in each of these graphs.

Graph of Cost against Age

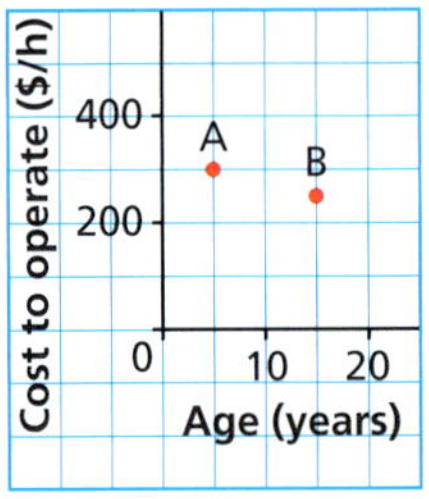

Graph of Maximum Speed against Number of Seats

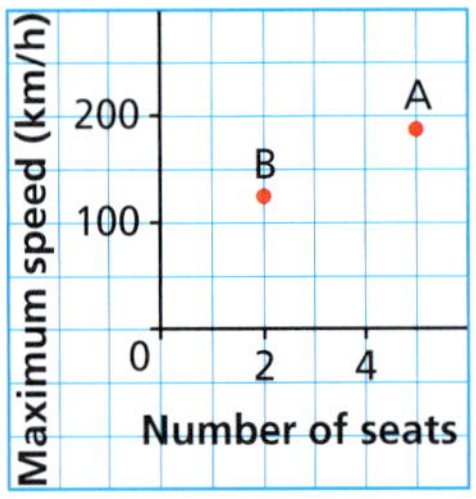

Which statements are true? Justify your answers.

a) The older helicopter is cheaper to operate.

b) The helicopter with more seats has the lower maximum speed.

c) The helicopter with the lower maximum speed is cheaper to operate.

d) The helicopter with the greater maximum speed is older.

e) The helicopter with fewer seats is newer.

9. a) Describe what is happening for each line segment in this graph.

Volume of Gas in a Snowmobile

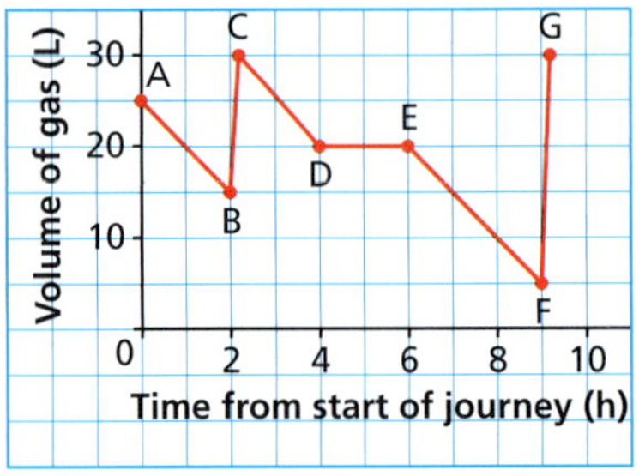

b) How much gas was in the tank at the start of the journey? Was the tank full at this time? Explain.

10. An oven is turned on at a room temperature of 20°C and it takes 10 min to reach a temperature of 190°C. A tray of cookies is placed in the oven to bake for 10 min. The oven is then turned off and returns to room temperature after 15 min. Sketch a graph of temperature as a function of time. Label each section of the graph and explain what it represents.

11. Write all that you know about a person's drive to work from this graph.

A Person's Drive to Work

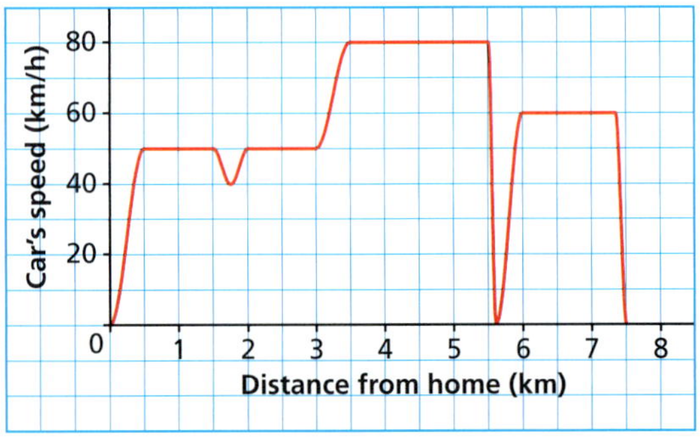

12. A school vending machine sells cartons of milk and juice. On a typical day:

- No cartons are sold between 7 A.M. and 8 A.M., or from 5 P.M. onward.
- The machine has a capacity of 100 cartons. At 7 A.M., it is three-quarters full.
- From 8 A.M. to 10 A.M., 10:15 A.M. to noon, and from 1 P.M. to 3 P.M. the students are in class.
- The machine is filled at 11 A.M. and at 4 P.M.

Sketch a graph of the number of cartons in the vending machine as a function of time. Explain what each section of the graph represents.

13. A student drew a graph to represent this situation.

"Jonah is watching television. After 3 min his mom enters the room to ask him a question. He turns the volume down a bit, answers his mom, then turns the volume back up. Two minutes later, Jonah's dad turns on the dishwasher so Jonah gradually turns up the volume. After a further 3 min, a commercial comes on so Jonah presses the mute button."

Describe any errors in the student's graph.

Volume of a Television

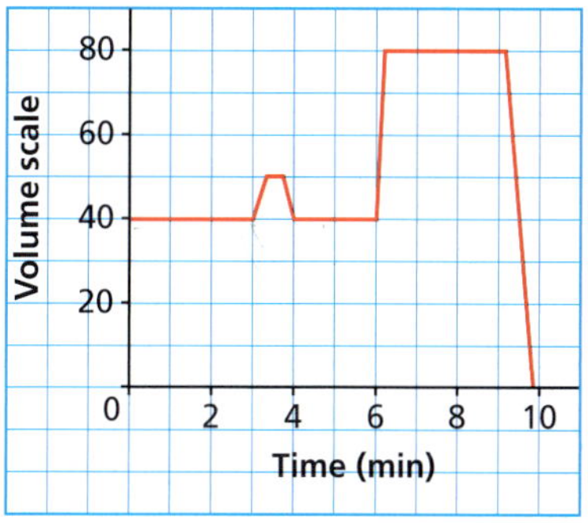

14. The two graphs below have the same shape, but different vertical axes. Copy each graph and include numbers and units on both axes. Write and justify a possible situation that it represents.

a) **Graph A**

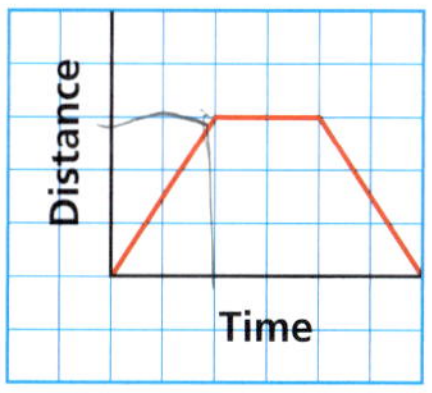

b) **Graph B**

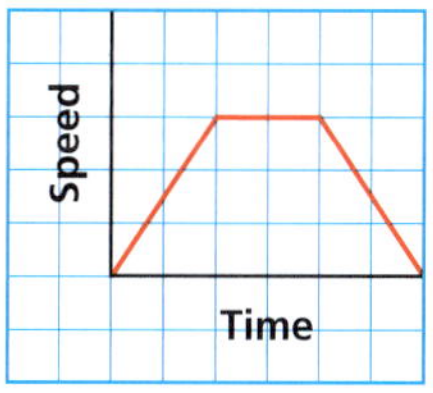

15. Each graph shows a quantity as a function of time. Choose a dependent variable for each graph, and suggest a possible situation that it represents. Copy the graph and include numbers on the axes.

a)

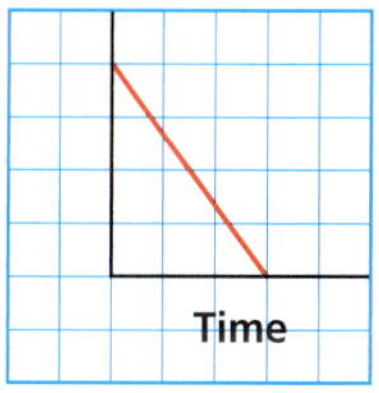

b)

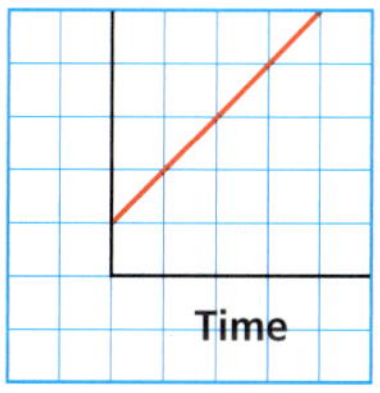

C

16. Chad goes bungee jumping.

a) Sketch each graph of his jump.

i) the distance above the ground as a function of time

ii) the speed as a function of time

b) Explain the similarities and differences between the two graphs.

17. For each graph, choose a dependent variable and an independent variable, and suggest a possible situation that it represents. Describe the significance of any key points or changes in the graph.

a)

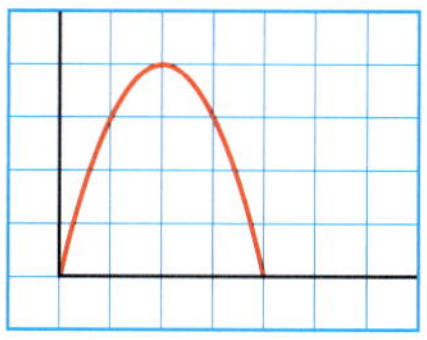

b)

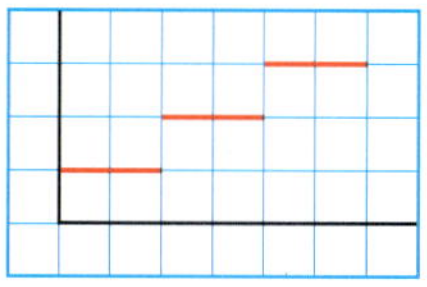

c)

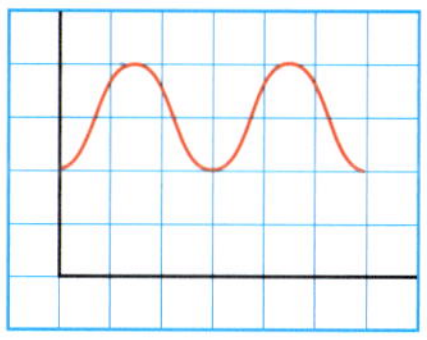

18. The diagrams below show cross-sections of swimming pools that will be filled with water at the same constant rate. Sketch two graphs on the same grid to represent the depth of water in each pool as a function of time. Label the axes. Justify the shape of each graph.

a)

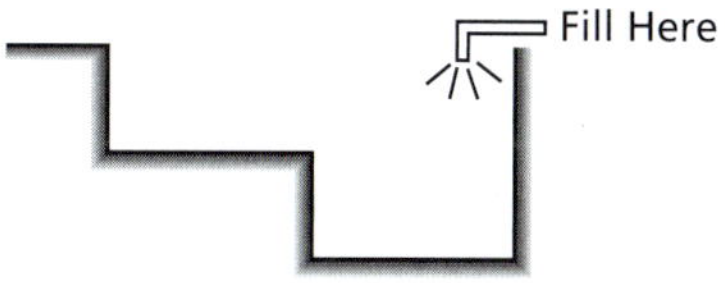

b)

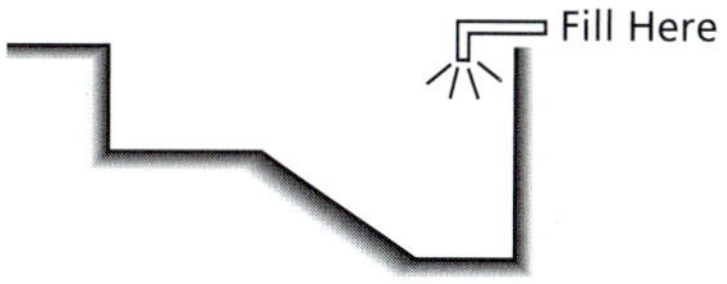

Reflect

When you describe a possible situation for a given graph, what features of the graph do you have to use in your description and how do you use them? Include a sketch of a graph in your explanation.

MATH LAB
5.4 Graphing Data

LESSON FOCUS

Graph data and investigate the domain and range when the data represent a function.

Make Connections

To rent a car for less than one week from Ace Car Rentals, the cost is \$65 per day for the first three days, then \$60 a day for each additional day.

Number of Days Car Is Rented	Total Cost (\$)
1	65
2	130
3	195
4	255
5	315
6	375

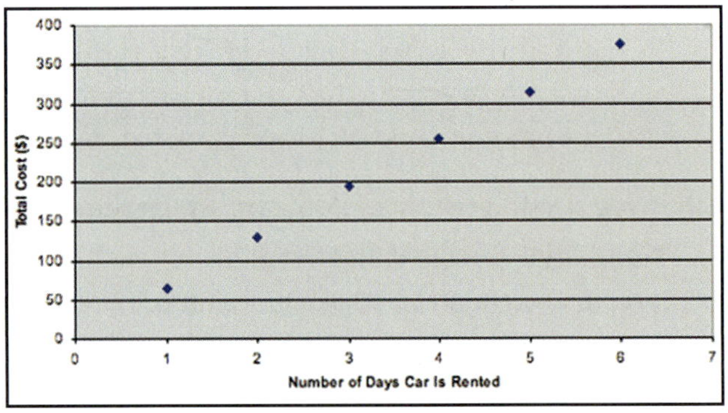

Why are the points on the graph not joined?

Is this relation a function? How can you tell?

What is the domain? What is the range?

Construct Understanding

TRY THIS

Work with a partner.

You will need:

- a length of rope
- a metre stick
- grid paper, a graphing calculator, or a computer with graphing software

When you tie knots in a rope, the length of the rope is related to the number of knots tied.

A. You will investigate the relation between the number of knots and the length of rope.

- Measure the length of the rope without any knots. Tie a knot in the rope. Measure the length of the rope with the knot.
- Repeat the measurements for up to 5 knots. Try to tie the knots so they are all the same size and tightness.
- Record the number of knots and the length of the rope in a table.

Number of Knots	Length of Rope (cm)

B. Graph the data.

- How did you determine on which axis to plot each variable?
- How did you choose the scale for each axis so the data fit on the axes?
- Did you join the points? Justify your answer.

C. If you used a graphing calculator, sketch the graph. If you used a computer, print the graph.

- Is the length of the rope a function of the number of knots? Explain. If your answer is yes, list the set of ordered pairs. What is the domain? What is the range?
- Would it make sense to extend the graph to the right? To the left? If your answer is yes, how far could you extend it? What is the new domain? What is the new range? If your answer is no, what restrictions are there on the domain and range?

Suppose you used another piece of rope with the same length. Would the length of the rope after each number of knots be the same as that which you first recorded? Why or why not?

D. Suppose you combined your data with those of 4 pairs of classmates.

- When you graph all the data, does the graph represent a function? Justify your answer.
- Suppose you calculated the mean rope length for each number of knots, then graphed the data. Would the graph represent a function? Justify your answer.

Assess Your Understanding

1. For each table of values below:

i) Graph the data. Will you join the points? Justify your answer.

ii) Does the graph represent a function? Explain.

a) At a constant pressure, the speed of sound in air is related to the air temperature.

Air Temperature (°C)	Speed of Sound (m/s)
0	331
5	334
10	337
15	340
20	343

b) The recommended daily dose of vitamin C is related to a female's age in years.

Age (years)	Dose of Vitamin C Tablet (mg
3	15
6	25
9	45
12	45
15	65
18	65
21	75

2. Graph the data in these tables of values from Lesson 5.2, question 9. Decide whether to join the points.
How can you tell from each graph that the relation is a function?

a)

Number of Cans of Juice Purchased, n	Cost, C ($)
1	2.39
2	4.00
3	6.39
4	8.00
5	10.39
6	12.00

b)

Altitude, A (m)	Temperature, T (°C)
610	15.0
1220	11.1
1830	7.1
2440	3.1
3050	−0.8
3660	−4.8

5.5 Graphs of Relations and Functions

LESSON FOCUS

Determine the properties of the graphs of relations and functions.

The great horned owl is Alberta's provincial bird.

Make Connections

In an environmental study in Northern Alberta, Joe collected data on the numbers of different species of birds he heard or saw in a 1-h period every 2 h for 24 h. Alice collected data on the temperature in the area at the end of each 1-h period. They plotted their data:

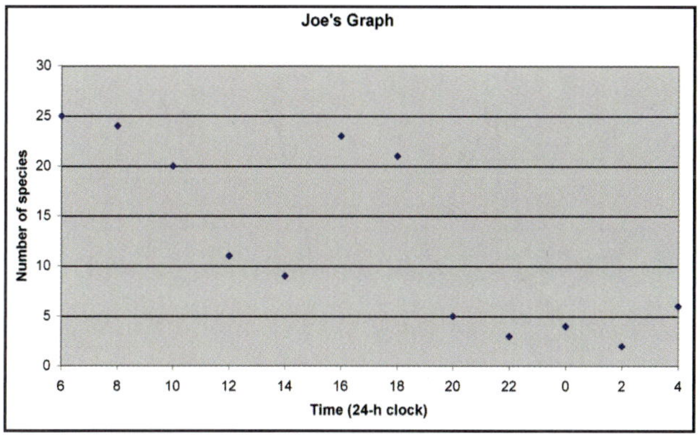

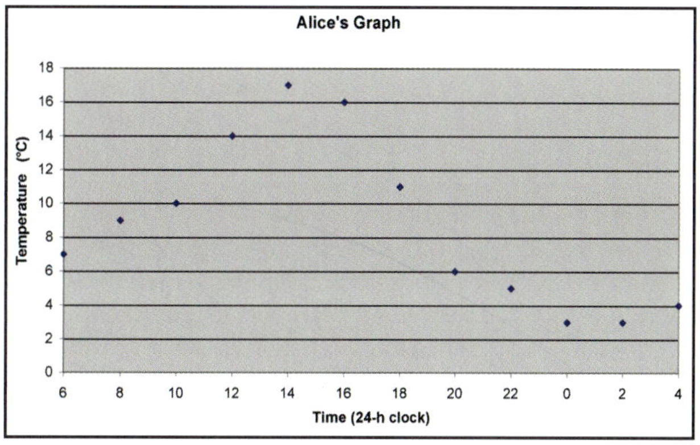

Does each graph represent a relation? A function? How can you tell?

Which of these graphs should have the data points connected? Explain.

Construct Understanding

TRY THIS

Work with a partner.

You will need grid paper.

A. Each of you chooses one of these tasks:

- A sugar cube has a volume of 5 cm^3 and a mass of 4 g. Graph the mass of sugar as a function of the number of sugar cubes from 0 to 5 sugar cubes.
- Five cubic centimetres of loose sugar also has a mass of 4 g. Graph the mass of sugar as a function of the volume of sugar from 0 to 25 cm^3 of loose sugar.

B. Share your results. How are your graphs alike? How are they different?

C. Work together:

- Identify the dependent variable and independent variable for each function. How did you decide on which axis to graph each variable?
- How did you decide whether to connect the points?
- Are there any restrictions on the domain and range? Explain.

We can represent the function that associates every whole number with its double in several ways.

Using a table of values:

Whole Number, x	Double the Number, y
0	0
1	2
2	4
3	6
4	8

The table continues for all whole numbers.
The domain is the set of whole numbers.
The range is the set of even whole numbers.

Using a graph:

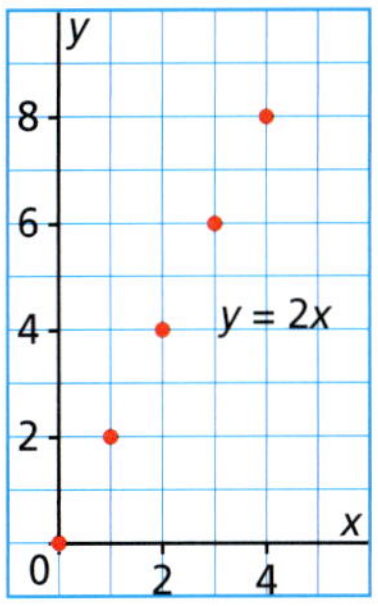

How would the graph change if both x and y were real numbers?

How can you tell the domain and range from the graph?

We know the relation $y = 2x$ is a function because each value of x associates with exactly one value of y, and each ordered pair has a different first element.

The *domain* of a function is the set of values of the independent variable; for the graph above, the domain is the x-values.

The *range* of a function is the set of values of the dependent variable; for the graph above, the range is the y-values.

When the domain is restricted to a set of discrete values, the points on the graph are not connected.

A relation that is not a function has two or more ordered pairs with the same first coordinate. So, when the ordered pairs of the relation are plotted on a grid, a vertical line can be drawn to pass through more than one point.

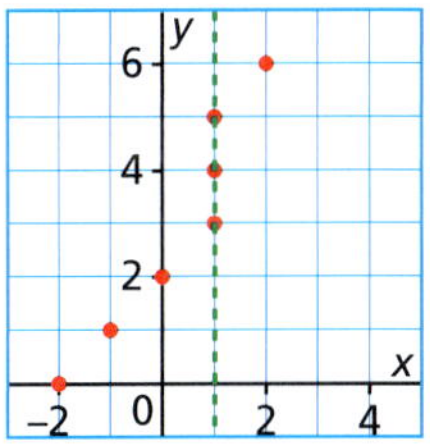

A function has ordered pairs with different first coordinates. So, when the ordered pairs of the function are plotted on a grid, any vertical line drawn will always pass through no more than one point.

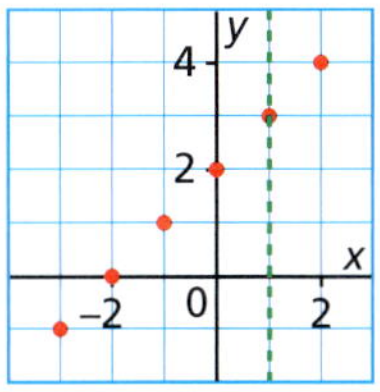

Vertical Line Test for a Function

A graph represents a function when no two points on the graph lie on the same vertical line.
Place a ruler vertically on a graph, then slide the ruler across the graph. If one edge of the ruler always intersects the graph at no more than one point, the graph represents a function.

Example 1 Identifying whether a Graph Represents a Function

Which of these graphs represents a function? Justify the answer.

a) Height against Shoe Size

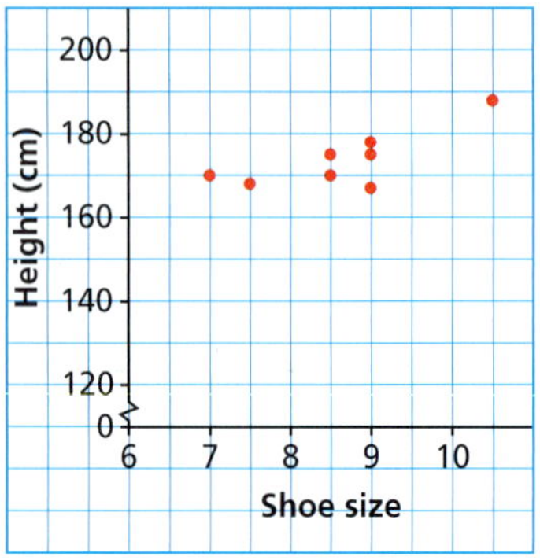

b) World Population

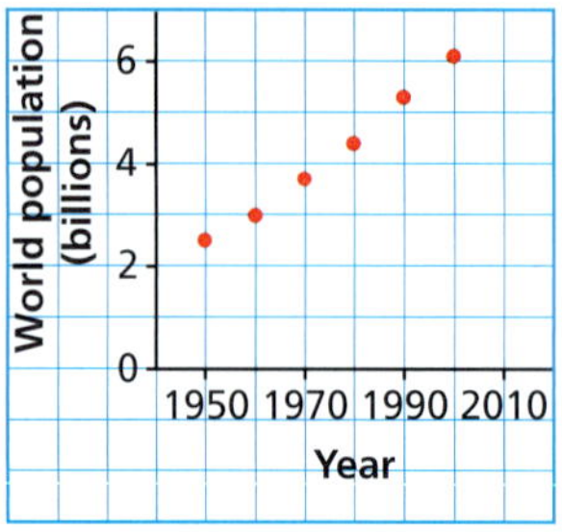

SOLUTION

Use the vertical line test for each graph.

a) This graph does not represent a function because two points lie on the same vertical line.

Height against Shoe Size

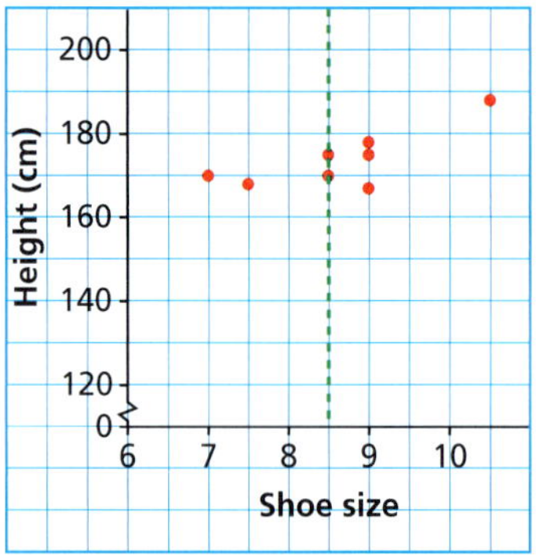

b) This graph does represent a function.
Any vertical line drawn on the graph passes through 0 points or 1 point.

World Population

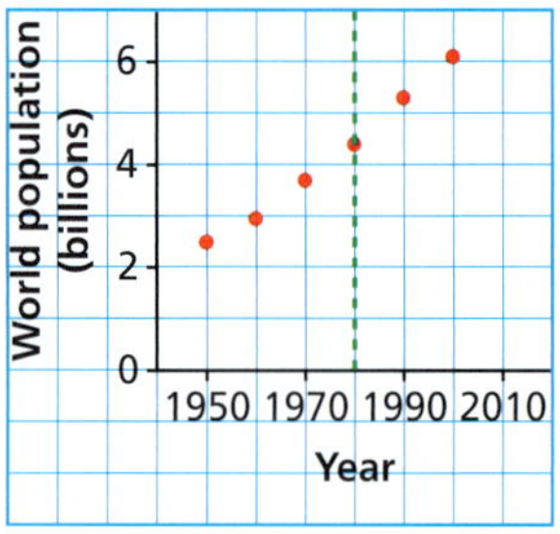

CHECK YOUR UNDERSTANDING

1. Which of these graphs represents a function? Justify your answer.

a) Outside Temperature over a 24-h Period

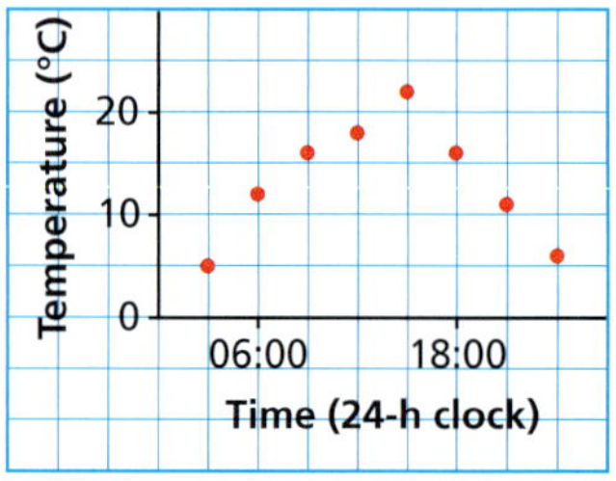

b) Masses of Students against Height

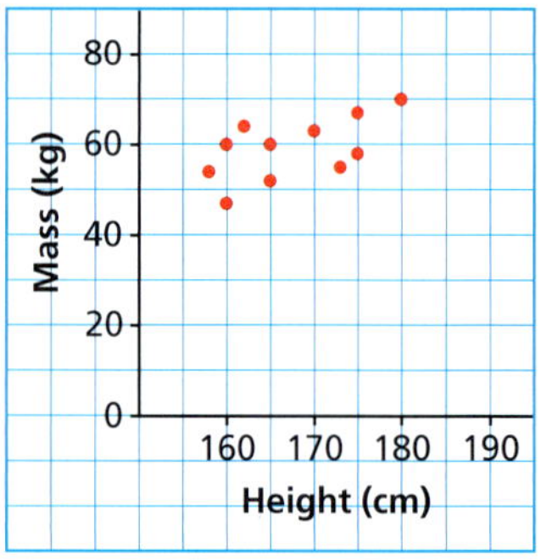

[Answers: a) function
b) not a function]

How does the vertical line test relate to the definition of a function?

Example 2 Determining the Domain and Range of the Graph of a Function

Determine the domain and range of the graph of each function.

a)

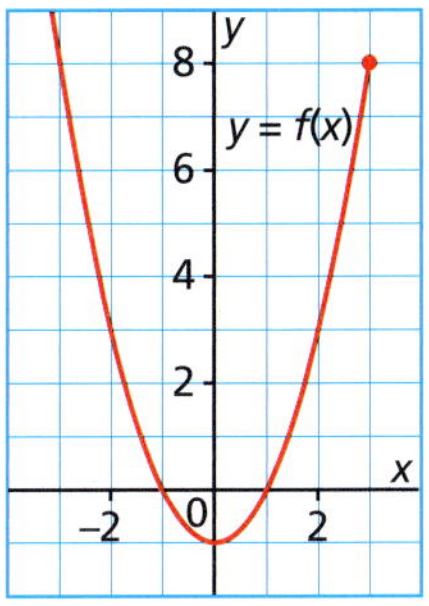

b)

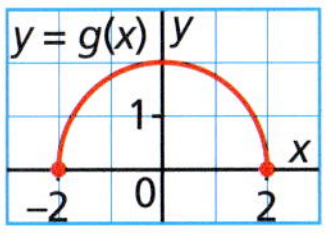

SOLUTION

a) The dot at the right end of the graph indicates that the graph stops at that point.

There is no dot at the left end of the graph, so the graph continues to the left.

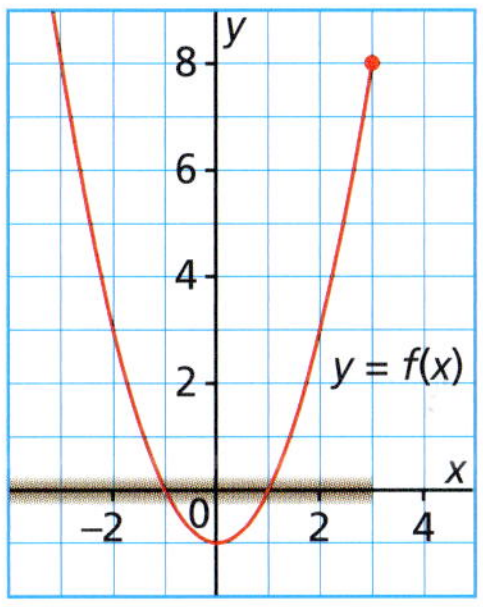

The domain is the set of x-values of the function.
Visualize the shadow of the graph on the x-axis.
The domain is the set of all real numbers less than or equal to 3; that is, $x \leq 3$.

The range is the set of y-values of the function.
Visualize the shadow of the graph on the y-axis.
The range is the set of all real numbers greater than or equal to -1; that is, $y \geq -1$.

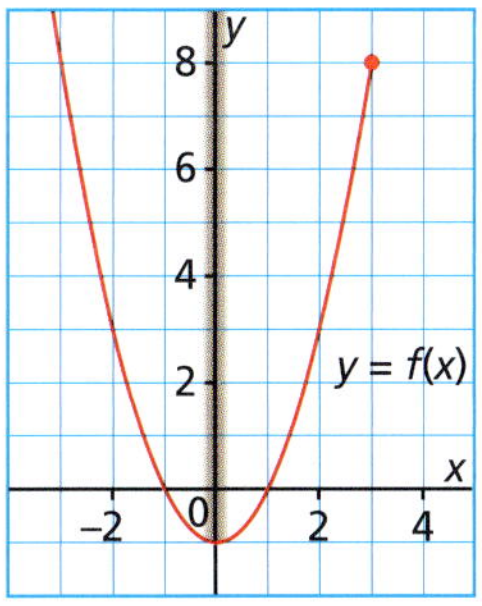

b) The dot at each end of the graph indicates that the graph stops at that point.

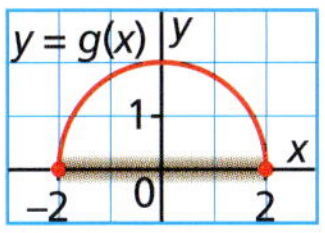

The domain is the set of x-values of the function.
Visualize the shadow of the graph on the x-axis.
The domain is the set of real numbers between -2 and 2, including these numbers; that is, $-2 \leq x \leq 2$.

We say: "x is greater than or equal to -2 and less than or equal to 2."

(Solution continues.)

CHECK YOUR UNDERSTANDING

2. Determine the domain and range of the graph of each function.

a)

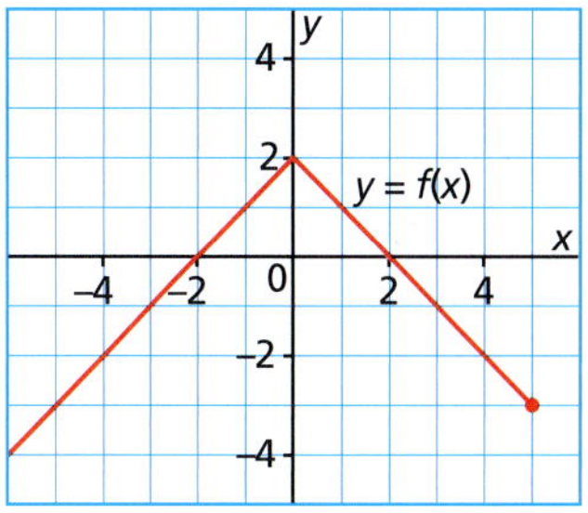

b)

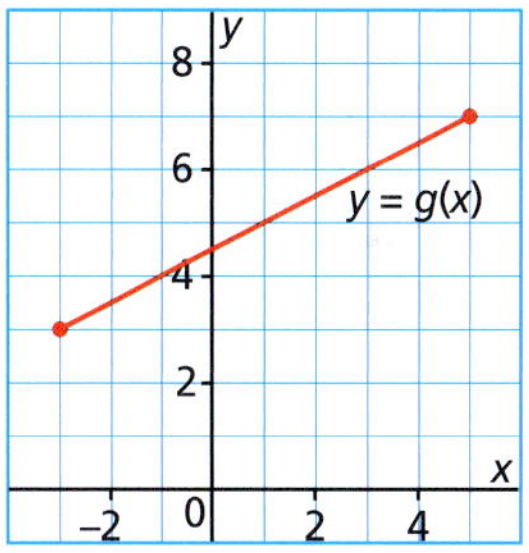

[Answers: a) $x \leq 5$; $y \leq 2$
b) $-3 \leq x \leq 5$; $3 \leq y \leq 7$]

When data are not discrete, we use inequality symbols to indicate the domain and range.

The range is the set of y-values of the function. Visualize the shadow of the graph on the y-axis. The range is the set of real numbers between 0 and 2, including these numbers; that is, $0 \le y \le 2$.

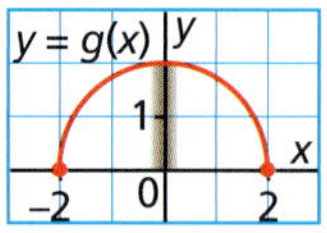

Example 3 Determining the Domain and Range of the Graph of a Situation

This graph shows the number of fishing boats, n, anchored in an inlet in the Queen Charlotte Islands as a function of time, t.

Number of Fishing Boats Anchored in an Inlet

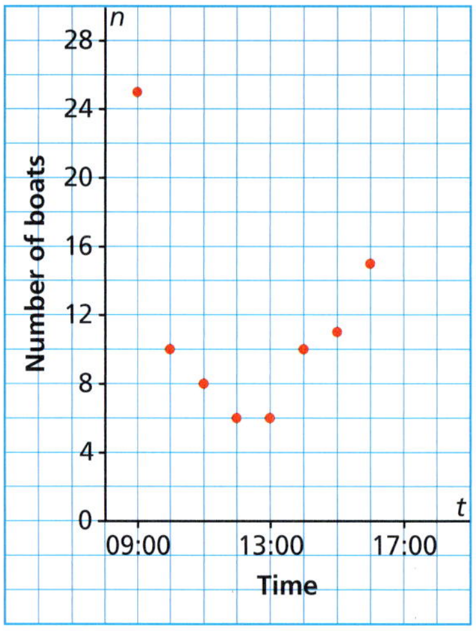

a) Identify the dependent variable and the independent variable. Justify the choices.

b) Why are the points on the graph not connected? Explain.

c) Determine the domain and range of the graph.

SOLUTION

a) The number of fishing boats is a function of time. Since the number of boats, n, depends on the time of day, the dependent variable is n and the independent variable is t.

b) The points on the graph are not connected because the number of boats is restricted to a whole number. This means that most values between the points are not valid; for example, between 10:00 and 11:00, the number of boats decreases from 10 to 8. We may plot a point at $n = 9$, if we know a corresponding time, but no other point is valid between 10 and 8 because we cannot have a fractional number of boats.

c) The domain is the set of times; that is, {09:00, 10:00, 11:00, 12:00, 13:00, 14:00, 15:00, 16:00}

The range is the set of the numbers of boats; that is, {6, 8, 10, 11, 15, 25}

CHECK YOUR UNDERSTANDING

3. This graph shows the approximate height of the tide, h metres, as a function of time, t, at Port Clements, Haida Gwaii on June 17, 2009.

Height of Tide at Port Clements, June 17, 2009

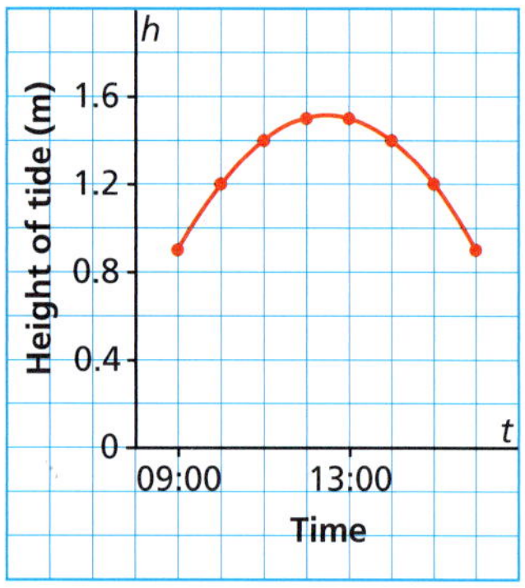

a) Identify the dependent variable and the independent variable. Justify your choices.

b) Why are the points on the graph connected? Explain.

c) Determine the domain and range of the graph.

[Answers: a) h, t
c) $09{:}00 \le t \le 16{:}00$;
$0.9 \le h \le 1.5$]

Example 4 Determining Domain Values and Range Values from the Graph of a Function

Here is a graph of the function $f(x) = -3x + 7$.

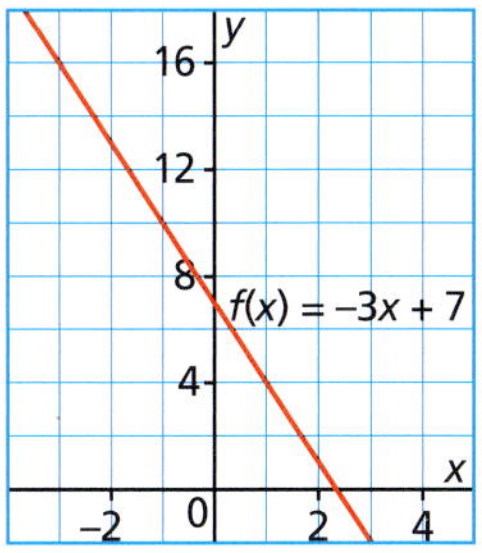

a) Determine the range value when the domain value is -2.

b) Determine the domain value when the range value is 4.

SOLUTION

The domain value is a value of x. The range value is a value of $f(x)$.

a) To determine the value of $f(x)$ when $x = -2$:

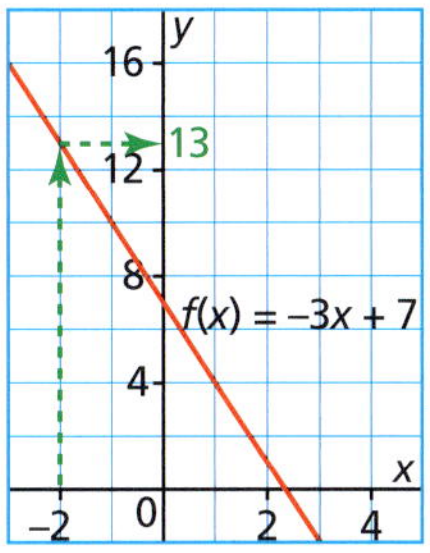

Begin at $x = -2$ on the x-axis.

Draw a vertical line to the graph, then a horizontal line to the y-axis.

The line appears to intersect the y-axis at 13.

So, $f(-2) = 13$

When the domain value is -2, the range value is 13.

b) To determine the value of x when $f(x) = 4$:

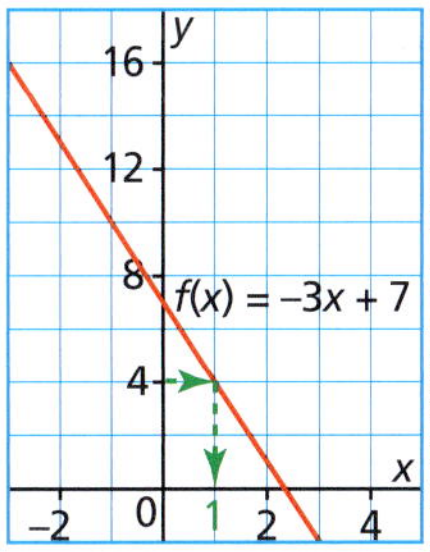

Since $y = f(x)$, begin at $y = 4$ on the y-axis.

Draw a horizontal line to the graph, then a vertical line to the x-axis.

The line intersects the x-axis at 1.

So, when $f(x) = 4$, $x = 1$

When the range value is 4, the domain value is 1.

CHECK YOUR UNDERSTANDING

4. Here is a graph of the function $g(x) = 4x - 3$.

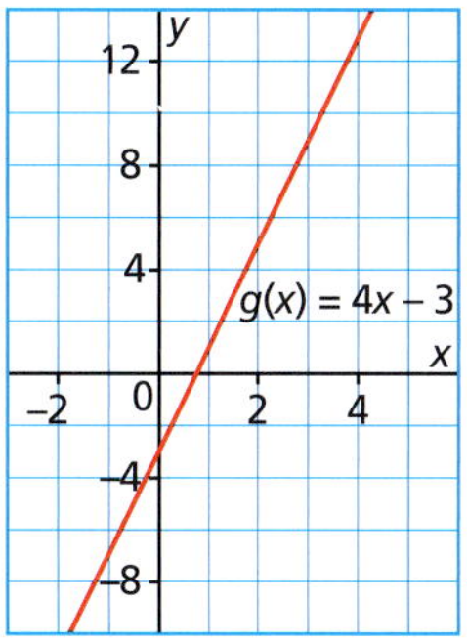

a) Determine the range value when the domain value is 3.

b) Determine the domain value when the range value is -7.

[Answers: a) 9 b) -1]

Discuss the Ideas

1. How do you decide whether to connect the points you plot for a graph?
2. What can you tell about the domain and range of a function from its graph?
3. How can you identify whether a graph represents a function?

Exercises

A

4. List the domain and the range of the graph of each function.

a)

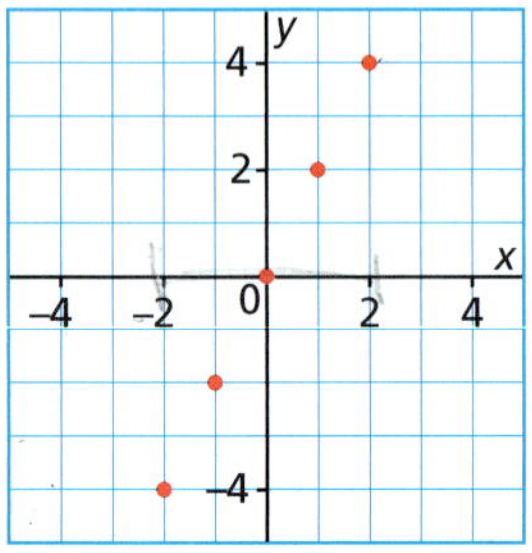

b)

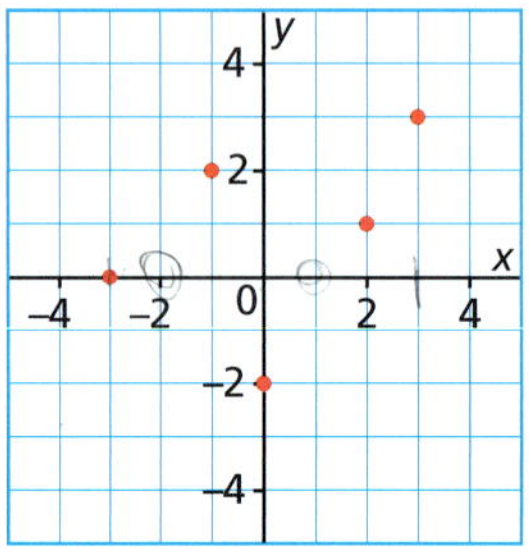

c)

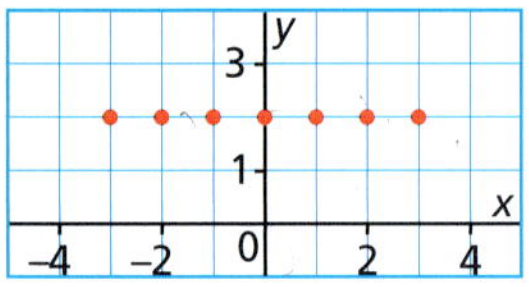

5. How can you tell that each graph in question 4 represents a function?

6. Which of these graphs represents a function? Justify your answer.

a)

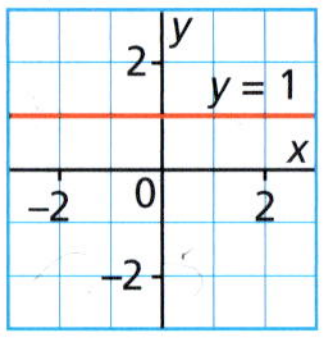

b)

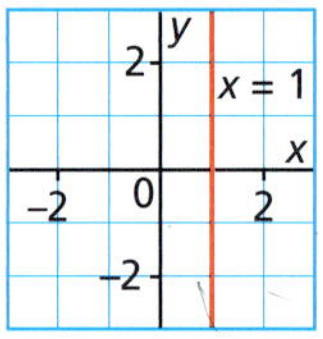

7. Match the graph of each function to its domain and range listed below.

a)

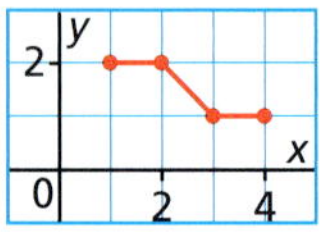

b)

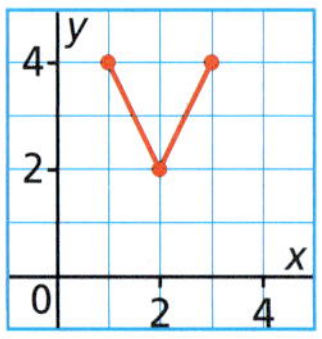

c)

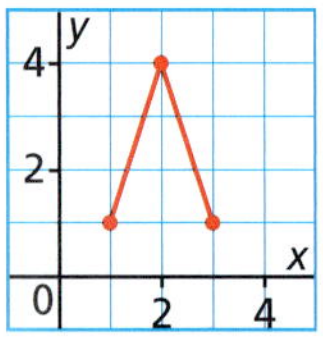

d)

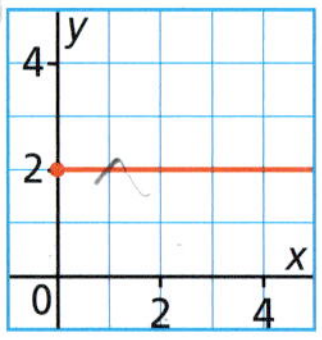

i) domain: $1 \leq x \leq 3$; range: $2 \leq y \leq 4$

ii) domain: $1 \leq x \leq 3$; range: $1 \leq y \leq 4$

iii) domain: $x \geq 0$; range: $y = 2$

iv) domain: $1 \leq x \leq 4$; range: $1 \leq y \leq 2$

B

8. Which of these graphs represents a function? Justify your answer.
Write the domain and range for each graph.

a)

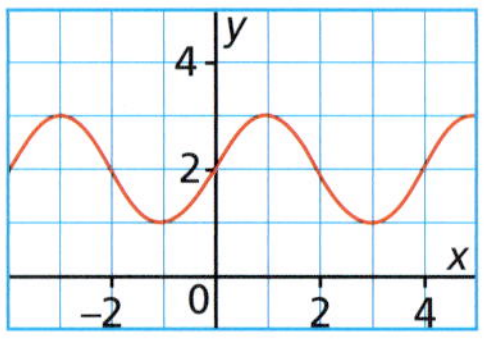

b)

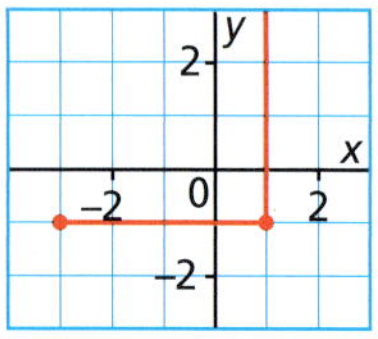

c)

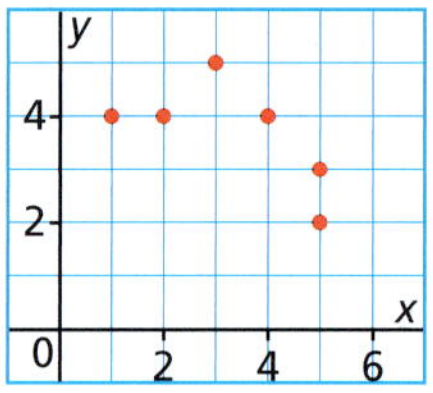

d)

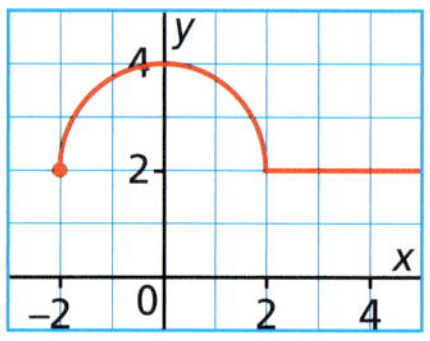

e)

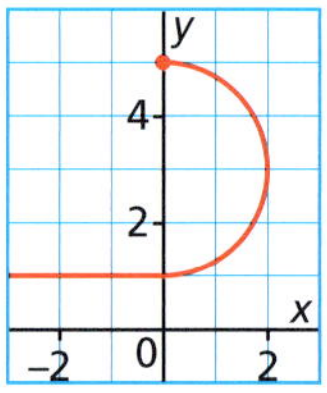

9. Determine the domain and range of the graph of each function.

a)

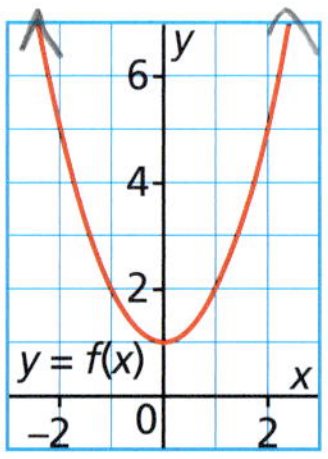

b)

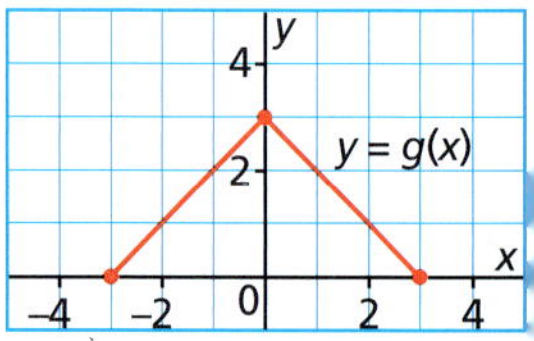

c)

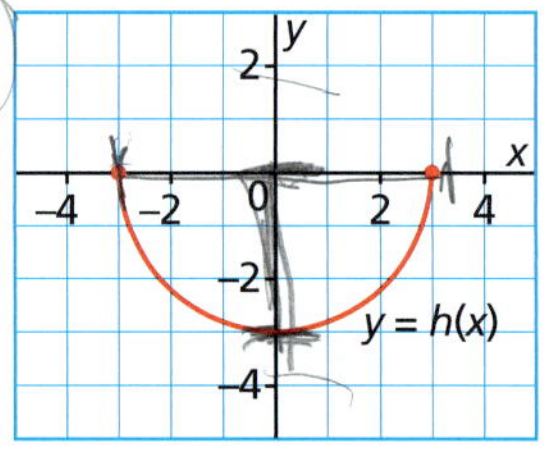

d)

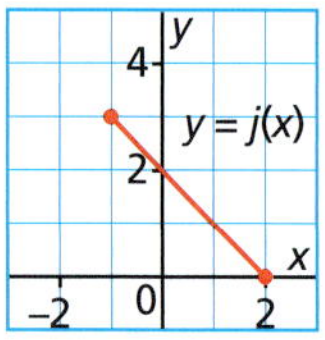

10. Suppose a student drew a graph of each function described below. For which graphs should the student connect the points? Justify your answers.

a) The cost of a custom-made T-shirt is a function of the number of letters on the T-shirt.

b) The altitude of a plane is a function of the time it is in the air.

c) The mass of a baby is a function of her age.

d) The cube root of a real number is a function of the number.

11. a) What do the data in each graph represent?

i) **Graph A**

Distance of School Bus from School

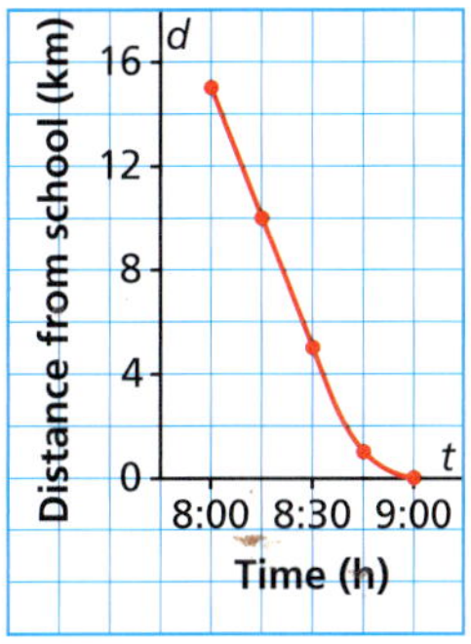

ii) **Graph B**

Number of Students on a School Bus

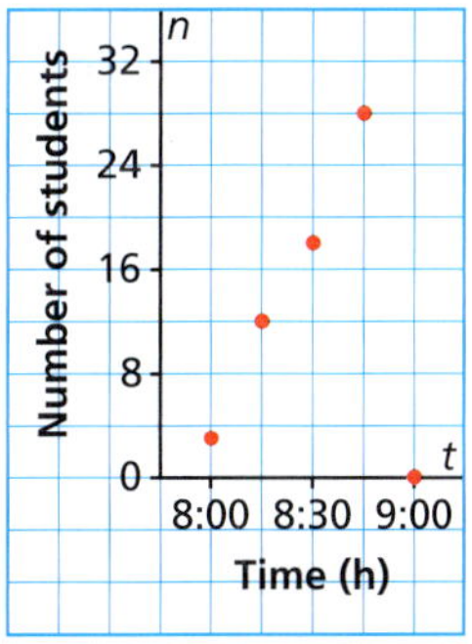

b) Identify the independent and dependent variables.

c) Why are the points connected on one graph but not on the other?

12. When police officers investigate a car crash, they can estimate the speed the car was travelling by measuring the skid distance.

Skid Distance of a Car

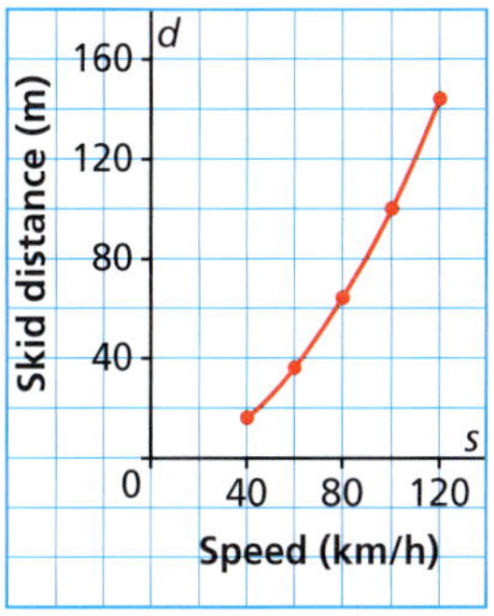

a) Why are the points on the graph connected?

b) Estimate the domain and range of the graph. Are there any restrictions on the domain and range? Explain.

13. This graph shows the number of cars, n, in the school parking lot as a function of time, t.

Number of Cars in the School Parking Lot

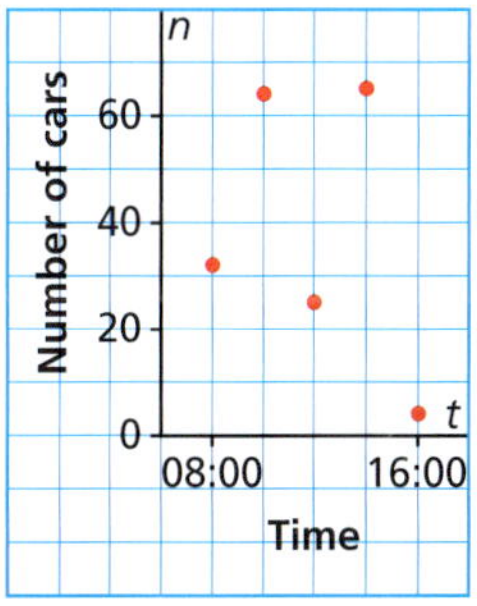

a) Identify the independent and dependent variables. Justify your choices.

b) Why are the points on the graph not connected?

c) Estimate the domain and range of the graph. Are there any restrictions on the domain and range? Explain.

14. Paulatuuq is north of the Arctic Circle. The table shows the number of hours, h, the sun is above the horizon every 60 days from January 1st, which is day 0.

Day	h
0	0
60	9.7
120	18.5
180	24.0
240	15.9
300	7.4
360	0

a) Identify the independent variable and the dependent variable. Justify your choices.
b) Graph the data in the table. Did you connect the points? Why or why not?
c) Use the table of values and the graph to explain why this relation is a function.

15. One litre of latex paint covers approximately 8.5 m^2 and costs \$12.
a) Copy and complete this table.

Volume of Paint, p (L)	0	2	4	6	8
Cost, c (\$)	0	24			
Area Covered, A (m^2)	0	17			

b) Graph the area covered as a function of the volume of paint.
c) Graph the area covered as a function of the cost.
d) Write the domain and range of the functions in parts b and c.

16. This is a graph of the function $f(x) = 2x - 1$.

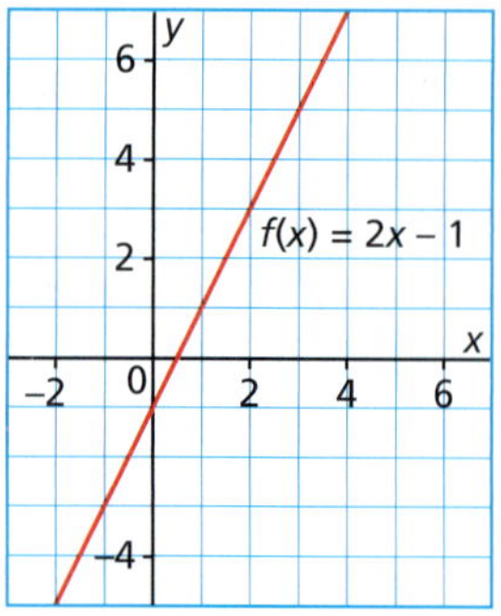

a) Determine the range value when the domain value is 0.
b) Determine the domain value when the range value is 5.

17. This is a graph of the function $g(x) = -x + 3$.

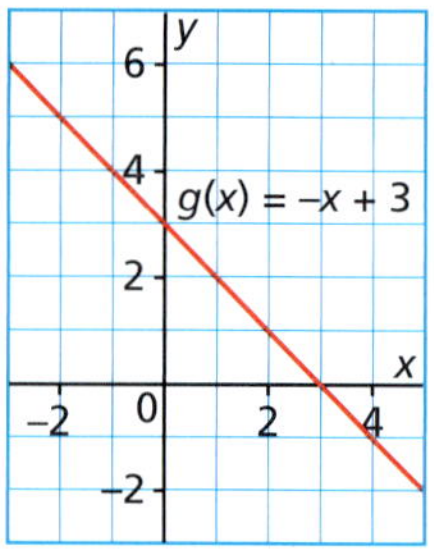

a) Determine the range value when the domain value is -2.
b) Determine the domain value when the range value is 0.

18. Draw a graph of a function on a grid. Write the domain and range of the function. Exchange graphs with a classmate, and check that the domain and range of your classmate's graph are correct. If they are not, correct them, then explain your corrections to your classmate.

19. Sketch a graph of a function that has each domain and range.
a) domain: $-2 \leq x \leq 3$; range: $1 \leq y \leq 5$
b) domain: $x \geq 1$; range: $-1 \leq y \leq 1$

20. One planetary year is the time it takes for a planet to travel once around the sun. Since the planets take different times to travel around the sun, one year on each planet is different. The distance from Earth to the sun is 1 astronomical unit. Other distances in the solar system are compared to the distance from Earth to the sun.

	Earth	Jupiter	Saturn	Uranus
Distance from Sun (astronomical units)	1	5	10	19
Planetary Year (Earth years)	1	12	29	84

a) Graph planetary year as a function of distance from the sun. Did you connect the points? Explain.

b) Write the domain and range of this function.

C

21. This table shows the costs to send letters within Canada in 2009.

Mass of Letter	Cost ($)
Up to 30 g	0.54
Greater than 30 g and up to 50 g	0.98
Greater than 50 g and up to 100 g	1.18
Greater than 100 g and up to 200 g	1.96
Greater than 200 g and up to 500 g	2.75

a) Graph the cost of sending a letter as a function of its mass. Did you connect the points? Explain.

b) Write the domain and range of this function.

22. A hospital patient has his temperature taken every hour.

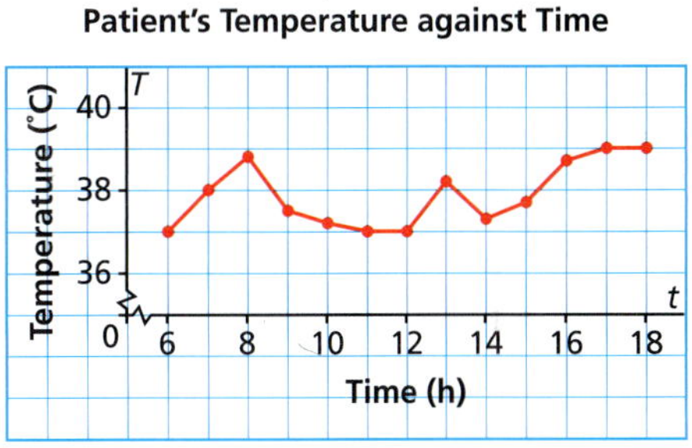

Should the points have been connected? Give reasons for your answer.

23. Is this statement true?
A measure of time can be any real number, so any graph with time as its independent variable should have its points connected.
Explain your answer with examples.

24. Payment scheme 1: A person receives 1¢ on day 1, then each day the payment is doubled.
Payment Scheme 2: A person receives $10 each day.
For both payments, the total money received is a function of the number of days.

a) Make a table of values for each payment scheme.

b) Graph the data.

c) Which payment scheme would you choose if you were receiving the money for 30 days? Explain.

Reflect

Generalize and explain rules for determining whether a graph represents a function. How do you determine the domain and range of a function from its graph? Include examples in your explanation.

CHECKPOINT 2

Connections

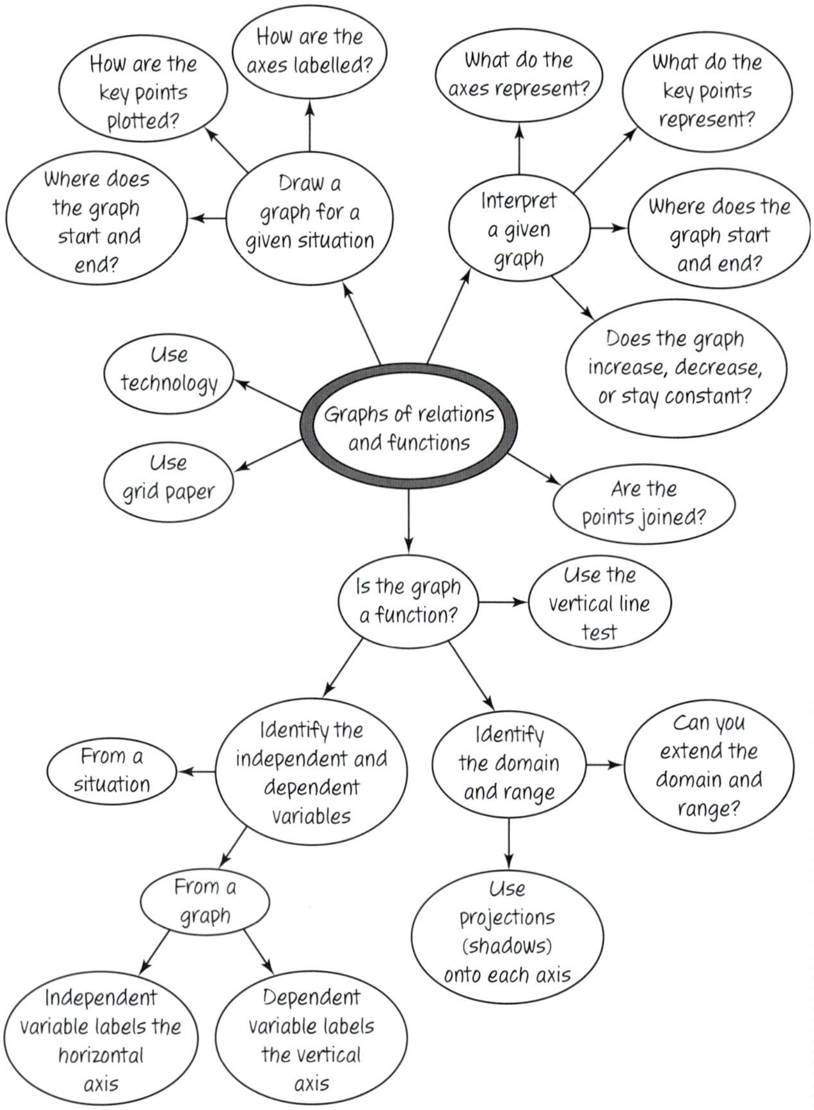

Concept Development

- **In Lesson 5.3**
  - You applied what you know about functions to interpret graphs that represent different situations.
  - You applied what you know about functions to sketch graphs that represent different situations.
- **In Lesson 5.4**
  - You generated data for a relation, then graphed and analyzed the data.
- **In Lesson 5.5**
  - You used the vertical line test on graphs to identify functions.
  - You identified the independent and dependent variables of a function.
  - You graphed tables of values for functions and identified their domains and ranges.
  - You connected points on a graph if all real-number values of the variables were permitted.

Assess Your Understanding

5.3

1. Copy the graph below. Choose labels for each axis, then describe a situation the graph could represent. Justify your description.

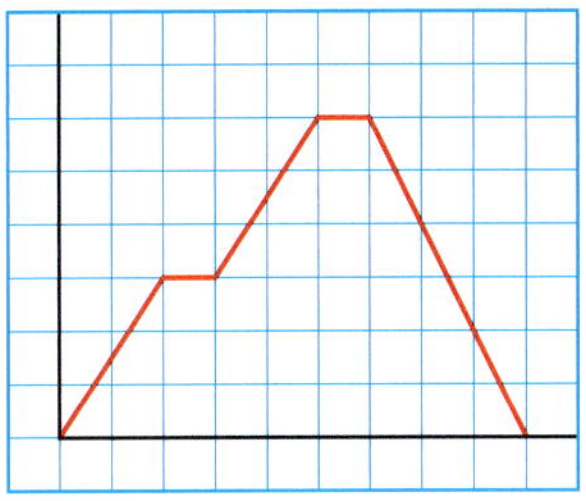

5.4

2. a) Use technology or grid paper to graph these data for people up to the age of 18.

b) Should you join the points? Explain your reasoning.

c) What are the domain and range of these data?

d) Suppose data for more people, up to the age of 18, with different masses were graphed. Would there be any restrictions on the domain and range? If your answer is yes, state the restrictions. If your answer is no, explain why no restrictions exist.

Age (years)	Mass (kg)
14	45
14	50
15	56
15	64
17	65
18	90

5.5

3. Which graphs represent functions? Justify your answer. Write the domain and range of each graph.

a)

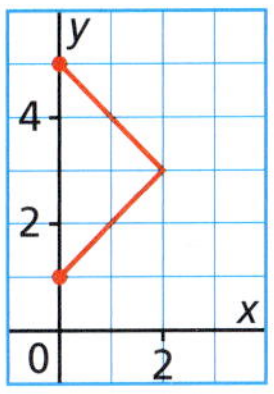

b)

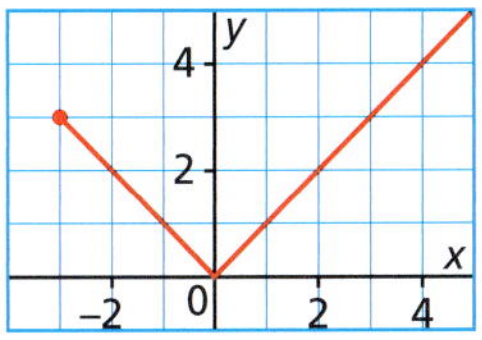

c)

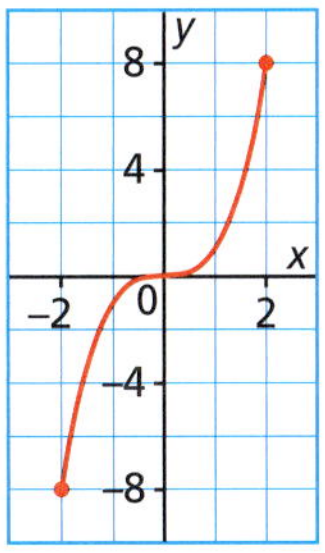

5.6 Properties of Linear Relations

LESSON FOCUS

Identify and represent linear relations in different ways.

Make Connections

The table of values and graph show the cost of a pizza with up to 5 extra toppings.

Number of Extra Toppings	Cost ($)
0	12.00
1	12.75
2	13.50
3	14.25
4	15.00
5	15.75

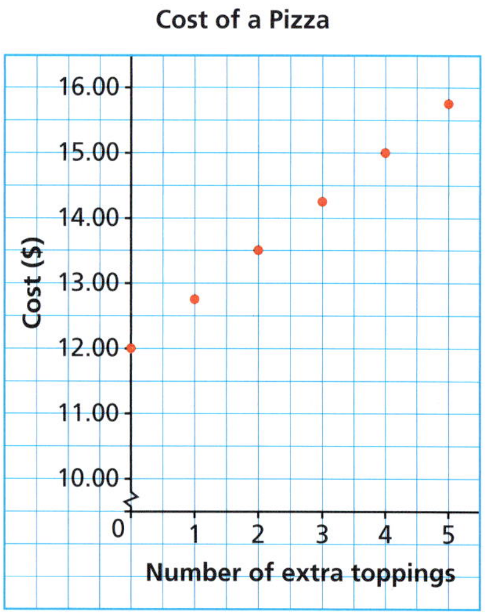

What patterns do you see in the table?

Write a rule for the pattern that relates the cost of a pizza to the number of its toppings.

How are the patterns in the table shown in the graph?

How can you tell from the table that the graph represents a linear relation?

Construct Understanding

TRY THIS

Work with a partner.

You will need 1-cm grid paper.

Use this pattern of rectangles.
This pattern continues.

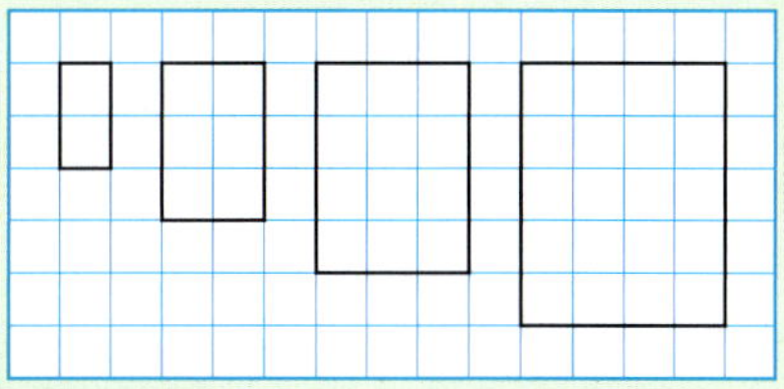

A. Draw the next two rectangles in the pattern.
Copy and complete each table of values for the 6 rectangles.

Width of Rectangle (cm)	Area (cm^2)
1	
2	

Width of Rectangle (cm)	Perimeter (cm)
1	
2	

B. Which table of values represents a linear relation? How can you tell?

C. Graph the data in each table of values.
Does each graph represent a linear relation?
How do you know?

The cost for a car rental is \$60, plus \$20 for every 100 km driven.
The independent variable is the distance driven and the dependent variable is the cost.
We can identify that this is a linear relation in different ways.

- a table of values

Independent variable → Distance (km); Dependent variable → Cost (\$)

Distance (km)	Cost (\$)
0	60
100	80
200	100
300	120
400	140

Distance: +100, +100, +100, +100; Cost: +20, +20, +20, +20

For a linear relation, a constant change in the independent variable results in a constant change in the dependent variable.

Why is it important that the ordered pairs are listed so their first elements are in numerical order?

The graph of a linear relation is a straight line.

- a set of ordered pairs

+100 +100 +100 +100

$\{(0, 60), (100, 80), (200, 100), (300, 120), (400, 140)\}$

+20 +20 +20 +20

- a graph

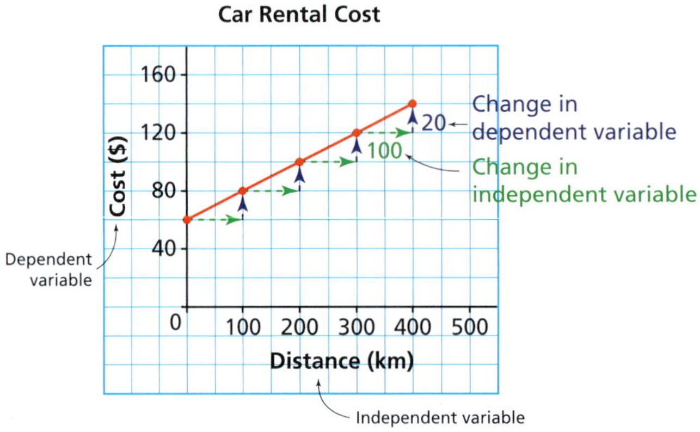

We can use each representation above to calculate the **rate of change**.
The rate of change can be expressed as a fraction:

$$\frac{\text{change in dependent variable}}{\text{change in independent variable}} = \frac{\$20}{100 \text{ km}}$$

$$= \$0.20/\text{km}$$

The rate of change is $0.20/km; that is, for each additional 1 km driven, the rental cost increases by 20¢. The rate of change is constant for a linear relation.

We can determine the rate of change from the equation that represents the linear function.
Let the cost be C dollars and the distance driven be d kilometres.
An equation for this linear function is:

$C = 0.20d + 60$

- 60: initial amount
- d: independent variable
- 0.20: rate of change
- C: dependent variable

Example 1 Determining whether a Table of Values Represents a Linear Relation

Which table of values represents a linear relation? Justify the answer.

a) The relation between temperature in degrees Celsius, *C*, and temperature in degrees Fahrenheit, *F*

C	*F*
0	32
5	41
10	50
15	59
20	68

b) The relation between the current, *I* amps, and power, *P* watts, in an electrical circuit

I	*P*
0	0
5	75
10	300
15	675
20	1200

SOLUTION

The terms in the first column are in numerical order. So, calculate the change in each variable.

a)

C	Change in *C*	*F*	Change in *F*
0		32	
5	$5 - 0 = 5$	41	$41 - 32 = 9$
10	$10 - 5 = 5$	50	$50 - 41 = 9$
15	$15 - 10 = 5$	59	$59 - 50 = 9$
20	$20 - 15 = 5$	68	$68 - 59 = 9$

Since the changes in both variables are constant, the table of values represents a linear relation.

b)

I	Change in *I*	*P*	Change in *P*
0		0	
5	$5 - 0 = 5$	75	$75 - 0 = 75$
10	$10 - 5 = 5$	300	$300 - 75 = 225$
15	$15 - 10 = 5$	675	$675 - 300 = 375$
20	$20 - 15 = 5$	1200	$1200 - 675 = 525$

The changes in *I* are constant, but the changes in *P* are not constant. So, the table of values does not represent a linear relation.

CHECK YOUR UNDERSTANDING

1. Which table of values represents a linear relation? Justify your answer.

a) The relation between the number of bacteria in a culture, *n*, and time, *t* minutes.

t	*n*
0	1
20	2
40	4
60	8
80	16
100	32

b) The relation between the amount of goods and services tax charged, *T* dollars, and the amount of the purchase, *A* dollars

A	*T*
60	3
120	6
180	9
240	12
300	15

[Answers: a) not linear b) linear]

What other strategies could you use to check whether each table of values represents a linear relation?

When an equation is written using the variables x and y, x represents the independent variable and y represents the dependent variable.

Example 2 Determining whether an Equation Represents a Linear Relation

a) Graph each equation.

i) $y = -3x + 25$ ii) $y = 2x^2 + 5$

iii) $y = 5$ iv) $x = 1$

b) Which equations in part a represent linear relations? How do you know?

SOLUTION

a) Create a table of values, then graph the relation.

i) $y = -3x + 25$

x	y
−2	31
−1	28
0	25
1	22
2	19

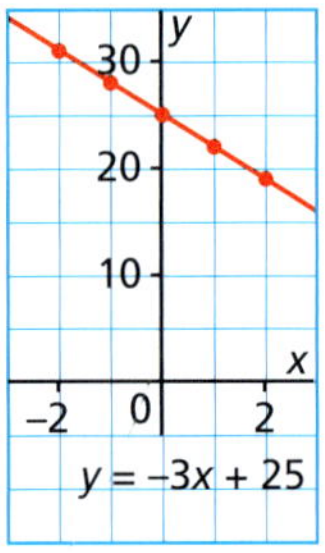

ii) $y = 2x^2 + 5$

x	y
−2	13
−1	7
0	5
1	7
2	13

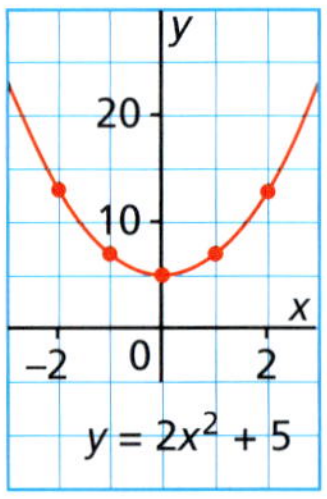

iii) $y = 5$

x	y
0	5
1	5
2	5

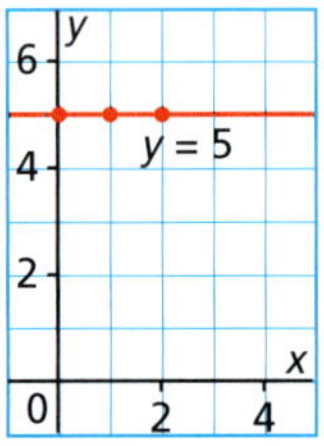

iv) $x = 1$

x	y
1	−1
1	0
1	1

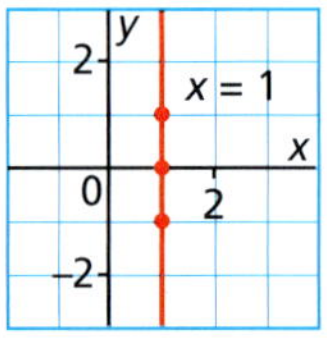

b) The graphs in parts i, iii, and iv are straight lines, so their equations represent linear relations; that is, $y = -3x + 25$, $y = 5$, and $x = 1$.
The graph in part ii is not a straight line, so its equation does not represent a linear relation.

CHECK YOUR UNDERSTANDING

2. a) Graph each equation.
i) $x = -2$
ii) $y = x + 25$
iii) $y = 25$
iv) $y = x^2 + 25$

b) Which equations in part a represent linear relations? How do you know?

[Answers: b) $x = -2$; $y = x + 25$; $y = 25$]

Example 3 Identifying a Linear Relation

Which relation is linear? Justify the answer.

a) A new car is purchased for $24 000. Every year, the value of the car decreases by 15%. The value is related to time.

b) For a service call, an electrician charges a $75 flat rate, plus $50 for each hour he works. The total cost for service is related to time.

SOLUTION

Create a table of values, then check to see if the relation is linear.

a) Every year, the value decreases by 15%.
The value of the car is:
100% − 15% = 85% of its previous value
So, multiply each value by 0.85.

Change	Time (years)	Value ($)	Change
	0	24 000	
+1	1	20 400	−3600
+1	2	17 340	−3060
+1	3	14 739	−2601

There is a constant change of 1 in the 1st column, but the differences in the 2nd column are not constant. So, the relation is not linear.

b) After the first hour, the cost increases by $50 per hour.

Change	Time (h)	Cost ($)	Change
	0	75	
+1	1	125	+50
+1	2	175	+50
+1	3	225	+50
+1	4	275	+50

There is a constant change of 1 in the 1st column and a constant change of 50 in the 2nd column, so the relation is linear.

CHECK YOUR UNDERSTANDING

3. Which relation is linear? Justify your answer.

a) A dogsled moves at an average speed of 10 km/h along a frozen river. The distance travelled is related to time.

b) The area of a square is related to the side length of the square.

[Answers: a) linear
b) not linear]

What equation could you write for the linear relation in part b?

Example 4 Determining the Rate of Change of a Linear Relation from Its Graph

A water tank on a farm near Swift Current, Saskatchewan, holds 6000 L.
Graph A represents the tank being filled at a constant rate.
Graph B represents the tank being emptied at a constant rate.

Graph A
Filling a Water Tank

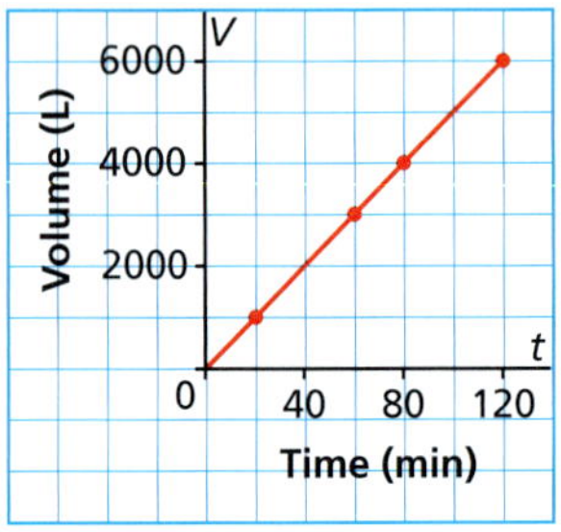

Graph B
Emptying a Water Tank

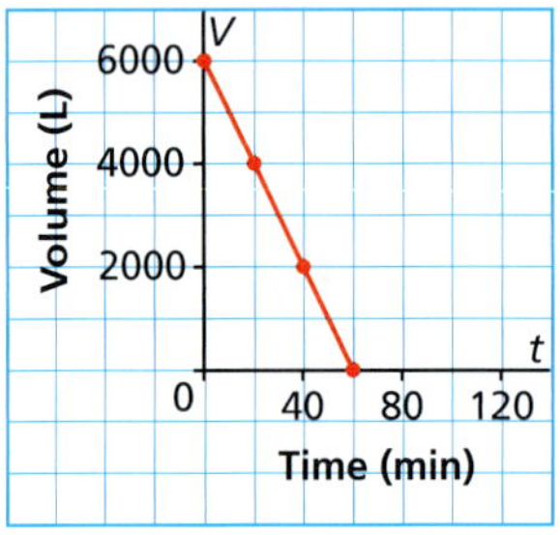

a) Identify the independent and dependent variables.

b) Determine the rate of change of each relation, then describe what it represents.

SOLUTION

For Graph A

a) The independent variable is the time, t.
The dependent variable is the volume, V.

b) Choose two points on the line. Calculate the change in each variable from one point to the other.

Graph A
Filling a Water Tank

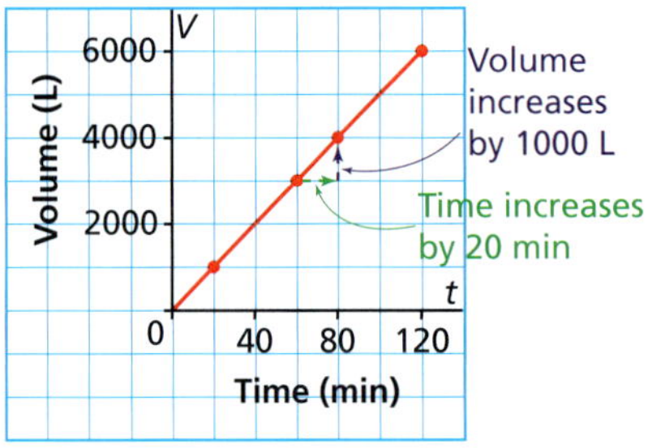

Change in volume:
4000 L − 3000 L = 1000 L

Change in time:
80 min − 60 min = 20 min

Rate of change: $\frac{1000 \text{ L}}{20 \text{ min}} = 50$ L/min

The rate of change is positive so the volume is increasing with time.
Every minute, 50 L of water are added to the tank.

CHECK YOUR UNDERSTANDING

4. A hot tub contains 1600 L of water. Graph A represents the hot tub being filled at a constant rate. Graph B represents the hot tub being emptied at a constant rate.

Graph A
Filling a Hot Tub

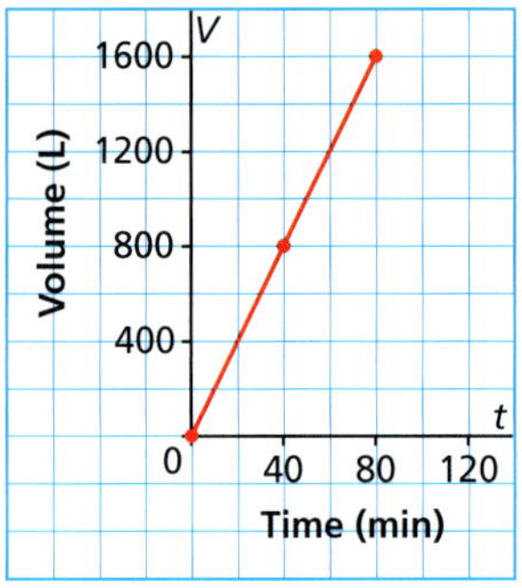

Graph B
Emptying a Hot Tub

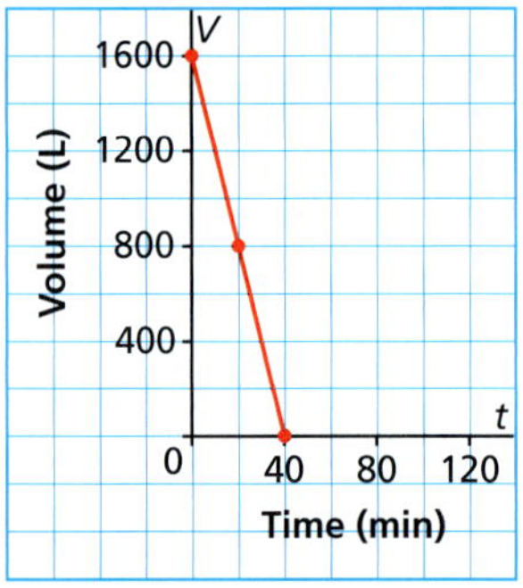

a) Identify the dependent and independent variables.

b) Determine the rate of change of each relation, then describe what it represents.

[Answers: Graph A a) V, t b) 20 L/min Graph B a) V, t b) −40 L/min]

For Graph B

a) The independent variable is the time, t.
The dependent variable is the volume, V.

b) Choose two points on the line.
Calculate the change in each variable from one point to the other.

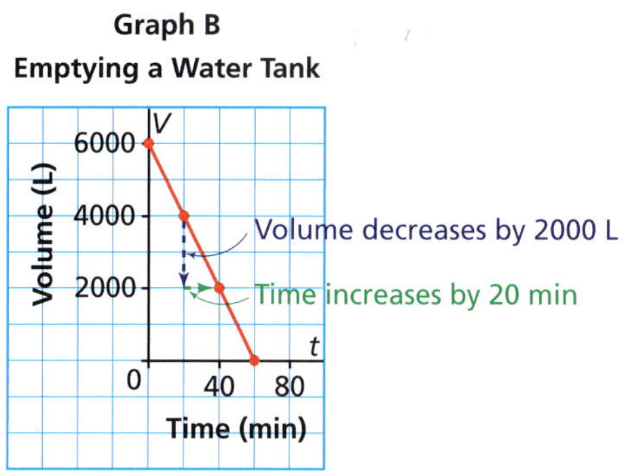

Change in volume: 2000 L − 4000 L = −2000 L
Change in time: 40 min − 20 min = 20 min

Rate of change: $\frac{-2000 \text{ L}}{20 \text{ min}} = -100$ L/min

The rate of change is negative so the volume is decreasing with time.
Every minute, 100 L of water are removed from the tank.

Discuss the Ideas

1. How can you tell from each format whether a relation is linear?
   - a description in words
   - a set of ordered pairs
   - a table of values
   - an equation
   - a graph

2. What is "rate of change"? How can you use each format in question 1 to determine the rate of change of a linear relation?

Exercises

A

3. Which tables of values represent linear relations? Explain your answers.

a)

Time (min)	Distance (m)
0	10
2	50
4	90
6	130

b)

Time (s)	Speed (m/s)
0	10
1	20
2	40
3	80

c)

Speed (m/s)	Time (s)
15	7.5
10	5
5	2.5
0	0

d)

Distance (m)	Speed (m/s)
4	2
16	4
1	1
9	3

4. Which sets of ordered pairs represent linear relations? Explain your answers.

a) $\{(3, 11), (5, 9), (7, 7), (9, 5)\}$
b) $\{(-2, 3), (0, 1), (2, -3), (4, -7)\}$
c) $\{(1, 1), (1, 3), (2, 1), (2, 3)\}$

5. Which graphs represent linear relations? How do you know?

a)

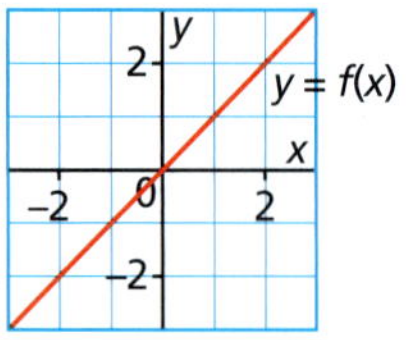

b)

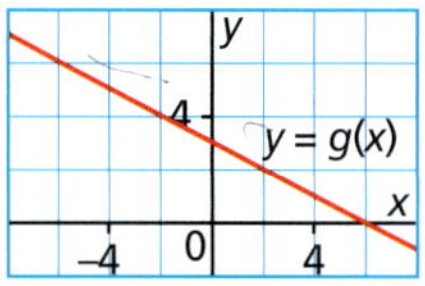

c)

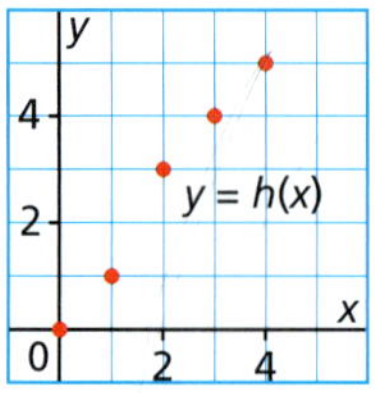

d)

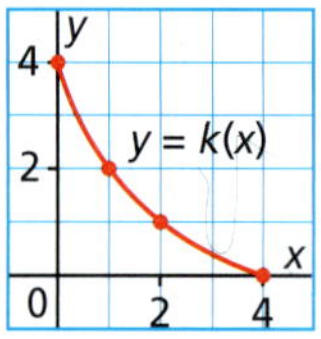

B

6. a) Create a table of values when necessary, then graph each relation.

i) $y = 2x + 8$ ii) $y = 0.5x + 12$
iii) $y = x^2 + 8$ iv) $y = 2x$
v) $x = 7$ vi) $x + y = 6$

b) Which equations in part a represent linear relations? How do you know?

7. For each relation below:

i) Identify the dependent and independent variables.
ii) Use the table of values to determine whether the relation is linear.
iii) If the relation is linear, determine its rate of change.

a) The distance required for a car to come to a complete stop after its brakes are applied is the *braking distance*. The braking distance, *d* metres, is related to the speed of the car, *s* kilometres per hour, when the brakes are first applied.

s (km/h)	*d* (m)
50	13
60	20
70	27
80	35

b) The altitude of a plane, *a* metres, is related to the time, *t* minutes, that has elapsed since it started its descent.

t (min)	*a* (m)
0	12 000
2	11 600
4	11 200
6	10 800
8	10 400

8. In a hot-air balloon, a chart shows how the distance to the horizon, d kilometres, is related to the height of the balloon, h metres.

h (m)	d (km)
5	8
10	11
30	20
50	25
100	36

a) Graph these data.
b) Is the relation linear? What strategy did you use?

9. Earth rotates through approximately 360° every 24 h. The set of ordered pairs below describes the rotation. The first coordinate is the time in hours, and the second coordinate is the approximate angle of rotation in degrees. Describe two strategies you could use to determine if this relation is linear.
{(0, 0), (6, 90), (12, 180), (18, 270), (24, 360)}

10. Sophie and 4 of her friends plan a trip to the Edmonton Chante for one night. The hotel room is $95 for the first 2 people, plus $10 for each additional person in the room. The total cost is related to the number of people. Is the relation linear? How do you know?

11. A skydiver jumps from an altitude of 3600 m. For the first 12 s, her height in metres above the ground is described by this set of ordered pairs:
{(0, 3600), (4, 3526), (8, 3353.5), (12, 3147.5)}
For the next 21 s, her height above the ground is described by this set of ordered pairs:
{(15, 2988.5), (21, 2670.5), (27, 2352.5), (33, 2034.5)}
Determine whether either set of ordered pairs represents a linear relation. Explain.

12. The cost, C dollars, to rent a hall for a banquet is given by the equation $C = 550 + 15n$, where n represents the number of people attending the banquet.
a) Explain why the equation represents a linear relation.
b) State the rate of change. What does it represent?

13. A safety flare is shot upward from the top of a cliff 200 m above sea level. An equation for the height of the flare, d metres, above sea level t seconds after the flare is fired, is given by the equation $d = -4.9t^2 + 153.2t + 200$. Describe two strategies you could use to determine whether this relation is linear.

14. This graph represents Jerome's long distance phone call to his pen pal in Nunavut. Jerome is charged a constant rate.

The Cost of Jerome's Phone Call

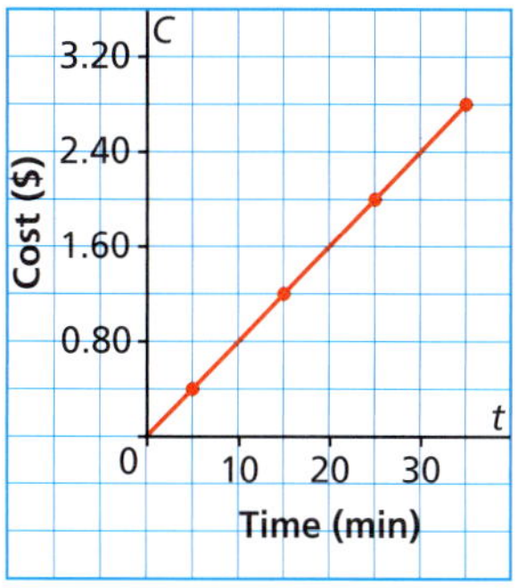

a) Identify the dependent and independent variables.
b) Determine the rate of change, then describe what it represents.

15. Kashala takes a cross-country trip from her home in Lethbridge through the United States. In Illinois, she drives on a toll highway. This graph represents the cost of Kashala's drive on the toll highway. She is charged a constant amount at each toll booth and she starts with US$10 in change. Determine the rate of change, then describe what it represents.

Kashala's Drive on the Toll Highway

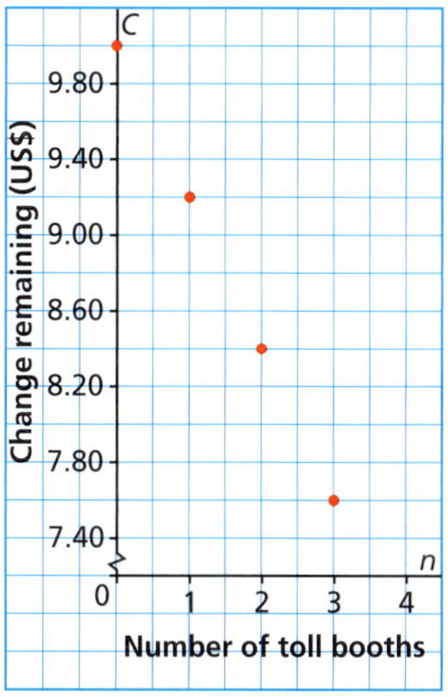

16. Match each description of a linear relation with its equation and set of ordered pairs below. Explain your choices.
   a) The amount a person earns is related to her hourly wage.
   b) The cost of a banquet is related to a flat fee plus an amount for each person who attends.
   c) The volume of gas in a car's gas tank is related to the distance driven since the time when the tank was filled.

   Equation 1: $y = 500 + 40x$
   Equation 2: $y = 35 - 0.06x$
   Equation 3: $y = 20x$
   Set A: {(100, 29), (200, 23), (300, 17), (400, 11)}
   Set B: {(1, 20), (5, 100), (10, 200), (15, 300)}
   Set C: {(0, 500), (40, 2100), (80, 3700), (100, 4500)}

17. a) Which situations represent linear relations? Explain how you know.
      i) A hang glider starts her descent at an altitude of 2000 m. She descends at a constant speed to an altitude of 1500 m in 10 min.
      ii) A population of bacteria triples every hour for 4 h.
      iii) A taxi service charges a $5 flat fee plus $2 for each kilometre travelled.
      iv) The cost to print each yearbook is $5. There is a start up fee of $500 to set up the printing press.
      v) An investment increases in value by 12% each year.
   b) For each linear relation in part a, identify:
      - the dependent and independent variables
      - the rate of change and explain what it represents

C

18. Identify the measurement formulas that represent linear relations. Explain how you know.
   a) Perimeter, P, of an equilateral triangle with side length s: $P = 3s$
   b) Surface area, A, of a cube with edge length s: $A = 6s^2$
   c) Volume, V, of a sphere with radius r: $V = \frac{4}{3}\pi r^3$
   d) Circumference, C, of a circle with diameter d: $C = \pi d$
   e) Area, A, of a circle with radius r: $A = \pi r^2$

19. Here are two equations that can be used to model the value, V dollars, of a $24 000 truck as it depreciates over n years:
   $V = 24\,000 - 2000n$ and $V = 24\,000(0.2^n)$
   a) Which equation represents a linear relation? Justify your answer.
   b) For the linear relation, state the rate of change. What does it represent?

20. You can estimate the distance in kilometres between you and a distant storm by measuring the time in seconds between seeing a lightning flash and hearing the thunder, then dividing by 3. This works because sound travels at approximately 0.3 km/s. Is this relation between distance and time linear? Justify your answer.

21. A berry patch is to be harvested. Is the relation between the time it will take to harvest the patch and the number of pickers needed linear? Justify your answer.

22. Which statements are true? Use examples to justify your answers.
   a) A relation described by exactly two ordered pairs is always linear.
   b) An equation of the form $Ax + By = C$ for non-zero constants, A, B, and C, always represents a linear function.
   c) An equation of the form $y = Cx^2$ for a non-zero constant C, always represents a linear function.
   d) An equation of the form $x = C$ for a constant C, always represents a linear relation.
   e) A linear relation is always a linear function.

Reflect

List three different strategies you can use to tell whether a relation is linear. Include an example with each strategy.

5.7 Interpreting Graphs of Linear Functions

LESSON FOCUS

Use intercepts, rate of change, domain, and range to describe the graph of a linear function.

Make Connections

Float planes fly into remote lakes in Canada's Northern wilderness areas for ecotourism. This graph shows the height of a float plane above a lake as the plane descends to land.

Height of a Float Plane

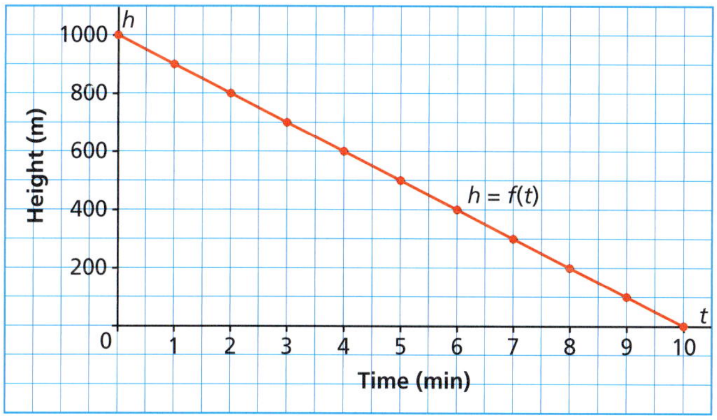

Where does the graph intersect the vertical axis? What does this point represent?

Where does the graph intersect the horizontal axis?
What does this point represent?

What is the rate of change for this graph? What does it represent?

Construct Understanding

TRY THIS

Work in a group.

You will need grid paper.

Dogsled tours are run between Armstrong cabin and Irving cabin. The cabins are 100 km apart.

Dogsled team 1 travels at an average speed of 20 km/h and starts its tour at Armstrong cabin.

Dogsled team 2 travels at an average speed of 25 km/h and starts its tour at Irving cabin.

One pair of students chooses team 1 and the other pair chooses team 2.

A. Copy and complete the table to show the distance from Irving cabin at different times on the tour.

Team 1

Time (h)	Distance from Irving Cabin (km)
0	100
1	

Team 2

Time (h)	Distance from Irving Cabin (km)
0	0
1	

B. Draw a graph to show the distance from Irving cabin as a function of time.

C. Share your results with the other pair of students.

- How are the graphs the same? How are they different?
- Identify where each graph intersects the vertical and horizontal axes. What do these points represent?
- Determine the rate of change for each graph. What does it represent?
- What are the domain and range for each graph?

Any graph of a line that is not vertical represents a function. We call these functions **linear functions**.

Each graph below shows the temperature, T degrees Celsius, as a function of time, t hours, for two locations.

Temperature in Location A

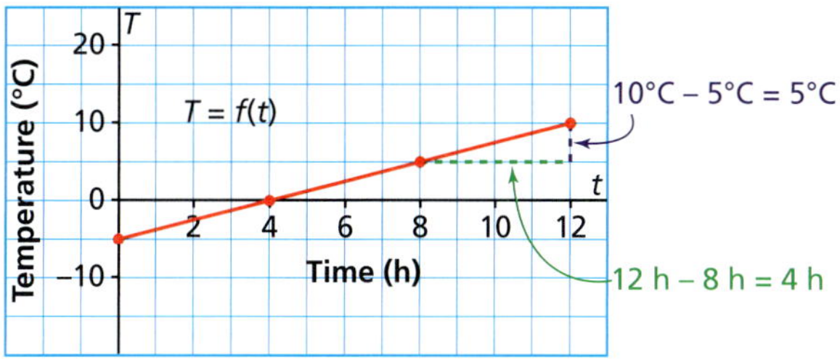

The point where the graph intersects the horizontal axis has coordinates (4, 0). The **horizontal intercept** is 4. This point of intersection represents the time, after 4 h, when the temperature is 0°C.

The point where the graph intersects the vertical axis has coordinates (0, –5). The **vertical intercept** is –5. This point of intersection represents the initial temperature, –5°C.

The *domain* is: $0 \leq t \leq 12$
The *range* is: $-5 \leq T \leq 10$
The *rate of change* is: $\dfrac{\text{change in } T}{\text{change in } t} = \dfrac{5°\text{C}}{4\,\text{h}}$

$= 1.25°\text{C/h}$

The rate of change is positive because the temperature is increasing over time.

Temperature in Location B

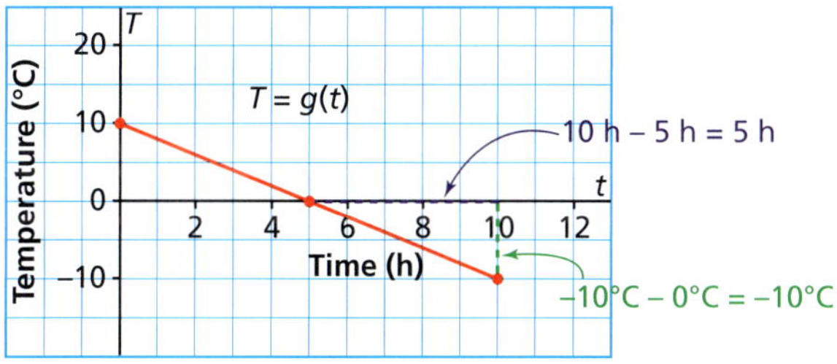

The point where the graph intersects the horizontal axis has coordinates (5, 0). The *horizontal intercept* is 5. This point of intersection represents the time, after 5 h, when the temperature is 0°C.

The point where the graph intersects the vertical axis has coordinates (0, 10). The *vertical intercept* is 10. This point of intersection represents the initial temperature, 10°C.

The *domain* is: $0 \leq t \leq 10$
The *range* is: $-10 \leq T \leq 10$

The *rate of change* is: $\dfrac{\text{change in } T}{\text{change in } t} = \dfrac{-10°\text{C}}{5\,\text{h}}$

$= -2°\text{C/h}$

The rate of change is negative because the temperature is decreasing over time.

Example 1 Determining Intercepts, Domain, and Range of the Graph of a Linear Function

This graph shows the fuel consumption of a scooter with a full tank of gas at the beginning of a journey.

Volume of Gas in a Scooter

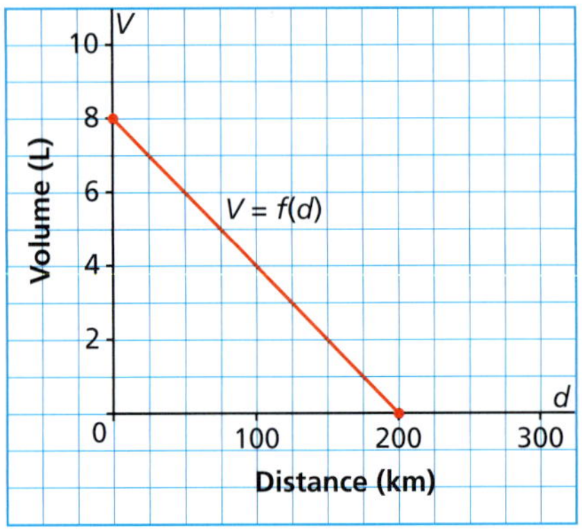

a) Write the coordinates of the points where the graph intersects the axes. Determine the vertical and horizontal intercepts. Describe what the points of intersection represent.

b) What are the domain and range of this function?

SOLUTION

a) On the vertical axis, the point of intersection has coordinates (0, 8). The vertical intercept is 8. This point of intersection represents the volume of gas in the tank when the distance travelled is 0 km; that is, the capacity of the gas tank: 8 L

On the horizontal axis, the point of intersection has coordinates (200, 0). The horizontal intercept is 200. This point of intersection is the distance travelled until the volume of gas is 0 L; that is, the distance the scooter can travel on a full tank of gas: 200 km

b) The domain is the set of possible values of the distance travelled:
$0 \leq d \leq 200$
The range is the set of possible values of the volume of fuel:
$0 \leq V \leq 8$

CHECK YOUR UNDERSTANDING

1. This graph shows how the height of a burning candle changes with time.

Height of a Burning Candle

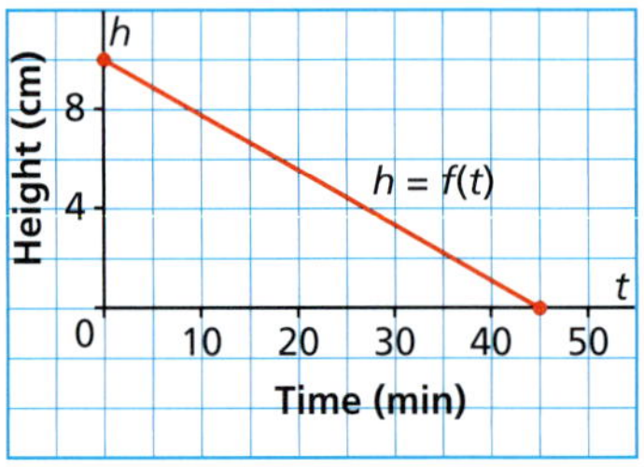

a) Write the coordinates of the points where the graph intersects the axes. Determine the vertical and horizontal intercepts. Describe what the points of intersection represent.

b) What are the domain and range of this function?

[Answers: a) (0, 10), 10; (45, 0), 45 b) domain: $0 \leq t \leq 45$; range: $0 \leq h \leq 10$]

Are there any restrictions on the domain and range? Explain.

What is the fuel consumption in litres per 100 km?

We can use the intercepts to graph a linear function written in function notation.
To determine the y-intercept, evaluate $f(x)$ when $x = 0$; that is, evaluate $f(0)$.
To determine the x-intercept, determine the value of x when $f(x) = 0$.

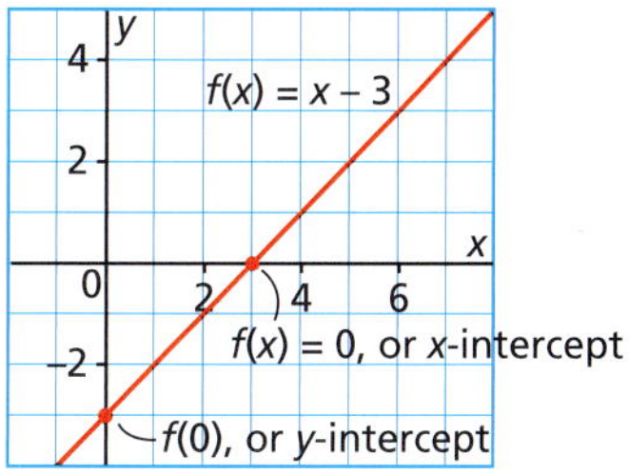

The x-coordinate of the point where a graph intersects the x-axis is called the ***x*-intercept**, or the **horizontal intercept**.

The y-coordinate of the point where a graph intersects the y-axis is called the ***y*-intercept**, or the **vertical intercept**.

Example 2 Sketching a Graph of a Linear Function in Function Notation

Sketch a graph of the linear function $f(x) = -2x + 7$.

SOLUTION

$f(x) = -2x + 7$

Since the function is linear, its graph is a straight line.

Determine the y-intercept:

When $x = 0$,

$f(0) = -2(0) + 7$

$f(0) = 7$

Determine the x-intercept:

When $f(x) = 0$,

$0 = -2x + 7$

$-7 = -2x + 7 - 7$

$-7 = -2x$

$x = \frac{-7}{-2}$

$x = \frac{7}{2}$

Determine the coordinates of a third point on the graph.

When $x = 1$,

$f(1) = -2(1) + 7$

$f(1) = 5$

Plot the points $(0, 7)$, $\left(\frac{7}{2}, 0\right)$, and $(1, 5)$, then draw a line through them.

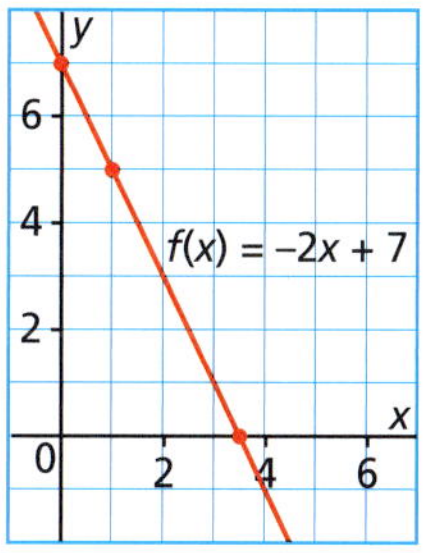

CHECK YOUR UNDERSTANDING

2. Sketch a graph of the linear function $f(x) = 4x - 3$.

Answer:

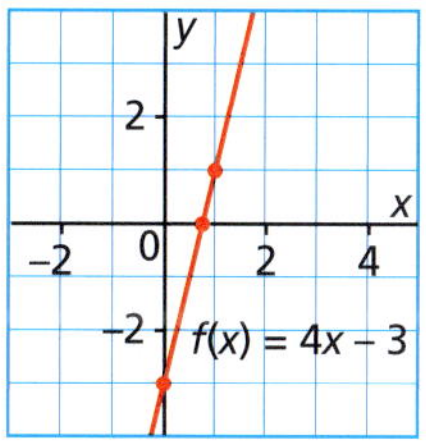

What other strategy could you use to graph the function? Which strategy would be more efficient?

Example 3 Matching a Graph to a Given Rate of Change and Vertical Intercept

Which graph has a rate of change of $\frac{1}{2}$ and a vertical intercept of 6? Justify the answer.

a)

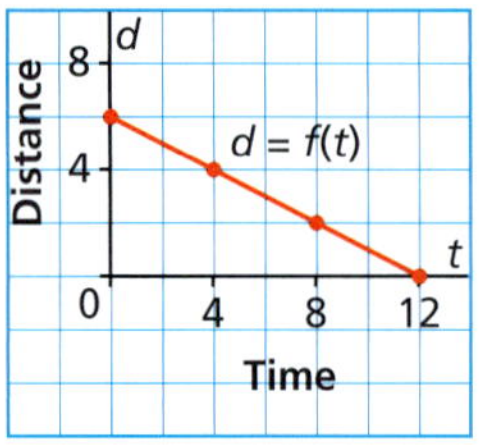

b)

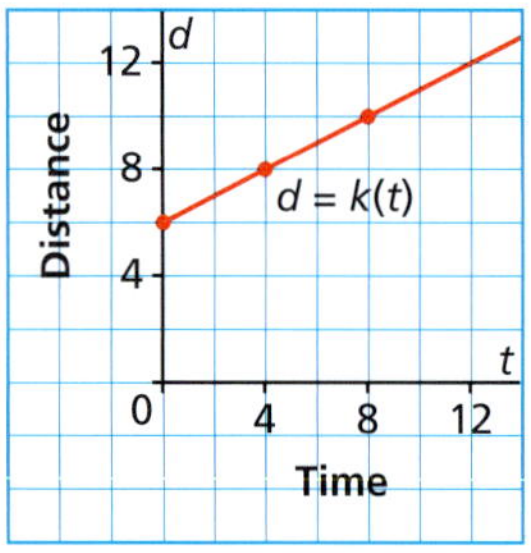

SOLUTION

a) The graph of $d = f(t)$ has a vertical intercept of 6.

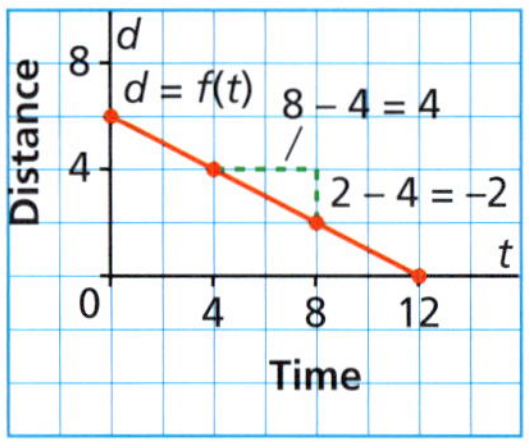

The rate of change is: $\frac{-2}{4} = -\frac{1}{2}$

So, it is not the correct graph.

b) The graph of $d = k(t)$ has a vertical intercept of 6.

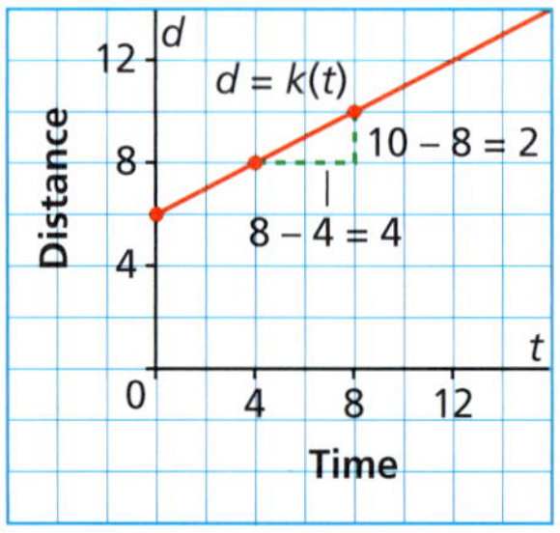

The rate of change is: $\frac{2}{4} = \frac{1}{2}$

So, this is the correct graph.

CHECK YOUR UNDERSTANDING

3. Which graph has a rate of change of -5 and a vertical intercept of 100? Justify your answer.

a)

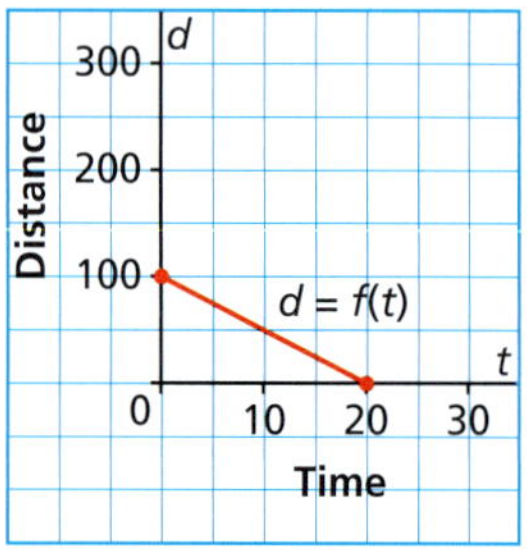

b)

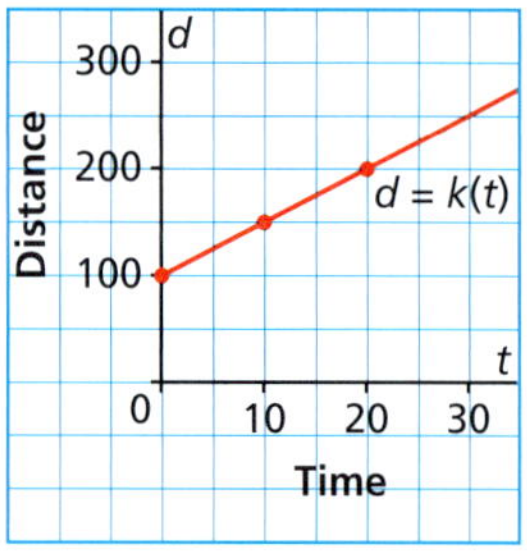

[Answer: the graph in part a]

Example 4 Solving a Problem Involving a Linear Function

This graph shows the cost of publishing a school yearbook for Collège Louis-Riel in Winnipeg.

Cost of Publishing a Yearbook

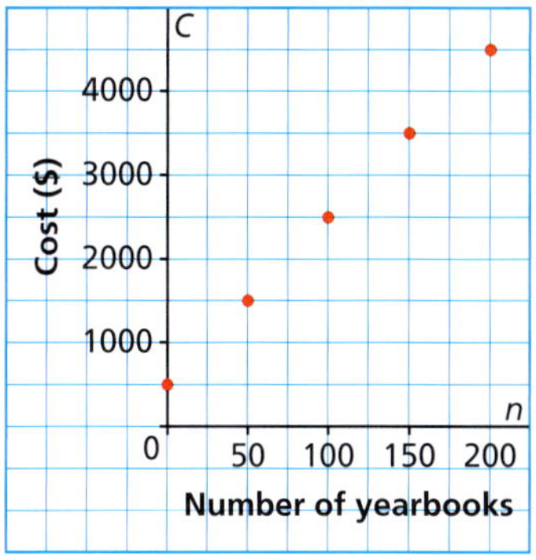

The budget for publishing costs is $4200. What is the maximum number of books that can be printed?

SOLUTIONS

Method 1

To estimate the number of yearbooks that can be printed for $4200, use the graph.

From 4200 on the C-axis, draw a horizontal line to the graph, then a vertical line to the n-axis.

Cost of Publishing a Yearbook

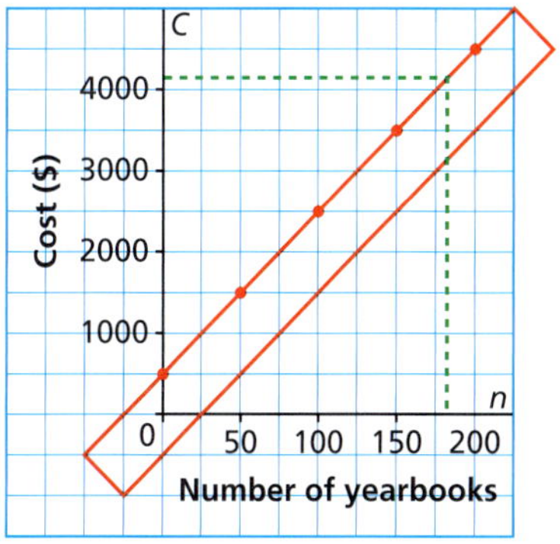

Use a straightedge to help.

From the graph, about 180 yearbooks can be printed.

(Solution continues.)

CHECK YOUR UNDERSTANDING

4. This graph shows the total cost for a house call by an electrician for up to 6 h work.

Cost of an Electrician's House Call

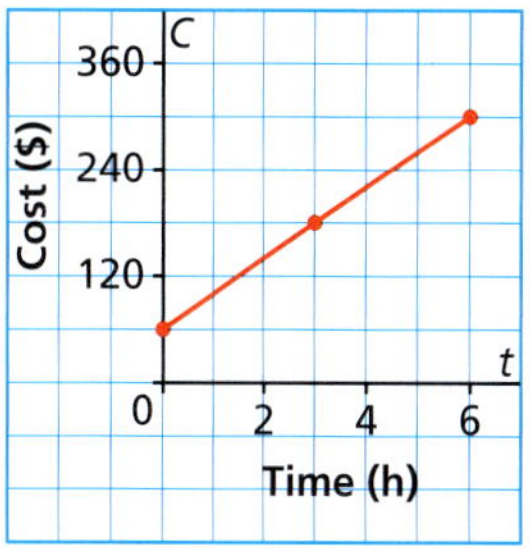

The electrician charges $190 to complete a job. For how many hours did she work?

[Answer: $3\frac{1}{4}$ h]

Why are the points on this graph not joined?

What are the domain and range of this function?

Method 2

The set-up cost is the cost when the number of books printed is 0. This is the vertical intercept of the graph, which is 500.
The set-up cost is \$500.

The increase in cost for each additional book printed is the rate of change of the function. Determine the change in each variable.

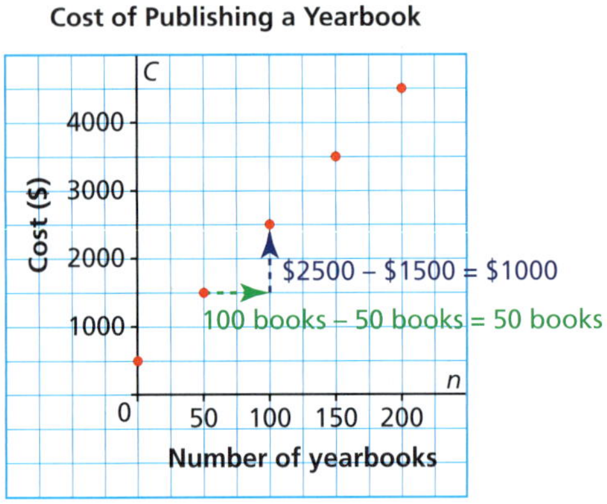

The graph shows that for every 50 books printed, the cost increases by \$1000.

The rate of change is: $\frac{\$1000}{50\text{ books}} = \$20/\text{book}$

The increase in cost for each additional book published is \$20.

An equation that represents this situation is: $C = 20n + 500$

To determine the maximum number of yearbooks that can be printed, use the equation:

$$C = 20n + 500 \quad \text{Substitute: } C = 4200$$
$$4200 = 20n + 500 \quad \text{Solve for } n.$$
$$4200 - 500 = 20n + 500 - 500$$
$$3700 = 20n$$
$$\frac{3700}{20} = \frac{20n}{20}$$
$$185 = n$$

The maximum number of yearbooks that can be printed is 185.

What is an advantage of using each method?

Discuss the Ideas

1. What information do the vertical and horizontal intercepts provide about a linear function? Use an example to explain.

2. How can you tell from a graph whether a linear function has a positive or negative rate of change?

3. When a situation can be described by a linear function, why doesn't it matter which pair of points you choose to determine the rate of change?

Exercises

A

4. Each graph below shows distance, *d* kilometres, as a function of time, *t* hours. For each graph:
   i) Determine the vertical and horizontal intercepts. Write the coordinates of the points where the graph intersects the axes.
   ii) Determine the rate of change.
   iii) Determine the domain and range.

a)

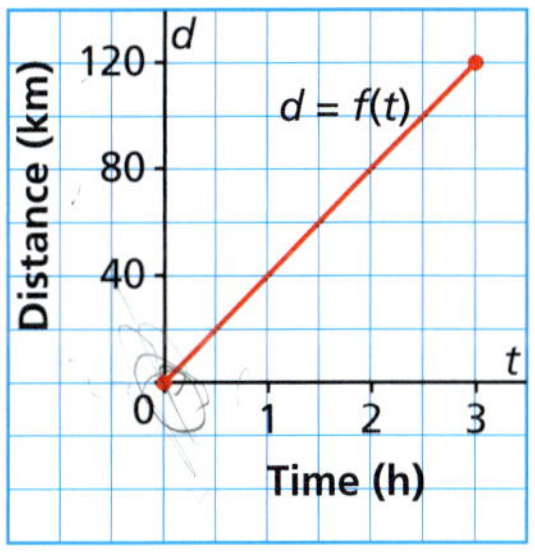

b)

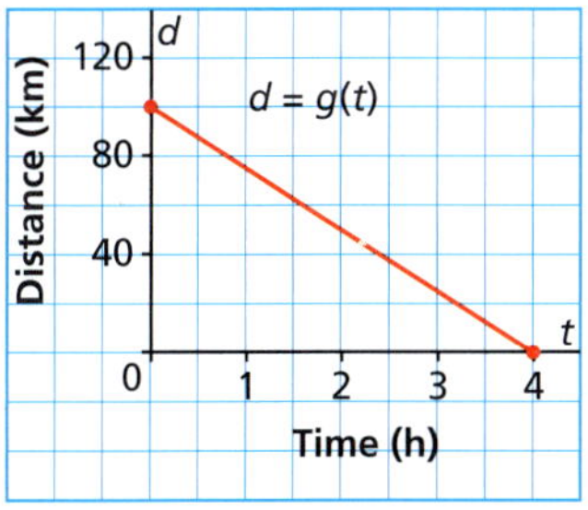

5. Each graph shows the altitude, *A* feet, of a small plane as a function of time, *t* minutes.
For each graph:
   i) Determine the vertical intercept. Write the coordinates of the point where the graph intersects the axis.
   ii) Determine the rate of change.
   iii) Determine the domain and range.

a)

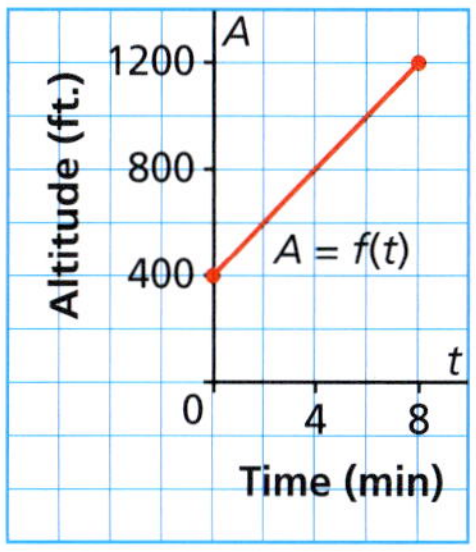

b)

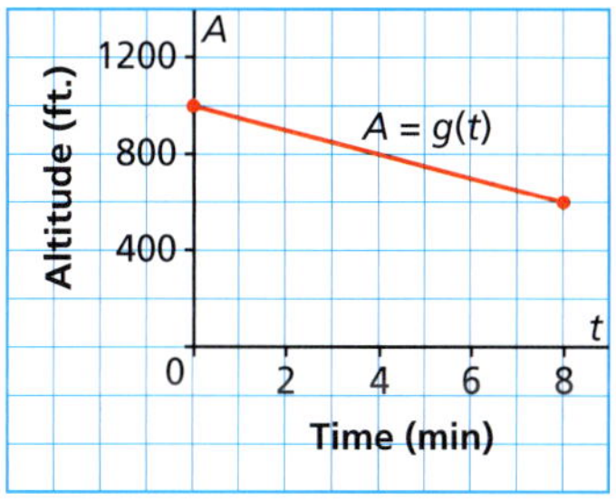

B

6. Sketch a graph of each linear function.
   a) $f(x) = 4x + 3$
   b) $g(x) = -3x + 5$
   c) $h(x) = 9x - 2$
   d) $k(x) = -5x - 2$

7. This graph shows the area, *A* square metres, that paint covers as a function of its volume, *V* litres.

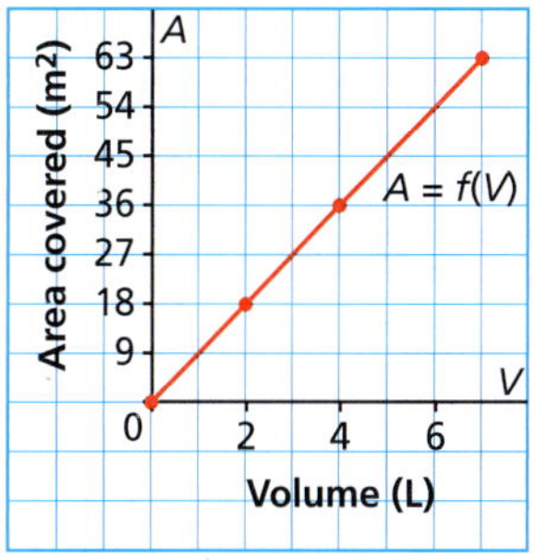

   a) What is the rate of change? What does it represent?
   b) What area is covered by 6 L of paint?
   c) What volume of paint would cover 45 m^2?

8. The graphs below show the temperature, T degrees Celsius, as a function of time, t hours, at different locations.

a) Which graph has a rate of change of 5°C/h and a vertical intercept of −10°C?

b) Which graph has a rate of change of −10°C/h and a vertical intercept of 20°C?

i)

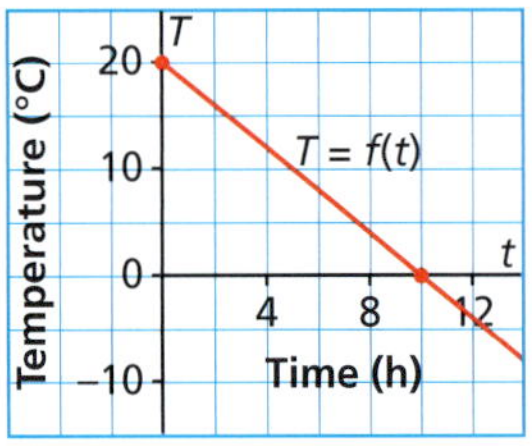

ii)

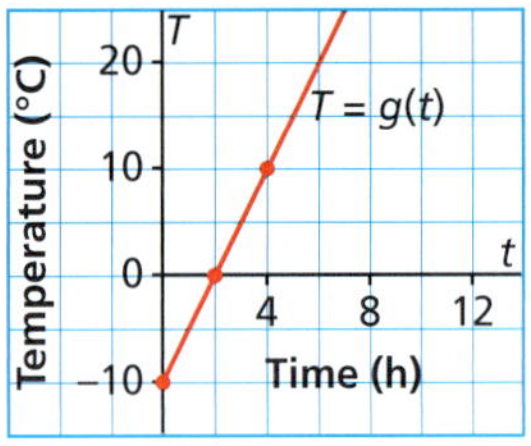

iii)

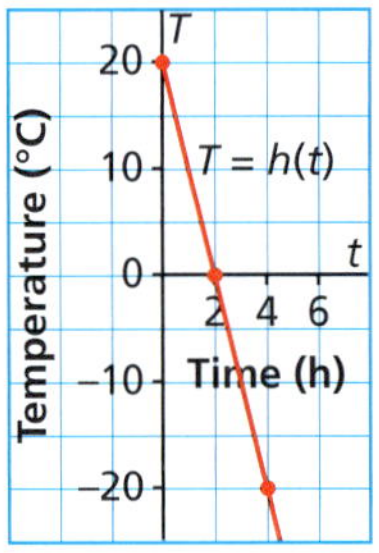

iv)

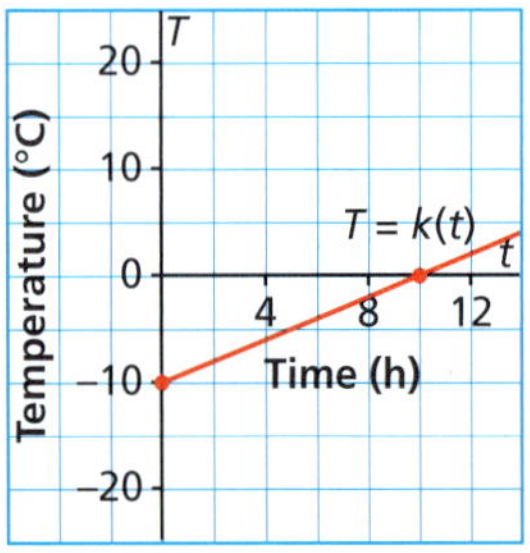

9. St. Adolphe, Manitoba, is located in the flood plain of the Red River. To help prevent flooding, backhoes were used to build dikes around houses and farms in the town. This graph shows the labour costs for running a backhoe.

Cost of Running a Backhoe

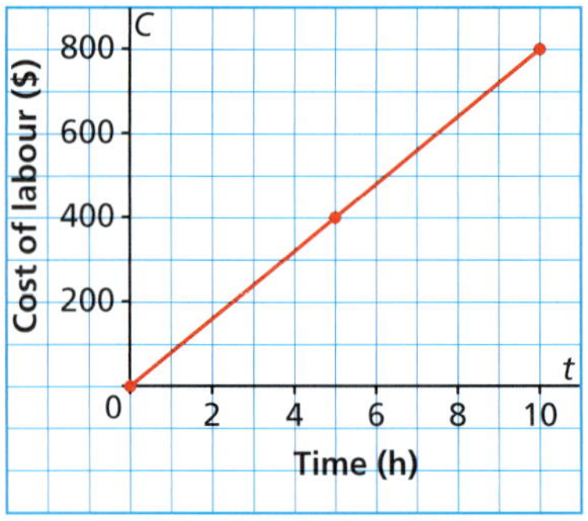

a) Determine the vertical and horizontal intercepts. Write the coordinates of the point where the graph intersects the axes. Describe what the point represents.

b) Determine the rate of change. What does it represent?

c) Write the domain and range.

d) What is the cost to run the backhoe for 7 h?

e) For how many hours is the backhoe run when the cost is $360?

10. This graph shows the cost for a cab at Eagle Taxi Cabs. The cost, C dollars, is a function of the distance travelled, d kilometres.

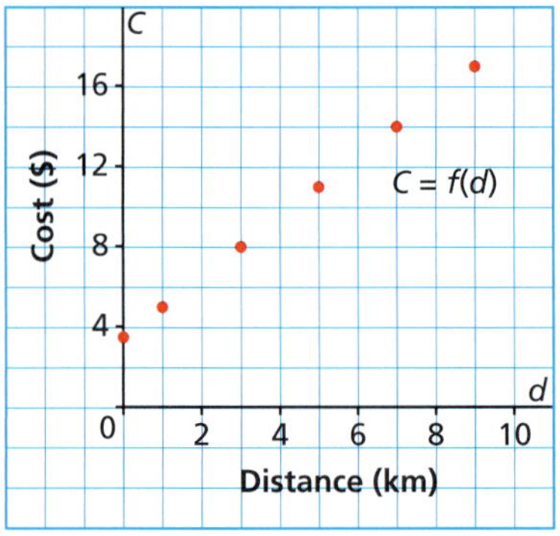

a) Determine the rate of change. What does it represent?

b) What is the cost when the distance is 7 km?

c) What is the distance when the cost is $9.50?

11. A Smart car and an SUV have full fuel tanks, and both cars are driven on city roads until their tanks are nearly empty. The graphs show the fuel consumption for each vehicle.

Fuel Consumption of a Smart Car

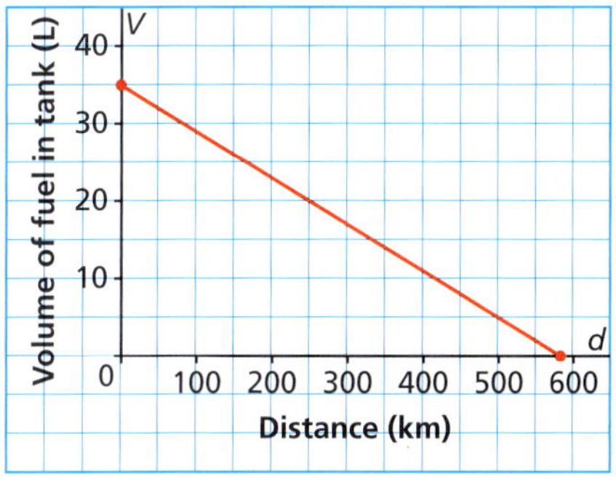

Fuel Consumption of an SUV

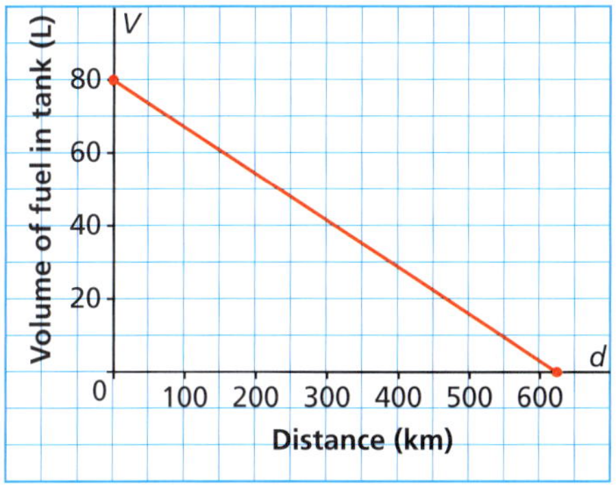

Use the graphs to explain why the Smart car is more economical to drive than the SUV.

12. This graph shows the distance to the finish line, d kilometres, as a function of time, t hours, for one dogsled in a race near Churchill, Manitoba.

Dogsled Race

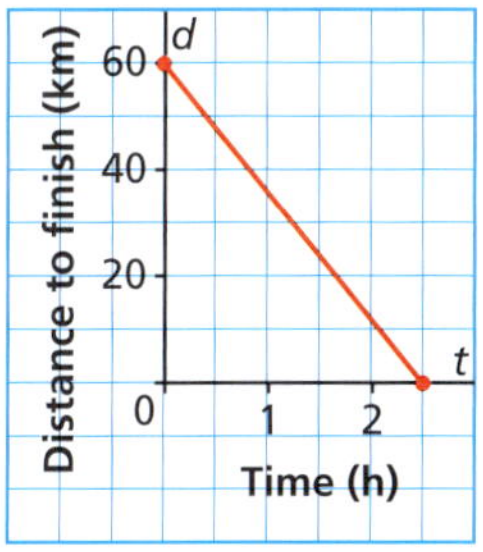

a) What was the length of time it took the dogsled to finish the race?

b) What was the average speed of the dogsled?

c) How long was the race in kilometres?

d) What time did it take for the dogsled to complete $\frac{2}{3}$ of the race?

13. The capacity of each of 2 fuel storage tanks is 100 m^3. Graph A represents the volume of fuel in one tank as a function of time as the tank is filled. Graph B represents the volume of fuel in another tank as a function of time as the tank is emptied.

Graph A

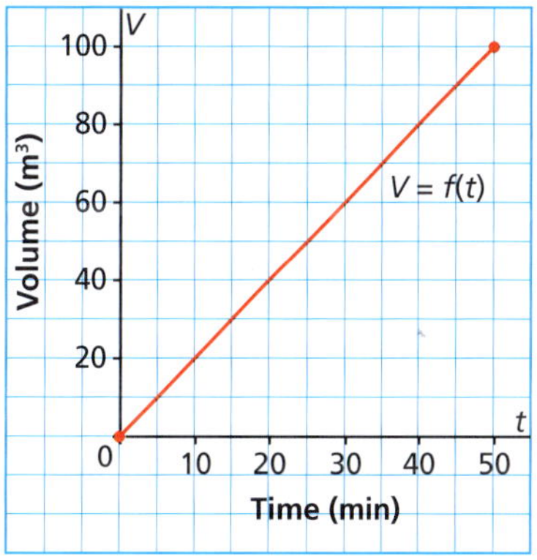

Graph B

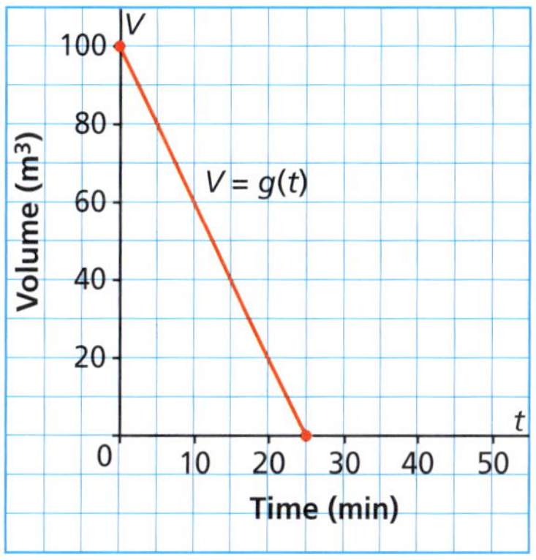

a) Does it take longer to fill the empty tank or empty the full tank? How do you know?

b) In the time it takes for one tank to be half empty, about how much fuel would be in a tank that was being filled from empty?

14. Ballenas School places an order for school sweatshirts with its logo of a killer whale on the back. This graph shows the cost of the sweatshirts, C dollars, as a function of the number ordered, n.

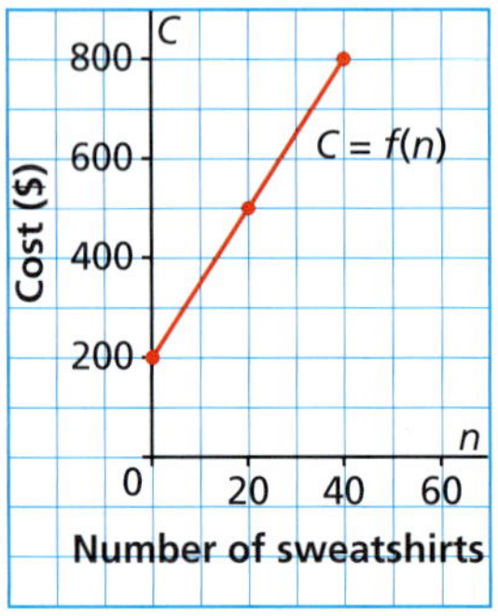

a) The number of sweatshirts cannot be a fraction or decimal. Why do you think the points on the graph are joined?

b) i) About how many sweatshirts can be bought for $700?

ii) Suppose one more sweatshirt was ordered. What would be the increase in cost?

15. Sketch a graph of each linear function for positive values of the independent variable.

a) $f(x) = 5 - 2.5x$ b) $g(t) = 85t$

c) $h(n) = 750 + 55n$ d) $V(d) = 55 - 0.08d$

16. Northlands School Outdoor Club had a fund-raiser to help purchase snowshoes. The club had 300 power bars to sell. This graph shows the profit made from selling power bars.

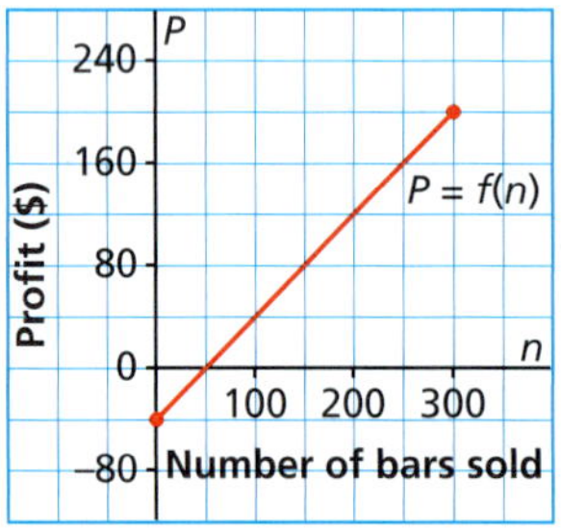

a) What is the profit on each bar sold? How do you know?

b) Determine the intercepts. What does each represent?

c) Describe the domain and range for the function. Why would you not want to list all the values in the range?

17. This graph shows the recommended maximum heart rate of a person, R beats per minute, as a function of her or his age, a years, for a stress test.

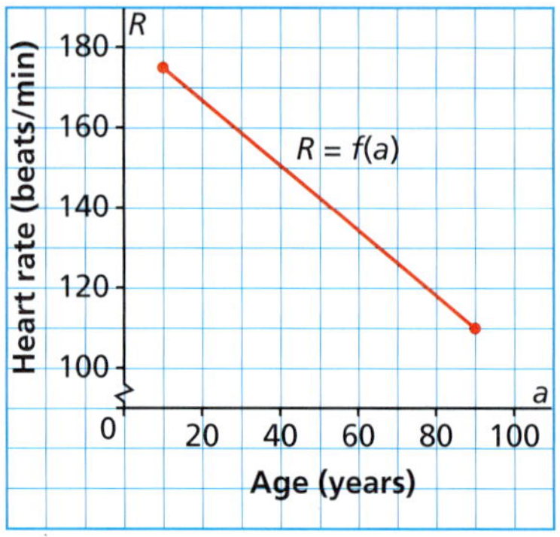

a) Why are there no intercepts on this graph?

b) What is the rate of change? What does it represent?

c) At what age is the recommended maximum heart rate 120 beats/min?

d) What is the approximate recommended maximum heart rate for a person aged 70?

C

18. Two graphs that relate two real numbers x and y in different ways are shown below.

For each graph:

i) State the x- and y-intercepts.

ii) Use the intercepts to describe how x and y are related.

a)

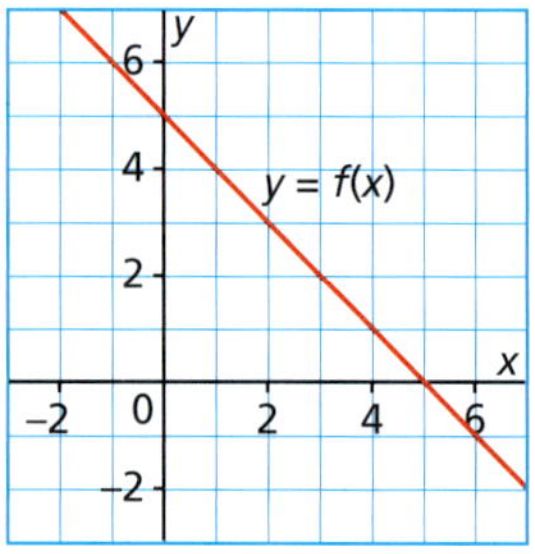

b)

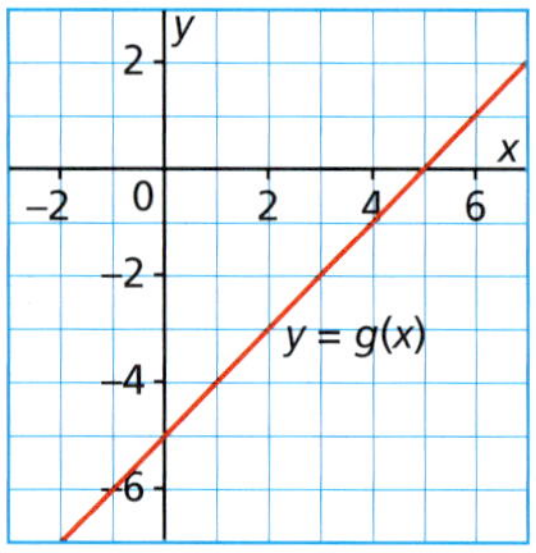

19. **a)** Sketch a graph of the linear function $d = f(t)$ that satisfies these conditions: $f(1.5) = 127.5$ and $f(3.5) = 297.5$

b) Determine $f(5)$.

c) Determine t when $f(t) = 212.5$.

d) Suggest a context for this linear function.

20. The distance between Parksville and the Duke Point Ferry Terminal on Vancouver Island is 50 km. A person drives from Parksville to the ferry terminal.

Distance from Parksville and to Duke Point

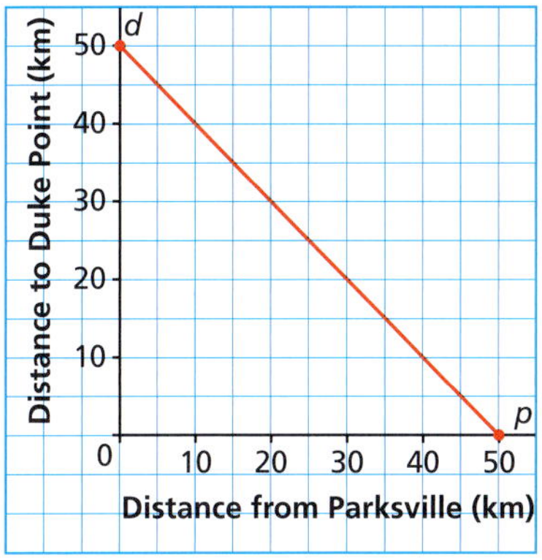

a) What do the intercepts represent? Why are they equal?

b) What is the rate of change? Why does it not have units? What does it indicate?

c) How would interchanging the dependent and independent variables change the graph?

d) Suppose the distance between two towns A and B is k kilometres. Describe the graph of the function, "Distance to A as a function of distance from B". State the intercepts, domain and range, and the rate of change.

Reflect

Explain why knowing the intercepts and the rate of change of the graph of a linear function may be helpful when you solve problems. Include examples in your explanation.

THE WORLD OF MATH

Historical Moment: Theano

Theano was one of the first known woman mathematicians. Her husband was Pythagoras, perhaps the most famous mathematician of all time. Theano lived in the 6th century B.C.E. in what is now southern Italy. She wrote many articles on mathematics, as well as on physics, medicine, astronomy, and child psychology. Her most famous work was on the development of the golden ratio and the golden rectangle.

STUDY GUIDE

CONCEPT SUMMARY

Big Ideas	Applying the Big Ideas
■ A relation associates the elements of one set with the elements of another set.	This means that: ■ A relation may be represented as: a rule, a table, a set of ordered pairs, an arrow diagram, and a graph. The set of first elements is the domain and the set of related second elements is the range.
■ A function is a special type of relation for which each element of the first set is associated with a unique element of the second set.	■ For a function, each element of the domain is associated with exactly one element of the range.
■ A linear function has a constant rate of change and its graph is a non-vertical straight line.	■ For a linear function, a constant change in the independent variable results in a constant change in the dependent variable, and any vertical line drawn through the graph intersects the graph at no more than one point.

Reflect on the Chapter

- What is a relation? What is a function? Create a graphic organizer to show their common characteristics, and those that are unique.
- How can the properties of linear functions be used to solve real-world problems? Include examples with your explanation.

SKILLS SUMMARY

Skill	Description	Example

Skill: Determine the domain and range of a function. [5.2, 5.4, 5.5, 5.7]

Description: The domain is the set of first elements of the ordered pairs. The range is the set of second elements.

For a graph, the domain is the set of values of the independent variable. The range is the set of values of the dependent variable.

Example: $\{(-1, 3), (0, 5), (1, 7), (2, 9), (3, 11)\}$

For this set of ordered pairs,
the domain is: $\{-1, 0, 1, 2, 3\}$;
the range is: $\{3, 5, 7, 9, 11\}$

For the graph below:
The domain is all possible times in one day.
The range is: $-4 \leq T \leq 10$

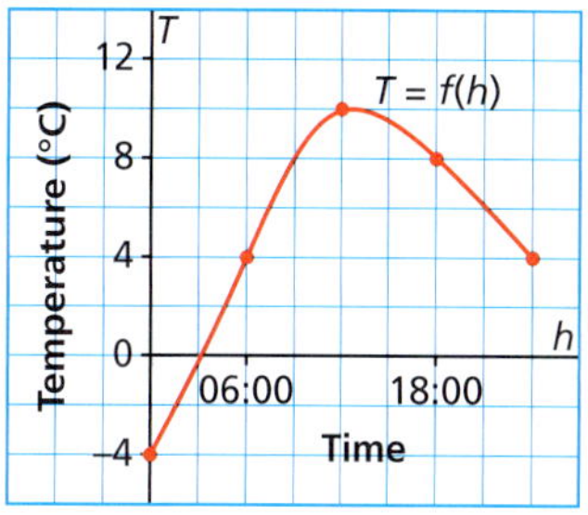

Skill: Determine the rate of change of the graph of a linear function. [5.6, 5.7]

Description: The rate of change is:

$$\frac{\text{change in dependent variable}}{\text{change in independent variable}}$$

The rate of change is positive when the graph goes up to the right. The rate of change is negative when the graph goes down to the right.

Example:

Distance against Time

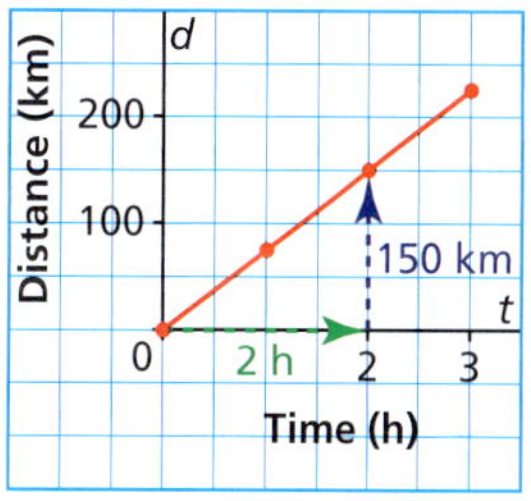

The rate of change is:

$$\frac{150 \text{ km}}{2 \text{ h}} = 75 \text{ km/h}$$

Skill: Determine the intercepts of the graph of a linear function. [5.7]

Description: The x-intercept is the value of x when y or $f(x)$ is 0.

The y-intercept is the value of y when x is 0.

Example: For the linear function
$f(x) = -2x + 5$,
When $f(x) = 0$:
$0 = -2x + 5$
$2x = 5$
$x = 2.5$
The x-intercept is 2.5.
When $x = 0$:
$f(0) = -2(0) + 5$
$f(0) = 5$
The y-intercept is 5.

REVIEW

5.1

1. This table shows some Northwest Coast artists and their cultural heritage.

Artist	Heritage
Bob Dempsey	Tlingit
Dorothy Grant	Haida
Bill Helin	Tsimshian
John Joseph	Squamish
Judith P. Morgan	Gitxsan
Bill Reid	Haida
Susan Point	Salish

 a) Describe the relation in words.
 b) Represent this relation:
  i) as a set of ordered pairs
  ii) as an arrow diagram

2. Here is a list of some chemical elements and their atomic numbers:
hydrogen (1), oxygen (8), iron (26), chlorine (17), carbon (6), silver (47)
For each association below, use these data to represent a relation in different ways.
 a) has an atomic number of
 b) is the atomic number of

5.2

3. Which sets of ordered pairs represent functions? What strategies did you use to find out?
 a) $\{(4, 3), (4, 2), (4, 1), (4, 0)\}$
 b) $\{(2, 4), (-2, 4), (3, 9), (-3, 9)\}$
 c) $\{(2, 8), (3, 12), (4, 16), (5, 20)\}$
 d) $\{(5, 5), (5, -5), (-5, 5), (-5, -5)\}$

4. Write in function notation.
 a) $y = -4x + 9$ b) $C = 12n + 75$
 c) $D = -20t + 150$ d) $P = 4s$

5. The function $P(n) = 5n - 300$ describes the profit, P dollars, for a school dance when n students attend.
 a) Write the function as an equation in 2 variables.
 b) Identify the independent variable and the dependent variable. Justify your choices.
 c) Determine the value of $P(150)$. What does this number represent?
 d) Determine the value of n when $P(n) = 700$. What does this number represent?

5.3

6. a) Laura cycles home from school, then walks back to school. Which graph best matches this situation? Explain your choice.

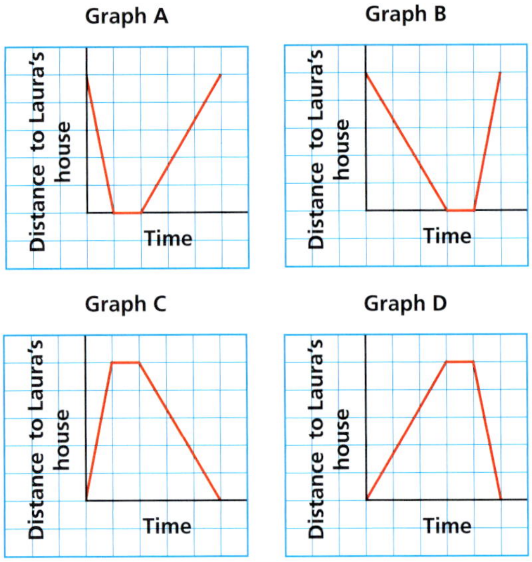

 b) Choose one of the graphs in part a that did not describe Laura's journey. Describe a possible situation for the graph.

7. This graph shows the volume of water in Liam's flask as he hikes the Trans Canada trail.

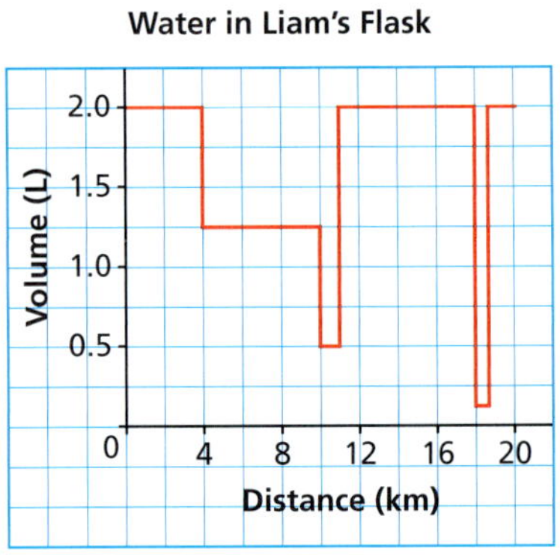

 a) Describe what is happening for each line segment of the graph.
 b) How many times did Liam fill his flask?

c) How much water was in Liam's flask at the start of his hike?

d) Identify the dependent and independent variables.

5.4

8. The data below show how the temperature of boiling water as it cools is related to time.

a) Graph the data. Did you join the points? Why or why not?

b) Does the graph represent a function? How can you tell?

Time (min)	Temperature (°C)
0	89
5	78
10	69
15	62
20	57
25	53
30	50

5.5

9. Which of these graphs represents a function? Justify your answer.
Write the domain and range for each graph.

a) **Heights and Ages of 8 Students**

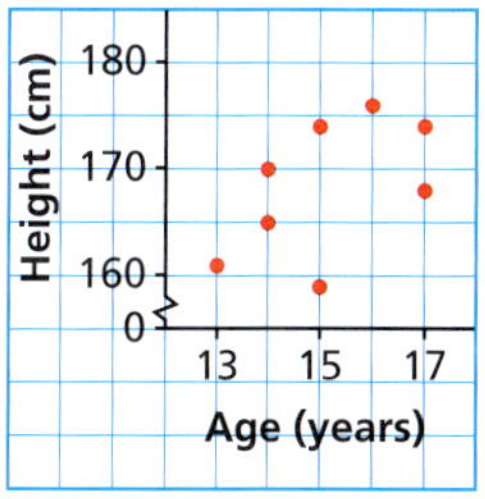

b) **Number of Bicycles at School**

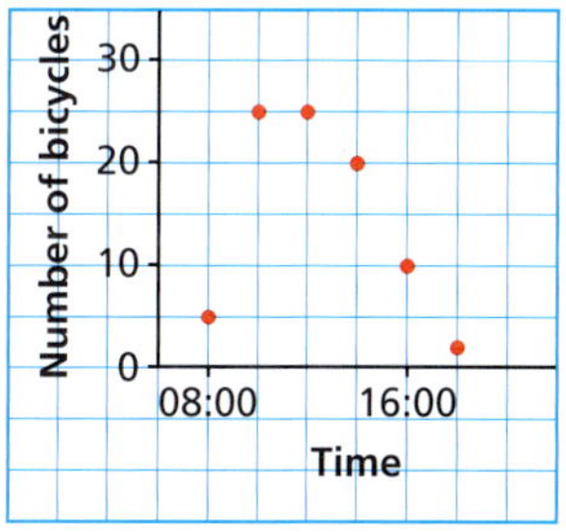

10. For the graphs below:

a) What does each graph represent?

b) Identify the independent and dependent variables.

c) Write the domain and range for each graph. Estimate when necessary. Are there any restrictions on the domain and range? Explain.

d) Why are the points joined on one graph but not on the other?

i) **Graph A**

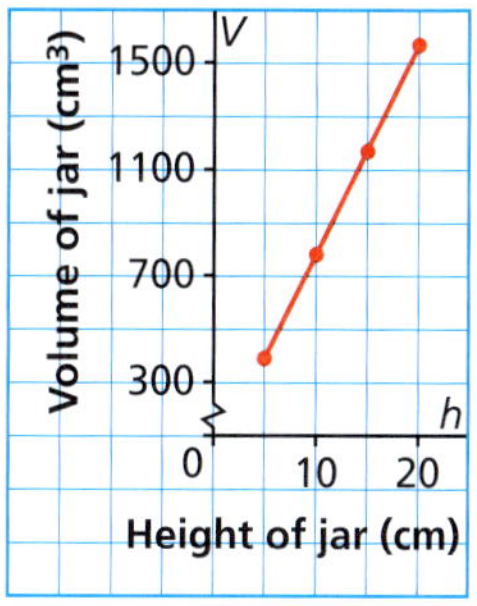

ii) **Graph B**

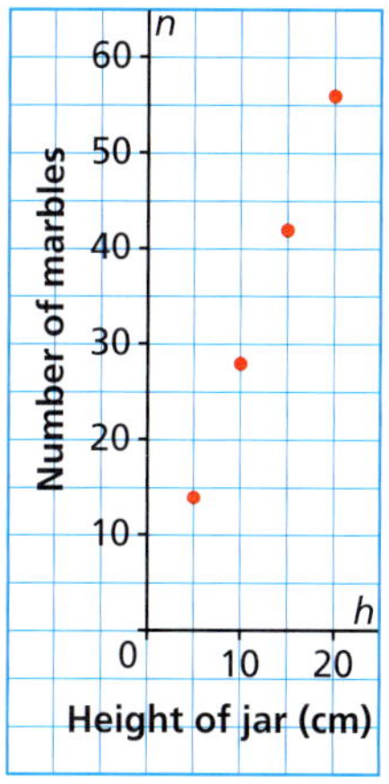

11. This is a graph of the function $f(x) = -3x + 1$.

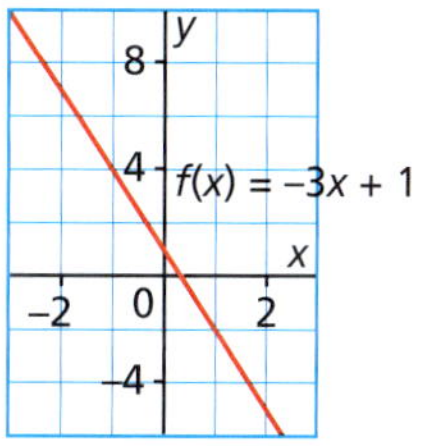

a) Determine the range value when the domain value is 1.

b) Determine the domain value when the range value is 4.

12. Sketch a graph of a function that has each domain and range.

a) domain: $-1 \leq x \leq 5$; range: $0 \leq y \leq 3$

b) domain: $x \leq 1$; range: $-2 \leq y \leq 2$

5.6

13. Which sets of ordered pairs represent linear relations? Explain your answers.

a) $\{(1, 5), (5, 5), (9, 5), (13, 5)\}$

b) $\{(1, 2), (1, 4), (1, 6), (1, 8)\}$

c) $\{(-2, -3), (-1, -2), (2, 1), (4, -3)\}$

14. **a)** For each equation, create a table of values when necessary, then graph the relation.

i) $x = 3$

ii) $y = 2x^2 + 3$

iii) $y = 2x + 3$

iv) $y = 3$

v) $y = 3x$

vi) $x + y = 3$

b) Which equations in part a represent linear relations? How do you know?

15. Isabelle manages her diabetes by taking insulin to control her blood sugar. The number of units of insulin taken, N, is given by the equation $N = \frac{1}{15}g$, where g represents the number of grams of carbohydrates consumed.

a) Explain why the equation represents a linear relation.

b) State the rate of change. What does it represent?

5.7

16. This graph shows the distance, d metres, travelled by Jadan on her bicycle as a function of the number of wheel revolutions, n, as she rode from Whitehorse to the Grey Mountain Road lookout in the Yukon.

Jadan's Bicycle Trip

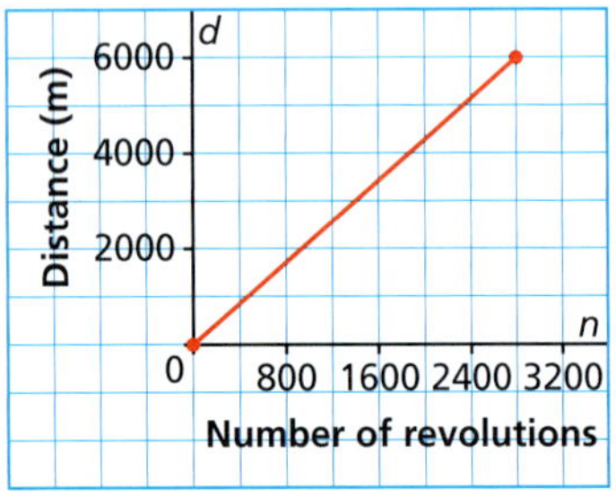

a) How far was Jadan from the lookout when she started her bicycle trip?

b) Write the domain and range.

c) Determine the rate of change. What does it represent?

d) Use your answer to part c to determine the diameter of a bicycle wheel.

17. These graphs show the temperature, T degrees Celsius, as a function of time, t hours. Match each graph with its vertical intercept and rate of change.

a)

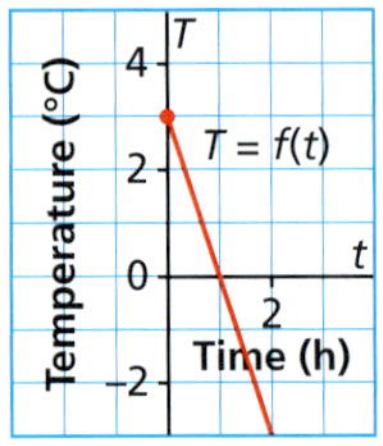

b)

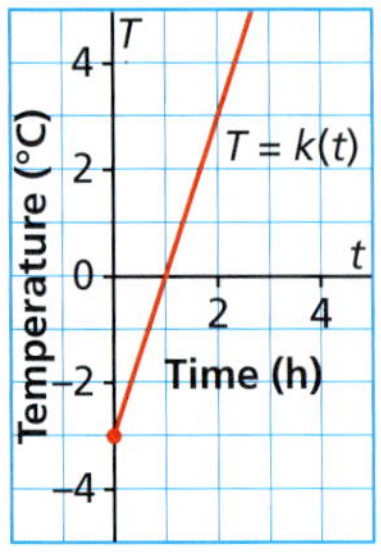

c)

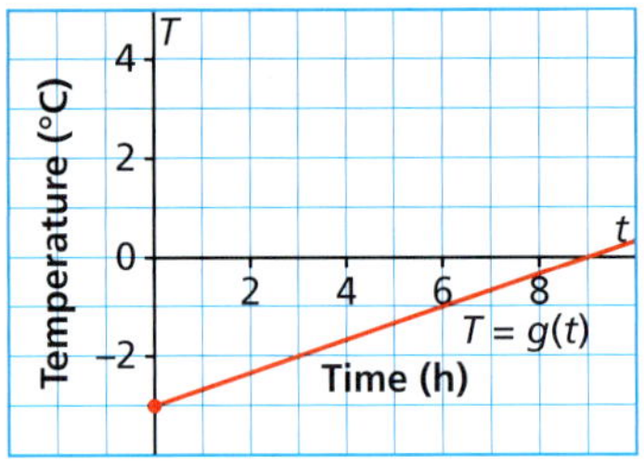

i) $-3°C; \frac{1}{3}°C/h$

ii) $3°C; -3°C/h$

iii) $-3°C; 3°C/h$

18. This graph shows the profit, P dollars, on a company's sale of n baseball caps.

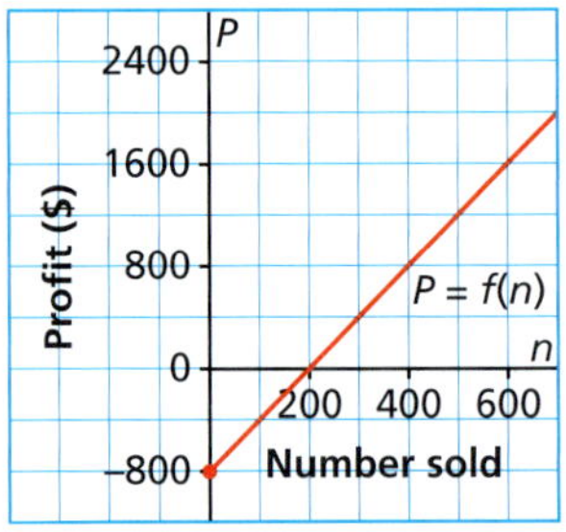

a) How many baseball caps have to be sold before the company begins to make a profit?

b) What is the profit on the sale of each baseball cap?

c) How many caps have to be sold to make each profit?

i) \$600 **ii)** \$1200

d) In part c, when the profit doubles why does the number of baseballs caps sold not double?

PRACTICE TEST

For questions 1 and 2, choose the correct answer: A, B, C, or D

1. For the function $f(x) = 3 - 6x$, what is the value of $f(-3)$?

A. 1 **B.** 21 **C.** -15 **D.** 0

2. Which equation does *not* represent a linear function?

A. $f(x) = 5$ **B.** $f(x) = 5x$ **C.** $f(x) = 5x^2$ **D.** $f(x) = -5$

3. For each relation represented below:

i) State whether it is a function and how you know.

ii) If the relation is a function:
State its domain and range.
Represent the function in a different way.
State whether it is a linear function and how you know.

iii) If the relation is a linear function:
Identify the dependent and independent variables.
Determine the rate of change.

a) $\{(2, 5), (-3, 6), (1, 5), (-1, 4), (0, 2)\}$

b)

n	*s*
2	4
−1	1
1	1
−3	9

c)

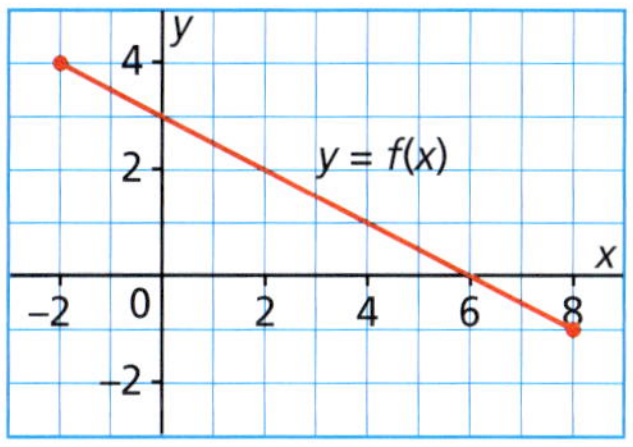

4. Describe a possible situation for this graph.
Label the axes and give the graph a title.
Justify your description.

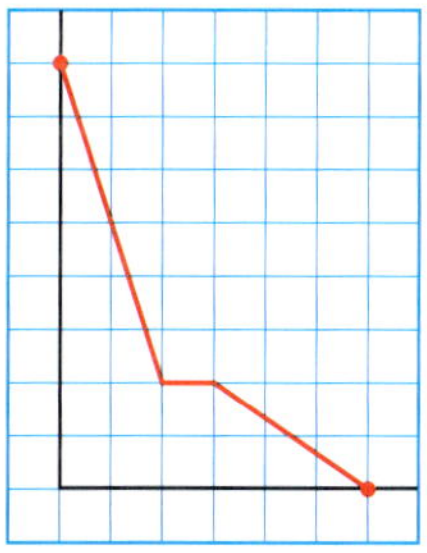

5. This table of values shows how the time to cook a turkey is related to its mass.

a) Why is this relation a function?

b) Identify the dependent and the independent variables. Justify your choice.

c) Graph the data. Did you connect the points? Explain.

d) Determine the domain and range of the graph. Could you extend the graph? Identify and explain any restrictions on the domain and range. Explain.

e) Determine the rate of change for this function. What does it represent?

f) For how long should you cook a turkey with mass 7 kg?

Mass (kg)	Time (h)
4	2.5
6	3.0
8	3.5
10	4.0

6 Linear Functions

BUILDING ON

- graphing linear relations
- recognizing the properties of linear relations
- solving linear equations

BIG IDEAS

- The graph of a linear function is a non-vertical straight line with a constant slope.
- Certain forms of the equation of a linear function identify the slope and y-intercept of the graph or the slope and the coordinates of a point on the graph.

NEW VOCABULARY

slope
rise
run
negative reciprocals
slope-intercept form
slope-point form
general form

POTASH MINING *Saskatchewan currently provides almost $\frac{1}{4}$ of the world's potash, which is an ingredient of fertilizer. Sales data are used to predict the future needs for potash.*

6.1 Slope of a Line

LESSON FOCUS

Determine the slope of a line segment and a line.

Make Connections

The town of Falher in Alberta is known as *la capitale du miel du Canada*, the Honey Capital of Canada. It has the 3-story slide in the photo above. How could you describe the steepness of the slide?

Construct Understanding

TRY THIS

Work with a partner.

This diagram shows different line segments on a square grid.

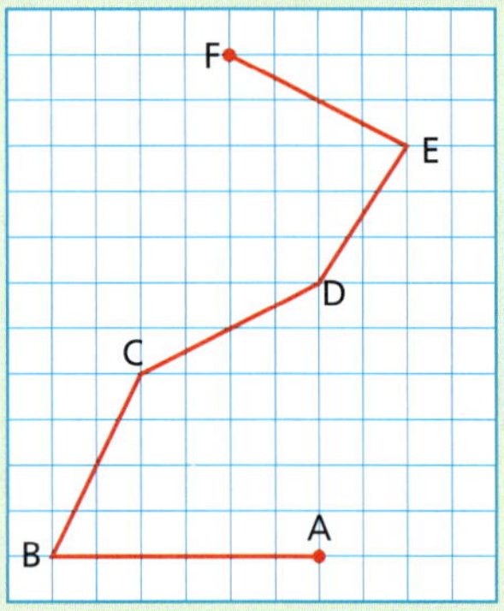

A. Think of a strategy to calculate a number to represent the steepness of each line segment.

B. Which is the steepest line segment? How does your number show that?

C. Which segment is the least steep? How does its number compare with the other numbers?

D. On a grid, draw a line segment that is steeper than segment CD, but not as steep as segment BC. Use your strategy to calculate a number to represent its steepness.

E. How are line segments CD and EF alike and different? How do the numbers for their steepnesses compare?

F. What number would you use to describe the steepness of a horizontal line?

Some roofs are steeper than others. Steeper roofs are more expensive to shingle.

Roof A

Roof B

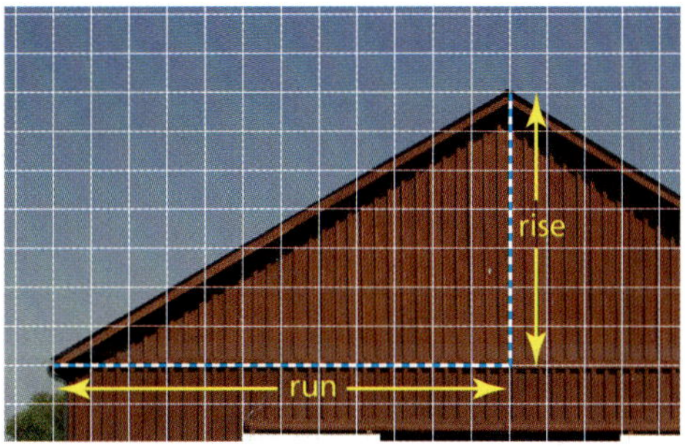

Roof C

The steepness of a roof is measured by calculating its **slope.**

$$\text{Slope} = \frac{\text{rise}}{\text{run}}$$

The **rise** is the vertical distance from the bottom of the edge of the roof to the top.
The **run** is the corresponding horizontal distance.
For each roof above, we count units to determine the rise and the run.

For Roof A

$$\text{Slope} = \frac{\text{rise}}{\text{run}}$$

$$\text{Slope} = \frac{13}{13}$$

$$\text{Slope} = 1$$

For Roof B

$$\text{Slope} = \frac{\text{rise}}{\text{run}}$$

$$\text{Slope} = \frac{7}{12}$$

$$\text{Slope} = 0.58\overline{3}$$

For Roof C

$$\text{Slope} = \frac{\text{rise}}{\text{run}}$$

$$\text{Slope} = \frac{14}{8}$$

$$\text{Slope} = 1.75$$

Roof C is the steepest because its slope is the greatest.
Roof B is the least steep because its slope is the least.

The slope of a line segment on a coordinate grid is the measure of its rate of change. From Chapter 5, recall that:

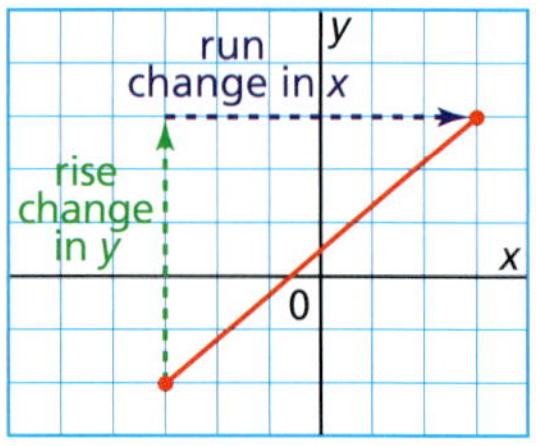

$$\text{Rate of change} = \frac{\text{change in dependent variable}}{\text{change in independent variable}}$$

$$\text{Rate of change} = \frac{\text{change in } y}{\text{change in } x}$$

The change in y is the rise.
The change in x is the run.

$$\text{So, slope} = \frac{\text{rise}}{\text{run}}$$

Example 1 Determining the Slope of a Line Segment

Determine the slope of each line segment.

a) 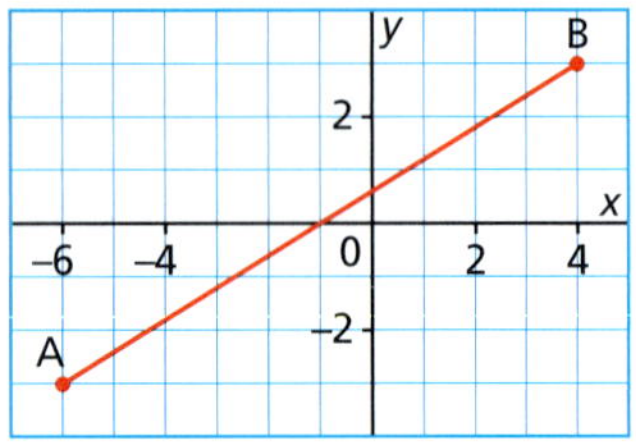

b) 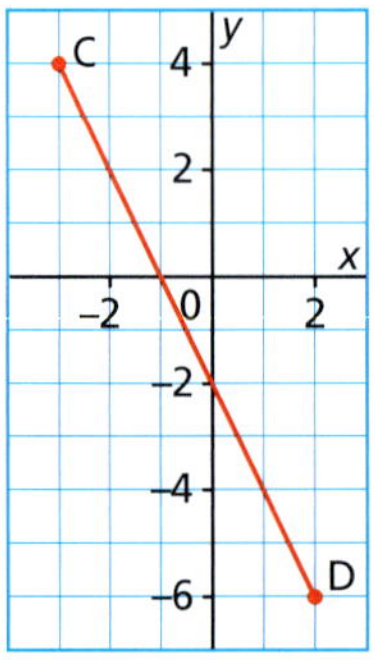

SOLUTION

Count units to determine the rise and run.

a) From A to B, both x and y are increasing, so the rise is 6 and the run is 10.

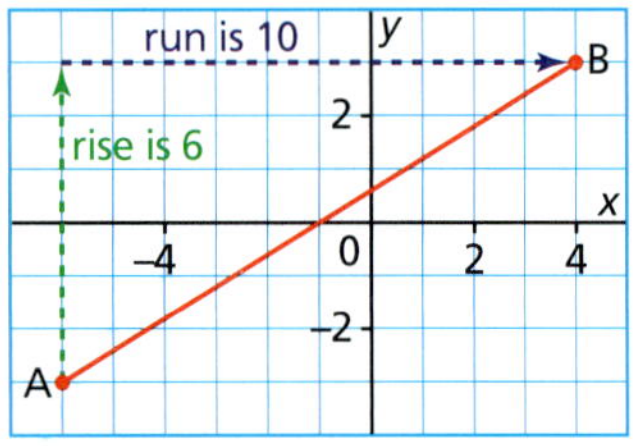

$$\text{Slope} = \frac{\text{rise}}{\text{run}}$$

$$\text{Slope} = \frac{6}{10}$$ Write the fraction in simplest form.

$$\text{Slope} = \frac{3}{5}$$

Line segment AB has slope $\frac{3}{5}$.

CHECK YOUR UNDERSTANDING

1. Determine the slope of each line segment.

a) 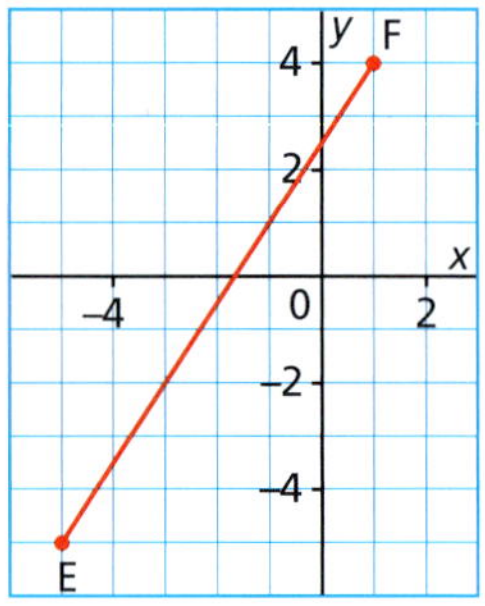

b) 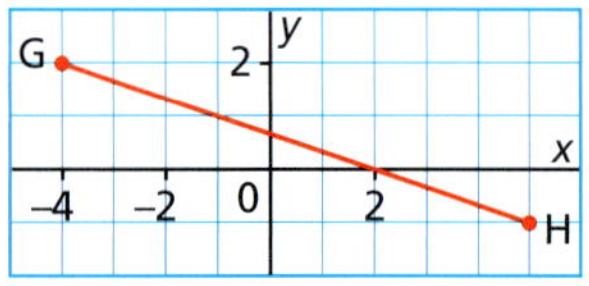

[Answers: a) $\frac{3}{2}$ b) $-\frac{1}{3}$]

b) From C to D, y is decreasing, so the rise is -10; x is increasing, so the run is 5.

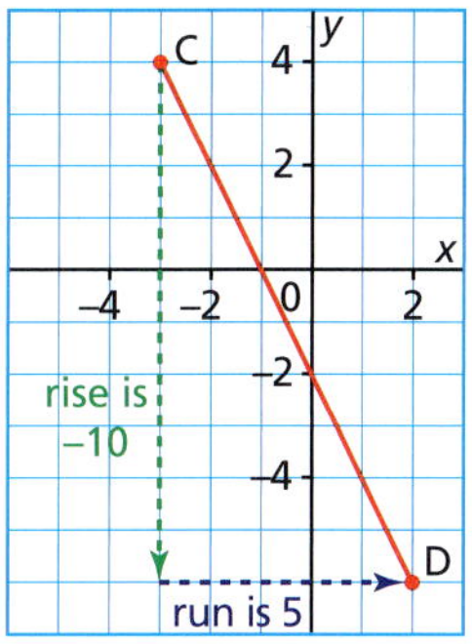

$$\text{Slope} = \frac{\text{rise}}{\text{run}}$$

$$\text{Slope} = \frac{-10}{5}$$

Write the fraction in simplest form.

Slope $= -2$

Line segment CD has slope -2.

Why does calculating the slope of the line segment joining D to C produce the same result as calculating the slope of the segment from C to D?

Suppose the slope is an integer. How do you identify the rise and the run?

When a line segment goes up to the right, both y and x increase; both the rise and run are positive, so the slope of the segment is positive.

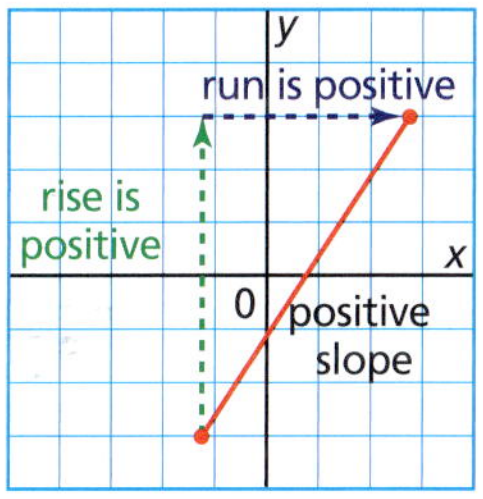

When a line segment goes down to the right, y decreases and x increases; the rise is negative and the run is positive, so the slope of the segment is negative.

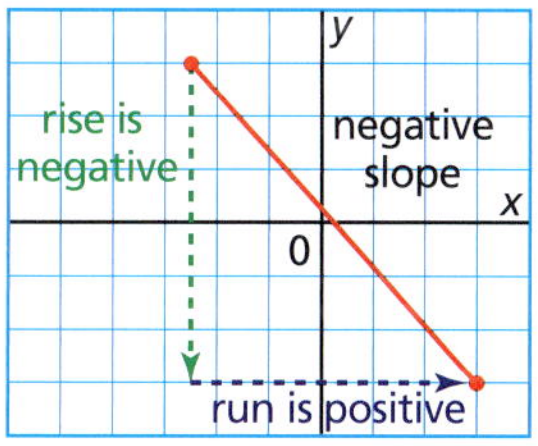

For a horizontal line segment, the change in y is 0 and x increases. The rise is 0 and the run is positive.

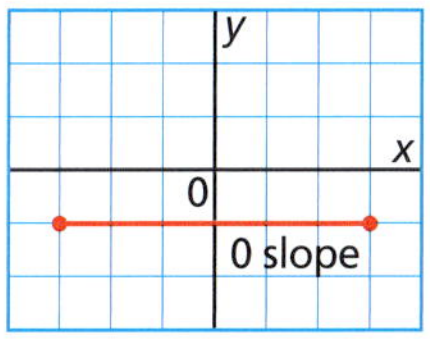

$$\text{Slope} = \frac{\text{rise}}{\text{run}}$$

$$\text{Slope} = \frac{0}{\text{run}}$$

Slope $= 0$

So, any horizontal line segment has slope 0.

For a vertical line segment, y increases and the change in x is 0. The rise is positive and the run is 0.

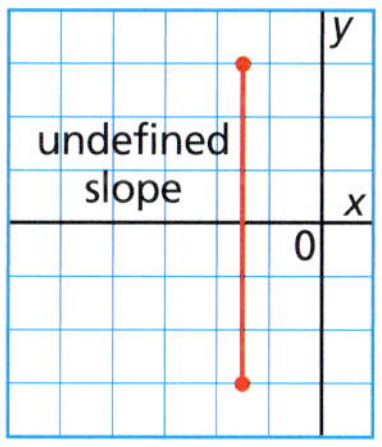

$$\text{Slope} = \frac{\text{rise}}{\text{run}}$$

$$\text{Slope} = \frac{\text{rise}}{0}$$

A fraction with denominator 0 is not defined.

So, any vertical line segment has a slope that is undefined.

For a vertical line segment, y could decrease and the rise would be negative.

Example 2 Drawing a Line Segment with a Given Slope

Draw a line segment with each given slope.

a) $\frac{7}{5}$ b) $-\frac{3}{8}$

SOLUTION

a) A line segment with slope $\frac{7}{5}$ has a rise of 7 and a run of 5. Choose any point R on a grid. From R, move 7 units up and 5 units right. Label the point S. Join RS.

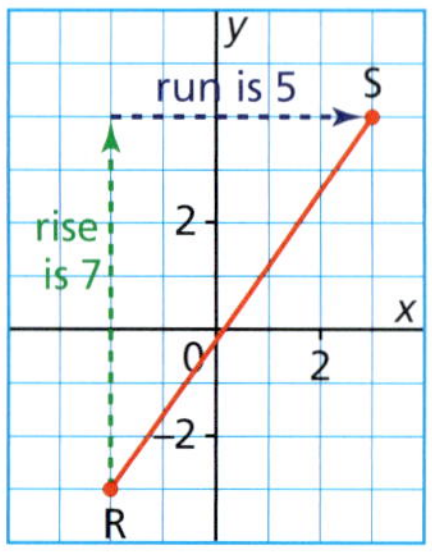

Line segment RS has slope $\frac{7}{5}$.

b) The slope $-\frac{3}{8}$ can be written as $\frac{-3}{8}$.

A line segment with slope $\frac{-3}{8}$ has a rise of -3 and a run of 8. Choose any point T on a grid. From T, move 3 units down and 8 units right. Label the point U. Join TU.

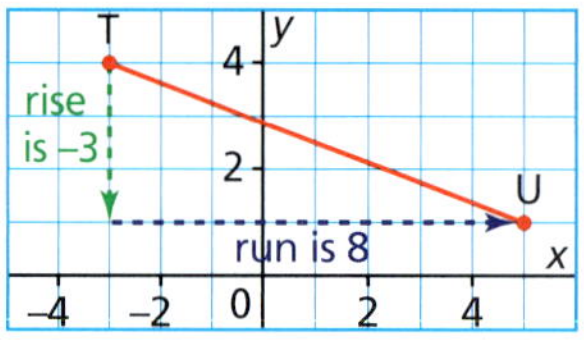

Line segment TU has slope $-\frac{3}{8}$.

CHECK YOUR UNDERSTANDING

2. Draw a line segment with each slope.

a) $\frac{4}{9}$ b) $-\frac{8}{3}$

Sample Answers:

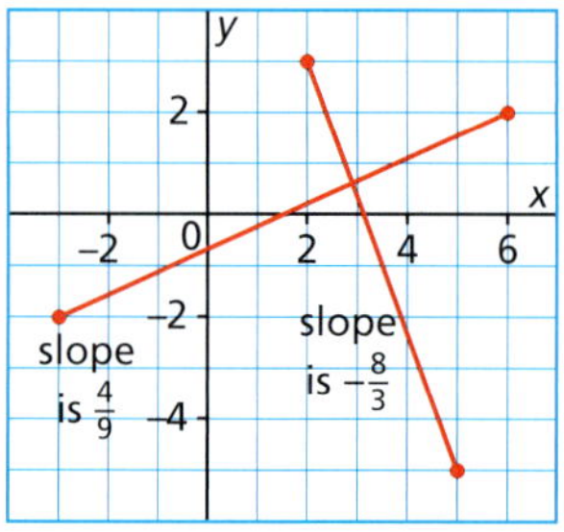

Why can we choose any point on the grid as one endpoint of the line segment?

Suppose the slope was written as $\frac{3}{-8}$. How would you draw the line segment?

We can show that the slopes of all segments of a line are equal.
On line MT, vertical and horizontal segments are drawn for the rise and run.
These segments form right triangles. Consider the lengths of the legs of these right triangles.

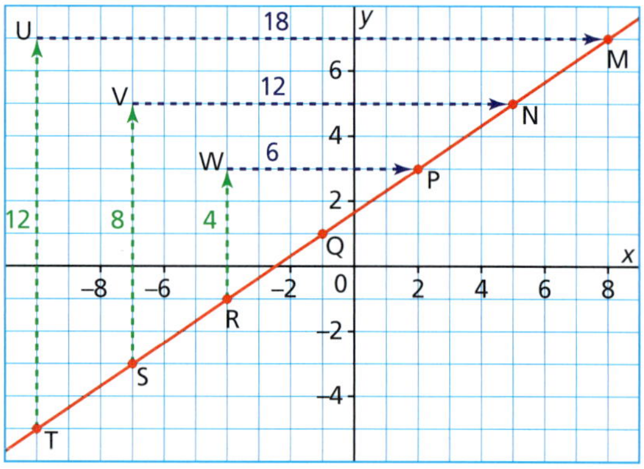

$\frac{TU}{UM} = \frac{12}{18}$ $\frac{SV}{VN} = \frac{8}{12}$ $\frac{RW}{WP} = \frac{4}{6}$

$\frac{TU}{UM} = \frac{2}{3}$ $\frac{SV}{VN} = \frac{2}{3}$ $\frac{RW}{WP} = \frac{2}{3}$

The lengths of the legs have the same ratio.
So, the triangles are similar.

Any right triangle drawn with its hypotenuse on line MT will have legs in the ratio $\frac{2}{3}$. So it does not matter which points we choose on the line; the slope of the line is the slope of any segment of the line. For example,

Slope of segment PQ $= \frac{2}{3}$ Slope of segment NR $= \frac{6}{9}$, or $\frac{2}{3}$

So, the slope of line MT is $\frac{2}{3}$.

Example 3 Determining Slope Given Two Points on a Line

Determine the slope of the line that passes through C(–5, –3) and D(2, 1).

SOLUTION

Sketch the line.
Subtract corresponding coordinates to determine the change in x and in y.

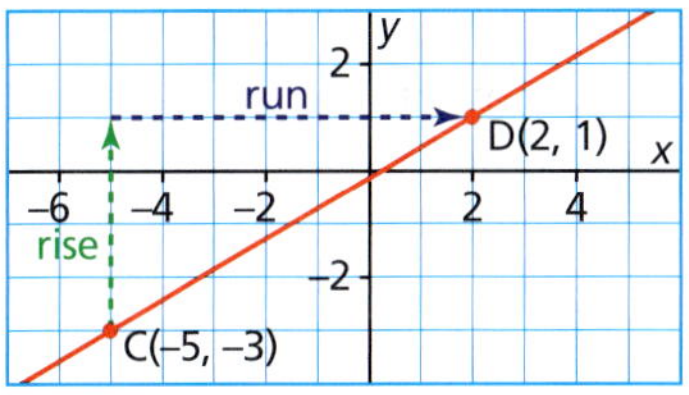

From C to D:
The rise is the change in y-coordinates.
Rise $= 1 - (-3)$
The run is the change in x-coordinates.
Run $= 2 - (-5)$

$$\text{Slope of CD} = \frac{1 - (-3)}{2 - (-5)}$$

$$\text{Slope of CD} = \frac{4}{7}$$

CHECK YOUR UNDERSTANDING

3. Determine the slope of the line that passes through E(4, –5) and F(8, 6).

[Answer: $\frac{11}{4}$]

How could you use slope to verify that three points lie on the same line?

Example 3 leads to a formula we can use to determine the slope of any line.

Slope of a Line

A line passes through $A(x_1, y_1)$ and $B(x_2, y_2)$.

$$\text{Slope of line AB} = \frac{y_2 - y_1}{x_2 - x_1}$$

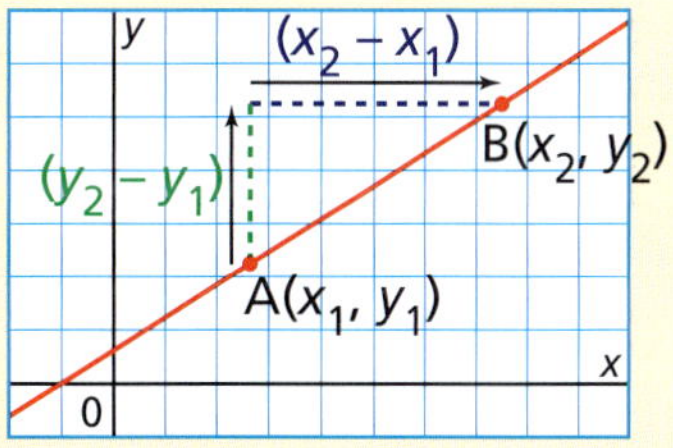

Example 4 Interpreting the Slope of a Line

Yvonne recorded the distances she had travelled at certain times since she began her cycling trip along the Trans Canada Trail in Manitoba, from North Winnipeg to Grand Beach. She plotted these data on a grid.

Graph of a Bicycle Ride

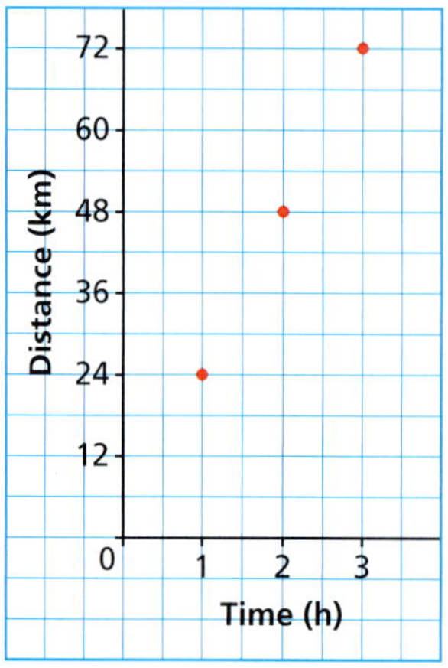

a) What is the slope of the line through these points?

b) What does the slope represent?

c) How can the answer to part b be used to determine:

  i) how far Yvonne travelled in $1\frac{3}{4}$ hours?

  ii) the time it took Yvonne to travel 55 km?

SOLUTION

a) Choose two points on the line, such as P(1, 24) and Q(3, 72). Label the axes x and y. Use this formula:

$$\text{Slope of PQ} = \frac{y_2 - y_1}{x_2 - x_1}$$

Substitute: $y_2 = 72$, $y_1 = 24$, $x_2 = 3$, and $x_1 = 1$

$$\text{Slope of PQ} = \frac{72 - 24}{3 - 1}$$

$$\text{Slope of PQ} = \frac{48}{2}$$

Slope of PQ = 24
The slope of the line is 24.

Graph of a Bicycle Ride

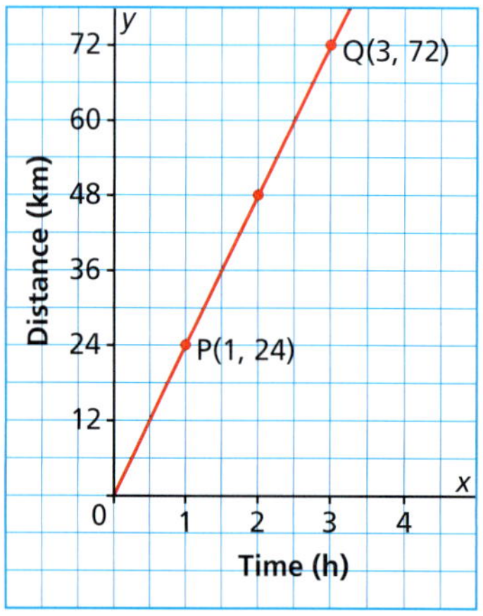

b) The values of y are distances in kilometres.
The values of x are time in hours.
So, the slope of the line is measured in kilometres per hour;
this is Yvonne's average speed for her trip.
Yvonne travelled at an average speed of 24 km/h.

CHECK YOUR UNDERSTANDING

4. Tom has a part-time job. He recorded the hours he worked and his pay for 3 different days. Tom plotted these data on a grid.

Graph of Tom's Pay

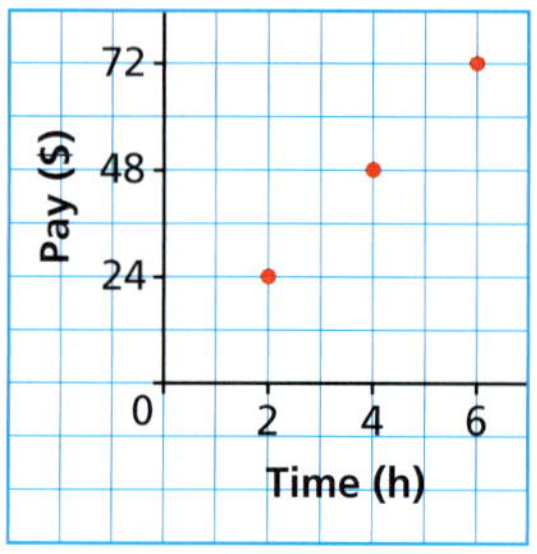

a) What is the slope of the line through these points?

b) What does the slope represent?

c) How can the answer to part b be used to determine:

  i) how much Tom earned in $3\frac{1}{2}$ hours?

  ii) the time it took Tom to earn $30?

[Answers: a) 12 b) Tom's hourly rate of pay: $12/h c) i) $42 ii) $2\frac{1}{2}$ hours]

c) i) In 1 h, Yvonne travelled approximately 24 km.

So, in $1\frac{3}{4}$ hours, Yvonne travelled: $\left(1\frac{3}{4}\right)(24 \text{ km}) = 42 \text{ km}$

In $1\frac{3}{4}$ hours, Yvonne travelled approximately 42 km.

ii) Yvonne travelled approximately 24 km in 1 h, or 60 min.

To travel 1 km, Yvonne took: $\frac{60 \text{ min}}{24} = 2.5 \text{ min}$

So, to travel 55 km, Yvonne took:
55(2.5 min) = 137.5 min, or 2 h 17.5 min
Yvonne took approximately 2 h 20 min to travel 55 km.

Discuss the Ideas

1. When you look at a line on a grid, how can you tell whether its slope is positive, negative, 0, or not defined? Give examples.
2. Why can you choose any 2 points on a line to determine its slope?
3. When you know the coordinates of two points E and F, and use the formula to determine the slope of EF, does it matter which point has the coordinates (x_1, y_1)? Explain.

Exercises

A

4. Determine the slope of the road in each photo.

a)

b)

5. For each line segment, is its slope positive, negative, zero, or not defined?

a)

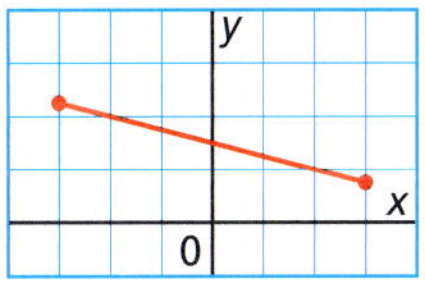

b)

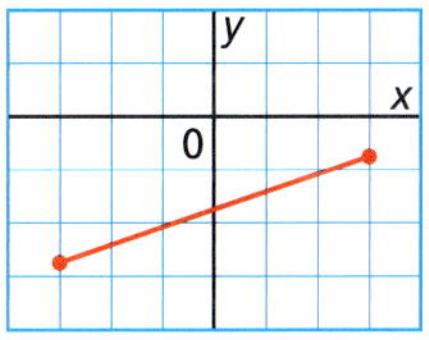

c)

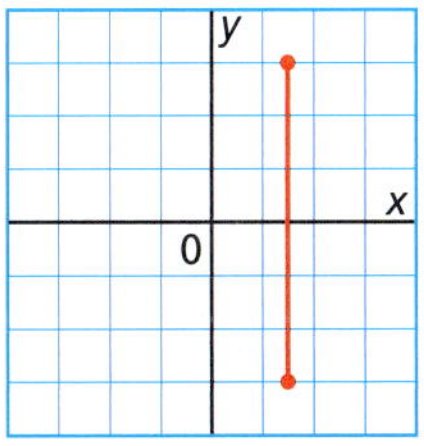

d)

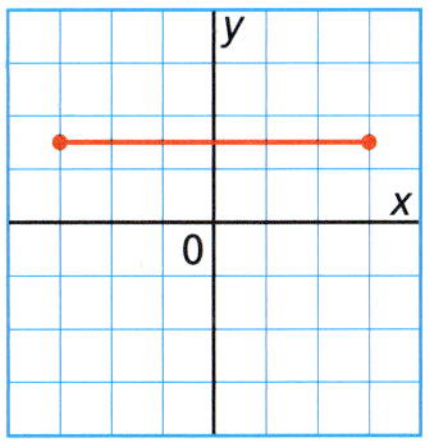

6. For each line segment, determine its rise, run, and slope.

a)

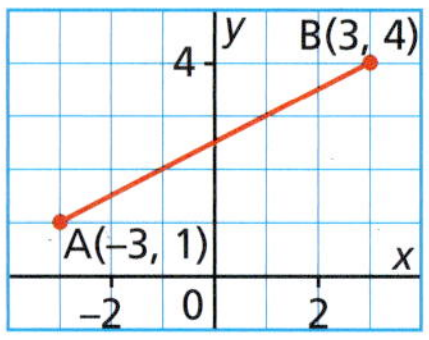

b)

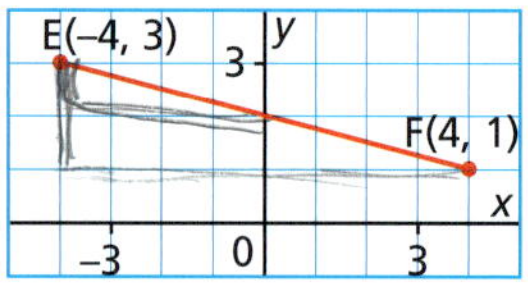

c)

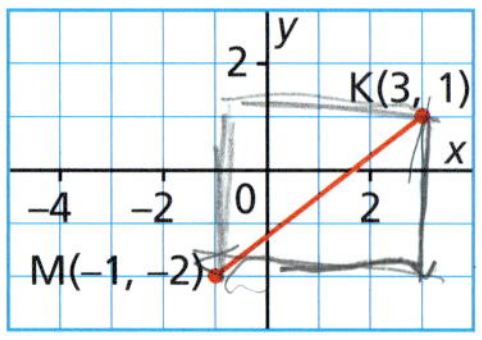

d)

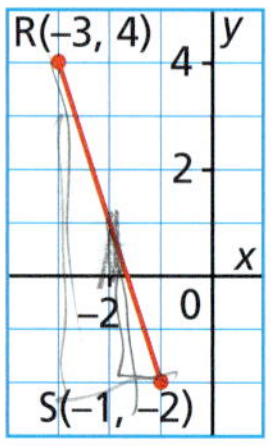

7. Determine the slope of each line described below.
   a) As x increases by 1, y increases by 3.
   b) As x increases by 2, y decreases by 7.
   c) As x decreases by 4, y decreases by 2.
   d) As x decreases by 2, y increases by 1.

8. Sketch a line whose slope is:
   a) positive
   b) zero
   c) negative
   d) not defined

9. Draw a line segment that has one endpoint at the origin and whose slope is:
   a) $\frac{2}{3}$ b) $-\frac{2}{5}$ c) 4 d) $-\frac{4}{3}$

10. To copy a picture by hand, an artist places a square grid over the picture. The artist then copies the image on a different grid, making sure corresponding grid squares match.
   a) How would determining the slopes of lines in the picture help a person to copy the picture?

   b) Copy the picture above, using the strategy you described in part a.

B

11. a) Choose two points on line segment DE. Use these two points to determine the slope of the line segment.

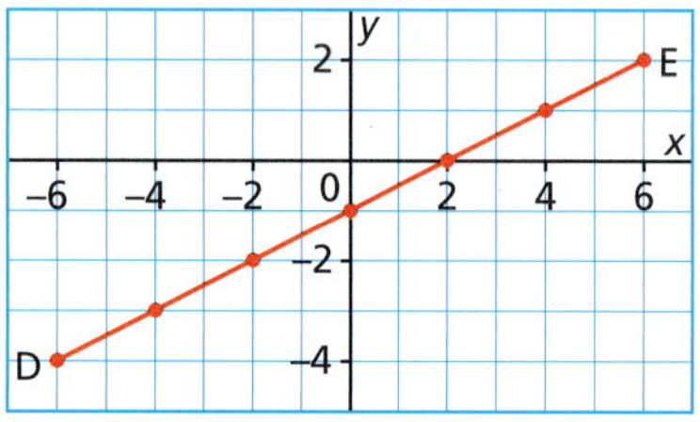

   b) Choose two different points on segment DE and calculate its slope.
   c) Compare the slopes you calculated in parts a and b. Explain the results.

12. a) Draw 2 different line segments with slope $\frac{7}{5}$.
   b) How are the line segments in part a the same? How are they different?

13. a) Determine the slope of the line that passes through each pair of points.
   i) P(1, 2) and Q(3, 6)
   ii) S(0, 1) and T(8, 5)
   iii) V(−1, 4) and R(3, −8)
   iv) U(−12, −7) and W(−6, −5)
   b) Explain what each slope tells you about the line.

14. a) On a grid, draw a line that passes through 3 points. Label the points C, D, and E.
   b) Determine the slope of each segment.
   i) CD ii) DE iii) CE
   What do you notice?

15. a) A treadmill is set with a rise of 6 in. and a run of 90 in. What is the slope of the treadmill?

   b) The treadmill is set at its maximum slope, 0.15. The run is 90 in. What is the rise?

16. A trench is to be dug to lay a drainage pipe. To ensure that the water in the pipe flows away, the trench must be dug so that it drops 1 in. for every 4 ft. measured horizontally.

a) What is the slope of the trench?

b) Suppose the trench drops $6\frac{1}{2}$ in. from beginning to end. How long is the trench measured horizontally?

c) Suppose the trench is 18 ft. long measured horizontally. By how much does it drop over that distance?

17. Match each line below with a slope. Explain your choices.

a) slope: –2

b) slope: $\frac{1}{2}$

c) slope: $-\frac{1}{2}$

d) slope: 2

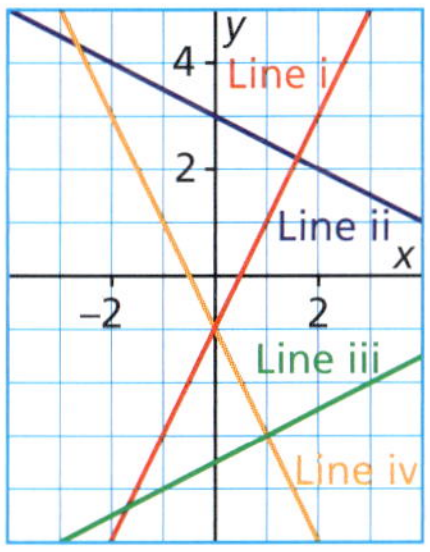

18. a) Draw the line through each pair of points. Determine the slope of the line.

i) B(0, 3) and C(5, 0)

ii) D(0, –3) and C(5, 0)

iii) D(0, –3) and E(–5, 0)

iv) B(0, 3) and E(–5, 0)

b) How are the slopes of the lines in part a related?

19. a) Explain why the slope of a horizontal line is zero.

b) Explain why the slope of a vertical line is undefined.

20. Four students determined the slope of the line through B(6, −2) and C(−3, −5). Their answers were: 3, −3, $\frac{1}{3}$, and $-\frac{1}{3}$

a) Which number is correct for the slope of line BC? Give reasons for your choice.

b) For each incorrect answer, explain what the student might have done wrong to get that answer.

21. a) On a grid, sketch each line:

i) a line that has only one intercept

ii) a line that has two intercepts

iii) a line that has more intercepts than you can count

b) How many lines could you draw in each of part a? What is the slope of each line?

22. A hospital plans to build a wheelchair ramp. Its slope must be less than $\frac{1}{12}$. The entrance to the hospital is 70 cm above the ground. What is the minimum horizontal distance needed for the ramp? Justify your answer.

23. Draw the line through G(−5, 1) with each given slope. Write the coordinates of 3 other points on the line. How did you determine these points?

a) 4

b) −1

c) $-\frac{1}{3}$

d) $\frac{7}{4}$

24. **a)** For each line described below, is its slope positive, negative, zero, or undefined? Justify your answer.

i) The line has a positive x-intercept and a negative y-intercept.

ii) The line has a negative x-intercept and a positive y-intercept.

iii) Both intercepts are positive.

iv) The line has an x-intercept but does not have a y-intercept.

b) Sketch each line in part a.

25. Tess conducted an experiment where she determined the masses of different volumes of aluminum cubes. Here are her data:

Volume of Aluminum (cm^3)	Mass of Aluminum (g)
64	172.8
125	337.5
216	583.2

a) Graph these data on a grid.

b) Calculate the slope of the line through the points.

c) What does the slope represent?

d) How could you use the slope to determine the mass of each volume of aluminum? Explain your strategy.

i) 50 cm^3 **ii)** 275 cm^3

e) What is the approximate volume of each mass of aluminum?

i) 100 g **ii)** 450 g

26. This graph shows the cost for text messages as a function of the number of text messages.

Cost for Text Messages

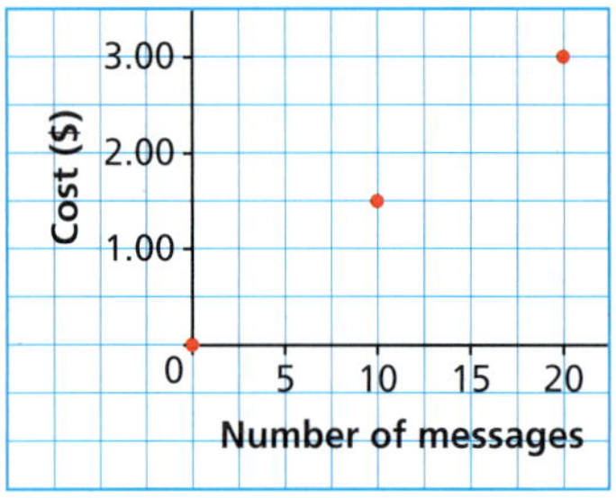

a) Why is a line not drawn through the points on the graph?

b) What is the cost for one text message? How do you know?

c) Determine the cost to send 33 text messages.

d) How many messages can be sent for $7.20?

e) What assumptions did you make when you completed parts c and d?

27. Charin saves the same amount of money each month. This table shows how his savings account balance is changing.

Months Saved	Account Balance ($)
2	145
5	280

a) How much money does Charin save each month? How could you use the concept of slope to determine this?

b) Determine how much money Charin will have saved after 10 months.

c) Determine how much money Charin had in his account when he started saving money each month. Explain your strategy.

d) What assumptions did you make when you answered parts a to c?

28. *Pitch* is often used to measure the steepness of a roof.

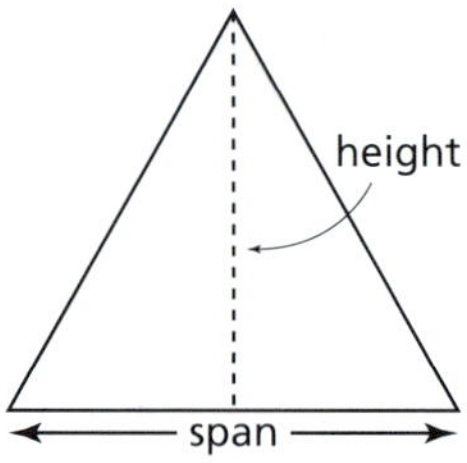

a) For a *full pitch* roof, the height and span are equal. A full pitch roof has a span of 36 ft. What is the slope of this roof?

b) For a *one-third pitch* roof, the height is one-third the span. A one-third pitch roof has a span of 36 ft. What is the slope of this roof?

C

29. On July 23, 1983, a Boeing 767 travelling from Montreal to Edmonton ran out of fuel over Red Lake, Ontario, and the pilot had to glide to make an emergency landing in Gimli, Manitoba. When the plane had been fuelled, imperial units instead of metric units were used for the calculations of the volume of fuel needed. Suppose the plane glided to the ground at a constant speed. The altitude of the plane decreased from 7000 m to 5500 m in a horizontal distance of 18 km. The plane was at an altitude of 2600 m when it was 63 km away from Winnipeg. Could this plane reach Winnipeg? Explain.

30. Use grid paper.
   a) Plot point O at the origin, point B(2, 4), and any point A on the positive x-axis.
   b) Determine the slope of segment OB and tan $\angle$AOB.
   c) Repeat parts a and b for B(5, 2).
   d) How is the slope of a line segment related to the tangent of the angle formed by the segment and the positive x-axis?

31. a) Construct an angle of 30° at the origin, with one arm along the positive x-axis. Determine the slope of the other arm of the angle.
   b) Repeat part a for an angle of 60°.
   c) For an angle with one arm horizontal, when the angle doubles does the slope of the other arm double? Justify your answer.

Reflect

Describe the types of slope a line may have. How is the slope of a line related to rate of change? Include examples in your explanation.

THE WORLD OF MATH

Profile: The Slope of a Road

The slope of a road is called the *grade* of the road, which is the fraction $\frac{\text{rise}}{\text{run}}$ expressed as a percent. When a grade is greater than 6%, a sign is erected by the side of the road to warn traffic travelling downhill. Trucks may have to gear down to travel safely. What are the rise and the run of a road with slope 6%?

6.2 Slopes of Parallel and Perpendicular Lines

LESSON FOCUS

Use slope to determine whether two lines are parallel or perpendicular.

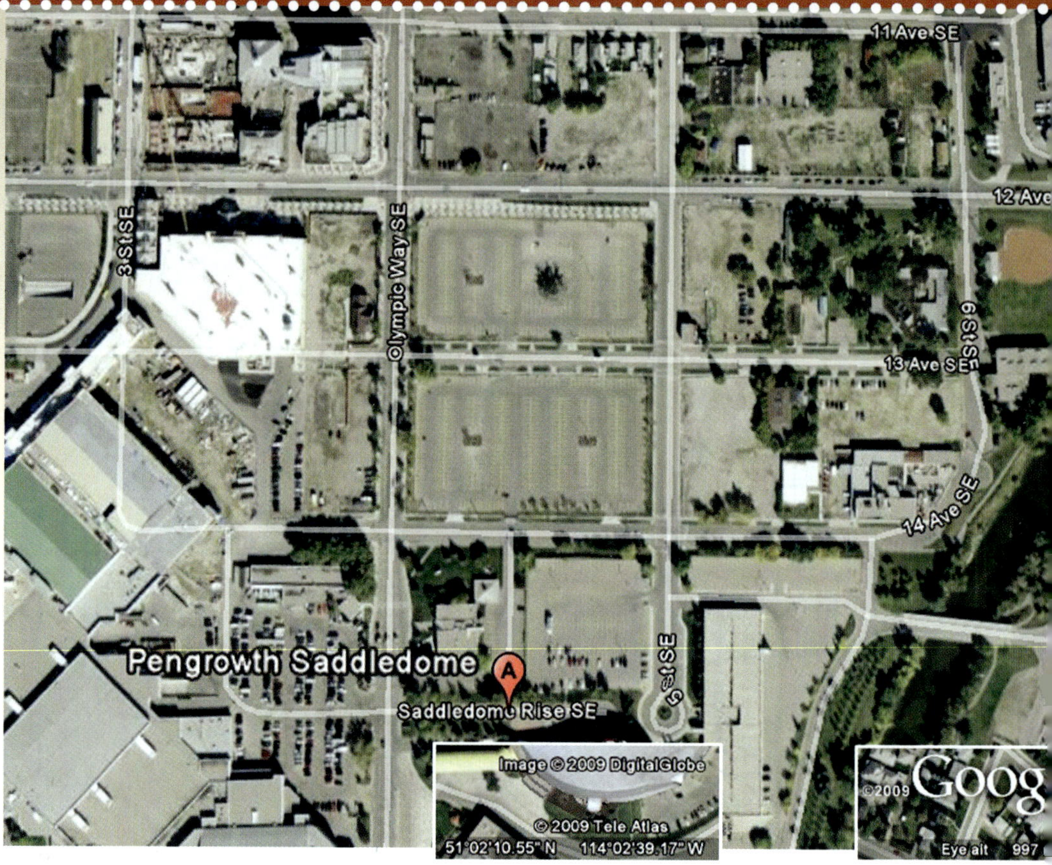

This map of Calgary shows the area close to the Saddledome.

Make Connections

Look at the map above.
Which streets are parallel to 11th Avenue?
Which streets are perpendicular to 11th Avenue? How could you verify this?

Construct Understanding

TRY THIS

Work on your own.

You will need grid paper and a ruler.

A. On a coordinate grid, draw 2 squares with different orientations.

B. For each square, determine the slope of each side.
- What do you notice about the slopes of parallel line segments?
- What do you notice about the slopes of perpendicular line segments?

C. Compare your results with those of 3 classmates. Do the relationships you discovered in Step B seem to be true in general? Justify your answer.

When two lines have the same slope, congruent triangles can be drawn to show the rise and the run.
Lines that have the some slope are parallel.

Slope of AB $= \frac{7}{5}$

Slope of CD $= \frac{7}{5}$

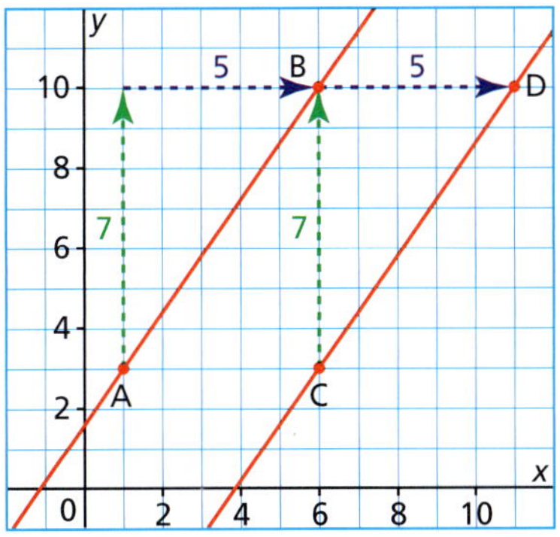

Since the slope of AB is equal to the slope of CD, line AB is parallel to line CD.

Example 1 Identifying Parallel Lines

Line GH passes through G(−4, 2) and H(2, −1). Line JK passes through J(−1, 7) and K(7, 3). Line MN passes through M(−4, 5) and N(5, 1). Sketch the lines. Are they parallel? Justify the answer.

SOLUTION

Use the formula for the slope of a line through points with coordinates (x_1, y_1) and (x_2, y_2):

Slope $= \frac{y_2 - y_1}{x_2 - x_1}$

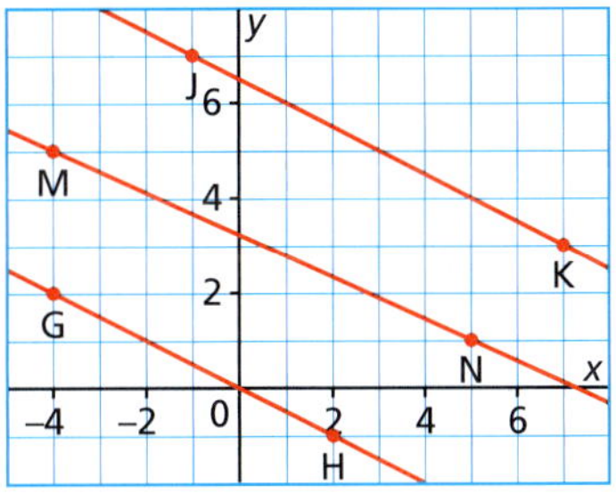

Slope of GH $= \frac{-1 - 2}{2 - (-4)}$

Slope of GH $= \frac{-3}{6}$, or $-\frac{1}{2}$

Slope of JK $= \frac{3 - 7}{7 - (-1)}$

Slope of JK $= \frac{-4}{8}$, or $-\frac{1}{2}$

Slope of MN $= \frac{1 - 5}{5 - (-4)}$

Slope of MN $= \frac{-4}{9}$, or $-\frac{4}{9}$

Since the slopes of GH and JK are equal, the two lines are parallel. Since the slope of MN is different from the slopes of GH and JK, MN is not parallel to those lines.

CHECK YOUR UNDERSTANDING

1. Line EF passes through E(−3, −2) and F(−1, 6). Line CD passes through C(−1, −3) and D(1, 7). Line AB passes through A(−3, 7) and B(−5, −2). Sketch the lines. Are they parallel? Justify your answer.

[Answer: The slopes of the lines are not equal, so the lines are not parallel.]

Non-parallel lines in the same plane have different slopes. Perpendicular lines are not parallel, so they have different slopes.

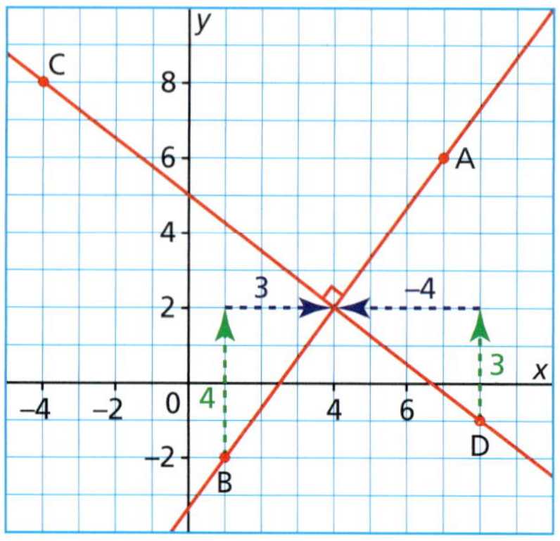

Lines AB and CD are drawn perpendicular.

Slope of AB $= \frac{\text{rise}}{\text{run}}$ Slope of CD $= \frac{\text{rise}}{\text{run}}$

Slope of AB $= \frac{4}{3}$ Slope of CD $= \frac{3}{-4}$

Slope of CD $= -\frac{3}{4}$

Two real numbers, *a* and *b*, are **negative reciprocals** if $ab = -1$.

The rise of AB is the opposite of the run of CD.
The run of AB is equal to the rise of CD.

$-\frac{3}{4}$ is the *negative reciprocal* of $\frac{4}{3}$.

And, $\left(-\frac{3}{4}\right)\left(\frac{4}{3}\right) = -1$

The relationship between the slopes of AB and CD is true for any two oblique perpendicular lines. Horizontal and vertical lines are an exception.

The slope of a horizontal line is 0. The slope of a vertical line is $\frac{1}{0}$, which is not defined. So, the slopes of horizontal and vertical lines are not negative reciprocals.

Slopes of Perpendicular Lines

The slopes of two oblique perpendicular lines are negative reciprocals; that is, a line with slope a, $a \neq 0$, is perpendicular to a line with slope $-\frac{1}{a}$.

Example 2 Examining Slopes to Compare Lines

Line PQ passes through P(−7, 2) and Q(−2, 10).
Line RS passes through R(−3, −4) and S(5, 1).

a) Are these two lines parallel, perpendicular, or neither? Justify the answer.

b) Sketch the lines to verify the answer to part a.

CHECK YOUR UNDERSTANDING

2. Line ST passes through S(−2, 7) and T(2, −5). Line UV passes through U(−2, 3) and V(7, 6).

a) Are these two lines parallel, perpendicular, or neither? Justify your answer.

b) Sketch the lines to verify your answer to part a.

[Answer: a) The two lines are perpendicular.]

SOLUTION

a) Slope of PQ $= \dfrac{10 - 2}{-2 - (-7)}$ Slope of RS $= \dfrac{1 - (-4)}{5 - (-3)}$

Slope of PQ $= \dfrac{8}{5}$ Slope of RS $= \dfrac{5}{8}$

The two slopes are not equal, so the lines are not parallel. The two slopes are reciprocals, but not negative reciprocals, so the lines are not perpendicular.
So, the two lines are neither parallel nor perpendicular.

b)

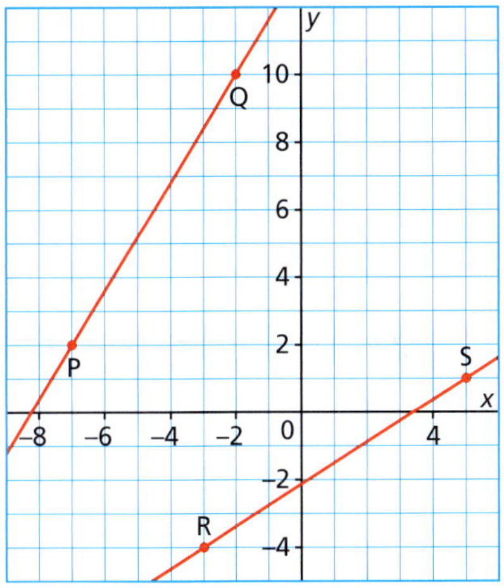

Example 3 Identifying a Line Perpendicular to a Given Line

a) Determine the slope of a line that is perpendicular to the line through E(2, 3) and F(−4, −1).

b) Determine the coordinates of G so that line EG is perpendicular to line EF.

SOLUTION

a) Determine the slope of EF.

Slope of EF $= \dfrac{-1 - 3}{-4 - 2}$

Slope of EF $= \dfrac{-4}{-6}$

Slope of EF $= \dfrac{2}{3}$

The slope of a line perpendicular to EF is the negative reciprocal of $\frac{2}{3}$, which is $-\frac{3}{2}$.

The slope of a line perpendicular to EF is $-\frac{3}{2}$.

(Solution continues.)

CHECK YOUR UNDERSTANDING

3. a) Determine the slope of a line that is perpendicular to the line through G(−2, 3) and H(1, −2).

b) Determine the coordinates of J so that line GJ is perpendicular to line GH.

[Answers: a) $\frac{3}{5}$ b) sample answer: J(3, 6)]

b) Draw line EF.

The slope of line EG is $-\frac{3}{2}$, so for each rise of -3 units, there is a run of 2 units. From point E, move 3 units down and 2 units right. Mark point G. Its coordinates are G(4, 0). Draw a line through EG. Line EG is perpendicular to line EF.

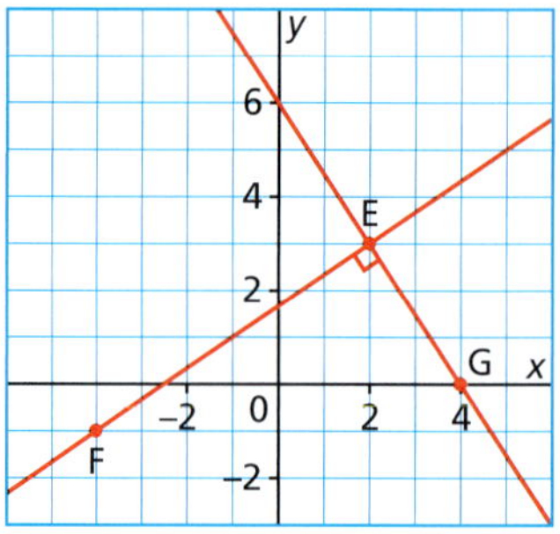

Why do the slopes of oblique perpendicular lines have opposite signs?

What are some other possible coordinates for G?

Example 4 Using Slope to Identify a Polygon

ABCD is a parallelogram. Is it a rectangle? Justify the answer.

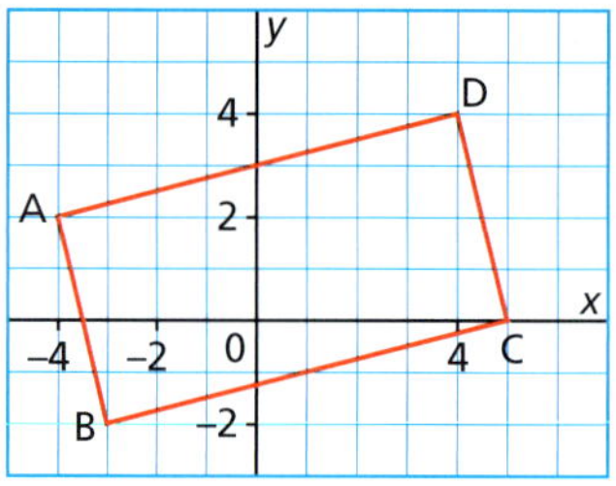

SOLUTION

A parallelogram has opposite sides equal.
It is a rectangle if its angles are right angles.
To check whether ABCD is a rectangle, determine whether two intersecting sides are perpendicular.
Determine whether AB is perpendicular to BC.
From the diagram, the rise from A to B is -4 and the run is 1.

Slope of AB $= \frac{-4}{1}$

From the diagram, the rise from B to C is 2 and the run is 8.

Slope of BC $= \frac{2}{8}$, or $\frac{1}{4}$

Since the slopes of AB and BC are negative reciprocals, AB and BC are perpendicular.
This means that $\angle$ABC is a right angle and that ABCD is a rectangle.

CHECK YOUR UNDERSTANDING

4. EFGH is a parallelogram. Is it a rectangle? Justify your answer.

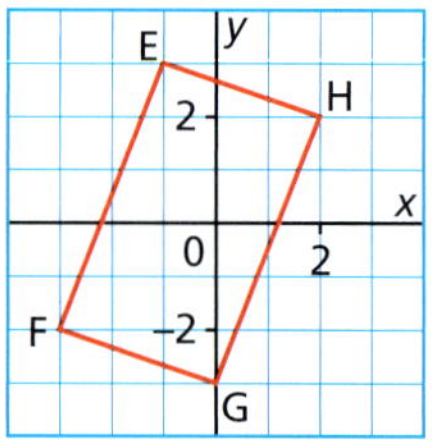

[Answer: No, EFGH is not a rectangle.]

Why didn't we need to check that all the angles of parallelogram ABCD were right angles?

Why didn't we write the slope of AB as -4?

Discuss the Ideas

1. How do you determine whether two lines are parallel?

2. How do you determine whether two lines are perpendicular?

Exercises

A

3. The slopes of lines are given below. For each line, what is the slope of a parallel line?

a) $\frac{4}{5}$ b) $-\frac{4}{3}$

c) 3 d) 0

4. The slopes of lines are given below. For each line, what is the slope of a perpendicular line?

a) $\frac{7}{6}$ b) $-\frac{5}{8}$

c) 9 d) -5

5. The slopes of two lines are given. Are the two lines parallel, perpendicular, or neither?

a) 4, 4 b) $\frac{1}{6}$, 6

c) $\frac{7}{8}$, $-\frac{7}{8}$ d) $\frac{1}{10}$, -10

6. The slopes of lines are given below. What is the slope of a line that is:

i) parallel to each given line?

ii) perpendicular to each given line?

a) $-\frac{4}{9}$ b) 5 c) $\frac{7}{3}$ d) -4

B

7. This golfer is checking his set-up position by holding his club to his chest and looking to see whether it is parallel to an imaginary line through the tips of his shoes.

Is this golfer set up correctly? How did you find out?

8. For each grid below:

i) Write the coordinates of the 2 labelled points on each line.

ii) Are the two lines parallel, perpendicular, or neither? Justify your answer.

a)

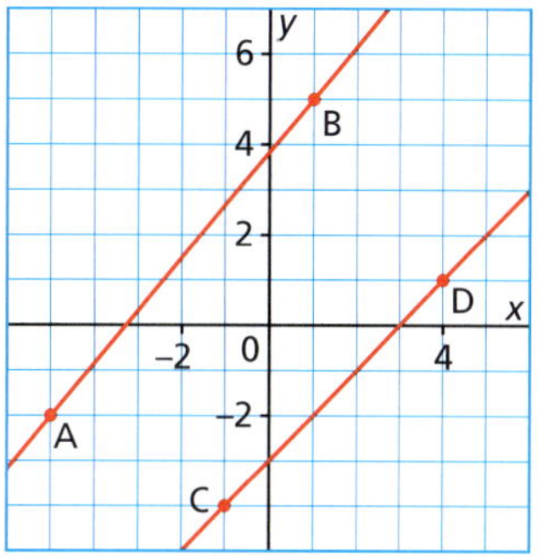

b)

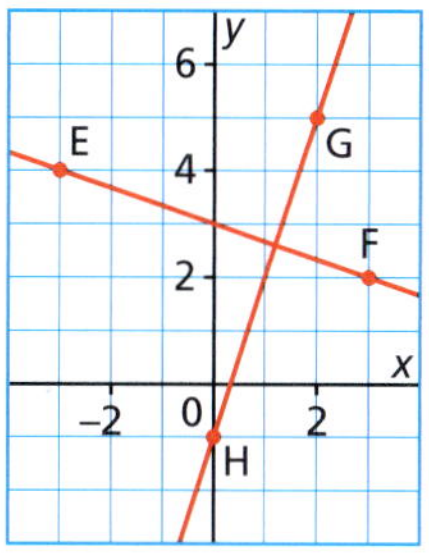

c)

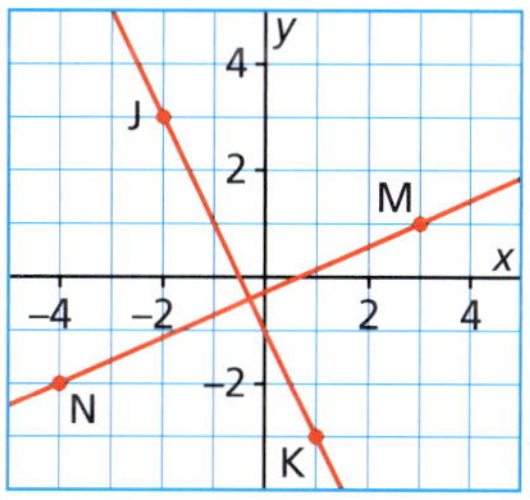

d)

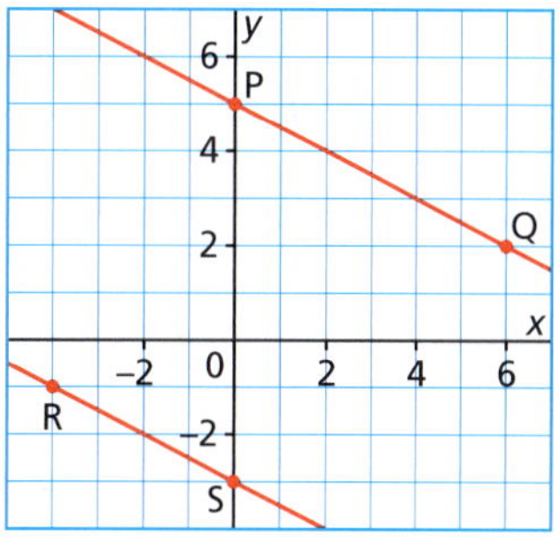

9. The coordinates of the endpoints of segments are given below. Are the two line segments parallel, perpendicular, or neither? Justify your answer.

a) S(-4, -1), T(-1, 5) and U(1, 1), V(5, -1)

b) B(-6, -2), C(-3, 3) and D(2, 0), E(5, 5)

c) N(-6, 2), P(-3, -4) and Q(1, -3), R(3, 4)

d) G(-2, 5), H(4, 1) and J(1, -4), K(7, 0)

10. How are the lines in each pair related? Justify your answer.

a) DE has an x-intercept of 4 and a y-intercept of -6.
FG has an x-intercept of -6 and a y-intercept of 4.

b) HJ has an x-intercept of -2 and a y-intercept of 3.
KM has an x-intercept of -9 and a y-intercept of 6.

11. A line passes through A$(-3, -2)$ and B$(1, 4)$.

a) On a grid, draw line AB and determine its slope.

b) Line CD is parallel to AB. What is the slope of CD?

c) Point C has coordinates $(-1, -1)$. Determine two sets of possible coordinates for D. Why might your answers be different from those of a classmate?

d) Line AE is perpendicular to AB. What is the slope of AE?

e) Determine two sets of possible coordinates for E.

12. A line passes through A$(5, -2)$ and B$(3, 2)$.

a) Draw line AB on a grid and determine its slope.

b) Line CD is parallel to AB. What is the slope of CD?

c) Given that Q$(1, -4)$ lies on CD, draw line CD. Determine the coordinates of its x- and y-intercepts.

d) Line EF is perpendicular to AB. What is the slope of EF?

e) Given that R$(-4, -4)$ lies on EF, draw line EF. Determine the coordinates of its x- and y-intercepts.

13. HJKM is a quadrilateral.

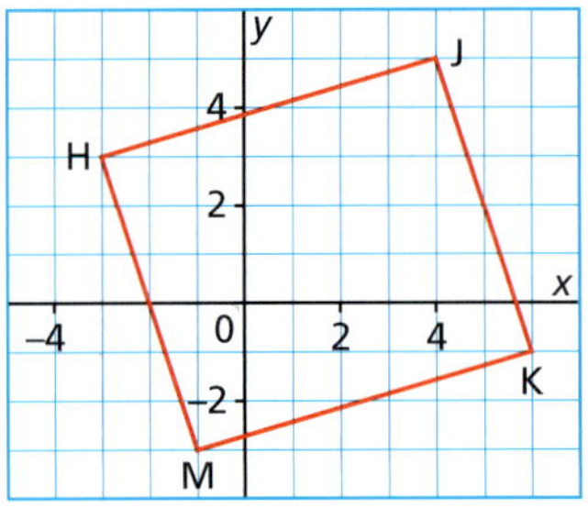

a) Is HJKM a parallelogram? Justify your answer.

b) Is HJKM a rectangle? Justify your answer.

14. Which type of quadrilateral is DEFG? Justify your answer.

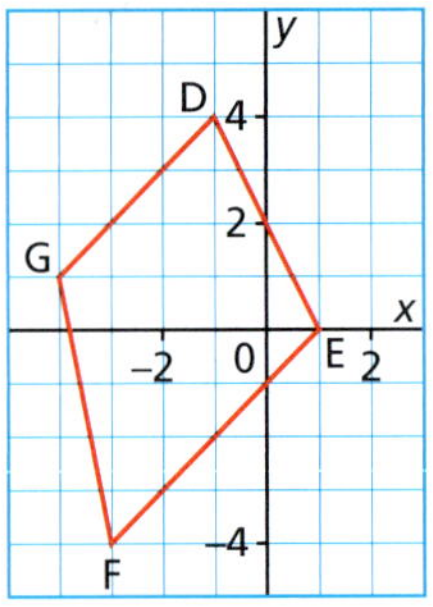

15. QRST is a rectangle with Q$(-2, 4)$ and R$(1, 1)$. Do you have enough information to determine the coordinates of S and T? Explain.

16. The coordinates of the vertices of $\triangle$ABC are A$(-3, 1)$, B$(6, -2)$, and C$(3, 4)$. How can you tell that $\triangle$ABC is a right triangle?

17. The coordinates of the vertices of $\triangle$DEF are D$(-3, -2)$, E$(1, 4)$, and F$(4, 2)$. Is $\triangle$DEF a right triangle? Justify your answer.

18. Draw a triangle on a grid.

a) Determine the slope of each side of the triangle.

b) Join the midpoints of the sides. Determine the slope of each new line segment formed.

c) What relationship do you notice between the slopes in parts a and b?

19. ABCD is a parallelogram. Three vertices have coordinates A(−4, 3), B(2, 4), and C(4, 0).
  a) Is ABCD a rectangle? Justify your answer.
  b) Determine the coordinates of D. Explain your answer.
  c) What other strategy could you use to determine the coordinates of D? Explain.

20. The coordinates of two of the vertices of △RST are R(−3, 4) and S(0, −2).
Determine possible coordinates for T so that △RST is a right triangle. Explain your strategy.

C

21. On a grid, draw several different rhombuses. Use slopes to determine the relationship between the diagonals.

22. Determine the value of c so that the line segment with endpoints B(2, 2) and C(9, 6) is parallel to the line segment with endpoints D(c, −7) and E(5, −3).

23. Given A(3, 5), B(7, 10), C(0, 2), and D(1, a), determine the value of a for which:
  a) Line AB is parallel to line CD.
  b) Line AB is perpendicular to line CD.

24. a) On grid paper, construct a square with side length 4 units and one vertex at the origin. Verify that the diagonals of this square are perpendicular.
  b) Repeat part a for a square with side length a units.

Reflect What have you learned about perpendicular lines and parallel lines? Include examples in your answer.

THE WORLD OF MATH

Historical Moment: Agnes Martin

Agnes Martin was born in Macklin, Saskatchewan, and lived from 1912 to 2004. She was an artist who used parallel lines and grids in her artwork. Before Agnes began a painting, she calculated the distances between pairs of parallel lines or bands. She then drew each line by hand, using a string stretched tightly across the surface to guide her, and a ruler to draw the line.

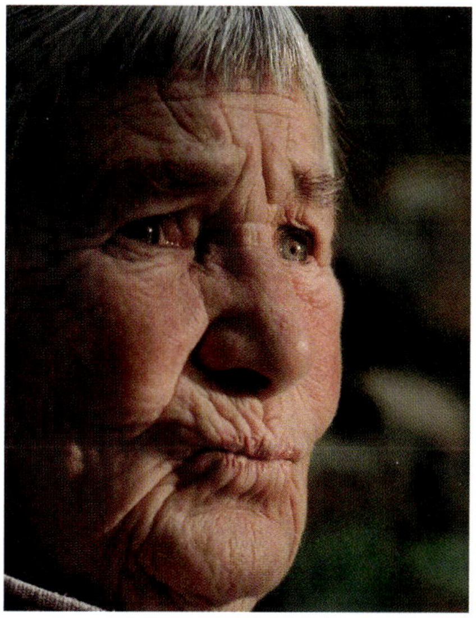

CHECKPOINT 1

Connections

Definition

The slope of a line is the measure of its rate of change.

$$\text{Slope} = \frac{\text{rise}}{\text{run}}$$

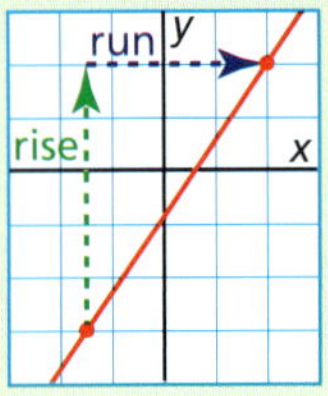

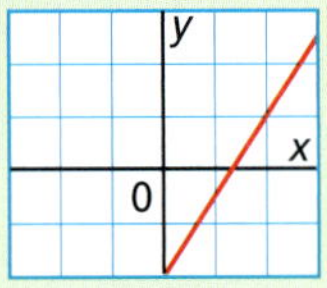

positive slope

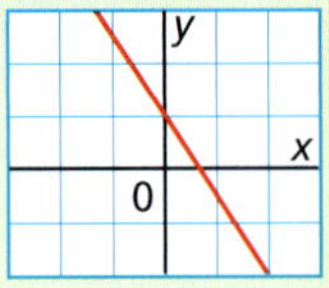

negative slope

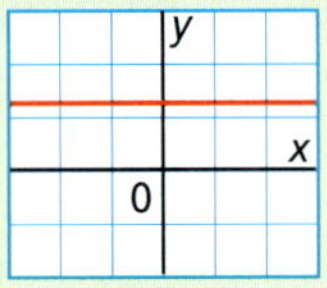

0 slope

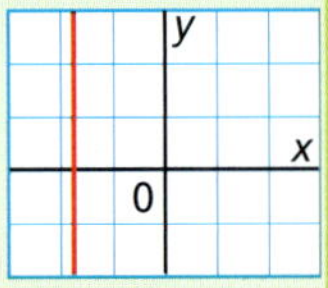

undefined slope

The slope of a line through $P(x_1, y_1)$ and $Q(x_2, y_2)$ is:

$$\text{Slope} = \frac{y_2 - y_1}{x_2 - x_1}$$

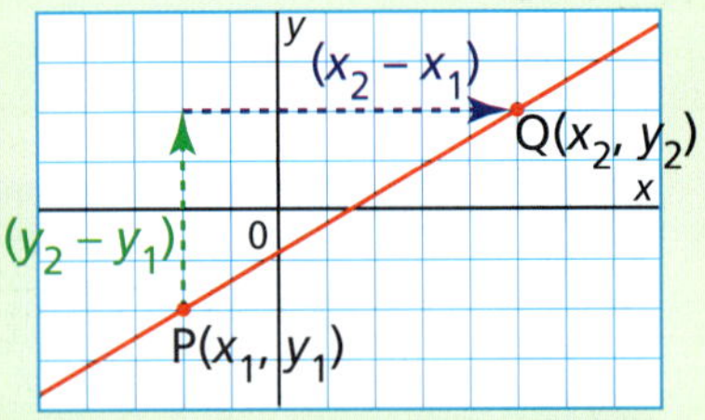

Two lines are parallel when they have equal slopes.

Slope of EF $= -\frac{1}{2}$

Slope of GH $= -\frac{1}{2}$

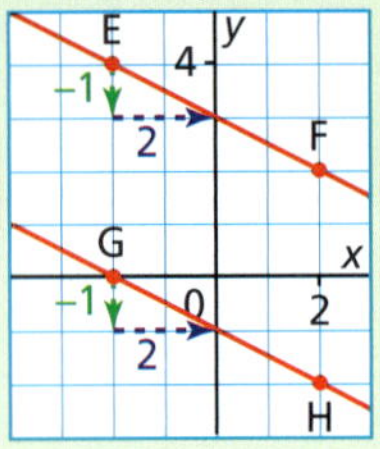

Two lines are perpendicular when their slopes are negative reciprocals.

Slope of MN = 3

Slope of JK $= -\frac{1}{3}$

$$(3)\left(-\frac{1}{3}\right) = -1$$

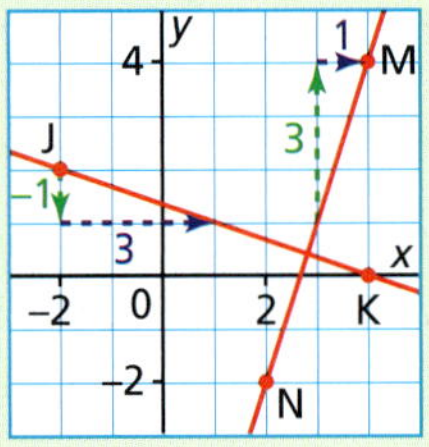

Concept Development

- **In Lesson 6.1**
  - You defined the slope of a line segment and the slope of a line as rate of change.
  - You determined the slope of a line segment and the slope of a line from measurements of the rise and run.
  - You showed that the slope of a line is equal to the slope of any segment of the line.
  - You determined the slope of a line segment given the coordinates of the endpoints of the segment, and the slope of a line given the coordinates of two points on the line.
  - You explained the meaning of the slope of a horizontal line and a vertical line.
  - You drew a line, given its slope and a point on the line.
  - You determined the coordinates of a point on a line, given its slope and another point on the line.
  - You solved contextual problems involving slope.

- **In Lesson 6.2**
  - You generalized and applied rules for determining whether two lines are parallel or perpendicular.
  - You drew lines that were parallel or perpendicular to a given line.

Assess Your Understanding

6.1

1. Determine the slopes of line segments AB and CD.

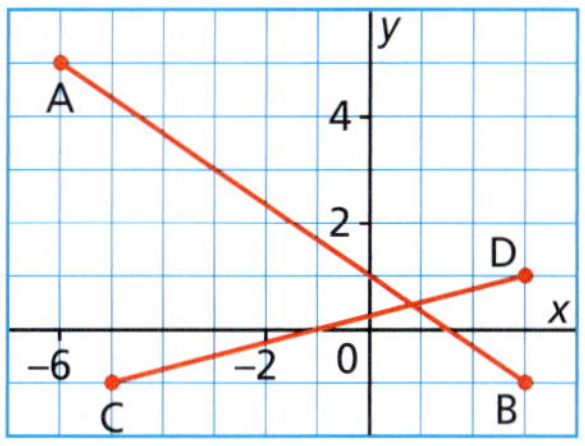

2. Determine the slope of the line that passes through each pair of points.
  a) Q(−2, 5) and R(2, −10)
  b) an x-intercept of 3 and a y-intercept of −5

3. Why can the slope of a line be determined by using any two points on the line?

4. Jordan recorded the distances he had travelled at certain times since he began his snowmobile trip along the Overland Trail from Whitehorse to Dawson in the Yukon. He plotted these data on a grid.
  a) What is the slope of the line through these points? What does it represent?
  b) How far did Jordan travel in $1\frac{1}{4}$ hours?
  c) How long did it take Jordan to travel 65 km?

Jordan's Snowmobile Journey

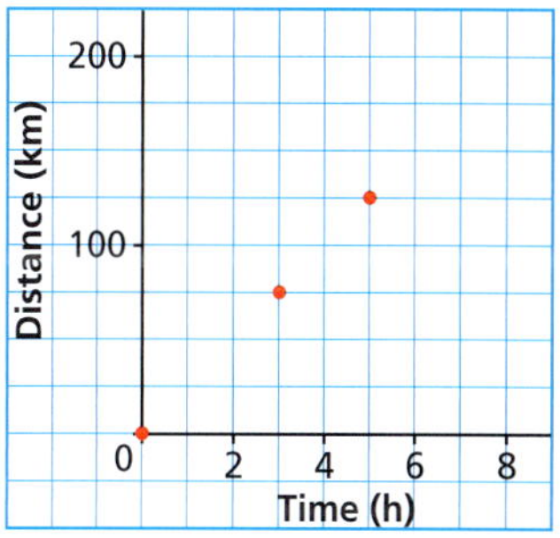

6.2

5. Draw lines with the given slopes. Are the lines parallel, perpendicular, or neither? Justify your answers.

  a) $\frac{2}{5}, \frac{5}{2}$ **b)** $-\frac{1}{4}, 4$ **c)** $\frac{9}{7}, \frac{18}{14}$

6. A line passes through D(−6, −1) and E(2, 5).
  a) Determine the coordinates of two points on a line that is parallel to DE.
  b) Determine the coordinates of two points on a line that is perpendicular to DE.
  Describe the strategies you used to determine the coordinates.

7. The vertices of a triangle have coordinates A(−1, 5), B(−5, −6), and C(3, 1). Is △ABC a right triangle? Justify your answer.

8. Two vertices of right △MNP have coordinates M(−3, 6) and P(3, −3). Point N lies on an axis. Determine two possible sets of coordinates for N. Explain your strategy.

MATH LAB

6.3 Investigating Graphs of Linear Functions

LESSON FOCUS

Investigate the relationship between the graph and the equation of a linear function.

Make Connections

Alimina purchased an mp3 player and downloaded 3 songs.
Each subsequent day, she downloads 2 songs.
Which graph represents this situation? Explain your choice.

Graph A

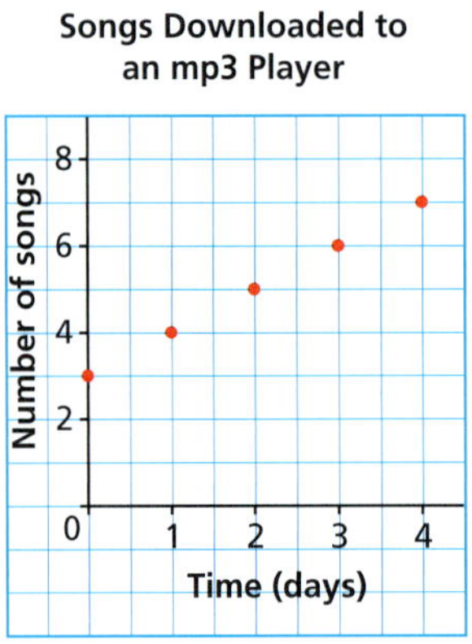

Graph B

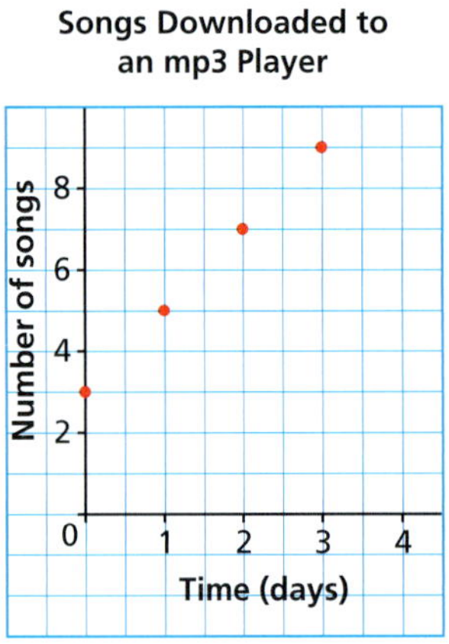

Graph C

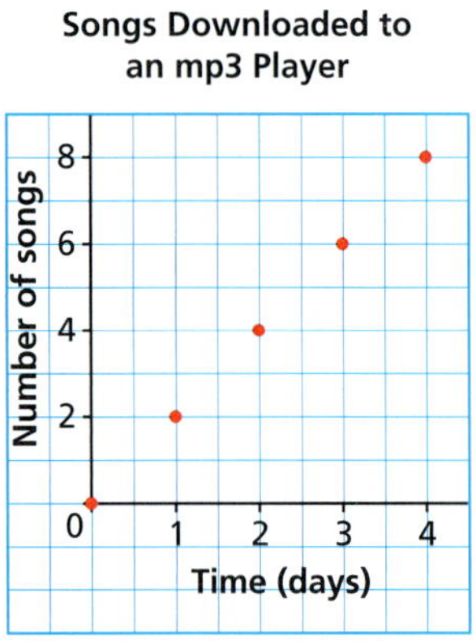

Construct Understanding

TRY THIS

Work with a partner.

Use a graphing calculator or a computer with graphing software.

A. Graph $y = mx + 6$ for different values of m.
Include values of m that are negative and 0.
Use a table to record your results.

Equation	Value of m	Sketch of the Graph	Slope of the Graph	x-intercept	y-intercept
$y = x + 6$	1				

B. How does changing the value of m change the appearance of the graph?
What does m represent?

C. Graph $y = 2x + b$ for different values of b.
Include values of b that are negative and 0.
Use a table to record your results.

Equation	Value of b	Sketch of the Graph	Slope of the Graph	x-intercept	y-intercept
$y = 2x + 6$	6				

D. How does changing the value of b change the appearance of the graph?
What does b represent?

E. Predict the appearance of the graph of $y = -2x + 4$.
Verify your prediction by graphing.

Suppose you are given the graph of a linear function. How could you use what you learned in this lesson to determine an equation for that function?

Assess Your Understanding

1. In the screens below, each mark on the x-axis and y-axis represents 1 unit. What is the equation of each line?

   a) The slope of each line is $\frac{1}{2}$.

   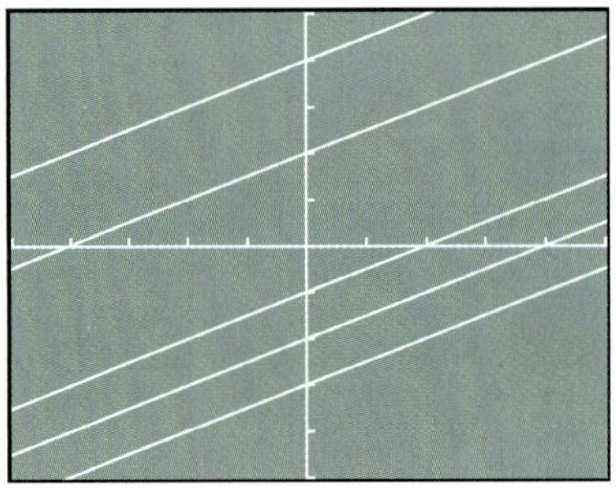

   b) The slope of each line is $-\frac{1}{3}$.

   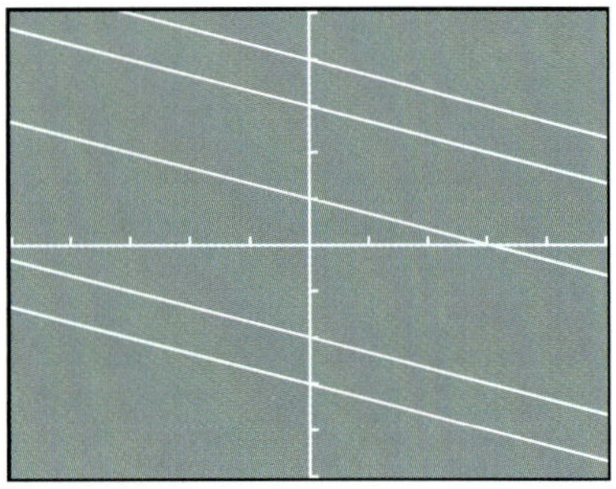

2. A linear function is written in the form $y = mx + b$. Use your results from *Try This* to suggest what the numbers m and b represent. Explain how you could use this information to graph the function.

3. Describe the graph of the linear function whose equation is $y = -3x + 6$. Draw this graph without using technology.

4. a) Predict what will be common about the graphs of these equations.
   i) $y = x - 1$ ii) $y = 2x - 1$
   iii) $y = -3x - 1$ iv) $y = -2x - 1$
   b) Graph the equations to check your prediction.

5. a) Predict what will be common about the graphs of these equations.
   i) $y = x - 3$ ii) $y = x - 2$
   iii) $y = x$ iv) $y = x + 3$
   b) Graph the equations to check your prediction.

6. Graph each equation on grid paper without using a table of values. Describe your strategy.
   a) $y = 3x + 5$ b) $y = -3x + 5$
   c) $y = 3x - 5$ d) $y = -3x - 5$

7. In Lesson 5.6, question 12, page 309, the cost, C dollars, to rent a hall for a banquet is given by the equation $C = 550 + 15n$, where n represents the number of people attending the banquet.
   a) Graph this equation on grid paper.
   b) Compare the equation above with the equation $y = mx + b$. What do m and b represent in this context?

6.4 Slope-Intercept Form of the Equation for a Linear Function

LESSON FOCUS

Relate the graph of a linear function to its equation in slope-intercept form.

Make Connections

This graph shows a cyclist's journey where the distance is measured from her home.

Graph of a Bicycle Journey

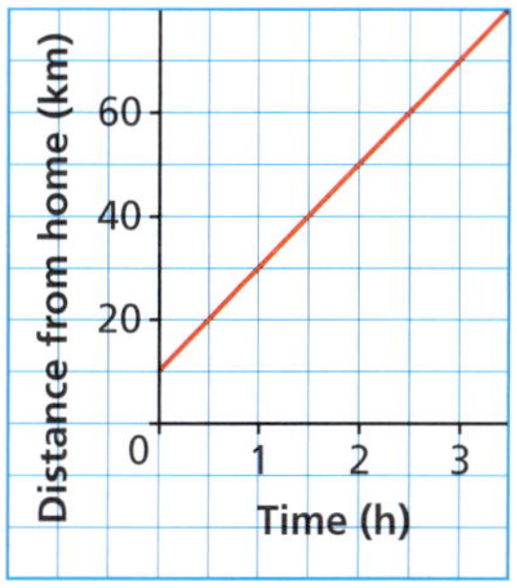

What does the vertical intercept represent?
What does the slope of the line represent?

Construct Understanding

THINK ABOUT IT

Work with a partner.

A cell phone plan charges a monthly fee that covers the costs of the first 300 min of phone use. This graph represents the cost of the plan based on the time beyond 300 min.

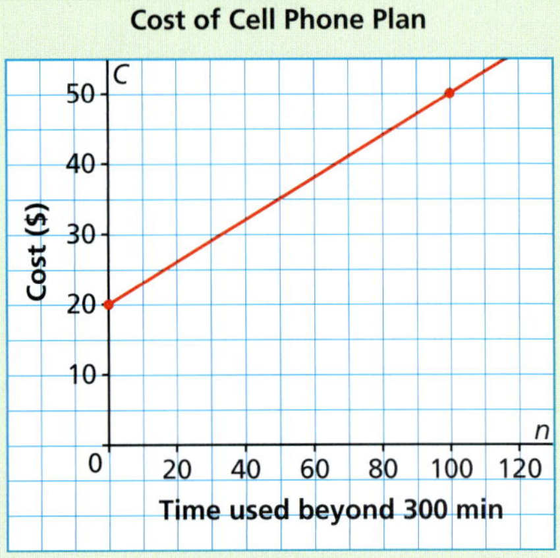

How do you know this is the graph of a linear function?
What does the slope of the graph represent?
Write an equation to describe this function.
Verify that your equation is correct.

In Chapter 5, Lesson 5.6, we described a linear function in different ways. The linear function below represents the cost of a car rental.

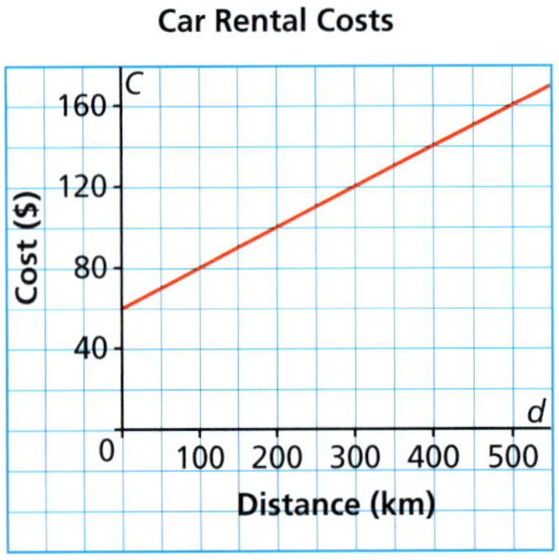

An equation of the function is:
$C = 0.20d + 60$

The number, 0.20, is the rate of change, or the slope of the graph. This is the cost in dollars for each additional 1 km driven.

The number, 60, is the vertical intercept of the graph. This is the cost in dollars that is independent of the distance driven – the initial cost for renting the car.

In general, any linear function can be described in **slope-intercept form.**

Slope-Intercept Form of the Equation of a Linear Function

The equation of a linear function can be written in the form $y = mx + b$, where m is the slope of the line and b is its y-intercept.

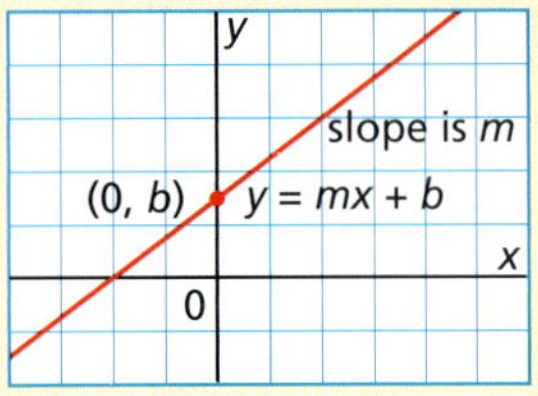

Example 1 Writing an Equation of a Linear Function Given Its Slope and *y*-Intercept

The graph of a linear function has slope $\frac{3}{5}$ and y-intercept -4. Write an equation for this function.

SOLUTION

Use:

$y = mx + b$ Substitute: $m = \frac{3}{5}$ and $b = -4$

$y = \frac{3}{5}x - 4$

An equation for this function is: $y = \frac{3}{5}x - 4$

CHECK YOUR UNDERSTANDING

1. The graph of a linear function has slope $-\frac{7}{3}$ and y-intercept 5. Write an equation for this function.

[Answer: $y = -\frac{7}{3}x + 5$]

Can you write an equation for a linear function when you know its slope and x-intercept? How would you do it?

Example 2 Graphing a Linear Function Given Its Equation in Slope-Intercept Form

Graph the linear function with equation: $y = \frac{1}{2}x + 3$

SOLUTION

Compare: $y = \frac{1}{2}x + 3$

with: $y = mx + b$

The slope of the graph is $\frac{1}{2}$.

The y-intercept is 3, with coordinates (0, 3).
On a grid, plot a point at (0, 3).
The slope of the line is:

$\frac{\text{rise}}{\text{run}} = \frac{1}{2}$

So, from (0, 3), move 1 unit up and 2 units right, then mark a point.
Draw a line through the points.

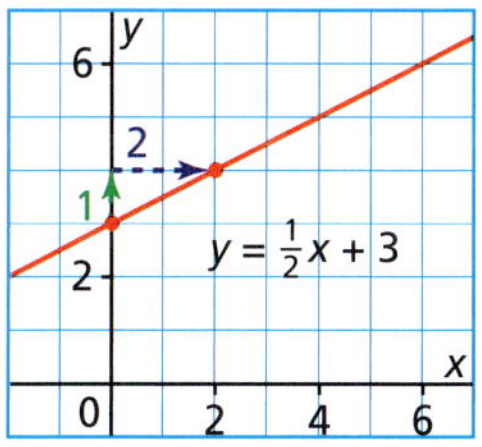

CHECK YOUR UNDERSTANDING

2. Graph the linear function with equation: $y = -\frac{3}{4}x + 2$

Answer:

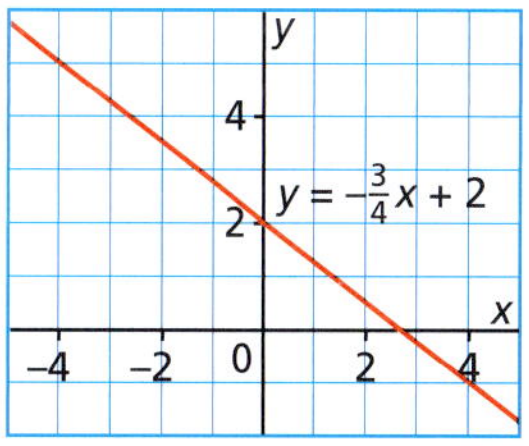

What other strategy could you use to graph this linear function?

Example 3 Writing the Equation of a Linear Function Given Its Graph

Write an equation to describe this function.
Verify the equation.

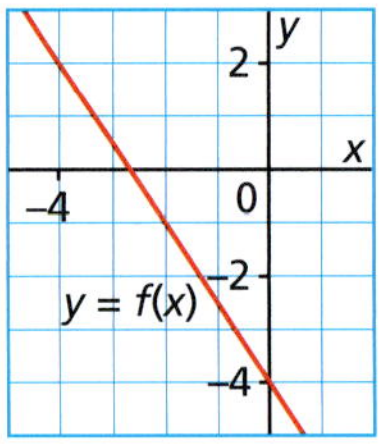

SOLUTION

Use the equation: $y = mx + b$
To write the equation of a linear function, determine the slope of the line, m, and its y-intercept, b.
The line intersects the y-axis at -4; so, $b = -4$.
From the graph, the rise is -3 when the run is 2.

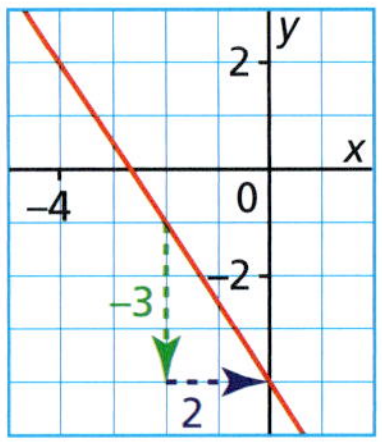

So, $m = \frac{-3}{2}$, or $-\frac{3}{2}$

Substitute for m and b in $y = mx + b$.

$y = -\frac{3}{2}x - 4$

An equation for the function is: $y = -\frac{3}{2}x - 4$

To verify the equation, substitute the coordinates of a point on the line into the equation. Choose the point $(-2, -1)$.

Substitute $x = -2$ and $y = -1$ into the equation: $y = -\frac{3}{2}x - 4$

$$\text{L. S.} = y = -1$$

$$\text{R. S.} = -\frac{3}{2}x - 4 = -\frac{3}{2}(-2) - 4 = 3 - 4 = -1$$

Since the left side is equal to the right side, the equation is correct.

CHECK YOUR UNDERSTANDING

3. Write an equation to describe this function. Verify the equation.

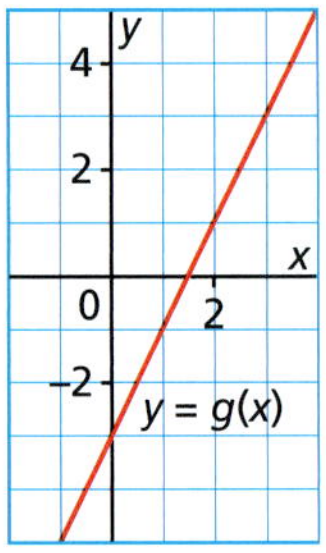

[Answer: $y = 2x - 3$]

Can the graph of a linear function be described by more than one equation of the form $y = mx + b$? Explain.

THE WORLD OF MATH

Historical Moment: Why Is *m* Used to Represent Slope?

Some historians have researched the works of great mathematicians from many different countries over the past few hundred years to try to answer this question. Others have attempted to identify words that could be used to refer to the slope of a line. The choice of the letter *m* may come from the French word *monter,* which means to climb. However, the French mathematician René Descartes did not use *m* to represent slope. At this time, historians cannot answer this question; it remains a mystery.

Example 4 Using an Equation of a Linear Function to Solve a Problem

The student council sponsored a dance. A ticket cost $5 and the cost for the DJ was $300.

a) Write an equation for the profit, P dollars, on the sale of t tickets.

b) Suppose 123 people bought tickets. What was the profit?

c) Suppose the profit was $350. How many people bought tickets?

d) Could the profit be exactly $146? Justify the answer.

SOLUTION

a) The profit is: income − expenses
When t tickets are sold, the income is: $5t$ dollars
The expenses are $300.
So, an equation is: $P = 5t - 300$

b) Use the equation:

$P = 5t - 300$ Substitute: $t = 123$

$P = 5(123) - 300$ Simplify.

$P = 615 - 300$

$P = 315$

The profit was $315.

c) Use the equation:

$P = 5t - 300$ Substitute: $P = 350$

$350 = 5t - 300$ Collect like terms.

$350 + 300 = 5t - 300 + 300$

$650 = 5t$ Solve for t.

$$\frac{650}{5} = \frac{5t}{5}$$

$130 = t$

One hundred thirty people bought tickets.

d) Use the equation:

$P = 5t - 300$ Substitute: $P = 146$

$146 = 5t - 300$ Simplify.

$146 + 300 = 5t - 300 + 300$

$446 = 5t$ Solve for t.

$$\frac{446}{5} = \frac{5t}{5}$$

$89.2 = t$

Since the number of tickets sold is not a whole number, the profit cannot be exactly $146.

CHECK YOUR UNDERSTANDING

4. To join the local gym, Karim pays a start-up fee of $99, plus a monthly fee of $29.

a) Write an equation for the total cost, C dollars, for n months at the gym.

b) Suppose Karim went to the gym for 23 months. What was the total cost?

c) Suppose the total cost was $505. For how many months did Karim use the gym?

d) Could the total cost be exactly $600? Justify your answer.

[Answers: a) $C = 29n + 99$ b) $766 c) 14 months d) no]

Suppose you graphed the linear relation. What would the slope and vertical intercept be?

Discuss the Ideas

1. When a real-world situation can be modelled by a linear function, what do the slope and vertical intercept usually represent?

2. When you are given the graph of a linear function, how can you determine an equation that represents that function?

3. When you are given an equation of a linear function in slope-intercept form, how can you quickly sketch the graph?

Exercises

A

4. For each equation, identify the slope and y-intercept of its graph.
   a) $y = 4x - 7$ b) $y = x + 12$
   c) $y = -\frac{4}{9}x + 7$ d) $y = 11x - \frac{3}{8}$
   e) $y = \frac{1}{5}x$ f) $y = 3$

5. Write an equation for the graph of a linear function that:
   a) has slope 7 and y-intercept 16
   b) has slope $-\frac{3}{8}$ and y-intercept 5
   c) passes through H(0, −3) and has slope $\frac{7}{16}$
   d) has y-intercept −8 and slope $-\frac{6}{5}$
   e) passes through the origin and has slope $-\frac{5}{12}$

6. Graph the line with each y-intercept and slope.
   a) y-intercept is 1, slope is $\frac{1}{2}$
   b) y-intercept is −5, slope is 2
   c) y-intercept is 4, slope is $-\frac{2}{3}$
   d) y-intercept is 0, slope is $\frac{4}{3}$

B

7. Graph each equation on grid paper. Explain the strategy you used.
   a) $y = 2x - 7$ b) $y = -x + 3$
   c) $y = -\frac{1}{4}x + 5$ d) $y = \frac{5}{2}x - 4$
   e) $V = -100t + 6000$ f) $C = 10n + 95$

8. For a service call, an electrician charges an \$80 initial fee, plus \$50 for each hour she works.
   a) Write an equation to represent the total cost, C dollars, for t hours of work.
   b) How would the equation change if the electrician charges \$100 initial fee plus \$40 for each hour she works?

9. The total fee for withdrawing money at an ATM in a foreign country is a \$3.50 foreign cash withdrawal fee, plus a 2% currency conversion fee. Write an equation to represent the total fee, F dollars, for withdrawing d dollars.

10. Use a graphing calculator or a computer with graphing software. Graph each equation. Explain the strategy you used. Sketch or print the graph.
    a) $f(x) = -\frac{3}{13}x + \frac{4}{11}$ b) $g(x) = 3.75x - 2.95$
    c) $C(n) = 0.45n + 25.50$ d) $F(c) = \frac{9}{5}c + 32$

11. A student said that the equation of this graph is $y = -3x + 4$.
    a) What mistakes did the student make?
    b) What is the equation of the graph?

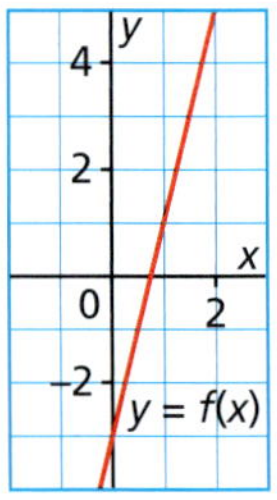

12. For each graph that follows:
    i) Determine its slope and y-intercept.
    ii) Write an equation to describe the graph, then verify the equation.
    iii) Use the equation to calculate the value of y when $x = 10$.

a)

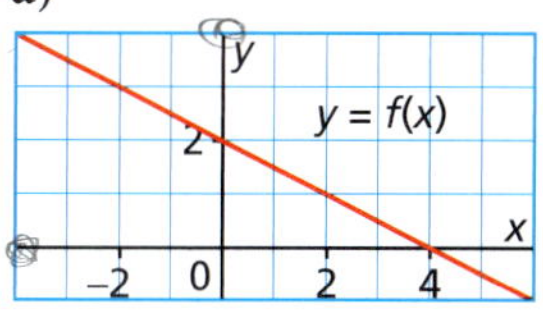

b)

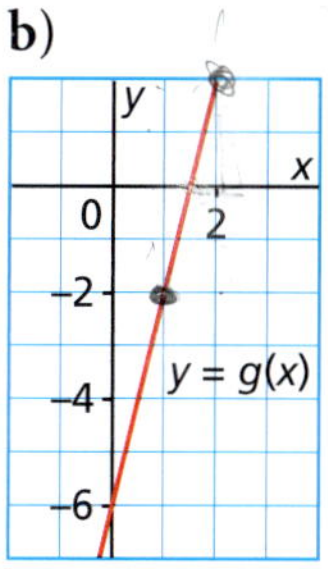

c)

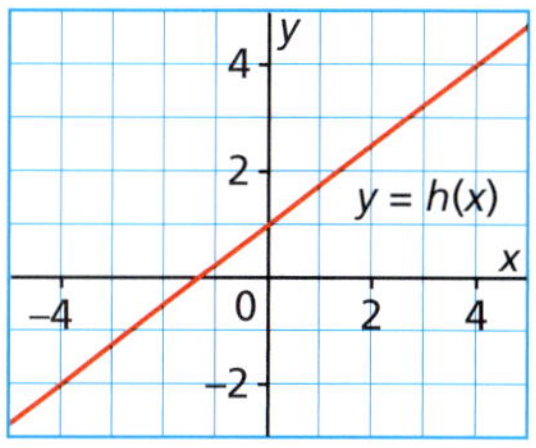

d)

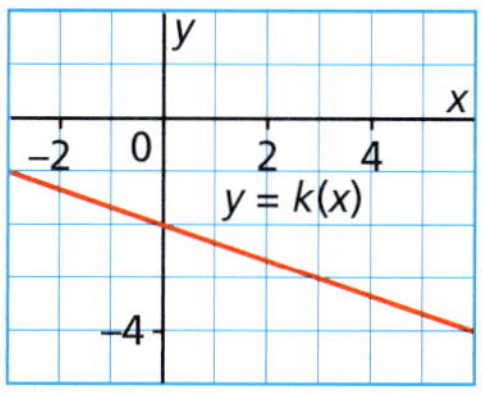

13. This graph represents the height of a float plane above a lake as the plane descends to land.

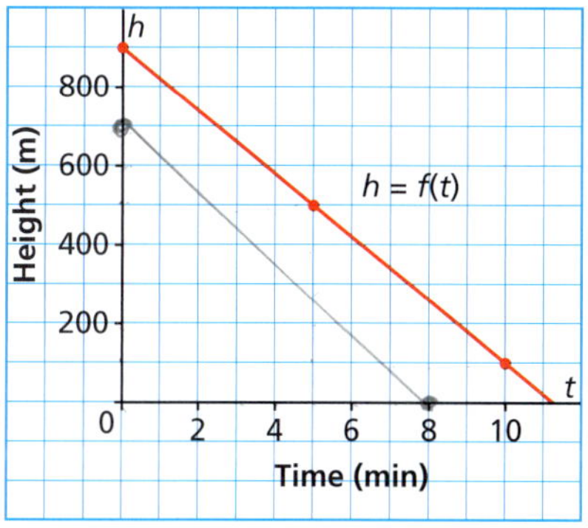

a) Determine the slope and the h-intercept. What do they represent?

b) Write an equation to describe the graph, then verify the equation.

c) Use the equation to calculate the value of h when $t = 5.5$ min.

d) Suppose the plane began its descent at 700 m and it landed after 8 min.

i) How would the graph change?

ii) How would the equation change?

14. An online music site charges a one-time membership fee of \$20, plus \$0.80 for every song that is downloaded.

a) Write an equation for the total cost, C dollars, for downloading n songs.

b) Jacques downloaded 109 songs. What was the total cost?

c) Michelle paid a total cost of \$120. How many songs did she download?

15. a) How can you use the slope-intercept form of an equation, $y = mx + b$, to graph the horizontal line $y = 2$?

b) How can you graph the vertical line $x = 2$? Explain your answers.

16. Alun has a part-time job working as a bus boy at a local restaurant. He earns \$34 a night plus 5% of the tips.

a) Write an equation for Alun's total earnings, E dollars, when the tips are t dollars.

b) What will Alun earn when the tips are \$400? Explain your strategy.

c) What were the nightly tips when Alun earned \$64? Explain your strategy.

17. Which equation matches each given graph? Justify your choice.

a) $y = x + 4$

$y = 4x + 1$

$y = x - 4$

$y = -4x + 1$

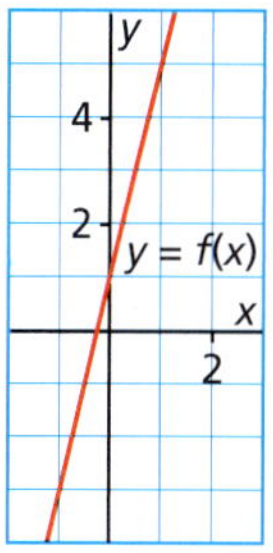

b) $y = \frac{3}{2}x - 1$

$y = -\frac{2}{3}x + 1$

$y = \frac{2}{3}x - 1$

$y = -x + \frac{2}{3}$

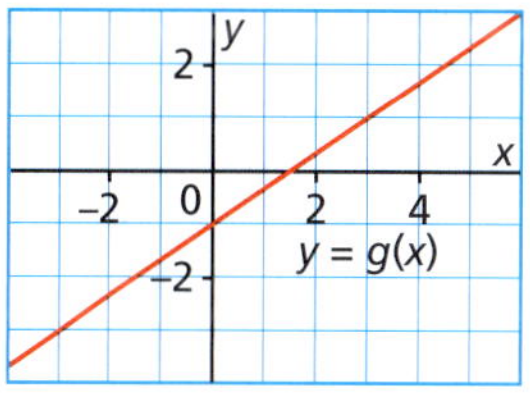

c) $y = \frac{5}{3}x + 7$

$y = -\frac{3}{5}x - 7$

$y = -7x - \frac{5}{3}$

$y = -\frac{5}{3}x - 7$

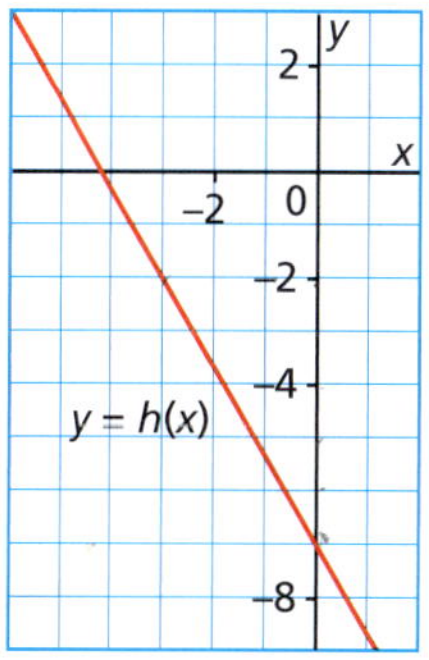

18. Match each equation with its graph. How did you decide on the equation for each graph?

a) $y = 2x - 1$ b) $y = 3x - 1$

c) $y = -x - 1$ d) $y = \frac{1}{3}x - 1$

Graph A

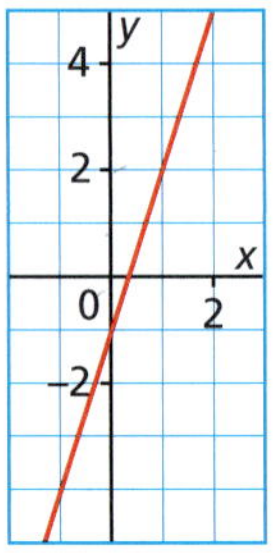

Graph B

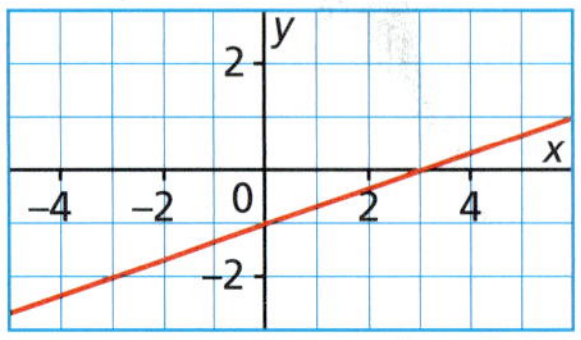

Graph C

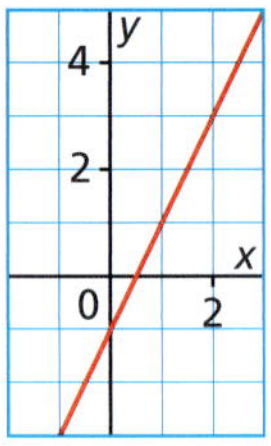

Graph D

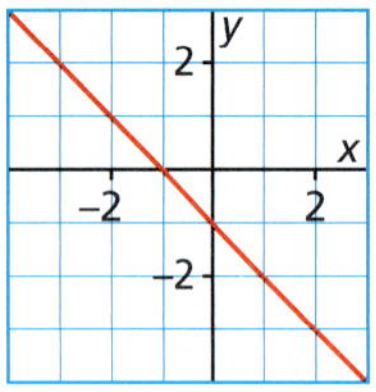

19. Match each equation with its graph. Compare the graphs. What do you notice?

a) $f(x) = -x - 4$ b) $f(x) = -x + 1$

c) $f(x) = x + 3$ d) $f(x) = x - 1$

Graph A

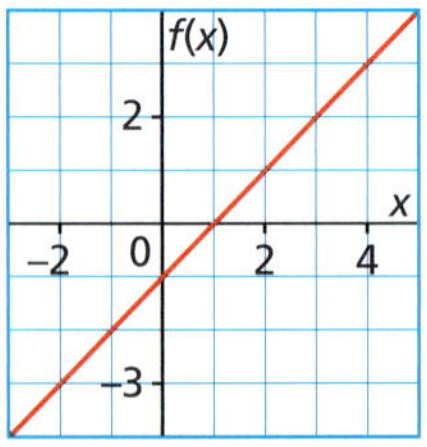

Graph B

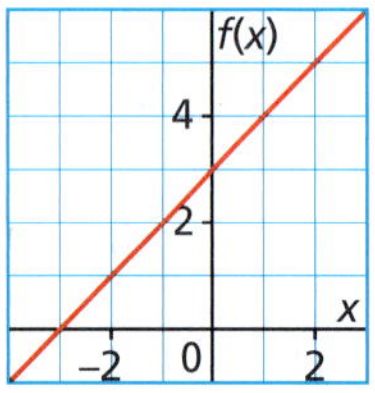

Graph C

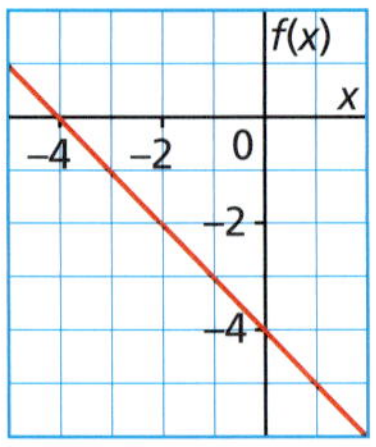

Graph D

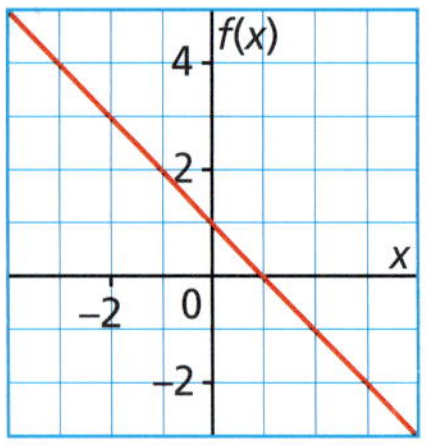

20. Identify the graph below that corresponds to each given slope and y-intercept.

a) slope 3; y-intercept 2

b) slope $\frac{1}{3}$; y-intercept -2

c) slope -3; y-intercept -2

d) slope $-\frac{1}{3}$, y-intercept 2

Graph A

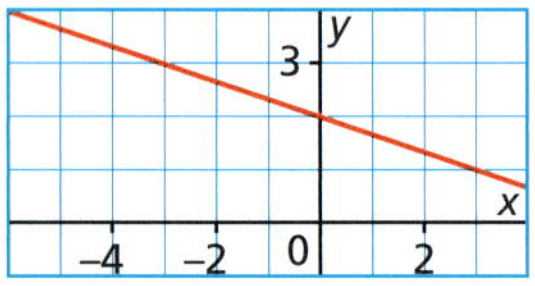

Graph B

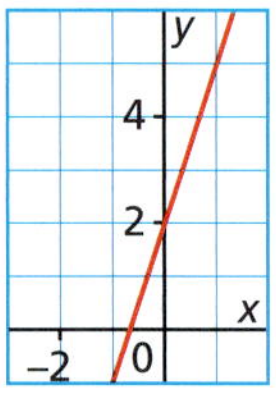

Graph C

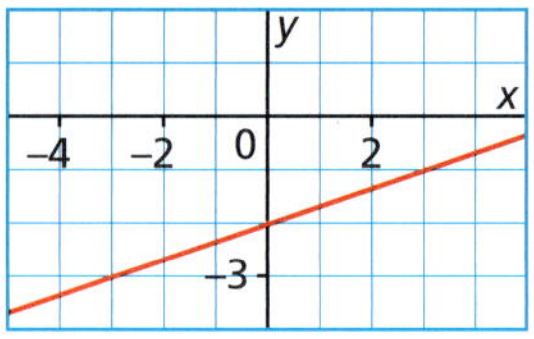

Graph D

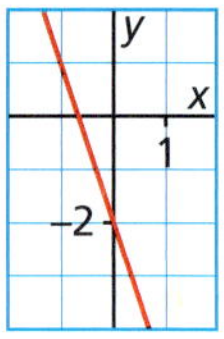

21. Consider these equations:

$y = -5x - 7$, $y = 5x + 15$,

$y = \frac{1}{5}x + 9$, $y = -\frac{1}{5}x + 15$,

$y = \frac{1}{5}x + 21$, $y = -5x + 13$,

$y = 5x + 24$, $y = -\frac{1}{5}x$

Which equations represent parallel lines? Perpendicular lines? How do you know?

C

22. Write an equation of a linear function that has y-intercept 4 and x-intercept 3. Describe the steps you used to determine the equation.

23. An equation of a line is $y = \frac{5}{3}x + c$. Determine the value of c when the line passes through the point F(4, -6). Describe your strategy.

24. An equation of a line is $y = mx - \frac{7}{8}$. Determine the value of m when the line passes through the point E(-3, 5).

Reflect

How do the values of m and b in the linear equation $y = mx + b$ relate to the graph of the corresponding linear function? Include an example.

6.5 Slope-Point Form of the Equation for a Linear Function

LESSON FOCUS

Relate the graph of a linear function to its equation in slope-point form.

Make Connections

This graph shows the height of a candle as it burns.
How would you write an equation to describe this line?
Suppose you could not identify the h-intercept.
How could you write an equation for the line?

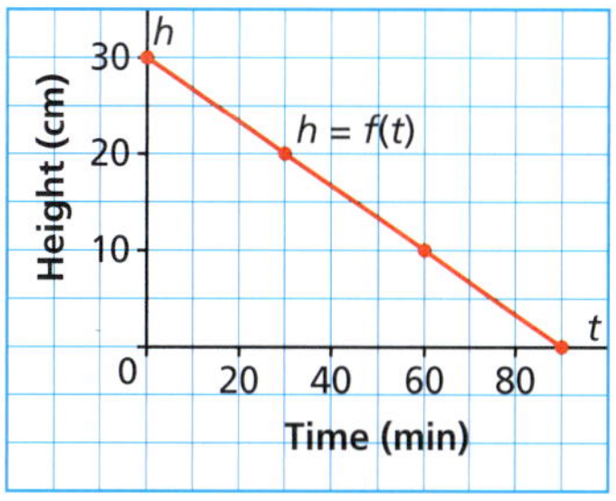

Construct Understanding

THINK ABOUT IT

Work with a partner.

Determine an equation for this line.
How many different ways can you do this?
Compare your equations and strategies.
Which strategy is more efficient?

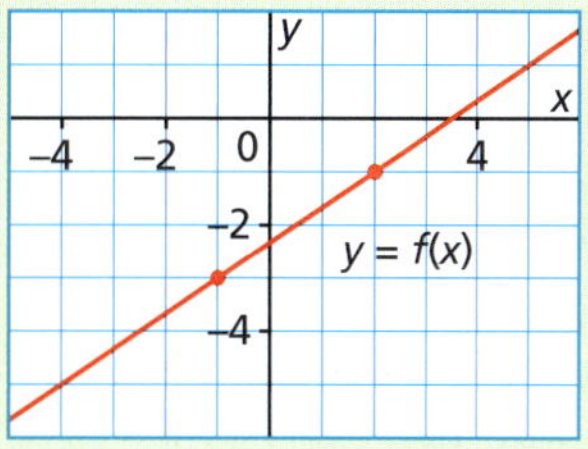

When we know the slope of a line and the coordinates of a point on the line, we use the property that the slope of a line is constant to determine an equation for the line.

This line has slope -3 and passes through P$(-2, 5)$. We use any other point Q(x, y) on the line to write an equation for the slope, m:

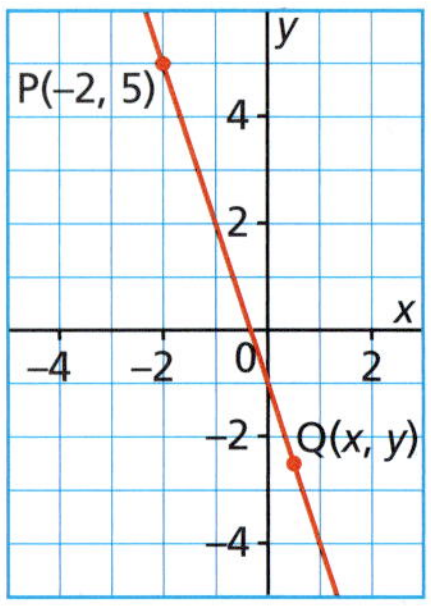

$$\text{Slope} = \frac{\text{rise}}{\text{run}}$$

$$m = \frac{y - 5}{x - (-2)}$$

$$m = \frac{y - 5}{x + 2}$$ Substitute: $m = -3$

$$-3 = \frac{y - 5}{x + 2}$$ Multiply each side by $(x + 2)$.

$$-3(x + 2) = (x + 2)\left(\frac{y - 5}{x + 2}\right)$$ Simplify.

$$-3(x + 2) = y - 5$$

$$y - 5 = -3(x + 2)$$

This equation is called the **slope-point form;** both the slope and the coordinates of a point on the line can be identified from the equation.

We can use this strategy to develop a formula for the slope-point form for the equation of a line.

This line has slope m and passes through the point P(x_1, y_1).
Another point on the line is Q(x, y).

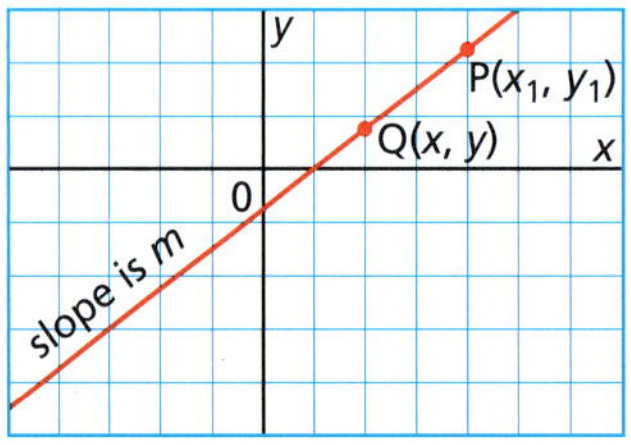

The slope, m, of the line is:

$$m = \frac{\text{rise}}{\text{run}}$$

$$m = \frac{y - y_1}{x - x_1}$$ Multiply each side by $(x - x_1)$.

$$m(x - x_1) = (x - x_1)\left(\frac{y - y_1}{x - x_1}\right)$$ Simplify.

$$m(x - x_1) = y - y_1$$

$$y - y_1 = m(x - x_1)$$

Slope-Point Form of the Equation of a Linear Function

The equation of a line that passes through $P(x_1, y_1)$ and has slope m is:
$y - y_1 = m(x - x_1)$

Example 1 Graphing a Linear Function Given Its Equation in Slope-Point Form

a) Describe the graph of the linear function with this equation:

$$y - 2 = \frac{1}{3}(x + 4)$$

b) Graph the equation.

SOLUTION

a) Compare the given equation with the equation in slope-point form.

$$y - y_1 = m(x - x_1)$$
$$y - 2 = \frac{1}{3}(x + 4)$$

To match the slope-point form, rewrite the given equation so the operations are subtraction.

$$y - 2 = \frac{1}{3}[x - (-4)]$$
$$y - y_1 = m(x - x_1)$$

So, $y_1 = 2$

$m = \frac{1}{3}$

$x_1 = -4$

The graph passes through $(-4, 2)$ and has slope $\frac{1}{3}$.

b) Plot the point $P(-4, 2)$ on a grid and use the slope of $\frac{1}{3}$ to plot another point. Draw a line through the points.

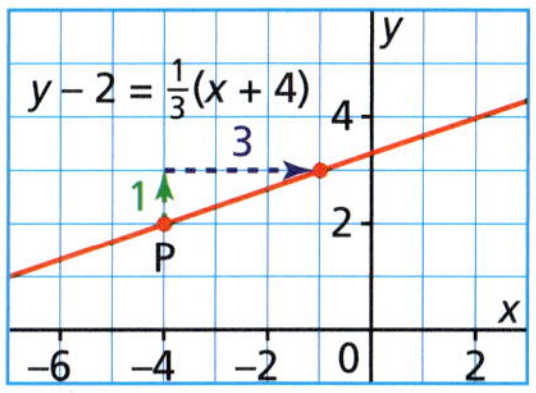

CHECK YOUR UNDERSTANDING

1. a) Describe the graph of the linear function with this equation:

$$y + 1 = -\frac{1}{2}(x - 2)$$

b) Graph the equation.

[Answer: a) slope $-\frac{1}{2}$; passes through $(2, -1)$]

Example 2 Writing an Equation Using a Point on the Line and Its Slope

a) Write an equation in slope-point form for this line.

b) Write the equation in part a in slope-intercept form. What is the y-intercept of this line?

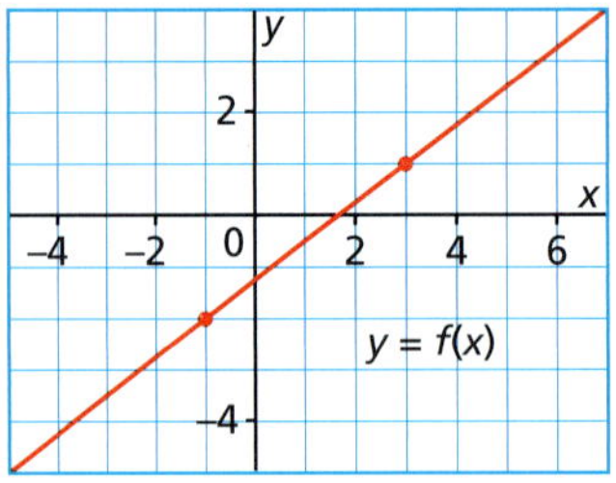

SOLUTION

a) Identify the coordinates of one point on the line and calculate the slope.
The coordinates of one point are $(-1, -2)$.
To calculate the slope, m, use:

$$m = \frac{\text{rise}}{\text{run}}$$

$$m = \frac{3}{4}$$

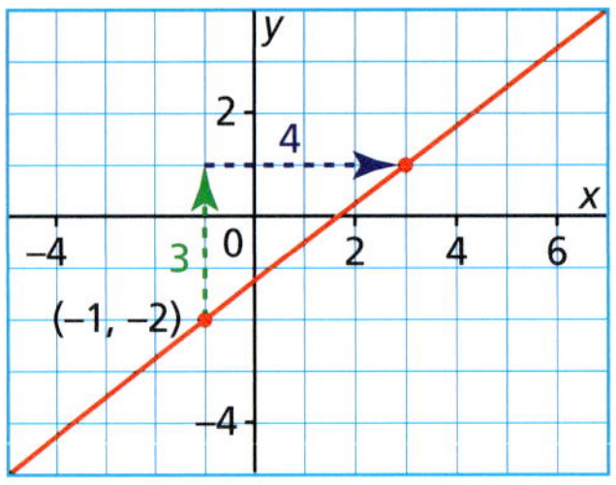

Use the slope-point form of the equation.

$$y - y_1 = m(x - x_1)$$ Substitute: $y_1 = -2$, $x_1 = -1$, and $m = \frac{3}{4}$

$$y - (-2) = \frac{3}{4}[x - (-1)]$$

$$y + 2 = \frac{3}{4}(x + 1)$$

In slope-point form, the equation of the line is:

$$y + 2 = \frac{3}{4}(x + 1)$$

b) $y + 2 = \frac{3}{4}(x + 1)$ Remove brackets.

$$y + 2 = \frac{3}{4}x + \frac{3}{4}$$ Solve for y.

$$y = \frac{3}{4}x + \frac{3}{4} - 2$$ Simplify.

$$y = \frac{3}{4}x - \frac{5}{4}$$

In slope-intercept form, the equation of the line is: $y = \frac{3}{4}x - \frac{5}{4}$

From the equation, the y-intercept is $-\frac{5}{4}$.

CHECK YOUR UNDERSTANDING

2. a) Write an equation in slope-point form for this line.

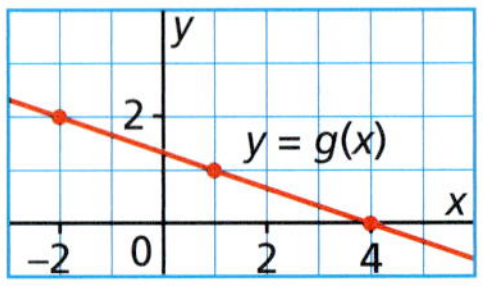

b) Write the equation in part a in slope-intercept form. What is the y-intercept of this line?

[Answers: a) sample answer: $y - 1 = -\frac{1}{3}(x - 1)$
b) $y = -\frac{1}{3}x + \frac{4}{3}$; $\frac{4}{3}$]

The coordinates of another point on the line are (3, 1). Show that these coordinates produce the same equation in slope-intercept form.

Explain how the general expression for the slope of a line can help you remember the equation $y - y_1 = m(x - x_1)$.

We can use the coordinates of two points that satisfy a linear function, $P(x_1, y_1)$ and $Q(x_2, y_2)$, to write an equation for the function.

We write the slope of the graph of the function in two ways:

$$m = \frac{y - y_1}{x - x_1} \quad \text{and} \quad m = \frac{y_2 - y_1}{x_2 - x_1}$$

So, an equation is: $\frac{y - y_1}{x - x_1} = \frac{y_2 - y_1}{x_2 - x_1}$

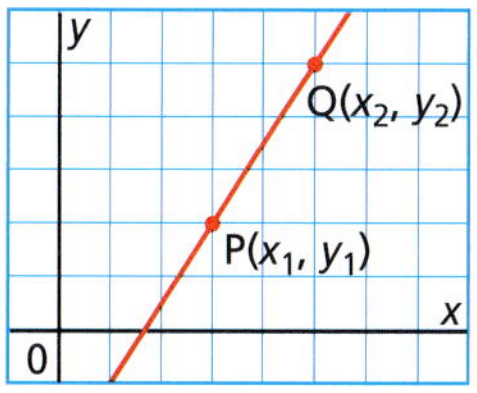

Example 3 Writing an Equation of a Linear Function Given Two Points

The sum of the angles, s degrees, in a polygon is a linear function of the number of sides, n, of the polygon. The sum of the angles in a triangle is 180°. The sum of the angles in a quadrilateral is 360°.

a) Write a linear equation to represent this function.

b) Use the equation to determine the sum of the angles in a dodecagon.

SOLUTION

a) $s = f(n)$, so two points on the graph have coordinates T(3, 180) and Q(4, 360)

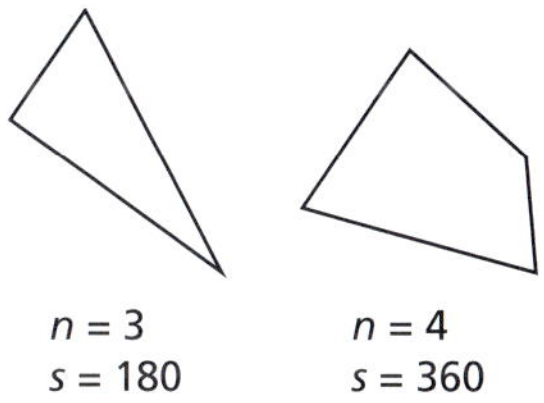

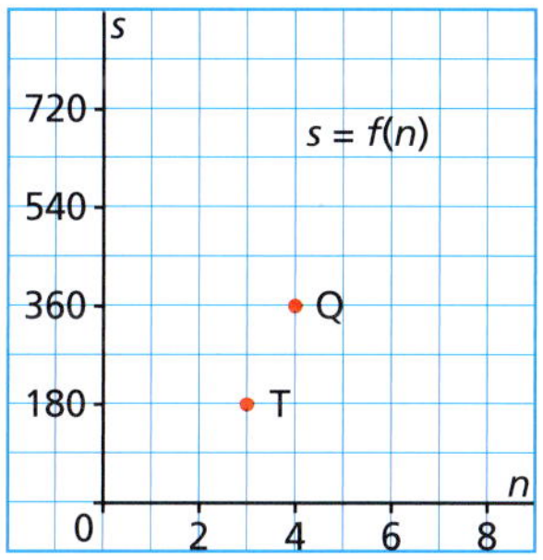

Use this form for the equation of a linear function:

$$\frac{s - s_1}{n - n_1} = \frac{s_2 - s_1}{n_2 - n_1}$$ Substitute: $s_1 = 180$, $n_1 = 3$, $s_2 = 360$, and $n_2 = 4$

$$\frac{s - 180}{n - 3} = \frac{360 - 180}{4 - 3}$$ Simplify.

$$\frac{s - 180}{n - 3} = 180$$ Multiply each side by $(n - 3)$.

$$(n - 3)\left(\frac{s - 180}{n - 3}\right) = 180(n - 3)$$

$$s - 180 = 180(n - 3)$$ This is the slope-point form of the equation. Simplify.

$$s - 180 = 180n - 540$$

$$s = 180n - 360$$ This is the slope-intercept form of the equation.

(Solution continues.)

CHECK YOUR UNDERSTANDING

3. A temperature in degrees Celsius, c, is a linear function of the temperature in degrees Fahrenheit, f. The boiling point of water is 100°C and 212°F. The freezing point of water is 0°C and 32°F.

a) Write a linear equation to represent this function.

b) Use the equation to determine the temperature in degrees Celsius at which iron melts, 2795°F.

[Answers: a) $c - 100 = \frac{5}{9}(f - 212)$, or $c = \frac{5}{9}f - \frac{160}{9}$ b) 1535°C]

Why is it possible for equations of a linear function to look different but still represent the same function?

b) A dodecagon has 12 sides.
Use:
$s = 180n - 360$ Substitute: $n = 12$
$s = 180(12) - 360$
$s = 1800$
The sum of the angles in a dodecagon is 1800°.

In part b, why does it make sense to use the slope-intercept form instead of the slope-point form?

Example 4 Writing an Equation of a Line That Is Parallel or Perpendicular to a Given Line

Write an equation for the line that passes through R(1, −1) and is:

a) parallel to the line $y = \frac{2}{3}x - 5$

b) perpendicular to the line $y = \frac{2}{3}x - 5$

SOLUTION

Sketch the line with equation: $y = \frac{2}{3}x - 5$, and mark a point at R(1, −1).

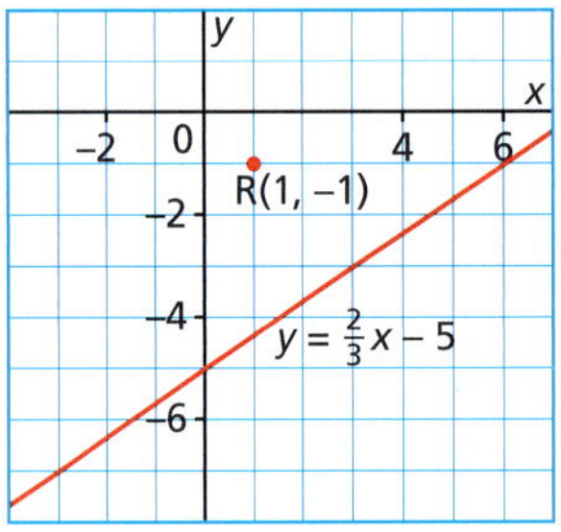

Compare the equation: $y = \frac{2}{3}x - 5$ with the equation: $y = mx + b$

The slope of the line is $\frac{2}{3}$.

a) Any line parallel to $y = \frac{2}{3}x - 5$ has slope $\frac{2}{3}$.

The required line passes through R(1, −1).

Use:

$y - y_1 = m(x - x_1)$ Substitute: $y_1 = -1$, $x_1 = 1$, and $m = \frac{2}{3}$

$y - (-1) = \frac{2}{3}(x - 1)$ Simplify.

$y + 1 = \frac{2}{3}(x - 1)$

The line that is parallel to the line $y = \frac{2}{3}x - 5$ and passes through R(1, −1) has equation: $y + 1 = \frac{2}{3}(x - 1)$

CHECK YOUR UNDERSTANDING

4. Write an equation for the line that passes through S(2, −3) and is:

a) parallel to the line $y = 3x + 5$

b) perpendicular to the line $y = 3x + 5$

[Answers: a) $y + 3 = 3(x - 2)$
b) $y + 3 = -\frac{1}{3}(x - 2)$]

What other strategies could you use to write an equation for each line?

Write each equation in slope-intercept form.

b) Any line perpendicular to $y = \frac{2}{3}x - 5$ has a slope that is the negative reciprocal of $\frac{2}{3}$; that is, its slope is $-\frac{3}{2}$.

The required line passes through R(1, −1).

Use:

$y - y_1 = m(x - x_1)$ Substitute: $y_1 = -1$, $x_1 = 1$, and $m = -\frac{3}{2}$

$y - (-1) = -\frac{3}{2}(x - 1)$ Simplify.

$y + 1 = -\frac{3}{2}(x - 1)$

The line that is perpendicular to the line $y = \frac{2}{3}x - 5$ and passes through the point R(1, −1) has equation: $y + 1 = -\frac{3}{2}(x - 1)$

To graph the equation of a linear function using technology, the equation needs to be rearranged to isolate y on the left side of the equation; that is, it must be in the form $y = f(x)$. So, if an equation is given in slope-point form, it must be rearranged before graphing. Here is the graph from *Example 4*, part a, on a graphing calculator and on a computer with graphing software.

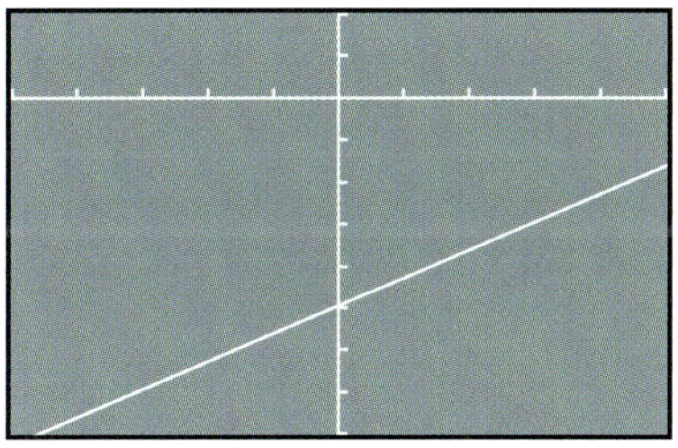

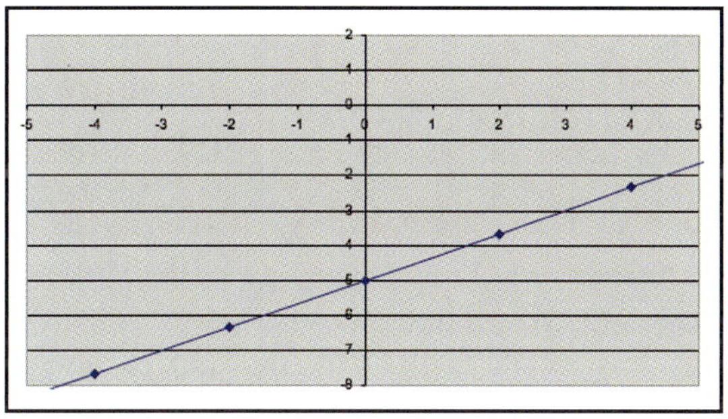

Discuss the Ideas

1. How does the fact that the slope of a line is constant lead to the slope-point form of the equation of a line?

2. How can you use the slope-point form of the equation of a line to sketch a graph of the line?

3. How can you determine the slope-point form of the equation of a line given a graph of the line?

Exercises

A

4. For each equation, identify the slope of the line it represents and the coordinates of a point on the line.

a) $y - 5 = -4(x - 1)$
b) $y + 7 = 3(x - 8)$
c) $y + 11 = (x + 15)$
d) $y = 5(x - 2)$
e) $y + 6 = \frac{4}{7}(x + 3)$
f) $y - 21 = -\frac{8}{5}(x + 16)$

5. Write an equation for the graph of a linear function that:

a) has slope -5 and passes through $P(-4, 2)$
b) has slope 7 and passes through $Q(6, -8)$
c) has slope $-\frac{3}{4}$ and passes through $R(7, -5)$
d) has slope 0 and passes through $S(3, -8)$

6. Graph each line.

a) The line passes through $T(-4, 1)$ and has slope 3.
b) The line passes through $U(3, -4)$ and has slope -2.
c) The line passes through $V(2, 3)$ and has slope $-\frac{1}{2}$.
d) The line has x-intercept -5 and slope $\frac{3}{4}$.

B

7. Describe the graph of the linear function with each equation, then graph the equation.

a) $y + 2 = -3(x - 4)$
b) $y + 4 = 2(x + 3)$
c) $y - 3 = (x + 5)$
d) $y = -(x - 2)$

8. A line passes through $D(-3, 5)$ and has slope -4.

a) Why is $y - 5 = -4(x + 3)$ an equation of this line?
b) Why is $y = -4x - 7$ an equation of this line?

9. a) For each line, write an equation in slope-point form.

i)

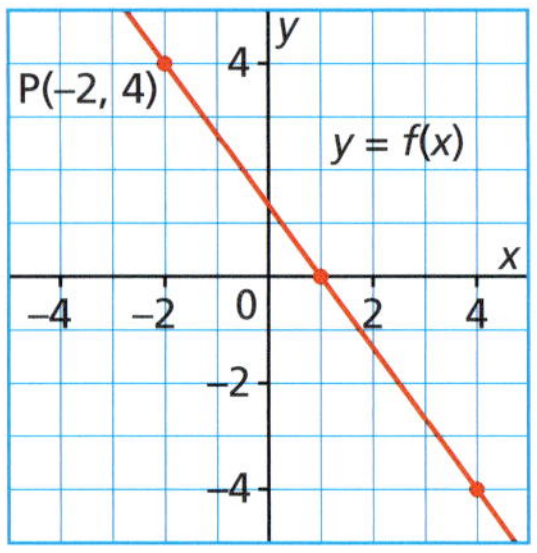

ii)

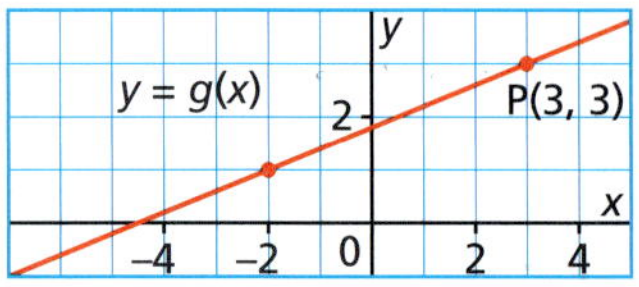

iii)

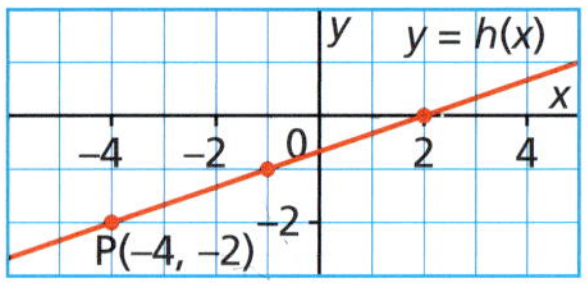

iv)

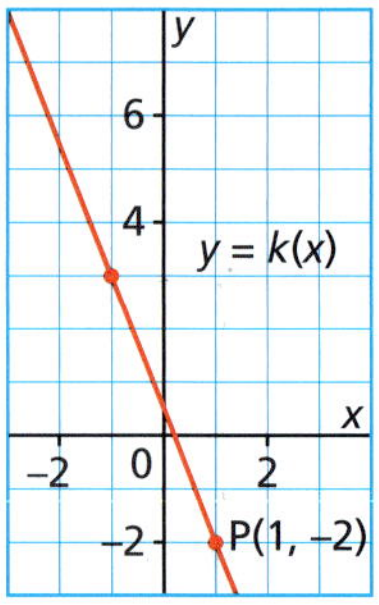

b) Write each equation in part a in slope-intercept form, then determine the x- and y-intercepts of each graph.

10. The speed of sound in air is a linear function of the air temperature. When the air temperature is 10°C, the speed of sound is 337 m/s. When the air temperature is 30°C, the speed of sound is 349 m/s.

a) Write a linear equation to represent this function.
b) Use the equation to determine the speed of sound when the air temperature is 0°C.

11. Write an equation for the line that passes through each pair of points. Write each equation in slope-point form and in slope-intercept form.

a) $B(-2, -5)$ and $C(1, 1)$
b) $Q(-4, 7)$ and $R(5, -2)$
c) $U(-3, -7)$ and $V(2, 8)$
d) $H(-7, -1)$ and $J(-5, -5)$

12. Which equation matches each graph? Describe each graph in terms of its slope and y-intercept.

a) $y + 3 = 2(x - 1)$ **b)** $y - 3 = (x - 2)$

c) $y - 3 = 2(x + 1)$ **d)** $y + 3 = -(x + 2)$

Graph A

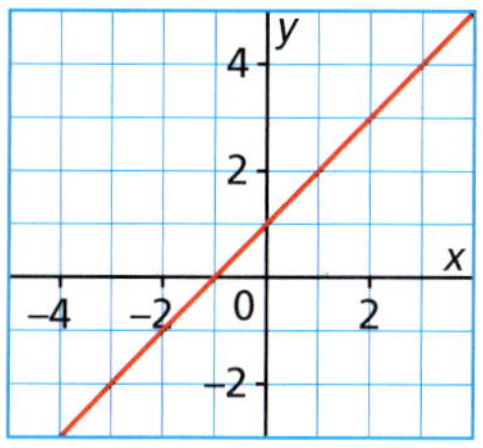

Graph B

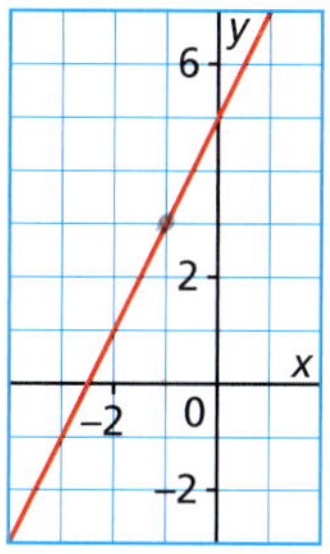

Graph C

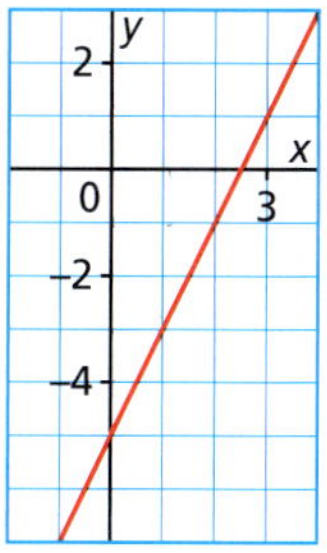

Graph D

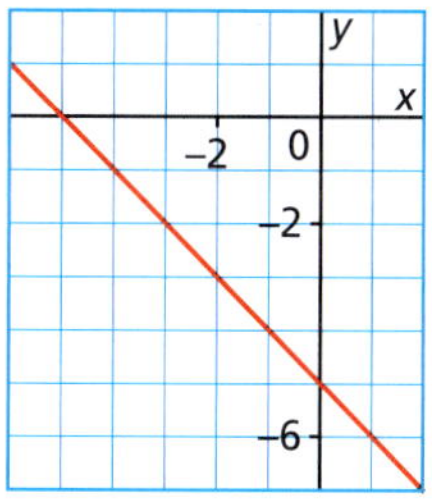

13. How does the graph of $y + y_1 = m(x + x_1)$ compare with the graph of $y - y_1 = m(x - x_1)$? Include examples in your explanation.

14. Match each graph with its equation. Justify your choice.

a)

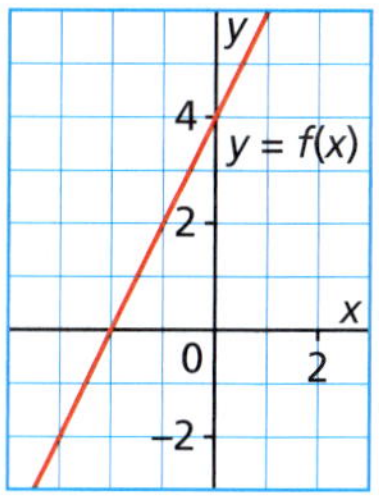

$y + 1 = 2(x - 2)$

$y + 2 = 2(x - 1)$

$y - 2 = 2(x + 1)$

$y + 1 = -2(x - 2)$

b)

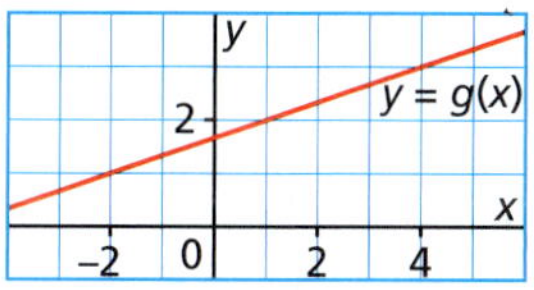

$y - 1 = \frac{1}{3}(x - 2)$

$y + 2 = \frac{1}{3}(x + 1)$

$y - 1 = 3(x - 2)$

$y - 2 = \frac{1}{3}(x - 1)$

c)

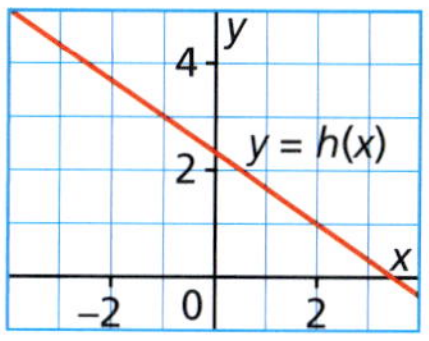

$y - 1 = \frac{2}{3}(x - 2)$

$y - 1 = \frac{3}{2}(x - 2)$

$y - 1 = -\frac{2}{3}(x - 2)$

$y - 2 = -\frac{2}{3}(x - 1)$

15. Use a graphing calculator or a computer with graphing software. Graph each equation. Sketch or print the graph. Write instructions that another student could follow to get the same display.

a) $y + \frac{2}{7} = \frac{3}{8}(x - 5)$

b) $y - \frac{10}{3} = -\frac{2}{9}(x + 11)$

c) $y + 1.4 = 0.375(x + 4)$

d) $y - 2.35 = -0.5(x - 6.3)$

16. Chloé conducted a science experiment where she poured liquid into a graduated cylinder, then measured the mass of the cylinder and liquid. Here are Chloé's data.

Volume of Liquid (mL)	Mass of Cylinder and Liquid (g)
10	38.9
20	51.5

a) When these data are graphed, what is the slope of the line and what does it represent?

b) Choose variables to represent the volume of the liquid, and the mass of the cylinder and liquid. Write an equation that relates these variables.

c) Use your equation to determine the mass of the cylinder and liquid when the volume of liquid is 30 mL.

d) Chloé forgot to record the mass of the empty graduated cylinder. Determine this mass. Explain your strategy.

17. In 2005, the Potash Corporation of Saskatchewan sold 8.2 million tonnes of potash. In 2007, due to increased demand, the corporation sold 9.4 million tonnes. Assume the mass of potash sold is a linear function of time.

a) Write an equation that describes the relation between the mass of potash and the time in years since 2005. Explain your strategy.

b) Predict the sales of potash in 2010 and 2015. What assumptions did you make?

18. In Alberta, the student population in francophone schools from January 2001 to January 2006 increased by approximately 198 students per year. In January 2003, there were approximately 3470 students enrolled in francophone schools.

a) Write an equation in slope-point form to represent the number of students enrolled in francophone schools as a function of the number of years after 2001.

b) Use the equation in part a to estimate the number of students in francophone schools in January 2005. Use a different strategy to check your answer.

19. A line passes through G(−3, 11) and H(4, −3).

a) Determine the slope of line GH.

b) Write an equation for line GH using point G and the slope.

c) Write an equation for line GH using point H and the slope.

d) Verify that the two equations are equivalent. What strategy did you use? What different strategy could you have used to verify that the equations are equivalent?

20. a) Write an equation for the line that passes through D(−5, −3) and is:

i) parallel to the line $y = -\frac{4}{3}x + 1$

ii) perpendicular to the line $y = -\frac{4}{3}x + 1$

b) Compare the equations in part a. How are they alike? How are they different?

21. Write an equation for the line that passes through C(1, −2) and is:

a) parallel to the line $y = 2x + 3$

b) perpendicular to the line $y = 2x + 3$

22. Write an equation for the line that passes through E(2, 6) and is:

a) parallel to the line $y - 3 = -\frac{5}{2}(x + 2)$

b) perpendicular to the line $y - 3 = -\frac{5}{2}(x + 2)$

How do you know your equations are correct?

23. Write an equation for each line.

a) The line has x-intercept 4 and is parallel to the line with equation $y = \frac{3}{5}x - 7$.

b) The line passes through F(4, −1) and is perpendicular to the line that has x-intercept −3 and y-intercept 6.

24. Two perpendicular lines intersect on the y-axis. One line has equation $y - 3 = \frac{2}{9}(x + 5)$. What is the equation of the other line?

25. Two perpendicular lines intersect at K(−2, −5). One line has equation $y = -\frac{5}{3}x - \frac{25}{3}$. What is the equation of the other line?

C

26. Two perpendicular lines intersect at M(3, 5). What might their equations be? How many possible pairs of equations are there?

27. The slope-intercept form of the equation of a line is a special case of the slope-point form of the equation, where the point is at the y-intercept. Use the slope-point form to show that a line with slope m and intersecting the y-axis at b has equation $y = mx + b$.

Reflect

How is the slope-point form of the equation of a line different from the slope-intercept form? How would you use each form to graph a linear function? Include examples in your explanation.

CHECKPOINT 2

Connections

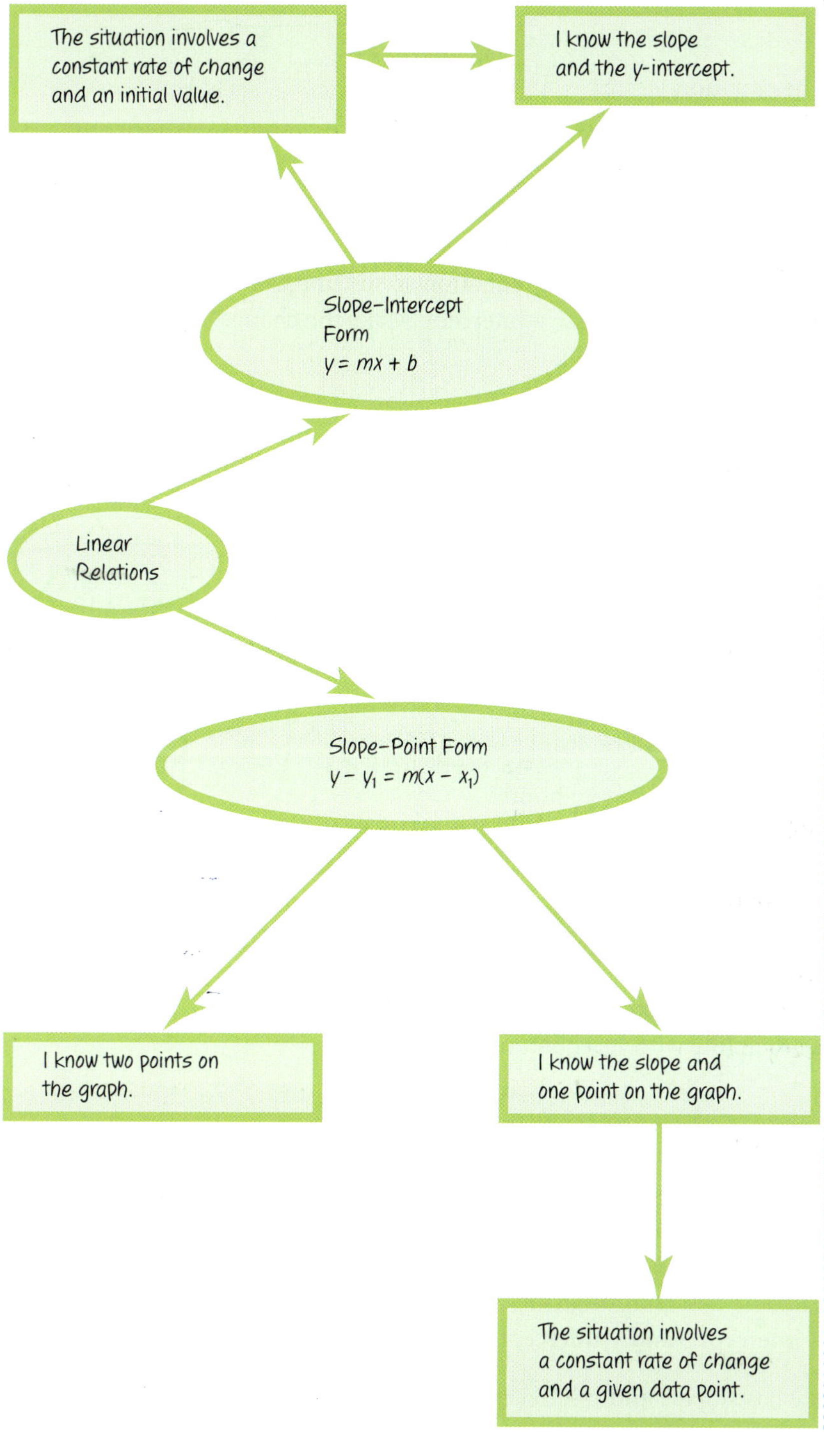

Concept Development

- **In Lesson 6.3**
  - You used technology to explore how changes in the constants m and b in the equation $y = mx + b$ affect the graph of the function.

- **In Lesson 6.4**
  - You used the slope and y-intercept of the graph of a linear function to write the equation of the function in slope-intercept form.
  - You graphed a linear function given its equation in slope-intercept form.
  - You used the graph of a linear function to write an equation for the function in slope-intercept form.

- **In Lesson 6.5**
  - You developed the slope-point form of the equation of a linear function.
  - You graphed a linear function given its equation in slope-point form.
  - You wrote the equation of a linear function after determining the slope of its graph and the coordinates of a point on its graph.
  - You wrote the equation of a linear function given the coordinates of two points on its graph.
  - You rewrote the equation of a linear function from slope-point form to slope-intercept form.

Assess Your Understanding

6.3

1. For the equation $y = \frac{3}{2}x - 4$:

a) Use a graphing calculator or a computer with graphing software to graph it.

b) Explain how to change the equation so the line will have a greater slope, then a lesser slope. Make the change.

c) Explain how to change the equation so the line will have a greater y-intercept, then a lesser y-intercept. Make the change.

Sketch or print each graph.

6.4

2. This graph represents Eric's snowmobile ride.

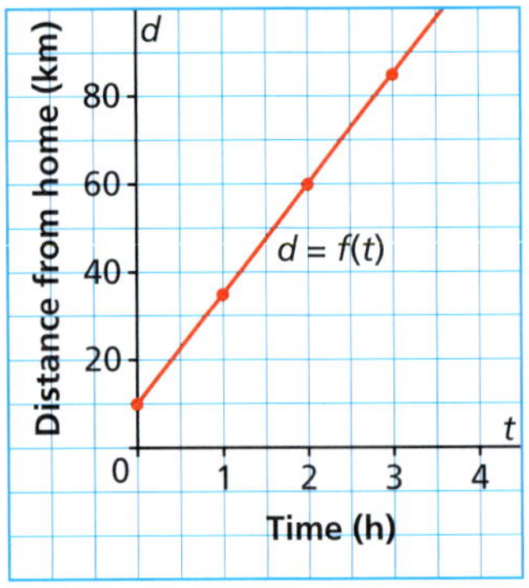

a) Determine the slope and d-intercept. What does each represent?

b) Write an equation to represent the graph, then verify the equation.

c) Use the equation to answer each question below.

i) How far was Eric from home after he had travelled $2\frac{1}{4}$ hours?

ii) How long did it take Eric to travel 45 km from home?

6.5

3. Graph each line. Explain your strategy. Label each line with its equation.

a) $y + 2 = 3(x - 4)$

b) $y - 2 = -\frac{1}{2}(x - 6)$

c) The line passes through D$(-4, 7)$ and E$(6, -1)$.

d) The line passes through F$(4, -3)$ and is perpendicular to the line with equation $y + 4 = 2(x + 2)$.

e) The line passes through G$(-7, -2)$ and is parallel to the line that has x-intercept 5 and y-intercept 3.

4. A line has slope 2 and y-intercept 3.

a) Write an equation for this line using the slope-intercept form.

b) Write an equation for the line using the slope-point form.

c) Compare the two equations. How are they alike? How are they different?

6.6 General Form of the Equation for a Linear Relation

LESSON FOCUS

Relate the graph of a linear function to its equation in general form.

Make Connections

A softball team may field any combination of 9 female and male players. There must be at least one female and one male on the field at any time. What are the possible combinations for female and male players on the field?

Construct Understanding

TRY THIS

Work with a partner.

Holly works in a furniture plant. She takes 30 min to assemble a table and 15 min to assemble a chair. Holly works 8 h a day, not including meals and breaks.

A. Make a table of values for the possible numbers of tables and chairs that Holly could assemble in one day.

Number of Tables	Number of Chairs

B. Graph the data. Use graphing technology if it is available. Describe the graph. What type of relation have you graphed? How do you know?

C. What do the intercepts represent?

D. Choose variables to represent the number of tables and number of chairs. Write an equation for your graph.

E. Suppose you interchanged the columns in the table, then graphed the data. How would the graph change? How would the equation change?

This graph is described by the equation $2x - 3y = 12$.

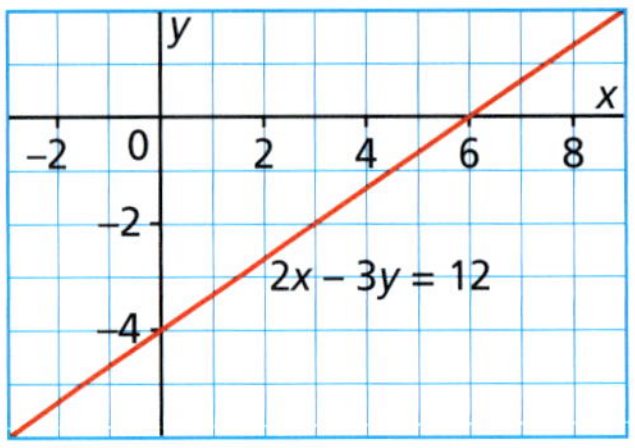

The equation $2x - 3y = 12$ is written in *standard form.*
The coefficients and constant terms are integers.
The x- and y-terms are on the left side of the equation, and the constant term is on the right side.
We may move the constant term to the left side of the equation:

$$2x - 3y = 12$$
$$2x - 3y - 12 = 12 - 12$$
$$2x - 3y - 12 = 0$$

The equation is now in **general form.**

What values of A, B, C, would produce a vertical line? A horizontal line?

General Form of the Equation of a Linear Relation

$Ax + By + C = 0$ is the general form of the equation of a line, where A is a whole number, and B and C are integers.

Consider what happens to the general form of the equation in each of the following cases:

- When $A = 0$:
  $Ax + By + C = 0$ becomes
  $By + C = 0$ Solve for y.
  $By = -C$ Divide each side by B.
  $y = \frac{-C}{B}$

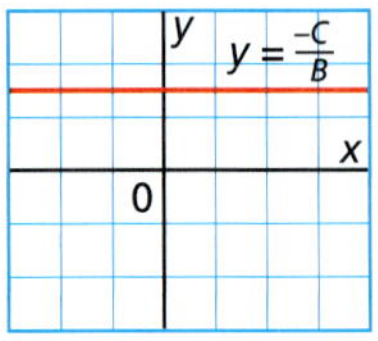

$\frac{-C}{B}$ is a constant, and the graph of $y = \frac{-C}{B}$ is a horizontal line.

- When $B = 0$:

$Ax + By + C = 0$ becomes

$$Ax + C = 0 \quad \text{Solve for } x.$$
$$Ax = -C \quad \text{Divide each side by } A.$$
$$x = \frac{-C}{A}$$

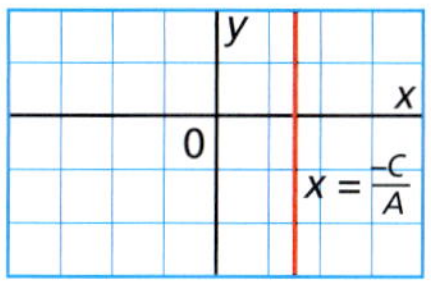

$\frac{-C}{A}$ is a constant, and the graph of $x = \frac{-C}{A}$ is a vertical line.

Example 1 Rewriting an Equation in General Form

Write each equation in general form.

a) $y = -\frac{2}{3}x + 4$

b) $y - 1 = \frac{3}{5}(x + 2)$

SOLUTION

a)

$$y = -\frac{2}{3}x + 4 \quad \text{Multiply each side by 3.}$$

$$3y = 3\left(-\frac{2}{3}x + 4\right) \quad \text{Remove the brackets.}$$

$$3y = 3\left(-\frac{2}{3}x\right) + 3(4)$$

$$3y = -2x + 12 \quad \text{Collect all the terms on the left side of the equation.}$$

$$2x + 3y - 12 = 0 \quad \text{This is the general form of the equation.}$$

b)

$$y - 1 = \frac{3}{5}(x + 2) \quad \text{Multiply each side by 5.}$$

$$5(y - 1) = 5\left(\frac{3}{5}\right)(x + 2) \quad \text{Remove the brackets.}$$

$$5y - 5 = 3(x + 2)$$

$$5y - 5 = 3x + 6 \quad \text{Collect like terms.}$$

$$5y = 3x + 11 \quad \text{Collect all the terms on the right side of the equation.}$$

$$0 = 3x - 5y + 11$$

The general form of the equation is: $3x - 5y + 11 = 0$

CHECK YOUR UNDERSTANDING

1. Write each equation in general form.

a) $y = -\frac{1}{4}x + 3$

b) $y + 2 = \frac{3}{2}(x - 4)$

[Answers: a) $x + 4y - 12 = 0$
b) $3x - 2y - 16 = 0$]

For the two equations, why were the terms collected on different sides of the equation?

When an equation of a line is written in general form, can all the terms be positive? Can all the terms be negative? Explain.

Example 2 Graphing a Line in General Form

a) Determine the x- and y-intercepts of the line whose equation is: $3x + 2y - 18 = 0$

b) Graph the line.

c) Verify that the graph is correct.

SOLUTION

a) To determine the x-intercept:

$$3x + 2y - 18 = 0 \quad \text{Substitute: } y = 0$$
$$3x + 2(0) - 18 = 0 \quad \text{Solve for } x.$$
$$3x = 18$$
$$\frac{3x}{3} = \frac{18}{3}$$
$$x = 6$$

The x-intercept is 6 and is described by the point (6, 0).

To determine the y-intercept:

$$3x + 2y - 18 = 0 \quad \text{Substitute: } x = 0$$
$$3(0) + 2y - 18 = 0 \quad \text{Solve for } y.$$
$$2y = 18$$
$$\frac{2y}{2} = \frac{18}{2}$$
$$y = 9$$

The y-intercept is 9 and is described by the point (0, 9).

b) On a grid, plot the points that represent the intercepts. Draw a line through the points.

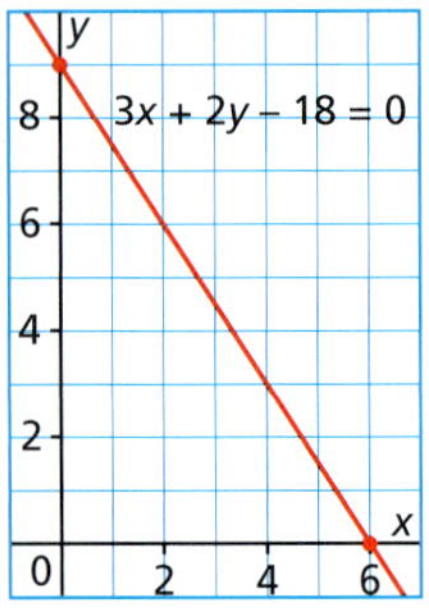

CHECK YOUR UNDERSTANDING

2. a) Determine the x- and y-intercepts of the line whose equation is: $x + 3y + 9 = 0$

b) Graph the line.

c) Verify that the graph is correct.

[Answer: a) −9, −3]

Why is it a good idea to check that the graph is correct when you use the intercepts to draw the graph?

c) The point T(2, 6) appears to be on the graph.
Verify that T(2, 6) satisfies the equation.
Substitute $x = 2$ and $y = 6$ in the equation $3x + 2y - 18 = 0$.

$$\begin{aligned} \text{L.S.} &= 3x + 2y - 18 \qquad\qquad \text{R.S.} = 0 \\ &= 3(2) + 2(6) - 18 \\ &= 6 + 12 - 18 \\ &= 0 \end{aligned}$$

Since the left side is equal to the right side, the point satisfies the equation and the graph is probably correct.

Example 3 Determining the Slope of a Line Given Its Equation in General Form

Determine the slope of the line with this equation:
$3x - 2y - 16 = 0$

SOLUTION

Rewrite the equation in slope-intercept form.

$$\begin{aligned} 3x - 2y - 16 &= 0 && \text{Solve for } y\text{. Subtract } 3x \text{ from each side.} \\ -2y - 16 &= -3x && \text{Add 16 to each side.} \\ -2y &= -3x + 16 && \text{Divide each side by } -2. \\ y &= \frac{-3x}{-2} + \frac{16}{-2} \\ y &= \frac{3}{2}x - 8 \end{aligned}$$

From the equation, the slope of the line is $\frac{3}{2}$.

CHECK YOUR UNDERSTANDING

3. Determine the slope of the line with this equation:
$5x - 2y + 12 = 0$

[Answer: $\frac{5}{2}$]

If an equation is given in general form, it must be rearranged to the form $y = f(x)$ before graphing using technology. Here is the graph from *Example 3* on a graphing calculator and on a computer with graphing software.

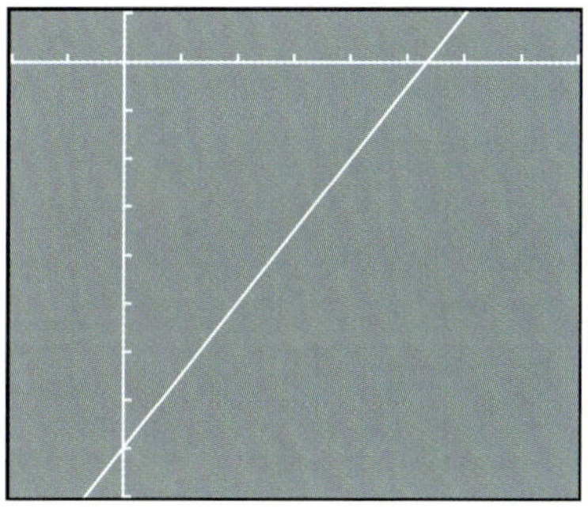

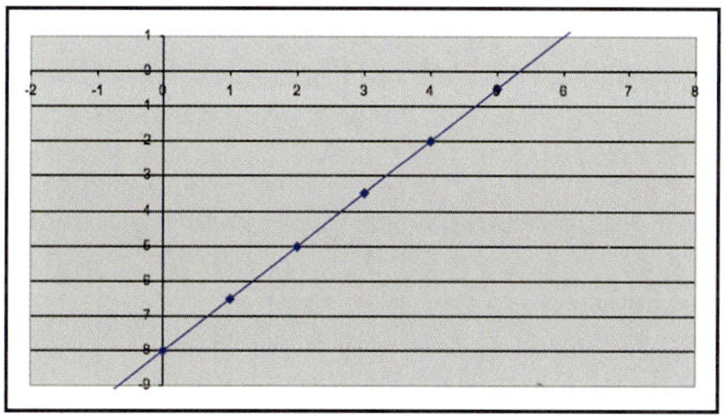

Example 4 Determining an Equation from a Graph of Generated Data

Peanuts cost \$2 per 100 g and raisins cost \$1 per 100 g. Devon has \$10 to purchase both these items.

a) Generate some data for this relation.

b) Graph the data.

c) Write an equation for the relation in general form.

d) i) Will Devon spend exactly \$10 if she buys 300 g of peanuts and 400 g of raisins?

ii) Will Devon spend exactly \$10 if she buys 400 g of peanuts and 300 g of raisins?

Use the graph and the equation to justify the answers.

SOLUTION

a) If Devon buys only peanuts at \$2 for 100 g, she can buy 500 g. If Devon buys only raisins at \$1 for 100 g, she can buy 1000 g. If Devon buys 200 g of peanuts, they cost \$4; so she can buy 600 g of raisins for \$6.

Mass of Peanuts, p (g)	Mass of Raisins, r (g)
500	0
0	1000
200	600

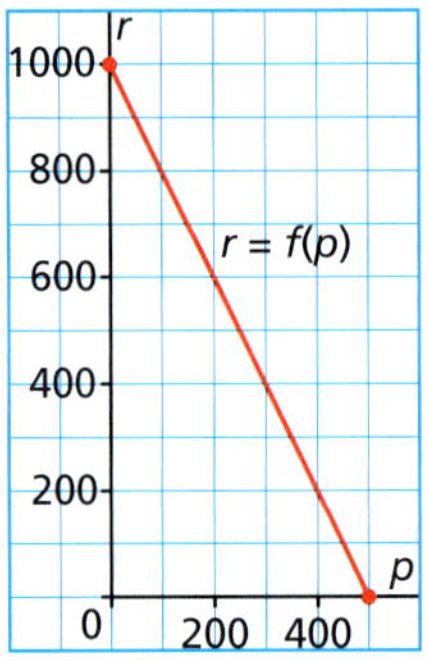

b) Join the points because Devon can buy any mass of items she likes.

c) Use the coordinates of two points on the line: (500, 0) and (0, 1000) Use the slope-point form with these coordinates:

$$\frac{r - r_1}{p - p_1} = \frac{r_2 - r_1}{p_2 - p_1}$$

Substitute: $r_1 = 0$, $p_1 = 500$, $r_2 = 1000$, and $p_2 = 0$

$$\frac{r - 0}{p - 500} = \frac{1000 - 0}{0 - 500}$$

$$\frac{r}{p - 500} = -2$$

Multiply each side by $(p - 500)$.

$$r = -2(p - 500)$$

$$r = -2p + 1000$$

Collect all the terms on the left side of the equation.

$$2p + r - 1000 = 0$$

CHECK YOUR UNDERSTANDING

4. Akeego is making a ribbon shirt. She has 60 cm of ribbon that she will cut into 5 pieces with 2 different lengths: 2 pieces have the same length and the remaining 3 pieces also have equal lengths.

a) Generate some data for this relation showing the possible lengths of the pieces.

b) Graph the data.

c) Write an equation for the relation in general form.

d) i) Can each of 2 pieces be 18 cm long and each of 3 pieces be 3 cm long?

ii) Can each of 2 pieces be 3 cm long and each of 3 pieces be 18 cm long?

Use the graph and the equation to justify your answers.

[Sample Answers: a) (2, 27), (4, 24), (6, 21) c) $3x + 2y - 60 = 0$ d) i) no ii) yes]

What other strategies could you use to determine the equation of the line?

Suppose you interchanged the coordinates and graphed $p = f(r)$. How would the graph change? How would the equation change?

d) i) Use the graph to determine whether Devon will spend exactly \$10 if she buys 300 g of peanuts and 400 g of raisins.
300 g of peanuts and 400 g of raisins are represented by the point (300, 400).
Plot this point on the grid. Since this point lies on the line, Devon can buy these masses of peanuts and raisins.

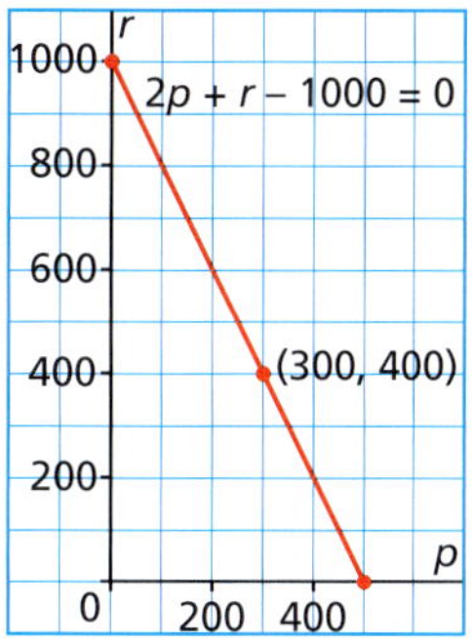

Check whether the point (300, 400) satisfies the equation:
$2p + r - 1000 = 0$
Substitute: $p = 300$ and $r = 400$

$$\begin{aligned} \text{L.S.} &= 2p + r - 1000 \qquad\qquad \text{R.S.} = 0 \\ &= 2(300) + 400 - 1000 \\ &= 0 \end{aligned}$$

Since the left side is equal to the right side, the point (300, 400) does satisfy the equation.

ii) Use the graph to determine whether Devon will spend exactly \$10 if she buys 400 g of peanuts and 300 g of raisins.
400 g of peanuts and 300 g of raisins are represented by the point (400, 300). Plot this point on the grid. Since this point does not lie on the line, Devon cannot buy these masses of peanuts and raisins.

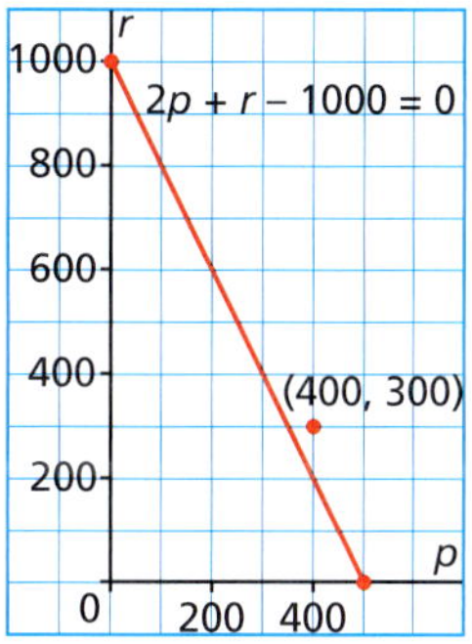

Check whether the point (400, 300) satisfies the equation:
$2p + r - 1000 = 0$
Substitute: $p = 400$ and $r = 300$

$$\begin{aligned} \text{L.S.} &= 2p + r - 1000 \qquad\qquad \text{R.S.} = 0 \\ &= 2(400) + 300 - 1000 \\ &= 100 \end{aligned}$$

Since the left side is not equal to the right side, the point (400, 300) does not satisfy the equation.

Discuss the Ideas

1. What steps would you use to sketch the graph of a linear relation in general form?
2. Is it easier to graph a linear relation with its equation in general form or slope-intercept form? Use examples to support your opinion.
3. An equation in general form may be rewritten in slope-intercept form. How is this process like solving a linear equation?

Exercises

A

4. In which form is each equation written?
   a) $8x - 3y = 52$
   b) $9x + 4y + 21 = 0$
   c) $y = 4x + 7$
   d) $y - 3 = 5(x + 7)$

5. Determine the x-intercept and the y-intercept for the graph of each equation.
   a) $8x - 3y = 24$
   b) $7x + 8y = 56$
   c) $4x - 11y = 88$
   d) $2x - 9y = 27$

6. Write each equation in general form.
   a) $4x + 3y = 36$
   b) $2x - y = 7$
   c) $y = -2x + 6$
   d) $y = 5x - 1$

7. Graph each line.
   a) The x-intercept is 2 and the y-intercept is -3.
   b) The x-intercept is -6 and the y-intercept is 2.

B

8. a) Explain how you can tell that each equation is not written in general form.
      i) $-2x + 3y + 42 = 0$
      ii) $4y - 5x = 100$
      iii) $\frac{1}{2}x - \frac{1}{2}y + 1 = 0$
      iv) $5y + 9x - 20 = 0$
   b) Write each equation in part a in general form.

9. For each equation below:
      i) Determine the x- and y-intercepts of the graph of the equation.
      ii) Graph the equation.
      iii) Verify that the graph is correct.
   a) $3x - 4y = 24$
   b) $6x - 5y = -60$
   c) $3x - 2y = 24$
   d) $5x - y = 10$

10. Two numbers, f and s, have a sum of 12.
   a) Generate some data for this relation.
   b) Graph the data. Should you join the points? Explain.
   c) Write an equation in general form to relate f and s.
   d) Use the graph to list 6 pairs of integers that have a sum of 12.

11. Rebecca makes and sells Nanaimo bars. She uses pans that hold 12 bars or 36 bars. Rebecca uses these pans to fill an order for 504 Nanaimo bars.
   a) Generate some data for this relation, then graph the data.
   b) Choose letters to represent the variables, then write an equation for the relation.

12. Write each equation in slope-intercept form.
   a) $4x + 3y - 24 = 0$
   b) $3x - 8y + 12 = 0$
   c) $2x - 5y - 15 = 0$
   d) $7x + 3y + 10 = 0$

13. Determine the slope of the line with each equation. Which strategy did you use each time?
   a) $4x + y - 10 = 0$
   b) $3x - y + 33 = 0$
   c) $5x - y + 45 = 0$
   d) $10x + 2y - 16 = 0$

14. Graph each equation on grid paper. Which strategy did you use each time?
   a) $x - 2y + 10 = 0$
   b) $2x + 3y - 15 = 0$
   c) $7x + 4y + 4 = 0$
   d) $6x - 10y + 15 = 0$

15. A pipe for a central vacuum is to be 96 ft. long. It will have s pipes each 6 ft. long and e pipes each 8 ft. long. This equation describes the relation: $6s + 8e = 96$
   a) Suppose 4 pieces of 6-ft. pipe are used. How many pieces of 8-ft. pipe are needed?
   b) Suppose 3 pieces of 8-ft. pipe are used. How many pieces of 6-ft. pipe are needed?
   c) Could 3 pieces of 6-ft. pipe be used? Justify your answer.
   d) Could 4 pieces of 8-ft. pipe be used? Justify your answer.

16. Pascal saves loonies and toonies. The value of his coins is $24.
   a) Generate some data for this relation.
   b) Graph the data. Should you join the points? Explain.
   c) Write an equation to relate the variables. Justify your choice for the form of the equation.
   d) i) Could Pascal have 6 toonies and 8 loonies?
      ii) Could Pascal have 6 loonies and 8 toonies?
   Use the graph and the equation to justify your answers.

17. Use a graphing calculator or a computer with graphing software. Graph each equation. Sketch or print the graph.

a) $x - 22y - 15 = 0$ b) $15x + 13y - 29 = 0$
c) $33x + 2y + 18 = 0$ d) $34x - y + 40 = 0$

18. Write each equation in general form.

a) $y = \frac{1}{3}x - 4$ b) $y - 2 = \frac{1}{3}(x + 5)$
c) $y + 3 = -\frac{1}{4}(x - 1)$ d) $y = -\frac{3}{2}x + \frac{4}{3}$

19. Choose one equation from question 18. Write it in 2 different forms. Graph the equation in each of its 3 forms. Compare the graphs.

20. Describe the graph of $Ax + By + C = 0$, when $C = 0$. Include a sketch in your answer.

21. a) How are the x- and y-intercepts of this line related to the slope of the line? Justify your answer.

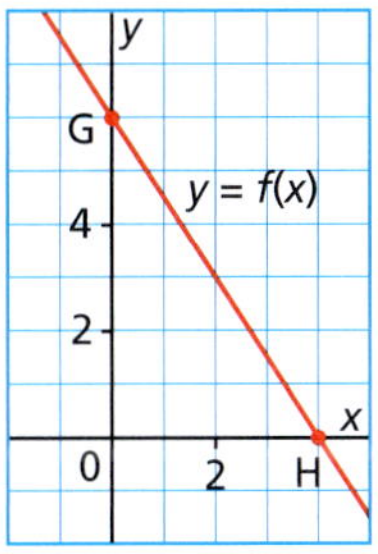

b) Is the relationship in part a true for all lines? Explain how you know.

22. Match each equation with its graph. Justify your answer.

a) $2x + 3y - 6 = 0$ b) $2x - 3y + 6 = 0$

Graph A

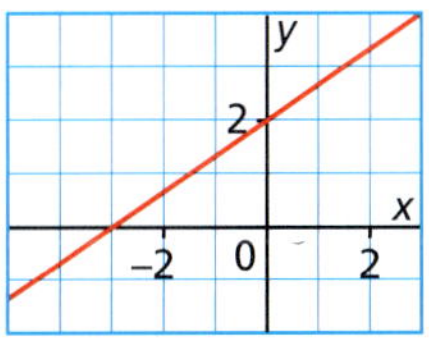

Graph B

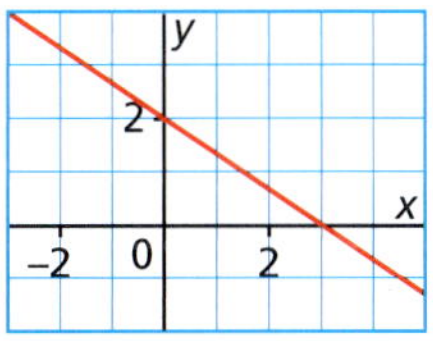

23. a) Why can't you use intercepts to graph the equation $4x - y = 0$?
b) Use a different strategy to graph the equation. Explain your steps.

24. Which equations below are equivalent? How did you find out?

a) $y = 3x + 6$ b) $2x - 3y - 3 = 0$
c) $y - 2 = \frac{2}{3}(x - 2)$ d) $3x - y - 6 = 0$
e) $y = \frac{2}{3}x - 1$ f) $y - 3 = 3(x - 3)$
g) $y - 1 = \frac{2}{3}(x - 3)$ h) $y + 3 = 3(x - 1)$

25. a) Write the equation of a linear function in general form that would be difficult to graph by determining its intercepts. Why is it difficult?
b) Use a different strategy to graph your equation. How did your strategy help you graph the equation?

C

26. If an equation of a line cannot be written in general form, the equation does not represent a linear function. Write each equation in general form, if possible. Indicate whether each equation represents a linear function.

a) $\frac{x}{4} + \frac{y}{3} = 1$
b) $y = \frac{10}{x}$
c) $y = 2x(x + 4)$
d) $y = \frac{x + y}{4} + 2$

27. Suppose you know the x- and y-intercepts of a line. How can you write an equation to describe the line without determining the slope of the line? Use the line with x-intercept 5 and y-intercept -3 to describe your strategy.

28. The general form for the equation of a line is: $Ax + By + C = 0$

a) Write an expression for the slope of the line in terms of A, B, and C.
b) Write an expression for the y-intercept in terms of A, B, and C.

Reflect

Describe a situation that can be most appropriately modelled with the equation of a linear relation in general form. Show that different forms of this equation represent the same graph.

STUDY GUIDE

CONCEPT SUMMARY

Big Ideas	Applying the Big Ideas
■ The graph of a linear function is a non-vertical straight line with a constant slope.	This means that: ■ The slope of a line is equal to the slope of any segment of the line. ■ When we know the slope of a line, we also know the slope of a parallel line and a perpendicular line.
■ Certain forms of the equation of a linear function identify the slope and *y*-intercept of the graph, or the slope and the coordinates of a point on the graph.	■ When the equation is written in the form $y = mx + b$, the slope of the line is m and its y-intercept is b. ■ When the equation is written in the form $y - y_1 = m(x - x_1)$, the slope of the line is m and the coordinates of a point on the line are (x_1, y_1). ■ Any equation can be written in the general form $Ax + By + C = 0$, where A is a whole number, and B and C are integers.

Reflect on the Chapter

- What information do you need to know about a linear function to be able to write an equation to describe it? Include examples in your explanation.
- For each form of the equation of a linear function, describe how you would graph the function.

THE WORLD OF MATH

Careers: Marketing

Marketing involves understanding consumers' needs and buying habits. For a company to be successful, it must ensure that its product meets consumers' needs and can be produced and sold at prices that ensure the company makes a profit. To understand the market, research is conducted, then data are analyzed and used to make predictions. Often, these data will be used to produce linear models to solve problems.

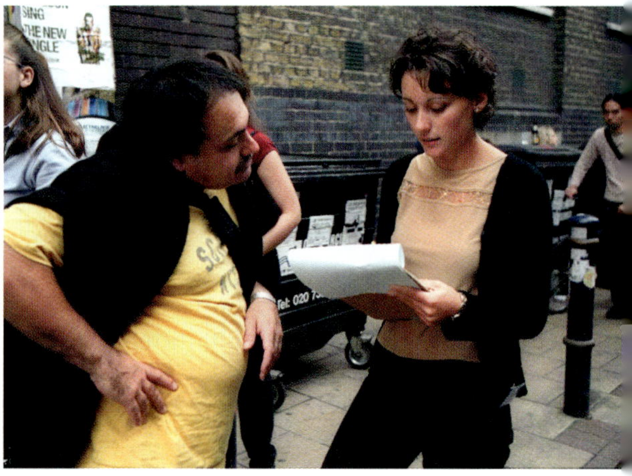

SKILLS SUMMARY

Skill	Description	Example
Determine the slope of a line and identify parallel lines and perpendicular lines. [6.1, 6.2]	A line that passes through $P(x_1, y_1)$ and $Q(x_2, y_2)$ has slope, m, where: $m = \frac{y_2 - y_1}{x_2 - x_1}$	For $P(-2, 4)$ and $Q(2, -1)$: $m = \frac{-1-4}{2-(-2)}$, or $-\frac{5}{4}$ The slope of a line parallel to PQ is $-\frac{5}{4}$. The slope of a line perpendicular to PQ is $\frac{4}{5}$.
Write the equation of a line in slope-intercept form. [6.4]	A line with slope, m, and y-intercept, b, has equation: $y = mx + b$	For a line with slope $-\frac{5}{4}$ and y-intercept 3, an equation is: $y = -\frac{5}{4}x + 3$
Write the equation of a line in slope-point form. [6.5]	A line with slope, m, and passing through $P(x_1, y_1)$, has equation: $y - y_1 = m(x - x_1)$	A line with slope $\frac{4}{5}$ and passing through $P(-2, 4)$ has equation: $y - 4 = \frac{4}{5}(x - (-2))$, or $y - 4 = \frac{4}{5}(x + 2)$
Graph a linear relation in general form. [6.6]	The general form of the equation is: $Ax + By + C = 0$ Determine intercepts by substituting: $x = 0$, and solving for y, then $y = 0$, and solving for x. Plot points at the intercepts, then draw a line through the points.	A line has equation: $3x + 4y + 12 = 0$ For the y-intercept: $3(0) + 4y + 12 = 0$; $4y = -12$; $y = -3$ For the x-intercept: $3x + 4(0) + 12 = 0$; $3x = -12$; $x = -4$ 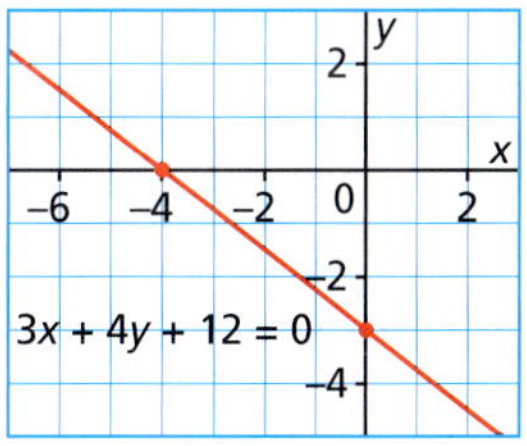

REVIEW

6.1

1. Determine the slope of each line.

a)

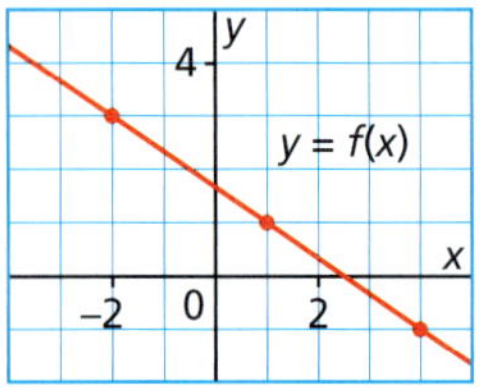

b)

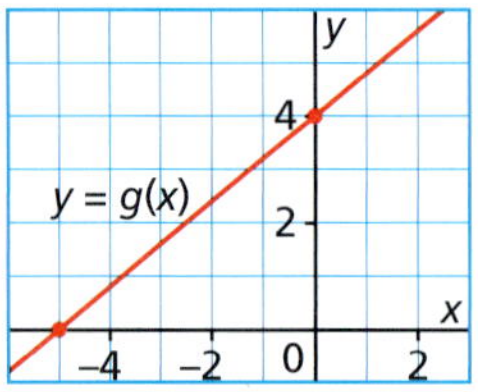

2. For each line described below, is its slope positive, negative, zero, or undefined? Justify your answer.
   a) As x increases by 3, y decreases by 2.
   b) The line has a negative x-intercept and a negative y-intercept.
   c) The line has a y-intercept but does not have an x-intercept.

3. A line passes through A$(-3, 1)$. For each slope given below:
   i) Sketch the line through A with that slope.
   ii) Write the coordinates of three other points on the line.

   a) -1 b) $\frac{1}{4}$ c) $-\frac{3}{2}$

4. Determine the slope of a line that passes through each pair of points. What strategy did you use?
   a) B$(-6, 8)$ and C$(-1, -2)$
   b) D$(-3, 7)$ and E$(5, -5)$

5. Gabrielle likes to jog and has a pedometer to measure how far she runs. She checks her pedometer periodically and records its readings. Gabrielle plotted these data on a grid.

Graph of Gabrielle's Run

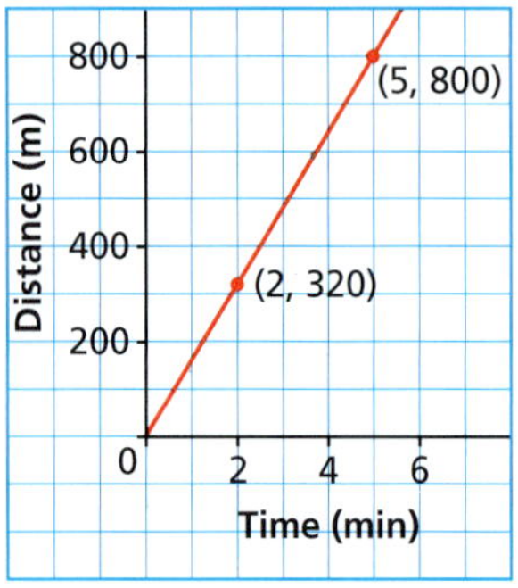

   a) What is the slope of the line and what does it represent?
   b) How is slope related to rate of change?
   c) Assume Gabrielle continues to run at the same rate.
      i) How far did Gabrielle jog in 4 min?
      ii) How long will it take Gabrielle to jog 1000 m?

6.2

6. The slope of line FG is given. What is the slope of a line that is:
   i) parallel to FG? ii) perpendicular to FG?

   a) 3 b) $-\frac{6}{5}$ c) $\frac{11}{8}$ d) 1

7. The coordinates of two points on two lines are given. Are the two lines parallel, perpendicular, or neither? Justify your choice.
   a) H$(-3, 3)$, J$(-1, 7)$ and K$(-1, 2)$, M$(5, -1)$
   b) N$(-4, -2)$, P$(-1, 7)$ and Q$(2, 5)$, R$(4, -1)$

8. Is quadrilateral STUV a parallelogram? Justify your answer.

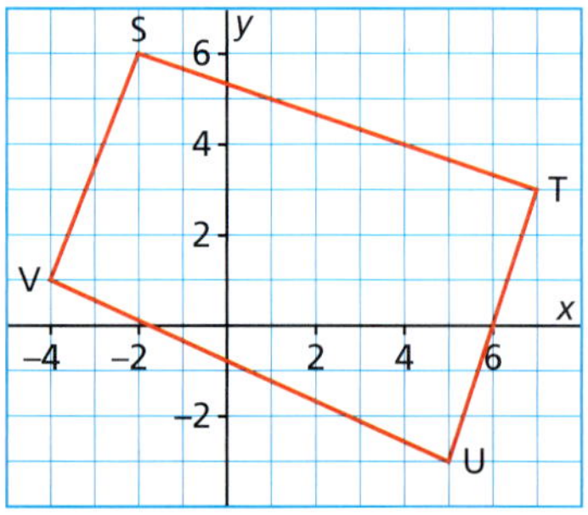

9. Triangle ABC has vertices A$(-1, -1)$, B$(2, 5)$, and C$(6, 3)$. Is $\triangle$ABC a right triangle? Justify your answer.

6.3

10. Sketch graphs to help explain what happens to the graph of $y = 3x + 4$ when:
   a) the coefficient of x increases by 1 each time until the coefficient is 6
   b) the constant term decreases by 1 each time until it is -4

6.4

11. For each equation, identify the slope and y-intercept of its graph, then draw the graph.

a) $y = -3x + 4$ b) $y = \frac{3}{4}x - 2$

12. For each graph below:

i) Determine its slope and y-intercept.
ii) Write an equation that describes the graph.
iii) Verify your equation.

a)
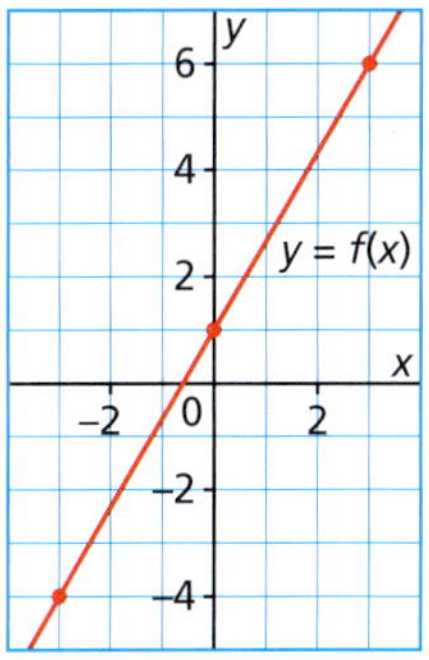

b)
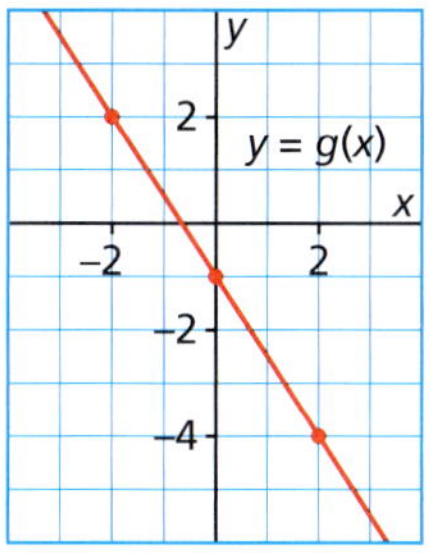

13. Match each equation with its graph. Explain your strategy.

a) $y = \frac{1}{2}x - 3$ b) $y = -3x - 2$

c) $y = 2x + 3$ d) $y = -2x + 3$

Graph A

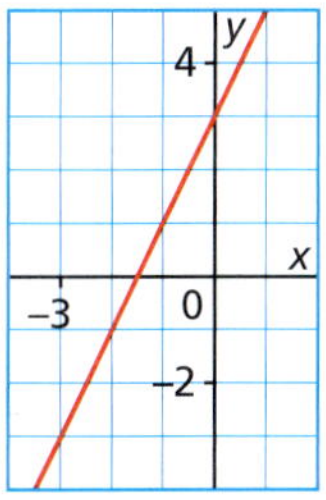

Graph B

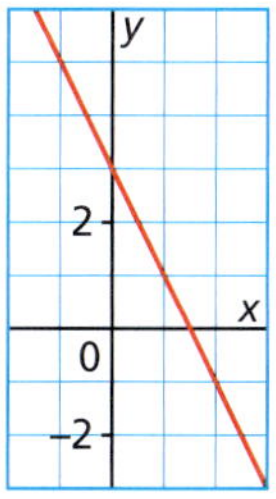

Graph C

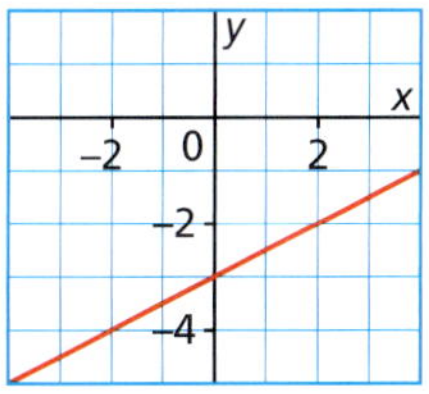

Graph D

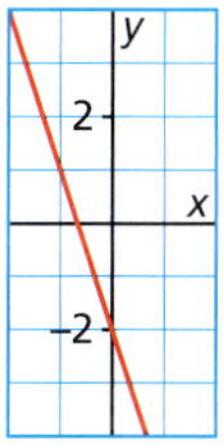

14. Mason had $40 in his bank account when he started to save $15 each week.

a) Write an equation to represent the total amount, A dollars, he had in his account after w weeks.
b) After how many weeks did Mason have $355 in his account?
c) Suppose you graphed the equation you wrote in part a. What would the slope and the vertical intercept of the graph represent?

15. Consider the graph of $y = \frac{4}{7}x - 5$.

a) Write 2 equations that describe 2 different lines that are parallel to this line. How do you know all 3 lines are parallel?
b) Write 2 equations that describe 2 different lines that are perpendicular to this line. How do you know that the 2 new lines are perpendicular to the original line?

6.5

16. Line DE passes through F(−2, 3) and is perpendicular to the line described by the equation $y = 2x + 1$. Write an equation for line DE.

17. For each equation below:

i) Identify the slope of its graph and the coordinates of a point on the graph.
ii) Graph the equation.
iii) Choose a different point on the graph, then write its equation in a different way.

a) $y + 4 = 2(x + 3)$

b) $y - 1 = -\frac{1}{3}(x - 4)$

18. Write an equation for each graph. Describe your strategy. Verify that the equation is correct.

a)
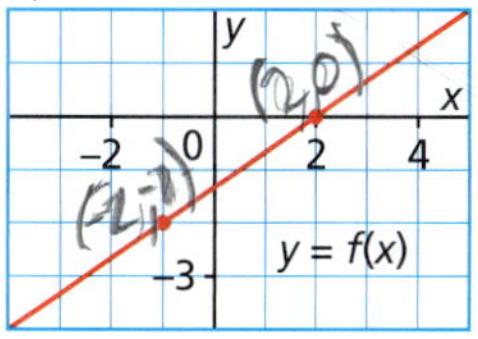

b)
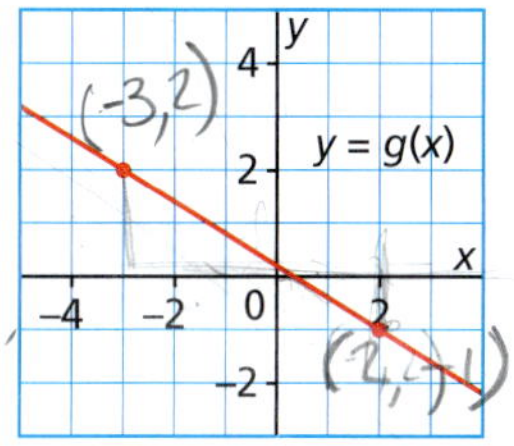

19. a) Write an equation for the line that passes through each pair of points. Describe your strategy.
  i) G(−3, −7) and H(1, 5)
  ii) J(−3, 3) and K(5, −1)
b) Use each equation you wrote in part a to determine the coordinates of another point on each line.

20. Two families went on a traditional nuuchahnulth dugout canoe tour in Tofino harbour, B.C. One family paid $220 for 5 people. The other family paid $132 for 3 people.
a) Choose variables, then write an equation for the cost as a function of the number of people. Explain your strategy.
b) What is the cost per person? How can you determine this from the equation?
c) A third family paid $264. How many people went on the tour?

6.6

21. a) Why is each equation not in general form?
  i) $4y - 5x - 40 = 0$ ii) $\frac{1}{3}x + y = 4$
  iii) $y - 2 = \frac{1}{3}(x + 4)$ iv) $y = \frac{1}{5}x + 3$
b) Write each equation in part a in general form.

22. a) Graph each equation. Describe the strategies you used.
  i) $3x - 4y - 24 = 0$ ii) $x - 3y + 12 = 0$
b) What is the slope of each line in part a? How did you determine the slopes?

23. Write the equation of a line in general form that you could not easily graph by using intercepts. Choose another strategy to graph the equation, and explain why you used that strategy.

24. The difference between two numbers, g and l, is 6.
a) Generate some data for this relation, then graph the data.
b) Write an equation in general form to relate g and l.
c) Use the graph to list 5 pairs of numbers that have a difference of 6.

25. Which equations are equivalent? How did you determine your answers?
a) $y = \frac{2}{5}x + 1$ b) $y - 3 = \frac{2}{5}(x - 4)$
c) $y - 1 = \frac{2}{5}(x - 1)$ d) $y - 3 = \frac{2}{5}(x - 5)$
e) $2x - 5y + 7 = 0$ f) $2x - 5y - 5 = 0$

26. Match each equation with its graph below. Justify each choice.
a) $y = -\frac{4}{5}x + 3$ b) $y - 3 = -\frac{4}{5}(x + 3)$
c) $5x + 4y - 15 = 0$

Graph A

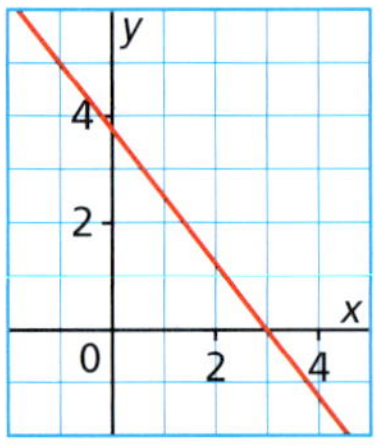

Graph B

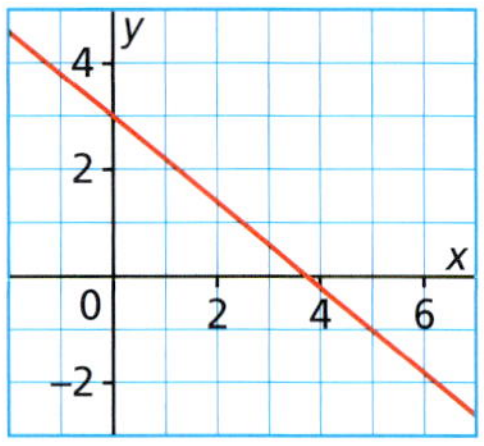

Graph C

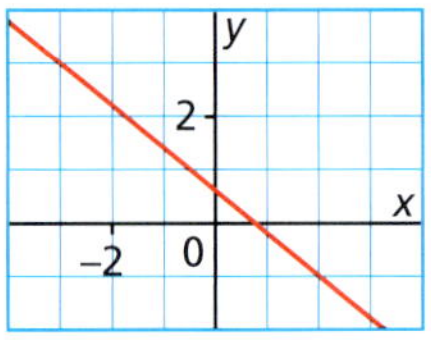

27. Max babysits for 2 families. One family pays him $5 an hour, the other family pays $4 an hour. Last week, Max earned $60.
a) Generate some data for this relation, then graph the data.
b) Write an equation for the relation. Explain what each variable represents.

28. A video store charges $5 to rent a new release and $3 to rent an older movie. Kylie spent $45 renting movies last month.
a) Generate some data for this relation, graph the data, then write an equation.
b) i) Could Kylie have rented 5 new releases and 6 old movies?
  ii) Could Kylie have rented 6 new releases and 5 old movies?
Justify your answers.

PRACTICE TEST

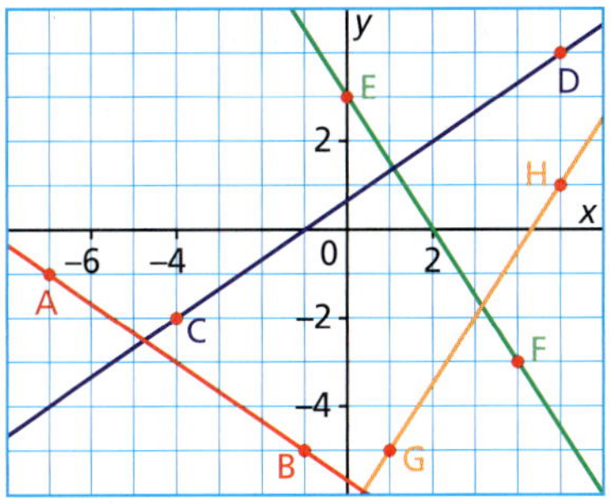

For questions 1 and 2, choose the correct answer: A, B, C, or D

1. Which line at the right has slope $-\frac{3}{2}$?

A. AB **B.** CD **C.** EF **D.** GH

2. Which line at the right has equation $2x - 3y + 2 = 0$?

A. AB **B.** CD **C.** EF **D.** GH

3. a) Graph each line. Explain your strategies.

i) $y = -\frac{3}{2}x + 5$ **ii)** $y - 3 = \frac{1}{3}(x + 2)$ **iii)** $3x - 4y - 12 = 0$

b) Determine an equation of the line that is parallel to the line with equation $y = -\frac{3}{2}x + 5$, and passes through A(6, 2). Explain how you know your equation is correct.

c) Determine an equation of the line that is perpendicular to the line with equation $y - 3 = \frac{1}{3}(x + 2)$, and passes through B(−1, 2). Write the new equation in general form.

d) Determine the coordinates of a point P on the line with equation $3x - 4y - 12 = 0$. Do not use an intercept. Write an equation of the line that passes through P and Q(1, 5). Write the new equation in slope-intercept form.

4. Write the equation of each line in the form that you think best describes the line. Justify your choice.

a)

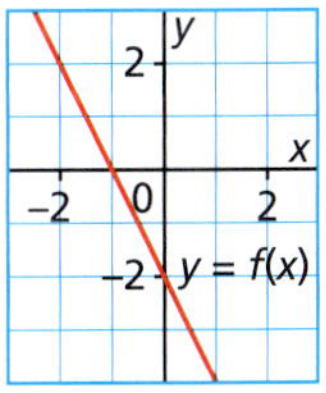

b)

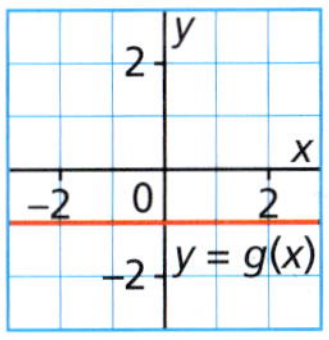

c)

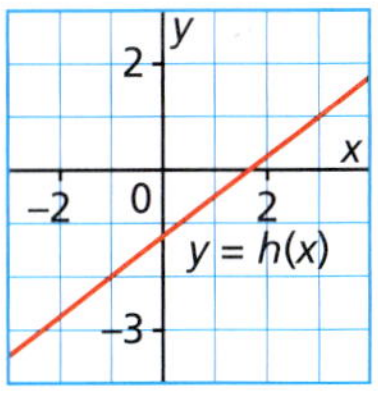

5. Sophia is planning the graduation banquet. The caterer charges a fixed amount plus an additional charge for each person who attends. The banquet will cost \$11 250 if 600 people attend and \$7650 if 400 people attend.

a) Suppose 340 people attend the banquet. What will the total cost be?

b) The total cost was \$9810. How many people attended the banquet?

c) What strategies did you use to answer parts a and b?

7 Systems of Linear Equations

BUILDING ON

- modelling problems using linear relations
- graphing linear functions
- solving linear equations

BIG IDEAS

- A system of two linear equations is solved when the set of ordered pairs that satisfies both equations is determined.
- Multiplying or dividing the equations in a linear system by a non-zero number, or adding or subtracting the equations, produces an equivalent system.
- A system of two linear equations may have one solution, infinite solutions, or no solution.

NEW VOCABULARY

system of linear equations, linear system
solving by substitution
equivalent systems
solving by elimination
infinite
coincident lines

POLAR BEARS In Nunavut, scientists collected data on the numbers of polar bears they encountered, and the bears' reactions. When we know some of these data, we can write, then solve, related problems using linear systems.

7.1 Developing Systems of Linear Equations

LESSON FOCUS

Model a situation using a system of linear equations.

Make Connections

Which linear equation relates the masses on these balance scales?

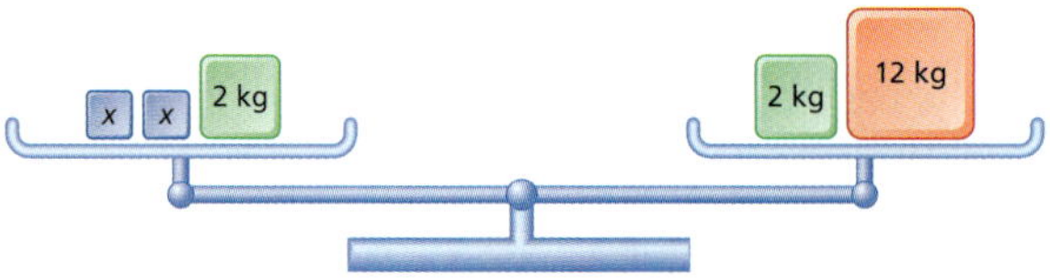

Which linear equation relates the masses on these balance scales?

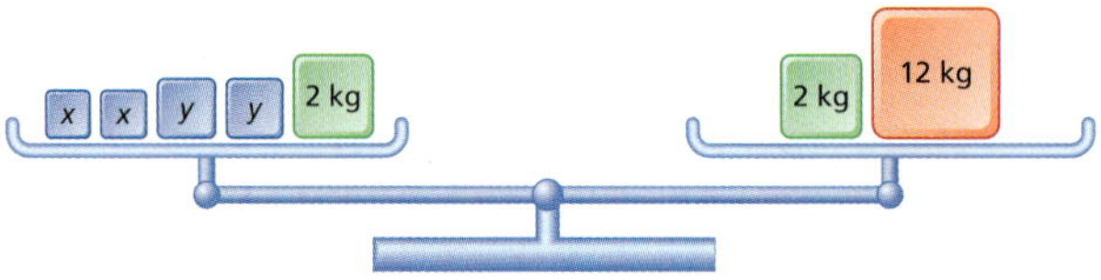

How are the two equations the same? How are they different?

What do you know about the number of solutions for each equation?

Construct Understanding

THINK ABOUT IT

Work with a partner.

A game uses a spinner with the number 1 or 2 written on each sector.

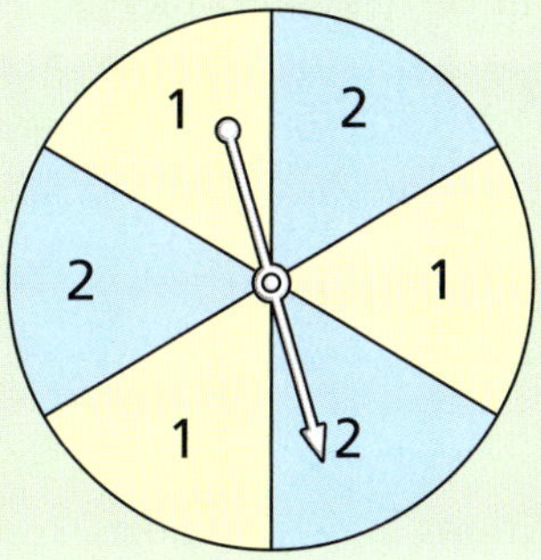

Each player spins the pointer 10 times and records each number.
The sum of the 10 numbers is the player's score.
One player had a score of 17.
How many times did the pointer land on 1 and land on 2?
Write two equations that model this situation.

Why do you need two equations to model this situation?
Is a solution of one equation also a solution of the other equation?
Explain.

A school district has buses that carry 12 passengers and buses that carry 24 passengers. The total passenger capacity is 780. There are 20 more small buses than large buses.

To determine how many of each type of bus there are, we can write two equations to model the situation.
We first identify the unknown quantities.
There are some small buses but we don't know how many.
Let s represent the number of small buses.

There are some large buses but we don't know how many.
Let l represent the number of large buses.
The total passenger capacity is 780.
Each small bus carries 12 people and each large bus carries 24 people.
So, this equation represents the total capacity: $12s + 24l = 780$
There are 20 more small buses than large buses.
So, this equation relates the numbers of buses: $s = l + 20$

Why can we also write the first equation as:
$s + 2l = 65$?
Why might it be better to write this equation as:
$12s + 24l = 780$?

These two linear equations model the situation:
$12s + 24l = 780$
$s = l + 20$

These two equations form a **system of linear equations** in two variables, s and l.
A system of linear equations is often referred to as a **linear system.**
A *solution* of a linear system is a pair of values of s and l that satisfy both equations.

Suppose you are told that there are 35 small buses and 15 large buses.
To verify that this is the solution, we compare these data with the given situation.
The difference in the numbers of small and large buses is: $35 - 15 = 20$
Calculate the total capacity of 35 small buses and 15 large buses.

$$\begin{aligned}\text{Total capacity} &= 35(12) + 15(24)\\ &= 420 + 360\\ &= 780\end{aligned}$$

The difference in the numbers of small and large buses is 20 and the total passenger capacity is 780. This agrees with the given data, so the solution is correct.

We can also verify the solution by substituting the known values of s and l into the equations.
In each equation, substitute: $s = 35$ and $l = 15$

$12s + 24l = 780$

$$\begin{aligned}\text{L.S.} &= 12s + 24l\\ &= 12(35) + 24(15)\\ &= 420 + 360\\ &= 780\\ &= \text{R.S.}\end{aligned}$$

$s = l + 20$

$$\begin{aligned}\text{L.S.} &= s\\ &= 35\end{aligned}$$

$$\begin{aligned}\text{R. S.} &= l + 20\\ &= 15 + 20\\ &= 35\\ &= \text{L.S.}\end{aligned}$$

For each equation, the left side is equal to the right side. Since $s = 35$ and $l = 15$ satisfy each equation, these numbers are the solution of the linear system.

Example 1 Using a Diagram to Model a Situation

a) Create a linear system to model this situation:
The perimeter of a Nunavut flag is 16 ft.
Its length is 2 ft. longer than its width.

b) Denise has determined that the Nunavut flag is 5 ft. long and 3 ft. wide.
Use the linear system from part a to verify that Denise is correct.

SOLUTION

a) Draw a rectangle to represent the flag.
Use the variables l and w to represent the dimensions of the flag in feet.

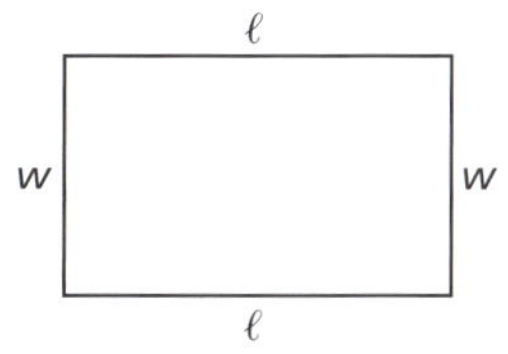

The perimeter of the flag is 16 ft.
The perimeter is: $l + l + w + w = 2l + 2w$
So, this equation represents the perimeter: $2l + 2w = 16$
The length of the flag is 2 ft. more than the width.
So, this equation relates the dimensions: $l = w + 2$

A linear system that models the situation is:
$2l + 2w = 16$
$l = w + 2$

b) The flag is 5 ft. long and 3 ft. wide.
To verify this solution:
The measurements above confirm that the length is 2 ft. longer than the width.
Calculate the perimeter.
Perimeter = twice the length plus twice the width
= 2(5 ft.) + 2(3 ft.)
= 10 ft. + 6 ft.
= 16 ft.
This confirms that the perimeter is 16 ft.
So, the solution is correct.

CHECK YOUR UNDERSTANDING

1. a) Create a linear system to model this situation:
The stage at the Lyle Victor Albert Centre in Bonnyville, Alberta, is rectangular.
Its perimeter is 158 ft.
The width of the stage is 31 ft. less than the length.

b) Sebi has determined that the stage is 55 ft. long and 24 ft. wide. Use the linear system from part a to verify that Sebi is correct.

[Answer: a) $2l + 2w = 158$; $w = l - 31$]

How could you use guess and test to solve the problem?

Example 2 Using a Table to Create a Linear System to Model a Situation

a) Create a linear system to model this situation:
In Calgary, a school raised \$195 by collecting 3000 items for recycling.
The school received 5¢ for each pop can and 20¢ for each large plastic bottle.

b) The school collected 2700 pop cans and 300 plastic bottles.
Use the linear system to verify these numbers.

SOLUTION

a) Choose a variable to represent each unknown number.
Let c represent the number of cans, and let b represent the number of bottles.
Use this information to create a table.

	Refund per Item (\$)	Number of Items	Money Raised (\$)
Can	0.05	c	$0.05c$
Bottle	0.20	b	$0.20b$
Total		3000	195

The third column in the table shows that the total number of items collected can be represented by this equation:
$c + b = 3000$
The fourth column in the table shows that the money raised can be represented by this equation: $0.05c + 0.20b = 195$
So, a linear system that models the situation is:
$c + b = 3000$
$0.05c + 0.20b = 195$

b) To verify the solution:
In each equation, substitute: $c = 2700$ and $b = 300$

$c + b = 3000$
$$\begin{aligned}\text{L.S.} &= c + b\\ &= 2700 + 300\\ &= 3000\\ &= \text{R.S.}\end{aligned}$$

$0.05c + 0.20b = 195$
$$\begin{aligned}\text{L.S.} &= 0.05c + 0.20b\\ &= 0.05(2700) + 0.20(300)\\ &= 135 + 60\\ &= 195\\ &= \text{R.S.}\end{aligned}$$

For each equation, the left side is equal to the right side.
Since $c = 2700$ and $b = 300$ satisfy each equation, these numbers are the solution of the linear system.

CHECK YOUR UNDERSTANDING

2. a) Create a linear system to model this situation:
A school raised \$140 by collecting 2000 cans and glass bottles for recycling.
The school received 5¢ for a can and 10¢ for a bottle.

b) The school collected 1200 cans and 800 bottles.
Use the linear system to verify these numbers.

[Answer: a) $0.05c + 0.10b = 140$; $c + b = 2000$]

What other linear system could model this situation? Would the solution be different? Explain.

For this situation:

A store display had packages of 8 batteries and packages of 4 batteries.
The total number of batteries was 320.
There were 1.5 times as many packages of 4 batteries as packages of 8 batteries.

Cary wrote this linear system:

$8e + 4f = 320$

$1.5f = e$

where e represents the number of packages of 8 batteries and f represents the number of packages of 4 batteries.

Cary's classmate, Devon, said that the solution of the linear system was:
There are 30 packages of 8 batteries and 20 packages of 4 batteries.

To verify the solution, in each equation Cary substituted: $e = 30$ and $f = 20$

$8e + 4f = 320$

$$\begin{aligned} \text{L.S.} &= 8e + 4f \\ &= 8(30) + 4(20) \\ &= 240 + 80 \\ &= 320 \\ &= \text{R.S.} \end{aligned}$$

$1.5f = e$

$$\begin{aligned} \text{L.S.} &= 1.5f \\ &= 1.5(20) \\ &= 30 \end{aligned} \qquad \begin{aligned} \text{R.S.} &= e \\ &= 30 \\ &= \text{L.S.} \end{aligned}$$

Cary said that since the left side is equal to the right side for each equation, the solution is correct.

But when Devon used the problem to verify the solution, she realized that there should be more packages of 4 batteries than packages of 8 batteries, so the solution was wrong.

This illustrates that it is better to consider the given data to verify a solution rather than substitute in the equations. There could be an error in the equations that were written to represent the situation.

What are the correct equations for this situation?

Example 3 Relating a Linear System to a Problem

A store sells wheels for roller skates in packages of 4 and wheels for inline skates in packages of 8.

Create a situation about wheels that can be modelled by the linear system below. Explain the meaning of each variable. Write a related problem.

$8i + 4r = 440$

$i + r = 80$

SOLUTION

$8i + 4r = 440$ ①

$i + r = 80$ ②

We number the equations in a linear system to be able to refer to them easily.

In equation ①:

The variable i is multiplied by 8, which is the number of inline skate wheels in a package.
So, i represents the number of packages of inline skate wheels in the store.
The variable r is multiplied by 4, which is the number of roller skate wheels in a package.
So, r represents the number of packages of roller skate wheels in the store.

Then, equation ① could represent the total number of wheels in all these packages in the store.
And, equation ② could represent the total number of packages of inline skate and roller skate wheels in the store.

A possible problem is:

A store has 80 packages of wheels for inline skates and roller skates.
Inline skate wheels come in packages of 8.
Roller skate wheels come in packages of 4.
The total number of these wheels in all packages is 440.
How many packages of inline skate wheels and how many packages of roller skate wheels are in the store?

CHECK YOUR UNDERSTANDING

3. A bicycle has 2 wheels and a tricycle has 3 wheels.

Create a situation about wheels that can be modelled by the linear system below. Explain the meaning of each variable. Write a related problem.

$2b + 3t = 100$

$b + t = 40$

[Sample Answer: A possible problem is: There are 40 bicycles and tricycles in a department store. The total number of wheels on all bicycles and tricycles in the store is 100. How many bicycles and how many tricycles are in the store?]

Discuss the Ideas

1. When you write a linear system to model a situation, how do you decide which parts of the situation can be represented by variables?

2. What does the *solution* of a linear system mean?

3. How can you verify the solution of a linear system?

Exercises

A

4. Which system of equations is *not* a linear system?

a) $2x + y = 11$
$x = 13 + y$

b) $2x = 11 - y$
$4x - y = 13$

c) $-\frac{1}{2}x - y = \frac{3}{4}$
$\frac{3}{2}x + 2 = -\frac{7}{8}$

d) $-x^2 + y = 10$
$x + y = 5$

5. Which linear systems have the solution $x = -1$ and $y = 2$?

a) $3x + 2y = -1$
$2x - y = 1$

b) $3x - y = -1$
$-x - y = -1$

c) $-3x + 5y = 13$
$4x - 3y = -10$

B

6. Match each situation to a linear system below. Justify your choice. Explain what each variable represents.

a) During a clothing sale, 2 jackets and 2 sweaters cost \$228. A jacket costs \$44 more than a sweater.

b) The perimeter of a standard tennis court for doubles is 228 ft. The width is 42 ft. less than the length.

c) At a cultural fair, the Indian booth sold chapatti and naan breads for \$2 each. A total of \$228 was raised. Forty more chapatti breads than naan breads were sold.

i) $2x + 2y = 228$
$x - y = 42$

ii) $2x + 2y = 228$
$x - y = 40$

iii) $2x + 2y = 228$
$x - y = 44$

7. a) Create a linear system to model this situation:
Two different lengths of pipe are joined, as shown in the diagrams.

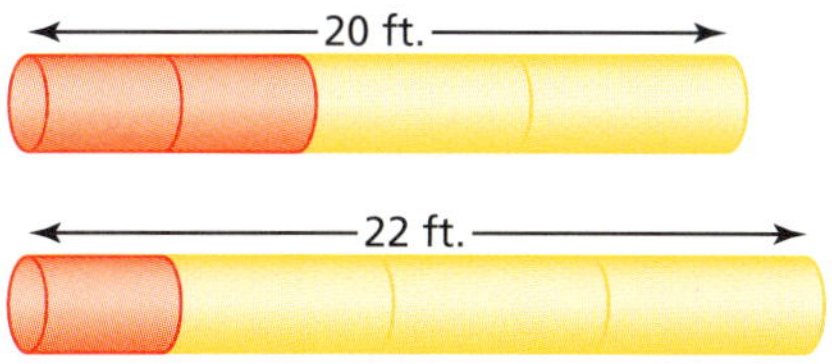

b) Verify that the shorter pipe is 4 ft. long and the longer pipe is 6 ft. long.

8. a) Create a linear system to model this situation:
The perimeter of an isosceles triangle is 24 cm. Each equal side is 6 cm longer than the shorter side.

b) Verify that the side lengths of the triangle are: 10 cm, 10 cm, and 4 cm

9. Teri works in a co-op that sells small and large bags of wild rice harvested in Saskatchewan.

a) These balance scales illustrate the two different sizes of bags of rice: x represents the mass of a large bag and y represents the mass of a small bag. Write a linear system to model the two balance scales.

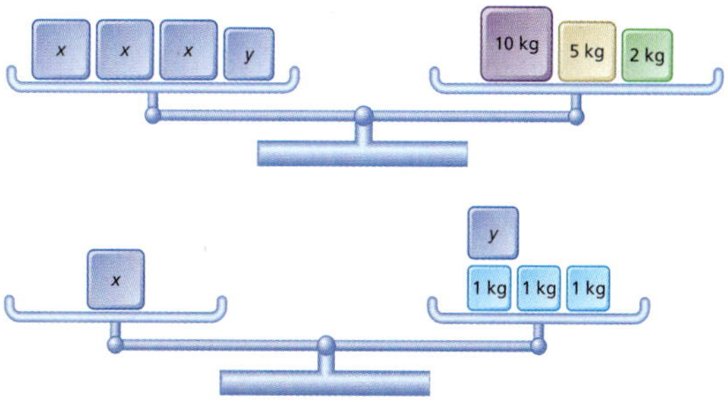

b) Use the diagrams of the balance scales to verify that a small bag of rice has a mass of 2 kg and a large bag has a mass of 5 kg.

c) Use the linear system to verify the masses of the bags in part b.

For questions 10 and 11, write a linear system to model each situation. Then verify which of the given solutions of the related problem is correct.

10. A dogsled team travelled a total distance of 25 km from home to three cabins and then back home. All distances are measured along the trail. The distance from home to cabin 2 is 13 km. What is the distance from home to cabin 1? What is the distance from cabin 1 to cabin 2? (*Solution A*: The distance from home to cabin 1 is 7 km. The distance from cabin 1 to cabin 2 is 6 km. *Solution B*: The distance from home to cabin 1 is 6 km. The distance from cabin 1 to cabin 2 is 7 km.)

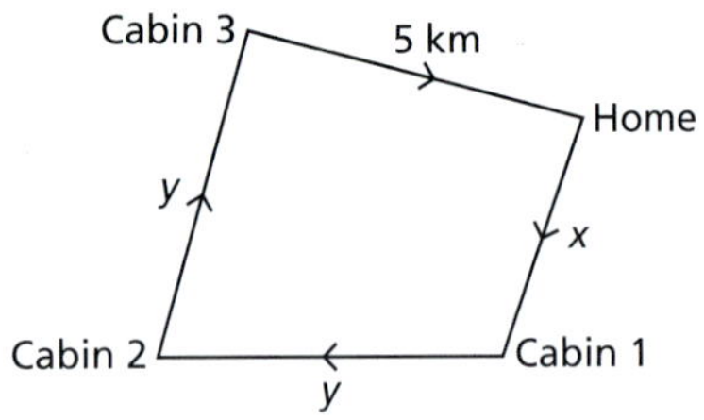

11. Padma walked and jogged for 1 h on a treadmill. She walked 10 min more than she jogged. For how long did Padma walk? For how long did she jog? (*Solution A*: Padma walked for 35 min and jogged for 25 min. *Solution B*: Padma jogged for 35 min and walked for 25 min.)

12. Shen used this linear system to represent a situation involving a collection of \$2 and \$1 coins.

$2t + l = 160$

$t + l = 110$

a) What problem might Shen have solved?

b) What does each variable represent?

13. Jacqui wrote a problem about the costs of tickets for a group of adults and children going to a local fair. She modelled the situation with this linear system.

$5a + 2c = 38$

$a - c = 2$

a) What problem might Jacqui have written? Justify your answer.

b) What does each variable represent?

14. Write a situation that can be modelled by this linear system. Explain what each variable means, then write a related problem.

$x + y = 100$

$x - y = 10$

C

15. Any linear system in two variables can be expressed as:

$Ax + By = C$

$Dx + Ey = F$

a) What do you know about the coefficients B, E, C, and F when the solution is the ordered pair $(0, y)$?

b) What do you know about the coefficients A, D, C, and F when the solution is the ordered pair $(x, 0)$?

16. Show how this system can be written as a linear system.

$$\frac{-3x + 24}{x + y} = -6$$

$$-\frac{x}{5} - \frac{y}{3} = x + y$$

17. **a)** Write a linear system that has the solution $x = 1$ and $y = 1$. Explain what you did.

b) Why is there more than one linear system with the same solution?

18. **a)** Without solving this system, how do you know that $y = 2$ is part of the solution of this linear system?

$x + 2y = 7$

$x + 3y = 9$

b) Solve the system for x. Explain what you did.

Reflect

What do you need to consider when you write a linear system to model a situation? Use one of the exercises to explain.

7.2 Solving a System of Linear Equations Graphically

LESSON FOCUS

Use the graphs of the equations of a linear system to estimate its solution.

The town of Kelvington, Saskatchewan, erected 6 large hockey cards by a highway to celebrate the town's famous hockey players. One player is Wendel Clark.

Make Connections

Two equations in a linear system are graphed on the same grid.

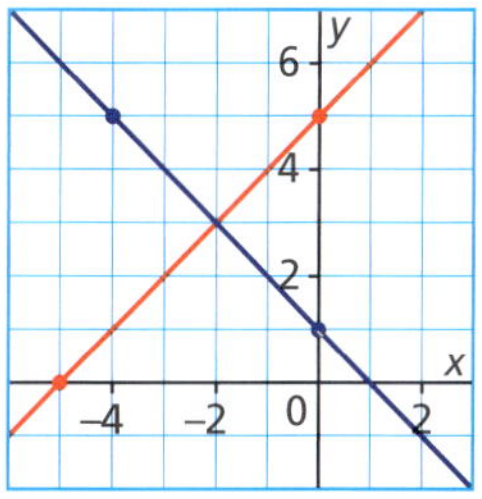

What are the equations of the graphs? Explain your reasoning.
What are the coordinates of the point of intersection of the two lines?
Explain why these coordinates are the solution of the linear system.

Construct Understanding

TRY THIS

Work with a partner.
You will need grid paper and a ruler.

Here is a problem about the hockey cards in Kelvington.

> The perimeter of each large hockey card is 24 ft.
> The difference between the height and width is 4 ft.
> What are the dimensions of each card?

A. Create a linear system to model this situation.

B. Graph the equations on the same grid.

C. What are the coordinates of the point of intersection, P, of the two lines?

D. Why must the coordinates of P be a solution of each equation in the linear system?

E. What are the side lengths of each large hockey card in Kelvington?

How did you decide on which axis each variable should be graphed?

The solution of a linear system can be estimated by graphing both equations on the same grid. If the two lines intersect, the coordinates (x, y) of the point of intersection are the solution of the linear system.
Each equation of this linear system is graphed on a grid.

$3x + 2y = -12$ ①
$-2x + y = 1$ ②

How could you verify that the graphs represent the equations in the linear system?

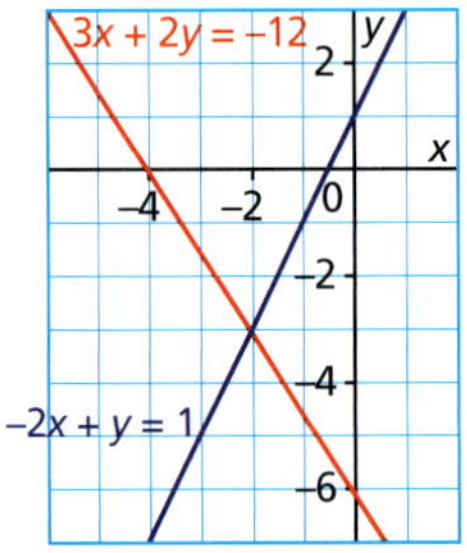

We can use the graphs to estimate the solution of the linear system.
The set of points that satisfy equation ① lie on its graph.
The set of points that satisfy equation ② lie on its graph.
The set of points that satisfy both equations lie where the two graphs intersect.
From the graphs, the point of intersection appears to be $(-2, -3)$.
To verify the solution, we check that the coordinates $(-2, -3)$ satisfy both equations.

In each equation, we substitute: $x = -2$ and $y = -3$:

$3x + 2y = -12$
L.S. $= 3x + 2y$
$= 3(-2) + 2(-3)$
$= -6 - 6$
$= -12$
= R.S.

$-2x + y = 1$
L.S. $= -2x + y$
$= -2(-2) - 3$
$= 4 - 3$
$= 1$
= R.S.

Why must the solution satisfy both equations?

For each equation, the left side is equal to the right side.
Since $x = -2$ and $y = -3$ satisfy each equation, these numbers are the solution of the linear system.

Example 1 Solving a Linear System by Graphing

Solve this linear system.
$x + y = 8$
$3x - 2y = 14$

SOLUTION

$x + y = 8$ ①
$3x - 2y = 14$ ②

Determine the x-intercept and y-intercept of the graph of equation ①.
Both the x- and y-intercepts are 8.
Write equation ② in slope-intercept form.

$3x - 2y = 14$
$-2y = -3x + 14$ Divide by -2 to solve for y.
$y = \frac{3}{2}x - 7$

The slope of the graph of equation ② is $\frac{3}{2}$, and its y-intercept is -7.
Graph each line.
The point of intersection appears to be (6, 2).

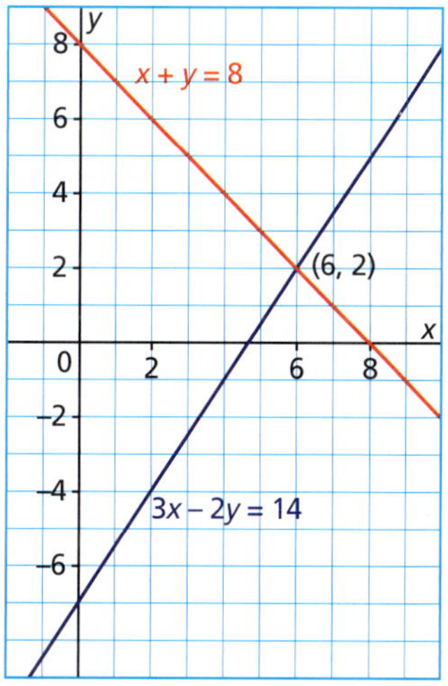

Verify the solution. In each equation, substitute: $x = 6$ and $y = 2$

$x + y = 8$
L. S. $= x + y$
$= 6 + 2$
$= 8$
= R.S.

$3x - 2y = 14$
L.S. $= 3x - 2y$
$= 3(6) - 2(2)$
$= 18 - 4$
$= 14$
= R.S.

For each equation, the left side is equal to the right side.
So, $x = 6$ and $y = 2$ is the solution of the linear system.

CHECK YOUR UNDERSTANDING

1. Solve this linear system.
$2x + 3y = 3$
$x - y = 4$
[Answer: (3, –1)]

What other strategy could you use to graph the equations?

Example 2 Solving a Problem by Graphing a Linear System

One plane left Regina at noon to travel 1400 mi. to Ottawa at an average speed of 400 mph. Another plane left Ottawa at the same time to travel to Regina at an average speed of 350 mph. A linear system that models this situation is:

$d = 1400 - 400t$

$d = 350t$

where d is the distance in miles from Ottawa and t is the time in hours since the planes took off

a) Graph the linear system above.

b) Use the graph to solve this problem: When do the planes pass each other and how far are they from Ottawa?

SOLUTION

The planes pass each other when they have been travelling for the same time and they are the same distance from Ottawa.

a) Solve the linear system to determine values of d and t that satisfy both equations.

$d = 1400 - 400t$ ①

$d = 350t$ ②

Each equation is in slope-intercept form.
For the graph of equation ①, the slope is −400 and the vertical intercept is 1400.
For the graph of equation ②, the slope is 350 and the vertical intercept is 0.
Graph the equations.

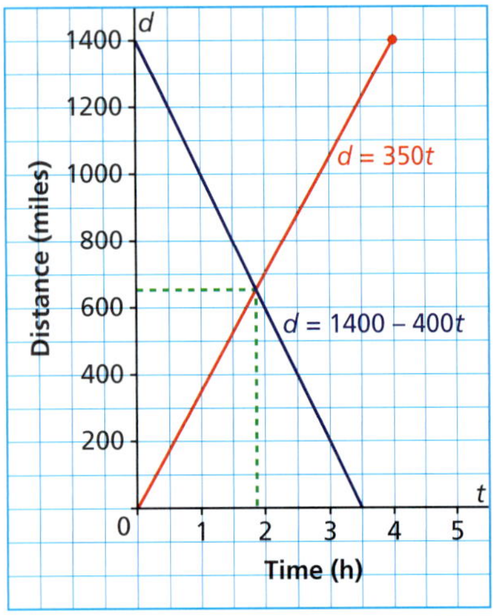

CHECK YOUR UNDERSTANDING

2. Jaden left her cabin on Waskesiu Lake, in Saskatchewan, and paddled her kayak toward her friend Tyrell's cabin at an average speed of 4 km/h. Tyrell started at his cabin at the same time and paddled at an average speed of 2.4 km/h toward Jaden's cabin. The cabins are 6 km apart. A linear system that models this situation is:

$d = 6 - 4t$

$d = 2.4t$

where d is the distance in kilometres from Tyrell's cabin and t is the time in hours since both people began their journey

a) Graph the linear system above.

b) Use the graph to solve this problem: When do Jaden and Tyrell meet and how far are they from Tyrell's cabin?

[Answer: b) after travelling for approximately 54 min and at approximately 2.3 km from Tyrell's cabin]

How would the equations in the linear system change if you wanted to determine when the planes meet and how far they are from Regina? Explain.

b) The graphs appear to intersect at (1.9, 650); that is, the planes appear to pass each other after travelling for 1.9 h and at a distance of 650 mi. from Ottawa.
To verify the solution, use the given information.
The plane travelling from Regina to Ottawa travels at 400 mph.
So, in 1.9 h, it will travel: $400(1.9)$ mi. $= 760$ mi.
So, it will be: $(1400 - 760)$ mi., or 640 mi. from Ottawa.
The plane travelling from Ottawa to Regina travels at 350 mph.
So, in 1.9 h, its distance from Ottawa will be:
$350(1.9)$ mi. $= 665$ mi.
The time and distance are approximate because these measures cannot be read accurately from the graph.
0.9 h is $60(0.9)$ min $= 54$ min
The planes pass each other after travelling for approximately 1 h 54 min and when they are approximately 650 mi. from Ottawa.

How could you solve the problem without using a linear system?

Example 3 Solving a Problem by Writing then Graphing a Linear System

a) Write a linear system to model this situation:
To visit the Head-Smashed-In Buffalo Jump interpretive centre near Fort Macleod, Alberta, the admission fee is \$5 for a student and \$9 for an adult. In one hour, 32 people entered the centre and a total of \$180 in admission fees was collected.

b) Graph the linear system then solve this problem: How many students and how many adults visited the centre during this time?

SOLUTION

a) Use a table to help develop the equations.

Given:	Creating a Linear System
There are students and adults.	Let s represent the number of students. Let a represent the number of adults.
There are 32 people.	One equation is: $s + a = 32$
Cost per student is \$5.	$5s$ dollars represents the total cost for the students.
Cost per adult is \$9.	$9a$ dollars represents the total cost for the adults.
Cost for all the people is \$180.	Another equation is: $5s + 9a = 180$

(Solution continues.)

CHECK YOUR UNDERSTANDING

3. a) Write a linear system to model this situation:
Wayne received and sent 60 text messages on his cell phone in one weekend. He sent 10 more messages than he received.

b) Graph the linear system then solve this problem: How many text messages did Wayne send and how many did he receive?

[Answers: a) $s + r = 60$; $s - r = 10$
b) 35 sent and 25 received]

The linear system is:

$s + a = 32$ ①

$5s + 9a = 180$ ②

b) Use intercepts to graph each line.

Equation	*a*-intercept	*s*-intercept
$s + a = 32$	32	32
$5s + 9a = 180$	20	36

Since the data are discrete, place a straightedge through the intercepts of each line and plot more points on each line.

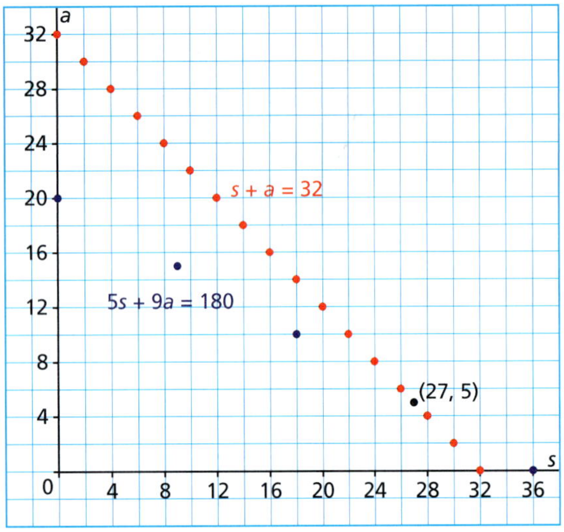

The point of intersection appears to be (27, 5).
Verify this solution.
Determine the cost for 27 students at \$5 each and 5 adults at \$9 each:

27 students at \$5 each	= \$135
+ 5 adults at \$9 each	= \$45
32 people for	\$180

The total number of people is 32 and the total cost is \$180, so the solution is correct.

Twenty-seven students and 5 adults visited the centre.

Suppose the equations had been graphed with *s* on the vertical axis and *a* on the horizontal axis. Would the graphs have been different? Would the solution have been different? Explain.

Discuss the Ideas

1. What steps do you follow to solve a system of linear equations by graphing?
2. What are some limitations to solving a linear system by graphing?

Exercises

A

3. Determine the solution of each linear system.

a)

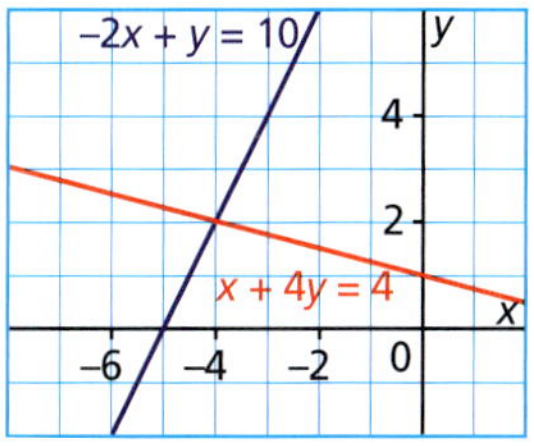

b)

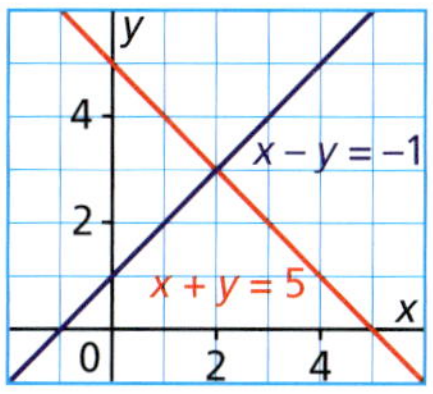

c)

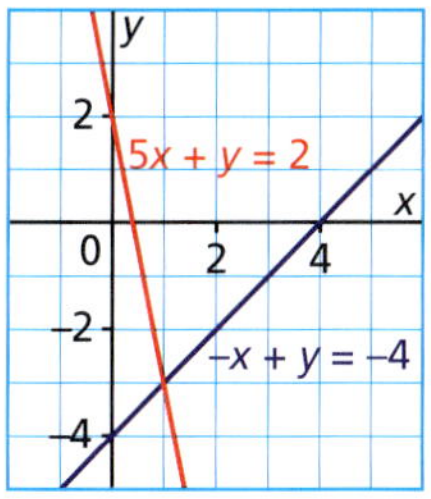

d)

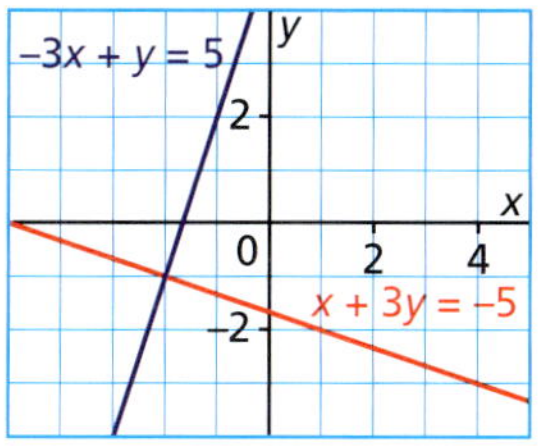

B

4. For each linear system, use the graphs to determine the solution. Explain how you know whether the solution is exact or approximate.

a)

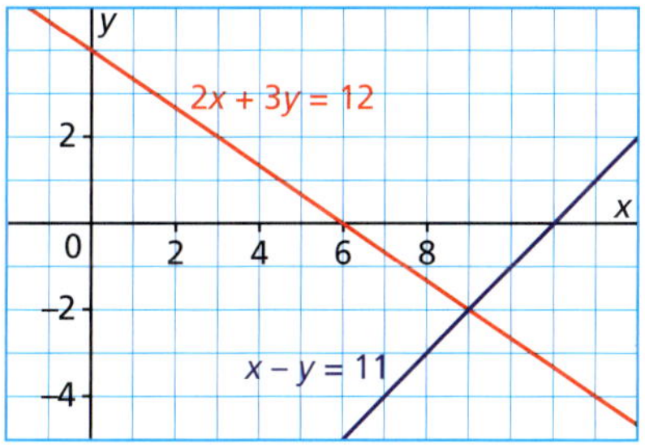

b)

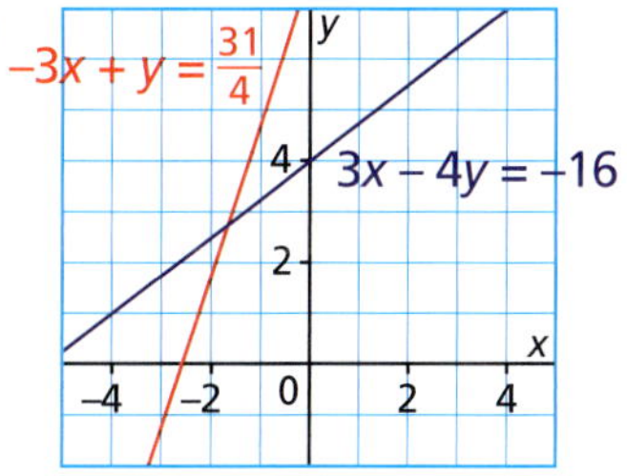

5. a) Solve each linear system.

i) $x + y = 7$
$3x + 4y = 24$

ii) $x - y = -1$
$3x + 2y = 12$

iii) $5x + 4y = 10$
$5x + 6y = 0$

iv) $x + 2y = -1$
$2x + y = -5$

b) Choose one linear system from part a. Explain the meaning of the point of intersection of the graphs of a system of linear equations.

6. Emil's solution to this linear system was (500, 300). Is his solution exact or approximate? Explain.

$3x - y = 1149$
$-x + 2y = 142$

7. Solve each linear system.

a) $2x + 4y = -1$
$3x - y = 9$

b) $5x + 5y = 17$
$x - y = -1$

c) $x + y = \frac{23}{4}$
$x - y = \frac{3}{4}$

d) $3x + y = 6$
$x + y = -\frac{4}{3}$

8. Two companies charge these rates for printing a brochure:
Company A charges \$175 for set-up, and \$0.10 per brochure.
Company B charges \$250 for set-up, and \$0.07 per brochure.
A linear system that models this situation is:
$C = 175 + 0.10n$
$C = 250 + 0.07n$
where C is the total cost in dollars and n is the number of brochures printed

a) Graph the linear system above.

b) Use the graph to solve these problems:

i) How many brochures must be printed for the cost to be the same at both companies?

ii) When is it cheaper to use Company A to print brochures? Explain.

9. Part-time sales clerks at a computer store are offered two methods of payment:
Plan A: \$700 a month plus 3% commission on total sales
Plan B: \$1000 a month plus 2% commission on total sales.
A linear system that models this situation is:
$P = 700 + 0.03s$
$P = 1000 + 0.02s$
where P is the clerk's monthly salary in dollars and s is the clerk's monthly sales in dollars

a) Graph the linear system above.

b) Use the graph to solve these problems:

i) What must the monthly sales be for a clerk to receive the same salary with both plans?

ii) When would it be better for a clerk to choose Plan B? Explain.

For questions 10 to 13, write a linear system to model each situation. Solve the related problem. Indicate whether your solution is exact or approximate.

10. The area of Stanley Park in Vancouver is 391 hectares. The forested area is 141 hectares more than the rest of the park. What is the area of each part of the park?

11. In the American Hockey League, a team gets 2 points for a win and 1 point for an overtime loss. In the 2008–2009 regular season, the Manitoba Moose had 107 points. They had 43 more wins than overtime losses. How many wins and how many overtime losses did the team have?

12. Annika's class raised $800 by selling $5 and $10 movie gift cards. The class sold a total of 115 gift cards. How many of each type of card did the class sell?

13. A group of adults and students went on a field trip to the Royal Tyrell Museum, near Drumheller, Alberta. The total admission fee was $152. There were 13 more students than adults. How many adults and how many students went on the field trip?

14. a) Write a linear system to model this situation: A box of 36 golf balls has a mass of 1806 g. When 12 balls are removed, the mass is 1254 g.

b) Use a graph to solve this problem: What is the mass of the box and the mass of one golf ball?

c) Why was it difficult to determine a solution?

15. The home plate in a baseball diamond is a pentagon with perimeter 58 in. Each shorter side, x, is $3\frac{1}{2}$ in. less than each longer side, y. What are the values of x and y?

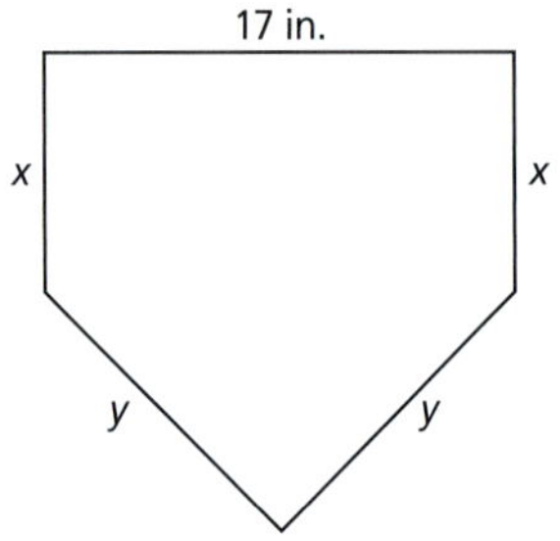

16. a) Solve this linear system by graphing.

$2x + 7y = 3$

$4x + 3y = 7$

b) Why is the solution approximate?

C

17. Emma solved a linear system by graphing. She first determined the intercepts of each line.

Equation	x-intercept	y-intercept
1	5	5
2	4	6

a) Write a linear system that Emma could have solved. Explain your work.

b) Draw the graphs to determine the solution.

18. One equation of a linear system is $y = 2x + 1$. The solution of the linear system is in the third quadrant. What might the second equation be? Explain how you determined the equation.

19. a) Suppose you want to solve this linear system by graphing. How do you know that the lines are perpendicular?

$2x + 3y = -5$

$\frac{x}{2} - \frac{y}{3} = 2$

b) Create another linear system where the lines are perpendicular. Explain what you did.

Reflect

When you solve a linear system graphically, how can you determine whether the solution is approximate or exact?

MATH LAB

7.3 Using Graphing Technology to Solve a System of Linear Equations

LESSON FOCUS

Determine and verify the solution of a linear system using graphing technology.

Make Connections

In 2006, the population of Canada was 31 612 897. The population of the eastern provinces was 12 369 487 more than the population of the territories and western provinces.

What linear system models this situation?
How could you determine the population of the territories and western provinces?
How could you determine the population of the eastern provinces?
Why can't you determine an exact solution by graphing on grid paper?

Construct Understanding

TRY THIS

Work with a partner.
You will need:

- a graphing calculator or computer with graphing software

Léa's school had a carnival to celebrate *Festival du Voyageur*.
The school raised $1518.75 by charging an adult $3.75 and a student $2.50.
The total attendance was 520.
How many adults and how many students attended?

A. Write a linear system to model this situation.

B. Express each equation in slope-intercept form. Graph each line.

> Before you graph, how can you tell in which quadrant the point of intersection lies?

C. Determine the coordinates of the point of intersection of the lines. Are these coordinates exact or approximate? Explain.

D. How could you verify the solution in Step C by using tables of values?

> What table settings would you use? Why did you choose these?

E. Verify your solution by using the data in the given problem.

F. How can you use your results to determine the number of adults and the number of students who attended the carnival?

Assess Your Understanding

1. To solve this linear system:
$x + 2y = 8$
$3x + 4y = 20$
Gerard entered each equation into his graphing calculator in this form:

```
Plot1 Plot2 Plot3
\Y1 = -X/2+4
\Y2 = -3X/4+5
\Y3 =
\Y4 =
\Y5 =
\Y6 =
\Y7 =
```

Gerard created a table of values for these equations.

X	Y1	Y2
0	4	5
1	3.5	4.25
2	3	3.5
3	2.5	2.75
4	2	2
5	1.5	1.25
6	1	.5

X=0

a) How could Gerard use the table to determine the solution of the linear system?
b) Describe a different strategy Gerard could use to solve this linear system.

2. a) Explain how you would use graphing technology to determine the solution of this linear system.

$3x - 6y = 14$

$x + y = \frac{7}{6}$

b) What is the solution?

3. A community group purchased 72 cedar tree and spruce tree seedlings to plant for an Earth Day project. The number of cedar trees was twice the number of spruce trees. How many of each type of tree seedling did the group purchase?

4. a) Each linear system below contains the equation $x + 2y = 3$. Solve each system by graphing.

i) $x + 2y = 3$
$2x - y = 1$

ii) $x + 2y = 3$
$2x - y = 6$

iii) $x + 2y = 3$
$2x - y = 11$

iv) $x + 2y = 3$
$2x - y = 16$

b) What patterns are there in the linear systems and their solutions? Use the patterns to predict another linear system that would extend the pattern. Explain your prediction.

c) Solve the linear system to check your prediction.

5. When you graph to solve a linear system that contains fractional coefficients, will you always get an approximate solution? Use the linear systems below to explain.

System A

$\frac{1}{2}x + y = 3$

$x + \frac{1}{2}y = 3$

System B

$2x + y = \frac{23}{6}$

$\frac{x}{3} + \frac{y}{2} = \frac{55}{36}$

CHECKPOINT 1

Connections

Given this Situation and Related Problem

A store has boxes containing 1500 golf balls.
There are 5 more boxes containing 12 balls than boxes containing 24 balls.
How many of each size of box does the store have?

Identify the Variables

Let x represent the number of boxes with 12 balls.

Let y represent the number of boxes with 24 balls.

Model the Situation with a Linear System

$12x + 24y = 1500$

$x - y = 5$

Graph to Locate the Point of Intersection

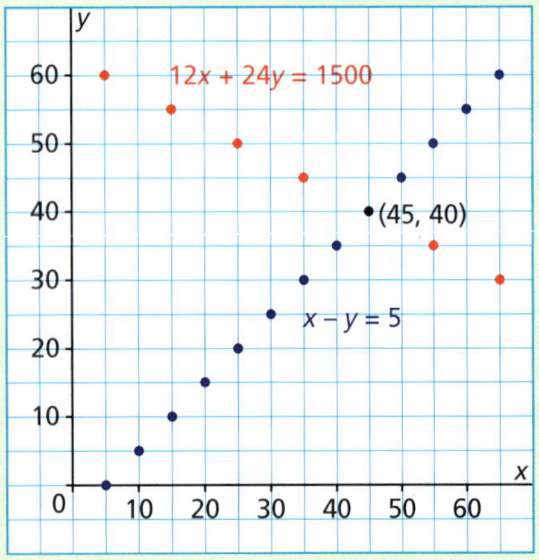

Identify the Solution

$x = 45$

$y = 40$

Use the equations to verify the solution.

Use the problem to verify the solution.

Concept Development

- **In Lesson 7.1**
  - You defined a linear system, wrote linear systems to model problems, and related linear systems to problems.
- **In Lesson 7.2**
  - You solved a linear system by graphing the linear equations on grid paper and determining the coordinates of their point of intersection.
  - You identified whether a solution to a linear system was exact or approximate.
- **In Lesson 7.3**
  - You solved linear systems using graphing technology by first expressing each equation in the form $y = f(x)$.
  - You used technology to determine whether the solution of a linear system was exact or approximate.
  - You verified the solution of a linear system by examining tables of values.

Assess Your Understanding

7.1

1. a) Create a linear system to model this situation:
   The Commonwealth stadium in Edmonton, Alberta, has the largest video screen JumboTron in the world. Its perimeter is 128 ft. Its width is 16 ft. less than its length.
   b) The length of the screen is 40 ft. and its width is 24 ft.
      i) Use the equations to verify these dimensions.
      ii) Use the problem to verify these dimensions.

2. Create a situation that can be modelled by this linear system, then write a related problem.
   $10x + 5y = 850$
   $x - y = 10$

7.2

3. Solve this linear system by graphing on grid paper. Describe your strategy.
   $2x + y = 1$
   $x + 2y = -1$

4. A fitness club offers two payment plans:
   Plan A: an initiation fee of \$75 plus a user fee of \$5 per visit
   Plan B: a user fee of \$10 per visit
   A linear system that models this situation is:
   $F = 75 + 5v$
   $F = 10v$
   where F is the total fee in dollars and v is the number of visits
   a) Graph this linear system.
   b) Under what conditions is Plan A cheaper? Justify your answer.

5. a) Write a linear system to model this situation:
   A group of students and adults went to the Vancouver Aquarium in B.C. The admission fee was \$21 for a student and \$27 for an adult. The total cost for 18 people was \$396.
   b) Use a graph to solve this problem:
   How many students and how many adults went to the aquarium?

7.3

6. a) Write a linear system to model this situation:
   A large tree removes 1.4 kg of pollution from the air each year. A small tree removes 0.02 kg each year. An urban forest has 15 000 large and small trees. Together, these trees remove 7200 kg of pollution each year.
   b) Use graphing technology to solve this problem: How many of each size of tree are in the forest?

7.4 Using a Substitution Strategy to Solve a System of Linear Equations

LESSON FOCUS

Use the substitution of one variable to solve a linear system.

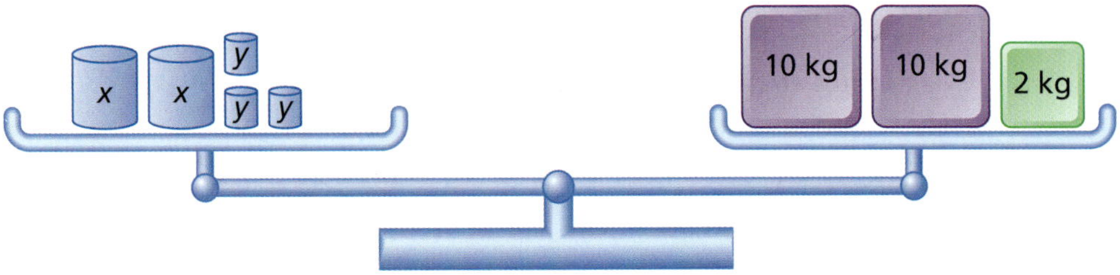

Make Connections

Look at the picture above.
Is there enough information to determine the masses of the container labelled x and the container labelled y? Explain.
How would your answer change if you knew that each container labelled x had a mass of 5 kg? Explain.

Construct Understanding

THINK ABOUT IT

Work with a partner.

Solve each linear system without graphing.

- $3x + 5y = 6$
  $x = -4$
- $2x + y = 5$
  $y = -x + 3$

What strategies did you use?
How can you check that each solution is correct?

In Lessons 7.2 and 7.3, you solved linear systems by graphing. This strategy is time-consuming even when you use graphing technology, and you can only approximate the solution. We use algebra to determine an exact solution. One algebraic strategy is called **solving by substitution.** By using substitution, we transform a system of two linear equations into a single equation in one variable, then we use what we know about solving linear equations to determine the value of that variable.

Consider this linear system.

$3x + 4y = -4$ ①

$x + 2y = 2$ ②

In equation ②, the variable x has coefficient 1. So, solve equation ② for x.

$x + 2y = 2$ ②

$x = -2y + 2$

Why did we solve for x instead of for y?

Since the solution of the linear system is the point of intersection of the graphs of the two lines, the x-coordinate must satisfy both equations. We substitute the expression for x in the other equation.

Substitute $x = -2y + 2$ in equation ①.

$3x + 4y = -4$ ①

$3(-2y + 2) + 4y = -4$ Use the distributive property to simplify.

$-6y + 6 + 4y = -4$ Collect like terms.

$-2y = -10$ Solve for y.

$y = 5$

When we know the value of one variable, we substitute for that variable in one of the original equations then solve that equation for the other variable.

Would we get the same solution if we solved equation ② for y instead of for x? Explain.

Substitute $y = 5$ in equation ②.

$x + 2y = 2$ ②

$x + 2(5) = 2$

$x + 10 = 2$ Solve for x.

$x = -8$

To verify the solution is correct, we substitute for both variables in the original equations.

In each equation, substitute: $x = -8$ and $y = 5$

$3x + 4y = -4$ ①

L.S. $= 3x + 4y$

$= 3(-8) + 4(5)$

$= -24 + 20$

$= -4$

$=$ R.S.

$x + 2y = 2$ ②

L.S. $= x + 2y$

$= -8 + 2(5)$

$= -8 + 10$

$= 2$

$=$ R.S.

Would we get the same solution if we substituted $y = 5$ in equation ① instead of equation ②? Explain.

For each equation, the left side is equal to the right side, so the solution is: $x = -8$ and $y = 5$

Here is the graphical solution for the linear system on page 417:

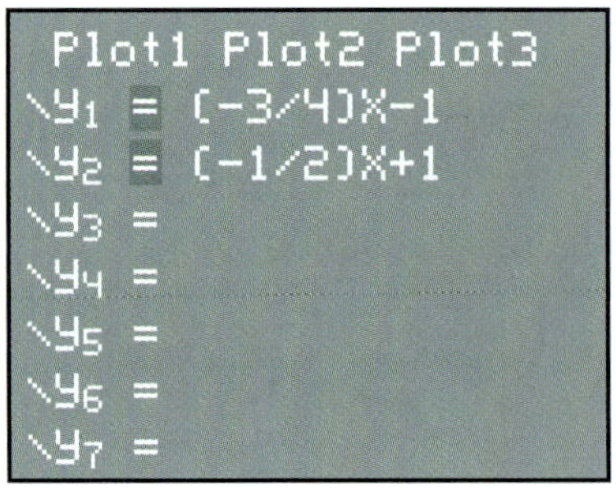

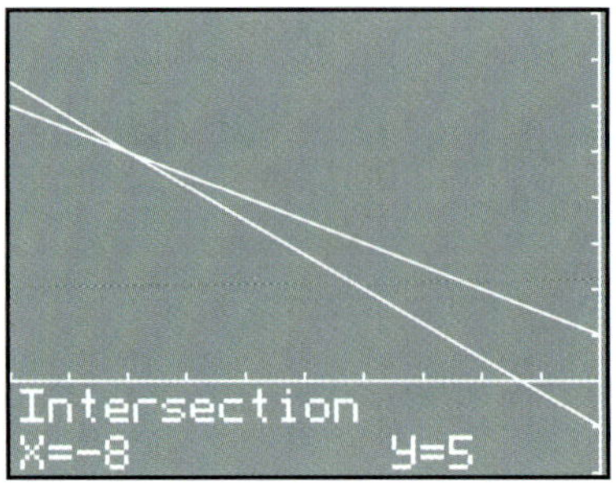

Example 1 Solving a Linear System by Substitution

Solve this linear system.

$2x - 4y = 7$

$4x + y = 5$

SOLUTIONS

Method 1

$2x - 4y = 7$ ①

$4x + y = 5$ ②

Solve equation ② for y.

$4x + y = 5$ ②

$y = 5 - 4x$

Substitute $y = 5 - 4x$ in equation ①.

$2x - 4y = 7$ ①

$2x - 4(5 - 4x) = 7$ Simplify, then solve for x.

$2x - 20 + 16x = 7$

$18x = 27$

$x = 1.5$

Substitute $x = 1.5$ in equation ②.

$4x + y = 5$ ②

$4(1.5) + y = 5$ ②

$6 + y = 5$

$y = -1$

CHECK YOUR UNDERSTANDING

1. Solve this linear system.

   $5x - 3y = 18$

   $4x - 6y = 18$

   [Answer: $x = 3$ and $y = -1$]

Method 2

When no equation in a linear system has a variable with coefficient 1, it is helpful if there are two like terms where one term is a multiple of the other term.

$2x - 4y = 7$ ①

$4x + y = 5$ ②

In equation ②, the term $4x$ can be written as $2(2x)$:

$2(2x) + y = 5$ ③

When we change the form of an equation, we label it with a different number.

Solve equation ① for $2x$.

$2x - 4y = 7$ ①

$2x = 7 + 4y$

Substitute $2x = 7 + 4y$ in equation ③.

$2(2x) + y = 5$ ③

$2(7 + 4y) + y = 5$

$14 + 8y + y = 5$

$9y = -9$

$y = -1$

Simplify, then solve for y.

Substitute $y = -1$ into equation ①.

$2x - 4y = 7$

$2x - 4(-1) = 7$

$2x + 4 = 7$

$2x = 3$

$x = 1.5$

Solve for x.

Verify the solution.
In each equation, substitute: $x = 1.5$ and $y = -1$

$2x - 4y = 7$ ①

L.S. $= 2x - 4y$
$= 2(1.5) - 4(-1)$
$= 3 + 4$
$= 7$
$=$ R.S.

$4x + y = 5$ ②

L.S. $= 4x + y$
$= 4(1.5) - 1$
$= 6 - 1$
$= 5$
$=$ R.S.

For each equation, the left side is equal to the right side, so the solution is: $x = 1.5$ and $y = -1$

Why did we write $4x = 2(2x)$ and not $4y = 2(2y)$?

Verify that we get the same solution when we substitute $y = -1$ into equation ②.

Example 2 Using a Linear System to Solve a Problem

a) Create a linear system to model this situation:
Nuri invested \$2000, part at an annual interest rate of 8% and the rest at an annual interest rate of 10%. After one year, the total interest was \$190.

b) Solve this problem: How much money did Nuri invest at each rate?

SOLUTIONS

a) Use a table to help develop the equations.

Given:	Creating a Linear System
There are two investments.	Let x dollars represent the amount invested at 8%. Let y dollars represent the amount invested at 10%.
The total investment was \$2000.	One equation is: $x + y = 2000$
x dollars at 8%	The interest is 8% of x dollars: $0.08x$
y dollars at 10%	The interest is 10% of y dollars: $0.10y$
The total interest is \$190.	Another equation is: $0.08x + 0.10y = 190$

The linear system is:

$x + y = 2000$ ①

$0.08x + 0.10y = 190$ ②

b) **Method 1**

Because the coefficients of x and y in equation ① are 1, use substitution to solve the linear system.

Solve for y in equation ①.

$x + y = 2000$ ①

$y = -x + 2000$

Substitute $y = -x + 2000$ in equation ②.

$0.08x + 0.10y = 190$ ②

$0.08x + 0.10(-x + 2000) = 190$ Use the distributive property.

$0.08x - 0.10x + 200 = 190$ Collect like terms.

$-0.02x + 200 = 190$

$-0.02x = -10$ Divide each side by -0.02 to solve for x.

$x = 500$

Substitute $x = 500$ in equation ①.

$x + y = 2000$

$500 + y = 2000$ Solve for y.

$y = 1500$

Nuri invested \$500 at 8% and \$1500 at 10%.

CHECK YOUR UNDERSTANDING

2. a) Create a linear system to model this situation:
Alexia invested \$1800, part at an annual interest rate of 3.5% and the rest at an annual interest rate of 4.5%. After one year, the total interest was \$73.

b) Solve this problem: How much money did Alexia invest at each rate?

[Answers: a) $x + y = 1800$; $0.035x + 0.045y = 73$
b) Alexia invested \$800 at 3.5% and \$1000 at 4.5%.]

Why might you want to multiply equation ② by 100?

Method 2

Use graphing technology to solve the system and the problem.
Express each equation in slope-intercept form.

$x + y = 2000$ $\qquad$ $0.08x + 0.10y = 190$

$y = -x + 2000$ $\qquad$ $0.10y = -0.08x + 190$

$y = -0.8x + 1900$

Graph each equation.

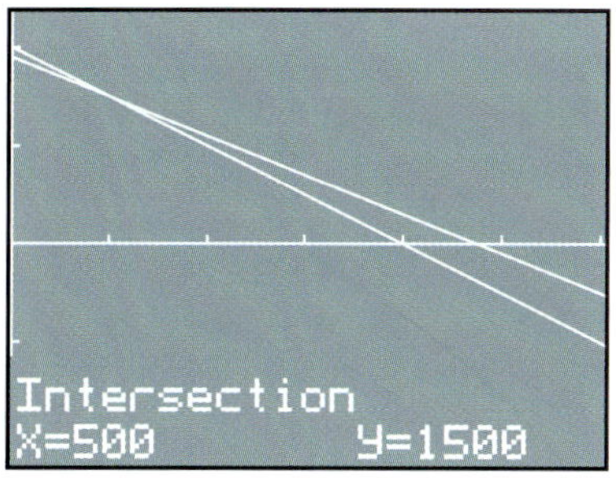

The lines intersect at: (500, 1500)
The solution is: $x = 500$ and $y = 1500$
So, Nuri invested $500 at 8% and $1500 at 10%.
To verify the solution, use the data in the given problem.
Add the amounts: $500 + $1500 = $2000, which is the total amount invested
8% of 500 is $40 and 10% of $1500 is $150. Add the interest.
The total interest is: $40 + $150 = $190
These numbers match those given in the problem, so the solution is correct.

These two linear systems have the same graphs and the same solution $x = 1$ and $y = 2$.

System A

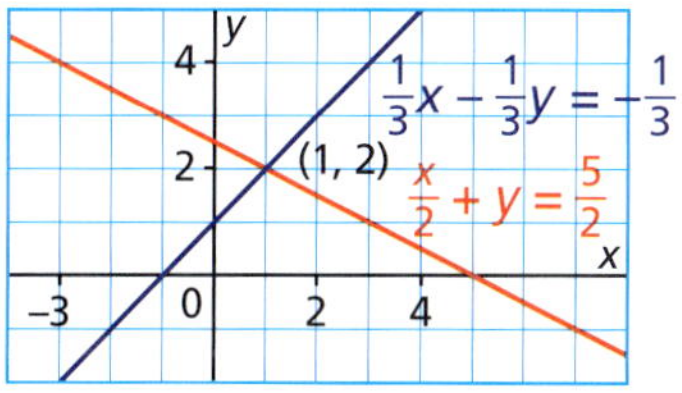

System B

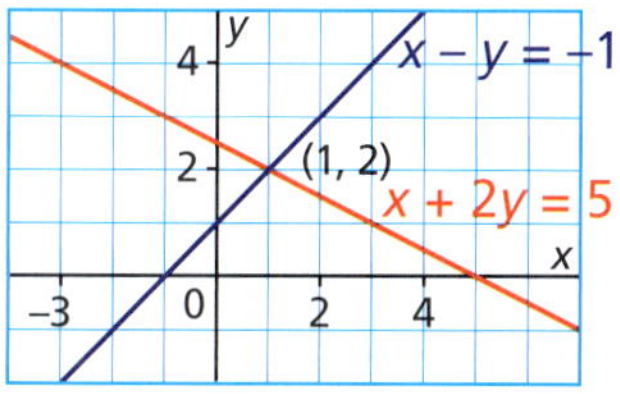

In System A, we can multiply the first equation by 2, and the second equation by 3 to write equivalent equations with integer coefficients. The result is the equations in System B.

System A			System B	
$\frac{x}{2} + y = \frac{5}{2}$	①	Multiply each term by 2.	$x + 2y = 5$	③
$\frac{1}{3}x - \frac{1}{3}y = -\frac{1}{3}$	②	Multiply each term by 3.	$x - y = -1$	④

The two linear systems have the same solution $x = 1$ and $y = 2$ because the corresponding equations are equivalent; that is, equation ① is equivalent to equation ③, and equation ② is equivalent to equation ④.
Multiplying or dividing the equations in a linear system by a non-zero number does not change the graphs. So, their point of intersection, and hence, the solution of the linear system is unchanged.

A system of equivalent equations is called an **equivalent linear system** and has the same solution as the original system.

When an equation in a linear system has coefficients or a constant term that are fractions, we can multiply by a common denominator to write an equivalent equation with integer coefficients.

Example 3 Solving a Linear System with Fractional Coefficients

Solve this linear system by substitution.

$$\frac{1}{2}x + \frac{2}{3}y = -1$$

$$y = \frac{1}{4}x - \frac{5}{3}$$

SOLUTIONS

Method 1

$$\frac{1}{2}x + \frac{2}{3}y = -1 \quad ①$$

$$y = \frac{1}{4}x - \frac{5}{3} \quad ②$$

Write an equivalent system with integer coefficients.
For equation ①:

$$\frac{1}{2}x + \frac{2}{3}y = -1$$ Multiply each term by 6.

$$6\left(\frac{1}{2}x\right) + 6\left(\frac{2}{3}y\right) = 6(-1)$$ Simplify.

$$3x + 4y = -6 \quad ③$$

For equation ②:

$$y = \frac{1}{4}x - \frac{5}{3}$$ Multiply each term by 12.

$$12(y) = 12\left(\frac{1}{4}x\right) - 12\left(\frac{5}{3}\right)$$ Simplify.

$$12y = 3x - 20 \quad ④$$

CHECK YOUR UNDERSTANDING

3. Solve this linear system by substitution.

$$\frac{1}{2}x - \frac{4}{5}y = -2$$

$$y = \frac{1}{4}x - \frac{3}{8}$$

[Answer: $x = -\frac{23}{3}$ and $y = -\frac{55}{24}$]

Why did we multiply equation ① by 6 and equation ② by 12?

Solve equation ③ for $3x$.

$3x + 4y = -6$ ③

$3x = -4y - 6$

Equations ③ and ④ form a linear system that is equivalent to the linear system formed by equations ① and ②.

Substitute for $3x$ in equation ④.

$12y = 3x - 20$ ④

$12y = (-4y - 6) - 20$

$12y = -4y - 26$ — Solve for y.

$16y - -26$

$y = -\frac{26}{16}$, or $-\frac{13}{8}$

Substitute $y = -\frac{13}{8}$ into equation ④.

$12y = 3x - 20$ ④

$12\left(-\frac{13}{8}\right) = 3x - 20$ — Solve for x.

$-\frac{39}{2} = 3x - 20$

$20 - \frac{39}{2} = 3x$

$\frac{40}{2} - \frac{39}{2} = 3x$

$\frac{1}{2} = 3x$ — Divide by 3.

$x = \frac{1}{6}$

Method 2

$\frac{1}{2}x + \frac{2}{3}y = -1$ ①

$y = \frac{1}{4}x - \frac{5}{3}$ ②

Since equation ② is solved for y, substitute for y in equation ①.

$\frac{1}{2}x + \frac{2}{3}y = -1$ ①

$\frac{1}{2}x + \frac{2}{3}\left(\frac{1}{4}x - \frac{5}{3}\right) = -1$ — Use the distributive property.

$\frac{1}{2}x + \frac{1}{6}x - \frac{10}{9} = -1$ — Collect like terms.

$\frac{2}{3}x - \frac{10}{9} = -1$ — Solve for x.

$\frac{2}{3}x = -1 + \frac{10}{9}$

$\frac{2}{3}x = \frac{1}{9}$ — Divide by $\frac{2}{3}$.

$x = \frac{1}{9}\left(\frac{3}{2}\right)$

$x = \frac{1}{6}$

(Solution continues.)

Substitute $x = \frac{1}{6}$ in equation ②.

$y = \frac{1}{4}x - \frac{5}{3}$ ②

$y = \frac{1}{4}\left(\frac{1}{6}\right) - \frac{5}{3}$

$y = \frac{1}{24} - \frac{5}{3}$

$y = \frac{1}{24} - \frac{40}{24}$

$y = -\frac{39}{24}$, or $-\frac{13}{8}$

Verify the solution.

In each equation, substitute: $x = \frac{1}{6}$ and $y = -\frac{13}{8}$

$\frac{1}{2}x + \frac{2}{3}y = -1$ ①

L.S. $= \frac{1}{2}\left(\frac{1}{6}\right) + \frac{2}{3}\left(-\frac{13}{8}\right)$

$= \frac{1}{12} - \frac{13}{12}$

$= -1$

$=$ R.S.

$y = \frac{1}{4}x - \frac{5}{3}$ ②

L.S. $= -\frac{13}{8}$

R.S. $= \frac{1}{4}\left(\frac{1}{6}\right) - \frac{5}{3}$

$= \frac{1}{24} - \frac{5}{3}$

$= \frac{1}{24} - \frac{40}{24}$

$= -\frac{39}{24}$, or $-\frac{13}{8}$

$=$ L.S.

For each equation, the left side is equal to the right side, so the solution is:

$x = \frac{1}{6}$ and $y = -\frac{13}{8}$

Discuss the Ideas

1. When you have a system of linear equations, how can you form an equivalent linear system?
2. When you want to write an equivalent equation with integer coefficients, how do you decide which number to multiply by? Use an example to explain.
3. What are some advantages of solving a linear system using the substitution strategy rather than graphing?

Exercises

A

4. Use substitution to solve each linear system.

a) $y = 9 - x$
$2x + 3y = 11$

b) $x = y - 1$
$3x - y = 11$

c) $x = 7 + y$
$2x + y = -10$

d) $3x + y = 7$
$y = x + 3$

5. Solve each linear system.

a) $2x + 3y = 11$
$4x - y = -13$

b) $4x + y = -5$
$2x + 3y = 5$

c) $x + 2y = 13$
$2x - 3y = -9$

d) $3x + y = 7$
$5x + 2y = 13$

B

6. a) In each linear system, identify two like terms and say how they are related.

i) $2x - 3y = 2$
$4x - 4y = 2$

ii) $40x + 10y = 10$
$3x + 5y = 5$

iii) $-3x + 6y = 9$
$5x - 2y = -7$

iv) $-3x + 4y = 6$
$9x + 3y = 27$

b) Solve each linear system in part a.

7. a) Suppose you wanted to solve a linear system in the fewest steps. Which of these systems would you choose? Why?

i) $x - y = -5$
$x = -1$

ii) $x - y = -5$
$-x - y = 3$

iii) $2x - 3y = 7$
$x - 2y = 3$

b) Solve each linear system in part a. Explain what you did.

8. a) For each equation, identify a number you could multiply each term by to ensure that the equation has only integer coefficients and constants. Explain why you chose that number. Create an equivalent linear system.

$$\frac{x}{3} - \frac{y}{2} = 2$$

$$\frac{5x}{6} + \frac{3y}{4} = 1$$

b) Verify that both linear systems in part a have the same solution.

9. a) For each equation, choose a divisor. Create an equivalent linear system by dividing each term in the equation by that divisor.

$2x + 2y = -4$
$-12x + 4y = -24$

b) Show that both linear systems in part a have the same solution.

For questions 10 to 18, write a linear system to model each situation. Solve the linear system to solve the related problem.

10. A study recorded the reactions of 186 polar bears as they were approached by a tundra buggy. Some bears did not appear to respond, while others responded by sitting, standing, walking away, or running away. There were 94 more bears that did not respond than did respond. How many bears responded and how many bears did not respond?

11. Louise purchased a Métis flag whose length was 90 cm longer than its width. The perimeter of the flag was 540 cm. What are the dimensions of the flag?

12. Forty-five high school students and adults were surveyed about their use of the internet. Thirty-one people reported a heavy use of the internet. This was 80% of the high school students and 60% of the adults. How many students and how many adults were in the study?

13. Many researchers, such as those at the Canadian Fossil Discovery Centre at Morden, Manitoba, involve students to help unearth fossil remains of 80 million-year-old reptiles. Forty-seven students are searching for fossils in 11 groups of 4 or 5. How many groups of 4 and how many groups of 5 are searching?

14. An art gallery has a collection of 85 Northwest Coast masks of people and animals. Sixty percent of the people masks and 40% of the animal masks are made of yellow cedar. The total number of yellow cedar masks is 38. How many people masks and how many animal masks are there?

15. Sam scored 80% on part A of a math test and 92% on part B of the math test. His total mark for the test was 63. The total mark possible for the test was 75. How many marks is each part worth?

16. Five thousand dollars was invested in two savings bonds for one year. One bond earned interest at an annual rate of 2.5%. The other bond earned 3.75% per year. The total interest earned was $162.50. How much money was invested in each bond?

17. Tess has a part-time job at an ice-cream store. On Saturday, she sold 76 single-scoop cones and 49 double-scoop cones for a total revenue of $474.25. On Sunday, Tess sold 54 single-scoop cones and 37 double-scoop cones for a total revenue of $346.25. What is the cost of each cone?

18. Joel has a part-time job that pays him $40 per weekend. Sue has a part-time job that paid a starting bonus of $150, then $30 per weekend. For how many weekends would Joel have to work before he earns the same amount as Sue? Justify your answer.

19. Solve each linear system.

a) $\frac{1}{2}x + \frac{2}{3}y = 1$
$\frac{1}{4}x - \frac{1}{3}y = \frac{5}{2}$

b) $\frac{3}{4}x + \frac{1}{2}y = -\frac{7}{12}$
$x - y = -\frac{4}{3}$

c) $\frac{1}{3}x - \frac{3}{8}y = 1$
$-\frac{1}{4}x - \frac{1}{8}y = \frac{3}{2}$

d) $\frac{7}{4}x + \frac{4}{3}y = 3$
$\frac{1}{2}x - \frac{5}{6}y = 2$

20. This linear system was used to solve a problem about the cost of buying reams of printer paper and ink cartridges for a school computer lab:
$7.50r + 45c = 375$
$r - c = 15$

a) Create a situation that can be modelled using the linear system. Write a related problem.
b) Solve the system and the problem.

21. Create a situation that can be modelled by this linear system. Write a related problem. Solve the system and the problem.
$2x + 4y = 98$
$x + y = 27$

22. a) Write a linear system that is equivalent to this system. Explain what you did.
$2x - y = -4$
$3x + 2y = 1$
b) Solve each linear system. How do your solutions show that the systems are equivalent?

C

23. One weekend, members of a cycling club rode on the KVR trail (Kettle Valley Railway) uphill from Penticton in Okanagan, B.C. The uphill climb reduced the cyclists' usual average speed by 6 km/h and they took 4 h to get to Chute Lake. On the return trip, the downhill ride increased the cyclists' usual average speed by 4 km/h. The return trip took 2 h.

a) What is the usual average speed?
b) What is the distance from Penticton to Chute Lake?

24. Researchers at the Nk'Mip Desert and Heritage Centre in Osoyoos, B.C., measured the masses of 45 female rattlesnakes and 100 male rattlesnakes as part of a study. The mean mass of all the snakes was 194 g. The mean mass of the males was 37.7 g greater than the mean mass of the females. What was the mean mass of the males and the mean mass of the females? Show your work.

25. After an airplane reached its cruising altitude, it climbed for 10 min. Then it descended for 15 min. Its current altitude was then 1000 m below its cruising altitude. The difference between the rate of climb and the rate of descent was 400 m/min. What were the rate of climb and the rate of descent?

26. Explain why x will always equal y in the solution of this linear system for any non-zero values of A, B, and C; $A \neq B$.

$Ax + By = C$
$Bx + Ay = C$

27. The solution of this linear system is (–2, 3). What are the values of A and B? Show your work.

$Ax + By = -17$
$Bx + Ay = 18$

Reflect

When you use the substitution strategy to solve a linear system, which do you choose first: the equation you start with or the variable you solve for? Use an example to justify your answer.

THE WORLD OF MATH

Careers: Electronics Technician

An electronics technician assembles, installs, troubleshoots, and repairs electronic equipment used by consumers, business, and industry. A technician can use a solution of a linear system to determine the current flowing through an electrical circuit and the voltage across the circuit.

7.5 Using an Elimination Strategy to Solve a System of Linear Equations

LESSON FOCUS

Use the elimination of one variable to solve a linear system.

Make Connections

A carpenter placed two identical plywood sheets end to end and measured their perimeter.

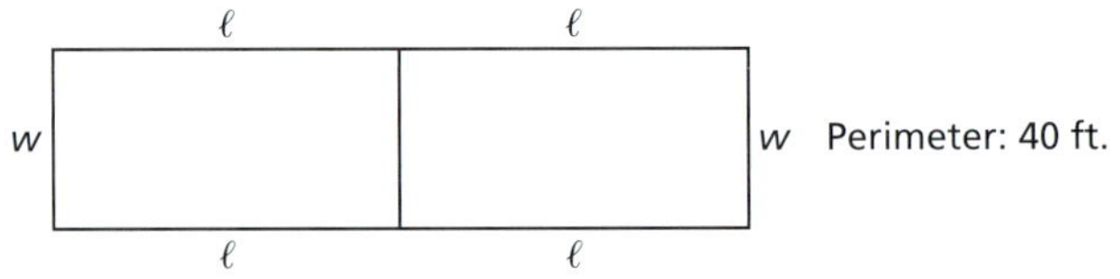

The carpenter placed the sheets side to side and measured their perimeter.

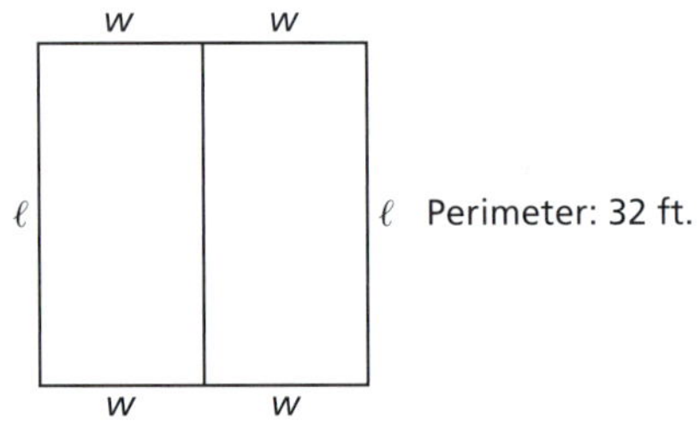

Suppose you wanted to determine the dimensions of a piece of this plywood.
Which linear system would model the situation?
How would you solve the linear system?

Construct Understanding

TRY THIS

Work with a partner.
Use graphing technology if it is available.

Use this linear system:

$x + 2y = 10$ ①

$x + y = 7$ ②

A. Create equation ③ by adding like terms in equation ① and equation ②. Graph all three equations on the same screen or grid. What do you notice?

B. Create equation ④ by subtracting equation ② from equation ①. Graph all four equations on the same screen or grid. What do you notice?

C. How would subtracting equation ② from equation ① help you solve the system? Would adding the two equations help you solve the system? Explain.

D. Create and solve your own linear system where each equation has the same y-coefficient. Add and subtract the equations to create two other linear equations. Graph all four equations. What do you notice?

E. How does adding or subtracting equations help you solve a linear system?

Why does adding or subtracting the like terms in two linear equations always result in another linear equation?

In Lesson 7.4, you learned that multiplying or dividing each equation in a linear system by a non-zero number does not change the solution because the linear systems that are formed are equivalent.

Similarly, adding or subtracting the two equations in a linear system produces equivalent linear systems. We use this property to solve a linear system by first eliminating one variable by adding or subtracting the two equations. This is called **solving by elimination.**

Why did we put brackets around equation ② when we subtracted it?

Consider this linear system.

$2x + y = -7$ ①

$x + y = -4$ ②

Because the coefficients of y are equal, we can eliminate y by subtracting the equations.

Subtract equation ② from equation ① to determine the value of x.

$$\begin{aligned} 2x + y &= -7 \quad ① \\ -(x + y &= -4) \quad ② \\ \hline 2x + y - x - y &= -7 - (-4) \\ x &= -3 \end{aligned}$$

Collect like terms.

Substitute $x = -3$ into equation ① to determine the value of y.

$$\begin{aligned} 2x + y &= -7 \quad ① \\ 2(-3) + y &= -7 \\ -6 + y &= -7 \\ y &= -1 \end{aligned}$$

Solve for y.

Verify the solution. In each equation, substitute: $x = -3$ and $y = -1$

$2x + y = -7$ ①

$$\begin{aligned} \text{L.S.} &= 2x + y \\ &= 2(-3) + (-1) \\ &= -6 - 1 \\ &= -7 \\ &= \text{R.S.} \end{aligned}$$

$x + y = -4$ ②

$$\begin{aligned} \text{L.S.} &= x + y \\ &= -3 + (-1) \\ &= -4 \\ &= \text{R.S.} \end{aligned}$$

For each equation, the left side is equal to the right side, so the solution is: $x = -3$ and $y = -1$

We may need to multiply one or both equations by constants before we can eliminate a variable by adding or subtracting.

Example 1 Solving a Linear System by Subtracting to Eliminate a Variable

Solve this linear system by elimination.

$3x - 4y = 7$

$5x - 6y = 8$

SOLUTION

$3x - 4y = 7$ ①

$5x - 6y = 8$ ②

No like terms have equal coefficients.

CHECK YOUR UNDERSTANDING

1. Solve this linear system by elimination.

$2x + 7y = 24$

$3x - 2y = -4$

[Answer: $x = 0.8$ and $y = 3.2$]

Consider the x-terms.
Their least common multiple is 15.
To make these terms equal, multiply equation ① by 5 and multiply equation ② by 3.

5 × equation ①: $5(3x - 4y = 7) \rightarrow 15x - 20y = 35$ ③
3 × equation ②: $3(5x - 6y = 8) \rightarrow 15x - 18y = 24$ ④

These equations form an equivalent linear system.

To solve this linear system, subtract equation ④ from equation ③ to eliminate x.

$$\begin{aligned} 15x - 20y &= 35 \quad ③ \\ -(15x - 18y &= 24) \quad ④ \\ \hline -20y - (-18y) &= 35 - 24 \\ -2y &= 11 \\ y &= -5.5 \end{aligned}$$

Substitute $y = -5.5$ in equation ①.

$$\begin{aligned} 3x - 4y &= 7 \quad ① \\ 3x - 4(-5.5) &= 7 \quad \text{Solve for } x. \\ 3x + 22 &= 7 \\ 3x &= -15 \\ x &= -5 \end{aligned}$$

Verify the solution.
In each equation, substitute: $x = -5$ and $y = -5.5$

$3x - 4y = 7$ ①

$$\begin{aligned} \text{L.S.} &= 3x - 4y \\ &= 3(-5) - 4(-5.5) \\ &= -15 + 22 \\ &= 7 \\ &= \text{R.S.} \end{aligned}$$

$5x - 6y = 8$ ②

$$\begin{aligned} \text{L.S.} &= 5x - 6y \\ &= 5(-5) - 6(-5.5) \\ &= -25 + 33 \\ &= 8 \\ &= \text{R.S.} \end{aligned}$$

For each equation, the left side is equal to the right side, so the solution is:
$x = -5$ and $y = -5.5$

What number would you multiply each equation by to be able to eliminate y by subtracting?

In a linear system, we may have to write equivalent equations with integer coefficients before we apply the elimination strategy.

Example 2 Solving a Linear System by Adding to Eliminate a Variable

Use an elimination strategy to solve this linear system.

$$\frac{2}{3}x - \frac{1}{2}y = 4$$
$$\frac{1}{2}x + \frac{1}{4}y = \frac{5}{2}$$

SOLUTION

$$\frac{2}{3}x - \frac{1}{2}y = 4 \quad ①$$
$$\frac{1}{2}x + \frac{1}{4}y = \frac{5}{2} \quad ②$$

Multiply each equation by a common denominator.

$6 \times$ equation ①: $6\left(\frac{2}{3}x - \frac{1}{2}y = 4\right)$

$$6\left(\frac{2}{3}x\right) - 6\left(\frac{1}{2}y\right) = 6(4)$$
$$4x - 3y = 24 \quad ③$$

$4 \times$ equation ②: $4\left(\frac{1}{2}x + \frac{1}{4}y = \frac{5}{2}\right)$

$$4\left(\frac{1}{2}x\right) + 4\left(\frac{1}{4}y\right) = 4\left(\frac{5}{2}\right)$$
$$2x + y = 10 \quad ④$$

An equivalent linear system is:

$4x - 3y = 24$ ③
$2x + y = 10$ ④

To eliminate y, multiply equation ④ by 3 so both y-terms have the numerical coefficient, 3.

$3 \times$ equation ④: $3(2x + y = 10) \rightarrow 6x + 3y = 30$ ⑤

An equivalent linear system is:

$6x + 3y = 30$ ⑤
$4x - 3y = 24$ ③

CHECK YOUR UNDERSTANDING

2. Use an elimination strategy to solve this linear system.

$$\frac{3}{4}x - y = 2$$
$$\frac{1}{8}x + \frac{1}{4}y = 2$$

[Answer: $x = 8$ and $y = 4$]

Suppose you multiplied equation ① by $\frac{1}{2}$. How would that help you eliminate one variable?

Add:

$$\begin{aligned} 6x + 3y &= 30 \quad ⑤ \\ +\ (4x - 3y &= 24) \quad ③ \\ \hline 10x \quad &= 54 \\ x \quad &= 5.4 \end{aligned}$$

Solve for *x*.

Substitute $x = 5.4$ in equation ①.

$$\frac{2}{3}x - \frac{1}{2}y = 4 \quad ①$$

$$\frac{2}{3}(5.4) - \frac{1}{2}y = 4$$

$$3.6 - \frac{1}{2}y = 4$$

Collect like terms.

$$-\frac{1}{2}y = 4 - 3.6$$

$$-\frac{1}{2}y = 0.4$$

Multiply each side by -2 to solve for *y*.

$$y = -2(0.4)$$

$$y = -0.8$$

Verify the solution.
In each equation, substitute: $x = 5.4$ and $y = -0.8$

$$\frac{2}{3}x - \frac{1}{2}y = 4 \quad ①$$

$$\begin{aligned} \text{L.S.} &= \frac{2}{3}x - \frac{1}{2}y \\ &= \frac{2}{3}(5.4) - \frac{1}{2}(-0.8) \\ &= 3.6 + 0.4 \\ &= 4 \\ &= \text{R.S.} \end{aligned}$$

$$\frac{1}{2}x + \frac{1}{4}y = \frac{5}{2} \quad ②$$

$$\begin{aligned} \text{L.S.} &= \frac{1}{2}x + \frac{1}{4}y \\ &= \frac{1}{2}(5.4) + \frac{1}{4}(-0.8) \\ &= 2.7 - 0.2 \\ &= 2.5 \\ &= \text{R.S.} \end{aligned}$$

For each equation, the left side is equal to the right side, so the solution is:
$x = 5.4$ and $y = -0.8$

What other strategy could you use to solve this linear system?

Example 3 Using a Linear System to Solve a Problem

a) Write a linear system to model this situation:
An alloy is a mixture of metals. An artist was commissioned to make a 100-g bracelet with a 50% silver alloy. He has a 60% silver alloy and a 35% silver alloy.

b) Solve this problem:
What is the mass of each alloy needed to produce the desired alloy?

SOLUTION

a) Let s grams represent the mass of 60% alloy and let t grams represent the mass of 35% alloy.
Sketch a diagram.

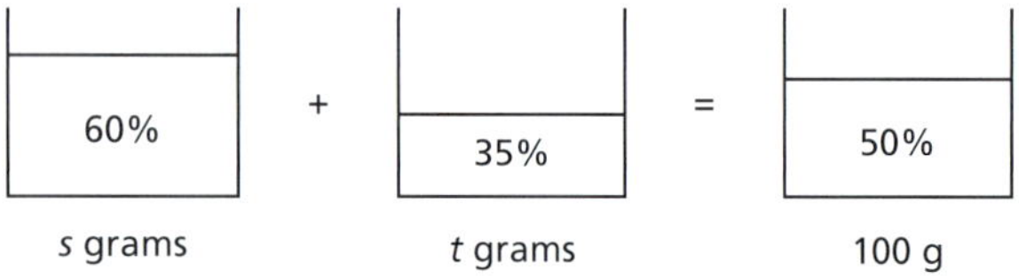

From the diagram:
The 100-g mass of the bracelet is the sum of mass s grams of 60% alloy and mass t grams of 35% alloy.
So, the first equation is: $s + t = 100$

The mass of silver in the bracelet is 50% of 100 g:
$0.50(100 \text{ g}) = 50 \text{ g}$
This 50 g of silver is made up of 60% of s plus 35% of t.
So, the second equation is: $0.60s + 0.35t = 50$

The linear system is:
$s + t = 100$ ①
$0.60s + 0.35t = 50$ ②

CHECK YOUR UNDERSTANDING

3. a) Write a linear system to model this situation:
An artist was commissioned to make a 625-g statue of a raven with a 40% silver alloy. She has a 50% silver alloy and a 25% silver alloy.

b) Solve this problem: What is the mass of each alloy needed to produce the desired alloy?

[Answers: a) $f + t = 625$; $0.50f + 0.25t = 250$
b) 375 g of the 50% alloy; 250 g of the 25% alloy]

b) Multiply equation ① by 0.60, then subtract to eliminate s.

0.60 × equation ①: $0.60(s + t = 100)$

$0.60s + 0.60t = 60$ ③

Use the distributive property.

Subtract equation ③ from equation ②.

$$\begin{array}{rl} 0.60s + 0.35t = 50 & ② \\ -(0.60s + 0.60t = 60) & ③ \\ \hline -0.25t = -10 & \\ t = 40 & \end{array}$$

Divide each side by −0.25 to solve for t.

Substitute $t = 40$ in equation ①.

$$\begin{array}{rl} s + t = 100 & ① \\ s + 40 = 100 & \\ s = 60 & \end{array}$$

Sixty grams of 60% silver alloy and 40 g of 35% silver alloy are needed. To verify the solution, use the given data.
The bracelet has a mass of 100 g; and 60 g + 40 g = 100 g.
60 g of 60% alloy was used in the bracelet.
So, the mass of silver in the bracelet from this alloy is:
60% of 60 g = 36 g
40 g of 35% alloy was used in the bracelet.
So, the mass of silver in the bracelet from this alloy is:
35% of 40 g = 14 g
The mass of silver in the bracelet is 36 g + 14 g = 50 g, which is 50% of the mass of the 100-g bracelet.
So, 60 g of 60% silver alloy and 40 g of 35% silver alloy are needed.

Why couldn't you determine a solution if the bracelet was made with a 25% silver alloy?

THE WORLD OF MATH

Math Fact: A Linear System with Three Variables

We can use both the substitution and elimination strategies to solve a linear system with three equations in three variables:

$$\begin{array}{ll} x + 4y + 3z = 5 & ① \\ x + 3y + 2z = 4 & ② \\ x + y - z = -1 & ③ \end{array}$$

We can begin by eliminating the variable x. Subtract equation ② from equation ①, then subtract equation ③ from equation ②.

$$\begin{array}{rl} x + 4y + 3z = 5 & ① \\ -(x + 3y + 2z = 4) & ② \\ \hline y + z = 1 & ④ \end{array} \qquad \begin{array}{rl} x + 3y + 2z = 4 & ② \\ -(x + y - z = -1) & ③ \\ \hline 2y + 3z = 5 & ⑤ \end{array}$$

The result is equations ④ and ⑤, which form a linear system in two variables.
Solve the linear system for y and z. Then solve for x.
Verify your solution.

Example 4 Solving by Determining the Value of Each Variable Independently

Solve this linear system.

$2x + 3y = 8$

$5x - 4y = -6$

SOLUTION

$2x + 3y = 8$ ①

$5x - 4y = -6$ ②

Eliminate x first. The least common multiple of the coefficients of x is 10.

Multiply equation ① by 5 and equation ② by 2, then subtract.

5 × equation ①: $10x + 15y = 40$

2 × equation ②: $-(10x - 8y = -12)$

$$23y = 52$$

$$y = \frac{52}{23}$$

Eliminate y next. The least common multiple of the coefficients of y is 12.

Multiply equation ① by 4 and equation ② by 3, then add.

4 × equation ①: $8x + 12y = 32$

3 × equation ②: $+(15x - 12y = -18)$

$$23x = 14$$

$$x = \frac{14}{23}$$

Verify the solution.

In each equation, substitute: $x = \frac{14}{23}$ and $y = \frac{52}{23}$

$2x + 3y = 8$ ①

$$\begin{aligned}\text{L.S.} &= 2\left(\frac{14}{23}\right) + 3\left(\frac{52}{23}\right)\\ &= \frac{28}{23} + \frac{156}{23}\\ &= \frac{184}{23}\\ &= 8\\ &= \text{R.S.}\end{aligned}$$

$5x - 4y = -6$ ②

$$\begin{aligned}\text{L.S.} &= 5\left(\frac{14}{23}\right) - 4\left(\frac{52}{23}\right)\\ &= \frac{70}{23} - \frac{208}{23}\\ &= -\frac{138}{23}\\ &= -6\\ &= \text{R.S.}\end{aligned}$$

For each equation, the left side is equal to the right side, so the solution is: $x = \frac{14}{23}$ and $y = \frac{52}{23}$

CHECK YOUR UNDERSTANDING

4. Solve this linear system.

$3x + 9y = 5$

$9x - 6y = -7$

[Answer: $x = -\frac{1}{3}$ and $y = \frac{2}{3}$]

What is an advantage of not substituting $y = \frac{52}{23}$ into one of the equations to determine x?

Discuss the Ideas

1. When you use the elimination strategy to solve a linear system, how can you tell whether you will add equations or subtract them?

2. When you use the elimination strategy to solve a linear system, how do you know when you need to begin by multiplying?

Exercises

A

3. Use an elimination strategy to solve each linear system.

a) $x - 4y = 1$
$x - 2y = -1$

b) $3a + b = 5$
$9a - b = 15$

c) $3x - 4y = 1$
$3x - 2y = -1$

d) $3x - 4y = 0$
$5x - 4y = 8$

4. For each linear system, write an equivalent linear system where both equations have:

i) the same x-coefficients
ii) the same y-coefficients

a) $x - 2y = -6$
$3x - y = 2$

b) $15x - 2y = 9$
$5x + 4y = 17$

c) $7x + 3y = 9$
$5x + 2y = 7$

d) $14x + 15y = 16$
$21x + 10y = -1$

5. Solve each linear system in question 4.

B

6. Use an elimination strategy to solve each linear system.

a) $2x + y = -5$
$3x + 5y = 3$

b) $3m - 6n = 0$
$9m + 3n = -7$

c) $2s + 3t = 6$
$5s + 10t = 20$

d) $3a + 2b = 5$
$2a + 3b = 0$

7. Solve each linear system. Explain what you did for part d.

a) $8x - 3y = 38$
$3x - 2y = -1$

b) $2a - 5b = 29$
$7a - 3b = 0$

c) $18a - 15b = 4$
$10a + 3b = 6$

d) $6x - 2y = 21$
$4x + 3y = 1$

For questions 8 to 11, model each situation with a linear system then solve the problem.

8. The mean attendance at the Winnipeg Folk Festival for 2006 and 2008 was 45 265. The attendance in 2008 was 120 more than the attendance in 2006. What was the attendance in each year?

9. Talise folded 545 metal lids to make cones for jingle dresses for herself and her younger sister. Her dress had 185 more cones than her sister's dress. How many cones are on each dress?

10. Years ago, people bought goods with beaver pelts instead of cash. Two fur traders purchased some knives and blankets from the Hudson's Bay Company store at Fort Langley, B.C. The items and the cost in beaver pelts for each fur trader are shown below:
10 knives + 20 blankets = 200 beaver pelts
15 knives + 25 blankets = 270 beaver pelts
What is the cost, in beaver pelts, of one knife and of one blanket?

11. Bernard used an electronic metronome to help him keep time to a guitar piece he was learning to play. He played at a moderate tempo for 4.5 min and at a fast tempo for 30 s. Bernard played a total of 620 beats on the metronome. The rate for the moderate tempo was 40 beats/min less than the rate for the fast tempo. What is the rate in beats per minute for each tempo?

12. Solve each linear system. Explain what you did for part a.

a) $\frac{a}{2} + \frac{b}{3} = 1$
$\frac{a}{4} - \frac{2b}{3} = -1$

b) $\frac{x}{2} + \frac{y}{2} = 7$
$3x + 2y = 48$

c) $0.03x + 0.15y = 0.027$
$-0.5x - 0.5y = 0.05$

d) $-1.5x + 2.5y = 0.5$
$2x + y = 1.5$

13. The 2008–09 Edmonton Oilers had 25 players, 17 of whom were over 6 ft. tall. Seven-ninths of the Canadian players were over 6 ft. tall. Three-sevenths of the foreign players were over 6 ft. tall. How many players were Canadian and how many were foreign?

14. Melody surveyed the 76 grade 10 students in her school to find out who played games online. One-quarter of the girls and $\frac{3}{4}$ of the boys said they played online games with someone over the weekend. Thirty-nine students played online games that weekend. How many girls and how many boys did Melody survey?

15. a) Which linear system is modelled by these two balance scales?

Balance scales 1

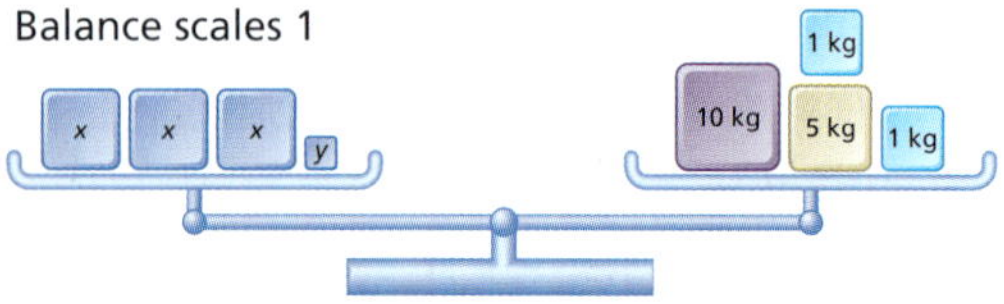

Balance scales 2

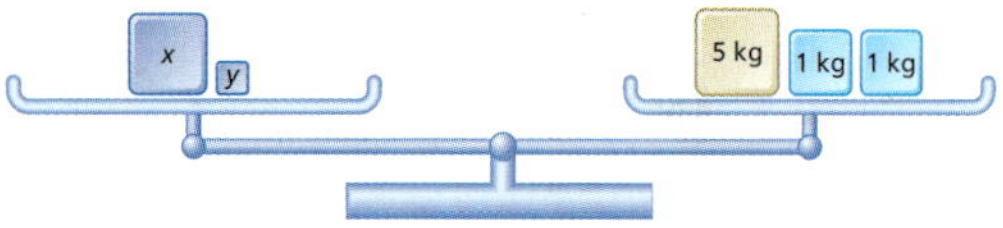

b) From Balance scales 1, suppose you remove mass x and mass y from the left side and 7 kg from the right side. How do you know that the scales will still be balanced?

c) How does this process help you determine the value of x and the value of y?

d) How is this process related to the elimination strategy for solving a linear system?

16. To visit the Manitoba Children's Museum in Winnipeg:

- One adult and 3 children pay \$27.75.
- Two adults and 2 children pay \$27.50.

Which ticket is more expensive? Justify your answer.

17. A co-op that sells organic food made 25 kg of soup mix by combining green peas that cost \$5/kg with red lentils that cost \$6.50/kg. This mixture costs \$140. What was the mass of peas and the mass of lentils in the mixture?

18. This linear system models a problem about a pentagon.
$3x + 2y = 21$
$x - y = 2$
What might the problem be? Solve the problem you suggest.

19. a) Write a problem that can be modelled by this linear system. Explain how you created the problem.
$3x + y = 17$
$x + y = 7$

b) Solve the problem you created.

20. Suppose you want to eliminate one variable in the linear system below by adding.

a) What are two different ways to eliminate a variable?
$3x + 4y = 29$
$2x - 5y = -19$

b) Solve the system using the two ways you described in part a.

21. This table shows the numbers of males and females in a study of colour blindness.

	Female	Male	Total
Colour blind	2	12	14
Not colour blind	98	88	186
Total	100	100	200

a) Use the data in the table to create a situation that can be modelled by a linear system.
b) Pose and solve a related problem.

C

22. Cam invested in a stock and a bond for one year. At the end of the year, the stock had lost 10.5% and the bond had gained 3.5%. The total loss for both investments was $84. If Cam had invested the bond amount into the stock and the stock amount into the bond, he would have lost only $14. How much money did Cam invest in the stock and in the bond?

23. In the equation $2x + 5y = 8$, the difference in consecutive coefficients and constant term is 3.
a) Write another equation whose coefficients and constant differ by 3. Solve the linear system formed by these equations.
b) Write, then solve two different systems of linear equations for which the coefficients and constant term in each equation differ by 3.
c) Compare your solutions in parts a and b.
d) Use algebra to verify that when the coefficients and constant term in the linear equations differ by a constant in this way, then the solution of the linear system will always be the same.

24. A farmer in Saskatchewan harvested 1 section (which is 640 acres) of wheat and 2 sections of barley. The total yield of grain for both areas was 99 840 bushels. The wheat sold for $6.35/bushel and the barley sold for $2.70/bushel. The farmer received $363 008 for both crops.
a) What was the yield of each section in bushels/acre?
b) Some farmers use hectares instead of acres or sections to measure area. One acre is 0.4047 ha. Would you have to write and solve a different linear system to determine the yield in bushels/hectare? Explain.

Reflect

You have used graphing, substitution, and elimination to solve a linear system. For each strategy, give an example of a linear system that you think would be best solved using that strategy. Justify your choices.

CHECKPOINT 2

Connections

Linear System

$3x + y = 7$

$2x - y = 3$

Solve by graphing

Use graphing software, a graphing calculator, or grid paper.

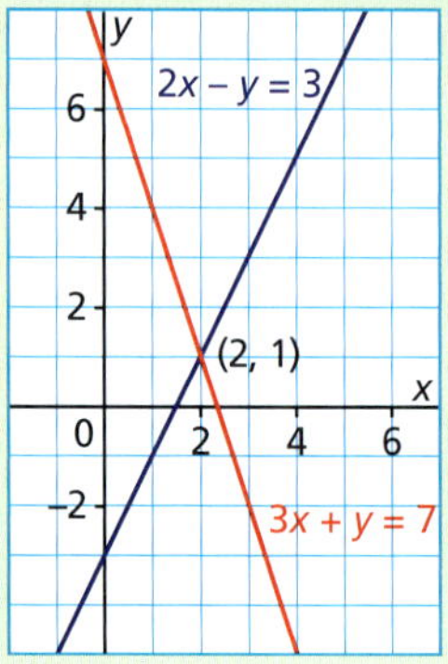

Solve by substitution

$3x + y = 7$ ①

$2x - y = 3$ ②

Solve equation ① for y.

$y = -3x + 7$

Substitute for y in equation ②.

$2x - (-3x + 7) = 3$

$5x - 7 = 3$

$5x = 10$

$x = 2$

Substitute for x in equation ①.

$3(2) + y = 7$

$6 + y = 7$

$y = 1$

Solution: $x = 2$ and $y = 1$

Solve by elimination

$3x + y = 7$ ①

$2x - y = 3$ ②

Add the equations to eliminate y.

$5x = 10$

$x = 2$

Substitute for x in equation ①.

$3(2) + y = 7$

$6 + y = 7$

$y = 1$

Solution: $x = 2$ and $y = 1$

Verify the solution.

Substitute for x and y in each equation to check that the values satisfy the equations.

$3x + y = 7$ ①

L.S. $= 3x + y$

$= 3(2) + 1$

$= 7$

$=$ R.S.

$2x - y = 3$ ②

L.S. $= 2x - y$

$= 2(2) - 1$

$= 3$

$=$ R.S.

Since the left side is equal to the right side for each equation, the solution is: $x = 2$ and $y = 1$

Concept Development

- **In Lesson 7.4**
  - You solved linear systems by using the substitution strategy.
  - You created equivalent equations by multiplying or dividing each term in an equation by a non-zero number.
- **In Lesson 7.5**
  - You solved linear systems by using the elimination strategy.
  - You created an equivalent linear system by adding or subtracting the two equations in a linear system.

Assess Your Understanding

7.4

1. Solve each linear system by substitution.

a) $5x + y = 4$
$x + y = 2$

b) $3x - y = 1$
$2x + y = -1$

c) $\frac{x}{3} + \frac{y}{4} = -\frac{9}{4}$
$\frac{5x}{6} - \frac{3y}{4} = -\frac{17}{4}$

2. a) Write a linear system to model this situation:
A store sold Inukshuk replicas made with either 6 or 7 stones.
The total number of stones in all Inukshuit sold was 494. The store sold 13 more Inukshuit made with 6 stones than those made with 7 stones.
b) Solve this problem: How many of each type of replicas were sold?

3. One thousand dollars was invested in two savings bonds for one year. One bond earned interest at an annual rate of 5.5%. The other bond earned 4.5% per year. The total interest earned was $50. How much money was invested in each bond?

7.5

4. Solve each linear system by elimination.

a) $3x - y = -11$
$-x + y = -1$

b) $\frac{1}{3}x + \frac{5}{6}y = \frac{8}{3}$
$\frac{1}{4}x - \frac{3}{4}y = -\frac{17}{8}$

c) $0.5x - 0.3y = 0.15$
$-0.3x + 0.5y = -0.65$

d) $x + 2y = -2$
$-2x + y = 6$

5. Each time Trisha went to the school cafeteria, she bought either a bowl of soup for $1.75 or a main course for $4.75. During the school year, she spent $490 and bought 160 food items. How many times did Trisha buy soup? How many times did she buy a main course? Justify your answers.

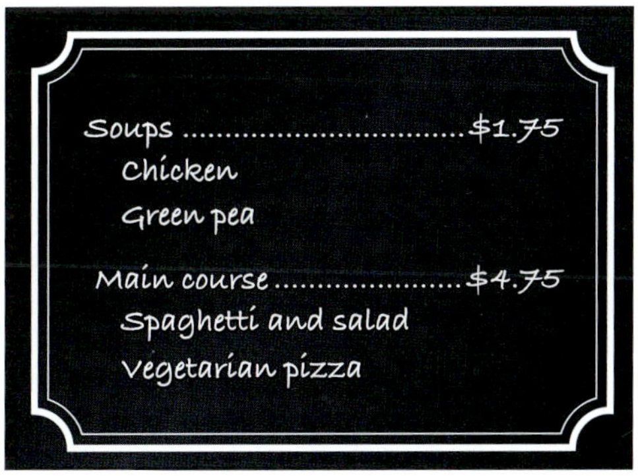

6. The volumes of two acid solutions differed by 1000 mL. The larger volume contained 5.5% acid. The smaller volume contained 4.5% acid. The total volume of acid in both solutions was 100 mL. What was the volume of each solution?

7. Determine the values of x and y in this diagram. How can you check that your answers are correct?

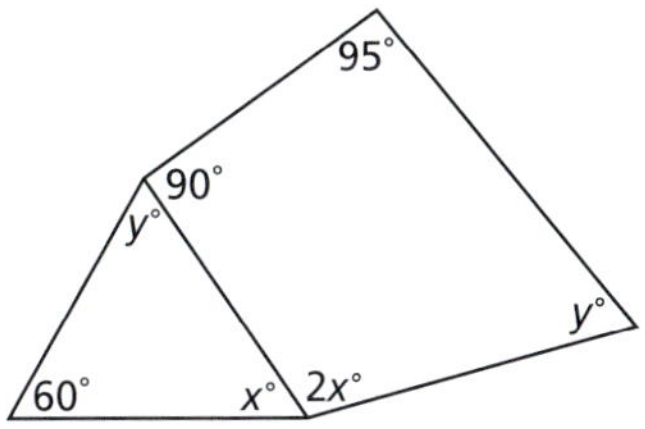

7.6 Properties of Systems of Linear Equations

LESSON FOCUS

Determine the numbers of solutions of different types of linear systems.

Make Connections

Phil was teased by his grandparents to determine their ages given these clues.

The sum of our ages is 151.

Add our two ages. Double this sum is 302.

What are our ages?

Can Phil determine his grandparents' ages given these clues? Why or why not?

Construct Understanding

THINK ABOUT IT

Work in a group of 3.
Use graphing technology if it is available.

Each linear system below contains the equation: $-2x + y = 2$
Solve each linear system by graphing.

System 1	**System 2**	**System 3**
$-2x + y = 2$	$-2x + y = 2$	$-2x + y = 2$
$2x + y = 2$	$-2x + y = 4$	$-4x + 2y = 4$

Share your results with your group.
How many solutions does each linear system have?

All the linear systems you studied in earlier lessons have had exactly one solution.
We can graph a linear system to determine how many solutions it has.

- Here are the graphs of the linear system:
  $x + y = -3$
  $-2x + y = 3$
  The graphs intersect at $(-2, -1)$.
  So, there is only one solution: $x = -2$ and $y = -1$
  Because the slopes of the lines are different, the lines intersect at exactly one point.

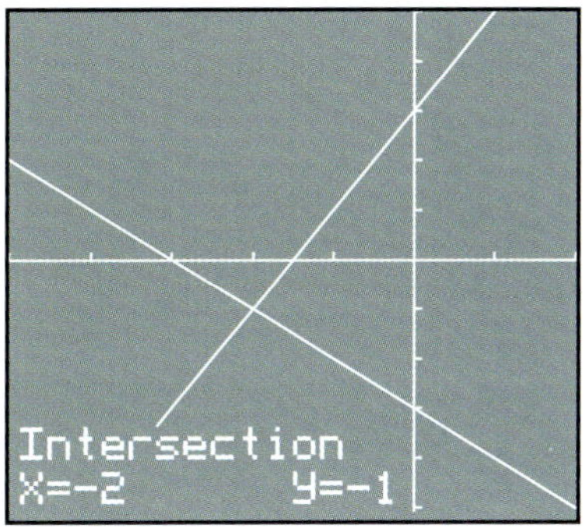

- Here are the graphs of the linear system:
  $-4x + 2y = 8$
  $-2x + y = -2$

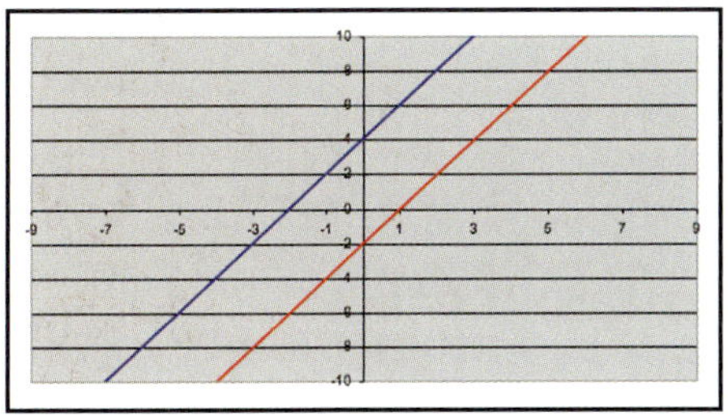

How can you tell from the equations that the lines are parallel?

The graphs do not intersect.
So, there is no solution.
Because the slopes of the lines are equal, the lines are parallel.

- Here are the graphs of the linear system:
  $2x + y = -1$
  $4x + 2y = -2$

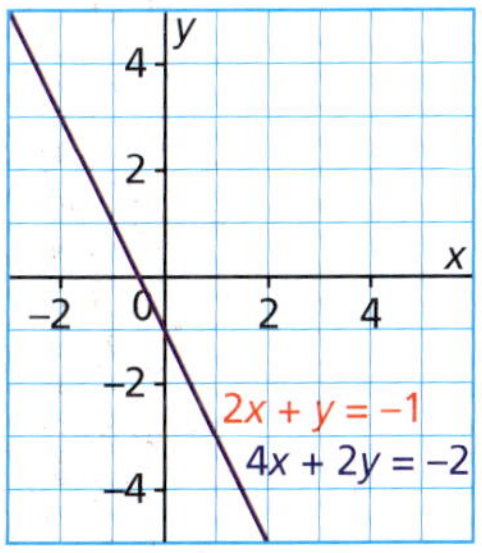

How can you tell from the equations that they represent the same line?

Since the graphs coincide, every point on one line is also a point on the other line; so all the points on the line are solutions.
So, there are **infinite** solutions.
Because the lines have equal slopes and the same y-intercept, they are **coincident lines.**

Infinite means unlimited or without bound.

When lines coincide, they are **coincident.**

Example 1 Determining the Number of Solutions of a Linear System

Determine the number of solutions of each linear system.

a) $x + y = -2$
$-2x - 2y = 4$

b) $4x + 6y = -10$
$-2x - y = -1$

c) $3x + y = -1$
$-6x - 2y = 12$

SOLUTION

Write each equation in slope-intercept form to identify the slope and y-intercept of each line.

a) $x + y = -2$ ①
$-2x - 2y = 4$ ②

For equation ①:
$x + y = -2$ Subtract x from each side.
$y = -x - 2$ ③
The slope is -1 and the y-intercept is -2.

For equation ②:
$-2x - 2y = 4$ Add $2x$ to each side.
$-2y = 2x + 4$ Divide by -2 to solve for y.
$$\frac{-2y}{-2} = \frac{2x}{-2} + \frac{4}{-2}$$
$y = -x - 2$ ④
Equation ④ is the same as equation ③, so the slope is -1 and the y-intercept is -2.
The slope-intercept forms of both equations are the same, so the lines are coincident and the linear system has infinite solutions.

b) $4x + 6y = -10$ ①
$-2x - y = -1$ ②

For equation ①:
$4x + 6y = -10$ Subtract $4x$ from each side.
$6y = -4x - 10$ Divide by 6 to solve for y.
$$\frac{6y}{6} = \frac{-4x}{6} - \frac{10}{6}$$
$y = -\frac{2}{3}x - \frac{5}{3}$ ③
The slope is $-\frac{2}{3}$ and the y-intercept is $-\frac{5}{3}$.

CHECK YOUR UNDERSTANDING

1. Determine the number of solutions of each linear system.

a) $x + y = 3$
$-2x - y = -2$

b) $4x + 6y = -10$
$-2x - 3y = 5$

c) $2x - 4y = -1$
$3x - 6y = 2$

[Answers: a) one solution
b) infinite solutions
c) no solution]

For equation ②:

$-2x - y = -1$ Add $2x$ to each side.

$-y = 2x - 1$ Multiply each side by -1 to solve for y.

$y = -2x + 1$ ④

The slope is -2 and the y-intercept is 1.

Because the slopes are different, the lines intersect at exactly one point and the linear system has one solution.

Why don't you need to identify the y-intercepts to show there is only one solution?
What is the solution?

c) $3x + y = -1$ ①

$-6x - 2y = 12$ ②

For equation ①:

$3x + y = -1$ Subtract $3x$ from each side.

$y = -3x - 1$ ③

The slope is -3 and the y-intercept is -1.

For equation ②:

$-6x - 2y = 12$ Add $6x$ to each side.

$-2y = 6x + 12$ Divide each side by -2 to solve for y.

$$\frac{-2y}{-2} = \frac{6x}{-2} + \frac{12}{-2}$$

$y = -3x - 6$ ④

The slope is -3 and the y-intercept is -6.

Because the slopes are equal and the y-intercepts are different, the lines are parallel and the linear system has no solution.

Why is it important to identify the y-intercepts when the equations in a linear system have the same slope?

When you attempt to solve a linear system of two equations in two variables, there are only three possibilities. You can determine the number of solutions using different methods.

Possible Solutions for a Linear System

Intersecting Lines

One solution

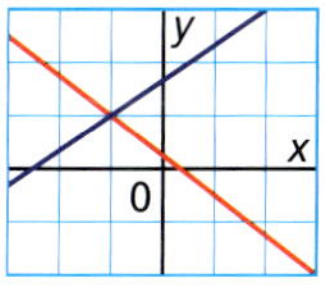

Parallel Lines

No solution

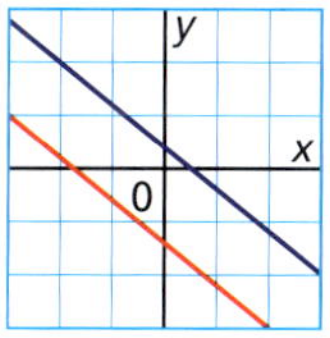

Coincident Lines

Infinite solutions

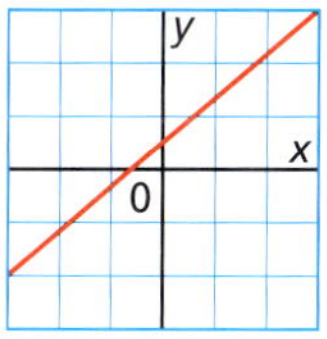

Example 2 Creating a Linear System with 0, 1, or Infinite Solutions

Given the equation $-2x + y = 4$, write another linear equation that will form a linear system with:

a) exactly one solution

b) no solution

c) infinite solutions

SOLUTION

a) For a linear system with one solution, the lines must have different slopes so they can intersect.
Write the given equation in slope-intercept form to identify its slope.

$-2x + y = 4$ Add $2x$ to each side.

$y = 2x + 4$

The slope of the line is 2.
Let the second line have slope 3 and any y-intercept, such as 2.
Then its equation is:
$y = 3x + 2$
A possible linear system with exactly one solution is:
$y = 2x + 4$
$y = 3x + 2$

b) For a linear system with no solution, the lines must be parallel but not coincident so there is no point of intersection.
The lines must have equal slopes but different y-intercepts.
From part a, the given equation is equivalent to $y = 2x + 4$, with slope 2.
The second line must also have slope 2.
Let its y-intercept be 5.
Then its equation is:
$y = 2x + 5$
A possible linear system with no solution is:
$y = 2x + 4$
$y = 2x + 5$

CHECK YOUR UNDERSTANDING

2. Given the equation $-6x + y = 3$, write another linear equation that will form a linear system with:

a) exactly one solution

b) no solution

c) infinite solutions

[Sample Answers: a) $y = 2x + 4$ b) $y = 6x - 3$ c) $-12x + 2y = 6$]

c) For a linear system with infinite solutions, the lines must be coincident so they intersect at every possible point.
The equations must be equivalent.
The given equation is: $-2x + y = 4$
To determine an equivalent equation, multiply each term by a non-zero number, such as -3.
$(-3)(-2x) + (-3)(y) = (-3)(4)$ Simplify.
$6x - 3y = -12$
A possible linear system with infinite solutions is:
$6x - 3y = -12$
$-2x + y = 4$

How is a linear system with infinite solutions like a linear system with no solution?
How are the systems different?

Discuss the Ideas

1. Without solving a linear system, what strategies could you use to determine how many solutions it has? Use an example to explain.
2. Why do you get the equation of a coincident line when you multiply or divide each term of the equation of a linear function by a non-zero number?
3. How can you use the slopes of the lines in a linear system to determine the number of possible solutions? How can you use the intercepts?

THE WORLD OF MATH

Historical Moment: Linear Systems and the Babylonians

Babylon was a city-state, the remains of which are in Iraq. The Babylonians had a superior knowledge of mathematics including the ability to solve problems that can be modelled by linear systems. Some of these problems are preserved on clay tablets. For example, a tablet dating from around 300 BCE contains a problem similar to this:

Two fields have a total area of 1800 square units. One field produces grain at the rate of $\frac{2}{3}$ of a bushel per square unit while the other field produces grain at the rate of $\frac{1}{2}$ of a bushel per square unit.
The total yield is 1100 bushels. What is the area of each field?

How would you solve this problem?

Exercises

A

4. a) Without graphing, determine the slope of the graph of each equation.
   i) $-x + y = 5$
   ii) $-x - y = 10$
   iii) $-2x + 2y = 10$
   iv) $x + y = 5$
   b) Which lines in part a are parallel?
   c) Which lines in part a intersect?

5. The graphs of three lines are shown below.

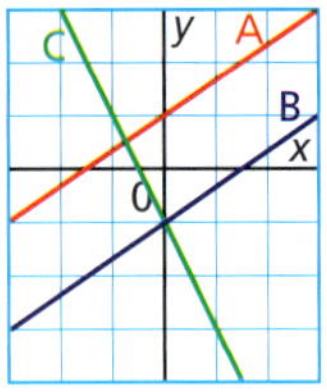

   a) Identify two lines that form a linear system with exactly one solution.
   b) Identify two lines that form a linear system with no solution.

6. Use these 6 equations:
   $4x + 2y = 20$ $x - 3y = 12$
   $5x - 15y = -60$ $2x + y = 10$
   $6x + 3y = 5$ $2x - 6y = 24$
   Write a linear system that has:
   a) no solution
   b) exactly one solution
   c) infinite solutions

B

7. Determine the number of solutions of each linear system.
   a) $x + 2y = 6$
   $x + y = -2$
   b) $3x + 5y = 9$
   $6x + 10y = 18$
   c) $2x - 5y = 30$
   $4x - 10y = 15$
   d) $\frac{x}{2} + \frac{y}{3} = \frac{1}{2}$
   $\frac{x}{2} + \frac{y}{3} = \frac{1}{4}$

8. The first equation of a linear system is given. Write a second equation to form a linear system that satisfies each condition. Explain your reasoning.
   a) The second line intersects the line $-2x + y = 1$ in the first quadrant.
   b) The second line does not intersect the line $-2x + y = 1$.
   c) The second line coincides with the line $-2x + y = 1$.

9. The table below shows some properties of the graphs of 3 linear equations. For the linear system formed by each pair of equations, how many solutions are there? Explain your reasoning.
   a) A and B
   b) A and C
   c) B and C

Equation	Slope	*y*-intercept
A	−0.5	4
B	−0.5	2
C	0.5	4

10. Marc wrote the two equations in a linear system in slope-intercept form. He noticed that the signs of the two slopes were different. How many solutions will this linear system have? Explain.

11. Two lines in a linear system have the same slope. What information do you need to determine whether the linear system has no solution or infinite solutions?

12. Use the equation $3x - 4y = 12$ as an equation in three different linear systems. Write a second equation so that each system has a different number of solutions. Explain what you did for each system.

For questions 13 to 17, tell whether the linear system that models each problem has one solution, no solution, or infinite solutions. Justify your answer. You do not have to solve the problems.

13. What are the masses of a large container and a small container?

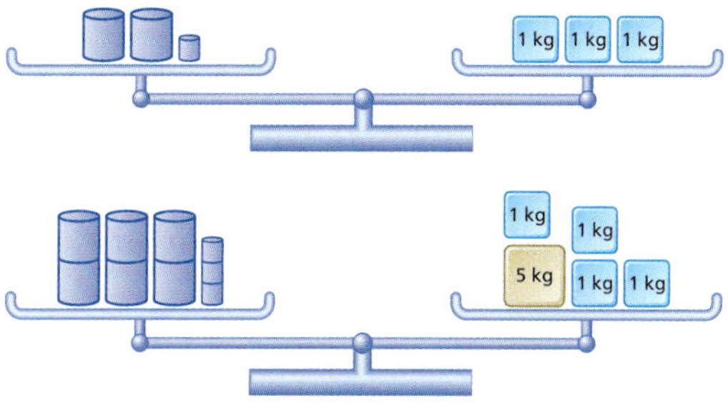

14. Nadine has a cup of nickels and a cup of dimes. The total number of coins is 300 and their value is \$23.25. How many coins are in each cup?

15. Prana has a savings account and a chequing account with a total balance of \$85. His parents doubled the amount in each account and the new total balance is \$170. How much money does Prana have in each account?

16. The total attendance at a weekend Pow Wow was 568. There were 44 more people on Sunday than on Saturday. What was the attendance for each day?

17. Tickets for a guided tour of La Maison Gabrielle-Roy in Saint-Boniface, Manitoba, cost \$5 for an adult and \$3 for a student. Seventy-five tickets were sold for \$275. How many adults and how many students visited La Maison Gabrielle-Roy?

18. Use the terms "slope" and "y-intercept" to describe the conditions for two lines to have 0, 1, or infinite points of intersection.

19. **a)** Write a linear system that has infinite solutions.

b) Explain what happens when you try to solve the system using elimination.

20. **a)** Write a linear system that has no solution.

b) Explain what happens when you try to solve the system using elimination.

21. Given the graph of a linear system, is it always possible to determine the number of solutions of the linear system? Use examples to explain your reasoning.

C

22. **a)** Determine the number of solutions of each system.

i) $2x + 3y = 4$
$4x + 6y = 8$

ii) $2x + 3y = 4$
$4x + 6y = 7$

iii) $2x + 3y = 4$
$4x + 5y = 8$

b) How can you compare corresponding coefficients to help you determine whether a system has no solution, one solution, or infinite solutions?

23. In the linear system below, $AE - DB = 0$; show that the system does not have exactly one solution.

$Ax + By = C$
$Dx + Ey = F$

24. **a)** For what values of k does the linear system below have:

i) exactly one solution?

ii) infinite solutions?

$$\frac{1}{2}x + \frac{5}{3}y = 2$$

$$kx + \frac{5}{2}y = 3$$

b) Explain why there is no value of k for which the linear system has no solution.

Reflect

Use examples to explain why the only possible solutions of a linear system are: no solution, one solution, or infinite solutions.

STUDY GUIDE

CONCEPT SUMMARY

Big Ideas	Applying the Big Ideas
■ A system of two linear equations is solved when the set of ordered pairs that satisfies both equations is determined.	This means that: ■ Substituting (x, y) into the two equations of a linear system determines whether the ordered pair is a solution. You can determine this solution using graphs, or algebraic strategies.
■ Multiplying or dividing the equations in a linear system by a non-zero number, or adding or subtracting the equations produces an equivalent system.	■ You can create an equivalent system by multiplying or dividing each term in a linear equation by a constant. The solution of the new system is the same as the original solution. You can create an equivalent system by adding or subtracting the like terms in the equations of a linear system. The solution of the new system is the same as the original system.
■ A system of two linear equations may have one solution, infinite solutions, or no solution.	■ You can determine the number of solutions by graphing or by comparing the slopes and y-intercepts of the graphs of the linear equations.

[illegible]pter

- How do you determine the number of solutions of a linear system?
- What are some different strategies you can use to solve a linear system?
- Why does multiplying or dividing each term in each equation or adding or subtracting the equations not change the solution of a linear system?

SKILLS SUMMARY

Skill	Description	Example
Solve a linear system by graphing. [7.2, 7.3]	To solve a linear system by graphing: **1.** Draw the graphs after determining their intercepts, or their slopes and y-intercepts. **2.** The coordinates of the point of intersection are the solution of the linear system. **3.** Verify the solution by substituting the coordinates into the equations.	For this linear system: $2x - y = -5$ $4x + y = -7$ 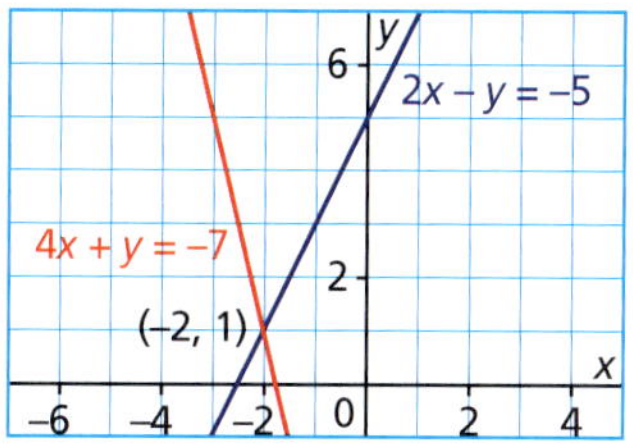 The solution is: $x = -2$ and $y = 1$
Solve a linear system algebraically. [7.4, 7.5]	To solve a linear system algebraically: **1.** Use substitution or elimination. **2.** Verify the solution by substituting for x and y in both equations to check that the coordinates of the point of intersection satisfy both equations.	For this linear system: $2x - y = -5$ ① $4x + y = -7$ ② Use elimination. Add the equations. $6x = -12$ $x = -2$ Substitute for x in equation ①. $2(-2) - y = -5$ $y = 1$ The solution is: $x = -2$ and $y = 1$
Determine the number of solutions of a linear system. [7.6]	To determine the number of solutions in a linear system, use Step 1 or Step 2: **1.** Compare the graphs of the equations. **2.** Compare the slopes and y-intercepts of the lines.	The graphs of the linear system above have different slopes, so there is exactly one solution. The graphs of the linear system below have the same slope and the same y-intercept, so there are infinite solutions: $2x + 4y = 6$ $4x + 8y = 12$ The graphs of the linear system below have the same slope and different y-intercepts, so there is no solution: $2x + 4y = 6$ $4x + 8y = 10$

REVIEW

7.1

For questions 1 and 2, create a linear system to model the situation, then identify which is the correct solution for the related problems. Justify your choice.

1. **a)** The situation is:
In 2009, the Bedford Road Invitational Tournament (BRIT) in Saskatoon, Saskatchewan, held its 41st annual basketball tournament. Teams from outside Saskatchewan have won the tournament 17 more times than teams from Saskatchewan.

b) The related problems are:
How many times have teams from Saskatchewan won the BRIT? How many times have teams from outside Saskatchewan won the BRIT? (*Solution A*: teams from Saskatchewan have won 29 times and teams from outside Saskatchewan have won 12 times. *Solution B*: teams from Saskatchewan have won 12 times and teams from outside Saskatchewan have won 29 times.)

2. **a)** The situation is:
Yvette operates a snow-blowing business. She charges \$15 for a small driveway and \$25 for a large driveway. One weekend, Yvette made \$475 by clearing snow from 25 driveways.

b) The related problems are:
How many small driveways did Yvette clear? How many large driveways did she clear? (*Solution A*: Yvette cleared 10 small driveways and 15 large driveways.
Solution B: Yvette cleared 15 small driveways and 10 large driveways.)

3. Kyle wrote this linear system to model a problem he created about the cost of tickets and popcorn for a group of people to go to a movie theatre. What problem might he have written?
$9.95t + 5.50p = 76.20$
$t - p = 3$

7.2

4. **a)** Which linear system is modelled by this graph? Explain how you know.

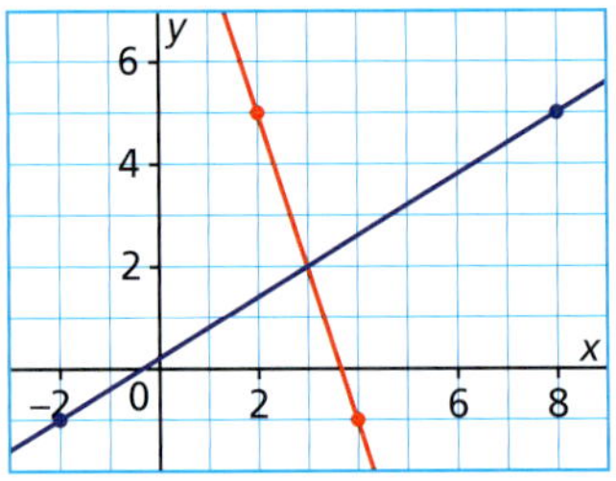

b) What is the solution of the linear system? Is it exact or approximate? How do you know?

5. To solve the linear system below by graphing, George and Sunita started with different steps:
$-x + 4y = 10$ ①
$4x - y = -10$ ②
George's Method
Equation ①: plot (0, 2.5) and (–10, 0)
Equation ②: plot (0, 10) and (–2.5, 0)

Sunita's Method
Equation ①: graph $y = \frac{1}{4}x + 2.5$
Equation ②: graph $y = 4x + 10$

a) Explain what each student will probably do next.

b) Choose either method. Solve the linear system by graphing.

6. Explain how you would solve this linear system by graphing on grid paper. You do not have to draw the graphs.
$x - y = 15$
$2x + y = 6$

7. **a)** Graph to solve this linear system.
$4x - 2y = 1$
$3x - 4y = 16$

b) Tell whether the solution is exact or approximate, and how you know.

7.3

8. a) Write a linear system to model this situation: Table salt contains 40% sodium, and health experts recommend that people limit their sodium intake. For breakfast, Owen ate 2 bowls of cereal and 4 slices of bacon that contained a total of 940 mg of sodium. Natalie ate 1 bowl of cereal and 3 slices of bacon that contained a total of 620 mg of sodium.

b) This graph represents a linear system for the situation in part a. What does each line in the graph represent?

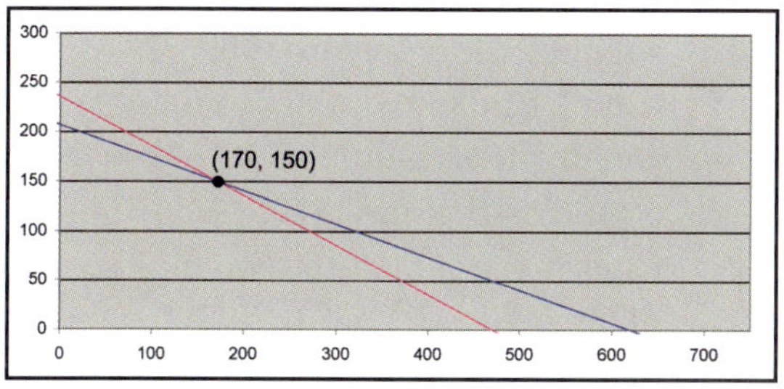

c) Solve this related problem: How much sodium is in 1 bowl of cereal and in 1 slice of bacon? Is the solution exact or approximate? How could you find out?

9. Use graphing technology to solve each linear system.

a) $2x + 3y = 13$
$5x - 2y = 1$

b) $y = \frac{1}{6}x - 2$
$y = -\frac{1}{6}x + 2$

c) $4x - 5y = 20$
$8x + 5y = 19$

d) $\frac{x}{2} + \frac{3y}{4} = -\frac{25}{16}$
$-2x + 4y = 20$

7.4

10. Solve each linear system by substitution.

a) $x + y = -5$
$x + 3y = -15$

b) $7x + y = 10$
$3x - 2y = -3$

c) $\frac{1}{2}x + 3y = \frac{5}{6}$
$\frac{1}{3}x - 5y = \frac{16}{9}$

d) $0.6x - 0.2y = -0.2$
$-0.03x - 0.07y = 0.17$

11. a) Why did Laura multiply equation ① by 4 and equation ② by 6 before she solved this linear system?

$-\frac{3}{2}x - \frac{1}{4}y = -\frac{1}{2}$ ①

$\frac{1}{3}x + \frac{5}{6}y = \frac{19}{3}$ ②

b) Why will the new linear system have the same solution as the original system?

c) Solve the linear system.

12. a) Write a linear system to model this situation: Paul made bannock to celebrate National Aboriginal Day. He measured $5\frac{3}{4}$ cups of flour using a $\frac{1}{4}$ cup measure and a $\frac{2}{3}$ cup measure. Paul used 1 more $\frac{1}{4}$ cup measure than $\frac{2}{3}$ cup measure.

b) Solve this related problem: How many measures of each size did Paul use?

13. When 30 identical rectangular tables are placed end to end, their perimeter is 306 ft. When the same tables are placed side by side, their perimeter is 190 ft.

a) Draw a diagram of the first 3 tables to illustrate each arrangement.

b) Write a linear system to model the situation.

c) Solve the linear system to solve this related problem: What is the width and length of each table?

14. Sofia sketched a design for a blanket. She made the design with 150 shapes that were equilateral triangles and squares. Eighty-three of the shapes were blue. Forty percent of the triangles and 60% of the squares were blue. How many triangles and how many squares were in the design?

7.5

15. Solve each system by elimination.

a) $-3x - y = 5$
$2x + y = -5$

b) $2x - 4y = 13$
$4x - 5y = 8$

16. a) In the linear system below, which number would you multiply one equation by to help you eliminate y in the next step? Explain.

$3x - 4y = 8.5$ ①
$4x + 2y = 9.5$ ②

b) What would be your next step in solving the linear system?

c) Solve the linear system.

17. The key in one type of basketball court has the shape of a rectangle and a semicircle, with perimeter approximately $68\frac{5}{6}$ ft. The length of the rectangular part of the key is 7 ft. longer than its width.

a) Write a linear system to model the situation above.

b) Solve this related problem: To the nearest foot, what are the length and the width of the rectangular part?

7.6

18. a) Write two linear systems where one system has infinite solutions and the other system has no solution.

b) How can you use graphs to show the number of solutions of each linear system?

c) How can comparing the slope-intercept forms for the equations in the linear system help you determine the number of solutions?

19. Grace and Olivia have 2-digit numbers on their hockey jerseys. They wrote three sets of clues to help some friends identify these numbers.

Clue 1: The difference between the two numbers is 33. When you triple each player's number then subtract, the difference is 99.

Clue 2: The sum of the two numbers is 57. When you divide each number by 3 then add the quotients, the sum is 20.

Clue 3: The sum of the two numbers is 57. Their difference is 33.

a) Which clues do not provide sufficient information to identify the two numbers? Explain.

b) Identify the numbers using the clues that are sufficient. Verify that you are correct.

20. Determine the number of solutions for each linear system. Describe the strategies you used.

a) $-x + 5y = 8$
$2x - 10y = 7$

b) $-\frac{3}{2}x + \frac{1}{4}y = -\frac{1}{4}$
$\frac{3}{4}x - \frac{y}{8} = \frac{1}{8}$

c) $0.5x + y = 0.3$
$-x + 2y = 0.6$

d) $2x - y = -5$
$6x - 3y = 15$

21. a) Explain how calculating the slopes of the graphs of the equations of a linear system helps you determine whether the system has only 1 solution. Use an example to explain.

b) Are the slopes of the graphs sufficient information to help you distinguish between a system that has no solution and a system that has infinite solutions?
Use an example to explain.

PRACTICE TEST

For questions 1 and 2, choose the correct answer: A, B, C, or D

1. Which statement below is true for this linear system?

$3x - 2y = 4.5$ ①

$-x + \frac{y}{2} = -1.25$ ②

A. If you multiply equation ① by 3, then add the new equation to equation ②, you can eliminate x.

B. There is one solution because the slopes of the lines are different.

C. If you replace equation ② with $4x - 2y = -5$, the new system will have the same solution as the original system.

D. The solution of the linear system is: $x = 1$ and $y = -0.75$

2. Which system has exactly one solution?

A. $y = 3x - 2$
$y = -4x + 5$

B. $4x - 2y = -0.2$
$-x + 0.5y = 0.05$

C. $y = 3x - 2$
$y = 3x + 2$

D. $\frac{1}{3}x + \frac{1}{2}y = \frac{1}{6}$
$\frac{1}{6}x + \frac{1}{4}y = \frac{1}{6}$

3. Use the linear systems in question 2 as examples to help you explain why a linear system may have no solution, exactly one solution, or infinite solutions.

4. Liam created a problem about a group of students and adults planning to travel on the Light Rail Transit (LRT) in Calgary, Alberta. He wrote this linear system to model the situation.

$1.75s + 2.50a = 15.50$

$s - a = 4$

a) Write a problem that can be modelled by the linear system above.

b) Solve your problem. Show how you know your solution is correct.

5. a) Solve each linear system.

i) $-3x - 4y = -2$
$x + 2y = 3$

ii) $-0.5x + 0.2y = -1$
$0.3x - 0.6y = -1.8$

iii) $x - \frac{1}{3}y = \frac{4}{3}$
$\frac{5}{6}x + \frac{1}{2}y = \frac{3}{2}$

b) Use one linear system from part a to explain the meaning of the point of intersection of the graphs of the equations of a linear system.

6. a) Write a linear system to model this situation:
A stained glass design was made of yellow squares, each with area 25 cm^2; and red right triangles, each with area 12.5 cm^2. The design used 90 shapes and covered an area of 1500 cm^2.

b) Solve this related problem: How many squares and how many triangles were used?

Exercise Mind and Body

Cross training involves varying the types of exercises you do in each workout, to use different muscles and different amounts of energy. For example, you might run and lift weights in one workout, then swim in the next workout.

Stationary bike: energy used – 420 Calories per hour

Swimming: energy used – 480 Calories per hour

PART A: INVESTIGATING RELATIONS

This table shows the approximate rate at which energy is used, in Calories per hour, for three physical activities. The rate at which energy is used is related to the mass of the person doing the activity.

Activity	Mass (kg)	Rate of Energy Use (Cal/h)	Mass (kg)	Rate of Energy Use (Cal/h)	Mass (kg)	Rate of Energy Use (Cal/h)	Mass (kg)	Rate of Energy Use (Cal/h)
Stationary bike	50	350	60	420	70	490	80	560
Swimming	50	400	60	480	70	560	80	640
Walking uphill	50	300	60	360	70	420	80	480

- Choose one physical activity from the table. Write four ordered pairs for this activity. Graph the ordered pairs. Use graphing technology if it is available. Is there a linear relationship between mass and the rate at which energy is used? How do you know?

- Write an equation to represent the relation between mass and the rate at which energy is used. Use the slope-intercept form of the equation. Explain what you did.
- Write an equation to represent the relation between mass and the rate at which energy is used for each of the other activities in the table.
- Use your equations to create a table of values for a mass that is not listed in the table above.
- Alex has a mass of 60 kg. He used 345 Calories in 45 min by riding a stationary bike followed by a swim.

  Create a linear system to represent this situation.

  Use the linear system to solve this problem:
  How much time did Alex spend on each activity?

PART B: INVESTIGATING OTHER LINEAR RELATIONS

- Do some research about other physical activities that are not listed in the table in Part A. Determine the rate at which energy is used in Calories per unit time.
- Conduct investigations, create situations, then pose problems that involve: linear relations or functions; linear systems; graphing; points of intersection; and so on.

PROJECT PRESENTATION

Your completed project can be presented in a written or an oral format but should include:

- A list of investigations you conducted, the situations you created, and the problems you posed, along with explanations of your strategies for solving the problems
- A display of the graphs that you made, including an explanation of how and why you created them and how you interpreted them

EXTENSION

Because exercise and nutrition play an important role in the health of people, much research has been conducted in these areas. Many linear relations have been discovered during these studies.

- Investigate other linear relations related to exercise, nutrition, and physical activities.
- Identify different types of energy and how they are measured. You might use an internet search using key words such as: joule, kilojoule, calorie, and kilocalorie.
- Write a brief report on the linear relations you discovered and how you know they are linear.

CUMULATIVE REVIEW Chapters 1–7

1

1. Convert each measurement.
 a) 290 cm to feet and the nearest inch
 b) 5 yd. to the nearest centimetre
 c) 8 km to miles and the nearest yard
 d) 6500 in. to the nearest metre
 e) 82 000 mm to feet and the nearest inch
 f) 16 mi. to the nearest hundredth of a kilometre

2. For each object, calculate the surface area to the nearest square unit, and the volume to the nearest cubic unit.
 a) right square pyramid

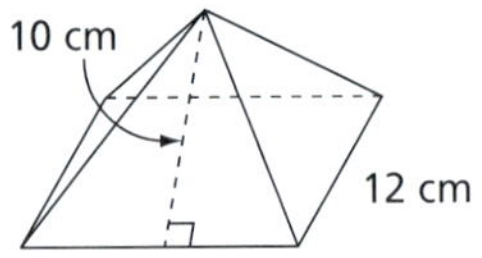

 b) right cone

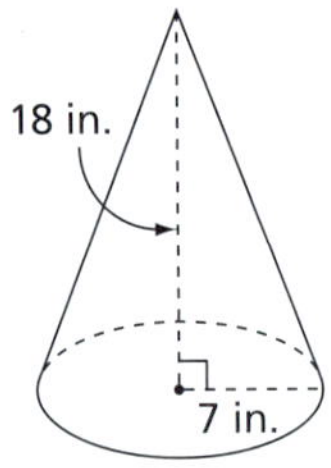

 c) sphere

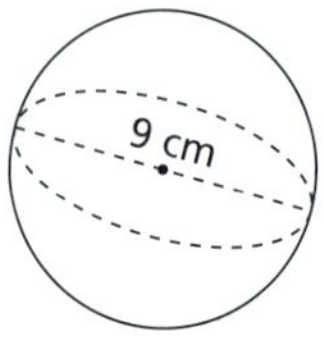

2

3. A tree is supported by a set of four guy wires. All the guy wires are anchored to the ground at points 3 m from the base of the tree. The guy wires are attached to the tree at a height of 4.5 m above the ground. To the nearest tenth of a degree, calculate the measure of the angle of inclination of a guy wire.

4. An equilateral triangle is inscribed in a circle. The radius of the circle is 21 in. Determine the side length of the triangle to the nearest tenth of an inch.

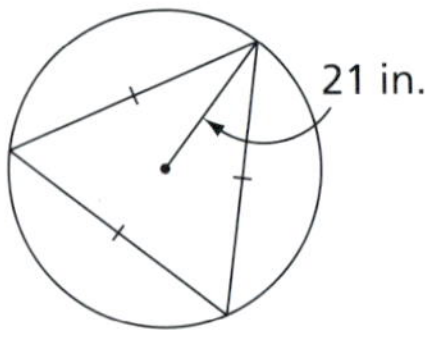

3

5. Expand and simplify.
 a) $(9 + s)(9 + s)$
 b) $(3a - 5)(2a - 3)$
 c) $(2n + 3p)(5n - 4p)$
 d) $(8s - t)(8s + t)$
 e) $(w + 4)(-2w^2 + 7w - 8)$
 f) $(4 + 3x - 2x^2)(-2 + 2x + 3x^2)$

6. Find and correct the errors in each factorization.
 a) $14a^3b^2 - 28b^3c^2 + 21a^2c^3 = 7b^2(2a^3 - 4bc^2 + 3a^2c^3)$
 b) $n^2 - n - 12 = (n + 4)(n - 3)$
 c) $36r^2 - 64s^2 = (6r + 8s)(6r - 8s)$
 d) $6m^2 + 23m - 18 = (6m - 9)(m + 2)$
 e) $w^2 - 22wx + 121x^2 = (w + 11x)^2$
 f) $30c^2 + 11cd - 30d^2 = (5c - 5d)(6c + 6d)$

4

7. a) Write each radical in simplest form.
 i) $\sqrt{45}$ **ii)** $\sqrt[3]{128}$ **iii)** $\sqrt[4]{932}$ **iv)** $\sqrt{539}$
 b) Write each mixed radical as an entire radical.
 i) $12\sqrt{3}$ **ii)** $3\sqrt[3]{7}$ **iii)** $2\sqrt[5]{15}$ **iv)** $5\sqrt{17}$

8. Simplify. Show your work.
 a) $(a^{-1}b^{-2})^2(a^4b^{-1})$
 b) $\left(\dfrac{c^{-2}d^{11}}{c^4d^{-4}}\right)^{-\frac{1}{3}}$
 c) $\dfrac{13x^3yz^{-2}}{-52x^{-2}y^4z^2}$
 d) $\dfrac{-18a^{-\frac{1}{2}}b^{-5}}{3a^{\frac{5}{2}}b^{-3}}$

9. Evaluate. Show your work.

a) $\left(\frac{3}{4}\right)^{\frac{5}{3}}\left(\frac{3}{4}\right)^{\frac{1}{3}}$

b) $\dfrac{(-3.5)^{-\frac{7}{2}}}{(-3.5)^{-\frac{11}{2}}}$

c) $\left[\left(-\frac{5}{6}\right)^{8}\right]^{\frac{1}{4}}$

d) $\dfrac{(0.064)^{\frac{5}{3}}(0.064)^{\frac{8}{3}}}{(0.064)(0.064)^{\frac{11}{3}}}$

5

10. This table represents a relation.

Name	**Sport**
Perdita Felicien	track
Donovan Bailey	track
Nancy Greene	skiing
Annamay Pierse	swimming
Justin Morneau	baseball
Steve Nash	basketball

a) Describe the relation in words.

b) Represent this relation as:

i) a set of ordered pairs

ii) an arrow diagram

11. a) Explain why the table of values below represents a function.

Volume of Gasoline (L), *v*	**Cost, *C* ($)**
1	1.09
2	2.18
3	3.27
4	4.36

b) Identify the independent variable and the dependent variable. Justify your choices.

c) Write the domain and range.

d) Write an equation for this function in function notation.

e) Determine the value of $C(25)$. What does this number represent?

f) Determine the value of v when $C(v) = 50$. What does this number represent?

12. These graphs give information about two students.

Height against Age

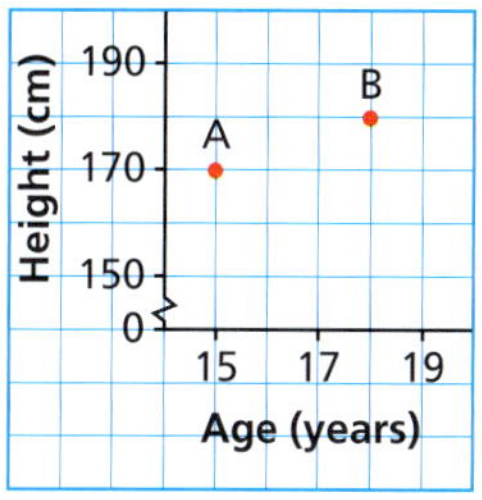

Hair Length against Mass

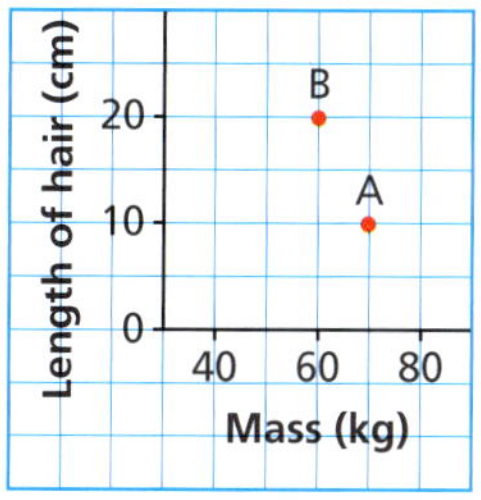

Which statements are true? Justify your answers.

a) The older student is shorter.

b) The student with the lesser mass has longer hair.

c) The older student has longer hair.

d) The shorter student has the lesser mass.

13. a) After playing basketball in the park, Yoshi walks home. He has a snack, then goes back to the park on his skateboard. Which graph best matches this situation? Explain your choice.

Graph A

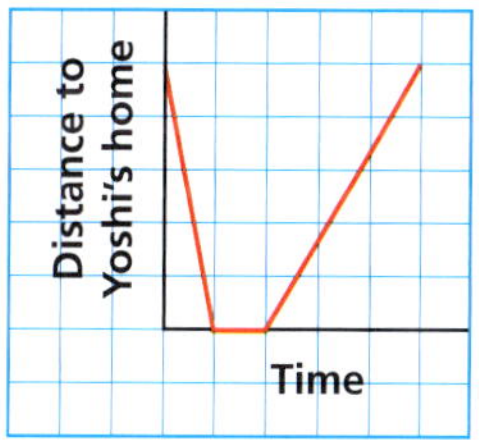

Graph B

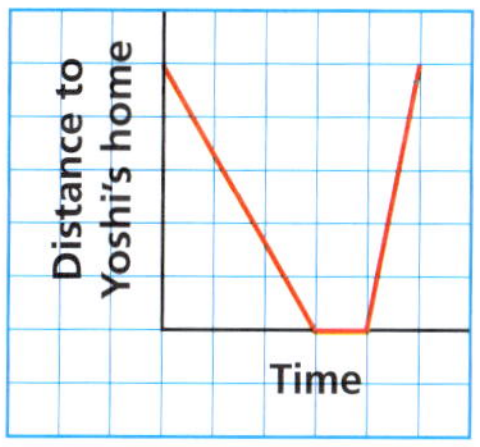

Graph C

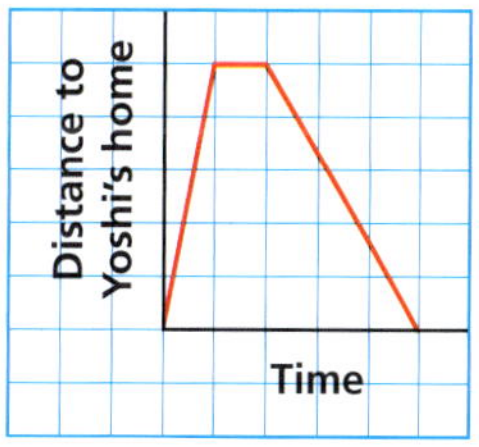

Graph D

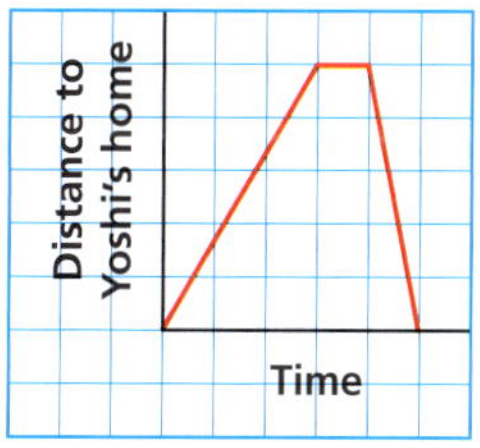

b) Choose one of the graphs in part a that did not describe Yoshi's journey. Describe a possible situation for the graph.

14. Determine the domain and range of the graph of each function.

a) 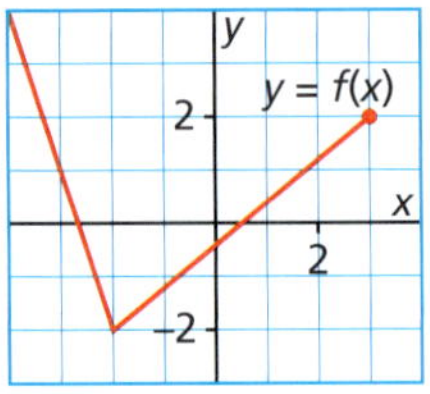

b) 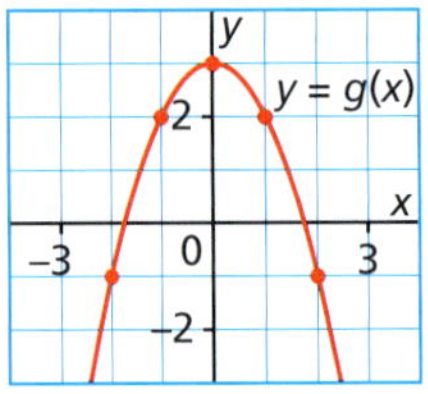

15. **a)** For each equation, create a table of values when necessary, then graph the relation.

i) $y = 4$ **ii)** $y = -2x + 1$

iii) $y = x^2 - 2$ **iv)** $x = 2$

v) $x + 2y = 6$ **vi)** $x - y^2 = 1$

b) Which equations in part a represent linear relations? How do you know?

16. This graph shows the cost for a banquet room rented for a birthday party. The cost, C dollars, is a function of the number of people, n, who attend.

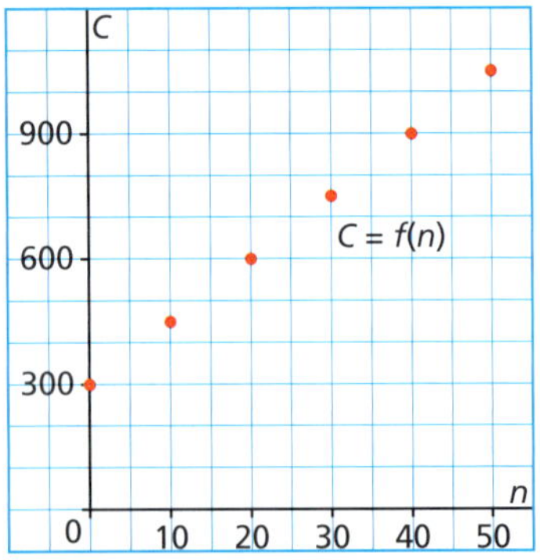

a) Determine the vertical intercept. Write the coordinates of the point where the graph intersects the axis. Describe what this point represents.

b) Determine the rate of change. What does it represent?

c) Identify the domain and range. Are there any restrictions? Explain.

d) What is the cost when 50 people attend the birthday party?

e) How many people can attend the party for a cost of \$675?

6

17. Draw the line through P(−1, 3) with each given slope. Write the coordinates of 3 other points on each line. How did you determine these points?

a) 2 **b)** −3 **c)** $\frac{3}{4}$ **d)** $-\frac{2}{5}$

18. The coordinates of two points on two different lines are given. Are the two lines parallel, perpendicular, or neither? Justify your choice.

a) W(−3, 5), X(8, 3) and C(6, 6), D(1, 8)

b) J(3, −4), K(9, 2) and P(5, −4), Q(2, −1)

c) R(−3, 2), S(1, −6) and E(−2, 1), F(−5, 7)

d) G(2, −5), H(2, 3) and M(3, −3), N(0, −3)

19. **a)** Graph these equations on the same grid without using a table of values.

i) $y = x - 5$

ii) $y = \frac{1}{3}x - 5$

iii) $y = -\frac{3}{2}x - 5$

iv) $y = -4x - 5$

b) Each equation in part a is written in the form $y = mx - 5$. When you change the value of m, how does it affect the graph?

20. A student said that the equation of this line is $y = \frac{1}{2}x - 3$.

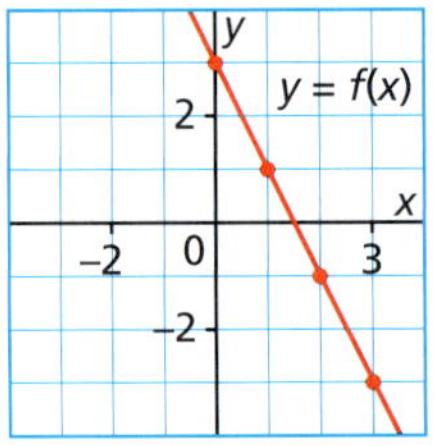

a) What mistakes did the student make?

b) What is the correct equation of the line?

21. **a)** For each line, write an equation in slope-point form.

i)

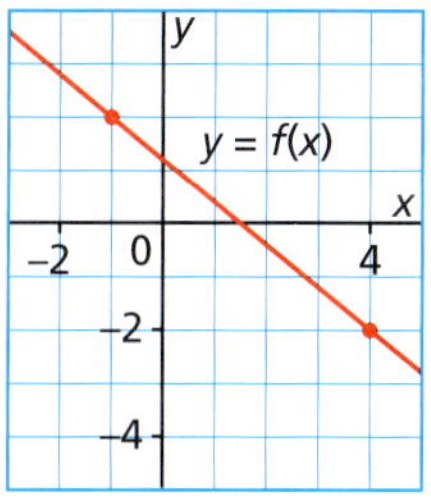

ii)

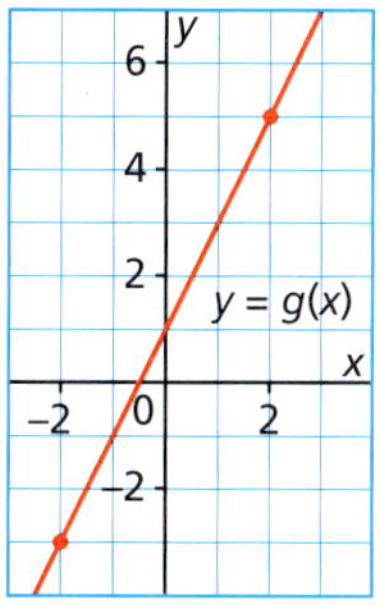

b) Write each equation in part a in slope-intercept form, then determine the x- and y-intercepts of each graph.

22. Loretta works as a cook in northern Saskatchewan. She is paid \$14 an hour plus \$200 a week for working in a remote location. Let t represent the time in hours Loretta works each week and let d represent her weekly pay in dollars.

a) Write an equation that relates d and t.

b) What will Loretta's weekly earnings be when she works 35 h?

c) For how many hours did Loretta work when her weekly pay was \$718?

d) Can Loretta earn exactly \$600 in one week? Explain.

23. **a)** Use intercepts to graph each equation.

i) $7x + y + 14 = 0$ **ii)** $2x - 5y - 20 = 0$

b) What is the slope of each line in part a? What strategy did you use?

24. **a)** Write each equation in general form.

i) $y = \frac{5}{4}x - \frac{3}{5}$ **ii)** $y + 4 = \frac{2}{3}(x - 1)$

b) For each of the 3 forms of the equation of a linear relation, describe when each form may be the best representation.

7

25. A store sells a 1-L can of paint for \$9.60 and a 4-L can of paint for \$20.80. The store has 140 cans of paint, for a total selling price of \$2206.40. Write a linear system that models this situation.

26. Tickets for the school play cost \$8 for an adult and \$5 for a student. The total revenue for one performance was \$1122, with 32 more students than adults in the audience.

a) Write a linear system that models this situation.

b) Solve the linear system in part a by graphing.

27. Use graphing technology to solve this linear system.

$$\frac{5}{2}x + \frac{4}{3}y = 7\frac{4}{9}$$
$$1.5x - 4.8y = 1.2$$

28. Arne scored 87.5% on part A of a math exam and 75% on part B of this exam. His total mark for the exam was 87. The total mark possible for the exam was 108. How many marks was each part worth?

29. Use an elimination strategy to solve each linear system.

a) $4x - 3y = 10$
$6x + 2y = 11$

b) $3x + 4y = 1$
$2x - 6y = -21$

30. Use $5x + 3y = 15$ as an equation in 3 different linear systems. Write the second equation so that each system has a different number of solutions. Explain what you did for each system.

31. Explain why Problem 1 has no solution and Problem 2 has infinite solutions.

Problem 1
The difference between two numbers is 75.
Triple each number. Subtract the products.
The difference is 200.
What are the two numbers?

Problem 2
The sum of two numbers is 40.
Divide each number by 2. Add the quotients.
The sum is 20.
What are the two numbers?

Answers

Chapter 1 Measurement, page 2

1.1 Imperial Measures of Length, page 11

3. Answers may vary. For example:
a) Foot **b)** Inch
c) Foot **d)** Inch
e) Mile

4. a) Inch

5. Answers may vary. For example:
a) Foot

7. a) 36 in. **b)** 189 ft.
c) 4 ft.

8. a) 10 560 ft. **b)** 15 yd. 2 ft. 10 in.
c) 1 mi. 703 yd. 1 ft.

9. 165 in. = 4 yd. 1 ft. 9 in.

10. a) 52 ft. = 17 yd. 1 ft. **b)** $197.82

11. a) 24 mats

12. No; 21 ft. 9 in. = 7 yd. 9 in.

13. 10 in.

14. a) 39 ft. 2 in. **b)** 4 rolls
c) $49.96

15. a) $119.99 **b)** $18.59

16. 1062 ft.

17. 62 mi.

18. 28 tulip bulbs

19. 2 mi. 80 yd.

20. 1:2 349 000

21. a) $351 000

22. $158 400 000

1.2 Math Lab: Measuring Length and Distance, page 15

3. Calipers require a steady hand to ensure an accurate reading. Calipers cannot be used for large measures.

1.3 Relating SI and Imperial Units, page 22

Answers will vary depending on the conversion ratios used.

4. a) 40.6 cm **b)** 1.2 m
c) 4.6 m **d)** 1.5 km
e) 9.7 km **f)** 50.8 mm

5. a) 1 in. **b)** 8 ft.
c) 11 yd. **d)** 93 mi.

6. a) 55.9 cm **b)** 256.5 cm
c) 9.6 m

7. a) i) 2 ft. 6 in. **ii)** 3 yd.
iii) 6 mi.

8. 100.6 m by 54.9 m

9. Tennessee River

10. The odometer is accurate; 142 km is close to 87 mi.

11. a) The warehouse

12. a) Michael

13. a) CN Tower: approximately 1815 ft.;
Willis Tower: approximately 442.3 m
b) CN Tower **c)** 111 m; 364 ft.

14. 144 sections of casing

15. 28 in.

16. Yes; approximately 8 cm

17. 7 homes

18. a) Approximately 65 hectares
b) Approximately 259 hectares

Chapter 1: Checkpoint 1, page 25

3. a) 26 yd. 2 ft. **b)** 5280 yd.
c) 84 in.

4. Sidney

7. Answers will vary depending on the conversion ratios used.
a) 14 yd. 1 ft. **b)** 122 cm
c) 1 mi. 427 yd. **d)** 273 yd. 1 ft. 3 in.
e) 330.2 m **f)** 5 ft. 9 in.

8. 10 ft. of laminate

1.4 Surface Areas of Right Pyramids and Right Cones, page 34

4. a) 132 in.^{2} **b)** 220 cm^2

5. a) 168 in.^{2} **b)** 294 cm^2

6. a) 101 in.^{2} **b)** 1649 cm^2

7. a) 151 in.^{2} **b)** 2356 cm^2

8. a) 896 cm^2 **b)** 628 yd.^{2}

9. a)

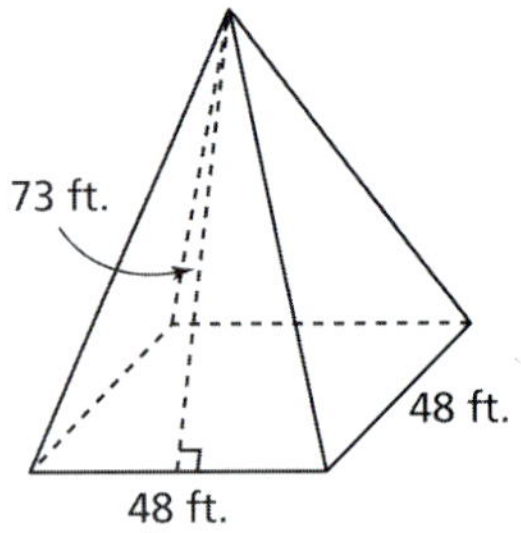

b) 7008 ft.^{2}

10. 923 285 ft.^{2}

11. a) 2261.9 cm^2

b) $11.94

12. 1520 cm^2

13. a) 87 m^2

b) 176 ft.^{2}

14. 2.0 m^2; I assumed the hides had equal areas.

15. 188 ft.^{2}

16. a) 69.0 mm

b) 7.6 m

17. a) Right square pyramid and right cone

b) Right rectangular prism

18. The Louvre

19. a) 193.7 cm^2

b) 34.9 m^2

20. 61 ft.^{2}

21. 16.0 cm

1.5 Volumes of Right Pyramids and Right Cones, page 42

4. a) 288 yd.^{3}

b) 1920 ft.^{3}

5. a) 96 yd.^{3}

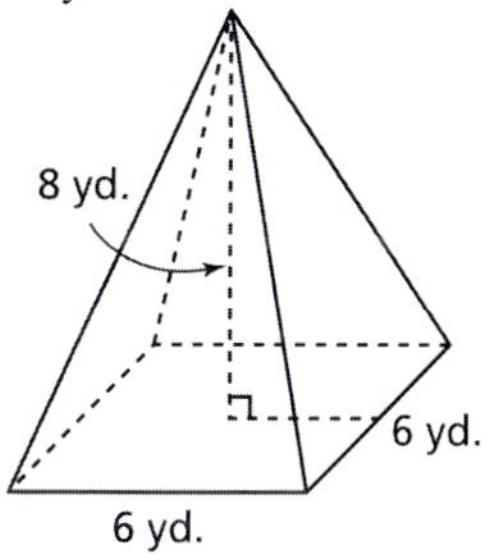

b) 640 ft.^{3}

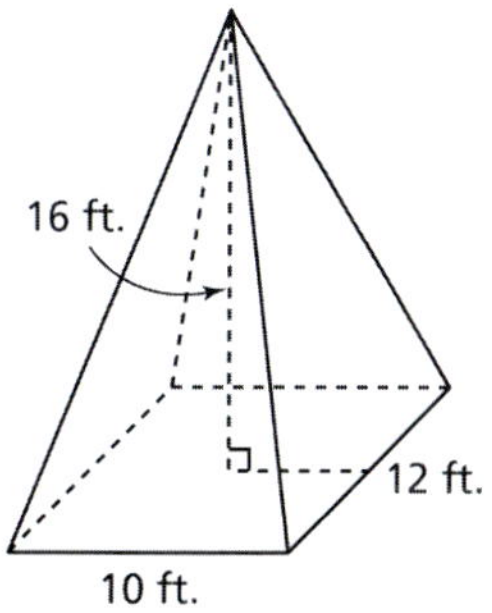

6. a) 1571 cm^3

b) 804 m^3

7. a) 524 cm^3

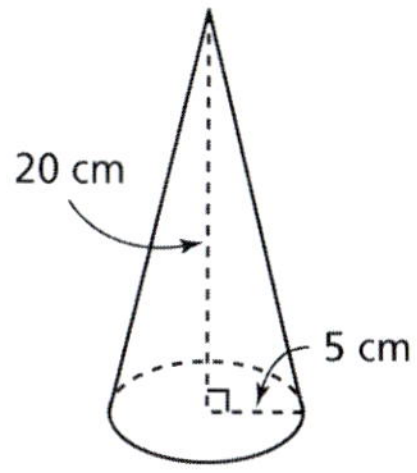

b) 268 m^3

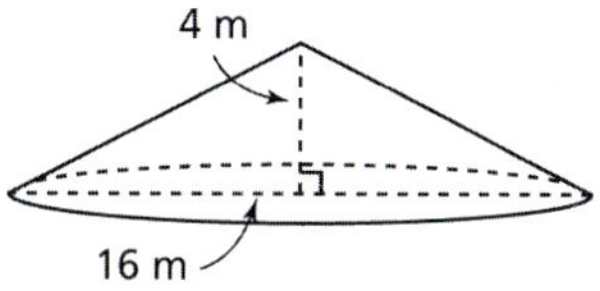

8. a) 18 m^3

b) 168 yd.^{3}

9. a) 37.7 m^3

b) 2948.9 cm^3

10. a)

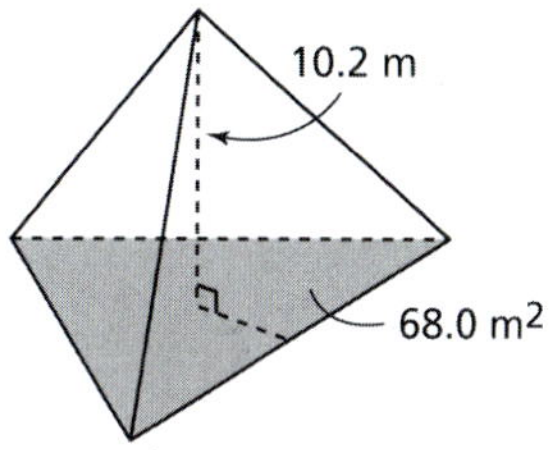

b) 231.2 m^3

11. a)

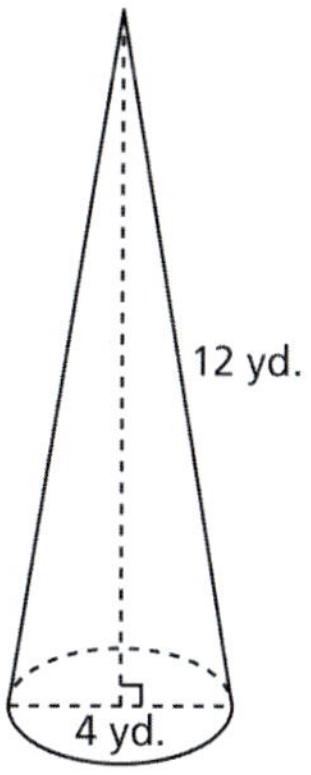

b) 50 yd.^{3}

12. 0.3 m^3

13. b) 441.2 cm^3

14. a) 5 in.^{3}

b) $3.33

c) Approximately 7 in.^{3}

15. **a)**

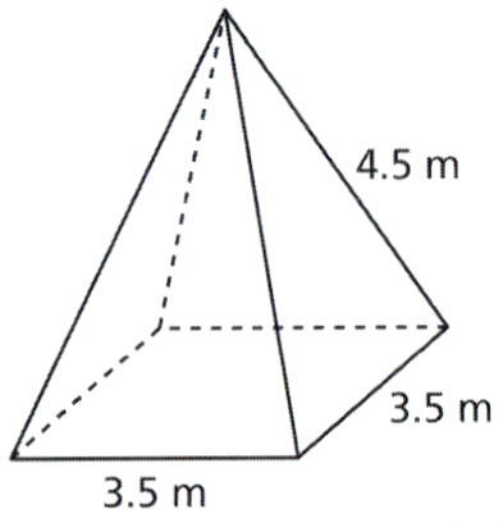

b) 3.8 m **c)** 15.3 m^3

16. 401 $ft.^3$

17. **a)** 15 cm^2 **b)** 23 cm^3
c) No, there is also some air inside the tea bag.

18. **a)** 4.7 cm **b)** 10.5 m
c) 3.3 m **d)** 7.4 cm

19. **b)** 8.0 cm

20. **a)** 22.9 kL **b)** Approximately 8.3 kL

21. 10 yd.

22. 49.6 m^3

1.6 Surface Area and Volume of a Sphere, page 51

3. **a)** 314 cm^2 **b)** 32 m^2
c) 201 $ft.^2$ **d)** 99 cm^2

4. **a)** 524 cm^3 **b)** 17 m^3
c) 268 $ft.^3$ **d)** 92 cm^3

5. **a)** 339 m^2, 452 m^3 **b)** 191 $yd.^2$, 191 $yd.^3$

7. 886.7 m, 2482.7 m^3

8. 3.2 cm

9. 12 in.

10. **a)** 2.1 L **b)** 8 cups

11. **a)** Hemisphere **b)** Hemisphere

12. **a)** 784 m^2 **b)** 2065 kL

13. **a)** 511 185 933 km^2
b) 357 830 153 km^2
c) 1 086 781 293 000 km^3
d) 1 078 037 876 000 km^3

14. Approximately 1 082 696 932 000 km^3; approximately 1 093 440 264 000 km^3

15. 239 spheres

16. **a)** 11 cm; 5 in. **b)** 1387 cm^2; 277 $in.^2$
c) 4855 cm^3; 434 $in.^3$ **d)** Basketball

17. **a)** 16.4 m^3 **b)** 1.0 m^2

18. 529.6 m^2; 882.2 m^3

19. 42 pumps

20. 45 cookies

21. **a)** Approximately 69%
b) Assumptions: Ball is created from one solid piece and has greatest possible diameter.

22. $SA = \pi d^2$; $V = \frac{1}{6}\pi d^3$

23. Approximately 5 in.

24. **a)** Inflated balloon's circumference is 3 times as great
b) Inflated balloon's surface area is 9 times as great
c) Inflated balloon's volume is 27 times as great

Chapter 1: Checkpoint 2, page 54

1. **a)** 80 $ft.^2$ **b)** 21 m^2
c) 1127 m^2

2. 425 m^2

3. 183 $in.^2$

4. **a)** 41 $ft.^3$ **b)** 6 m^3
c) 1947 m^3

5. **a)** 9.5 cm **b)** 2.7 m
c) 17.4 cm

6. **a)** 973.1 km^2, 2854.5 km^3
b) 109.0 cm^2, 82.3 cm^3

7. 7946 cm^2.

1.7 Solving Problems Involving Objects, page 59

3. **a)** 170 cm^2 **b)** 1040 $ft.^2$
c) 95 $in.^2$ **d)** 314 $in.^2$

4. **a)** Object in part c **b)** Approximately 38 $in.^3$

5. **a)** 273.3 cm^2, 353.4 cm^3 **b)** 12.0 m^2, 2.5 m^3

6. **a)** $5\frac{4}{5}$ in. **b)** 6.7 cm

7. **a)**

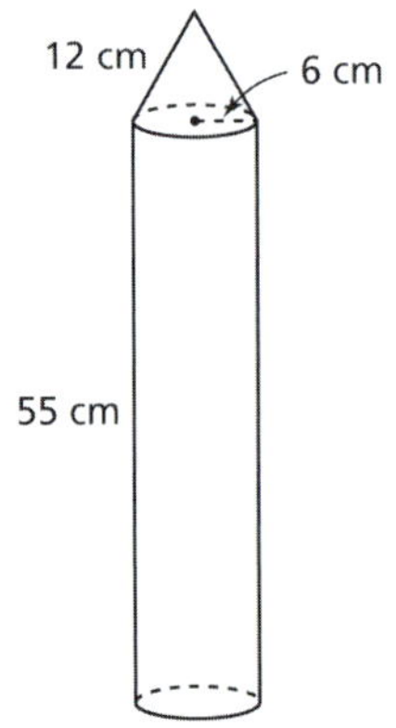

b) 2413 cm^2 **c)** 6612 cm^3
d) Approximately 2204 cm^3, or 2204 mL

8. 93 cm^3

9. a) Circular-based bin

b) Square-based bin

10. a) 1300.0 cm^3 **b)** 6.2 m^3

11. a) 856.2 cm^2 **b)** 24.2 m^2

12. Approximately 26.4 m^2

13. a) 1060 $in.^3$ **b)** 15 in. by 15 in. by 12 in.

c) 1820 $in.^3$

Chapter 1: Review, page 64

1. Answers may vary. For example:

a) Inch **b)** Foot

c) Yard

3. a) 42 ft. **b)** 8800 yd.

c) 75 in. **d)** 3 yd. 1 ft. 3 in.

4. 320 in., or 8 yd. 2 ft. 8 in.

6. Answers will vary depending on the conversion ratios used.

a) 8 ft. 7 in. **b)** 136 yd. 2 ft. 1 in.

c) 3 mi. 1282 yd. **d)** 1 ft. 2 in.

7. Answers will vary depending on the conversion ratios used.

a) 12.5 m **b)** 6.8 km

c) 48.3 cm **d)** 215.9 mm

8. Answers will vary depending on the conversion ratio used. 670 750 strides

9. a) 75 $ft.^2$ **b)** 85 cm^2

c) 898 mm^2 **d)** 192 m^2

10. 160 $yd.^2$

11. a)

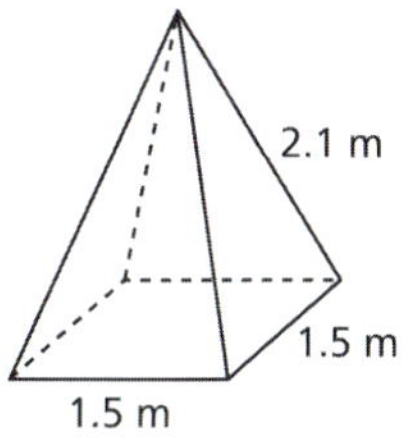

b) 2.0 m

c) 6 m^2

12. a) $8\frac{7}{10}$ in. **b)** 173 $in.^2$

13. 125.8 cm^2

14. 5810 $ft.^2$

15. a) 11 m^3 **b)** 8822 $in.^3$

c) 7 $ft.^3$ **d)** 221 mm^3

16. No; approximately 132.7 cm^3

17. 12 cm

18. a) 24 $in.^3$ **b)** 6 in.

19. a) 2.1 m **b)** 2.3 cm

20. a) 254 $in.^2$, 382 $in.^3$

b) 133 m^2, 144 m^3

21.

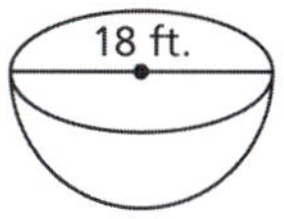

a) 763 $ft.^2$ **b)** 1527 $ft.^3$

22. $4\frac{3}{5}$ in.

23. Approximately 98 cm^3

24. 523 $in.^3$

25. a) 480 cm^2, 595 cm^3 **b)** 108 $ft.^2$, 84 $ft.^3$

26. a) 113 981 cm^3 **b)** 11 878 cm^2

27. a) 8 cm **b)** 10 mm

Chapter 1: Practice Test, page 67

1. B

2. C

3. The volume of the right cylinder is 3 times the volume of the right cone.

4. a) 28.3 cm^3, 69.3 cm^2

b) 1215.8 m^3, 647.2 m^2

5. a) A ruler with inches marked

6. 5.8 cm

Chapter 2 Trigonometry, page 68

2.1 The Tangent Ratio, page 75

3. a) $\tan A = \frac{6}{7}$; $\tan C = \frac{7}{6}$

b) $\tan D = \frac{3}{2}$; $\tan F = \frac{2}{3}$

c) $\tan H = \frac{5}{4}$; $\tan J = \frac{4}{5}$

d) $\tan K = \frac{5}{7}$; $\tan M = \frac{7}{5}$

4. a) 14° **b)** 51°

c) 68° **d)** 87°

5. a) 27° **b)** 45°

c) 61° **d)** 69°

6. Sketches will vary. For example:

a)

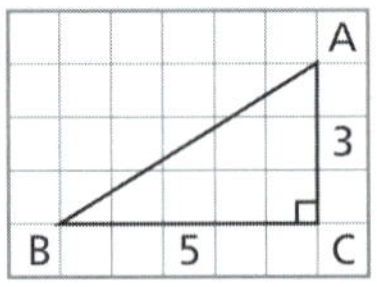

b)

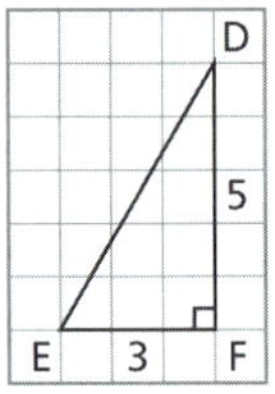

c)

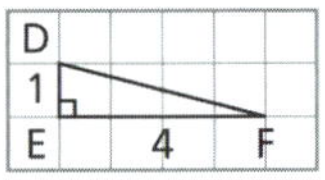

d)

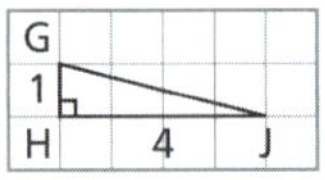

e)

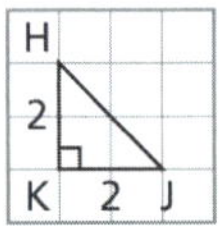

f)

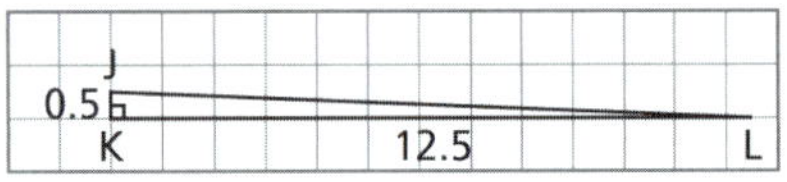

7. **a)** tan 60° > 1 **b)** tan 30° < 1

8. **a)** 36.4° **b)** 68.0°

9. **b)** **i)** ∠A ≐ 26.6°; ∠B ≐ 63.4°
   ii) ∠D ≐ 63.4°; ∠F ≐ 26.6°
   iii) ∠G ≐ 63.4°; ∠H ≐ 26.6°
   c) No

10. **a)** 36.0° **b)** 49.1°
    c) 20.3° **d)** 82.4°

11. **a)** 11° **b)** 14°
    c) 6° **d)** 9°

12. Whitehorse

13. ∠P = ∠RQS ≐ 67.4°, ∠R = ∠PQS ≐ 22.6°

14. 22°

15. 20.6°; 69.4°

16. The side opposite the acute angle has the same length as the side adjacent to the angle.

17. 25°

18. 22°

19. 146°

20. 76°

21. ∠X ≐ 50.1°, ∠Y = ∠Z ≐ 64.9°

22. **a)** There is no least possible value; the tangent can be arbitrarily close to zero.
    b) There is no greatest possible value; the tangent can be arbitrarily large.

23. **a)** 1; $\frac{1}{\sqrt{2}}$; $\frac{1}{\sqrt{3}}$; $\frac{1}{\sqrt{4}}$, or $\frac{1}{2}$; $\frac{1}{\sqrt{5}}$
    b) $\frac{1}{\sqrt{100}}$, or $\frac{1}{10}$

2.2 Using the Tangent Ratio to Calculate Lengths, page 82

3. **a)** 2.5 cm **b)** 1.4 cm
   c) 5.0 cm **d)** 7.5 cm

4. **a)** 2.2 cm **b)** 2.8 cm
   c) 2.8 cm

5. **a)** 5.6 cm **b)** 4.1 cm
   c) 3.8 cm

6. 22.8 m

7. 3.8 m

8. 187 m

9. **a)** 3.6 cm **b)** 10.0 cm

10. Approximately 30 m

11. **a)**

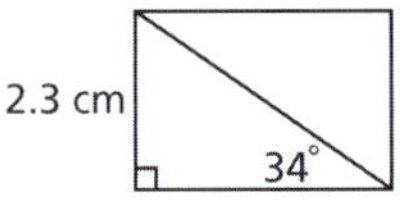

    b) 3.4 cm

12. 40.3 cm^2

13. Approximately 60 m

14. Approximately 58 m, assuming the balloon is directly over the store

15. ∠QRT = ∠SRT = 26.5°, ∠QRS = 53.0°,
    ∠QPT = ∠SPT = 56.3°, ∠QPS = 112.6°,
    ∠RQT = ∠RST = 63.5°,
    ∠PQT = ∠PST = 33.7°,
    ∠PQR = ∠PSR = 97.2°,
    ∠PTQ = ∠PTS = ∠QTR = ∠RTS = 90.0°
    PQ = PS ≐ 3.6 cm, QR = SR ≐ 6.7 cm

16. **a)** Approximately 38.7°
    b) Approximately 63.4°

2.3 Math Lab: Measuring an Inaccessible Height, page 86

1. The sum of the angle shown on the protractor and the angle of inclination is 90°.
2. 13.5 m
3. 25 m

Chapter 2: Checkpoint 1, page 88

1. a) 14° b) 56°
   c) 53°
3. 11.5°
4. a) 11.2 cm b) 7.3 cm
   c) 11.7 cm
5. Approximately 23.7 m

2.4 The Sine and Cosine Ratios, page 95

4. a) i) Opposite: GH; adjacent: AG; hypotenuse: AH
   ii) Opposite: TK; adjacent: AK; hypotenuse: AT
   b) i) sin A = 0.60; cos A = 0.80
   ii) sin A = 0.28; cos A = 0.96
5. a) sin 57° ≐ 0.84; cos 57° ≐ 0.54
   b) sin 5° ≐ 0.09; cos 5° ≐ 1.00
   c) sin 19° ≐ 0.33; cos 19° ≐ 0.95
   d) sin 81° ≐ 0.99; cos 81° ≐ 0.16
6. a) 14° b) 50°
   c) 33° d) 39°
7. a) 34° b) 35°
   c) 39° d) 33°
8. a) 41° b) 78°
   c) 26° d) 66°
9. Sketches will vary. For example:
   a)

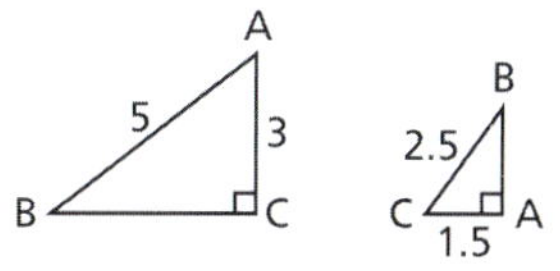

   b)

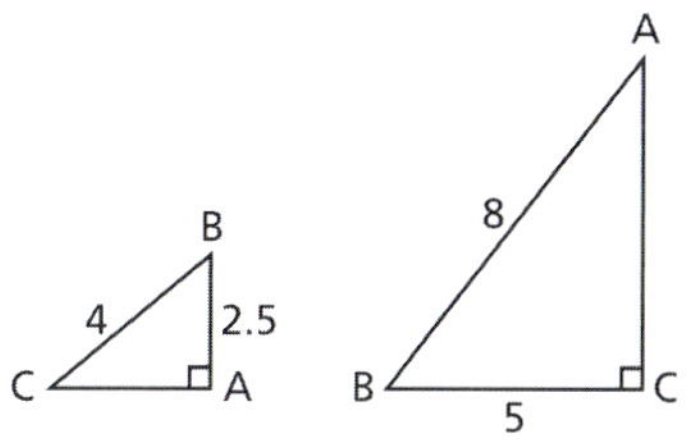

   c)

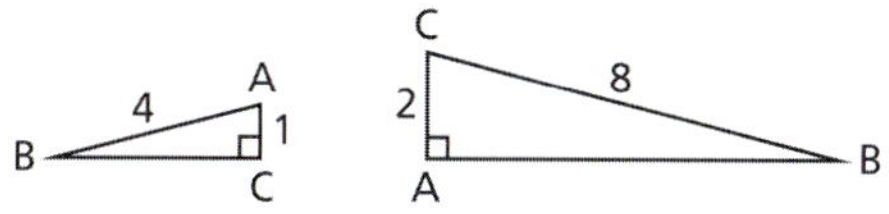

   d)

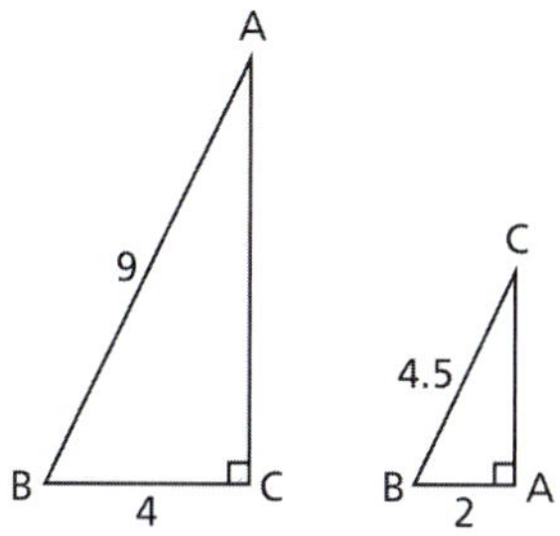

10. a) ∠C ≐ 16.3°, ∠D ≐ 73.7°
    b) ∠F ≐ 63.9°, ∠H ≐ 26.1°
    c) ∠J ≐ 38.0°, ∠K ≐ 52.0°
    d) ∠P ≐ 49.3°, ∠Q ≐ 40.7°
11. 1.3°
12. 79.4°
13. 61°
14. 31°
15. a) i) 0.1736… ii) 0.3420…
    iii) 0.6427… iv) 0.7660…
    v) 0.8660… vi) 0.9848…
16.

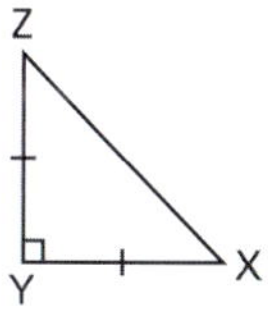

The opposite and adjacent sides of an acute angle have the same length, so $\frac{\text{opposite}}{\text{hypotenuse}} = \frac{\text{adjacent}}{\text{hypotenuse}}$.

17. 40°
18. a) i) 1 ii) 0
    iii) 0 iv) 1

2.5 Using the Sine and Cosine Ratios to Calculate Lengths, page 101

3. a) 3.1 cm b) 1.5 cm
   c) 1.5 cm d) 3.7 cm
4. a) 1.7 cm b) 3.2 cm
   c) 5.4 cm d) 7.9 cm
5. a) 25.3 cm b) 8.0 cm
   c) 7.7 cm d) 12.4 cm

6. 29.7 m
7. a) 48.3 m
   b) The surveyor could use the tangent ratio or the Pythagorean Theorem.
8. 4.0 km
9. 2813 m
10. 18.3 cm by 4.6 cm
11. a) 423 cm   b) 272 cm
12. a) i) 21.0 cm   ii) 15.1 cm
13. 186 mm
14. a) Approximately 139 ft.
    b) 17 407 $ft.^2$

Chapter 2: Checkpoint 2, page 104

1. a) 30°   b) 48°
   c) 56°
2. 13°
3. a) i) 0.9848...   ii) 0.9396...
   iii) 0.8660...   iv) 0.7660...
   v) 0.6427...   vi) 0.5
   vii) 0.3420...   viii) 0.1736...
4. a) 4.2 cm   b) 2.7 cm
   c) 14.0 cm
5. Approximately 3.2 km

2.6 Applying the Trigonometric Ratios, page 111

3. a) Sine   b) Tangent
   c) Cosine   d) Tangent
4. a) 4.6 cm; cosine   b) 4.7 cm; tangent
   c) 11.8 cm; sine   d) 14.5 cm; cosine
5. a) Pythagorean Theorem   b) Sine ratio
   c) Pythagorean Theorem   d) Pythagorean Theorem
6. a) $\angle T = 57°$, $TU \doteq 23.0$ cm, $VU \doteq 19.2$ cm
   b) $\angle Y = 43°$, $WY \doteq 8.7$ cm, $XY \doteq 6.3$ cm
   c) $ZB \doteq 11.3$ cm, $\angle B \doteq 60.3°$, $\angle Z \doteq 29.7°$
   d) $\angle E = 61°$, $CD \doteq 12.0$ cm, $CE \doteq 6.6$ cm
7. a) 1147 cm   b) 1144 cm
8. 173 ft.
9. a) 68 km   b) 31°
10. a) 4°   b) 15.0 m
11. a) 31°   b) 118°
12. a) 13.5 cm; 7.8 cm^2 b) 28.9 cm; 47.5 cm^2
13. 7.3 cm
14. a) 3 $in.^2$ b) 15 $in.^3$
15. 36 cm
16. 15.6 cm; 11.6 cm^2

2.7 Solving Problems Involving More than One Right Triangle, page 118

3. a) 6.0 cm   b) 6.0 cm
   c) 4.3 cm   d) 3.6 cm
4. a) 5.7 cm   b) 4.9 cm
   c) 5.7 cm
5. a) 93.2°   b) 123.7°
   c) 11.1°   d) 15.0°
6. 15 m, 19 m
7. 51°, 65°, 65°
8. a) 19 ft.   b) 21 ft.
9. 35 m, 58 m
10. Approximately 126°, approximately 54°
11. 4.5 m
12. a) 53 m   b) 29 m
    c) 50 m
13. a) 5.0 m   b) 51.3°
    c) 2.4 m
14. a) 23 m   b) 20 m
16. a)

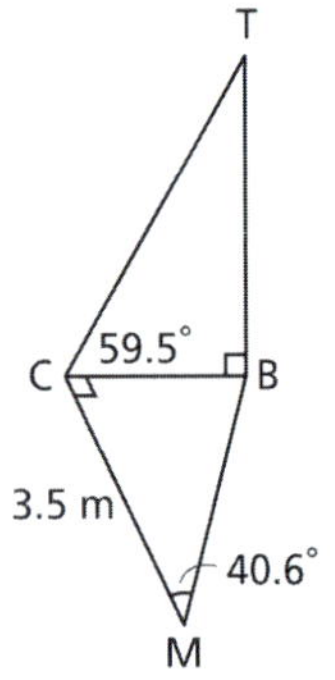

    b) 5.1 m
17. a) 98.1°, 51.7°, 105.1°, 105.1°
    b) 100 mm
18. a)

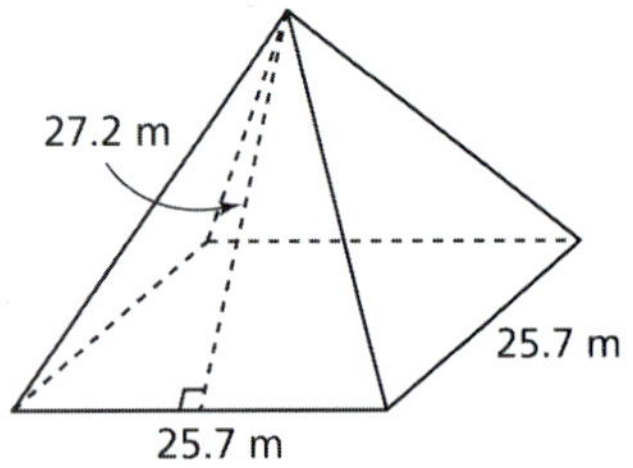

    b) 24.0 m
19. a) 5.4 cm   b) 33.9°
20. Approximately 8.3 m
21. Approximately 18 in.

Chapter 2: Review, page 124

1. a) 35° **b)** 65°

2. a) $\tan 20° < 1$ **b)** $\tan 70° > 1$

3. 6°

4. The triangle is an isosceles right triangle.

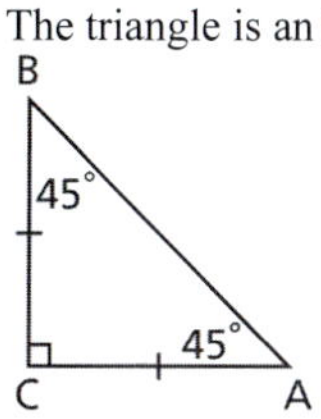

5. a) i) 3.7 cm
ii) 3.0 cm
b) Could also use trigonometric ratios
i) Approximately 4.2 cm
ii) Approximately 4.0 cm

6. 327 m

7. a) 11.7 cm **b)** 13.0 cm

8. 17.5 m

9. 30 m

11. a) 73°; cosine **b)** 28°; sine

12.

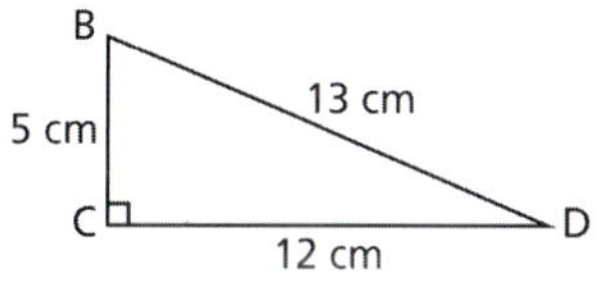

a) i) $\frac{5}{13}$ **ii)** $\frac{12}{13}$
iii) $\frac{5}{13}$ **iv)** $\frac{12}{13}$
b) $\sin D = \cos B$; $\sin B = \cos D$

13. 64.2°

14. 36.9°

15. a) 3.9 cm; cosine
b) 4.4 cm; sine
c) 4.7 cm; sine
d) 4.5 cm; cosine

16. 6.0 km

17. 1.6 cm by 2.8 cm

18. a) $CE \doteq 5.0$ cm, $\angle E \doteq 57.3°$, $\angle C \doteq 32.7°$
b) $\angle H = 52°$, $GH \doteq 2.7$ cm, $FH \doteq 4.3$ cm
c) $\angle K = 63°$, $JM \doteq 3.9$ cm, $KM \doteq 2.0$ cm

19. 85.9°

20. a) 35.5 cm; 52.1 cm^2
b) 13.0 cm; 10.2 cm^2

21. a) 3.2 m **b)** 8.2 m

22. a) 13.6 cm **b)** 11.3 cm
c) 21.0°

23. 2316 ft.

Chapter 2: Practice Test, page 127

1. B

2. C

4. $\angle D = 27.0°$, $DE \doteq 6.9$ cm, $EF \doteq 3.5$ cm

5. 203 cm

6. 75.5 m

Cumulative Review Chapters 1 and 2, page 130

1. a) 23 yd. 1 ft. **b)** $59.76

2. 276 km

4. Answers will vary depending on the conversion ratios used.
a) 823 cm **b)** 279 400 m
c) 3 mi. **d)** 5 ft. 3 in.

5. Answers will vary depending on the conversion ratio used. The road above The Narrows is higher by approximately 5 ft., or 1.5 m.

6. a) 342 m^2 **b)** 208 $ft.^2$

7. 192 $ft.^3$

8. Approximately 6 yd.

9. No

10. a) Hemisphere; 138 $in.^2$
b) Sphere; 3824 $in.^3$

11. 191 m^2, 170 m^3

12. 4478 $in.^2$

13. 222.1 mm^2, 239.6 mm^3

14. a) 31.0° **b)** 62.5°

15. 26 yd.

16. 201 ft.

17. a) 61.9° **b)** 68.4°

18. 22°

19. 50 ft. by 94 ft.

20. a) $\angle S = 24.0°$, $RT \doteq 6.4$ m, $RS \doteq 14.4$ m
b) $\angle M = 46.0°$, $MN \doteq 7.1$ cm, $MP \doteq 10.3$ cm

21. 59°

22. $x = 20.0$ cm; $y \doteq 40.0$ cm;
$\angle PRQ = 46.4°$; $\angle PRS = 133.6°$;
$\angle PSR = 31.7°$; $\angle QPR = 43.6°$;
$\angle QPS = 58.3°$; $\angle QRS = 180.0°$;
$\angle RPS = 14.7°$

Chapter 3 Factors and Products, page 132

3.1 Factors and Multiples of Whole Numbers, page 140

3. a) 6, 12, 18, 24, 30, 36
b) 13, 26, 39, 52, 65, 78
c) 22, 44, 66, 88, 110, 132
d) 31, 62, 93, 124, 155, 186
e) 45, 90, 135, 180, 225, 270
f) 27, 54, 81, 108, 135, 162

4. a) 2, 5 **b)** 3, 5
c) 3 **d)** 2, 3, 5
e) 2, 5, 7 **f)** 2, 3

5. a) $3 \cdot 3 \cdot 5$, or $3^2 \cdot 5$
b) $2 \cdot 2 \cdot 2 \cdot 2 \cdot 5$, or $2^4 \cdot 5$
c) $2 \cdot 2 \cdot 2 \cdot 2 \cdot 2 \cdot 3$, or $2^5 \cdot 3$
d) $2 \cdot 61$
e) $2 \cdot 2 \cdot 2 \cdot 2 \cdot 2 \cdot 5$, or $2^5 \cdot 5$
f) $3 \cdot 5 \cdot 13$

6. a) $2^3 \cdot 3 \cdot 5^2$ **b)** $2 \cdot 5^2 \cdot 23$
c) $2 \cdot 7 \cdot 73$ **d)** $2 \cdot 3^2 \cdot 5^3$
e) $2^2 \cdot 3^2 \cdot 5^3$ **f)** $5^3 \cdot 7^2$

8. a) 2 **b)** 2^3, or 8
c) 3^3, or 27 **d)** 2^2, or 4
e) 2^5, or 32 **f)** $2^2 \cdot 5$, or 20

9. a) 5 **b)** $2^3 \cdot 5$, or 40
c) $2 \cdot 3 \cdot 7$, or 42 **d)** 2^2, or 4

10. a) $2^2 \cdot 3 \cdot 7$, or 84 **b)** $3^2 \cdot 5 \cdot 7$, or 315
c) $2^2 \cdot 3^2 \cdot 5$, or 180 **d)** $2 \cdot 3 \cdot 7 \cdot 19$, or 798
e) $2^5 \cdot 3^2 \cdot 5$, or 1440 **f)** $2^2 \cdot 7 \cdot 13$, or 364

11. a) $2^2 \cdot 3^2 \cdot 5 \cdot 19$, or 3420
b) $2^5 \cdot 3 \cdot 5 \cdot 11$, or 5280
c) $2^2 \cdot 3^2 \cdot 5^2$, or 900
d) $2^3 \cdot 3^3 \cdot 5$, or 1080

12. Greatest common factor: 2;
least common multiple: $2^2 \cdot 3 \cdot 7$, or 84

13. $2 \cdot 3$, or 6

14. The greatest common factor of the two numbers is 1.

15. a) $\frac{37}{65}$ **b)** $\frac{17}{19}$
c) $\frac{13}{18}$ **d)** $\frac{42}{61}$
e) $\frac{49}{110}$ **f)** $\frac{33}{17}$

16. a) $\frac{149}{112}$ **b)** $\frac{65}{60}$, or $\frac{13}{12}$
c) $\frac{43}{264}$ **d)** $\frac{304}{210}$, or $\frac{152}{105}$
e) $\frac{121}{600}$ **f)** $\frac{239}{90}$
g) $\frac{27}{20}$ **h)** $\frac{77}{12}$

17. 800 m

18. No; 1 does not have any prime factors.

19. a) 72 cm by 72 cm **b)** Yes

20. a) Yes **b)** Yes
c) 660 feet

21. Yes

22. 30 cm

3.2 Perfect Squares, Perfect Cubes, and Their Roots, page 146

4. a) 14 **b)** 16
c) 19 **d)** 17
e) 21

5. a) 7 **b)** 8
c) 10 **d)** 11
e) 15

6. a) Perfect square
b) Perfect square and perfect cube
c) Neither
d) Perfect square
e) Perfect square and perfect cube
f) Perfect cube

7. a) 22 mm **b)** 42 yd.

8. a) 18 in. **b)** 25 ft.

9. 96 ft.^{2}

10. 35 937 ft.^{3}

11. No; 2000 is not a perfect cube.

12. These answers assume that the endpoints of each range are included in the range.
a) Perfect squares: 324, 361; perfect cube: 343
b) Perfect squares: 676, 729; perfect cube: 729
c) Perfect squares: 841, 900
d) Perfect squares: 1225, 1296; perfect cube: 1331

13. The first 5 are: 0, 1, 64, 729, 4096

14. 12 ft.

15. a) $\frac{45x^2}{8}$ **b)** $x = 4$

16. Edge length: 6 units

17. a) $11x^2y$ b) $4x^2y$

18. $1^3 + 12^3$, $9^3 + 10^3$

Chapter 3: Checkpoint 1, page 149

1. a) $2^2 \cdot 3^2 \cdot 5 \cdot 7$ b) $2^7 \cdot 3 \cdot 11$
   c) $2^3 \cdot 3^2 \cdot 5 \cdot 17$ d) $5 \cdot 11 \cdot 19$
   e) $2^4 \cdot 3^3 \cdot 7$ f) $3 \cdot 5^2 \cdot 7^2$
2. a) 2^3, or 8 b) $2^2 \cdot 3$, or 12
   c) 5 d) 2^4, or 16
   e) 2^3, or 8 f) 5^2, or 25
3. a) $2^2 \cdot 3 \cdot 5 \cdot 7$, or 420
   b) $2^5 \cdot 3 \cdot 5$, or 480
   c) $2^3 \cdot 3^2 \cdot 5$, or 360
   d) $2^5 \cdot 3 \cdot 5$, or 480
   e) $2^6 \cdot 7^2$, or 3136
   f) $2 \cdot 3 \cdot 5^2 \cdot 11$, or 1650
4. a) $\frac{103}{33}$ b) $\frac{71}{35}$
   c) $\frac{27}{70}$
5. 18 980 days; 52 years
6. a) 20 b) 28
   c) 24 d) 33
   e) 39 f) 55
7. a) 12 b) 15
   c) 20 d) 18
   e) 22 f) 21
8. a) Neither
   b) Perfect square
   c) Perfect square and perfect cube
   d) Perfect square
   e) Perfect cube
   f) Neither
9. a) Perfect squares: 400, 441, 484
   b) Perfect squares: 900, 961; perfect cube: 1000
   c) Perfect square: 1156
10. 26 cans

3.3 Common Factors of a Polynomial, page 155

Gray algebra tiles represent positive tiles and black tiles represent negative algebra tiles.

4. a) $3x + 12$; 3, $x + 4$
   b) $4x^2 + 10x$; $2x$, $2x + 5$
   c) $12x^2 - 8x + 16$; 4, $3x^2 - 2x + 4$
5. a) 3 b) m
6. a) i) $3(2 + 5n)$ ii) $3(2 - 5n)$
   iii) $3(5n - 2)$ iv) $3(-5n + 2)$
   b) i) $m(4 + m)$ ii) $m(m + 4)$
   iii) $m(4 - m)$ iv) $m(m - 4)$
7. a) $5(y + 2)$

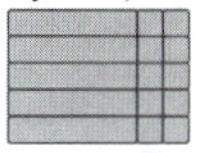

   b) $6(1 + 2x^2)$

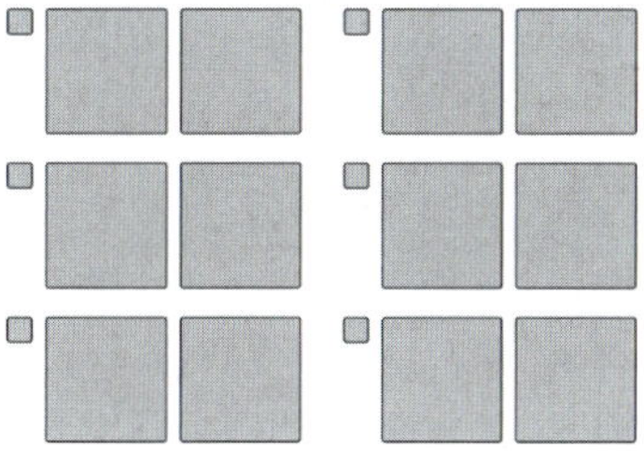

   c) $3(3k + 2)$

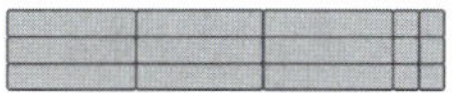

   d) $2s(2s + 7)$

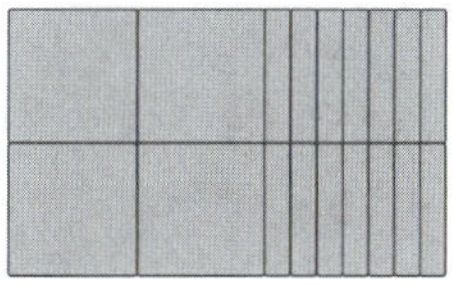

   e) $y(1 + y)$

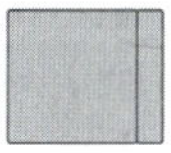

   f) $h(3 + 7h)$

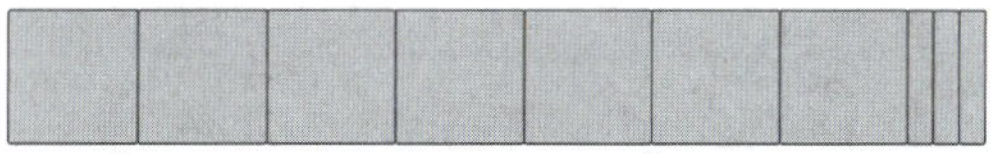

8. a) $3b^2(3 - 4b)$ b) $12(4s^3 - 1)$
   c) $-a^2(1 + a)$ d) $3x^2(1 + 2x^2)$
   e) $4y(2y^2 - 3)$ f) $-7d(1 + 2d^3)$
9. a) $3(x^2 + 4x - 2)$

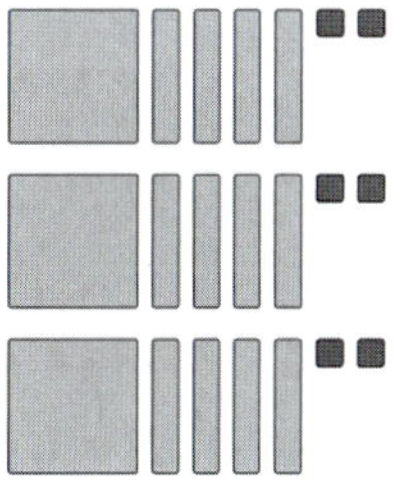

b) $2(2 - 3y - 4y^2)$

c) $-7(m + m^2 + 2)$

d) $2(5n - 3 - 6n^2)$

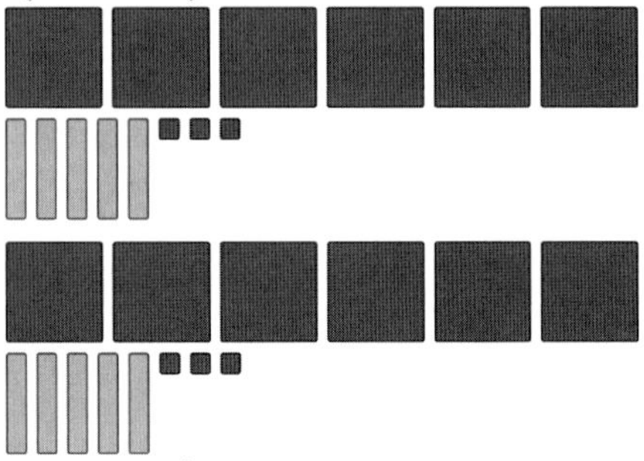

e) $2(4 + 5x + 3x^2)$

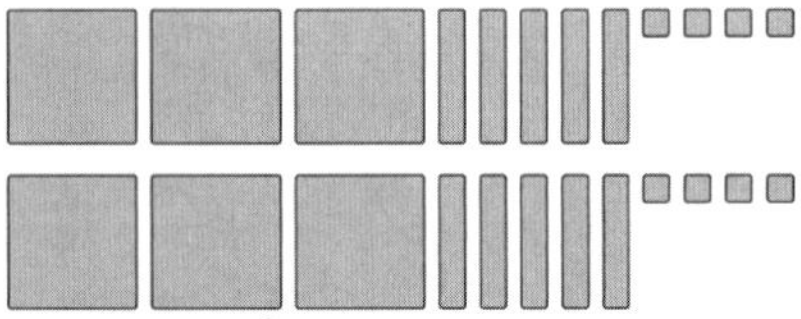

f) $-3(3 - 4b - 2b^2)$

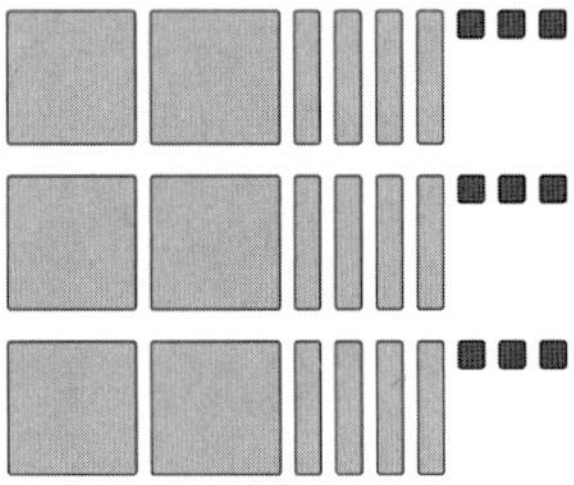

10. a) $5(1 + 3m^2 - 2m^3)$ **b)** $9(3n + 4 - 2n^3)$
c) $v(6v^3 + 7 - 8v^2)$ **d)** $-c^2(3 + 13c^2 + 12c)$
e) $6x(4 + 5x - 2x^3)$ **f)** $s(s^3 + s - 4)$

11. a) $-12x^2 + 20x$
b) $4x$ and $(-3x + 5)$
c) The factors are the dimensions of the rectangle.

12. a) **i)** $3m(m + 3m^2 - 1)$
ii) $-4(4 - 2n + n^3)$
b) Expanded his solutions

13. The monomial is 1 when the term is the common factor. The monomial is –1 when the term has the opposite sign of the common factor.

14. a) $4x - 4 = 4(x - 1)$
b) $16m^2 - 24m - 16 = 8(2m^2 - 3m - 2)$
c) $-8n^3 - 6n^2 - 10n = -2n(4n^2 + 3n + 5)$

15. a) **i)** $2 \cdot 2 \cdot s \cdot t \cdot t$, or $4st^2$
ii) $a \cdot a \cdot b$, or a^2b
iii) $2 \cdot 2 \cdot 3 \cdot x \cdot x \cdot y \cdot y$, or $12x^2y^2$
b) **i)** $4st^2(s + 3st + 9)$
ii) $4st^2(3st - s - 9)$
iii) $-a^2b(3a + 9a^2 - 8)$
iv) $a^2b(9a^2 + 3a - 8)$
v) $12x^2y^2(3y^2 + x + x^2y)$
vi) $-12x^2y^2(3y^2 + x^2y + x)$

16. a) $5x(5y + 3x - 6xy^2)$
b) $3mn(17m + 13n - 24)$
c) $3p^2q^2(3p^2 - 2pq + 4q^2)$
d) $a^2b^2(10a + 12b^2 - 5)$
e) $4cd(3d - 2 - 5c)$
f) $7rs^2(r^2s + 2r - 3)$

17. a) $SA = 2\pi r(r + h)$
b) Approximately 2639 cm^2

18. a) $SA = \pi r(r + s)$
b) Approximately 679 cm^2

19. a) Assume the area of the base of the silo is not included in the surface area. $SA = 2\pi rh + 2\pi r^2$; $SA = 2\pi r(h + r)$; approximately 603 m^2
b) $V = \pi r^2 h + \frac{2}{3}\pi r^3$; $V = \pi r^2\left(h + \frac{2}{3}r\right)$; approximately 1583 m^3

20. Yes

21. a) $\frac{2\pi rh}{2\pi r^2 + 2\pi rh}$ **b)** $\frac{h}{r + h}$

22. a) 2; 3
b) $n - 3$
c) $\frac{n^2}{2} - \frac{3n}{2} = \frac{n}{2}(n - 3)$

3.4 Math Lab: Modelling Trinomials as Binomial Products, page 158

1. a) Can be represented

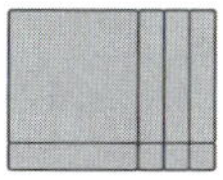

b) Can be represented

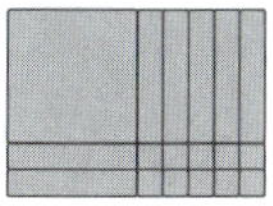

c) Cannot be represented

d) Cannot be represented

e) Cannot be represented

f) Cannot be represented

2. a) Can be represented

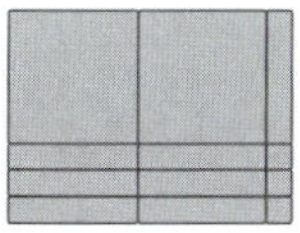

b) Can be represented

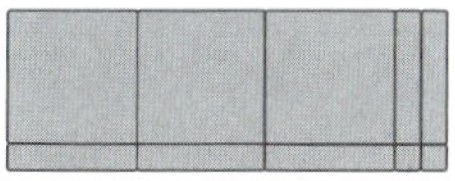

c) Cannot be represented

d) Cannot be represented

e) Cannot be represented

f) Can be represented

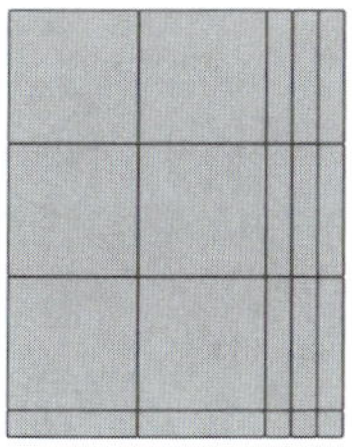

3. 7, 8, 13

4. 4, 7, 9, 10

3.5 Polynomials of the Form $x^2 + bx + c$, page 166

4. a) $(x+1)(x+3) = x^2 + 4x + 3$

b) $(x+2)(x+4) = x^2 + 6x + 8$

c) $(x+5)(x+5) = x^2 + 10x + 25$

d) $(x+3)(x+6) = x^2 + 9x + 18$

5. a) $b^2 + 7b + 10$

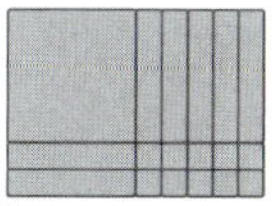

b) $n^2 + 11n + 28$

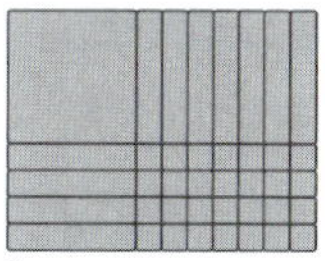

c) $h^2 + 11h + 24$

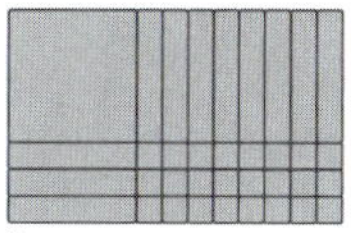

d) $k^2 + 7k + 6$

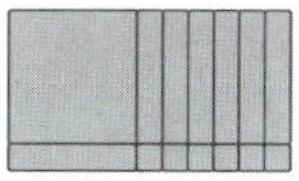

6. a) i) $x^2 + 4x + 4$

ii)

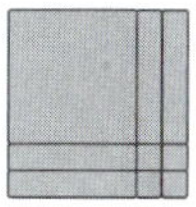

iii) $(x+2)(x+2)$

b) i) $x^2 + 5x + 4$

ii)

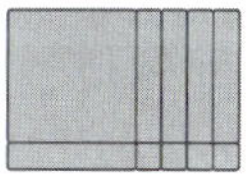

iii) $(x+1)(x+4)$

c) i) $x^2 + 6x + 8$

ii)

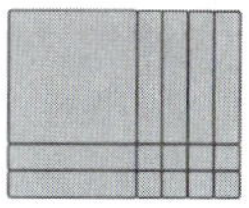

iii) $(x+2)(x+4)$

d) i) $x^2 + 7x + 12$

ii)

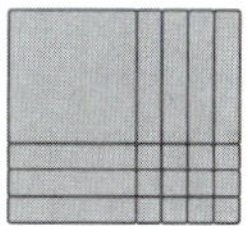

iii) $(x+3)(x+4)$

7. a) i) 1, 2 **ii)** 2, 3
iii) 1, 9 **iv)** 2, 5
v) 3, 4 **vi)** 3, 5

b) i) $(v + 1)(v + 2)$ **ii)** $(w + 2)(w + 3)$
iii) $(s + 1)(s + 9)$ **iv)** $(t + 2)(t + 5)$
v) $(y + 3)(y + 4)$ **vi)** $(h + 3)(h + 5)$

8. a) i) $(v + 1)(v + 1)$

ii) $(v + 2)(v + 2)$

iii) $(v + 3)(v + 3)$

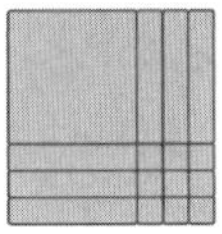

iv) $(v + 4)(v + 4)$

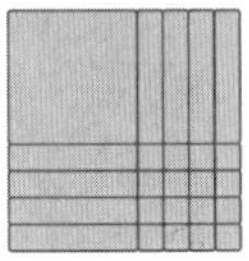

b) The rectangles are squares; the binomial factors are the same.

c) $v^2 + 10v + 25 = (v + 5)(v + 5)$;
$v^2 + 12v + 36 = (v + 6)(v + 6)$;
$v^2 + 14v + 49 = (v + 7)(v + 7)$

9. Area models and/or rectangle diagrams may vary. For example:

a) $m^2 + 13m + 40$

	m	8
m	$(m)(m) = m^2$	$(m)(8) = 8m$
5	$(5)(m) = 5m$	$(5)(8) = 40$

b) $y^2 + 12y + 27$

	y	3
y	$(y)(y) = y^2$	$(y)(3) = 3y$
9	$(9)(y) = 9y$	$(9)(3) = 27$

c) $w^2 + 18w + 32$

	w	16
w	$(w)(w) = w^2$	$(w)(16) = 16w$
2	$(2)(w) = 2w$	$(2)(16) = 32$

d) $k^2 + 14k + 13$

	k	1
k	$(k)(k) = k^2$	$(k)(1) = k$
13	$(13)(k) = 13k$	$(13)(1) = 13$

10. a) $(w + 3)(w + 2) = w^2 + 5w + 6$
b) $(x + 5)(x + 2) = x^2 + 7x + 10$
c) $(y + 10)(y + 2) = y^2 + 12y + 20$

11. a) $(x + 4)(x + 6)$ **b)** $(m + 2)(m + 8)$
c) $(p + 1)(p + 12)$ **d)** $(s + 2)(s + 10)$
e) $(n + 1)(n + 11)$ **f)** $(h + 2)(h + 6)$
g) $(q + 1)(q + 6)$ **h)** $(b + 2)(b + 9)$

12. a) $g^2 + 4g - 21$

	g	7
g	$(g)(g) = g^2$	$(g)(7) = 7g$
-3	$(-3)(g) = -3g$	$(-3)(7) = -21$

b) $h^2 - 5h - 14$

	h	-7
h	$(h)(h) = h^2$	$(h)(-7) = -7h$
2	$(2)(h) = 2h$	$(2)(-7) = -14$

c) $22 - 13j + j^2$

	2	$-j$
11	$(11)(2) = 22$	$(11)(-j) = -11j$
$-j$	$(-j)(2) = -2j$	$(-j)(-j) = j^2$

d) $k^2 + 8k - 33$

	k	11
k	$(k)(k) = k^2$	$(k)(11) = 11k$
-3	$(-3)(k) = -3k$	$(-3)(11) = -33$

e) $84 - 5h - h^2$

	7	$-h$
12	$(12)(7) = 84$	$(12)(-h) = -12h$
h	$(h)(7) = 7h$	$(h)(-h) = -h^2$

f) $m^2 - 81$

	m	9
m	$(m)(m) = m^2$	$(m)(9) = 9m$
-9	$(-9)(m) = -9m$	$(-9)(9) = -81$

g) $n^2 - 18n + 56$

	n	-4
n	$(n)(n) = n^2$	$(n)(-4) = -4n$
-14	$(-14)(n) = -14n$	$(-14)(-4) = 56$

h) $p^2 - 11p - 102$

	p	-17
p	$(p)(p) = p^2$	$(p)(-17) = -17p$
6	$(6)(p) = 6p$	$(6)(-17) = -102$

13. a) $r^2 - 9r - 52$
b) $s^2 - 20s + 75$

14. a) $(b - 1)(b + 20)$ **b)** $(t - 3)(t + 18)$
c) $(x - 2)(x + 14)$ **d)** $(n + 3)(n - 8)$
e) $(a + 4)(a - 5)$ **f)** $(y + 6)(y - 8)$
g) $(m - 5)(m - 10)$ **h)** $(a - 6)(a - 6)$

15. a) $(1 + k)(12 + k)$ **b)** $(2 + g)(-8 + g)$
c) $(5 + y)(12 + y)$ **d)** $(9 + z)(8 - z)$

16. a) i) $x^2 + 3x + 2$; 132
ii) $x^2 + 4x + 3$; 143
b) The coefficients of the terms of the polynomial are the digits in the product of integers.

17. a) $(m + 5)(m - 12)$
b) $(w - 5)(w - 9)$
c) $(b - 3)(b + 12)$

18. a) i) $t^2 + 11t + 28$ **ii)** $t^2 - 11t + 28$
iii) $t^2 + 3t - 28$ **iv)** $t^2 - 3t - 28$
b) i) Because the constant terms in the binomials have the same sign
ii) Because the constant terms in the binomials have opposite signs
iii) Add the constant terms in the binomials

19. a) $\pm7, \pm11$; 4 integers
b) $0, \pm8$; 3 integers
c) $\pm6, \pm9$; 4 integers
d) $\pm1, \pm4, \pm11$; 6 integers
e) $\pm9, \pm11, \pm19$; 6 integers
f) $0, \pm6, \pm15$; 5 integers

20. Infinitely many integers are possible. For example:

a) 0, –2, –6, –12, –20, –30, …
b) 0, –2, –6, –12, –20, –30, …
c) 1, 0, –3, –8, –15, –24, –35, …
d) 1, 0, –3, –8, –15, –24, –35, …
e) 2, 0, –4, –10, –18, –28, –40, …
f) 2, 0, –4, –10, –18, –28, –40, …

21. a) $4(y-7)(y+2)$ **b)** $-3(m+2)(m+4)$
c) $4(x-3)(x+4)$ **d)** $10(x+2)(x+6)$
e) $-5(n-1)(n-7)$ **f)** $7(c-2)(c-3)$

23. a) i) $(h+2)(h-12)$ **ii)** $(h-2)(h+12)$
iii) $(h-4)(h-6)$ **iv)** $(h+4)(h+6)$
b) The first 6 are:
$h^2 \pm 13h \pm 30$, $h^2 \pm 15h \pm 54$, $h^2 \pm 17h \pm 60$,
$h^2 \pm 25h \pm 84$, $h^2 \pm 20h \pm 96$, $h^2 \pm 26h \pm 120$

3.6 Polynomials of the Form $ax^2 + bx + c$, page 177

5. a) $(2m+1)(m+3) = 2m^2 + 7m + 3$
b) $(3p+2)(p+4) = 3p^2 + 14p + 8$
c) $(3w+1)(2w+1) = 6w^2 + 5w + 1$
d) $(4v+3)(3v+2) = 12v^2 + 17v + 6$

6. a) $2v^2 + 7v + 6$ **b)** $3r^2 + 13r + 4$
c) $6g^2 + 13g + 6$ **d)** $8z^2 + 26z + 15$
e) $9t^2 + 24t + 16$ **f)** $4r^2 + 12r + 9$

7. a) i) $2x^2 + 5x + 2$
ii)

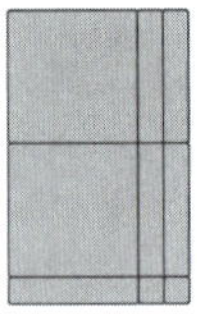

iii) $(2x+1)(x+2)$

b) i) $3x^2 + 11x + 6$
ii)

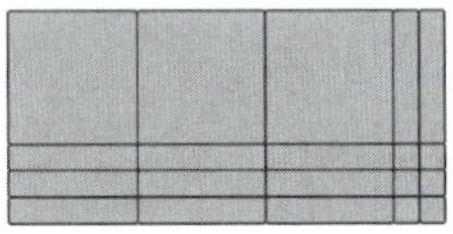

iii) $(x+3)(3x+2)$

c) i) $3x^2 + 8x + 4$
ii)

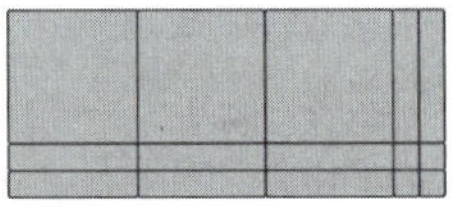

iii) $(x+2)(3x+2)$

d) i) $4x^2 + 9x + 2$
ii)

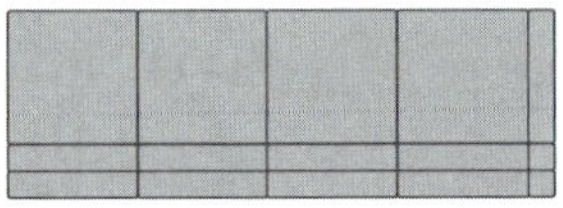

iii) $(x+2)(4x+1)$

8. a) $(2w+1)(w+6) = 2w^2 + 13w + 6$
b) $(2g-5)(3g-3) = 6g^2 - 21g + 15$
c) $(-4v-3)(-2v-7) = 8v^2 + 34v + 21$

9. a) $15 + 23f + 4f^2$ **b)** $15 - 29t + 12t^2$
c) $90 + 11r - 2r^2$ **d)** $36 - 24m + 4m^2$
e) $-24 + 50x + 14x^2$ **f)** $-36 + 60n - 25n^2$

10. a) $6c^2 + 23c + 20$ **b)** $-21t^2 - 32t + 5$
c) $32r^2 + 48r - 14$ **d)** $5t^2 + 46t + 9$
e) $35h^2 + 29h - 30$ **f)** $-36y^2 + 84y - 49$

11. a) i) $(t+1)(3t+1)$

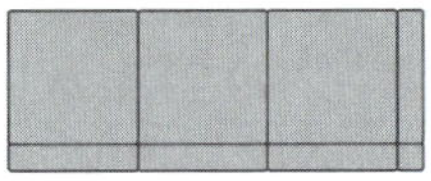

ii) $(t+2)(3t+2)$

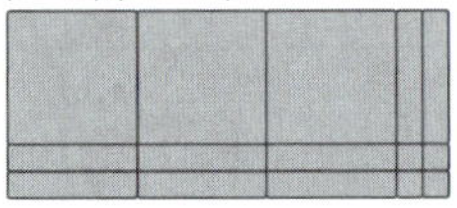

iii) $(t+3)(3t+3)$

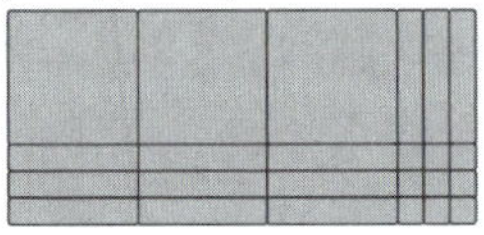

iv) $(t+4)(3t+4)$

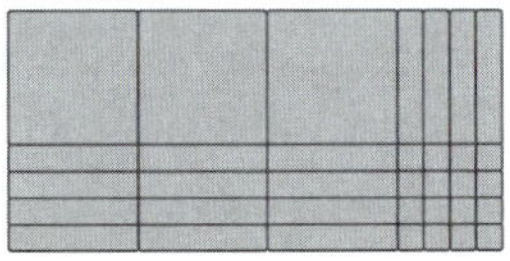

b) The side lengths increase by 1 each time; the constant terms in the binomial factors increase by 1 each time.
c) $3t^2 + 20t + 25 = (t+5)(3t+5)$;
$3t^2 + 24t + 36 = (t+6)(3t+6)$;
$3t^2 + 28t + 49 = (t+7)(3t+7)$

12. a) i) $(n+6)(2n+1)$ **ii)** $(n-6)(2n-1)$
b) i) $(n+6)(2n-1)$ **ii)** $(n-6)(2n+1)$
c) i) $(n+2)(2n+3)$ **ii)** $(n-2)(2n-3)$
The trinomials in each pair have middle terms with the same value, but opposite signs. The constant terms in the binomial factors have opposite signs.

13. a) $(y + 2)(2y + 1)$ **b)** $(a + 4)(2a + 3)$
c) $(k + 5)(2k + 3)$ **d)** $(m - 4)(2m - 3)$
e) $(k - 3)(2k - 5)$ **f)** $(m + 7)(2m + 1)$
g) $(g + 6)(2g + 3)$ **h)** $(n + 6)(2n - 3)$

14. a) i) 1, 15 **ii)** 2, 12
iii) 3, 5 **iv)** 3, 4
v) 1, 12 **vi)** 3, 8

b) i) $(v + 5)(3v + 1)$
ii) $(m + 4)(3m + 2)$
iii) $(b + 1)(3b + 5)$
iv) $(a + 1)(4a + 3)$
v) $(d + 3)(4d + 1)$
vi) $(v + 2)(4v + 3)$

15. a) $(a - 2)(5a + 3)$ **b)** $(y - 5)(3y + 2)$
c) $(s + 4)(5s - 1)$ **d)** $(2c - 3)(7c + 1)$
e) $(2a + 5)(4a - 1)$ **f)** $(2r - 3)(4r - 1)$
g) $(d + 1)(6d - 5)$ **h)** $(3e - 2)(5e + 1)$

16. a) $(2u + 7)(3u - 2)$
b) $(3k - 10)(k + 3)$
c) $(4v - 5)(v - 4)$

17. $(3g + 7)(5g - 6)$

18. a) $10(r + 2)(2r + 3)$ **b)** $5(a - 4)(3a - 1)$
c) $3(2h + 3)(3h - 2)$ **d)** $6(2u - 3)(2u - 3)$
e) $4(m - 5)(3m + 2)$ **f)** $2(3g + 5)(4g - 7)$

19. a) $(2y - 1)(7y - 3)$ **b)** $(p - 2)(10p + 3)$
c) $(2r - 7)(5r + 1)$ **d)** $(3g + 1)(5g - 2)$
e) $(2x - 3)(2x + 5)$ **f)** $(3d - 4)(3d - 4)$
g) $(3t + 2)(3t + 2)$ **h)** $(5y + 2)(8y - 3)$
i) $(2c + 3)(12c - 5)$ **j)** $(2x + 5)(4x - 3)$

20. These answers do not include cases where there is a common constant factor among the terms of the polynomial.
a) ±7, ±8, ±13; 6 integers
b) ±20, ±25, ±29, ±52, ±101; 10 integers
c) ±3, ±15, ±25, ±53; 8 integers
d) ±22, ±23, ±26, ±29, ±34, ±43, ±62, ±121; 16 integers
e) ±6, ±10; 4 integers
f) ±1; 2 integers

21. a) i) $(r + 1)(4r - 5)$
ii) Cannot be factored
iii) Cannot be factored
iv) $(w - 2)(2w - 1)$
v) $(h - 3)(3h + 1)$
vi) Cannot be factored

22. a) i) $(n + 2)(3n + 5)$ **ii)** $(n - 2)(3n - 5)$
iii) $(n + 1)(3n + 10)$ **iv)** $(n - 1)(3n - 10)$
v) $(n + 5)(3n + 2)$ **vi)** $(n - 5)(3n - 2)$

b) Yes; $3n^2 + 31n + 10$ and $3n^2 - 31n + 10$

23. $9m^2 \pm 24m + 16$, $9m^2 \pm 25m + 16$, $9m^2 \pm 26m + 16$, $9m^2 \pm 30m + 16$, $9m^2 \pm 40m + 16$, $9m^2 \pm 51m + 16$, $9m^2 \pm 74m + 16$, $9m^2 \pm 145m + 16$

Chapter 3: Checkpoint 2, page 180

1. a) $6x + 15$; 3 and $(2x + 5)$

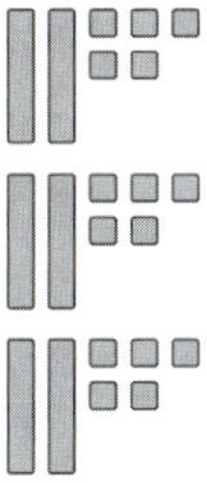

b) $4x + 12$; 4 and $(x + 3)$

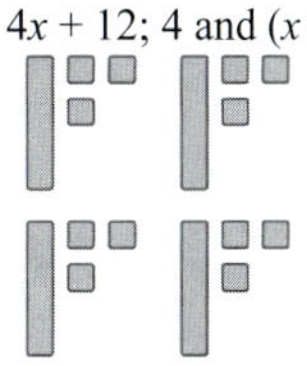

2. a) i) $4(a + 2)$

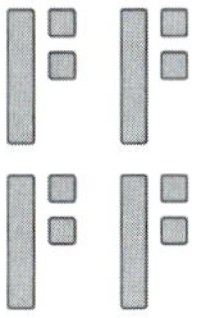

ii) $3(c - 2)$

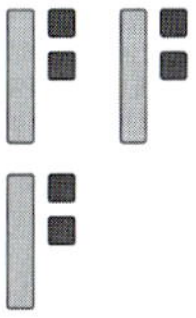

iii) $-v(2v + 5)$

iv) $2(x^2 + 7x + 3)$

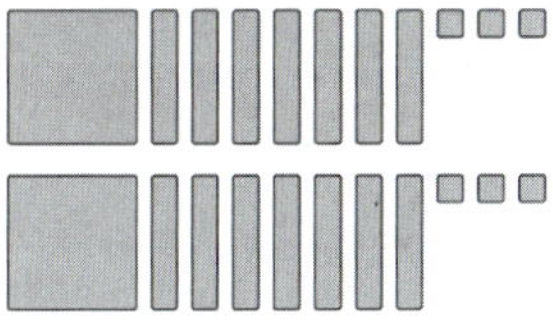

v) $-3(r^2 - 5r + 1)$

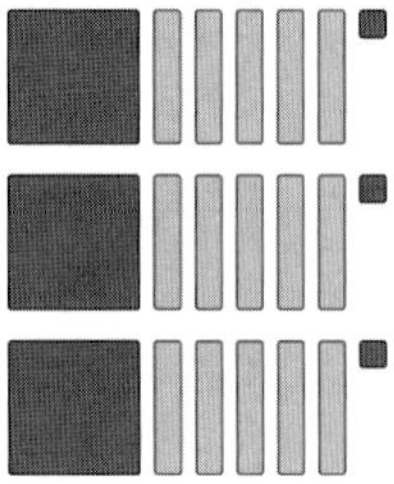

vi) $3a(5a^2 - ab - 2b^2)$

vii) $4(3 - 8x + 2x^2)$

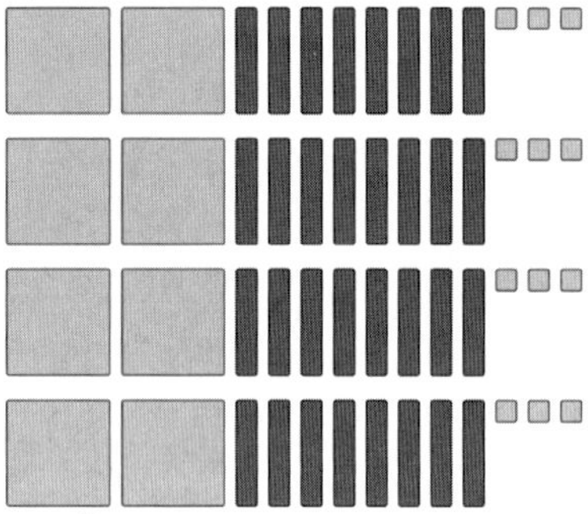

viii) $4y(3x^2 - 2x - 4)$

b) The polynomials in part vi and part viii

3. Answers will vary. For example:
$x^2 + 5x + 6 = (x + 3)(x + 2)$

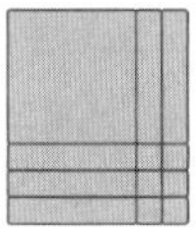

4. Answers will vary. For example:
$3x^2 + 10x + 8 = (x + 2)(3x + 4)$

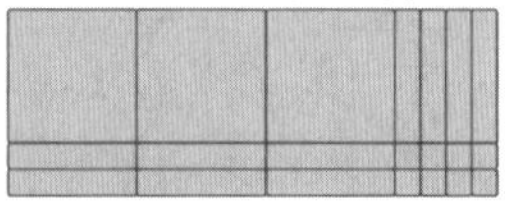

5. Area models and rectangle diagrams may vary. For example:

a) $x^2 + 5x + 4$

	x	4
x	$(x)(x) = x^2$	$(x)(4) = 4x$
1	$(1)(x) = x$	$(1)(4) = 4$

b) $d^2 + d - 6$

	d	3
d	$(d)(d) = d^2$	$(d)(3) = 3d$
−2	$(-2)(d) = -2d$	$(-2)(3) = -6$

c) $x^2 - 6x + 8$

	x	−2
x	$(x)(x) = x^2$	$(x)(-2) = -2x$
−4	$(-4)(x) = -4x$	$(-4)(-2) = 8$

d) $30 - r - r^2$

	6	r
5	$(5)(6) = 30$	$(5)(r) = 5r$
$-r$	$(-r)(6) = -6r$	$(-r)(r) = -r^2$

e) $g^2 + 4g - 5$

	g	−1
g	$(g)(g) = g^2$	$(g)(-1) = -g$
5	$(5)(g) = 5g$	$(5)(-1) = -5$

f) $20 - 12t + t^2$

	10	$-t$
2	$(2)(10) = 20$	$(2)(-t) = -2t$
$-t$	$(-t)(10) = -10t$	$(-t)(-t) = t^2$

6. a) $(s + 5)(s + 6)$ **b)** $(n + 5)(n - 6)$
c) $(4 - b)(5 - b)$ **d)** $-(1 + t)(11 - t)$
e) $(z + 3)(z + 10)$ **f)** $-(k - 3)(k - 6)$

7. a) $3(x - 2)(x + 7)$ **b)** $-2(y - 3)(y - 8)$
c) $-(3 + m)(8 + m)$ **d)** $(2 - y)(25 + y)$

8. a) $2c^2 + 7c + 3$ **b)** $-4m^2 + 21m - 5$
c) $9f^2 - 9f - 4$ **d)** $12z^2 - 20z + 3$
e) $30 - 8r - 6r^2$ **f)** $8 + 20h + 8h^2$

9. a) $(j + 4)(2j + 5)$ **b)** $(v + 2)(3v - 5)$
c) $(k - 4)(5k - 3)$ **d)** $(3h + 2)(3h + 4)$
e) $(2y - 1)(4y + 1)$ **f)** $(3 - 4u)(2 - 5u)$

3.7 Multiplying Polynomials, page 186

4. a) $g^3 + 3g^2 + 5g + 3$
b) $2 + 7t + 6t^2 + 4t^3 + t^4$
c) $2w^3 + 11w^2 + 26w + 21$
d) $12 + 29n + 22n^2 + 8n^3 + n^4$

5. a) $6z^2 + 5zy + y^2$
b) $12f^2 + 4f - 25fg - 3g + 12g^2$
c) $8a^2 + 22ab + 15b^2$
d) $12a^2 + 4a - 31ab - 5b + 20b^2$
e) $4r^2 + 4rs + s^2$
f) $9t^2 - 12tu + 4u^2$

6. a) i) $4x^2 + 4xy + y^2$
ii) $25r^2 + 20rs + 4s^2$
iii) $36c^2 + 60cd + 25d^2$
iv) $25v^2 + 70vw + 49w^2$
v) $4x^2 - 4xy + y^2$
vi) $25r^2 - 20rs + 4s^2$
vii) $36c^2 - 60cd + 25d^2$
viii) $25v^2 - 70vw + 49w^2$
b) i) $p^2 + 6pq + 9q^2$
ii) $4s^2 - 28st + 49t^2$
iii) $25g^2 + 40gh + 16h^2$
iv) $100h^2 - 140hk + 49k^2$

7. a) i) $x^2 - 4y^2$ **ii)** $9r^2 - 16s^2$
iii) $25c^2 - 9d^2$ **iv)** $4v^2 - 49w^2$
b) i) $121g^2 - 25h^2$ **ii)** $625m^2 - 49n^2$

8. a) $3y^3 + y^2 - 26y + 16$
b) $4r^3 - 7r^2 - 14r - 3$
c) $2b^3 + 17b^2 - 13b + 2$
d) $3x^3 + 11x^2 - 39x - 7$

9. a) $x^2 + 3x + 2xy + 3y + y^2$
b) $x^2 + 3x + xy + 2y + 2$
c) $a^2 + 2ab + b^2 + ac + bc$
d) $3s + st + 5t + t^2 + 6$

10. a) $x^2 - x - 2y - 4y^2$
b) $2c^2 + 2c - cd - 3d - 3d^2$
c) $a^2 - 4a - 3ab + 20b - 10b^2$
d) $p^2 + 2pq - 8q^2 - pr + 2qr$

11. $2r^2 - 13rs + 12r + 15s^2 - 18s$

12. $x^3 + 10x^2 + 23x + 14$

13. a) $4r^4 + 13r^3 + 12r^2 + 5r + 2$
b) $2d^4 + 14d^3 + 19d^2 + 12d + 3$
c) $-4c^4 + 26c^3 - c^2 - 22c - 6$
d) $8n^4 - 18n^3 - 7n^2 + 16n - 3$

14. $-3g^4 - 7g^3 + 10g^2 + 18g - 8$

15. a) $9s^2 + 41s + 52$
b) $13x^2 + 4x + 40$
c) $18m^2 - 2m - 42mn - 4n$
d) 0
e) $3x^2 - 28x + 10$
f) $7a^2 + 2a - 7$

16. a) $20 - 2x$
b) $10 - 2x$
c) $4x^2 - 60x + 200$
d) $4x^3 - 60x^2 + 200x$

17. a) $27x^2 + 43x + 16$
b) $x^2 + 2x - 2$

18. a) $x^3 - 6x^2 + 12x - 8$
b) $8y^3 + 60y^2 + 150y + 125$
c) $64a^3 - 144a^2b + 108ab^2 - 27b^3$
d) $c^3 + 3c^2d + 3cd^2 + d^3$

19. a) $12a^3 + 2a^2 - 4a$
b) $-6r^3 + 3r^2 + 3r$
c) $40x^4 - 50x^3 + 15x^2$
d) $-8x^3y - 10x^2y + 25xy$
e) $4b^3 + 2b^2c - 2bc^2$
f) $y^6 - y^2$

20. a) $(2x + 3)^3 = 8x^3 + 36x^2 + 54x + 27$
b) $6(2x + 3)^2 = 24x^2 + 72x + 54$

21. a) $6x^3 + 2x^2 - 128x - 160$
b) $3b^3 - b^2 - 172b + 224$
c) $18x^3 + 3x^2 - 88x - 80$
d) $50a^3 - 235a^2 + 228a - 63$
e) $8k^3 + 12k^2 - 18k - 27$

22. a) $x^3 + 3x^2y + 3xy^2 + y^3 + 3x^2 + 6xy + 3y^2 + 3x + 3y + 1$
b) $x^3 - 3x^2y + 3xy^2 - y^3 - 3x^2 + 6xy - 3y^2 + 3x - 3y - 1$
c) $x^3 + 3x^2y + 3xy^2 + y^3 + 3x^2z + 6xyz + 3y^2z + 3xz^2 + 3yz^2 + z^3$
d) $x^3 - 3x^2y + 3xy^2 - y^3 - 3x^2z + 6xyz - 3y^2z + 3xz^2 - 3yz^2 - z^3$

3.8 Factoring Special Polynomials, page 194

4. a) $x^2 + 4x + 4$ **b)** $9 - 6y + y^2$
c) $25 + 10d + d^2$ **d)** $49 - 14f + f^2$
e) $x^2 - 4$ **f)** $9 - y^2$
g) $25 - d^2$ **h)** $49 - f^2$

5. a) Difference of squares
b) Neither
c) Neither
d) Perfect square trinomial

6. a) $(x+7)(x-7)$ b) $(b+11)(b-11)$
c) $(1+q)(1-q)$ d) $(6+c)(6-c)$

7. a) i) $(a+5)^2$ ii) $(b-6)^2$
iii) $(c+7)^2$ iv) $(d-8)^2$
v) $(e+9)^2$ vi) $(f-10)^2$
b) $g^2+22g+121=(g+11)^2$;
$h^2-24h+144=(h-12)^2$;
$i^2+26i+169=(i+13)^2$;
$j^2-28j+196=(j-14)^2$

8. a) $(2x-3)^2$ b) $(3+5n)^2$
c) $(9-2v)^2$ d) $(5+4h)^2$
e) $(3g+8)^2$ f) $(7r-2)^2$

9. a) $x^2; y^2; x^2-y^2$
b) $(x-y)$ and $(x+y)$; $(x-y)(x+y)$

10. a) $(3d+4f)(3d-4f)$
b) $(5s+8t)(5s-8t)$
c) $(12a+3b)(12a-3b)$, or $9(4a+b)(4a-b)$
d) $(11m+n)(11m-n)$
e) $(9k+7m)(9k-7m)$
f) $(10y+9z)(10y-9z)$
g) $(v+6t)(v-6t)$
h) $(2j+15h)(2j-15h)$

11. a) $(y+2z)(y+5z)$ b) $(2w+3x)(2w-7x)$
c) $(3s-u)(4s-u)$ d) $(t-v)(3t-4v)$
e) $(2r+3s)(5r-3s)$ f) $(2p+7q)(4p-5q)$

12. Trinomials in parts a, c, and d are perfect squares.
a) $(2x+7y)^2$ b) $(3m-n)(5m+4n)$
c) $(4r+t)^2$ d) $(3a-7b)^2$
e) $(3h+4k)(4h+3k)$ f) $(3f-5g)(5f-2g)$

13. a) $8(m+3n)(m-3n)$
b) $2(2z+y)^2$
c) $3(2x+3y)(2x-3y)$
d) $2(2p+5q)^2$
e) $-3(2u-v)(4u+3v)$
f) $-2(3b+8c)(3b-8c)$

14. a)

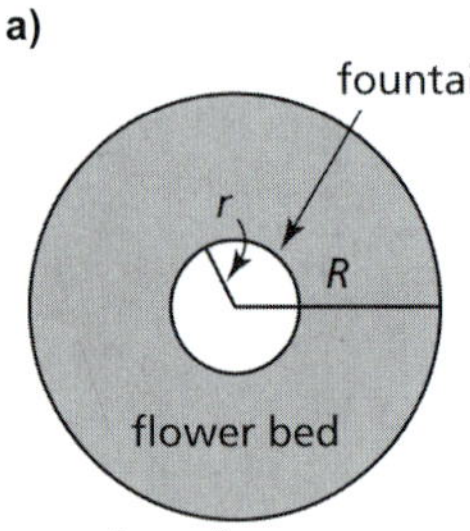

b) $\pi R^2-\pi r^2=\pi(R+r)(R-r)$
c) Approximately 314 159 cm^2

15. a) i) ±14 ii) 25
iii) 9
b) i) 2 integers ii) 1 integer
iii) 1 integer

16. –2, –1, 0; –1, 0, 1; 2 possibilities

17. 39 999

18. $5x^2+34x+24$

19. a) i) Neither
ii) Difference of squares
iii) Difference of squares
iv) Perfect square trinomial
b) ii) $(-10+r)(10+r)$
iii) $(9ab+1)(9ab-1)$
iv) $(4s^2+1)^2$

20. a) $(x+2)(x-2)(x+3)(x-3)$
b) $(a+1)(a-1)(a+4)(a-4)$
c) $(y+1)(y-1)(y+2)(y-2)$

21. a) $8(d+2e)(d-2e)$
b) $\frac{1}{4}(10m+n)(10m-n)$, or $\left(5m+\frac{1}{2}n\right)\left(5m-\frac{1}{2}n\right)$
c) $2y^2(3x+5y)(3x-5y)$
d) Cannot be factored
e) Cannot be factored
f) $\frac{1}{196}(7x+2y)(7x-2y)$, or $\left(\frac{x}{4}+\frac{y}{7}\right)\left(\frac{x}{4}-\frac{y}{7}\right)$

Chapter 3: Review, page 198

1. a) 2, 3, 11; $2 \cdot 3^3 \cdot 11$
b) 2, 3, 5, 7; $2^2 \cdot 3 \cdot 5^2 \cdot 7$
c) 3, 5, 13; $3 \cdot 5^3 \cdot 13$
d) 3, 7, 11, 13; $3^2 \cdot 7 \cdot 11 \cdot 13$

2. a) $2^2 \cdot 5$, or 20 b) $5 \cdot 7$, or 35
c) 2^4, or 16 d) 2^2, or 4

3. a) $2^2 \cdot 3^2 \cdot 5 \cdot 7$, or 1260
b) $2^3 \cdot 3 \cdot 5 \cdot 13 \cdot 103$, or 160 680
c) $2^3 \cdot 5^3$, or 1000
d) $2^4 \cdot 3^2 \cdot 5 \cdot 17$, or 12 240

4. 61 beads

5. a) $\frac{7}{9}$ b) $\frac{11}{17}$
c) $\frac{13}{15}$ d) $\frac{247}{576}$
e) $\frac{20}{27}$ f) $\frac{23}{160}$

6. a) 28 in. b) 32 cm

7. a) 12 cm **b)** 14 ft.

8. a) Perfect square; $\sqrt{256} = 16$

b) Perfect square; $\sqrt{324} = 18$

c) Perfect square and perfect cube; $\sqrt{729} = 27$; $\sqrt[3]{729} = 9$

d) Neither

e) Perfect square; $\sqrt{1936} = 44$

f) Perfect cube; $\sqrt[3]{9261} = 21$

9. 540 ft.

10. 44 cm

11. a) $4m(2 - m)$ **b)** $-3(1 - 3g^2)$

c) $7a^2(4 - a)$ **d)** $3a^2b^2c(2b - 5c)$

e) $-6mn(4m + n)$ **f)** $7b^2(2bc^2 - 3a^3)$

Algebra tiles could be used to factor the binomials in parts a and b

12. a) $3(4 + 2g - g^2)$ **b)** $d(3c^2 - 10c - 2)$

c) $4mn(2n - 3 - 4m)$ **d)** $y(y^3 - 12y + 24)$

e) $10x^2y(3 - 2y + xy)$ **f)** $-4b(2b^2 - 5b + 1)$

13. a) $4x(2x - 3)$ **b)** $3y(y^2 - 4y + 5)$

c) $2b(2b^2 - 1 - 3b)$ **d)** $6m(m^2 - 2 - 4m)$

14. a) $5q(3p^2 + 5pq - 7q^2)$ **b)** $-3(4mn - 5m^2 - 6n^2)$

15. a)

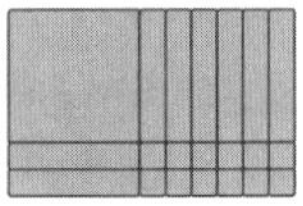

b)

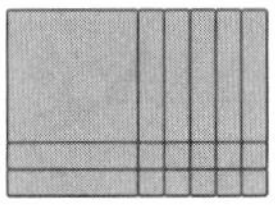

c) Cannot be arranged as a rectangle

d)

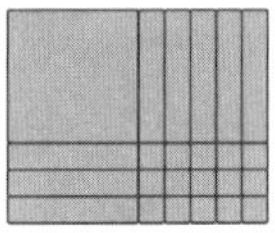

16. a) Cannot be arranged as a rectangle

b)

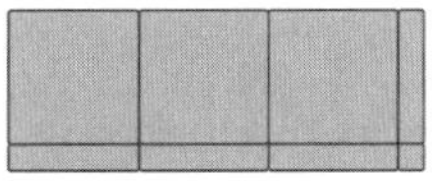

c)

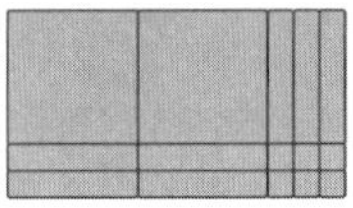

d) Cannot be arranged as a rectangle

17. 6 x-tiles

18. a) $g^2 + g - 20$

	g	-4
g	$(g)(g) = g^2$	$(g)(-4) = -4g$
5	$(5)(g) = 5g$	$(5)(-4) = -20$

b) $h^2 + 14h + 49$

	h	7
h	$(h)(h) = h^2$	$(h)(7) = 7h$
7	$(7)(h) = 7h$	$(7)(7) = 49$

c) $k^2 + 7k - 44$

	k	11
k	$(k)(k) = k^2$	$(k)(11) = 11k$
-4	$(-4)(k) = -4k$	$(-4)(11) = -44$

d) $81 - s^2$

	9	$-s$
9	$(9)(9) = 81$	$(9)(-s) = -9s$
s	$(s)(9) = 9s$	$(s)(-s) = -s^2$

e) $144 - 24t + t^2$

	12	$-t$
12	$(12)(12) = 144$	$(12)(-t) = -12t$
$-t$	$(-t)(12) = -12t$	$(-t)(-t) = t^2$

f) $42 - r - r^2$

	6	$-r$
7	$(7)(6) = 42$	$(7)(-r) = -7r$
r	$(r)(6) = 6r$	$(r)(-r) = -r^2$

g) $y^2 - 14y + 33$

	y	-11
y	$(y)(y) = y^2$	$(y)(-11) = -11y$
-3	$(-3)(y) = -3y$	$(-3)(-11) = 33$

h) $x^2 - 25$

	x	5
x	$(x)(x) = x^2$	$(x)(5) = 5x$
-5	$(-5)(x) = -5x$	$(-5)(5) = -25$

19. a) $(q + 2)(q + 4)$ **b)** $(n + 5)(n - 9)$
c) $(6 - s)(9 - s)$ **d)** $(k + 6)(k - 15)$
e) $(x + 4)(x - 5)$ **f)** $(3 - y)(4 - y)$

20. a) i) $(m + 3)(m + 4)$ **ii)** $(m + 2)(m + 6)$
iii) $(m + 1)(m + 12)$ **iv)** $(m - 3)(m - 4)$
v) $(m - 2)(m - 6)$ **vi)** $(m - 1)(m - 12)$
b) No

21. a) $(u - 3)(u - 9)$ **b)** $(v + 4)(v - 5)$
c) $(w - 2)(w + 12)$

22. a) $2h^2 + 10h + 8$

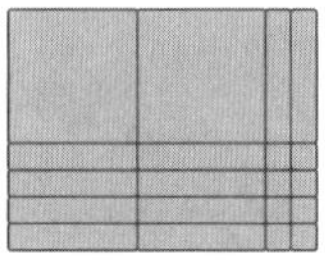

b) $3j^2 + 16j + 5$

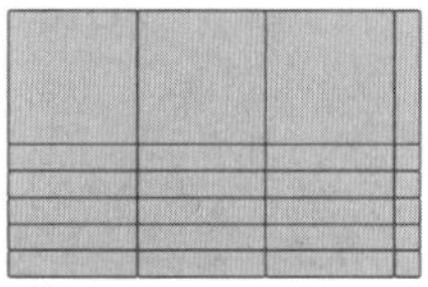

c) $6k^2 + 7k + 2$

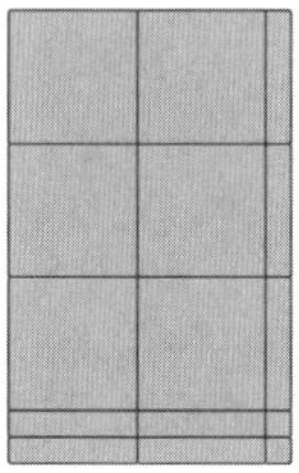

d) $8m^2 + 14m + 3$

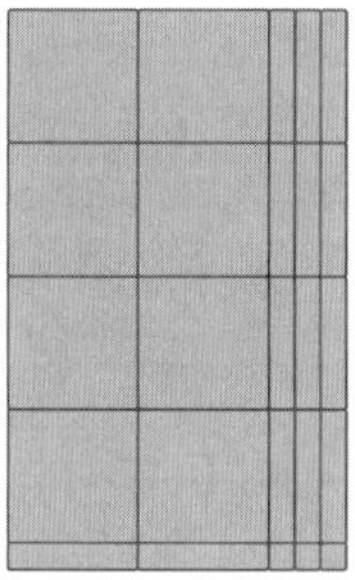

23. a) i) $2x^2 + 5x + 3$
ii)

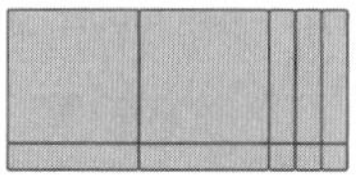

iii) $(x + 1)(2x + 3)$

b) i) $3x^2 + 10x + 8$
ii)

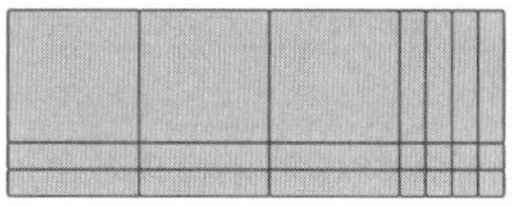

iii) $(x + 2)(3x + 4)$

24. a) $6r^2 + 31r + 35$

	$3r$	5
$2r$	$(2r)(3r) = 6r^2$	$(2r)(5) = 10r$
7	$(7)(3r) = 21r$	$(7)(5) = 35$

b) $9y^2 - 80y - 9$

	y	-9
$9y$	$(9y)(y) = 9y^2$	$(9y)(-9) = -81y$
1	$(1)(y) = y$	$(1)(-9) = -9$

c) $4a^2 - 26a + 42$

	$2a$	-6
$2a$	$(2a)(2a) = 4a^2$	$(2a)(-6) = -12a$
-7	$(-7)(2a) = -14a$	$(-7)(-6) = 42$

d) $9w^2 - 9w + 2$

	$3w$	-1
$3w$	$(3w)(3w) = 9w^2$	$(3w)(-1) = -3w$
-2	$(-2)(3w) = -6w$	$(-2)(-1) = 2$

e) $16p^2 + 40p + 25$

	$4p$	5
$4p$	$(4p)(4p) = 16p^2$	$(4p)(5) = 20p$
5	$(5)(4p) = 20p$	$(5)(5) = 25$

f) $3y^2 - 2y - 1$

	$-3y$	-1
$-y$	$(-y)(-3y) = 3y^2$	$(-y)(-1) = y$
1	$(1)(-3y) = -3y$	$(1)(-1) = -1$

25. a) $(k - 1)(4k - 3)$
b) $(3c + 1)(2c - 5)$
c) $(b - 2)(4b + 3)$
d) $(a - 5)(6a - 1)$
e) $(4x - 1)(7x + 4)$
f) $(3x + 2)(7x - 2)$

26. a) $(2m - 3)(3m + 7)$
b) $(4n + 1)(3n - 5)$
c) $(4p - 5)(5p + 4)$

27. a) $c^3 + 4c^2 + 5c + 2$
b) $8r^3 - 22r^2 - 9r + 30$
c) $-2j^3 - 5j^2 + 35j + 11$
d) $6x^3 + 5x^2 - 17x - 6$

28. a) $16m^2 - 8mp + p^2$
b) $9g^2 - 24gh + 16h^2$
c) $y^2 - yz - 2z^2 - 2y + 4z$
d) $-18c^2 + 39cd - 20d^2 + 21c - 28d$

29. a) $2m^4 + 7m^3 + 12m^2 + 17m + 10$
b) $5 - 11x - 3x^2 + 11x^3 - 2x^4$
c) $-6k^4 + 25k^3 + 10k^2 - 33k - 18$
d) $3 + 2h - 10h^2 - 3h^3 + 2h^4$

30. a) $22a^2 + 3a + 7$
b) $23c^2 - 10c - 53$

31. a) $n + 2, n + 4$
b) $n(n + 2)(n + 4) = n^3 + 6n^2 + 8n$

32. a) $(9 + 2b)(9 - 2b)$
b) $(4v + 7)(4v - 7)$
c) $16(2g + h)(2g - h)$
d) $2(3m + n)(3m - n)$

33. a) $(m - 7)^2$ **b)** $(n + 5)^2$
c) $(2p + 3)^2$ **d)** $(4 - 5q)^2$
e) $(2r + 7)^2$ **f)** $(6 - 11s)^2$

34. a) $(g + 3h)^2$ **b)** $(4j - 3k)^2$
c) $(5t + 2u)^2$ **d)** $(3v - 8w)^2$

35. $3x^2 + 14x + 16$

Chapter 3: Practice Test, page 201

1. A
2. C
3. 900; 5
4. a) i) 20: 5, 20, 45, 80, 125, …
45: 5, 20, 45, 80, 125, …
50: 2, 8, 18, 32, 50, …
ii) 20: 50, 400, 1350, 3200, 6250, …
45: 75, 600, 2025, 4800, 9375, …
50: 20, 160, 540, 1280, 2500, …

5. a) $6c^2 + 19c + 10$

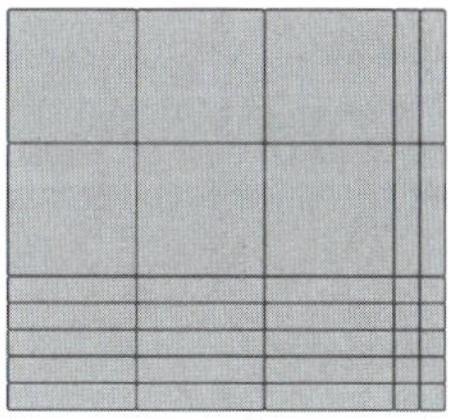

b) $72 + 86r + 24r^2$

	8	$6r$
9	$(9)(8) = 72$	$(9)(6r) = 54r$
$4r$	$(4r)(8) = 32r$	$(4r)(6r) = 24r^2$

c) $12t^2 + 13t - 35$

	$3t$	7
$4t$	$(4t)(3t) = 12t^2$	$(4t)(7) = 28t$
-5	$(-5)(3t) = -15t$	$(-5)(7) = -35$

6. a) $2p^3 + 3p^2 - 16p + 7$
b) $3e^3 + 6e^2f + 2ef^2 + 4f^3 + 5ef + 10f^2$
c) $-7y^2 + 60yz - 16z^2$

7. a) $(f + 1)(f + 16)$
b) $(c - 2)(c - 11)$
c) $(t + 4)(4t - 7)$
d) $(2r + 5s)^2$
e) $(2x - 5y)(3x - y)$
f) $(h + 5j)(h - 5j)$

8. $6r^3 + 11r^2 + 6r + 1$

9. $8t^2 \pm 25t + 3$; $8t^2 \pm 14t + 3$; $8t^2 \pm 11t + 3$; $8t^2 \pm 10t + 3$

Chapter 4 Roots and Powers, page 202

4.1 Math Lab: Estimating Roots, page 206

1. Answers will vary. For example:
a) $\sqrt{25}$, $\sqrt[3]{19}$, $\sqrt[4]{37}$, $\sqrt[5]{3}$
b) For $\sqrt{25}$, the radicand is 25 and the index is 2.
For $\sqrt[3]{19}$, the radicand is 19 and the index is 3.
For $\sqrt[4]{37}$, the radicand is 37 and the index is 4.
For $\sqrt[5]{3}$, the radicand is 3 and the index is 5.
c) The index tells which root to take.

2. a) 6; $36 = (6)(6)$
b) 2; $8 = (2)(2)(2)$
c) 10; $1000 = (10)(10)(10)(10)$
d) -2; $(-2)(-2)(-2)(-2)(-2) = -32$
d) $\frac{3}{5}$; $\left(\frac{3}{5}\right)\left(\frac{3}{5}\right)\left(\frac{3}{5}\right) = \frac{27}{125}$
e) 1.5; $(1.5)(1.5) = 2.25$
f) 0.5; $(0.5)(0.5)(0.5) = 0.125$
g) 5; $(5)(5)(5)(5) = 625$

3. a) 2.8 **b)** 2.1
c) 1.8 **d)** 3.6
e) 2.5 **f)** 2.0
g) 4.4 **h)** 2.7

4. a) The calculator returns an error message; the square of a real number will always be positive.
b) Any non-zero even index
c) i) Any odd index
ii) Any even index

5. a) i) $\sqrt{4}$ **ii)** $\sqrt[3]{8}$
iii) $\sqrt[4]{16}$
b) i) $\sqrt{9}$ **ii)** $\sqrt[3]{27}$
iii) $\sqrt[4]{81}$
c) i) $\sqrt{16}$ **ii)** $\sqrt[3]{64}$
iii) $\sqrt[4]{256}$
d) i) $\sqrt{100}$ **ii)** $\sqrt[3]{1000}$
iii) $\sqrt[4]{10\ 000}$
e) i) $\sqrt{0.81}$ **ii)** $\sqrt[3]{0.729}$
iii) $\sqrt[4]{0.6561}$
f) i) $\sqrt{0.04}$ **ii)** $\sqrt[3]{0.008}$
iii) $\sqrt[4]{0.0016}$

6. Answers will vary. For example:
a) $\sqrt[3]{216} = 6$ **b)** $\sqrt[3]{-343} = -7$
c) $\sqrt[4]{\frac{81}{16}} = \frac{3}{2}$ **d)** $\sqrt{17} \doteq 4.1$

4.2 Irrational Numbers, page 211

3. a) Irrational
b) Rational
c) Irrational
d) Rational
e) Irrational
f) Rational

4. a) 7, $\sqrt[3]{27}$
b) -5, 7, $\sqrt[3]{27}$
c) $\frac{4}{3}$, $0.3\overline{4}$, -5, -2.1538, $\sqrt[3]{27}$, 7
d) $\sqrt[4]{9}$

5. a) $\sqrt{49} = 7$; $\sqrt[4]{16} = 2$
b) $\sqrt{21}$ and $\sqrt[3]{36}$ cannot be written as a terminating or repeating decimals.

6. a) Rational
b) Irrational

7. a), b)

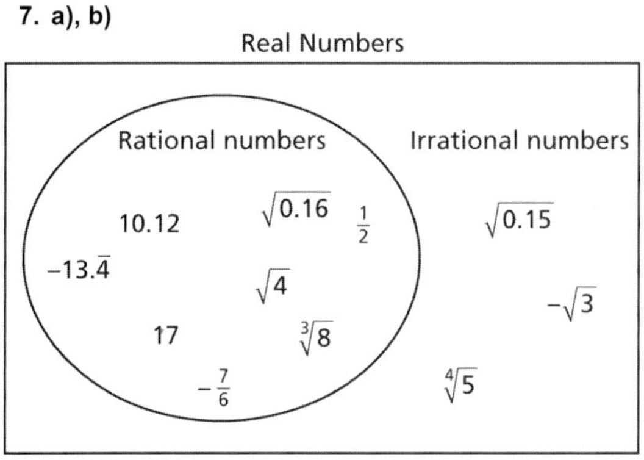

8. The cubes roots of the numbers in parts c and d will be irrational.

9. a)

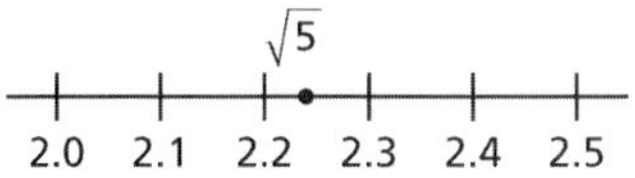

b)

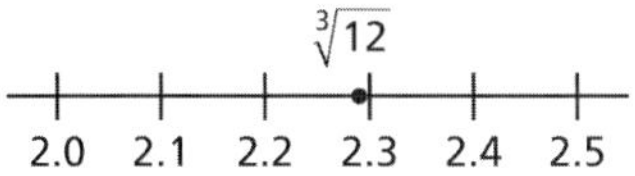

c)

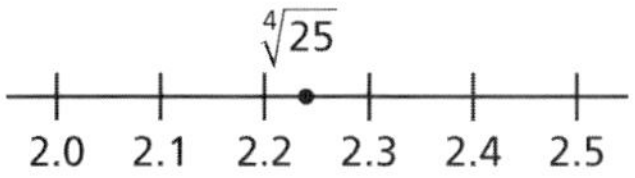

d)

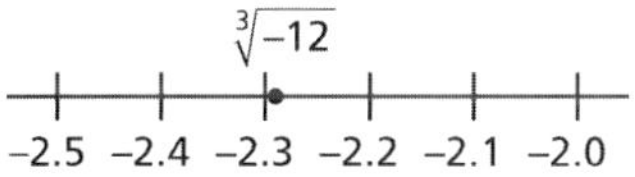

10. a) $\sqrt[3]{400}$, $\sqrt{50}$, $\sqrt[3]{70}$, $\sqrt[4]{100}$

b) $\sqrt{89}$, $\sqrt[3]{150}$, $\sqrt[4]{250}$, $\sqrt[3]{-150}$

11. $\sqrt[3]{98}$, $\sqrt{40}$, $\sqrt[3]{300}$, $\sqrt[3]{500}$, $\sqrt{75}$, $\sqrt{98}$

12. $\frac{-14}{5}$, $\sqrt[3]{-10}$, -2, $\frac{123}{99}$, $\sqrt{4}$;

irrational: $\sqrt[3]{-10}$; rational: $\frac{-14}{5}$, -2, $\frac{123}{99}$, $\sqrt{4}$

13. $\sqrt{5^2+3^2} = \sqrt{34}$, which is an irrational number.

14. a) i) True **ii)** True

iii) False **iv)** False

v) True

b) iii) 0 **iv)** π

15. Answers will vary. For example:

a) 075 **b)** 0

c) $\sqrt{7}$

16. Additional numbers may vary. For example:

a), b)

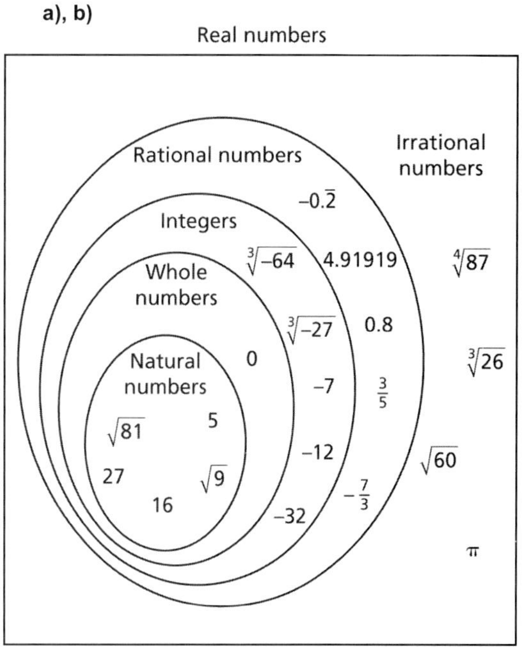

17. Answers may vary. For example:

a) 21 **b)** 125

18. a) 1.6

b)

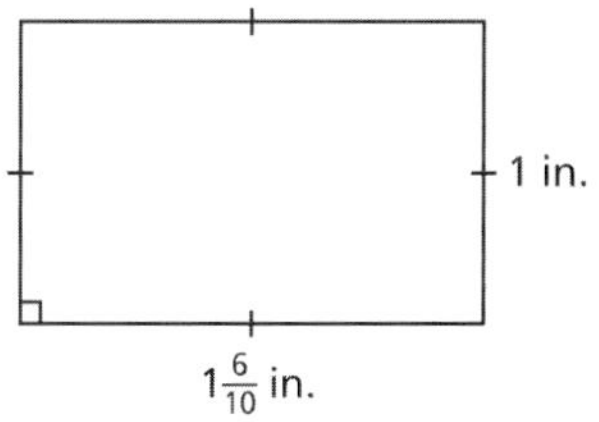

19. 755:481 is approximately equivalent to 1.6:1, and $\frac{1+\sqrt{5}}{2}$ is approximately 1.6.

20. a) Irrational number

b) Rational number

21. Each prime factor occurs a multiple of n times.

22. Triangles will vary. For example:

a) Side lengths: 3 units, 4 units, 5 units

b) Side lengths: 1 unit, $\sqrt{3}$ units, 2 units

c) Side lengths: 1 unit, $\sqrt{2}$ units, $\sqrt{3}$ units

d) Side lengths: $\sqrt{2}$ units, $\sqrt{3}$ units, $\sqrt{5}$ units

23. a) Yes **b)** No

24. Take rational numbers to the 12th power.

4.3 Mixed and Entire Radicals, page 218

3.

Perfect square	Square root
1	1
4	2
9	3
16	4
25	5
36	6
49	7
64	8
81	9
100	10
121	11
144	12
169	13
196	14
225	15
256	16
289	17
324	18
361	18
400	20

4. a) $2\sqrt{2}$ **b)** $2\sqrt{3}$
c) $4\sqrt{2}$ **d)** $5\sqrt{2}$
e) $3\sqrt{2}$ **f)** $3\sqrt{3}$
g) $4\sqrt{3}$ **h)** $5\sqrt{3}$

5. a) $\sqrt{50}$ **b)** $\sqrt{72}$
c) $\sqrt{98}$ **d)** $\sqrt{128}$
e) $\sqrt{75}$ **f)** $\sqrt{108}$
g) $\sqrt{147}$ **h)** $\sqrt{192}$

6. a)

Perfect cube	Cube root
1	1
8	2
27	3
64	4
125	5
216	6
343	7
512	8
729	9
1000	10

b)

Perfect fourth power	Fourth root
1	1
16	2
81	3
256	4
625	5

9. 25 is a perfect square, but neither 10 nor 5 is a perfect square.

10. a) $3\sqrt{10}$ **b)** Cannot be simplified
c) $6\sqrt{3}$ **d)** $10\sqrt{6}$
e) $3\sqrt{6}$ **f)** Cannot be simplified
g) $2\sqrt{7}$ **h)** Cannot be simplified
i) $4\sqrt{7}$

11. a) $2\sqrt[3]{2}$ **b)** $3\sqrt[3]{3}$
c) $4\sqrt[3]{4}$ **d)** $4\sqrt[3]{2}$
e) Cannot be simplified **f)** $4\sqrt[3]{3}$
g) $3\sqrt[3]{5}$ **h)** Cannot be simplified
i) $5\sqrt[3]{4}$ **j)** $5\sqrt[3]{3}$

12. a) $\sqrt{18}$ **b)** $\sqrt{32}$
c) $\sqrt{180}$ **d)** $\sqrt{150}$
e) $\sqrt{343}$ **f)** $\sqrt[3]{16}$
g) $\sqrt[3]{81}$ **h)** $\sqrt[3]{192}$
i) $\sqrt[3]{250}$ **j)** $\sqrt[3]{72}$

13. a) Yes
b) No

14. $6\sqrt{7}$ ft.

15. $2\sqrt[3]{25}$ cm

16. $12\sqrt{6}$ in.

17. a) $2\sqrt[4]{3}$ **b)** $3\sqrt[4]{5}$
c) $5\sqrt[4]{2}$ **d)** $2\sqrt[4]{11}$

18. a) $\sqrt[4]{3888}$ **b)** $\sqrt[4]{4802}$
c) $\sqrt[5]{972}$ **d)** $\sqrt[5]{3072}$

19. a) $\sqrt{2}$, $\sqrt{3}$, $\sqrt{4}$, $\sqrt{5}$, $\sqrt{6}$, $\sqrt{7}$, $\sqrt{8}$, $\sqrt{9}$, $\sqrt{10}$, $\sqrt{11}$, $\sqrt{12}$, $\sqrt{13}$, $\sqrt{14}$
b) i) The radicands start at 2 and increase by 1 each time.
ii) $\sqrt{51}$
iii) 30

20. $\sqrt[3]{1024}$

21. $4\sqrt{6}$

22. a) $8\sqrt{3}$, $9\sqrt{2}$, $4\sqrt{5}$, $6\sqrt{2}$, $2\sqrt{6}$
b) $8\sqrt{3}$, $6\sqrt{5}$, $4\sqrt{7}$, $2\sqrt{13}$
c) $9\sqrt{2}$, $3\sqrt{17}$, $5\sqrt{6}$, $7\sqrt{3}$, $\sqrt{103}$

23. a) 2, 20, 200;
$\sqrt{4\ 000\ 000}$, $\sqrt{400\ 000\ 000}$
b) 3, 30, 300;
$\sqrt[3]{27\ 000\ 000\ 000}$, $\sqrt[3]{27\ 000\ 000\ 000\ 000}$
c) $2\sqrt{2}$, $20\sqrt{2}$, $200\sqrt{2}$;
$\sqrt{8\ 000\ 000}$, $\sqrt{800\ 000\ 000}$
d) $2\sqrt[3]{3}$, $20\sqrt[3]{3}$, $200\sqrt[3]{3}$;
$\sqrt[3]{24\ 000\ 000\ 000}$, $\sqrt[3]{24\ 000\ 000\ 000\ 000}$

24. $4\sqrt{2}$ cm, 32 cm^2; 4 cm, 16 cm^2

25. a) i) 14.142
ii) 141.42
b) i) 2.8284
ii) 4.2426
iii) 5.6568
iv) 7.071

Chapter 4: Checkpoint 1, page 221

1. a) 9 **b)** –5
c) 4 **d)** 3

2. a) 3.16 **b)** 2.47
c) 1.73 **d)** 1.87

3. Neither

4. a) Irrational **b)** Irrational
c) Irrational **d)** Rational
e) Rational **f)** Irrational

5. a)

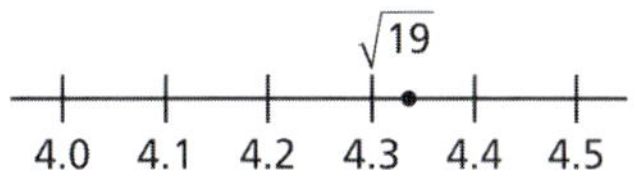

b)

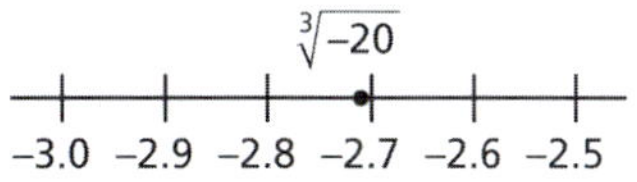

c)

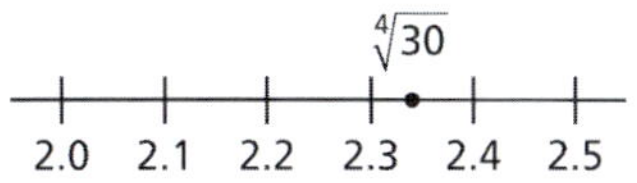

d)

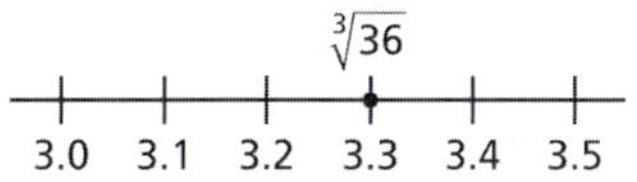

6. a), b) Additional numbers may vary. For example:

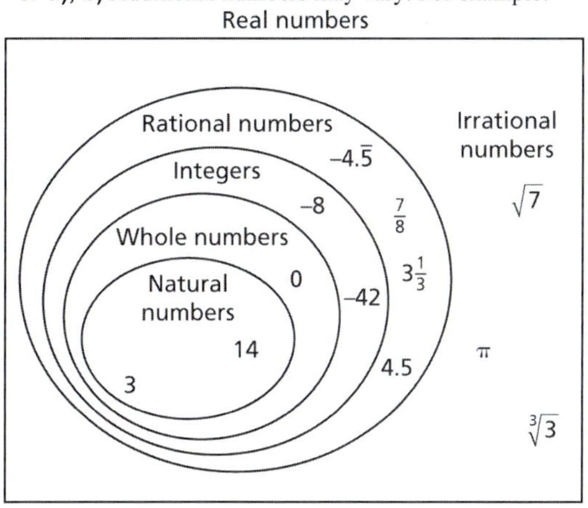

7. a)

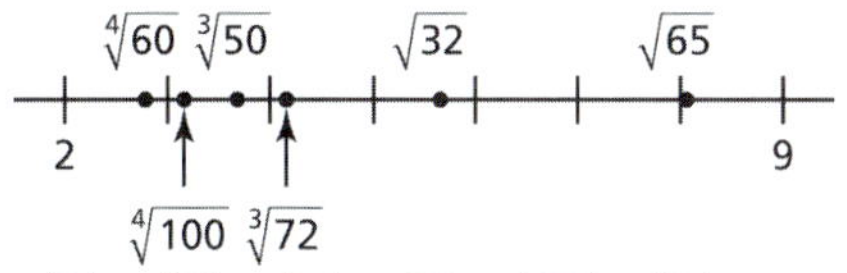

b) $\sqrt{65}$, $\sqrt{32}$, $\sqrt[3]{72}$, $\sqrt[3]{50}$, $\sqrt[4]{100}$, $\sqrt[4]{60}$

8. Areas of squares may vary. For example:

a)

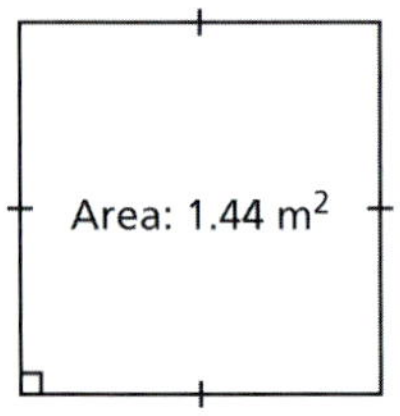

b)

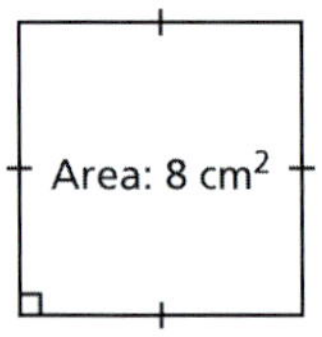

9. a) $3\sqrt{5}$ b) $2\sqrt[3]{12}$
   c) Cannot be simplified   d) $2\sqrt[4]{3}$
   e) $2\sqrt[3]{10}$ f) Cannot be simplified

11. a) $\sqrt{63}$ b) $\sqrt[3]{32}$
    c) $\sqrt{147}$ d) $\sqrt[4]{192}$
    e) $\sqrt[3]{270}$ f) $\sqrt{396}$

4.4 Fractional Exponents and Radicals, page 227

3. a) 4   b) 6
   c) 4   d) 2
   e) –3   f) –10
4. a) 10   b) 3
   c) 4   d) –2
5. a) $\sqrt[3]{36}$ b) $\sqrt{48}$
   c) $\sqrt[5]{-30}$
6. a) $39^{\frac{1}{2}}$ b) $90^{\frac{1}{4}}$
   c) $29^{\frac{1}{3}}$ d) $100^{\frac{1}{5}}$
7. a) 1   b) 2
   c) 4   d) 8
   e) 16   f) 32
8. a) $\sqrt[3]{4^2}$, or $\left(\sqrt[3]{4}\right)^2$
   b) $\sqrt[5]{(-10)^3}$, or $\left(\sqrt[5]{-10}\right)^3$
   c) $\sqrt{2.3^3}$, or $\left(\sqrt{2.3}\right)^3$
9. $\sqrt[3]{350}$ cm, $350^{\frac{1}{3}}$ cm

10. a) $\sqrt[3]{48^2}$, or $\left(\sqrt[3]{48}\right)^2$
    b) $\sqrt[3]{(-1.8)^5}$, or $\left(\sqrt[3]{-1.8}\right)^5$
    c) $\sqrt{\left(\frac{3}{8}\right)^5}$, or $\left(\sqrt{\frac{3}{8}}\right)^5$
    d) $\sqrt[4]{0.75^3}$, or $\left(\sqrt[4]{0.75}\right)^3$
    e) $\sqrt[5]{\left(-\frac{5}{9}\right)^2}$, or $\left(\sqrt[5]{-\frac{5}{9}}\right)^2$
    f) $\sqrt{1.25^3}$, or $\left(\sqrt{1.25}\right)^3$
11. a) $3.8^{\frac{3}{2}}$, or $3.8^{1.5}$ b) $(-1.5)^{\frac{2}{3}}$
    c) $\left(\frac{9}{5}\right)^{\frac{5}{4}}$, or $\left(\frac{9}{5}\right)^{1.25}$ d) $\left(\frac{3}{8}\right)^{\frac{4}{3}}$
    e) $\left(\frac{5}{4}\right)^{\frac{3}{2}}$, or $\left(\frac{5}{4}\right)^{1.5}$ f) $(-2.5)^{\frac{3}{5}}$, or $(-2.5)^{0.6}$
12. a) 27   b) $\frac{9}{4}$
    c) 9   d) 0.216
    e) 16   f) $\frac{8}{125}$
13. a) $4^{\frac{1}{2}}$, $\sqrt{4}$ b) $16^{\frac{1}{2}}$, $\sqrt{16}$
    c) $100^{\frac{1}{2}}$, $\sqrt{100}$ d) $9^{\frac{1}{2}}$, $\sqrt{9}$
    e) $25^{\frac{1}{2}}$, $\sqrt{25}$
14. a) $(-1)^{\frac{1}{3}}$, $\sqrt[3]{-1}$ b) $8^{\frac{1}{3}}$, $\sqrt[3]{8}$
    c) $27^{\frac{1}{3}}$, $\sqrt[3]{27}$ d) $(-64)^{\frac{1}{3}}$, $\sqrt[3]{-64}$
    e) $64^{\frac{1}{3}}$, $\sqrt[3]{64}$
15. $\left(\frac{1}{4}\right)^{\frac{3}{2}}$, $\sqrt[3]{4}$, $4^{\frac{3}{2}}$, 4^2
16. a) i) 64   ii) 27
       iii) 16   iv) 5.9160…
       v) 1.331   vi) 0.8414…
    b) i, ii, iii, v
17. Approximately 76 m
18. 2.744
19. Approximately 1.3 m^2

20. a) Approximately 93%
b) Approximately 81%
c) 5 h

21. Mars; period of Earth: approximately 363.8 Earth days; period of Mars: approximately 688.5 Earth days

22. Karen

4.5 Negative Exponents and Reciprocals, page 233

3. a) $\frac{1}{5^4} = 5^{-4}$ b) $\left(-\frac{1}{2}\right)^{-3} = (-2)^3$
c) $\frac{1}{3^{-2}} = 3^2$ d) $\frac{1}{4^{-2}} = 4^2$

4. a) $16, \frac{1}{16}$ b) $16, \frac{1}{16}$
c) $6, \frac{1}{6}$ d) $64, \frac{1}{64}$

5. $\frac{1}{1024}$

6. a) $\frac{1}{2^3}$
b) $\frac{1}{3^5}$
c) $\frac{1}{(-7)^2}$, or $\frac{1}{7^2}$

7. a) 2^2
b) $\left(\frac{3}{2}\right)^3$
c) $\left(-\frac{5}{6}\right)^4$, or $\left(\frac{5}{6}\right)^4$

8. a) $\frac{1}{9}$ b) $\frac{1}{16}$
c) $-\frac{1}{32}$ d) 27
e) $\frac{9}{4}$ f) 125

9. a) $\frac{1}{2}$ b) $\frac{10}{3}$
c) $\frac{1}{3}$ d) $-\frac{1}{4}$
e) $\frac{100}{9}$ f) $\frac{1}{4}$
g) $\frac{1}{27}$ h) 125

10. Answers may vary. For example:
a) 3^{-2}
b) $25^{-\frac{1}{2}}$
c) $\left(\frac{1}{2}\right)^{-2}$
d) $\left(\frac{1}{-27}\right)^{-\frac{1}{3}}$

11. \$2651.56

12. $-\frac{3125}{1024}$

13. a) $\frac{1}{81}$ b) $\frac{1}{64}$
c) $\frac{1}{4}$ d) $\frac{9}{4}$
e) $\frac{8}{27}$ f) $\frac{32}{243}$

14. \$1266.57

15. Approximately 0.19%

16. 5^{-2}; $\frac{1}{25} > \frac{1}{32}$

17. a) The numbers at the left are divided by 2 each time. The exponents in the powers at the right decrease by 1 each time.
b) $2 = 2^1$; $1 = 2^0$; $\frac{1}{2} = 2^{-1}$; $\frac{1}{4} = 2^{-2}$; $\frac{1}{8} = 2^{-3}$

18. 3^8, or 6561 times as great

19. a) The exponent is positive.
b) The exponent is negative.
c) The exponent is 0.

20. No; if the base is between 0 and 1, the power will be greater than 1. For example: $\left(\frac{1}{2}\right)^{-1} = 2$

21. a) Approximately 2.0×10^{20} N
b) Answers may vary depending on researched values. For example: approximately 1.9×10^{20} N

Chapter 4: Checkpoint 2, page 236

1. a) 2 b) 7
c) 16 d) $\frac{343}{27}$
e) –32

2. a) i) $\sqrt[3]{35^2}$, or $\left(\sqrt[3]{35}\right)^2$

ii) $\sqrt{32^3}$, or $\left(\sqrt{32}\right)^3$

iii) $\sqrt[5]{(-32)^2}$, or $\left(\sqrt[5]{-32}\right)^2$

iv) $\sqrt{400^3}$, or $\left(\sqrt{400}\right)^3$

v) $\sqrt[3]{-125}$

vi) $\sqrt[3]{\left(\frac{8}{125}\right)^2}$, or $\left(\sqrt[3]{\frac{8}{125}}\right)^2$

b) iii) 4 iv) 8000

v) –5 vi) $\frac{4}{25}$

3. a) $4^{\frac{1}{3}}$

b) $9^{\frac{1}{2}}$, or $9^{0.5}$

c) $18^{\frac{1}{4}}$, or $18^{0.25}$

d) $10^{\frac{3}{2}}$, or $10^{1.5}$

e) $(-10)^{\frac{2}{3}}$

4. Approximately 53 s

5. $\sqrt[3]{3}$, $3^{\frac{2}{3}}$, $\left(\sqrt[3]{3}\right)^4$, $3^{\frac{3}{2}}$, $\left(\sqrt{3}\right)^5$

6. $\sqrt[3]{421\,875}$ mm, $421\,875^{\frac{1}{3}}$ mm, 75 mm

7. a) $\frac{81}{16}$ b) 4

c) $\frac{1}{100}$ d) 2

e) 100 f) 625

8. \$4589.06

4.6 Applying the Exponent Laws, page 241

3. a) x^7 b) $\frac{1}{a^3}$

c) b^2 d) $\frac{1}{m}$

4. a) 0.5^5 b) 0.5^{-1}

c) 0.5^{-1} d) 0.5^5

5. a) x^2 b) $\frac{1}{x^3}$

c) n d) $\frac{1}{a^4}$

6. a) n^6 b) $\frac{1}{z^6}$

c) n^{12} d) $\frac{1}{c^4}$

7. a) $\left(\frac{3}{5}\right)^{12}$ b) $\left(\frac{3}{5}\right)^{-12}$

c) $\left(\frac{3}{5}\right)^{12}$ d) $\left(-\frac{3}{5}\right)^{12}$

8. a) $\frac{a^2}{b^2}$ b) $\frac{n^6}{m^3}$

c) $\frac{d^8}{c^8}$ d) $\frac{4b^2}{25c^2}$

e) a^2b^2 f) n^6m^3

g) $\frac{1}{c^{12}d^8}$ h) $\frac{x^3}{y^3}$

9. a) x; product of powers law

b) a^{-5}; product of powers law

c) b^3; product of powers law

d) 1; product of powers law

e) $\frac{1}{x^7}$; quotient of powers law

f) s^{10}; quotient of powers law

g) $\frac{1}{b^5}$; quotient of powers law

h) 1; quotient of powers law

10. a) 2.25 b) $\frac{9}{16}$

c) 0.36 d) 1

e) $\frac{5}{3}$ f) $-\frac{3}{8}$

g) $\frac{1000}{343}$ h) $\frac{3}{10}$

11. a) x^3y^6 b) $\frac{a^4}{4b^4}$

c) $\frac{1}{64m^6n^9}$ d) $\frac{16m^8n^{12}}{81}$

12. 10.6 cm

13. 251 ft.^{2}

14. a) $\frac{a^5}{b}$ b) $\frac{d^4}{c^2}$

15. a) –32 b) $-\frac{1}{8}$

c) $-\frac{1}{32}$ d) $\frac{1}{1024}$

16. a) m^2

b) $\frac{1}{x^{\frac{5}{4}}}$

c) $-\frac{3b^{\frac{1}{2}}}{a^6}$

d) $-\frac{4c^2b^{\frac{1}{6}}}{a^3}$

17. a) $\frac{x^{\frac{5}{2}}}{y^4}$

b) $\frac{b}{25a^4}$

19. a) $\frac{m^8}{n^2}$

b) $\frac{r^{\frac{1}{2}}}{s^{\frac{5}{4}}}$

20. a) i) Dimensions, in millimetres: $\frac{1000}{2^{\frac{7}{4}}}$ by $\frac{1000}{2^{\frac{5}{4}}}$; 297 mm by 420 mm

ii) Dimensions, in millimetres: $\frac{1000}{2^{\frac{9}{4}}}$ by $\frac{1000}{2^{\frac{7}{4}}}$; 210 mm by 297 mm

iii) Dimensions, in millimetres: $\frac{1000}{2^{\frac{11}{4}}}$ by $\frac{1000}{2^{\frac{9}{4}}}$; 149 mm by 210 mm

b) i) Dimensions, in millimetres: $\frac{1000}{2^{\frac{9}{4}}}$ by $\frac{1000}{2^{\frac{7}{4}}}$

ii) Dimensions, in millimetres: $\frac{1000}{2^{\frac{11}{4}}}$ by $\frac{1000}{2^{\frac{9}{4}}}$

iii) Dimensions, in millimetres: $\frac{1000}{2^{\frac{13}{4}}}$ by $\frac{1000}{2^{\frac{11}{4}}}$

c) A piece of A4 paper has the same dimensions as a folded piece of A3 paper; a piece of A5 paper has the same dimensions as a folded piece of A4 paper.

21. a) $\frac{a^{16}c^3}{b^7}$

b) $\frac{c^{14}}{64a^2b^{10}}$

22. a) $\frac{1}{a^{\frac{10}{9}}}$

b) $\frac{1}{a^{\frac{7}{2}}}$

23. For example:

a) $x^1 \cdot x^{\frac{1}{2}}$, $x^{\frac{3}{4}} \cdot x^{\frac{3}{4}}$, $x^2 \cdot x^{-\frac{1}{2}}$

b) $x^2 \div x^{\frac{1}{2}}$, $x^{\frac{5}{2}} \div x^1$, $x^{-1} \div x^{-\frac{5}{2}}$

c) $\left(x^{\frac{1}{2}}\right)^3$, $\left(x^6\right)^{\frac{1}{4}}$, $\left(x^{-\frac{1}{3}}\right)^{-\frac{9}{2}}$

24. $\frac{1}{2}\left(\frac{3}{2}\right)^{\frac{1}{2}}$ cm, or approximately 0.6 cm

Chapter 4: Review, page 246

1. a) 10

b) 0.9

c) 2

d) $\frac{3}{5}$

2. The index tells which root to take.

3. a) 3.3

b) –2.3

c) 2.0

4. a) 25

b) 216

c) 2401

5. Neither

6. a) Rational

b) Rational

c) Rational

d) Irrational

e) Rational

f) Rational

g) Rational

h) Irrational

i) Irrational

7. Approximately 4.8 cm

8. a) Rational

b) Irrational

9. $\sqrt[3]{-30}$, $\sqrt[4]{10}$, $\sqrt[4]{18}$, $\sqrt[3]{30}$, $\sqrt{20}$, $\sqrt{30}$

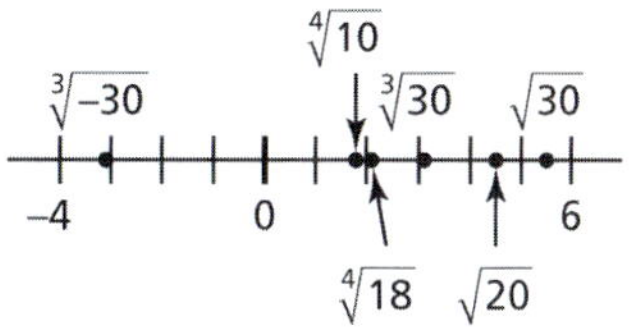

10. 1 s

11. a) $5\sqrt{6}$

b) $3\sqrt[3]{5}$

c) $4\sqrt{7}$

d) $3\sqrt[4]{2}$

12. a) $\sqrt{180}$

b) $\sqrt{126}$

c) $\sqrt[3]{192}$

d) $\sqrt[4]{32}$

13. Approximately 1.0 cm

15. $6\sqrt{2}$, $3\sqrt{6}$, $5\sqrt{2}$, $4\sqrt{3}$, $2\sqrt{7}$

17. a) $\sqrt[4]{12}$

b) $\sqrt[3]{(-50)^5}$, or $\left(\sqrt[3]{-50}\right)^5$

c) $\sqrt{1.2}$

d) $\sqrt[3]{\frac{3}{8}}$

18. a) $1.4^{\frac{1}{2}}$

b) $13^{\frac{2}{3}}$

c) $2.5^{\frac{4}{5}}$

d) $\left(\frac{2}{5}\right)^{\frac{3}{4}}$

19. a) 2

b) 1.2

c) –32

d) $\frac{27}{64}$

20. Approximately 35%

21. $\left(\sqrt{5}\right)^3$, $5^{\frac{3}{4}}$, $5^{\frac{2}{3}}$, $\sqrt[3]{5}$, $\sqrt[4]{5}$

22. a) Approximately 7122 Calories/day

b) Approximately 4 Calories/day

23. a) The numbers at the left are divided by 3 each time; the exponents in the powers at the right decrease by 1 each time.

b) $3 = 3^1$; $1 = 3^0$; $\frac{1}{3} = 3^{-1}$; $\frac{1}{9} = 3^{-2}$; $\frac{1}{27} = 3^{-3}$

24. a) $\frac{1}{4}$ b) $\frac{27}{8}$

c) $\frac{125}{8}$

25. \$908.51

26. 18.0 cm

27. 262 Hz

28. a) $9m^8n^2$ b) $\frac{1}{x^4y^6}$

c) $\frac{1}{4ab^3}$ d) $\frac{1}{r^{\frac{10}{3}}s^{\frac{2}{3}}}$

29. a) a^2b^5 b) $\frac{x^2}{y}$

c) $\frac{1}{a^5}$ d) $x^{\frac{3}{2}}y^3$

30. a) $\frac{9}{4}$ b) 30.25

c) $\frac{144}{25}$ d) 0.4

31. Approximately 6.4 cm

32. a) $s^3t^{\frac{10}{3}}$

b) $\frac{d^9}{64c}$

Chapter 4: Practice Test, page 249

1. B

2. A

3. a) $5\sqrt{3}$; $5\sqrt{3} = \sqrt{75}$

b)

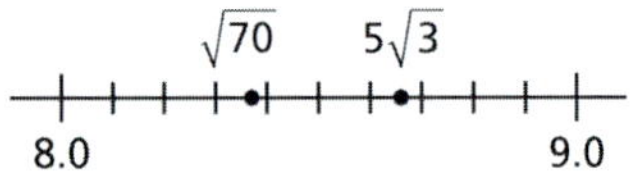

4. a) $\frac{4}{3}$ b) $\frac{1}{16}$

c) 0.729 d) $\frac{1}{4}$

5. $2\sqrt{11}$

6. $\frac{y^5}{x^2}$

7. a) $\frac{1}{p^2q}$ b) $\frac{1}{cd^{\frac{1}{3}}}$

8. Approximately 29 L

Cumulative Review Chapters 1–4, page 252

1. 117 m^2

2. 236 $in.^3$

3 a) 5.2 cm b) 1 in.

4. 28 ft.

5. 64.2°

6. a) $9\frac{7}{10}$ in. b) 4 $in.^2$

7. a) 9; 585

b) 14; 924

c) 3; 3150

d) 2; 4620

8. 8214 $in.^2$

9. a) 1, 4, 9, 16, 25, 36, 49, 64, 81, 100

b) 1, 8, 27, 64, 125, 216, 343, 512, 729, 1000

c) 1, 64, 729

10. a) $3a(5a - 9)$ b) $2p(2 + 6p^2 - 3p)$

c) $-2d(4d^3 + 7)$ d) $7(3w - 4 + 2w^2)$

e) $2x^2y^2(9x^2 - 2xy + 5y^2)$ f) $11np^2(3n^3p + n - 11p^2)$

11. The trinomials that can be represented as a rectangle of algebra tiles can be factored.

a) Can be represented b) Cannot be represented

c) Cannot be represented d) Can be represented

12. a) $d^2 + 2d - 15$

	d	-3
d	$(d)(d) = d^2$	$(d)(-3) = -3d$
5	$(5)(d) = 5d$	$(5)(-3) = -15$

b) $45 - 14s + s^2$

	9	$-s$
5	$(5)(9) = 45$	$(5)(-s) = -5s$
$-s$	$(-s)(9) = -9s$	$(-s)(-s) = s^2$

c) $-49 + 16g^2$

	7	4g
−7	(−7)(7) = −49	(−7)(4g) = −28g
4g	(4g)(7) = 28g	(4g)(4g) = $16g^2$

d) $6k^2 + 13k - 63$

	2k	9
3k	(3k)(2k) = $6k^2$	(3k)(9) = 27k
−7	(−7)(2k) = −14k	(−7)(9) = −63

13. Answers may vary. For example, one of these:
a) 15, −15, 9, −9
b) 6, 4, 0, −6, −14, −24, −36, …
c) 17, −17, 7, −7, 3, −3
d) 4, 3, 0, −5, −12, −21, −32, …

14. a) $(n + 11)(n - 2)$
b) $(4 - m)(15 - m)$
c) $(2r + 5)(3r + 4)$
d) $(2n + 1)(5n - 2)$

15. a) $3(c - 10)(c + 2)$
b) $-5(h + 7)(h - 3)$
c) $3(8c + 3)(c - 4)$
d) $5(4 - 3a)(5 - 4a)$
e) $4(t - 6)^2$
f) $2(4 + w)(8 - w)$
g) $3(6r - 7s)(6r + 7s)$
h) $-2(5x - 3y)(7x + 2y)$

16. a) $2x^3 + 3x^2 - 19x + 15$
b) $2a^2 - ab - 6a - 10b^2 - 12b$
c) $12 - t - t^2 + 9s - 3st$
d) $2n^4 + 3n^3 - 8n^2 - 7n + 4$

17. a) $5c^2 + 23c - 42$
b) $-2t^2 - 33t + 30$
c) $-4w^2 + 53w + 46$
d) $3d^2 + 12d - 25$

18. a) $(5n + 4)^2$
b) $(6v - w)(4v + 3w)$
c) $(9c - 13d)(9c + 13d)$
d) $(3a - 5b)^2$

19. 3.42

20. $\sqrt[3]{-90}$, $\sqrt[4]{150}$, $\sqrt[4]{250}$, $\sqrt[3]{90}$, $\sqrt{30}$

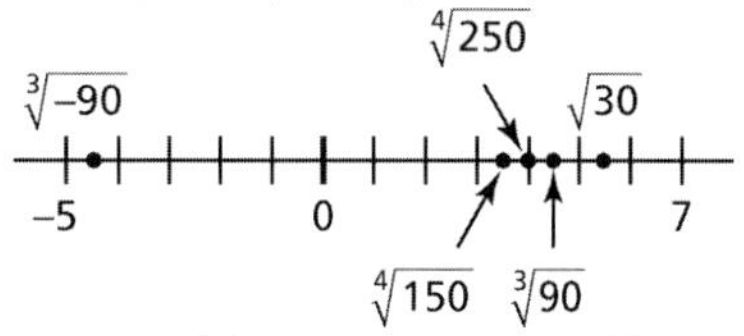

21. a) i) $4\sqrt{6}$ **ii)** $3\sqrt[3]{4}$
iii) $2\sqrt[4]{9}$ **iv)** $5\sqrt{17}$
v) $6\sqrt[3]{3}$ **vi)** $2\sqrt[4]{22}$
b) i) $\sqrt{75}$ **ii)** $\sqrt[3]{40}$
iii) $\sqrt[4]{29\,282}$ **iv)** $\sqrt{63}$
v) $\sqrt[3]{2916}$ **vi)** $\sqrt[5]{96}$

22. a) i) $\sqrt[4]{50^3}$, or $\left(\sqrt[4]{50}\right)^3$
ii) $\sqrt[3]{(-2.5)^2}$, or $\left(\sqrt[3]{-2.5}\right)^2$
iii) $\sqrt[5]{\left(\frac{3}{4}\right)^8}$, or $\left(\sqrt[5]{\frac{3}{4}}\right)^8$
b) i) $8.9^{\frac{2}{3}}$ **ii)** $\left(\frac{7}{4}\right)^{\frac{3}{4}}$
iii) $(-4.8)^{\frac{6}{5}}$

23. a) 27 **b)** $\frac{216}{343}$
c) −0.002 43 **d)** $\frac{81}{16}$
e) $\frac{1}{8}$ **f)** $\frac{512}{125}$
g) 27 **h)** $\frac{25}{4}$, or 6.25
i) $\frac{1331}{343}$

24. $24 895.92

25. a) $\frac{4}{25}$ **b)** 0.25
c) $\frac{5}{3}$ **d)** $-\frac{1}{2}$

26. a) a^3b^2 **b)** $\frac{16x^{24}}{y^8}$
c) $\frac{-3b^{\frac{5}{2}}}{a^{\frac{3}{2}}}$ **d)** $\frac{-5z}{x^2y^3}$

Chapter 5 Relations and Functions, page 254

5.1 Representing Relations, page 262

3. a) i) The relation shows the association "has a value, in dollars, of" from a set of coins to a set of numbers.

ii) As a set of ordered pairs:
{(penny, 0.01), (nickel, 0.05), (dime, 0.10), (quarter, 0.25), (loonie, 1.00), (toonie, 2.00)}
As an arrow diagram:

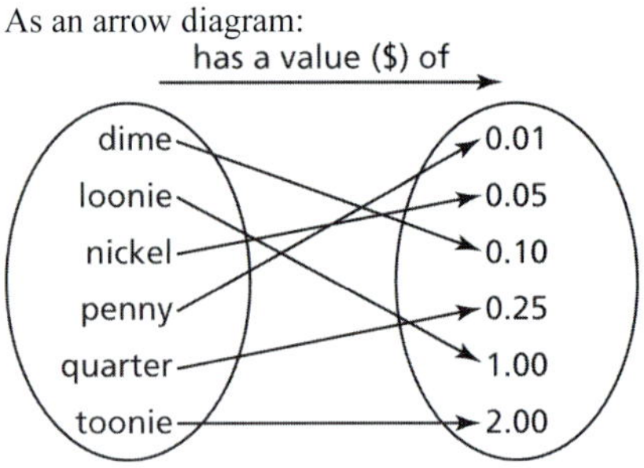

b) i) The relation shows the association "is played with a" from a set of sports to a set of equipment.

ii) As a set of ordered pairs:
{(badminton, racquet), (badminton, shuttlecock), (hockey, puck), (hockey, stick), (tennis, ball), (tennis, racquet), (soccer, ball)}
As an arrow diagram:

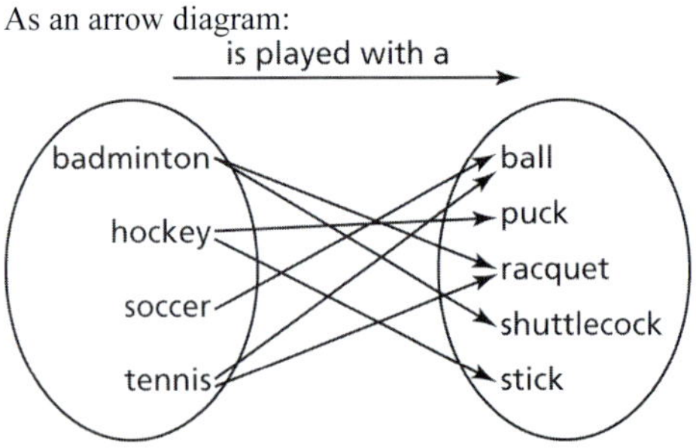

4. a) As a table:

Word	Number of Letters
blue	4
green	5
orange	6
red	3
yellow	6

b) As an arrow diagram:

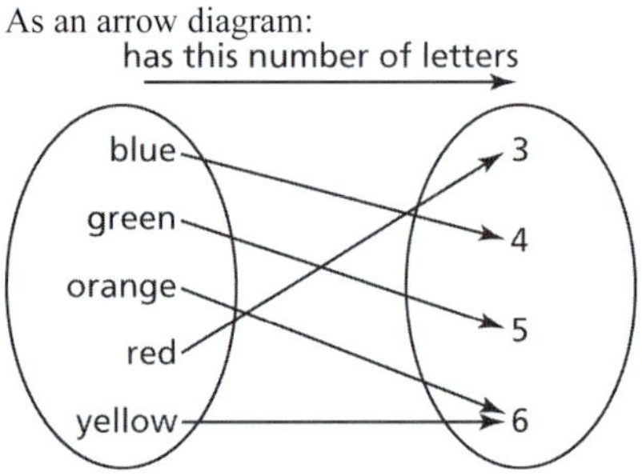

5. a) The relation shows the association "creates art using the medium of" from a set of francophone artists from Manitoba to a set of artistic mediums.

b) i) As a set of ordered pairs:
{(Gaëtanne Sylvester, sculpture), (Hubert Théroux, painting), (Huguette Gauthier, stained glass), (James Culleton, painting), (Nathalie Dupont, photography), (Simone Hébert Allard, photography)}

ii) As an arrow diagram:

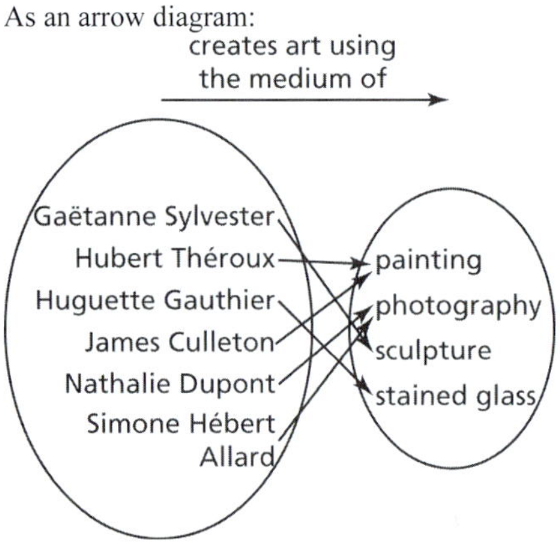

6. a) The relation shows the association "has a typical mass, in kilograms, of" from a set of salmon species to a set of masses.

b) As a set of ordered pairs:
{(Chinook, 13), (Chum, 9), (Coho, 5), (Pink, 3), (Sockeye, 6)}

c) As an arrow diagram:

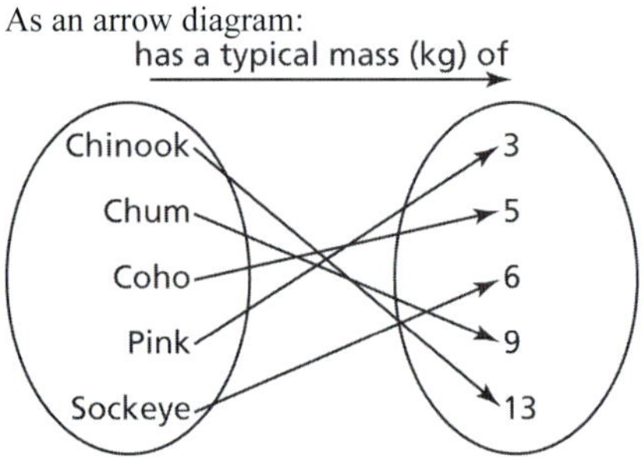

7. a) The arrow diagram shows a relation with the association "is the number of letters in" from a set of numbers to a set of words beginning with the letter Z.

b) As a set of ordered pairs:
{(3, Zen), (4, zany), (4, zero), (5, zebra), (6, zombie), (7, Zamboni), (8, zeppelin)}

As a table:

Number	Word beginning with Z
3	Zen
4	zany
4	zero
5	zebra
6	zombie
7	Zamboni
8	zeppelin

c) Chosen words and representations may vary. For example:

As an arrow diagram:

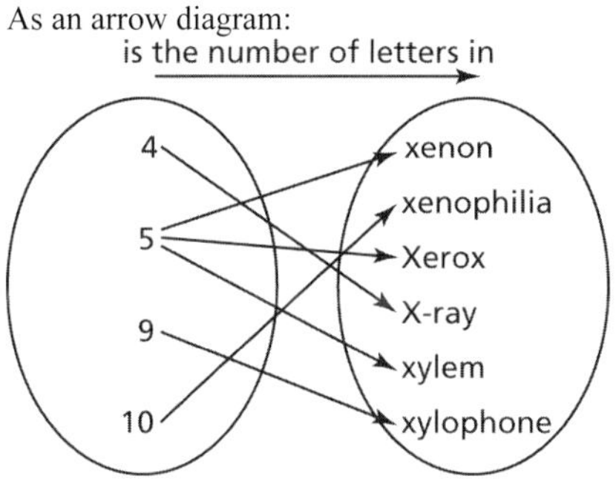

As a set of ordered pairs:
{(4, X-ray), (5, xenon), (5, Xerox), (5, xylem), (9, xylophone), (10, xenophilia)}

As a table:

Number	Word beginning with X
4	X-ray
5	xenon
5	Xerox
5	xylem
9	xylophone
10	xenophilia

8. a) The diagram shows a relation with the association "translates to" from the set of French words to the set of English words.

b) Answers may vary. For example: Two ordered pairs that satisfy the relation are: (oui, yes) and (et, and)

9. a) {(0, 6), (1, 2), (2, 5), (3, 5), (4, 4), (5, 5), (6, 6), (7, 3), (8, 7), (9, 6)} Some digital clocks may show the number 9 with 5 line segments.

b) Representations may vary. For example:

As an arrow diagram:

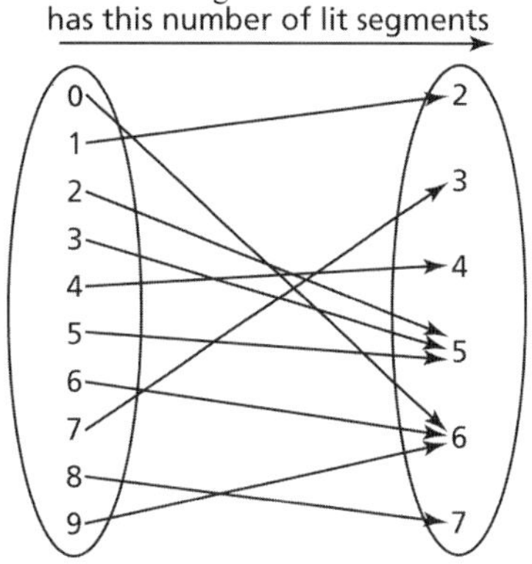

As a table of values:

Digit	Number of lit segments
0	6
1	2
2	5
3	5
4	4
5	5
6	6
7	3
8	7
9	6

10. a) As an arrow diagram:

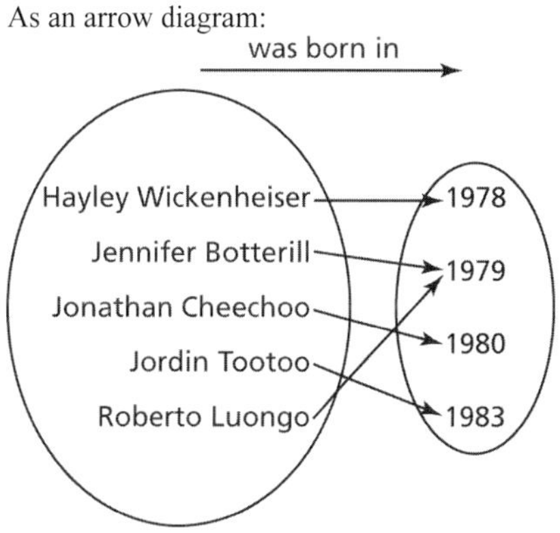

As a set of ordered pairs:
{(Hayley Wickenheiser, 1978), (Jennifer Botterill, 1979), (Jonathan Cheechoo, 1980), (Jordin Tootoo, 1983), (Roberto Luongo, 1979)}

As a table:

Hockey Player	Birth Year
Hayley Wickenheiser	1978
Jennifer Botterill	1979
Jonathan Cheechoo	1980
Jordin Tootoo	1983
Roberto Luongo	1979

b) As an arrow diagram:

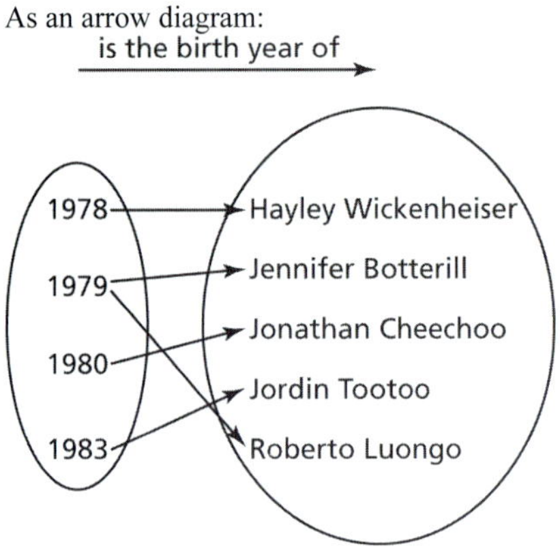

As a set of ordered pairs:
{(1978, Hayley Wickenheiser),
(1979, Jennifer Botterill),
(1979, Roberto Luongo),
(1980, Jonathan Cheechoo),
(1983, Jordin Tootoo)}

As a table:

Birth Year	Hockey Player
1978	Hayley Wickenheiser
1979	Jennifer Botterill
1979	Roberto Luongo
1980	Jonathan Cheechoo
1983	Jordin Tootoo

11. Answers may vary. For example:

a) Ordered pairs should be in the form: (older person, younger person)

b) Other associations include: "is taller than"
"is involved in more school groups than"
"usually wakes up earlier than"

12. a) **i)** {(1, 1), (1, 3), (1, 5), (2, 2), (2, 4), (2, 6), (3, 1), (3, 3), (3, 5), (4, 2), (4, 4), (4, 6), (5, 1), (5, 3), (5, 5), (6, 2), (6, 4), (6, 6)}

ii) {(1, 3), (1, 4), (1, 6), (2, 4), (2, 5), (3, 1), (3, 5), (3, 6), (4, 1), (4, 2), (4, 6), (5, 2), (5, 3), (6, 1), (6, 3), (6, 4)}

b) No

13. a) 6 children **b)** 4 parents

c) 2 grandparents

14. a) 2 females **b)** 3 males

5.2 Properties of Functions, page 270

4. a) Function

b) Not a function

c) Function

5. a) Function; domain: {1, 2, 3, 4}; range: {3, 6, 9, 12}

b) Not a function; domain: {–1, 0, 1}; range: {–1, 0, 1}

c) Function; domain: {2, 4, 6, 8}; range: {3, 5, 7, 9}

d) Not a function; domain: {0, 1, 2}; range: {1, 2, 3}

6. a) $C(n) = 20n + 8$ **b)** $P(n) = n - 3$

c) $t(d) = 5d$ **d)** $f(x) = -x$

7. a) $d = 3t - 5$ **b)** $y = -6x + 4$

c) $C = 5n$ **d)** $P = 2n - 7$

8. a) Function; domain: {1, 2, 3, 4}; range: {1, 8, 27, 64}

b) Not a function; domain: {3}; range: {4, 5, 6, 7}

9. a) **i)** Function

ii) Dependent variable: C; independent variable: n

iii) Domain: {1, 2, 3, 4, 5, 6, …};
range: {2.39, 4.00, 6.39, 8.00, 10.39, 12.00, …}

b) **i)** Function

ii) Dependent variable: T; independent variable: A

iii) Domain: {610, 1220, 1830, 2440, 3050, 3660, …};
range: {15.0, 11.1, 7.1, 3.1, –0.8, –4.8, …}

10. a) Not a function **b)** Function

c) Part a: domain: {3, 4, 5, 6}; range: { equilateral triangle, hexagon, isosceles triangle, parallelogram, pentagon, rectangle, rhombus, right triangle, scalene triangle, square, trapezoid}
Part b: domain: {equilateral triangle, hexagon, isosceles triangle, parallelogram, pentagon, rectangle, rhombus, right triangle, scalene triangle, square, trapezoid}; range: {3, 4, 5, 6}

11. Answers may vary. For example:

a) Functions:

Name	From
Marie	Edmonton
Gabriel	Falher
Élise	Bonnyville
Christophe	Calgary
Jean	Edmonton
Mélanie	Edmonton
Nicole	Red Deer
Marc	Légal

Name	Age
Marie	13
Gabriel	16
Élise	14
Christophe	13
Jean	15
Mélanie	15
Nicole	17
Marc	13

b) Not functions:

Age	Name
13	Marie
16	Gabriel
14	Élise
13	Christophe
15	Jean
15	Mélanie
17	Nicole
13	Marc

From	Age
Edmonton	13
Falher	16
Bonnyville	14
Calgary	13
Edmonton	15
Edmonton	15
Red Deer	17
Légal	13

12. The statement in part a is true.

13. a)

Letter	Number
A	1
D	2
F	4
G	2
M	3
Q	10
T	1
X	8
Z	10

Number	Letter
1	A
1	T
2	D
2	G
3	M
4	F
8	X
10	Q
10	Z

b) The first table represents a function.

14. a) $f(1) = 6$

b) $f(-3) = 26$

c) $f(0) = 11$

d) $f(1.2) = 5$

15. a) i) $n = 9$

ii) $n = \frac{1}{2}$, or 0.5

b) i) $x = -8$

ii) $x = \frac{17}{5}$, or 3.4

16. a) $C = 2.54i$

b) $C(12) = 30.48$; a length of 12 in. is equal to a length of 30.48 cm.

c) $i = 39.3700\ldots$; a length of 100 cm is approximately equal to a length of 39 in.

17. a) $D(t) = -80t + 300$

b) 300 km

18. a) i) $f(15) = 112.785$; a female whose humerus is 15 cm long will be approximately 113 cm tall.

ii) $m(20) = 128.521$; a male whose humerus is 20 cm long will be approximately 129 cm tall.

b) i) $l = 25.6082\ldots$; a female who is 142 cm tall will have a humerus length of approximately 26 cm.

ii) $l = 42.6257\ldots$; a male who is 194 cm tall will have a humerus length of approximately 43 cm.

19. a) i) $C(50) = 10$

ii) $C(-13) = -25$

b) i) $f = 68$

ii) $f = -31$

c) i) $C(32) = 0$

ii) $C(212) = 100$

iii) $C(356) = 180$

20. Variables may differ. Let c represent a temperature in degrees Celsius. Let F represent the same temperature in degrees Fahrenheit. $F(c) = \frac{9}{5}c + 32$

21. $P(l) = 2l + \frac{18}{l}$

22. $l(w) = 6 - w$; domain: $0 < w < 6$; range: $0 < l < 6$

23. $t(s) = 11 - 2s$; domain: $1.5 < s < 3$; range: $5 < t < 8$

Chapter 5: Checkpoint 1, page 275

1. a) In words:

This relation shows the association "is used to make" from a set of materials to a set of objects.

As an arrow diagram:

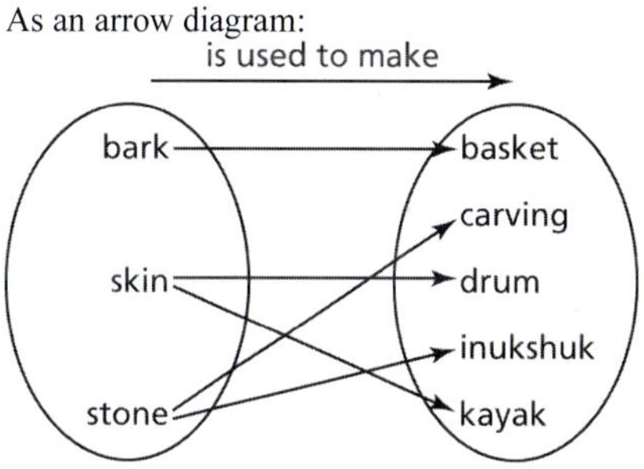

As a table:

Material	Object
bark	basket
skin	drum
skin	kayak
stone	carving
stone	inukshuk

b) In words:

This relation shows the association "has this many factors" from the natural numbers from 1 to 4 to a set of natural numbers.

As a set of ordered pairs:

{(1, 1), (2, 2), (3, 2), (4, 3)}

As an arrow diagram:

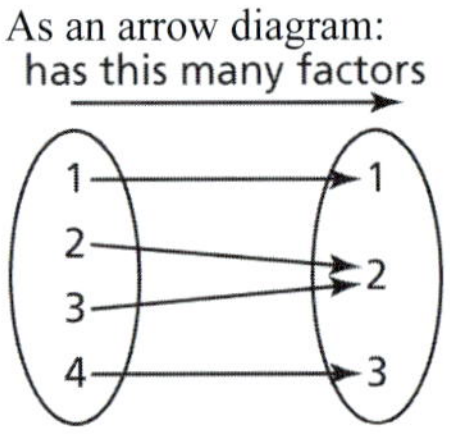

c) In words:

This relation shows the association "is usually coloured" from a set of objects to a set of colours.

As a set of ordered pairs:

{(grass, green), (sea, blue), (sky, blue), (snow, white)}

As a table:

Object	Colour
grass	green
sea	blue
sky	blue
snow	white

d) As a set of ordered pairs:

{(2, 1), (3, 1), (3, 2), (4, 1), (4, 2), (4, 3)}

As an arrow diagram:

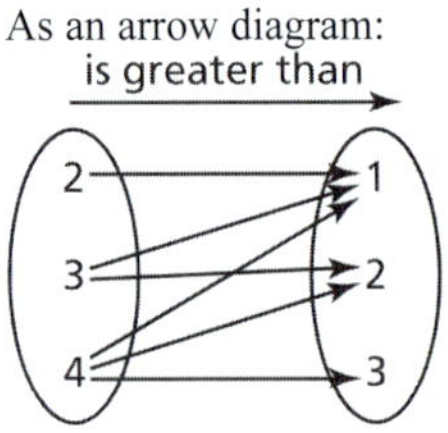

As a table:

Number	Number
2	1
3	1
3	2
4	1
4	2
4	3

2. a) The relations in parts b and c are functions.

b) Part b: domain: {1, 2, 3, 4}; range: {1, 2, 3}

Part c: domain: {grass, sea, sky, snow};

range: {blue, green, white}

3. Answers may vary. For example:

a) i) {(1, 1), (1, 3), (1, 5), (1, 7)}

ii) {(1, 1), (3, 3), (5, 5), (7, 7)}

b) i) As an arrow diagram:

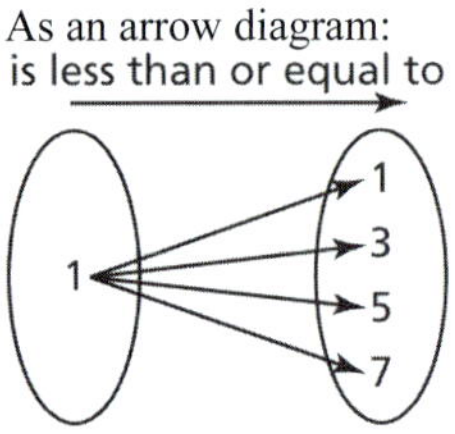

As a table of values:

Number	Number
1	1
1	3
1	5
1	7

ii) As an arrow diagram:

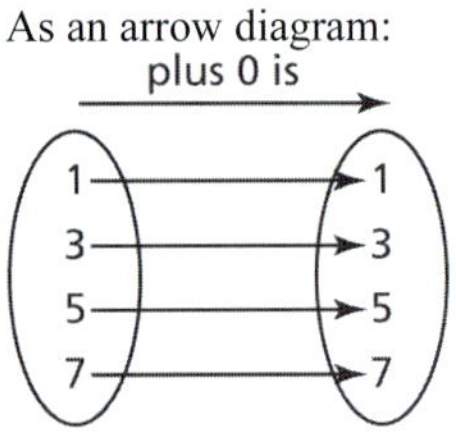

As a table of values:

Number	Number
1	1
3	3
5	5
7	7

4. a) Dependent variable: T; independent variable: d

b) $T = 10d + 20$

c) $T(5) = 70$; At a depth of 5 km below Earth's surface, the temperature is 70°C.

d) $d = 3$; A temperature of 50°C occurs at a depth of 3 km below Earth's surface.

5.3 Interpreting and Sketching Graphs, page 281

3. a) Bear F; approximately 650 kg

b) Bear A; approximately 0.7 m

c) Bears D and E; 400 kg

d) Bears D and H; approximately 2.25 m

4. a) 8 m; 06:00 and 18:00

b) 2 m; 00:00 (midnight), 12:00 (noon), and 24:00 (midnight)

c) Approximately 6.5 m

d) At approximately 02:20, 09:40, 14:20, and 21:40

5. Graph B

8. a) True **b)** False
c) True **d)** False
e) False

9. b) 25 L; no

10.

Temperature of an Oven

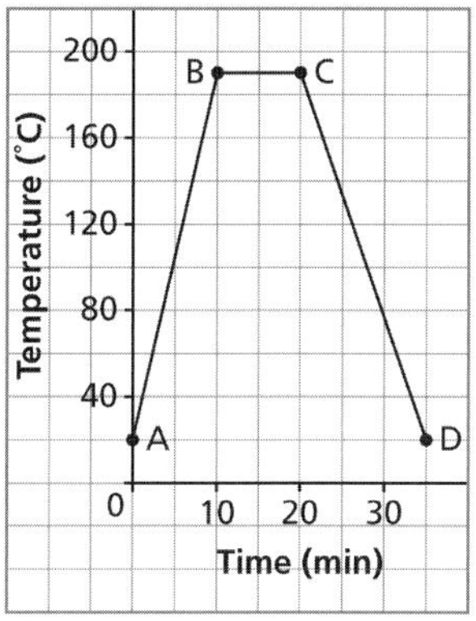

12.

Number of Cartons in the School Vending Machine

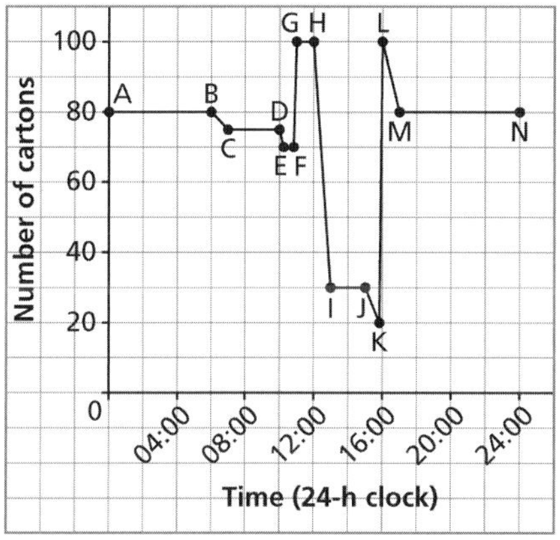

13. From 3 min to 4 min, the volume should be below 40 because Jonah turns the volume down.
At 9 min, the graph should be a vertical line from 80 to 0 because the mute button immediately silences the television.

14. Answers may vary. For example:

a)

Distance from Home

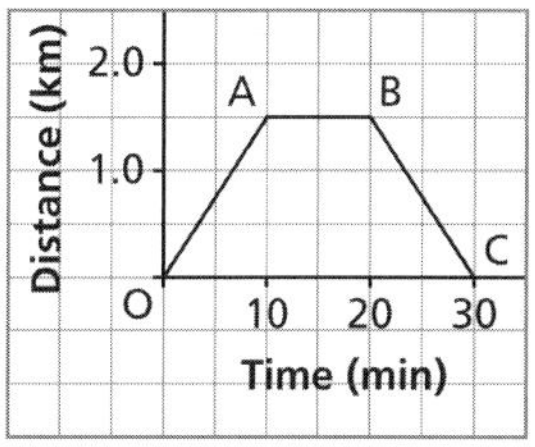

Situation: A person walks from home to a park 1.5 km away in 10 min. He sits on a park bench and reads for 10 min. Then he walks home.

b)

Speed while Sprinting

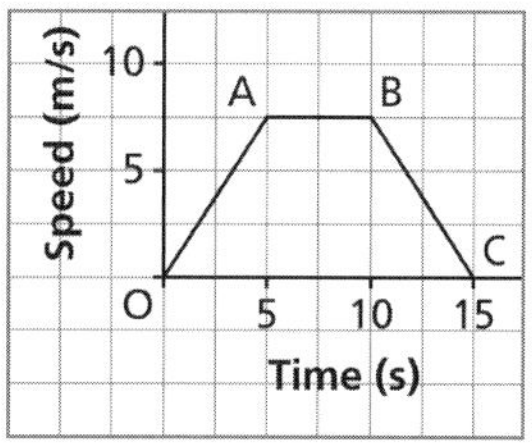

Situation: A person sprints down a street starting from a standstill. It takes the person 5 s to reach a speed of 7.5 m/s. After 5 s of running at 7.5 m/s, the person slows down and stops in 5 s.

15. Answers may vary. For example:

a)

Emptying a Watering Can

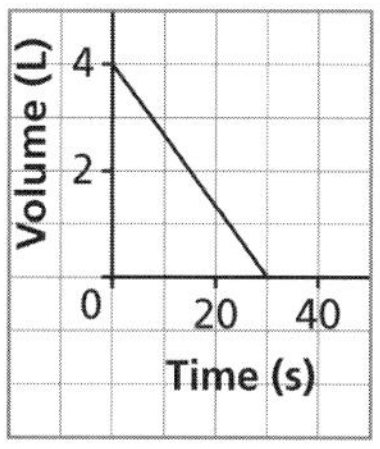

Situation: A watering can contains 4 L of water. The water is poured at a steady rate so the watering can is empty after 30 s.

b)

Height of a Helium Balloon

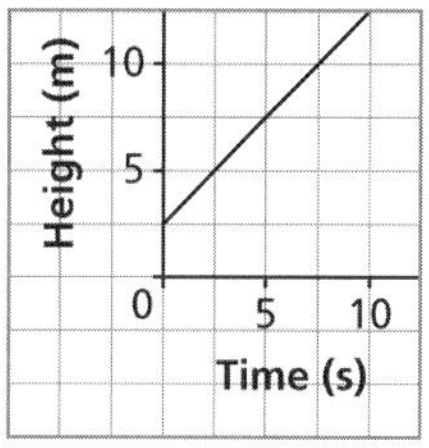

Situation: A person lets go of a helium balloon. The balloon starts at a height of 2.5 m above the ground. After 10 s, it is at a height of 12.5 m above the ground.

16. Answers may vary. For example:

a) i)

Distance above the Ground while Bungee Jumping

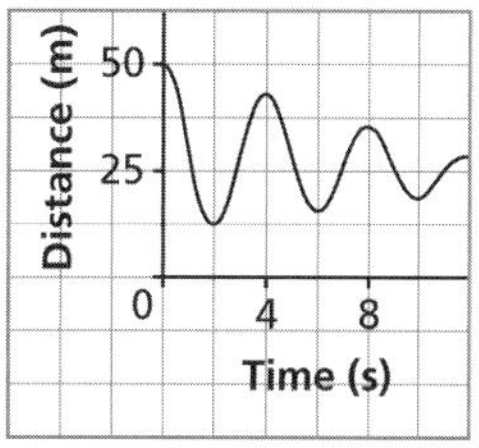

ii)

Speed while Bungee Jumping

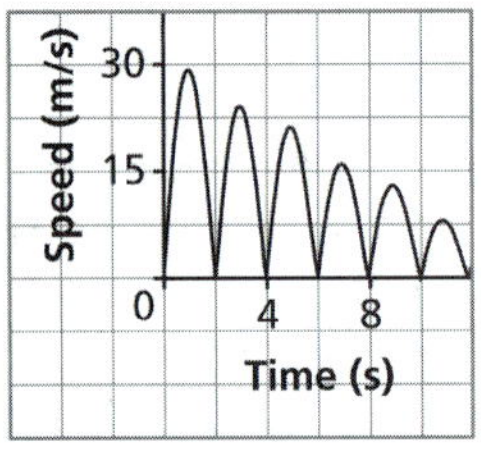

17. a)

Height of a Jump

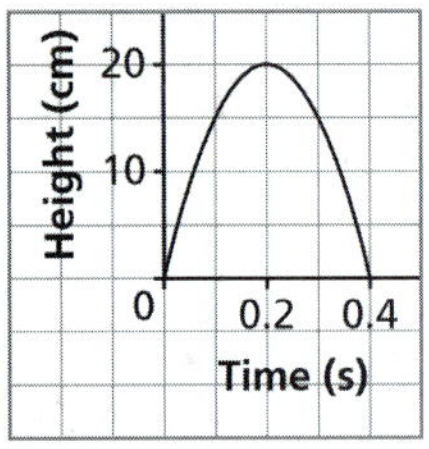

Situation: The height of a grasshopper during one hop. It takes 0.2 s for a grasshopper to jump 20 cm high, and another 0.2 s for it to return to the ground.

b)

Cost of Parking in a Parking Garage

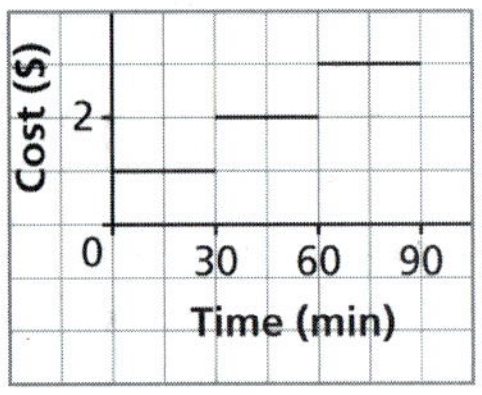

Situation: The cost of parking in a parking garage. It costs $1 to park for up to 30 min, $2 to park from 30 min to 60 min, and $3 to park from 60 min to 90 min.

c)

Height of a Point on the Rim of a Tire

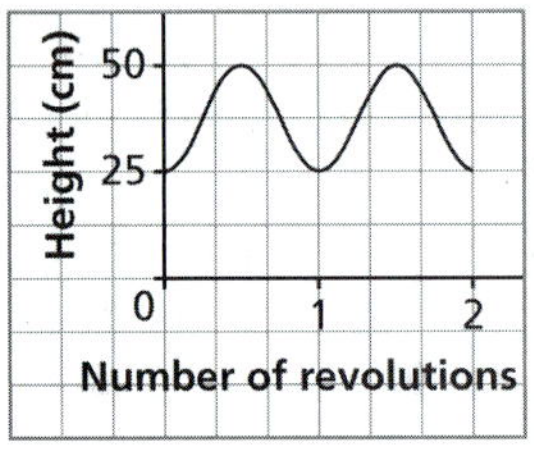

Situation: The height of a point on the rim of a tire on a truck over time. The point starts at the lowest point on the rim, 25 cm above the ground.
As the wheel goes around, the point moves up to a maximum height of 50 cm, then down, then up again.

18.

Depth of Water in Two Pools

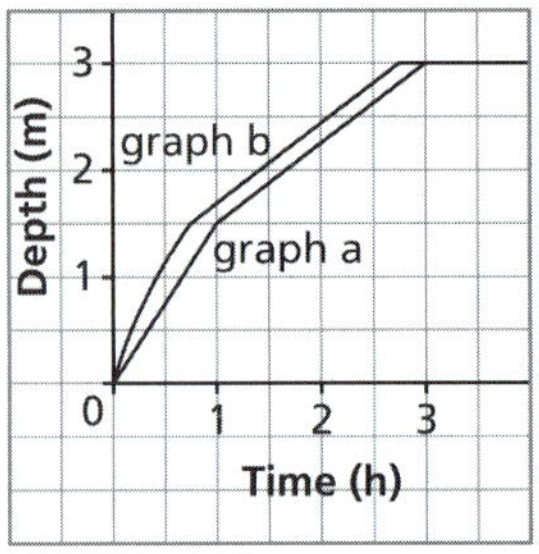

5.4 Math Lab: Graphing Data, page 286

1. a) i) The points are joined because air temperature and speed can have any numerical value between those indicated by the points on the graph.

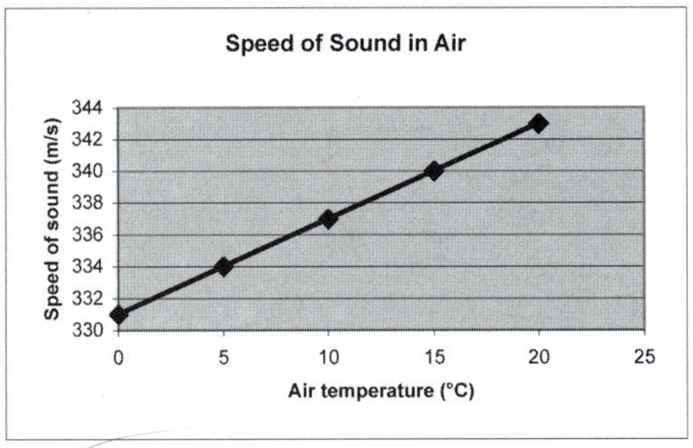

ii) Yes

b) i) The points are not joined because the data are only valid for whole numbers of years.

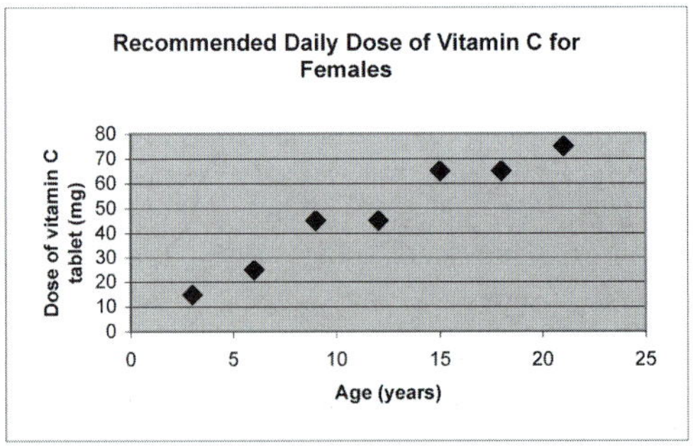

ii) Yes

2. a) The points are not joined because only whole numbers are permissible for the number of juice cans purchased.

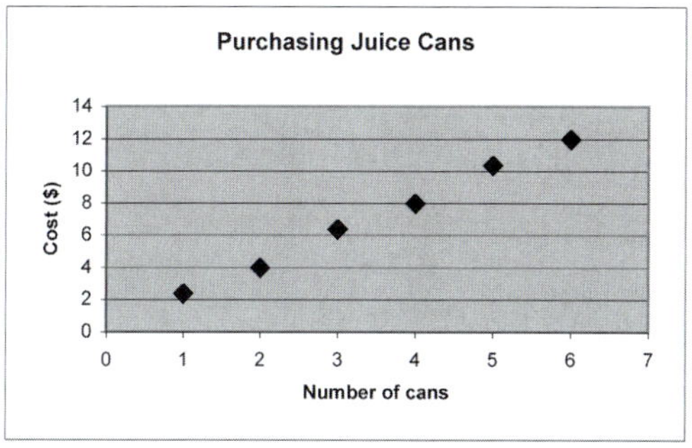

The relation is a function because there is only one cost for each number of cans.

b) The points are joined because all values of altitude and temperature are permissible between those plotted.

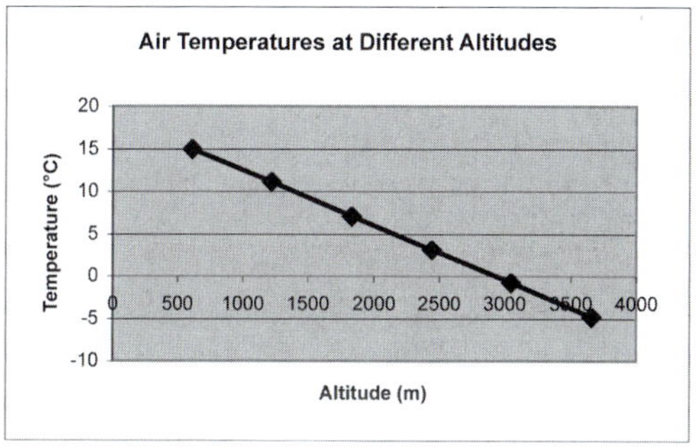

The relation is a function because there is only one value of temperature for each altitude.

5.5 Graphs of Relations and Functions, page 294

4. a) Domain: {–2, –1, 0, 1, 2}; range: {–4, –2, 0, 2, 4}
b) Domain: {–3, –1, 0, 2, 3}; range: {–2, 0, 1, 2, 3}
c) Domain: {–3, –2, –1, 0, 1, 2, 3}; range: {2}

5. A vertical line drawn on each graph intersects the graph at 0 points or 1 point.

6. a) Yes; each point on the line has a different x-coordinate.
b) No; each point on the line has the same x-coordinate, 1.

7. a) iv **b)** i
c) ii **d)** iii

8. a) Function; domain: all real numbers; range: $1 \le y \le 3$
b) Not a function; domain: $-3 \le x \le 1$; range: $y \ge -1$
c) Not a function; domain: {1, 2, 3, 4, 5}; range: {2, 3, 4, 5}
d) Function; domain: $x \ge -2$; range: $2 \le y \le 4$
e) Not a function; domain: $x \le 2$; range: $1 \le y \le 5$

9. a) Domain: all real numbers; range: $y \ge 1$
b) Domain: $-3 \le x \le 3$; range: $0 \le y \le 3$
c) Domain: $-3 \le x \le 3$; range: $-3 \le y \le 0$
d) Domain: $-1 \le x \le 2$; range: $0 \le y \le 3$

10. a) The points on the graph should not be connected.
b) The points on the graph should be connected.
c) The points on the graph should be connected.
d) The points on the graph should be connected.

11. a) i) The distance of a school bus from the school from 8:00 to 9:00.
ii) The number of students on a school bus from 8:00 to 9:00.
b) i) Independent variable: time; dependent variable: distance from the school
ii) Independent variable: time; dependent variable: number of students
c) Graph A: points are connected because all values of time and distance are permissible between the indicated plotted points.
Graph B: points are not connected because it is impossible to have only part of a student on a bus.

12. a) The points on the graph are connected because the car's speed and skid length can be any positive number of kilometres per hour and metres, respectively, between the plotted points.
b) Exact numbers for the range may vary. For example: domain: $40 \le s \le 120$; range: $16 \le d \le 144$
Restrictions: the domain and range cannot contain negative numbers because it is impossible to have a negative skid distance or a negative speed.
The domain is also restricted because the relationship shown on the graph may not be true for speeds less than 40 km/h and greater than 120 km/h.

13. a) Independent variable: t; dependent variable: n
b) The points are not connected because it is impossible to have part of a car in a parking lot.
c) Exact numbers for the range may vary. For example: domain: {8:00, 10:00, 12:00, 14:00, 16:00}; range: {4, 25, 31, 64, 65}
Restrictions: the domain can be any time between 00:00 and 24:00, all the possible times in one day.
The range can be any whole number up to the number of parking spaces in the lot.

14. a) Independent variable: number of days after January 1; dependent variable: number of hours the sun is above the horizon, h

b) Answers may vary. For example:

Number of Hours the Sun Is above the Horizon in Paulatuuq

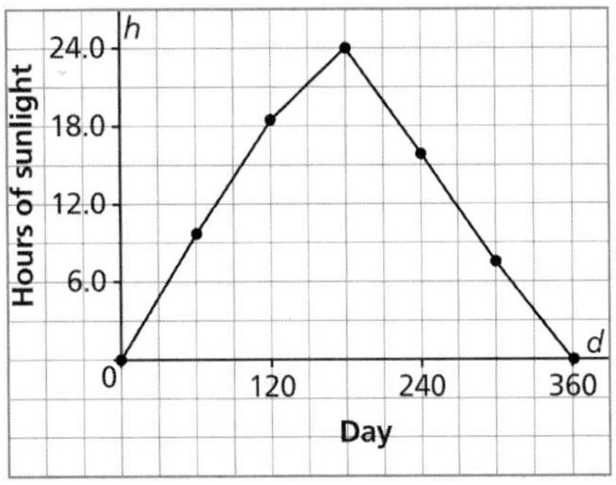

I connected the points because the relationship shown on the graph is true for days represented by points between the ones plotted.

The data are discrete, but the scale is so small that if all the points were plotted, they would make a line segment.

c) From the table: the relation is a function because each number in the first column is different.

From the graph: the relation is a function because a vertical line drawn on the graph would intersect the graph in only 1 point.

15. a)

Volume of Paint, *p* (L)	0	2	4	6	8
Cost, *c* ($)	0	24	48	72	96
Area Covered, *A* (m^2)	0	17	34	51	68

b)

Area Covered by Paint

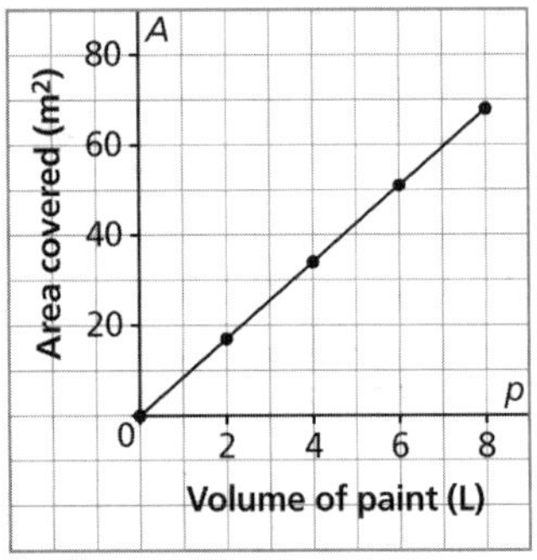

c)

Area that Can Be Covered for a Given Cost

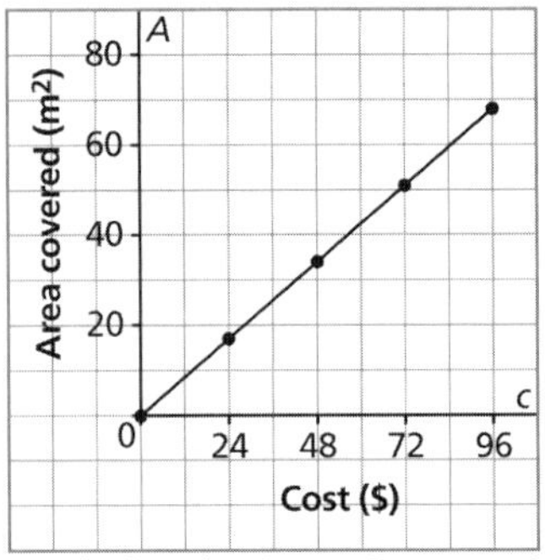

d) Part b: domain: $0 \leq p \leq 8$; range: $0 \leq A \leq 68$

Part c: domain: $0 \leq c \leq 96$; range: $0 \leq A \leq 68$

16. a) −1

b) 3

17. a) 5

b) 3

18. Answers may vary. For example:

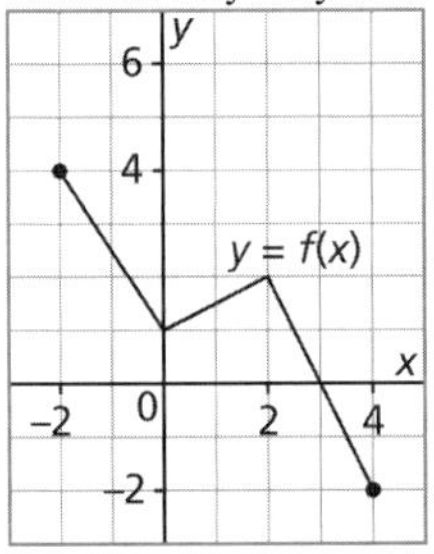

Domain: $-2 \leq x \leq 4$; range: $-2 \leq y \leq 4$

19. a)

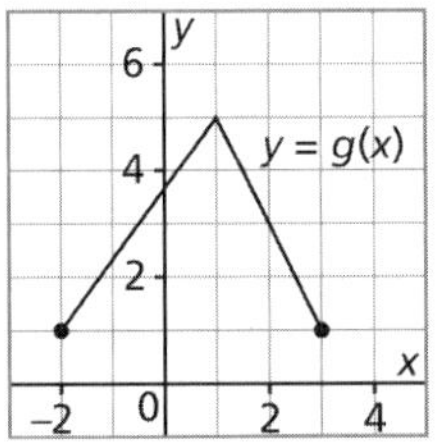

b)

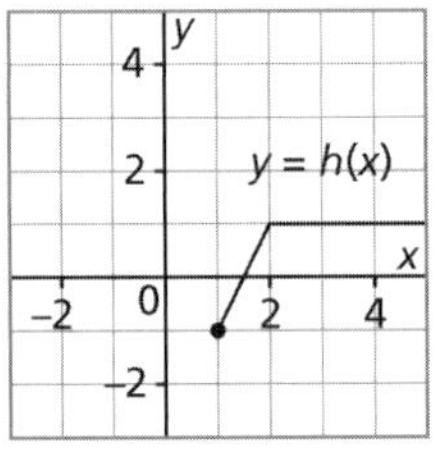

20. a)

Planetary Years as a Function of Distance from the Sun

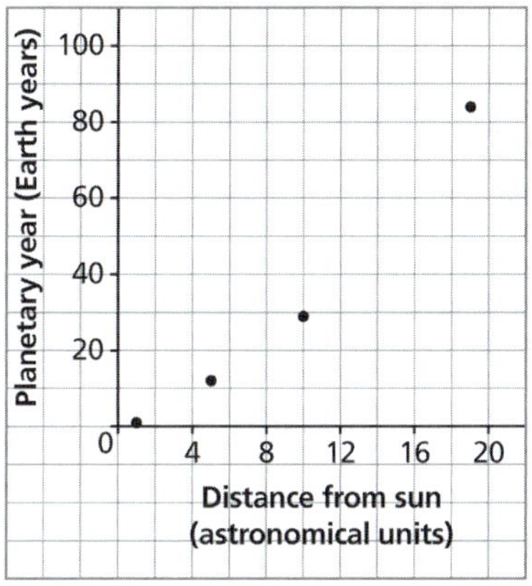

The points are not joined because each point represents a planet and their number is limited.

b) Domain: {1, 5, 10, 19}; range: {1, 12, 29, 84}

21. a)

Cost of Sending a Letter in 2009

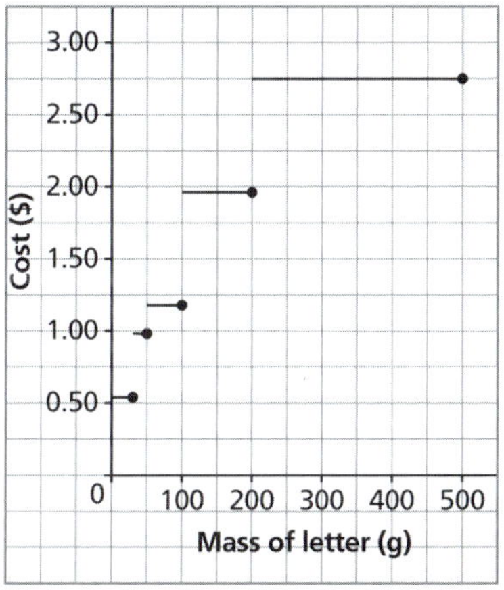

b) Domain: all real numbers greater than 0 and less than or equal to 500; range: {0.54, 0.98, 1.18, 1.96, 2.75}

22. Yes

23. The statement is false.

24. a)

Payment Scheme 1	
Day	Total money received ($)
1	0.01
2	0.03
3	0.07
4	0.15
5	0.31
6	0.63
7	1.27
8	2.55
9	5.11
10	10.23
11	20.47
12	40.95
13	81.91
14	163.83
15	327.67

Payment Scheme 2	
Day	Total money received ($)
1	10
2	20
3	30
4	40
5	50
6	60
7	70
8	80
9	90
10	100
11	110
12	120
13	130
14	140
15	150

b)

Total Money Received Under Two Payment Schemes

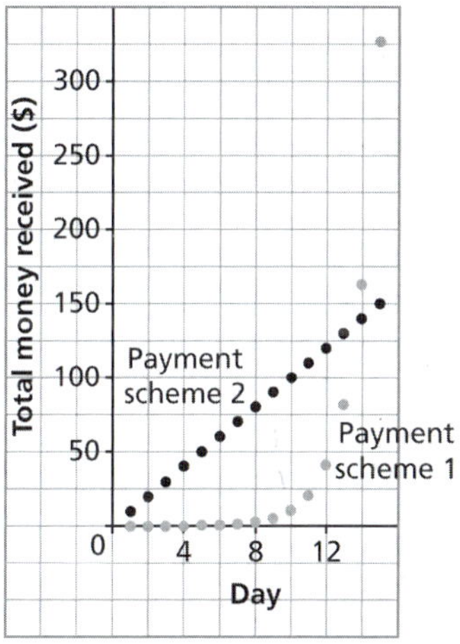

c) I would choose Payment Scheme 1 because after 13 days, the money received is greater and increases at a faster rate.

Chapter 5: Checkpoint 2, page 299

1. Answers may vary. For example:

Paula's Distance from Home

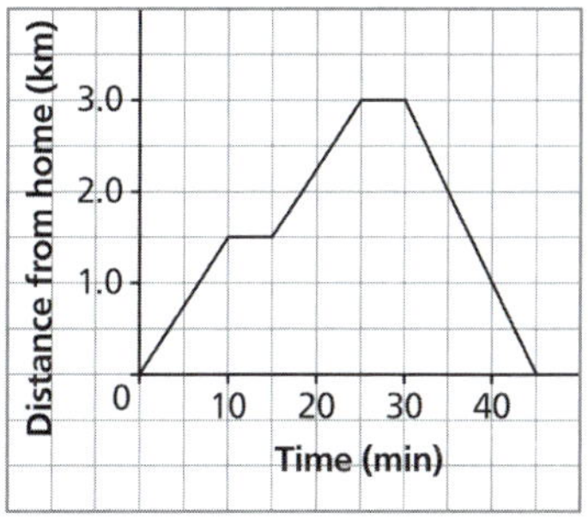

2. a)

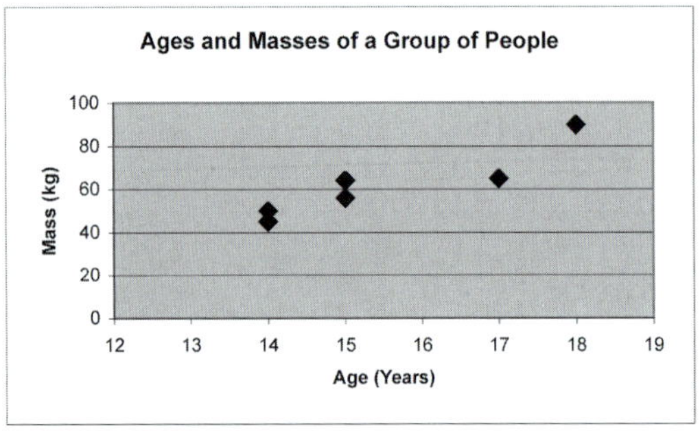

b) No

c) Domain: {14, 15, 17, 18};
range: {45, 50, 56, 64, 65, 90}

3. a) Not a function; domain: $0 \le x \le 2$; range: $1 \le y \le 5$

b) Function; domain: $x \ge -3$; range: $y \ge 0$

c) Function; domain: $-2 \le x \le 2$; range: $-8 \le y \le 8$

5.6 Properties of Linear Relations, page 308

3. a) Linear relation **b)** Not a linear relation

c) Linear relation **d)** Not a linear relation

4. a) Linear relation **b)** Not a linear relation

c) Not a linear relation

5. a) Linear relation **b)** Linear relation

c) Not a linear relation **d)** Not a linear relation

6. a) Tables of values may vary. For example:

i)

x	y
–2	4
–1	6
0	8
1	10
2	12

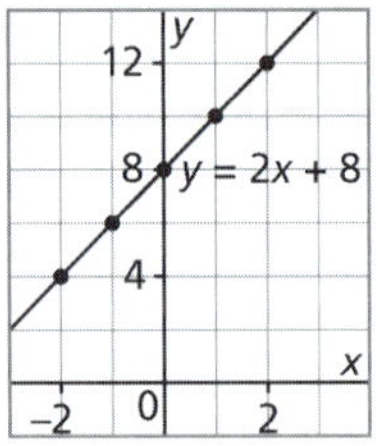

ii)

x	y
–2	11
–1	11.5
0	12
1	12.5
2	13

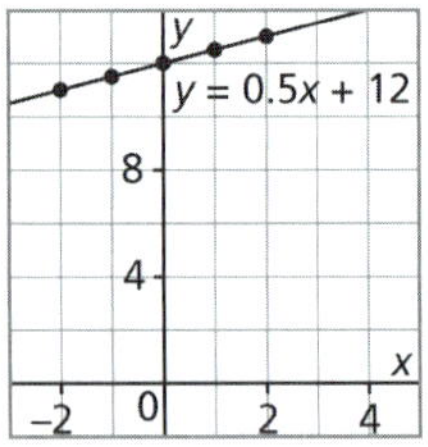

iii)

x	y
–2	12
–1	9
0	8
1	9
2	12

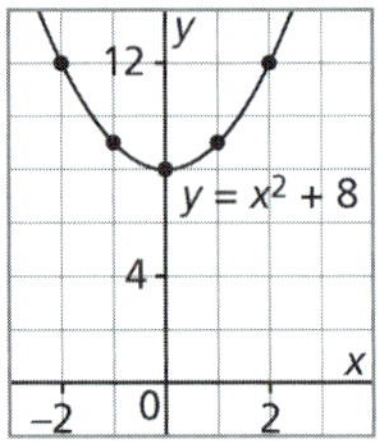

iv)

x	y
–2	–4
–1	–2
0	0
1	2
2	4

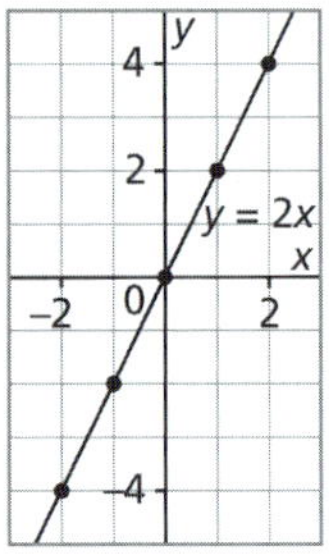

v)

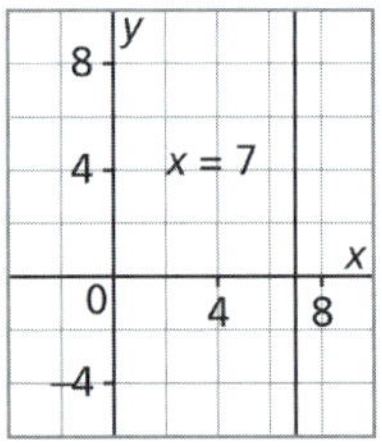

vi)

x	y
–2	8
0	6
2	4
4	2
6	0

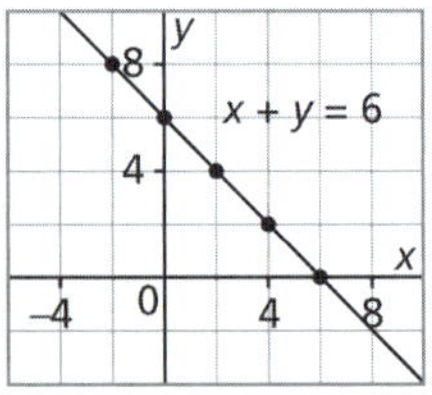

b) The relations in part a, i, ii, iv, v, and vi are straight lines, so they are linear relations.

7. a) i) Independent variable: *s*; dependent variable: *d*

ii) Not linear

b) i) Independent variable: *t*; dependent variable: *a*

ii) Linear

iii) –200 m/min

8. a)

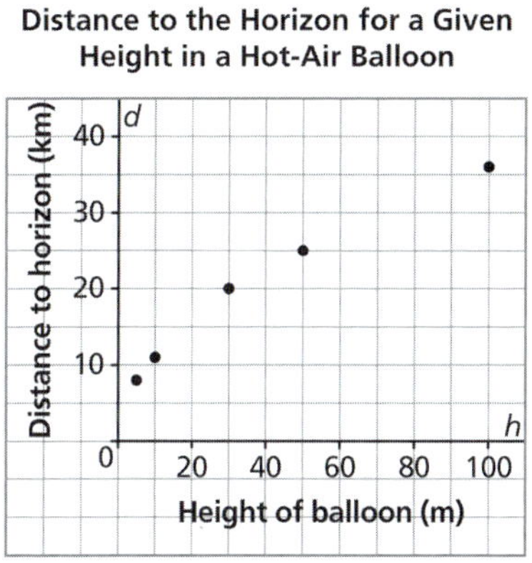

b) The relation is not linear because the points on the graph do not lie on a straight line.

9. Answers may vary. For example:
I could examine the change in the first and second coordinates. If both changes are constant, the relation is linear.
I could also graph the ordered pairs. If the points lie on a straight line, the relation is linear.

10. Yes

11. The first set of ordered pairs does not represent a linear relation. The second set of ordered pairs represents a linear relation.

12. a) Answers may vary. For example: The equation relates the dependent variable, C, to the rate of change, 15, times the independent variable, n, plus a constant, 550.

b) 15; cost per guest

13. Answers may vary. For example:
Create a table of values for the relation. Then, either check the differences in the numbers in each column or plot the points. If the differences are constant or the points lie along a line, the relation is linear. Otherwise, it is not linear.

14. a) Independent variable: t; dependent variable: C

b) \$0.08/min; every minute, the cost of the phone call increases by \$0.08.

15. –\$0.80/booth; at every toll booth, Kashala pays \$0.80.

16. a) Equation 3 and Set B

b) Equation 1 and Set C

c) Equation 2 and Set A

17. a) i) Linear **ii)** Not linear

iii) Linear **iv)** Linear

v) Not linear

b) i) Independent variable: time since the hang glider started her descent; dependent variable: hang glider's altitude; rate of change: –50 m/min; every minute, the hang glider's altitude decreases by 50 m.

iii) Independent variable: distance travelled; dependent variable: taxi fee; rate of change: \$2/km; every kilometre, the fee increases by \$2.

iv) Independent variable: number of yearbooks to be printed; dependent variable: fee; rate of change: \$5/yearbook; for every yearbook to be printed, the fee increases by \$5.

18. a) Linear

b) Not linear

c) Not linear

d) Linear

e) Not linear

19. a) The equation $V = 24\,000 - 2000n$ is linear.
The equation $V = 24\,000(0.2^n)$ is not linear.

b) –\$2000/year; every year, the value of the truck depreciates by \$2000

20. Yes; the relation is linear.

21. No; the relation is not linear.

22. a) True

b) True

c) False

d) True

e) False

5.7 Interpreting Graphs of Linear Functions, page 319

4. a) i) Vertical intercept: 0; horizontal intercept: 0; (0, 0); (0, 0)

ii) 40 km/h

iii) Domain: $0 \le t \le 3$; range: $0 \le d \le 120$

b) i) Vertical intercept: 100; horizontal intercept: 4; (0, 100); (4, 0)

ii) –25 km/h

iii) Domain: $0 \le t \le 4$; range: $0 \le d \le 100$

5. a) i) 400; (0, 400)

ii) 100 ft./min

iii) Domain: $0 \le t \le 8$; range: $400 \le A \le 1200$

b) i) 1000; (0, 1000)

ii) –50 ft./min

iii) Domain: $0 \le t \le 8$; range: $600 \le A \le 1000$

6. a)

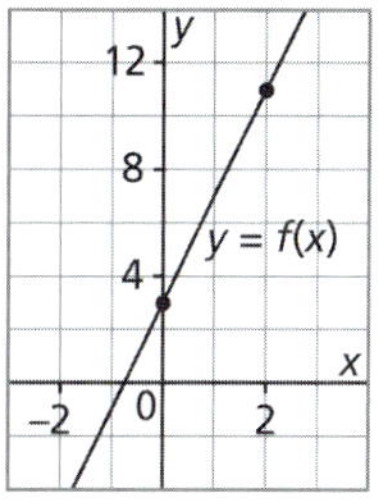

b)

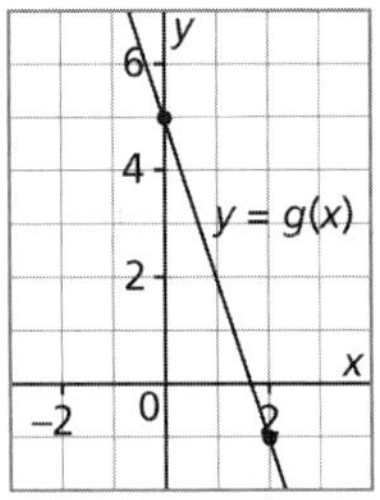

c)

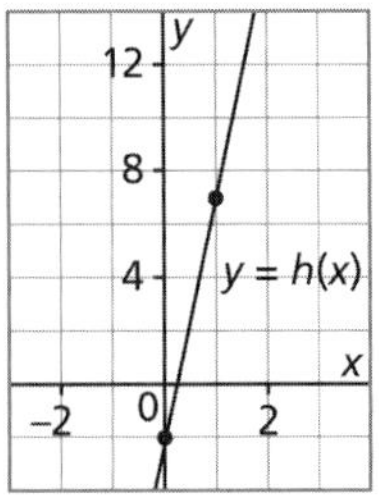

d)

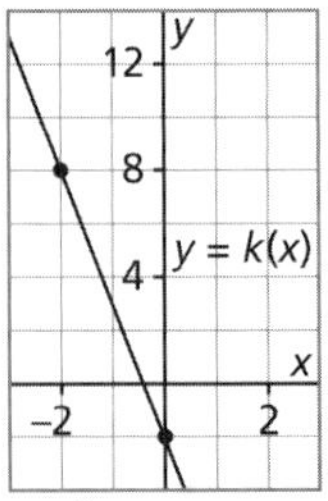

7. a) 9 m^2/L; every litre of paint covers an area of 9 m^2.

b) 54 m^2

c) 5 L

8. a) ii

b) iii

9. a) Vertical intercept: 0; horizontal intercept: 0; (0, 0); the cost of running the backhoe for 0 h is $0.

b) $80/h; each hour that the backhoe is run increases the cost by $80.

c) Domain: $0 \le t \le 10$; range: $0 \le C \le 800$

d) $560

e) 4.5 h

10. a) $1.50/km; every kilometre driven costs an additional $1.50.

b) $14

c) 4 km

11. Estimates may vary. Smart car: approximately 0.06 L/km; SUV: approximately 0.128 L/km; the Smart car uses less fuel per kilometre.

12. a) 2.5 h, or 2 h 30 min

b) 24 km/h

c) 60 km

d) $1\frac{2}{3}$ h, or 1 h 40 min

13. a) It takes longer to fill the empty tank.

b) 25 m^3 of fuel

14. a) Answers may vary. For example:
The scale on the axes is so small that it would be impossible to distinguish every point on the graph.

b) i) Approximately 33 sweatshirts

ii) $15

15. a)

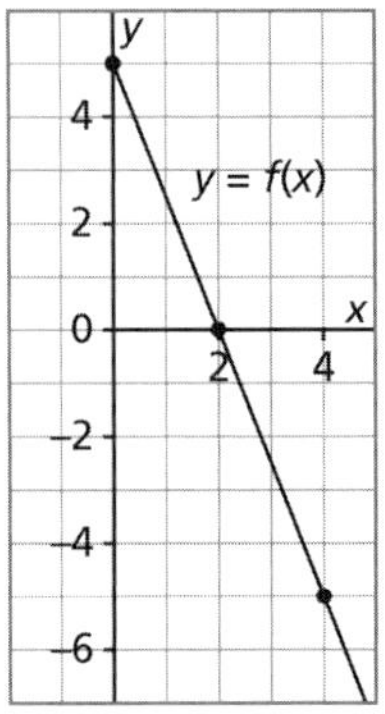

b)

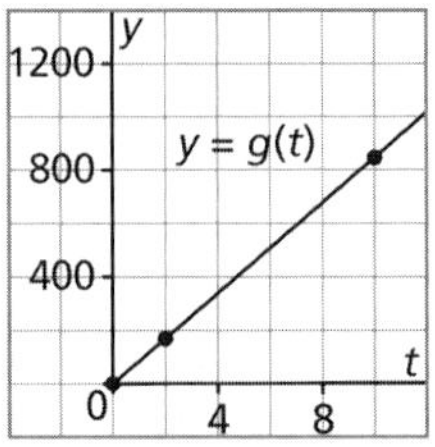

c)

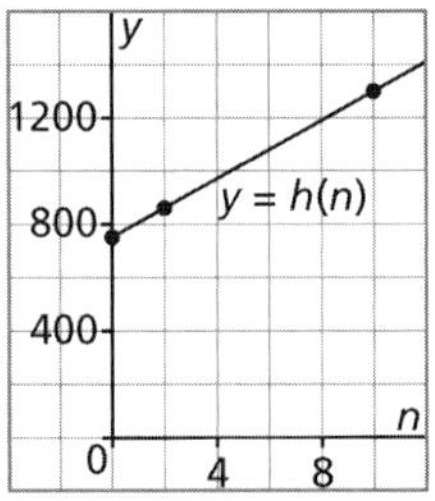

d)

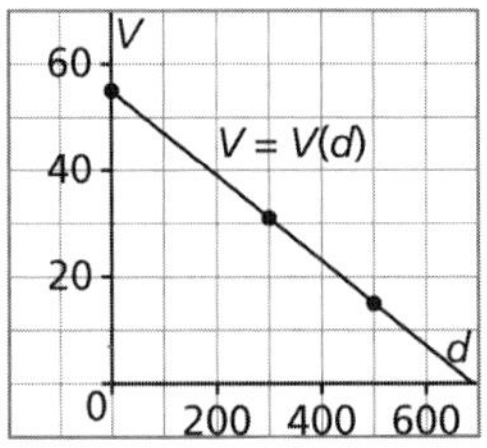

16. a) $0.80 per bar sold

b) Vertical intercept: –40; it represents the loss when 0 bars are sold: $40; horizontal intercept: 50; it represents the number of bars that must be sold to reach the break-even point, when no profit is made and there is no loss: 50 bars

c) Domain: $0 \le n \le 300$, where n is a whole number; range: all multiples of 0.80 from –40 to 200; I wouldn't want to list all the values in the range because there are 301 of them.

17. a) Answers may vary. For example:
There are no intercepts on the graph because the relation does not apply to people less than 10 years of age and older than 90 years of age.

b) Approximately –0.8 (beats/min)/year; for every additional year of age, the recommended maximum heart rate decreases by approximately 1 beat/min.

c) Approximately 77 years of age

d) Approximately 126 beats/min

18. a) i) x-intercept: 5; y-intercept: 5

ii) $x + y = 5$

b) i) x-intercept: 5; y-intercept: –5

ii) $x - y = 5$

19. a)

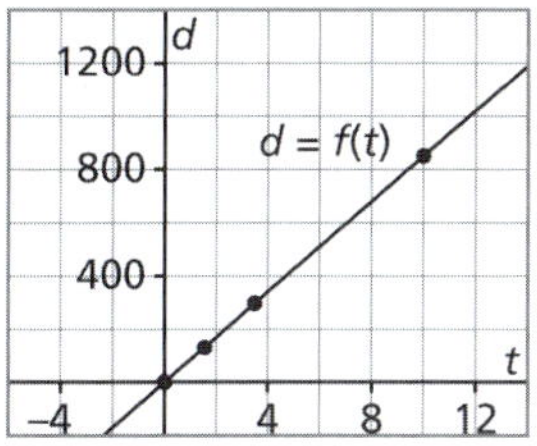

b) $f(5) = 425$

c) $t = 2.5$

d) Contexts may vary. For example: A car's distance from home as it travels away at an average speed of 85 km/h. In this context, only the 1st quadrant of the graph is relevant.

20. a) The vertical intercept represents the person's distance from Duke Point when starting the journey at Parksville.
The horizontal intercept represents the person's distance from Parksville after completing the journey at Duke Point.
The distance between the two locations doesn't change, so the intercepts have the same value.

b) –1; for every 1 km the car moves away from Parksville, it moves 1 km closer to Duke Point.

c) Interchanging the dependent and independent variables would interchange the labels on the axes, but the line on the graph would stay the same.

Chapter 5: Review, page 326

1. a) The table shows a relation with the association "has this cultural heritage" from a set of artists to a set of First Nations heritages.

b) i) As a set of ordered pairs:
{(Bob Dempsey, Tlingit), (Dorothy Grant, Haida), (Bill Helin, Tsimshian), (John Joseph, Squamish), (Judith P. Morgan, Gitxsan), (Bill Reid, Haida), (Susan Point, Salish)}

ii) As an arrow diagram:

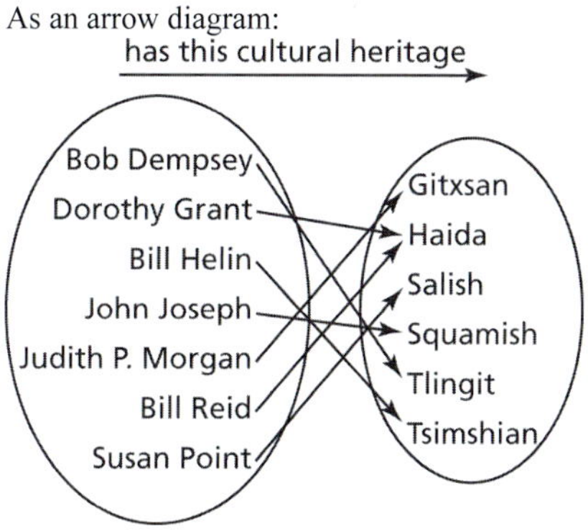

2. Representations may vary. For example:

a) As a table:

Element	Atomic Number
carbon	6
chlorine	17
hydrogen	1
iron	26
oxygen	8
silver	47

As an arrow diagram:

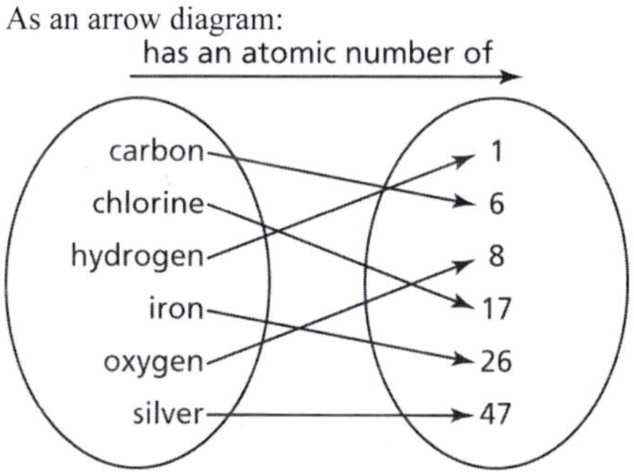

As a set of ordered pairs:
{(carbon, 6), (chlorine, 17), (hydrogen, 1), (iron, 26), (oxygen, 8), (silver, 47)}

b) As a table:

Atomic Number	Element
1	hydrogen
6	carbon
8	oxygen
17	chlorine
26	iron
47	silver

As an arrow diagram:

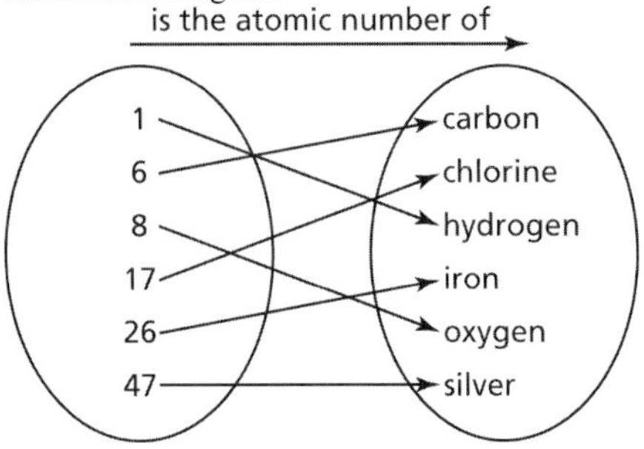

As a set of ordered pairs:
{(1, hydrogen), (6, carbon), (8, oxygen), (17, chlorine), (26, iron), (47, silver)}

3. a) Not a function
b) Function
c) Function
d) Not a function

4. a) $f(x) = -4x + 9$
b) $C(n) = 12n + 75$
c) $D(t) = -20t + 150$
d) $P(s) = 4s$

5. a) $P = 5n - 300$
b) Independent variable: n; dependent variable: P
c) $P(150) = 450$; if 150 students attend the dance, the profit is $450.
d) $n = 200$; the profit is $700 when 200 students attend the dance.

6. a) Graph A
b) Answers may vary. For example:
Graph D could represent Laura's journey to school to pick up her bike. She walks to school, then picks up her bicycle and rides home.

7. b) 2 times
c) 2.0 L of water
d) Dependent variable: volume of water in Liam's flask; independent variable: distance Liam hikes

8. a) I joined the points because all times between 0 min and 30 min are permissible and all temperatures between 50°C and 89°C are permissible.

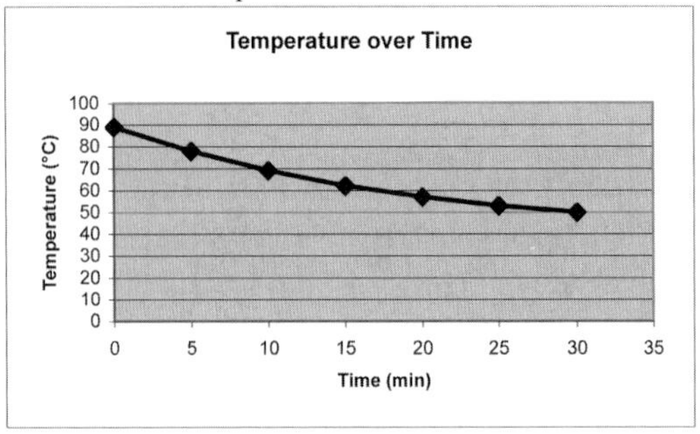

b) The graph represents a function because a vertical line drawn on the graph passes through one point.

9. Estimates may vary.
a) Not a function; domain: {13, 14, 15, 16, 17}; range: {159, 161, 165, 168, 170, 174, 176}
b) Function; domain: {08:00, 10:00, 12:00, 14:00, 16:00, 18:00}; range: {2, 5, 10, 20, 25}

10. a) i) Graph A represents the volume of a jar, in cubic centimetres, as a linear function of its height, in centimetres.
ii) Graph B represents the number of marbles in a jar as a linear function of the jar's height, in centimetres.
b) i) Independent variable: height of the jar, h; dependent variable: volume of the jar, V
ii) Independent variable: height of the jar, h; dependent variable: number of marbles in the jar, n
c) i) Estimates may vary. For example: Domain: $5 \le h \le 20$; range: approximately $400 \le V \le 1575$
ii) Domain: {5, 10, 15, 20}; range: {14, 28, 42, 56}
d) The points are joined in Graph A because it is possible for a jar to have any height between 5 cm and 20 cm and any volume between 400 cm^3 and 1575 cm^3. The points are not joined in Graph B because only whole numbers of marbles are permissible.

11. a) –2
b) –1

12. Graphs may vary. For example:
a)

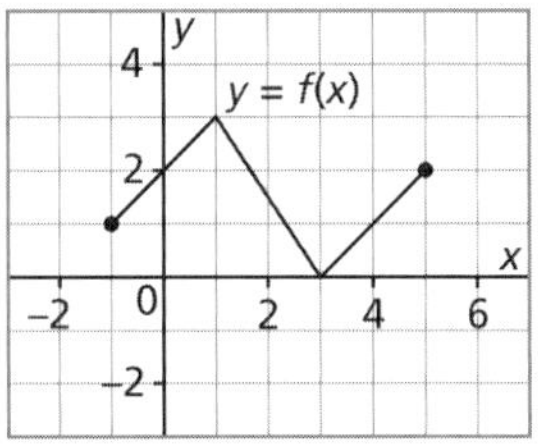

b)

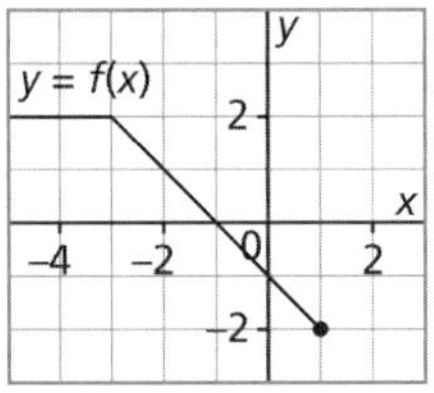

13. a) Linear relation **b)** Linear relation
c) Not a linear relation

14. Tables of values may vary. For example:
a) i)

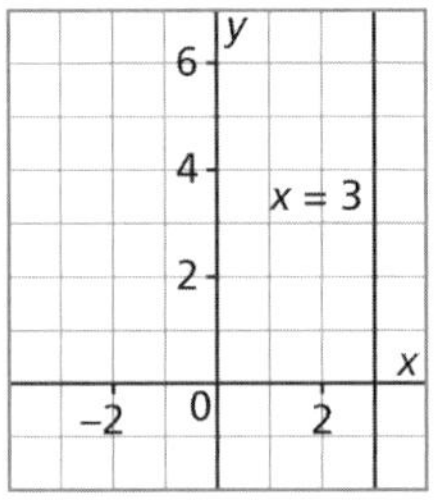

ii) Table:

x	y
–2	11
–1	5
0	3
1	5
2	11

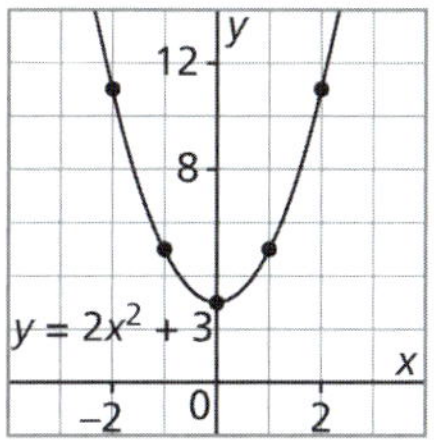

iii)

x	y
–2	–1
–1	1
0	3
1	5
2	7

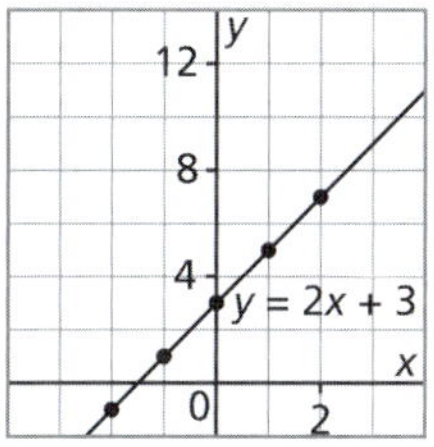

iv)

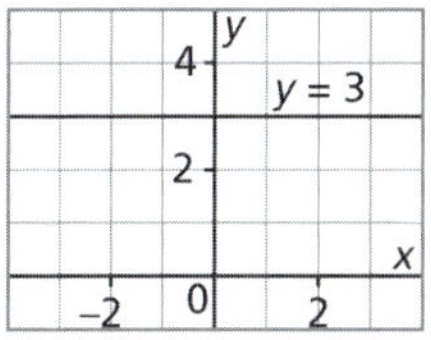

v)

x	y
–2	–6
–1	–3
0	0
1	3
2	6

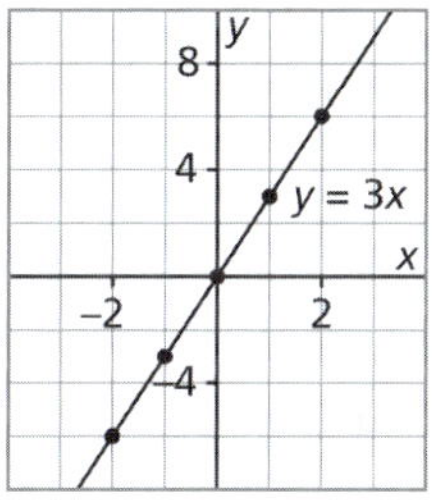

vi)

x	y
–1	4
0	3
1	2
2	1
3	0

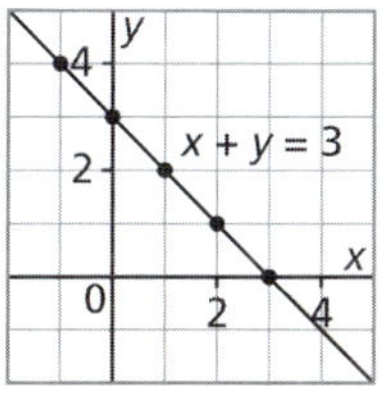

b) i, iii, iv, v, vi

15. a) The equation represents a linear relation because, when g changes by 1, N changes by $\frac{1}{15}$.

b) $\frac{1}{15}$; For every 1 g of carbohydrate that Isabelle consumes, she gives herself $\frac{1}{15}$ of a unit of insulin.

16. a) 6000 m, or 6 km

b) Domain: $0 \le n \le 2800$; range: $0 \le d \le 6000$

c) Approximately 2.1 m/revolution; in one revolution of the wheel, the bicycle covers a distance of approximately 2 m.

d) Approximately 0.68 m, or 68 cm

17. a) ii

b) iii

c) i

18. a) 201 caps

b) \$4

c) **i)** 350 caps

ii) 500 caps

d) The profit depends on the sale of caps and the initial cost of \$800 to buy or make the caps. So, doubling the number of caps does not double the profit.

Chapter 5: Practice Test, page 329

1. B

2. C

3. a) **i)** Function

ii) Representations may vary. For example:
Domain: {–3, –1, 0, 1, 2}; range: {2, 4, 5, 6}
As a graph:

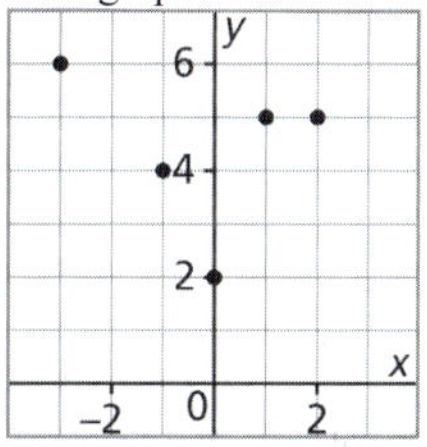

The function is not linear because the points on the graph do not lie on a line.

b) **i)** Function

ii) Representations may vary. For example:
Domain: {–3, –1, 1, 2, …}; range: {1, 4, 9, …}
As a graph:

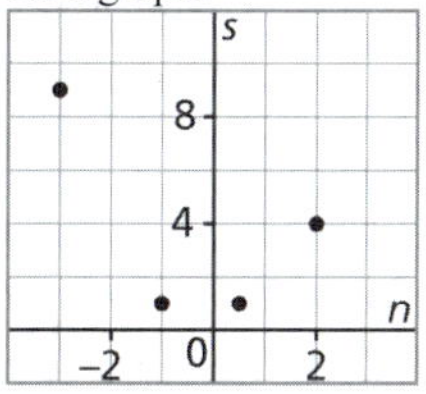

The function is not linear because the points on the graph do not lie on a line.

c) **i)** Function

ii) Representations may vary. For example:
Domain: $-2 \le x \le 8$; range: $-1 \le y \le 4$

As an equation:

$y = -\frac{1}{2}x + 3$, for $-2 \le x \le 8$

The function is linear because the graph is a non-vertical line.

iii) Independent variable: x; dependent variable: y; rate of change: $-\frac{1}{2}$

4. Situation: Jamie's school is 20 km from her home. Jamie rides her friend's bike from school to her friend's home, which is 4 km from her own home. She arrives at her friend's home 20 min after she left school. She talks to her friend for 10 min, then walks the remaining 4 km home in 30 min.

Jamie's Journey Home

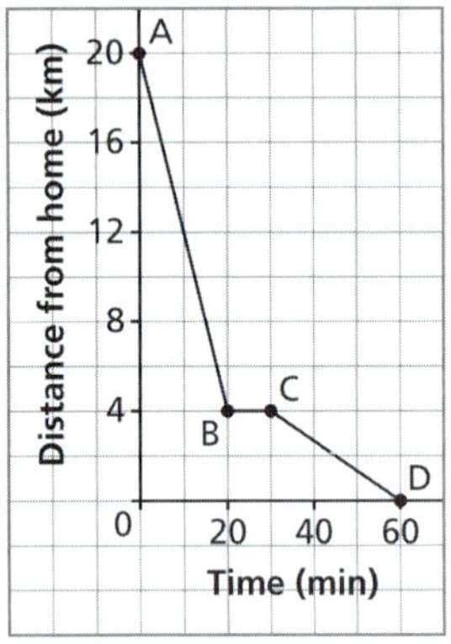

5. a) The relation is a function because no number is repeated in the first column.

b) Dependent variable: time; independent variable: mass

c)

Time Needed to Cook a Turkey

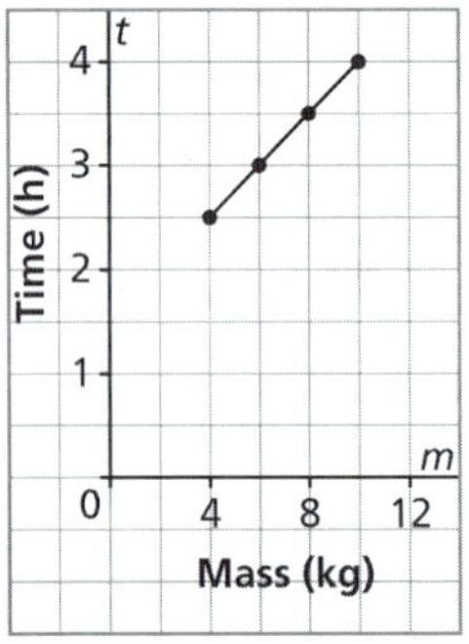

I connected the points because both time and mass are not discrete data.

d) Domain: $4 \le m \le 10$; range: $2.5 \le t \le 4.0$

e) 0.25 h/kg; for every additional kilogram, the time needed to cook the turkey increases by 0.25 h.

f) 3.25 h or 3 h 15 min

Chapter 6 Linear Functions, page 330

6.1 Slope of a Line, page 339

4. a) $\frac{2}{11}$ **b)** $\frac{2}{7}$

5. a) Negative

b) Positive

c) Not defined

d) Zero

6. a) Rise: 3; run: 6; slope: $\frac{1}{2}$

b) Rise: –2; run: 8; slope: $-\frac{1}{4}$

c) Rise: 3; run: 4; slope: $\frac{3}{4}$

d) Rise: –6; run: 2; slope: –3

7. a) 3

b) $-\frac{7}{2}$

c) $\frac{1}{2}$

d) $-\frac{1}{2}$

8. Sketches may vary. The lines may be in different positions on the grid but they should have the same orientations as those shown.

a)

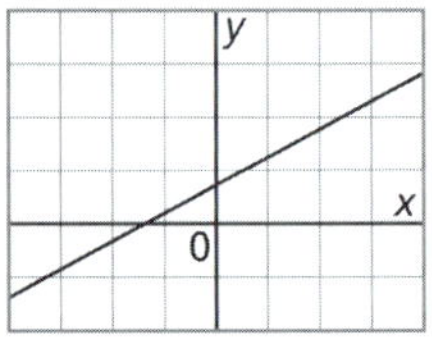

b)

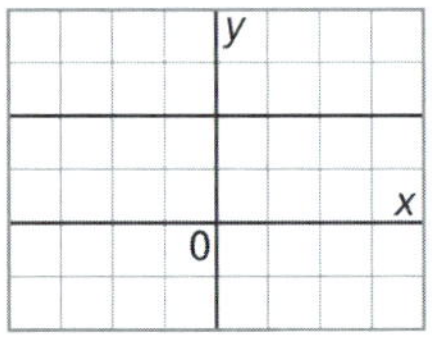

c)

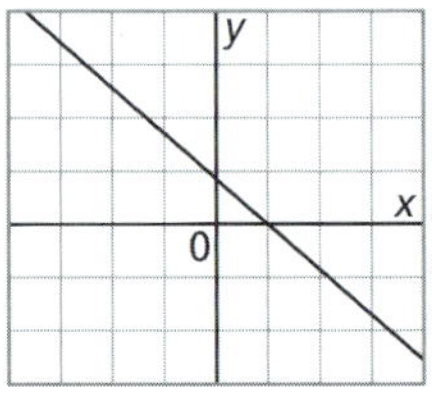

d)

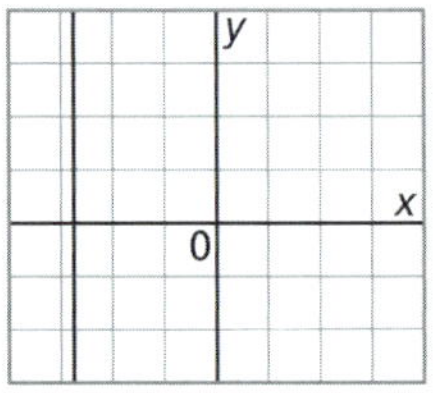

9. Sketches may vary. The line segments may have different lengths but they should have the same orientations as those shown.

a)

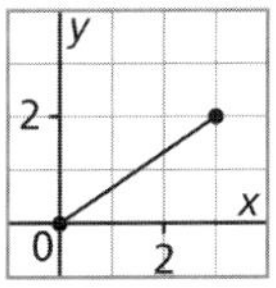

b)

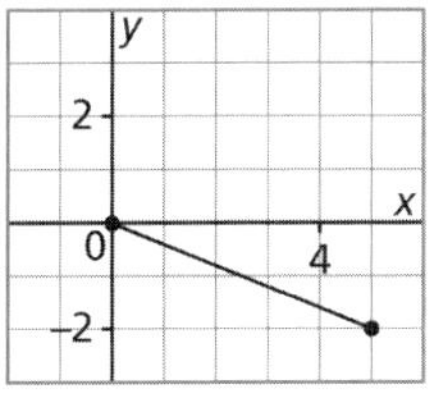

c)

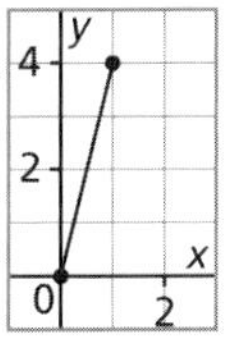

d)

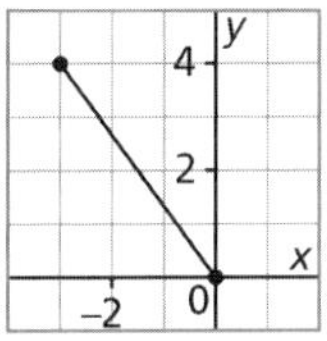

11. a) $\frac{1}{2}$

b) $\frac{1}{2}$

c) The slopes in parts a and b are equal.

12. Diagrams may vary. For example:

a)

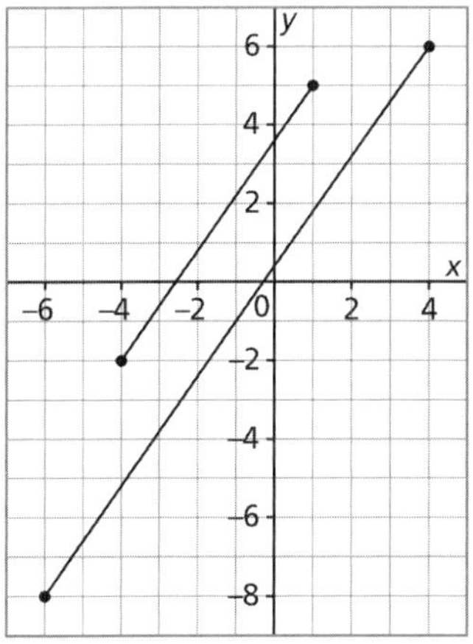

b) Similarities: the line segments have the same slope; differences: they pass through different points

13. a) i) 2 **ii)** $\frac{1}{2}$

iii) –3 **iv)** $\frac{1}{3}$

b) i) As x increases by 1, y increases by 2.

ii) As x increases by 2, y increases by 1.

iii) As x increases by 1, y decreases by 3.

iv) As x increases by 3, y increases by 1.

14. a) Diagrams may vary.

b) i) The slopes of the segments are equal; all segments on the same line have the same slope.

15. a) $\frac{1}{15}$, or $0.0\overline{6}$

b) $13\frac{1}{2}$ in.

16. a) $-\frac{1}{48}$

b) 312 in., or 26 ft.

c) $4\frac{1}{2}$ in.

17. a) Line iv

b) Line iii

c) Line ii

d) Line i

18. a) i) $-\frac{3}{5}$

ii) $\frac{3}{5}$

iii) $-\frac{3}{5}$

iv) $\frac{3}{5}$

b) The slopes of BC and ED are equal. The slopes of BE and CD are equal. The two different slopes are opposites.

19. a) The slope of a horizontal line is 0 because its rise is 0, and the quotient of 0 and any number is zero.

b) The slope of a vertical line is undefined because its run is 0, and the quotient of any number and 0 is undefined; that is, I cannot divide by 0.

20. a) $\frac{1}{3}$

21. Positions of lines on the grid may vary. For example:

a) i)

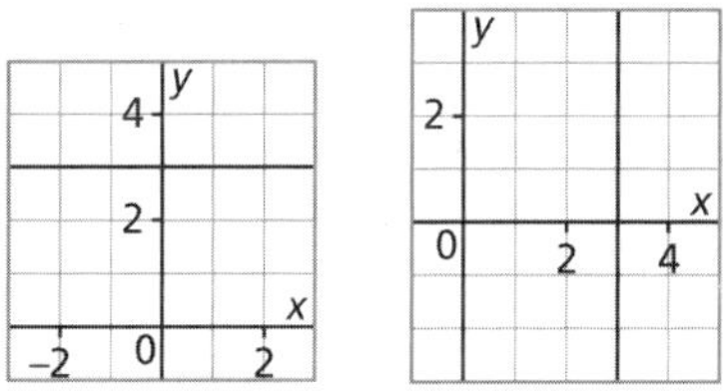

ii)

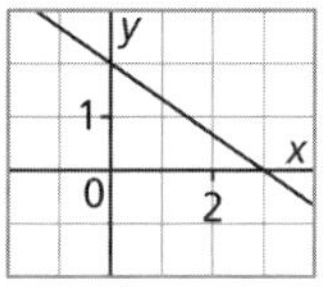

iii)

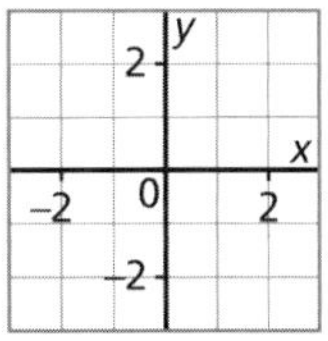

22. 840 cm, or 8.4 m

23. Coordinates may vary.

For example:

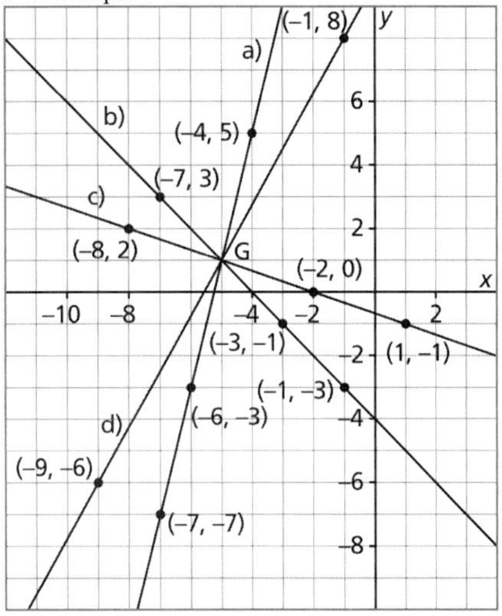

a) (−4, 5), (−6, −3), (−7, −7)

b) (−7, 3), (−3, −1), (−1, −3)

c) (−8, 2), (−2, 0), (1, −1)

d) (−1, 8), (−9, −6), (−13, −13)

24. a) **i)** Positive

ii) Positive

iii) Negative

iv) Not defined

b) Sketches may vary.

For example:

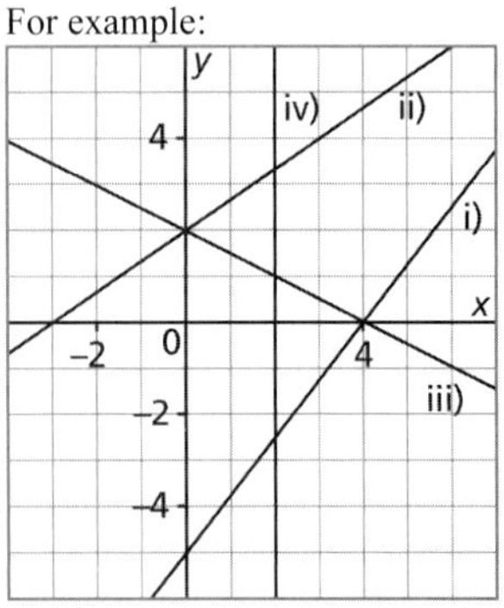

25. a)

Mass and Volume of Aluminum

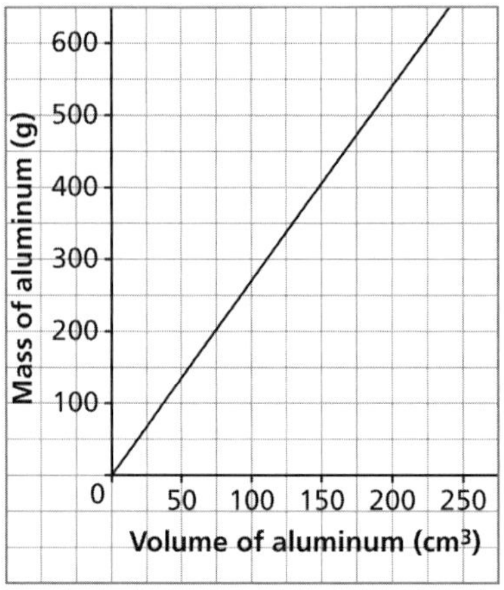

b) 2.7 g/cm^3

c) The slope shows that for every 1 cm^3 increase in the volume of an aluminum cube, the mass of the cube increases by 2.7 g.

d) **i)** 135 g **ii)** 742.5 g

e) **i)** Approximately 37 cm^3

ii) Approximately 167 cm^3

26. a) The number of text messages is restricted to whole numbers.

b) $0.15, or 15¢ **c)** $4.95

d) 48 text messages

e) Assumptions may vary. For example: I assumed that all messages cost the same.

27. a) $45/month **b)** $505

c) $55

d) Assumptions may vary. For example: I assumed that Charin continues to save the same amount each month after the 5th month and that the savings account did not earn any interest.

28. a) 2 **b)** $\frac{2}{3}$

29. No

30. a) Positions of point A may vary. For example:

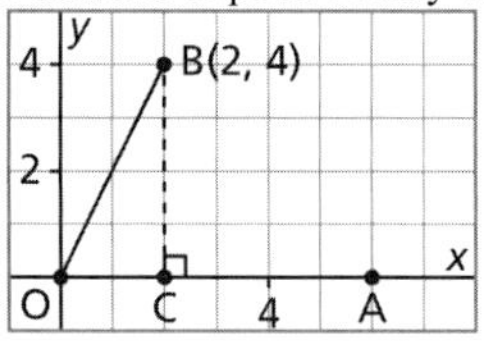

b) Slope of OB is 2; tan∠AOB = 2

c)

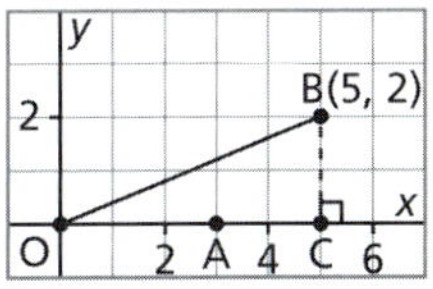

Slope of OB is $\frac{2}{5}$; $\tan\angle AOB = \frac{2}{5}$

d) The slope of a line segment is equal to the tangent of the angle formed by the segment and the positive x-axis. Both the slope and the tangent are equal to the quotient of the same two numbers.

31. a) The slope is tan 30°, or approximately 0.6.

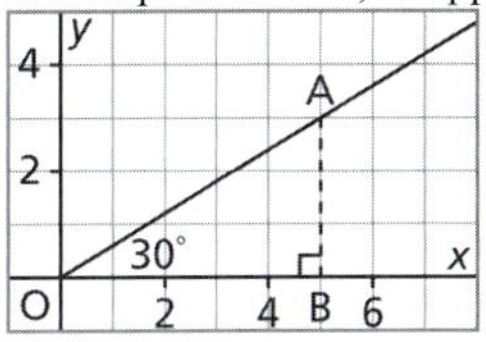

b) The slope is tan 60°, or approximately 1.7.

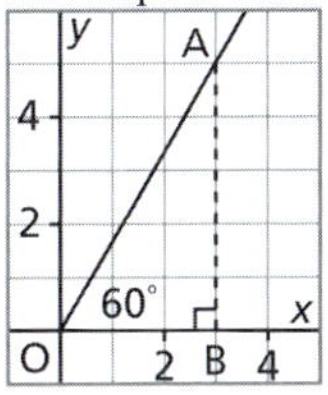

c) No

6.2 Slopes of Parallel and Perpendicular Lines, page 349

3. a) $\frac{4}{5}$

b) $-\frac{4}{3}$

c) 3

d) 0

4. a) $-\frac{6}{7}$

b) $\frac{8}{5}$

c) $-\frac{1}{9}$

d) $\frac{1}{5}$

5. a) Parallel **b)** Neither

c) Neither **d)** Perpendicular

6. a) i) $-\frac{4}{9}$ **ii)** $\frac{9}{4}$

b) i) 5

ii) $-\frac{1}{5}$

c) i) $\frac{7}{3}$

ii) $-\frac{3}{7}$

d) i) –4

ii) $\frac{1}{4}$

7. Yes; the slope of the line through the golfer's club and the slope of the line through the golfer's feet are the same: approximately $-\frac{1}{6}$

8. a) i) A(–5, –2), B(1, 5) and C(–1, –4), D(4, 1)

ii) Neither

b) i) E(–3, 4), F(3, 2) and G(2, 5), H(0, –1)

ii) Perpendicular

c) i) J(–2, 3), K(1, –3) and M(3, 1), N(–4, –2)

ii) Neither

d) i) P(0, 5), Q(6, 2) and R(–4, –1), S(0, –3)

ii) Parallel

9. a) Perpendicular

b) Parallel

c) Neither

d) Neither

10. a) Both lines have positive slopes, which are reciprocals.

b) Both lines have positive slopes, which are reciprocals.

11. a) Slope of AB is $\frac{3}{2}$, or 1.5.

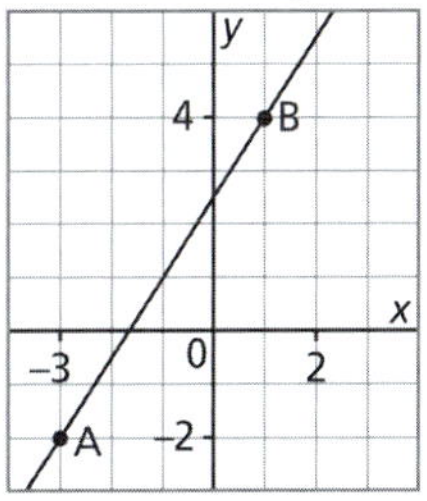

b) Slope of CD is $\frac{3}{2}$, or 1.5.

c) Answers may vary. For example: (1, 2), (3, 5)

d) Slope of AE is $-\frac{2}{3}$.

e) Answers may vary. For example: (0, –4), (3, –6)

12. a) Slope of AB is –2.

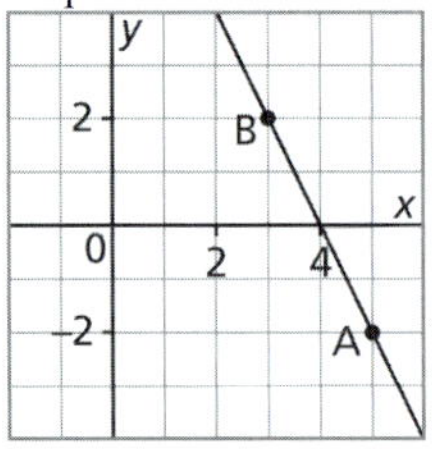

b) Slope of CD is –2.

c) (–1, 0) and (0, –2)

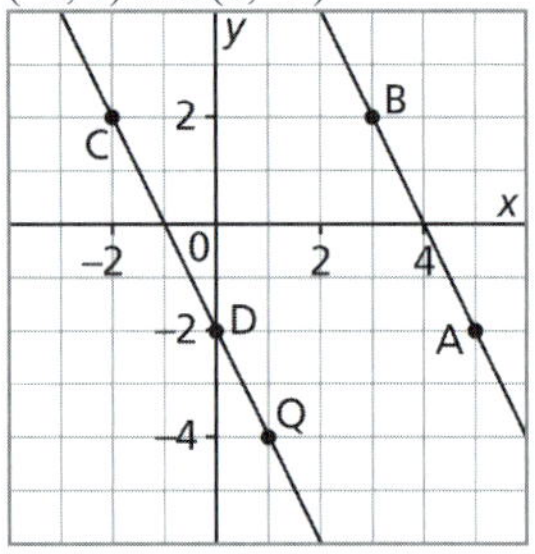

d) Slope of EF is $\frac{1}{2}$, or 0.5.

e) (4, 0) and (0, –2)

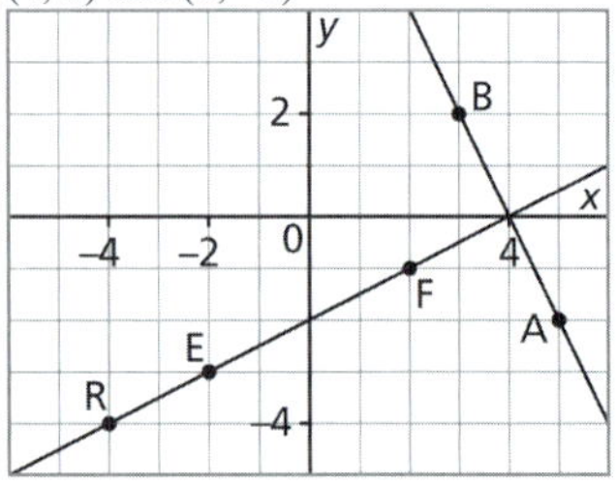

13. a) Yes **b)** No

14. Trapezoid

15. No

16. The slopes of BC and AC are negative reciprocals, so BC and AC are perpendicular: slope of BC: –2; slope of AC: $\frac{1}{2}$

17. Yes; The slopes of DE and EF are negative reciprocals, so DE and EF are perpendicular: slope of DE: $\frac{3}{2}$; slope of EF: $-\frac{2}{3}$

18. Triangles may vary.

c) In each case, the line segment that joins the midpoints of two sides of a triangle is parallel to the third side of the triangle.

19. a) No; no pairs of slopes are negative reciprocals.

b) D(–2, –1)

20. Coordinates may vary. For example: (3, 7), (–9, 1), (6, 1), (–6, –5)

21. Rhombuses may vary. The diagonals intersect at right angles.

22. $c = -2$

23. a) $a = 3\frac{1}{4}$, or 3.25

b) $a = 1\frac{1}{5}$, or 1.2

Chapter 6: Checkpoint 1, page 353

1. Slope of AB: $-\frac{2}{3}$; slope of CD: $\frac{1}{4}$

2. a) $-\frac{15}{4}$

b) $\frac{5}{3}$

3. Answers may vary. For example: The slope of a line is equal to the slope of any segment of the line, so we can use any two points that form that segment to determine the slope of the line.

4. a) 25 km/h; Jordan's average speed

b) Approximately 31 km

c) 2.6 h, or 2 h 36 min

5. The positions of the lines on the grids and their labels may vary. For example:

a) Neither

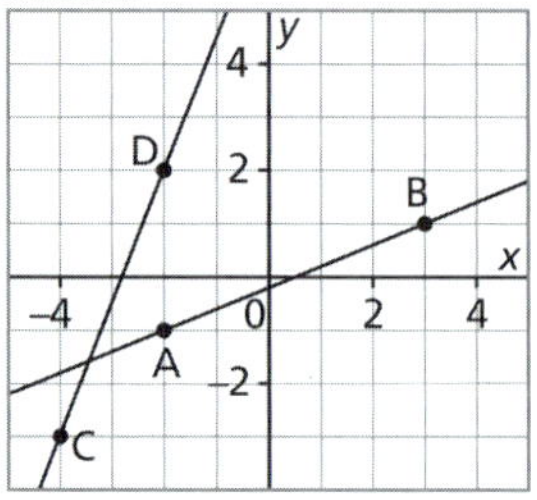

b) Perpendicular

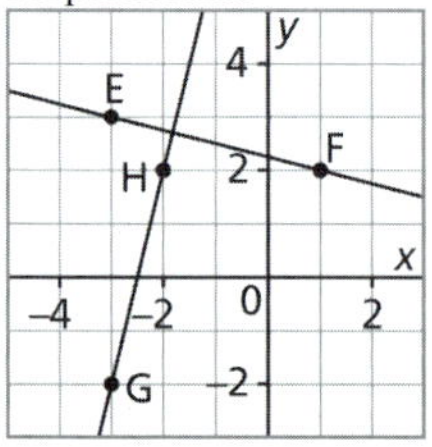

c) Parallel

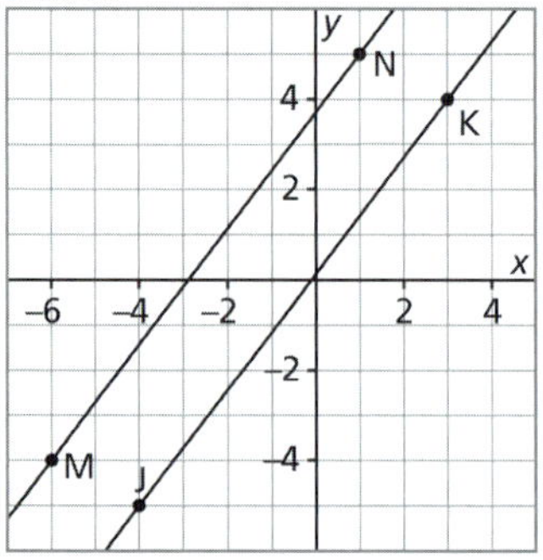

6. Coordinates may vary. For example:

a) (2, –2), (6, 1)

b) (5, –2), (2, 2)

7. No, no two of the three slopes of the sides of the triangle are negative reciprocals.
8. Answers may vary. For example: (–12, 0), (0, –5)

6.3 Math Lab: Investigating Graphs of Linear Functions, page 356

1. a) From top to bottom:

$y=\frac{1}{2}x+4$, $y=\frac{1}{2}x+2$, $y=\frac{1}{2}x-1$,

$y=\frac{1}{2}x-2$, $y=\frac{1}{2}x-3$

b) From top to bottom:

$y=-\frac{1}{3}x+4$, $y=-\frac{1}{3}x+3$, $y=-\frac{1}{3}x+1$,

$y=-\frac{1}{3}x-2$, $y=-\frac{1}{3}x-3$

2. m represents the slope and b represents the y-intercept of the line. I could plot the y-intercept, then plot a point using the slope.
3. The graph has a slope of –3 and a y-intercept of 6.

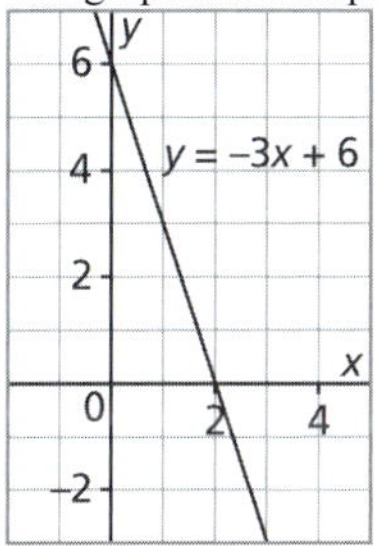

4. a) All the graphs have y-intercept –1.

b)

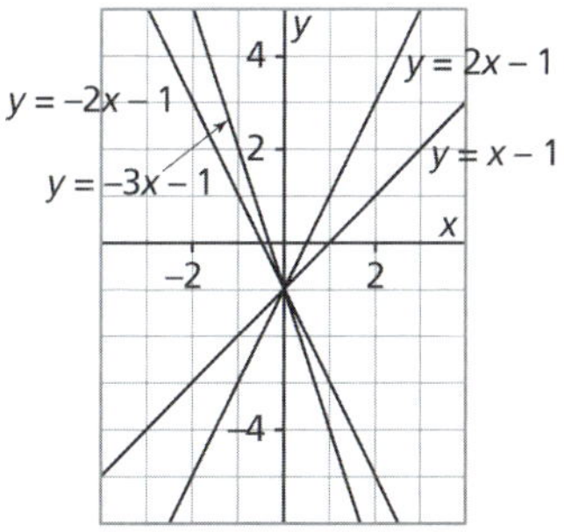

5. a) All the graphs have slope 1.

b)

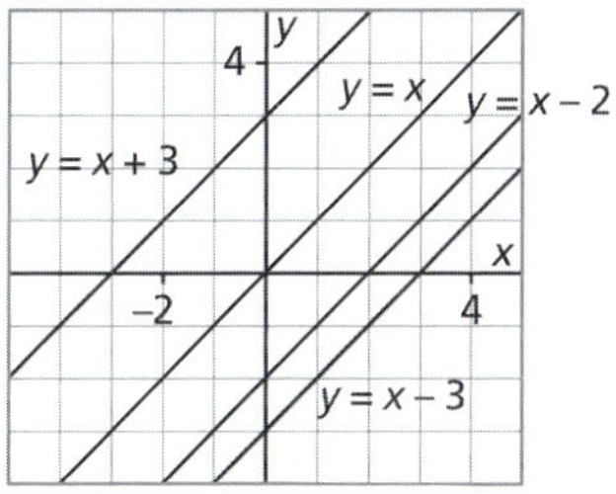

6. a), b)

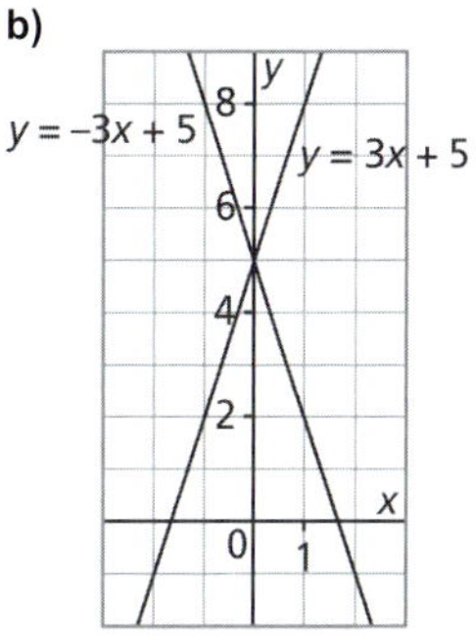

c), d)

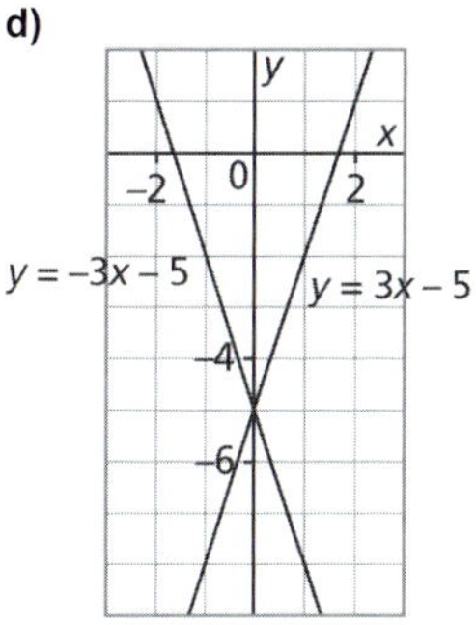

7. a)

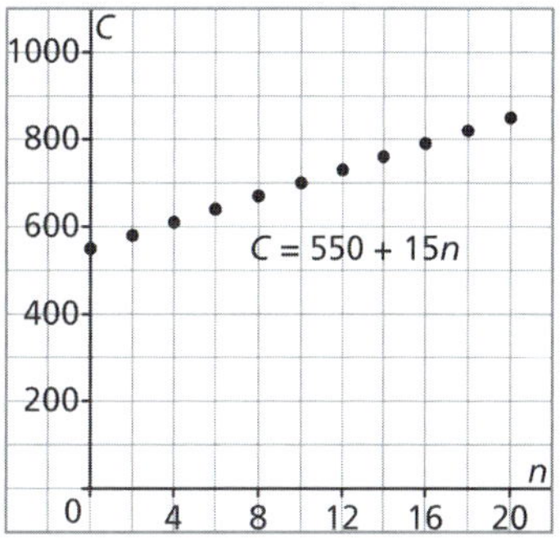

b) m represents the slope or rate of change; that is, \$15 per person. b represents the initial cost of \$550 to rent the hall.

6.4 Slope-intercept Form of the Equation for a Linear Function, page 362

4. a) Slope: 4; y-intercept: –7

b) Slope: 1; y-intercept: 12

c) Slope: $-\frac{4}{9}$; y-intercept: 7

d) Slope: 11; y-intercept: $-\frac{3}{8}$

e) Slope: $\frac{1}{5}$; y-intercept: 0

f) Slope: 0; y-intercept: 3

5. **a)** $y = 7x + 16$

b) $y = -\frac{3}{8}x + 5$

c) $y = \frac{7}{16}x - 3$

d) $y = -\frac{6}{5}x - 8$

e) $y = -\frac{5}{12}x$

6. Sketches may vary. For example:

a)

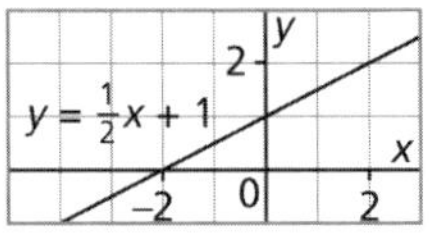

b)

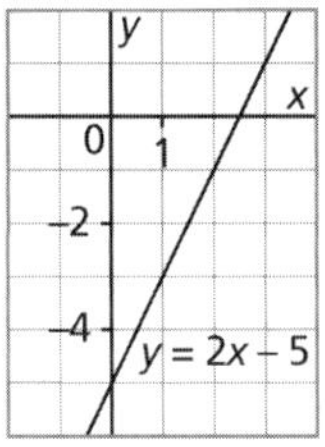

c)

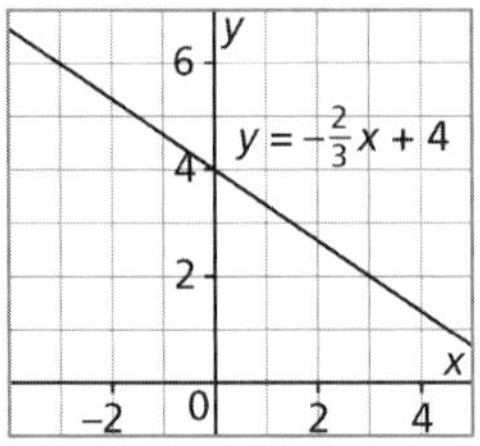

d)

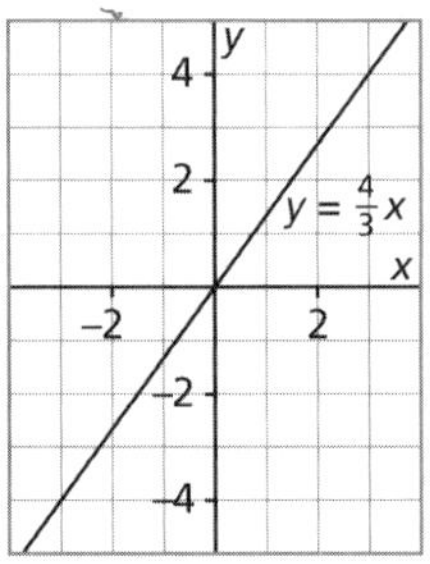

7. **a)**

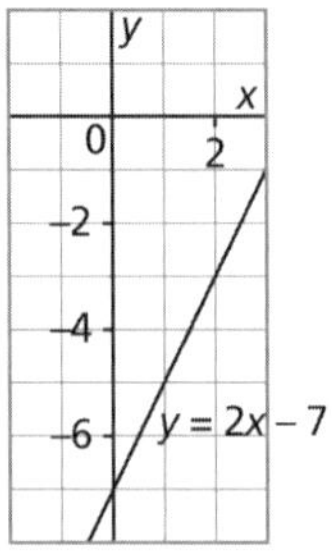

b)

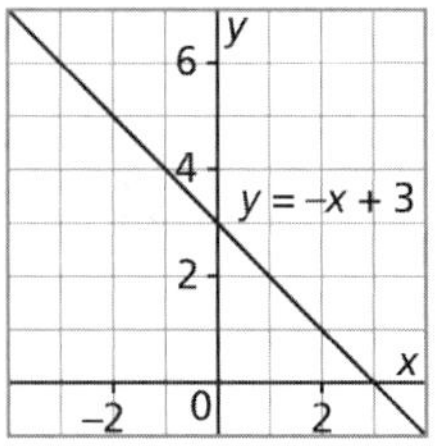

c)

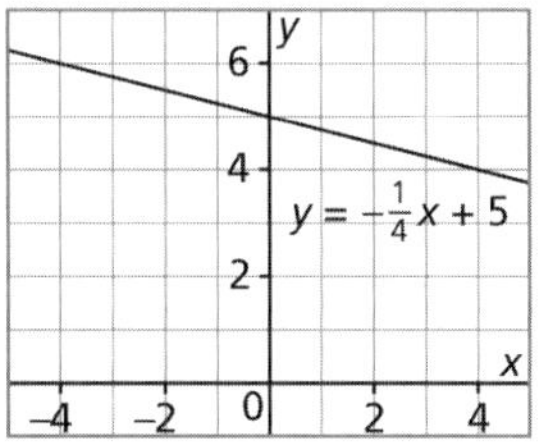

d)

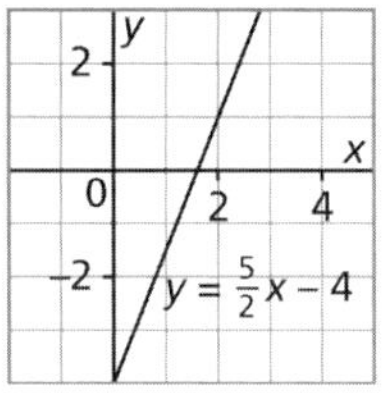

e)

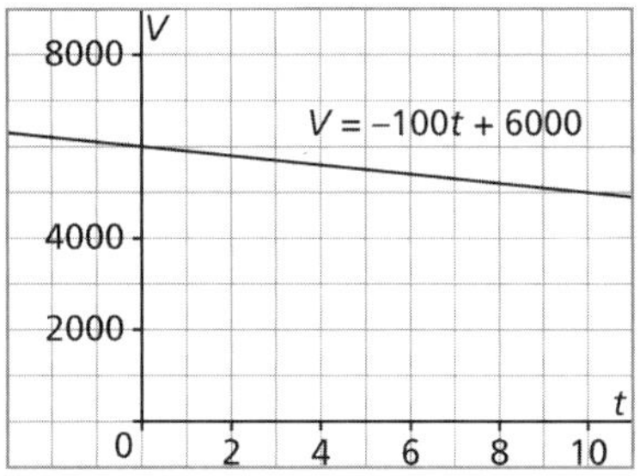

f)

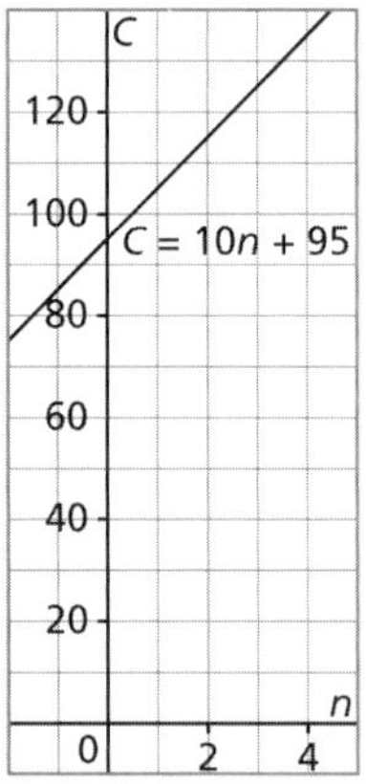

8. **a)** $C = 50t + 80$ **b)** $C = 40t + 100$

9. $F = 0.02d + 3.50$

10. a)

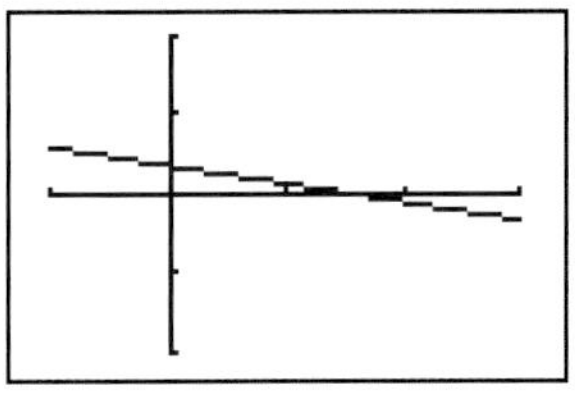

b)

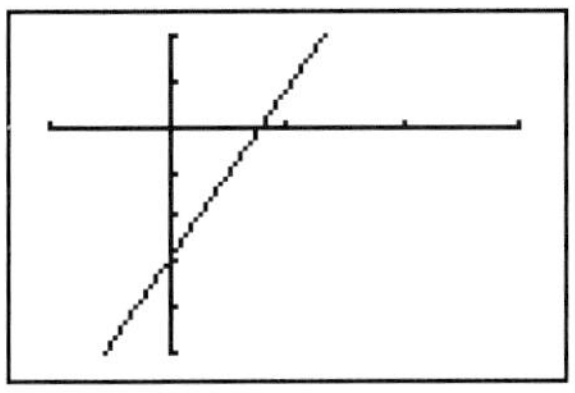

c)

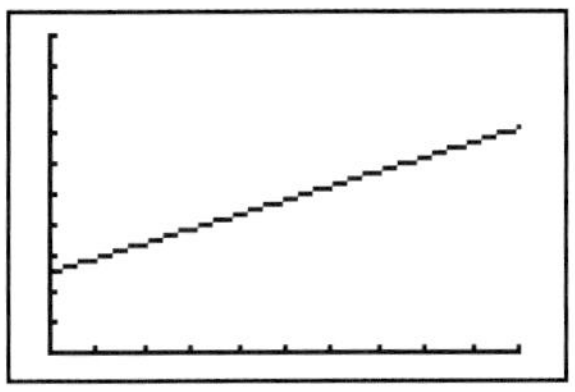

d)

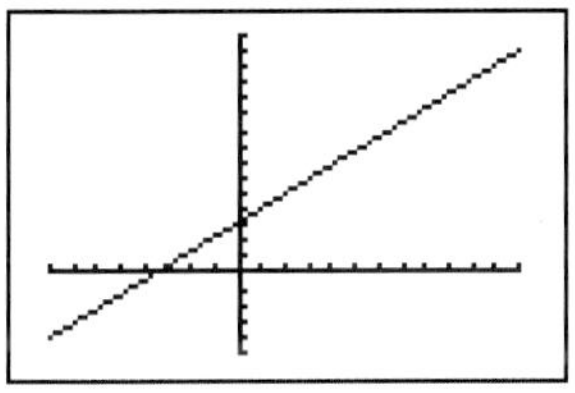

11. a) The student may have confused the values of the slope and the y-intercept.

b) $y = 4x - 3$

12. a) i) Slope: $-\frac{1}{2}$; y-intercept: 2

ii) $y = -\frac{1}{2}x + 2$

iii) $y = -3$

b) i) Slope: 4; y-intercept: –6

ii) $y = 4x - 6$

iii) $y = 34$

c) i) Slope: $\frac{3}{4}$; y-intercept: 1

ii) $y = \frac{3}{4}x + 1$

iii) $y = 8.5$

d) i) Slope: $-\frac{1}{3}$; y-intercept: –2

ii) $y = -\frac{1}{3}x - 2$

iii) $y = -\frac{16}{3}$, or $-5\frac{1}{3}$

13. a) Slope: –80; the plane is descending at a speed of 80 m/min. h-intercept: 900; when the plane begins its descent, it is 900 m above the lake.

b) $h = -80t + 900$

c) 460 m

d) i) The graph would be a line joining (0, 700) and (8, 0).

ii) $h = -87.5t + 700$

14. a) $C = 0.80n + 20$

b) \$107.20

c) 125 songs

16. a) $E = 0.05t + 34$

b) \$54

c) \$600

17. a) $y = 4x + 1$

b) $y = \frac{2}{3}x - 1$

c) $y = -\frac{5}{3}x - 7$

18. a) Graph C **b)** Graph A

c) Graph D **d)** Graph B

19. a) Graph C **b)** Graph D

c) Graph B **d)** Graph A

20. a) Graph B **b)** Graph C

c) Graph D **d)** Graph A

21. Parallel lines:

$y = -5x - 7$ and $y = -5x + 13$;

$y = 5x + 15$ and $y = 5x + 24$;

$y = \frac{1}{5}x + 9$ and $y = \frac{1}{5}x + 21$;

$y = -\frac{1}{5}x + 15$ and $y = -\frac{1}{5}x$

Perpendicular lines:

$y = -5x - 7$ and $y = \frac{1}{5}x + 9$;

$y = -5x - 7$ and $y = \frac{1}{5}x + 21$;

$y = -5x + 13$ and $y = \frac{1}{5}x + 9$;

$y = -5x + 13$ and $y = \frac{1}{5}x + 21$;

$y = 5x + 15$ and $y = -\frac{1}{5}x + 15$;

$y = 5x + 15$ and $y = -\frac{1}{5}x$;

$y = 5x + 24$ and $y = -\frac{1}{5}x + 15$;

$y = 5x + 24$ and $y = -\frac{1}{5}x$

22. $y = -\frac{4}{3}x + 4$

23. $c = -\frac{38}{3}$, or $-12\frac{2}{3}$

24. $m = -\frac{47}{24}$, or $-1\frac{23}{24}$

6.5 Slope-Point Form of the Equation for a Linear Function, page 372

4. Coordinates may vary. For example:

a) Slope: –4; (1, 5)
b) Slope: 3; (8, –7)
c) Slope: 1; (–15, –11)
d) Slope: 5; (2, 0)
e) Slope: $\frac{4}{7}$; (–3, –6)
f) Slope: $-\frac{8}{5}$; (–16, 21)

5. a) $y-2=-5(x+4)$
b) $y+8=7(x-6)$
c) $y+5=-\frac{3}{4}(x-7)$
d) $y+8=0$, or $y=-8$

6. a)

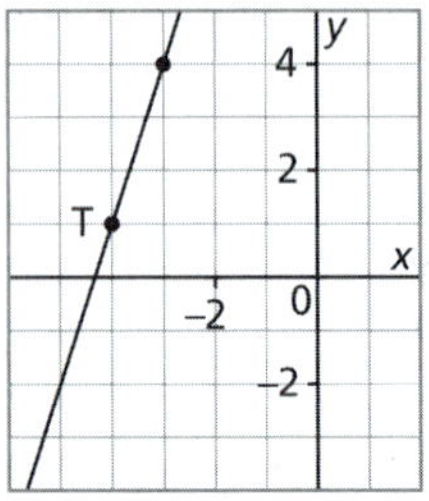

b)

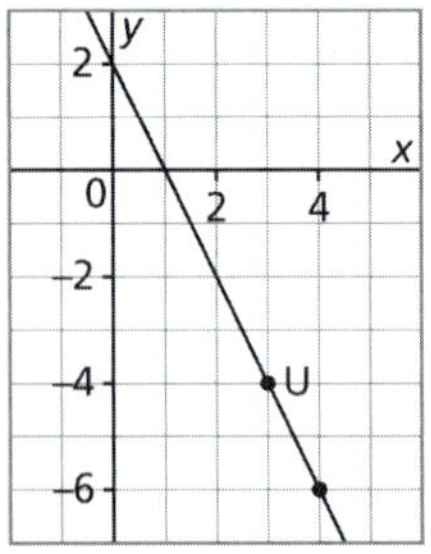

c)

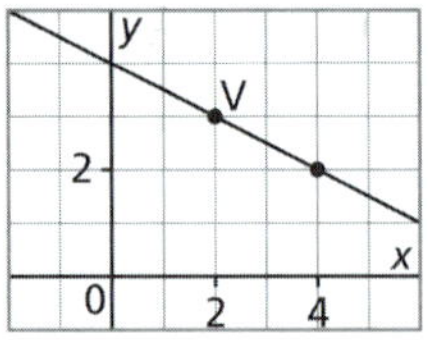

d)

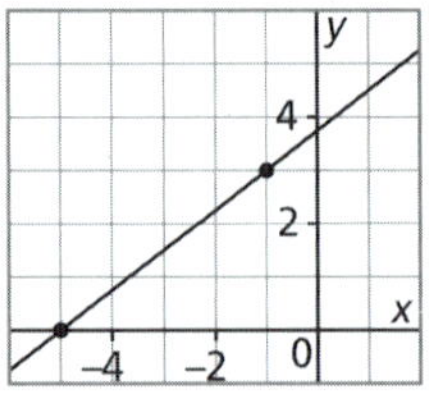

7. a) The graph is a line through (4, –2) with slope –3.

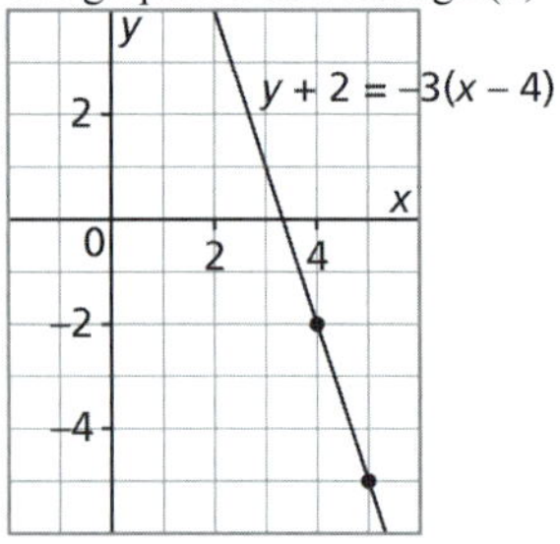

b) The graph is a line through (–3, –4) with slope 2.

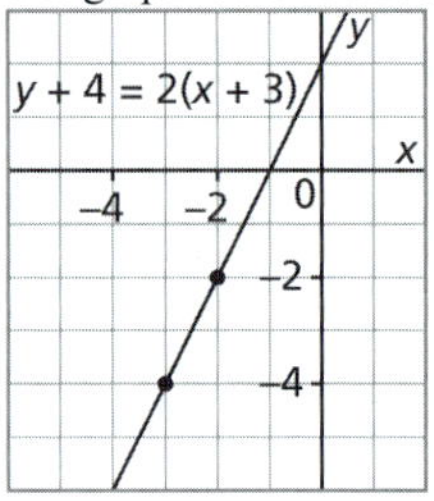

c) The graph is a line through (–5, 3) with slope 1.

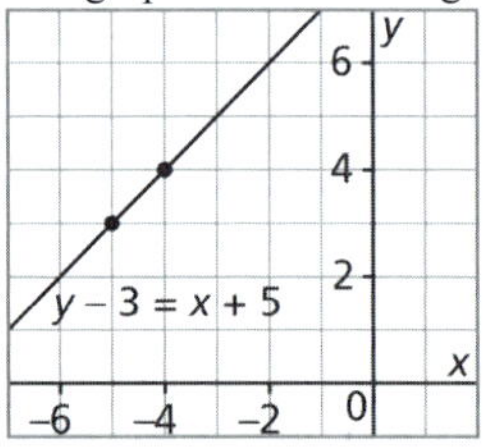

d) The graph is a line through (2, 0) with slope –1.

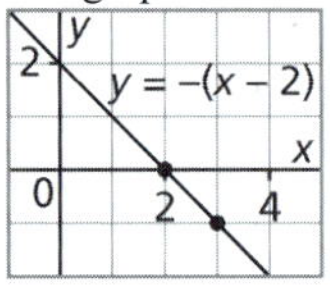

9. Equations may be written in different forms.

a) i) $y-4=-\frac{4}{3}(x+2)$ **ii)** $y-3=\frac{2}{5}(x-3)$

iii) $y+2=\frac{1}{3}(x+4)$ **iv)** $y+2=-\frac{5}{2}(x-1)$

b) i) $y=-\frac{4}{3}x+\frac{4}{3}$; x-intercept: 1; y-intercept: $\frac{4}{3}$

ii) $y=\frac{2}{5}x+\frac{9}{5}$; x-intercept: $-\frac{9}{2}$, or -4.5;
y-intercept: $\frac{9}{5}$

iii) $y=\frac{1}{3}x-\frac{2}{3}$; x-intercept: 2; y-intercept: $-\frac{2}{3}$

iv) $y=-\frac{5}{2}x+\frac{1}{2}$; x-intercept: $\frac{1}{5}$, or 0.2;
y-intercept: $\frac{1}{2}$, or 0.5

10. Different variables may be used.

a) Let s represent the speed of sound and t represent the air temperature: $s - 337 = 0.6(t - 10)$

b) 331 m/s

11. Slope-point forms of equations may vary. For example:

a) $y - 1 = 2(x - 1)$, or $y + 5 = 2(x + 2)$; $y = 2x - 1$

b) $y + 2 = -(x - 5)$, or $y - 7 = -(x + 4)$; $y = -x + 3$

c) $y - 8 = 3(x - 2)$, or $y + 7 = 3(x + 3)$; $y = 3x + 2$

d) $y + 5 = -2(x + 5)$, or $y + 1 = -2(x + 7)$; $y = -2x - 15$

12. a) Graph C: slope 2 and y-intercept –5

b) Graph A: slope 1 and y-intercept 1

c) Graph B: slope 2 and y-intercept 5

d) Graph D: slope –1 and y-intercept –5

13. The graphs are parallel. The graph of $y - y_1 = m(x - x_1)$ passes through the point $P(x_1, y_1)$, and the graph of $y + y_1 = m(x + x_1)$ passes through the point $Q(-x_1, -y_1)$.

14. a) $y - 2 = 2(x + 1)$

b) $y - 2 = \frac{1}{3}(x - 1)$

c) $y - 1 = -\frac{2}{3}(x - 2)$

15. Graphs may also be produced on a computer with graphing software. Graphs may show different windows.

a)

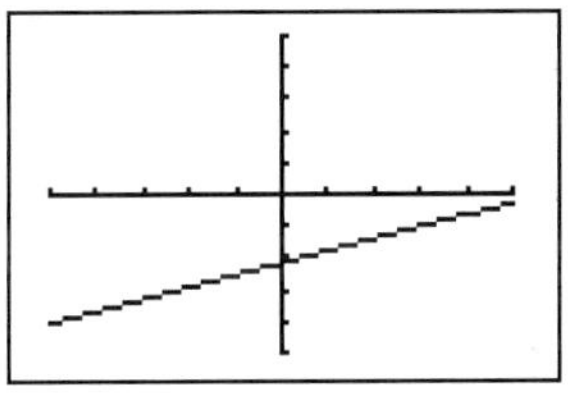

b)

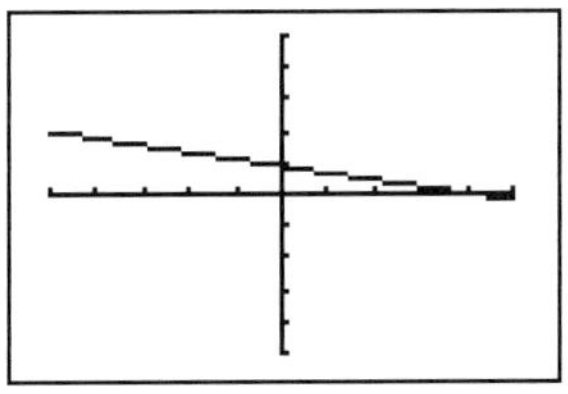

c)

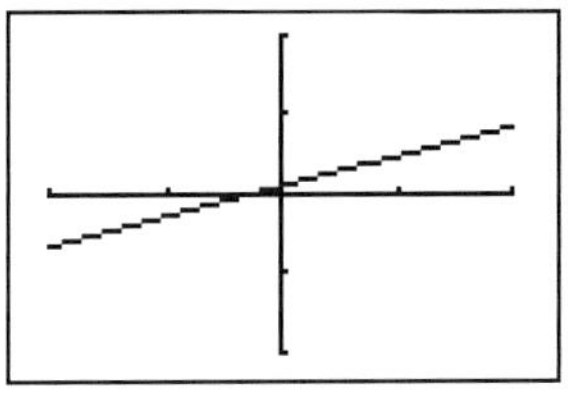

d)

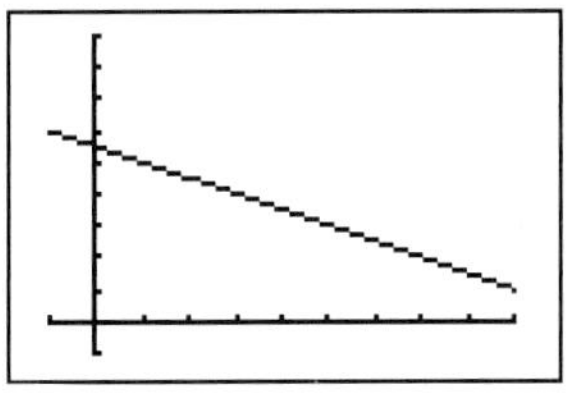

16. a) 1.26 g/mL; For every 1 mL of liquid that is poured into the cylinder, the mass of the cylinder and the liquid increases by 1.26 g.

b) Variables and form of the equation may vary. For example: Let v millilitres represent the volume of the liquid, and M grams represent the mass of the cylinder and liquid; $M - 51.5 = 1.26(v - 20)$

c) 64.1 g

d) 26.3 g

17. a) Variables and form of the equation may vary. For example: Let M represent the mass of potash in millions of tonnes, and t represent the time in years since 2005; $M = 0.6t + 8.2$

b) 11.2 million tonnes; 14.2 million tonnes; Assumption: I assume that the relation continues for times beyond 2007 and remains linear.

18. a) Variables and form of the equation may vary. For example: Let p represent the number of students enrolled in francophone schools, and t represent the time, in years, since 2001; $p - 3470 = 198(t - 2)$

b) Approximately 3866 students

19. a) –2 **b)** $y - 11 = -2(x + 3)$

c) $y + 3 = -2(x - 4)$

20. a) i) $y + 3 = -\frac{4}{3}(x + 5)$

ii) $y + 3 = \frac{3}{4}(x + 5)$

21. a) $y + 2 = 2(x - 1)$ **b)** $y + 2 = -\frac{1}{2}(x - 1)$

22. a) $y - 6 = -\frac{5}{2}(x - 2)$ **b)** $y - 6 = \frac{2}{5}(x - 2)$

23. a) $y = \frac{3}{5}(x - 4)$

b) $y + 1 = -\frac{1}{2}(x - 4)$

24. Form of the equation may vary.

$y = -\frac{9}{2}x + \frac{37}{9}$

25. Form of the equation may vary.

$y + 5 = \frac{3}{5}(x + 2)$

Chapter 6: Checkpoint 2, page 376

1. Screens may vary.

a)

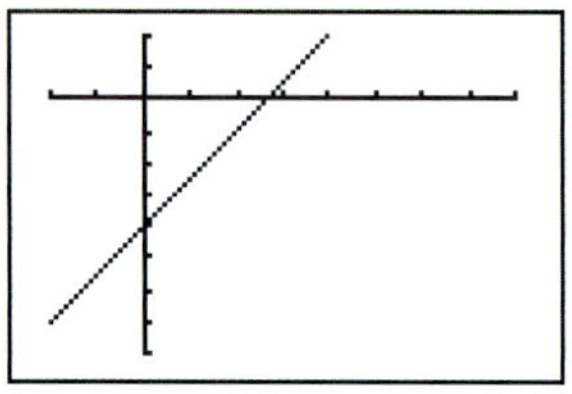

b) Increase the value of m to get a line with a greater slope. Decrease the value of m to get a line with a lesser slope.

c) Increase the value of b to get a line with a greater y-intercept. Decrease the value of b to get a line with a lesser y-intercept.

2. a) Slope: 25; d-intercept: 10; 25 km/h is Eric's average speed; d-intercept: 10 km is Eric's distance from home at the start of his ride.

b) $d = 25t + 10$

c) i) 66.25 km

ii) 1.4 h, or 1 h 24 min

3. a)

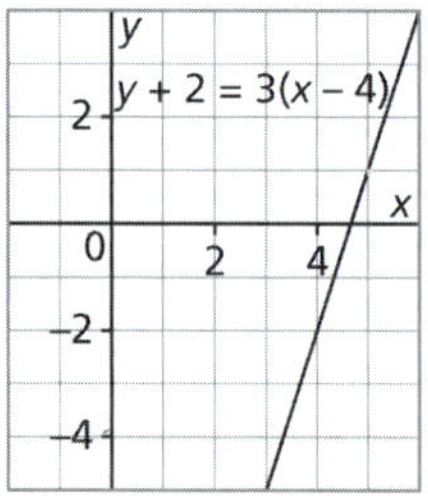

b)

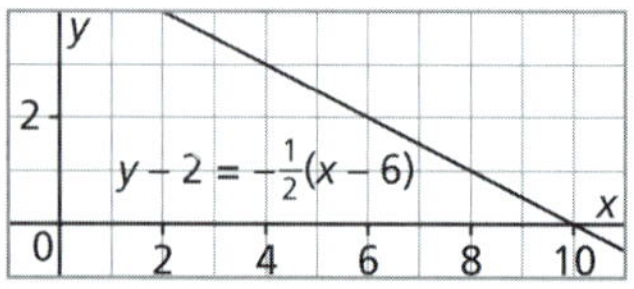

c)

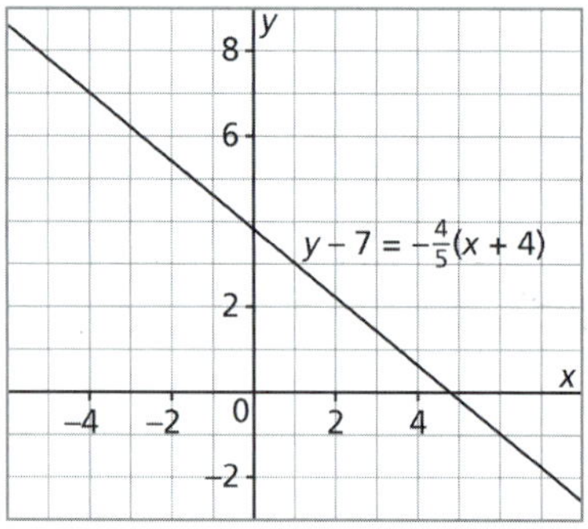

d)

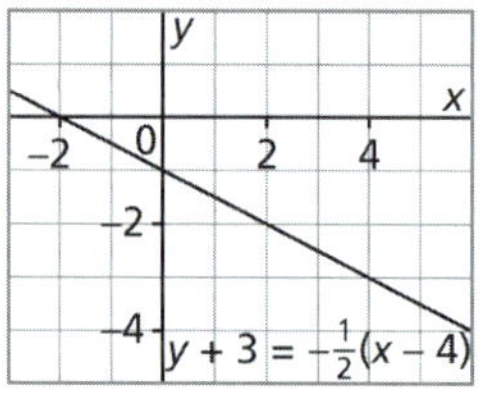

e)

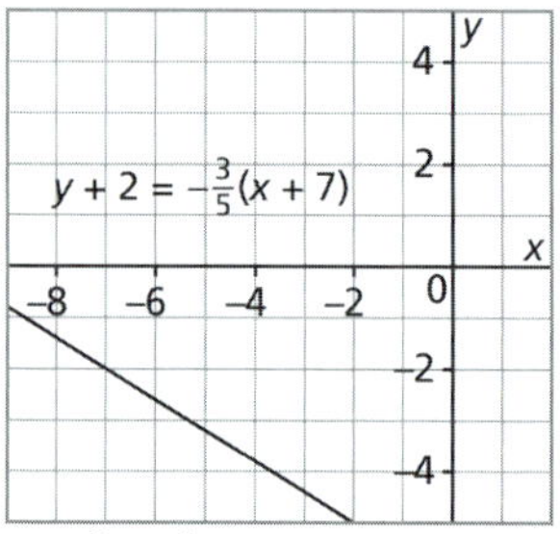

4. a) $y = 2x + 3$

b) Equations may have different forms. For example: $y - 5 = 2(x - 1)$

6.6 General Form of the Equation for a Linear Relation, page 384

4. a) Standard form

b) General form

c) Slope-intercept form

d) Slope-point form

5. a) x-intercept: 3; y-intercept: –8

b) x-intercept: 8; y-intercept: 7

c) x-intercept: 22; y-intercept: –8

d) x-intercept: 13.5; y-intercept: –3

6. a) $4x + 3y - 36 = 0$

b) $2x - y - 7 = 0$

c) $2x + y - 6 = 0$

d) $5x - y - 1 = 0$

7. a)

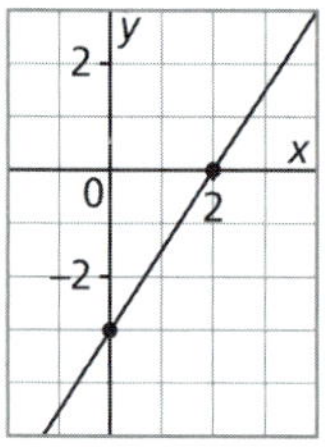

b)

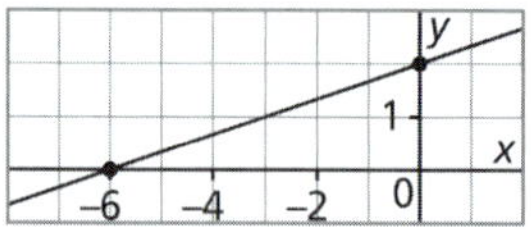

8. a) **i)** The coefficient of x is negative.

ii) Neither side of the equation is 0.

iii) The coefficient of x is not a whole number.

iv) The x-term should come before the y-term.

b) **i)** $2x - 3y - 42 = 0$

ii) $5x - 4y + 100 = 0$

iii) $x - y + 2 = 0$

iv) $9x + 5y - 20 = 0$

9. a) **i)** x-intercept: 8; y-intercept: –6

ii)

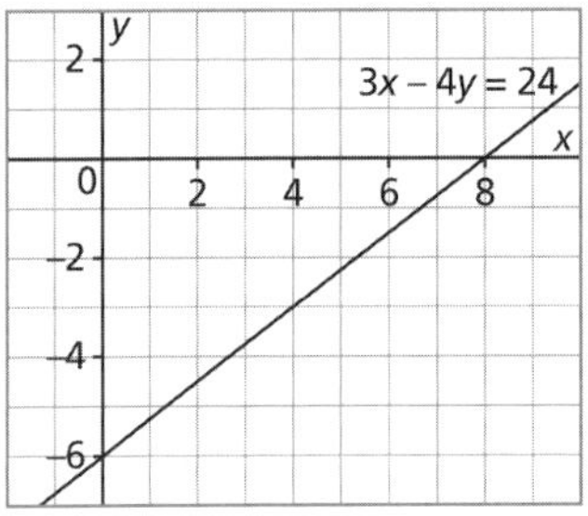

b) **i)** x-intercept: –10; y-intercept: 12

ii)

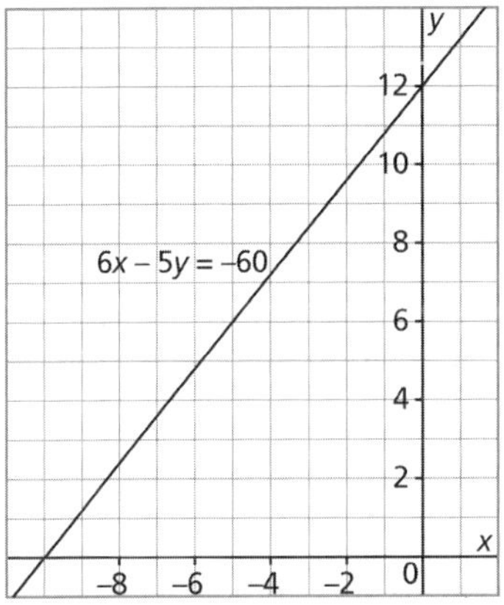

c) **i)** x-intercept: 8; y-intercept: –12

ii)

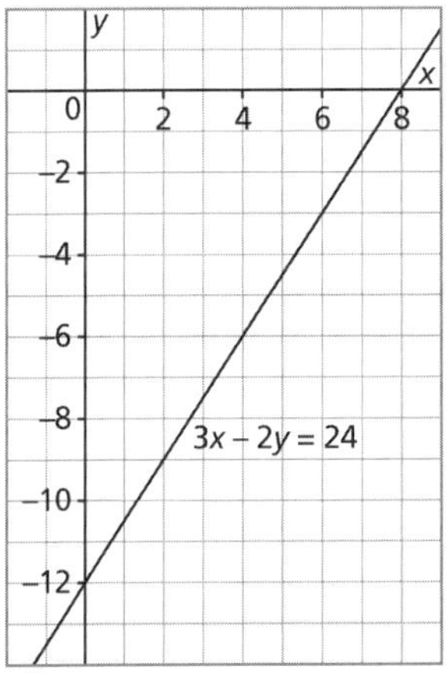

d) **i)** x-intercept: 2; y-intercept: –10

ii)

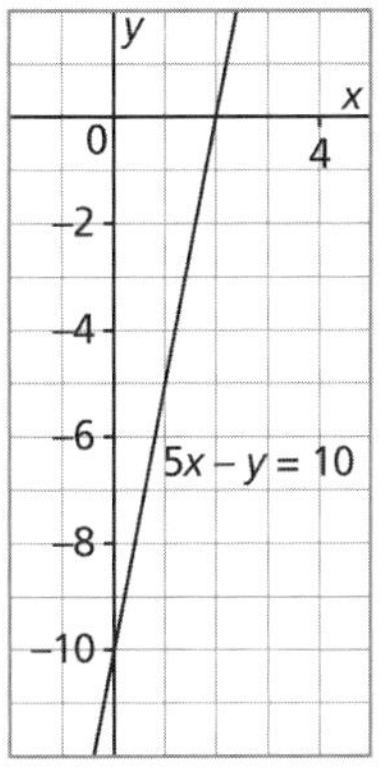

10. b)

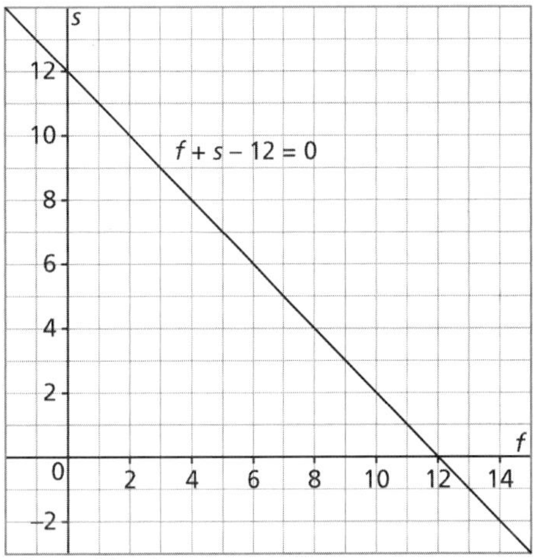

c) $f + s - 12 = 0$

d) Pairs of integers may vary. For example: 0 and 12; 5 and 7; 3 and 9; 13 and –1; 14 and –2; 15 and –3

11. a), b) Letters for the variables may differ.

Let s represent a small pan, and l represent a large pan.

$12s + 36l = 504$

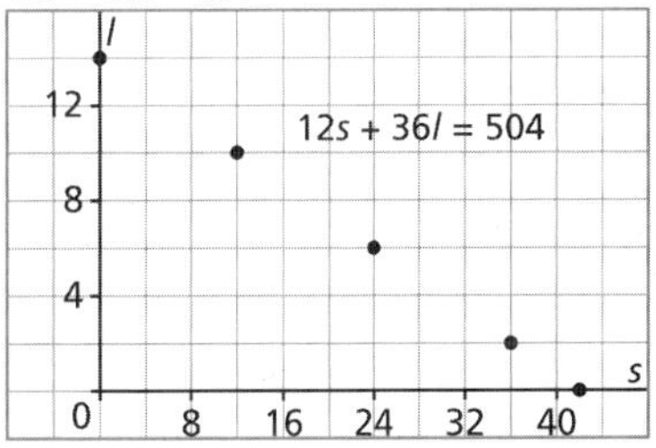

12. a) $y = -\frac{4}{3}x + 8$

b) $y = \frac{3}{8}x + \frac{3}{2}$

c) $y = \frac{2}{5}x - 3$

d) $y = -\frac{7}{3}x - \frac{10}{3}$

13. a) –4

b) 3

c) 5

d) –5

14. a)

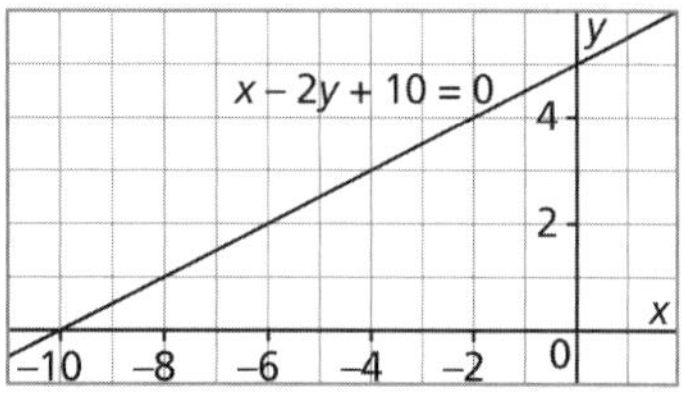

b)

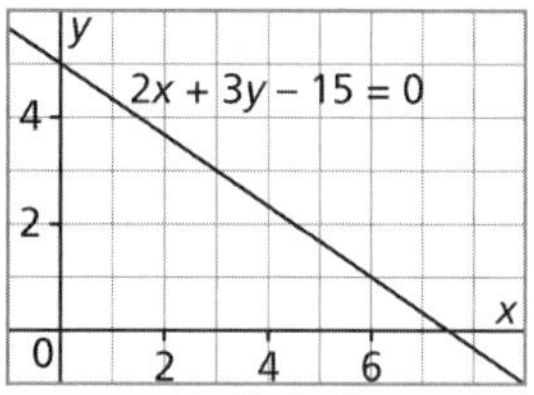

c)

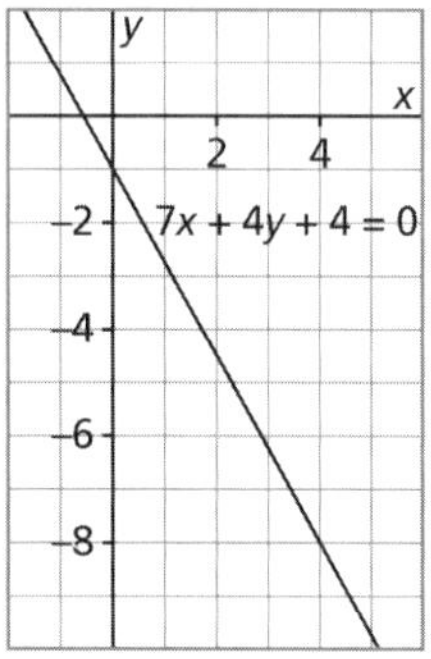

d)

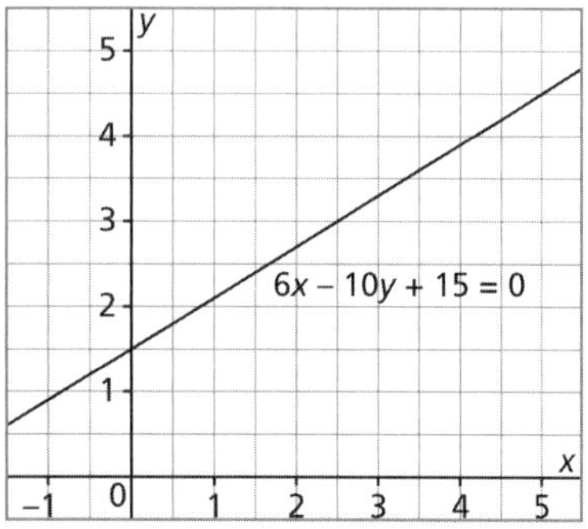

15. a) 9 pieces of 8-ft. pipe

b) 12 pieces of 6-ft. pipe

c) No; 9.75 pieces of 8-ft. pipe would be needed

d) No; $10\frac{2}{3}$ pieces of 6-ft. pipe would be needed

16. Graphs may have variables on different axes; and variables may be different. Let *l* represent the number of loonies and *t* represent the number of toonies.

b), c) $2t + l = 24$

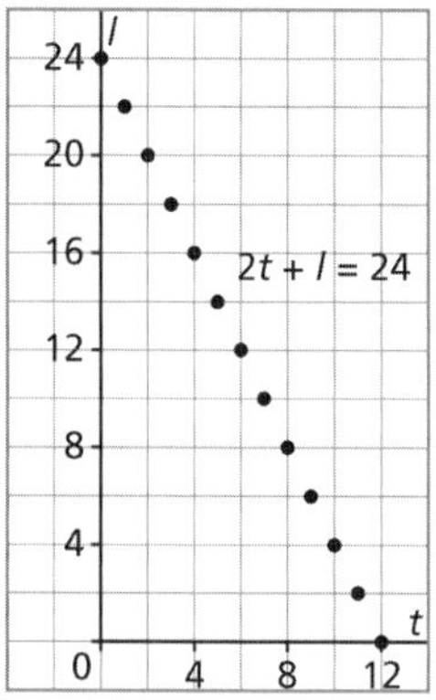

d) i) No

ii) No

17. Screens may vary.

a)

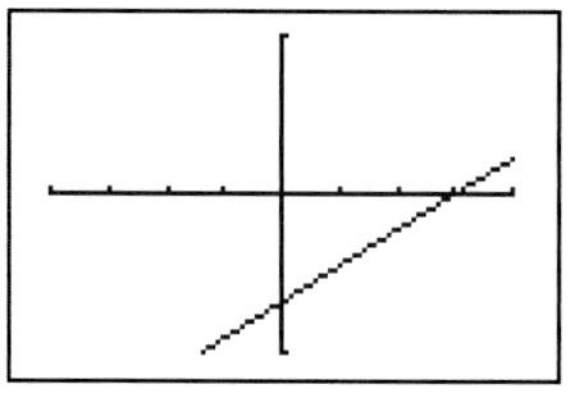

b)

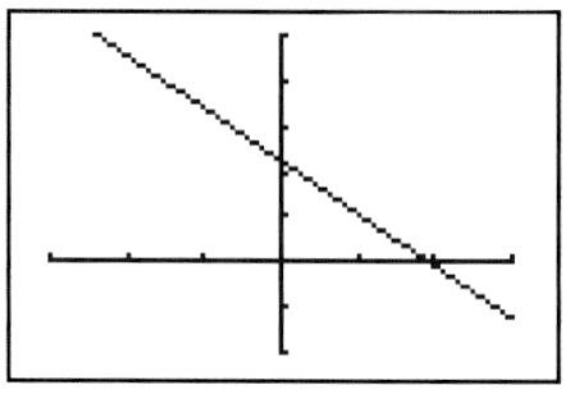

c)

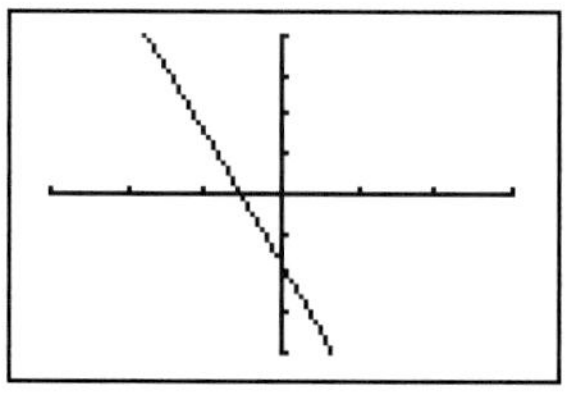

d)

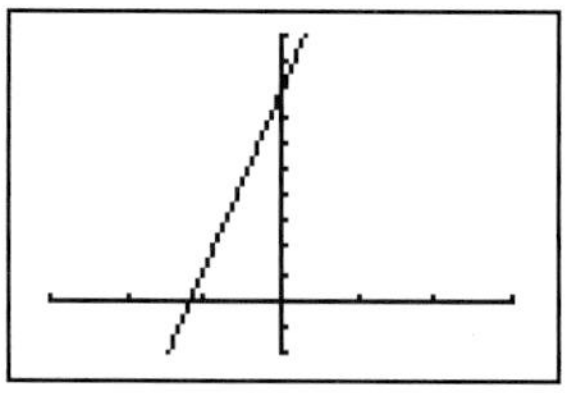

18. a) $x - 3y - 12 = 0$

b) $x - 3y + 11 = 0$

c) $x + 4y + 11 = 0$

d) $9x + 6y - 8 = 0$

19. Forms of the equations may vary. For example:

a) $y = \frac{1}{3}x - 4$; $x - 3y - 12 = 0$; $y + 3 = \frac{1}{3}(x - 3)$

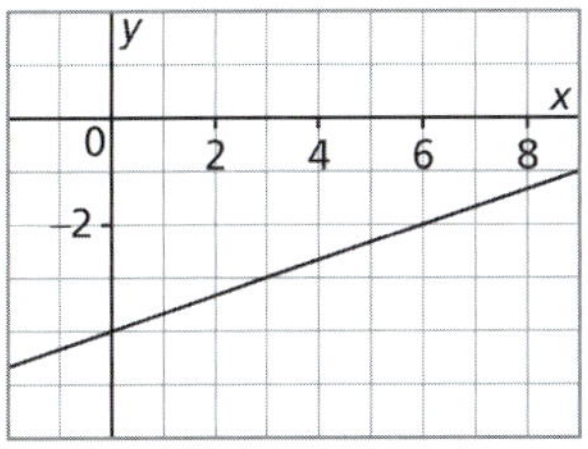

b) $y - 2 = \frac{1}{3}(x + 5)$; $x - 3y + 11 = 0$; $y = \frac{1}{3}x + \frac{11}{3}$

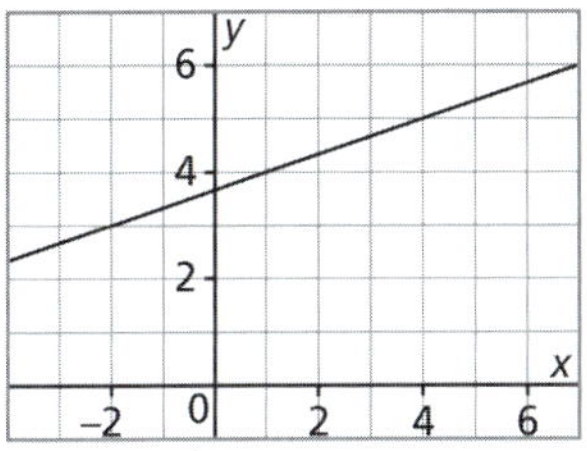

c) $y + 3 = -\frac{1}{4}(x - 1)$; $x + 4y + 11 = 0$; $y = -\frac{1}{4}x - \frac{11}{4}$

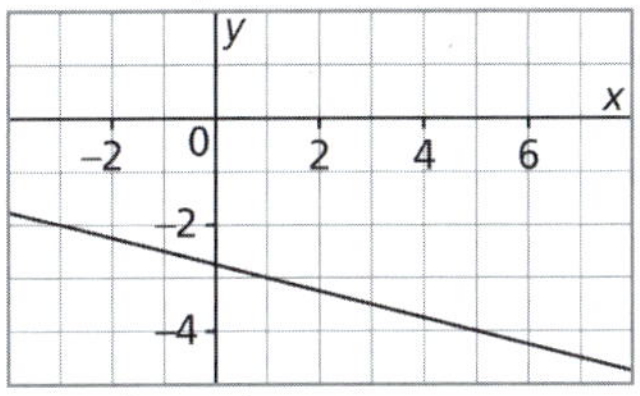

d) $y = -\frac{3}{2}x + \frac{4}{3}$; $9x + 6y - 8 = 0$; $y + \frac{1}{6} = -\frac{3}{2}(x - 1)$

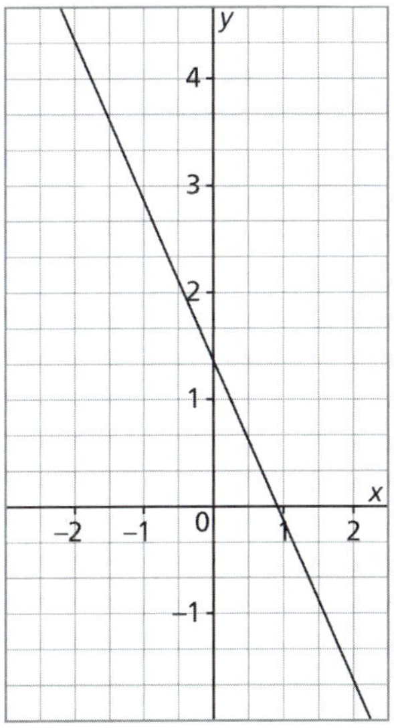

22. a) Graph B

b) Graph A

23. b)

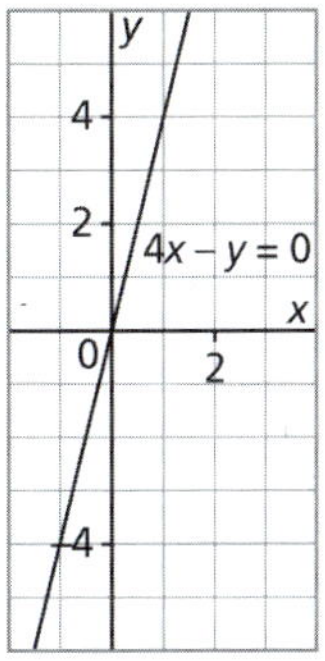

24. Equations in parts b, e, and g are equivalent.
Equations in parts d, f, and h are equivalent.

26. a) $3x + 4y - 12 = 0$; linear function

b) Not a linear function

c) Not a linear function

d) $x - 3y + 8 = 0$; linear function

28. a) $B \neq 0 : -\frac{A}{B}$

b) $B \neq 0 : -\frac{C}{B}$

Chapter 6: Review, page 388

1. a) $-\frac{2}{3}$

b) $\frac{4}{5}$

2. a) Negative

b) Negative

c) Zero

3. Sketches and coordinates may vary.

a) i)

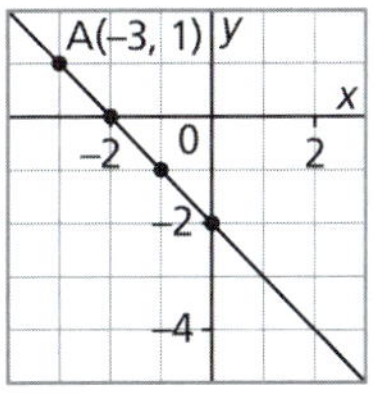

ii) (–2, 0), (–1, –1), (0, –2)

b) i)

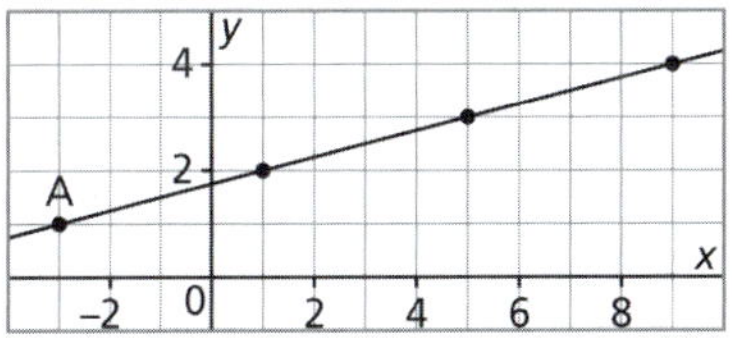

ii) (1, 2), (5, 3), (9, 4)

c) i)

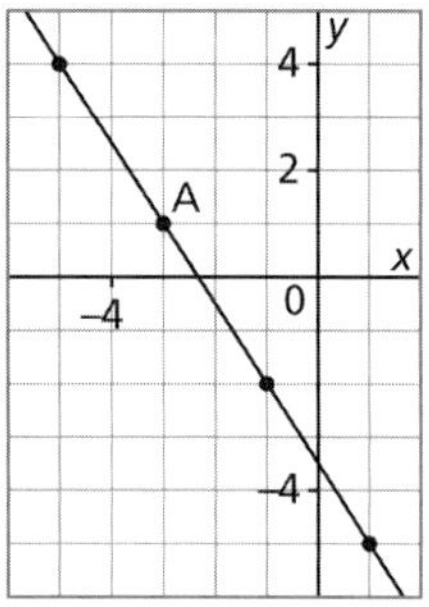

ii) (–5, 4), (–1, –2), (1, –5)

4. a) –2 **b)** $-\frac{3}{2}$

5. a) 160; for every 1 min Gabrielle jogs, she covers a distance of 160 m.

b) Slope is equal to the rate of change.

c) i) 640 m

ii) 6.25 min, or 6 min 15 s

6. a) i) 3 **ii)** $-\frac{1}{3}$

b) i) $-\frac{6}{5}$ **ii)** $\frac{5}{6}$

c) i) $\frac{11}{8}$ **ii)** $-\frac{8}{11}$

d) i) 1 **ii)** –1

7. a) Perpendicular; slope of JH: 2; slope of KM: $-\frac{1}{2}$

b) Neither; slope of NP: 3; slope of QR: –3

8. No; slope of ST: $-\frac{1}{3}$; slope of TU: 3; slope of UV: $-\frac{4}{9}$;

slope of SV: $\frac{5}{2}$

9. Yes; The slopes of AB and BC are negative reciprocals, so AB and BC are perpendicular.

Slope of AB: 2; slope of BC: $-\frac{1}{2}$

11. a) Slope: –3; y-intercept: 4

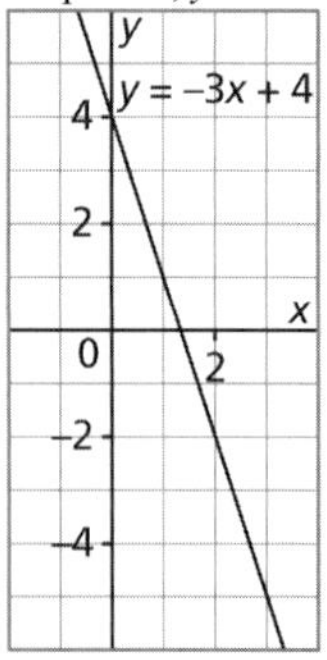

b) Slope: $\frac{3}{4}$; y-intercept: –2

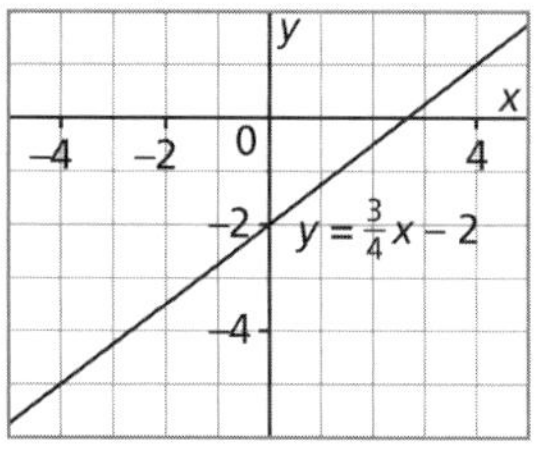

12. a) i) Slope: $\frac{5}{3}$; y-intercept: 1

ii) $y = \frac{5}{3}x + 1$

b) i) Slope: $-\frac{3}{2}$; y-intercept: –1

ii) $y = -\frac{3}{2}x - 1$

13. a) Graph C

b) Graph D

c) Graph A

d) Graph B

14. a) $A = 15w + 40$

b) 21 weeks

c) The slope would represent the amount Mason saved each week: $15; the vertical intercept would represent the amount in his bank account when he started saving: $40

15. Equations may vary. For example:

a) $y = \frac{4}{7}x + 1$ and $y = \frac{4}{7}x - 10$

b) $y = -\frac{7}{4}x + 1$ and $y = -\frac{7}{4}x - 10$

16. $y - 3 = -\frac{1}{2}(x + 2)$

17. Coordinates and forms of the equation may vary.

a) i) 2; (–3, –4)

ii)

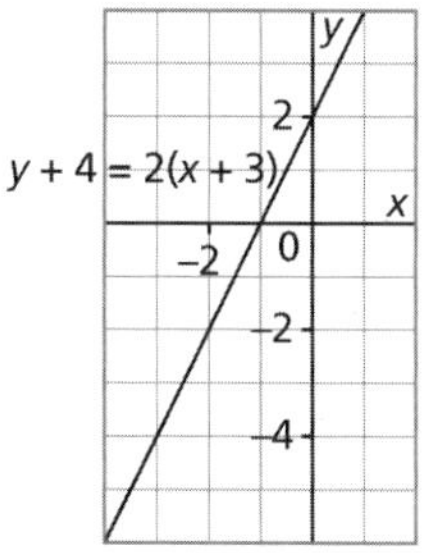

iii) $y + 2 = 2(x + 2)$

b) i) $-\frac{1}{3}$; (4, 1)

ii)

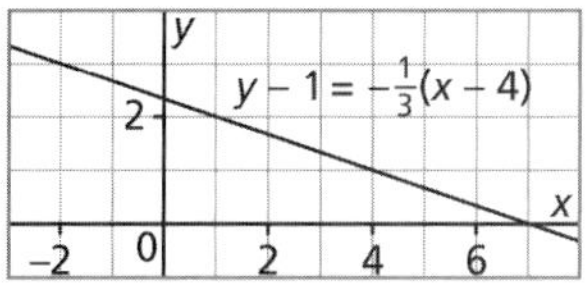

iii) $y - 2 = -\dfrac{1}{3}(x - 1)$

18. Forms of the equation may vary. For example:

a) $y = \dfrac{2}{3}(x - 2)$

b) $y - 2 = -\dfrac{3}{5}(x + 3)$

19. Forms of the equation may vary.

a) **i)** $y - 5 = 3(x - 1)$ or $y + 7 = 3(x + 3)$

ii) $y + 1 = -\dfrac{1}{2}(x - 5)$ or $y - 3 = -\dfrac{1}{2}(x + 3)$

b) Coordinates may vary. For example:

i) (2, 8)

ii) (1, 1)

20. Variables may differ. For example:

a) Let *C* represent the cost, and *p* represent the number of people: $C = 44p$

b) $44

c) 6 people

21. b) **i)** $5x - 4y + 40 = 0$

ii) $x + 3y - 12 = 0$

iii) $x - 3y + 10 = 0$

iv) $x - 5y + 15 = 0$

22. a) **i)**

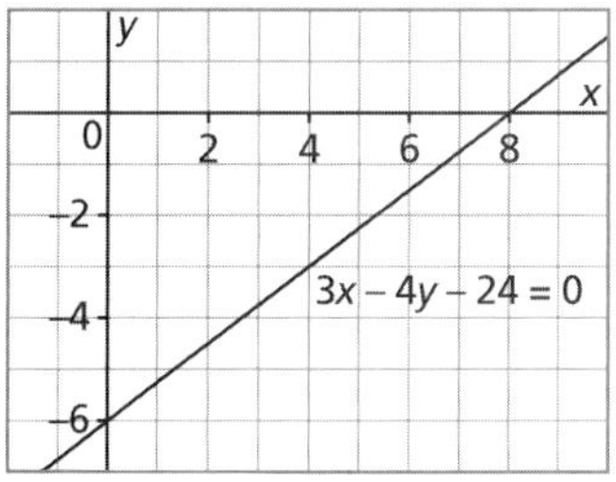

ii)

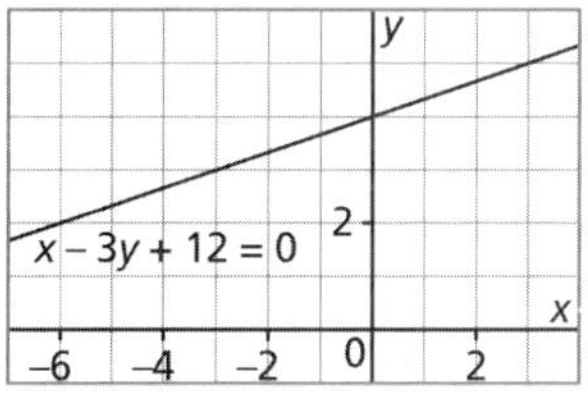

b) **i)** $\dfrac{3}{4}$ **ii)** $\dfrac{1}{3}$

24. a), b) $g - l - 6 = 0$

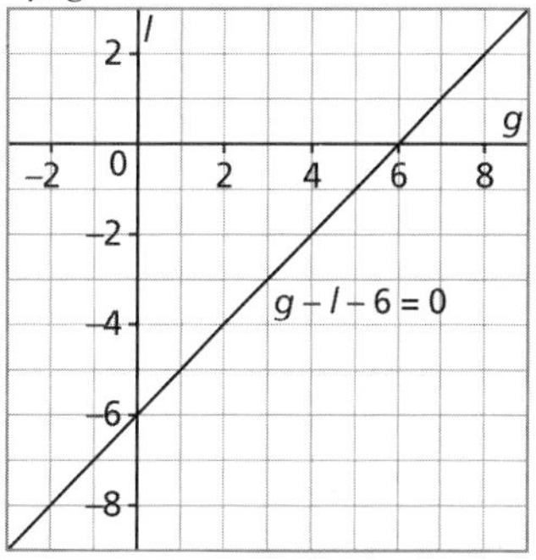

c) Pairs of integers may vary. For example: 8 and 2; 7 and 1; 6 and 0; 5 and –1; 4 and –2

25. Equations in parts a and d are equivalent. Equations in parts b and e are equivalent.

26. a) Graph B

b) Graph C

c) Graph A

27. Variables may differ. Let *a* represent the number of hours Max babysits for the first family, and *b* represent the number of hours he babysits for the second family.

a), b) $5a + 4b = 60$

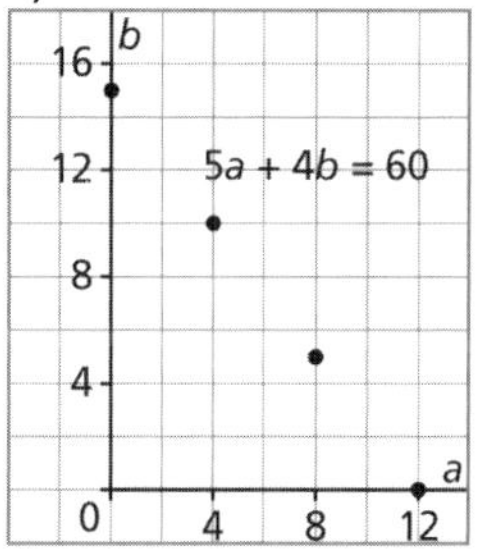

28. Variables may differ. Let *n* represent the number of new releases and *m* represent the number of old movies Kylie rents:

a) $5n + 3m = 45$

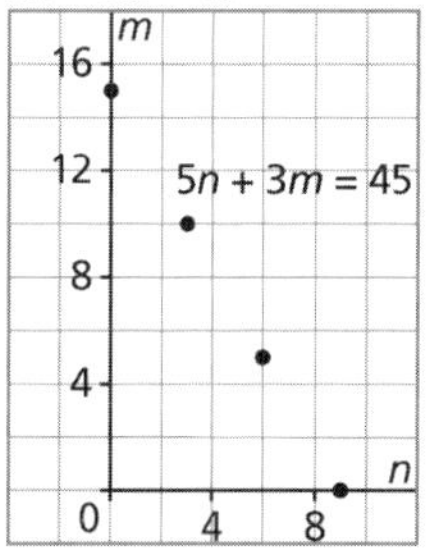

b) **i)** No

ii) Yes

Chapter 6: Practice Test, page 391

1. C

2. B

3. a) i)

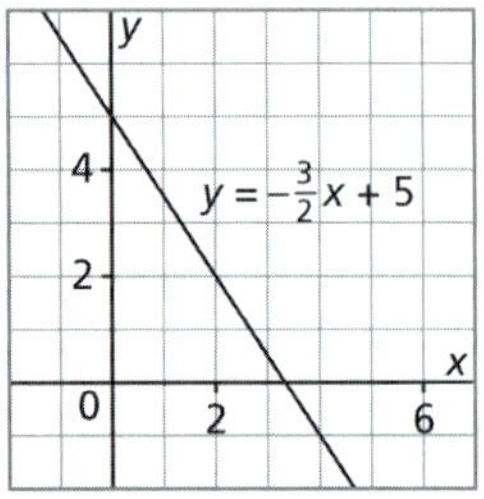

ii)

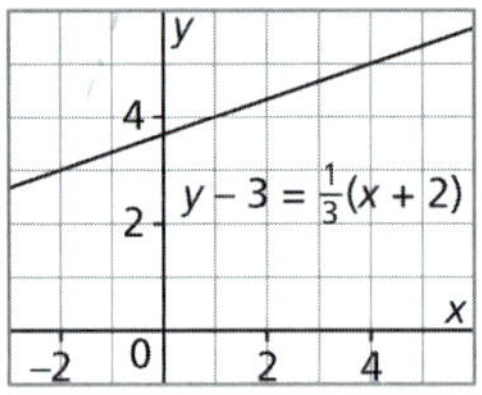

iii)

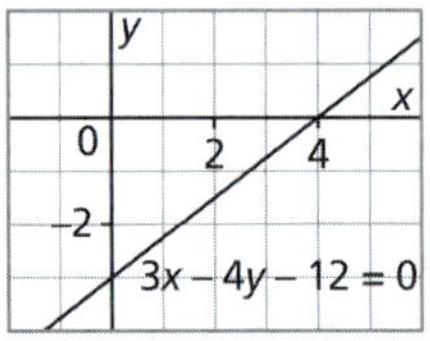

b) $y - 2 = -\frac{3}{2}(x - 6)$

c) $3x + y + 1 = 0$

d) Coordinates and equations may vary. For example:

P(8, 3) and $y = -\frac{2}{7}x + \frac{37}{7}$

4. Answers and forms of equations may vary. For example:

a) Slope-intercept form: $y = -2x - 2$

b) General form: $y + 1 = 0$

c) Slope-point form: $y - 1 = \frac{3}{4}(x - 3)$

5. a) \$6570

b) 520 people

Chapter 7 Systems of Linear Equations

7.1 Developing Systems of Linear Equations, page 401

4. d

5. c

6. a) iii; x dollars represents the cost of a jacket and y dollars represents the cost of a sweater.

b) i; x represents the length in feet and y represents the width in feet.

c) ii; x represents the number of chapatti breads sold and y represents the number of naan breads sold.

7. Variables may differ.

a) $2s + 2l = 20$ and $s + 3l = 22$

8. Variables may differ.

a) $2l + s = 24$ and $l - s = 6$

9. a) $3x + y = 17$ and $x = y + 3$

10. $x + 2y = 20$ and $x + y = 13$; Solution B

11. Variables may differ.

$w + j = 60$ and $w - j = 10$; Solution A

15. a) $\frac{C}{B} = \frac{F}{E}$

b) $\frac{C}{A} = \frac{F}{D}$

16. $x + 2y = -8$ and $9x + 10y = 0$

17. a) For example, $3x + 2y = 5$ and $-2x + 3y = 1$

18. b) $x = 3$

7.2 Solving a System of Linear Equations Graphically, page 409

3. a) $x = -4, y = 2$

b) $x = 2, y = 3$

c) $x = 1, y = -3$

d) $x = -2, y = -1$

4. a) $x = 9, y = -2$; exact

b) $x = -1\frac{3}{4}, y = 2\frac{3}{4}$; approximate

5. a) i) $x = 4, y = 3$

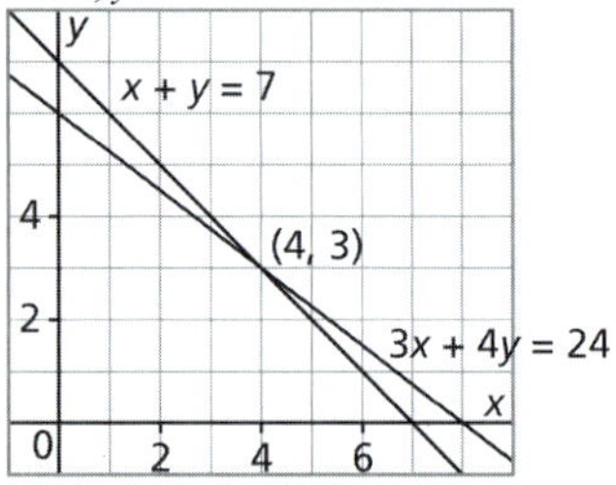

ii) $x = 2, y = 3$

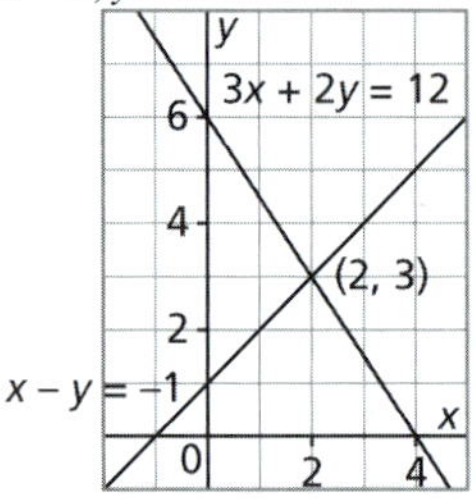

iii) $x = 6, y = -5$

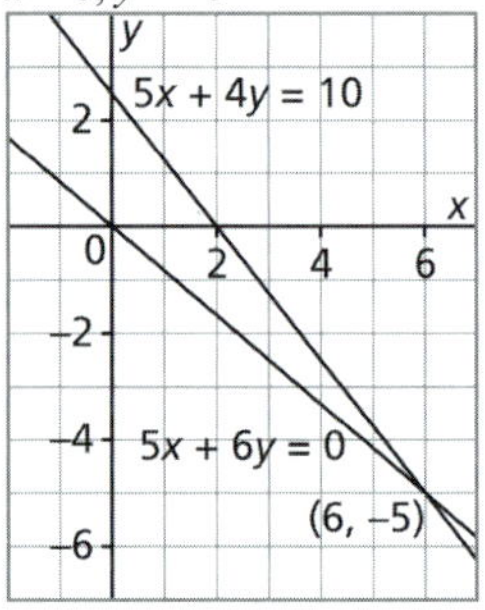

iv) $x = -3, y = 1$

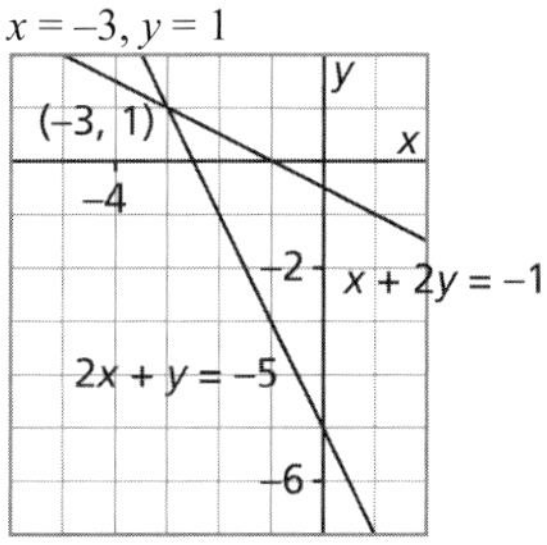

b) The coordinates of the point of intersection represent the solution of the linear system.

6. Approximate

7. Approximations may vary.

a) $x = 2.5, y = -1.5$

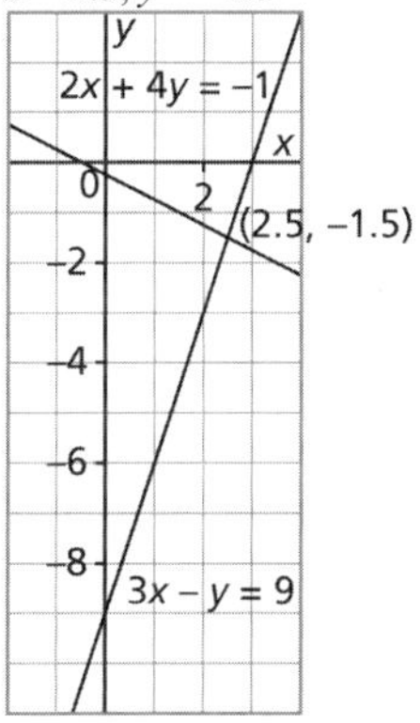

b) $x = 1.2, y = 2.2$

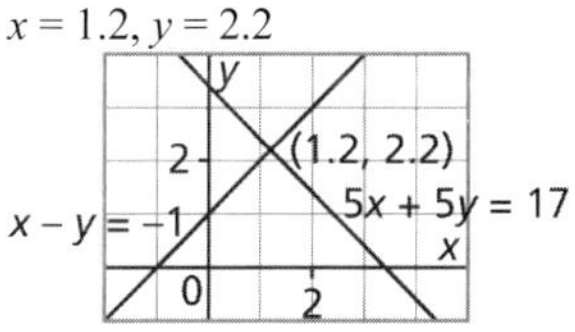

c) $x = 3.2, y = 2.5$

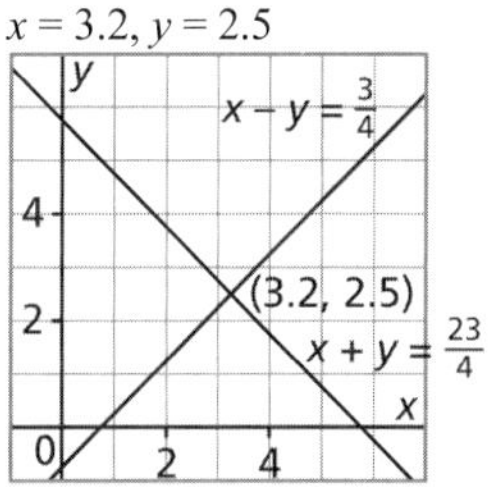

d) $x = 3.7, y = -5$

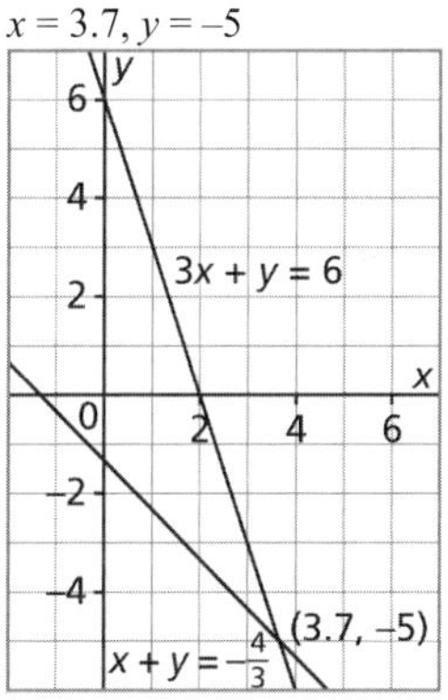

8. a)

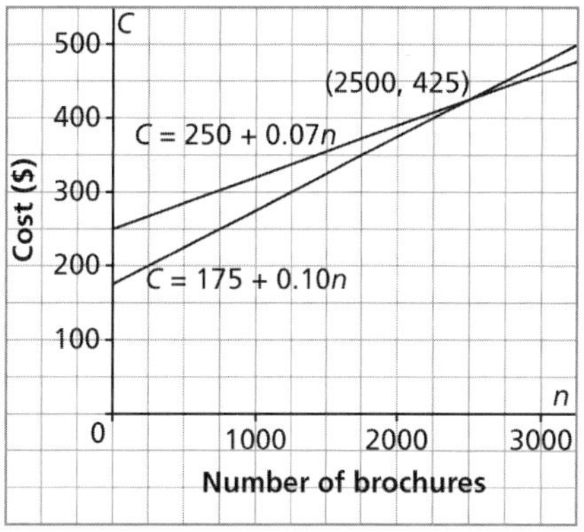

b) i) 2500 brochures

ii) It is cheaper to use Company A when fewer than 2500 brochures are printed.

9. a)

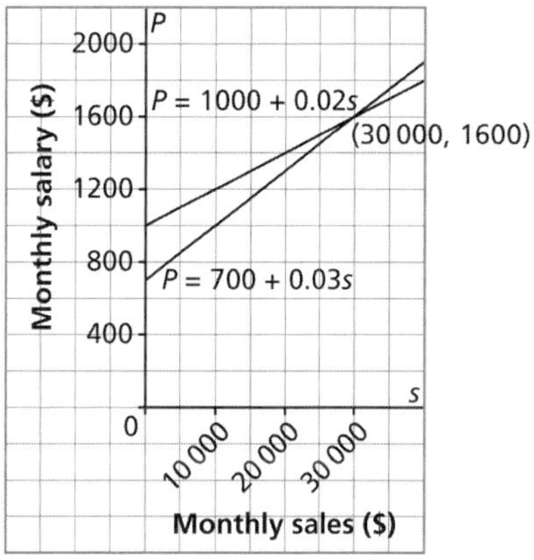

b) i) $30 000

ii) It would be better to choose Plan B when the clerk's monthly sales are less than $30 000.

10. Variables may differ. $f + r = 391$ and $f - r = 141$

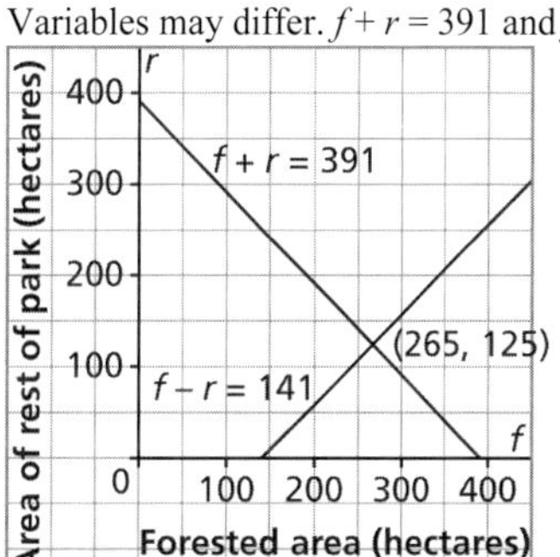

Approximations may vary. For example,
forested area: about 265 hectares;
the rest of the park: about 125 hectares; approximate

11. Variables may differ. $w - l = 43$ and $2w + l = 107$

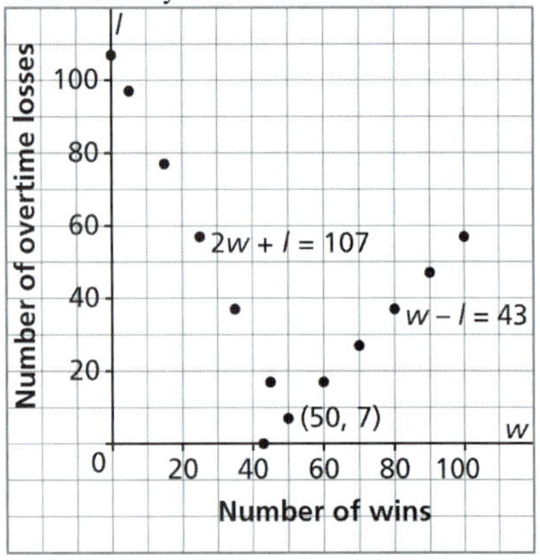

50 wins and 7 overtime losses; exact

12. Variables may differ. $f + t = 115$ and $5f + 10t = 800$

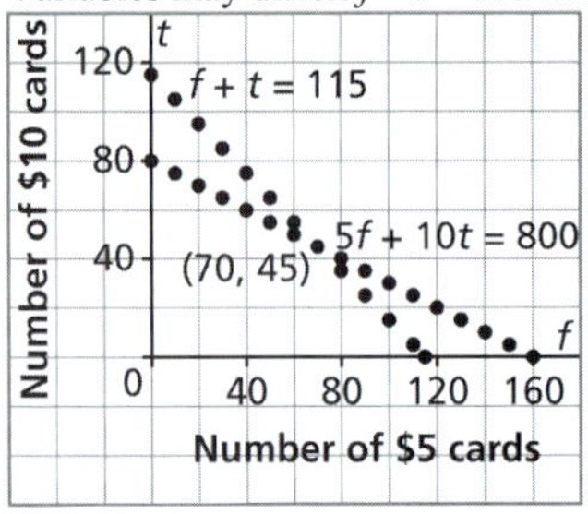

Seventy $5 gift cards and forty-five $10 gift cards; exact

13. Variables may differ.

$4.8s + 8.0a = 152$ and $s - a = 13$

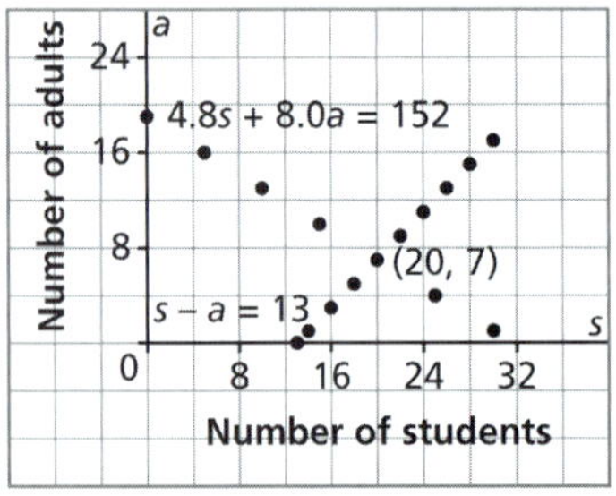

7 adults and 20 students; exact

14. Variables may differ.

a) $b + 36g = 1806$ and $b + 24g = 1254$

b)

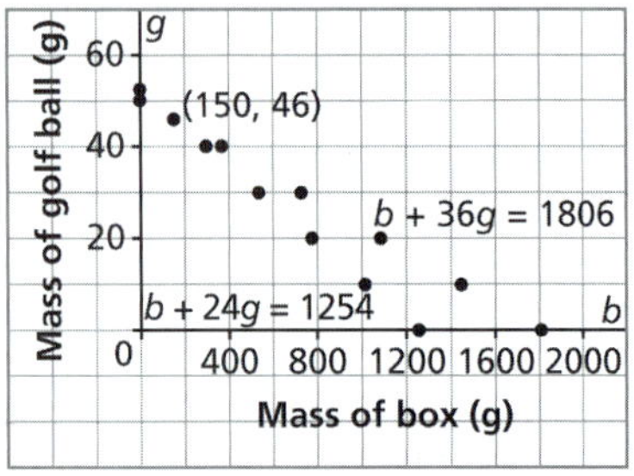

Approximations may vary. For example, mass of box: 150 g; mass of one golf ball: 46 g; approximate

15. $x = 8\frac{1}{2}$ in. and $y = 12$ in.

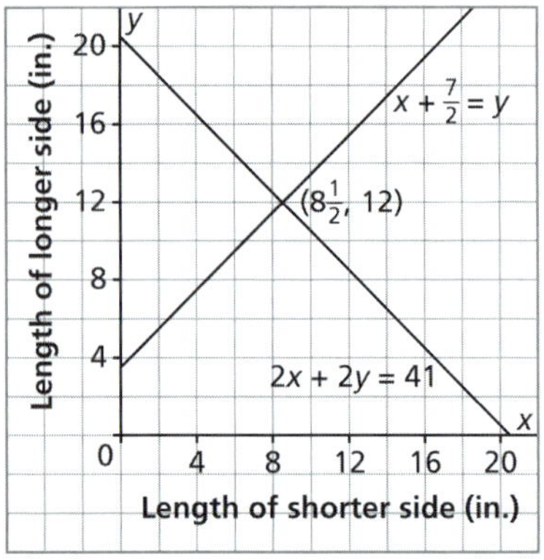

16. a) For example, $x = 1.8$ and $y = -0.1$; approximate

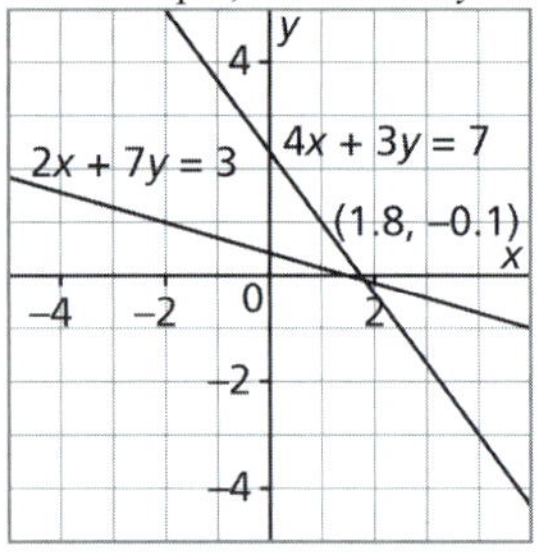

17. a) For example, $y = -x + 5$ and $y = -\frac{3}{2}x + 6$

b) $x = 2$ and $y = 3$

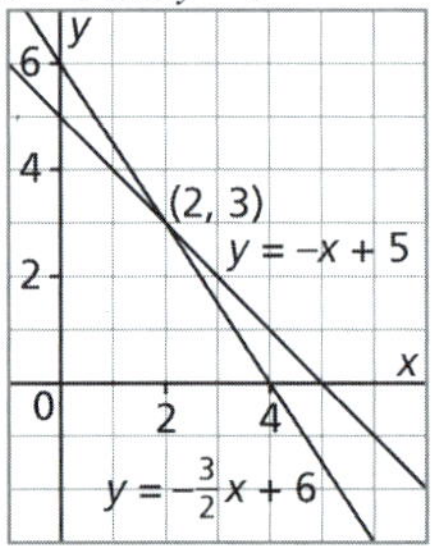

18. Equations may vary. For example, $y = -2x - 7$

19. a) The slopes are negative reciprocals: $-\frac{2}{3}$ and $\frac{3}{2}$

b) Answers may vary. For example,

$y = 4x + 5$ and $y = -\frac{1}{4}x - 2$

7.3 Math Lab: Using Graphing Technology to Solve a System of Linear Equations, page 412

1. a) Look for equal values of Y_1 and Y_2, then the corresponding X-value: $x = 4$, $y = 2$

b) Graph each line, then determine the coordinates of the point of intersection of the lines.

2. b) $x = 2.\overline{3}$ and $y = -1.1\overline{6}$

3. 48 cedar tree and 24 spruce tree seedlings

4. a) **i)** $x = 1$ and $y = 1$

ii) $x = 3$ and $y = 0$

iii) $x = 5$ and $y = -1$

iv) $x = 7$ and $y = -2$

b) $x + 2y = 3$ and $2x - y = 21$

c) $x = 9$ and $y = -3$

5. No

Chapter 7: Checkpoint 1, page 415

1. Variables may differ.

a) $2l + 2w = 128$ and $l - w = 16$

3. $x = 1$ and $y = -1$

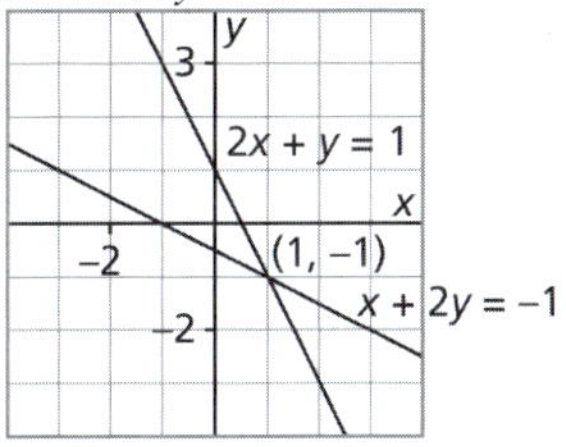

4. a)

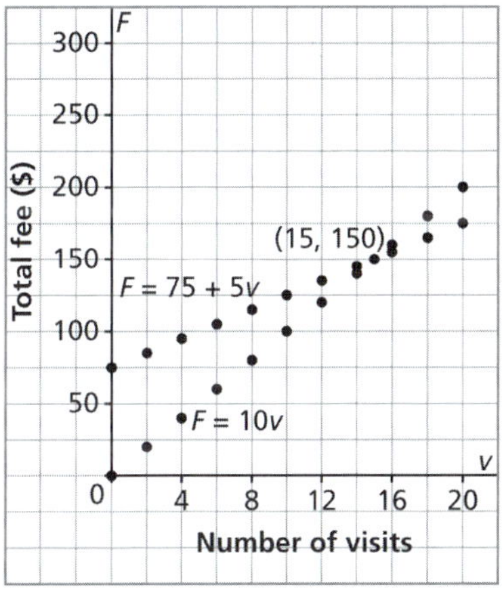

b) Plan A is cheaper when the number of visits is greater than 15.

5. Variables may differ.

a) $21s + 27a = 396$ and $s + a = 18$

b) 15 students and 3 adults

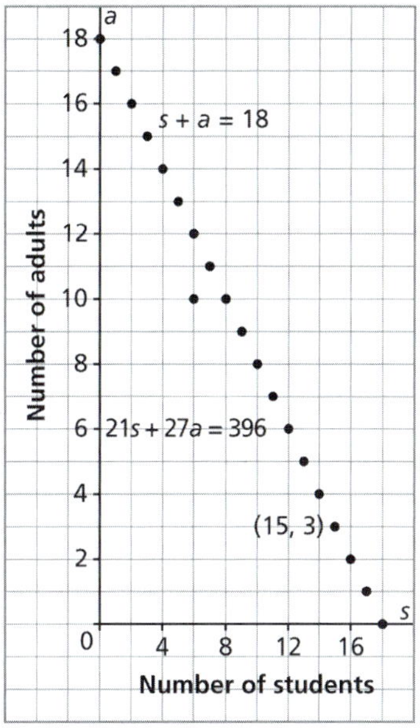

6. Variables may differ.

a) $l + s = 15\,000$ and $1.4l + 0.02s = 7200$

b) 5000 large trees and 10 000 small trees

7.4 Using a Substitution Strategy to Solve a System of Linear Equations, page 425

4. a) $x = 16, y = -7$ **b)** $x = 6, y = 7$

c) $x = -1, y = -8$ **d)** $x = 1, y = 4$

5. a) $x = -2, y = 5$ **b)** $x = -2, y = 3$

c) $x = 3, y = 5$ **d)** $x = 1, y = 4$

6. a) **i)** $2x$, $4x$; $4x = 2(2x)$

ii) $10y$, $5y$; $10y = 2(5y)$

iii) $6y$, $-2y$; $6y = -3(-2y)$

iv) $-3x$, $9x$; $9x = -3(-3x)$

b) **i)** $x = -\frac{1}{2}, y = -1$ **ii)** $x = 0, y = 1$

iii) $x = -1, y = 1$ **iv)** $x = 2, y = 3$

7. a) i

b) **i)** $x = -1, y = 4$ **ii)** $x = -4, y = 1$

iii) $x = 5, y = 1$

8. a) For example, multiply each term in the first equation by 6: $2x - 3y = 12$

For example, multiply each term in the second equation by 12: $10x + 9y = 12$

b) $x = 3, y = -2$

9. a) For example, divide each term in the first equation by 2: $x + y = -2$

For example, divide each term in the second equation by 4: $-3x + y = -6$

b) $x = 1, y = -3$

10. Variables may differ.
$r + n = 186$ and $n - r = 94$
46 bears responded; 140 bears did not respond.

11. Variables may differ.
$2l + 2w = 540$ and $l - w = 90$
Length: 180 cm; width: 90 cm

12. Variables may differ.
$s + a = 45$ and $0.8s + 0.6a = 31$
20 students and 25 adults

13. Variables may differ.
$x + y = 11$ and $4x + 5y = 47$
8 groups of 4 and 3 groups of 5

14. Variables may differ.
$p + a = 85$ and $0.6p + 0.4a = 38$
20 people masks; 65 animal masks

15. Variables may differ.
$0.80A + 0.92B = 63$ and $A + B = 75$
Part A: 50 marks; part B: 25 marks

16. Variables may differ.
$x + y = 5000$ and $0.025x + 0.0375y = 162.50$
Two thousand dollars in the 2.5% bond; $3000 in the 3.75% bond

17. Variables may differ.
$76s + 49d = 474.25$ and $54s + 37d = 346.25$
Single-scoop cone: $3.50; double-scoop cone: $4.25

18. Joel would have to work 15 weekends before he earns the same amount as Sue.

19. **a)** $x = 6, y = -3$ **b)** $x = -1, y = \frac{1}{3}$
c) $x = -\frac{42}{13}, y = -\frac{72}{13}$ **d)** $x = \frac{124}{51}, y = -\frac{16}{17}$

20. **b)** $r = 20, c = 5$

21. $x = 5, y = 22$

22. **a)** For example: $4x - 2y = -8$ and $9x + 6y = 3$
b) $x = -1, y = 2$; the systems have the same solution.

23. **a)** 16 km/h
b) 40 km

24. Mean mass of males: 205.7 g; mean mass of females: 168 g

25. Rate of climb: 200 m/min; rate of descent: –200 m/min

27. $A = 4, B = -3$

7.5 Using an Elimination Strategy to Solve a System of Linear Equations, page 437

3. **a)** $x = -3, y = -1$ **b)** $a = \frac{5}{3}, b = 0$
c) $x = -1, y = -1$ **d)** $x = 4, y = 3$

4. **a)** **i)** $3x - 6y = -18$ and $3x - y = 2$
ii) $x - 2y = -6$ and $6x - 2y = 4$
b) **i)** $15x - 2y = 9$ and $15x + 12y = 51$
ii) $-30x + 4y = -18$ and $5x + 4y = 17$
c) **i)** $35x + 15y = 45$ and $35x + 14y = 49$
ii) $14x + 6y = 18$ and $15x + 6y = 21$
d) **i)** $42x + 45y = 48$ and $42x + 20y = -2$
ii) $28x + 30y = 32$ and $63x + 30y = -3$

5. **a)** $x = 2, y = 4$ **b)** $x = 1, y = 3$
c) $x = 3, y = -4$ **d)** $x = -1, y = 2$

6. **a)** $x = -4, y = 3$ **b)** $m = -\frac{2}{3}, n = -\frac{1}{3}$
c) $s = 0, t = 2$ **d)** $a = 3, b = -2$

7. **a)** $x = \frac{79}{7}, y = \frac{122}{7}$ **b)** $a = -3, b = -7$
c) $a = \frac{1}{2}, b = \frac{1}{3}$ **d)** $x = \frac{5}{2}, y = -3$

8. Variables may differ.
$x + y = 90\ 530$ and $y - x = 120$
2006 attendance: 45 205; 2008 attendance: 45 325

9. Variables may differ.
$t + s = 545$ and $t - s = 185$
Talise's dress: 365 cones; her sister's dress: 180 cones

10. Variables may differ.
$10k + 20b = 200$ and $15k + 25b = 270$
1 knife: 8 beaver pelts; 1 blanket: 6 beaver pelts

11. Variables may differ.
$4.5m + 0.5f = 620$ and $f - m = 40$
Moderate tempo: 120 beats/min; fast tempo: 160 beats/min

12. **a)** $a = \frac{4}{5}, b = \frac{9}{5}$ **b)** $x = 20, y = -6$
c) $x = -0.35, y = 0.25$ **d)** $x = 0.5, y = 0.5$

13. 18 Canadian; 7 foreign

14. 36 girls; 40 boys

15. **a)** $3x + y = 17$ and $x + y = 7$
b) From Balance scales 2, the sum of mass x and mass y is 7 kg. The same mass is being removed from each pan. So, the scales will still be balanced.
c) Two x-masses equal 10 kg. So, mass x is 5 kg. Remove mass x from the left side of Balance scales 2 and 5 kg from the right side. Then mass y balances 2 kg.
d) When I remove the x mass, y mass, and 7 kg from Balance scales 1, it is like subtracting the second equation from the first equation to eliminate y.

16. An adult pays $6.75 and a child pays $7. So, a child's ticket is more expensive.

17. 15 kg of green peas; 10 kg of red lentils

18. Problems may vary. $x = 5, y = 3$

19. **b)** $x = 5, y = 2$

20. **a)** For example, multiply equation 1 by –2 and equation 2 by 3, then add to eliminate x.
Multiply equation 1 by 5 and equation 2 by 4, then add to eliminate y.
b) $x = 3, y = 5$

22. $950 in the stock; $450 in the bond

23. **a)** For example, $3x + 6y = 9$; $x = -1, y = 2$

b) The solution to each system is: $x = -1, y = 2$

c) The solutions are the same.

24. a) 40 bushels/acre for wheat; 58 bushels/acre for barley

b) No, I could use the solution to part a and proportions to determine the yield in bushels/hectare.

Chapter 7: Checkpoint 2, page 441

1. a) $x = \frac{1}{2}, y = \frac{3}{2}$ **b)** $x = 0, y = -1$

c) $x = -6, y = -1$

2. a) Variables may differ.

$6x + 7y = 494$ and $x - y = 13$

b) 45 replicas with 6 stones; 32 replicas with 7 stones

3. \$500 was invested in each bond.

4. a) $x = -6, y = -7$ **b)** $x = \frac{1}{2}, y = 3$

c) $x = -0.75, y = -1.75$ **d)** $x = -\frac{14}{5}, y = \frac{2}{5}$

5. Soup: 90 times; a main course: 70 times

6. Larger volume: 1450 mL; smaller volume: 450 mL

7. $x = 55°; y = 65°$

7.6 Properties of Systems of Linear Equations, page 448

4. a) i) 1 **ii)** –1

iii) 1 **iv)** –1

b) i and iii; ii and iv

c) i and ii; i and iv; ii and iii; iii and iv

5. a) A and C; B and C **b)** A and B

6. a) For example, $x - 3y = 12$ and $5x - 15y = -60$

b) For example, $6x + 3y = 5$ and $2x - 6y = 24$

c) For example, $4x + 2y = 20$ and $2x + y = 10$

7. a) One solution

b) Infinite solutions

c) No solution **d)** No solution

8. a) For example, $y = x + 2$

b) For example, $y = 2x + 2$

c) For example, $-4x + 2y = 2$

9. a) No solution **b)** One solution

c) One solution

10. One solution

11. I need to know whether the y-intercepts are the same or different.

12. For example:

One solution: $-3x - 4y = 12$

No solution: $3x - 4y = 8$

Infinite solutions: $6x - 8y = 24$

13. Infinite solutions

14. One solution

15. Infinite solutions

16. One solution

17. One solution

18. 0 points of intersection: slopes of the lines are equal and their y-intercepts are different.

1 point of intersection: slopes of the lines are different.

Infinite points of intersection: slopes of the lines are equal and their y-intercepts are equal.

19. a) For example: $x + y = 5$ and $2x + 2y = 10$

b) When I try to eliminate one variable, I also eliminate the other variable and the constant.

20. a) For example: $x + y = 4$ and $2x + 2y = 6$

b) When I try to eliminate one variable, I also eliminate the other variable.

22. a) i) Infinite solutions

ii) No solution **iii)** One solution

24. a) i) $k \neq \frac{3}{4}$ **ii)** $k = \frac{3}{4}$

Chapter 7: Review, page 452

1. a) Variables may differ.

$o + s = 41$ and $o - s = 17$

b) Solution B

2. a) Variables may differ.

$s + l = 25$ and $15s + 25l = 475$

b) Solution B

4. a) $3x + y = 11$ and $3x - 5y = -1$

b) $x = 3, y = 2$; exact

5. a) George: draw a line through each pair of points, then determine the coordinates of the point of intersection.

Sunita: plot each y-intercept, then use the slope to mark another point on each line.

b) $x = -2, y = 2$

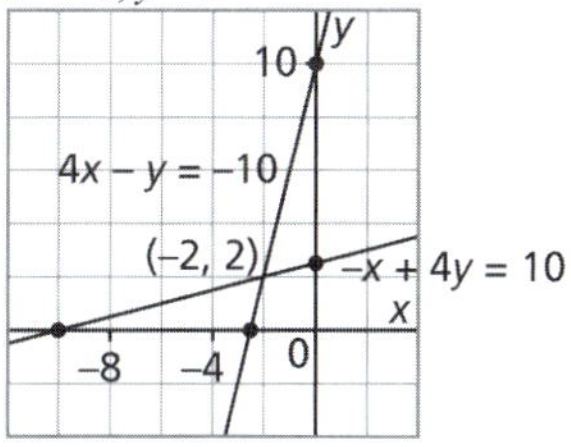

7. a)

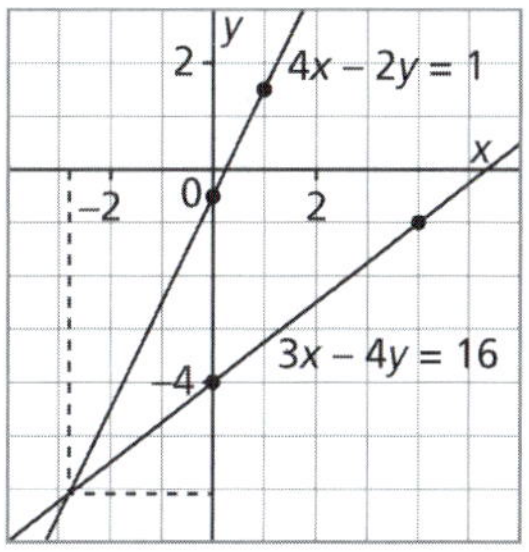

The graphs appear to intersect at (–2.8, –6.1).

b) Exact; when (–2.8, –6.1) is substituted into each equation, the left side equals the right side.

8. a) Variables may differ.

$2c + 4b = 940$ and $c + 3b = 620$

b) Each line represents one of the equations in the linear system.

c) One bowl of cereal has 170 mg of sodium and 1 slice of bacon has 150 mg of sodium; exact solution.

9. Where necessary, the answers have been written to 3 decimal places.

a) $x \doteq 1.526$, $y \doteq 3.316$ b) $x = 12, y = 0$

c) $x = 3.25, y = -1.4$

d) $x \doteq -6.071$, $y \doteq 1.964$

10. a) $x = 0, y = -5$ b) $x = 1, y = 3$

c) $x = \frac{19}{7}, y = -\frac{11}{63}$ d) $x = -1, y = -2$

11. c) $x = -1, y = 8$

12. a) Variables may differ.

$\frac{1}{4}x + \frac{2}{3}y = 5\frac{3}{4}$ and $x - y = 1$

b) 7 one-quarter cup measures; 6 two-third cup measures

13. a)

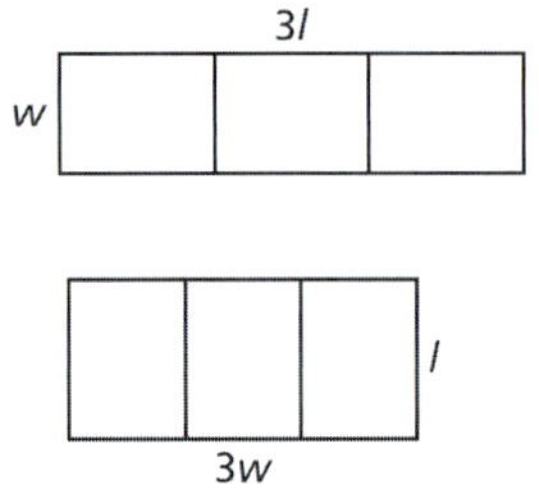

b) Variables may differ.

$60l + 2w = 306$ and $2l + 60w = 190$

c) Width: 3 ft.; length: 5 ft.

14. 35 triangles; 115 squares

15. a) $x = 0, y = -5$ b) $x = \frac{11}{2}, y = -6$

16. c) $x = 2.5, y = -0.25$

17. a) $2l + \left(1 + \frac{1}{2}\pi\right)w = 68\frac{5}{6}$ and $l - w = 7$

b) Length: 19 ft.; width: 12 ft.

18. a) Infinite solutions, for example:

$x + y = -1$ and $2x + 2y = -2$

No solution, for example: $2x + 2y = 5$ and $4x + 4y = -5$

19. a) Clue 1 and Clue 2 b) 45 and 12

20. a) No solution

b) Infinite solutions

c) One solution d) No solution

Chapter 7: Practice Test, page 455

1. B

2. A

4. b) $s = 6, a = 2$

5. a) i) $x = -4, y = \frac{7}{2}$ ii) $x = 4, y = 5$

iii) $x = \frac{3}{2}, y = \frac{1}{2}$

b) The solution of a linear system is the coordinates of the point of intersection of the graphs of the lines.

6. a) Variables may differ.

$y + r = 90$ and $25y + 12.5r = 1500$

b) 30 squares and 60 triangles

Cumulative Review Chapters 1–7, page 458

1. Answers may vary. These answers are calculated using exact conversions.

a) 9 ft. 6 in. b) 457 cm

c) 4 mi. 1709 yd. d) 165 m

e) 269 ft. f) 25.75 km

2. a) 384 cm^2; 384 cm^3 b) 579 in.^{2}; 924 in.^{3}

c) 254 cm^2; 382 cm^3

3. 56.3°

4. $36\frac{4}{10}$ in.

5. a) $81 + 18s + s^2$ b) $6a^2 - 19a + 15$

c) $10n^2 + 7np - 12p^2$ d) $64s^2 - t^2$

e) $-2w^3 - w^2 + 20w - 32$

f) $-6x^4 + 5x^3 + 22x^2 + 2x - 8$

6. a) $7(2a^3b^2 - 4b^3c^2 + 3a^2c^3)$

b) $(n - 4)(n + 3)$

c) $4(3r + 4s)(3r - 4s)$ d) $(2m + 9)(3m - 2)$

e) $(w - 11x)^2$ f) $(5c + 6d)(6c - 5d)$

7. a) i) $3\sqrt{5}$ ii) $4\sqrt[3]{2}$

iii) $\sqrt[4]{932}$ iv) $7\sqrt{11}$

b) i) $\sqrt{432}$ ii) $\sqrt[3]{189}$

iii) $\sqrt[5]{480}$ iv) $\sqrt{425}$

8. a) $\frac{a^2}{b^5}$ b) $\frac{c^2}{d^5}$

c) $-\frac{x^5}{4y^3z^4}$ d) $-\frac{6}{a^3b^2}$

9. a) $\frac{9}{16}$ b) 12.25

c) $\frac{25}{36}$ d) 2.5

10. a) The relation shows the association "participates in" from a set of athletes to a set of sports.

b) i) {(Perdita Felicien, track), (Donovan Bailey, track), (Nancy Greene, skiing), (Annamay Pierse, swimming), (Justin Morneau, baseball), (Steve Nash, basketball)}

ii)

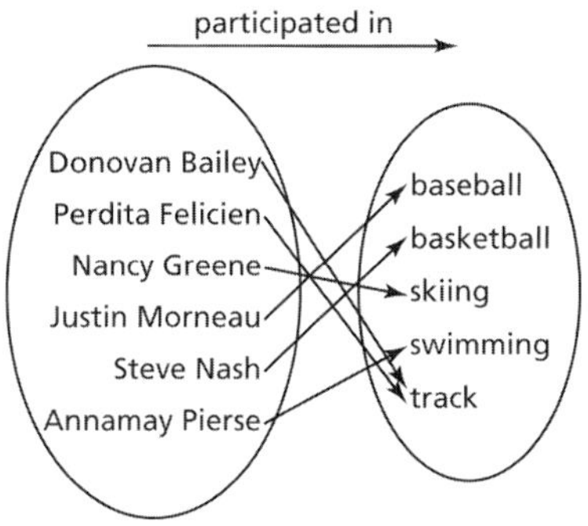

11. a) Each number in the first column of the table appears exactly once.

b) Independent variable: v; dependent variable: C

c) Domain: $\{1, 2, 3, 4, \ldots\}$; range: $\{1.09, 2.18, 3.27, 4.36, \ldots\}$

d) $C(v) = 1.09v$

e) $C(25) = 27.25$; the cost of 25 L of gasoline is $27.25.

f) $v \doteq 46$; with $50, approximately 46 L of gasoline can be purchased.

12. a) False **b)** True

c) True **d)** False

13. a) Graph B

14. a) Domain: $x \leq 3$; range: $y \geq -2$

b) Domain: all real numbers; range: $y \leq 3$

15. a) Tables of values and sketches may vary. For example:

i) A horizontal line that passes through (0, 4)

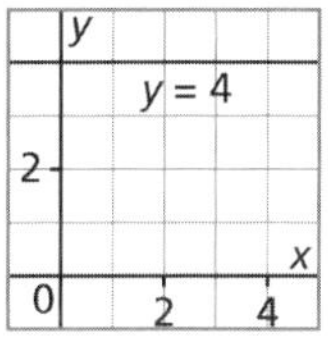

ii)

x	y
–2	5
–1	3
0	1
1	–1
2	–3

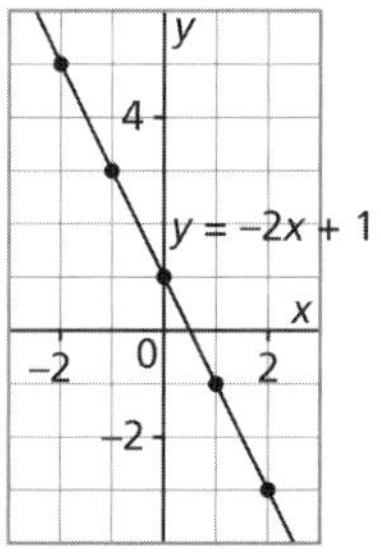

iii)

x	y
–2	2
–1	–1
0	–2
1	–1
2	2

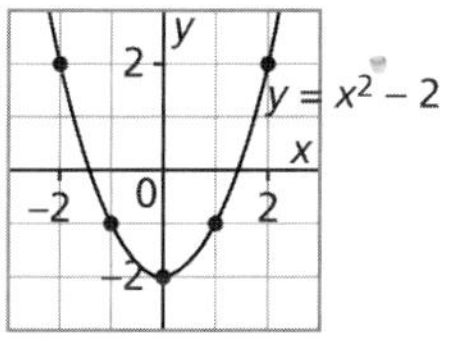

iv) A vertical line that passes through (2, 0)

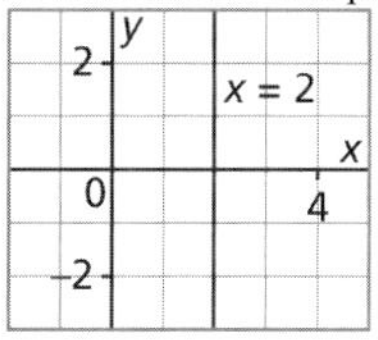

v)

x	y
–2	4
0	3
2	2
4	1
6	0

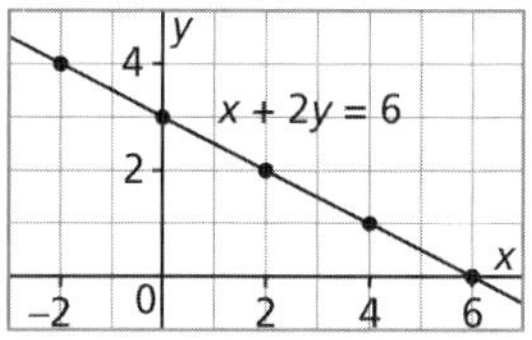

vi)

x	y
1	0
2	1
2	–1
5	2
5	–2

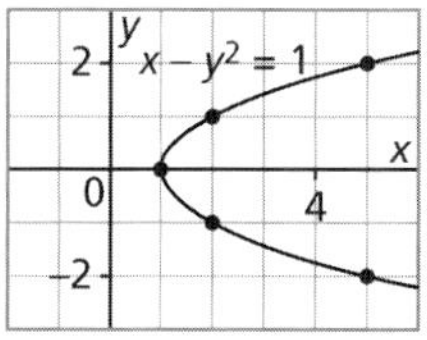

b) i, ii, iv, and v; the graphs are straight lines.

16. a) 300; (0, 300); the fixed cost of renting the banquet room is $300.

b) $15/person; for each additional person who attends, the cost increases by $15.

c) Domain: $\{0, 1, 2, 3, 4, 5, \ldots\}$; range: $\{300, 315, 330, 345, 360, 375, \ldots\}$; The domain can be any whole number up to the number of people the banquet room can hold. The range can be any multiple of 15 greater than or equal to 300, up to a number that depends on the maximum capacity of the room.

d) $1050 **e)** 25 people

17. Points and sketches may vary. For example:

a) (–3, –1), (–2, 1), (0, 5)

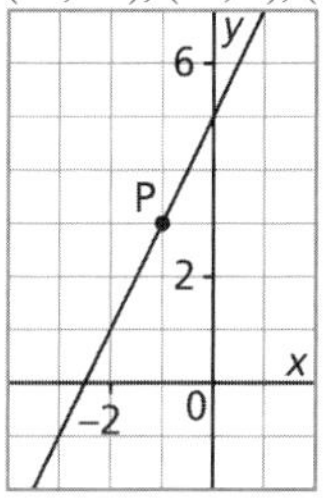

b) (–2, 6), (0, 0), (1, –3)

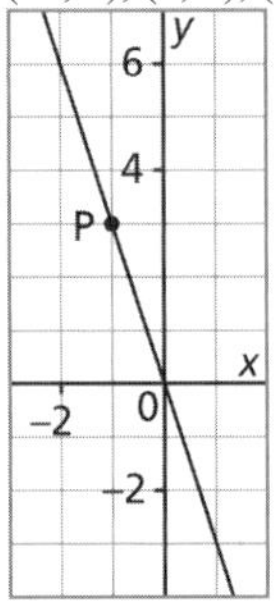

c) (–5, 0), (3, 6), (7, 9)

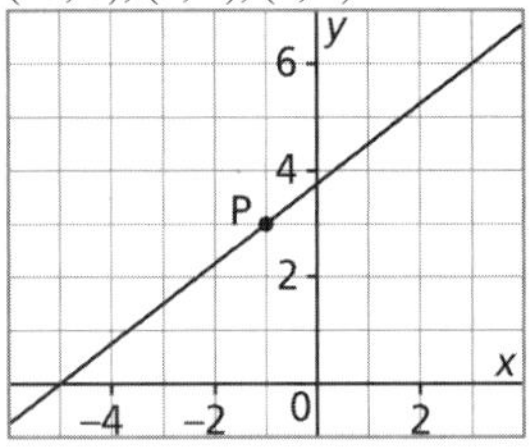

d) (–6, 5), (4, 1), (9, –1)

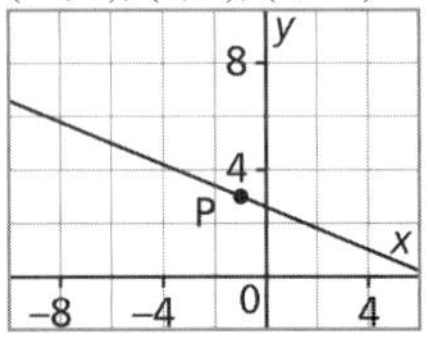

18. a) Neither **b)** Perpendicular

c) Parallel **d)** Perpendicular

19. a)

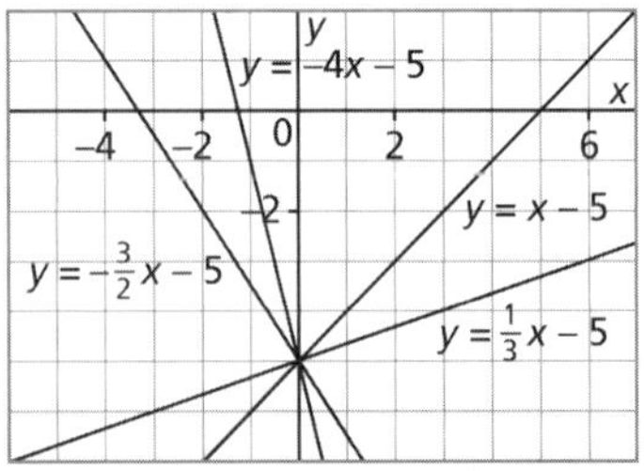

b) Changing the value of m changes the steepness of the graph.

20. a) The student wrote the slope as $\frac{1}{2}$ instead of –2, and the y-intercept as –3 instead of 3.

b) $y = -2x + 3$

21. a) Equations may vary. For example:

i) $y - 2 = -\frac{4}{5}(x + 1)$

ii) $y + 3 = 2(x + 2)$

b) i) $y = -\frac{4}{5}x + \frac{6}{5}$; x-intercept: $\frac{3}{2}$; y-intercept: $\frac{6}{5}$

ii) $y = 2x + 1$; x-intercept: $-\frac{1}{2}$; y-intercept: 1

22. a) $d = 14t + 200$ **b)** $690

c) 37 h **d)** No

23. a) Sketches may vary. For example:

i)

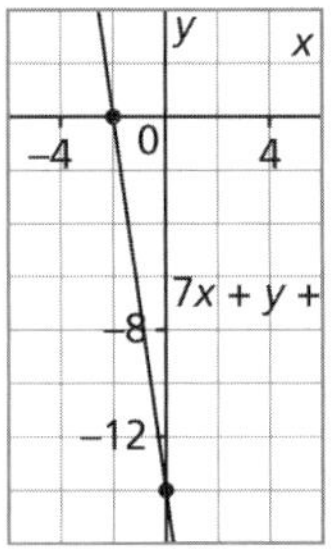

ii)

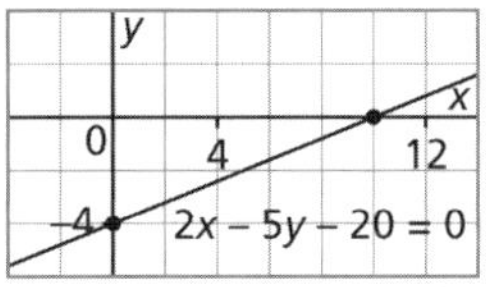

b) i) –7 **ii)** $\frac{2}{5}$

24. a) i) $25x - 20y - 12 = 0$

ii) $2x - 3y - 14 = 0$

25. Variables may differ.

$9.60s + 20.80l = 2206.40$ and $s + l = 140$

26. a) Forms of equations in the system may vary. For example:

$8a + 5s = 1122$ and $s - a = 32$

b) Answers may vary. For example:

75 adults and 105 students; approximate

(Actual answer: 74 adults and 106 students)

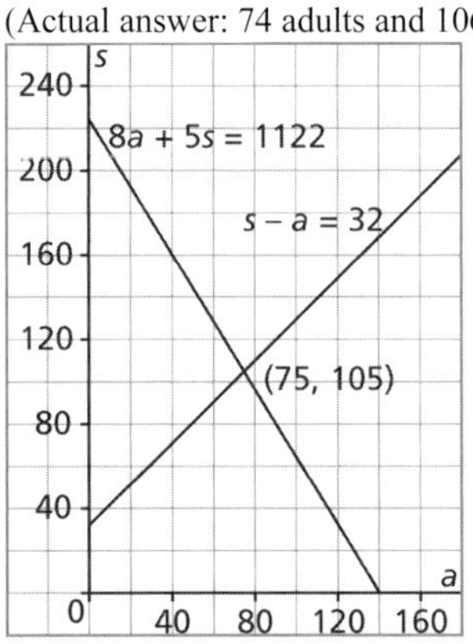

27. $x = \frac{8}{3}$; $y = \frac{7}{12}$

28. Part A: 48 marks; Part B: 60 marks

29. a) $x = \frac{53}{26}$, $y = -\frac{8}{13}$

b) $x = -3$, $y = \frac{5}{2}$

30. Equations may vary. For example:

One solution: $x - y = 1$

No solution: $5x + 3y = 1$

Infinite solutions: $10x + 6y = 30$

Glossary

acute angle: an angle measuring less than 90°

acute triangle: a triangle with three acute angles

algebraic expression: a mathematical expression containing a variable: for example, $6x - 4$

angle of depression: the angle between the horizontal through eye level and a line of sight to a point below eye level

angle of elevation: the angle between the horizontal through eye level and a line of sight to a point above eye level

angle of inclination: the acute angle between the horizontal and a line or line segment

apex: the vertex farthest from the base of an object

approximate: a number close to the exact value of an expression; the symbol $\doteq$ means "is approximately equal to"

area: a measure of the number of square units needed to cover a region

arithmetic operations: the operations of addition, subtraction, multiplication, and division

arrow diagram: used to represent a relation; the ovals show the sets, and the arrows associate elements of the first set with elements of the second set

average: a single number that represents a set of numbers (see *mean*)

bar graph: a graph that displays data by using horizontal or vertical bars

bar notation: the use of a horizontal bar over a decimal digit to indicate that it repeats; for example, $1.\overline{3}$ means 1.333 333 ...

base: the side of a polygon or the face of an object from which the height is measured

base of a power: see *power*

binomial: a polynomial with two terms; for example, $3x - 8$

calipers: a tool used to measure the diameter or thickness of an object

capacity: the amount a container can hold

central angle: an angle whose arms are radii of a circle

circumference: the distance around a circle, also the perimeter of the circle

clinometer: a tool used to measure an angle above or below the horizontal

coefficient: the numerical factor of a term; for example, in the terms $3x$ and $3x^2$, the coefficient is 3

common factor: a number that divides into each number in a set; for example, 3 is a common factor of 15, 9, and 21. An expression that divides into each term of a given polynomial; for example, $4y$ is a common factor of $8x^2y + 4xy + 12y$

common multiple: a number that is a multiple of each number in a set; for example, 6 is a common multiple of 2 and 3

composite number: a number with three or more factors; for example, 8 is a composite number because its factors are 1, 2, 4, and 8

composite object: the result of combining two or more objects to make a new object

cone: see *right cone*

congruent: shapes that match exactly, but do not necessarily have the same orientation

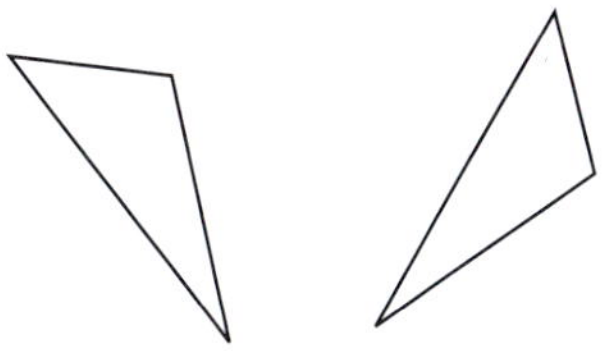

consecutive numbers: integers that come one after the other without any integers missing; for example, 34, 35, 36 are consecutive numbers, so are $-2, -1, 0$, and 1

constant term: the term in an expression or equation that does not change; for example, in the expression $4x + 3$, 3 is the constant term

conversion factor: a number used to multiply or divide a quantity to convert from one unit of measure to another

coordinate axes: the horizontal and vertical axes on a grid

coordinates: the numbers in an ordered pair that locate a point on a coordinate grid (see *ordered pair, x-coordinate, y-coordinate*)

corresponding angles: matching angles in similar polygons

corresponding lengths: matching lengths on an original diagram and its scale diagram

corresponding sides: matching sides of similar polygons

cosine ratio: for an acute ∠A in a right triangle, the ratio of the length of the side adjacent to ∠A to the length of the hypotenuse; written cos A

$$\cos A = \frac{\text{length of side adjacent to } \angle A}{\text{length of hypotenuse}}$$

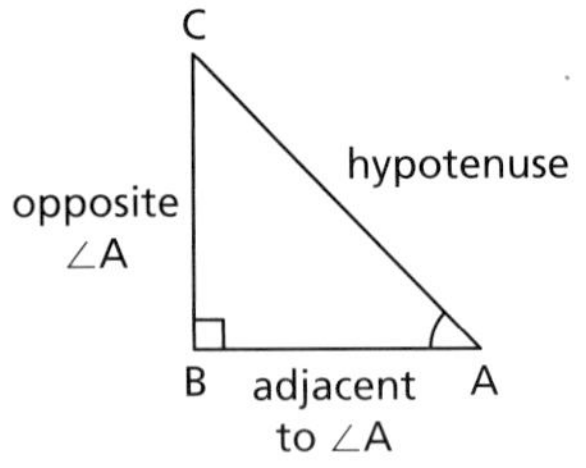

cube: an object with six congruent square faces

cube number: a number that can be written as a power with an integer base and exponent 3; for example, $8 = 2^3$

cube root: a number which, when raised to the exponent 3, results in a given number; for example, 5 is the cube root of 125

cubic units: units that measure volume

decagon: a polygon with 10 sides

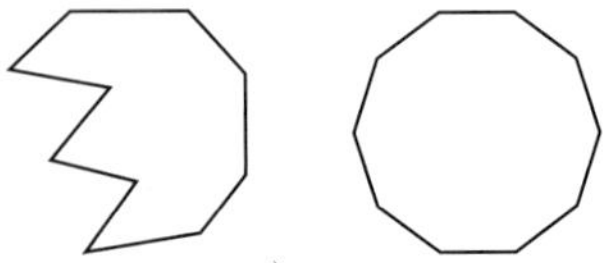

denominator: the term below the line in a fraction

dependent variable: a variable whose value is determined by the value of another (the independent) variable

diagonal: a line segment that joins two vertices of a shape, but is not a side

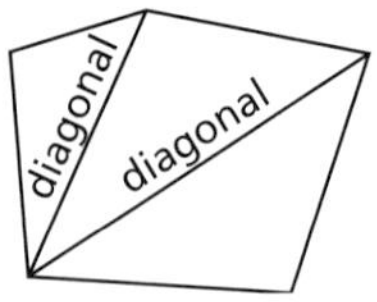

diameter: the distance across a circle, measured through its centre; or the line segment that joins two points on the circle and passes through its centre

difference of squares: a binomial of the form $a^2 - b^2$; it can be factored as $(a - b)(a + b)$

digit: any of the symbols used to write numerals; for example, 0, 1, 2, 3, 4, 5, 6, 7, 8, and 9

dimensions: measurements such as length, width, and height

direct measurement: a measurement made using a measuring instrument or by counting

displacement: the volume of water moved or displaced by an object put in the water; the volume of the object is equal to the volume of water displaced

distributive property: the property stating that a product can be written as a sum or difference of two products; for example, $a(b + c) = ab + ac$

divisor: the number that divides into another number

domain: the set of first elements of a relation

edge: two faces of an object meet at an edge

element: an element of a set is one object in the set

entire radical: a radical sign and the number under it; for example, $\sqrt[5]{32}$

equation: a mathematical statement that two expressions are equal

equilateral triangle: a triangle with 3 equal sides

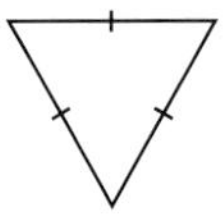

equivalent: having the same value; for example, $\frac{1}{2}$ and $\frac{2}{4}$; 3:4 and 9:12

estimate: a reasoned guess that is close to the actual value, without calculating it exactly

evaluate: to determine the value of a numerical expression

even integer: a number that has 2 as a factor; for example, 2, 4, 6

expanding an expression: writing a product of polynomial factors as a polynomial

exponent: see *power*

exponent laws: the rules that describe how combinations of powers can be written differently

expression: a mathematical statement made up of numbers and/or variables connected by operations

face: a flat surface of an object

factor: to factor means to write as a product; for example, $20 = 2 \cdot 2 \cdot 5$

factor tree: a branching diagram with a number at the top and its prime factors at the bottom

factored fully: factoring a polynomial so each factor cannot be factored further

factoring a polynomial: writing a polynomial as a product of its factors

factoring by decomposition: factoring a trinomial after writing the middle term as a sum of two terms, then determining a common binomial factor from the two pairs of terms formed

factors: numbers or algebraic expressions that are multiplied to get a product; for example, 3 and 7 are factors of 21, and $x + 1$ and $x + 2$ are factors of $x^2 + 3x + 2$

formula: a rule that is expressed as an equation

fraction: an indicated quotient of two quantities

function: a relation where each element in the first set is associated with exactly one element in the second set

function notation: notation used to show the independent variable in a function; for example, $f(x)$ means that the value of the function f depends on the value of the independent variable x.

general form: the equation of a line in the form $Ax + By + C = 0$, where A is a whole number, and B and C are integers

greatest common factor (GCF): the greatest number that divides into each number in a set; for example, 5 is the greatest common factor of 10 and 15

height: the perpendicular distance from the base of a shape to the opposite side or vertex; the perpendicular distance from the base of an object to the opposite face or vertex

hemisphere: half a sphere

hexagon: a polygon with 6 sides

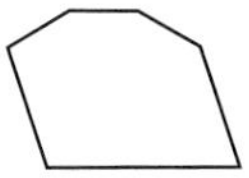

horizontal axis: see *x-axis*

horizontal intercept: see *x-intercept*

horizontal line: a line parallel to the horizon

hypotenuse: the side opposite the right angle in a right triangle

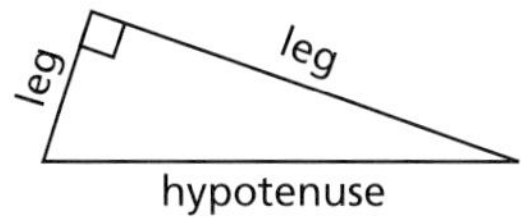

imperial units: measurement units such as the mile, yard, foot, and inch commonly used in the United States and in some industries in Canada

independent variable: a variable whose value is not determined by the value of another variable, and whose value determines the value of another (the dependent) variable

index: in a radical, the number above the radical symbol that indicates which root is to be taken; for example, 3 is the index in the radical $\sqrt[3]{81}$; if the index is not written, it is assumed to be 2

indirect measurement: a measurement made using a ratio, formula, or other mathematical reasoning

integers: the set of numbers $\ldots -3, -2, -1, 0, 1, 2, 3, \ldots$

inverse operation: an operation that reverses the result of another operation; for example, subtraction is the inverse of addition, and division is the inverse of multiplication

irrational number: a number that *cannot* be written in the form $\frac{m}{n}$, $n \neq 0$, where m and n are integers

isometric: equal measure; on isometric dot paper, the line segments joining 2 adjacent dots in any direction are equal

isosceles trapezoid: a trapezoid with 2 equal, non-parallel sides

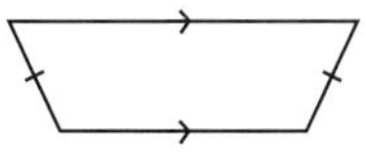

isosceles triangle: a triangle with 2 equal sides

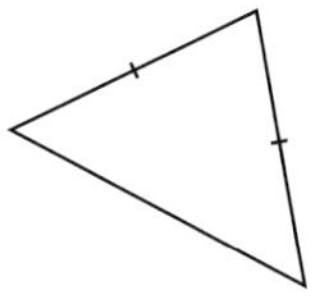

kite: a quadrilateral with two pairs of adjacent sides equal

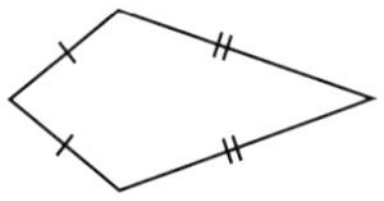

lateral area: the surface area of an object, not including the area of its bases

least common multiple (LCM): the least multiple that is the same for two numbers; for example, the least common multiple of 12 and 21 is 84

legs: the sides of a right triangle that form the right angle (see *hypotenuse*)

like terms: terms that have the same variables raised to the same powers; for example, $4x$ and $-3x$ are like terms

line segment: the part of a line between two points on the line

linear function: a linear relation whose graph is not a vertical line

linear relation: a relation that has a straight-line graph

linear system: see *system of linear equations*

mass: the amount of matter in an object

mean: the sum of a set of numbers divided by the number of numbers in the set

midpoint: the point that divides a line segment into two equal parts

mixed radical: a number written as a product of another number and a radical; for example, $3\sqrt{5}$

monomial: a polynomial with one term; for example, 14 and $5x^2$ are monomials

multiple: the product of a given number and a natural number; for example, some multiples of 8 are 8, 16, 24, …

natural numbers: the set of numbers 1, 2, 3, 4, 5, …

negative number: a number less than 0

negative reciprocals: two numbers whose product is -1; for example, $-\frac{3}{7}$ and $\frac{7}{3}$

numerator: the term above the line in a fraction

numerical coefficient: see *coefficient*

object: a solid or shell that has 3 dimensions

obtuse triangle: a triangle with one angle greater than 90°

octagon: a polygon with 8 sides

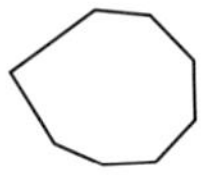

operation: a mathematical process or action such as addition, subtraction, multiplication, division, or raising to a power

opposites: two numbers with a sum of 0; for example, 2.4 and -2.4 are opposite numbers

order of operations: the rules that are followed when simplifying or evaluating an expression

ordered pair: two numbers in order, for example, (2, 4); on a coordinate grid, the first number is the horizontal coordinate of a point, and the second number is the vertical coordinate of the point

origin: the point where the horizontal axis and the vertical axis intersect

parallel lines: lines on the same flat surface that do not intersect

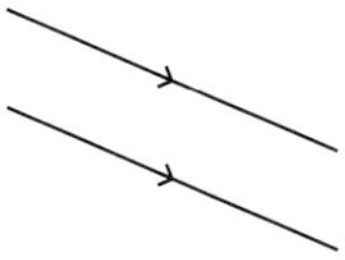

parallelogram: a quadrilateral with opposite sides parallel and opposite angles equal

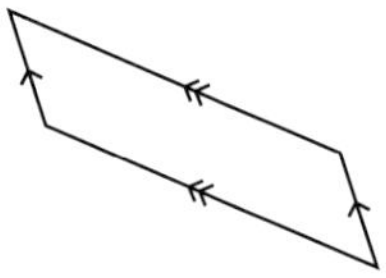

pentagon: a polygon with 5 sides

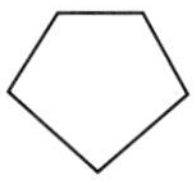

percent: the number of parts per 100; the numerator of a fraction with denominator 100

perfect cube: see *cube number*

perfect square: see *square number*

perfect square trinomial: a trinomial of the form $a^2 + 2ab + b^2$; it can be factored as $(a + b)^2$

perimeter: the distance around a closed shape

perpendicular: lines or line segments that intersect at right angles

pi (π): the ratio of the circumference of a circle to its diameter; $\pi = \dfrac{\text{circumference}}{\text{diameter}}$

point of intersection: the point where two graphs intersect

polygon: a closed shape that consists of line segments; for example, triangles and quadrilaterals are polygons

polyhedron (*plural*, **polyhedra**): an object with faces that are polygons

polynomial: one term or the sum of terms whose variables have whole-number exponents; for example, $x^2 + 3xy - 2y^2 + 5x$

power: an expression of the form a^n, where a is the base and n is the exponent; it represents a product of equal factors; for example, $4 \cdot 4 \cdot 4$ can be written as 4^3

primary trigonometric ratios: three ratios involving sides in right triangles (see *cosine ratio*, *sine ratio*, and *tangent ratio*)

prime factor: a prime number that is a factor of a number; for example, 5 is a prime factor of 30

prime factorization: writing a number as a product of its prime factors; for example, the prime factorization of 20 is $2 \cdot 2 \cdot 5$, or $2^2 \cdot 5$

prime number: a whole number with exactly two factors, itself and 1; for example, 2, 3, 5, 7, 11, 29, 31, and 43

prism: an object with 2 bases (see *right prism*)

product: the result when two or more numbers are multiplied; or the expression of one number multiplied by another

proportion: a statement that two ratios are equal; for example, $r{:}24 = 3{:}4$

proportional reasoning: the ability to understand and compare quantities that are related multiplicatively

Pythagorean Theorem: the rule that states that, for any right triangle, the area of the square on the hypotenuse is equal to the sum of the areas of the squares on the legs

quadrilateral: a polygon with 4 sides

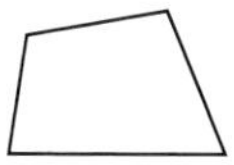

quotient: the result when one number is divided by another; or the expression of one number divided by another

radical: an expression consisting of a radical sign, a radicand, and an index; for example, $\sqrt[3]{64}$

radicand: the number under a radical sign; for example, 81 is the radicand in $\sqrt{81}$

radius (*plural*, **radii**): the distance or line segment from the centre of a circle to any point on the circle

range: the set of second elements associated with the first elements (domain) of a relation

rate: a comparison of two quantities measured in different units

rate of change: the change in one quantity with respect to the change in another quantity (see *slope*)

ratio: a comparison of two or more quantities with the same unit

rational number: any number that can be written in the form $\frac{m}{n}$, $n \neq 0$, where m and n are integers

real number: any number that is a rational number or an irrational number; a member of the set of numbers that have a decimal representation

reciprocals: two numbers whose product is 1; for example, $\frac{2}{3}$ and $\frac{3}{2}$

rectangle: a quadrilateral that has four right angles

rectangular prism: see *right rectangular prism*

rectangular pyramid: see *right rectangular pyramid*

referent: used to estimate a measure; for example, a referent for a length of 1 mm is the thickness of a dime

regular polygon: a polygon that has all sides equal and all angles equal

regular polyhedron: a polyhedron with congruent faces, each of which is a regular polygon

regular prism: a prism with regular polygons as bases; for example, a cube

regular pyramid: a pyramid with a regular polygon as its base

regular tetrahedron: an object with four congruent equilateral triangular faces; a regular triangular pyramid

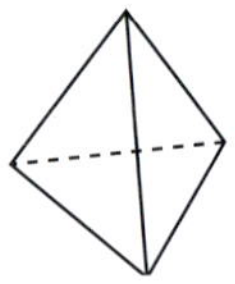

relation: a rule that associates the elements of one set with the elements of another set

repeating decimal: a decimal with a repeating pattern in the digits to the right of the decimal point; it is written with a bar above the repeating digits; for example, $0.\overline{3} = 0.333\ 333\ \ldots$

rhombus: a parallelogram with four equal sides

right angle: a 90° angle

right cone: an object with one circular base and one vertex; the line through the vertex and the centre of the base is perpendicular to the base

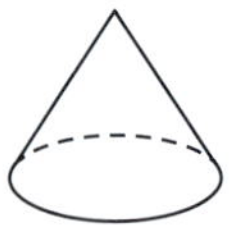

right cylinder: an object with two parallel, congruent, circular bases; the line through the centres of the bases is perpendicular to the bases

right prism: an object that has two congruent and parallel faces (the *bases*), and other faces that are rectangles

right pyramid: an object that has one face that is a polygon (the *base*), and other faces that are triangles with a common vertex; the line through the vertex and the centre of the base is perpendicular to the base

right rectangular prism: a prism that has rectangular faces

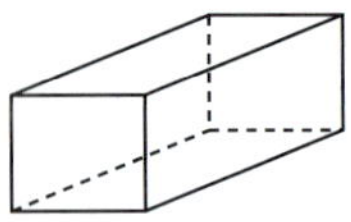

right rectangular pyramid: a pyramid that has a rectangular base; the line through the vertex and the centre of the base is perpendicular to the base

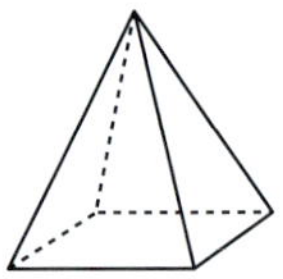

right triangle: a triangle that has one right angle

rise: the vertical distance between two points; see *slope*

run: the horizontal distance between two points; see *slope*

scale: the numbers on the axes of a graph

scale factor: the ratio of corresponding lengths of two similar shapes

set: a collection of distinct objects

SI system of measures: a system of units based on powers of 10; the fundamental unit: of length is the metre (m); of mass is the kilogram (kg); and of time is the second (s).

similar polygons: polygons with the same shape; one polygon is an enlargement or a reduction of the other polygon

simplest form: a ratio with terms that have no common factors, other than 1; a fraction with numerator and denominator that have no common factors, other than 1

sine ratio: for an acute ∠A in a right triangle, the ratio of the length of the side opposite ∠A to the length of the hypotenuse; written sin A

$$\sin A = \frac{\text{length of side opposite } \angle A}{\text{length of hypotenuse}}$$

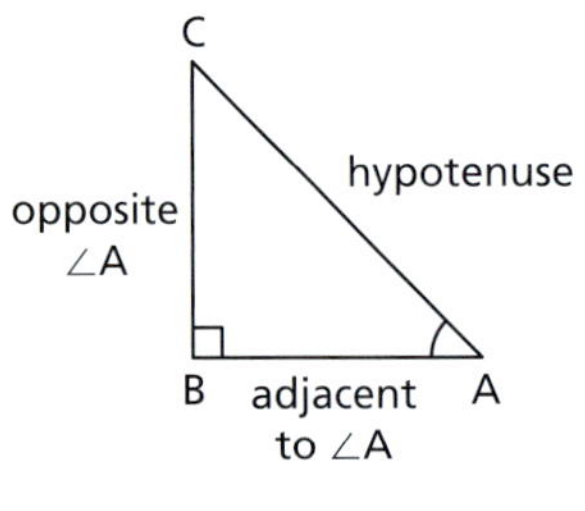

slant height: the distance from a point on the perimeter of the base of a cone to the apex of the cone; the distance from the midpoint of the base of one triangular face of a regular pyramid to the apex of the pyramid

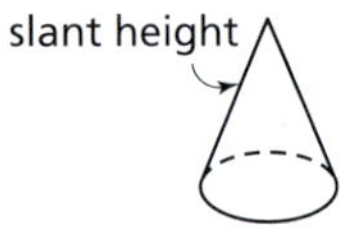

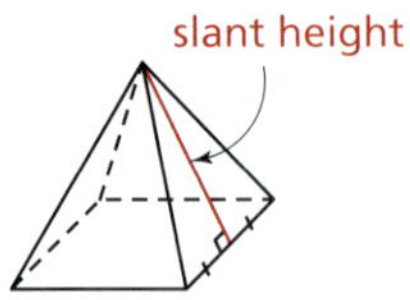

slope: a measure of how one quantity changes with respect to the other; it can be determined by calculating $\frac{\text{rise}}{\text{run}}$

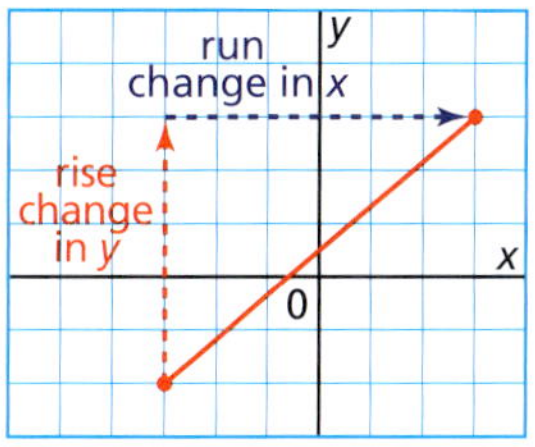

slope-intercept form: the equation of a line in the form $y = mx + b$, where m is the slope of the line, and b is its y-intercept

slope-point form: the equation of a line in the form $y - y_1 = m(x - x_1)$, where m is the slope of the line, and the line passes through point $P(x_1, y_1)$

solving a triangle: determining the measure of each angle in a triangle and the length of each side of the triangle

sphere: an object where every point on the surface of the object is the same distance from the centre of the object

square: a rectangle with 4 equal sides

square number: a number that can be written as a power with an integer base and exponent 2; for example, $49 = 7^2$

square root: a number which, when multiplied by itself, results in a given number; for example, 5 is a square root of 25

square units: units that measure area

standard form: the equation of a line in the form $Ax + By = C$, where A, B, and C are integers

substituting into an equation: in an equation of a linear function, replacing one variable with a number or an expression

surface area: the total area of the surface of an object

system of linear equations: two equations of linear functions in the same two variables

tangent ratio: for an acute $\angle A$ in a right triangle, the ratio of the length of the side opposite $\angle A$ to the length of the side adjacent to $\angle A$; written tan A

$$\tan A = \frac{\text{length of side opposite } \angle A}{\text{length of side adjacent to } \angle A}$$

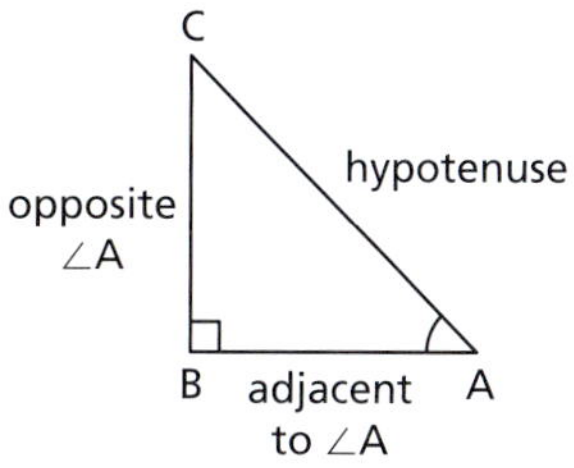

term: a number, a variable, or the product of numbers and variables; for example, -5, y, $7a^2$

terminating decimal: a decimal with a certain number of digits after the decimal point; for example, 0.125

tetrahedron: a pyramid that has a triangular base

three-dimensional: having length, width, and depth or height

trapezoid: a quadrilateral with exactly 1 pair of parallel sides

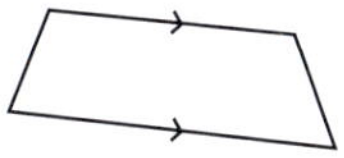

triangle: a polygon with 3 sides

triangular prism: a prism with triangular bases

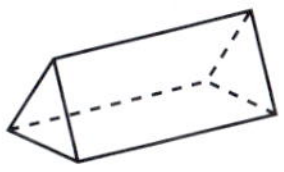

trigonometry: the study of the properties and applications of triangles

trinomial: a polynomial with three terms; for example, $3x^2 + 5x - 8$

unit analysis: a method of converting a measure in a given unit to a measure in a different unit by multiplying the measure by a conversion factor

variable: a letter or symbol representing a quantity that can vary

vertex (*plural*, **vertices**): the point where 2 sides of a shape meet, or the point where 3 or more edges of an object meet

vertical axis: see *y-axis*

vertical intercept: see *y-intercept*

vertical line: a line perpendicular to the horizontal

volume: the amount of space occupied by an object

whole numbers: the set of numbers 0, 1, 2, 3, …

***x*-axis:** the horizontal number line on a coordinate grid

***x*-coordinate:** on a coordinate grid, the first number in an ordered pair

***x*-intercept:** the *x*-coordinate of a point where a graph intersects the *x*-axis

***y*-axis:** the vertical number line on a coordinate grid

***y*-coordinate:** on a coordinate grid, the second number in an ordered pair

***y*-intercept:** the *y*-coordinate of a point where a graph intersects the *y*-axis

Zero Principle: the property of addition that states that adding 0 to a number does not change the number; for example, $3 = 0 + 3$

Index

Acknowledgments

The publisher wishes to thank the following sources for photographs, illustrations, and other materials used in this book. Every reasonable effort has been made to find copyright holders of the material in this text. The publisher will gladly receive information enabling us to rectify any errors or omissions in credits.

Photography

pp. 2–3 © Lone Pine Photo; p. 4 (top) © Raymond Gehman/CORBIS; p. 4 (bottom) Ian Crysler; p. 5 Ian Crysler; p. 6 (top) Ian Crysler; p. 6 (bottom) Dave Starrett; p. 11 (right) © GLEB GARANICH/ Reuters/Corbis; p. 11 (left) © AP Photo/Phil Meyers/THE CANADIAN PRESS; p. 13 (top) © A.G.E. Foto Stock/First Light; p. 13 (bottom) Ian Crysler; p. 14 Ian Crysler; p. 15 © Peter de Clercq/Alamy; p. 16 (top) © Stefano Paltera/Handout/Reuters/Corbis; p. 16 (bottom) Ian Crysler; p. 17 Ian Crysler; p. 23 © Mike Grandmaison/AllCanadaPhotos.com; p. 26 © Maksym Gorpenyuk/Shutterstock; p. 35 (left) © Burton Zaro/Alamy; p. 35 (right) © Barrett & MacKay/ AllCanadaPhotos.com; p. 36 Ian Crysler; p. 44 © Construction Photography/Corbis; p. 45 © North End Water Pollution Control Centre; p. 46 Ian Crysler; p. 47 © Lawrence Manning/Corbis; p. 49 © Milos Luzanin/ Shutterstock; p. 52 © Denis Beauvais; p. 55 © Milos Luzanin/Shutterstock; p. 61 (top) © Doug Allan/ The Image Bank/Getty Images; p. 61 (bottom) © Dave Reede/First Light; p. 65 © Summerhill Pyramid Winery; pp. 68–69 © Mike Zens/CORBIS; p. 70 © Steven J. Kazlowski/Alamy; p. 76 (left) © Mike Sturk/Alamy; p. 76 (right) © Ronnie Howard/Shutterstock; p. 77 © Jacek Chabraszewski/Shutterstock; p. 78 Bernard Chong; p. 83 (left) © Roy Ooms/Masterfile; p. 83 (right) © Tibor Bognar/Alamy; p. 84 © Mike Hayward/ photoshropshire.com/Alamy; p. 85 Dave Starrett; p. 88 (top) © Larry Mayer/Creatas Images/Jupiterimages; p. 88 (bottom) © Courtesy of the Royal Alberta Museum, Edmonton, Alberta; p. 89 © David R. Spencer; p. 96 (top) © Robert Kyllo/Shutterstock; p. 96 (bottom) © Rob Allen/First Light; p. 97 © Purestock/Alamy; p. 102 © David Nunuk /AllCanadaPhotos.com; p. 104 © David Nunuk/AllCanadaPhotos.com; p. 105 © Courtesy of BC Transit; p. 110 © John Kirinic/Shutterstock; p. 112 © Alan Marsh/First Light; p. 113 © Paul A. Souders/ CORBIS; p. 119 © Brian Sytnyk/Masterfile; p. 120 © Headline Photo Agency/Alamy; p. 121 © Mary Evans Picture Library/Alamy; p. 124 © Trevor Payne/Alamy; p. 126 © Cosmo Condina Western Europe/Alamy; p. 128 (top) © Huntstock, Inc/Alamy; p. 128 (bottom) Bernard Chong; p. 129 © superclic/Alamy; pp. 132–133 © Brian Sytnyk/Masterfile; p. 134 (left) © MacBride Museum of Yukon History 1993.48.46; p. 134 (right) © MacBride Museum of Yukon History 1977.1.133; p. 142 (top) © Manu Martinez & Balestra Berlin; p. 142 (bottom) © AFP/Getty Images; p. 147 (left) © Gerry Fox; p. 147 (right) © Stan Milosevic; p. 150 Ian Crysler; p. 157 Ian Crysler; p. 158 © Bildarchiv Preussischer Kulturbesitz/ Art Resource, NY; p. 159 Ian Crysler; p. 162 Bernard Chong; p. 168 Ian Crysler; p. 179 © TWPhoto/Corbis; p. 181 © Bettmann/CORBIS; p. 182 art by Deborah Crowle; p. 188 © Dave Reede/AllCanadaPhotos.com; pp. 202–203 © imagebroker/Alamy; p. 204 Ian Crysler; p. 207 © Stan Milosevic; p. 212 © David H. Seymour/ Shutterstock; p. 213 © Mary Louise Metz, Indiana University of Pennsylvania; p. 222 © Supri Suharjoto/Shutterstock; p. 229 © Louie Psihoyos/ CORBIS; p. 234 Bernard Chong; p. 236 © Percussa Bvba; p. 237 Steven Daniel; p. 244 © Ariel Skelley/CORBIS; p. 246 (top) © ACE STOCK LIMITED/Alamy; p. 246 (bottom) © Legal Alfalfa Products Ltd; p. 248 © Ferdinand Knab/The Bridgeman Art Library/Getty Images; p. 250 (top) © REUTERS/ Vijay Mathur (INDIA); p. 250 (centre) © AFP/Getty Images; p. 251 (top) Ian Crysler; p. 251 (bottom) © The Bodleian Library; pp. 254–255 © Parks Canada; p. 256 © Hans Blohm/Masterfile; p. 261 (left) © Qyd; p. 261 (right) © Carla Victor, Mountain View Publishing; p. 262 © James Culleton; p. 272 © Mybaitshop/Dreamstime.com; p. 273 © Chung Sung-Jun/Getty Images; p. 276 © Poelzer Wolfgang/Alamy; p. 282 © AP Photo/The Canadian Press/Jonathan Hayward; p. 284 © Corbis Premium RF/Alamy; p. 287 © James Urbach/MaXx Images; p. 295 © Stephen Aaron Rees/Shutterstock; p. 296 © 2009 Jupiterimages Corporation; p. 297 © MOODBOARD/MaXx Images; p. 300 © 2009 Jupiterimages Corporation; p. 302 © Don Wilkie/istockphoto.com; p. 307 © JoLi/ Shutterstock; p. 311 © Wave Royalty Free/Alamy; p. 318 © DAN ROSENSTRAUCH/Keystone Press; p. 320 © Dave Reede/First Light; p. 321 (left) © Transtock/Corbis; p. 321 (right) © iztok noc/ istockphoto.com; p. 323 (top) © Ken Walker; p. 323 (bottom) ArtPlus; pp. 330–331 © Michael Christopher Brown/Corbis; p. 332 © Richard Magleo; p. 333 (left) © Mirenska Olga/Shutterstock; p. 333 (centre) © Casper Voogt/Shutterstock; p. 333 (right) © Ingram Publishing/MaXx Images; p. 339 (top) © Zoomstock/Masterfile; p. 339 (bottom) © Aflo Foto Agency/Alamy; p. 340 (left) © Dave Reede/Getty Images; p. 340 (right) © Tomasz Trojanowski/ Shutterstock; p. 341 (left) © BORTEL Pavel/ Shutterstock; p. 341 (right) © nicobatista/Shutterstock;

p. 342 © Masterfile; p. 343 (top) © THE CANADIAN PRESS/Winnipeg Free Press – Wayne Glowacki; p. 343 (bottom) © Tom Oliveira/Shutterstock; p. 349 © Golf Digest; p. 351 (right) © AP Photo/Eric Draper; p. 351 (left) © Art Resource; p. 354 © JAUBERT BERNARD/Alamy; p. 355 Ian Crysler; p. 357 © Stephen Matera/Aurora Photos/Corbis; p. 365 © T.W. van Urk/ Shutterstock; p. 376 © Jon Faulknor/istockphoto.com; p. 377 © moodboard/Corbis; p. 386 © Janine Wiedel Photolibrary/Alamy; pp. 392–393 © Louise Murray/ Alamy; p. 394 © Martin Nemec/Shutterstock; p. 395 © Michael Layefsky/Getty Images; p. 397 © Joggi2002/Dreamstime.com; p. 399 © Ronen/ Shutterstock; p. 401 © Nativestock.com/Marilyn Angel Wynn/Getty Images; p. 403 © MARK DUFFY/Alamy; p. 411 © AP Photo/Jacquelyn Martin; p. 413 © Tim Pannell/Corbis; p. 415 © AP Photo/Thomas Kienzle; p. 425 © CP PHOTO/ EdmontonSun – David Bloom; p. 426 © THE CANADIAN PRESS/John Woods; p. 427 (top) © Gunter Marx/Alamy; p. 427 (bottom) © J.R. Bale/Alamy; p. 428 © Rick Gomez/Masterfile; p. 434 © David Sutherland/Alamy; p. 437 (top) © Emily Riddell/Alamy; p. 437 (bottom) © Ekays/ Dreamstime.com; p. 438 © Rolf Hicker/ AllCanadaPhotos.com; p. 439 © Pixart/ Dreamstime.com; p. 441 © Shutterstock; p. 442 © Brian Summers/First Light; p. 447 © Iraq Museum, Baghdad/The Bridgeman Art Library; p. 449 © Stan Milosevic/Manitoba Photos; p. 453 Courtesy of Janice Ealey; p. 454 © AP Photo/Andy Wong/The Canadian Press; p. 456 (left) © Corbis Super RF/Alamy; p. 456 (right) © Schmid Christophe/Shutterstock

Illustrations

ArtPlus Limited
Deborah Crowle
Lapiz Digital Services

Texas Instruments images used with permission.

78.700

76

73.800